With the purchase of a new Book*

You Can Access the Real Financial Data that the Experts Use!

*If you purchased a used book, see other side for access information

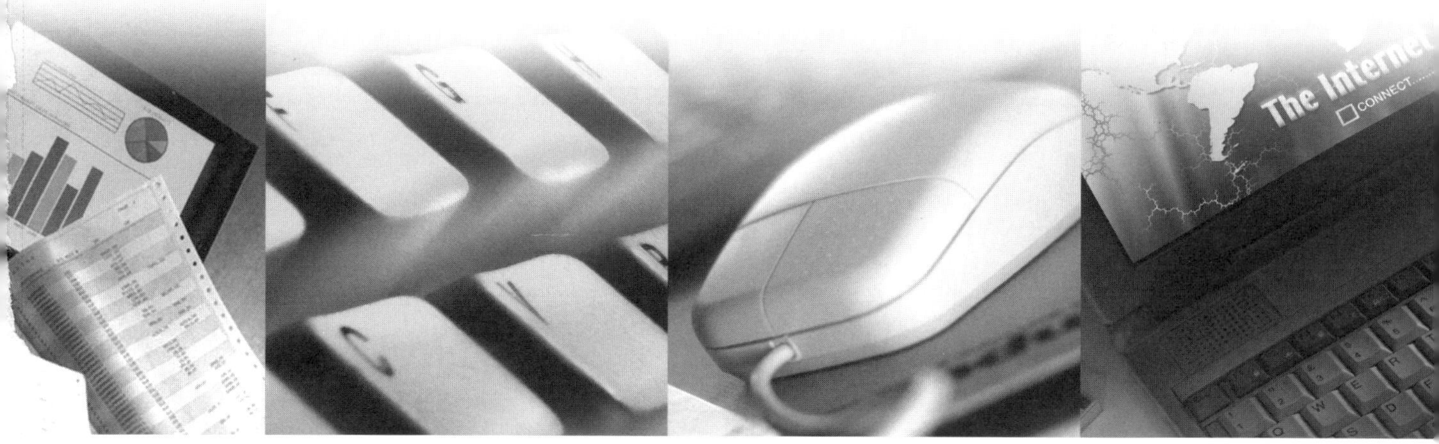

This card entitles the purchaser of a new textbook to a semester of access to the Educational Version of Standard & Poor's Market Insight®, a rich online resource featuring hundreds of the most-often researched companies in the Market Insight database.

For over 1000 Canadian, U.S., and international companies, this Web site provides you:

- Access to six years' worth of fundamental financial data from the renowned Standard & Poor's COMPUSTAT® database
- 12 Excel Analytics Reports, including annual and quarterly balance sheets, income statements, ratio reports, and cash flow statements; daily, weekly, and monthly adjusted price reports, and profitability; forecasted values and monthly valuation data reports
- Access to Financial Highlights Reports including key ratios
- S&P Stock Reports offering fundamental, quantitative, and technical analysis
- Industry Surveys, written by S & P's Equity analysts
- Charting, providing powerful, interactive JavaCharts with price and volume data, incorporating over 100 different technical studies, user-specific watch lists, easy-to-customize parameters and drawing tools. Delayed real-time pricing available.
- News feeds (updated hourly) for companies and industries

STANDARD
&POOR'S

McGraw-Hill Ryerson

See other side for your unique site ID access code.

Welcome to the Educational Version of Market Insight!

1. To get started, use your web browser to go to **www.mcgrawhill.ca/edumarketinsight**
2. Enter your site ID exactly as it appears below.
3. You may be prompted to enter the site ID for future use—please keep this card

Your site ID is: AD14Z616

If you purchased a used book, this site ID may have expired. For new password purchase, please go to **www.mcgrawhill.ca/edumarketinsight**. Password activation is good for a six month duration.

Fifth Canadian Edition

INVESTMENTS

ZVI BODIE
BOSTON UNIVERSITY

ALEX KANE
UNIVERSITY OF CALIFORNIA, SAN DIEGO

ALAN J. MARCUS
BOSTON COLLEGE

STYLIANOS PERRAKIS
JOHN MOLSON SCHOOL OF BUSINESS
CONCORDIA UNIVERSITY

PETER J. RYAN
UNIVERSITY OF OTTAWA

McGraw-Hill Ryerson

Toronto Montréal Boston Burr Ridge, IL Dubuque, IA Madison, WI New York San Francisco St. Louis Bangkok Bogotá Caracas Kuala Lumpur Lisbon London Madrid Mexico City Milan New Delhi Santiago Seoul Singapore Sydney Taipei

The McGraw·Hill Companies

McGraw-Hill Ryerson

Investments
Fifth Canadian Edition

ISBN: 0-07-089503-1

1 2 3 4 5 6 7 8 9 10 TCP 0 9 8 7 6 5

Executive Sponsoring Editor: Lynn Fisher
Developmental Editor: Daphne Scriabin
Senior Marketing Manager: Kelly Smyth
Senior National Sales Manager: Megan Farrell
Manager, Editorial Services: Kelly Dickson
Supervising Editor: Joanne Limebeer
Copy Editor: Rodney Rawlings
Senior Production Coordinator: Madeleine Harrington
Editorial Associate: Stephanie Hess
Page Layout: Lynda Powell
Cover Design: Sharon Lucas
Cover Photo: Charlie Newham/Alamy Images
Printer: Transcontinental Printing Group
Printed in Canada

National Library of Canada Cataloguing in Publication Data

Investments / Zvi Bodie ... [et al.]. — 5th Canadian ed.

Includes bibliographical references and index.
ISBN 0-07-089503-1

1. Investments—Textbooks. 2. Portfolio management—Textbooks.
I. Bodie, Zvi

HG4521.I548 2005 332.63'2 C2005-900179-8

ZVI BODIE

BOSTON UNIVERSITY

Zvi Bodie is professor of finance and economics at Boston University School of Management. He holds a Ph.D. from the Massachusetts Institute of Technology and has served on the finance faculty at Harvard Business School and MIT's Sloan School of Management. Professor Bodie has published widely on pension finance and investment strategy in leading professional journals. His books include *Worry-Free Investing: A Safe Approach to Achieving Your Lifetime Financial Goals* and *Foundations of Pension Finance.* Professor Bodie is a managing director of Integrated Finance Limited, a specialized investment bank and financial engineering company. He is also a member of the Advisory Board of the Pension Research Council.

ALEX KANE

UNIVERSITY OF CALIFORNIA, SAN DIEGO

Alex Kane is professor of finance and economics at the Graduate School of International Relations and Pacific Studies at the University of California, San Diego. He has been visiting professor at the Faculty of Economics, University of Tokyo; Graduate School of Business, Harvard; and Kennedy School of Government, Harvard; and a research associate at the National Bureau of Economic Research. An author of many articles in finance and management journals, Professor Kane's research is mainly in corporate finance, portfolio management, and capital markets, most recently in the measurement of market volatility and pricing of options.

ALAN J. MARCUS

BOSTON COLLEGE

Alan Marcus is professor of finance in the Wallace E. Carroll School of Management at Boston College. He received his Ph.D. in economics from MIT. Professor Marcus has been a visiting professor at the Athens Laboratory of Business Administration and at MIT's Sloan School of Management and has served as a research associate at the National Bureau of Economic Research. Professor Marcus has published widely in the fields of capital markets and portfolio management. His consulting work has ranged from new product development to provision of expert testimony in utility rate proceedings. He also spent two years at the Federal Home Loan Mortgage Corporation (Freddie Mac), where he developed models of mortgage pricing and credit risk. He currently serves on the Research Foundation Advisory Board of the CFA Institute.

STYLIANOS PERRAKIS

JOHN MOLSON SCHOOL OF BUSINESS
CONCORDIA UNIVERSITY

Stylianos Perrakis is Professor of Finance at the John Molson School of Business of Concordia University. He is the author of many articles published in leading academic and professional journals in economics and finance, especially in the areas of industrial organization, corporate finance, and option pricing. Professor Perrakis has served as a consultant to many private and governmental organizations, including the Institute of Canadian Bankers and the World Bank. He is also the author of *Canadian Industrial Organization* and has taught as a visiting professor in universities in Switzerland, France, and the United States.

PETER J. RYAN

UNIVERSITY OF OTTAWA

Peter Ryan is Professor of Finance at the University of Ottawa, School of Management. He received a Ph.D. in operations research from Stanford University. Professor Ryan's research interests include both contingent claims in general and the incentive effects of financial claims in corporate structures. His articles on the subject of options and financial instruments have been published in a number of international journals in finance and management science. He has recently been involved in developing the course material for the Canadian Securities Institute. Professor Ryan also serves as an expert witness on the execution of responsibilities by financial advisors.

CONTENTS IN BRIEF

Preface xiii

PART ONE
INTRODUCTION 1

1 The Investment Objective 2
2 Markets and Instruments 27
3 How Securities Are Traded 60
4 Mutual Funds and Institutional Environment 99

PART TWO
PORTFOLIO THEORY 143

5 Concepts and Issues: Return, Risk, and Risk Aversion 144
6 Portfolio Selection 194

PART THREE
EQUILIBRIUM IN CAPITAL MARKETS 251

7 The Capital Asset Pricing Model 252
8 Index Models and the Arbitrage Pricing Theory 284
9 Market Efficiency 322
10 Empirical Evidence on Security Returns 361

PART FOUR
FIXED-INCOME SECURITIES 391

11 Bond Prices and Yields 392
12 The Term Structure of Interest Rates 430
13 Managing Bond Portfolios 458

PART FIVE
EQUITIES 502

14 Security Analysis 503
15 Financial Statement Analysis 568
16 Technical Analysis 610

PART SIX
DERIVATIVE ASSETS 638

17 Options and Other Derivatives: Introduction 639
18 Option Valuation 683
19 Futures and Forward Markets 727

PART SEVEN
ACTIVE PORTFOLIO MANAGEMENT 779

20 Active Management and Performance Measurement 780
21 Portfolio Management Techniques 825
22 International Investing 853

APPENDIX A
Quantitative Review *Available on the Bodie Online Learning Centre at www. mcgrawhill.ca/college/bodie*

APPENDIX B
Solutions to Concept Checks *Available on the Bodie Online Learning Centre at www. mcgrawhill.ca/college/bodie*

Glossary 891
Name Index 904
Subject Index 906

CONTENTS

Preface xiii

PART ONE
INTRODUCTION 1

CHAPTER 1
THE INVESTMENT OBJECTIVE 2

1.1 A Short History of Investing 3
1.2 Investors and the Need for Capital 4
Real Investment Versus Financial Investment 6
The Sectors of the Economic System 7
Individuals and Financial Objectives 8
1.3 Financial Intermediaries and Innovation 10
Financial Intermediation 10
Investment Banking and Brokerage Services 11
Financial Engineering 12
1.4 Analysts, Auditors, and the Agency Problem 16
1.5 The Right Approach 21
Diversification 22
Information and Patience 23

CHAPTER 2
MARKETS AND INSTRUMENTS 27

2.1 The Money Market 28
Treasury Bills 28
Certificates of Deposit and Bearer Deposit Notes 29
Commercial Paper 29
Bankers' Acceptances 29
Eurodollars 30
Repos and Reverses 30
Brokers' Call Loans 30
The LIBOR Market 30
Yields on Money Market Instruments 31
2.2 The Fixed-Income Capital Market 33
Government of Canada Bonds 33
Provincial and Municipal Bonds 36
Corporate Bonds 36
Mortgages and Mortgage-Backed Securities 37
2.3 Equity Securities 39
Common Stock as Ownership Shares 39
Characteristics of Common Stock 40
Stock Market Listings 40
Preferred Stock 42
Income Trusts 42
2.4 Stock and Bond Market Indices 43
Stock Market Indices 43
Foreign and International Stock Market Indices 48
Bond Market Indicators 48
2.5 Derivative Markets 50
Options 50
Futures Contracts 52
Other Derivative Assets: Warrants, Swaps, and Hybrid Securities 54

CHAPTER 3
HOW SECURITIES ARE TRADED 60

3.1 How Firms Issue Securities 61
Investment Bankers 61
Short-Form Prospectus System 62
Initial Public Offerings 62
3.2 Where Securities Are Traded 66
The Secondary Markets 67
The Over-the-Counter Market 70
The Third and Fourth Markets 71
Foreign Markets 72
Derivatives Markets 73
3.3 Trading on Exchanges 73
The Participants 73
Types of Orders 74
The Execution of Trades 76
Block Sales 77
The SuperDOT System 77
Settlement 78
Trading on the OTC Market 78
3.4 Trading with Margin 79
Buying on Margin 80
Short Sales 82
3.5 Trading Costs 84
Internet Investing 87

3.6 Regulation of Securities Markets 88
Self-Regulation and Circuit Breakers 89
Insider Trading 91
Appendix 3A: Detailed Margin Position 97

CHAPTER 4
MUTUAL FUNDS AND THE INSTITUTIONAL ENVIRONMENT 99
4.1 Management by Institutions 100
Institutions and Their Objectives 100
Constraints 102
Unique Needs 103
4.2 Investment Companies 104
Other Investment Organizations 106
4.3 Mutual Funds 108
Investment Policies 110
Taxation of Mutual Fund Proceeds 112
Information on Mutual Funds 112
4.4 Costs of Investing in Mutual Funds 115
Fee Structure 115
Fees and Mutual Fund Returns 116
4.5 Mutual Fund Investment Performance 117
Persistence in Performance 119
Exchange-Traded Funds—Superior Performance 121
Appendix 4A: Taxation and Tax Sheltering 129
Appendix 4B: Pension Funds 137

PART TWO
PORTFOLIO THEORY 143

CHAPTER 5
CONCEPTS AND ISSUES: RETURN, RISK, AND RISK AVERSION 144
5.1 Determinants of the Level of Interest Rates 145
Real and Nominal Rates of Interest 146
The Equilibrium Real Rate of Interest 147
The Equilibrium Nominal Rate of Interest 148
Bills and Inflation, 1957–2003 148
Taxes and the Real Rate of Interest 149
5.2 Risk and Risk Premiums 149
5.3 The Historical Record 151
Bills, Bonds, and Stocks, 1957–2003 151
5.4 Real Versus Nominal Risk 156
5.5 Return Distributions and Value at Risk 157
5.6 A Global View of the Historical Record 159
5.7 Forecasts for the Long Haul 161
5.8 Risk and Risk Aversion 162
Risk with Simple Prospects 162
Risk, Speculation, and Gambling 163
Risk Aversion and Utility Values 164
5.9 Portfolio Risk 169
Asset Risk Versus Portfolio Risk 169
A Review of Portfolio Mathematics 169
Appendix 5A: Continuous Compounding 181
Appendix 5B: A Defence of Mean-Variance Analysis 183
Appendix 5C: Risk Aversion and Expected Utility 189

CHAPTER 6
PORTFOLIO SELECTION 194
6.1 Capital Allocation Across Risky and Risk-Free Portfolios 195
6.2 The Risk-Free Asset 198
6.3 Portfolios of One Risky Asset and One Risk-Free Asset 199
6.4 Risk Tolerance and Asset Allocation 203
6.5 Passive Strategies: The Capital Market Line 206
6.6 Diversification and Portfolio Risk 207
6.7 Portfolios of Two Risky Assets 209
6.8 Asset Allocation with Stocks, Bonds, and Bills 217
The Optimal Risky Portfolio with Two Risky Assets and a Risk-Free Asset 217
6.9 The Markowitz Portfolio Selection Model 222
Security Selection 222
6.10 A Spreadsheet Model 227
Calculation of Expected Return and Variance 227
Capital Allocation and Separation Property 231
Asset Allocation and Security Selection 232
6.11 Optimal Portfolios with Restrictions on the Risk-Free Asset 233
Appendix 6A: The Power of Diversification 246
Appendix 6B: The Insurance Principle: Risk-Sharing Versus Risk-Pooling 248

PART THREE
EQUILIBRIUM IN CAPITAL MARKETS 251

CHAPTER 7
THE CAPITAL ASSET PRICING MODEL 252

7.1 The Capital Asset Pricing Model 253
Why Do All Investors Hold the Market Portfolio? 254
The Passive Strategy Is Efficient 255
The Risk Premium of the Market Portfolio 256
Expected Returns on Individual Securities 256
The Security Market Line 260
7.2 Extensions of the CAPM 262
The CAPM with Restricted Borrowing: The Zero-Beta Model 262
Lifetime Consumption: The CAPM with Dynamic Programming 267
7.3 The CAPM and Liquidity: A Theory of Illiquidity Premiums 267
Appendix 7A: Demand for Stocks and Equilibrium Prices 279

CHAPTER 8
INDEX MODELS AND THE ARBITRAGE PRICING THEORY 284

8.1 A Single-Index Security Market 285
Systematic Risk Versus Firm-Specific Risk 285
Estimating the Index Model 288
The Index Model and Diversification 290
8.2 The Industry Version of the Index Model 293
Company Beta Estimates 293
8.3 Index Models and Tracking Portfolios 296
8.4 Multifactor Models 298
A Multifactor Security Market Line 299
8.5 Arbitrage Pricing Theory 301
Arbitrage, Risk Arbitrage, and Equilibrium 301
Well-Diversified Portfolios 302
Betas and Expected Returns 304
The Security Market Line 306
8.6 Individual Assets and the APT 307
The APT and the CAPM 307
8.7 A Multifactor APT 308
8.8 Where Should We Look for Factors? 310
8.9 A Multifactor CAPM 312

CHAPTER 9
MARKET EFFICIENCY 322

9.1 Random Walks and the Efficient Market Hypothesis 323
Competition as a Source of Efficiency 323
Versions of the Efficient Market Hypothesis 324
9.2 Implications of the EMH for Investment Policy 325
Technical Analysis 325
Fundamental Analysis 326
Active Versus Passive Portfolio Management 326
The Role of Portfolio Management in an Efficient Market 327
9.3 Event Studies 329
9.4 Are Markets Efficient? 333
The Issues 333
Weak-Form Tests: Patterns in Stock Returns 335
Semistrong Tests: Market Anomalies 338
Strong-Form Tests: Inside Information 342
Interpreting the Evidence 343
9.5 A Behavioural Interpretation 345
Information Processing 345
Behavioural Biases 347
Limits to Arbitrage 348
Evaluating the Behavioural Critique 348
9.6 Mutual Fund Performance 349
So Are Markets Efficient? 353

CHAPTER 10
EMPIRICAL EVIDENCE ON SECURITY RETURNS 361

10.1 The Index Model and the Single-Factor APT 362
The Expected Return–Beta Relationship 362
Tests of the CAPM 364
Estimating Index Models for Canadian Stocks 364
Thin Trading 365
The Market Index 366
Measurement Error in Beta 368
The EMH and the CAPM 371
Accounting for Human Capital and Cyclical Variations in Asset Betas 371
10.2 Tests of Multifactor CAPM and APT 373
A Macro Factor Model 373
10.3 The Fama-French Three-Factor Model 375

10.4 Time-Varying Volatility 378
10.5 The Equity Premium Puzzle 381
Expected Versus Realized Returns 382
Survivorship Bias 383
10.6 Survivorship Bias and Tests of Market Efficiency 384

PART FOUR
FIXED-INCOME SECURITIES 391

CHAPTER 11
BOND PRICES AND YIELDS 392
11.1 Bond Characteristics 393
Canada Bonds 393
Corporate Bonds 395
Preferred Stock 397
Other Issuers 397
International Bonds 397
Innovation in the Bond Market 398
11.2 Bond Pricing 399
Review of the Present Value Relationship 399
An Example: Bond Pricing 400
Bond Pricing Between Coupon Dates 403
11.3 Bond Yields 404
Yield to Maturity 404
Yield to Call 405
Realized Compound Yield Versus Yield to Maturity 407
11.4 Bond Prices over Time 408
Yield to Maturity Versus Holding Period Return 410
Zero-Coupon Bonds 410
After-Tax Returns 411
11.5 Default Risk 412
Junk Bonds 413
Determinants of Bond Safety 414
Bond Indentures 417
Yield to Maturity and Default Risk 419

CHAPTER 12
THE TERM STRUCTURE OF INTEREST RATES 430
12.1 The Term Structure Under Certainty 431
Bond Pricing 431
Bond Stripping and Pricing of Coupon Bonds 434
Holding-Period Returns 435
Forward Rates 436
12.2 Interest Rate Uncertainty and Forward Rates 437
12.3 Theories of the Term Structure 439
The Expectations Hypothesis 439
Liquidity Preference 440
12.4 Interpreting the Term Structure 440
12.5 Forward Rates as Forward Contracts 445
12.6 Measuring the Term Structure 447

CHAPTER 13
MANAGING BOND PORTFOLIOS 458
13.1 Interest Rate Risk 459
Interest Rate Sensitivity 459
Duration 462
13.2 Convexity 469
Why Do Investors Like Convexity? 471
Duration and Convexity of Callable Bonds 472
13.3 Passive Bond Management 474
Bond Index Funds 474
Immunization 475
Cash Flow Matching and Dedication 482
Other Problems and Conventional Immunization 483
13.4 Active Bond Management 484
Sources of Potential Profit 484
Horizon Analysis 486
Contingent Immunization 486
13.5 Interest Rate Swaps 488
13.6 Financial Engineering and Interest Rate Derivatives 490

PART FIVE
EQUITIES 502

CHAPTER 14
SECURITY ANALYSIS 503
14.1 Valuation by Comparables 504
The Balance Sheet Approach 505
Intrinsic Value Versus Market Price 507
14.2 Dividend Discount Models 508
Stock Prices and Investment Opportunities 509
Life Cycles and Multistage Growth Models 512

14.3 Earnings, Growth, and Price-Earnings Ratios 516
P/E Ratios and Stock Risk 520
Pitfalls in P/E Analysis 520
Combining P/E Analysis and the DDM 525
Other Comparative Valuation Ratios 526
14.4 Growth or Value Investing 527
The Graham Technique 528
14.5 Corporate Finance and the Free Cash Flow Approach 529
14.6 Inflation and Equity Valuation 531
14.7 Macroeconomic Analysis 534
The Global Economy 534
The Macro Economy 536
Demand and Supply Shocks and Government Policy 537
The Business Cycle 538
14.8 The Aggregate Stock Market 541
Explaining Past Behaviour 541
Forecasting the Stock Market 541
14.9 Industry Analysis 542
Defining an Industry 544
Sensitivity to the Business Cycle 545
Sector Rotation 547
Industry Life Cycles 548
Appendix 14A: Derivation of the Dividend Discount Model 564
Appendix 14B: Contingent Claims Approach to Equity Valuation 567

CHAPTER 15
FINANCIAL STATEMENT ANALYSIS 568
15.1 The Major Financial Statements 569
The Income Statement 569
The Balance Sheet 569
The Statement of Changes in Financial Position 571
15.2 Accounting Versus Economic Earnings 573
Analysts' Forecasts and Stock Returns 575
15.3 Return on Equity 577
Past Versus Future ROE 577
Financial Leverage and ROE 577
15.4 Ratio Analysis 580
Decomposition of ROE 580
Turnover and Other Asset Utilization Ratios 582
Liquidity and Coverage Ratios 583
Market Price Ratios 584
Choosing a Benchmark 586
15.5 Economic Value Added 588
15.6 An Illustration of Financial Statement Analysis 589
15.7 Comparability Problems 591
Inventory Valuation 591
Depreciation 592
Inflation and Interest Expense 592
Quality of Earnings 593
International Accounting Conventions 594
Limitations 597

CHAPTER 16
TECHNICAL ANALYSIS 610
16.1 Technical Analysis 611
16.2 Charting 613
The Dow Theory 613
Other Charting Techniques 616
A Warning 619
16.3 Technical Indicators 622
Sentiment Indicators 622
Flow of Funds 624
Market Structure 624
16.4 Technical Analysis for Canadian Investors 627
16.5 The Value Line System 629
16.6 Can Technical Analysis Work in Efficient Markets? 631
Self-Destructing Patterns 631
A New View of Technical Analysis 633

PART SIX
DERIVATIVE ASSETS 638

CHAPTER 17
OPTIONS AND OTHER DERIVATIVES: INTRODUCTION 639
17.1 The Option Contract 640
Options Trading 642
American and European Options 643
Adjustments in Option Contract Terms 643
The Option Clearing Corporation 645
Other Listed Options 646
17.2 Values of Options at Expiration 649
Call Options 649
Put Options 650
Options Versus Stock Investments 651

17.3 Option Strategies 653
Protective Put 653
Covered Call 655
Straddle 657
Spreads 658
Collars 660
17.4 The Put-Call Parity Relationship 660
17.5 Option-Like Securities 663
Callable Bonds 663
Convertible Securities 664
Warrants 666
Collateralized Loans 667
Levered Equity and Risky Debt 669
17.6 Financial Engineering 669
17.7 Exotic Options 671
Asian Options 671
Barrier Options 672
Lookback Options 672
Currency-Translated Options 673
Binary Options 673

CHAPTER 18
OPTION VALUATION 683
18.1 Option Valuation: Introduction 684
Intrinsic and Time Values 684
Determinants of Option Values 685
18.2 Restrictions on Option Values 686
Restrictions on the Value of a Call Option 687
Early Exercise and Dividends 688
Early Exercise of American Puts 689
18.3 Black-Scholes Option Valuation 690
Dividends and Call Option Valuation 695
Put Option Valuation 696
18.4 Using the Black-Scholes Formula 697
Hedge Ratios and the Black-Scholes Formula 697
Portfolio Insurance 699
Hedging Bets on Mispriced Options 702
18.5 Binomial Option Pricing 707
Two-State Option Pricing 707
Generalizing the Two-State Approach 710
18.6 Multinomial Option Pricing 714
Complete and Incomplete Markets 714
Generalizing the Binomial Option Pricing Model 715
18.7 Empirical Evidence 716

CHAPTER 19
FUTURES AND FORWARD MARKETS 727
19.1 The Futures Contract 728
The Basics of Futures Contracts 728
Existing Contracts 731
19.2 Mechanics of Trading in Futures Markets 733
The Clearinghouse and Open Interest 733
Marking to Market and the Margin Account 734
Cash Versus Actual Delivery 737
Regulations 737
Taxation 738
19.3 Futures Markets Strategies 738
Hedging and Speculating 738
Basis Risk and Hedging 740
Other Hedging Strategies 741
19.4 The Determination of Futures Prices 741
The Spot-Futures Parity Theorem 741
Spreads 744
Forward Versus Futures Pricing 745
19.5 Commodity Futures Pricing 746
Pricing with Storage Costs 746
Discounted Cash Flow Analysis for Commodity Futures 748
Futures Prices Versus Expected Spot Prices 751
Expectations Hypothesis 751
Normal Backwardation 752
Contango 752
Modern Portfolio Theory 752
19.6 Stock Index Futures 753
The Contracts 753
Creating Synthetic Stock Positions: An Asset Allocation Tool 753
Empirical Evidence on Pricing of Stock Index Futures 756
Index Arbitrage and the Triple Witching Hour 758
19.7 Foreign Exchange Futures 759
The Markets 759
Interest Rate Parity 760
19.8 Interest Rate Futures 763
The Markets 763
Hedging Interest Rate Risk 764
Other Interest Rate Futures 764
19.9 Swaps 765
Credit Risk in the Swap Market 768
Swap Variations 769

PART SEVEN
ACTIVE PORTFOLIO MANAGEMENT 779

CHAPTER 20
ACTIVE MANAGEMENT AND PERFORMANCE MEASUREMENT 780

20.1 The Objective of Active Management 781
Performance Measurement Under Active Management 783
20.2 Risk-Adjusted Performance Measures 786
Measuring Returns 786
Risk Adjustment Techniques 787
The M^2 Measure of Performance 789
Relationships Between the Measures 790
Sharpe's Measure as the Criterion for Overall Portfolios 791
Appropriate Performance Measures in Three Scenarios 792
Actual Performance Measurement: An Example 794
Realized Returns Versus Expected Returns 795
20.3 Alternatives to Mean-Variance Measures 797
Morningstar's Risk-Adjusted Rating 797
Style Analysis 798
Alternative Performance Measures 800
20.4 Market Timing 802
The Value of Imperfect Forecasting 804
Identifying Timing Ability 804
20.5 Performance Evaluation 806
Empirical Studies of Canadian Performance 808
Appendix 20A: Measuring Investment Returns 817
Appendix 20B: Option Pricing of Timing Ability 823

CHAPTER 21
PORTFOLIO MANAGEMENT TECHNIQUES 825

21.1 Indexing 826
21.2 Asset Allocation 827
21.3 Security Selection: The Treynor-Black Model 830
Overview of the Treynor-Black Model 830
Portfolio Construction 831
Imperfect Forecasts of Alpha Values 836
21.4 Hedging 838
Hedging Systematic Risk 838
Hedging Interest Rate Risk 840
21.5 Performance Attribution Procedures 842
Asset Allocation Decisions 844
Sector and Security Allocation Decisions 845
Summing Up Component Contributions 846
Appendix 21A: Multifactor Models and Active Portfolio Management 851

CHAPTER 22
INTERNATIONAL INVESTING 853

22.1 International Investments 854
The World Equity Portfolio 854
International Diversification 854
Market Capitalization and GDP 858
Techniques for Investing Internationally 859
22.2 Risk Issues in International Investing 862
Country-Specific Risk 863
Exchange Rate Risk 866
Using Futures to Manage Exchange Rate Risk 869
Diversification of Risk 871
22.3 Measurement of International Investing 876
Passive and Active International Investing 876
Factor Models and International Investing 879
Equilibrium in International Capital Markets 881
22.4 Integration with International Markets 882
Integration Versus Segmentation in Markets 882
Integration of Canadian and U.S. Markets 884

APPENDIX A
Quantitative Review *Available on the Bodie Online Learning Centre at www. mcgrawhill.ca/college/bodie*

APPENDIX B
Solutions to Concept Checks *Available on the Bodie Online Learning Centre at www.mcgrawhill.ca/college/bodie*

Glossary 891
Name Index 904
Subject Index 906

PREFACE

The first Canadian edition of this text was written fifteen years ago. The intervening years have been a period of rapid and profound change in the investments industry. This is due in part to an abundance of newly designed securities, in part to the creation of new trading strategies that would have been impossible without concurrent advances in computer technology, and in part to rapid advances in the theory of investments that have come out of the academic community. In no other field, perhaps, is the transmission of theory to real-world practice as rapid as is now commonplace in the financial industry. These developments place new burdens on practitioners and teachers of investments far beyond what was required only a short while ago.

Investments, Fifth Canadian Edition, is intended primarily as a textbook for courses in investment analysis. Our guiding principle has been to present the material in a framework that is organized by a central core of consistent fundamental principles. We make every attempt to strip away unnecessary mathematical and technical detail, and we have concentrated on providing the intuition that may guide students and practitioners as they confront new ideas and challenges in their professional lives.

This text will introduce you to major issues currently of concern to all investors. It can give you the skills to conduct a sophisticated assessment of current issues and debates covered by both the popular media as well as more specialized finance journals. Whether you plan to become an investment professional, or simply a sophisticated individual investor, you will find these skills essential.

Our primary goal is to present material of practical value, but all five of us are active researchers in the science of financial economics and find virtually all of the material in this book to be of great intellectual interest. Fortunately, we think, there is no contradiction in the field of investments between the pursuit of truth and the pursuit of money. Quite the opposite. The capital asset pricing model, the arbitrage pricing model, the efficient markets hypothesis, the option-pricing model, and the other centrepieces of modern financial research are as much intellectually satisfying subjects of scientific inquiry as they are of immense practical importance for the sophisticated investor.

In our effort to link theory to practice, we also have attempted to make our approach consistent with that of the Institute of Chartered Financial Analysts (ICFA), a subsidiary of the CFA Institute. In addition to fostering research in finance, the CFA and ICFA administer an education and certification program to candidates seeking the title of chartered financial analyst (CFA). The CFA curriculum represents the consensus of a committee of distinguished scholars and practitioners regarding the core of knowledge required by the investment professional.

There are many features of this text that make it consistent with and relevant to the CFA curriculum. The end-of-chapter problem sets contain questions from past CFA exams, and for students who will be taking the exam, each CFA question in the text and the exam from which it has been taken is listed at this book's Web site at www.mcgrawhill.ca/college/bodie. There are also topics covered in the Canadian Securities Course, given by the Canadian Securities Institute (CSI) as part of the Canadian certification process for financial professionals. Much of the material in the book parallels the content of more advanced courses designed and offered by the CSI to develop portfolio management skills.

Standard & Poor's questions have been added to the end-of-chapter material with a link available to the Web site. E-Investments exercises are now also included to help students find financial data on the Internet.

In the Fifth Edition, we have introduced a systematic collection of Excel spreadsheets that give students tools to explore concepts more deeply than was previously possible. These spreadsheets are available through the book's Web site at www.mcgrawhill.ca/college/bodie, and provide a taste of the sophisticated analytic tools available to professional investors.

UNDERLYING PHILOSOPHY

Of necessity, our text has evolved along with the financial markets. In the Fifth Canadian Edition, we address many of the changes in the investment environment.

At the same time, a few basic *principles* remain important. We believe that attention to these can simplify the study of otherwise difficult material and that they should organize and motivate all study. These principles are crucial to understanding the securities already traded in financial markets and in understanding new securities that will be introduced in the future. For this reason, we have made this book thematic, meaning we never offer rules of thumb without reference to the central tenets of the modern approach to finance.

The theme unifying this book is that *security markets are nearly efficient*, meaning most securities are usually priced appropriately given their risk and return attributes. Underlying this theme is perhaps the most fundamental principle in finance—that of the *single-price law*. This principle, alternatively known as *the Law of One Price*, insists that the same price must apply to any two financial instruments, or combinations of instruments, that offer identical payment streams. This leads to the notion of arbitrage and the avoidance of arbitrage that drives prices to their appropriate values. Arbitrage profits are popularly described as "free lunches," and there are few free lunches found in markets as competitive as the financial market. This simple observation is remarkably powerful in its implications for the design of investment strategies; as a result, our discussions of strategy are always guided by the implications of the efficient markets hypothesis. While the degree of market efficiency is, and always will be, a matter of debate, we hope our discussions throughout the book convey a good dose of healthy criticism concerning much conventional wisdom.

Distinctive Features

Investments is designed to emphasize several important aspects of making investment decisions.

The central principle is the existence of near-informational-efficiency of well-developed security markets such as ours, and the general awareness that competitive markets do not offer arbitrage opportunities or free lunches to participants.

A second aspect of investing is the risk-return tradeoff. This too is a no-free-lunch notion, holding that in competitive security markets, higher expected returns come only at a price: the need to bear greater investment risk. However, this notion leaves several questions unanswered. How should one measure the risk of an asset? What should be the quantitative tradeoff between risk (properly measured) and expected return? The approach we present to these issues is known as *modern portfolio theory (MPT)*. Modern portfolio theory focuses on the techniques and implications of *efficient diversification*, and we devote considerable attention to the effect of diversification on portfolio risk as well as the implications of efficient diversification for the proper measurement of risk and the risk-return relationship.

This text puts greater emphasis on asset allocation than most of its competitors. We prefer this emphasis for two important reasons. First, it corresponds to the procedure that most individuals actually follow. Typically, you start with all of your money in a bank account, only then considering how much to invest in something riskier that might offer a higher expected return. The logical step at this point is to consider other risky asset classes, such as stock, bonds, or real estate.

This is an asset allocation decision. Second, in most cases, the asset allocation choice is far more important in determining overall investment performance than is the set of security selection decisions. Asset allocation is the primary determinant of the risk-return profile of the investment portfolio, and so it deserves primary attention in a study of investment policy.

The text examines the evidence on market efficiency and uses the results to motivate the traditional forms of investment analysis used to identify superior investment opportunities. The dilemma of the apparent futility of conducting expensive analyses in the face of efficient markets is resolved by explaining the value of the analysis and the need for it to arrive at efficient pricing. The usual issues of pricing and portfolio management in the fixed-income arena and fundamental, statement and technical analysis of equities are supplemented by a broader and deeper treatment of derivative securities than offered by most investments texts. Markets for derivatives, including options, futures and more complex instruments, have become both crucial and integral to the financial universe and are the major sources of innovation in that universe. Your only choice is to become conversant in these markets—whether you are to be a finance professional or simply a sophisticated individual investor.

NEW IN THE FIFTH EDITION

All chapters have had various additions and deletions or rewriting of text in order to make the material both timely and efficiently presented. The major general change has been to identify and highlight specific examples in numbered Example sections. As well, new and updated material has been selected from other media to illustrate the concepts with practical examples or discussions. Specific changes include:

Chapter 2 contains revised descriptions of domestic and international indices, and a discussion of income trusts.

Chapter 4 has added material on hedge funds. The chapter reflects more of a focus on mutual funds, with new material added on exchange-traded funds (ETFs) and coverage of taxation moved to the appendix.

Chapter 5 has additional sections on value at risk using historic returns as a guideline, as well as on international comparisons of risk and return.

Chapter 8 has been largely rewritten, with a new section on tracking portfolios and an expanded treatment of multifactor models as a means to understand and measure various risk exposures.

Chapter 9 contains a much-expanded section on behavioural finance and its implications for security pricing, in which behavioural hypotheses have been linked to empirical evidence.

Chapter 10 has an updated and expanded discussion of the Fama-French three-factor model, with an emphasis on its size and value effects.

Chapter 11 contains new spreadsheet material helpful in analyzing bond prices and yields, which also allows students to price bonds between coupon dates.

Chapter 14 has substantially revised the treatment of industry analysis and enhanced the introduction to the fundamental valuation relationship in the first section.

Chapter 15 includes new material on quality of earnings; the sections on EVA and an illustration of the analysis process have been reorganized.

Chapter 16 enhances the description of the more recent charting techniques, as displayed by online charting services.

Chapter 18 contains an extended treatment of the binomial option pricing model in a multi-period context.

Chapter 20 provides more focus on alternative performance measures, now presented in a separate subsection.

Chapter 22 has received a substantial reorganization. The second section on risk issues has been expanded to include extensive new material on country/political risk, followed by material on exchange rate risk and hedging, and a new treatment of diversification and correlation.

ORGANIZATION AND CONTENT

This Canadian edition is both an adaptation of the U.S. text for a Canadian audience and an extension of the material to incorporate several topics of specific Canadian interest. The adaptation has changed the presentation and examples of the basic material with respect to currency, macroeconomic environment, tax rates and legislation, and other legal and institutional features of the Canadian economy. Substantial information about the U.S. institutions is included, as much of the investment activity by Canadian investors takes place in U.S. markets, implying that Canadian investment professionals cannot afford to ignore the situation south of their country's border. Not only does the U.S. market set the standards for most of the financial innovation and research in Canada, but it also paces many of the economic developments that underlie the performance of the Canadian financial system. Nevertheless, several Canadian financial aspects are unique and deserve more extended coverage in their theoretical and empirical aspects.

Part One: Introduction

The first four chapters motivate the study of investing and include a description of the markets, instruments, and institutions that are specific to the Canadian environment, as well as a summary description of the same concepts in the U.S. context. The material includes detailed descriptions of financial instruments and how to trade them in the markets. The fourth chapter is nominally an introduction to how individuals interact with institutions in the investment industry. It explains how consumption needs and taxes motivate investment choices, but its primary emphasis is on the most popular vehicle used by investors to participate in financial markets—the mutual fund. There is a detailed presentation of the mutual fund industry and its results in meeting investors' concerns, including tax consequences.

Parts Two & Three: Portfolio Theory & Equilibrium in Capital Markets

These together present the core of modern portfolio theory. Chapter 5 starts with a review of the historical returns to various classes of Canadian instruments and continues with an introduction to the risk-return tradeoff. The text then moves from the issue of capital allocation between cash and equities, through portfolio diversification, to the development of the capital market line in Chapter 6. The next two chapters treat the development of the CAPM and its extensions and alternative models, such as the arbitrage pricing theory. Then Chapter 9 addresses the issues of market efficiency, with evidence for and against it such as anomalies. Chapter 10 reviews empirical evidence on security returns, including tests of the CAPM and other studies in the context of market efficiency.

Part Four: Fixed-Income Securities

Part Four is the first of three parts on security valuation. This Part treats fixed-income securities—bond pricing (Chapter 14), term structure relationships (Chapter 15), and interest-rate risk management (Chapter 16). The next two Parts deal with equity securities and derivative securities. For a course emphasizing security analysis and excluding portfolio theory, one may proceed directly from Part One to Part Four with no loss in continuity.

Part Five: Equities

The three chapters of this Part are devoted to the popular forms of security analysis—fundamental, statement and technical. Fundamental analysis treats refinements of the dividend discount model as well as macroeconomic analysis, while statement analysis presents the traditional accounting approach to assessing value. Technical analysis includes only a brief and critical presentation of some popular techniques.

Part Six: Derivative Assets

Chapters 17 and 18 describe options, beginning with a description of the instruments, their payoffs, and the markets in which they trade, and then continuing to the details of models for valuation. Chapter 19 presents similar material for futures and forward contracts. Together these chapters describe how risk management can be achieved.

Part Seven: Active Portfolio Management

This section presents active management as an alternative to passive acceptance of efficient markets. It describes how to measure the performance of individuals and institutions who attempt to time markets or select portfolios, and how they can practise the techniques such as selective indexing, or inclusion of active portfolio components; finally, it addresses international investing as an added component of portfolios.

WALKTHROUGH

NEW AND ENHANCED PEDAGOGY

This book contains several features designed to make it easy for the student to understand, absorb, and apply the concepts and techniques presented.

Current Event Boxes

Short articles from business periodicals are included in boxes throughout the text. The articles are chosen for relevance, clarity of presentation, and consistency with good sense.

TORONTO EXCHANGE TO PHASE IN U.S. DOLLAR TRADING

TSX Group Inc. said on Monday it will allow U.S. dollar-denominated trading of certain stocks on the Toronto Stock Exchange as early as next month as it tries to grab a larger share of companies listed in both Canada and the United States.

TSX Group, which operates Canada's senior bourse and the junior TSX Venture Exchange, said it will start its U.S.-dollar book with 12 companies, adding it might expand the list by the Feb. 2 start date if enough demand exists.

The TSX said it surveyed broker-dealers and institutional investors to determine which companies to list first, and said it could eventually end up with 50 or more companies trading in U.S. dollars by the end of the year.

"Right now we've got way over 100 interlisted companies that trade on the TSX and on a U.S. marketplace, so that's sort of our primary target audience," said Rik Parkhill, senior vice-president at TSX Markets.

"We think that by making the foreign exchange process more transparent, that we'll make the market more efficient as

Angiotech Pharmaceuticals Inc., methanol producer Methanex Corp. and Wheaton River Minerals Ltd. round out the stocks that will be offered, identified by a ".U" after their trading symbol.

All 12 stocks are also listed on U.S. exchanges.

The TSX said it decided to offer the services after complaints about the specialist-based system on the New York Stock Exchange, which critics say is less efficient than electronic trading systems such as the TSX.

The NYSE is facing regulatory scrutiny over the system, under which auctioneers put up their own capital in order to reduce volatility, using a mix of manual and automated trades.

"On fast moving markets, if you're an institutional investor, that tends to be a fairly inefficient way to trade, and the price point that you thought you could get executed sometimes turns out not to be the case, because the specialist has held up that trade," said Rik Parkhill.

The TSX hopes it will be seen as a more palatable option to

Excel Applications

The Fifth Edition has expanded the boxes featuring Microsoft® Excel® spreadsheet applications. A sample spreadsheet is presented in the text with an interactive version and related questions available on the book Web site at www.mcgrawhill.ca/college/bodie.

EXCEL APPLICATIONS

BUYING ON MARGIN

The spreadsheet shown here can be used to measure the return on investment for buying stocks on margin. The model is set up to allow the holding period to vary. The model also calculates the price at which you would get a margin call based on a specified minimum (maintenance) margin and presents return analysis for a range of ending stock prices. Additional problems using this spreadsheet are available at www.mcgrawhill.ca/college/bodie.

	A	B	C	D	E
1					
2	Buying on Margin			Ending	Return on
3				St Price	Investment
4	Initial Equity Investment	10,000.00			−42.00%
5	Amount Borrowed	10,000.00		20	−122.00%
6	Initial Stock Price	50.00		25	−102.00%
7	Shares Purchased	400		30	−82.00%
8	Ending Stock Price	40.00		35	−62.00%

Concept Check

A unique feature of this book is the inclusion of Concept Checks in the body of the text. These self-test questions and problems enable the student to determine whether he or she has understood the preceding material. Detailed solutions are provided in Appendix B, which is available on the Online Learning Centre at www.mcgrawhill.ca/college/bodie.

CONCEPT CHECK

6. What would be the profit or loss per share of stock to an investor who bought the October 2004 maturity Bank of Nova Scotia call option with exercise price $72.50 on March 11, 2004, if the stock price at the expiration of the option was $75? What about a purchaser of the put option with the same maturity?

6. The payoff to the option is $2.5 per share at maturity. The option costs $1.5 per share. The dollar profit per share of stock is therefore $1. The exercise price of the put option with the same maturity is $70, so it expires worthless. Therefore the investor's loss is the cost of the put, or $3.50.

Examples

Separate called-out examples are integrated into the chapters.

EXAMPLE 3.2 Using Margin for Leverage

Let us suppose that an investor is bullish (optimistic) on Brascan stock, which is currently selling at $100 per share. The investor has $10,000 to invest and expects Brascan stock to go up in price by 30 percent during the next year. Ignoring any dividends, the expected rate of return would thus be 30 percent if the investor spent only $10,000 to buy 100 shares.

But now let us assume that the investor also borrows another $10,000 from the broker and invests it in Brascan also. The total investment in Brascan would thus be $20,000 (for 200 shares). Assuming an interest rate on the margin loan of 9 percent per year, what will be the investor's rate of return now (again ignoring dividends) if Brascan's stock does go up 30 percent by year's end?

The 200 shares will be worth $26,000. Paying off $10,900 of principal and interest on the margin loan leaves $15,100 ($26,000 – $10,900). The rate of return therefore will be

$$\frac{\$15,100 - \$10,000}{\$10,000} = 51\%$$

Summary and End-of-Chapter Problems

At the end of each chapter, a detailed Summary outlines the most important concepts presented. The Problems that follow the Summary progress from simple to challenging. Many of them are taken from CFA examinations and from the Canadian Securities Course, and represent the kinds of questions professionals in the field believe are relevant to the "real world"; they are indicated by an icon in the left margin.

SUMMARY

1. When discussing the principles of portfolio management, it is useful to distinguish seven clas of investors:
   a. Individual investors and personal trusts
   b. Mutual funds

CFA® PROBLEMS

27. According to the theory of arbitrage,
   a. High-beta stocks are consistently overpriced
   b. Low-beta stocks are consistently overpriced
   c. Positive alpha stocks will quickly disappear
   d. Rational investors will arbitrage consistent with their risk tolerance

CFA® PROBLEMS

28. A zero investment portfolio with a positive alpha could arise if
   a. The expected return of the portfolio equals zero

/college/bodi

CSI

The following questions are adapted from the Canadian Securities Course.

32. Which of the following statements regarding long-term debt is correct?
   a. Bonds are usually secured by real assets.
   b. Subordinated debentures rank behind some other long-term debt security.
   c. A collateral trust bond is usually secured by financial assets.
   d. A unit is a package of two or more corporate securities for sale at an overall price.

Internet Exercises: *E-Investments*

These exercises provide students with a structured set of steps to finding financial data on the Internet. Easy-to-follow instructions and questions are presented so students can utilize what they've learned in class in today's Web-driven world.

> **E-INVESTMENTS**
> **Security Prices and Returns**
>
> Go to **www.cbs.marketwatch.com**. What was the return on the S&P/TSX today? Chart its value over the last day and the last year. What is the current yield on 10-year maturity Treasury bonds? At what price is Nortel stock selling? Find the price of the nearest-to-maturity Nortel call option with exercise price equal to Nortel's stock price rounded down to the nearest $5. What was the return on the following indices: Nikkei 225, FTSE 100, DAX? (*Hint:* Use NT for US$ and CA:NT for C$.)

Standard & Poor's Problems

New to this edition! Relevant chapters contain problems directly incorporating the Educational Version of Market Insight, a service based on Standard & Poor's renowned COMPUSTAT® database. These problems provide you with an easy method of including current real-world data into your course.

> STANDARD &POOR'S
>
> Enter the Market Insight database at **www.mcgrawhill.ca/edumarketinsight** and click on *Educational Version of Market Insight*. After logging in, go to the *Company* tab, then click the *Population* button. Select a company of interest to you and go to the *Company Research* page with a menu of company information reports on the left. Select the *Company Profile* report and review the information provided. In what market is your company's stock traded? What is the stock ticker symbol? (Remember the ticker to access company information quickly on financial Web sites.) Finally, what is the industry classification of your company and its major competitors?

TECHNOLOGY SOLUTIONS

Online Learning Centre

More and more students are studying online. That is why we offer an Online Learning Centre (OLC) that follows *Investments* chapter by chapter. You do not have to build or maintain anything, and it is ready to go the moment you and your students type in this URL:

www.mcgrawhill.ca/college/bodie

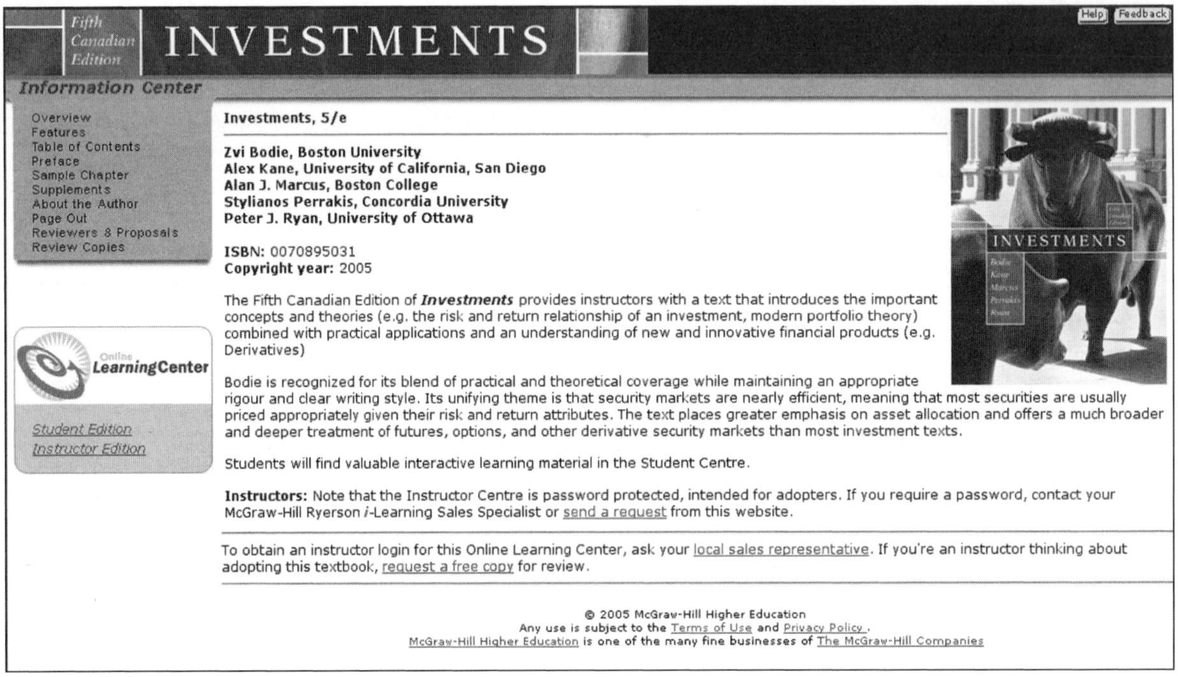

As your students study, they can refer to the OLC site for such benefits as:

- Online Quizzes
- *Globe and Mail* Newsfeeds
- Annotated Web Links
- Internet Exercises
- Finance Around the World
- Study To Go
- Excel Problems
- Excel Templates
- Chapter Overviews
- Glossary and Key Terms
- Chapter Summaries
- Appendix A (Quantitative Review)
- Appendix B (Solutions to Concept Checks)
- Link to Standard & Poor's Educational Version of Market Insight

Remember, the *Investments* OLC content is flexible enough to use with any course management platform currently available. If your department or school is already using a platform, we can help. For information on our course management services, contact your *i*Learning Sales Specialist, or see under "Superior Service" on page xxiv.

Classroom Performance System (CPS) by eInstruction

Bring interactivity into the classroom or lecture hall.

CPS, by eInstruction, is a student response system using wireless connectivity. It gives instructors and students immediate feedback from the entire class. The response pads are remotes that are easy to use and engage students.

- CPS helps you to **increase student preparation, interactivity, and active learning** so you can get immediate feedback and know what students understand.
- CPS allows you to **administer quizzes and tests**, and **provide immediate grading**.
- With CPS you can **create lecture questions** that can be multiple-choice, true/false, or subjective. You can even **create questions on the fly** and **conduct group activities**.
- CPS not only allows you to **evaluate classroom attendance, activity, and grading** for your course as a whole, but CPS Online allows you to **provide students with an immediate study guide**. All results and scores can easily be imported into Excel and can be used with various classroom management systems.

CPS-ready content is available for use with this text. Please contact your *i*Learning Sales Specialist for more information on how you can integrate CPS into your classroom.

Mobile Learning

Study To Go

The businesses and companies of today want their new employees to be adept in all aspects of the changing business environment. They are quick to tell us they want graduates with the skills of tomorrow … today. From laptops to cell phones to PDAs, the new medium is mobility.

As a leader in technology and innovation, McGraw-Hill Ryerson has developed material providing students with optimum flexibility for use anytime, anywhere they need to study—whether with a laptop, PDA, or tablet. These innovations provide instructors with a number of exciting ways to integrate technology into the learning process.

With **Study To Go** we have introduced wireless activities as a part of our Online Learning Centre. Now, whether you are waiting in line, riding on transit, or just filling some spare time, homework and practice are just a click away.

PowerWeb and PowerWeb To Go

Keeping your course current can be a job in itself, and now McGraw-Hill Ryerson can do it for you. **PowerWeb** extends the learning experience beyond the core textbook by offering all the latest news and developments pertinent to your course via the Internet, without all the clutter and dead links of a typical online search.

PowerWeb offers current articles related to investments, weekly updates with assessment tools, informative and timely world news culled by a finance expert, refereed Web links, and more. In addition, PowerWeb provides an array of helpful learning aids, including self-grading quizzes and interactive glossaries and exercises. Students may also access study tips, conduct online research, and learn about different career paths. Visit the PowerWeb site at **dushkin.com/powerweb** and see firsthand what PowerWeb can mean to your course.

PowerWeb To Go is a new McGraw-Hill content offering designed specifically for use on handheld devices. PowerWeb To Go content consists of current news stories, weekly updates, and magazine articles developed specifically for the study of investments. It is revised daily, giving you the most up-to-date, course-specific information available, and is easily loaded onto your Pocket PC or Palm OS handheld device. Visit the PowerWeb To Go site at **www.powerwebtogo.com** for information on how you can sign up today.

Course Management

McGraw-Hill Ryerson's course management system, **PageOut**, is the easiest way to create a Web site for your investments course. There is no need for HTML coding, graphic design, or a thick how-to book. Just fill in a series of boxes in plain English and click on one of our professional designs. In no time, your course is online!

For the integrated instructor, we offer *Investments* content for complete online courses. Whatever your needs, you can customize the *Investments* Online Learning Centre content and author your own online course materials. It is entirely up to you. You can offer online discussion and message boards that will complement your office hours and reduce the lines outside your door.

Content cartridges are also available for course management systems, such as **WebCT** and **Blackboard**. Ask your *i*Learning Sales Specialist for details.

SUPERIOR SERVICE

Service takes on a whole new meaning with McGraw-Hill Ryerson and *Investments*. More than just bringing you the textbook, we have consistently raised the bar in terms of innovation and educational research—both in finance and in education generally. These investments in learning and the education community have helped us understand the needs of students and educators across the country and allowed us to foster the growth of truly innovative, integrated learning.

Integrated Learning

Your Integrated Learning Sales Specialist is a McGraw-Hill Ryerson representative who has the experience, product knowledge, training, and support to help you assess and integrate any of the above-noted products, technology, and services into your course for optimum teaching and learning performance. Whether it's helping your students improve their grades or putting your entire course online, your *i*Learning Sales Specialist is there to help you do it. Contact your *i*Learning Sales Specialist today to learn how to maximize all of McGraw-Hill Ryerson's resources!

iLearning Services

McGraw-Hill Ryerson offers a unique *i*Services package designed for Canadian faculty. Our mission is to equip providers of higher education with superior tools and resources required for excellence in teaching.

For additional information, visit www.mcgrawhill.ca/highereducation/iservices.

Teaching, Technology & Learning Conference Series

The educational environment has changed tremendously in recent years, and McGraw-Hill Ryerson continues to be committed to helping you acquire the skills you need to succeed in this new milieu. Our innovative Teaching, Technology & Learning Conference Series brings faculty together from across Canada with 3M Teaching Excellence award winners to share teaching and learning best practices in a collaborative and stimulating environment. Preconference workshops on general topics, such as teaching large classes and technology integration, will also be offered. We can work with you at your own institution to customize workshops that best suit the needs of your faculty.

Research Reports into Mobile Learning and Student Success

We offer landmark reports, undertaken in conjunction with academic and private sector advisory boards, that are the result of research studies into the challenges professors face in helping students succeed and the opportunities new technology presents to impact teaching and learning.

COMPREHENSIVE TEACHING AND LEARNING PACKAGE

For the Instructor

Instructor Online Learning Centre (www.mcgrawhill.ca/college/bodie) The Online Learning Centre includes a password-protected Web site for instructors. The site contains downloadable instructor supplements; solutions to the Excel spreadsheets; and PageOut, the McGraw-Hill Ryerson course Web site development centre.

Instructor's CD-ROM including:

Instructor's Manual Each chapter includes the following, prepared by the authors and William Lim (York University): a chapter overview, a review of learning objectives, an annotated chapter outline, teaching tips and insights, and a detailed solution to each of the end-of-chapter problems.

Test Bank The Test Bank has been revised to increase the quantity and variety of questions. Short-answer essay questions are also provided for each chapter to further test student comprehension and critical thinking abilities.

Microsoft® PowerPoint® Presentation Software These presentation slides, updated by the authors, follow the order of the chapters.

For the Student

Student Online Learning Centre (www.mcgrawhill.ca/college/bodie), prepared by William Lim (York University), includes quiz material, Internet exercises, Web links, Study To Go, *Globe and Mail* Newsfeeds, a searchable glossary, Excel applications, Excel Problems, Appendix A (Quantitative Review), Appendix B (Solutions to Concept Checks), and a link to S&P's Educational Version of Market Insight©. There is also a link to Finance Around the World, a tremendous resource that takes students to important and popular finance Web sites throughout the world.

ONLINE RESOURCES

Educational Version of Standard & Poor's Market Insight

STANDARD &POOR'S

McGraw-Hill Ryerson and the Institutional Market Services division of Standard & Poor's is pleased to announce an exclusive partnership that, with each new textbook, offers instructors and students *free* access to the Educational Version of Standard & Poor's Market Insight, a rich online resource that provides six years of fundamental financial data for over 1,000 Canadian, U.S., and international companies in the database. S&P-specific problems can be found at the end of almost all chapters in this text. For more details, please see the bound-in card inside the front cover of this text, or visit **www.mcgrawhill.ca/edumarketinsight**.

ACKNOWLEDGMENTS

We Canadian authors first would like to express our gratitude to Professors Bodie, Kane, and Marcus for their continued improvement to what has been an outstanding text. Also, we appreciate their agreement to join in our production of a Canadian edition.

We would like to note, as well, the extensive contributions and comments of our Canadian reviewers; most of their suggestions were incorporated into the final draft, as they led to clarifications and more effective presentations. These reviewers were:

Ben Amoako-Adu, *Wilfrid Laurier University*
Abraham Brodt, *Concordia University*
Edward Blinder, *Ryerson University*
Alex Faseruk, *Memorial University*
Lawrence Gould, *University of Manitoba*
Kris Jacobs, *McGill University*
Eric Kirzner, *Rotman School of Management, University of Toronto*
Patrick Latham, *Northern Alberta Institute of Technology*
William Lim, *York University*
Allan Marshall, *York University, Atkinson*
David Pearce, *University of Alberta*
Helen Prankie, *Canadian Securities Institute*
Charles Schell, *University of Northern British Columbia*
Francis Tapon, *University of Guelph*
George Ye, *St. Mary's University*

For granting permission to include many of their examination questions in the text, we are grateful to the Institute of Chartered Financial Analysts and the Canadian Securities Institute. We are grateful also to Bogdan Campianu for his invaluable help in preparing the ancillary material for this edition. Much material and information was contributed by Melanie Moore of Scotia Capital. We are also grateful to BMO Nesbitt Burns for providing us with material on their beta estimates. Helen Prankie, of the Canadian Securities Institute, has been especially helpful with many technical details of Canadian markets, and in reviewing the revisions.

Many of the tables and graphs have been compiled from information provided through the cooperation of Statistics Canada. Readers wishing to obtain further information may contact Statistics Canada's Regional Offices, its World Wide Web site at www.statcan.ca, and its toll-free access number 1-800-263-1136. Much credit also is due to the development and production team at McGraw-Hill Ryerson: our special thanks go to Lynn Fisher, Executive Sponsoring Editor; Daphne Scriabin, Developmental Editor; Joanne Limebeer, Supervising Editor; and the rest of the development team.

Stylianos Perrakis
Peter J. Ryan

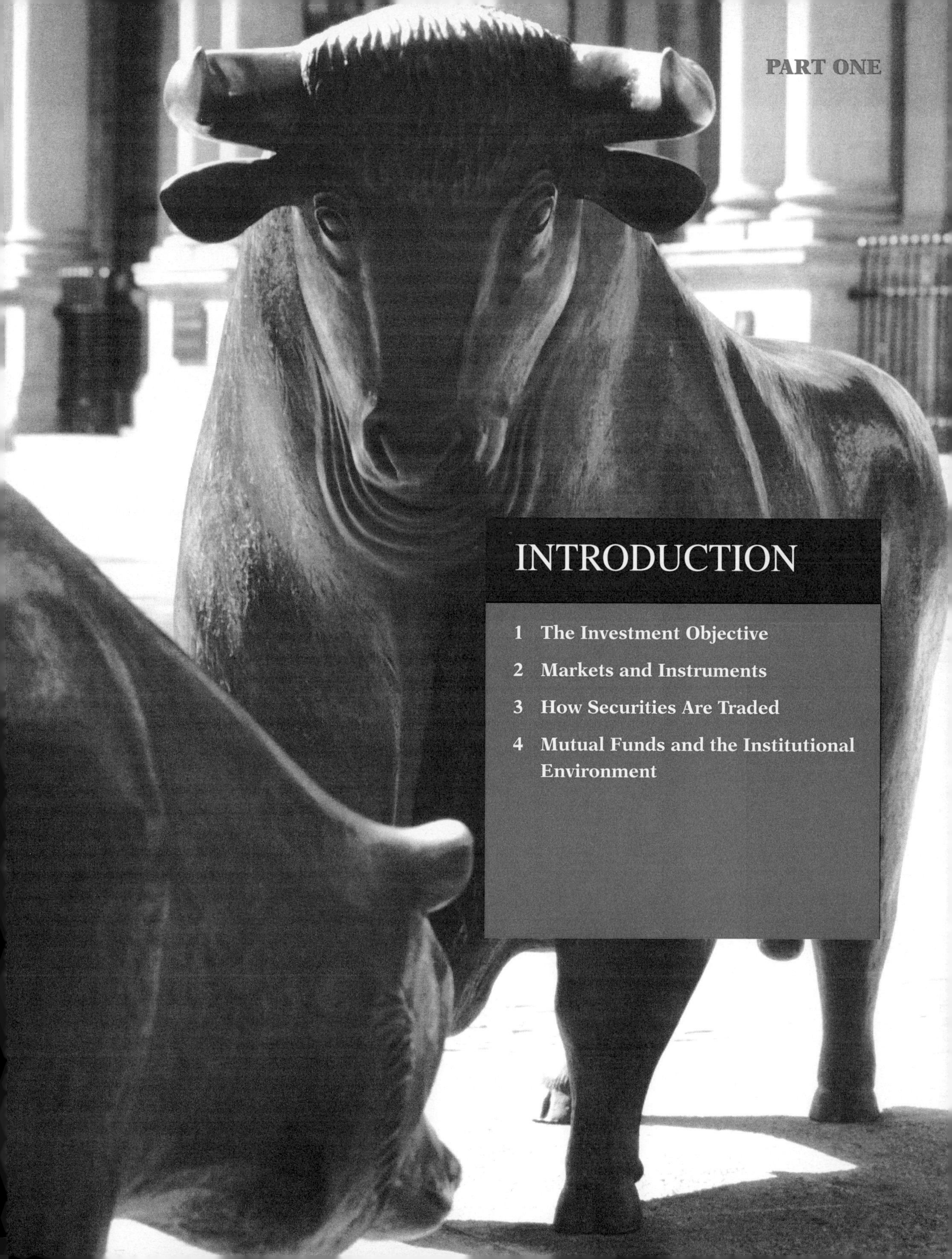

PART ONE

INTRODUCTION

1 The Investment Objective

2 Markets and Instruments

3 How Securities Are Traded

4 Mutual Funds and the Institutional Environment

CHAPTER ONE

THE INVESTMENT OBJECTIVE

The world of investing looks much like a jungle to the uninitiated—a dangerous and exotic place, and definitely unfamiliar territory. Competent and intelligent professionals from other fields such as medicine and law react to this prospect in a perfectly rational way; just as they are hired for their expertise, they expect to need a professional financial advisor to guide them around the pitfalls. With a thorough understanding of the concepts in this book, they would find themselves quite capable of an enlightened discussion with such an advisor. By contrast, a representative of the accounting or financial profession would be far less comfortable discussing a legal case or operating procedure with the benefit of a single text on law or medicine.

This chapter introduces the environment of investing. Capital investment, with its need for funds, gives rise to capital markets. Fortunately, individuals have excess funds and regularly provide them to institutions that require those funds. The process is complex and highly organized. Capital markets exist for a complex array of financial instruments that meet the precise needs of investors and users of capital; each of those instruments, starting with stocks and bonds, has evolved in response to those needs. We examine this system from all angles, the individuals and the institutions and their respective requirements, and the financial intermediaries which serve to bring the two together.

We begin with a short presentation of the turbulent history of North American markets. This is followed by an examination of the markets and their participants—the process of capital formation, the economic sectors that form the market, and individual investors and their investment-consumption patterns. After this, we describe the system of financial intermediaries and how these have created instruments responsive to the needs of the participants. Finally, we discuss how the market turbulence represents a failure of the financial system to fulfill its purpose—determining the value of financial assets through the sale and purchase of financial instruments.

1.1 A SHORT HISTORY OF INVESTING

Investing has been a priority for as long as individuals realized that current needs had to be balanced with future needs. Once society had progressed from a truly hand-to-mouth existence, food and other assets have been stored for later consumption. The creation of coinage as a means of exchange enabled individuals with surplus assets to store their wealth in a currency and transform it into an investment in assets of other varieties. Over the millennia, the economic system has developed to direct the surplus wealth of some individuals into needed areas of production.

By the twenty-first century, this evolution has culminated in a vast array of financial contracts made between individuals and institutions, each specifying how an initial investment will yield payment flows over a period of time. That period ranges from a day to eternity, even if neither party to the contract is likely to last very long. All of these contracts have evolved from more primitive forms that might have existed for centuries or more. The refinement of the contracts reflects the attempt to satisfy the specific needs of the one party requiring funds for a purpose and a time, and with a vision of when returns from the investment of those funds are likely to occur. On the other side, the investing party has needs for a specific pattern of payments for future consumption or for reinvestment in other contracts.

The fascination of the public with the investment world varies in intensity, with a general lack of interest in this poorly understood and not very newsworthy subject—except occasionally when stock market activity and results capture media attention. This was the case during the 1920s, as fortunes were rapidly made by supposedly brilliant investors; in those days, "elevator boys" and cab drivers overhearing the Wall Street financiers in their discussions participated in the public mania for investing. The result was a phenomenal rise in the stock market averages and the Crash of 1929, which appeared to precipitate the Great Depression.

Near the end of the century, the Crash of 1987 attracted universal interest by the one-day panic in the stock market. Unlike in 1929, however, no economic collapse followed. This may well have been due to more enlightened financial response by monetary officials; but the economic situation was markedly different. So was the financial environment, as 1987 turned out to be a neutral year for investors from January to December. Once out of the way, with confidence restored, the 1987 crash set the stage for the economic and financial boom of the 1990s.

The 1990s were also a period of public interest in the stock market, with nightly news reports on the levels of the market indices—the Dow and the TSX—on both television and radio. The last five years of the millennium witnessed another phenomenal rise in the markets, although the vast majority of this increase was confined to the technology arena. Small companies such as Dell Computer and Cisco Systems grew at incredible rates. The measurement of their sizes is a detail that needs to be examined. One measure is the value of sales, an indicator of the production of the company; another is the value of the share price and what we call the market capitalization, which indicate the investing public's appraisal of value of the current and future production and profits. The market capitalization of Dell grew by thousands of percentage points over the decade; such increases are relatively rare in history, though not unprecedented.

The problem with the rapid growth in share values in technology is that it spurred increasing attention by unsophisticated investors, individuals who had no experience with the stock market. Such individuals were seduced by the media attention revealing the fortunes that were being made so quickly, with results as high as 100 percent gains overnight. An indication of the media effect is that the U.S. financial news network CNBC apparently became the most watched program on television, outstripping all those soap operas, game shows, and sitcoms that used to be more entertaining.

The growth in the technology companies, measured globally by the value of the Nasdaq market index, was being described as a "bubble," a term used many times before in history to describe the unwarranted inflation in asset values. Inevitably bubbles are punctured, and the most naïve investors lose the most money in the collapse, as they enter the bubbling market long after the initial gains have been made, just in time to watch their capital evaporate in the relentless return to pre-bubble prices. In this case, however, even experienced investors insisted on staying in the market, afraid to lose the opportunity to participate in the gains. By the time the euphoria of the new millennium had ended, the Nasdaq and its most overpriced stocks began their decline and the acceptance that it had indeed been a bubble became universal. What was surprising to many was the extent of the collapse; even those predicting a return to more rational and defensible valuation were amazed by the declines in the shares of highly profitable companies, Nortel being a prime example. As the market fell, the debate switched to whether the good companies were now bargains or still overpriced; those with the latter view proved to be correct for over a year. In market parlance, the great "bull market" of the 1990s turned into the "bear market" of the new millennium. (See the extract from an interview with Burton Malkiel here for comments on the bubble and the difference between professional and individual investors.)

Beneath this general account of the market's behaviour lies a complex subject that must be examined closely, with a variety of issues that will be addressed in this book. The end of the twentieth century revealed a number of major mistakes by individual investors and by professionals, mistakes in the sense of their not following the precepts of investment analysis. This book will present the major concerns in investing, and how those concerns should be addressed. Much of it is theory and much is practice. Very often, the market will appear to contradict theoretical predictions, but over the long run most of the theory holds up well. Even if investors appear to ignore theory, if fortunes can be made by defying theory, and, worse yet, if some theories might prove to be inaccurate, it is essential to understand them. Much of professional practice pays more than lip service to the theoretical results of academic research. Careers in finance require familiarity with the theories, if only to realize how and when they are not being followed.

1.2 INVESTORS AND THE NEED FOR CAPITAL

Many naïve observers of the market can observe that professionals and individuals appear to be buying and selling shares in major corporations whose names are familiar as producers of common items or providers of services. They may then presume that every time such a trade occurs, these shares are sold or bought by those same corporations. If they followed this line of thought further, they might realize the enormity of such a process and then begin to understand why something quite different is happening.

When investors buy or sell stocks they are rarely trading with the company that issued the shares. Instead the trade is made with another investor, one who has an opposite idea of what the value of the company is—buyers think value is higher than the share price, and sellers think the opposite. The price in the market is crucial to establishing a fair market valuation of the shares. This ultimately becomes relevant to the corporation when it needs to issue new shares at a fair price, which only occurs when it requires new capital. The company itself is fairly remote from the trading, its interest lying only in what the trade price says about investor sentiment for its perceived financial prospects. The company gets involved in trading its own shares only when it makes an issue of stock to the public in order to raise capital, or when, having excess capital, it might decide to repurchase its own shares.

Shares in companies exist because those companies need capital in order to expand and purchase physical assets. Companies must raise this capital from the investing public because they do not have sufficient funds to make all the investments in plant and equipment required for their growth. Investors have this capital because, in general, individuals have more funds than required by immediate needs; they can and wish to postpone their current consumption to save and build capital for later consumption.

A RANDOM TALK WITH BURTON MALKIEL

How Will the Technology Bubble Be Remembered?

Historians will record the Internet bubble of the late 1990s as one of the greatest bubbles of all time. Valuations became truly unbelievable. During the Nifty Fifty craze, the well-known growth stocks may have sold at 60-, 70- or even 80-times earnings. During the Internet bubble, stocks would sell at 60-, 70- or 80-times sales. Priceline.com, one of the Internet companies that sold discounted airline tickets, was valued at one time with a market capitalization that was larger than the combined market capitalizations of Delta Airlines, American Airlines and United Airlines. At its low, Priceline sold for about a dollar a share. You even had enormous multi-billion dollar capitalizations from companies that had essentially no sales at all. They were just selling on a promise.

People confused the correct idea that the Internet was real, that it was going to mean some profound changes in the way we live and shop and get information, to saying that the ordinary rules of valuation didn't apply. Whatever business you are in, an asset can only be worth the present value of the cash flows that are going to be generated in the future.

Look at reports that were issued by Wall Street firms. You find statements such as "the old metrics are different this time." That has certainly proved to be wrong. Most of these Internet stocks today are selling at a tiny fraction of their high market valuations. It is not clear that any of them have a business model that is going to allow them to make money. In one sense, Amazon.com is a very successful company. But they have yet to show that they are able to make any money.

To be sure, the same thing happened in our past history. There were many people who laid railroad tracks during the railroad-ization of North America. There was overbuilding and most of them collapsed. We had hundreds of automobile manufacturers at one time.

But what didn't happen in the past were the market valuations assigned to these companies. Why did firms like Morgan Stanley and Merrill Lynch put out buy recommendations on all of these stocks when they were at or near their peaks? The real problem is that their well-known analysts were paid a lot of money, not necessarily to make correct judgments about whether stocks were good buys or not, but rather based on their success in bringing investment banking clients into the firm. Who knows whether they knew better or not? But there was a clear conflict of interest.

Here's another thing—the CNBC effect. You had people talking about these extraordinary gains, and [producers] didn't want a fuddy duddy value manager being interviewed on CNBC. [They] wanted the person who said Amazon.com has a price target of $500 a share. Those were the people who got on those shows. That fed the public enthusiasm. There were some people who got it right. They were generally the value managers who actually underperformed the market as a whole very badly during that period.

How Did Institutional Investors Compare to Retail Investors?

The retail investors probably did a bit worse. Some of the institutional investors were sucked up in the enthusiasm and probably did overweight some of these stocks. But I think the real damage occurred with individual investors. It really worries me how sensitive the public money flows are to recent performance.

Having said that, everyone is ranked each quarter in the institutional business versus everyone else. The institutions—not quite to the extent that the public is—are not immune at all. Presumably the savvy institutions should be precisely the ones who lean against the wind. But if you look at the cash balances of mutual fund managers and institutional money managers, you find almost invariably their lowest cash balances are just at the peak of the market. They're almost perfect contrarian indicators.

I can remember arguments that I had with institutional investors in 1999, when I'd talk about the Pricelines of the world. People would say "You don't understand the value of the first mover. What a brilliant idea Priceline has. Don't worry that they're losing money now." Very clearly, there is soul searching to be done by the institutions.

Source: Interview by Kevin Press, *CIR* 14, no. 2 (Summer 2001), pp. 23–24+.

In order to obtain capital, those with a deficit must issue securities, which are bought by those with excess funds. The types of securities or financial instruments involved will be defined formally in the following chapter, but we can begin by talking about stocks and bonds, issued by private corporations. Bonds are notes that acknowledge indebtedness and specify the terms of repayment; stocks are instruments that convey ownership rights to their holders, with no guarantee of any fixed, or even positive, return. Stocks enable investors to participate in business activities while being protected from the major drawbacks of individual ownership or partnership; they are relatively liquid, enabling the investor to extract the true value of the shares fairly quickly, and they offer limited liability, so that the greatest loss to be suffered is the investment itself, in the case of a catastrophe in the business.

Real Investment Versus Financial Investment

The investment by individuals in stocks and bonds of corporations is identified as **financial investment**. For the most part, this occurs as investors enter the securities markets and exchange cash for the financial instruments. Since the cash is exchanged between investors and no new capital reaches the corporations, no **real investment** occurs as a result of this activity. Real investment only occurs when a corporation takes capital and invests it in productive assets; this may come about as a result of reinvested profits, but major real investment requires the issuance of new debt or equity instruments.

Real investment is channelled into **real assets**, which determine the productive capacity of the economy. These real assets are the land, buildings, and machines, even the knowledge, necessary to produce goods, together with the workers and their skills in operating those resources. In contrast to real assets are **financial assets**, such as stocks or bonds. These assets, per se, do not represent a society's wealth. For example, shares of stock represent only ownership rights to assets; they do not directly contribute to the productive capacity of the economy. Financial assets instead contribute to the productive capacity of the economy *indirectly*, because they allow for separation of the ownership and management of the firm and facilitate the transfer of funds to enterprises with attractive investment opportunities. Financial assets certainly contribute to the wealth of the individuals or firms holding them, because they are claims on the income generated by real assets or on income from the government.

When the real assets used by a firm ultimately generate income, that income is allocated to investors according to their ownership of financial assets, or securities, issued by the firm. Bondholders, for example, are entitled to a flow of income based on the interest rate and par value of the bond. Equity holders or stockholders are entitled to any residual income after bondholders and other creditors are paid. In this way the values of financial assets are derived from and depend on the values of the underlying real assets of the firm.

Real assets are income-generating assets, whereas financial assets define the allocation of income or wealth among investors. Individuals can choose between consuming their current endowments of wealth today and investing for the future. When they invest for the future, they may choose to hold financial assets. The money a firm receives when it issues securities (sells them to investors) is used to purchase real assets. Ultimately, then, the returns on a financial asset come from the income produced by the real assets financed by the issuance of the security. In this way, it is useful to view financial assets as the means by which individuals hold their claims on real assets in well-developed economies. Most of us cannot personally own a bank, but we can hold shares of the Royal Bank or the Bank of Nova Scotia, which provide us with income derived from providing banking services.

An operational distinction between real and financial assets involves the balance sheets of individuals and firms in the economy. Real assets appear only on the asset side of the balance sheet. In contrast, financial assets always appear on both sides of balance sheets. Your financial claim on a firm is an asset for you, but the firm's issuance of that claim is the firm's liability. When we aggregate over all balance sheets, financial assets will cancel out, leaving only the sum of real assets as the net wealth of the aggregate economy. Another way of distinguishing between financial and real assets is to note that financial assets are created and destroyed in the ordinary course of doing business. For example, when a loan is paid off, both the creditor's claim (a financial asset) and the debtor's obligation (a financial liability) cease to exist. In contrast, real assets are destroyed only by accident or by wearing out over time.

CONCEPT CHECK

1. Are the following assets real or financial?
   a. Patents
   b. Lease obligations
   c. Customer goodwill
   d. A university education
   e. A $5 bill

CONCEPT CHECK

2. Explain how a car loan from a bank creates both financial assets and financial liabilities.

The Sectors of the Economic System

The distinction between the providers and users of capital is characterized in economics by defining three sectors in the economy: household, corporate, and government. (One can also consider the fairly important roles played by not-for-profit organizations and by the foreign sector in a trading nation such as Canada.) Because of its particular needs for the timing of cash flows, each sector requires a different mix of financial assets.

Households, with their surplus of funds, are potentially interested in a wide array of assets, and the assets that are attractive can vary considerably depending on each household's economic situation. Even a limited consideration of taxes and risk preferences can lead to widely varying asset demands.

Taxes lead to varying asset demands because people in different tax brackets "transform" before-tax income into after-tax income at different rates. For example, income from dividends and capital gains is taxed at a lower rate than interest income. High-tax-bracket investors will naturally seek securities that generate income from capital gains and dividends, in contrast with low-tax-bracket investors, who may prefer fully taxable interest-bearing instruments. A desire to minimize taxes also leads to demand for portfolios of such securities. In other words, differential tax status creates "tax clienteles" that in turn give rise to demand for a range of assets with a variety of tax implications.

Risk considerations also create demand for a diverse set of investment alternatives. Differences in risk tolerance create demand for assets with a range of risk and return levels. Investment demands are also determined by individual hedging requirements, that is, needs to offset particular risks. For example, a resident of Toronto planning to retire in Vancouver in 15 years might search for instruments whose values are tied to real estate valuation in Vancouver. A real estate limited partnership, as described in Chapter 4, with a portfolio based in British Columbia, might serve that end.

Aversion to risk also leads to demand for ways that investors can easily diversify their portfolios and even out their risk exposure. We will see that these diversification motives inevitably give rise to mutual funds, which are discussed in Chapter 4; these offer small individual investors the ability to invest in a wide range of stocks, bonds, precious metals, and virtually all other financial instruments.

Whereas household financial decisions are concerned with how to invest money, businesses typically need to raise money to finance their investments in real assets: plant, equipment, technological know-how, and so forth. Broadly speaking, there are two ways for private businesses to raise money—they can borrow it, either from banks or directly from households by issuing bonds, or they can "take in new partners" by issuing stocks, which are ownership shares in the firm.

Businesses issuing securities to the public have several objectives. First, they want to get the best price possible for their securities. Second, they want to market the issues to the public at the lowest possible cost. Hence, businesses might want to farm out the marketing of their securities to firms that specialize in such security issuance, because it is unlikely that any single firm is in the market often enough to justify a full-time security issuance division. The process of issuing securities requires immense effort. The security issue must be brought to the attention of the public. Buyers then must subscribe to the issue, and records of subscriptions and deposits must be kept. The allocation of the security to each buyer must be determined, and subscribers finally must exchange money for the securities. These activities clearly call for specialists. The complexities of security issuance have been the catalyst for creation of an investment banking industry catering to business demands. The lowest-cost securities to issue are simple instruments that may not match the household sector's demand; transforming simple instruments to match householders' needs is the role of yet other financial intermediaries.

Like businesses, governments often need to finance their expenditures by borrowing. Unlike businesses, governments cannot sell equity shares; they are restricted to borrowing to raise funds when tax revenues are not sufficient to cover expenditures. The federal government can also print money, of course, but this source of funds is limited by its inflationary implications, and so most national governments usually try to avoid excessive use of the printing press.

Governments have a special advantage in borrowing money because their taxing power makes them very creditworthy and therefore able to borrow at the lowest rates. The federal government has special powers not available to the other levels, through its control over the Bank of Canada. The latter is the main institution responsible for Canada's monetary policy. This policy is a major determinant of Canada's economic performance, including output growth, price level, and interest rates.

Bank of Canada www.bankofcanada.ca

A second, special role of the government is to regulate the financial environment. This is fulfilled in Canada by both federal and provincial governments, resulting in a fragmented regulatory system. Since trading in Canadian financial markets often transcends interprovincial borders, the fragmentation of the regulatory system has at times created inefficiencies and problems of law enforcement.

Some government regulations are relatively innocuous. For example, the Ontario Securities Commission is responsible for **disclosure** laws that are designed to enforce truthfulness in various financial transactions that take place in that province. Other types of government intervention in the financial markets, however, have been more controversial. For instance, both federal and provincial governments have instituted programs to encourage investment in certain sectors. Programs to stimulate resource development, research, and small business creation (as in Ontario and Quebec) have led to inefficient investment, as the focus on tax reduction has overshadowed the need for determining good investment prospects.

Individuals and Financial Objectives

The reader of a book on investments presumably has a good idea of what the objective of investing is—making a return on capital. This broad statement, however, encompasses a range of possibilities for the kind of return expected, from a safe, guaranteed percentage each year to a chance at a quick and large profit. (In the investment world, phrases such as *preservation of capital* and *speculation* may be used to describe these objectives.) Different kinds of investors will be attracted to strategies from the very conservative to the very risky, and at times to combinations of them, on the basis of their future needs. How much, how safely, and how quickly they want their return on capital, together with their personal tolerances for risk, will dictate the kinds of investments they are likely to make at different stages of their lives.

Investment choices must be linked directly to the question of the timing of consumption. An investor chooses to exchange current consumption for later wealth available for future consumption. This reflects current needs and the anticipation of future needs. In theory, the choice will be made so as to maximize the utility for consumption over the investor's lifetime. The choice also must respect the risk posed by certain types of investments and its effect on necessary consumption in the near future.

Investors are a very diverse group. Some of them are content with a fixed return if the principal is guaranteed; these investors usually place funds in a savings account. Others are looking for opportunities to double their investment in a matter of days. Neither of these extremes is of much interest to the subject of this book; some might label these individuals as "hoarders" or "speculators" rather than investors. There is a place, however, for both of these behaviours within the overall investment plan of an investor, provided this is part of a portfolio of investments. At times, cash may rightfully be hoarded in some safe form with virtually no return, while highly risky (speculative) investments offering extravagant returns can also be justified in other circumstances.

The first significant investment decision for most individuals concerns education, building up their human capital. The major asset most people have during their early working years is the earning power that draws on their human capital. In these circumstances, the risk of illness or injury is far greater than the risk associated with their financial wealth. The most direct way of hedging human capital risk is to purchase insurance. Life insurance is a hedge against the complete loss of income as a result of the death of any of the family's income earners. Insurance is not limited to covering loss of life and income, however; besides insuring personal assets and health, insurance can be used to accumulate retirement savings and to do so in a way that has tax benefits.

The first major economic asset acquired by most people is a personal residence. This is a financial investment that requires an evaluation of potential appreciation in residential values in the light of rental expense. When we consider real estate investment as a diversifying alternative, it is important to recognize the degree of direct exposure from a personal residence; in many cases, a personal portfolio may be over-weighted in real estate.

The risk in this area is correlated to risk in human capital. Individuals are first exposed to the risk of a downturn in their employer's industry or factors affecting the firm itself. Should the individual lose his or her job, the necessity of moving, with associated expenses and the risk of housing prices, presents itself. Hence, the investment portfolio should attempt to diversify away from the industry sector and real estate, if the latter is over-weighted.

Other personal assets also can be considered. Art, jewellery, and cars may represent possibilities to individuals. Because of the illiquidity of these assets, however, investment should only be made if there is also a great degree of personal satisfaction associated with the objects.

People save and invest money to provide for future consumption and leave an estate. The primary aim of lifetime savings is to allow maintenance of the customary standard of living after retirement. Life expectancy, when one makes it to retirement at age 65, approaches 85 years, so the average retiree needs to prepare a 20-year nest egg and sufficient savings to cover unexpected health-care costs. Investment income also may increase the welfare of one's heirs, favourite charity, or both.

The consumption enabled by investment income depends on the degree of risk the household is willing to take with its investment portfolio. Empirical observation summarized in Table 1.1 indicates how a person's age and stage in the life cycle affects attitude toward risk. The evidence in the table supports the life-cycle view of investment behaviour. Questionnaires suggest that attitudes shift away from risk tolerance and toward risk aversion as investors near retirement age.

Table 1.1 Amount of Risk That Investors Said They Were Willing to Take (by age)

	Under 35	35–54	55 and Over
No risk	54%	57%	71%
A little risk	30	30	21
Some risk	14	13	8
A lot of risk	2	1	1

Source: *Market Facts, Inc.*, Chicago, IL. Reprinted by permission.

With age, individuals lose the potential to recover from a disastrous investment performance. When they are young, investors can respond to a loss by working harder and saving more of their income. But as retirement approaches, investors realize there will be less time to recover; hence the shift to safe assets.

CONCEPT CHECK

3. *a.* Think about the financial circumstances of your closest relative in your parents' generation (preferably your parents' household, if you are fortunate enough to have them around). Write down the objectives and constraints for their investment decisions.
   b. Now consider the financial situation of your closest relative who is in his or her 30s. Write down the objectives and constraints that would fit his or her investment decision.
   c. How much of the difference between the two statements is due to the age of the investors?

1.3 FINANCIAL INTERMEDIARIES AND INNOVATION

When enough clients demand and are willing to pay for a service, it is likely in a capitalistic economy that a profit-seeking supplier will find a way to provide and charge for that service. This is the mechanism that leads to the diversity of financial markets. Let us consider the market responses to the disparate demands of the three sectors.

Financial Intermediation

Direct investment in businesses that need to finance real investments is intrinsically difficult for most households, small as they are. Thus **financial intermediaries**, such as banks, have naturally evolved to bring the two sectors together. Financial intermediaries sell their own liabilities to raise funds that are used to purchase liabilities of other corporations. For example, a bank raises funds by taking in deposits and lending that money to other borrowers. The spread between the rates paid to depositors and the rates charged to borrowers is the source of the bank's profit, earned as a reward for the convenience and cost savings that it provides both types of clients. The problem of matching lenders with borrowers is solved when each comes independently to the common intermediary. Thus, the problem of coordination creates a market niche for the bank as an intermediary.

Other examples of financial intermediaries are investment companies, insurance companies, and credit unions. All these firms offer similar advantages, in addition to playing a middleman role. First, by pooling the resources of many small investors, they are able to lend considerable sums to large borrowers. Second, by lending to many borrowers, intermediaries achieve significant diversification, meaning they can accept loans that individually might be risky. Third, intermediaries build expertise through the volume of business they do. One individual trying to borrow or lend directly would have much less specialized knowledge of how to structure and execute the transaction with another party.

Economies of scale give rise to **mutual funds**, as most household portfolios are not large enough to be spread over a wide variety of securities. It is very expensive in terms of brokerage fees to purchase one or two shares of many different firms, and it is clearly more economical for stocks and bonds to be purchased and sold in large blocks.

Scale economies also explain the proliferation of analytic services available to investors. Newsletters, databases, and brokerage house research services all exploit the fact that the expense of collecting information is best borne by having a few agents engage in research to be sold to a large client base. This setup arises naturally. Investors clearly want information, but with only small portfolios to manage, it is not economical to incur the expense of collecting it. Hence, a profit opportunity emerges: a firm can perform this service for many clients and charge for it.

Investment Banking and Brokerage Services

Economies of scale and specialization also create profit opportunities for firms that offer services to businesses. We said before that firms raise much of their capital by selling securities such as stocks and bonds to the public. Because these firms do not do so frequently, however, investment banking firms that specialize in such activities are able to offer their services at a cost below that of running an in-house security issuance division.

Investment bankers—or, as they are known in Canada, **investment dealers**—such as Scotia Capital, RBC Investments, or BMO Nesbitt Burns, advise the issuing firm on the prices it can charge for the securities issued, market conditions, appropriate interest rates, and so forth. Ultimately, the investment dealer handles the marketing of the security issue to the public.

Investment bankers can provide more than just expertise to security issuers. Because investment bankers are constantly in the market, assisting one firm or another to issue securities, it is in the banker's interest to protect and maintain its reputation for honesty. The investment banker will suffer along with investors if it turns out that securities it has underwritten have been marketed to the public with overly optimistic or exaggerated claims, for the public will not be so trusting the next time that investment banker participates in a security sale. As we have seen, this lesson was relearned with considerable pain in the boom years of the late 1990s and the subsequent high-tech crash of 2000–2002. Too many investment bankers seemed to get caught up in the flood of money that could be made by pushing stock issues to an overly eager public. The failure of many of these offerings soured the public on both the stock market and the firms managing the IPOs. At least some on Bay Street belatedly recognize that they squandered a valuable asset—reputational capital—and there are signs that they recognize as well that the conflicts of interest that engendered these deals are not only wrong but bad for business as well.

The investment banker's effectiveness and ability to command future business thus depends on the reputation it has established over time. The economic incentives to maintain a trustworthy reputation are not nearly as strong for firms that plan to go to the securities markets only once or very infrequently. Therefore, investment bankers (whose reputations are intact) can provide a certification role—a "seal of approval"—to security issuers. Their investment in reputation is another type of scale economy that arises from frequent participation in the capital markets.

These same dealers are also involved in the retail business of trading for clients on the stock exchanges, although some may identify different niches for their emphasis. As part of the service of advising customers of investment opportunities, large stockbrokers have extensive in-house analysis departments. As an alternative, information and analysis may be carried out by independent firms, so as to avoid public distrust of the dealers' recommendations. In parallel, a growing volume of trading is executed by discount brokers who have no analysis departments and offer investment advice provided by the independents only for a fee, if at all.

Financial Engineering

The investment diversity desired by households is far greater than most businesses have a desire to satisfy. Most firms find it simpler to issue "plain vanilla" securities, leaving exotic variants to others who specialize in financial markets. This, of course, creates a profit opportunity for innovative security design and repackaging that investment dealers are only too happy to fill. The process of designing and issuing innovative securities is known as **financial engineering**. Financial engineers regard securities as bundles of cash flows that may be carved up and rearranged according to the needs or desires of traders in the security markets. An important process known as **securitization** converts non-marketable assets, such as receivables held by a firm, into traded securities by issuing claims against the firm backed by the original assets. This process creates a new class of negotiable securities offering reliable credit quality to investors, and provides cash advances to the issuing firm, with financial intermediaries handling the issue.

Canada Mortagage and Housing Corporation www.cmhc-schl.gc.ca

One widely used but little-known instrument is the **mortgage-backed security (MBS)**. These were first created in the United States, then came to Canada in 1986 under the Canada Mortgage and Housing Corporation (CMHC), which insures and guarantees pools of mortgages issued by banks and trust companies; the securities granting an interest in the payments on the mortgages (both principal and interest) to their holders are MBSs. These were a tremendous innovation in mortgage markets.[1] The securitization of mortgages meant that mortgages could be traded just like other securities in national financial markets. Availability of funds no longer depended on local credit conditions; with mortgage **pass-through securities** trading in national markets, mortgage funds could flow from any region to wherever demand was greatest.

In contrast to the long-term MBS market, short-term loans are also subject to securitization by investment bankers. The major asset-backed securities are issued for credit card debt, automobile loans, home equity loans, and student loans. In these cases, the regular payments made by the borrowers to the original grantors of the credit are passed through to the holders of the securities. The security for the paper is the underlying pool of loans and the security associated with them. The pooling and issuing by the investment banker makes these illiquid small instruments negotiable. The process enables the borrower (the original holder of the paper) to enjoy the use of the funds, while the lenders receive a superior return on those funds.

Although these securities are relatively complex, the message here is that security demand elicited a market response. The waves of product development in the past three decades are responses to perceived profit opportunities created by as-yet-unsatisfied demands for securities with particular risk, return, tax, and timing attributes. As the investment banking industry becomes even more sophisticated, security creation and customization become more routine. A Wall Street joke asks how many investment bankers it takes to sell a light bulb. The answer is one hundred—1 to break the bulb and 99 to sell off the individual fragments.

This discussion leads to the notion of primitive versus derivative securities. A **primitive security** offers returns only on the basis of the status of the issuer, who is generally a corporation or government. For example, corporate bonds make stipulated interest payments depending only on the solvency of the issuing firm. Dividends paid to shareholders depend as well on the board of directors' assessment of the firm's financial position. In contrast, **derivative securities** yield returns that depend on additional factors pertaining to the prices of other assets. In its simplest form, the value of a derivative depends on the price of the underlying security, which is the common term for the primitive security. For example, the payoff to stock options depends on the price of the underlying stock and not on the financial conditions of the writer (issuer) of the option. In our mortgage examples, the derivative mortgage-backed securities offer payouts that depend on the original mortgages, which are the primitive securities. **Swaps**, by which firms

[1]These were followed by **collateralized mortgage obligations (CMOs)** with different effective times to maturity.

arrange to exchange loan payments, have rapidly grown to prominence among derivative instruments. Much of the innovation in security design may be viewed as the continual creation of new types of derivative securities from the available set of primitive securities.

Derivatives have become an integral part of the investment environment. The primary role of derivatives is to hedge risks, but they also are used to take highly speculative positions. Through the misunderstanding of complex derivatives and their correct use, however, firms may be increasing their exposure to risk when they believe that they are hedging. In the 1990s, spectacular examples such as the $157 million loss of Procter & Gamble on interest rate derivatives and the $700 million loss in Piper Jaffray Companies' fixed-income portfolio were probably cases of misunderstanding about hedging; the bankruptcy of Barings, on the other hand, was due to the speculation of one of its traders, Nick Leeson. Despite these losses, derivatives play a legitimate role in the financial system and in portfolio management.

CONCEPT CHECK

4. If you take out a car loan, is the loan a primitive security or a derivative security?

Many financial innovations are direct responses to government attempts either to regulate or to tax investments of various sorts. The money market industry developed as a result of earlier U.S. banking regulations that capped interest rates on bank deposits. These caps on domestic rates, and the requirement for reserve deposits against domestic bank accounts, also led to the creation of U.S. dollar–denominated time deposits in foreign accounts, popularly known as *Eurodollar accounts.* The market for **Eurodollars** and other Eurocurrencies (referring to accounts in major currencies held outside the particular country) has undergone phenomenal growth since then, even though the motivating U.S. regulations have been changed.

The long-term deep-discount, or zero-coupon, bond is another innovation largely attributable to tax avoidance motives. These bonds pay little or no interest, instead providing most or all of the return to investors through a redemption price that is higher than the initial sales price. Corporations were allowed, under U.S. tax regulations, to impute an implied interest expense based on this built-in price appreciation. Originally, the technique for imputing tax-deductible interest expenses was excessively advantageous to corporations, resulting in a large number of issues of these bonds; ultimately, the interest imputation procedures were amended, and the issue of "zeros" for tax purposes ended.

Meanwhile, however, the financial markets had discovered that zeros were useful ways to lock in a long-term investment return. When the supply of *primitive* zero-coupon bonds ended, financial innovators created *derivative* zeros by purchasing Government of Canada bonds, "stripping" off the coupons, and selling them separately as zeros. The major Canadian investment dealers combined to institutionalize these stripped bonds by selling claims against a pool of government bonds under the name of Sentinels.

Another tax-induced innovation is the **split share**. With deferred taxes for capital gains, high-tax-bracket investors prefer growth to income while tax-exempt investors prefer the opposite. Rather than choosing stocks that offer these characteristics, investors can buy shares in reliable high-yielding but growing industries, such as communications and banking, that have been split into income and capital shares. Essentially, the income portion returns the original investment plus a stream of dividends, while the capital portion pays the capital gain since the creation of the split share. The underlying shares are bought by the financial engineer, who splits them into the two components and issues these against the original holding for a span of several years. Examples of these have included shares in Bell Canada Enterprises, the major chartered banks, and even a portfolio of these same banks.

Creative security design often calls for **bundling** primitive and derivative securities into one composite security. The long-established example of this is the convertible preferred share or bond, by which the holder has the right to exchange the convertible for a number of common shares in the company; this usually is done when the converted value is higher than the value of the original instrument as a fixed-income security.

Export Development Canada
www.edc.ca

Canada's Export Development Corporation (EDC) provides some interesting examples of derivatives produced by bundling securities. Figure 1.1 reproduces the announcement of EDC's issue of a dual currency bond, with payment in either Australian dollars or Japanese yen, at the option of the holder. These obviously will have appeal to Australian and Japanese investors; however, they also provide an opportunity to Canadian or other investors to speculate on the appreciation of either

Figure 1.1
Derivative securities: A dual-currency bond issue.

This announcement appears as a matter of record only. *September, 1990*

Export Development Corporation

¥20,000,000,000

Dual Currency
Japanese Yen/Australian Dollar
Bonds—First Series (1990)

Issue Price: 99.3% Coupon Rate: 8.0% (A$335.75)
Maturity Date: September 5, 2000

Daiwa Securities Co. Ltd.

The Nikko Securities Co., Ltd. The Nomura Securities Co., Ltd. Yamaichi Securities Company, Limited

New Japan Securities Co., Ltd.

KOKUSAI Securities Co., Ltd. The Nippon Kangyo Kakumaru Securities Co., Ltd.

Sanyo Securities Co., Ltd. Universal Securities Co., Ltd.

Cosmo Securities Co., Ltd. Dai-ichi Securities Co., Ltd. Marusan Securities Co., Ltd.

Okasan Securities Co., Ltd. Taiheiyo Securities Co., Ltd. Tokyo Securities Co., Ltd.

Toyo Securities Co., Ltd. Wako Securities Co., Ltd. Yamatane Securities Co., Ltd.

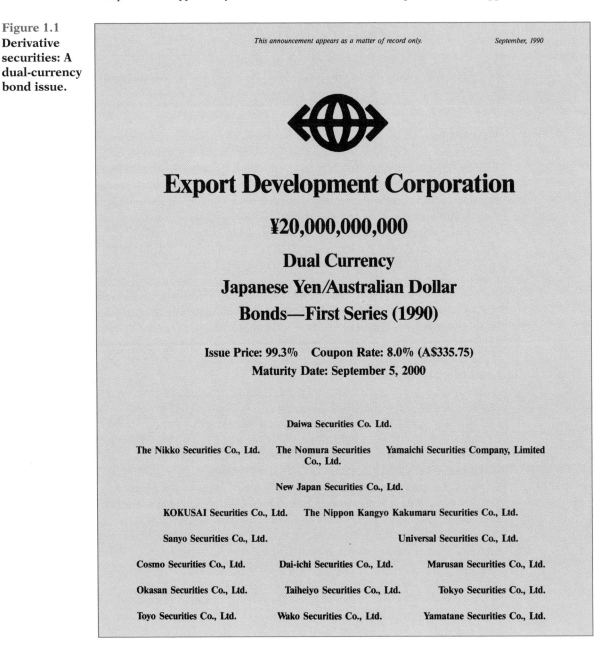

of the currencies against the dollar. Figure 1.2 displays the cover page of the prospectus for PINs, or protected index notes. Each PIN on issue cost $10 in U.S. dollars and promised, at the option of the holder, to repay the $10 upon maturity after five-and-a-half years, or, at any time up to maturity, an amount based on the value of the S&P 500 index relative to its value at issue. The holder is guaranteed a minimum repayment of the initial investment without interest but also can participate in any appreciation in the U.S. equity market—in both cases speculating on the exchange rate.

Figure 1.2 **Derivative securities: Prospectus for a minimum-return index investment.**

Offering Circular dated June 25, 1991

This Offering Circular constitutes a public offering of these securities only in those jurisdictions where they may be lawfully offered for sale. No securities commission nor similar authority in Canada has in any way passed upon the merits of the securities offered hereunder and any representation to the contrary is an offence.

Export Development Corporation

(An agent of Her Majesty in right of Canada)

Société pour l'expansion des exportations

(Mandataire de Sa Majesté du chef du Canada)

U.S.$75,000,000

S&P 500® Protected Index Notes Due 1997 ("PINS")

The S&P 500 Protected Index Notes Due 1997 (the "Notes") offered hereby will mature on January 3, 1997 (the "Stated Maturity"). The Notes may not be called for redemption by Export Development Corporation ("EDC") prior to Stated Maturity. Each Note will have a principal amount of U.S.$10 and all payments with respect to the Notes will be denominated in U.S. dollars. At Stated Maturity, a holder of each Note (a "Holder") will receive in respect of each Note held by such Holder the greater of (A) U.S.$10 or (B) the Repurchase Price which will be computed by reference to the Standard & Poor's 500 Composite Stock Price Index (the "S&P 500 Index"). The repurchase price of each Note (the "Repurchase Price") will equal U.S.$10 multiplied by the Spot S&P Index (as hereinafter defined) for the applicable Valuation Date (as hereinafter defined) divided by the Strike S&P Index (as hereinafter defined) (rounded down to the nearest cent). The Strike S&P Index will equal 105% of the Initial S&P Index (as hereinafter defined). No interest will be paid on the Notes, except to the extent that the Repurchase Price exceeds U.S.$10 upon exercise of the Repurchase Option or at Stated Maturity. The Repurchase Price will not exceed U.S.$10 unless the S&P 500 Index increases to a level greater than the Strike S&P Index. Prior to 10:00 a.m. on the sixteenth Business Day immediately preceding the Stated Maturity, a Holder will have the option (the "Repurchase Option") to require EDC to repurchase any Notes held by such Holder at the Repurchase Price. If a Holder exercises the Repurchase Option prior to January 3, 1992, the amount payable to the Holder will be equal to 95% of the Repurchase Price.

The valuation and payment of the Repurchase Price may be postponed as a result of a Market Disruption Event (as hereinafter defined). In such event the Holder will receive the Repurchase Price determined as of a later date, except that Notes tendered for repurchase that become subject to such postponed valuation and payment will not be repurchased if the Holder elects in the Repurchase Notice that the Note Agent withdraw the Repurchase Notice (a "Withdrawal Election") in the event of a Market Disruption Event (as hereinafter defined).

PRICE: U.S.$10.00 per Note

Minimum Subscription: 100 Notes

	Price to the Public (1)(2)	Agents' Commission	Proceeds to EDC (3)
Per Note	U.S.$10.00	U.S.$0.30	U.S.$9.70
Total Offering (4)	U.S.$75,000,000	U.S.$2,250,000	U.S.$72,750,000

Notes:

(1) The subscription price has been determined by negotiation between EDC and the Agents (as hereinafter defined).

(2) On June 24, 1991, the Canadian dollar purchase price of each Note would have been C$11.43 based on the noon exchange rate of C$1.1427 for each U.S.$1.00.

(3) The expenses of the issue of approximately C$350,000 are being borne by the Issuer and the Agents.

(4) EDC has granted to the Agents an overallotment option, exercisable from time to time up to the Date of Closing (as hereinafter defined) with the concurrence of EDC, to distribute an additional 1,000,000 Notes on the same terms and conditions as the other Notes offered hereby. To the extent such option is exercised, the Agents will offer to the public such additional Notes at the price shown above.

Investment in the Notes is speculative and a Holder may sustain a substantial loss of its investment if such Holder elects to exercise the Repurchase Option and the Notes are repurchased prior to Stated Maturity. Since the return to a Holder on exercise of the Repurchase Option or at Stated Maturity is determined solely by reference to the S&P 500 Index, the Notes are not suitable for persons unfamiliar with the risks of investing in equity securities. (See "Risk Factors".) In order for a Holder to avoid a loss of principal on the Notes, the level of the S&P 500 Index must increase to the Breakeven Point (as hereinafter defined) or the Notes must be held to Stated Maturity. (See "Description of Notes — Breakeven Point" and "Description of the Notes — Repurchase Price".) The Notes will constitute direct unsecured obligations of EDC and, as such, will constitute direct obligations of Her Majesty in right of Canada. (See "Description of the Notes — Status".)

The Repurchase Option will be exercisable on any Business Day (as hereinafter defined) after the Date of Closing and will expire at 10:00 a.m. on the sixteenth Business Day immediately preceding the Stated Maturity of the Notes. Any Holder who does not exercise the Repurchase Option will receive in respect of each Note held by such Holder the greater of (A) U.S.$10 or (B) the Repurchase Price, at the Stated Maturity. The Repurchase Option may not be exercised by or on behalf of any Holder in respect of fewer than 100 Notes or integral multiples thereof. (See "Description of the Notes — Repurchase Option".)

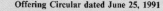

Quite often, creating a security that appears to be attractive requires the **unbundling** of an asset. An example is given by strip bonds—the composite bond cash flow of regular interest payments and principal is unbundled into single payments. Other examples of unbundling include CMOs and split shares; both permit investors to concentrate on the payment stream, and its risk, which appeal to their particular interests.

Most examples of innovative instruments are responses to U.S. tax or regulatory restrictions, reflecting the dominance of the U.S. financial markets. Eurobonds and financial futures are products that have left their U.S. origins behind and become international, now serving a far more diverse purpose than escaping U.S. taxes or regulations. The process continues as unanticipated financial innovations are created to evade the government's efforts to obtain fiscal revenues; as the government reacts to these innovations, even more instruments are designed.

These innovations are a small sample of the product of financial engineering in recent decades. Essentially, they are derivatives of familiar instruments such as deposits, stocks, and bonds. The original derivatives, namely options and futures, are described in detail in Part Six. The creation of options and futures on stock indices and for interest rates has led to the development of techniques to hedge portfolios against market risk; this area, often known as **portfolio insurance**, is explored in Chapter 21, where the process of portfolio management is presented.

CONCEPT CHECK

5. How can tax motives contribute to the desire for unbundling?

1.4 ANALYSTS, AUDITORS, AND THE AGENCY PROBLEM

The bubble and ensuing collapse in the high-tech market at the end of the millennium are fundamentally the result of the age-old economic phenomenon of supply and demand. During the bubble, the demand for shares exceeded the supply and forced the price up, as investors saw increasing value behind the shares; subsequently, supply greatly exceeded demand, as cash appeared to hold more value. In financial market parlance, greed overcame fear, until the reverse occurred.

The underlying question is why. Why did investors believe that the potential profits of fibre optic technology could justify not just high P/E ratios, but price-to-operating-revenue ratios when earnings were negative, price-to-sales ratios when there were no operating earnings, and price-to-ideas when there were no sales? Why did the public embrace the "dot com" mania so enthusiastically? Answers include naïveté, the herd instinct, and media attention; but a major factor was that respected analysts (of varying age and experience) recommended these and other stocks, and, in particular, placed one-year target prices that were 50 to 100 percent higher than the current price. Since their advice to buy these stocks had been so right in the recent past, it was presumed to be as good for the future. Since these stocks could rise by 500 or more percent in a year, it was hard to justify not owning them and "missing the boat."

On what analysis did the analysts base their opinions? As you will see in Chapter 14 on security analysis, it should have been a process consisting of the following:

1. Estimation of the potential size of the product market
2. Estimation of the potential share of the market for the company
3. Estimation of the profit margins
4. Estimation of an appropriate P/E ratio for when the earnings appeared
5. Discounting of the future price to the present

This process is not easy to accomplish under normal conditions; it becomes even more difficult when the technology and the growth are relatively unprecedented.

As the bubble inflated, it became apparent that the best source for growth projections was from the companies themselves. They would predict their sales in following quarters and inform the analysts; the analysts would adjust these predictions as they saw fit and pass on the good news. The analysts became expert at predicting extremely accurate sales and earnings figures for each quarter. Any time an event would cause the estimate to need revision, the companies would inform the analysts and their official estimates would be modified. The general result was that companies actually reported results that were right in line with expectations.

In selected cases, companies would regularly beat the predicted figures by a small percentage. Despite having informed analysts of their best predictions shortly before the official reports, they still managed to beat their best estimates; this caused a satisfactory jump in the price at the "surprise" good news. The investing public grew to expect the good news, and companies that failed to beat their own predictions, via the analysts, would be punished by a price fall.

Eventually, the story ended. The economic realism behind the past sales growth and the tightening by the Federal Reserve of the money supply to avoid inflation combined to impress the investing public, and even the analysts, that there could be no more such growth in the immediate future; and the market fell—sharply and relentlessly. Canada's Nortel was a major player in the collapse, as it continued to predict growth in sales after the inevitable slowdown in tech spending began, in defiance of the monetary actions of the Fed. That shares of small companies with no sales could lose most of their value in the market fall was no surprise; that Nortel and Cisco, market leaders and huge companies with real sales and operating profits, could also was a definite shock. Nortel fell from a high of $124 to 70 cents, an incredible loss of 99.4 percent in value in two years, without going bankrupt. Cisco lost only 90 percent in value as it fell from $80 to $8, while maintaining a multibillion-dollar net income except in 2001. Even the realists who recognized the extreme overvaluation could not have predicted such a correction in value.

Nortel Networks
www.nortelnetworks.com

By 2002, the market continued to doubt the prospects for companies that had unique and valuable technologies. Analysts had reversed their enthusiastic appraisals, forecast continued depressed sales, and estimated that many high-tech shares had no bottoms. Those same analysts who found ABC shares a "strong buy" at $100 in 2000, reevaluated them as "holds" or "sells" at $20 two years later. For the future, one must hope that advisors will provide better service to investors.

How could investors have avoided these losses? The simple answer is by taking profits near the top—shortly after the millennium celebrations had ended. This is also a very incomplete answer; it implies that one can and should try to exit at the right time. A wealth of evidence indicates that this is impossible, and that trying to do so results in missing many of the market's gains. Conservative and experienced investors would have taken gains on companies such as Dell much earlier in the decade; younger companies would have been dropped after the first few doubles in value. Such early exits would have missed almost all of the stupendous gains that followed. In fact, buying early and staying in through the collapse still left many investors with more than 100 percent gains in less than five years in many cases; this record should be recognized as excellent in a historical context.

An even better scenario could have occurred. Seasoned advisors should have counselled investors to take their profits much earlier; the final year of bubble would then not have developed, and the magnitude of the collapse would have been avoided. Traditional evaluation methods certainly indicated the overpriced situation, and many advisors stressed this. Investors, however, were more interested in following the momentum of the market, believing either that it would never end, or, equally foolishly, that they would be able to recognize the top and take their profits then. Many analysts and advisors cautioned against the overvaluation and excess hopes, and the media presented the conservative view as well; but, on the whole, the public and the media preferred the positive note. Too few professionals did anything to correct the problem, and many happily participated in magnifying it.

How are you supposed to know whether to trust analysts in the absence of full disclosure? Get this. Robert Millham, a veteran analyst at Research Capital Corp., issued a "speculative buy" rating on Wi-LAN Inc. in early February (2001). You've heard about Wi-LAN, the brainchild of Hatim Zaghloul and Michel Fattouche, those wonder boys of wireless in Calgary. Like most of the overhyped, overvalued technology firms that haven't earned dollar one, Wi-LAN wooed investors, its stock reaching a high of $87.50 last year. The party didn't last. By the time Millham's report came out on Feb. 9, Wi-LAN's shares had shrivelled to $8.40. (They've sunk even further since.)

While Wi-LAN was flat-lining, Millham had the gumption to issue a $50 price target—an astounding 495% return. But he hemmed and hawed in his report, cautioning investors that Wi-LAN "will have a hard time meeting 2001 revenue expectations." Read further, and it seems Millham's three-page report, despite the hefty price target, is chock-full of speculation about industry spending on wireless technology and Wi-LAN enlisting European customers. Buried near the end is this curious boilerplate: "Research Capital has acted as an underwriter and/or provided financial advice to Wi-LAN within the past three years."

Actually, it was in January—less than a month before Millham's report—that Research Capital, along with CIBC World Markets Inc., handled a $13-million offering of Wi-LAN shares and warrants. (Units of one common share and one-half of a warrant were offered for $7.75 apiece.) Research Capital and CIBC took a 6% cut for underwriting fees. Fair enough. But here's the rub: Wi-LAN gave Research Capital and CIBC the option of buying 10% of shares sold in the offering. Anytime in the next two years, they could purchase common shares for $7.75. Put all the pieces together, and it's plain that Millham is mixed up in a major conflict of interest: first, he recommended Wi-LAN—and set an exorbitant price target for its stock—although Wi-LAN is a client of Research Capital; and second, his firm stands to profit from endorsing Wi-LAN shares. Sadly, this is not an isolated incident.

Millham maintains he has not been involved in a conflict of interest. On March 13, he told Canadian Business that he dropped his Wi-LAN price target to $30 because the market took a nosedive. (Still, $30 would be a 323% projected return from Wi-LAN's share price of $7.10 at that time.) "It's still an extremely high return from the current level," he agrees, "but if there's one thing we've seen in the history of Wi-LAN, it is that it's volatile and is able to go up several-fold in a very short period of time." Fine. But is he pressured by Research Capital's corporate finance department to slap an outrageous price target on Wi-LAN's shares to earn—and keep—the company's patronage? "It's our hope that any companies I cover from a research perspective, we'll also develop a relationship with from a corporate finance perspective," he replies. But Millham insists he's made unpopular calls before. "There are a number of companies that I've changed my opinion on, that we're probably gonna kiss goodbye in terms of any future corporate finance," he says. Still, Millham concedes: "I suspect that ultimately, whether it's corporate finance or research, everybody wants to give clients, you know, winning strategies and winning stocks, always."

"Sunshine is the best antiseptic to conflicts of interest," says John Richardson, vice-president at Lincluden Management Ltd. Investment firms are already required to reveal their relationships to the companies covered in research reports. But that's not enough, because the ownership stake of the analyst or his investment firm is rarely disclosed. Investors should be able to see the number of shares owned by the investment firm and when—and at what price—its interest was acquired. "If you do that and nothing else, you will clean up 75% of the problems with respect to conflicts of interest," says Jason Donville of Lightyear Capital.

Better disclosure might shed some light on why Todd Coupland, an analyst at CIBC World Markets, slapped a "speculative strong buy" rating on Wi-LAN on May 31, 2000. Coupland issued an aggressive 12-month price target of $200, more than seven times what the stock was trading for at the time. On May 8, Wi-LAN issued a prospectus for the offering of 600,000 shares through the exercise of special warrants. Four underwriters, including CIBC, handled the distribution. How can we not question Coupland's optimism?

The Toronto Stock Exchange, Canadian Venture Exchange and the Investment Dealers Association of Canada (IDA) are finally taking notice. They've struck the Securities Industry Committee on Analyst Standards, which will release draft recommendations in mid-April. It's rumoured that the standards will improve disclosure of conflicts of interest, establish an analyst code of conduct and suggest educational and competency standards. Analyst rules are long overdue; there are no nationwide, mandatory standards, which leaves investors at the mercy of countless shenanigans.

Egged on until lately by a seemingly unstoppable bull market, investors poured billions into stocks. Interest in investing has reached a fever pitch, and the opinions of analysts have assumed shaman-like importance. Investors are inundated with analyst predictions through the media. Analysts must be trusted experts, investors assume. Not necessarily. It's not that all analysts are misinformed, crooked or unethical. But the dynamics of the securities industry discourages good research and compromises analysts' objectivity.

Investment firms now see underwriting—not trading stocks or providing research—as the road to riches. After all, brokerage commissions have fallen from about 20 cents a share to 3 cents a share, Palmer estimates. "You can make a hell of a lot more money taking a dollar-a-share commission on corporate finance deals," he says. John Richardson of Lincluden puts it best: "Brokerage analysts are hired by their employers to generate revenue and profit—not to provide a public service."

Analysts are tangled in a catch-22. They're compelled to compliment companies who've done business with their firms through, say, an IPO or bond issue. Otherwise, the firms might be passed over for future underwriting deals. It's also common for investment banks to hold stock in their clients' companies, so coverage by cooing analysts can wow investors, boost shares and turn a tidy profit for the firm. Why is it so hard to find research on small- and mid-cap companies? Analysts focus on popular stocks that generate large volumes of trading revenue (and commissions), or companies that regularly issue more stock, which keeps corporate finance departments busy.

Many analysts blew it when evaluating Nortel Networks Corp. Although the company hasn't made a dime since John Roth took over in 1997, it kept trumpeting "earnings from operations," which excluded the cost of Nortel's acquisitions. Tom Astle, an analyst with Merrill Lynch & Co. Inc., issued a long-term buy recommendation on Nortel in mid-January, with a 12-month "price objective" of $60. In his report, Astle cited earnings per share figures of 52 cents in 1999 and earnings estimates of 74 cents per share for 2000 and 98 cents for 2001. His report gave the impression that Nortel was turning a profit. In fact, it was losing money—a lot of it.

"Now here's a company that was reporting a loss under Generally Accepted Accounting Principles," Palmer seethes. "Nortel just invents some number, the Street goes along with it, the media goes along and, all of a sudden, Nortel is reporting earnings that don't exist."

Source: Keith Kalawsky, *Canadian Business* 74, no. 6 (April 2, 2001), pp. 66–69.

After the collapse, fingers were pointed at three players: investment dealers and their analysts, multinational auditors, and corporate executives. A common term used was *disclosure*, or the failure of it. The accusation of inadequate disclosure was directed at

- Investment dealers who failed to disclose the conflict of interest between their banking divisions and their analyst sections, despite the potential for biased recommendations
- Accounting audits that failed to disclose enough information about the cash flows, the risky assets and the alternative definitions of income (before and after different potential write-offs)
- Managers who failed to disclose their own investment or disinvestment in company shares through incentive plans based on stock options or loans

Fingers should also have been pointed at the investors themselves. Quite possibly, the disclosure was not so inadequate on the part of everyone; rather, the shareholders failed to inform themselves of the available facts, interpret them correctly, and act accordingly. (See the article "Hidden Agendas" here.)

As the bear market progressed in the new millennium and markets began their recovery, blame was fixed on greedy executives, compliant and negligent directors, discriminatory and criminal actions by investment bankers, and inadequate audits. Major American and international players included auditors Arthur Andersen, investment bankers such as Salomon Smith Barney and CSFB, and major corporations such as Tyco, Enron, Worldcom, and Parmalat, whose executives were accused of looting the firm's assets and/or misrepresenting accounting statements to conceal irregularities and inflate assets and profits. Although the investment bankers were generally engaged in conflicts of interest leading to inaccurate appraisals of IPOs and were assessed huge fines, the more significant problem was the failure of directors and auditors to monitor and restrain the actions of corporate managers. Excessively generous compensation packages were awarded without question on the excuse of being competitive and needed for incentives. As well, and the problem has not been resolved, executives in the high-tech industry, in particular, insisted on their right to award option-based bonuses to key employees without recognizing the bonuses as expenses in the income statement. Pro forma financial statements have continued to be issued and accepted as accurate portrayals of the state of corporations' financial health.

The public reaction was more pronounced to the instances of fraud or grossly exaggerated compensation, particularly when the results were massive losses in equity value. Canadians have displayed far more tolerance of the stock profits taken by more Nortel's former chief executive before the price collapsed than have American investors in similar cases. True to form, regulators responded to this outrage by pursuing executives and employees of investment bankers, with fines to the parent corporations in the latter cases. The losers in all these scandals have been the shareholders of the corporations, even if a few executives face fines and prison sentences. Exchange directors, regulators, and accounting bodies have moved for tighter regulations and control through more independence on boards of directors and in auditors to escape conflicts of interest. There is no evidence that executive salaries are falling, however, and the long-run effects of more public scrutiny remain to be seen.

The economic problem linked to disclosure is analyzed under the name of **agency theory**. This refers to the principal-agent relationship when employees are hired to represent the interests of owners. Shareholders are principals in corporations; management is the agent of the owners. Auditors are agents of the shareholders; their duty is to ensure that management provides all the relevant information in a clear and unambiguous manner. Analysts are also agents, whose compensation comes from the salaries earned from firms that are paid commissions to engage in investment banking activities; but the ultimate payer is the investor who purchases shares.

The recognized problem is that the agent tends to further his or her own interests rather than those of the principal. Corporate executives are receiving regular compensation ranging from $100,000 in very small companies to the $10 million level at large corporations; this is augmented by performance bonuses on a similar scale and options as incentives for higher performance. (For the CEO of Nortel, this amounted to $100 million.) These incentives are designed to ensure that management takes actions "aligned with shareholder interests," that is, actions that will maximize share price; options clearly fulfill that objective—except to the extent that the aggregate resulting share issues are highly dilutive to the stock value. It is curious to consider that executives will not make all possible efforts to earn their base salary of $10 million, but require added inducement. If financial results are sufficiently poor, executives will lose all of these rewards.

Management pays the board of directors to watch over itself and the company. Director compensation includes an annual fee plus attendance fees, plus further payments for additional duties; it often includes a pension for service (i.e., after being a highly paid and successful executive elsewhere, with a pension, a director receives a further pension for the many years of valuable service on the board). Directors who do not cooperate with the executives on the board are likely to lose their seats; yet they can be held responsible if they do not protect their shareholders' interests.

The board of directors pays auditors to ensure that financial information is correctly presented to the investors. Auditors are highly paid to provide this service, but their firms also derive large revenues from providing consulting services. Auditors do not want to jeopardize a relationship by displeasing the board with an audit that differs from the management view. At the same time, if an auditor's reputation suffers from inadequate representation of investors, the widespread loss of business is far greater.

Management pays investment dealers to issue securities on behalf of the firm. The commissions on these operations are extremely large. At the same time, these same investment dealers are in the retail business acting for individuals; besides trading for them, they advise on investment opportunities, with in-house analysis departments providing the information. This merging of the two sides of the securities industry gives rise to two problems. In order to serve their corporate clients, the investment bankers may not divulge an impending issue to the trading public; furthermore, keeping that corporate business involves not giving advice that would tend to lower the share price. This leads to the creation of an artificial barrier within the securities firm between the brokerage and investment banking departments; on the other hand, that barrier is breached to the extent that negative forecasts by the analysis department are likely to be softened. The absorption of most securities dealers by the chartered banks, who must satisfy the other financing needs of the same corporate clients, puts the banks in a unique position. It also limits the availability of independent financial advice.

Consequently, one may suspect that investors receive from management the true story on neither the operating and financial prospects nor results. Financial results are modified and presented, with the approval of the auditors, to satisfy management's wishes as to how the results should appear. Directors do not question the actions of the executive in presenting information, nor question the compensation paid to the executives. Analysts dispute neither management's projections nor their directions to avoid offending management by making negative recommendations and jeopardizing investment banking activities.

Such a bleak picture is grossly overstated most of the time, but all too likely an explanation for the end-of-century bubble. It probably serves to explain the failure of the financial industry to arrive at realistic estimates of stock values. In fact, the normal situation has analysts reacting quite skeptically to optimistic management projections. The regulators and securities industry itself in both Canada and the United States have taken aggressive steps to ensure better and ethical behaviour by the professionals, with regulations for analyst conflict disclosure, corporate announcements, and auditor independence.[2]

Finally, the investor must be wary. "He who pays the piper calls the tune." It appears here that the audience is using intermediaries to hire the musicians, buy the tickets, and broadcast the music. The impression left is that the concert is not quite what it should be, yet the audience cannot directly arrange for the performance. Individual investors ultimately pay for the concert and have the right to be satisfied with what they hear; to that end, they must learn to recognize the quality of the music. Unless individuals are capable of investigating their own company results, they must rely on those agents whose advice has proven fallible in the past.

1.5 THE RIGHT APPROACH

The twenty-first century investor plays the same role as always: to help determine the true current value of equities and bonds. This is part of the essential process of raising capital for real investment through the intermediation of several types of institutions. Compared to his or her twentieth-century predecessor, the modern investor faces a broader array of financial instruments with which to establish the value of the basic corporate issues. The derivative securities at hand present more choice and complicate the process to some degree. Yet all these are ultimately intended to suit more precisely the needs and tastes of the investor; and, fundamentally, the values of all of the available instruments depend on the individual's perception of the value of the firm that issues the primary instruments.

The lesson from the end of the century is that investors collectively and drastically failed in determining the firms' prospects for the near future. With the dubious benefit of professional advice, many investors found their portfolio values decimated after a concentration in high-risk assets whose prices soared and then collapsed. The attraction of these particular assets was their recent ascent in price. This approach to portfolio selection, described as "momentum investing," coincided with a focus on so-called "growth stocks." Analysts and fund managers with this style were paraded as heroes, and rewarded with substantial bonuses. Many other investors and portfolio managers rejected the temptation to follow the momentum and opted for the alternative of "value investing." These latter were usually disappointed in the last five years of the 1990s; what normal investment analysis

[2]See the document "Setting Analyst Standards" published jointly by the TSE, Canadian Venture Exchange, and the Investment Dealers Association in 2001. Note also the SEC investigation of sources of audit conflict resulting from the Enron collapse and its business relationship to Andersen.

would identify as bargain stocks became better bargains. Finally they had their vindication in the high-tech collapse. Yet even these could not escape the final market fall in 2001 and 2002.

Diversification

The protection from the disappointment for value investors in the high-tech boom and from the calamity for growth investors that followed lies in the well-understood principle of diversification. By holding both kinds of stocks, investors could have mitigated the losses, or failures to gain, in one part of the portfolio with the other part's successes. Diversification entails the design of a portfolio that generally offsets some gains with other losses, and in the long run grows at a fairly predictable rate. This is achieved to a great extent by selecting assets with interests in different sectors of the economy, which react differently to economic conditions and cycles. (We shall see in Part Two that modern portfolio design takes a more statistical approach to this problem.) Even a diversified portfolio, however, must rise and fall in value with the whole market trend. Hence an economic slowdown will be correlated with a portfolio loss.

Solutions to the macroeconomic vulnerability of a portfolio have emerged from two recent developments. One is the use of the financial derivatives previously mentioned; these are used to hedge the value of the portfolio and can greatly reduce the risk in a portfolio at the cost of lower returns. The second approach lies in further diversification. One method of this is by a balanced portfolio made up of both equities and bonds, a cash position, and other, less liquid assets. Another is to follow the trend toward **globalization**, which refers to the increasingly international focus of business and finance; we devote Chapter 22 to this subject.

Investors can increase their diversification by taking positions in assets located in other countries. In this way, the effects of an economic downturn domestically can be offset by the continued boom in other parts of the world. This may occur when a foreign country benefits from increased export sales due to a better economic policy, leading to more competitive prices and increased production; this is quite possibly related to the mentioned decline in one's domestic economy. A portfolio with assets in the home and the foreign countries will find the combined effect less variable.

Opportunities for benefiting from international assets can be found in several ways. Multinational corporations based in one's home country will have both sales and production facilities in worldwide locations; this leads to net revenues that depend on the economic conditions in each of these countries, and which eventually are likely to be smoothed across local fluctuations. Besides American corporations, firms based in other countries (also likely to be multinationals) can often be bought as easily as domestic corporations, particularly if traded on U.S. exchanges. These latter are often listed as **ADRs (American Depository Receipts)**, which are U.S. securities representing a claim to one or more share certificates in corporations foreign to the United States.

Canadian governments, both federal and provincial, their agencies, and major Canadian corporations often issue debt instruments denominated in foreign currencies; these are usually issued in the countries of those currencies and aimed at the investors of those countries to assist them in their diversification efforts. Also, the major Canadian banks have issued preferred shares denominated in U.S. dollars, but eligible for Canadian issuer tax treatment (the dividend tax credit) and traded on the Toronto Stock Exchange. Both the debt and the preferred instruments allow Canadian holders to hedge against the depreciation of the Canadian dollar relative to the American.

The only drawback to international diversification is the increasing interconnection of the economies of the world. To the extent that a global economy develops, the effects of a slowdown in one major nation are felt globally. Already, the introduction of the Euro as a currency and the development of a common economic policy for the Euro zone have reduced the diversification possibilities for European markets. There is increasing evidence of three zones of economic activity—American, European, and Asian—which are highly dependent internally, but also interdependent. This too is a manifestation of globalization.

Information and Patience

One of the ironies of the 1990s bubble is that the result of constructing a portfolio by modern principles would have resulted in an uncomfortable concentration in stocks such as Nortel, Cisco, and Dell. The theory prescribes that a portfolio should be invested in stocks according to their market value. Since these three stocks rose from modest values to immense values, investors were supposed to have large holdings in them; those holdings would have then collapsed after the bubble burst. An alternative strategy would have prescribed reducing the holdings to maintain a more equally balanced portfolio. If that had been followed, the portfolio would never have risen to anything approaching the value of the buy-and-hold strategy at the end of the decade. No credible approach pretends to dictate that good stocks be held until they reach their maximum value, and then promptly sold. Such prescience is both invaluable and impossible. Hence no ideal resolution of the investor's dilemma exists.

The solution for investors is finally to be diversified, to be informed, and to be patient. A program of investing in a well-chosen portfolio, characterized by diverse asset holdings selected after consulting reliable sources of information, will lead in time to returns that are superior to alternatives. Concentrated investments, and those based on tips, may often lead to quick gains; over an extended period, the associated risk can be expected to cause major losses. Inexperienced investors tend to sell poor investments after losses are experienced and then fail to benefit from recoveries, if not having suffered irreparable losses to their wealth.

The purpose of a book on investing is to present the techniques that have the highest expectation of success, while showing the pitfalls of alternative approaches. One thing, however, should be clear. Chance plays a major role in any uncertain outcome such as investing. Someone must always come out ahead; after the fact, some investor who did not diversify will inevitably have a better return than the great majority that did. Finally, it is better to be lucky. Since one cannot count on good fortune, it is far wiser to be informed and diversified, and then let time work for you.

SUMMARY

1. Real investment creates real assets that are used to produce the goods and services created by an economy. Financial investment is in financial assets, which are claims to the income generated by real assets. Securities are financial assets. Financial assets are part of an investor's wealth, but not part of national wealth. Instead, financial assets determine how the "national pie" is split up among investors.
2. Financial instruments such as stocks and bonds are issued by firms to investors who buy and sell them in markets; except on the initial issue, they do not directly affect the capital and production of the issuing firms.
3. The financial environment is composed of three sectors: household, business, and government. Households decide on investing their funds; businesses and government, in contrast, typically need to raise funds.
4. The life-cycle approach to the management of an individual's investment portfolio views the individual as passing through a series of stages, becoming more risk-averse in later years. The rationale underlying this approach is that as we age, we use up our human capital and have less time remaining to recoup possible portfolio losses through increased labour supply.
5. People buy life and disability insurance during their prime earning years to hedge against the risk associated with loss of their human capital, that is, their future earning power.
6. Investors select investments that will provide them with the kind of returns that will suit their needs and preferences. Their investment opportunities correspond to the need for funds by corporations and governments. The after-tax returns that accompany the various types of financial instruments guide investors' choices.

Visit us at www.mcgrawhill.ca/college/bodie

7. The excess funds of investors are channelled to businesses for investment purposes through financial intermediaries such as banks, investment bankers, mutual funds, and insurance companies. Economies of scale and specialization are factors supporting the investment banking industry.
8. The diverse task and risk preferences of households create a demand for a wide variety of securities. In contrast, businesses typically find it more efficient to offer relatively uniform forms of securities. This conflict gives rise to an industry that creates complex derivative securities from primitive ones.
9. Some of the recent techniques for financial engineering include issuing derivative securities (especially by bundling and unbundling), securitization, and credit enhancement.
10. Overvaluation of financial assets occurs when information is not properly disclosed by insiders, or analyzed by investors and by financial advisors. Faulty disclosure is a prime example of a market failure due to the agency problem between principals and agents.
11. Successful investing requires diversification across domestic assets and internationally, in addition to efficient processing of information. Finally, the passage of time is necessary for expected results to follow from good investment techniques.

KEY TERMS

financial investment 6
real investment 6
real assets 6
financial assets 6
disclosure 8
financial intermediaries 10
mutual funds 11
investment dealers 11
financial engineering 12
securitization 12
mortgage-backed security (MBS) 12
pass-through securities 12
primitive security 12
derivative securities 12
swaps 12
Eurodollars 13
split share 13
bundling 14
unbundling 16
portfolio insurance 16
agency theory 20
globalization 22
ADRs (American Depository Receipts) 22

SELECTED READINGS

An excellent discussion of financial innovation may be found in:

Miller, Merton H. "Financial Innovation: The Last Twenty Years and the Next." *Journal of Financial and Quantitative Analysis* 21 (December 1986), pp. 459–471.

Detailed discussions of a variety of financial markets and market structures are provided in:

Garbade, Kenneth D. *Securities Markets*. New York: McGraw-Hill, 1982.

Wood, John H., and Norm L. Wood. *Financial Markets*. San Diego: Harcourt Brace Jovanovich, 1985.

Several trends in the capital market are discussed in:

Recent Innovations in International Banking. Basel: Bank for International Settlements, 1986.

A broad range of non-technical articles on the subject of investing in Canada and by Canadians appear quarterly in the Canadian Investment Review *(*CIR*). These articles are usually organized by theme. Some examples of interest to our discussion would be:*

"Market Innovation in Canada." *CIR* 3, no. 2 (Fall 1990).

"Investment Perspectives on Ethics, Ownership and Control." *CIR* 4, no. 2 (Fall 1991).

Poapst, James V. "Households as Financial Managers: An Assessment." *CIR* 2, no. 2 (Fall 1989).

Irvine, Paul J. A. "Do Analysts Generate Trade for Their Firms? Evidence from the Toronto Stock Exchange." *CIR* 14, no. 3 (Fall 2001).

For information on self-regulation of securities analysts:

"Setting Analyst Standards: Recommendations for the Supervision and Practice of Canadian Securities Industry Analysts." (PDF.) Final Report—SICAS (Securities Industry Committee on Analyst Standards), October 2001. Available tse.com/en/pdf/SICAS-FinalReport.pdf. Accessed September 4, 2004.

PROBLEMS

1. Suppose you discover a treasure chest of $10 billion in cash.
   a. Is this a real or financial asset?
   b. Is society any richer for the discovery?
   c. Are you wealthier?
   d. Can you reconcile your answers to (*b*) and (*c*)? Is anyone worse off as a result of the discovery?
2. Lanni Products is a start-up computer software development firm. It currently owns computer equipment worth $30,000 and has cash on hand of $20,000 contributed by Lanni's owners. For each of the following transactions, identify the real and/or financial assets that trade hands. Are any financial assets created or destroyed in the transaction?
   a. Lanni takes out a bank loan. It receives $50,000 in cash and signs a note promising to pay back the loan over three years.
   b. Lanni uses the cash from the bank plus $15,000 of its own funds to finance the development of new financial planning software.
   c. Lanni sells the software product to Microsoft, which will market it to the public under the Microsoft name. Lanni accepts payment in the form of 1,500 shares of Microsoft stock.
   d. Lanni sells the shares of stock for $80 per share and uses part of the proceeds to pay off the bank loan.
3. Reconsider Lanni Products from problem 2.
   a. Prepare Lanni's balance sheet just after it gets the bank loan. What is the ratio of real assets to financial assets?
   b. Prepare the balance sheet after Lanni spends the $65,000 to develop the product. What is the ratio of real assets to total assets?
   c. Prepare the balance sheet after Lanni accepts payment of shares from Microsoft. What is the ratio of real assets to total assets?
4. In the 1960s, the U.S. government instituted a 30 percent withholding tax on interest payments on bonds sold in the United States to overseas investors. (It has since been repealed.) What connection does this have to the contemporaneous growth of the huge Eurobond market, where U.S. firms issue dollar-denominated bonds overseas?
5. Why would you expect securitization to take place only in highly developed capital markets?
6. Suppose that you are an executive of Ford Motors Canada, and that a large share of your potential income is derived from year-end bonuses that depend on your firm's annual profits.
   a. Would purchase of Ford Canada's stock be an effective hedging strategy if you are worried about the uncertainty surrounding your bonus?
   b. Would purchase of Toyota stock be an effective hedging strategy?
7. Consider the Ford executive in problem 6. In light of the fact that the design of the annual bonus exposes the executive to risk that you would like to shed, why doesn't Ford instead pay you a fixed salary that doesn't entail this uncertainty?
8. What is the relationship between securitization and the role of financial intermediaries in the economy? What happens to financial intermediaries as securitization progresses?
9. Many investors would like to invest part of their portfolios in real estate, but obviously cannot on their own purchase office buildings or strip malls. Explain how this situation creates a profit incentive for investment firms that can sponsor REITs (real estate investment trusts).
10. Financial engineering has been disparaged as nothing more than paper shuffling. Critics argue that resources that go to *rearranging wealth* (i.e., bundling and unbundling financial assets) might better be spent on *creating* wealth (i.e., creating real assets). Evaluate this criticism. Are there any benefits realized by creating an array of derivative securities from various primary securities?

11. Although we stated that real assets make up the true productive capacity of an economy, it is hard to conceive of a modern economy without well-developed financial markets and security types. How would the productive capacity of the Canadian economy be affected if there were no markets in which one could trade financial assets?

12. Why does it make sense that the first futures markets introduced in nineteenth-century America were for trades in agricultural products? For example, why did we not see instead futures markets for goods such as paper or pencils?

13. Discuss the advantages and disadvantages of the following forms of managerial compensation in terms of mitigating agency problems, that is, potential conflicts of interest between managers and shareholders.

a. A fixed salary

b. Stock in the firm

c. Call options on shares of the firm

14. Oversight by large institutional investors or creditors is one mechanism to reduce agency problems. Why don't individual investors in the firm have the same incentive to keep an eye on management?

CHAPTER TWO

MARKETS AND INSTRUMENTS

This chapter covers a range of financial securities and the markets in which they trade. Our goal is to introduce you to the features of various security types. This foundation will be necessary to understand the more analytic material that follows in later chapters.

We refer to the traditional classification of securities into money market instruments or capital market instruments. The **money market** includes short-term, marketable, liquid, low-risk debt securities. Money market instruments are sometimes called *cash equivalents* because of their safety and liquidity. **Capital markets**, in contrast, include longer-term and riskier securities. Securities in the capital market are much more diverse than those found within the money market. For this reason, we will subdivide the capital market into four segments. This chapter therefore contains a discussion of five markets overall: the money market, longer-term fixed-income capital markets, equity markets, and the two so-called derivative markets—options and futures markets.

We first describe money market instruments and how to measure their yields. We then move on to fixed-income and equity securities. We explain the structure of various stock market indices in this chapter because market benchmark portfolios play an important role in portfolio construction and evaluation. Finally, we survey the derivative security markets for options and futures contracts.

2.1 THE MONEY MARKET

The money market is a subsector of the fixed-income market. It consists of very short-term debt securities that usually are highly marketable. Many of these securities trade in large denominations and so are out of reach of individual investors. Money market funds, however, are easily accessible to small investors. These mutual funds pool the resources of many investors and purchase a wide variety of money market securities on their behalf.

Figure 2.1 is a reprint of a money rates listing from *The Globe and Mail*. It includes the various instruments of the money market that we will describe in detail. Trading in and issues of money market instruments are rising but remain far below the levels of ten years ago.[1]

Treasury Bills

Treasury bills (T-bills) are the most marketable of all Canadian money market instruments. T-bills represent the simplest form of borrowing: the government raises money by selling bills to the public. Investors buy the bills at a discount from the stated maturity value. At the bill's maturity, the holder receives from the government a payment equal to the face value of the bill. The difference between the purchase price and ultimate maturity value constitutes the investor's earnings.

T-bills with initial maturities of 3, 6, and 12 months are issued biweekly. Sales are conducted via auction, at which chartered banks and authorized dealers can submit only *competitive* bids. A competitive bid is an order for a given quantity of bills at a specific offered price. The order is filled only if the bid is high enough relative to other bids to be accepted. By contrast, a noncompetitive bid is an unconditional offer to purchase at the average price of the successful competitive bids; such bids can be submitted only for bonds. The government rank-orders bids by offering price and accepts bids in order of descending price until the entire issue is absorbed. Competitive bidders face two dangers: they may bid too high and overpay for the bills, or they may bid too low and be shut out of the auction.

Figure 2.1
Rates on money market securities.

MONEY RATES

ADMINISTERED	
Bank of Canada	2.25%
Target overnight rate	2.25%
Central bank call range	2.25-2.75%
Canadian prime	4.00%
MONEY MARKET	
(for transactions of $1-million or more)	
3-mo. treasury bills	2.21%
6-mo. treasury bills	2.20%
1-year treasury bills	2.24%
10-year Canada bonds	4.38%
30-year Canada bonds	5.04%
1-mo. banker's accept.	2.29%
2-mo. banker's accept.	2.27%
3-mo. banker's accept.	2.26%
Commercial Paper (R-1 Low)	
1-mo.	2.28%
3-mo.	2.25%
Call money	2.25%

Bloomberg News

UNITED STATES

NEW YORK (AP) – Money rates for Thursday as reported by Moneyline Telerate:

Prime Rate: 4.00.

Discount Rate Primary: 2.00.

Discount Rate Secondary: 2.50.

Broker call loan rate: 2.75.

Federal funds market rate: High 1.0; Low 1.0; Last 1.0.

Dealers commercial paper: 30-180 days: 0.96-1.03.

Commercial paper by finance company: 30-270 days: 1.08-1.12.

Bankers acceptances dealer indications: 30 days, 1.04; 60 days, 1.05; 90 days, 1.06; 120 days, 1.08; 150 days, 1.10; 180 days, 1.13.

Certificates of Deposit Primary: 30 days, 0.90; 90 days, 0.75; 180 days, 0.89.

Certificates of Deposit by dealer: 30 days, 1.02; 60 days, 1.03; 90 days, 1.04; 120 days, 1.06; 150 days, 1.08; 180 days, 1.11.

Eurodollar rates: Overnight, 1.00-1.06; 1 month, 0.94-1.06; 3 months, 1.00-1.13; 6 months, 1.06-1.19; 1 year, 1.31-1.44.

London Interbank Offered Rate: 3 months, 1.12; 6 months, 1.19; 1 year, 1.42.

Treasury Bill auction results: average discount rate: 3-month as of Mar. 1: 0.940; 6-month as of Mar. 1: 0.990.

Treasury Bill annualized rate on weekly average basis, yield adjusted for constant maturity, 1-year, as of Mar. 1: 1.22.

Treasury Bill market rate, 6 Mos: 1.00-0.99.

Treasury Note market rate, 10-year as of 4 pm: 4.02.

Source: Report on Business, *The Globe and Mail*, March 5, 2004, p. B16. Reprinted with permission of The Globe and Mail.

[1]An excellent overview as well as statistics of the money markets (and other debt and equity markets) are given by the Investment Dealers Association of Canada's *Securities Industry & Capital Markets Developments Chartbook*, published annually and available online at www.ida.ca.

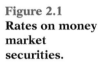

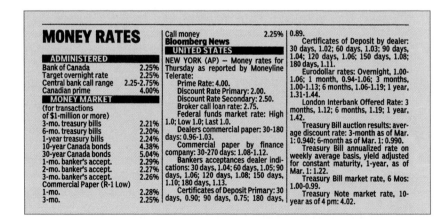

T-bills are purchased primarily by chartered banks, by investment dealers, by the Bank of Canada (as part of its monetary policy), and by individuals who obtain them on the secondary market from a government securities dealer. T-bills are highly liquid; that is, they are easily converted to cash and sold at low transaction cost with not much price risk. Unlike most other money market instruments, which sell in minimum denominations of $100,000, T-bills are offered in denominations of $1,000, $5,000, $25,000, $100,000 and $1 million.

Certificates of Deposit and Bearer Deposit Notes

A **certificate of deposit (CD)** is a time deposit with a chartered bank. Time deposits may not be withdrawn on demand. The bank pays interest and principal to the depositor only at the end of the fixed term of the deposit. A similar time deposit for smaller amounts is known as a **guaranteed investment certificate (GIC)**.

Although both CDs and GICs are nontransferable in Canada, some bank time deposits issued in denominations greater than $100,000 are negotiable; that is, they can be sold to another investor if the owner needs to cash in the deposit before its maturity date. In Canada these marketable CDs are known as **bearer deposit notes (BDNs)**. By contrast, a CD in the United States is a marketable instrument, similar to BDNs. Some trust companies also have issued transferable GICs as well as GICs with variable rates or with payoffs linked to equity indices. CDs and GICs are treated as bank deposits by the Canada Deposit Insurance Corporation (CDIC), so they are insured for up to $60,000 in the event of a bank insolvency.

Commercial Paper

Large, well-known companies often issue their own short-term unsecured debt notes rather than borrow directly from banks. These notes are called **commercial paper**. Very often, commercial paper is backed by a bank line of credit, which gives the borrower access to cash that can be used (if needed) to pay off the paper at maturity. Commercial paper maturities range up to one year; longer maturities would require registration under the Ontario Securities Act and so are almost never issued. Most often, commercial paper is issued with maturities of less than one or two months and minimum denominations of $50,000. Therefore, small investors can invest in commercial paper only indirectly, via money market mutual funds. Almost all commercial paper today is rated for credit quality by the major rating agencies.

Commercial paper is considered to be a fairly safe asset, because a firm's condition presumably can be monitored and predicted over a term as short as one month. Many firms issue commercial paper intending to roll it over at maturity, that is, issue new paper to obtain the funds necessary to retire the old paper. If in the meantime there are doubts raised about their creditworthiness, then the borrowers may be forced to turn to other, more expensive, sources of financing. For instance, in March 1992, Olympia and York was forced to retire its outstanding commercial paper several weeks before it became insolvent.

Bankers' Acceptances

A **bankers' acceptance** starts as an order to a bank by a bank's customer to pay a sum of money at a future date, typically within six months. At this stage, it is similar to a postdated cheque. In return for a stamping fee, the bank endorses the order for payment as "accepted"; it thereby assumes responsibility for ultimate payment to the holder of the acceptance, making the instrument second only to T-bills in terms of default security. At this point, the acceptance may be traded in secondary markets like any other claim on the bank. Bankers' acceptances are considered very safe assets because traders can substitute the bank's credit standing for their own. They are used widely in foreign trade where the creditworthiness of one trader is unknown to the trading partner. Acceptances sell at a discount from the face value of the payment order, just as T-bills sell at a discount from par value, with a similar calculation for yield.

Eurodollars

Eurodollars are U.S. dollar–denominated deposits at foreign banks or foreign branches of American banks. By locating outside the United States, these banks escape regulation by the Federal Reserve Board. Despite the tag "Euro," these accounts need not be in European banks, although that is where the practice of accepting dollar-denominated deposits outside the United States began.

Most Eurodollar deposits are for large sums, and most are time deposits of less than six months' maturity. A variation on the Eurodollar time deposit is the Eurodollar certificate of deposit. A Eurodollar CD resembles a U.S. domestic bank CD, except that it is the liability of a non-U.S. branch of a bank (typically a London branch). The advantage of Eurodollar CDs over Eurodollar time deposits is that the holder can sell the asset to realize its cash value before maturity. Eurodollar CDs are considered less liquid and riskier than U.S. domestic CDs, however, and thus offer higher yields. Firms also issue Eurodollar bonds, which are dollar-denominated bonds in Europe, although bonds are not a money market investment because of their long maturities.

All of the above instruments—time deposits, CDs, and bonds—also exist denominated in all major currencies; these are labelled Eurocurrency instruments when located outside the country of currency. When issued in Canadian dollar denominations then they are referred to as *Euro-Canadian* dollars; these constitute a minor portion of the Eurocurrency market, which is dominated by Eurodollar trading.

Repos and Reverses

Dealers in government securities use **repurchase agreements** (also called **repos** or **RPs**) as a form of short-term, usually overnight, borrowing. The dealer sells government securities to an investor on an overnight basis, with an agreement to buy back those securities the next day at a slightly higher price. The increase in the price is the overnight interest. The dealer thus takes out a one-day loan from the investor, and the securities serve as collateral.

A *term repo* is essentially an identical transaction, except that the term of the implicit loan can be 30 days or more. Repos are considered very safe in terms of credit risk because the loans are backed by the government securities. A *reverse repo* is the mirror image of a repo. Here, the dealer finds an investor holding government securities and buys them, agreeing to sell them back at a specified higher price on a future date.

Brokers' Call Loans

Individuals who buy stocks on margin borrow part of the funds to pay for the stocks from their broker. The broker in turn may borrow the funds from a bank, agreeing to repay the bank immediately (on call) if the bank requests it. Chartered banks make such call loans to investment firms that use them to finance their inventory of securities. The rate paid on these loans is usually closely related to the rate on short-term T-bills.

The LIBOR Market

The **London Interbank Offered Rate (LIBOR)** is the rate at which large banks in London are willing to lend money among themselves. This rate has become the premier short-term interest rate quoted in the European money market, and it serves as a reference rate for a wide range of transactions. For example, a corporation might borrow at a rate equal to LIBOR plus 2 percent.

Yields on Money Market Instruments

Although most money market securities are of low risk, they are not risk-free. For example, as we noted earlier, the U.S. commercial paper market was rocked by the Penn Central bankruptcy, which precipitated a default on $82 million of commercial paper. Money market investors in that country became more sensitive to creditworthiness after this episode, and the yield spread between low- and high-quality paper widened.

The securities of the money market do promise yields greater than those on default-free T-bills, at least in part because of greater relative riskiness. In addition, many investors require more liquidity; thus they will accept lower yields on securities such as T-bills that can be quickly and cheaply sold for cash. Figure 2.2 shows that commercial paper, for example, has consistently paid a risk premium over T-bills of approximately equal maturity. Moreover, that risk premium increased with economic crises, such as the energy price shocks associated with the two OPEC disturbances, even though it has been lower overall in more recent years, as compared to earlier periods.

T-Bill Yields T-bill yields are not quoted in the financial pages as effective annual rates of return. Instead, the **bond equivalent yield** is used. To illustrate this method, consider a $1,000 par value T-bill sold at $960 with a maturity of a half-year, or 182 days. With the bond equivalent

Figure 2.2 Yield spread between 3-month corporate paper and T-bills.

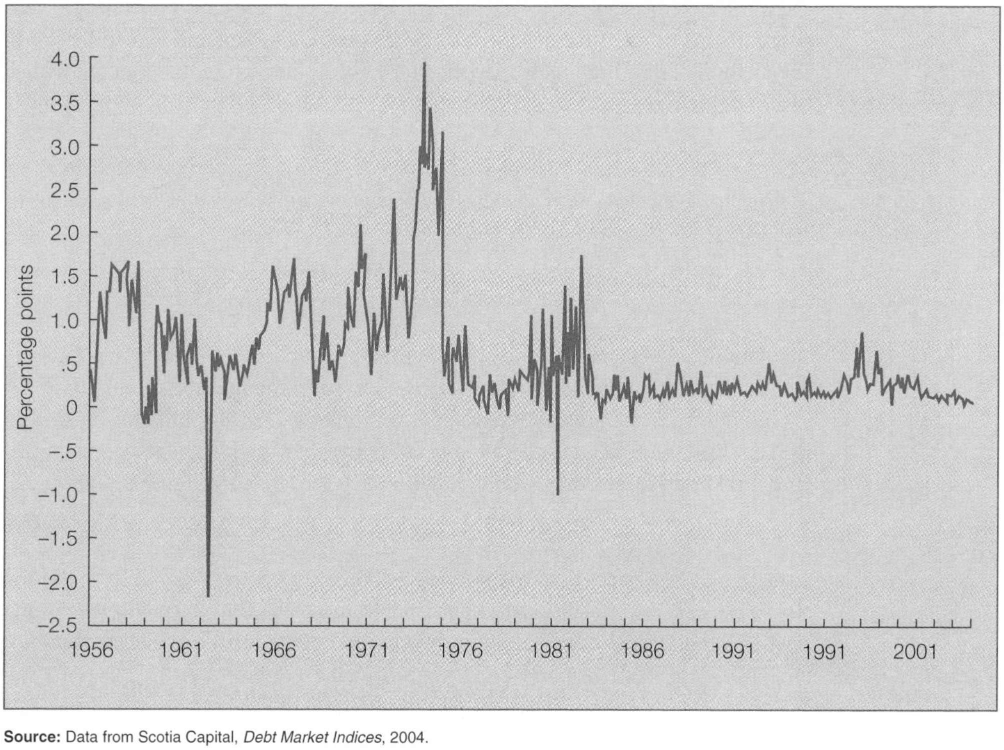

Source: Data from Scotia Capital, *Debt Market Indices*, 2004.

yield method, the bill's discount from par value, which here equals \$40, is "annualized" based on a 365-day year. The \$40 discount is annualized as

$$\$40 \times (365/182) = \$80.22$$

The result is divided by the \$960 purchase price to obtain a bond equivalent yield of 8.356 percent per year. Rather than report T-bill prices, the financial pages report these bond equivalent yields.

The bond equivalent yield is not an accurate measure of the effective annual rate of return. To see this, note that the half-year holding period return on the bill is 4.17 percent: the \$960 investment provides \$40 in earnings, and 40/960 = .0417. The compound interest annualized rate of return, or **effective annual yield**, is therefore

$$(1.0417)^2 - 1 = .0851 = 8.51\%$$

We can highlight the source of the discrepancy between the bond equivalent yield and the effective annual yield by examining the bond equivalent yield formula:

$$r_{\text{BEY}} = \frac{1{,}000 - P}{P} \times \frac{365}{n} \qquad (2.1)$$

where P is the bond price, n is the maturity of the bill in days, and r_{BEY} is the bond equivalent yield. The bond equivalent formula thus takes the bill's discount from par as a fraction of price and then annualizes by the factor $365/n$. The annualization technique uses simple interest rather than compound interest. Multiplication by $365/n$ does not account for the ability to earn interest on interest, which is the essence of compounding. The discrepancy is, therefore, greater for a 91-day bill and disappears for a one-year bill.

The quoted yields for U.S. T-bills use a formula similar to that in equation 2.1, with a 360-day year and the par value of 1,000 in the denominator instead of P. The resulting yield is known as the **bank discount yield**. As a result, the quoted U.S. rate for the example would have been 7.912 percent. Part of the difference in yields between Canadian and U.S. bills can thus be attributed to the method of quoting yields. A convenient formula relating the bond equivalent yield to the bank discount yield is

$$r_{\text{BEY}} = \frac{365 \times d}{360 - (d \times n)}$$

where d is the discount yield. Suppose $d = .07912$; then

$$r_{\text{BEY}} = \frac{365 \times .07912}{360 - (.07912 \times 182)} = .08356$$

the previously derived yield. Hence, in this case, about .4 percentage points of the differential between Canadian and U.S. quoted yields stem from the method of calculation.

In Figure 2.1, the money market listings include Treasury bills for closing prices on August 21, 2001. Three-month T-bills show a bond equivalent yield of 3.94 percent. To determine a bill's true market price, we must solve equation 2.1 for P. Rearranging equation 2.1, we obtain

$$P = 1{,}000/[1 + r_{\text{BEY}} \times (n/365)] \qquad (2.2)$$

Equation 2.2 in effect first "deannualizes" the bond equivalent yield to obtain the actual proportional interest rate, then discounts the par value of \$1,000 to obtain the T-bill's sale price. In the case at hand, $n = 91$ days, and the yield is 3.94 percent for the bill, so that the price is

$$\$1{,}000/[1 + .0394 \times (91/365)] = \$990.27$$

CONCEPT CHECK

1. Find the price of the six-month bill from Figure 2.1.

The bond equivalent yield is the bill's yield over its life, assuming that it is purchased for the auction bid price and annualized using simple interest techniques. Note that this yield uses a simple interest procedure to annualize, also known as *annual percentage rate* (APR), and so there are problems in comparing yields on bills with different maturities. Nevertheless, yields on most securities with less than a year to maturity are annualized using a simple interest approach.

Finally, the effective annual yield on the quoted bill based on the market price, \$990.27, is 4.00 percent. The bond's 91-day return equals (1,000 – \$990.27)/\$990.27 or .9826 percent. Annualizing this return, we obtain $(1.009826)^{365/91} = 1.04$, implying an effective annual interest rate of 4.00 percent.

2.2 THE FIXED-INCOME CAPITAL MARKET

Bond Market Canada www.bondcan.com

The fixed-income capital market is composed of longer-term borrowing instruments than those that trade in the money market. This market includes Government of Canada bonds, provincial and municipal bonds, corporate bonds, and mortgage securities. Bonds can be **callable** during a given period; this feature allows the issuer to redeem the bond at par value, or at a stated premium prior to maturity.

The title "fixed-income" is given to these securities because most of them promise either a fixed stream of income or a stream of income that is determined according to a specified formula. Payments are administered by the issuer or a banking agent on the issuer's behalf. These payments are fixed unless the issuer is declared bankrupt.

Government of Canada Bonds

The Canadian government borrows funds in large part by selling both nonmarketable and marketable debt securities. The nonmarketable securities are known as Canada Savings Bonds (CSBs) or Canada Premium Bonds (CPBs); they are issued every year starting November 1, with a sale period of a few months. Although these bonds are nontransferable, they bear little interest rate risk. The CSBs are perfectly liquid, since they can be cashed any time prior to maturity at face value plus accrued interest. The CPBs can only be cashed in November of succeeding years, so they are somewhat like 365-day term deposits; interest rates also rise if the realized holding period is longer. Because of the redemption feature, the valuation of CSBs is quite complex and transcends the level of this text. These instruments are more accurately described as savings certificates than bonds. See the boxed article for the latest twist.

Government of Canada Bonds, also known as *Canadas* or *Canada Bonds,* are longer-term marketable debt securities issued by the Canadian federal government. These bonds have varying maturities at issue date, ranging up to 40 years. They are considered part of the money market when their term becomes less than three years. Canada bonds are generally noncallable and make semiannual coupon payments that are set at a competitive level designed to ensure their issue at or near par value.

www.theglobeandmail.com

Figure 2.3 shows a listing of actively traded Canada bonds as they appear in *The Globe and Mail.* Under the "Government of Canada and Agencies" section, note the bond that matures in September 2006 (*highlighted*). The coupon income, or interest, paid by the bond is 5.75 percent of par value,

SAVING FALLS SHORT OF INVESTING

The first new product in five years was unveiled by the federal government's retail debt agency yesterday—Canada Investment Bonds (CIBs). Think of them as "locked-in Canada Savings Bonds," suggests Warren Baldwin, regional vice president for Toronto-based T. E. Financial Consultants Ltd. As a pilot project available only through investment dealers, CIBs pay a fixed 3% rate each year over a three-year term to maturity. While not redeemable, the 3% yields more than regular CSBs or Canada Premium Bonds over that time. Sadly, CIBs do nothing to protect investors from inflation or taxes.

A press backgrounder describes CIBs as "transferable but not redeemable before maturity." That means that, unlike the older bonds, ownership can be transferred to others. The government expects a secondary market to develop in them, says Jacqueline Orange, president of Canada Investing & Savings. However, they cannot be redeemed, except in cases of hardship. It's just as well these locked-in bonds pay more interest because the first-year rate on the new series of CSBs that went on sale yesterday is just 1.75%. That's low but better than the all-time low of 1.3% that CSBs paid in the first quarter of 2002.

CSBs should be considered an alternative to money market mutual funds, most of which also pay less than 2%. However, treasury bills pay 2.56%. Most high-yield savings accounts will beat the CSB and have equal liquidity, says Rob Whipp, branch manager for Toronto-based Fiscal Agents. ING Direct pays 2.5% and President's Choice 2.25%.

With CSBs for ready cash and CIBs as the higher-yielding locked-in version, CPBs become the middle-of-the-road compromise in yield and liquidity. Cashable once a year, they were introduced in 1998. The new series of CPBs which went on sale yesterday pay 2.45% in Year 1, rising each year to reach 5% in Year 5, for a blended yield of 3.34% over the five years.

However, CPBs pay slightly less than comparable bank escalator GICs, says David Newman, Fiscal Agents' director of information services. Thus, BMO's five-year Rate Riser GIC pays 3% in the first year, rises 25 basis points each year till Year 4, and pays 5.5% in the fifth, for a blended yield of 3.8%. TD Canada Trust's five-year Stepper GIC pays only 2.25% in Year 1, but jumps to 3.3% in Year 2 and 6% in Year 5, for a blended yield of 3.81%.

CI&S does a better job of competing against the three-year GICs of the banks with its new CIBs. TD Canada Trust three-year GICs pay just 2.45%, while comparable products at three other big banks pay 2.35%, all less than the 3% of the CIB. However, the CIB pays less than some of the independents like ING Direct's 3.5% or Community Trust's 3.6%, Whipp says.

Questioned as to the accuracy of describing a savings vehicle as an investment, Orange says the banks use similar terminology in their Guaranteed Investment Certificates. Besides, the name Canada Investment Bonds tested well in focus groups. Orange laughs off the suggestion CIBs should be renamed the "Barely Break Even After Inflation Bonds." As predicted earlier this week, the new product does nothing to address taxes or inflation. There is some precedent for the former. The Ontario Opportunity Bonds issued in the spring paid 4.25% for a five-year term and are free of Ontario income taxes payable.

As for inflation, Orange's view is it will stay within the government-mandated range of 1% to 3% per year, which goes "hand in hand" with the low interest rates that have prevailed so far this century. Those concerned about inflation can buy Real Return Bonds from brokers, but something like America's Inflation Bonds would have been a welcome addition to the CI&S stable.

For many CSB investors, the year 2001 was a big shock as older maturing CSBs paying 5.5% were replaced by issues paying just 1.8%. "There was a lot of sticker shock there," Orange says. "I personally feel that, like it or not, we Canadians have become resigned to lower rates. They're not a flash in the pan." Even so, CSB sales have stayed steady the last four years. Sales to the first quarter of 2003 were $3.5-billion, up 29% from $2.8-billion to the first quarter of 2002. Total sales in fiscal 2001 were $3.3-billion and in 2000 [were] $2.9-billion.

For the well-heeled, the agency has raised the maximum which can be invested "per registration" to $500,000 from the previous $200,000. But it's hard to believe such clients wouldn't also welcome innovative new CSBs that protected them from the ravages of taxes and inflation.

Source: Jonathan Chevreau, "Personal Finance," Financial Post Investing, *National Post*, October 2, 2003, p. IN.01.F. © National Post 2003. Don Mills, ON.

meaning that for a $1,000 face value bond, $57.50 in annual interest payments will be made in two semiannual installments of $28.75 each. In the trading of a security, bid and ask prices are quoted; these represent, respectively, the price at which an investor can sell or buy the asset. The bid-side price given here shows $107.18, denoting a percentage of par value. Thus, the price shown should be interpreted as 107.18 percent of par, or $1,071.80 for a $1,000 face value bond. Finally, the yield to maturity on the bond is 2.73 percent at the ask, which is a decrease of .006 (.6 basis points) from the previous close.

The quotations also highlight the benchmarks for standard-length Canada bonds and for key international government issues. Also, actively traded provincials, corporates, and strips are shown. Note as well the real return bond quotations and the Scotia Capital Bond Indices.

Figure 2.3
Canadian bond quotations.

CANADIAN BONDS

Bond quotations supplied by CBID Markets Inc. Closing prices and yields as of 4:00 PM yesterday. Most active based on volume traded. Yields are semi-annual compound to maturity. "Yield Chg" is the change in ask yield from the previous close.

Issuer	Coupon	Maturity Date	Bid Price	Ask Price	Bid Yld	Ask Yld	Yield Chg
GOVERNMENT OF CANADA BENCHMARKS							
2 Year	3.000	2005-Dec-01	100.91	100.93	2.46	2.45	+0.003
5 Year	4.250	2008-Sep-01	103.15	103.20	3.48	3.47	-0.005
10 Year	5.250	2013-Jun-01	106.50	106.60	4.39	4.37	0.000
20 Year	8.000	2023-Jun-01	137.83	137.91	4.93	4.93	-0.008
30 Year	5.750	2029-Jun-01	110.05	110.15	5.04	5.03	-0.010
ACTIVE PROVINCIALS AND AGENCIES							
Ontario	5.850	2033-Mar-08	105.78	105.97	5.45	5.44	-0.007
Ontario	3.500	2006-Sep-08	101.53	101.58	2.86	2.84	-0.016
Ontario	4.750	2013-Jun-02	100.79	100.84	4.64	4.64	+0.005
Quebec	6.000	2029-Oct-01	106.51	106.64	5.52	5.51	-0.003
Ontario	4.400	2008-Nov-19	103.06	103.12	3.68	3.67	-0.005
ACTIVE CORPORATES							
BNS	4.295	2008-Aug-22	102.28	102.36	3.73	3.71	+0.015
Telus Corp	7.500	2006-Jun-01	108.50	108.75	3.50	3.39	+0.007
Bombard Cap	6.600	2004-Nov-29	101.70	102.20	4.18	3.48	-0.011
Ford Cr Cda	5.800	2006-Sep-26	103.29	103.67	4.42	4.26	+0.009
Bell CDA	6.250	2012-Apr-12	109.40	109.65	4.83	4.80	+0.003
ACTIVE STRIPS (COUPONS AND RESIDUALS)							
Quebec	0.000	2005-Jun-01		97.05		2.45	+0.006
Canada	0.000	2008-Dec-01	83.86	84.25	3.76	3.66	0.000
Canada	0.000	2011-Dec-01	70.80	71.33	4.52	4.42	-0.002
Canada	0.000	2007-Oct-01	88.93	89.25	3.32	3.22	0.000
Ontario	0.000	2009-Jun-02	80.89	81.91	4.10	3.85	-0.001
GOVERNMENT OF CANADA AND AGENCIES							
BusDevBk Cda	5.650	2005-Aug-17	104.55	104.62	2.42	2.37	-0.004
CMHC	5.750	2004-Dec-01	102.60	102.65	2.15	2.08	+0.019
CMHC	5.300	2007-Dec-03	106.94	106.95	3.31	3.31	0.000
CMHC	5.500	2012-Jun-01	107.53	107.63	4.40	4.38	0.000
Canada	13.500	2004-Jun-01		102.64		1.96	+0.012
Canada	3.500	2004-Jun-01	100.30	100.33	2.17	2.03	+0.004
Canada	6.500	2004-Jun-01	100.99	101.02	2.15	2.02	-0.002
Canada	5.000	2004-Sep-01	101.32	101.34	2.21	2.17	+0.020
Canada	10.500	2004-Oct-01		104.66		2.16	+0.019
Canada	4.250	2004-Dec-01	101.50	101.56	2.18	2.10	+0.010
Canada	9.000	2004-Dec-01	104.94	104.95	2.15	2.14	+0.042
Canada	6.000	2005-Sep-01	105.23	105.28	2.39	2.35	+0.009
Canada	8.750	2005-Dec-01	110.62	110.64	2.45	2.44	-0.005
Canada	5.750	2006-Sep-01	107.18	107.20	2.74	2.73	-0.006
Canada	7.000	2006-Dec-01	110.84	110.88	2.84	2.83	-0.008
Canada	7.250	2007-Jun-01	112.89	112.93	3.03	3.01	-0.005
Canada	4.500	2007-Sep-01	104.47	104.51	3.13	3.12	-0.005
Canada	6.000	2008-Jun-01	110.13	110.18	3.41	3.39	-0.005
Canada	4.250	2008-Sep-01	103.15	103.20	3.48	3.47	-0.005
Canada	5.500	2009-Jun-01	108.47	108.53	3.70	3.69	-0.006
Canada	5.500	2010-Jun-01	108.51	108.55	3.94	3.94	+0.001
Canada	6.000	2011-Jun-01	111.56	111.63	4.13	4.12	+0.001
Canada	5.250	2012-Jun-01	106.71	106.80	4.27	4.26	+0.002
Canada	5.250	2013-Jun-01	106.50	106.60	4.39	4.37	0.000
Canada	8.000	2023-Jun-01	137.83	137.91	4.93	4.93	-0.008
Canada	8.000	2027-Jun-01	140.40	140.52	5.03	5.02	-0.012
Canada	5.750	2029-Jun-01	110.05	110.15	5.04	5.03	-0.010
Canada	5.750	2033-Jun-01	111.21	111.33	5.01	5.01	-0.012
Cda House Tr	5.527	2006-Jun-15	106.15	106.21	2.71	2.69	+0.009
Cda House Tr	4.750	2007-Mar-15	104.93	104.98	3.03	3.01	-0.008
Cda House Tr	5.100	2007-Sep-15	106.15	106.20	3.23	3.22	-0.005
Exp Dev Cda	5.500	2004-Jun-18	100.90	100.92	2.19	2.12	+0.021
Exp Dev Cda	5.750	2011-Jun-01	109.22	109.26	4.25	4.25	-0.002
Exp Dev Cda	5.800	2012-Dec-03	109.41	109.57	4.49	4.46	+0.003
Farm Cr Cda	5.750	2004-Apr-15		100.38		1.85	+0.004
PROVINCIALS AND AGENCIES							
Alberta	6.375	2004-Jun-01		100.99		1.98	-0.004
Alberta	5.750	2004-Dec-01	102.56	102.60	2.19	2.13	0.000
Alberta	5.650	2007-Oct-01		108.11		3.22	0.000
AltaCapFinAu	5.850	2012-Jun-01		109.75		4.42	-0.001
BC	9.000	2004-Jun-21		101.97		1.96	+0.020
BC	8.000	2005-Aug-23	107.92	108.01	2.44	2.38	-0.003
BC	5.250	2006-Dec-01	106.00	106.04	2.94	2.93	-0.001
BC	6.000	2008-Jun-09	109.62	109.65	3.54	3.53	-0.005
BC	5.700	2009-Jun-01	108.67	108.70	3.85	3.85	-0.003
BC	6.250	2009-Dec-01	111.53	111.59	3.98	3.97	-0.006
BC	6.375	2010-Aug-23	112.40	112.46	4.17	4.16	+0.001
BC	5.750	2012-Jan-09	108.77	108.79	4.41	4.41	+0.009
BC	8.500	2013-Aug-23	129.54	129.66	4.61	4.60	0.000
BC	7.500	2014-Jun-09	122.86	123.05	4.67	4.65	0.000
BC	8.000	2023-Sep-08		133.79		5.22	-0.008
BC	6.150	2027-Nov-19		111.02		5.33	-0.008
BC	5.700	2029-Jun-18	104.27	104.46	5.39	5.37	-0.007
BC	6.350	2031-Jun-18	113.74	113.89	5.38	5.37	-0.005
BC MFA	8.500	2005-Apr-12		106.69		2.26	0.000
BC MFA	7.750	2005-Dec-01	108.74	108.76	2.55	2.54	+0.009
BC MFA	7.250	2006-Sep-25		110.54		2.92	+0.009
Fin Quebec	6.300	2006-Jun-01		107.73		2.70	+0.009
Fin Quebec	5.750	2008-Dec-01	108.73	108.87	3.72	3.69	-0.005
Hydro-Quebec	8.500	2005-Aug-15	108.55	108.62	2.41	2.36	+0.002
Hydro-Quebec	7.000	2007-Feb-15		111.20		2.99	+0.009
Hydro-Quebec	6.500	2011-Feb-15	113.00	113.21	4.31	4.28	-0.005
Hydro-Quebec	10.000	2011-Sep-26		135.80		4.38	0.000
Hydro-Quebec	6.500	2035-Feb-15	114.03	114.69	5.55	5.51	0.000
Manitoba	5.650	2004-Jul-15	101.17	101.21	2.30	2.17	+0.007
Manitoba	9.375	2004-Nov-15	104.74	104.79	2.34	2.27	+0.020
Manitoba	6.250	2005-Jun-22	104.93	105.00	2.33	2.29	+0.002
Manitoba	5.100	2006-Dec-01		105.70		2.91	+0.009
Manitoba	6.625	2007-May-16		110.44		3.15	0.000
Manitoba	5.750	2008-Jun-02	108.60	108.78	3.54	3.50	-0.005
Manitoba	5.850	2011-Jan-25		109.62		4.22	-0.005
NB MFA	5.625	2004-Aug-25		101.58		2.18	-0.009
NB MFA	6.250	2005-Aug-10		105.15		2.54	+0.002
NS MFC	8.000	2004-Nov-14		103.83		2.30	0.000
NewBrunswick	5.400	2004-Jun-09		100.86		1.92	-0.002
NewBrunswick	8.750	2005-Apr-19	107.09	107.17	2.25	2.18	+0.020
NewBrunswick	7.500	2005-Dec-15	108.46	108.55	2.57	2.52	+0.009
NewBrunswick	7.100	2006-Oct-16		110.51		2.88	+0.007
NewBrunswick	5.700	2008-Jun-02		108.41		3.54	-0.005
NewBrunswick	5.250	2009-Jun-02		106.45		3.87	-0.001
NewBrunswick	10.250	2009-Jun-22	130.01	130.14	3.91	3.89	-0.003
NewBrunswick	5.850	2011-Dec-01	109.13	109.20	4.44	4.43	+0.007
NewBrunswick	5.875	2012-Dec-06	108.99	109.11	4.61	4.60	+0.005
NewBrunswick	5.650	2028-Dec-27		102.80		5.44	-0.008
Nfld MFC	10.000	2004-Dec-15		105.80		2.33	-0.001
Nfld MFC	6.000	2009-Sep-20		109.98		3.97	0.000
NfldLabHydro	5.050	2006-Dec-01		105.31		3.01	+0.006
NfldLabHydro	5.500	2008-Apr-30	107.41	107.54	3.56	3.53	-0.005
Nova Scotia	6.250	2004-Dec-01	102.78	102.85	2.38	2.29	+0.019
Ont Elec Fin	7.750	2005-Nov-03	108.42	108.48	2.51	2.47	+0.009
Ont Elec Fin	5.600	2008-Jun-02	108.00	108.01	3.55	3.54	+0.008
Ont Elec Fin	10.750	2021-Aug-06		162.73		5.22	-0.008
Ontario	4.875	2004-Jun-02	100.62	100.64	2.13	2.08	+0.019
Ontario	9.000	2004-Sep-15	103.43	103.50	2.27	2.15	+0.020
Ontario	6.250	2005-Mar-08	103.90	103.93	2.27	2.25	+0.020
Ontario	8.250	2005-Dec-01	109.60	109.62	2.53	2.53	+0.006
Ontario	7.500	2006-Jan-19	108.86	108.89	2.59	2.58	+0.009
Ontario	5.900	2006-Mar-08	106.31	106.34	2.64	2.62	-0.008
Ontario	7.750	2006-Jul-24	111.27	111.32	2.81	2.79	+0.003
Ontario	5.200	2007-Mar-08	106.09	106.12	3.06	3.05	-0.005
Ontario	6.125	2007-Sep-12	109.42	109.47	3.26	3.25	-0.005
Ontario	5.700	2008-Dec-01	108.63	108.70	3.69	3.68	-0.008
Ontario	6.200	2009-Nov-19	111.19	111.20	3.98	3.98	-0.003
Ontario	6.100	2010-Nov-19	110.84	110.90	4.22	4.21	+0.008
Ontario	6.100	2011-Dec-02	110.94	110.96	4.41	4.41	+0.009
Ontario	5.375	2012-Dec-02	105.70	105.76	4.57	4.57	+0.005
Ontario	8.100	2023-Sep-08	134.03	134.06	5.28	5.28	-0.008
Ontario	7.600	2027-Jun-02	128.90	129.10	5.40	5.39	-0.004
Ontario	6.500	2029-Mar-08	114.30	114.44	5.45	5.44	-0.006
Ontario	6.200	2031-Jun-02	110.70	110.88	5.44	5.43	-0.008
Quebec	6.500	2005-Dec-01	106.61	106.69	2.57	2.52	+0.009
Quebec	7.750	2006-Mar-30	110.11	110.18	2.66	2.64	+0.009
Quebec	9.500	2006-May-01		114.22		2.63	+0.006
Quebec	6.500	2007-Oct-01	110.73	110.78	3.28	3.27	-0.006
Quebec	5.500	2009-Jun-01	107.60	107.64	3.88	3.87	-0.003
Quebec	10.000	2010-Jun-28		132.44		4.10	-0.001
Quebec	6.250	2010-Dec-01	111.50	111.55	4.26	4.26	+0.003
Quebec	6.000	2012-Oct-01	109.82	109.86	4.60	4.59	+0.004
Quebec	9.375	2023-Jan-16		148.66		5.27	-0.048
Quebec	8.500	2026-Apr-01	138.96	139.00	5.44	5.44	-0.005
Quebec	6.000	2029-Oct-01	106.51	106.64	5.52	5.51	-0.003
Quebec	6.250	2032-Jun-01	110.44	110.48	5.52	5.51	-0.001
Saskatchewan	9.500	2004-Aug-16		103.16		2.24	+0.020
Saskatchewan	9.625	2004-Dec-30		105.97		2.14	+0.020
Saskatchewan	7.500	2005-Dec-19		108.60		2.52	+0.007
Saskatchewan	4.750	2006-Dec-01		104.89		2.87	+0.006
Saskatchewan	6.250	2007-Mar-09	109.01	109.18	3.08	3.02	+0.009
Saskatchewan	5.000	2007-Sep-06		105.76		3.24	-0.006
Saskatchewan	5.500	2008-Jun-02	107.63	107.66	3.54	3.53	-0.005
Saskatchewan	6.500	2009-Nov-12	112.62	112.75	3.99	3.97	-0.003
Saskatchewan	6.150	2010-Sep-01		111.17		4.16	0.000
Saskatchewan	10.250	2014-Apr-10		144.45		4.67	0.000
CORPORATES							
407 Intl	6.050	2009-Jul-27		109.13		4.14	0.000
Aliant Telec	6.450	2004-Oct-15		102.48		2.26	+0.021
Aliant Telec	6.700	2005-Nov-24		106.68		2.67	+0.009
Aliant Telec	5.350	2007-Jan-15		105.76		3.22	+0.009
BC Gas Inc	6.300	2008-Dec-01		109.57		4.05	-0.005
BCE Inc.	7.350	2009-Oct-30		115.56		4.22	-0.008
BMO	7.000	2010-Jan-28	114.90	115.20	4.12	4.07	-0.006
BMO Cap Tr	6.685	2011-Dec-31	112.02	112.25	4.82	4.79	+0.004
BNS	5.750	2009-May-12		108.13		3.99	-0.005
Bell CDA	6.500	2005-May-09		104.66		2.42	+0.002
Bell CDA	8.800	2005-Aug-17		108.82		2.53	-0.003
Bell CDA	6.700	2007-Jun-28	110.38	110.56	3.35	3.30	0.000
Bell CDA	6.250	2008-Jan-18	109.30	109.55	3.64	3.58	-0.005
Bell CDA	6.150	2009-Jun-15	109.48	109.67	4.13	4.09	-0.001
Bell CDA	10.350	2009-Dec-15		131.32		4.18	-0.005
Bell CDA	5.500	2010-Aug-12		106.19		4.38	0.000
Bell CDA	6.900	2011-Dec-15		114.34		4.67	+0.004
Bell CDA	6.250	2012-Apr-12	109.40	109.65	4.83	4.80	+0.003
Bell CDA	6.550	2029-May-01		106.97		6.01	-0.008
Bombard Cap	6.600	2004-Nov-29	101.70	102.20	4.18	3.48	-0.011

Source: Report on Business, *The Globe and Mail*, March 5, 2004, p. B14. Reprinted with permission of The Globe and Mail.

The **yield to maturity** reported in the financial pages is calculated by determining the semi annual yield and then doubling it, rather than compounding it for two half-year periods. This use of a simple interest technique to annualize means that the yield is quoted on an annual percentage rate (APR) basis, rather than as an effective annual yield. The APR method in this context is also called the *bond equivalent yield.* From Figure 2.3 we can see that the yields on Government of Canada bonds are generally rising with term to maturity; this is not true uniformly, due to the different coupons of bonds with similar maturities. Listings for callable bonds trading at a premium (selling above par value) show the yield calculated to the first call date, while for discount bonds the yield is calculated to the redemption date. (No such callable bonds appear in Figure 2.3.)

CONCEPT CHECK

2. Why does it make sense to calculate yields on discount bonds to maturity and yields on premium bonds to the first call date?

The current yield on a bond is annual coupon income per dollar invested in the bond. For this Canada 5.75 percent bond, the current yield is then

$$\text{Current yield} = \frac{\text{Annual coupon income}}{\text{Price}} = \frac{5.75}{107.18} = .0536 \text{ or } 5.36 \text{ percent}$$

Provincial and Municipal Bonds

Figure 2.3 shows a representative sample of bonds issued by provincial governments and by provincial Crown corporations; the latter are generally guaranteed by the corresponding provincial government. All these bonds are similar in their characteristics to federal government issues, with a variety of maturities and coupon rates, and are available to investors at any given time. These securities are considered extremely safe assets, even though not as safe as comparable Government of Canada bonds. Consequently, a small yield spread can be observed in Figure 2.3 between Government of Canada bonds and provincial bonds, as well as between the bonds of the various provinces. For instance, bonds maturing in September 2007 yield 3.12 percent for Canada's, and 3.25 percent for Ontario's. British Columbia's December 2009 bonds yield .10 percentage points more than Quebec's June 2009 bonds.

U.S. municipal bonds are exempt from federal income tax and from state and local tax in the issuing state. Hence, the quoted yield is an after-tax yield, which should be compared with after-tax yields on other bonds. This explains why the quoted yields on municipals are lower than the quoted (before-tax) yields on other, comparable bonds. Since the tax advantage is not available to Canadian investors, U.S. municipal bonds generally would not be attractive to them.

Corporate Bonds

Corporate bonds enable private firms to borrow money directly from the public. These bonds are similar in structure to government issues—they typically pay semiannual coupons over their lives and return the face value to the bondholder at maturity. They differ most importantly from government bonds in degree of risk. Default risk is a real consideration in the purchase of corporate bonds, and Chapter 11 discusses this issue in considerable detail. For now, we distinguish only between *secured bonds*, which have specific collateral backing them in the event of firm bankruptcy, unsecured bonds called **debentures**, which have no collateral, and **subordinated debentures**, which have a lower priority claim to the firm's assets in the event of bankruptcy. Referring to Figure 2.3 again, we see a BCE bond (*highlighted*) maturing in 2009 and paying a coupon of 7.35 percent; its yield of 4.22 percent compares with the above-mentioned government bonds with yields ranging from 3.12 percent to 3.25 percent.

Corporate bonds usually come with options attached. **Callable bonds** give the firm the option to repurchase the bond from the holder at a stipulated call price. **Retractable** and **extendible bonds** give the holder the option, respectively, to redeem the bonds earlier and later than the stated maturity date. **Convertible bonds** give the bondholder the option to convert each bond into a stipulated number of shares of stock. These options are treated in more detail in Chapter 11.

Mortgages and Mortgage-Backed Securities

An investments text of 30 years ago probably would not include a section on mortgage loans, since at that time investors could not invest in them. Now, because of the explosion in mortgage-backed securities, almost anyone can invest in a portfolio of mortgage loans, and these securities have become a major component of a fixed-income market.

Home mortgages are usually written with a long-term (25-to-30-year maturity) amortization of the principal. Until the 1970s, almost all such mortgages had a fixed interest rate over the life of the loan, with equal fixed monthly payments. Since then these so-called conventional mortgages have become renewable at one-to-five-year intervals, at which point their interest rates may be renegotiated. More recently, a diverse set of alternative mortgage designs has been developed.

Fixed-rate mortgages pose difficulties to banks in years of increasing interest rates because of the mismatching of the maturities of assets and liabilities. Banks commonly issue short-term liabilities (the deposits of their customers) and hold long-term assets such as fixed-rate mortgages. Hence, they suffer losses when interest rates increase: the rates they pay on deposits increase while their mortgage income remains fixed. The five-year renewal period helps to alleviate this problem.

A more recent introduction is the **variable rate mortgage**. These mortgages require the borrower to pay an interest rate that varies with some measure of the current market interest rate. For example, the interest rate might be set at two points above the current rate on one-year Treasury bills and might be adjusted once a year. Often, a contract sets a limit, or cap, on the maximum size of an interest rate change within a year and over the life of the contract. The variable rate contract shifts the risk of fluctuations in interest rates from the lender to the borrower.

Because of the shifting of interest rate risk to their customers, banks are willing to offer lower rates on variable rate mortgages than on conventional fixed-rate mortgages. This proved to be a great inducement to borrowers during a period of high interest rates in the early 1980s. As interest rates fell, however, conventional mortgages appeared to regain popularity.

A *mortgage-backed security* (MBS) is either an ownership claim in a pool of mortgages or an obligation that is secured by such a pool. These claims represent securitization of mortgage loans. Mortgage lenders originate loans and then sell packages of these loans in the secondary market. Specifically, they sell their claim to the cash inflows from the mortgages as those loans are paid off. The mortgage originator continues to service the loan, collecting principal and interest payments, and passes these payments along to the purchaser of the mortgage. For this reason, these mortgage-backed securities are called **pass-throughs**.

For example, suppose that ten 30-year mortgages, each with a principal value of $100,000, are grouped into a million-dollar pool. If the mortgage rate is 10 percent, then the first month's payment for each loan would be $877.57, of which $833.33 would be interest and

Figure 2.4 Mortgage-backed securities.

MORTGAGE-BACKED SECURITIES

List provided by CIBC World Markets Inc. and shows the gross bid price for transactions of at least $1-million at Friday's close. Indicated yields assume no prepayments. All are priced to weighted average maturity date.

fund	issuer	maturity	coupon	price	yield
PREPAYABLE					
97002190	TD Bank	Jun.04	5.000	100.33300	2.60
96413562	Alberta Motor	Jun.05	6.100	103.55771	2.73
96413760	Alberta Motor	Oct.06	4.800	103.59147	3.03
97003263	CIBC	Jun.07	4.500	102.75716	3.22
96413836	Alberta Motor	Jan.07	4.850	103.71937	3.14
97500557	Royal Bank	Mar.07	4.750	103.76810	3.25
97003917	BNS	Feb.08	4.650	103.06484	3.43
96414073	Alberta Motor	Mar.08	4.350	102.56207	3.50
96413323	MRS Trust	Dec.08	5.700	105.46175	3.93
96413463	MRS Trust	Oct.09	5.750	105.56861	4.06
NONPREPAYABLE					
99008534	TD Bank	Mar.05	3.875	101.25720	2.52
99008294	TD Bank	Sep.05	5.750	104.42957	2.67
96600804	Maritime Life	Nov.05	5.000	103.15441	2.71
96501606	Equitable Tr	Sep.06	4.800	103.75360	3.13
99008443	TD Bank	Sep.06	5.000	104.45157	3.04
99008526	TD Bank	Mar.07	4.625	103.65471	3.25
96601091	Peoples	Oct.08	5.200	105.04518	3.89
99008005	BMO	Apr.09	5.375	106.12343	3.91
99008641	BNS	Dec.12	4.900	101.32902	4.66
99008682	BNS	Jul.13	4.050	95.15036	4.75

Source: Report on Business, *The Globe and Mail*, February 9, 2004, p. B10. Reprinted with permission of The Globe and Mail.

$44.24 would be principal repayment. The holder of the mortgage pool would receive a payment in the first month of $8,775.70, the total payments of all 10 of the mortgages in the pool.[2] In addition, if one of the mortgages happens to be paid off in any month, the holder of the pass-through security also receives that payment of principal. In future months, of course, the pool will comprise fewer loans, and the interest and principal payments will be lower. The prepaid mortgage in effect represents a partial retirement of the pass-through holder's investment. Mortgage-backed pass-through securities were first introduced in Canada by the Canada Mortgage and Housing Corporation (CMHC, a federal Crown corporation) in 1987. CMHC pass-throughs carry a federal government guarantee under the National Housing Act (NHA), which ensures the timely payment of principal and interest. Thus, the cash flow can be considered risk-free even if individual borrowers default on their mortgages. This guarantee increases the marketability of the pass-through. Therefore, investors can buy or sell NHA MBSs like any other bond.

Although pass-through securities often guarantee payment of interest and principal, they do not guarantee the rate of return. Holders of mortgage pass-throughs therefore can be severely disappointed in their returns in years when interest rates drop significantly. This is because homeowners usually have an option to prepay, or pay ahead of schedule, up to 10 percent of the remaining principal outstanding on their mortgages. This right is essentially an option held by the borrower to "call back" the loan for the remaining principal balance, quite analogous to the option held by government or corporate issuers of callable bonds. The prepayment option gives the borrower the right to buy back the loan at the outstanding principal amount rather than at the present discounted value of the *scheduled* remaining payments. The exercise of this option usually requires the payment of a penalty or bonus by the borrower,

[2]Actually, the institution that services the loan and the pass-through agency that guarantees the loan each retain a portion of the monthly payment as a charge for their services. Thus, the interest rate received by the pass-through investor is a bit less than the interest rate paid by the borrower. For example, although the ten homeowners together make total monthly payments of $8,775.70, the holder of the pass-through security may receive a total payment of only $8,740.

which also is passed through to the MBS investors; prepayments also may occur due to the sale of the underlying property. When interest rates fall, causing the present value of the scheduled mortgage payments to increase, the borrower may choose to take out a new loan at today's lower interest rate and use the proceeds of the loan to prepay or retire the outstanding mortgage. This refinancing may disappoint pass-through investors, who are liable to "receive a call" just when they might have anticipated capital gains from interest rate declines. Figure 2.4 shows a recent listing from *The Globe and Mail* of both prepayable and nonprepayable MBSs. In 2003, MSBs constituted 65 percent of the $92 billion market for asset-backed securities.

2.3 EQUITY SECURITIES

Common Stock as Ownership Shares

Common stocks, also known as *equity securities* or **equities**, represent ownership shares in a corporation. Each share of common stock entitles its owner to one vote on any matters of corporate governance that are put to a vote at the corporation's annual meeting, as well as to a share in the financial benefits of ownership.

The corporation is controlled by a board of directors elected by the shareholders. The board, which meets only a few times each year, selects managers who actually run the corporation on a day-to-day basis. Managers have the authority to make most business decisions without the board's specific approval. The board's mandate is to oversee the management to ensure that it acts in the best interests of shareholders.

The members of the board are elected at the annual meeting. Shareholders who do not attend the annual meeting can vote by **proxy**, empowering another party to vote in their name. Management usually solicits the proxies of shareholders and normally gets a vast majority of these proxy votes. Thus, management usually has considerable discretion to run the firm as it sees fit—without daily oversight from the equityholders who actually own the firm.

We noted in Chapter 1 that such separation of ownership and control can give rise to "agency problems," in which managers pursue goals not in the best interests of shareholders. However, there are several mechanisms designed to alleviate these agency problems. Among these are: compensation schemes that link the success of the manager to that of the firm; oversight by the board of directors as well as outsiders such as security analysts, creditors, or large institutional investors; the threat of a proxy contest in which unhappy shareholders attempt to replace the current management team; or the threat of a takeover by another firm.

Several Canadian firms have at times issued a special type of common stock (**restricted shares**) that has no voting rights, or only restricted voting rights, but otherwise participates fully in the financial benefits of share ownership. For instance, a company may issue two classes of shares, only one of which has the right to vote; alternatively, the senior class may have five votes and the subordinate class only one vote per share. Such shares are issued by firms that want to expand without diluting the holdings of a controlling group. Occasionally, restricted shares are issued to comply with regulatory requirements, such as those restricting foreign ownership in Canadian broadcasting.

Restricted shares sometimes carry different (generally higher) financial benefits for their holders than regular common stock. Otherwise, the loss of the right to vote should be reflected in a lower market value for restricted than for ordinary shares; this loss is the market value of the right to vote. Restricted shareholders also have some legal protection in case of tender offers. Several studies have examined this value of the voting rights, as well as other implications of restricted shares.[3]

The common stock of most large corporations can be bought or sold freely on one or more stock exchanges. A corporation whose stock is not publicly traded is said to be *closely held.* In most closely held corporations, the owners of the firm also take an active role in its management. Takeovers, therefore, are generally not an issue.

Characteristics of Common Stock

The two most important characteristics of common stock as an investment are its **residual claim** and **limited liability** features.

Residual claim means that shareholders are the last in line of all those who have a claim on the assets and income of the corporation. In a liquidation of the firm's assets, the shareholders have a claim to what is left after all other claimants, such as the tax authorities, employees, suppliers, bondholders, and other creditors, have been paid. For a firm not in liquidation, shareholders have claim to the part of operating income left over after interest and taxes have been paid. Management either can pay this residual as cash **dividends** to shareholders or reinvest it in the business to increase the value of the shares.

Limited liability means that the greatest amount shareholders can lose in event of failure of the corporation is their original investment. Unlike owners of unincorporated businesses, whose creditors can lay claim to the personal assets of the owner (e.g., house, car, furniture), corporate shareholders may at worst have worthless stock. They are not personally liable for the firm's obligations.

CONCEPT CHECK

3. a. If you buy 100 shares of Alcan stock, to what are you entitled?

b. What is the most money you can make on this investment over the next year?

c. If you pay $50 per share, what is the most money you could lose over the year?

Stock Market Listings

Toronto Stock Exchange www.tsx.ca

Figure 2.5 shows a partial listing from *The Globe and Mail*'s weekly report of stocks traded on the Toronto Stock Exchange (TSX). The TSX is the major Canadian market in which investors may buy or sell shares of stock. We will examine securities markets in detail in Chapter 3.

To interpret the information provided for each traded stock, consider the two listings for Canadian Tire, "Cdn Tire" and "Cdn Tir." These two shares are identical, except that the second or class A listing has no voting rights; for this reason, its quoted prices are lower than those of CTR, with the difference representing a large premium for the voting privilege. For the class A shares, the first two columns provide the highest and lowest price at which the stock has traded in the last 52 weeks, 44.73 and 28.70, respectively. The .40 figure following the name means that the dividend payout to its shareholders in each class over the last quarter was $.40 per share on an annual basis. Thus, Canadian Tire class A stock, which is selling at 43.85 (the last recorded, or *close* price, in the

[3]See, for instance, Vijay Jog and Allan Riding, "Price Effects of Dual-Class Shares," *Financial Analysts Journal,* January/February 1986, and "Market Reactions of Return, Risk, and Liquidity to the Creation of Restricted Voting Shares," *Canadian Journal of Administrative Sciences* 6, no. 1 (March 1989); Elizabeth Maynes, Chris Robinson, and Alan White, "How Much Is a Share Vote Worth?" *Canadian Investment Review* 3, no. 1 (Spring 1990); Chris Robinson and Alan White, "Empirical Evidence on the Relative Valuation of Voting and Restricted Voting Shares," *Canadian Journal of Administrative Sciences* 7, no. 4 (December 1990); and Elizabeth Maynes, "Evidence on the Value of a Stock Exchange Listing," *Canadian Journal of Administrative Sciences* 8, no. 3 (September 1991). There are also non-Canadian studies on restricted shares; see, for instance, M. Partch, "The Creation of a Class of Limited Voting Common Stock and Shareholder Wealth," *Journal of Financial Economics* 18, no. 2 (June 1987).

Figure 2.5 Stock market listings.

Yesterday's activity

	365-day high	365-day low	stock	sym	div	high	low	close	chg	vol 100s	yld	p/e ratio
A-B												
	0.58	.055	01 Commu	ONE		0.45	.425	.445	-.015	626		
	27.00	25.25	5Ban	FBS.PR.A	1.375	25.99	25.85	25.91	+0.04	21	5.3	
	6.40	**3.42**	**724 Solution**	**SVN**		**5.70**	**5.06**	**5.35**	**+0.35**	**3929**		
	3.70	**1.30**	**ACD Systm**	**ASA**		**1.75**	**1.62**	**1.73**	**+0.09**	**731**		**20.4**
	6.00	3.00	♣ AD OPT	AOP	0.08	5.45	5.45	5.45		59	1.5	30.3
	0.55	.165	ADB Syst	ADY		.415	.405	.405	-0.01	1246		
	1.39	0.36	♣ ADF Grp	DRX		0.64	0.61	0.63	-0.01	197		
	2.84	1.60	ADS Inc	AAL.A	0.05	1.64	1.60	1.60	-0.05	62	3.1	26.7
	19.45	11.45	AGF Man	AGF.B	0.32	18.25	17.60	18.00	+0.40	29696	1.8	37.5
↑	25.00	16.00	AIC Diversi	ADC		25.00	24.60	25.00	+1.00	10		
	3.95	0.92	AMR Tech	AMR		2.55	2.41	2.50	-0.08	211		89.3
	4.23	1.55	ART Adva	ARA		2.07	2.01	2.01	-0.06	687		
	24.00	5.83	ATI Tech	ATY		20.76	20.14	20.58	+0.28	10914		48.0
	15.80	8.10	ATS Autom	ATA		11.75	11.31	11.52	-0.13	1176		
	21.00	12.11	Aastra Tech	AAH		20.05	19.80	19.80	-0.03	333		13.1
	52.50	25.35	Aber Diam	ABZ		44.70	44.30	44.50	-0.30	1418		65.4
	9.56	8.30	♣ Aberdeen	FAP	0.72	9.44	9.27	9.40	+0.12	601	7.7	11.0
	11.34	8.22	Abitibi Consl	A	0.10	10.89	10.55	10.60	-0.27	16518	0.9	25.9
	7.45	5.15	Acetex	ATX		5.64	5.50	5.64	+0.13	43		
	0.65	0.15	Adeptron Tc	ATQ		0.55	0.52	0.55	+0.03	260		
	0.84	0.30	♣ Adherex	AHX		0.65	0.64	0.65	+0.01	1919		
	0.84	0.06	Adrian Res	ADL		0.60	0.60	0.60		160		
	.245	.065	Advantex	ADX		0.16	.145	0.16	+0.01	265		
	5.85	**3.70**	**Aecon Grp**	**ARE**	**0.03**	**5.55**	**5.30**	**5.30**	**-0.28**	**111**	**0.6**	
	10.00	3.52	Aeterna	AEL		8.73	8.45	8.50	-0.11	1015		
	1.41	0.53	Afriore	AFO		0.87	0.81	0.81	-0.06	656		
	20.77	13.40	♣ Agnico-Ea	AGE	0.04	18.75	18.25	18.72	+0.27	1669	0.2	
	9.99	3.60	♣ Agricore	AU	0.03	8.81	8.81	8.81	-0.24	17	0.3	
	15.25	12.50	♣ Agricor	AU.PR.A	1.00	14.80	15.25	14.80		z 21	6.8	
	21.81	14.20	Agrium	AGU	.147	19.34	19.15	19.22	+0.02	2477	0.8	
	29.25	2.75	Ainsworth	ANS		28.00	27.02	28.00	+0.71	86		3.3
	3.08	0.56	Air Canada	AC		1.50	1.47	1.49		5716		
	1.75	0.12	Air Canada	AC.A		0.47	.455	0.46	-0.01	507		
	2.89	1.51	AirBoss	BOS		2.10	2.01	2.10	-0.04	2650		23.3
	0.77	.155	♣ AirIQ	IQ		0.58	0.55	0.55	-0.01	392		
	26.50	18.75	♣ Akita	AKT.A	0.40	26.15	26.15	26.15	+0.03	4	1.5	13.6
	4.10	1.26	AlarmForce	AF		3.74	3.60	3.60	-0.10	359		25.7
	66.08	38.77	Alcan	AL	.803	63.61	62.39	63.30	+0.44	10478	1.3	41.0
	25.60	21.05	Alcan	AL.PR.F	.845	25.30	25.00	25.30		14	3.3	
	27.10	25.20	Alcan	AL.PR.E	1.125	26.75	26.60	26.60	-0.15	15	4.2	
↑	24.15	9.05	Alcatel Cda	AT	.223	24.15	23.49	24.10	+0.95	131	0.9	
	0.25	0.06	Algo Grp	AO		.105	.125	0.12		z 5		
	64.00	41.10	♣ Algoma C	ALC	1.00	60.00	60.00	60.00		35	1.7	19.9
	9.95	1.01	Algoma St	AGA		9.60	9.40	9.45	-0.05	1279		28.6
	34.70	26.80	♣ Aliant	AIT	1.10	32.65	32.35	32.48	-0.17	353	3.4	15.0
	27.24	25.00	♣ Aliant	AIT.PR.A	1.362	26.82	26.82	26.82	-0.03	3	5.1	
	31.25	13.00	Alimentat	ATD.A		28.75	28.29	28.63	+0.23	120		32.5
↑	29.00	12.00	Alimentat	ATD.B		29.00	28.35	28.80	+0.55	2203		32.7
	78.50	43.01	Allbanc	ABK.A		74.95	73.99	74.95	+0.95	4		
	66.00	60.90	Allban	ABK.PR.C	3.04	61.85	61.80	61.80	+0.05	14	4.9	
	23.50	11.51	♣ AlianAt	AAC.B		22.25	22.01	22.05	-0.05	424		
	75.00	31.94	♣ Allstream	ALR.A	3.50	69.00	69.97	69.30		z 70	5.0	
	2.75	0.61	Almaden	AMM		2.39	2.20	2.20		444		
	20.16	9.37	AltaGas	ALA	0.44	19.78	19.30	19.78	+0.28	2284	2.2	23.6
	0.62	0.20	Altarex	ALT		0.36	.355	0.36	-0.01	2564		
	0.15	.025	Alternative	ATF		.075	0.07	0.07		866		
	2.50	0.36	America Mi	AMZ		2.05	2.00	2.00	+0.02	999		
	3.50	2.00	♣ Amica	ACC		3.36	3.30	3.35	+0.10	32		67.0
	8.25	5.10	Amisco Ind	IAC	0.40	8.25	8.06	8.15	-0.10	217	4.9	9.1
	1.33	0.60	Amisk	AS.A		1.00	1.00	1.00		65		
	12.44	5.75	Amvescap	AVZ	.272	11.19	10.80	11.00	-0.08	252	2.5	17.6
	24.00	16.02	Andre	ADW.A	.644	22.20	22.05	22.20	-0.21	10	2.9	11.0
	24.45	18.50	Andres	ADW.B	0.56	22.85	25.00	22.44		z 50	2.5	11.5
	39.00	13.87	Angiotech	ANP		33.81	33.13	33.40	-0.10	713		
	6.25	2.30	Anormed	AOM		6.25	5.90	5.99	+0.09	1688		
	1.90	0.70	Anthony Cl	ACL		1.40	1.40	1.40	-0.05	20		
	1.40	0.69	♣ Antrim	AEN		1.37	1.27	1.31	+0.06	638		
	3.60	1.85	♣ Apollo Gl	APG		2.82	2.69	2.75	+0.10	1385		
	12.20	9.15	Bus Devl	BDB.J		11.65	11.65	11.65	-0.05	5		
	10.80	10.00	BusnsDv	BDB.X		10.66	10.66	10.66	+0.05	52		
	11.85	9.60	Business	BDB.A		11.85	11.75	11.75	-0.10	57		
	9.00	7.90	BusinDvl	BDB.G		8.50	8.46	8.46	-0.04	25		
	8.70	7.65	Busines	BDB.M		8.52	8.52	8.52	-0.07	4		
	10.80	9.50	BusinDvl	BDB.S		10.80	10.80	10.80	+0.05	4		
	11.80	9.90	BusnsDv	BDB.Y		10.80	10.80	10.80		1		
C-E												
	2.75	1.50	C1 Energy	CTT		1.80	1.65	1.75	-0.02	1725		
	6.79	2.76	♣ CAE Inc	CAE	0.12	6.39	6.30	6.31	-0.01	5505	1.9	19.1
	21.10	16.25	CCL Inds	CCL.B	0.36	19.43	19.06	19.30	+0.10	113	1.9	11.8
	0.85	0.10	♣ CCR Tec	CRL		0.74	0.70	0.74	+0.04	371		19.0
	4.10	2.61	CE Franklin	CFT		4.00	4.00	4.00		2		
	15.45	7.92	♣ CFM Crp	CFM		10.45	10.28	10.28	-0.03	535		16.4
	9.29	6.45	CGI	GIB.A		8.68	8.53	8.60	+0.03	2406		18.3
↑	38.30	21.64	CHC He	FLY.A	0.50	38.30	37.70	38.21	+0.56	385	1.3	13.1
	16.30	9.25	CI Fund Ma	CIX	0.50	15.90	15.61	15.65	-0.22	6582	3.2	41.2
	7.24	4.86	CPI Plastics	CPI		5.70	5.61	5.65	-0.10	150		9.7
	3.68	1.19	CSI Wirlss	CSY		3.24	3.15	3.23	+0.04	191		
	0.18	.025	Cable Sa	CSQ.A		.065	0.06	.065		1176		
	0.20	0.06	Caldera	CDR		0.14	.135	.135		2243		
	1.89	1.33	Caldwell	CWL.A		1.85	1.80	1.80		241		22.5
	0.48	.215	Caledonia	CAL		.355	0.34	.355	+.015	803		
	14.75	5.66	Calian Tec	CTY	0.20	14.30	13.80	14.10	-0.04	115	1.4	21.0
	6.10	1.35	Call-Net	FON		4.35	4.35	4.35		3		
	6.25	1.25	Call-Net	FON.B		4.44	4.31	4.40	+0.13	33		
	4.95	1.51	Cambior	CBJ		3.62	3.50	3.55	-0.01	5034		
	78.00	29.00	♣ Cameco	CCO	0.60	63.35	62.52	62.80	-0.28	2349	1.0	17.2
	1.11	0.33	Campbell	CCH		0.81	0.79	0.79		392		
	14.40	5.49	CanW	CGS.S		13.00	12.54	12.95	-0.05	238		58.9
	14.27	5.52	CanWest	CGS.A		12.98	12.78	12.78	-0.07	24		44.1
	28.25	21.94	Cda Bread	CBY	0.24	25.50	25.30	25.50		77	0.9	18.0
	8.33	3.52	♣ Cda Southn	CSW		6.95	6.94	6.95	+0.05	9		5.4
	2.95	1.65	Cdn Bnk No	CBK		2.55	2.55	2.55	-0.13	10		12.1
	45.51	29.50	Cdn Financ	CFC	.404	45.10	44.95	45.10	+0.83	6	0.9	
	14.88	7.70	♣ Cdn Gnrl	CGI	0.60	14.39	14.01	14.35	+0.10	43	4.2	
	8.40	2.75	♣ CdnGn	CGI.WT		8.40	8.40	8.40		10		
	27.71	25.30	Cdn Gen	CGI.PR.B	1.162	26.80	26.80	26.80	-0.20	10	4.3	
	1.25	.325	Cdn Gold	CGH		0.88	0.85	0.85	-0.02	128		
	2.49	1.60	♣ Cdn Hydro	KHD		2.49	2.40	2.49	+0.01	255		49.8
↑	70.15	44.85	CIBC	CM	2.00	70.15	69.00	69.01	+0.01	17893	2.9	12.2
	28.20	26.20	CIBC	CM.PR.A	1.325	28.10	27.95	28.10	+0.10	24	4.7	
	27.39	25.30	CIBC	CM.PR.B	1.50	27.26	27.20	27.20	-0.05	30	5.5	
	27.44	25.20	CIBC	CM.PR.C	1.50	27.39	27.20	27.39	+0.19	99	5.5	
	27.45	25.05	CIBC	CM.PR.D	1.437	27.10	26.90	27.00		100	5.3	
	27.10	25.02	CIBC	CM.PR.E	1.40	26.90	26.76	26.90	+0.13	15	5.2	
	27.60	26.00	CIBC	CM.PR.M	1.412	26.50	26.46	26.50	+0.05	11	5.3	
	27.46	25.71	CIBC	CM.PR.N	1.362	26.45	26.45	26.45	+0.20	8	5.2	
	27.48	24.08	CIBC	CM.PR.P	1.375	26.99	26.73	26.90	+0.08	31	5.1	
	27.95	25.62	CIBC	CM.PR.R	1.237	27.75	27.75	27.75		15	4.5	
	29.00	27.10	CIBC	CM.PR.T	1.50	28.05	28.03	28.03		10	5.3	
x	55.63	39.40	CN Rail	CNR	0.78	52.73	51.81	52.03	-0.12	4811	1.5	20.3
	75.84	46.55	♣ Cdn Naturl	CNQ	0.80	73.90	72.10	72.51	-0.89	7417	1.1	6.9
	80.43	62.01	Cdn Pacific	HCH	1.123	79.08	78.56	78.56	-0.51	8	1.4	
	38.65	27.98	CP Railway	CP	0.51	33.30	32.90	33.00	+0.24	10603	1.6	13.2
	30.64	17.20	♣ CP Ships	TEU	.214	25.13	24.15	24.22	-0.71	2302	0.9	20.1
	4.88	1.24	Cdn Superi	SNG		4.35	4.06	4.18	-0.02	9995		
	54.00	35.60	♣ Cdn Tire	CTR	0.40	53.00	52.00	52.00		9	0.8	17.0
↑	44.73	28.70	♣ CdnTir	CTR.A	0.40	44.73	43.85	43.85	-0.16	1999	0.9	14.3
	27.90	24.35	Cdn Utili	CU.PR.A	1.45	27.50	27.50	27.50	+0.20	5	5.3	
	60.25	45.10	Cdn Util	CU	2.12	60.00	59.50	59.75	-0.10	427	3.5	14.6
	60.00	45.50	Cdn Util	CU.X	2.12	59.63	59.63	59.63	-0.37	4	3.6	15.4
	27.99	24.90	Cdn Utili	CU.PR.B	1.50	27.37	26.94	27.00	-0.39	32	5.6	
	25.75	23.50	Cdn Uti	CU.PR.V	1.325	25.45	25.25	25.45		4	5.2	
↑	43.98	25.80	♣ Cdn WBk	CWB	0.60	43.98	43.10	43.41	+0.56	464	1.4	14.6
	2.04	0.09	♣ Cdn Zinc	CZN		1.54	1.47	1.48	-0.02	4072		
	5.90	3.28	Cana	CAM.A		4.40	4.25	4.25		83		
	1.34	0.35	♣ Canarc	CCM		1.00	0.97	0.97	-0.02	625		
	28.00	25.75	Canc	CAC.PR.A	1.35	27.00	27.00	27.00	-0.06	7	5.0	
	14.70	7.60	Canfor	CFP		14.50	14.09	14.16	-0.29	13033		7.8
	13.00	9.75	♣ Cangene	CNJ		11.59	11.15	11.35	-0.10	2115		15.3
	16.10	4.15	Canico	CNI		13.65	13.00	13.15	-0.30	6869		
	2.30	**1.10**	**Canico**	**CNI.WT.A**		**1.61**	**1.51**	**1.51**	**-0.29**	**320**		
	0.11	0.04	Canlan Ice	ISE		0.07	.065	.065	-.015	38		
	18.25	16.00	Capital Ga	CGQ		17.74	17.66	17.66	+0.09	72		
	15.40	11.51	CapitlGa	CGO.E	1.05	14.69	14.40	14.69	+0.34	20	7.2	

Source: Report on Business, *The Globe and Mail*, March 5, 2004, p. B12. Reprinted with permission of The Globe and Mail.

eighth column), has a dividend yield of .40/43.85 = .0091, or .91 percent; this is higher than the yield on the voting shares, .77 percent of the price of $52. A cursory analysis of the stock listings shows that dividend yields vary widely among firms. It is important to recognize that high-yield dividend stocks are not necessarily better investments than low-yield stocks. Total return to an investor comes from dividends and **capital gains**, or appreciation in the value of the stock. Low-yield dividend firms presumably offer greater prospects for capital gains, or investors would not be willing to hold the low-yield firms in their portfolios.

The P/E ratio, or **price/earnings ratio**, is the ratio of the closing stock price to last year's earnings per share. The P/E ratio tells us how much stock purchasers must pay per dollar of earnings that the firm generates. The P/E ratio also varies widely across firms. Where neither dividend yield nor P/E ratio are reported in Figure 2.5, the firms have zero dividends, or zero or negative earnings. We shall have much to say about P/E ratios in Chapter 15.

The sales column shows that 199,900 shares of the stock were traded. Shares commonly are traded in **board lots** of 100 shares each; however, a board lot consists of 1,000 shares for stocks selling below $5, while it falls to 25 shares for stocks above $100. Investors who wish to trade in smaller, odd lots may pay higher commissions to their stockbrokers, although many brokers are not charging an odd-lot differential in order to attract the small investor. The commission structure actually makes trading in a small number of higher-priced stocks (say 25 shares at $120) cheaper on a percentage basis than the same value of a low-priced stock (say 1,000 shares at $3). The highest price and lowest price per share at which the stock traded in that day were 44.73 and 43.85, respectively. The last, or closing, price of 43.85 was down .16 from the closing price of the previous day, and was right at the low of the day.

Preferred Stock

Preferred stock has features similar to both equity and debt. Like a bond, it promises to pay to its holder a fixed amount of income each year. In this sense, preferred stock is similar to an infinite-maturity bond, that is, a perpetuity. It also resembles a bond in that it does not convey voting power regarding the management of the firm. Preferred stock is an equity investment, however, in the sense that failure to pay the dividend does not precipitate corporate bankruptcy. Instead, preferred dividends are usually *cumulative*; that is, unpaid dividends cumulate and must be paid in full before any dividends may be paid to holders of common stock.

Preferred stock also differs from bonds in terms of its tax treatment for the firm. Because preferred stock payments are treated as dividends rather than interest, they are not tax-deductible expenses for the firm. This disadvantage is offset somewhat by the fact that corporations may exclude dividends received from domestic corporations in the computation of their taxable income. Preferred stocks, therefore, make desirable fixed-income investments for some corporations. Similarly, preferred dividends are taxed like common dividends for individual investors, which confers them a higher after-tax yield than bonds with the same pretax yield. Hence, even though they rank after bonds in the event of corporate bankruptcy, preferred stocks generally sell at lower yields than corporate bonds.

Preferred stock is issued in variations similar to those of corporate bonds. It can be callable by the issuing firm, in which case it is said to be *redeemable*. It also can be convertible into common stock at some specified conversion ratio. A firm often issues different series of preferreds, with different dividends, over time. For example, in Figure 2.5, there are three different issues of Canadian Utilities preferreds (Cdn Util), in addition to two classes of common. One innovation in the market is variable rate preferred stock, which, similarly to variable rate mortgages, ties the dividend rate to current market interest rates.

Income Trusts

Income trusts also are instruments with debt and equity features. An income trust holds an underlying asset or group of assets that generate income, most of which is distributed to unitholders. This is a variation on the structure of an REIT or a royalty trust. REITs derive their income from holdings in real estate, while the source for royalty trusts is royalties in the oil and gas industry. The notion has been expanded to industries where income is considered to be reliable and predictable and there are minimal capital spending requirements that would act as a drain on cash flow; these might include the hotel or food service industries among others. The trusts are likely to be formed by an existing company that identifies an operating division as a source of revenue.

Instead of using alternatives such as equity carve-outs or spinoffs offered directly to investors, the parent corporation would cooperate in the creation of a trust that issues units to the public. Proceeds from the unit sales are used to purchase common shares and debt that represent the capital base of the operating division.

The principal motive for the creation of the trust is the tax treatment, which is favourable to both investors and the underlying operating division. The income generated is flowed through to investors virtually tax-free. Use of high leverage, and hence high-yield debt, is typically part of the design, implying a degree of risk that may not be recognized by investors. The issue of trust units is similar to that of equity issues, with a prospectus preceding the primary issue. Secondary trading occurs on stock exchanges, after the units are listed. The trust functions like a closed-end mutual fund (see Chapter 4), which protects against the need to sell assets to cover redemptions.

The major attraction to investors is the promise of a high yield; recent low yields on debt instruments have increased the appeal of trust units, and investors' appetites have been strong. There were about 75 income trusts of various types available in Canada by mid-2004. At the end of 2003, there was close to $18 billion in new issues of trust units, up from less than $2 billion in 1999; the three most popular issues were made by the resources sector, followed by the financial and services sectors with approximately 30 percent, 27 percent, and 22 percent respectively of the total issues.

Although there is a perception of guaranteed cash flow, the payouts depend on the operating results of the underlying business. Frequently, the cash flow involves also a repayment of capital to unitholders. For this reason, the initial level of payments may be impossible to maintain for a lengthy period and many income trusts have suffered losses on the order of 50 percent in a few years. One risky variety entails the trading of derivatives based on an underlying portfolio in order to generate the promised payouts.

2.4 STOCK AND BOND MARKET INDICES

Stock Market Indices

The daily performance of the Dow Jones Industrial Average and the Toronto Stock Exchange (TSX) Composite Index are staple portions of the Canadian evening news report. Although these indices are, respectively, the best-known measures of the performances of the U.S. and Canadian stock markets, they are only two of several indicators of stock market performance in the two countries. Other indices are computed and published daily. In addition, several indices of bond market performance are widely available.

The ever-increasing role of international trade and investments has made indices of foreign financial markets part of the general news. Thus, foreign stock exchange indices, such as the Nikkei Average of Tokyo and the Financial Times Index of London, are fast becoming household names.

Toronto Stock Exchange Indices. The S&P/TSX Composite Index is Canada's best-known stock market indicator. It contains over 220 of the largest securities (in terms of market value) traded on the TSX, regardless of industry group, but excluding control blocks composed of more than 20 percent of outstanding shares. The TSX Composite is a **market-value-weighted index** based on a very broad set of companies. It is constructed to reflect an investment in each company proportional to its total market capitalization, giving considerably more weight to large, highly valued stocks.

The TSX Composite is computed by calculating the total market value of the stocks in the index and the total market value of those stocks on the previous day of trading, always excluding the control blocks. The percentage increase in the total market value from one day to the next represents the increase in the index. The rate of return of the index therefore equals the rate of return that would be earned by an investor holding a portfolio of all stocks in the index in proportion to their market value, except that the index does not reflect cash dividends paid out by those stocks.

To illustrate, suppose that there are only two companies in the market—ABC with 20 million shares at $25 and XYZ with 1 million shares at $100; then the index would be set at the combined market values of the companies of $600 million divided by the arbitrary divisor of 10, giving a

Table 2.1 Stock Market Index Calculation

Stock	No. of Shares	Initial Price	Market Value	Final Price	Market Value
ABC	20M	$ 25	$500M	$30	$600M
XYZ	1M	$100	$100M	$90	$90M
Initial	Value-weighted average = (500 + 100)/10 = 60				
	Price-weighted average = (25 + 100)/2 = 62.5				
Final	Value-weighted average = (600 + 90)/10 = 69		Percentage gain = (69 – 60)/60 = 15%		
	Price-weighted average = (30 + 90)/2 = 60		Percentage gain = (60 – 62.5)/62.5 = –4%		

level of 60. (Initially an index is likely to be set at a round number such as 100 or 1,000, by dividing the opening value by 6 or .6 in this case.) ABC has five times the weight of XYZ in the index. Table 2.1 shows how the index changes value with the individual stock movements; as ABC rises to $30 and XYZ falls to $90, the index value changes to 69, and rising by 15 percent.

CONCEPT CHECK

4. Suppose that shares of XYZ increase in price to $110 while shares of ABC fall to $20. Find the percentage change in the market-value-weighted average of these two stocks. Compare that to the percentage return of a portfolio that holds $500 of ABC for every $100 of XYZ, that is, an index portfolio.

S&P's Institutional Market Services www.compustat.com

The Toronto Stock Exchange is described by a variety of indices, all calculated by S&P, including capped indices and 14 indices based on narrow industry groupings, such as energy, financials, and gold, which are the constituents of the main index. The narrower TSX 60 represents the 60 most important companies, while the TSX MidCap and TSX SmallCap reflect the performance of smaller companies. Both the TSX 60 and the Composite index are recalculated as capped indices by limiting the contribution of each component to a maximum of 10 percent of the index value. The associated TSX Venture Exchange, for smaller Canadian companies not listed on the TSX, is described by the S&P/TSX Venture Index. Total return indices are also calculated; these include the value of dividends paid by constituent companies in the returns on the indices. In addition, Dow-Jones has computed a DJ Canada 40 Index. Figure 2.6 reproduces an extract from the report of The Globe and Mail on the performance of the various indices.

Suppose now that a two-for-one stock split occurs in XYZ, giving shareholders a total of two million shares valued at $50. Since the total market value of XYZ and of the market are unchanged, the value of the index remains unaffected, as can be seen by examining Table 2.2. This characteristic is a considerable advantage in the calculation and maintenance of a value-weighted index.

Market value weighting corresponds to the theoretical solution to portfolio construction presented in Chapter 6. It also corresponds to a buy-and-hold strategy based on an initial portfolio that is value-weighted. Unfortunately, it can have a very distorting effect on the index. The market appreciation of Nortel gave it a total capitalization of $367.2 billion in July 2000, representing 36.5 percent of the then TSE 300. For mutual funds limited to maximum holdings in a single security,

Table 2.2 Stock Market Index Calculation After a Stock Split

Stock	No. of Shares	Initial Price	Market Value	Final Price	Market Value
ABC	20M	$25	$500M	$30	$600M
XYZ	2M	$50	$100M	$45	$ 90M
Initial	Value-weighted average = (500 + 100)/10 = 60				
	Price-weighted average = (25 + 50)/1.2 = 62.5				
Final	Value-weighted average = (600 + 90)/10 = 69		Percentage gain = (69 – 60)/60 = 15%		
	Price-weighted average = (30 + 45)/1.2 = 62.5		Percentage gain = (62.5 – 62.5)/62.5 = 0		

Figure 2.6
Canadian stock indices.

TORONTO STOCK EXCHANGE

52-week high	low	index	high	low	close	chg	% chg	vol (100s)	div yield	avg p/e	total return
8878.53	5678.60	S&P/TSX composite	8827.82	8773.27	8773.27	−22.42	−0.2				
495.36	353.43	S&P/TSX 60	491.00	486.58	486.58	−2.29	−0.5				
1292.59	930.72	DJ Canada 40	1284.43	1272.29	1272.32	−6.21	−0.5				
595.91	389.51	S&P Cdn Mid Cap	595.91	592.83	594.93	+1.75	+0.3				
629.71	402.36	S&P Cdn Small Cap	629.71	625.72	628.81	+2.98	+0.5				

TSX Venture Exchange

| 1933.49 | 1026.05 | S&P/TSX Venture | 1893.83 | 1884.00 | 1890.98 | −1.30 | −0.1 | 51967285 | | | |

CANADIAN INDEXES
S&P/TSX composite subgroups

index	high	low	close	chg	vol	index	high	low	close	chg	vol
Energy	170.20	166.94	167.42	−1.52	12791599	Materials	155.54	154.47	154.89	−0.15	35371638
Financials	141.85	140.76	140.76	−0.17	20509007	Telecom	68.66	67.94	68.42	+0.48	5055384
Info Tech	35.58	35.30	35.40	+0.10	18719318	Utilities	154.70	153.97	154.27	+0.30	3436408
Consmr Discretion	90.77	89.83	89.83	−0.45	4213647	Gold	212.61	209.51	210.48	+0.69	19855671
Consumer Staples	178.49	176.90	176.90	−0.47	4431524	Metals & Mining	229.77	227.08	228.86	−0.71	6916332
Healthcare	71.34	70.63	71.04	−0.20	6878955	Real Estate	161.89	159.84	161.55	+0.76	65288
Industrials	79.57	78.81	78.91			Income Trust	124.87	124.48	124.71	−0.02	7018550

The day's S&P/TSX composite
The S&P/TSX composite index through the day yesterday, showing the change each hour from the previous day's close

| 9:45 a.m. | 8819.92 | +24.92 | 11 a.m. | 8803.55 | +8.55 | 1 p.m. | 8809.42 | +14.42 | 3 p.m. | 8779.08 | −15.92 |
| 10 a.m. | 8824.84 | +29.84 | Noon | 8813.56 | +18.56 | 2 p.m. | 8788.55 | −6.45 | 4 p.m. | 8773.27 | −21.73 |

Source: Report on Business, *The Globe and Mail*, March 5, 2004, p. B11. Reprinted with permission of The Globe and Mail.

this made matching the index performance impossible. By August 13, 2001 it had fallen to $35.6 billion in value, or 5.01 percent of the TSE 300; at this point it was passed by Royal Bank at $36 billion. For all but Nortel investors this was considered to be a much healthier scenario.

Investors today can purchase shares in mutual funds that hold shares in proportion to their representation in the S&P/TSX Composite. These **index funds** yield a return equal to that of the TSX index and so provide a low-cost passive investment strategy for equity investors. The topic of index funds and exchange-traded funds is developed in Chapter 4.

Dow Jones Averages The Dow Jones Industrial Average (DJIA) of 30 large blue-chip corporations has been computed since 1896. Its long history probably accounts for its preeminence in the public mind. (The average covered only 20 stocks until 1928.) The Dow is a **price-weighted average**, which means that it is computed by adding the prices of the 30 companies and dividing by a certain number.

Originally, the divisor was simply 20 when 20 stocks were included in the index; thus, the index was no more than the average price of the 20 stocks. This makes the index performance a measure of the performance of a particular portfolio strategy that buys one share of each firm in the index. Therefore, the weight of each firm in the index is proportional to the share price rather than the total outstanding market value of the shares. In the case of the firms ABC and XYZ above, the "Dow portfolio" would have four times as much invested in XYZ as in ABC ($100 as against $25), as Table 2.1 also shows. Although the market-value-weighted index increased by 15 percent, the price-weighted average drops by 4 percent, due to the reliance on the high-priced XYZ that loses value. A price-weighted average reflects the performance of a portfolio that holds an equal number of shares in each of the companies in the index; unfortunately, the capital invested in each stock is arbitrarily determined by when and to what level each stock has last split.

Dow Jones Indexes indexes.dow jones.com

CONCEPT CHECK

5. Reconsider the changes to the stocks, as in question 4. Calculate the percentage change in the price-weighted index. Compare that to the rate of return of a portfolio that holds one share in each company.

As stocks are added to or dropped from the average, or stocks split over time, the Dow divisor is continually adjusted to leave the average unaffected by the change. The treatment of a stock split is more complicated, as we would not want the average to fall because of a company's decision to split when no change in actual value has occurred. Following a split, the divisor must be reduced to a value that leaves the average unaffected by the split. Table 2.2 illustrates this point. The initial share price of XYZ, which was $100 in Table 2.1, falls to $50 if the stock splits at the beginning of the period. Notice that the number of shares outstanding doubles, leaving the market value of total shares unaffected. The divisor, d, which originally was 2.0 when the two-stock average was initiated, must be reset to a value that leaves the average unchanged. Because the sum of the post-split stock price is 75 and the pre-split average price was 62.5, we calculate the new value of d by solving $75/d = 62.5$. The value of d therefore falls from its original value of 2.0 to $75/62.5 = 1.20$, and the initial value of the average is indeed unaffected by the split: $75/1.20 = 62.5$. At period-end, shares of ABC will sell for $30, while shares of XYZ will sell for $45, representing the same negative 10 percent return it was assumed to earn in Table 2.1. The new value of the price-weighted average is $(30 + 45)/1.20 = 62.5$, and the rate of return on the average is $62.5/62.5 - 1 = 0$. Notice that this return is greater than the –4 percent calculated in Table 2.1. The relative weight of XYZ, which is the poorer-performing stock, is lower after the split because its price is lower; the performance of the average therefore improves. This example illustrates again that the implicit weighting scheme of a price-weighted average is somewhat arbitrary, being determined by the prices rather than the outstanding market values of the shares in the average.

In the same way that the divisor is updated for stock splits, if one firm is dropped from the average and another firm with a different price is added, the divisor has to be updated to leave the average unchanged by the substitution. By now, the divisor for the Dow Jones Industrial Average has fallen to a value of about .17.

Dow Jones & Company also computes a Transportation Average of 20 airline, trucking, and railroad stocks; a Public Utility Average of 15 electric and natural gas utilities; and a Composite Average combining the 65 firms of the three separate averages. Each is a price-weighted average, and thus over-weights the performance of high-priced stocks.

Figure 2.7 reproduces some of the data reported on the TSX Index and the Dow Jones Industrial Average from *The Globe and Mail*. The vertical bars show the range of values assumed by the average on each day, with the crossbar indicating the closing value.

www.nyse.com

Other U.S. Market-Value Indices The New York Stock Exchange publishes a market-value-weighted composite index of all NYSE-listed stocks, in addition to subindexes for industrial, utility, transportation, and financial stocks. These indices are even more broadly based than the S&P 500. The National Association of Securities Dealers publishes an index of 4,000 over-the-counter (OTC) firms traded on the Nasdaq market.

www.nasdaq.com

The ultimate U.S. equity index so far computed is the Wilshire 5000 index of the market value of all NYSE and American Stock Exchange (Amex) stocks plus actively traded Nasdaq stocks. Despite its name, the index actually includes about 7,000 stocks. Figure 2.8 reproduces a *Globe and Mail* listing of U.S. stock index performance. Vanguard offers an index mutual fund, the Total Stock Market Portfolio, that enables investors to match the performance of the Wilshire 5000 index, and a small stock portfolio that matches the MSCI U.S. small-capitalization 1750 index.

Equally Weighted Indices Market performance sometimes is measured by an equally weighted average of the returns of each stock in an index. Such an averaging technique, by placing equal weight on each return, corresponds to an implicit portfolio strategy that places equal dollar values on each stock. This is in contrast to both price-weighting (which requires equal numbers of shares of each stock) and market-value-weighting (which requires investments in proportion to outstanding value).

Figure 2.7 TSX and Dow Jones Industrial indices.

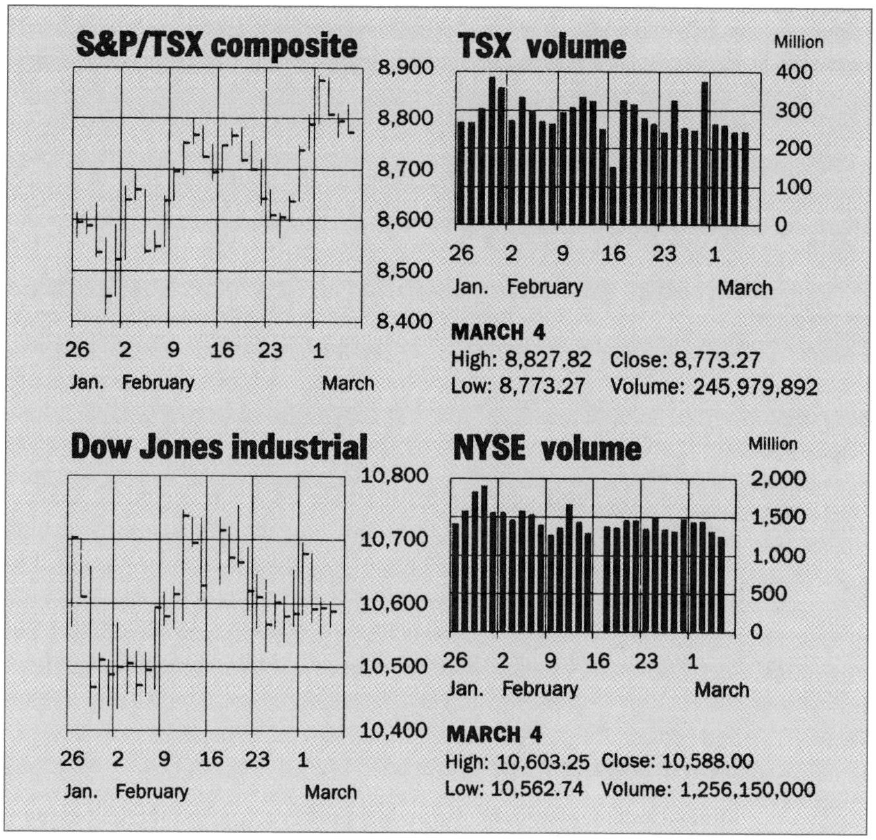

Source: Report on Business, *The Globe and Mail,* March 5, 2004, p. B11. Reprinted with permission of The Globe and Mail.

Figure 2.8 Performance of U.S. stock indices.

NEW YORK STOCK EXCHANGE

52-week high	low	index	high	low	close	chg	% chg	vol (100s)
10753.63	7416.64	DJ Industrials-A	10473.86	10284.67	10296.89	−160.07	−1.5	2590030
3090.07	1918.12	DJ Transport-A	2838.08	2786.61	2788.48	−45.82	−1.6	357705
281.63	194.85	DJ Utilities-A	280.55	276.88	277.03	−2.86	−1.0	199188
3067.64	2085.03	DJ 65 Composit-A	2985.03	2936.26	2938.31	−43.40	−1.5	3147555
181.00	161.33	DJ Bond			181.00			
573.44	400.24	S&P 100	561.38	552.01	552.80	−8.10	−1.4	
618.46	381.82	S&P 400 MidCap	605.95	594.68	594.72	−10.46	−1.7	
1163.23	788.90	S&P 500	1141.45	1122.53	1123.89	−16.69	−1.5	

U.S. INDEXES

New York

index	close	chg
NYSE Composite	6591.72	−106.35
NYSE US 100	5738.21	−86.07
NYSE Healthcare	5975.69	−100.75
NYSE Finance	6931.48	−106.90
NYSE Energy	6508.00	−71.92

Nasdaq

index	high	low	close	chg	% chg
Nasdaq comp	2007.25	1963.13	1964.15	−31.01	−1.6
Nasdaq 100	1447.71	1417.18	1417.50	−19.97	−1.4
NNM Composite	905.30	885.40	885.90	−13.90	−1.5
NNM Industrial	678.60	663.70	664.00	−11.30	−1.7

American

index	high	low	close	chg	% chg
Amer Biotech	544.20	530.24	532.44	−10.93	−2.0
Amex Composi	1259.97	1242.39	1242.66	−16.85	−1.3
Institutional	580.66	571.63	572.38	−7.80	−1.3
Japan Index	120.39	120.39	120.39	−1.04	−0.9
Major market	1077.21	1059.00	1060.55	−13.08	−1.2
Oil and gas	604.79	595.37	595.62	−6.14	−1.0

New York odd lots

Odd-lot trades made Tuesday The New York Stock Exchange:

Customer purchases	10,520,822	Short sales	1,046,689
Other sales	10,640,520	Total sales	11,687,209

Source: Report on Business, *The Globe and Mail,* March 11, 2004, p. B15. Reprinted with permission of The Globe and Mail.

Unlike price- or market-value-weighted indices, equally weighted indices do not correspond to buy-and-hold portfolio strategies. Suppose that you start with equal dollar investments in the two stocks of Table 2.1, ABC and XYZ. Because ABC increases in value by 20 percent over the year while XYZ increases by only 10 percent, your portfolio no longer is equally weighted; it is now more heavily invested in ABC. To reset the portfolio to equal weights, you would need to rebalance: sell off some ABC stock and/or purchase more XYZ stock. Such rebalancing would be necessary to align the return on your portfolio with that on the equally weighted index.

Foreign and International Stock Market Indices

Development in financial markets worldwide includes the construction of indices for these markets as mentioned in the earlier boxed article. The popular indices are broader than the Dow Jones average and most are value-weighted.

The most important are the Nikkei, FTSE (pronounced "footsie"), and DAX. The Nikkei 225 is a price-weighted average of the largest Tokyo Stock Exchange (TSE) stocks. The Nikkei 300 is a value-weighted index. FTSE is published by the *Financial Times* of London and is a value-weighted index of 100 of the largest London Stock Exchange corporations. The DAX index is the premier German stock index. Figure 2.9 shows the list of foreign stock exchange indices published by *The Globe and Mail*. More details on international indices are provided in Chapter 22.

The leading compendium of international indices is produced by MSCI (Morgan Stanley Capital International), which computes over 50 country indices and several regional indices. Table 2.3 presents a sample of MSCI indices.

Bond Market Indicators

Just as stock market indices provide guidance concerning the performance of the overall stock market, bond market indicators measure the performance of various categories of bonds. Scotia Capital publishes the main Canadian bond market indices, while in the United States the three most well-known groups of indices are those of Merrill Lynch, Lehman Brothers, and Salomon Brothers. Table 2.4 lists some of the indices compiled by Scotia Capital, as well as their average values as of June 2004.

Figure 2.9 Listing of foreign stock exchange indices.

Overseas Indexes

	yesterday	previous	2003/04 high	2003/04 low
Amsterdam AEX	354.52	355.50	364.80	340.17
Brussels	2477.03	2481.30	2517.28	2270.71
Frankfurt DAX	4044.70	4087.55	4151.83	3995.34
Hong Kong	13214.20	13397.25	14058.21	12763.10
London FT 250	6301.6	6359.3	6388.8	5834.1
FT-SE 100	4545.3	4542.0	4559.1	4357.4
Mexico City	9978.71	10079.20	10196.17	8818.19
Milan	21054	21061	21129	20173
Paris CAC-40	3758.09	3737.03	3785.36	3560.10
Sydney All ord	3414.3	3427.2	3427.2	3274.9
Tokyo	11433.24	11532.04	11537.29	10299.43
Zurich SMI	5877.1	5858.8	5934.4	5487.8

Emerging Markets

	close	chg		close	chg
Athens	2469.92	-11.16	Madrid	869.06	+1.65
Bangkok	705.29	−5.37	Manila	1455.67	−0.08
Bombay	5759.29	-91.32	Santiago	7693.02	+30.90
Buenos Aires	1239.67	+22.64	Sao Paulo	21670.28	-1003.48
Caracas	27686.36	−0.96	Seoul	876.02	-15.56
Jakarta	760.32	-10.75	Shanghai B	116.68	+2.62
Johannesburg	10896.26	−103.85	Singapore	1875.02	-10.18
Karachi	4883.62	-26.37	Taipei	6874.91	-98.99
Kuala Lumpur	875.83	−7.13	Turkey	19798.79	+310.32

Source: Report on Business, *The Globe and Mail,* March 11, 2004, p. B25. Reprinted with permission of The Globe and Mail.

Table 2.3 Sample of MSCI Stock Indices

Regional Indices		Countries	
Developed Markets	**Emerging Markets**	**Developed Markets**	**Emerging Markets**
EAFE (Europe, Australia, Far East)	**Emerging Markets (EM)**	Australia	Argentina
EASEA (EAFE ex Japan)	EM Asia	Austria	Brazil
Europe	EM Far East	Belgium	Chile
European Monetary Union (EMU)	EM Latin America	Canada	China
Far East		Denmark	Colombia
Kokusai (World ex Japan)	**Emerging Markets Free (EMF)**	Finland	Czech Republic
Nordic Countries	EMF Asia	France	Egypt
North America	EMF Eastern Europe	Germany	Greece
Pacific	EMF Europe	Hong Kong	Hungary
The World Index	EMF Europe & Middle East	Ireland	India
G7 countries	EMF Far East	Italy	Indonesia
World ex U.S.	EMF Latin America	Japan	Israel
		Netherlands	Jordan
		New Zealand	Korea
		Norway	Malaysia
		Portugal	Mexico
		Singapore	Morocco
		Spain	Pakistan
		Sweden	Peru
		Switzerland	Philippines
		U.K.	Poland
		U.S.	Russia
			South Africa
			Sri Lanka
			Taiwan
			Thailand
			Turkey
			Venezuela

Source: MSCI site, www.msci.com.

Table 2.4 Scotia Capital Universe Bond Index

				Total Returns (percentage change)		
	Avg. Yield (%)	Price Index	Total Return Index	Last 1 Year	Last 10 Years	Sector Weight
Federal	4.27	115.88	512.35	2.94	8.61	46.83
Provincials	4.96	120.40	573.13	2.45	9.41	24.63
Municipals	4.79	120.30	616.13	2.69	9.72	1.30
All governments	**4.51**	**117.39**	**531.99**	**2.78**	**8.85**	**72.77**
AAA/AA	4.24	120.38	543.30	3.47	8.93	5.98
A	5.06	123.41	589.46	4.46	9.69	16.68
BBB	4.98	118.74	604.15	7.04	9.42	4.58
All corporates	**4.87**	**122.06**	**573.19**	**4.69**	**9.44**	**27.23**
Overall	**4.61**	**118.36**	**539.63**	**3.29**	**8.96**	**100.00**

Source: Adapted from Scotia Capital, Inc., *Debt Market Indices*, June 30, 2004. Risk premium constructed by subtracting the T-bill yield from the stock yield and then computing the means and the standard deviations. Reprinted with permission of The Globe and Mail.

The indices all are computed monthly, and all measure total returns as the sum of capital gains plus interest income derived from the bonds during the month. Any intra-month cash distributions received from the bonds are assumed to be reinvested weekly during the month back into the bond market.

The major problem with these indices is that true rates of return on many bonds are difficult to compute because the infrequency with which the bonds trade make reliable up-to-date prices difficult to obtain. In practice, prices must often be estimated from bond valuation models. These "matrix" prices may differ substantially from true market values.

2.5 DERIVATIVE MARKETS

One of the most significant developments in financial markets in recent years has been the growth of futures and options markets. These instruments provide payoffs that depend on the values of other assets, such as commodity prices, bond and stock prices, or market index values. For this reason, these instruments sometimes are called **derivative assets**, or **contingent claims**. Their values derive from or are contingent on the values of other assets.

Options

A **call option** gives its holder the right to purchase an asset for a specified price, called the **exercise** or **strike price**, on or before a specified expiration date. For example, a February call option on Alcan Aluminum stock with an exercise price of $40 entitles its owner to purchase Alcan stock for a price of $40 at any time up to and including the expiration date in February. Each option contract is for the purchase of 100 shares. However, quotations are made on a per-share basis. The holder of the call need not exercise the option; it will be profitable to exercise only if the market value of the asset that may be purchased exceeds the exercise price.

When the market price exceeds the exercise price, the option holder may "call away" the asset for the exercise price and reap a profit equal to the difference between the stock price and the exercise price. Otherwise, the option will be left unexercised. If not exercised before the expiration date of the contract, the option simply expires and no longer has value. Calls therefore provide greater profits when stock prices increase and thus represent bullish investment vehicles.

In contrast, a **put option** gives its holder the right to sell an asset for a specified exercise price on or before a specified expiration date. A February put on Alcan with an exercise price of $40 thus entitles its owner to sell Alcan stock ("put the stock") to the put writer at a price of $40 at any time before expiration in February, even if the market price of Alcan is lower than $40. Whereas profits on call options increase when the asset increases in value, profits on put options increase when the asset value falls. The put is exercised only if its holder can deliver an asset worth less than the exercise price in return for the exercise price.

Canadian Derivatives Exchange www.m-x.ca/accueil_en.php

Figure 2.10 gives listed stock option quotations from *The Globe and Mail*. The quotations cover trading on the Montreal Exchange. Locate the option listed in the table for shares of Barrick. The number on the same line as the company name indicates that the closing price for Barrick stock was $27.88 per share. The total number of all option contracts on Barrick traded the previous day is given next. Options were traded on Barrick with exercise prices of $22.50 to $32.50. (Options with other exercise prices might exist but were not traded the previous day.) These values, the exercise price or strike price, are given in the second column of numbers, after the expiration month.

The next three columns of numbers provide the bid, ask, and last trade prices of call options on Barrick shares with expiration dates of March, April, July, and October. The prices of call options decrease in successive rows for a given expiration date, corresponding to progressively

Figure 2.10 Canadian equity options market listings.

EQUITY OPTIONS

Trading in Canadian equity options on the Montreal Exchange. P is a put.

FIVE MOST ACTIVE

	Volume	Op Int
Nortel Netwk	13596	239437
TransCanad	2389	15678
Placer Do	2161	24315
Inco	2085	12913
Bombr B	1998	116149

TRADES

stock series		bid	close ask	tot vol last	vol	tot o.i. op int
ATI Tech			**18.98**	**485**		**8638**
Mar04	19.00p	0.55	0.75	0.25	10	22
	20.00	0.25	0.30	0.30	223	251
	20.00p	1.20	1.40	0.65	10	218
	22.00	0.05	0.10	0.10	14	1739
	22.00p	3.00	3.20	2.25	10	243
Apr04	20.00	0.70	0.85	0.85	98	989
	20.00p	1.75	1.90	1.65	11	143
	22.00	0.35	0.40	0.40	30	861
	22.00p	3.20	3.45	3.10	3	172
	24.00p	5.10	5.30	4.30	20	40
Jul04	17.00p	1.05	1.10	1.10	10	14
	22.00	0.95	1.15	1.35	5	276
	26.00p	7.20	7.40	7.15	10	25
Oct04	20.00	2.25	2.50	2.45	10	0
	22.00	1.55	1.80	1.65	21	24
Abitibi Consl			**9.96**	**422**		**9130**
Mar04	10.00	0.10	0.30	0.20	118	535
Apr04	10.00	0.40	0.50	0.45	30	40
	10.00p	0.30	0.55	0.35	57	0
Jun04	9.00	1.20	1.40	1.35	10	139
	11.00	0.20	0.40	0.40	110	2556
	11.00p	1.15	1.35	1.25	10	55
Sep04	9.00	1.55	1.65	1.70	10	40
	9.00p	0.35	0.50	0.35	57	0
	10.00	0.85	1.00	1.00	10	179
	10.00p	0.80	1.00	0.80	10	145
Agnico-Ea			**18.60**	**135**		**6603**
Mar04	15.00	3.45	3.70	3.75	5	84
	18.00	0.70	0.90	1.10	80	479
	20.00	0.10	0.15	0.20	10	154
Apr04	20.00	0.30	0.50	0.55	10	72
Jun04	20.00	0.90	1.05	1.05	30	319
Air Canada			**1.36**	**1843**		**20802**
Mar04	2.00p	0.65	0.75	0.70	60	350
	3.00p	1.65	1.75	1.70	20	0
Apr04	2.00	0.01	0.10	0.01	982	4075
	2.00p	0.85	1.00	0.95	256	1976
Jul04	2.00	0.05	0.10	0.05	500	11211
	2.00p	1.25	1.40	1.35	15	2100
	5.00p	4.25	4.45	4.30	10	260
Alcan			**57.00**	**1848**		**20945**
Mar04	55.00	2.35	2.60	2.50	20	70
	57.50	0.80	0.95	0.95	200	1885
	57.50p	1.15	1.35	1.20	202	103
	60.00	0.15	0.30	0.35	67	1172
	60.00p	2.95	3.20	2.15	120	454
	62.50		0.15	0.10	6	702
	62.50p	5.30	5.60	4.30	20	247
Apr04	52.50	5.10	5.35	7.20	10	207
	52.50p	0.40	0.55	0.45	40	170
	55.00	3.20	3.40	4.10	16	1715
	55.00p	1.05	1.25	1.25	126	420
	57.50	1.80	2.00	2.00	71	595
	57.50p	2.10	2.30	2.10	16	403
	60.00	0.90	1.10	1.25	84	928
	60.00p	3.70	3.90	3.60	72	127
	62.50	0.40	0.55	0.55	39	524
	65.00	0.15	0.30	0.25	37	518
	65.00p	7.90	8.20	7.00	3	42
	67.50	0.01	0.15	0.15	10	557
Jul04	50.00p	1.05	1.20	1.10	2	213
	52.50p	1.70	1.90	1.60	120	312
	55.00	5.00	5.10	5.00	10	306
	57.50	3.55	3.75	3.85	22	162
	57.50p	3.75	4.00	3.75	25	315
	60.00	2.50	2.70	2.70	120	486
	60.00p	5.25	5.45	4.70	10	326
	62.50	1.70	1.90	1.95	32	314
	65.00	1.15	1.35	1.70	37	336
	67.50	0.75	0.85	1.00	162	737
	67.50p	10.90	11.15	9.00	10	41
	70.00	0.45	0.60	0.70	3	204
	70.00p	13.10	13.35	11.05	10	1
Oct04	55.00	6.05	6.30	7.40	10	0
	55.00p	3.70	3.95	3.50	40	0
	57.50	4.80	5.10	5.05	3	4
	57.50p	4.90	5.15	5.00	10	16
	60.00	3.70	4.00	4.00	5	31
	[illegible]	[illegible]	[illegible]	2.90	[illegible]	36
	27.50p	1.20	1.30	1.30	10	950
	30.00	1.10	1.20	1.05	8	1675
Jan06	25.00p	1.45	1.65	1.45	4	249
	27.50p	2.35	2.60	2.35	3	337
Ballard			**12.95**	**132**		**5484**
Mar04	10.00	2.90	3.05	3.20	10	10
	12.50	0.60	0.75	0.75	5	74
	15.00		0.05	0.05	10	220
Apr04	15.00p	2.10	2.20	2.00	4	217
Jul04	17.50	0.25	0.30	0.30	40	205
	20.00	0.05	0.15	0.10	50	400
Oct04	12.50	1.95	2.15	2.30	3	93
	15.00	0.95	1.15	1.15	10	20
Bnk of Mtl			**53.55**	**825**		**30125**
Apr04	54.00	0.85	1.10	1.15	30	1166
	56.00	0.20	0.45	0.40	10	750
Jul04	54.00	1.90	2.00	2.10	5	284
	56.00	0.95	1.15	1.20	753	574
	58.00	0.55	0.70	0.65	20	916
Jan05	50.00	5.40	5.70	5.80	5	1215
Jan06	50.00	6.60	7.50	7.55	2	207
Bank of NS			**69.47**	**348**		**32652**
Mar04	67.50	1.95	2.05	1.95	30	168
	70.00	0.25	0.30	0.45	50	1798
	70.00p	0.80	0.95	0.80	70	1182
Apr04	67.50	2.20	2.40	2.30	52	3949
Jul04	70.00	1.65	1.80	1.80	2	6667
	75.00	0.30	0.45	0.40	4	40
Oct04	62.50	7.30	7.65	7.60	5	60
	70.00p	3.20	3.45	3.50	15	0
	72.50	1.40	1.60	1.50	10	40
Jan05	60.00	10.00	10.10	10.00	20	684
	65.00p	1.80	2.00	2.05	10	495
	70.00	2.95	3.20	3.30	10	1088
Jan06	55.00	15.30	15.80	16.00	22	237
	65.00	8.20	8.60	8.20	42	163
	65.00p	4.20	4.35	4.25	6	307
Barrick			**27.88**	**677**		**55169**
Mar04	25.00	2.80	2.90	3.35	40	123
	27.50	0.70	0.80	0.85	75	2121
	27.50p	0.35	0.45	0.30	60	610
	30.00		0.05	0.05	146	439
	30.00p	2.10	2.25	2.20	10	60
Apr04	27.50	1.35	1.40	1.40	42	3580
	27.50p	0.90	1.05	0.90	10	2747
	30.00p	2.45	2.60	2.10	12	169
Jul04	22.50	5.65	5.80	6.20	10	240
	25.00p	0.85	0.95	0.75	25	5686
	27.50	2.30	2.35	2.40	15	2305
	27.50p	1.85	2.00	1.80	30	910
	30.00	1.25	1.35	1.30	45	6114
	32.50	0.65	0.75	0.75	70	1932
Oct04	25.00p	1.30	1.35	1.20	50	60
	27.50p	2.40	2.60	2.40	10	15
Jan05	20.00	8.30	8.55	8.50	10	1347
	27.50p	2.90	3.10	2.95	10	365
Jan06	22.50p	1.90	2.05	1.90	7	175
Biovail			**22.80**	**280**		**13033**
Mar04	22.50	0.80	1.00	0.90	5	81
	22.50p	0.45	0.60	0.60	20	520
	27.50p	4.50	4.90	4.45	18	83
Apr04	22.50	1.60	1.65	1.65	5	103
	22.50p	1.20	1.45	1.30	10	163
	25.00	0.70	0.85	0.75	8	381
	25.00p	2.70	3.05	2.65	8	283
	27.50	0.35	0.45	0.45	7	368
	30.00	0.10	0.25	0.20	10	867
	30.00p	7.05	7.55	7.15	10	248
Jul04	20.00	4.50	4.60	4.75	15	82
	20.00p	1.35	1.55	1.35	20	108
	22.50	2.90	3.20	3.00	12	47
	25.00p	3.70	4.10	4.00	30	388
	27.50	1.15	1.35	1.20	40	233
	30.00	0.80	0.90	0.95	10	374
	30.00p	7.55	8.00	7.30	10	102
Oct04	20.00	4.95	5.35	5.25	10	28
	22.50	3.65	3.95	4.00	2	72
	25.00p	4.40	4.75	4.40	10	40
	32.50	0.90	1.15	1.15	20	23
Bombr B			**6.43**	**1998**		**116149**
Mar04	6.00	0.40	0.50	0.50	10	2802
	6.50p	0.20	0.30	0.20	50	420
	7.00	0.02	0.05	0.05	43	8566
Apr04	5.00	1.40	1.50	1.55	25	3789
	5.00p		0.05	0.05	100	2658
	6.00	0.60	0.65	0.65	237	6662
	6.00p	0.15	0.25	0.20	300	4293
	6.50	0.30	0.35	0.30	510	228
	7.00	0.10	0.20	0.20	20	6685
	7.50	0.03	0.08	0.09	30	150
Jul04	3.00	3.35	3.50	3.60	20	180
	5.00	1.50	1.60	1.65	10	706
	5.50p	0.25	0.35	0.25	45	60
	6.00	0.85	0.95	0.95	10	4862
	[illegible]	0.40	[illegible]	[illegible]	[illegible]	[illegible]
Sep04	42.50	6.45	7.20	7.55	6	181
	45.00p	1.15	1.60	1.30	10	0
CAE Inc			**5.92**	**536**		**13329**
Mar04	6.00	0.10	0.20	0.15	111	2558
	6.00p	0.15	0.30	0.20	60	622
Apr04	6.00	0.25	0.35	0.30	30	105
	6.00p	0.25	0.40	0.40	30	60
Jun04	6.00	0.35	0.50	0.40	45	1951
	6.00p	0.45	0.50	0.50	105	612
	7.00p	1.10	1.30	1.15	10	250
	8.00p	2.00	2.20	2.00	6	91
Sep04	6.00	0.60	0.70	0.65	69	516
	6.00p	0.65	0.70	0.60	10	355
	7.00	0.25	0.30	0.30	25	709
	8.00	0.10	0.25	0.15	35	194
CGI			**8.31**	**125**		**7932**
May04	8.00	0.65	0.80	0.75	100	1086
	9.00p	0.75	0.90	0.75	20	142
Aug04	9.00	0.40	0.50	0.45	5	778
CI Fund Ma			**15.40**	**10**		**1193**
Apr04	14.00	1.30	1.55	1.60	10	63
CIBC			**68.40**	**199**		**27320**
Mar04	67.50p	0.30	0.40	0.40	40	290
	70.00	0.15	0.25	0.20	35	2065
	70.00p	1.65	1.75	1.45	27	692
Apr04	65.00	3.65	3.85	4.20	31	306
Jul04	72.50	0.95	1.15	1.10	10	2139
Oct04	70.00	2.60	2.85	2.60	34	20
Jan05	45.00	23.45	23.70	24.00	20	284
	60.00	9.40	9.75	10.30	2	366
CN Rail			**50.75**	**40**		**5037**
Mar04	52.00	0.10	0.40	0.35	10	0
Apr04	52.00	0.75	1.00	0.85	10	23
Jun04	50.00p	1.55	1.90	1.50	10	160
	55.00	0.55	0.80	0.80	10	85
Cdn Naturl			**72.20**	**323**		**5551**
Mar04	70.00	2.65	2.80	3.85	10	312
	70.00p	0.35	0.50	0.25	14	122
	75.00	0.25	0.45	0.90	45	295
	75.00p	3.00	3.20	2.10	13	75
Apr04	65.00	7.60	7.90	7.40	42	2
	70.00	3.80	4.05	5.10	46	102
	70.00p	1.45	1.65	1.35	3	88
May04	55.00	17.40	17.70	18.80	1	10
	60.00	12.55	12.90	14.95	5	171
	65.00	8.20	8.45	8.35	11	231
	70.00	4.70	4.95	4.85	30	266
	70.00p	2.20	2.45	2.10	2	78
	75.00	2.35	2.55	2.55	20	481
	80.00	0.95	1.15	1.15	20	188
Aug04	60.00	13.35	13.70	15.00	1	53
	65.00p	1.90	2.15	1.65	50	197
	85.00	1.30	1.50	1.50	10	11
CP Railway			**31.40**	**323**		**15227**
Mar04	32.50	0.05	0.20	0.15	160	428
	32.50p	1.05	1.20	0.85	19	123
Apr04	30.00	1.75	1.80	1.75	7	73
	32.50	0.40	0.50	0.45	20	360
	32.50p	1.40	1.55	1.30	20	324
Jul04	32.50p	1.85	2.00	1.85	45	1403
Oct04	27.50	4.50	4.70	4.60	5	22
	30.00	2.65	2.85	2.70	2	90
	32.50	1.30	1.50	1.50	15	121
	32.50p	2.20	2.35	2.05	5	1060
	35.00	0.60	0.75	0.70	25	81
CP Ships			**22.95**	**184**		**3899**
Apr04	20.00	2.95	3.20	3.00	4	0
	24.00	0.40	0.60	0.55	6	124
	26.00	0.05	0.20	0.10	1	1402
Jul04	26.00	0.45	0.70	0.70	5	167
Oct04	22.00p	1.35	1.40	1.35	120	70
	26.00	0.90	1.10	0.95	10	57
	28.00	0.45	0.65	0.45	38	25
Celestica			**21.40**	**475**		**15938**
Mar04	20.00	1.50	1.60	1.80	28	190
	20.00p	0.20	0.30	0.25	10	441
	22.50	0.20	0.25	0.50	35	609
	22.50p	1.30	1.35	1.40	48	229
	25.00p	3.60	3.65	3.85	13	141
	27.50p	6.10	6.20	5.90	5	65
Apr04	19.00	2.75	2.90	3.20	10	10
	20.00p	0.70	0.80	0.65	25	100
	22.50	0.80	0.95	1.00	8	43
	22.50p	1.90	2.00	1.90	20	72
	25.00	0.30	0.35	0.40	65	330
Jun04	20.00	2.80	2.90	3.30	5	69
	20.00p	1.25	1.40	1.20	10	285
	22.50	1.60	1.75	1.70	35	353
	25.00	0.85	1.00	1.00	68	660
	30.00	0.15	0.30	0.25	10	455
	32.50	0.05	0.15	0.15	10	114
Sep04	22.50p	3.30	3.45	3.40	20	60
	[illegible]	[illegible]	1.70	[illegible]	[illegible]	[illegible]
	40.00p	5.85	6.05	4.95	5	0
Apr04	38.00p	3.90	4.10	3.10	5	0
	40.00p	5.80	6.00	4.90	5	0
Jun04	32.00	2.90	3.10	3.75	5	77
	34.00	1.70	1.80	2.35	5	96
	40.00p	6.05	6.20	5.25	5	32
EnCana Crp			**56.11**	**735**		**39971**
Mar04	50.00	5.95	6.10	6.00	20	137
	55.00	1.25	1.35	1.20	60	5203
	55.00p	0.25	0.40	0.25	10	162
	57.50	0.20	0.25	0.25	159	2049
	57.50p	1.70	1.80	1.30	20	464
	62.50p	6.50	6.65	6.50	10	10
Apr04	42.50	13.45	13.70	13.30	10	93
	45.00	11.00	11.20	10.90	14	409
	47.50	8.50	8.70	9.50	11	555
	50.00	6.10	6.25	6.05	20	716
	52.50p	0.30	0.40	0.25	32	328
	55.00	2.05	2.20	2.10	81	1045
	55.00p	0.95	1.10	0.90	10	323
	57.50	0.90	1.00	1.20	20	1359
	57.50p	2.25	2.40	2.35	46	149
	60.00	0.30	0.40	0.35	20	1120
	62.50	0.06	0.15	0.10	10	199
Jul04	42.50	13.70	13.90	14.75	10	47
	50.00	6.90	7.05	7.70	40	12113
	55.00	3.40	3.60	3.55	9	2888
	55.00p	2.10	2.30	2.10	10	1204
	60.00	1.45	1.55	1.45	10	821
Oct04	50.00	7.60	7.85	7.85	80	22
	57.50	3.15	3.40	3.25	10	115
	60.00	2.20	2.45	2.70	10	183
	62.50	1.50	1.70	1.50	3	203
Fairmont Ho			**33.45**	**120**		**1466**
Mar04	37.50p	3.85	4.10	3.95	10	10
Apr04	30.00	3.60	3.90	3.75	10	3
	37.50p	3.90	4.10	4.00	40	50
Jul04	27.50	6.20	6.50	6.40	10	0
	35.00	1.10	1.35	1.35	10	87
	37.50p	4.15	4.40	4.10	40	15
Falconbridge			**32.60**	**551**		**3024**
Mar04	32.00	1.30	1.50	1.65	10	45
	34.00p	1.55	1.75	1.45	8	50
	36.00	0.05	0.20	0.30	10	171
Apr04	30.00p	0.60	0.80	0.65	30	61
	32.00	2.20	2.45	2.45	25	256
	34.00	1.30	1.50	1.35	25	291
	34.00p	2.40	2.65	2.25	6	194
	36.00	0.70	0.90	0.90	85	922
	40.00	0.15	0.35	0.35	30	72
May04	30.00p	1.25	1.35	1.15	20	30
	32.00	2.90	3.15	3.00	12	0
	32.00p	2.10	2.20	2.05	8	75
	34.00	2.20	2.30	2.35	104	7
	36.00	1.35	1.60	1.55	120	92
	38.00	0.95	1.10	1.20	58	78
Goldcorp			**17.75**	**412**		**17741**
Mar04	18.00	0.30	0.40	0.40	80	1182
Apr04	16.00	2.00	2.15	2.40	95	572
	18.00	0.80	0.95	0.90	81	890
	20.00	0.25	0.35	0.40	16	1640
	22.00	0.05	0.15	0.10	50	917
Jul04	14.00p	0.35	0.40	0.40	10	373
	16.00	2.70	2.90	2.95	13	107
	20.00	0.95	1.10	1.10	5	1005
	26.00	0.10	0.20	0.20	5	440
Oct04	14.00	4.40	4.65	5.00	30	3
	18.00	2.05	2.25	2.10	22	50
	22.00	0.85	1.05	1.00	5	22
Great Wst			**51.40**	**10**		**1763**
Jul04	54.00	0.85	1.10	0.85	10	205
iUnits Ind			**47.76**	**531**		**29790**
Mar04	40.00	7.75	7.90	7.95	10	643
	46.00	1.75	1.90	2.25	5	162
	47.00	0.85	1.00	1.10	16	154
	48.00	0.30	0.40	0.50	10	1317
	48.00p	0.45	0.50	0.40	100	1275
	50.00p	2.15	2.30	1.65	40	94
Apr04	45.00	2.80	2.95	3.00	70	70
	46.00	1.90	2.10	2.25	10	150
	48.00	0.55	0.75	0.65	47	68
	49.00	0.30	0.35	0.40	105	222
May04	46.00	2.15	2.35	2.35	30	0
Jun04	45.00	3.20	3.40	3.75	8	76
	48.00	1.10	1.35	1.40	20	85
	49.00p	1.85	2.10	1.85	5	13
	50.00	0.35	0.55	0.65	9	103
Sep04	49.00	1.20	1.45	1.50	6	41
Mar05	42.50	6.30	6.60	6.70	10	2531
	50.00p	3.70	4.00	3.70	20	40
Mar06	52.50	2.05	2.30	2.10	10	0
iUnits Enr			**41.55**	**102**		**6264**
Apr04	40.00p	0.30	0.55	0.50	40	40
	43.00	0.30	0.60	0.60	50	20
Jun04	43.00	1.05	1.35	1.00	7	0
Sep04	37.00	5.25	5.70	5.20	5	5
iUnits Gold			**52.61**	**60**		**6506**
Mar04	50.00p	0.15	0.25	0.20	40	178
Apr04	53.00	1.85	2.10	2.15	10	202
Jun04	[illegible]	[illegible]	8.75	9.60	1	86

Source: Report on Business, *The Globe and Mail*, March 11, 2004, p. B23. Reprinted by permission from the Toronto Stock Exchange and the Montreal Exchange. Reprinted with permission of The Globe and Mail.

higher exercise prices. This makes sense, because the right to purchase a share at a given exercise price is worth less as the exercise price increases. For example, with an exercise price of $22.50, the July call lists for $6.20 per share, whereas the option to purchase the stock for an exercise price of $27.50 is worth only $2.40. The exercise price indicates the range of prices at which the stock has traded during the life of the option; thus, we see that Barrick has had a price in the $22–$32 range in the past six months. The last two columns give an indication of the liquidity of the option as they record the volume traded and the "open interest," which refers to the total number of contracts outstanding in that option.

Put options, with various strike prices and times to maturity, are denoted with a "p" next to the exercise price. Put prices, of course, increase with the exercise price. The right to sell a share of Barrick at a price of $25 is less valuable than the right to sell it at $30.

Note that option prices increase with time to expiration. Clearly, the right to buy Barrick at $27.50 (or sell at $27.50) until July is worth less than the same right until October. (Check the prices for calls with the same exercise price in successive months.)

Most options have relatively short expiration dates, that is, less than one year. For some firms, however, there is a class of options called LEAPS (long-term equity anticipation securities) with much longer expiration dates, of two to three years at issue. LEAPS exist for several large Canadian companies, such as Bank of NS, Barrick, and Bombardier. See, for instance, the January 2005 and 2006 options for Barrick Gold in Figure 2.10.

CONCEPT CHECK

6. What would be the profit or loss per share of stock to an investor who bought the October 2004 maturity Bank of Nova Scotia call option with exercise price $72.50 on March 11, 2004, if the stock price at the expiration of the option was $75? What about a purchaser of the put option with the same maturity?

Futures Contracts

The **futures contract** calls for delivery of an asset or its cash value at a specified delivery or maturity date for an agreed-upon price, called the **futures price**, to be paid at contract maturity. The *long position* is held by the trader who commits to purchasing the commodity on the delivery date. The trader who takes the *short position* commits to delivering the commodity at contract maturity.

Figure 2.11 illustrates the listing of several futures financial contracts as they appear in *The Globe and Mail*. The listings include futures on bankers' acceptances, bonds, stock indices, and individual stocks, as well as options on futures on acceptances. The top line in boldface type gives the contract name and size. Thus, the first contract listed on the left is for three-month bankers' acceptances. Each contract calls for delivery of $1 million in acceptances.

The next eight rows detail price data for contracts expiring on various dates. The March 2004 maturity contract's highest futures price during the day was 97.80, the lowest was 97.78, and the settlement price (a representative trading price during the last few minutes of trading) was 97.79. The settlement price was unchanged from the previous trading day. The highest and lowest futures prices over the contract's life to date have been 97.80 and 97.75, respectively. Finally, open interest was 50,396. Corresponding information is given for the other maturity dates.

The trader holding the long position profits from price increases. Suppose that at expiration acceptances are priced at 97.92. The long-position trader who entered the contract at the futures price of 97.78 on March 11 would pay the previously agreed-upon 97.78 for each unit of the index, which at contract maturity would be worth 97.92. Because each contract calls for delivery of $1 million in acceptances, ignoring brokerage fees, the profit to the long position would equal $1 million × (.9792 – .9778) = $1,400. Conversely, the short position must deliver $1 million in

Figure 2.11 Montreal Exchange futures and future options.

MONTREAL EXCHANGE FUTURES & OPTIONS

r = not traded; s = no option offered

Futures

sea hi	sea lo	mth.	open	high	low	settle	chg.	op int
3-month bankers' acceptances $1M, pts. of 100%								
97.80	97.75	Mar04	97.79	97.80	97.78	97.79		50396
97.97	97.81	Jun04	97.94	97.95	97.93	97.94	−0.01	123259
97.95	97.70	Sep04	97.94	97.94	97.92	97.93	−0.01	54457
97.85	97.59	Dec04	97.83	97.83	97.79	97.80	−0.03	23931
97.65	97.52	Mar05	97.61	97.62	97.57		−0.04	10903
97.37	97.30	Jun05	97.35	97.35	97.30	97.33	−0.04	4723
97.08	97.02	Sep05	97.03	97.03	97.02	97.02	−0.04	1935
96.57	96.48	Mar06	96.50	96.50	96.48	96.50	−0.07	1543

Est sales	Prv sales	Open Int	Chg
32944	19583	272629	−5975

10-year Cda bonds $100K, pts of 100%, 1 pt = $10

sea hi	sea lo	mth.	open	high	low	settle	chg.	op int
112.51	110.84	Jun04	112.23	112.35	112.02	112.19	−0.05	98656

Est sales	Prv sales	Open Int	Chg
5408	4746	110768	−4155

S&P/TSX 60 200 X index pts, pts of 100%, 5 pts=$10

sea hi	sea lo	mth.	open	high	low	settle	chg.	op int
492.40	474.70	Mar04	483.60	483.60	474.70	474.80	−9.60	108548
492.40	474.80	Jun04	483.30	483.30	474.80	474.70	−9.70	29466

Est sales	Prv sales	Open Int	Chg
15515	24672	138014	+6973

S&P/TSX Info Tech Index 500 X index pts, pts of 100%, 5 pts=$10

Est sales	Prv sales	Open Int	Chg
		25	+0

S&P/TSX Energy Index 200 X index pts, pts of 100%, 1 pt=$20

Est sales	Prv sales	Open Int	Chg
		132	+0

S&P/TSX Financial Index 200 X index pts, pts of 100%, 1 pt=$20

Est sales	Prv sales	Open Int	Chg
		0	+0

S&P/TSX Gold Index 200 X index pts, pts of 100%, 1 pt=$20

Est sales	Prv sales	Open Int	Chg
		1	+0

Nortel 100 shares, pts of 100%, 1 pt=$1

Est sales	Prv sales	Open Int	Chg
		0	+0

30-day Overnight repo rate $5M, pts of 100%, 1 pt=$41.10

Est sales	Prv sales	Open Int	Chg
		0	+0

Options

3-mo. bankers' acceptances futures$1M,pts of 100%

price	calls-last			puts-last		
	Mar	Jun	Sep	Mar	Jun	Sep
9625.00	.075	0.08	0.08	r	r	r
9637.00	0.07	.075	.075	r	r	r
9650.00	0.06	0.07	0.07	r	r	r
9675.00	0.05	.055	.055	r	r	r
9700.00	.035	.045	.045	r	r	r
9712.00	0.03	0.04	0.04	r	r	r
9725.00	.025	0.03	.035	r	r	r
9737.00	0.02	r	.025	r	r	r
9750.00	0.01	0.02	0.02	r	r	r
9775.00	r	0.01	0.01	r	r	.005
9800.00	r	r	.005	0.01	.005	0.01
9812.00	r	r	r	.015	0.01	0.01
9825.00	r	r	r	0.02	.015	.015
9837.00	r	r	r	.025	0.02	0.02
9850.00	r	r	r	.035	.025	.025

Prev day call vol	820	Open Int	30050
Prev day put vol	0	Open Int	18637

Source: Report on Business, *The Globe and Mail,* March 11, 2004, p. B23. Reprinted with permission of The Globe and Mail.

acceptances for the previously agreed-upon futures price. The short position's loss equals the long position's profit.

In addition to futures contracts, there are also stock index options. Several call and put option contracts are quoted on the S&P/TSX 60 stock index. Index options differ from stock options because they are **cash settlement** options. If the value of the index rises above the exercise price, then the holder of a call option on the S&P/TSX 60 index receives, upon exercise, a cash amount equal to $500 times the difference between the stock index and exercise price. Conversely, the put option holder would exercise the option only when the index falls below the exercise price.

Stock index options are listed as Canadian equity options. (There are also U.S. index options on the Dow, S&P 500, S&P 100, and NASDAQ 100.) Index options are not to be confused with index futures or with options on futures (which are more complex), both shown in Figure 2.11.

Futures are also quoted on commodities such as grains, meats, fruits, fuels, and base and precious metals in Winnipeg, New York, Chicago, and other locations. Figure 2.12 shows listings from the Winnipeg Commodity Exchange for canola and other agricultural commodity futures. In addition, the listings show cash or spot prices for grain and precious metals; **spot prices** are current rather than future.

The right to purchase the asset at an agreed-upon price, as opposed to the obligation, distinguishes call options from long positions in futures contracts. A futures contract *obliges* the long position to purchase the asset at the futures price; the call option, in contrast, *conveys the right* to purchase the asset at the exercise price. The purchase will be made only if it yields a profit.

Clearly, a holder of a call has a better position than the holder of a long position on a futures contract with a futures price equal to the option's exercise price. This advantage, of course, comes only at a price. Call options must be purchased; futures investments may be entered into without cost. The purchase price of an option is called the **premium**. It represents the compensation the holder of the call must pay for the ability to exercise the option only when it is profitable to do so. Similarly, the difference between a put option and a short futures position is the right, as opposed to the obligation, to sell an asset at an agreed-upon price.

Figure 2.12
Futures and cash prices for commodities.

WINNIPEG FUTURES

r = not traded; s = no option offered

CANOLA 20 tonnes $Cdn/tonne

sea hi	sea lo	mth.	open	high	low	settle	chg.	op int
420.40	348.00	May04	411.50	418.50	408.50	409.10	−4.00	33514
421.40	347.50	Jul04	414.00	420.50	411.50	412.00	−3.50	14276
378.90	331.20	Nov04	371.00	375.50	370.70	370.80	−2.20	19827

Est sales	Prv sales	Open Int	Chg
		67793	+1295

FLAXSEED 20 tonnes $US/tonne

Est sales	Prv sales	Open Int	Chg
		0	+0

WESTERN BARLEY 20 tonnes $Cdn/tonne

sea hi	sea lo	mth.	open	high	low	settle	chg.	op int
153.00	133.50	May04	142.50	142.50	141.70	142.20	−0.70	3717
148.80	135.50	Jul04	144.00	144.00	143.00	143.80	−0.60	1107
146.00	136.00	Oct04	144.00	144.20	144.00	144.20	−0.50	834

Est sales	Prv sales	Open Int	Chg
		5870	−25

WHEAT 20 tonnes $Cdn/tonne

sea hi	sea lo	mth.	open	high	low	settle	chg.	op int
151.00	136.50	May04	149.00	149.00	146.90	148.00	−1.40	2292
151.00	139.00	Jul04	151.00	151.00	149.50	150.20	−0.80	684
151.50	136.00	Oct04	151.00	151.50	151.00	151.50		829

Est sales	Prv sales	Open Int	Chg
		4048	+348

GRAIN

PARRISH & HEIMBECKER
Domestic 1 cw 13.5 wheat, Thunder Bay, $218.68; Export 1 cw 13.5 wheat St. Lawrence, $244.07; Export 1 cw durum, St. Lawrence, $296.60.
Domestic milling wheat CIF Bayports: 1 cw durum wheat $271.01, 1 cw 14.5 wheat, $239.89; 1 cw 13.5 wheat, $234.95; 2 cw 13.5 wheat, $234.95, 2 cw 12.5 wheat, $234.95, 2 cw 12.5 wheat, $234.95.
FEEDING GRADES
Wheat DGC $199.00, 2 cw oats $225.00; 1 cw barley $168.00; 1 feed screening $175.00.
ONTARIO GRAIN
Approximate bid price track shipping point: 2 white oats $140.00; Ontario feed oats $100.00; Ontario barley $150.00; 2 winter wheat milling $177.97; 2 soybeans $453.78, 2 rye $160.00; 2 yellow corn $156.88; 3 yellow corn $155.70.
(Prices quoted in tonnes)
WINNIPEG CASH
Feed wheat: Track Thunder Bay 3 cwrs: $165.00.
Flax: 1 cw: $280.30; 2 cw: $278.30.
Canola: Track Thunder Bay No. 1 Canada: unavailable; In store Vancouver No.1 Canada $426.10.
WHEAT BOARD
Wheat, St. Lawrence: 1 cw 1.00 pct $244.07; 1 durum $296.60.
Malting barley (domestic), Thunder Bay: Special Select 6-row $207.00; Select 6-row $204.50; Special select 2-row $219.00; Select 2-row $216.50.

GOLD

CANADIAN SILVER
Handy and Harman of Canada's silver quotation $9.823 oz., $315.81 kg.
CIBC GOLD AND SILVER
Closing quotes, in U.S. funds, from Canadian Imperial Bank of Commerce on March 10 gold bid at $399.50, asked $400.50 for standard bars of 400 ounces. Silver bid $7.14 asked $7.16 for standard bars of 1,000 ounces.

SCOTIABANK GOLD AND SILVER
The Bank of Nova Scotia quoted on March 10 at 4:00 p.m. gold bid $399.95 (U.S.) a fine ounce, $400.65 asked for standard bars of 400 ounces. Closing prices for silver in standard bars of 1,000 ounces were $7.12 (U.S.) an ounce bid, $7.14 asked.
IN EUROPE
LONDON _ The morning fixing for gold on the European market was $400.80 ($U.S.) a fine ounce, compared with $401.20 Tuesday. The afternoon fixing was $400.25.

Source: Report on Business, *The Globe and Mail*, March 11, 2004, p. B20. Reprinted with permission of The Globe and Mail.

Other Derivative Assets: Warrants, Swaps, and Hybrid Securities

In addition to options and futures, there are other contingent claims traded in Canadian financial markets. We list briefly the most important of them, which will be discussed in more detail in Chapters 17 to 19.

Warrants are like call options, with the difference being that the holder receives the shares upon exercise from the firm that issued them, rather than from another investor. For this reason, unlike call options, the exercise of warrants increases the number of outstanding shares of a corporation and its capital, while diluting the equity of its shareholders. Warrants also trade on the regular stock exchanges and have much longer expiration dates than normal stock options.

A **swap** is an agreement between two parties to exchange a set of liabilities, like the obligation to pay a stream of future interest payments in a given currency and rate. For instance, in an interest rate swap, one party trades its fixed interest payments against the other party's payments at a rate that varies with a benchmark rate, like LIBOR. Swaps are brokered by intermediaries, and the terms of representative agreements are quoted in the over-the-counter market.

Last, some firms have issued instruments that are essentially a combination of a bond and a call option on a stock index. Most such instruments are traded in the over-the-counter market, but a couple of them trade on the TSX. We shall return to them in Chapter 17.

SUMMARY

1. Money market securities are very-short-term debt obligations. They are usually highly marketable and have relatively low credit risk. Their low maturities and low credit risk ensure minimal capital gains or losses. These securities trade in large denominations but may be purchased indirectly through money market funds.
2. Much of the Canadian government borrowing is in the form of Canada bonds. These are coupon-paying bonds usually issued at or near par value. Canada bonds are similar in design to coupon-paying corporate bonds. Provincial governments and Crown corporations also issue similar default-free coupon-paying bonds.
3. Mortgage pass-through securities are pools of mortgages sold in one package. Owners of pass-throughs receive all principal and interest payments made by the borrower. The originator that issued the mortgage merely services the mortgage, simply "passing through" the payments to the purchasers of the mortgage. The government guarantees the timely payment of interest and principal on mortgages pooled into these pass-through securities.
4. Common stock is an ownership share in a corporation. Each voting share entitles its owner to a vote on matters of corporate governance and to a prorated share of the dividends paid to shareholders. Restricted shares have a lower number of votes, or no right to vote. Stock, or equity, owners are the residual claimants on the income earned by the firm.
5. Preferred stock usually pays fixed dividends for the life of the firm; it is a perpetuity. A firm's failure to pay the dividend due on preferred stock, however, does not precipitate corporate bankruptcy. Instead, unpaid dividends simply cumulate. New varieties of preferred stock include convertible and variable rate issues.
6. Many stock market indices measure the performance of the overall market in Canada and the United States. The Dow Jones Averages, the oldest and best-known indicators, are U.S. price-weighted indices. Today, many broad-based market value-weighted indices are computed daily. These include the main Canadian index, S&P/TSX Composite stock index, as well as the S&P/TSX 60, the U.S. Standard & Poor's 500 stock index, the NYSE and AMEX indices, the Nasdaq index, and the Wilshire 5000 index.
7. A call option is a right to purchase an asset at a stipulated exercise price on or before a maturity date. A put option is the right to sell an asset at some exercise price. Calls increase in value while puts decrease in value as the value of the underlying asset increases.
8. A futures contract is an obligation to buy or sell an asset at a stipulated futures price on a maturity date. The long position, which commits to purchasing, gains if the asset value increases, while the short position, which commits to delivering the asset, loses.

KEY TERMS

money market 27
capital markets 27
Treasury bills (T-bills) 28
certificate of deposit (CD) 29
guaranteed investment certificate (GIC) 29
bearer deposit notes (BDNs) 29
commercial paper 29
bankers' acceptance 29
Eurodollars 30
repurchase agreement (repo *or* RP) 30
London Interbank Offered Rate (LIBOR) 30
bond equivalent yield 31
effective annual yield 32
bank discount yield 32
callable 33
yield to maturity 36
debentures 36
subordinated debentures 36
callable bonds 37
retractable bonds 37
extendible bonds 37
convertible bonds 37
variable rate mortgage 37
pass-through 37
common stocks 39
equities 39
proxy 39
restricted shares 39
residual claim 40
limited liability 40
dividends 40
capital gains 41
price/earnings ratio 41
board lots 42
preferred stock 42

Visit us at www.mcgrawhill.ca/college/bodie

income trusts 42
market-value-weighted index 43
index funds 45
price-weighted average 45
derivative assets 50
contingent claims 50
call option 50
exercise price 50
strike price 50
put option 50
futures contract 52
futures price 52
cash settlement 53
spot price 53
premium 53
warrant 54
swap 54

SELECTED READINGS

The standard reference to the securities, terminology, and organization of the U.S. money market is:

Stigum, Marcia. *The Money Market*, Homewood, IL: Dow Jones-Irwin, 1983.

A good survey of a wide variety of U.S. financial markets and instruments is:

Logue, Dennis E. (ed.). *The WG&L Handbook of Financial Markets*. Cincinnati, OH: Warren, Gorham, & Lamont, 1995.

The Canadian money market is described in:

Sarpkaya, S. *The Money Market in Canada*, 4th ed. Toronto, ON: CCH Canadian, 1989.

A reference to Canadian and international fixed-income instruments is the annual publication:

Guide to International Investing. Toronto, ON: CCH Canadian.

An extended coverage of restricted-voting shares is in:

Smith, Brian, and Ben Amoako-Adu. *Financing Canadian Corporations with Restricted Shares* (monograph). London, ON: National Centre for Management Research and Development, University of Western Ontario, 1990.

Institutional details of the Canadian Derivatives Exchange can be found at:

Montreal Exchange site, www.m-x.ca.

Institutional features of futures markets are provided by:

Hore, John E. *Trading on Canadian Futures Markets*, 4th ed. Toronto, ON: The Canadian Securities Institute, 1989.

PROBLEMS

1. The following multiple-choice problems are based on questions that have appeared in past CFA examinations.

a. A firm's preferred stock often sells at yields below its bonds because

i. Preferred stock generally carries a higher agency rating.
ii. Owners of preferred stock have a prior claim on the firm's earnings.
iii. Owners of preferred stock have a prior claim on a firm's assets in the event of liquidation.
iv. Corporations owning stock may exclude from income taxes most of the dividend income they receive.

b. Which is the *most risky* transaction to undertake in the stock index option markets if the stock market is expected to increase substantially after the transaction is completed?

i. Write a call option.
ii. Write a put option.
iii. Buy a call option.
iv. Buy a put option.

2. The investment manager of a corporate pension fund has purchased a Treasury bill with 182 days to maturity at a price of $9,600 per $10,000 face value. The manager has computed the bank discount yield at 8 percent.

a. Calculate the bond equivalent yield for the Treasury bill. Show your calculations.

b. Briefly state two reasons why a Treasury bill's bond equivalent yield is always different from the discount yield.

3. A bill has a bank discount yield of 6.81 percent based on the ask price, and 6.90 percent based on the bid price. The maturity of the bill (already accounting for skip-day settlement) is 61 days. Find the bid and ask prices of the bill.

4. Reconsider the T-bill of problem 3. Calculate its bond equivalent yield and effective annual yield on the basis of the ask price. Confirm that these yields exceed the discount yield.

5. The bond equivalent yield of a 91-day T-bill is 5 percent. What is the price of the bill for a $10,000 face value?

6. *a.* Which security offers a higher effective annual yield?

i. A three-month bill selling at $9,764

ii. A six-month bill selling at $9,539

b. Calculate the bank discount yield on each bill.

7. A U.S. Treasury bill with 90-day maturity sells at a bank discount yield of 3 percent.

a. What is the price of the bill?

b. What is the 90-day holding period return of the bill?

c. What is the bond equivalent yield of the bill?

d. What is the effective annual yield of the bill?

8. Find the price of a six-month (180-day) U.S. T-bill with a par value of $100,000 and a bank discount yield of 9.18 percent.

9. Find the after-tax return to a corporation that buys a share of preferred stock at $40, sells it at year-end at $40, and receives a $4 year-end dividend. The firm is in the 25 percent tax bracket.

10. Consider the following data for the three stocks that make up the market:

Stock	P_0	Q_0	P_1
A	$60	200	$70
B	$80	500	$70
C	$20	600	$25

a. What is the single-period return on the price-weighted index constructed from the three stocks?

b. What is the single-period return on the value-weighted index constructed from the three stocks using a divisor of 100?

c. What is the single-period return on the price-weighted index constructed from the three stocks if stocks A and B were to split 2 for 1 and 4 for 1, respectively, after period 0?

d. What is the single-period return on the value-weighted index constructed from the three stocks if stocks A and B were to split 2 for 1 and 4 for 1, respectively, after period 0?

11. Consider the three stocks in the following table. P_t represents price at time t, and Q_t represents shares outstanding at time t. Stock C splits two for one in the last period.

	P_0	Q_0	P_1	Q_1	P_2	Q_2
A	90	100	95	100	95	100
B	50	200	45	200	45	200
C	100	200	110	200	55	400

a. Calculate the rate of return on a price-weighted index of the three stocks for the first period ($t = 0$ to $t = 1$).

b. What must happen to the divisor for the price-weighted index in year 2?

c. Calculate the price-weighted index for the second period ($t = 1$ to $t = 2$).

12. Using the data in problem 11, calculate the first period rates of return on the following indices of the three stocks:

a. A market-value-weighted index

b. An equally weighted index

13. Which of the following securities should sell at a greater price?

a. A 10-year Canada bond with a 9 percent coupon rate versus a 10-year Canada bond with a 10 percent coupon rate

b. A three-month maturity call option with an exercise price of $40 versus a three-month call on the same stock with an exercise price of $35

c. A put option on a stock selling at $50, or a put option on another stock selling at $60 (all other relevant features of the stocks and options may be assumed to be identical)

d. A three-month T-bill with a discount yield of 6.1 percent versus a three-month bill with a discount yield of 6.2 percent

14. In what ways is preferred stock like long-term debt? In what ways is it like equity?

15. Why are money market securities sometimes referred to as "cash equivalents"?

16. Why do call options with exercise prices greater than the price of the underlying stock sell for positive prices?

17. Both a call and a put currently are traded on stock XYZ; both have strike prices of $50 and maturities of six months. What will be the profit to an investor who buys the call for $4 in the following stock price scenarios in six months?

a. $40

b. $45

c. $50

d. $55

e. $60

f. What will be the profit in each scenario to an investor who buys the put for $6?

18. Explain the difference between a put option and a short position in a futures contract.

CSI

19. Which of the following statements regarding stock indices and/or averages is/are correct?

a. An average is a time series of numbers that represent a combination of various stock's prices (or any numerical items) in such a manner that one can calculate a percentage change of this series over any period of time.

b. In Canada, the Toronto Stock Exchange and the Montreal Exchange compile and publish indices of stock prices for a variety of industry classifications.

c. The S&P/TSX Composite Index measures changes in the market value of a portfolio of over 200 stocks due to changes in the total market capitalization.

d. Criticism about the DJIA is periodically raised because so few companies are included in this average that it is not a truly representative indicator of broad market activity. Also, since it is price-weighted, distortion occurs when a higher-priced stock rises rather than a lower-priced one.

20. Examine the first 25 stocks listed in the stock market listings for TSX stocks in your local newspaper. For how many of these stocks is the 52-week high price at least 50 percent greater than the 52-week low price? What do you conclude about the volatility of prices on individual stocks?

21. Turn to Figure 2.5 and find the listing for Alcan.

a. What was the closing price for Alcan?

b. How many shares could you buy for $5,000?

c. What would be your annual dividend income from those shares?

d. What must be Alcan's earnings per share?

22. Turn to Figure 2.10 and find the options for Barrick. Suppose you buy a March call option with exercise price $27.50, and the stock price in March is $30.

a. Will you exercise your call? What are the profit and rate of return on your position?

b. What, if you had bought the call with exercise price $30, would be your revised answers?

c. Suppose you had bought a March put with exercise price $27.50. What would be your answers, if the price in March is $63?

23. Turn to Figure 2.11 and find the S&P 60 future.

a. Suppose you buy one contract for March delivery. If the contract closes in March at a price of 470, what will your profit be?

b. How many March contracts are outstanding? (*Hint:* Use the Montreal Exchange Web site for help.)

STANDARD &POOR'S

Enter the Market Insight database at **www.mcgrawhill.ca/edumarketinsight** and click on *Educational Version of Market Insight*. After logging in, go to the *Company* tab, then click the *Population* button. Select a company of interest to you and go to the *Company Research* page with a menu of company information reports on the left. Select the *Company Profile* report and review the information provided. In what market is your company's stock traded? What is the stock ticker symbol? (Remember the ticker to access company information quickly on financial Web sites.) Finally, what is the industry classification of your company and its major competitors?

E-INVESTMENTS
Security Prices and Returns

Go to **www.cbs.marketwatch.com**. What was the return on the S&P/TSX today? Chart its value over the last day and the last year. What is the current yield on 10-year maturity Treasury bonds? At what price is Nortel stock selling? Find the price of the nearest-to-maturity Nortel call option with exercise price equal to Nortel's stock price rounded down to the nearest $5. What was the return on the following indices: Nikkei 225, FTSE 100, DAX? (*Hint:* Use NT for US$ and CA:NT for C$.)

HOW SECURITIES ARE TRADED

The buying and selling of securities is, to the ordinary investor, a fairly simple procedure. A telephone call to the broker is all that is needed to place an order and cause a given number of shares or bonds to be traded. Behind the execution of that order, however, lies a complicated and efficient system; and even the statement of the order must follow one of a variety of forms, so that it will follow the investor's actual wishes. The creation or issuance of securities, and the subsequent exchange of them between investors, requires the participation of a large number of financial professionals, who are subject to precise regulations in their actions.

We examine in this chapter the institutional details and mechanics of making investments in securities. We see how firms issue securities in the primary market and then how investors trade in these securities in the secondary market. The secondary market is further specified, depending on the type and structure of the exchange where trading takes place. How the trading is handled varies with the type of exchange, but the details seen by the investor are similar. We explain the notion of trading using margin, in which security is provided for borrowed money or short sales. The cost of trading in securities is an important factor affecting returns, and it is related to the services provided to the investor. Finally, we present the subject of how securities markets are regulated by various bodies to protect the interests of investors by guaranteeing a degree of openness and fairness in trading.

3.1 HOW FIRMS ISSUE SECURITIES

When firms need to raise capital they may choose to sell (or **float**) new securities. These new issues of stock, bonds, or other securities typically are marketed to the public by investment bankers in what is called the **primary market**. Purchase and sale of already issued securities among private investors take place in the **secondary market**.

There are two types of primary market issues of common stock. **Initial public offerings**, or *IPOs*, are stocks issued by a formerly privately owned company selling stock to the public for the first time. **Seasoned new issues** are offered by companies that already have floated equity. A sale by Canadian Pacific of new shares of stock, for example, would constitute a seasoned new issue.

A **secondary offering** is a stock sale that has all the characteristics of a primary market issue but is in fact a secondary market transaction.[1] Although the number is falling, many foreign multinational firms have Canadian subsidiaries, with a fraction of the total equity traded on Canadian exchanges and the remaining holding retained by the parent. When a parent company or any company that holds a significant interest in another firm chooses to sell all or a part of that holding, a secondary offering results. The shares then are sold to the general public as in a new equity issue; however, the parent firm receives the cash proceeds and no new shares are issued.

In the case of bonds we also distinguish between two types of primary market issues. A **public offering** is an issue of bonds sold to the general investing public that can then be traded on the secondary market. A **private placement** is an issue that is sold to a few institutional investors at most and generally held to maturity. Both of these terms also apply to the issue of stock.

Investment Bankers

Public offerings of both stocks and bonds typically are marketed via an **underwriting** by **investment bankers**, often known in Canada as **investment dealers**. The major firms are subsidiaries of chartered banks such as Nesbitt Burns (BMO) or Scotia McLeod (Scotiabank). In fact, more than one investment dealer usually markets the securities. A lead firm forms an **underwriting syndicate** of other investment dealers to share the responsibility for the stock issue.

The bankers advise the firm regarding the terms, such as price and number of units, on which it should attempt to sell the securities. A preliminary registration statement describing the issue and the prospects of the company must be filed with the provincial securities commission in the provinces in which the securities will be offered for sale. This *preliminary prospectus* is known as a *red herring* because of a statement, printed in red, that the company is not attempting to sell the security before the registration is approved. When the statement is finalized and approved by the commission, it is called the **prospectus**. At this time, the price at which the securities will be offered to the public is announced.

In a typical underwriting arrangement the investment bankers purchase the securities from the issuing company and then resell them to the public. The issuing firm sells the securities to the underwriting syndicate for the public offering price less a spread that serves as compensation to the underwriters. This procedure is called a *firm commitment.* The underwriters receive the issue and assume the full risk that the shares cannot in fact be sold to the public at the stipulated offering price. Besides being compensated by the spread between the purchase price and the public offering price, the investment banker may receive shares of common stock or other securities of the firm. Figure 3.1 depicts the relationship between the firm issuing the security, the underwriting syndicate, and the public.

---

[1]Actually, in Canada a seasoned new issue is referred to as a "secondary offering," in addition to the secondary market transactions involving corporate holdings; the word "secondary" is used to indicate that it is not the "first" IPO.

Figure 3.1 Relationship between a firm issuing securities, the underwriters, and the public.

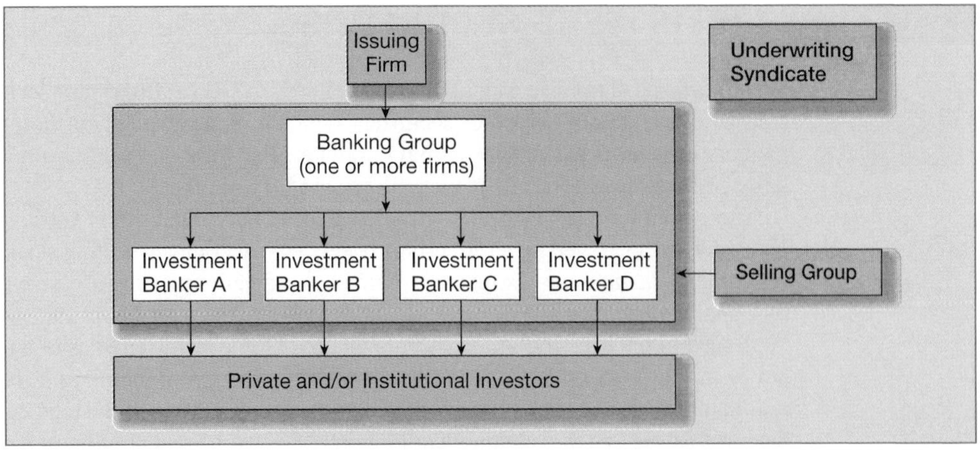

An alternative to this arrangement is the *best-efforts* agreement. In this case, the investment banker agrees to help the firm sell the issue to the public but does not actually purchase the securities. The banker simply acts as an intermediary between the public and the firm and thus does not bear the risk of being unable to resell purchased securities at the offering price.

Corporations engage investment bankers either by negotiation or by competitive bidding. Negotiation is more common. Besides being compensated by the spread between the purchase and public offering prices, an investment banker may receive shares of common stock or other securities of the firm. In the case of competitive bidding, a firm may announce its intent to issue securities and then invite investment bankers to submit bids for the underwriting. Such a bidding process may reduce the cost of the issue; however, it might also bring fewer services from the investment banker.

The immensely profitable business of IPOs is crucial to the financial success of the companies that conduct the investment dealer activity. In Canada, these are primarily the major banks that own securities dealers such as TD Waterhouse (TD Canada Trust) or Scotia Capital (Bank of Nova Scotia); these names are probably more familiar because of their "retail" business as stockbrokers.

Short Form Prospectus System (SFPD)

www.osc.gov.on.ca

The Ontario Securities Commission (OSC) permits the preparation of a prospectus for a new issue, with only minor additions to available financial information. This information, filed annually with the OSC, contains virtually all required information for a prospectus. The approval of the supplementary material requires only a few days instead of weeks, thus allowing the prompt placement of the issue with the underwriters; this is known as the *short form prospectus system* (SFPD).[2] This system reduces the underwriters' risk and makes bought deals more attractive. The sale to the public no longer requires a full prospectus.

Initial Public Offerings

Investment bankers manage the issuance of new securities to the public. Once the OSC has commented on the registration statement and a preliminary prospectus has been distributed to interested investors, the investment bankers organize road shows in which they travel around the country to publicize the imminent offering. These *road shows* serve two purposes. First, they attract potential

[2]The efficiency of the SFPD and the U.S. equivalent "shelf registration" have reduced the use of "rights" for secondary offerings since 1970; see Nancy D. Ursel and David J. Trepanier, "Securities Regulation Reform and the Decline of Rights Offerings," *Canadian Journal of Administrative Sciences* 18, no. 2 (June 2001), pp. 77–86.

investors and provide them information about the offering. Second, they collect for the issuing firm and its underwriters information about the price at which they will be able to market the securities. Large investors communicate their interest in purchasing shares of the IPO to the underwriters; these indications of interest are called a *book* and the process of polling potential investors is called *bookbuilding*. The book provides valuable information to the issuing firm because large institutional investors often will have useful insights about the market demand for the security as well as the prospects of the firm and its competitors. It is common for investment bankers to revise both their initial estimates of the offering price of a security and the number of shares offered based on feedback from the investing community.

Why would investors truthfully reveal their interest in an offering to the investment banker? Might they be better off expressing little interest in the hope that this will drive down the offering price? Truth is the better policy in this case because truth-telling is rewarded. Shares of IPOs are allocated to investors in part on the basis of the strength of each investor's expressed interest in the offering. If a firm wishes to get a large allocation when it is optimistic about the security, it needs to reveal its optimism. In turn, the underwriter needs to offer the security at a bargain price to these investors to induce them to participate in bookbuilding and share their information. Thus IPOs commonly are underpriced compared to the price at which they could be marketed. Such underpricing is reflected in price jumps on the date when the shares are first traded in public security markets. The most dramatic case of underpricing occurred in December 1999 when shares in VA Linux were sold in an IPO at $30 a share and closed on the first day of trading at $239.25, a 698 percent one-day return.

While the explicit costs of an IPO tend to be around 7 percent of the funds raised, such underpricing should be viewed as another cost of the issue. For example, if VA Linux had sold its shares for the $239.25 that investors obviously were willing to pay for them, its IPO would have raised eight times as much as it actually did. The money "left on the table" in this case far exceeded the explicit costs of the stock issue.

Figure 3.2 presents average first-day returns on IPOs of stocks across the world. The results consistently indicate that the IPOs are marketed to the investors at attractive prices. Underpricing

Figure 3.2
Average initial returns for IPOs in various countries.

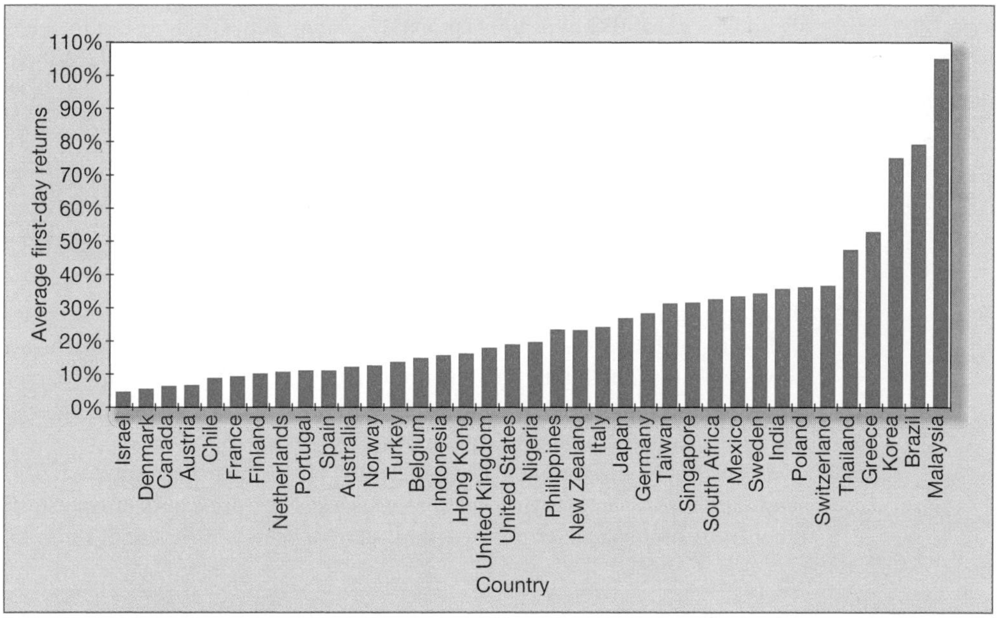

Source: Professor J. Ritter of the University of Florida, 2001. This is an updated version of the information contained in T. Loughran, J. Ritter, and K. Rydquist, "Initial Public Offerings," *Pacific-Basin Finance Journal* 2 (1994), pp. 165–99.

SPUN GOLD: DID WALL STREET FIRMS BRIBE BOSSES WITH SHARES?

Back in 1997, reports that Robertson Stephens, a Silicon Valley investment bank, was "spinning" IPO shares to executives who rewarded them with banking mandates prompted an SEC probe into the practice. The probe was soon abandoned. The practice boomed, becoming one of the more lucrative ways in which executives combined with Wall Street to abuse ordinary shareholders.

On August 30th Citigroup told congressional investigators that in 1997–2000 it had allocated IPO shares to Bernie Ebbers that had generated profits of $11m for the former boss of WorldCom, a telecoms firm which was a big Citigroup client, and is now bust thanks to fraud. Other WorldCom executives had also benefited. Citi claims that these allocations were not in return for investment-banking work; rather, they were a reward to the best customers of its private-banking arm. Underwriters and issuing firms are free to allocate shares however they wish, Citi notes—while in the same breath promising to change its allocation procedures.

Citigroup has yet to show that it was as generous to other private-banking clients who could not offer potential investment-banking business in return. Its "host of benign" explanations for why some shares were allocated retrospectively, giving executives a risk-free gain, seems thin. So does its claim that Jack Grubman, until last month the bank's top telecoms analyst, played no part in allocating shares to executives. Among the documents that Citigroup sent to Congress was a memo copied to Mr. Grubman that listed executives at several telecoms firms who had expressed interest in shares in IPOs.

Regulators and the courts will have to decide whether allocations of shares to executives were, in effect, bribes. If so, the punishment could be severe. Nor is Citi the only firm at risk. Credit Suisse First Boston gave shares in IPOs to executives minded to award it investment-banking business, via so-called "Friends of Frank" accounts, named after Frank Quattrone, its top technology investment banker.

CSFB and Goldman, Sachs now form part of the congressional investigation. And Morgan Stanley may soon face scrutiny over the role of Mary Meeker, formerly its top Internet analyst.

Source: Abridged from "Spun Gold...." *The Economist*, September 7, 2002.

of IPOs makes them appealing to all investors, yet institutional investors are allocated the bulk of a typical new issue. Some view this as unfair discrimination against small investors. However, our discussion suggests that the apparent discounts on IPOs may be no more than fair payments for a valuable service, specifically, the information contributed by the institutional investors. The right to allocate shares in this way may contribute to efficiency by promoting the collection and dissemination of such information.[3]

Both views of IPO allocations probably contain some truth. IPO allocations to institutions do serve a valid economic purpose as an information-gathering tool. Nevertheless, the system can be—and has been—abused. Part of the Wall Street scandals of 2000–2002 centred on the allocation of shares in IPOs. Some investment bankers used IPO allocations to corporate insiders to curry favour, in effect as implicit kickback schemes. Underwriters apparently would award generous IPO allocations to executives of particular firms in return for the firm's future investment banking business. In other cases, most notably at Credit Suisse First Boston, IPO allocations were awarded in return for a promise to direct excessive and expensive securities trading to the brokerage arm of the investment banking firm. The boxed article here discusses some of these practices.

Pricing of IPOs is not trivial, and not all IPOs turn out to be underpriced. Some stocks do poorly after the initial issue and others cannot even be fully sold to the market. Underwriters left with unmarketable securities are forced to sell them at a loss on the secondary market. Therefore, the investment banker bears the price risk of an underwritten issue.

Interestingly, despite their dramatic initial investment performance, IPOs have been poor long-term investments. Figure 3.3 compares the stock price performance of IPOs with shares of other firms of the same size for each of the five years after issue of the IPO. The year-by-year

[3]An elaboration of this point and a more complete discussion of the bookbuilding process is provided in Lawrence Benveniste and William Wilhelm, "Initial Public Offerings: Going by the Book," *Journal of Applied Corporate Finance* 9 (Spring 1997).

Figure 3.3 Long-term relative performance of initial public offerings.

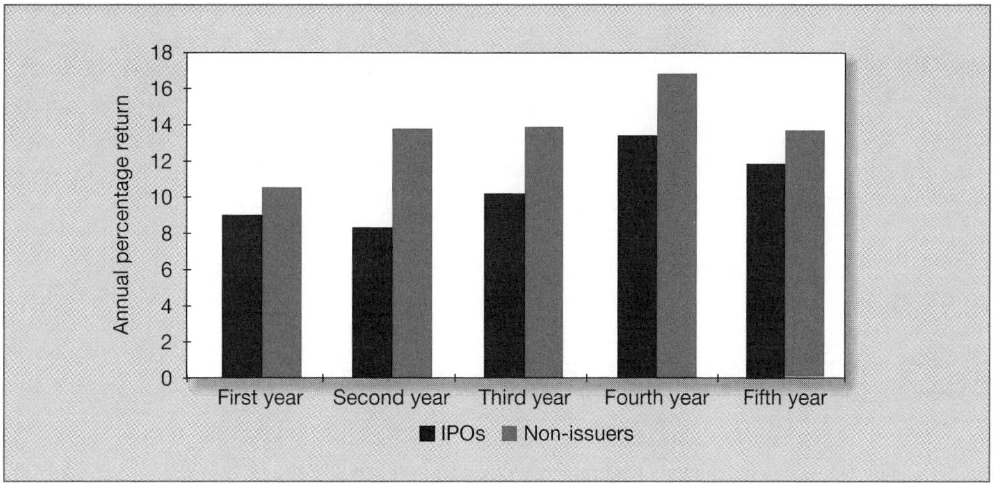

Source: Professor J. Ritter, University of Florida, 2001.

underperformance of the IPOs is dramatic, suggesting that on average, the investing public may be too optimistic about the prospects of these firms.[4]

IPOs can be expensive, especially for small firms. The landscape seemed to change in 1995 when Spring Street Brewing Company, which produces Wit beer, came out with an Internet IPO. It posted a page on the Web to let investors know of the stock offering and distributed the prospectus along with a subscription agreement as online word-processing documents. By the end of the year, the firm had sold 860,000 shares to 3,500 investors, and had raised $1.6 million, all without an investment banker. This was admittedly a small IPO, but a low-cost one that was well suited to such a small firm. Pursuant to this success, a new company named Wit Capital was formed, with the goal of arranging low-cost Web-based IPOs for other firms. Wit also participates in the underwriting syndicates of more conventional IPOs; unlike conventional investment bankers, it allocates shares on a first-come, first-served basis.

Another relatively new entry to the underwriting field is W. R. Hambrecht & Co., which also conducts IPOs on the Internet geared toward smaller, retail investors. Unlike typical investment bankers, which tend to favour institutional investors in the allocation of shares, and which determine an offer price through the bookbuilding process, Hambrecht conducts a "Dutch auction." In this procedure, which Hambrecht has dubbed OpenIPO, investors submit a price for a given number of shares. The bids are ranked in order of bid price, and shares are allocated to the highest bidders until the entire issue is absorbed. All shares are sold at an offer price equal to the highest price at which all the issued shares will be absorbed by investors. Those investors who bid below that cutoff price get no shares. By allocating shares based on bids, this procedure minimizes underpricing.

To date, however, upstarts like Wit Capital and Hambrecht have captured only a tiny share of the underwriting market. Their long-term prospects are still unclear.

Canadian underwriters have faced increasing competition from U.S. investment bankers for large offerings. Yet evidence indicates that Canadian costs are lower than U.S. costs, for small firms especially.[5] A comprehensive examination of the price behaviour of Canadian IPOs was

---

[4]It is worth noting in this regard that by December 2000, shares in VA Linux (now renamed VA Software) were selling for less than $9 a share, and by mid-2003 less than $2 a share. This example is extreme, but it is consistent with the generally poor long-term investment performance of IPOs.

[5]The relative cost structures examined in M. Kooli and J.-M. Suret, "How Cost Effective Are Canadian IPO Markets?" *CIRANO Working Papers*, April 2002.

presented by Chung et al.,[6] while Jog and Wang[7] traced the evolution through the 1990s of IPO underpricing and its link to volatility, finding that the latter has increased while the former has not. Recent Canadian research has examined the IPO issue with regard to special factors. For instance, Boabang[8] investigated the pricing of installment receipts; these are share issues in which only a portion of the price is paid initially, and the remainder is paid on one or more later dates (in installments). He found that IPOs of this type had a significant level of underpricing, associated with greater uncertainty about the underlying corporate value; the underpricing persisted throughout the first month of trading. Londerville[9] substantiated an earlier study showing evidence of underpricing of REITS using a Canadian sample from 1998.

3.2 WHERE SECURITIES ARE TRADED

Once securities have been issued to the public, investors may trade among themselves. This occurs in markets that have evolved to meet the needs of investors; consider what would happen if the organized markets did not exist. Investors seeking to sell would have to find potential buyers. To avoid a buyers' market, there would need to be a meeting place, which also would serve buyers who did not want to be at the mercy of sellers. Hence buyers and sellers would meet and bargain for satisfactory prices, or agents would undertake to match potential buyers and sellers; ideally, competition among agents would drive down their fees. Eventually, the meeting place would evolve into a financial market, as was the case for a pub called Lloyd's in London and a Manhattan curb on Wall Street. Without this evolution of the secondary market, the costs of selling shares would be extremely detrimental to the purchase of shares in the primary market; so an efficient secondary market, which determines a fair and accurate price and allows the relatively quick and cheap transfer of shares, is crucial to the raising of investment capital by businesses.

The markets that have evolved can be characterized as four types: direct search markets, brokered markets, dealer markets, and auction markets. The **direct search market** is what we have described above, where buyers and sellers must seek each other out directly. Such markets are characterized by sporadic participation and low-priced and nonstandard goods.

The next level of organization is a **brokered market**. If there is sufficient activity in trading a good, brokers can find it profitable to offer search services to buyers and sellers. Examples include the real estate market, as well as primary and secondary markets for security trading. Markets for large **block transactions** of shares have developed, since attempts to move them on the regular exchanges would cause major price movements; blocks are recorded as being "crossed" on the exchange by traders, who have located other large traders, even though the trade does not actually pass through the usual exchange process.

When trading activity in a particular type of asset increases, **dealer markets** arise. Here, dealers specialize in various commodities, purchase assets for their own inventory, and sell goods for a profit from their inventory. Dealers, unlike brokers, trade assets for their own accounts. The dealer's profit margin is the "bid-asked" spread, the difference between the price at which the dealer buys for and sells from inventory. Dealer markets save traders on search costs

---

[6]R. Chung, L. Kryzanowski, and I. Rakita, "The Relationship Between Overallotment Options, Underwriting Fees and Price Stabilization for Canadian IPOs," *Multinational Finance Journal* 4, nos. 1–2 (June 2000).

[7]V. Jog and L. Wang, "Aftermarket Volatility and Underpricing of Canadian Initial Public Offerings," *Canadian Journal of Administrative Sciences* 19, no. 3 (September 2002), pp. 231–248.

[8]F. Boabang, "The IPOs of Canadian Firms via Installment Receipts: The Opening Performance and Implications for the Short-Run Efficiency of the Canadian Market," *Canadian Journal of Administrative Sciences* 20, no. 3 (September 2003).

[9]J. Londerville, "Canadian Real Estate Investment Trusts: A Review of the IPO Literature and Preliminary Analysis of Canadian REIT IPO Pricing," *Canadian Journal of Administrative Sciences* 19, no. 4 (December 2002), pp. 359–368.

because market participants are easily able to look up the prices at which they can buy from or sell to dealers. Obviously, a fair amount of market activity is required before dealing in a market is an attractive source of income. The over-the-counter securities market is one example of a dealer market.

The most integrated market is an **auction market**, in which all transactors in a good converge at one place to bid on or offer a good. The New York Stock Exchange (NYSE) is an example of an auction market, as are all the major Canadian markets. An advantage of auction markets over dealer markets is that one need not search to find the best price for a good. If all participants converge, they can arrive at mutually agreeable prices and thus save the bid-asked spread. Continuous auction markets (as opposed to periodic auctions such as in the art world) require very heavy and frequent trading to cover the expense of maintaining the market. For this reason, larger exchanges set up listing requirements, which limit the shares traded on the exchange to those of firms in which sufficient trading interest is likely to exist.

CONCEPT CHECK

1. Many assets trade in more than one type of market. What types of markets do the following trade in?
   a. Used cars
   b. Paintings
   c. Rare coins

The Secondary Markets

www.tsx.com
www.me.com

Where previously there were five **stock exchanges** in Canada, with the largest in Toronto, Montreal and Vancouver, there is now one major exchange for equities, the TSX, with the Canadian Derivatives Exchange (CDE) handling derivative securities. In 2000, the TSX became a for-profit organization rather than a mutual body of member firms. The major consolidation began in 1999 with the division of trading and listing of large firms on the TSX and small firms on the Canadian Venture Exchange or CDNX; stocks listed on the Montreal Exchange (ME) moved to the TSX, or to the CDNX if small. All trading in financial derivatives moved to the ME from Toronto and Vancouver. The CDNX was formed from the trading in small and regional issues in Vancouver, Alberta, and Winnipeg.

Historically, an exchange provided a facility for its members to trade securities, with only members of the exchange allowed to trade there. Therefore memberships, or *seats*, on the exchange have been valuable assets. Brokerage firms are exchange members who own seats and advertise their willingness to execute trades for customers for a fee. The commissions that can be earned through this activity determine the market value of a seat. Hence, the price of a seat is taken as an indicator of the buoyancy of the market.

For instance, a seat on the New York Stock Exchange (NYSE), which sold for more than US$1 million prior to the October 1987 crash, was worth only US$625,000 by January 1988; ten years later the price was $2 million. The highest price of a seat on the TSE was $370,000 in 1987, but by 1996 it had fallen to $52,000.

Under its new structure, however, the TSE—now TSX—has no seats, only shares owned by participating organizations; these shares will sell at prices reflecting the buoyancy of the market. The realignment of the TSX is a consequence of the development of alternative trading systems (ATSs), particularly the electronic networks (ECNs) described below, by which traders can effect their investment decisions more efficiently or cheaply than under the traditional exchange-centred model. The TSX sees the NYSE, the Nasdaq, and the ATSs as its primary competition, and is trying to accommodate the ATSs within its new structure. Interlisting between exchanges exposes a stock to competition from both domestic and foreign equities, leading to greater efficiencies of

TORONTO EXCHANGE TO PHASE IN U.S. DOLLAR TRADING

TSX Group Inc. said on Monday it will allow U.S. dollar-denominated trading of certain stocks on the Toronto Stock Exchange as early as next month as it tries to grab a larger share of companies listed in both Canada and the United States.

TSX Group, which operates Canada's senior bourse and the junior TSX Venture Exchange, said it will start its U.S.-dollar book with 12 companies, adding it might expand the list by the Feb. 2 start date if enough demand exists.

The TSX said it surveyed broker-dealers and institutional investors to determine which companies to list first, and said it could eventually end up with 50 or more companies trading in U.S. dollars by the end of the year.

"Right now we've got way over 100 interlisted companies that trade on the TSX and on a U.S. marketplace, so that's sort of our primary target audience," said Rik Parkhill, senior vice-president at TSX Markets.

"We think that by making the foreign exchange process more transparent, that we'll make the market more efficient as well."

Companies that will be traded in both U.S. and Canadian dollars will include gold miners Barrick Gold Corp. and Placer Dome Inc., and energy producers Canadian Natural Resources Ltd., Precision Drilling Corp. and Suncor Energy Inc.

Nickel miner Inco Ltd. and aluminum producer Alcan Inc. will also be available in both currencies, as will wireless device manufacturer Research In Motion Ltd., and graphics chip maker ATI Technologies Inc.

Angiotech Pharmaceuticals Inc., methanol producer Methanex Corp. and Wheaton River Minerals Ltd. round out the stocks that will be offered, identified by a ".U" after their trading symbol.

All 12 stocks are also listed on U.S. exchanges.

The TSX said it decided to offer the services after complaints about the specialist-based system on the New York Stock Exchange, which critics say is less efficient than electronic trading systems such as the TSX.

The NYSE is facing regulatory scrutiny over the system, under which auctioneers put up their own capital in order to reduce volatility, using a mix of manual and automated trades.

"On fast moving markets, if you're an institutional investor, that tends to be a fairly inefficient way to trade, and the price point that you thought you could get executed sometimes turns out not to be the case, because the specialist has held up that trade," said Rik Parkhill.

The TSX hopes it will be seen as a more palatable option to the NYSE than is the electronic Nasdaq market.

The TSX, which has seen trading and listing revenues soar over the past year as stock prices surged more than 20 percent, has been trying to make itself more attractive to foreign investors and raise its share of trading in companies that are listed in both Canada and the United States.

Shares of TSX Group were up 45 Canadian cents at C$45.35 on Monday afternoon, after touching a record high of C$46 earlier in the session.

pricing.[10] It may also cause trading to shift from the domestic to a foreign exchange if the trading time is comparable. In particular, sufficient interest in the United States will divert trading from Canadian exchanges if there is greater liquidity, or higher trading volume, that leads to tighter spreads.[11] On the other hand, note the TSX's response to interlisting on U.S. exchanges described in the boxed article here.

Approximately 3,600 companies are listed by the TSX Group, of which about two-thirds are on the Venture exchange. Daily trading volume on the TSX averaged about 150 million shares in 2003. The value of shares traded in 2003 was $655 billion (US$475 billion), including an insignificant amount of Venture Exchange trading (around $3 billion); this is less than 5 percent of the NYSE value for the same period. Another measure of an exchange's importance is the total market capitalization; the TSX, at US$910 billion, ranks seventh in the world, up from eighth in 2002. On a worldwide basis, as shown in Table 3.1, the NYSE, Nasdaq, London, and

[10]For a detailed explanation of the reorganization of the TSX, its strategies, and its trading systems, refer to their Web site at www.tsx.com.

[11]For a discussion of the benefits of interlisting, see Usha Mittoo, "How Canadian Companies Win by Interlisting Shares on U.S. Exchanges," *Canadian Investment Review*, Winter 1993/1994. See also Lorne Switzer, "The Benefits and Costs of Listing Canadian Stocks in U.S. Markets," *Corporate Structure, Finance and Operations* 4 (1986), pp. 141–156.

Table 3.1 The Top Ten Stock Exchanges in the World, December 2003

	Market Capitalization (US$ millions)		Value of Trading (US$ millions)	
	2003	2002	2003	2002
1. NYSE	11,328,953	9,015,167	9,692,341	10,311,156
2. Tokyo	2,953,098	2,069,299	2,130,710	1,565,824
3. Nasdaq	2,844,193	1,994,494	7,068,213	7,254,595
4. London	2,425,822	1,785,199	3,624,009	3,998,462
5. Euronext*	2,076,410	1,538,654	1,905,398	1,987,199
6. Deutsche Börse	1,079,026	686,014	1,304,987	1,207,977
7. TSX Group	910,231	579,803	474,950	408,107
8. Swiss Exchange	727,103	612,667	609,002	600,067
9. Spanish Exchanges (BME)	726,243	461,560	938,720	654,743
10. Hong Kong	714,597	463,055	296,407	194,003

*Includes Amsterdam, Brussels, Lisbon, and Paris figures.

Source: World Federation of Exchanges.

Tokyo stock exchanges account for the majority of market capitalization. (Tokyo's capitalization and trading value have collapsed since 1987.)

World Federation of Exchanges www.fibv.com

The TSX is willing to list a stock (i.e., allow trading in that stock on the exchange) only if it meets certain criteria of size and stability. Table 3.2 gives the initial listing requirements of the TSX. Unlike the NYSE, the TSX has different requirements for the various kinds of companies. Besides industrials, the TSX also lists mining and energy companies; these are required to have both capital and either reserves of or potential for mineral production. These requirements ensure that a firm is of significant trading interest before the TSX will allocate facilities for it to be traded on the exchange. If a listed company suffers a decline and fails to meet the criteria in Table 3.2 (or those applicable), it may be "de-listed."

Although most common and preferred stocks are traded on the exchanges, bonds are not. Corporate and all federal, provincial, and municipal government bonds are traded only over the counter.

Table 3.2 Minimum Listing Requirements for the Toronto Stock Exchange (senior companies)

	Financial Requirements		
	Industrials*	Mining	Oil and Gas
Pre-tax cash flow in last year	$700K	$700K	$700K
Earnings before taxes in last year	300K	Positive	Positive
Net tangible assets	7.5M	$7.5M	
Adequate working capital	✓	✓	
Sufficient capital funds		✓	✓
Proven reserves			$7.5M
		Public Distribution	
Market value of publicly held stock	$4M	$4M	$4M
Shares publicly held	1M	1M	1M
Number of holders of board lot or more	300	300	300

*Alternative, stricter requirements for technology companies.

Source: Toronto Stock Exchange.

The Over-the-Counter Market

Several hundred issues are traded on the Canadian **over-the-counter (OTC) market** on a regular basis, and, in fact, any security may be traded there. The OTC market, however, is not a formal exchange; there are neither membership requirements for trading nor listing requirements for securities. In the OTC market, brokers registered with the provincial securities commission act as dealers in OTC securities. Security dealers quote prices at which they are willing to buy or sell securities. A broker can execute a trade by contacting a dealer listing an attractive quote.

The Canadian OTC market has developed similarly to that of the United States. Prior to automation, quotations of stock were recorded manually and published daily. The so-called "pink sheets" were the means by which dealers communicated their interest in trading at various prices. This was a cumbersome and inefficient technique, and published quotes were a full day out of date. In 1971, the U.S. National Association of Securities Dealers Automated Quotation system, or **Nasdaq**, began to offer immediate information on a computer-linked system of bid and asked prices for stocks offered by various dealers. The **bid price** is that at which a dealer is willing to purchase a security; the **asked price** is that at which the dealer is willing to sell a security. The system allows a dealer who receives a buy or a sell order from an investor to examine all current quotes, call the dealer with the best quote, and execute a trade. With over 6,000 firms listed, the system has grown in importance by providing real competition to the NYSE and has now come to be known as the Nasdaq Stock Market. Since 1998, the volume of trading has exceeded that on the NYSE, with the value of trading also higher despite the lower-priced securities found on the Nasdaq.

Nasdaq
www.nasdaq.com

The Nasdaq market is divided into two sectors, the Nasdaq National Market System and the Nasdaq SmallCap Market, the former having more restrictive listing requirements. For even smaller firms, Nasdaq maintains an electronic "OTC Bulletin Board," which allows brokers and dealers to use computerized posting; for the smallest firms, the traditional pink slips are used. Whether the term "over-the-counter" should still be applied is debatable, since the National Market System has all the appearances of a modern electronic exchange.

The Canadian OTC market parallels the U.S. situation, having another, smaller equity trading system. The TSX Venture Exchange was taken over by the TSE in 2001 as a vehicle for trading in stocks that do not qualify for TSX listing. The exchange is described as being designed for "emerging" companies, with a focus on venture capital investment; two tiers are established for companies, corresponding to their stage of development. Both tiers have separate standards for five categories of firms: mining, oil and gas, technology or industrial, research and development, and real estate or investment. Requirements vary, but they cover such items as net tangible assets, property or reserves (O&G), prior expenditures (R&D), working capital, pre-tax earnings, share issues (distribution, market capitalization, and float), and availability of financial statements, with lighter requirements for second-tier companies. The Venture Exchange identifies two types of affiliates, Member brokerage firms and Participating Organizations, the latter being defined as having trading access to the facilities of the Exchange.

Beyond the TSX Venture Exchange lie the NEX and the Canadian Unlisted Board (CUB), for the truly over-the-counter trading. The TSX Venture Exchange, in fact, describes itself as an alternative exchange and not an OTC market. Technically, those stocks that previously traded on the Canadian Dealer Network (CDN) were moved to the TSX Venture Exchange at Tier 2 if qualified. Those that did not qualify were listed as Tier 3, now the NEX or the CUB, although the CUB is restricted to Ontario companies. All three tiers are cleared and settled through the Canadian Depository for Securities. It should be borne in mind that, often, stocks trading on the OTC market are subject to manipulation by some small brokerage houses and promoters.

For bonds, the over-the-counter market is a loosely organized network of dealers linked by a computer quotation system for a number of bellwether bonds. In practice, the corporate bond market often is quite "thin," in that there are few investors interested in trading a particular bond at any particular time. The bond market is subject to a type of liquidity risk, because it can be difficult to sell holdings quickly if the need arises.

The Third and Fourth Markets

The **third market** refers to trading of exchange-listed securities on the OTC market. The development of this phenomenon followed its evolution in the United States. Until the 1970s, members of the NYSE were required to execute all their trades of NYSE-listed securities on the exchange itself and to charge commissions according to a fixed schedule. This schedule was disadvantageous to large traders, who were prevented from realizing economies of scale on large trades. The restriction led brokerage firms that were not members of the NYSE, and so not bound by its rules, to establish trading in the OTC market on large NYSE-listed firms. These trades took place at lower commissions than would have been charged on the NYSE, and the third market grew dramatically until 1975, when commissions on all orders became negotiable in the United States. Negotiated commissions became a common practice in Canada after April 1983, together with the growing popularity of discount brokerage houses.

The discount brokerage houses typically encourage investors, by lower commissions, to use online trading. This is not to be misunderstood as third-market trading, as orders are routed to the exchanges, even if they bypass a broker; in fact, special authorization is required to channel the order to the "floor" without review by a broker to ensure that it is a suitable trade for the account. The electronic nature of this order submission is quite distinct from the electronic networks (ECNs) that follow. Small investors *may* be using ECNs in trading through on-line discount brokers, but not necessarily so, and if so, at the brokers' initiative.

*E*Trade www.etrade.com*

The **fourth market** refers to direct trading between investors in exchange-listed securities without benefit of a broker. The direct trading among investors that characterizes the fourth market has exploded in recent years due to the advent of the **electronic communication network**, or **ECN**. The ECN is an alternative to either formal stock exchanges like the NYSE or dealer markets like Nasdaq for trading securities. These networks allow members to post buy or sell orders and to have those orders matched up or "crossed" with orders of other traders in the system. Both sides of the trade benefit because direct crossing eliminates the bid-ask spread that otherwise would be incurred. (Traders pay a small price per trade or per share rather than incurring a bid-ask spread, which tends to be far more expensive.) In addition to speed and cost savings, these systems provide traders greater anonymity than they could otherwise achieve. This is important since big traders do not want to publicly signal their desire to buy or sell large quantities of shares for fear of moving prices in advance of their trades. ECNs have been highly successful and have captured about 40 percent of the trading volume in Nasdaq-listed stocks.

The United States suffers from a fragmented market system, such as has been eliminated by the realignment of the TSX and the ME. A partial remedy has been the Intermarket Trading System (ITS), which links ten exchanges, displaying quotes from all, and allows cross-market trades.

While the ITS does much to unify markets, it has some important shortcomings. First, it does not provide for automatic execution in the market with the best price. The trade must be directed there by a market participant, who might find it inconvenient (or unprofitable) to do so. Moreover, some feel that the ITS is too slow to integrate prices off the NYSE. A logical extension of the ITS as a means to integrate securities markets would be the establishment of a central limit order book. Such an electronic "book" would contain all orders conditional on both prices and dates. All markets would be linked and all traders could compete for all orders.

Although market integration seems like an desirable goal, the recent growth of ECNs has led to some concern that markets are in fact becoming more fragmented. This is because participants in one ECN do not nesessarily know what prices are being quoted on other networks. ECNs do display their best-priced offers on the Nasdaq system, but other limit orders are not available. Only stock exchanges may participate in the Intermarket Trading System, which means that most ECNs are excluded. Moreover, during the after-hours trading enabled by ECNs, trades take place on these private networks while other, larger markets are closed and current prices for securities are harder to assess. In the wake of growing concern about market fragmentation, some big Wall Street brokerage houses have called for an electronically driven central limit order book, but full market integration has yet to be achieved.

Foreign Markets

An important development in trading is the cross-listing of major corporations on exchanges around the world. In particular, listing on the London, Euronext, Tokyo Stock Exchanges (TSE) permits traders to trade virtually at any hour of the day, if so inclined; in fact, the Frankfurt Exchange has an active market in major U.S. corporations prior to the New York opening. This has implications for valuation, as news can be received and traded upon immediately, leading to more pricing efficiency.

The structure of security markets varies considerably from one country to another. A full cross-country comparison is far beyond the scope of this text. Therefore, we instead briefly review three of the biggest non-U.S. stock markets: the London, Euronext, and Tokyo exchanges.

London Until 1997, trading arrangements in London were similar to those on Nasdaq. Competing dealers who wished to make a market in a stock would enter bid and asked prices into the Stock Exchange Automated Quotations (SEAQ) system. As in the United States, London security firms acted as both dealers and as brokerage firms, that is, both making a market in securities and executing trades for their clients.

In 1997, the London Stock Exchange introduced an electronic trading system dubbed SETS (Stock Exchange Electronic Trading Service). This is an electronic clearing system similar to ECNs in which buy and sell orders are submitted via computer networks and any buy and sell orders that can be crossed are executed automatically.

Most trading in London equities is now conducted using SETS, particularly for shares in larger firms. However, SEAQ continues to operate and may be more likely to be used for the "upstairs market" in large-block transactions or other less-liquid transactions.

Euronext Euronext was formed in 2000 by a merger of the Paris, Amsterdam, and Brussels exchanges. Euronext, like most European exchanges, uses an electronic trading system. Its system, called NSC (for Nouveau Système de Cotation, or New Quotation System), has fully automated order routing and execution. In fact, investors can enter their orders directly without contacting their brokers. An order submitted to the system is executed immediately if it can be crossed against an order in the public limit-order book; if it cannot be executed, it is entered into the limit-order book.

Euronext is in the process of establishing cross-trading agreements with several other European exchanges such as Helsinki or Luxembourg. In 2001, it also purchased LIFFE, the London International Financial Futures and Options Exchange.

Tokyo The Tokyo Stock Exchange (TSE) is the largest stock exchange in Japan, accounting for about 80 percent of total trading. There is no specialist system on the TSE. Instead, a *saitori* maintains a public limit-order book, matches market and limit orders, and is obliged to follow certain actions to slow down price movements when simple matching of orders would result in price changes greater than exchange-prescribed limits. In their clerical role of matching orders saitoris are somewhat similar to specialists on the NYSE. However, saitoris do not trade for their own accounts and therefore are quite different from either dealers or specialists in the United States.

Because the saitoris perform an essentially clerical role, there are no market-making services or liquidity provided to the market by dealers or specialists. The limit-order book is the primary provider of liquidity. In this regard, the TSE bears some resemblance to the fourth market in the United States in which buyers and sellers trade directly via ECNs. On the TSE, however, if order imbalances would result in price movements across sequential trades that are considered too extreme by the exchange, the saitori may temporarily halt trading and advertise the imbalance in the hope of attracting additional trading interest to the "weak" side of the market.

The TSE organizes stocks into two categories. The First Section consists of about 1,200 of the most actively traded stocks. The Second Section is for less actively traded stocks. Trading in the larger First Section stocks occurs on the floor of the exchange. The remaining securities in the First Section and the Second Section trade electronically.

Derivatives Markets

www.telenium.ca/WCE

Markets also exist in Canada for trading in options and futures. Unlike stocks, for which the primary markets exist to raise capital for the issuing firms, derivatives are created as contracts between investors; therefore, there is only a secondary market for them. Commodity futures for agricultural products are traded on the Winnipeg Commodity Exchange; options and financial futures, in T-bills for example, trade on the Canadian Derivatives Exchange. In addition, there are a number of options and futures that trade on U.S. or foreign exchanges. Because of the complexity of these derivatives, our discussion of these markets is given in Chapters 17 to 19. The mechanics of trading in derivatives are similar to stock trading, but there are far more complicated strategies. We describe these strategies in a later chapter.

3.3 TRADING ON EXCHANGES

Most of the material in this section applies to all securities traded on exchanges. Some of it, however, applies just to stocks, and in such cases we use the terms *stocks* or *shares*.

The Participants

When an investor instructs a broker to buy or sell securities, a number of players must act to consummate the trade. We start our discussion of the mechanics of exchange trading with a brief description of the potential parties to a trade.

The investor places an order with a broker. The latter contacts a brokerage firm owning a seat on the exchange (a *commission broker*) to execute the order. *Floor traders* (also known as floor attorneys) are representatives of members of the exchange charged with executing the trades on behalf of their firms' clients. In 1997, the physical "floor" of the Toronto Stock Exchange was replaced by automated trading.

Registered traders are floor traders entrusted with **market-making** in specific stocks. A registered trader, who is known as a *specialist* in the NYSE, is central to the trading process. Registered traders maintain a market in one or more listed securities. We will examine their role in detail shortly.

Types of Orders

Market Orders Market orders are simply buy or sell orders that are to be executed immediately at current market prices. For example, an investor might call his broker and ask for the market price of Inco. The retail broker will consult her screen for best current quotes. Finding that the current quotes are $48 per share bid and $48.20 asked, the investor might direct the broker to buy 100 shares "at market," meaning that he is willing to pay $48.20 per share for an immediate transaction. Similarly, an order to "sell at market" will result in stock sales at $48 per share. When a trade is executed, an order card will record the time, price, and quantity of shares traded, and the transaction is reported on the exchange's ticker tape.

There are two potential complications to this simple scenario, however. First, as noted earlier, the posted quotes of $48 and $48.20 actually represent commitments to trade up to a specified number of shares. If the market order is for more than this number of shares, the order may be filled at multiple prices. For example, if the asked price is good for orders of up to 600 shares, and the investor wishes to purchase 1,000 shares, it may be necessary to pay a slightly higher price for the last 400 shares than the quoted asked price.

The second complication arises from the possibility of trading "inside the quoted spread." If the broker who has received a market buy order for Inco meets another broker who has received a market sell order for Inco, they can agree to trade with each other at a price of $48.10 per share. By meeting in the middle of the quoted spread, both the buyer and the seller obtain "price improvement," that is, transaction prices better than the best quoted prices. Such "meetings" of brokers are more than accidental. Because all trading takes place at the specialist's post, floor brokers know where to look for counterparties to take the other side of a trade. One U.S. study[12] found that when the spread between the quoted bid and asked price was $.25 or greater, approximately one-half of trades on the NYSE were actually executed "inside the quotes."

Limit Orders Investors may also place **limit orders**, whereby they specify prices at which they are willing to buy or sell a security. If the stock falls below the limit on a *limit-buy order* then the trade is to be executed. If Inco is selling at $48 bid, $48.20 asked, for example, a limit-buy order may instruct the broker to buy the stock if and when the share price falls below $45. Correspondingly, a *limit-sell order* instructs the broker to sell as soon as the stock price goes above the specified limit.

Figure 3.4 is a portion of the limit-order book for shares in Intel on the Island exchange on one particular day. Notice that the best orders are at the top of the list: the offers to buy at the highest price and to sell at the lowest price. The buy and sell orders at the top of the list—$27.88 and $27.93—are called the *inside quotes*; they are the buy and sell orders with the closest prices. For Intel, the inside spread is only $.05 per share.

What happens if a limit order is placed between the quoted bid and ask prices? For example, suppose you have instructed your broker to buy Inco at a price of $48.10 or better. The order may not be executed immediately, since the quoted asked price for the shares is $48.20, which is more than you are willing to pay. However, your willingness to buy at $48.10 is better than the quoted bid price of $48 per share. Therefore, you may find that there are traders who were unwilling to sell their shares at the $48 bid price but are happy to sell shares to you at your higher bid price of $48.10.

Stop-loss orders are similar to limit orders in that the trade is not to be executed unless the stock hits a price limit. In this case, however, the stock is to be sold if its price falls *below* a

[12] K. Ross, J. Shapiro, and K. Smith, "Price Improvement of SuperDOT Market Orders on the NYSE," NYSE Working Paper 96-02, March 1996.

Figure 3.4 The limit-order book for Intel on the Island exchange, November 9, 2001.

refresh | island home | disclamer | help

INTC — GET STOCK [INTC] go

LAST MATCH		TODAY'S ACTIVITY	
Price	27.8900	Orders	16,774
Time	14:24:45	Volume	4,631,778

BUY ORDERS		SELL ORDERS	
Shares	Price	Shares	Price
100	27.8800	1,000	27.9300
500	27.8500	1,000	27.9690
200	27.8500	1,000	27.9800
1,000	27.8200	1,000	27.9900
3,300	27.8100	1,000	28.0000
300	27.8000	1,800	28.0600
75	27.7500	1,000	28.0800
101	27.7300	1,000	28.1000
5,000	27.7200	2,000	28.1100
1,000	27.72	1,000	28.1800
(416 more)		(395 more)	

stipulated level. As the name suggests, the order lets the stock be sold to stop further losses from accumulating. Symmetrically, *stop-buy orders* specify that the stock should be bought when its price rises above a given limit. These trades often accompany short sales, and they are used to limit potential losses from the short position. (Short sales are discussed in greater detail in Section 3.5.) A stop-loss at \$21.50 will be executed (a sale) if the price drops to \$21.50; however, the sale may only realize \$21.20 if that is the next limit-buy order. To prevent this a *stop limit* is needed; the arrival of the new low at \$21.50 triggers a limit order to sell at \$21.50. In this case, however, if the price immediately falls to \$21, there is no sale. Figure 3.5 organizes the types of orders in a simple matrix.

Orders also can be limited by a time period. Day orders, for example, expire at the close of the trading day. If it is not executed on that day, the order is cancelled. *Open or good-till-cancelled orders*, in contrast, remain in force for up to six months unless cancelled by the customer. At the other extreme, *fill or kill orders* expire if the broker cannot fill them immediately.

Figure 3.5 Limit orders.

ACTION \ CONDITION	Price ≤ The limit	Price = The limit	Price ≥ The limit
Buy	Limit-buy order	Stop-limit (buy) order	Stop-buy order
Sell	Stop-loss order	Stop-limit (sell) order	Limit-sell order

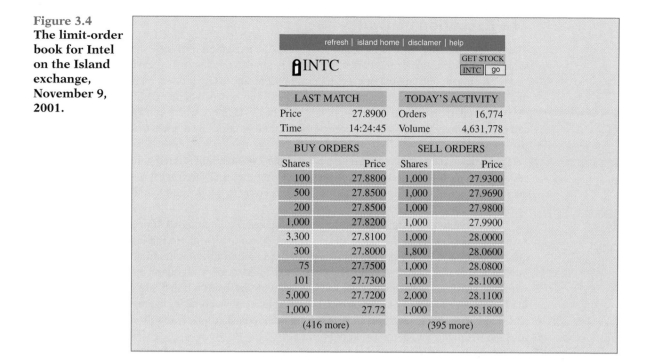

The Execution of Trades

The registered trader, who is the central figure in the execution of trades, makes a market in the shares of one or more firms. Part of this task is simply mechanical. It involves maintaining a "book" listing all outstanding unexecuted limit orders entered by brokers on behalf of clients. Actually, the book is now a computer console. When limit orders can be executed at market prices, the registered trader sees to the trade; in this role, he or she merely acts as a facilitator. As buy and sell orders at mutually agreeable prices cross the trading desk, the market-maker matches the two parties to the trade.

The registered trader is required to use the highest outstanding offered purchase price and lowest outstanding offered selling price when matching trades. Therefore, this system results in an auction market—all buy orders and all sell orders come to one location, and the best bids "win" the trades.

The more interesting function of the market-maker is to maintain a "fair and orderly market" by dealing personally in the stock. In return for the exclusive right to make the market in a specific stock on the exchange, the registered trader is required to maintain an orderly market by buying and selling shares from inventory. Registered traders maintain bid and asked prices, within a maximum spread specified by TSX regulations, at which they are obligated to meet at least a limited amount of market orders. If market buy orders come in, the registered traders must sell shares from their own accounts at the maintained asked price; if sell orders come in, they must be willing to buy at the listed bid price.

Ordinarily, in an active market registered traders can cross buy and sell orders without direct participation on their own accounts. That is, the trader's own inventory need not be the primary means of order execution. However, sometimes the market-maker's bid and asked prices will be better than those offered by any other market participant. Therefore, at any point, the effective asked price in the market is the lower of either the registered trader's offered asked price or the lowest of the unfilled limit-sell orders. Similarly, the effective bid price is the highest of unfilled limit-buy orders or the trader's bid. These procedures ensure that the registered trader provides liquidity to the market.

By standing ready to trade at quoted bid and asked prices, the market-maker is exposed somewhat to exploitation by other traders. Large traders with ready access to late-breaking news will trade with market-makers only if the latter's quoted prices are temporarily out of line with assessments based on the traders' (possibly superior) information. Registered traders who cannot match the information resources of large traders will be at a disadvantage when their quoted prices offer profit opportunities to better-informed traders.

You might wonder why market-makers do not protect their interests by setting a low bid price and a high asked price. A registered trader using that strategy would not suffer losses by maintaining a too-low asked price or a too-high bid price in a period of dramatic movements in the stock price. Traders who offer a narrow spread between the bid and the asked prices have little leeway for error and must constantly monitor market conditions to avoid offering other investors advantageous terms.

Large bid-asked spreads are not viable options for the specialist for two reasons. First, one source of the specialist's income is derived from frequent trading at the bid and asked prices, with the spread as the trading profit. A too-large spread would make the specialist's quotes noncompetitive with the limit orders placed by other traders. If the specialist's bid and asked quotes are consistently worse than those of public traders, it will not participate in any trades and will lose the ability to profit from the bid-asked spread.

An equally important reason that specialists cannot use large bid-ask spreads to protect their interests is that they are obligated to provide *price continuity* to the market. To illustrate the principle of price continuity, suppose that the highest limit-buy order for a stock is $30 while the lower limit-sell order is at $32. When a market buy order comes in, it is matched to the best limit-sell at $32. A market sell order would be matched to the best limit-buy at $30. As market buys and sells come to the floor randomly, the stock price would fluctuate between $30 and $32. The exchange would consider this excessive volatility, and the specialist would be expected to step in with bid and/or asked prices between these values to reduce the bid-asked spread to an acceptable level, typically less than $.15 for large firms.

Registered traders earn income both from commissions for acting as brokers for orders and from the spread between the bid and asked prices at which they buy and sell securities. It also appears that their "book" of limit orders gives them unique knowledge about the probable direction of price movement over short periods of time. For example, suppose the market-maker sees that a stock now selling for $45 has limit-buy orders for over 100,000 shares at prices ranging from $44.50 to $44.75. This latent buying demand provides a cushion of support, because it is unlikely that enough sell pressure could come in during the next few hours to cause the price to drop below $44.50. If there are very few limit-sell orders above $45, some transient buying demand could raise the price substantially. The trader in such circumstances realizes that a position in the stock offers little downside risk and substantial upside potential. Such unique access to the trading intentions of other market participants seems to allow a market-maker to earn substantial profits on personal transactions.

Specific regulations of the TSX govern the registered traders' ability to profit from their superior information and their responsibility to maintain an orderly market. Such a market should respond to changes in information affecting the value of the stock by adjusting the price without excessive fluctuations. The trader achieves this result by making *stabilizing* trades. As defined by the TSX, a stabilizing trade is one in which a purchase (sale) is made at a price lower (higher) than the last price on an *uptick* (*downtick*); an uptick is an upward move in the share price. Registered traders are required to make a minimum 70-30 superiority of stabilizing over destabilizing trades, where the latter is defined as the reverse of a stabilizing trade.[13]

There are also **desk traders** who engage only in executing trades for clients by transmitting orders to the exchange. These are precluded from executing trades for their firms, although they may enter personal orders.

Block Sales

Institutional investors frequently trade blocks of several thousand shares of stock. **Block transactions** of over 100,000 shares now account for about half of all trading on the TSX; on the NYSE, block trading also represents about one-half. Such transactions are often too large to be handled comfortably by registered traders, who do not wish to hold such large blocks of stock in their inventory.

In response to this problem, "block houses" have evolved in the United States to aid in the placement of block trades. Block houses are brokerage firms that help to find potential buyers or sellers of large block trades. With the absorption of independent major broker firms by the chartered banks in Canada, blocks are still handled by most large brokerages. Figure 3.6 shows an example of the daily report on block trading activity on the TSX.

The SuperDOT System

In the United States, SuperDOT enables exchange members to send orders directly to the specialist over computer lines. In 2001, SuperDOT processed an average of 2.7 million orders per day, with an average execution time for market orders of 18 seconds.

[13]*Toronto Stock Exchange Member's Manual*, Division G, Part XIX, p. G19-3.

Figure 3.6 The daily block trading report.

TSX BLOCKS *Trades of 100,000 or more shares worth at least $1-million.*

stock	sym	buyer	seller	vol '000s	price
ARC E	AET.UN	TD Securit	TD Securit	125	15.52
Abitibi Consl	A	TD Securit	TD Securit	100	10.06
Abitibi Consl	A	BMO Nesb	BMO Nesb	100	10.00
Agnico-Ea	AGE	Dundee	Dundee	102	18.75
Alimentat	ATD.B	Scotia Cptl	Scotia Cptl	150	29.05
AlianAt	AAC.B	Merrill Lyn	Merrill Lyn	198	21.00
Aurizon	ARZ	Sprott	Sprott	1000	1.51
Aurizon	ARZ	BMO Nesb	BMO Nesb	676	1.51
BCE Inc	BCE	Merrill Lyn	Merrill Lyn	100	29.02
BCE Inc	BCE	Scotia Cptl	Scotia Cptl	100	29.05
BCE Inc	BCE	TD Securit	TD Securit	100	29.09
BCE Inc	BCE	CSFB	CSFB	100	29.09
BCE Inc	BCE	Scotia Cptl	Scotia Cptl	100	29.20
BCE Inc	BCE	TD Securit	TD Securit	100	29.21
BCE Inc	BCE	Scotia Cptl	Scotia Cptl	100	29.20
BCE Inc	BCE	TD Securit	TD Securit	200	29.14
BCE Inc	BCE	Scotia Cptl	Scotia Cptl	100	29.14
BPO	BPP.PR.J	Scotia Cptl	Scotia Cptl	150	22.60
Bnk of Mtl	BMO	TD Securit	TD Securit	100	54.15
Bnk of Mtl	BMO	TD Securit	TD Securit	100	54.00
Barrick	ABX	RBC Domi	RBC Domi	100	28.36
Barrick	ABX	CSFB	CSFB	100	27.90
Barrick	ABX	RBC Domi	RBC Domi	171	27.95
Baytex	BTE.UN	TD Securit	TD Securit	100	10.45
Baytex	BTE.UN	TD Securit	TD Securit	136	10.45
BlackRock	BVI	GMP	GMP	400	4.95
Bom	BBD.PR.D	Scotia Cptl	Scotia Cptl	200	25.00

stock	sym	buyer	seller	vol '000s	price
Bombr B	BBD.B	Scotia Cptl	Scotia Cptl	250	6.53
Bombr B	BBD.B	Scotia Cptl	Scotia Cptl	298	6.50
Bombr B	BBD.B	UBS	UBS	500	6.50
BmbB	BBD.PR.B	Scotia Cptl	Scotia Cptl	185	25.00
Brascan	BNN.A	BMO Nesb	BMO Nesb	100	49.00
Brascan	BNN.A	RBC Domi	RBC Domi	100	48.90
CAE Inc	CAE	Scotia Cptl	Scotia Cptl	300	5.95
CAE Inc	CAE	Scotia Cptl	Scotia Cptl	246	5.95
CAE Inc	CAE	Scotia Cptl	Scotia Cptl	200	5.95
CAE Inc	CAE	GMP	GMP	244	5.95
CGI	GIB.A	CIBC World	CIBC World	203	8.30
CIBC	CM	CIBC World	CIBC World	250	69.00
CIBC	CM	CIBC World	CIBC World	200	69.00
CIBC	CM	CIBC World	CIBC World	200	69.05
CIBC	CM	Scotia Cptl	Scotia Cptl	100	69.25
CIBC	CM	CIBC World	CIBC World	200	69.05
CIBC	CM	CIBC World	CIBC World	179	69.05
CIBC	CM	CIBC World	CIBC World	169	69.05
CIBC	CM	CIBC World	CIBC World	200	68.70
CP Ships	TEU	RBC Domi	RBC Domi	100	22.95
Cdn Util	CU	Merrill Lyn	Merrill Lyn	107	60.00
Canfor	CFP	CIBC World	CIBC World	120	13.90
Cathedr	CET.UN	1st Assoc	1st Assoc	438	3.00
Cinram	CRW	CIBC World	CIBC World	100	26.50
Cinram	CRW	Merrill Lyn	Merrill Lyn	100	26.50
Cinram	CRW	Merrill Lyn	Merrill Lyn	100	27.50
Cinram	CRW	Merrill Lyn	Merrill Lyn	100	26.62

stock	sym	buyer	seller	vol '000s	price
Com Dev	CDV	Natl Bank	Natl Bank	500	2.45
Corus En	CJR.B	GMP	GMP	100	28.65
Dynatec	DY	GMP	GMP	2337	1.57
EnCana Crp	ECA	RBC Domi	RBC Domi	100	56.00
Enbridge	ENB	RBC Domi	RBC Domi	100	54.30
FNX Min	FNX	GMP	GMP	145	7.05
Falconbridge	FL	RBC Domi	RBC Domi	150	32.90
Falconbridge	FL	UBS	UBS	140	33.00
Falcon	FL.PR.A	BMO Nesb	BMO Nesb	100	24.60
Falconbr	FL.PR.B	Scotia Cptl	Scotia Cptl	200	26.00
Frt Ch	FCE.UN	BMO Nesb	BMO Nesb	112	11.05
Great Wst	GWO	CIBC World	CIBC World	100	51.50
High Point	HPR	1st Assoc	1st Assoc	594	2.25
Hip Interac	HP	Sprott	Sprott	700	3.00
Hollin	HLG.PR.B	Scotia Cptl	Scotia Cptl	207	11.15
Home Ca	HCG.B	Sprott	Sprott	105	26.65
iUnits Ind	XIU	RBC Domi	RBC Domi	195	48.53
Inco	N	Natl Bank	Natl Bank	200	44.00
Inco	N	CSFB	CSFB	100	44.00
Inco	N	Natl Bank	Natl Bank	100	44.00
Inex Pharm	IEX	RBC Domi	RBC Domi	300	7.95
Inex Pharm	IEX	RBC Domi	RBC Domi	200	8.00
Inex Pharm	IEX	RBC Domi	RBC Domi	281	8.00
Inmet	IMN	RBC Domi	RBC Domi	105	18.85
Intr Pipe	IPL.UN	TD Securit	TD Securit	179	8.55
Intertape	ITP	TD Securit	TD Securit	100	12.85
Intertape	ITP	Scotia Cptl	Scotia Cptl	100	12.80
Intrawest	ITW	Merrill Lyn	Merrill Lyn	105	25.10
Ivanhoe	IVN	Scotia Cptl	Scotia Cptl	145	7.50
Ketch Res	KER	GMP	GMP	100	10.30

Source: Report on Business, *The Globe and Mail*, March 11, 2004, p. B16. Reprinted with permission of The Globe and Mail.

SuperDOT is especially useful to program traders. A **program trade** is a coordinated purchase or sale of an entire portfolio of stocks. Many trading strategies (such as index arbitrage, a topic we will study in Chapter 19) require that an entire portfolio of stocks be purchased or sold simultaneously in a coordinated program. SuperDOT is the tool that enables the many trading orders to be sent out at once and executed almost simultaneously.

The vast majority of all U.S. orders are submitted through SuperDOT. However, these tend to be smaller orders, and in 2001 they accounted for about two-thirds of total trading volume.

Settlement

Since June 1995, an order executed on the exchange must be settled within three working days. This requirement is often called T + 3, for trade date plus three days. The purchaser must deliver the cash, and the seller must deliver the stock to his or her broker, who in turn delivers it to the buyer's broker. Transfer of the shares is made easier when the firm's clients keep their securities in **street name**, meaning that the broker holds the shares registered in the firm's own name on behalf of the client. This arrangement can speed security transfer. T + 3 settlement has made such arrangements more important: it can be quite difficult for a seller of a security to complete delivery to the purchaser within the three-day period if the stock is kept in a safety deposit box.

Settlement is simplified further by a clearinghouse. The trades of all exchange members are recorded each day, with members' transactions netted out, so that each member need only transfer or receive the net number of shares sold or bought that day. Each member settles only with the clearinghouse, instead of with each firm with whom trades were executed.

Trading on the OTC Market

On the exchanges all trading takes place through a specialist. Trades on the OTC market, however, are negotiated directly through dealers. Each dealer maintains an inventory of selected securities.

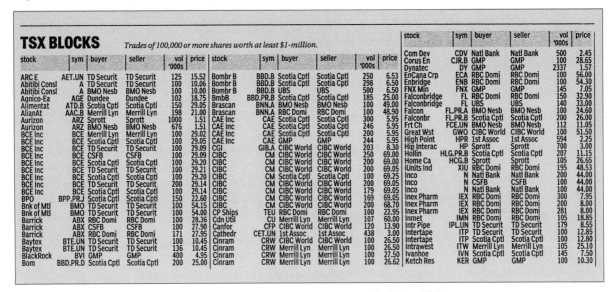

Dealers sell from their inventories at asked prices and buy for them at bid prices. Since there is no specialist, OTC trades do not require a centralized trading floor as do exchange-listed stocks. Dealers can be located anywhere, as long as they can communicate effectively with other buyers and sellers.

An investor who wishes to purchase or sell shares engages a broker, who tries to locate the dealer offering the best deal on the security. This contrasts with exchange trading, where all buy or sell orders are negotiated through the specialist, who arranges for the best bids to get the trade. In the OTC market brokers must search the offers of dealers directly to find the best trading opportunity. In this sense, Nasdaq is largely a price quotation, not a trading system. While bid and asked prices can be obtained from the Nasdaq computer network, the actual trade still requires direct negotiation between the broker and the dealer in the security.

One disadvantage of the decentralized dealer market is that the investing public is vulnerable to *trading through*, which refers to the practice of dealers to trade with the public at their quoted bid or asked prices even if other customers have offered to trade at better prices. For example, a dealer who posts a $20 bid and $20.30 asked price for a stock may continue to fill market buy orders at this asked price and market sell orders at this bid price, even if there are limit orders by public customers "inside the spread," for example, limit orders to buy at $20.10, or limit orders to sell at $20.20. This practice harms the investor whose limit order is not filled (is "traded through"), as well as the investor whose market buy or sell order is not filled at the best available price.

Trading through on Nasdaq sometimes results from imperfect coordination among dealers. A limit order placed with one broker may not be seen by brokers for other traders because computer systems are not linked and only the broker's own bid and asked prices are posted on the Nasdaq system. In contrast, trading through is strictly forbidden on the NYSE or Amex, where "price priority" requires that the specialist fill the best-priced order first. Moreover, because all traders in an exchange market must trade through the specialist, the exchange provides true *price discovery*, meaning that market prices reflect prices at which *all* participants at that moment are willing to trade. This is the advantage of a centralized auction market.

However, in the wake of the stock market crash of 1987, Nasdaq instituted a Small-Order Execution System (SOES), which is in effect a trading system. Under SOES, market makers in a security who post bid or asked prices on Nasdaq may be contacted over the network by other traders and are required to trade at the prices they currently quote. Dealers must accept SOES orders at their posted prices up to some limit, which may be 1,000 shares, but usually is smaller, depending on factors such as trading volume in the stock.

There is one Canadian phenomenon that deserves mention at this point. A number of brokerage houses act as exclusive market-makers for low-capitalization stocks. Under such circumstances the stocks are extremely illiquid, with bid-asked spreads as high as 50 percent of the asked value. These stocks are generally thought to be poor investment prospects, carrying what is later (in Section 7.3) referred to as an illiquidity premium.

3.4 TRADING WITH MARGIN

The concept of **margin** refers to the need for investors to provide security whenever they engage in a transaction in which the asset value of their accounts can fall beneath the value of the liabilities they have incurred. In this event, they—and failing them, their brokers—would be liable to pay the shortfall. This possibility arises if investors purchase shares without having the full purchase price available or if they short sell shares or derivative securities.

Buying on Margin

Investors who purchase stocks on margin borrow part of the purchase price of the stock from their brokers. The brokers in turn borrow money from banks using *brokers' call loans* at the call money rate to finance these purchases, then charge their clients that rate plus a service charge for the loan. All securities purchased on margin must be left with the brokerage firm in street name, because the securities are used as collateral for the loan.

The regulators of the various exchanges set limits on the extent to which stock purchases can be financed via margin loans. Currently, the margin is 30 percent for the most marginable stocks, meaning that, at most, 70 percent of the purchase price may be borrowed; however, this margin rises to as much as 100 percent on low-price stocks. Brokers are likely to require a higher margin to open a margin position so as to avoid an immediate drop in value below 30 percent.

The margin is defined as the ratio of the net worth, or "equity value" of the account, to the market value of the securities. To demonstrate, suppose that the investor initially pays $6,000 toward the purchase of $10,000 worth of stock (100 shares at $100 per share), borrowing the remaining $4,000 from the broker. The account will have a balance sheet as follows:

Assets		**Liabilities and Owner's Equity**	
Value of stock	$10,000	Loan from broker	$4,000
		Equity	$6,000

The initial margin is:

$$\text{Margin ratio} = \frac{\text{Equity value}}{\text{Market value of assets}} = \frac{\text{Market value of assets} - \text{Loan}}{\text{Market value of assets}}$$

$$= \frac{\$10{,}000 - \$4{,}000}{\$10{,}000} = .6 = 60\% \qquad (3.1)$$

If the stock's price declines to $70 per share, the account balance becomes:

Assets		**Liabilities and Owner's Equity**	
Value of stock	$7,000	Loan from broker	$4,000
		Equity	$3,000

The equity in the account falls by the full decrease in the stock value, and the margin is now

$$\text{Margin ratio} = \frac{\text{Equity in account}}{\text{Value of stock}} = \frac{\$3{,}000}{\$7{,}000} = .43\text{, or }43\%$$

If the stock value were to fall below $4,000, equity would become negative, meaning that the value of the stock is no longer sufficient collateral to cover the loan from the broker. To guard against this possibility, the margin must be maintained above the limit of 30 percent. If the percentage margin falls below this level, the broker will issue a *margin call*, requiring the investor to add new cash or securities to the margin account. If the investor does not act, the broker may sell the securities from the account to pay off enough of the loan to restore the percentage margin to an acceptable level.

Margin calls can occur with little warning. For example, on October 25, 2000, when the TSE index fell by 8.3 percent, the accounts of many investors who had purchased stock with borrowed funds fell afoul of their minimum margin requirements. Some brokerage houses, concerned about the incredible volatility in the market and the possibility that stock prices would fall below the point that remaining shares could cover the amount of the loan, gave their customers only a few hours or less to meet a margin call rather than the more typical notice of a few days. If customers could not come up with the cash, or were not at a phone to receive the notification of the margin call until later in the day, their accounts were sold out. In other cases, brokerage houses sold out accounts without notifying their customers.

EXAMPLE 3.1 Minimum Margin Level and Margin Calls

Let P be the price of the stock. The value of the investor's 100 shares is then $100P$, and the equity in his or her account is $100P$ – $4,000. The percentage margin is therefore (100P – $4,000)/$100P$. The price at which the percentage margin equals the minimum margin of .3 is found by solving the equation

$$\frac{100P - \$4{,}000}{100P} = .3$$

$$100P - \$4{,}000 = 30P$$

for

$$P = \$57.14$$

If the price of the stock were to fall below $57.14 per share, the investor would get a margin call.

CONCEPT CHECK

2. If the minimum margin in the above example were 40 percent, how far could the stock price fall before the investor would get a margin call?

Why do investors buy stock (or bonds) on margin? They do so when they wish to invest an amount greater than their own money alone would allow. Thus they can achieve greater upside potential, but they also expose themselves to greater downside risk.

EXAMPLE 3.2 Using Margin for Leverage

Let us suppose that an investor is bullish (optimistic) on Brascan stock, which is currently selling at $100 per share. The investor has $10,000 to invest and expects Brascan stock to go up in price by 30 percent during the next year. Ignoring any dividends, the expected rate of return would thus be 30 percent if the investor spent only $10,000 to buy 100 shares.

But now let us assume that the investor also borrows another $10,000 from the broker and invests it in Brascan also. The total investment in Brascan would thus be $20,000 (for 200 shares). Assuming an interest rate on the margin loan of 9 percent per year, what will be the investor's rate of return now (again ignoring dividends) if Brascan's stock does go up 30 percent by year's end?

The 200 shares will be worth $26,000. Paying off $10,900 of principal and interest on the margin loan leaves $15,100 ($26,000 – $10,900). The rate of return therefore will be

$$\frac{\$15{,}100 - \$10{,}000}{\$10{,}000} = 51\%$$

The investor has parlayed a 30 percent rise in the stock's price into a 51 percent rate of return on the $10,000 investment.

Doing so, however, magnifies the downside risk. Suppose that instead of going up by 30 percent the price of Brascan stock goes down by 30 percent to $70 per share. In that case, the 200 shares will be worth $14,000, and the investor is left with $3,100 after paying off the $10,900 of principal and interest on the loan. The result is a disastrous rate of return:

$$\frac{\$3,100 - \$10,000}{\$10,000} = -69\%$$

CONCEPT CHECK

3. Suppose that in the previous example the investor borrows only $5,000 at the same interest rate of 9 percent per year. What will be the rate of return if the price of Brascan stock goes up by 30 percent? If it goes down by 30 percent? If it remains unchanged?

Short Sales

A **short sale** allows investors to profit from a decline in a security's price. An investor borrows a share of stock from a broker and sells it. Later, the short-seller must purchase a share of the same stock in the market to replace the share that was borrowed. This is called *covering the short position*. Table 3.3 compares stock purchases to short sales.

The short-seller anticipates the stock price will fall, so that the share can be purchased at a lower price than it initially sold for; the short-seller will then reap a profit. Short-sellers must not only replace the shares but also pay the lender of the security any dividends paid during the short sale.

In practice, the shares loaned out for a short sale are typically provided by the short-seller's brokerage firm, which holds a wide variety of securities in street name. The owner of the shares will not even know that the shares have been lent to the short-seller. If the owner wishes to sell the shares, the brokerage firm will simply borrow shares from another investor. Therefore, the short sale may have an indefinite term. However, if the brokerage firm cannot locate new shares to replace the ones sold, the short-seller will need to repay the loan immediately by purchasing shares in the market and turning them over to the brokerage firm to close out the loan.

Exchange rules permit short sales only when the last recorded change in the stock price is positive. This rule apparently is meant to prevent waves of speculation against the stock. In other

Table 3.3 Cash Flows from Purchasing Versus Short Selling Shares of Stock

Time	Action	Cash Flow*
Purchase of Stock		
0	Buy share	– Initial price
1	Receive dividend, sell share	Ending price + Dividend
Profit = (Ending price + Dividend) – Initial price		
Short Sale of Stock		
0	Borrow share; sell it	+ Initial price
1	Repay dividend and buy share to replace the share originally borrowed	– (Ending price + Dividend)
Profit = Initial price – (Ending price + Dividend)		

*A negative cash flow implies a cash outflow.

words, the votes of "no confidence" in the stock that short sales represent may be entered only after a price increase.

Finally, exchange rules require that proceeds from a short sale must be kept on account with the broker. The short-seller, therefore, cannot invest these funds to generate income. However, large or institutional investors typically will receive some income from the proceeds of a short sale being held with the broker. In addition, short-sellers are required to post margin (which is essentially collateral) with the broker to ensure that the trader can cover any losses sustained should the stock price rise during the period of the short sale.[14]

EXAMPLE 3.3 Short Sales

www.brascancorp.com

To illustrate the actual mechanics of short selling, suppose that you are bearish (pessimistic) on Brascan stock, and that its current market price is $100 per share. You tell your broker to sell short 1,000 shares. The broker borrows 1,000 shares either from another customer's account or from another broker.

The $100,000 cash proceeds from the short sale are credited to your account. Suppose the broker has a 50 percent margin requirement on short sales. This means that you must have other cash or securities in your account worth at least $50,000 that can serve as margin (i.e., collateral) on the short sale. Let us suppose that you have $50,000 in Treasury bills. Your account with the broker after the short sale will then be:

Assets		**Liabilities and Owner's Equity**	
Cash	$100,000	Short position in Brascan stock (1,000 shares owed)	$100,000
T-bills	$ 50,000	Equity	$ 50,000

The 50 percent margin satisfies the requirement that your credit balance be at least 150 percent of the market value of borrowed stock, so that the margin ratio is the market value of assets in the account, $150,000, divided by the current value of the borrowed shares, $100,000. Initially,

$$\text{Margin ratio} = \frac{\text{Market value of assets}}{\text{Value of stock owed}} \tag{3.2}$$

$$= \frac{\$150{,}000}{\$100{,}000} = 150\%$$

If you are right, and Brascan stock falls to $70 per share, you can close out your position at a profit. To cover the short sale, you buy 1,000 shares to replace the borrowed shares for $70,000. Because your account was credited by $100,000 at the time of the short sale, your profit is $30,000, which is the decline in share price times the number of shares sold short.

On the other hand, if the price of Brascan rises while you are short, you may get a margin call. Using the minimum margin requirement of 30 percent for short sales, the equity in your account must be at least 30 percent of the value of your short position at all times. How far can the price of Brascan rise before you get a margin call?

Let P be the price of Brascan stock; then the value of the shares you must repay is $1{,}000P$, and the asset value in your account is $150,000. The critical value of P for a margin ratio of 130 percent is

[14]We should note that although we have been describing a short sale of a stock, bonds also may be sold short.

$$\frac{\text{Market value of assets}}{\text{Value of stock owed}} = \frac{\$150{,}000}{1{,}000P} = 1.3$$

or

$$P = \$115.38 \text{ per share}$$

If Brascan stock should rise above $115.38 per share, you will get a margin call and you will have to either put up additional cash or cover your short position.

You can see now why stop-buy orders often accompany short sales. You short-sold Brascan at $100 per share. If the share price falls, you will profit from the short sale. On the other hand, if the share price rises, let's say to $130, you will lose $30 per share. But suppose that when you initiate the short sale, you also enter a stop-buy order at $120. The stop-buy will be executed if the share price surpasses $120, thereby limiting your losses to $20 per share. (If the stock price drops, the stop-buy will never be executed.) The stop-buy order thus provides protection to the short-seller if the share price moves up.

CONCEPT CHECK

4. If the short-position minimum margin in the preceding example were 40 percent, how far could the stock price rise before the investor would get a margin call?

3.5 TRADING COSTS

Part of the cost of trading is the explicit payment to the broker of a commission. The size of this commission depends mostly on the choice between a full-service or discount broker. *Full-service brokers* provide a variety of services. Besides carrying out the basic services of executing orders, holding securities for safekeeping, extending margin loans, and facilitating short sales, normally they also provide information and advice relating to investment alternatives. Full-service brokers usually are supported by a research staff that issues analyses and forecasts of general economic, industry, and company conditions and often makes specific buy or sell recommendations. Some customers take the ultimate leap of faith and allow a full-service broker to make buy and sell decisions for them by establishing a **discretionary account**.[15] This step requires an unusual degree of trust on the part of the customer, because an unscrupulous broker can "churn" an account, that is, trade securities excessively in order to generate commissions.

Discount brokers are able to charge much lower commissions by restricting their services to execution of orders, holding securities for safekeeping, offering margin loans, and facilitating short sales. They provide the basic information of price quotations about indices and individual securities. The more comprehensive discounters also will offer analytical services of advice and software for an additional fee, these being provided by outside firms.

In recent years, discount brokerage services have become increasingly available, offered by both mutual fund management companies and chartered banks. With the chartered banks having bought up most of the independent full-service banks as well, we have banks such as the Royal Bank offering both full-service and discount brokerage subsidiaries to customers in an attempt to provide a full range of financial services. Customers are able to deposit cash with their banks,

[15]Certain individuals, such as politicians, are often required to place their investment assets in blind trusts that are managed in discretionary accounts.

BUYING ON MARGIN

The spreadsheet shown here can be used to measure the return on investment for buying stocks on margin. The model is set up to allow the holding period to vary. The model also calculates the price at which you would get a margin call based on a specified minimum (maintenance) margin and presents return analysis for a range of ending stock prices. Additional problems using this spreadsheet are available at www.mcgrawhill.ca/college/bodie.

	A	B	C	D	E
1					
2	**Buying on Margin**			**Ending**	**Return on**
3				**St Price**	**Investment**
4	Initial Equity Investment	10,000.00			−42.00%
5	Amount Borrowed	10,000.00		20	−122.00%
6	Initial Stock Price	50.00		25	−102.00%
7	Shares Purchased	400		30	−82.00%
8	Ending Stock Price	40.00		35	−62.00%
9	Cash Dividends During Hold Per.	0.50		40	−42.00%
10	Initial Margin Percentage	50.00%		45	−22.00%
11	Maintenance Margin Percentage	30.00%		50	−2.00%
12				55	18.00%
13	Rate on Margin Loan	8.00%		60	38.00%
14	Holding Period in Months	6		65	58.00%
15				70	78.00%
16	**Return on Investment**			75	98.00%
17	Capital Gains on Stock	−4,000.00		80	118.00%
18	Dividends	200.00			
19	Interest on Margin Loan	400.00			
20	Net Income	−4200.00			
21	Initial Investment	10,000.00			
22	Return on Investment	−42.00%			
23					
24	**Margin Call:**				
25	Margin Based on Ending Price	37.50%			
26	Price When Margin Call Occurs	$35.71			
27					
28					
29	Return on Stock Without Margin	−19.00%			

transfer it to pay for securities, and have interest and dividends either transferred back to their bank accounts or deposited in money market funds.

Faced with the competition of discount brokers, full-service brokers have turned to converting commission-based accounts into managed accounts that are fee-based, known as "wrap accounts." Annual fees typically are 2.5 to 3.5 percent of assets managed.

In addition to the explicit cost of commissions, there is an implicit cost deriving primarily from the **bid-asked spread**. If the broker for a trade is actually the dealer in the security, instead of a commission, the fee for purchase or sale will come entirely in the form of the bid-asked spread. With the dramatic reduction in commissions, the execution cost of the spread has become a far more significant component of trading costs. Another implicit cost of trading that some observers would distinguish is the price concession an investor may be forced to make for trading in any quantity that exceeds the quantity the dealer is willing to trade at the posted bid or asked price.

SHORT SALE

The spreadsheet below is set up to measure the return on investment from a short sale. It calculates the price at which additional margin would be required and presents return analysis for a range of ending stock prices.

	A	B	C	D	E	F
1						
2	**Short Sales**					
3						
4					**Ending**	**Return on**
5	Initial Investment	10,000.00			**St Price**	**Investment**
6	Beginning Share Price	100.00				60.00%
7	Number of Shares Sold Short	2,000.00			170	−140.00%
8	Ending Share Price	70.00			160	−120.00%
9	Dividends per Share	0.00			150	−100.00%
10	Initial Margin Percentage	50.00%			140	−80.00%
11	Maintenance Margin Percentage	30.00%			130	−60.00%
12					120	−40.00%
13	**Return on Short Sale**				110	−20.00%
14	Gain or Loss on Price	60,000.00			100	0.00%
15	Dividends Paid	0.00			90	20.00%
16	Net Income	60,000.00			80	40.00%
17	Return on Investment	60,00%			70	60.00%
18					60	80.00%
19					50	100.00%
20	**Margin Positions**				40	120.00%
21	Margin Based on Ending Price	114.29%			30	140.00%
22					20	160.00%
23	Price for Margin Call	115.38			10	180.00%

One continuing trend is toward online trading either through the Internet or through software that connects a customer directly to a brokerage firm. While there is little conceptual difference between placing your order using a phone call versus through a computer link, online brokerage firms can process trades more cheaply since they do not have to pay as many brokers. The average commission for an online trade is \$20–\$30, in contrast to perhaps \$100–\$300 at full-service brokers.

Moreover, these *e-brokers* are beginning to compete with some of the same services offered by full-service broker such as online company research and, to a lesser extent, the opportunity to participate in IPOs. The traditional full-service brokerage firms are responding to this competitive challenge by introducing online trading for their own customers. Some of these firms are charging by the trade; others plan to charge for such trading through fee-based accounts. in which the customer pays a percentage of assets in the account for the right to trade online.

An ongoing controversy is the extent to which better execution on a traditional market like the NYSE offsets the generally lower explicit costs of trading in other markets. Execution refers to the size of the effective bid-asked spread and the amount of price impact in a market. The NYSE believes that many investors focus too intently on the costs they can see, despite the fact that quality of execution can be a far more important determinant of total costs. Many trades on the NYSE are executed at a price inside the quoted spread. This can happen because floor brokers at the specialist's post can bid above or sell below the specialist's quote. In this way, two public orders cross without incurring the specialist's spread.

In contrast, in a dealer market such as Nasdaq, all trades go though the dealer, and all trades, therefore, are subject to a bid-asked spread. The client never sees the spread as an explicit cost, however. The price at which the trade is executed incorportates the dealer's spread, but this part of the trading cost is never reported to the investor.

A controversial practice related to the bid-asked spread and the quality of trade execution is "paying for order flow." This entails paying a broker a rebate for directing the trade to a particular dealer rather than to the NYSE. By bringing the trade to a dealer instead of to the exchange, however, the broker eliminates the possibility that the trade could have been executed without incurring a spread. Moreover, a broker that is paid for order flow might direct a trade to a dealer that does not even offer the most competitive price. (Indeed, the fact that dealers can afford to pay for order flow suggests that they are able to lay off the trade at better prices elsewhere and, therefore, that the broker also could have found a better price with some additional effort.) Many of the online brokerage firms rely heavily on payment for order flow, since their explicit commissions are so minimal. They typically do not actually execute orders, instead sending an order either to a market maker or to a stock exchange for some listed stocks.

Such practices raise serious ethical questions, because the broker's primary obligation is to obtain the best deal for the client. Payment for order flow might be justified if the rebate were passed along to the client either directly or through lower commisssions, but it is not clear that such rebates are passed through.

Online trading and electronic communications networks have already changed the landscape of the financial markets, and this trend can only be expected to continue. The boxed article that follows considers some of the implications of these new technologies for the future structure of financial markets. The threat they pose to the NYSE as it has been is but one of the problems faced by the TSX in its struggle against competing markets.

Internet Investing

Almost any kind of information on investments can be found via the Internet. This includes analysts' recommendations, financial statements, an assortment of charts, and economic projections; these are available either free or for a stated charge. Much of the information is distributed freely by financial news providers and by brokers, while more can be downloaded in conjunction with a brokerage account from the online brokers' sites; typically the latter may be free in limited quantities, with additional amounts earned by trading. Services provide an opportunity to record one's portfolio and have its value updated daily.

The trading itself is conducted by establishing an online account with the major brokers (usually their discount operations) or with a variety of cut-rate brokers offering trades for less than $10 (in U.S. dollars, as that is where the great majority of these services operate). With a secure connection and a password, trading on stocks, options, and futures is limited only by the traffic. (This latter qualification may be significant, but access to human voices may also be difficult at times of heavy volume.) Orders may be entered during trading hours or after, for execution upon opening; they may be limit or market orders. Essentially, for an experienced trader there is only one difference in trading online from what has been experienced in using a broker: the cost of trading is much lower.

Pre-market and post-market trading on ECNs is also handled through the Internet. Unfortunately, the lack of integration referred to in the boxed article and the current thinness of trading leads to poor execution of orders; prices are quite volatile and often not representative of the actual market.

SEC PREPARES FOR A NEW WORLD OF STOCK TRADING

What should our securities markets look like to serve today's investor best? Arthur Levitt, chairman of the Securities and Exchange Commission, recently addressed this question at Columbia Law School. He acknowledged that the costs of stock trading have declined dramatically, but expressed fears that technological developments may also lead to market fragmentation, so that investors are not sure they are getting the best price when they buy and sell.

Congress addressed this very question a generation ago, when markets were threatened with fragmentation from an increasing number of competing dealers and exchanges. This led the SEC to establish the national market system, which enabled investors to obtain the best quotes on stocks from any of the major exchanges.

Today it is the proliferation of electronic exchanges and after-hours trading venues that threatens to fragment the market. But the solution is simple, and would take the intermarket trading system devised by the SEC a quarter century ago to its next logical step. The highest bid and the lowest offer for every stock, no matter where they originate, should be displayed on a screen that would be available to all investors, 24 hours a day, seven days a week.

If the SEC mandated this centralization of order flow, competition would significantly enhance investor choice and the quality of the trading environment.

Would brokerage houses or even exchanges exist, as we now know them? I believe so, but electronic communication networks would provide the crucial links between buyers and sellers. ECNs would compete by providing far more sophisticated services to the investor than are currently available—not only the entering and execution of standard limit and market orders, but the execution of contingent orders, buys and sells dependent on the levels of other stocks, bonds, commodities, even indexes.

The services of brokerage houses would still be in much demand, but their transformation from commission-based to flat-fee or asset-based pricing would be accelerated. Although ECNs will offer almost costless processing of the basic investor transactions, brokerages would aid investors in placing more sophisticated orders. More importantly, brokers would provide investment advice. Although today's investor has access to more and more information, this does not mean that he has more understanding of the forces that rule the market or the principles of constructing the best portfolio.

As the spread between the best bid and offer price has collapsed to 1/16th of a point in many cases—decimalization of prices promises to reduce the spread even further—some traditional concerns of regulators are less pressing than they once were. Whether to allow dealers to step in front of customers to buy or sell, or allow brokerages to cross their orders internally at the best price, regardless of other orders at the price on the book, have traditionally been burning regulatory issues. But with spreads so small and getting smaller, these issues are of virtually no consequence to the average investor as long as the integrity of the order flow information is maintained. ...

Source: Jeremy J. Siegel, "The SEC Prepares for a New World of Stock Trading," *The Wall Street Journal,* September 27, 1999. Reprinted by permission of Dow Jones & Company, Inc. via Copyright Clearance Center, Inc.

3.6 REGULATION OF SECURITIES MARKETS

Trading in securities markets in Canada is regulated under a number of laws. Laws such as the federal Canada Business Corporations Act govern the conduct of business firms, while the various provincial securities acts regulate the trading of securities. Most legislation is at the provincial level, even though historically the first Canadian laws concerning securities were introduced at the federal level in the late nineteenth century. Provincial legislation in the Maritime provinces followed shortly thereafter, while the Ontario Companies Act was established in 1907. The Ontario Securities Act, Canada's first provincial securities act, was passed in 1945, and has been revised repeatedly since that time. Other provinces generally have tended to follow Ontario's lead. Although the federal government doesn't have a securities act, portions of the Criminal Code of Canada are specifically directed to securities trading.

In addition to the laws, there also is considerable self-regulation in the financial services industry. It takes place via regulations governing membership in various associations of professionals participating in the industry. Thus, the Investment Dealers Association of Canada encompasses stock exchange members and bond dealers, while the Mutual Fund Dealers Association is the association of Canadian mutual funds. Trading on the TSX is regulated by Market Regulation Services Inc.

The Investment Dealers Association and the stock exchanges have established the Canadian Investor Protection Fund (CIPF) to protect investors from losses if their brokerage firms fail. Just as the Canada Deposit Insurance Corporation provides federal protection to depositors against bank failure, the CIPF ensures that investors will receive the value of their accounts up to a maximum of $1 million. Securities held for their account in street name by the failed brokerage firm and cash balances will be replaced by equivalent securities, or by their cash value. The CIPF is financed by levying an "insurance premium" on its participating, or member, brokerage firms.

Provincial securities legislation exists in all Canadian provinces and territories, but not all have provincial securities commissions, which are responsible for administering and enforcing the provincial securities laws. In other cases, this responsibility is exercised within the justice departments. The key purpose of these laws is to protect investors from fraud. They achieve this by controlling (through registration) the people participating in the financial services industry and by ensuring that investors have all material facts at their disposal in order to make their own investment decisions. The approval, however, by a securities commission of a prospectus or financial report does not mean that it views the security as a good investment. The commission cares only that the relevant facts are disclosed; investors make their own evaluations of the security's value.

Relevant facts are revealed for prospective investors when a primary issue takes place, through the prospectus. Investors also must be kept informed, on a continuous basis, about all important changes to a company's status, such as changes in the control structure of the corporation, acquisitions or disposals of major assets, and proposed takeovers or mergers. Companies also must issue several financial reports on a quarterly basis and more complete reports annually.

Several problems are created by the fragmentation along provincial lines of the regulatory system for Canadian securities markets. Differences in provincial laws are an immediate cause, although the CSA (Canadian Securities Administrators) are taking steps to harmonize the legislation. Financial transactions in markets may involve parties residing in different provinces; for instance, a group of Ontario investors might purchase the shares of a Quebec company, traded on the TSX. Such a transaction would fall under the jurisdiction of two provinces' regulatory bodies, implying that it should simultaneously comply with the Quebec and Ontario regulatory regimes. Apart from the fact that this may create multiple (and costly) investigations of the same transaction, it also would generate uncertainty among the investors about the set of rules governing their investment.

Securities and Exchange Commission
www.sec.gov

Such problems are avoided in the United States, where the securities industry is regulated by national agencies. The most important of these is the Securities and Exchange Commission (SEC), established by the 1934 Securities Exchange Act, to ensure the full disclosure of relevant information relating to the issue of new securities and the periodic release of financial information for secondary trading. The act also empowered the SEC to register and regulate securities exchanges, OTC trading, brokers, and dealers. It thus established the SEC as the administrative agency responsible for broad oversight of the securities markets. The SEC, however, shares oversight with other regulatory bodies. For example, the Commodity Futures Trading Commission (CFTC) regulates trading in futures markets, whereas the Federal Reserve Bank ("the Fed") has broad responsibility for the health of the U.S. financial system. In this role, the Fed sets margin requirements on stocks and stock options and regulates bank lending to the securities markets' participants.

Self-Regulation and Circuit Breakers

Much of the securities industry relies on self-regulation, which is conducted by bodies known as self-regulatory organizations (SROs). These comprise the various exchanges and the Investment Dealers Association (IDA) representing the member firms. The policies of the IDA are intended to foster efficient markets by encouraging participation and ensuring integrity of the marketplace and protection of investors. The Canadian Securities Institute (CSI) serves these SROs (and others) by providing educational programs. Among these programs are the Conduct and Professional Handbook (CPH) Course, which presents to students the regulations as well as ethical and professional responsibilities regarding dealing with investors.

The collapse of markets around the world in October 1987 prompted a number of responses, starting with mechanisms to prevent panic selling exacerbated by program trading. "Circuit breakers" were instituted to close temporarily the markets when drastic losses occur as well as to limit extreme movements in either direction during periods of high volatility. These were imposed directly on the NYSE, but other exchanges have often chosen to key their regulations to the NYSE practice. Failing this, trading might easily move from the NYSE to other exchanges for products that might be expected to move in direct correlation with NYSE securities, as well as for securities actually traded on other exchanges.

The NYSE response is keyed to the level of the Dow Jones Industrial Average (DJIA), with circuit breaker thresholds for trading halts, based on 10, 20, and 30 percent of the DJIA of the previous month, and rounded to the nearest 50 points; these levels are reset every quarter. (For example, as of January 2, 2004 the triggering DJIA drops at each level were 1,000, 2,000, and 3,050 points.) The two most significant circuit breakers are:

- *Trading halts.* If the Dow Jones Industrial Average falls by 10 percent, trading will be halted for one hour if the drop occurs before 2:00 P.M. (Eastern Standard Time), for one-half hour if the drop occurs between 2:00 and 2:30, but not at all if the drop occurs after 2:30. If the Dow falls by 20 percent, trading will be halted for two hours if the drop occurs before 1:00 P.M., for one hour if the drop occurs between 1:00 and 2:00, and for the rest of the day if the drop occurs after 2:00. A 30 percent drop in the Dow would close the market for the rest of the day, regardless of the time.

- *Collars.* When the Dow moves about 2 percent in either direction from the previous day's close, Rule 80A of the NYSE requires that index arbitrage orders pass a "tick test." In a failing market, sell orders may be executed only at a plus tick or zero-plus tick, meaning that the trade may be done at a higher price than the last trade (a plus tick) or at the last price if the last recorded change in the stock price is positive (a zero-plus tick). The rule remains in effect for the rest of the day unless the Dow returns to within 1 percent of the previous day's close. (Collars apply only to program trading.)

The idea behind circuit breakers is that a temporary halt in trading during periods of very high volatility can help mitigate informational problems that might contribute to excessive price swings. For example, even if a trader is unaware of any specific adverse economic news, if she sees the market plummeting, she will suspect that there might be a good reason for the price drop and will become unwilling to buy shares. In fact, the trader might decide to sell shares to avoid losses. Thus feedback from price swings to trading behaviour can exacerbate market movements. Circuit breakers give participants a chance to assess market fundamentals while prices are temporarily frozen. In this way, they have a chance to decide whether price movements are warranted while the market is closed.

For the TSX, Market Regulation Services Inc. determines the circuit breaker mechanism in conjunction with the thresholds announced by the New York Stock Exchange. The TSX responds to the same levels 1, 2 and 3 above by imposing corresponding halts to trading as defined for the NYSE.

Insider Trading

One of the important restrictions on trading involves *insider trading*. It is illegal for anyone to transact in securities to profit from **inside information**, that is, private information held by officers, directors, or major stockholders that has not yet been divulged to the public. The difficulty is that the definition of *insiders* can be ambiguous. Although it is obvious that the chief financial officer of a firm is an insider, it is less clear whether the firm's biggest supplier can be considered an insider. However, the supplier may deduce the firm's near-term prospects from significant changes in orders. This gives the supplier a unique form of private information, yet the supplier does not necessarily qualify as an insider. These ambiguities plague security analysts, whose job is to uncover as much information as possible concerning the firm's expected prospects. The distinction between legal private information and illegal inside information can be fuzzy.

The OSC requires officers, directors, and major shareholders of all publicly held firms to report all of their transactions in their firm's stock within ten days of the occurrence of the transaction. A compendium of insider trades is published monthly in the OSC's insider trading bulletin, extracts of which are published promptly by *The Globe and Mail*. The idea is to inform the public of any implicit votes of confidence or no confidence made by insiders.

Do insiders exploit their knowledge? The answer seems to be, to a limited degree, yes. Two forms of evidence support this conclusion. First, there is massive evidence of "leakage" of useful information to some traders *before* any public announcement of that information. For example, share prices of firms announcing dividend increases (which the market interprets as good news concerning the firm's prospects) commonly increase in value a few days before the public announcement of the increase.[16] Clearly, some investors are acting on the good news before it is released to the public. Similarly, share prices tend to increase a few days before the public announcement of above-trend earnings growth.[17] At the same time, share prices still rise substantially on the day of the public release of good news, indicating that insiders, or their associates, have not fully bid up the price of the stock to the level commensurate with that news.

The second sort of evidence on insider trading is based on returns earned on trades by insiders. Researchers have examined the SEC's summary of insider trading to measure the performance of insiders. Muelbroek[18] investigated the contention by previous researchers that insider trading actually improves market efficiency by accelerating the price adjustment process, through the examination of SEC information on illegal trading activity. She found there to be no doubt that insider trading causes significant price adjustment to occur in advance of the public release of information and gave some support to the view that this "victimless crime" is actually beneficial. A Canadian study by Baesel and Stein[19] investigated the abnormal return on stocks over the months following purchases or sales by insiders. They found that a simulated policy of buying a portfolio of stocks purchased by insiders yielded an abnormal return in the following eight months of about 3.8 percent. If the insiders were also directors of Canadian banks (presumed to be even better informed), the abnormal return persisted for 12 months and rose to 7.8 percent. In both cases, the major part of the gain occurred after publication of the insiders' actions. Insider sales, however, did not generate information leading to abnormal gains.

---

[16]See, for example, J. Aharony and I. Swary, "Quarterly Dividend and Earnings Announcement and Stockholders' Return: An Empirical Analysis," *Journal of Finance* 35 (March 1980).

[17]See, for example, George Foster, Chris Olsen, and Terry Shevlin, "Earnings Releases, Anomalies, and the Behavior of Security Returns," *The Accounting Review*, October 1984.

[18]Lisa K. Muelbroek, "An Empirical Analysis of Illegal Insider Trading," *The Journal of Finance* 47, no. 5 (December 1992), pp. 1661–1699.

[19]Jerome Baesel and Garry Stein, "The Value of Information: Inferences from the Profitability of Insider Trading," *Journal of Financial and Quantitative Analysis*, September 1979. See also Jean-Marc Suret and Elise Cormier, "Insiders and the Stock Market," *Canadian Investment Review* 3, no. 2 (Fall 1990).

SUMMARY

1. Firms issue securities to raise the capital necessary to finance their investments. Investment bankers market these securities to the public on the primary market. Investment bankers generally act as underwriters who purchase the securities from the firm and resell them to the public at a markup. Before the securities may be sold to the public, the firm must publish a securities commission-approved prospectus that provides information on the firm's prospects.
2. Issued securities are traded on the secondary market, that is, on organized stock exchanges. Securities also trade on the over-the-counter market and, for large traders, through direct negotiation. Only members of exchanges may trade on the exchange. Brokerage firms holding seats on the exchange sell their services to individuals, charging commissions for executing trades on their behalf. The TSX has fairly strict listing requirements; the TSX Venture Exchange is much less restrictive, being designed for firms who do not meet the requirements of the TSX.
3. Trading of common stocks in exchanges takes place through registered traders or market-makers; these act to maintain an orderly market in the shares of one or more firms, maintaining "books" of limit-buy and limit-sell orders and matching trades at mutually acceptable prices. Market-makers also will accept market orders by selling from or buying for their own inventory of stocks when an imbalance of buy and sell orders exists.
4. The over-the-counter market is not a formal exchange but an informal network of brokers and dealers who negotiate sales of securities. When an individual wishes to purchase or sell a share, the broker can search the listing of offered bid and asked prices, call the dealer who has the best quote, and execute the trade.
5. Block transactions are a fast-growing segment of the securities market, which currently accounts for about one-half of trading volume. These trades often are too large to be handled readily by regular market-makers, and thus block houses have developed that specialize in these transactions, identifying potential trading partners for their clients.
6. Buying on margin means borrowing money from a broker in order to buy more securities. By buying securities on margin, an investor magnifies both the upside potential and the downside risk. If the equity in a margin account falls below the required maintenance level, the investor will get a margin call from the broker.
7. Short selling is the practice of selling securities that the seller does not own. The short seller borrows the securities sold through a broker and may be required to cover the short position at any time on demand. The cash proceeds of a short sale are always kept in escrow by the broker, and the broker usually requires that the short seller deposit additional cash or securities to serve as margin (collateral) for the short sale.
8. In addition to providing the basic services of executing buy and sell orders, holding securities for safekeeping, making margin loans, and facilitating short sales, full-service brokers offer investors information, advice, and even investment decisions. Discount brokers offer only the basic brokerage services but usually charge less.
9. Total trading costs consist of commissions, the dealer's bid-asked spread, and price concessions. These costs can represent as much as 30 percent of the value of the securities traded.
10. Securities trading is regulated by the provincial securities commissions and by self-regulation of the exchanges and the dealer associations. Many of the important regulations have to do with full disclosure of relevant information concerning the securities in question. Insider trading rules also prohibit traders from attempting to profit from inside information.

KEY TERMS

float 61
primary market 61
secondary market 61
initial public offering 61
seasoned new issue 61
secondary offering 61
public offering 61
private placement 61
underwriting 61
investment dealers (*or* bankers) 61
underwriting syndicate 61
prospectus 61
direct search market 66
brokered market 66
block transactions 66
dealer market 66
auction market 67
stock exchange 67
over-the-counter (OTC) market 70
Nasdaq 70
bid price 70
asked price 70
third market 71
fourth market 71
electronic communication network (ECN) 71
registered trader 73
market-making 73
limit order 74
stop-loss order 74
desk trader 77
block transactions 77
program trade 78
street name 78
margin 79
short sale 82
discretionary account 84
bid-asked spread 85
inside information 91

SELECTED READINGS

A good treatment of investment banking is found in:

Smith, Clifford W. "Investment Banking and the Capital Acquisition Process." *Journal of Financial Economics* 15 (January/February 1986).

An overview of securities markets is provided in:

Garbade, Kenneth D. *Securities Markets*. New York: McGraw-Hill, 1982.

The American specialist system is examined in:

Stoll, Hans R. "The Stock Exchange Specialist System: An Economic Analysis." *Monograph Series in Finance and Economics*, Graduate School of Business Administration, New York University, 1985.

An examination of market functioning during the October 1987 crash is:

The Brady Commission Report, or formally, the *Report of the Presidential Task Force on Market Mechanisms*. Washington, DC: United States Government Printing Office, 1988.

Material facts about listing and trading on Canadian markets are available in:

The Toronto Stock Exchange Fact Book, published annually, and *The TSX Review*, published monthly. Produced by the Toronto Stock Exchange, Toronto, ON.

Perspectives on trading appear in:

Kirzner, Eric. "Stock Markets of the Future—How Should Trading Be Conducted?" *Canadian Investment Review* 10, no. 4 (Winter 1997).

PROBLEMS

1. FBN, Inc. has just sold 100,000 shares in an initial public offering. The underwriter's explicit fees were $70,000. The offering price for the shares was $50, but immediately upon issue the share price jumped to $53.

a. What is your best guess as to the total cost to FBN of the equity issue?

b. Is the entire cost of the underwriting a source of profit to the underwriters?

2. Suppose that you sell short 100 shares of Alcan, now selling at $70 per share.

a. What is your maximum possible loss?

b. What happens to the maximum loss if you simultaneously place a stop-buy order at $78?

3. Dée Trader opens a brokerage account, and purchases 300 shares of Internet Dreams at $40 per share. She borrows $4,000 from her broker to help pay for the purchase. The interest rate on the loan is 8 percent.

a. What is the margin in Dée's account when she first purchases the stock?

b. If the price falls to $30 per share by the end of the year, what is the remaining margin in her account? If the maintenance margin requirement is 30 percent, will she receive a margin call?

c. What is the rate of return on her investment?

4. Old Economy Traders opened an account to short-sell 1,000 shares of Internet Dreams from the previous problem. The initial margin requirement was 50 percent. (The margin account pays no interest.) A year later, the price of Internet Dreams has risen from \$40 to \$50, and the stock has paid a dividend of \$2 per share.
   a. What is the remaining margin in the account?
   b. If the maintenance margin requirement is 30 percent, will Old Economy receive a margin call?
   c. What is the rate of return on the investment?
5. An expiring put will be exercised and the stock will be sold if the stock price is below the exercise price. A stop-loss order causes a stock sale when the stock price falls below some limit. Compare and contrast the two strategies of purchasing put options versus issuing a stop-loss order.
6. Compare call options and stop-buy orders.
7. Here is some price information on Barrick:

	Bid	Asked
Barrick	37.80	38.10

   You have placed a stop-loss order to sell at \$38. What are you telling your broker? Given market prices, will your order be executed?
8. Do you think it is possible to replace market-making specialists by a fully automated computerized trade-matching system?
9. Consider the following limit-order book of a market-maker. The last trade in the stock took place at a price of \$50.

Limit-Buy Orders		Limit-Sell Orders	
Price (\$)	**Shares**	**Price (\$)**	**Shares**
49.75	500	50.25	100
49.50	800	51.50	100
49.25	500	54.75	300
49.00	200	58.25	100
48.50	600		

   a. If a market-buy order for 100 shares comes in, at what price will it be filled?
   b. At what price would the next market-buy order be filled?
   c. If you were the specialist, would you desire to increase or decrease your inventory of this stock?
10. What purpose does the Designated Order Turnaround system (SuperDOT) serve on the New York Stock Exchange?
11. Who sets the bid and asked price for a stock traded over the counter? Would you expect the spread to be higher on actively or inactively traded stocks?
12. Suppose that BMO currently is selling at \$80 per share. You buy 250 shares, using \$15,000 of your own money and borrowing the remainder of the purchase price from your broker. The rate on the margin loan is 8 percent.
    a. What is the percentage increase in the net worth of your brokerage account if the price of BMO *immediately* changes to (i) \$88; (ii) \$80; (iii) \$72? What is the relationship between your percentage return and the percentage change in the price of BMO?
    b. If the minimum margin is 30 percent, how low can BMO's price fall before you get a margin call?

c. How would your answer to (*b*) change if you had financed the initial purchase with only $10,000 of your own money?

d. What is the rate of return on your margined position (assuming again that you invest $15,000 of your own money) if BMO is selling *after one year* at (i) $88; (ii) $80; (iii) $72? What is the relationship between your percentage return and the percentage change in the price of BMO? Assume that BMO pays no dividends.

e. Continue to assume that a year has passed. How low can BMO price fall before you get a margin call?

13. Suppose that you sell short 250 shares of BMO, currently selling for $80 per share, and give your broker $15,000 to establish your margin account.

a. If you earn no interest on the funds in your margin account, what will be your rate of return after one year if BMO stock is selling at (i) $88; (ii) $80; (iii) $72? Assume that BMO pays no dividends.

b. If the minimum margin is 30 percent, how high can BMO's price rise before you get a margin call?

c. Redo parts (*a*) and (*b*), now assuming that BMO's dividend (paid at year-end) is $2 per share.

14. Here is some price information on Fincorp stock. Suppose first that Fincorp trades in a dealer market.

Bid	Asked
55.25	55.50

a. Suppose you have submitted an order to your broker to buy at market. At what price will your trade be executed?

b. Suppose you have submitted an order to sell at market. At what price will your trade be executed?

c. Suppose an investor has submitted a limit order to sell at $55.40. What will happen?

d. Suppose another investor has submitted a limit order to buy at $55.40. What will happen?

15. Now reconsider the previous problem assuming that Fincorp sells in an exchange market like the TSX.

a. Is there any chance for price improvement in the market orders considered in parts (*a*) and (*b*)?

b. Is there any chance of an immediate trade at $55.40 for the limit-buy order in part (*d*)?

16. You are bullish on BCE stock. The current market price is $50 per share, and you have $5,000 of your own to invest. You borrow an additional $5,000 from your broker at an interest rate of 8 percent per year and invest $10,000 in the stock.

a. What will be your rate of return if the price of BCE stock goes up by 10 percent during the next year? (Ignore the expected dividend.)

b. How far does the price of BCE stock have to fall for you to get a margin call if the minimum margin is 30 percent?

17. You've borrowed $20,000 on margin to buy shares in Bombardier, which is now selling at $80 per share. Your account starts at the initial margin requirement of 50 percent. The minimum margin is 35 percent. Two days later, the stock price falls to $75 per share.

a. Will you receive a margin call?

b. How low can the price of Bombardier shares fall before you receive a margin call?

18. You are bearish on BCE stock and decide to sell short 100 shares at the current market price of $50 per share.

a. How much in cash or securities must you put into your brokerage account if the broker's initial margin requirement is 50 percent of the value of the short position?

b. How high can the price of the stock go before you get a margin call if the minimum margin is 30 percent of the value of the short position?

19. To cover the initial margin requirement of 60 percent, you deposited funds after short-selling 100 shares of common stock at $45 per share.

a. What is your rate of return if you cover at $50, assuming no dividends and no addition or removal of funds from the account?

b. At what price would you receive a margin call if the minimum margin requirement is 30 percent?

20. On January 1, you sold short one round lot (i.e., 100 shares) of Zenith stock at $14 per share. On March 1, a dividend of $2 per share was paid. On April 1, you covered the short sale by buying the stock at a price of $9 per share. You paid 50 cents per share in commissions for each transaction. What is the value of your account on April 1?

21. Call one full-service broker and one discount broker and find out the transaction costs of implementing the following strategies:

a. Buying 100 shares of BMO now and selling them six months from now.

b. Investing an equivalent amount in six-month "at-the-money" call options (calls with strike price equal to the stock price) on BMO stock now and selling them six months from now.

The following questions are from past CFA examinations:

CFA® PROBLEMS

22. If you place a stop-loss order to sell 100 shares of stock at $55 when the current price is $62, how much will you receive for each share if the price drops to $50?

a. $50

b. $55

c. $54.90

d. Cannot tell from the information given.

CFA® PROBLEMS

23. You wish to sell short 100 shares of XYZ Corporation stock. If the last two transactions were at 34.10 followed by 34.15, you only can sell short on the next transaction at a price of

a. 34.10 or higher

b. 34.15 or higher

c. 34.15 or lower

d. 34.10 or lower

CFA® PROBLEMS

24. Specialists on the New York Stock Exchange do all of the following except

a. Act as dealers for their own accounts

b. Execute limit orders

c. Help provide liquidity to the marketplace

d. Act as odd-lot dealers

CSI

The following questions are adapted from the Canadian Securities Course.

25. Which of the following statements is *not true* concerning primary issues?

a. The company may already have an issue of securities in the public's hands, but requires further funds.

b. The security may be a new issue of equity of a class never before issued.

c. The security being issued may be a reopening of an old issue that still meets current market requirements.

d. It is the sale of a security from an institution that held a control position.

26. Protective covenants appear in a legal instrument called a(n) ______________.

---

27. "Each preliminary prospectus is required to display in red on its front cover a statement, in approved form, to the effect that the preliminary prospectus has been filed but is not final. This is why it is called a 'red herring' prospectus." True or false?
28. The opposite of an agency deal or best efforts underwriting is a(n) ______________.
29. The opposite of an all or none order is a(n) ______________ order.
30. A(n) ______________ order is used to limit a loss or protect a profit on a short sale.

APPENDIX 3A: A DETAILED MARGIN POSITION

Examples 3.1, 3.2, and 3.3 in Section 3.4 show the basic margin analysis for buying and selling. The balance sheets showed a progression from the assets including only the purchased stock to having T-bills, which were needed for margin for the short position. Those T-bills could have been included in the first balance sheet, if you happened to hold them in your account. The assets provided for margin purposes can earn a return within the account. The balance sheet could, and would normally, also include other stocks in your portfolio. It is the aggregate value of the account that goes into the margin calculation. Table 3A.1 shows the balance sheet for a more complicated account, first at the time of opening the positions—a margin purchase of 500 shares of Brascan at $100 and a short sale of 300 shares of Alcan at $40—in addition to other assets, and then at a later date; we ignore any dividends or interest payments and suppose that no cash is advanced at the time of the opening trades.

If the margin position had come from all purchases or all short sales, the calculations would have been simple extensions of equations 3.1 and 3.2, where we aggregate long positions for market value, short positions for value owed, and the loan amounts. When we have both long and short positions, we have to calculate the exposure of the account on both long and short sides and sum the requirements to protect against both. If the equity in the account is sufficient to cover both sides, then margin has been met. The initial margin requirement for the margin purchase alone in this account is found by considering the market value of the account before the effect of the short sale, or $122,500 when we

Table 3A.1 Illustration of a Margined Account

Initial Account Position			
Assets		**Liabilities**	
Cash	$ 12,000	Alcan (300 @ $40) (short position)	$12,000
T-bills	30,000	Broker loan	50,000
Brascan (500 @ $100)	50,000	Equity	72,500
CIBC (1,000 @ $30)	30,000		
Noranda (500 @ $25)	12,500		
	$134,500		
Later Account Position			
Assets		**Liabilities**	
Cash	$ 12,000	Alcan (300 @ $50) (short position)	$ 15,000
T-bills	30,000	Broker loan	50,000
Brascan (500 @ $102)	51,000	Equity	71,000
CIBC (1,000 @ $28)	28,000		$136,000
Noranda (500 @ $30)	15,000		
	$136,000		

remove the \$12,000 short sale and cash proceeds; the equity value is found by subtracting the \$50,000 loan, which we then divide by the market value of the securities held long, or \$122,500, for a margin ratio of .59. The investor needs \$30,000 to establish margin of .3 and has \$42,500 excess equity.

For the short position alone, we remove the effect of the margin purchase from the market value; so the investor has \$84,500 as account value, which is divided by the short value of \$12,000 for a margin ratio of 7; but we have counted the same equity twice in arriving at the two satisfactory ratios. To cover the short sale margin requirement, the investor needs assets of V where V/\$12,000 must equal 1.3; solving for V yields \$15,600 as the asset requirement. Separately, there is plenty of excess equity in the account, but combined, the investor needs \$30,000 plus \$15,600, or \$45,600, equity in the account before making both the margin purchase and the short sale. There is an excess of only \$26,900; without the T-bills, the investor would have needed to find another \$3,100 to place on deposit.

In finding the amount of margin that the investor must provide, we have been using the following two formulas; for margin purchases, the market value of collateral required is

$$\text{Market value} = \text{Loan value}/(1 - \text{Margin ratio}) \qquad (3A.1)$$

and for short sales, the value of collateral required is

$$\text{Market value} = \text{Short value} \times \text{Margin ratio} \qquad (3A.2)$$

Using these equations, we can see that at the later date, the account easily satisfies the margin requirement of \$50,000/(1 – .3) = \$71,429 for the purchase plus \$15,000 × 1.3 = \$19,500 for the short sale, summing to \$90,929 against assets of \$136,000.

CONCEPT CHECK ?

3A.1. If at the later date in the preceding example the prices of Noranda and CIBC were the same as given but Brascan had fallen to \$80, how high could Alcan stock rise before a margin call would result? If instead Alcan rose to \$60, how low could Brascan fall before triggering a margin call?

CHAPTER FOUR

MUTUAL FUNDS AND THE INSTITUTIONAL ENVIRONMENT

The previous chapter introduced you to the mechanics of trading securities and the structure of the markets in which securities trade. Increasingly, however, individual investors are choosing not to trade securities directly for their own accounts, as this requires personal attention that many investors feel they have neither time nor expertise to give; rather, they entrust investment decisions to institutional management.

The investment decision hinges on the individual's needs for funds throughout the earning period and after retirement. Investment choices are also affected by the tax regime and how it affects the individual; in particular, tax rates on investment income are expected to be higher during earning years than during retirement years. Insurance companies and pension funds are institutions that participate in the investment process to help meet individual needs; indirectly, they are managing individual assets.

The most important institution to manage individual assets is the mutual fund industry, and this chapter focuses on this branch of professional investment management. We begin by giving a broad overview of institutional management, relating different types of institutions to individual needs, and how these needs impose constraints on institutional actions. We then turn to a classification of the variety of investment companies available to investors, before describing the particular form known as mutual funds. We categorize them according to their policies and styles, discuss how these affect the taxation of their results in investors' hands, and note where information may be obtained. Following this, we examine the expenses associated with management and how costs and fees affect the returns. This leads to the final topic of just how good is the performance of professional managers in directing mutual funds.

In Appendix 4A, we present a summary of the tax system, as it affects investing; this detail is essential for determining what investment promises to provide the highest risk-adjusted, after-tax returns. In Appendix 4B is a general overview of the pension fund industry with a focus on the defined benefit and defined contribution dichotomy.

4.1 MANAGEMENT BY INSTITUTIONS

Investors can be differentiated as individuals and institutions. A frequent lament is that individuals appear to be abandoning the markets to the institutions. As small investors, individuals are thought to provide liquidity to the market, which institutional portfolios are too large to do. Nevertheless, individuals provide the funds to the institutions to invest; although individuals have no immediate control over pension funds, mutual funds must respond by buying and selling as their investors add or withdraw cash. This process should still channel funds to the best investment opportunities.

Institutions must attempt to interpret and serve the requirements of households in making their investment decisions. Generally, the household sector equates to individuals, but occasionally there will be **personal trusts**.[1] The institutions that respond to household needs by investing in stock and bond markets include mutual funds, pension funds, endowment funds, and life insurance companies. Casualty insurance companies, like banks and trust companies, tend to have more conservative investments, with shorter maturities, due to the nature of their cash payouts. Each of the institutions must tailor its policies to the needs of its clients and the regulations or circumstances guiding it. We shall examine how these respond accordingly, with particular attention to mutual funds and pension funds.

www.cfainstitute.org

A formal process for making investment decisions has been established by the CFA Institute, formerly the Association for Investment Management and Research (AIMR), established by the merger of the Financial Analysts Federation (FAF) with the Institute of Chartered Financial Analysts (ICFA). The idea is to subdivide the major steps (objectives, constraints, and policies) into concrete considerations of the various aspects, making the process more tractable. The standard format appears in Table 4.1, and we shall discuss the three parts of the process in turn.

Institutions and Their Objectives

Portfolio objectives centre on the risk-return tradeoff between the expected return the investors want (*return requirements* in the first column of Table 4.1) and how much risk they are willing to assume (*risk tolerance*). Investment managers must know the level of risk that can be tolerated in the pursuit of a better rate of return. Table 4.2 lists factors governing return requirements and risk attitudes for each of the seven major investor categories discussed.

---

[1]These are established when an individual confers legal title to another person or institution (the trustee) to manage that property for one or more beneficiaries. The beneficiaries are of two types, essentially, those entitled to a life income and those entitled to the remaining principal upon death of the former. By definition of the objective of the trust, the options of the trustee are limited; the requirements have been made much clearer for the trustee than for individuals.

Table 4.1 Determination of Portfolio Policies

Objectives	Constraints	Policies
Return requirements	Liquidity	Asset allocation
Risk tolerance	Horizon	Diversification
	Regulations	Risk positioning
	Taxes	Tax positioning
	Unique needs	Income generation

For mutual funds, the objectives are spelled out precisely in the prospectus. Individuals and trustees can be guided by those statements, even if the objectives are not guaranteed to be met. A detailed discussion follows in the next section.

Pension funds are usually categorized as **defined-contribution plans** or **defined-benefit plans.** The former are, in effect, tax-deferred retirement savings accounts established by the firm in trust for its employees; the employees bear all the risk and receive all the return from the plans' assets. In the second form, the assets serve as collateral for the liabilities that the firm sponsoring the plan owes to the plan beneficiaries. The difference between the two is crucial to how the objective is defined and how the plan will be directed, as we see in Appendix 4B.

Endowment funds are organizations chartered to use their money for specific nonprofit purposes. They are financed by gifts from one or more sponsors and are typically managed by educational, cultural, and charitable organizations or by independent foundations established solely to carry out the fund's specific purposes. Generally, the investment objectives of an endowment fund are to produce a steady flow of income subject to only a moderate degree of risk. Trustees of an endowment fund, however, can specify other objectives as dictated by the circumstances of the particular endowment fund.

Life insurance companies generally try to invest so as to hedge their liabilities, which are defined by the policies they write. Thus, there are as many objectives as there are distinct types of policies. Until a decade or so ago there were only two types of life insurance policies available for individuals: whole-life and term. A **whole-life insurance policy** combines a death benefit with a kind of savings plan that provides for a gradual buildup of cash value that the policyholder can withdraw at a later point in life, usually at age 65. **Term insurance**, on the other hand, provides death benefits only, with no buildup of cash value.

Table 4.2 Matrix of Objectives

Type of Investor	Return Requirement	Risk Tolerance
Individual and personal trusts	Life cycle (education, children, retirement)	Life cycle (younger: more risk-tolerant)
Mutual funds	Variable	Variable
Pension funds	Assumed actuarial rate	Depends on proximity of payouts
Endowment funds	Determined by current income needs and need for asset growth to maintain real value	Generally conservative
Life insurance companies	Should exceed new money rate by sufficient margin to meet expenses and profit objectives; also actuarial rates important	Conservative
Nonlife insurance companies	No minimum	Conservative
Banks	Interest spread	Variable

The interest rate embedded in the schedule of cash value accumulation promised under a whole-life policy is a fixed rate; life insurance companies try to hedge this liability by investing in long-term bonds. Often, the insured individual has the right to borrow at a prespecified fixed interest rate against the cash value of the policy.

During the inflationary years of the 1970s and early 1980s, when many older whole-life policies carried contractual borrowing rates as low as 4 percent or 5 percent per year, policyholders borrowed heavily against the cash value to invest in money market mutual funds paying double-digit yields. Other actual and potential policyholders abandoned whole-life policies and took out term insurance, investing the difference in the premiums on their own.

In response to the public's change in tastes, the insurance industry came up with some new policy types, of which two are of particular interest to investors: **variable life** and **universal life**.[2] Under a variable life policy, the insured's premium buys a fixed death benefit plus a cash value that can be invested in a variety of mutual funds from which the policyholder can choose. With a universal life policy, policyholders can increase or reduce the premium or death benefit according to their changing needs. Furthermore, the interest rate on the cash value component changes with market interest rates. These two plans effectively unbundle the charges for insurance and savings. The great advantage of variable and universal life insurance policies is that earnings on the cash value are not taxed until the money is withdrawn.[3]

The life insurance industry also provides services or products in the pension area, these being the sale of annuities and pension fund management service. Prior to the introduction of the registered retirement savings plan (RRSP) for individual retirement planning, the monopolistic sale by insurance companies of annuities was a major source of income. The insurance industry must now compete with other financial intermediaries for the sale of RRSPs. The RRSP must, however, be collapsed into an annuity or a registered retirement income fund (RRIF); since RRIFs are less popular than annuities, which may only be offered by insurance companies, the industry has benefited from the wide adoption of RRSPs.

Since the cash flow characteristics of life insurance and pensions are quite similar, insurance companies have developed expertise in fund management that is transferable to the pension industry. One example of this is the **insured defined-benefit pension**. A firm sponsoring a pension plan enters into a contractual agreement by which an insurance company assumes all liability for the benefits accrued under the plan. This guarantee is given in return for an annual premium based on the benefit formula and the number and characteristics of the employees covered by the plan.

Constraints

Both households and institutional investors restrict their choice of investment assets. These restrictions arise from their specific circumstances. Identifying these restrictions/constraints will affect the choice of investment policy. Five common types of constraints are described below.

Liquidity is the ease (speed) with which an asset can be sold and still fetch a fair price. It is a relationship between the time dimension (how long will it take to dispose) and the price dimension (what discount from fair market price) of an investment asset.

When an actual concrete measure of liquidity is necessary, one thinks of the discount when an immediate sale is unavoidable.[4] Cash and money market instruments, such as Treasury bills and commercial paper, where the bid-asked spread is a fraction of 1 percent, are the most liquid assets,

---

[2]A third type was *adjustable life*, which enabled the policyholder to vary benefits and premiums according to his or her changing needs.

[3]Investment contracts with insurance features also may be protected against seizure in bankruptcy.

[4]In most cases, it is impossible to know the liquidity of an asset with certainty, before it is put up for sale. In dealer markets (described in Chapter 3), however, the liquidity of the traded assets can be observed from the bid-asked spread that is quoted by the dealers, that is, the difference between the "bid" quote (the lower price the dealer will pay the owner) and the "asked" quote (the higher price a buyer would have to pay the dealer).

and real estate is among the least liquid. Office buildings and manufacturing structures can easily be assessed a 50 percent liquidity discount.

Both individual and institutional investors must consider how likely they are to dispose of assets at short notice. From this likelihood, they establish the minimum level of liquid assets they want in the investment portfolio.

The **investment horizon** is the planned liquidation date of all or part of the investment; for example, it might be the time to fund college education or the retirement date for a wage earner. For a university endowment, an investment horizon could relate to the time needed to fund a major campus construction project. Horizon needs to be considered when investors choose between assets of various maturities, such as bonds, which pay off at specified future dates.

Only professional and institutional investors are constrained by *regulations*. First and foremost is the **prudent person** law. That is, professional investors who manage other people's money have a fiduciary responsibility to restrict investment to assets that would have been approved by a prudent investor. The law is purposefully nonspecific. Every professional investor must stand ready to defend an investment policy in a court of law, and interpretation may differ according to the standards of the times.

Also, specific regulations apply to various institutional investors. For instance, Canadian pension portfolios are limited to a 30 percent maximum holding of foreign assets, as are individual retirement portfolios. Similarly, provincial legislation governs mutual fund holdings, imposing a maximum on the percentage of ownership in a single corporation; this regulation keeps professional investors from getting involved in the actual management of corporations.

Tax consequences are central to investment decisions. The performance of any investment strategy should be measured by how much it yields in real, after-tax investment returns. For household and institutional investors who face significant tax rates, tax sheltering and deferral of tax obligations may be pivotal in their investment strategy.

Unique Needs

Virtually every investor faces special circumstances. Imagine husband-and-wife aeronautical engineers holding high-paying jobs in the same aerospace corporation. The entire human capital of that household is tied to a single player in a rather cyclical industry. This couple would need to hedge the risk (find investment assets that yield more when the risk materializes, thus partly insuring against the risk) of a deterioration in the economic well-being of the aerospace industry.

An example of a unique need for an institutional investor is a university whose trustees let the administration use only cash income from the endowment fund. This constraint would translate into a preference for high-dividend-paying assets.

Table 4.3 presents a summary of the importance of each of the general constraints to each of the seven types of investors.

Table 4.3 Matrix of Constraints

Type of Investor	Liquidity	Horizon	Regulatory	Taxes
Individuals and personal trusts	Variable	Life cycle	None	Variable
Mutual funds	Low	Short	Little	None
Pension funds	Young, low; mature, high	Long	Some (federal)	None
Endowment funds	Little	Long	Little	None
Life insurance companies	Low	Long	Complex	Yes
Nonlife insurance companies	High	Short	Little	Yes
Banks	Low	Short	Changing	Yes

4.2 INVESTMENT COMPANIES

Investment companies are financial intermediaries that collect funds from individual investors and invest those funds in a potentially wide range of securities or other assets. Pooling of assets is the key idea behind investment companies. Each investor has a claim to the portfolio established by the investment company in proportion to the amount invested. These companies thus provide a mechanism for small investors to "team up" to obtain the benefits of large-scale investing.

Investment companies perform several important functions for their investors:

1. *Record keeping and administration.* Investment companies issue periodic status reports, keeping track of capital gains distributions, dividends, investments, and redemptions, and they may reinvest dividend and interest income for shareholders.
2. *Diversification and divisibility.* By pooling their money, investment companies enable investors to hold fractional shares of many different securities. They can act as large investors even if any individual shareholder cannot.
3. *Professional management.* Many, but not all, investment companies have full-time staffs of security analysts and portfolio managers who attempt to achieve superior investment results for their investors. High individual search costs are reduced when institutional research is conducted.
4. *Lower transaction costs.* Because they trade large blocks of securities, investment companies can achieve substantial savings on brokerage fees and commissions.

While all investment companies pool assets of individual investors, they also need to divide claims to those assets among those investors. Investors buy shares in investment companies, and ownership is proportional to the number of shares purchased. The value of each share is called the **net asset value**, or **NAV**. Net asset value equals assets minus liabilities expressed on a per-share basis:

$$\text{Net asset value} = \frac{\text{Market value of assets minus liabilities}}{\text{Shares outstanding}}$$

Consider a mutual fund that manages a portfolio of securities worth \$120 million. Suppose the fund owes \$4 million to its investment advisers and owes another \$1 million for rent, wages due, and miscellaneous expenses. The fund has 5 million shareholders. Then

$$\text{Net asset value} = \frac{\$120 \text{ million} - \$5 \text{ million}}{5 \text{ million shares}} = \$23 \text{ per share}$$

CONCEPT CHECK

1. Consider these data from the December 31, 1996 balance sheet of the Index Trust 500 Portfolio mutual fund sponsored by the Vanguard Group. What was the net asset value of the portfolio?

Assets:	$105,496 million
Liabilities:	844 million
Shares:	773.3 million

Funds under the administration of investment companies are usually referred to as **managed funds**, so named because securities in their investment portfolios are continually being managed by purchase and sale.

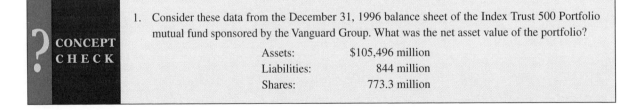

There are two types of managed companies: closed-end and open-end. In both cases, the fund's board of directors, which is elected by shareholders, hires a management company to manage the portfolio for an annual fee that typically ranges from .2 percent to 1.5 percent of assets. In many cases the management company is the firm that organized the fund. For example, AGF Management Limited sponsors many AGF mutual funds and is responsible for managing the portfolios. It assesses a management fee on each AGF fund. In other cases, a mutual fund will hire an outside portfolio manager. For example, AGF has hired Nomura Asset Management as the investment advisor for both its Japan and its China funds. Most management companies have contracts to manage several funds.

www.agf.com

Open-end funds stand ready to redeem or issue shares at their net asset value (although both purchases and redemptions may involve sales charges). When investors in open-end funds wish to "cash out" their shares, they sell them back to the fund at NAV. In contrast, **closed-end funds** do not redeem or issue shares. Investors in closed-end funds who wish to cash out must sell their shares to other investors. Shares of closed-end funds are traded on organized exchanges and can be purchased through brokers just like other common stock; their prices therefore can differ from NAV.

Figure 4.1 shows a listing of closed-end funds from *The Globe and Mail*. The first column after the name of the fund indicates its symbol and the exchange on which the shares trade (T means Toronto). The next three columns give the fund's most recent net asset value, the closing share price, and the percentage difference between the two, which is (Price – NAV)/NAV. Notice that there are more funds selling at discounts to NAV (indicated by negative differences) than premiums.

The common divergence of price from net asset value, often by wide margins, is a puzzle that has yet to be fully explained. To see why this is a puzzle, consider a closed-end fund that is selling at a discount from net asset value. If the fund were to sell all the assets in the portfolio, it would realize proceeds equal to net asset value. The difference between the market price of the fund and the fund's NAV would represent the per-share increase in the wealth of the fund's investors. Despite this apparent profit opportunity, sizable discounts seem to persist for long periods of time.

Interestingly, while many closed-end funds sell at a discount from net asset value, the prices of these funds when originally issued are typically above NAV. This is a further puzzle, as it is hard to explain why investors would purchase these newly issued funds at a premium to NAV when the shares tend to fall to a discount shortly after issue.

Many investors consider closed-end funds selling at a discount to NAV to be a bargain. Even if the market price never rises to the level of NAV, the dividend yield on an investment in the fund at this price would exceed the dividend yield on the same securities held outside the fund. To see this, imagine a fund with an NAV of $10 per share holding a portfolio that pays an annual dividend of $1 per share; that is, the dividend yield to investors that hold this portfolio directly is 10 percent. Now suppose that the market price of a share of this closed-end fund is $9. If management pays out dividends received from the shares as they come in, then the dividend yield to those that hold the same portfolio through the closed-end fund will be $1/$9, or 11.1 percent.

In contrast to closed-end funds, the price of open-end funds cannot fall below NAV, because these funds stand ready to redeem shares at NAV. The offering price will exceed NAV, however, if the fund carries a **load**. A load is, in effect, a sales charge, which is paid to the seller. Load funds are sold by securities brokers and directly by mutual fund groups.

Unlike closed-end funds, open-end mutual funds do not trade on organized exchanges. Instead, investors simply buy shares from and liquidate through the investment company at net asset value. Thus the number of outstanding shares of these funds changes daily.

Figure 4.1
Closed-end mutual funds.

FUND ASSET VALUES

Recent prices of closed investment funds supplied by Globe Interactive at 6:15 p.m. yesterday. Latest trading price represent values from GlobeInvestor.com. **NAV** *(Net Asset Value) represents the latest value reported to Globefund.com by the fund companies.* **Premium** *- represents percantage difference between the fund's trading price and the fund's NAV.* **Discount** *- represents percentage difference between the fund's NAV and the fund's trading price. All data is for information purposes only. Confirmation of prices should be obtained from the fund.*

fund name	symbol -exch.	latest reported NAV	latest trading price	prem /disc
5Banc Split Inc(03/04	FBS.A-T	70.22	70.03	-.27
AIC Diversified Canada Split Corp.(03/05	ADC-T	30.86	24.81	-19.60
Aberdeen Asia-Pacific(03/04	FAP-T	10.12	9.38	-7.31
Aberdeen G7 Trust(03/05	GSV.UN-T	10.17	10.81	6.29
Aberdeen SCOTS Trust(03/05	SCO.UN-T	21.68	21.00	-3.14
Acuity Growth & Income Trust(03/04	AIG.UN-T	10.76	10.11	-6.05
AllBanc Split Corp.(03/04	ABK.A-T	137.02	138.50	1.08
B Split II Corp.(03/04	BXN-T	29.04	28.99	-.17
BCX Split Corp.(03/04	BCX.A-T	28.92	29.25	1.14
BNS Split Corp.(03/04	BSN-T	69.23	70.30	1.55
BPI Global Opportunities II(03/10	BOI.UN-T	8.55	8.20	-4.09
Barclays Advant Equal Weighted(03/10	BAE.UN-T	10.49	10.85	3.45
Barclays Advantaged(03/10	BAI.UN-T	11.44	11.25	-1.64
Big 8 Split Inc(03/04	BIG.A-T	53.29	52.65	-1.20
BluMont Strategic Partners Hedge(03/10	BSP.UN-T	9.46	9.07	-4.16
Brascan Soundvest Diversified Inc.(03/05	BSI.UN-T	10.62	11.00	3.58
Brompton Equal Weight Income Fund(03/04	EWI.UN-T	11.23	10.75	-4.26
Brompton MVP Income Fund(03/04	MVP.UN-T	12.65	12.18	-3.75
Brompton Stable Income Fund(03/04	BSR.UN-T	12.20	12.03	-1.36
Brompton VIP Income Trust(03/04	VIP.UN-T	12.16	11.64	-4.29
Business Trust Equal Weight Income(03/04	BWI.UN-T	11.29	11.15	-1.23
COMPASS Income Fund(03/04	CMZ.UN-T	12.65	12.05	-4.74
Canada Trust Income Investments(03/04	CNN.UN-T	9.92	8.95	-9.76
Canadian Financial Services NT Corp(03/05	CFC-T	61.09	60.44	-1.07
Canadian General Investments Ltd.(03/10	CGI-T	18.60	14.30	-23.12
Canadian Resources Income Trust(03/04	RTU.UN-T	11.41	10.63	-6.84
Canadian World Fund Limited(03/10	CWF-T	5.23	3.95	-24.47
Casurina Performance(03/04	CAF.UN-T	31.54	32.71	3.72
Central Fund of Canada Ltd.(03/10	CEF.A-T	6.78	7.70	13.57
Central Gold-Trust(03/10	GTU.UN-T	20.78	22.20	6.83
Citadel Diversified Investm't Trust(03/04	CTD.UN-T	11.23	10.75	-4.27
Citadel Hytes Fund(03/04	CHF.UN-T	33.14	30.90	-6.76
Citadel Income & Equity Index(03/04	IEP.UN-T	9.46	9.95	5.18
Citadel Income & Growth(03/04	CIF.UN-T	10.67	10.41	-2.44
Citadel Multi-Sector Income Fund(03/04	CMS.UN-T	11.06	10.48	-5.24
Citadel S-1 Income Trust(03/04	SDL.UN-T	32.05	30.00	-6.40
Citadel SMaRT(03/04	CRT.UN-T	30.62	29.60	-3.33
Citadel Series S-1 Income Fund(03/04	SRC.UN-T	11.02	10.70	-2.90
Commerical & Indust Sec Inc Trust(03/04	COI.UN-T	24.93	24.05	-3.52
Connor Clark & Lunn PRINTS(03/09	CCP.UN-T	16.87	16.00	-5.13
Convertible & Yield Advantage Trust(03/10	CNV.UN-T	25.16	24.75	-1.63
Cyclical Split NT Corp.(03/05	CYC-T	57.35	54.51	-4.96
DDJ Canadian High Yield(03/10	HYB.UN-T	18.50	19.99	8.05
DDJ U.S. High Yield(03/10	DDJ.UN-T	9.69	10.13	4.54
DiversiTrust Income Fund(03/10	DTF.UN-T	12.90	12.24	-5.12
DiversiTrust Income Plus Fund(03/10	DTP.UN-T	9.59	10.05	4.80
DiversiTrust Stable Income(03/10	DTS.UN-T	10.76	10.40	-3.35
Diversified Income Trust II(03/04	DTT.UN-T	12.92	12.00	-7.14
Diversified Preferred Share Trust(03/03	DPS.UN-T	24.42	25.65	5.02
Diversified Utility Trust(03/04	DUT.UN-T	29.25	28.66	-2.02
Dundee Precious Metals Inc.(03/10	DPM.A-T	35.64	33.40	-6.29
Economic Investment Trust(03/04	EVT-T	76.60	50.75	-33.75
Energy Split Corp. Inc.(03/04	ES-T	49.77	51.27	3.01
Enervest Diversified Income Trust(03/09	EIT.UN-T	7.44	7.00	-5.91
Faircourt Income Split Trust(03/04	FCI.UN-T	22.72	21.00	-7.58
Faircourt Split Five Trust(03/04	FCF.UN-T	18.84	17.50	-7.10
First Asset Pref Securities Inc(03/10	PFS.UN-T	24.15	24.90	3.11
First Asset Yield Opportunity Trust(03/10	FAY.UN-T	25.25	25.40	.59
Health Care & Biotechnology Venture(03/05	HCB.UN-T	.45	.48	6.67
High Inc Principal & Yield Sec Cp E(03/05	PAY-T	18.09	18.10	.06
High Inc Principal & Yld Sec Cp PF(03/05	PAY.PR.A-T	25.00	26.70	6.80

Source: *The Globe and Mail,* March 11, 2004, p. B21. Reprinted with permission of The Globe and Mail.

Other Investment Organizations

There are intermediaries not formally organized or regulated as investment companies that nevertheless serve functions similar to investment companies. Four of the more important are commingled funds, real estate trusts, segregated funds, and hedge funds.

Commingled funds are partnerships of investors that pool their funds. The management firm that organizes the partnership, for example, a bank or insurance company, manages the funds for a fee. Typical partners in a commingled fund might be trust or retirement accounts which have portfolios that are much larger than those of most individual investors but are still too small to warrant managing on a separate basis.

Commingled funds are similar in form to open-end mutual funds. Instead of shares, though, the fund offers units, which are bought and sold at net asset value. A bank or insurance company may offer an array of different commingled funds from which trust or retirement accounts can choose. Examples are a money market fund, a bond fund, and a common stock fund. In certain cases, these funds may be formed as *unit investment trusts* as a means of avoiding realization of gains when assets are sold and the proceeds reinvested. The holding in the trust is not deemed to be realized, so that tax or other regulatory consequences can be avoided, but the composition of the portfolio can be adjusted to meet market conditions. (The concept of "unit investment trust" has another interpretation in the United States.)

A **real estate limited partnership** functions similarly to a closed-end mutual fund, using leverage to purchase real estate. Partnership units are sold to the public to raise equity capital, which is leveraged by borrowing from banks and issuing mortgages. **Mortgage funds** invest directly in mortgages by purchasing pass-through securities of different maturities; they tend to be managed by banks or trust companies. A limited partnership, by its very construction, pays no income taxes; all income or loss is recognized in the hands of its unitholders. The mortgage funds are treated as any other mutual fund, for tax purposes.

The equivalent U.S. institution occupies a significant niche in the market, responding to perceived inflation and interest rates. The real estate investment trust (REIT) can take the form of either an equity or a mortgage trust. REITs generally are established by banks, insurance companies, or mortgage companies, which then serve as investment managers to earn a fee.

Segregated funds are essentially mutual funds with an attached guarantee for a minimum value. They are typically sold by insurance companies, with estate planning aspects, tying the performance of a mutual fund to the payoff but allowing 75 or 100 percent of the initial investment (or a reset value at a later date) to be a guaranteed payout at maturity or upon death of the investor. The "reset" feature makes for difficult valuation of the product; high fees paid for funds management and the insurance guarantee make these funds far less attractive than they appear to be.

Like mutual funds, **hedge funds** are vehicles that allow private investors to pool assets to be invested by a fund manager. However, hedge funds are not registered as mutual funds and are not subject to the level of regulation that governs mutual funds. They are typically open only to wealthy or institutional investors. As hedge funds are only lightly regulated, their managers can pursue investment strategies not open to mutual fund managers, including, for example, heavy use of derivatives, short sales, and leverage.

Hedge funds typically attempt to exploit temporary misalignments in security valuations. For example, if the yield on mortgage-backed securities seems abnormally high compared to that on Treasury bonds, the hedge fund would buy mortgage-backed and short-sell Treasury securities. Notice that the fund is *not* betting on broad movement in the entire bond market; it buys one type of bond and sells another. By taking a long mortgage/short Treasury position, the fund "hedges" its interest rate exposure, while making a bet on the *relative* valuation across the two sectors. The idea is that when yield spreads converge back to their "normal" relationship, the fund will profit from the realignment regardless of the general trend in the level of interest rates. In this respect, it strives to be "market-neutral," which gives rise to the term "hedge fund."

Of course even if the fund's position is market-neutral, this does not mean that it is low-risk. The fund is still speculating on valuation differences across the two sectors, often taking a very large position, and this decision can turn out to be right or wrong. Because the funds often operate with considerable leverage, returns can be quite volatile.

After the consistent rise in equity markets in the 1990s, the recent modest returns have increased the attraction of hedge funds, now offered to smaller investors. This has led to increased regulation, whose amount varies by jurisdiction in Canada.

4.3 MUTUAL FUNDS

Mutual funds are by far the most popular form of investment vehicle open to individuals. The value of the funds under management by mutual funds grew immensely during the decade of the 1990s as investors recognized the unprecedented growth in equity values during that period. We shall see, however, that the general increase in market valuation has indicated to investors that the option of index funds has become an extremely attractive form of mutual fund that competes with the traditional forms. In what follows, the term "mutual fund" refers to open-ended investment companies.

By January 2004, there were 209 members in the Investment Funds Institute of Canada managing 1,887 mutual funds with assets of over $451 billion. Of these, money market funds held approximately one-eighth of the total assets. Figure 4.2 demonstrates the substantial growth that has occurred in the Canadian market, while Table 4.4 gives a breakdown of the types and sizes of mutual funds in December 2003. Figure 4.3 shows part of the listings for mutual funds published every weekday in *The Globe and Mail*, showing the value and the absolute and percentage changes from the previous trading period.

Table 4.4
Types and Assets of Mutual Funds, December 31, 2003

Fund Type	Total Assets ($000)	% Share of Market
Balanced	74,539,017	17.0%
Canadian common shares	100,070,612	22.8%
Foreign common shares	87,159,540	19.9%
Bond and income	40,657,464	9.3%
Foreign bond and income	4,657,949	1.1%
Dividend and income	39,060,692	8.9%
Mortgage	5,868,087	1.3%
Real estate	880,767	0.2%
U.S. common shares	31,453,710	7.2%
Subtotal	**384,347,838**	**87.7%**
Money market	52,107,071	11.9%
Foreign money market	2,410,013	0.5%
Subtotal (money market)	**54,517,084**	**12.4%**
All funds	438,864,922	100.0%

Source: Investment Funds Institute of Canada.

Figure 4.2
Growth of mutual fund assets in Canada, January 1994–2004.

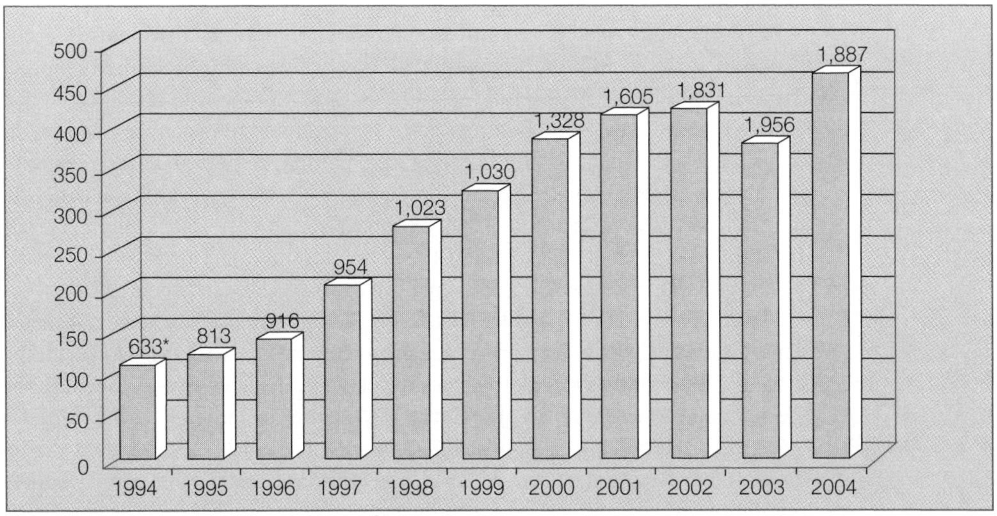

*Number of funds

Source: Data from the Investment Funds Institute of Canada.

Figure 4.3
Daily mutual funds listing.

CANADIAN MUTUAL FUNDS

YESTERDAY'S MOVERS

As of 6:15 p.m. yesterday. All prices show the % change from the previous day. Data supplied by Globe Interactive. Results in this table exclude offshore funds such as All Points Index Funds.

All funds

Dynamic Canadian Precious Metals	-3.63%
TD Precious Metals	-3.54%
Dynamic Global Resource	-3.46%
iUnits S&P/TSX Capped Gold	-3.44%
AGF Precious Metal	-3.37%

Canadian equity funds

Montrusco Bolton TSE 100 Momentum	-3.33%
Mavrix Canadian Strategic Equity	-3.23%
Mavrix Growth	-3.23%
IA Group CdnEquity (Knight Bain)	-2.82%
Altamira Special Growth	-2.80%

U.S. equity funds

Mavrix Enterprise	-3.07%
University Avenue Growth	-2.85%
Fidelity American Opportunities Cl	-2.37%
Fidelity American Opportunities-A	-2.32%
Fidelity RSP American Opport-A	-2.30%

Int'l equity funds

Fidelity Latin America-A	-2.99%
TD Latin American Growth	-2.66%
Fidelity RSP Europe-A	-2.56%
MLI Fidelity Europe GIF 1	-2.55%
Fidelity Europe Class	-2.55%

LATEST VALUES

Recent prices of investment funds supplied by Bell Globemedia Interactive at 6:15 p.m. yesterday. Prices reported by funds are the net asset value per share or unit last calculated and are for information purposes only. Confirmation of price should be obtained from the fund. Chg - $ change from last valuation; % Chg - 1 day percentage change; m -minimum purchase of $150,000; x - ex-dividend; (Date following fund denotes last valuation).

fund	valuation	chg	% chg
@RGENTUM MANAGEMENT C$			
Cdn Equity	7.92	-.14	-1.73
Cdn L/S Equ Po	10.32	-.15	-1.43
Cdn Perf Port.	14.65	-.26	-1.77
Discovery	13.73	-.30	-2.11
Income	7.53	-.08	-1.04
Int'l Master	5.44	-.04	-.70
Quebec Bal Port	10.26	-.13	-1.22
US Master	.22	-.00	-1.15
US Mkt Neutral	.62	+.00	+.75
@RGENTUM MANAGEMENT US$			
Int'l Master U$	4.10	-.05	-1.30
US Master U$	.16	-.00	-1.75
US Mkt Neut U$	.47	+.00	+.15
ABC FUNDS			
mAmer-Value 02/27	9.00	–	–
mFully-Mgd 02/27	10.10	–	–
mFund-Value 02/27	18.58	–	–
ACCUMULUS INVESTMENT MGMT			
Balanced - A	10.02	+.02	+.18
Balanced - I	10.00	unch	unch
Divers Mthly -A	10.02	+.02	+.18
Divers Mthly -I	10.00	unch	unch
Index Momentum	7.69	-.11	-1.46
Shrt-Trm Inc-A	10.01	+.01	+.11
Shrt-Trm Inc-I	10.00	unch	unch
Talisman - A	9.97	-.03	-.27
Talisman - I	9.97	-.03	-.26
ACKER FINLEY			
QSA Cdn Equ A	6.27	-.11	-1.73
QSA Cdn Equ B	13.28	-.23	-1.74
QSA Enterpr U$	8.08	-.13	-1.62
QSA US V50 C$	5.49	-.09	-1.62
QSA US Val C$	2.22	-.04	-1.79
Select Cdn Equ	8.10	-.14	-1.71
ACUITY MUTUAL FUNDS			
All Cap 30	18.01	-.26	-1.40
CE Balanced	12.13	-.10	-.85
CE Equity	12.20	-.17	-1.35
CE Glo Equity	6.14	-.10	-1.64
CE Sci & Tech	4.84	-.07	-1.49
Cdn Balanced	15.96	-.18	-1.13
Cdn Equity	19.44	-.39	-1.95
Fixed Income	10.55	-.02	-.17
G7 RSP Equity	7.55	-.10	-1.35
Global Equity	9.18	-.16	-1.69
Gwth and Inc	14.07	-.19	-1.32
High Income	14.36	-.17	-1.14
Income Trust	13.96	-.09	-.61
Social Val CdEq	14.01	-.22	-1.58
Social Val GlEq	8.08	-.14	-1.68
AIC INCOME GROUP			
Bond	5.63	unch	unch
Global Bond	5.88	-.04	-.68
AIC PRIVATE PORTFOLIO COUNSEL			
PCC Bond Pool	10.58	-.01	-.09
PCC Cdn Pool	11.72	-.07	-.59
PPC Glo Pool	11.21	-.08	-.71
PPC Glo Pool U$	8.47	-.06	-.75
PPC Inc Pool	10.48	unch	unch
PPC Inc Pool T	9.94	unch	unch
PPC RSP Gl Pool	10.87	-.08	-.73
AIM FUNDS C$			
Am MidCapGw Cl	6.84	-.07	-1.03
Amer Aggr Grwth	9.24	-.11	-1.13
Amer Growth	4.09	-.03	-.80
Cda Income Cl	4.40	-.06	-1.26
Cdn Balanced	21.96	-.24	-1.07
Cdn First Class	9.00	-.16	-1.78
Cdn Premier	13.85	-.27	-1.89
Cdn Premier Cl	9.29	-.18	-1.89
Euro Growth Cl	5.11	-.07	-1.37
European Growth	13.46	-.19	-1.38
Glo Fin Serv Cl	8.81	-.09	-.96
Glo Health Sci	14.28	-.13	-.89
Glo Hlth Sci Cl	6.42	-.06	-.88
Glo Technol Cl	2.60	-.04	-1.33
Glo Technology	13.06	-.16	-1.22
Glo Theme Cl	6.97	-.05	-.68
Indo-Pacific	4.61	-.03	-.73
Int'l Growth Cl	7.53	-.11	-1.43
RSP Amer Growth	3.68	-.03	-.78
RSP Euro Growth	5.08	-.07	-1.38
RSP Glo Fin Ser	8.92	-.09	-.95
RSP Glo Hth Sci	8.24	-.07	-.89
RSP Glo Technol	2.40	-.03	-1.24
RSP Glo Theme	7.48	-.05	-.68
RSP IndoPacific	3.60	-.03	-.74
RSP Int'l Grwth	7.54	-.11	-1.42
Sht-Tm Inc Cl A	5.82	unch	unch
Sht-Tm Inc Cl B	5.61	+.00	+.02
AIM FUNDS U$			
AmMidCapG Cl U$	5.16	-.09	-1.64
Amer Aggr Gw U$	6.96	-.12	-1.72
Amer Growth U$	3.08	-.04	-1.38
Euro Gwth Cl U$	3.85	-.08	-1.94
EuropeanGwth U$	10.15	-.20	-1.96
Glo FinSerCl U$	6.64	-.10	-1.54
Glo Hlth Sci U$	10.76	-.16	-1.48
Glo HthSciCl U$	4.84	-.07	-1.47
Glo Tech Cl U$	1.96	-.04	-1.90
Glo Technol U$	9.85	-.18	-1.81
iGold	52.61	-1.87	-3.44
iIT	8.15	-.18	-2.13
iIntR	20.36	-.18	-.86
iMidCap	58.62	-.98	-1.64
iREIT	11.90	-.19	-1.54
BEUTELGOODMAN			
Amer Equity	7.30	-.05	-.73
BG Cdn EquityPl	11.36	-.14	-1.19
BG Cdn Intrinsc	6.33	-.08	-1.28
Balanced	15.18	-.10	-.67
Cdn Dividend	5.53	-.04	-.79
Cdn Equity	20.28	-.28	-1.37
Income	11.74	-.00	-.02
Intl Equity	5.33	-.03	-.58
Small Cap	16.12	-.25	-1.53
BIOCAPITAL BIOTECHNOLOGY FUND			
Biocapital Fund	6.17	-.13	-2.09
BMO MUTUAL FUNDS			
Allocation	15.60	-.18	-1.16
Bond	13.32	-.01	-.04
Dividend	33.07	-.36	-1.09
Emerg Mkts	8.18	-.14	-1.73
Equity	23.66	-.50	-2.07
Equity Index	25.63	-.49	-1.87
European	15.46	-.12	-.79
Glo Bal Cl	7.17	-.05	-.68
Glo Bond	12.49	-.12	-.95
Glo Equity Cl	5.13	-.06	-1.12
Glo Sci&Tech	14.02	-.23	-1.59
Int'l Index RSP	7.93	-.01	-.09
Intl Bond	9.48	-.01	-.06
Intl Equity	12.55	-.11	-.83
Japanese	5.55	-.00	-.07
MM Reg Bal 1 02/27	5.08	–	–
MM Reg Bal 2 02/27	7.07	–	–
MM Reg Gth 1 02/27	9.81	–	–
MM Reg Gth 2 02/27	13.16	–	–
MM Reg Sec 1 02/27	1.54	–	–
MM Reg Sec 2 02/27	2.70	–	–
MM Str Bal 1 02/27	5.10	–	–
MM Str Bal 2 02/27	10.14	–	–
MM Str Gth 1 02/27	13.57	–	–
MM Str Gth 2 02/27	13.97	–	–
MM Str Sec 1 02/27	2.58	–	–
MM Str Sec 2 02/27	2.95	–	–
Monthly Income	9.73	-.06	-.66
Mort&Sh Term In	11.82	-.00	-.02
NAFTA Adv	15.80	-.18	-1.15
Prec Metals	12.56	-.33	-2.59
RSP Glo Sci&Tec	4.32	-.07	-1.59
Resource	17.72	-.54	-2.93
Short-Term Inc	11.03	-.00	-.02
Special Equity	21.42	-.39	-1.80
US Bond U$	10.41	-.00	-.04
US Equ Index	8.95	-.15	-1.66
US Equ Index U$	8.26	-.14	-1.69
US Growth	15.31	-.20	-1.31
US Spec Equity	19.72	-.37	-1.83
US Value	13.39	-.15	-1.14
BRANDES INVESTMENT PARTNERS			
Canadian Bal	12.82	-.10	-.81
Canadian Equity	13.46	-.14	-1.05
Emerging Mkt Eq	13.50	-.16	-1.19
Glo Sm Cap Eq	13.70	-.12	-.84
Global Balanced	11.38	-.12	-1.04
Global Equity	11.82	-.21	-1.74
Int'l Equity	11.64	-.13	-1.10
RSP Global Bal	11.36	-.12	-1.04
RSP Global Equ	12.73	-.23	-1.75
RSP Int'l Equ	12.89	-.14	-1.10
RSP U.S. Equity	12.87	-.27	-2.02
U.S. Equity	11.12	-.23	-2.02
U.S. Small Cap	11.99	-.16	-1.30
BRANDES INVSTMT PARTNERS US$			
Emerg MktEq U$	10.18	-.19	-1.79
Glo SmCapEq U$	10.33	-.15	-1.43
Global Bal U$	8.57	-.14	-1.63
Global EquityU$	8.91	-.21	-2.34
Int'l Equity U$	8.77	-.15	-1.70
U.S. Equity U$	8.39	-.22	-2.61
US SmallCap U$	9.04	-.17	-1.89
BULLION FUND			
BullionFund	6.82	+.09	+1.39
BURGEONVEST SECURITIES LTD.			
Canadian	19.09	-.48	-2.45
Cdn Demographic	10.62	-.05	-.49
Tactical Alloc	19.38	-.40	-2.02
CALDWELL			
America	4.86	-.05	-1.10
Balanced	5.93	-.05	-.79
Canada	3.46	-.02	-.54
Income	5.23	-.01	-.13
CAPITAL INTERNATIONAL FUND			
Global Disc	12.30	-.11	-.86
Global Equity	12.36	-.11	-.92
Global SmCap	13.11	-.13	-.96
Intl Equity	11.84	-.11	-.89
US Equity	11.80	-.10	-.85
CAPSTONE GROUP			
♣Balanced	8.73	-.07	-.80
Cdn Equity	13.82	-.24	-1.71
♣International	5.73	-.10	-1.72
CARTIER MULTIMANAGEMENT FUNDS			
Bond	5.15	-.00	-.06
Cdn Equity	7.45	-.12	-1.58
Glo Leaders RSP	4.06	-.05	-1.33

Source: *The Globe and Mail,* March 11, 2004, p B21. Reprinted with permission of The Globe and Mail.

Investment Policies

Every mutual fund has a specified investment policy, which is described in the fund's prospectus. For example, money market mutual funds hold the short-term, low-risk instruments of the money market (see Chapter 2 for a review of these securities), while bond funds hold fixed-income securities. Some funds have even more narrowly defined mandates. For example, some fixed-income funds will hold primarily government-issue bonds, others primarily mortgage-backed securities.

Management companies manage a family, or "complex," of mutual funds. They organize an entire collection of funds and then collect a management fee for operating them. By managing a collection of funds under one umbrella, these companies make it easy for investors to allocate assets across market sectors and to switch assets across funds while still benefiting from centralized record keeping.

Some of the more important fund types, classified by investment policy, are discussed next.

Money Market Funds These funds invest in money market securities. They usually offer cheque-writing features, and net asset value is fixed at $10 per share, so that there are no tax implications such as capital gains or losses associated with redemption of shares.

Fixed-Income Funds As the name suggests, these funds specialize in the fixed-income sector. Within that sector, however, there is considerable room for specialization. For example, various funds will concentrate on corporate bonds, Canada bonds, or mortgage-backed securities. Many funds will also specialize by the maturity of the securities, ranging from short-term to intermediate to long-term, or by the credit risk of the issuer, ranging from very safe to high-yield or "junk" bonds.

Balanced and Income Funds Some funds are designed to be candidates for an individual's entire investment portfolio. Therefore, they hold both equities and fixed-income securities in relatively stable proportions. According to Wiesenberger, such funds are classified as income or balanced funds. *Income funds* strive to maintain safety of principal consistent with "as liberal a current income from investments as possible," while *balanced funds* "minimize investment risks so far as this is possible without unduly sacrificing possibilities for long-term growth and current income." *Dividend funds* hold preferred shares and high-quality common shares that pay consistent dividends.

Asset Allocation Funds These funds are similar to balanced funds in that they hold both stocks and bonds. However, asset allocation funds may dramatically vary the proportions allocated to each market in accord with the portfolio manager's forecast of the relative performance of each sector. Hence these funds are engaged in market timing and are not designed to be low-risk investment vehicles.

Equity Funds Equity funds invest primarily in stock, although they may, at the portfolio manager's discretion, also hold fixed-income or other types of securities. Funds will commonly hold at least some money market securities to provide liquidity necessary to meet potential redemption of shares.

It is traditional to classify stock funds according to their emphasis on capital appreciation versus current income. Thus, *income funds* tend to hold shares of firms with high dividend yields, which provide high current income. *Growth funds* are willing to forgo current income, focusing instead on prospects for capital gains. While the classification of these funds is couched in terms of income versus capital gains, it is worth noting that in practice the more relevant distinction concerns the level of risk these funds assume. Growth stocks and therefore growth funds are typically riskier and respond far more dramatically to changes in economic conditions than do income funds.

Index Funds An **index fund** tries to match the performance of a broad market index. The fund buys shares in securities included in a particular index in proportion to the security's representation in that index. For example, CIBC's Canadian Index Fund is a mutual fund that replicates the composition of the TSX Composite Index. Because the TSX is a value-weighted index, the fund buys shares in each company in proportion to the market value of that company's outstanding equity. Investment in an index fund is a low-cost way for small investors to pursue a passive investment strategy—that is, to invest without engaging in security analysis. Of course, index funds can be tied to nonequity indices as well.

Specialized Sector Funds Some funds concentrate on a particular industry. For example, in the United States, Fidelity markets dozens of "select funds," each of which invests in a specific industry such as biotechnology, utilities, precious metals, or telecommunications. Other funds specialize in securities of particular countries. Emerging market, regional (e.g., Asian) or global funds have become increasingly popular as the importance of global diversification is realized.

Mutual funds are sold either directly by the management companies themselves (using an 800 telephone number for contact) or by brokers and agents who receive a commission for the sale. The commission is paid out of the load fee that is charged to the client. Brokers may also receive "trailer fees" from the mutual fund company for the continued investment by clients; that is, as long as the investor does not redeem the shares, the broker will receive what is effectively a deferred commission. For that reason, a broker's recommendation to retain a poor performer may not be entirely unbiased.

The larger of the 67 members of the Investment Funds Institute of Canada are likely to have approximately a hundred different types of funds under management. These different funds will include equity, income, money market, index, international, and other more narrowly focused funds of the types mentioned above; these may be managed internally or delegated to outside specialized professional managers. Table 4.5 lists the ten largest families and the assets under management as of December 2003. The total assets of $328 billion of these ten fund managers constitute about 75 percent of the total assets ($439 billion) managed by the 67 member firms.

Table 4.5
The Largest Canadian Mutual Fund Families—December 2003

Rank	Fund Family	Total Net Assets ($ millions)
1	RBC Asset Management Inc.	41,086
2	Investors Group	40,904
3	AIM Trimark Investments	38,037
4	CIBC Asset Management	37,592
5	Mackenzie Financial Corporation	33,591
6	C.I. Mutual Funds Inc.	32,279
7	TD Asset Management Inc.	31,990
8	Fidelity Investments Canada Limited	30,010
9	AGF Management Limited	23,977
10	Franklin Templeton Investments	18,056
	Total	**327,522**

Source: Investment Funds Institute of Canada.

Taxation of Mutual Fund Proceeds

Under the Canadian tax system, the returns on investment made by mutual funds is taxable in the hands of the investors and not to the management company or the fund, provided that the proceeds are paid out annually to the investors (hence being taxable for them). Every year, the mutual fund will issue a statement to the investor as to the amount of taxable capital gains and dividend or interest income that has been recognized. This practice can be viewed favourably as ensuring that there is no liability being built up for taxes, contingent upon disposal of the shares in the mutual fund; on the other hand, it is necessary to keep track of the accumulated annual declarations when the shares are finally sold. Typically, the recognized proceeds are not distributed but are reinvested in additional shares, even though the taxes must be paid annually. Consequently, the holding in the fund grows in keeping with its performance; however, the difference in value, as of disposition, from its original value does not reflect the recognizable gain that must be declared.

The pass-through of investment income has one important disadvantage for individual investors. If you manage your own portfolio, you decide when to realize capital gains and losses on any security; therefore, you can time those realizations to efficiently manage your tax liabilities. When you invest through a mutual fund, however, the timing of the sale of securities from the portfolio is out of your control, which reduces your ability to engage in tax management. Of course, if the mutual fund is held in a tax-deferred retirement account such as an RRSP account, these tax management issues are irrelevant.

A fund with a high portfolio turnover rate can be particularly "tax-inefficient." **Turnover** is the ratio of the trading activity of a portfolio to the assets of the portfolio. It measures the fraction of the portfolio that is "replaced" each year. For example, a $100 million portfolio with $50 million in sales of some securities with purchases of other securities would have a turnover rate of 50 percent. High turnover means that capital gains or losses are being realized constantly, and therefore that the investor cannot time the realizations to manage his or her overall tax obligation. The boxed article here focuses on the importance of turnover rates on tax efficiency.

CONCEPT CHECK

2. An investor's portfolio currently is worth $1 million. During the year, the investor sells 1,000 shares of Nortel at a price of $80 per share and 2,000 shares of Brascan at a price of $40 per share. The proceeds are used to buy 1,600 shares of Royal Bank at $100 per share.
   a. What was the portfolio turnover rate?
   b. If the shares in Nortel were originally purchased for $70 each and those in Brascan were purchased for $35, and the investor's tax rate on capital gains income is 20 percent, how much extra will the investor owe on this year's taxes as a result of these transactions?

Information on Mutual Funds

Beside the tax effects on mutual fund returns, which apply to all funds, there are two major issues that are particular to the choice of specified funds, namely the fees that are charged by the management companies and the success that they have in managing the funds. Both of these crucial pieces of information can be obtained *in one form or another*. That qualifying phrase is there to indicate that what funds may advertise about their fees and performance will tend to cast them in a favourable light that may omit some of the relevant factors; for example, the advertised return is likely to be for the best-performing funds without mention of the benchmark index or the risk involved. What is needed is an independent appraisal service that presents information in a consistent and complete manner.

LOW "TURNOVERS" MAY TASTE VERY GOOD TO FUND OWNERS

With lower capital-gains tax rates in store, mutual-fund investors are going to be rewarded by portfolio managers who believe in one of the stock market's most effective strategies: buy and hold.

This is because, under the new federal tax agreement, investors will face lower taxes from stock mutual funds that pay out little in the way of dividends and hold onto their gains for as long as they can.

So, how can you find such funds? The best way is to track a statistic called "turnover." Turnover rates are disclosed in a fund's annual report, prospectus and, many times, in the semi-annual report.

Turnover measures how much trading a fund does. A fund with 100% turnover is one that, on average, holds onto its positions for one year before selling them. A fund with a turnover of 50% "turns over" half of its portfolio in a year; that is, after six months it has replaced about half of its portfolio.

Funds with low turnover generate fewer taxes each year. Consider the nation's top two largest mutual funds, Fidelity Magellan and Vanguard Index Trust 500 Portfolio. The Vanguard fund, with an extremely low turnover rate of 5%, handed its investors less of an annual bill the past three years than Magellan, which had a turnover rate of 155%. Diversified U.S. stock funds on average have a turnover rate of close to 90%.

Vanguard Index Trust 500 Portfolio, at $42 billion the second-largest fund in the country, has low turnover, and as an index fund you'd expect it to stay that way. Index funds buy and hold a basket of stocks to try to match the performance of a market benchmark—in this case, the Standard & Poor's 500 Index.

But turnover isn't a constant. Though Fidelity Magellan, at $58 billion the largest fund in the nation, shows a high turnover rate of 155%, that's because its new manager Robert Stansky has been revamping the fund since he took over from Jeffrey Vinik last year. The turnover rate could well go down, along with Magellan's taxable distributions, as Mr. Stansky settles in.

It makes sense that turnover would offer clues about how much tax a fund would generate. Funds that just buy and hold stocks, such as index funds, aren't selling stocks that generate gains. So an investor has to pay taxes only when he sells the low-turnover fund, if the fund has appreciated in value.

On the other hand, a fund that trades in a frenzy could generate lots of short-term gains. For instance, a fund sells XYZ Corp. after three months, realizing a gain of $1 million. Then it buys ABC Corp., and sells it after two months, realizing a gain of, say $2 million. By law, these gains have to be distributed to investors, who then have to pay taxes on them, and since they're short-term gains, the tax rate is higher.

Fans of low-turnover funds say that, in general, such portfolios have had higher total returns than high-turnover funds. There are always exceptions, of course: Peter Lynch, former skipper of giant Fidelity Magellan fund, racked up huge returns while trading stocks like they were baseball cards. Still, one reason low-turnover funds might have higher returns is that they don't incur the hidden costs of trading, such as commissions paid to brokers, that can drain away a fund's returns.

Source: Robert McGough, "Low 'Turnovers' May Taste Very Good to Fund Owners in Wake of Tax Deal," *The Wall Street Journal,* July 31, 1997, p. C1. Reprinted by permission of The Wall Street Journal, © 1997 Down Jones & Company, Inc. All rights reserved worldwide.

Mutual Funds Performance
www.globefunds.com
www.morningstar.ca

The most widely available report on mutual funds is published regularly by the major financial newspapers in Canada. For example, *The Globe and Mail*'s Report on Business survey of mutual funds appears monthly and provides a summary of the realized performance of Canadian funds. In an attempt to provide meaningful comparisons, the funds are grouped by type, including: balanced, dividend (income), Canadian equity, U.S. equity, international equity, as well as money market, bond, mortgage, and real estate funds; the Canadian, U.S., and international equity funds ought to be growth-oriented by contrast with the balanced and dividend funds. The report also provides a measure of volatility on a one-to-five scale. The tables within the report list returns for periods ranging from three months to ten years, where these are net of management fees and include reinvestment of dividends. An average for the group is given in addition to other individual information of interest to investors, including details of sales commissions or "loads." Online sources include Globefunds.com and Morningstar.ca.

A far more informative appraisal is provided by firms whose primary purpose is to track performance of managers for funds who are their clients. Individual components of performance are measured to examine the success or failure of the manager in beating the index or the average of similar-objective funds. There are four major services that specialize in providing these analyses in Canada: SEI Financial Services, Comstat Capital Sciences, CTUCS, and Intersec Research Corp. Between them they track performance for over 2,000 investment portfolios.

www.morningstar.ca

Software providing similar information also is available to individuals to aid in the assessment of funds. For instance, Morningstar Canada provides statistical information about mutual funds on line through software called "PALTrak." The data provided include performance, management expense ratios and load structures, characterization as to purpose, asset allocation, NAV, dividend payouts, and other relevant material. Similar material on U.S. mutual funds is available in *Investment Companies* by Wiesenberger Investment Company Services and in Morningstar Inc's principle software. Figure 4.4 shows a sample of PALTrak analysis.

The PALTrak analysis comprises information of a tabular and graphical nature, with the latter including a comparative historical summary of the fund's returns, a breakdown of asset composition, and, in this example, a breakdown of the source of income. Tabular results include the major holdings and historical performance data such as returns and the net asset value. "General Information" summarizes the fees and MER, with a capsule description of the return and risk of

Figure 4.4 PALTrak analysis.

CI Signature Dividend

Benchmark : S&P/TSX 60
CIFSC Category : Canadian Dividend
Release date : November 30 2004

Morningstar Rating ★★★
Tax-Adjusted Ranking
Morningstar Style Box

Prepared by Isabell Grygianiec

Fund Summary

World Regions	% Assets
Canada	89.9
US	7.1
Latin America	0.0
Japan	0.0
Asia/Pac ex-Jap	0.0
UK	0.6
Europe ex-UK	2.4
Africa & MidEast	0.0
Other	0.0

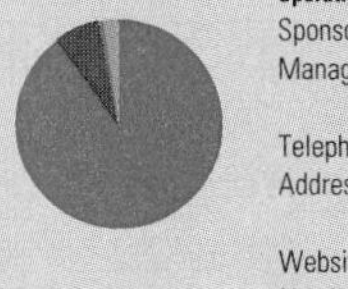

Operations	
Sponsor	CI Mutual Funds Inc.
Managers	Eric B. Bushell
	Benedict G. Cheng
Telephone	800 563 5181
Address	151 Yonge Street, 11th Floor,
	Toronto, ON, Canada, M5C 2W7
Website	http://www.cifunds.com
Net Assets	$1,601.26 mil

RRSP Eligibility	Yes
Minimum Initial Purchase	$500
Minimum RRSP Purchase	$500
Minimum Additional Purchase	$50
Sales Status	Open
Load	Deferred, Front, Low Load
Expense Ratio	1.96%
Management Fee	1.50%

Current Asset Weights

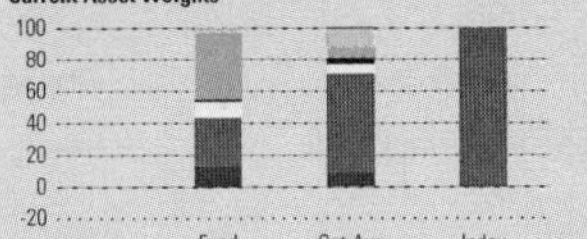

	Fund	Cat.Avg	Index
Cash	12.6	8.6	--
Cdn Eq	30.6	62.1	100.0
Fgn Eq	10.1	6.0	--
Cdn Bd	1.5	3.8	--
Fgn Bd	--	0.1	--
Other	0.9	0.0	--
Pref Eq	42.4	8.2	--
MBS	--	0.0	--
OtherDerivatives	--	0.0	--
Cdn In Trust	2.0	11.2	--
Fgn In Trust	--	0.0	--

Top Holdings as of 11-30-2004	% Assets
ABN Amro Bank Canada Short Term/D	12.24
Canadian Pac Rr Ltd Com	2.48
CIBC Pfd Cl A Ser 23	2.39
Toronto Dominion Ban Pfd 1st A Se	2.35
Manulife Financial C Common	2.34
Encana Corporation Common	2.34
Sun Life Financial I Common	2.33
Toronto Dominion Ban Common	2.05
Quebecor World Inc Pfd 1st Ser 3	1.83
BCE Inc Pfd 1st Ser Aa	1.59
Bnk of Montreal Common	1.57
Weston George Ltd Pfd Ser Ii	1.52
CIBC Pfd A Ser 22	1.44
Brascan Corp Pfd Cl-A Ser 2	1.42
Barrick Gold Corp Common	1.40
Total	39.28

Sector Weights as of 11-30-2004	Fund	Index
Information Economy	**3.2**	**14.4**
Software	--	0.6
Hardware	--	6.8
Media	--	1.5
Telecommunication	3.2	5.4
Service Economy	**45.2**	**44.2**
Healthcare Services	1.0	0.8
Consumer Services	--	2.8
Business Services	8.0	5.6
Financial Services	36.2	35.0
Manufacturing Economy	**51.6**	**41.4**
Consumer Goods	0.9	2.2
Industrial Goods	29.0	17.6
Energy	16.1	21.5
Utilities	5.6	--

Rolling History Table (Month End Values)

	Nov 04	Oct 04	Sep 04	Aug 04	Jul 04	Jun 04	May 04	Apr 04	Mar 04	Feb 04	Jan 04	Dec 03
NAVPS	12.970	12.780	12.720	12.550	12.540	12.510	12.420	12.337	12.690	12.740	12.550	12.530
Capital Gains	0.040	0.040	0.040	0.040	0.040	--	--	--	--	--	--	--
Dividends	--	--	--	--	--	0.040	0.040	0.040	0.040	0.040	0.040	0.040

Calendar Year Returns

CI Signature Dividend
Average Canadian Dividend - MF
S&P/TSX 60

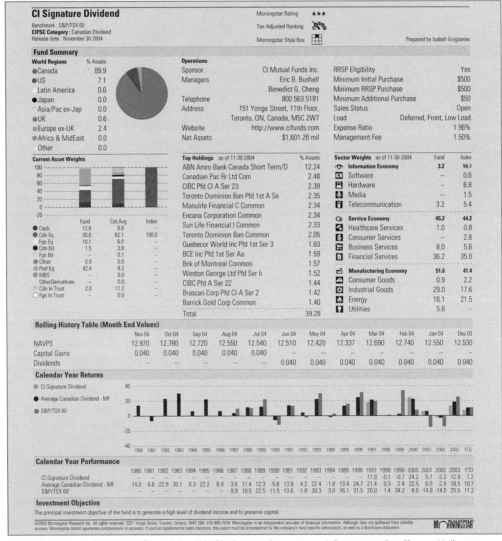

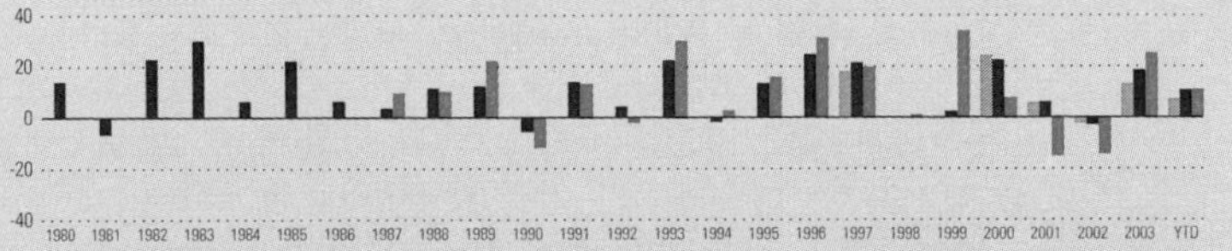

Calendar Year Performance

	1980	1981	1982	1983	1984	1985	1986	1987	1988	1989	1990	1991	1992
CI Signature Dividend	--	--	--	--	--	--	--	--	--	--	--	--	--
Average Canadian Dividend - MF	14.0	-6.6	22.9	30.1	6.3	22.2	6.4	3.6	11.4	12.3	-5.6	13.9	4.2
S&P/TSX 60	--	--	--	--	--	--	--	9.9	10.5	22.5	-11.5	13.6	-1.8

	1993	1994	1995	1996	1997	1998	1999	2000	2001	2002	2003	YTD
CI Signature Dividend	--	--	--	--	17.9	-0.1	-0.7	24.2	5.7	-2.3	12.9	7.2
Average Canadian Dividend - MF	22.4	-1.8	13.4	24.7	21.4	0.3	2.4	22.5	6.0	-2.9	18.5	10.7
S&P/TSX 60	30.3	3.0	16.1	31.5	20.0	1.4	34.2	8.0	-14.8	-14.0	25.5	11.2

Investment Objective

The principal investment objective of the fund is to generate a high level of dividend income and to preserve capital.

MORNINGSTAR

Source: Screen capture © Morningstar Research Inc., 2004. Morningstar makes no representations or warranties with respect to the accuracy, correctness, completeness, or timeliness of this publication or its content and any derivation thereof and specifically disclaims any implied or expressed warranties, including but not limited to any implied merchantability, fitness for a particular purpose, and accuracy of information content. Morningstar shall not be responsible for investment decisions, damages, or other losses resulting from the use of this book or its content. The advice and strategies contained herein may not be suitable for your situation. You should consult with a professional where applicable. Past performance of a mutual fund, stock, or other investment vehicle does not guarantee future performance.

the fund. Other fundamental analysis classifies ratios such as P/E and price to book in order to characterize the risk of the fund.

Morningstar Canada's parent, Morningstar Inc. issues reports on U.S. mutual funds that provide a more extensive range of useful information in descriptive, tabular and graphical form. One kind of information is qualitative, giving a narrative description of the type of securities held, the history, income strategy, and the investment policy; this can be far more informative than mere statistics. A list and analysis of the top holdings of the fund is also given. A number of key statistics are presented that help to identify the style of the fund, such as P/E and other price ratios, as well as capitalization of the holdings; these reveal the style with respect to size and to the value/growth dichotomy. Other information presented in tables and charts helps appraise the performance, both before and after expenses, and absolutely or relative to the benchmark index; both recent and long-run performance is shown.

A more ambitious section deals with the risk-return issue. Morningstar compares the returns of the fund with those of other funds having similar investment policies. The report also details how often the returns trail the T-bill rate as a measure of downside risk. Once again, this measure of risk performance is compared with the average of similar funds. Another interesting section considers the tax efficiency of the fund management by comparing after-tax and pretax returns and calculating their ratio as a measure. Finally, a tabulation of the associated expenses enables clear comparison with other funds.

4.4 COSTS OF INVESTING IN MUTUAL FUNDS

Fee Structure

Front- and Back-End Load These fees are paid to cover commissions for selling agents and to deter rapid switching in and out of funds, which is detrimental to keeping the assets fully invested in long-term assets. The front-end load typically can be as high as 8 percent, so that a $1,000 investment only leaves $920 invested in a portfolio; discount brokers will often cut their commission to lower the load fee to the investor, and larger investments rapidly lead to a lower charge. Back-end loads leave the initial investment intact but usually charge 6 percent in the first year, falling by a percent per year, for redemptions; the load may apply to the initial or the final asset value. In addition, there are many no-load funds, which appear to have no poorer performance than their costly cousins.

Operating Expenses These expenses refer to the costs incurred by the mutual fund in operating the portfolio, including administrative expenses and advisory fees paid to the investment manager. These expenses usually are expressed as a percent of total assets under management and may range from .2 to 2.5 percent. Funds may voluntarily lower the actual expenses charged to the portfolio if they are lower than specified by the prospectus. Shareholders do not receive an explicit bill for these operating expenses; however, the expenses are periodically deducted from the assets of the fund. Shareholders pay these expenses through the reduction in the value of their share of the fund portfolio.

Other Charges These refer to charges against the asset value for expenses due to distribution costs such as advertising, promotional literature including prospectuses and annual reports, and commissions paid to brokers (which may be alternative or additional to load fees and which include the trailer fees). (These are specifically referred to in the United States as "12b-1 charges.")

The combination of operating expenses and other charges is expressed as a ratio of total assets and is then referred to as the **management expense ratio**. Other expenses such as switching fees between funds in the family may be charged. The *Mutual Fund Sourcebook* published by Southam Information Products Ltd. provides data on fees for Canadian funds.

Fees and Mutual Fund Returns

The rate of return on an investment in a mutual fund is measured as the increase or decrease in net asset value plus income distributions such as dividends or distributions of capital gains expressed as a fraction of net asset value at the beginning of the investment period. If we denote the net asset value at the start and end of the period as NAV_0 and NAV_1, respectively, then

$$\text{Rate of return} = \frac{NAV_1 - NAV_0 + \text{Income and capital gain distributions}}{NAV_0}$$

For example, if a fund has an initial NAV of \$20 at the start of the month, makes income distributions of \$.15 and capital gain distributions of \$.05, and ends the month with NAV of \$20.10, the monthly rate of return is computed as

$$\text{Rate of return} = \frac{\$20.10 - \$20 + \$.15 + \$.05}{\$20} = 0.15, \text{ or } 1.5\%$$

Notice that this measure of the rate of return ignores any commissions such as front-end loads paid to purchase the fund.

On the other hand, the rate of return is affected by the fund's expenses and other fees. This is because such charges are periodically deducted from the portfolio, which reduces net asset value. Thus the rate of return on the fund equals the gross return on the underlying portfolio minus the total expense ratio.

To see how expenses can affect rate of return, consider a fund with \$100 million in assets at the start of the year and with 10 million shares outstanding. The fund invests in a portfolio of stocks that provides no income but increases in value by 10 percent. The expense ratio, including other charges, is 1 percent. What is the rate of return for an investor in the fund?

The initial NAV equals \$100 million/10 million shares = \$10 per share. In the absence of expenses, fund assets would grow to \$110 million and NAV would grow to \$11 per share, for a 10 percent rate of return. However, the expense ratio of the fund is 1 percent. Therefore, \$1 million will be deducted from the fund to pay these fees, leaving the portfolio worth only \$109 million, and NAV equal to \$10.90. The rate of return on the fund is only 9 percent, which equals the gross return on the underlying portfolio minus the total expense ratio.

Fees can have a big effect on performance. Table 4.6 considers an investor who starts with \$10,000 and can choose between three funds that all earn an annual 12 percent return on investment before fees but have different fee structures. The table shows the cumulative amount in each fund after several investment horizons. Fund A has total operating expenses of .5 percent, no load, and no other charges. This might represent an index fund. Fund B has no load but has 1 percent in management expenses and .5 percent in other charges. This level of charges is fairly typical of actively managed equity funds. Finally, Fund C has 1 percent in management expenses, no other charges, but assesses an 8 percent front-end load on purchases. Note the substantial return advantage of low-cost Fund A. Moreover, that differential is greater for longer investment horizons.

Although expenses can have a big impact on net investment performance, it is sometimes difficult for the investor in a mutual fund to measure true expenses accurately. This is because of the common practice of paying for some expenses in **soft dollars**. A portfolio manager earns soft-dollar credits with a stockbroker by directing the fund's trades to that broker. On the basis of those credits, the broker will pay for some of the mutual fund's expenses, such as databases, computer hardware, or stock quotation systems. The soft-dollar arrangement means that the stockbroker effectively returns part of the trading commission to the fund. The advantage of the mutual fund is that purchases made with soft dollars are not included in the fund's expenses, so the fund

Table 4.6 Impact of Costs on Investment Performance

	Cumulative Proceeds (all dividends reinvested)		
	Fund A	Fund B	Fund C
Initial investment*	$10,000	$10,000	$ 9,200
5 years	17,187	16,341	15,419
10 years	29,540	26,702	25,842
15 years	50,771	43,633	43,310
20 years	87,261	71,299	72,586

*After front-end load, if any.

Notes

1. Fund A is no-load with .5 percent expense ratio.
2. Fund B is no-load with 1.5 percent expense ratio.
3. Fund C has an 8 percent load on purchase and reinvested dividends, with a 1 percent expense ratio.
4. Gross return on all funds is 12 percent per year before expenses. Net returns are 1.12(1 – X%).

can advertise an unrealistically low expense ratio to the public. Although the fund may have paid the broker needlessly high commissions to obtain the soft-dollar "rebate," trading costs are not included in the fund's expenses. The impact of the higher trading commission shows up instead in net investment performance. Soft-dollar arrangements make it difficult for investors to compare fund expenses, and periodically these arrangements come under attack. Canadian regulations limit the soft-dollar arrangements that may be made.

CONCEPT CHECK

3. The Equity Fund sells Class A shares with a front-end load of 6 percent and Class B shares with other charges of .4 percent annually as well as back-end load fees that start at 5 percent and fall by 1 percent for each full year the investor holds the portfolio (until the fifth year). Assume the rate of return on the fund portfolio net of operating expenses is 10 percent annually. What will be the value of a $10,000 investment in Class A and Class B shares if the shares are sold after (*a*) one year, (*b*) four years, (*c*) eight years? Which fee structure provides higher net proceeds at the end of the investment horizon?

4.5 MUTUAL FUND INVESTMENT PERFORMANCE

We noted earlier that one of the benefits of mutual funds for the individual investor is the ability to delegate management of the portfolio to investment professionals. The investor retains control over the broad features of the overall portfolio through the asset allocation decision: each individual chooses the percentages of the portfolio to invest in bond funds versus equity funds versus money market funds, and so forth, but can leave the specific security selection decisions within each investment class to the managers of each fund. Shareholders hope that these portfolio managers can achieve better investment performance than they could obtain on their own.

What is the investment record of the mutual fund industry? This seemingly straightforward question is deceptively difficult to answer because we need a standard against which to evaluate performance. For example, we clearly would not want to compare the investment performance of an equity fund to the rate of return available in the money market. The vast differences in the risk of these two markets dictate that year-by-year as well as average performance will differ considerably. We would expect to find that equity funds outperform money market funds (on average) as compensation to investors for the extra risk incurred in equity markets. How then can we determine whether mutual fund portfolio managers are performing up to par *given* the level of risk they incur? In other words, what is the proper benchmark against which investment performance ought to be evaluated?

Measuring portfolio risk properly and using such measures to choose an appropriate benchmark is an extremely difficult task. We devote all of Parts Two and Three of the text to issues surrounding the proper measurement of portfolio risk and the tradeoff between risk and return. In this chapter, therefore, we will satisfy ourselves with a first look at the question of fund performance by using only very simple performance benchmarks and ignoring the more subtle issues of risk differences across funds. However, we will return to this topic in Chapter 20, where we take a closer look at mutual fund performance after adjusting for differences in the exposure of portfolios to various sources of risk.

www.nyse.com

Here[5] we use as a benchmark for the performance of equity fund managers the rate of return on the Wilshire 5000 Index. Recall from Chapter 2 that this is a value-weighted index of about 7,000 stocks that trade on the NYSE, Nasdaq, and Amex stock markets. It is the most inclusive index of the performance of U.S. equities. The performance of the Wilshire 5000 is a useful benchmark with which to evaluate professional managers because it corresponds to a simple passive investment strategy: buy all the shares in the index in proportion to their outstanding market value. Moreover, this is a feasible strategy for even small investors, because the Vanguard Group offers an index fund (its Total Stock Market Portfolio) designed to replicate the performance of the Wilshire 5000 Index. The expense ratio of the fund is extremely small by the standards of other equity funds, only .25 percent per year. Using the Wilshire 5000 Index as a benchmark, we may pose the problem of evaluating the performance of mutual fund portfolio managers this way: How does the typical performance of actively managed equity mutual funds compare to the performance of a passively managed portfolio that simply replicates the composition of a broad index of the stock market?

Casual comparisons of the performance of the Wilshire 5000 index versus that of professionally managed mutual fund portfolios show disappointing results for most fund managers. Figure 4.5 shows the percentage of mutual fund managers whose performance was inferior in each year to the Wilshire 5000. In more years than not, the Index has outperformed the median manager.[6] In fact, as

Figure 4.5 Percent of equity mutual funds outperformed by Wilshire 5000 Index, 1972–2001.

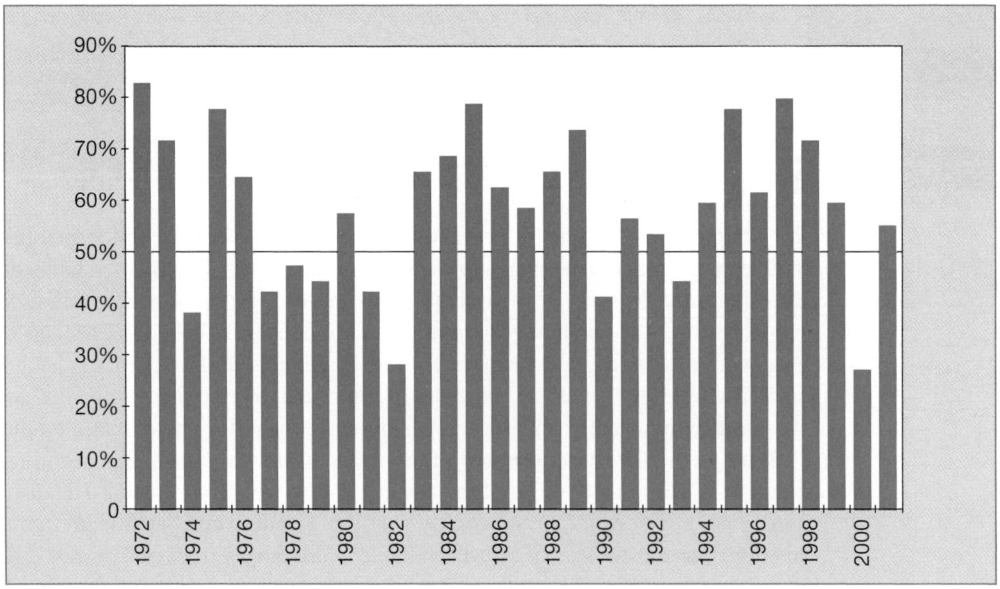

Source: The Vanguard Group.

[5] We use U.S. data here due to the extensive study conducted.

[6] Of course, actual funds incur trading costs while the Wilshire index does not. Vanguard's Wilshire 5000 fund charges an expense ratio of .20 percent, and, because it engages in little trading, it incurs low trading costs. To facilitate the comparison in Figure 4.5, the returns on the Wilshire 5000 Index were reduced by .30 percent.

Figure 4.6 shows, since 1971 the compound return of the Wilshire 5000 was 14.01 percent versus 12.44 percent for the average fund. The 1.57 percent margin is substantial.

This result may seem surprising to you. After all, it would not seem unreasonable to expect that professional money managers should be able to outperform a very simple rule such as "hold an indexed portfolio." As it turns out, however, there may be good reasons to expect such a result. We explore them in detail in Chapter 9, where we discuss the efficient market hypothesis.

Persistence in Performance

Of course, one might argue that there are good managers and bad managers, and that the good managers can, in fact, consistently outperform the index. To test this notion, we examine whether managers with good performance in one year are likely to repeat that performance in a following year. In other words, is superior performance in any particular year due to luck, and therefore random, or due to skill, and therefore consistent from year to year?

To answer this question, Goetzmann and Ibbotson[7] examined the performance of a large sample of equity mutual fund portfolios over the 1976–1985 period. Dividing the funds into two groups based on total investment return for different subperiods, they posed the question: "Do funds with investment returns in the top half of the sample in one two-year period continue to perform well in the subsequent two-year period?"

Panel A of Table 4.7 presents a summary of their results. The table shows the fraction of "winners" (i.e., top-half performers) in the initial period that turn out to be winners or losers in the following two-year period. If performance were purely random from one period to the next, there would be entries of 50 percent in each cell of the table, as top- or bottom-half performers would be equally likely to perform in either the top or the bottom half of the sample in the following period. On the other hand, if performance were due entirely to skill, with no randomness, we would expect to see entries of 100 percent on the diagonals and entries of 0 percent on the off-diagonals:

Figure 4.6
Growth of $1 invested in Wilshire 5000 Index Versus Average General Equity Fund.

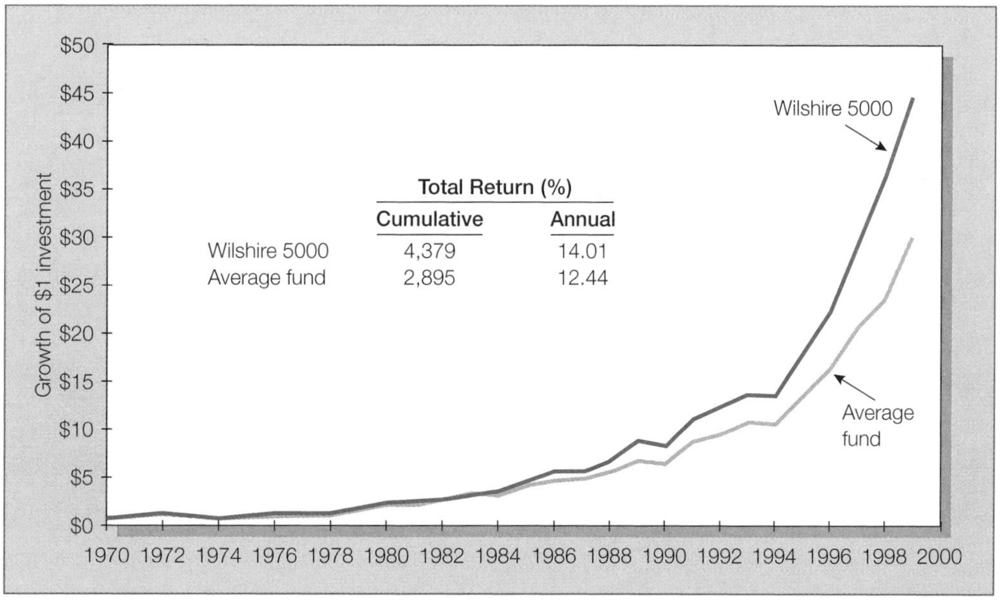

Source: The Vanguard Group.

[7] William N. Goetzmann and Roger G. Ibbotson, "Do Winners Repeat?" *Journal of Portfolio Management*, Winter 1994, pp. 9–18.

Table 4.7 Consistency of Investment Results

Initial-Period Performance	Successive-Period Performance (%) Top Half	Bottom Half
A. Goetzmann and Ibbotson study		
Top half	62.0	38.0
Bottom half	36.6	63.4
B. Malkiel study, 1970s		
Top half	65.1	34.9
Bottom half	35.5	64.5
C. Malkiel study, 1980s		
Top half	51.7	48.3
Bottom half	47.5	52.5

Source: Panel A: William N. Goetzmann and Roger G. Ibbotson, "Do Winners Repeat?" *Journal of Portfolio Management*, Winter 1994, pp. 9–18; Panels B and C: Burton G. Malkiel, "Returns from Investing in Equity Mutual Funds 1971–1991," *Journal of Finance* 50 (June 1995), pp. 549–572.

top-half performers would all remain in the top half while bottom-half performers similarly would all remain in the bottom half. In fact, the table shows that 62.0 percent of initial top-half performers fall in the top half of the sample in the following period, while 63.4 percent of initial bottom-half performers fall in the bottom half in the following period. This evidence is consistent with the notion that at least part of a fund's performance is a function of skill as opposed to luck, so that relative performance tends to persist from one period to the next.[8]

On the other hand, this relationship does not seem stable across different sample periods. Malkiel[9] uses a larger sample, but a similar methodology (except that he uses one-year instead of two-year investment returns) to examine performance consistency. He finds that while initial-year performance predicts subsequent-year performance in the 1970s (see Table 4.7, panel B), the pattern of persistence in performance virtually disappears in the 1980s (panel C).

To summarize, the evidence that performance is consistent from one period to the next is suggestive, but it is inconclusive. In the 1970s, top-half funds in one year were twice as likely in the following year to be in the top half as the bottom half of funds. In the 1980s, the odds that a top-half fund would fall in the top half in the following year were essentially equivalent to those of a coin flip.

There have been a number of studies of Canadian fund performance, which have focused on various effects such as size, inflation, performance in up and down markets, and signs of managerial expertise. Fund performance for the period 1967–1984 was analyzed by Bishara,[10] who concluded that Canadian funds could not outperform the market. He subdivided his fund universe into balanced, income, and growth funds and considered their returns over boom and recession periods. His findings concluded that while growth funds managed to match the index return, the balanced and income funds were inferior to the index over the whole period and during one boom. A study by Calvet and Lefoll[11] used 17 mutual funds and considered the effect of inflation. Only one of the funds was able to outperform the market by one measure of performance and none did by other traditional measures; inflation offered no explanation for the results.

[8]Another possibility is that performance consistency is due to variation in fee structure across funds. We return to this possibility in Chapter 9.

[9]Burton G. Malkiel, "Returns from Investing in Equity Funds 1971–1991," *Journal of Finance* 50 (June 1995), pp. 549–572.

[10]H. Bishara, "Evaluation of the Performance of Canadian Mutual Funds (1967–1984)," *Proceedings of the Administrative Sciences Association of Canada* 1, part 1 (1987), p. 18.

[11]A. L. Calvet and J. Lefoll, "The CAPM Under Inflation and the Performance of Canadian Mutual Funds," *Journal of Business Administration* 12, no. 1 (Fall 1980).

Other studies suggest that bad performance is more likely to persist than good performance. This makes some sense: it is easy to identify fund characteristics that will predictably lead to consistently poor investment performance, notably high expense ratios, and high turnover ratios with associated trading costs. It is far harder to identify the secrets of successful stock picking. (If it were easy, we would all be rich!) Thus the consistency we do observe in fund performance may be due in large part to the poor performers. On the other hand, the phenomenon of "survivorship bias"—the worst performers go out of business—implies that statistics based on surviving funds are upwardly biased. This suggests that the real value of past performance data is to avoid truly poor funds, even if identifying the future top performers is still a daunting task.

CONCEPT CHECK

4. Suppose you observe the investment performance of 200 portfolio managers and rank them by investment returns during the year. Of the managers in the top half of the sample, 40 percent are truly skilled, but the other 60 percent fell in the top half purely because of good luck. What fraction of these top-half managers would you expect to be top-half performers next year?

Exchange-Traded Funds—Superior Performance

Exchange-traded funds (ETFs) are products that allow investors to trade index portfolios just as they do shares of individual stocks. The first ETF was the TIP (Toronto Index Participation unit), which represented a share of the TSE 35 index value; this predated the first U.S. ETF known as the "spider," a nickname for SPDR or S&P Depositary Receipt, which was a unit investment trust holding a portfolio based on the S&P 500 index. TIPs were expanded by the creation of TIPs on the TSE 100, which is a closer approximation of a broad index such as the S&P 500.

These ETFs give investors the diversification advantage of a large mutual fund but allow trading throughout the day, like ordinary shares, rather than at the closing value like mutual funds. The U.S. market added to spiders by devising the "cubes" (from the symbol QQQ for the Nasdaq 100 index unit) and the "diamonds" (from DIA for the Dow-Jones Industrials); these permitted investments in either the technology-heavy Nasdaq or the conservative Dow. Cubes and spiders are consistently the most heavily traded securities on U.S. exchanges, with average daily volume of nearly 100 million and 40 million, respectively. For Canadian investors, these are excellent vehicles for U.S. diversification.

With the creation of the new S&P/TSX 60 Index, TIPs were replaced by iUnits, called the i60s. iUnits are index securities issued by BGI Canada (Barclays Global) based on the new S&P/TSX 60 Index and sub-indices. The i60, trading under the symbol XIU, is the basic index security for the TSX. Canadian ETFs include a variety of Barclays products with a capped index, portfolios of IT, financial, energy, and gold companies, fixed-income funds on 5- and 10-year Canadas, and a Canadian-listed S&P 500 fund. These have been designed to reflect the primary interests of Canadian investors.

Technically, ETFs are securities that participate in an open-ended fund. In the case of i60s, the fund is established by BGI and holds a portfolio of the 60 stocks in the index. They are listed like common shares and pay dividends, as well as being marginable. These units allow small investors to hold a portfolio of senior Canadian firms diversified across the economy, similarly to owning a mutual fund but escaping the management fee. Acceptance is high, with the i60 being the largest Canadian mutual fund for Canadian securities, and the fifth most actively traded security on the exchange in 2000.

Many other ETFs now exist. TD Asset Management has launched four ETFs capturing the composite index, a capped index, plus a value- and a growth-focused index. Foreign index shares can be bought as part of the S&P international index portfolio as iShares based on either S&P global funds or Morgan Stanley country indices (MSCI). Sectors of the U.S. market can be bought again as iShares linked to almost all the recognized U.S. indices, as SPDR Selects on industry groups, as Merrill Lynch HOLDRS, and as S&P Global industry sector indices. (See Table 4.8 for a list of some issuers and products.) In addition, chartered banks may trade their index funds as ETFs.

ETFs offer several advantages over conventional mutual funds. First, as we just noted, a mutual fund's net asset value is quoted—and therefore, investors can buy or sell their shares in the fund—only once a day. In contrast, ETFs trade continuously. Moreover, like other shares, but unlike mutual funds, ETFs can be sold short or purchased on margin.

ETFs also offer a potential tax advantage over mutual funds. When large numbers of mutual fund investors redeem their shares, the fund must sell securities to meet the redemptions. This can trigger large capital gains taxes, which are passed through to and must be paid by the remaining shareholders. In contrast, when small investors wish to redeem their position in an ETF, they simply sell their shares to other traders, with no need for the fund to sell any of the underlying portfolio. Again, a redemption does not trigger a stock sale by the fund sponsor.

ETFs are also cheaper than mutual funds. Investors who buy ETFs do so through brokers rather than buying directly from the fund. Therefore, the fund saves the cost of marketing itself directly to small investors. This reduction in expenses translates into lower management fees. For example, Barclays charges annual expenses of just over 9 basis points (i.e., .09 percent) of net asset value per year on its S&P 500 ETF, whereas Vanguard charges 18 basis points on its S&P 500 index mutual fund.

Table 4.8 ETF Sponsors and Products

A. ETF Sponsors

Sponsor	Product Name
Barclays Global Investors	i-Shares
Merrill Lynch	HOLDRS (Holding Company Depository Receipts: "Holders")
StateStreet/Merrill Lynch	Select Sector SPDRs (S&P Depository Receipts: "Spiders")
Vanguard	VIPER (Vanguard Index Participation Equity Receipts: "Vipers")

B. Sample of ETF Products

Name	Ticker	Index Tracked
Broad U.S. indices		
Spiders	SPY	S&P 500
Diamonds	DIA	Dow Jones Industrials
Cubes	QQQ	Nasdaq 100
iShares Russell 2000	IWM	Russell 2000
VIPERS	VTI	Wilshire 5000
Industry indices		
Energy Select Spider	XLE	S&P 500 energy companies
iShares Energy Sector	IYE	Dow Jones energy companies
Financial Sector Spider	XLF	S&P 500 financial companies
iShares Financial Sector	IYF	Dow Jones financial companies
International indices		
WEBS United Kingdom	EWU	MCSI U.K. Index
WEBS France	EWQ	MCSI France Index
WEBS Japan	EWJ	MCSI Japan Index

ETFS ARE SECURITIES, NOT MUTUAL FUNDS

One investment innovation that has proliferated in Canada recently is the exchange-traded fund, or ETF. Since 1999, no fewer than 16 ETFs have been introduced on to the Toronto Stock Exchange, and collectively they have grown to represent close to $5-billion in investor assets. Investors can now buy these funds based on global, U.S. or domestic stocks, bonds and even investment trusts. And they are as easy to buy as common shares.

Because they are relatively new, investors know little about the benefits or pitfalls of these funds. Like mutual funds, ETFs represent a pooled basket of securities. However, rather than requiring active management, these funds simply mimic the content, and hence the performance, of a particular market index or sub-index, such as the S&P/TSX 60. Like indexed mutual funds, this so-called passive investment provides the same yields as the index that is being followed. That is not bad, considering few fund managers ever beat the market averages with any consistency.

Indexation tends to be cheaper than active management (nothing to study or research—just copy the index), meaning investors keep more of their profits. Most actively managed Canadian equity mutual funds, for example, have management expense ratios, or MERs, ranging from 1.5% to 3% of total assets per year, whereas index funds have expense ratios of 0.3% to 1%.

ETFs tend to be even cheaper than index funds, with management fees capped at levels between 0.17% and 0.55%. That is largely because they are actual securities with value pegged to an index, rather than being an assemblage of stocks or other securities that must be maintained at all times to reflect the holdings that constitute the index. That MER differential can make an enormous difference in the long term. A $10,000 investment today in an equity fund earning an average annual compound yield of, say, 10%, with a MER of 2.5%, would grow to $20,610 (pre-tax) after 10 years; in an ETF earning 10% with a MER of 0.25% it would grow to $25,354.

Since ETFs are actual securities, they can be traded like stocks on a stock exchange. That means they can be bought or sold at market value anytime during trading hours, not just at the end of each day like many mutual funds. They also tend to track their indexes more accurately than indexed mutual funds. There are tax benefits as well. Foreign ETFs, such as the iUnits S&P 500 Index RSP Fund, are, as the name [implies], RRSP-eligible. ETFs also produce fewer taxable distributions to unitholders, since portfolios are adjusted only to reflect changes in the underlying index.

All of these features have led many Canadian investors to move at least some money into ETFs. But while the benefits are undeniable, there is a potential downside to ETFs and to passive investing in general.

Although investors never earn less than the market average, they also never earn more. During the recent market downturn, the S&P/TSX Composite index lost half its value, yet some Canadian equity funds actually continued to post modest annual gains, so there is something to be said for having an investment with active management. Many mutual fund managers outperform the markets at times, although few are able to do so consistently.

Ultimately, the choice between passive and active investment is a personal one. Many investors combine the two. Given their cost-efficiency, ETFs certainly merit consideration as a conservative component in any equity portfolio.

Source: Olev Edur, "ETFs Are Securities, Not Mutual Funds," Special Report, Financial Post, Investing Guide, *National Post*, October 30, 2003, p. SR-05. © National Post, Don Mills, ON.

There are some disadvantages to ETFs, however. Because they trade as securities, there is the possibility that their prices can depart by small amounts from net asset value. This discrepancy cannot be too large without giving rise to arbitrage opportunities for large traders, but even small discrepancies can easily swamp the cost advantage of ETFs over mutual funds. Second, while mutual funds can be bought at no expense from no-load funds, ETFs must be purchased from brokers for a fee. (See the boxed article.)

SUMMARY

1. When discussing the principles of portfolio management, it is useful to distinguish seven classes of investors:
   a. Individual investors and personal trusts
   b. Mutual funds
   c. Pension funds
   d. Endowment funds
   e. Life insurance companies
   f. Nonlife insurance companies
   g. Banks

   In general, these groups have somewhat different investment objectives, constraints, and portfolio policies.
2. To some extent, most institutional investors seek to match the risk and return characteristics of their investment portfolios to the characteristics of their liabilities.
3. As an alternative to investing in securities through a broker, many individuals invest in mutual funds and other investment companies. Mutual funds are classified according to whether they are open-end or closed-end, whether they are load or no-load, and by the type of securities in which they invest. Real estate limited partnerships are specialized investment companies that invest in real estate; mortgage funds invest in loans secured by real estate.
4. Net asset value equals the market value of assets held by a fund minus the liabilities of the fund divided by the shares outstanding.
5. Mutual funds free the individual from many of the administrative burdens of owning individual securities and offer professional management of the portfolio. They also offer advantages that are available only to large-scale investors, such as discounted trading costs. On the other hand, funds are assessed management fees and incur other expenses, which reduce the investor's rate of return. Funds also eliminate some of the individual's control over the timing of capital gains realizations.
6. Mutual funds are often categorized by investment policy. Major policy groups include money market funds; equity funds, which are further grouped according to emphasis on income versus growth; fixed-income funds; balanced and income funds; asset allocation funds; index funds; and specialized sector funds.
7. Costs of investing in mutual funds include front-end loads, which are sales charges; back-end loads, which are redemption fees or, more properly, contingent-deferred sales charges; fund operating expenses; and other charges, which are recurring fees used to pay for the expenses of marketing the fund to the public.
8. Income earned on mutual fund portfolios is not taxed at the level of the fund. Instead, as long as the fund meets certain requirements for pass-through status, the income is treated as being earned by the investors in the fund.
9. The average rate of return of the average equity mutual fund in the last 25 years has been below that of a passive index fund holding a portfolio to replicate a broad-based index like the TSX Composite, S&P 500, or Wilshire 5000. Some of the reasons for this disappointing record are the costs incurred by actively managed funds, such as the expense of conducting the research to guide stock-picking activities, and trading costs due to higher portfolio turnover. The record on the consistency of fund performance is mixed. In some sample periods, the better-performing funds continue to perform well in the following periods; in other sample periods they do not.
10. Exchange-traded funds (ETFs) are index securities trading on the exchanges that provide low-cost alternatives to mutual funds.

KEY TERMS

personal trusts 100
defined-contribution plans 101
defined-benefit plans 101
endowment funds 101
whole-life insurance policy 101
term insurance 101
variable life 102
universal life 102
insured defined-benefit pension 102
liquidity 102
investment horizon 103
prudent person 103
investment company 104
net asset value (NAV) 104
managed funds 104
open-end funds 105
closed-end funds 105
load 105
commingled funds 106
real estate limited partnership 107
mortgage funds 107
segregated funds 107
hedge funds 107
index fund 111
turnover 112
management expense ratio 115
soft dollars 116
exchange-traded funds (ETFs) 121

SELECTED READINGS

For a collection of essays presenting the Institute of Chartered Financial Analysts' approach to portfolio management, see:

Ambachtsheer, Keith P. "Strategic Approaches to Asset Allocation." *Asset Allocation for Institutional Portfolios*, The Institute of CFAs, 1988.

Maginn, John L., and David L. Tuttle (eds.). *Managing Investment Portfolios: A Dynamic Analysis*, 2nd edition. Boston: Warren, Gorham, & Lamont, 1990.

A number of interesting articles appear under the collective theme "Investment Management: A New Look" in the special edition of:

Canadian Investment Review IV, no. 1 (Spring 1991).

PROBLEMS

CFA® PROBLEMS

1. (Level I) Assume it is now 1998. Several discussion meetings have provided the following information about one of your firm's new advisory clients, a charitable endowment fund recently created by means of a one-time $10,000,000 gift:

   Objectives

   - *Return requirement.* Planning is based on a minimum total return of 8 percent per year, including an initial current income component of $500,000 (5 percent on beginning capital). Realizing this current income target is the endowment fund's primary return goal. (See "Unique needs.")

   Constraints

   - *Time horizon.* Perpetuity, except for requirement to make an $8,500,000 cash distribution on June 30, 1998. (See "Unique needs.")
   - *Liquidity needs.* None of a day-to-day nature until 1998. Income is distributed annually after year-end. (See "Unique needs.")
   - *Tax considerations.* None; this endowment fund is exempt from taxes.
   - *Legal and regulatory considerations.* Minimal, but the prudent man rule applies to all investment actions.
   - *Unique needs, circumstances, and preferences.* The endowment fund must pay out to another tax-exempt entity the sum of $8,500,000 in cash on June 30, 1998. The assets remaining after this distribution will be retained by the fund in perpetuity. The endowment fund has adopted a "spending rule" requiring a first-year current income payout of $500,000; thereafter, the annual payout is to rise by 3 percent in real terms. Until 1998, annual income in excess of that required by the spending rule is to be reinvested; after 1998, the spending rate will be reset at 5 percent of the then-existing capital.

With this information and information found in this chapter, do the following:

a. Formulate an appropriate investment policy statement for the endowment fund.

b. Identify and briefly explain three major ways in which your firm's initial asset allocation decisions for the endowment fund will be affected by the circumstances of the account.

CFA® PROBLEMS

2. (Level I) Your client says, "With the unrealized gains in my portfolio, I have almost saved enough money for my daughter to go to college in eight years, but educational costs keep going up." On the basis of this statement alone, which one of the following appears to be least important to your client's investment policy?

a. Time horizon

b. Purchasing power risk

c. Liquidity

d. Taxes

CFA® PROBLEMS

3. (Level I) The aspect least likely to be included in the portfolio management process is

a. Identifying an investor's objectives, constraints, and preferences

b. Organizing the management process itself

c. Implementing strategies regarding the choice of assets to be used

d. Monitoring market conditions, relative values, and investor circumstances

4. Would you expect a typical open-end fixed-income mutual fund to have higher or lower operating expenses than a fixed-income unit investment trust? Why?

5. An open-end fund has a net asset value of $10.70 per share. It is sold with a front-end load of 6 percent. What is the offering price?

6. If the offering price of an open-end fund is $12.30 per share and the fund is sold with a front-end load of 5 percent, what is its net asset value?

7. The composition of the Fingroup Fund portfolio is as follows:

Stock	Shares	Price ($)
A	200,000	35
B	300,000	40
C	400,000	20
D	600,000	25

The fund has not borrowed any funds, but its accrued management fee with the portfolio manager currently totals $30,000. There are 4 million shares outstanding. What is the net asset value of the fund?

8. Reconsider the Fingroup Fund in the previous problem. If during the year the portfolio manager sells all of the holdings of stock D and replaced it with 200,000 shares of stock E at $50 per share and 200,000 shares of stock F at $25 per share, what is the portfolio turnover rate?

9. The Closed Fund is a closed-end investment company with a portfolio currently worth $200 million. It has liabilities of $3 million and 5 million shares outstanding.

a. What is the NAV of the fund?

b. If the fund sells for $36 per share, what is the percentage premium or discount that will appear in the listings in the financial pages?

10. Corporate Fund started the year with a net asset value of $12.50. By year-end, its NAV equalled $12.10. The fund paid year-end distributions of income and capital gains of $1.50. What was the rate of return to an investor in the fund?

11. A closed-end fund starts the year with a net asset value of $12. By year-end, NAV equals $12.10. At the beginning of the year, the fund was selling at a 2 percent premium to NAV. By the end of the year, the fund is selling at a 7 percent discount to NAV. The fund paid year-end distributions of income and capital gains of $1.50.

a. What is the rate of return to an investor in the fund during the year?

b. What would have been the rate of return to an investor who held the same securities as the fund manager during the year?

12. What are some comparative advantages of investing in each of the following?

a. Closed-end mutual funds

b. Open-end mutual funds

c. Individual stocks and bonds that you choose for yourself

13. Open-end equity mutual funds find it necessary to keep a significant percentage of total investments, typically around 5 percent of the portfolio, in very liquid money market assets. Closed-end funds do not have to maintain such a position in "cash-equivalent" securities. What difference between open-end and closed-end funds might account for their differing policies?

14. Balanced funds and asset allocation funds invest in both the stock and the bond market. What is the difference between these types of funds?

15. *a.* Impressive Fund had excellent investment performance last year, with portfolio returns that placed it in the top 10 percent of all funds with the same investment policy. Do you expect it to be a top performer next year? Why or why not?

b. Suppose instead that the fund was among the poorest performers in its comparison group. Would you be more or less likely to believe its relative performance will persist into the following year? Why?

16. Consider a mutual fund with $200 million in assets at the start of the year and with 10 million shares outstanding. The fund invests in a portfolio of stocks that provides dividend income at the end of the year of $2 million. The stocks included in the fund's portfolio increase in price by 8 percent, but no securities are sold, and there are no capital gains distributions. The fund charges other fees of 1 percent, which are deducted from portfolio assets at year-end. What is net asset value at the start and end of the year? What is the rate of return for an investor in the fund?

17. The New Fund had average daily assets of $2.2 billion in 2000. The fund sold $400 million worth of stock and purchased $500 million during the year. What was its turnover ratio?

18. If New Funds' expense ratio was 1.1 percent and the management fee was .7 percent, what were the total fees paid to the fund's investment managers during the year? What were other administrative expenses?

19. You purchased 1,000 shares of the New Fund at a price of $20 per share at the beginning of the year. You paid a front-end load of 4 percent. The securities in which the fund invests increase in value by 12 percent during the year. The fund's expense ratio if 1.2 percent. What is your rate of return on the fund if you sell your shares at the end of the year?

20. The Investments Fund sells Class A shares with a front-end load of 6 percent and Class B shares with other charges of .5 percent annually as well as back-end load fees that start at 5 percent and fall by 1 percent for each full year the investor holds the portfolio (until the fifth year). Assume the portfolio rate of return net of operating expenses is 10 percent annually. If you plan to sell the fund after four years, are Class A or Class B shares the better choice for you? What if you plan to sell after 15 years?

21. Suppose you observe the investment performance of 350 portfolio managers for five years, and rank them by investment returns during each year. After five years, you find that 11 of the funds have investment returns that place the fund in the top half of the sample in each and every year of your sample. Such consistency of performance indicates to you that these must be the funds whose managers are in fact skilled, and you invest your money in these funds. Is your conclusion warranted?

22. You are considering an investment in a mutual fund with a 4 percent load and expense ratio of .5 percent. You can invest instead in a bank GIC paying 6 percent interest.

a. If you plan to invest for two years, what annual rate of return must the fund portfolio earn for you to be better off in the fund than in the GIC? Assume annual compounding of returns.

b. How does your answer change if you plan to invest for six years? Why does your answer change?

c. Now suppose that instead of a front-end load the fund assesses an other charge of .75 percent per year. What annual rate of return must the fund portfolio earn for you to be better off in the fund than in the GIC? Does your answer in this case depend on your time horizon?

23. Suppose that every time a fund manager trades stock, transaction costs such as commissions and bid-asked spreads amount to .4 percent of the value of the trade. If the portfolio turnover rate is 50 percent, by how much is the total return of the portfolio reduced by trading costs?

24. A front-end load mutual fund has a net asset value of $25 per share. It has a sales charge of 7 percent. Calculate the offering price and round your answer to two decimal places.

25. If an investor's investment objectives were protection of capital, cash flows and the possibility of capital gains, the investor would probably choose a

a. Money market fund

b. Dividend and income fund

c. Growth fund

d. Balanced fund

26. The following is a list of fund objectives. Identify the type of fund that best exemplifies each objective:

a. The focus is on income and safety, and the securities in which it invests give it less volatility than a bond fund.

b. The goal is to achieve the maximum in safety and liquidity.

c. The goal is income and safety, but investors should be aware that capital losses are possible when interest rates rise.

d. The goal is to provide income in a form that is subject to lower taxation.

e. These funds seek capital gains, and are willing to forgo broad diversification in an attempt to achieve above-average returns.

f. The goal is to provide a mixture of safety, income, and capital appreciation, and the fund manager shifts the weighting of different asset classes to achieve these goals.

g. The goal of fund is to limit investments to firms that produce socially responsible products and act in socially responsible ways.

h. These funds seek capital gains, but often rely on diversification to reduce nonsystematic risk.

27. For closed-end funds the purchase price

a. Is unlikely to be different from the fund's net asset value per share (NAVPS).

b. Depends on the number of sellers of shares relative to the number of buyers.

c. Is equal to the NAVPS less the broker's sales commission.

d. All of the above.

28. For closed-end funds, the investor wishing to sell her units does so

a. Usually in the open market to a willing buyer.

b. Usually to the fund itself.

c. To other unit holders of the same fund.

d. Usually to the company that set up the fund.

CSI

29. Given the following information about a mutual fund, calculate the NAVPS.

Current market value of the fund's portfolio of assets	$728,525,000
Number of shares outstanding	100,000,000
Unpaid bill for management fees	$1,500,000
Unpaid bill for fund auditor's fees	$25,000

E-INVESTMENTS
Choosing a Mutual Fund

Here are the Web sites for three of the largest mutual fund companies:

Fidelity Investments: **www.fidelity.ca**

Putnam Investments: **www.aimtrimark.com**

Vanguard Group: **www.investorsgroup.ca**

Pick three or four funds from one of these sites. What are the investment objectives of each fund? Find the expense ratio of each fund. Which fund has had the best recent performance? What are the major holdings of each fund? Compare your answers with information at www.morningstar.ca.

APPENDIX 4A: TAXATION AND TAX SHELTERING

The Canadian Tax System

Investment choice by individuals is a process of placing funds temporarily under the control of others in the hope of obtaining a future cash flow greater than the amount invested. Governments consider the increase in funds, or the return on investment, to be taxable, like earned income. For the investor, the return available after tax is what is relevant. Frequently, the tax payable may reflect the risk involved in the investment; hence, the government may encourage risky investments by exempting part, or even all, of their returns from income tax. In order to stimulate investment in certain areas or of certain types, the government may legislate particularly favourable tax treatment. Thus, tax policy is often (many would say always) a reflection of social policy.

In Canada, the three major characteristics of income tax that are relevant to investment are the treatment of interest, dividends, and capital gains. The receipt of interest is predictable and relatively certain (barring default by the borrower), leading the government to tax it as ordinary income. Since equity is more risky than debt for investors, but safer for corporations, equity investment is encouraged by offering a lower effective tax rate. Dividends being more assured than capital gains, we would expect a higher tax rate on dividends than on capital gains. Thus, the system rewards long-term equity investment for growth more than equity investment for dividend income, and in turn, dividend income more than interest income.

Although the system has changed extensively since the introduction of the capital gains tax in 1972, we now have a system that favours dividends through a complicated adjustment procedure and capital gains by exclusion of some of the gain from taxable income. Dividends are currently "grossed up" by increasing the actual amount by 25 percent and including this in taxable income; then a tax credit of $13\frac{1}{3}$ percent of the grossed-up amount is granted against taxes due. Actual capital gains are reduced by 50 percent and then included in taxable income.

Table 4A.1 Calculation of Tax Payable on Forms of Investment Income

Source	Interest	Dividend	Capital Gain
Income	1,000	1,000	1,000
Dividend gross-up (25%)		250	
Capital gain exclusion			(500)
Taxable income	1,000	1,250	500
Federal tax (29%)	(290)	(362.50)	(145.00)
Dividend tax credit (13.33%)		166.67	
Basic federal tax	(290)	(195.83)	(145.00)
Ontario tax (17.41%)	(174.10)	(217.62)	(87.05)
Dividend tax credit		100.04	
Ontario tax	(174.10)	(117.58)	(87.05)
Total tax	(464.10)	(313.42)	(232.05)
After-tax income	535.90	686.58	767.95
Retention ratio	53.59%	68.66%	76.80%

Capital losses are deductible against capital gains, and can be carried back and forward if insufficient gains exist in a year. One is hindered from taking losses as they occur by the **superficial loss rule**, which governs the sale of an asset at a loss within 30 days of purchase. Thus if a stock has been bought for $30 and is currently trading at $20, one can only recognize the loss of $10 provided that the stock is not re-bought within 30 days of the sale or even 30 days before (in anticipation of the sale); this prevents investors from taking the loss but maintaining a long-term position on the assumption that the stock price will rebound. If the stock were sold for $20 and re-bought a week later for $18, the cost base would be adjusted to $28 ($30 – $20 + $18) for determination of the effective gain or loss; that gain or loss is ultimately recognized when the stock is sold (and not re-bought during the 60-day window).

Table 4A.1 illustrates the calculation of taxes and the after-tax return for an income of $1,000 from the three types of investment income: interest, dividends, and capital gains. As we see in Table 4A.2, comparing the after-tax retention rates in Ontario, Quebec, and British Columbia, capital gains are currently taxed less than dividends, although the difference is small. The fact that capital gains can be accrued over a period of time, but are taxable only upon realization, causes their treatment to be even more favourable in reality. This makes ETFs even better investments relative to mutual funds; the latter must distribute annual capital gains on portfolio changes to unitholders, but ETFs have only minimal portfolio adjustments. Purchase of ETFs defers virtually all capital gains until the final sale.

Timing is an important detail in the effect of taxation. Generally, income is taxed in the year that it is received, although corporations may account for income on an accrual basis. Bond interest is then taxed when received, which is determined as the payment date by the issuer; similarly, dividends are taxed as of the payment date (not to be confused with the declaration or record

Table 4A.2 After-Tax Retention of Income from Interest, Dividends, and Capital Gains, 2003

	Ontario	Quebec	British Columbia
Combined federal and provincial tax rate	46.41%	48.2%	43.70%
Retention rate on:			
Interest	53.59	51.8	56.30
Dividend	68.66	67.2	68.50
Capital gains	76.80	75.9	78.15

Source: Deloitte & Touche.

dates). Capital gains are based on the years of purchase and sale; because of transfer delays, the date for tax purposes—the **settlement date**—is formally three business days after the actual trade date (this makes the days prior to Christmas an active period of trading, as annual gains and losses are established).

One exception to the actual receipt of cash occurs for so-called **zero-coupon bonds**, or **zeroes** (described in Section 1.3), and similarly for compound interest savings bonds. Although no actual interest is paid, interest is imputed from the increase in value over the life of the zero-coupon bond; similarly, the savings bonds' interest is not received until redemption. In both cases, the income tax is paid annually on the imputed interest, making these negative cash flow instruments. Note that the government is precluding the possibility of an investor claiming the increase in value of the zero, from its initial discounted value to its redemption value, as a capital gain to be taxed at the preferential rate.

Besides timing, location of the source of income is important. As international investments become more common, income from foreign sources is likely to become part of taxable income. It is fortunate that agreements between taxing authorities permit the recognition of foreign income tax as a credit against Canadian taxes, although only to the extent that that tax would have been charged under Canadian law. Note that it is the source of the income that causes a country to tax it first, that is, U.S.-source income will be taxed there. Capital gains on foreign assets, however, are taxable in Canada and generally are not taxable under the foreign tax regime.

The significance of the after-tax returns on different forms of investment is that the prices of financial assets are determined by the returns, on an after-tax basis, that are required by investors in recompense for the risks posed by the assets. Investment choices in response to tax policies must be made from the available set of instruments that are competitively priced to appeal to the investing public. As previously mentioned, occasionally governments may judge that the investment appeal of certain assets does not attract sufficient capital; in such cases, additional incentives may be offered to increase their appeal.

Tax Deferral and Shelters

There are four important tax-sheltering options that can radically affect the optimal asset allocation for individual investors. The first is the tax-deferral option, which arises from the fact that you do not have to pay tax on a capital gain until you choose to realize the gain. The second and third options are similar; they are called tax-deferred retirement plans, such as the registered retirement savings plan, and tax-deferred annuities, which are offered by life insurance companies. The fourth option is the class of investments known as tax shelters. We will discuss each of these options in more detail below.

A fundamental feature of the Income Tax Act is that tax on the capital gain of an asset is payable only when the asset is sold,[12] this is the **tax-deferral option**. The investor, therefore, can control the timing of the tax payment. From a tax perspective, this option makes stocks in general preferable to fixed-income securities.

To see this, compare BCE stock with a BCE bond. Suppose both offer an expected total return of 15 percent this year. The stock has a dividend yield of 5 percent and an expected appreciation in price of 10 percent, whereas the bond has an interest rate of 15 percent. The bond investor must pay tax on the bond's interest in the year it is earned, whereas the BCE shareholder pays tax only on the dividend and defers paying tax on the capital gain until the stock is sold.

[12]The only exception to this rule occurs in futures investing, where National Revenue treats a gain as taxable in the year it occurs, regardless of whether the investor closes the position. Note also that on pure discount bonds, imputed interest is taxable, even though no interest payment is received until sale or maturity (making these very popular in RRSPs). Additionally, note that there are capital gains exemptions for principal residences and small businesses.

Suppose the investor is investing $1,000 for five years and is in a 40 percent tax bracket. An investment in the bond will earn an after-tax return of 9.0 percent per year ($.60 \times 15$ percent). The yield after taxes at the end of five years is

$$\$1,000 \times 1.09^5 = \$1,538.62$$

For the stock, dividend yield after taxes will be 3.333 percent per year ($[1. - 1.25(.40 - .1333)] \times 5\%$).[13] Because no taxes are paid on the capital gain until year 5, the return before paying the capital gains tax is

$$\$1,000 \times (1 + .03333 + .10)^5 = \$1,000(1.1333)^5 = \$1,869.75$$

In year 5, the capital gain is

$$\$1,000(1.10^5 - 1) = \$1,610.51 - \$1,000 = \$610.51$$

Taxes due are $122.10, leaving $1,747.65 of the year 5 return, which is $209.03 more than the bond investment yields. Deferral of the capital gains tax allows the investment to compound at a faster rate until the tax is actually paid.

Note that the more of one's total return that is in the form of price appreciation, the greater the value of the tax-deferral option.

Recent years have seen the establishment of **tax-deferred retirement plans** in which investors can choose how to allocate assets. Such plans include self-directed RRSPs and employer-sponsored "tax-qualified" defined contribution plans. A feature they all have in common is that contributions and earnings are subject to neither federal nor provincial income tax until the individual withdraws them as benefits.

Typically, an individual may have some investment in the form of such qualified retirement accounts and some in the form of ordinary taxable accounts. The basic investment principle that applies is to keep whatever bonds you want to hold in the retirement account while placing equities in the ordinary account. You maximize the tax advantage of the retirement account by holding in it the security that is the least tax-advantaged.

To see this point, consider the following example. Suppose Eloise has $200,000 of wealth, $100,000 of it in a tax-qualified retirement account. She has decided to invest half of her wealth in bonds and half in stocks, so she allocates half of her retirement account and half of her nonretirement funds to each. By doing this, Eloise is not maximizing her after-tax returns. She could reduce her tax bill with no change in before-tax returns simply by shifting her bonds into the retirement account and holding all her stocks outside the retirement account.

? CONCEPT CHECK

A1. Suppose Eloise earns a 10 percent per year rate of interest on bonds and 15 percent per year on stocks, all in the form of price appreciation. In five years she will withdraw all her funds and spend them. By how much will she increase her final accumulation if she shifts all bonds into the retirement account and holds all stocks outside the retirement account? She is in a 28 percent tax bracket.

Deferred annuities are accounts offered by life insurance companies that combine the option of withdrawing one's funds in the form of a life annuity with some tax sheltering. Variable annuity contracts offer the additional advantage of mutual fund investing. One major difference between a RRSP and a variable annuity contract is that, whereas the amount one can contribute to a RRSP is tax-deductible and extremely limited as to maximum amount, the amount one can contribute to a deferred annuity is unlimited, but not tax-deductible.

[13] We have used .1333 as the dividend tax credit rate.

The defining characteristic of a life annuity is that its payments continue as long as the recipient is alive, although virtually all deferred annuity contracts have several withdrawal options, including a lump sum of cash paid out at any time. You need not worry about running out of money before you die. Like CPP, therefore, life annuities offer longevity insurance and would seem to be an ideal asset for someone in the retirement years. Indeed, theory suggests that where there are no bequest motives, it would be optimal for people to invest heavily in actuarially fair life annuities.[14]

There are two types of life annuities, **fixed annuities** and **variable annuities**. A fixed annuity pays a fixed nominal sum of money per period (usually each month), whereas a variable annuity pays a periodic amount linked to the investment performance of some underlying portfolio.

In pricing annuities, insurance companies use **mortality tables** that show the probabilities that individuals of various ages will die within a year. These tables enable the insurer to compute with reasonable accuracy how many of a large number of people in a given age group will die in each future year. If it sells life annuities to a large group, the insurance company can estimate fairly accurately the amount of money it will have to pay in each future year to meet its obligations.

Variable annuities are structured so that the investment risk of the underlying asset portfolio is passed through to the recipient, much as shareholders bear the risk of a mutual fund. There are two stages in a variable annuity contract: an accumulation phase and a payout phase. During the *accumulation* phase, the investor contributes money periodically to one or more open-end mutual funds and accumulates shares. The second, or *payout*, stage usually starts at retirement, when the investor typically has several options, including the following:

1. Taking the market value of the shares in a lump-sum payment
2. Receiving a fixed annuity until death
3. Receiving a variable amount of money each period that is computed according to a certain procedure

This procedure is best explained by the following example. Assume that, at retirement, John Shortlife has $100,000 accumulated in a variable annuity contract. The initial annuity payment is determined by setting an *assumed investment return* (AIR), 4 percent per year in this example, and an assumption about mortality probabilities. In Shortlife's case, we assume he will live for only three years after retirement and will receive three annual payments starting one year from now.

The benefit payment in each year, B_t, is given by the recursive formula

$$B_t = B_{t-1}[(1 + R_t)/(1 + \text{AIR})] \tag{4.1}$$

where R_t is the actual holding period return on the underlying portfolio in year t. In other words, each year the amount Shortlife receives equals the previous year's benefit multiplied by a factor that reflects the actual investment return compared with the assumed investment return. In our example, if the actual return equals 4 percent, the factor will be one, and this year's benefit will equal last year's. If R_t is greater than 4 percent, the benefit will increase, and if R_t is less than 4 percent, the benefit will decrease.

The starting benefit is found by computing a hypothetical constant payment with a present value of $100,000 using the 4 percent AIR to discount future values and multiplying it by the first year's performance factor. In our example, the hypothetical constant payment is $36,035.

The "Illustration of a Variable Annuity" box summarizes the computation and shows what the payment will be in each of three years if R_t is 6 percent, then 2 percent, and finally 4 percent. The last column shows the balance in the fund after each payment.

[14]For an elaboration of this point, see Laurence J. Kotlikoff and Avia Spivak, "The Family as an Incomplete Annuities Market," *Journal of Political Economy* 89 (April 1981).

This method guarantees that the initial $100,000 will be sufficient to pay all benefits due, regardless of what actual holding period returns turn out to be. In this way, the variable annuity contract passes all portfolio risk through to the annuitant.

By selecting an appropriate mix of underlying assets, such as stocks, bonds, and cash, an investor can create a stream of variable annuity payments with a wide variety of risk-return combinations. Naturally, the investor wants to select a combination that offers the highest expected level of payments for any specified level of risk.[15]

CONCEPT CHECK

A2. Assume Victor is now 75 years old and is expected to live until age 80. He has $100,000 in a variable annuity account. If the assumed investment return is 4 percent per year, what is the initial annuity payment? Suppose the annuity's asset base is the TSX Composite equity portfolio and its holding period return for the next five years is each of the following: 4 percent, 10 percent, –8 percent, 25 percent, and 0. How much would Victor receive each year? Verify that the insurance company would wind up using exactly $100,000 to fund Victor's benefits.

Variable life insurance is another tax-deferred investment vehicle offered by the life insurance industry. A variable life insurance policy combines life insurance with the tax-deferred annuities described earlier.

To invest in this product, you pay either a single premium or a series of premiums. In each case there is a stated death benefit, and the policyholder can allocate the money invested to several portfolios, which generally include a money market fund, a bond fund, and at least one common stock fund. The allocation can be changed at any time.

A variable life policy has a cash surrender value equal to the investment base minus any surrender charges. Typically, there is a surrender charge (about 5 percent of the purchase payments) if you surrender the policy during the first several years, but not thereafter. At policy surrender, income taxes become due on all investment gains.

Variable life insurance policies offer a death benefit that is the greater of the stated face value or the market value of the investment base. In other words, the death benefit may rise with favourable investment performance, but it will not go below the guaranteed face value. Furthermore, the surviving beneficiary is not subject to income tax on the death benefit.

The policyholder can choose from a number of income options to convert the policy into a stream of income, either on surrender of the contract or as a partial withdrawal. In all cases, income taxes are payable on the part of any distribution representing investment gains.

The insured can gain access to the investment without having to pay income tax by borrowing against the cash surrender value. Policy loans of up to 90 percent of the cash value are available at any time at a contractually specified interest rate.

Tax shelters are investment opportunities under which most, if not all, of the investment can be deducted from ordinary income over a few years' horizon. These generally are structured as *limited partnerships* (LP) for the investors, with a general partner who is usually related to the sponsor of the shelter. The advantage of this arrangement is that there is only minimal risk of any further assessment of liability against the limited partners, while a share of LP expenses are deductible against income; if the structure involved a limited liability corporation, these expenses would *not* be deductible. Tax regulations allow the write-off of these expenses over three years, typically, with administrative expenses of setting up and selling the LP requiring five years to write off.

[15]For an elaboration on possible combinations, see Zvi Bodie, "An Innovation for Stable Real Retirement Income," *Journal of Portfolio Management*, Fall 1980; and Zvi Bodie and James E. Pesando, "Retirement Annuity Design in an Inflationary Climate," Chapter 11 in Zvi Bodie and J. B. Shoven (eds.), *Financial Aspects of the United States Pension Systems* (Chicago: University of Chicago Press, 1983).

ILLUSTRATION OF A VARIABLE ANNUITY

Starting accumulation = \$100,000

R_t = Rate of return on underlying portfolio in year t

Assumes investment return (AIR) = 4 percent per year

B_t = Benefit received at end of year t

$$= B_{t-1} \frac{1 + R_t}{1 + \text{AIR}}$$

B_0 = \$36,035, the hypothetical constant payment, which has a present value of \$100,000, using a discount rate of 4 percent per year

A_t = Remaining balance after B_t is withdrawn

t	R_t	B_t	Remaining Balance = $A_t = A_{t-1} \times (1 + R_t) - B_t$
0			\$100,000
1	6%	36,728	69,272
2	2	36,022	34,635
3	4	36,022	0

The consequences of entering into an LP include the generation of a cash flow of income from the business for the life of the LP, often ten years or even much longer, against which the amortized expenses can be deducted for income tax purposes. If a partner wishes to sell his share, however, the adjusted cost basis is likely to be zero for the purpose of determining the taxable capital gain. Such a sale is further impeded by illiquidity in the (OTC) resale market, with large bid-asked spreads.

Shelters are created to raise capital to finance investment in various areas, including commercial real estate (such as multiple-unit residential buildings, or MURBs), filmmaking, and railroad boxcars. Two more popular forms have been the flow-through share program of the 1980s and mutual fund LPs, in favour until the mid-1990s.

Flow-through shares were issued to allow mining and energy companies to pass through their exploration and resource depletion expenses to shareholders who would be able to use the deduction against income; the companies themselves usually did not have enough taxable income to make use of the expenses. Companies were able to raise significant amounts of capital to finance resource exploration and development in this way. The federal government originally encouraged this arrangement to increase activity and employment in the mining and energy sectors. As capital was squandered on marginal prospects, and tax revenues suffered from helping in the financing, the government greatly reduced the attractiveness of the shares by reducing the write-off allowances; this virtually killed the program.

Mutual fund LPs raised capital to pay for the commissions paid to salespersons for back-end load funds. Since no front-end fee was collected, the fund managers did not have the cash to pay the commissions. In return for financing the commissions, partners were entitled to receive all the resulting back-end load fees, as well as a percentage of the regular management fees paid by mutual fund shareholders. This income was received for ten or more years through the LP. The load income and management fee income tend to offset each other as fund performance varies. Ultimately, the after-tax cash flow is correlated with the performance of the underlying mutual fund; having much lower risk, it dominates direct investment in the fund.[16] Resale of the LPs was costly, with many investors trying to sell after the three-year write-off period; attempts were made to improve liquidity by consolidating the partnerships into TSX-traded securities. The government again killed these shelters by disallowing write-offs.

Many tax shelters, such as MURB investments, have turned out to have very poor results. Although taxes were saved originally, little of the after-tax investment was returned. Although early

[16]See Peter J. Ryan, "Gimme More Than Shelter," *Canadian Investment Review*, Fall 1995, pp. 22–27.

flow-through share partnerships were extremely profitable, the later ones resulted in investment in low-quality mining companies and yielded little payoff. The saving of taxes must be a secondary consideration to the overall profitability of the investment when choosing a shelter. Given the complexity of the tax consequences, the advice of a tax accountant, rather than that of the selling broker, is strongly recommended to prospective investors. That advice ought to include some appraisal of the investment prospects, as well as tax planning.

PROBLEMS

1. Your neighbour has heard that you have just successfully completed a course in investments and has come to seek your advice. She and her husband are both 50 years old. They have just finished making their last payments for their condominium and their children's college education and are planning for retirement. Until now, neither of them has been able to set aside any savings for retirement, and so have not participated in their employers' voluntary tax-sheltered savings plan, nor have they opened RRSPs. Both of them work, and their combined after-tax income last year was $50,000. They are both in the 42 percent marginal tax bracket. They plan to retire at age 65 and would like to maintain the same standard of living in retirement as they enjoy now.
   a. Devise a simple plan for them on the assumption of a combined CPP income of $10,000 per year. How much should they start saving? (Assume they will live to age 80, can shelter as much retirement savings as they want from tax, and will earn a zero real rate of return.)
   b. Redo part (*a*) with the following changes:
      i. The real interest rate is assumed to be 3 percent per year.
      ii. Your neighbours are 40 years old instead of 50.
      iii. The tax bracket after retirement drops to 15 percent.
   c. What advice on investing their retirement savings would you give them? If they are very risk-averse, what would you advise?

The following problem is based on a question that appeared in past CFA examinations:

CFA® PROBLEMS

2. (Level I) Investors in high marginal tax brackets probably would be least interested in a
   a. Portfolio of diversified stocks
   b. Tax-deferred retirement fund
   c. Commodity pool
   d. High-income bond fund

CSI

The following questions are adapted from the Canadian Securities Course.

3. The taxable amount of a $352 dividend from a taxable Canadian corporation is about ______________ (round to the nearest whole number).
4. If an investor has capital gains and wishes to realize some capital losses from TSX-listed stocks to offset the gains, the last day to sell the stocks is ______________.
5. A Canadian resident in the 29 percent federal tax bracket receives $450 in dividends from a taxable Canadian corporation. The amount of basic federal tax payable is ______________.
6. A superficial loss is a paper loss. It occurs when the value of a portfolio is less than the original cost. True or false?
7. Which of the following investments is taxed at the lowest tax rate? An investment in
   a. A money market fund
   b. Preferred shares of an American company
   c. Units of a bond fund
   d. Units of a Canadian dividend fund

APPENDIX 4B: PENSION FUNDS

Defined-Contribution Versus Defined-Benefit Plans

Although employer pension programs vary in design, they usually are classified into two broad types: defined-contribution and defined-benefit. Under a *defined-contribution* (DC) plan, each employee has an account into which the employer and the employee (in a contributory plan) make regular contributions. Benefit levels depend on the total contributions and investment earnings of the accumulation in the account.

In a *defined-benefit* (DB) plan, the employee's pension benefit entitlement is determined by a formula that takes into account years of service for the employer and, in most cases, wage or salary. Many defined-benefit formulas also take into account the CPP (Canada Pension Plan) benefit to which an employee is entitled. These are called "integrated" plans.

The DC arrangement is conceptually the simpler of the two. The employer, and sometimes also the employee, makes regular contributions into the employee's retirement account. The contributions usually are specified as a predetermined fraction of salary, although that fraction need not be constant over the course of a career.

Contributions from both parties are tax-deductible, and investment income accrues tax-free. Often, the employee has some choice as to how the account is to be invested. In principle, contributions may be invested in any security, although in practice most plans limit investment options to various bond, stock, and money market funds. At retirement, the employee typically receives an annuity whose size depends on the accumulated value of the funds in the retirement account. The employee bears all the investment risk; the retirement account is by definition fully funded, and the firm has no obligation beyond making its periodic contribution.

A typical DB plan determines the employee's benefit as a function of both years of service and wage history. As a representative plan, consider one in which the employee receives retirement income equal to 1 percent of final salary multiplied by the number of years of service. Thus, an employee retiring after 40 years of service with a final salary of $15,000 per year would receive a retirement benefit of 40 percent of $15,000, or $6,000 per year.

The annuity promised to the employee is the employer's liability. The present value of this liability represents the amount of money that the employer must set aside today to fund the deferred annuity that commences upon the employee's retirement.

CONCEPT CHECK

B1. An employee is 40 years old and has been working for the firm for 15 years. If normal retirement age is 65, the interest rate is 8 percent, and the employee's life expectancy is 80, what is the present value of the accrued pension benefit?

Defined-benefit pension funds are pools of assets that serve as collateral for firms' pension liabilities. Traditionally, these funds have been viewed as separate from the corporation. Funding and asset allocation decisions are supposed to be made in the beneficiaries' best interests, regardless of the financial condition of the sponsoring corporation.

Beneficiaries presumably want corporate pension plans to be as well funded as possible. Their preferences with regard to asset allocation policy, however, are less clear. If beneficiaries could not share in any windfall gains—if the defined-benefit liabilities were really fixed in nominal terms—rationally, they would prefer that the funds be invested in the least risky assets. If beneficiaries had a claim on surplus assets, however, the optimal asset allocation could in principle include virtually any mix of stocks and bonds.

Pension Funds (Canada) www.benefitscanada.com/content/legacy/Content/1997/04-97

Another way to view the pension fund investment decision is as an integral part of overall corporate financial policy. Seen in this perspective, defined-benefit liabilities are part and parcel of the firm's other fixed financial liabilities, and pension assets are part of the firm's assets. From this point of view, any plan surplus or deficit belongs to the firm's shareholders. The firm thus manages an extended balance sheet, which includes both its normal assets and liabilities and its pension assets and liabilities, in the best interests of *shareholders.*

The special tax status of pension funds creates the same incentive for both defined-contribution and defined-benefit plans to tilt their asset mix toward assets with the largest spread between pretax and after-tax rates of return. In a defined-contribution plan, because the participant bears all of the investment risk, the optimal asset mix also depends on the risk tolerance of the participant.

In defined-benefit plans, optimal investment policy may be different because the sponsor absorbs the investment risk. If the sponsor has to share some of the upside potential of the pension assets with plan participants, there is an incentive to eliminate all investment risk by investing in securities that match the promised benefits. If, for example, the plan sponsor has to pay $100 per year for the next five years, it can provide this stream of benefit payments by buying a set of five zero-coupon bonds each with a face value of $100 and maturing sequentially. By so doing, the sponsor eliminates the risk of a shortfall. This is called **immunization** of the pension liability.

If the pension fund is overfunded, then a 100 percent fixed-income portfolio is no longer required to minimize the cost of the corporate pension guarantee. Management can invest surplus pension assets in equities, provided it reduces the proportion so invested when the market value of pension assets comes close to the value of the accumulated benefit obligation (ABO). Such an investment strategy is a type of portfolio insurance known as *contingent immunization.*

To understand how contingent immunization works, consider a simple version of it that makes use of a stop-loss order. Imagine that the ABO is $100 and that the fund has $120 of assets entirely invested in equities. The fund can protect itself against downside risk by maintaining a stop-loss order on all its equities at a price of $100. This means that should the price of the stocks fall to $100, the fund manager would liquidate all the stocks and immunize the ABO. A stop-loss order at $100 is not a perfect hedge because there is no guarantee that the sell order can be executed at a price of $100. The result of a series of stop-loss orders at prices starting well above $100 is even better protection against downside risk.

If the only goal guiding corporate pension policy were shareholder wealth maximization, it would be hard to understand why a financially sound pension sponsor would invest in equities at all. A policy of 100 percent bond investment would minimize the cost of guaranteeing the defined benefits.

In addition to the reasons given for a fully funded pension plan to invest only in fixed-income securities, there is a tax reason for doing so. The tax advantage of a pension fund stems from the ability of the sponsor to earn the pretax interest rate on pension investments. To maximize the value of this tax shelter, it is necessary to invest entirely in assets offering the highest pretax interest rate. Because capital gains on stocks can be deferred and dividends are taxed at a much lower rate than interest on bonds, corporate pension funds should invest entirely in taxable bonds and other fixed-income investments.

Yet we know that, in general, pension funds invest from 40 percent to 60 percent of their portfolios in equity securities. Even a casual perusal of the practitioner literature suggests that they do so for a variety of reasons—some right and some wrong. There are two possible correct reasons.

The first is that corporate management views the pension plan as a trust for the employees and manages fund assets as if it were a defined-contribution plan. It believes that a successful policy of investment in equities might allow it to pay extra benefits to employees and is therefore worth taking the risk. As explained before, if the plan is overfunded, then the sponsor can invest in stocks and still minimize the cost of providing the benefit guarantee by pursuing a contingent immunization strategy.

The second possible correct reason is that management believes that through superior market timing and security selection it is possible to create value in excess of management fees and expenses.

Many executives in nonfinancial corporations are used to creating value in excess of cost in their businesses. They assume that it also can be done in the area of portfolio management. Of course, if that is true, then one must ask why they do not do it on their corporate account rather than in the pension fund. That way, they could have their tax shelter "cake" and eat it, too. It is important to realize, however, that to accomplish this feat, the plan must beat the market, not merely match it.

Pension Fund Appraisal

Institutions operating pension funds for their employees can assess the performance both of their funds and of the professional managers they hire for portions of the funds. Several organizations, the largest being SEI, will evaluate performance by comparing the realized returns to benchmarks based on selected categories such as long-term bonds, small-cap equities, or market indices. The overall performance over various time periods can be compared to results of other institutions in general or of a similar type, such as universities or hospitals.

If an institution has been using a number of managers for different purposes, or if it is considering a change to other potential managers, it can obtain information about the results they have obtained. Combining the realized returns with the variability of results over different periods will permit the identification of managers who will satisfy the objectives of the pension fund.

SUMMARY

1. The Canadian tax system is designed to make investment in equity more favourable than investment in debt, by offering a dividend tax credit and excluding some of the capital gains from taxation. Capital gains and dividends are taxed at approximately the same effective rate.
2. There are four ways to shelter investment income from federal income taxes. The first is by investing in assets whose returns take the form of appreciation in value, such as common stocks or real estate. As long as capital gains taxes are not paid until the asset is sold, the tax can be deferred indefinitely. The second way of tax sheltering is through investing in tax-deferred retirement plans, such as RRSPs. The general investment rule is to hold the least tax-advantaged assets in the plan and the most tax-advantaged assets outside of it. The third way of sheltering is to invest in the tax-advantaged products offered by the life insurance industry—tax-deferred annuities and variable and universal life insurance. They combine the flexibility of mutual fund investing with the tax advantages of tax deferral. Finally, there are investments in tax shelters, which finance investment in mutual funds, real estate, or other assets. Poor prospects with tax benefits make bad investments.
3. Pension plans are either defined-contribution plans or defined-benefit plans. Defined-contribution plans are, in effect, retirement funds held in trust for the employee by the employer. The employees in such plans bear all the risk of the plan's assets and often have some choice in the allocation of those assets. Defined-benefit plans give the employees a claim to a money-fixed annuity at retirement. The annuity level is determined by a formula that takes into account years of service and the employee's wage or salary history.
4. If the only goal guiding corporate pension policy were shareholder wealth maximization, it is hard to understand why a financially sound pension sponsor would invest in equities at all. A policy of 100 percent bond investment would both maximize the tax advantage of funding the pension plan and minimize the cost of guaranteeing the defined benefits.

KEY TERMS

superficial loss rule 130
settlement date 131
zero-coupon bonds (zeroes) 131
tax-deferral option 131
tax-deferred retirement plans 132
deferred annuities 132
fixed annuities 133
variable annuities 133
mortality tables 133
tax shelters 134
immunization 138

SELECTED READINGS

For a further discussion of the theory and evidence regarding the investment policies of corporate defined-benefit pension plans, see:

Bodie, Z. "Managing Pension and Retirement Assets: An International Perspective." *Journal of Financial Services* Research, December 1990.

Bodie, Z., J. Light, R. Morck, and R. A. Taggart. "Corporate Pension Policy: An Empirical Investigation." *Financial Analysts Journal* 41, no. 5 (September/October 1985).

PROBLEMS

1. John Oliver, formerly a senior partner of a large management consulting firm, has been elected president of Mid-South Trucking Company. He has contacted you, a portfolio manager for a large investment advisory firm, to discuss the company's defined-benefit pension plans. Upon assuming his duties, Oliver learned that Mid-South's pension plan was 100 percent in bonds, with a maximum maturity of 10 years. He believes that "a pension plan should be managed so as to maximize return within well-defined risk parameters," and "anyone can buy bonds and sit on them." Mr. Oliver has suggested that he meet with you, as an objective advisor, and the plan's actuary to discuss possible changes in plan asset mix. To aid you in preparing for the meeting, Mr. Oliver has provided the current portfolio (Table 4B.1). He also has provided the following information about the company and its pension plans.

Company

Mid-South is the eighth largest domestic trucking company, with annual revenues of $500 million. Revenues have grown about 8 percent per year over the past five years, with one down year. The company employs about 7,000 people, as against 6,500 five years ago. The annual payroll is about $300 million. The average age of the workforce is 43 years. Company profits last year were $20 million, compared with $12 million five years ago.

Pension Plan

Mid-South's pension plan is a defined-benefit plan that was established in 1975. The company annually contributes 7 percent of payroll to fund the plan. During the past five years, portfolio income has been used to meet payments for retirees, while company contributions have been available for investment. Although the plan is adequately funded on a current basis, unfunded past service liabilities are equal to 40 percent of plan assets. The liability is to be funded over the next 35 years. Plan assets are valued annually on a rolling four-year average for actuarial purposes.

Whereas FASB No. 87 requires an annual reassessment of the assumed rate of return, for purposes of this analysis, Mid-South's management, in consultation with the actuary, has decided to use an assumed annual rate of 7 percent. This compares with actual plan results that have averaged 10 percent per year over the past 20 years. Wages and salaries are assumed to increase 5 percent per year, which is identical with past company experience.

Table 4B.1 Current Portfolio

	Cost	Market Value	Current Yield	Yield to Maturity
Short-term reserves	$ 10,000,000	$ 10,000,000	5.8%	5.8%
Notes, 90 days to 1 year	25,000,000	25,500,000	6.5	6.4
Notes, 1 to 5 years	110,000,000	115,000,000	8.0	7.8
Bonds, 5 to 10 years	115,000,000	127,500,000	8.8	8.5
Total	**$260,000,000**	**$278,000,000**	**8.1%**	**7.9%**

Before the meeting, you review your firm's investment projections, dated March 31, 1997. Your firm believes that continued prosperity is the most likely outlook for the next three to five years but has allowed for two alternatives, a return to high inflation or a move into deflation/depression. The details of the projections are shown in Table 4B.2.

a. Using this information, create an investment policy statement for the Mid-South Trucking Company's pension plan. On the basis of your policy statement and the expectations shown, recommend an appropriate asset allocation strategy for Mid-South Trucking Company's pension plan limited to the same asset classes shown. Justify your changes, if any, from the current portfolio. Your allocation must sum to 100 percent.

b. At the meeting, the actuary suggests that Mid-South consider terminating the defined-benefit plan, purchasing annuities for retirees and vested employees with the proceeds, and establishing a defined-contribution plan. The company would continue to contribute 7 percent of payroll to the defined-contribution plan.

Compare the key features of a defined-benefit plan and a defined-contribution plan. Assuming Mid-South were to adopt and retain responsibility for a defined-contribution plan, briefly explain any revisions to your asset allocation strategy developed in part (*a*) above. Again, your allocation must sum to 100 percent and be limited to the same asset classes shown.

CFA® PROBLEMS

2. You are Mr. R. J. Certain, a retired CFA, who formerly was the chief investment officer of a major investment management organization. Although you have over 30 years of experience in the investment business, you have kept up with the literature and developed a reputation for your knowledge and ability to blend modern portfolio theory and traditional portfolio methods.

The chairperson of the board of Morgan Industries has asked you to serve as a consultant to him and the other members of the board of trustees of the company's pension fund. Since you are interested in developing a consulting practice and in keeping actively involved in the investment management business, you welcome the opportunity to develop a portfolio management decision-making process for Morgan Industries that you could apply to all types of investment portfolios.

Table 4B.2 Investment Projections

Scenarios	Expected Annual Total Return (%)
Continued Prosperity (60% probability)	
Short-term reserves (Treasury bills)	6.0
Stocks (S&P 500 index)	12.0
Bonds (S&P high-grade bond index)	8.0
High-Inflation Scenario (25% probability)	
Short-term reserves (Treasury bills)	10.0
Stocks (S&P 500 index)	15.0
Bonds (S&P high-grade bond index)	3.0
Deflation/Depression Scenario (15% probability)	
Short-term reserves (Treasury bills)	2.0
Stocks (S&P 500 index)	–6.0
Bonds (S&P high-grade bond index)	12.0

Morgan Industries is a company in transition. Its long-established business, dating back to the early years of the century, is the production of steel. Since the 1960s, however, Morgan gradually has built a highly profitable stake in the domestic production of oil and gas.

Most of the company's 1982 sales of $4 billion were still derived from steel operations. Because Morgan occupies a relatively stable niche in a specialized segment of the steel industry, its losses on steel during the 1982 recession were moderate compared to industry experience. At the same time, profit margins for Morgan's oil and gas business remained satisfactory despite all the problems in the world oil market. This segment of the company's operations accounted for the entire 1982 net profit of $150 million. Even when steel operations recover, oil and gas operations are expected to contribute, on average, over half of Morgan's annual profits.

Judging from the combination of the two segments of the company's operations, the overall cyclicality of company earnings appears to be approximately the same as that of the S&P 500. Several well-regarded security analysts, citing the outlook for recovery in steel operations, as well as further gains in oil and gas production, project earnings progress for Morgan over the next five years at about the same rate as for the S&P 500. Debt makes up about 35 percent of the long-term capital structure, and the beta (market risk) for the company's common stock is also about the same as for the S&P 500.

Morgan's defined-benefit pension plan covers 25,000 active employees, vested and unvested, and 15,000 retired employees, with the latter projected to exceed 20,000 in five years. The burden of pension liabilities is large because the steel industry has long been labour-intensive and the company's current labour force in this area of operations is not as large as it was some years ago. Oil and gas operations, although growing at a significant rate, account for only 10 percent of the active plan participants and for even less of the retired beneficiaries.

Pension assets amounted to $1 billion of market value at the end of 1982. For the purpose of planning investment policy, the present value of the unfunded pension liability is calculated at $500 million. Although the company's outstanding debt is $600 million, it is clear that the unfunded pension liability adds significantly to the leverage in the capital structure.

Pension expenses charged to company income—and reflected in company contributions to the pension trust—were $80 million in 1982. The level of expenses, which are projected to rise with payroll, reflects current assumptions concerning inflation, the rate of return on pension assets, wage and salary increases, and benefits changes. If these assumptions were to prove completely correct, the current method of funding would amortize the unfunded pension liability over 20 years. Since assumptions are subject to change in the light of new information, they must be reviewed periodically. Revision by one percentage point in the assumed rate of investment return, for example, would require a current change in the level of pension expenses by $15 million before taxes, or about $7 million after taxes. The current actuarially assumed rate of return is 8.5 percent.

Pension investment policy, through its influence on pension expenses, unfunded pension liability, and the company's earnings progress, is a critical issue for Morgan's management. The chairperson is strongly committed to the corporate goal of achieving a total investment return for shareholders superior to that of other large industrial companies. He recognizes that a more aggressive pension investment policy—if successful—would facilitate attainment of the corporate goal through a significant reduction in pension expenses and unfunded pension liability. He also worries, however, that a significant drop in the market value of the company's pension fund—now $1 billion—could result in a major setback in the company's growth strategy. Current pension investment policy is based on an asset mix of approximately 50 percent common stocks and 50 percent fixed-income securities.

The chairperson is concerned about the overall investment management and direction of the pension fund and is very interested in your informed and objective evaluation.

What recommendations would you make and why?

PART TWO

PORTFOLIO THEORY

5 Concepts and Issues: Return, Risk, and Risk Aversion

6 Portfolio Selection

CONCEPTS AND ISSUES: RETURN, RISK, AND RISK AVERSION

This chapter introduces some key concepts and issues that are central to informed investment decision making. The material presented is basic to the development of portfolio theory in this and subsequent parts of the book.

The investment process consists of two broad tasks. One task is security and market analysis, by which we assess the risk and expected-return attributes of the entire set of possible investment vehicles. The second task is the formation of an optimal portfolio of assets. This task involves the determination of the best risk-return opportunities available from feasible investment portfolios and the choice of the best portfolio from that feasible set. This latter task is known as *portfolio theory*.

We start this chapter by presenting the basic components of the return of any financial asset: real and nominal interest rates and risk premiums on risky securities. Then, we present the historical record of rates of return on Treasury bills, bonds, and stocks. We measure the expected returns and volatilities of these financial instruments and review the performance of several portfolios of interest to provide a sense of the range of performance in the past several decades. These elements are basic tools of the security analysis task, to which we return in later chapters.

The remainder of this chapter introduces three themes in portfolio theory, all centring on risk.

The first is the basic tenet that investors avoid risk and demand a reward for engaging in risky investments. The reward is taken as a risk premium, an expected rate of return higher than that available on alternative risk-free investments.

The second theme allows us to summarize and quantify investors' personal tradeoffs between portfolio risk and expected return. To do this we introduce the utility function, which assumes that investors can assign a welfare, or "utility," score to any investment portfolio depending on its risk and return.

Finally, the third fundamental principle is that we cannot evaluate the risk of an asset separately from the portfolio of which it is a part; that is, the proper way to measure the risk of an individual asset is to assess its impact on the volatility of the entire portfolio of investments. Taking this approach, we find that seemingly risky securities may be portfolio stabilizers and actually low-risk assets.

Appendix 5A discusses continuous compounding. Appendix 5B describes the theory and practice of measuring portfolio risk by the variance or standard deviation of returns. We also discuss other potentially relevant characteristics of the probability distribution of portfolio returns, as well as the circumstances in which variance is sufficient to measure risk. Appendix 5C discusses the classical theory of risk aversion.

5.1 DETERMINANTS OF THE LEVEL OF INTEREST RATES

Interest rates and forecasts of their future values are among the most important inputs into an investment decision.

For example, suppose you have $10,000 in a savings account. The bank pays you a variable interest rate tied to some short-term reference rate such as the 30-day Treasury bill rate. You have the option of moving some or all of your money into a longer-term *guaranteed investment certificate* (GIC) that offers a fixed rate over the term of the deposit.

Your decision depends critically on your outlook regarding interest rates. If you think rates will fall, you will want to lock in the current higher rates by investing in a relatively long-term GIC. If you expect rates to rise, you will want to postpone committing any funds to long-term GICs.

Forecasting interest rates is one of the most notoriously difficult parts of applied macroeconomics. Nonetheless, we do have a good understanding of the fundamental factors that determine the level of interest rates:

1. The supply of funds from savers, primarily households
2. The demand for funds from businesses to be used to finance physical investments in plant, equipment, and inventories (real assets or capital formation)
3. The government's net supply and/or demand for funds as modified by actions of the monetary authority

Before we elaborate on these forces and resultant interest rates, we need to distinguish real from nominal interest rates.

Real and Nominal Rates of Interest

Bloomberg www.bloomberg.com/markets/rates

Suppose exactly one year ago you deposited \$1,000 in a one-year time deposit guaranteeing a rate of interest of 10 percent. You are about to collect \$1,100 in cash.

Is your \$100 return for real? That depends on what money can buy these days, relative to what you *could* buy a year ago. The consumer price index (CPI) measures purchasing power by averaging the prices of goods and services in the consumption basket of an average urban family of four. While this basket may not represent your particular consumption plan, suppose for now that it does.

Suppose the rate of inflation (percent change in the CPI, denoted by i) for the last year amounted to $i = 6$ percent. This tells you the purchasing power of money is reduced by 6 percent a year. The value of each dollar depreciates by 6 percent a year in terms of the goods it can buy. Therefore, part of your interest earnings are offset by the reduction in the purchasing power of the dollars you will receive at the end of the year. With a 10 percent interest rate, after you net out the 6 percent reduction in the purchasing power of money, you are left with a net increase in purchasing power of about 4 percent. Thus, we need to distinguish between a **nominal interest rate**—the growth rate of your money—and a **real interest rate**—the growth rate of your purchasing power. If we call R the nominal rate, r the real rate, and i the inflation rate, then we conclude

$$r \approx R - i$$

In words, the real rate of interest is the nominal rate reduced by the loss of purchasing power resulting from inflation.

In fact, the exact relationship between the real and nominal interest rate is given by

$$1 + r = \frac{1 + R}{1 + i}$$

This is because the growth factor of your purchasing power, $1 + r$, equals the growth factor of your money, $1 + R$, divided by the new price level, that is, $1 + i$ times its value in the previous period. The exact relationship can be rearranged to

$$r = \frac{R - i}{1 + i}$$

which shows that the approximation rule overstates the real rate by the factor $1/(1 + i)$.

For example, if the interest rate on a one-year GIC is 8 percent, and you expect inflation to be 5 percent over the coming year, then using the approximation formula, you expect the real rate to be $r = 8$ percent $- 5$ percent $= 3$ percent. Using the exact formula, the real rate is

$$r = \frac{.08 - .05}{1 + .05} = .0286$$

or 2.86 percent. Therefore, the approximation rule overstates the expected real rate by only .14 percent (14 basis points). The approximation rule is more exact for small inflation rates and is perfectly exact for continuously compounded rates. We discuss further details in Appendix 5A of this chapter.

Before the decision to invest, you would realize that conventional investment certificates offer a guaranteed *nominal* rate of interest. Thus, you can only infer the expected real rate by subtracting your expectation of the rate of inflation.

www.statcan.ca

It is always possible to calculate the real rate after the fact. The inflation rate is published by Statistics Canada. The future real rate, however, is unknown, and one has to rely on expectations. In other words, because future inflation is risky, the real rate of return is risky even if the nominal rate is risk-free.

The Equilibrium Real Rate of Interest

Three basic factors—supply, demand, and government actions—determine the *real* interest rate. The nominal interest rate, which is the rate we actually observe, is the real rate plus the expected rate of inflation. So a fourth factor affecting the interest rate is the expected rate of inflation.

Although there are many different interest rates economywide (as many as there are types of securities), economists frequently talk as if there were a single representative rate. We can use this abstraction to gain some insights into determining the real rate of interest if we consider the supply and demand curves for funds.

Figure 5.1 shows a downward-sloping demand curve and an upward-sloping supply curve. On the horizontal axis, we measure the quantity of funds, and on the vertical axis, we measure the real rate of interest.

The supply curve slopes up from left to right because the higher the real interest rate, the greater the supply of household savings. The assumption is that at higher real interest rates, households will choose to postpone some current consumption and set aside or invest more of their disposable income for future use.[1]

The demand curve slopes down from left to right because the lower the real interest rate, the more businesses will want to invest in physical capital. Assuming that businesses rank projects by the expected real return on invested capital, firms will undertake more projects the lower the real interest rate on the funds needed to finance those projects.

Equilibrium is at the point of intersection of the supply and demand curves, point *E* in Figure 5.1.

www.bankofcanada.ca

The government and the central bank (Bank of Canada) can shift these supply and demand curves either to the right or to the left through fiscal and monetary policies. For example, consider an increase in the government's budget deficit. This increases the government's borrowing demand and shifts the demand curve to the right, which causes the equilibrium real interest rate to rise to point *E′*. That is, a forecast that indicates higher than previously expected government borrowing increases expected future interest rates. The central bank can offset such a rise through an expansionary monetary policy, which will shift the supply curve to the right.

Thus, while the fundamental determinants of the real interest rate are the propensity of households to save and the expected productivity (or we could say profitability) of investment in physical capital, the real rate can be affected as well by government fiscal and monetary policies.

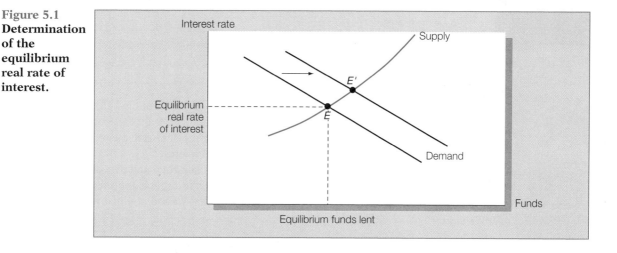

Figure 5.1 Determination of the equilibrium real rate of interest.

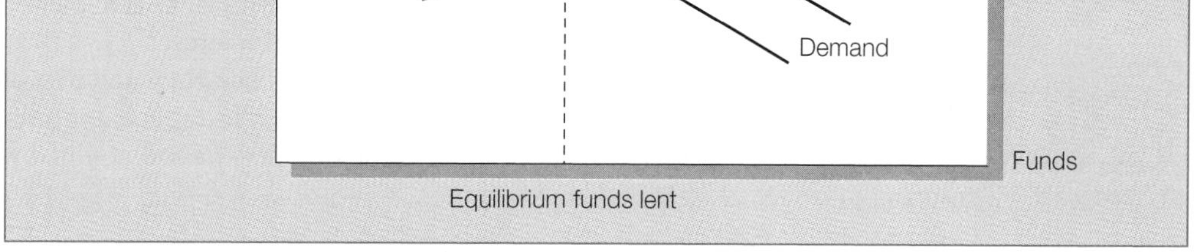

[1]There is considerable disagreement among experts on the issue of whether household saving does go up in response to an increase in the real interest rate.

The Equilibrium Nominal Rate of Interest

We've seen that the real rate of return of an asset is approximately equal to the nominal rate minus the inflation rate. Because investors should be concerned with their real returns—the increase in their purchasing power—we would expect that as the inflation rate increases, investors will demand higher nominal rates of return on their investments. This higher rate is necessary to maintain the expected real return offered by an investment.

Irving Fisher (1965) argued that the nominal rate ought to increase one for one with increases in the expected inflation rate. If we use the notation $E(i)$ to denote the current expectation of the inflation rate that will prevail over the coming period, then we can state the so-called Fisher equation formally as

$$R = r + E(i)$$

This relationship has been debated and empirically investigated. The equation implies that if real rates are reasonably stable, then increases in nominal rates ought to predict higher inflation rates. The results are mixed; while the data do not strongly support this relationship, nominal interest rates seem to predict inflation as well as alternative methods, in part because we are unable to forecast inflation well with any method.

One reason it is difficult to determine the empirical validity of the Fisher hypothesis that changes in nominal rates predict changes in future inflation rates is that the real rate also changes unpredictably over time. Nominal interest rates can be viewed as the sum of the required real rate on nominally risk-free assets, plus a "noisy" forecast of inflation.

In Part Four, we discuss the relationship between short- and long-term interest rates. Longer rates incorporate forecasts for long-term inflation. For this reason alone, interest rates on bonds of different maturities may diverge. In addition, we will see that prices of long-term bonds are more volatile than those of short-term bonds. This implies that expected returns on long-term bonds may include a risk premium, so that the expected real rate offered by bonds of varying maturity also may vary.

CONCEPT CHECK

1. *a.* Suppose the real interest rate is 3 percent per year and the expected inflation rate is 8 percent. What is the nominal interest rate?

   b. Suppose the expected inflation rate rises to 10 percent, but the real rate is unchanged. What happens to the nominal interest rate?

Bills and Inflation, 1957–2003

Inflation Calculator www.bankofcanada.ca/en/inflation_calc

The Fisher equation predicts a close connection between inflation and the rate of return on T-bills. This is apparent in Figure 5.2, which plots both time series on the same set of axes. Both series tend to move together, which is consistent with our previous statement that expected inflation is a significant force determining the nominal rate of interest.[2]

For a holding period of 30 days, the difference between actual and expected inflation is not large. The 30-day bill rate will adjust rapidly to changes in expected inflation induced by observed changes in actual inflation. It is not surprising that we see nominal rates on bills move roughly in tandem with inflation over time.

[2]See Nabil T. Khoury and Guy McLeod, "The Relationship Between the Canadian Treasury Bill Rate and Expected Inflation in Canada and the United States," *Canadian Journal of Administrative Sciences* 2, no. 1 (June 1985).

Figure 5.2 Rates of return, 1957–2003.

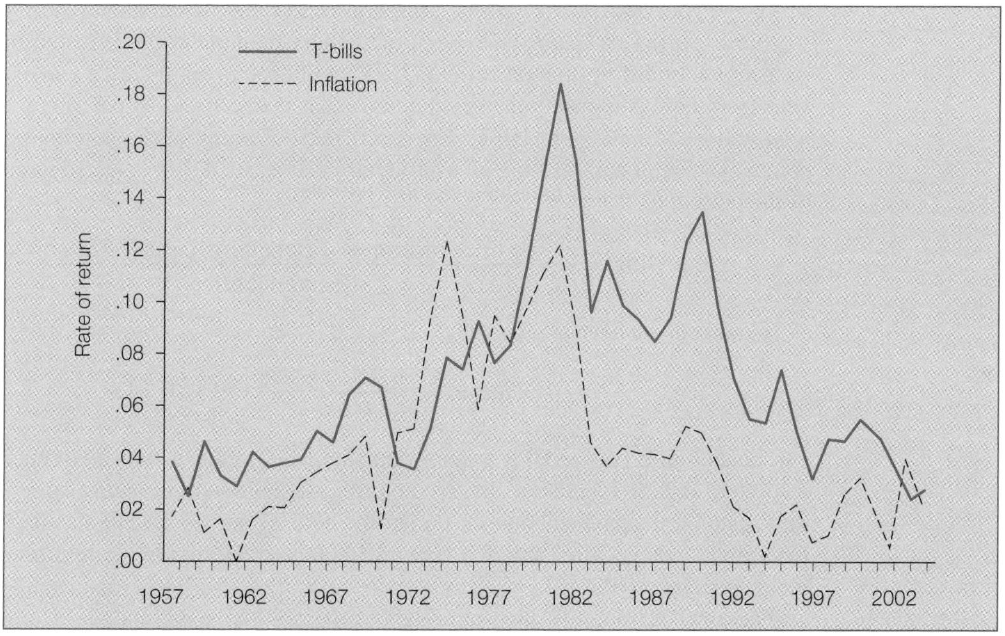

Source: Data from Scotia Capital's "Debt Market Indices," various years. Used by permission of Scotia Capital Markets Fixed Income Research.

Taxes and the Real Rate of Interest

Tax liabilities are based on *nominal* income and the tax rate determined by the investor's tax bracket. Parliament has recognized the resultant "bracket creep" (when nominal income grows due to inflation and pushes taxpayers into higher brackets) and has partially indexed tax brackets and exemptions since 1975.

Index-linked tax brackets do not provide relief from the effect of inflation on the taxation of savings, however. Given a tax rate (r) and a nominal interest rate (R), the after-tax interest rate is $R(1 - t)$. The real after-tax rate is approximately the after-tax nominal rate minus the inflation rate:

$$R(1 - t) - i = (r + i)(1 - t) - i = r(1 - t) - it$$

Thus the after-tax real rate of return falls as the inflation rate rises. Investors suffer an inflation penalty equal to the tax rate times the inflation rate. If, for example, you are in a 30 percent tax bracket and your investments yield 12 percent, while inflation runs at the rate of 8 percent, then your before-tax real rate is 4 percent, and you *should*, in an inflation-protected tax system, net after taxes 4(1 − .3) = 2.8 percent. But the tax code does not recognize that the first 8 percent of your return is no more than compensation for inflation—not real income—and hence your after-tax return is reduced by 8 percent × .3 = 2.4 percent, so that your after-tax real interest rate, at .4 percent, is almost wiped out.

5.2 RISK AND RISK PREMIUMS

Risk means uncertainty about future rates of return. We can quantify that uncertainty using probability distributions.

For example, suppose you are considering investing some of your money, now all invested in a bank account, in a stock market index fund. The price of a share in the fund is currently

\$100, and your *time horizon* is one year. You expect the cash dividend during the year to be \$4, so your expected *dividend yield* (i.e., dividends earned per dollar invested) is 4 percent.

Your total **holding-period return (HPR)** will depend on the price you expect to prevail one year from now. Suppose your best guess is that it will be \$110 per share. Then your *capital gain* will be \$10 and your HPR 14 percent. The definition of the holding period return in this context is capital gain income plus dividend income per dollar invested in the stock at the start of the period:

$$\text{HPR} = \frac{\text{Ending price of a share} - \text{Beginning price} + \text{Cash dividend}}{\text{Beginning price}}$$

In our case we have

$$\text{HPR} = \frac{\$110 - \$100 + \$4}{\$100} = .14, \text{ or } 14\%$$

This definition of the HPR assumes the dividend is paid at the end of the holding period. To the extent that dividends are received earlier, the HPR ignores reinvestment income between the receipt of the payment and the end of the holding period. Recall also that the percent return from dividends is called the dividend yield, and so the dividend yield plus the capital gains yield equals the HPR.

There is considerable uncertainty about the price of a share a year from now, however, so you cannot be sure about your eventual HPR. We can try to quantify our beliefs about the state of the economy and the stock market, however, in terms of three possible scenarios with probabilities as presented in Table 5.1.

How can we evaluate this probability distribution? Throughout this book we will characterize probability distributions of rates of return in terms of their **expected** or **mean return**, $E(r)$, and their **standard deviation**, σ. The expected rate of return is a probability-weighted average of the rates of return in all scenarios. Calling $p(s)$ the probability of each scenario and $r(s)$ the HPR in each scenario, where scenarios are labelled or "indexed" by the variable s, we may write the expected return as

$$E(r) = \sum_s p(s)r(s) \tag{5.1}$$

Applying this formula to the data in Table 5.1, we find that the expected rate of return on the index fund is

$$E(r) = .25 \times 44\% + .5 \times 14\% + .25 \times (-16\%) = 14\%$$

In Section 5.5 and in Appendix 5B, we argue that the standard deviation of the rate of return (σ) is a measure of risk. It is defined as the square root of the **variance**, which in turn is defined as the expected value of the squared deviations from the expected return. The higher the volatility in outcomes, the higher will be the average value of these squared deviations. Therefore, variance and standard deviation measure the uncertainty of outcomes. Symbolically,

$$\sigma^2 = \sum_s p(s)[r(s) - E(r)]^2 \tag{5.2}$$

Table 5.1 Probability Distribution of HPR on the Stock Market

State of the Economy	Probability	Ending Price	HPR
Boom	.25	\$140	44%
Normal growth	.50	110	14
Recession	.25	80	−16

Therefore, in our example,

$$\sigma^2 = .25(44 - 14)^2 + .5(14 - 14)^2 + .25(-16 - 14)^2 = 450$$

and

$$\sigma = 21.21\%$$

Clearly, what would trouble potential investors in the index fund is the downside risk of a –16 percent rate of return, not the upside potential of a 44 percent rate of return. The standard deviation of the rate of return does not distinguish between these two; it treats both as deviations from the mean. As long as the probability distribution is more or less symmetric about the mean, however, σ is an adequate measure of risk. In the special case where we can assume that the probability distribution is normal—represented by the well-known bell-shaped curve—$E(r)$ and σ are perfectly adequate to characterize the distribution.

Getting back to the example, how much, if anything, should you invest in the index fund? First, you must ask how much of an expected reward is offered for the risk involved in investing money in stocks.

Risk
www.contingencyanalysis.com/_x/fundamentals.htm

We measure the reward as the difference between the expected HPR on the index stock fund and the **risk-free rate**, that is, the rate you can earn by leaving money in risk-free assets such as T-bills, money market funds, or the bank. We call this difference the **risk premium** on common stocks. If the risk-free rate in the example is 6 percent per year, and the expected index fund return is 14 percent, then the risk premium on stocks is 8 percent per year. The difference between the actual rate of return on a risky asset and the risk-free rate is called **excess return**. Therefore, the risk premium is the expected excess return.

The degree to which investors are willing to commit funds to stocks depends on **risk aversion**. CFAs and financial analysts generally assume investors are risk-averse in the sense that, if the risk premium were zero, people would not be willing to invest any money in stocks. In theory then, there must always be a positive risk premium on stocks in order to induce risk-averse investors to hold the existing supply of stocks instead of placing all their money in risk-free assets. We explore their theory more systematically further on in this chapter.

Although this simple scenario analysis illustrates the concepts behind the quantification of risk and return, you still may wonder how to get a more realistic estimate of $E(r)$ and σ for common stocks and other types of securities. Here history has insights to offer.

5.3 THE HISTORICAL RECORD

Bills, Bonds, and Stocks, 1957–2003

The record of past rates of return is one possible source of information about risk premiums and standard deviations. We can estimate the historical risk premium by taking an average of the past differences between the HPRs on the asset type and the risk-free rate. Table 5.2 presents the annual HPRs on three asset classes for the period 1957–2003.

The first column shows the one-year HPR on a policy of "rolling-over" 91-day Treasury bills as they mature. Because this rate changes from month to month, it is risk-free only for a 91-day holding period. The second column presents the annual HPR an investor would have earned by investing in Canadian bonds with maturities higher than 10 years. The third column illustrates the HPR on the S&P/TSX Composite index of common stocks, which is a value-weighted stock portfolio of the largest corporations in Canada. (We discussed the S&P/TSX Composite stock index in Chapter 2.) Finally, the last column gives the annual inflation rate as measured by the rate of change in the consumer price index.

Table 5.2 Rates of Return, 1957–2003

Date	T-Bill	LT Bond	Stock	CPI Change
1957	0.038322	0.079399	−0.20584	0.02
1958	0.024373	0.019218	0.312471	0.028225
1959	0.046907	−0.05072	0.045861	0.010989
1960	0.033117	0.121918	0.017815	0.016304
1961	0.028913	0.091575	0.327455	0
1962	0.04215	0.050336	−0.07094	0.016043
1963	0.036342	0.045793	0.156011	0.021053
1964	0.037896	0.061609	0.254329	0.020619
1965	0.039237	0.00048	0.066819	0.030303
1966	0.050341	−0.01055	−0.07067	0.034314
1967	0.045931	−0.00484	0.180884	0.037915
1968	0.064439	0.021422	0.224451	0.041096
1969	0.070852	−0.0286	−0.00809	0.048246
1970	0.067002	0.163886	−0.03566	0.012552
1971	0.038069	0.148398	0.080077	0.049587
1972	0.035539	0.081131	0.273834	0.051181
1973	0.051114	0.019694	0.002736	0.093633
1974	0.078499	−0.04529	−0.25927	0.123288
1975	0.074074	0.080223	0.184831	0.094512
1976	0.092654	0.236358	0.110223	0.058496
1977	0.076564	0.090363	0.10706	0.094737
1978	0.083355	0.040958	0.297202	0.084135
1979	0.114118	−0.0283	0.447698	0.097561
1980	0.149736	0.021785	0.301336	0.111111
1981	0.184056	−0.02086	−0.10246	0.121818
1982	0.154204	0.458225	0.041367	0.092382
1983	0.096237	0.096088	0.373146	0.05
1984	0.115866	0.168962	−0.02393	0.04
1985	0.09878	0.266785	0.250654	0.043776
1986	0.0933	0.1721	0.08954	0.04194
1987	0.084789	0.017661	0.058788	0.041509
1988	0.094098	0.113011	0.110814	0.039855
1989	0.123613	0.151702	0.213728	0.052265
1990	0.134842	0.043231	−0.14798	0.049669
1991	0.098332	0.252962	0.120151	0.037855
1992	0.070764	0.115681	−0.01433	0.021277
1993	0.05509	0.220872	0.325476	0.016865
1994	0.053529	−0.07387	−0.00176	0.001951
1995	0.073925	0.263406	0.145294	0.017527
1996	0.050196	0.141839	0.283463	0.02201
1997	0.031974	0.184625	0.149776	0.007491
1998	0.047388	0.128441	−0.01584	0.010223
1999	0.04661	−0.05975	0.317142	0.025759
2000	0.054897	0.129673	0.074087	0.032287
2001	0.047231	0.060589	−0.12572	0.00695
2002	0.025224	0.110513	−0.12438	0.038827
2003	0.029114	0.090703	0.267249	0.019934
Mean	0.069864	0.090188	0.106487	0.04294
Variance	0.001392	0.01075	0.02718	0.001061
Standard deviation	0.037307	0.103682	0.164864	0.032568
Minimum	0.024373	−0.07387	−0.25927	0
Maximum	0.184056	0.458225	0.447698	0.123288

Source: Scotia Capital's "Debt Market Indices," various years. Used by permission of Scotia Capital Markets Fixed Income Research.

At the bottom of each column are five descriptive statistics. The first is the arithmetic mean or average HPR. For bills it is 6.99 percent, for bonds it is 9.02 percent, and for common stock it is 10.65 percent. These numbers imply an average risk premium of 2.03 percent per year on bonds and 3.66 percent on stocks (the average HPR less the risk-free rate of 6.99 percent).

The third statistic reported at the bottom of Table 5.2 is the standard deviation. The higher the standard deviation, the higher the variability of the HPR. This standard deviation is based on historical data rather than forecasts of *future* scenarios, as in equation 5.2. The formula for historical variance, however, is similar to equation 5.2. It is as follows:

$$\sigma^2 = \frac{n}{n-1} \sum_{t=1}^{n} \frac{(r_t - \bar{r})^2}{n} \tag{5.3}$$

Here each year's outcome is taken as a possible scenario.[3] Deviations are simply taken from the historical average, $\bar{r}$, instead of the expected value $E(r)$. Each historical outcome is taken as equally likely, and given a "probability" of $1/n$.

Figure 5.3 gives a graphical representation of the relative variabilities of the annual HPR on the three different asset classes. We have plotted the three time series on the same set of axes. Clearly, the annual HPR on stocks is the most variable series. The standard deviation of stock returns has been 16.49 percent, in contrast to 10.37 percent for bonds and 3.73 percent for bills. Here is evidence of the risk-return tradeoff that characterizes security markets: the markets with the highest average returns are also the most volatile.

Comparable figures for U.S. stocks show that they have both a higher return and a higher risk than their Canadian counterparts. Thus, over the period 1926–2002, the average annual HPR for the 500 stocks that made the S&P 500 index was 12.04 percent, with a standard deviation of 20.55

Figure 5.3 Rates of return on bills, bonds, and stocks, 1957–2003.

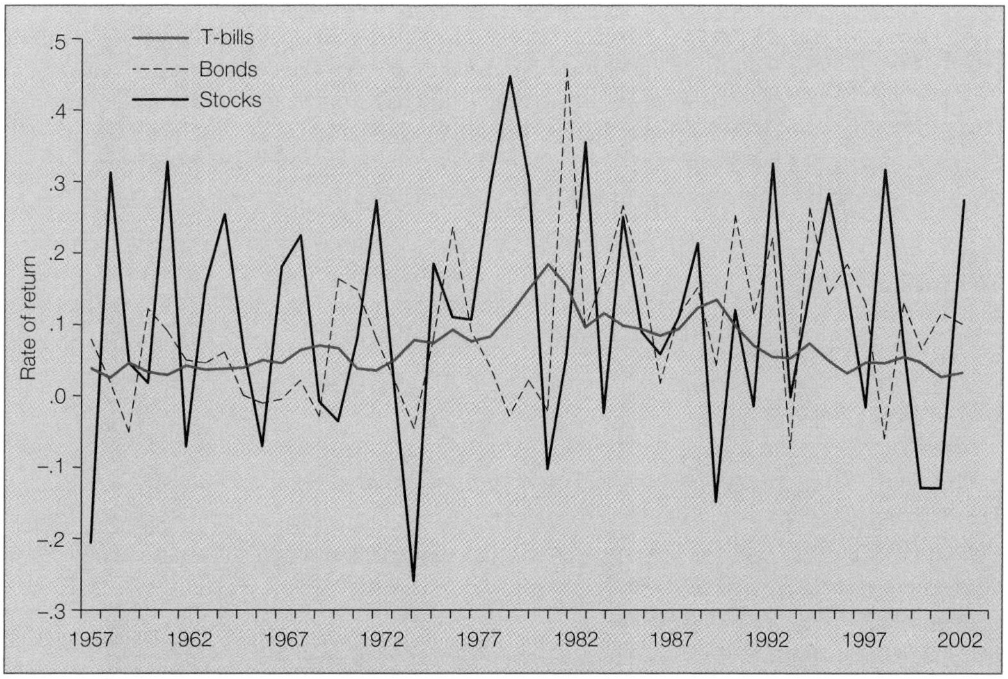

Source: Data from Scotia Capital's "Debt Market Indices," various years. Used by permission of Scotia Capital Markets Fixed Income Research.

[3]We multiply by $n/(n-1)$ in equation 5.3 to eliminate statistical bias in the estimate of variance.

percent. Similarly, a study by Roll[4] that used daily data covering the period April 1988–March 1991 gives average annual HPRs of 4.20 percent and 12.27 percent for Canada and the United States, with corresponding standard deviations of 9.97 percent and 14.37 percent. Part of the Canada-U.S. difference is due to the different industrial composition of their respective economies.

The other summary measures at the bottom of Table 5.2 show the highest and lowest annual HPR (the range) for each asset over the 45-year period. The size of this range is another possible measure of the relative riskiness of each asset class. It too confirms the ranking of stocks as the riskiest and bills as the least risky of the three asset classes.

An all-stock portfolio with a standard deviation of 16.49 percent would constitute a very volatile investment. For example, if stock returns are normally distributed with that standard deviation and an expected rate of return of 10.65 percent (the historical average), then in roughly one year out of three, returns will be less than –5.84 percent (10.65 percent – 16.49 percent) or greater than 27.14 percent (10.65 percent + 16.49 percent).

Figure 5.4 graphs the normal curve with a mean of 10.65 percent and a standard deviation of 16.4 percent. The graph shows the theoretical probability of rates of return within various ranges given these parameters.

Figures 5.5a and 5.5b present another view of the historical data, the actual frequency distribution of returns on various asset classes over the period 1957–2003. Notice the greater range of stock returns relative to bill or bond returns. Thus, the historical results are consistent with the risk-return tradeoff: riskier assets have provided higher expected returns.

Figure 5.6 presents graphs of wealth indexes for investments in three asset classes over the period 1957–2003. The plot for each asset class assumes that you invest $1 at year-end 1956 and traces the value of your investment in following years. The inflation plot demonstrates that to achieve the purchasing power represented by $1 in year-end 1956 one would require $7.06 at year-end 2003. One dollar continually invested in T-bills starting at year-end 1956 would have grown to $23.26 by year-end 2003, representing 3.29 times the original purchasing power (23.26/7.06 = 3.29). That same dollar invested in stocks would have grown to $68.51, representing 9.70 times the original purchasing power of the dollar invested, almost three times as much as the investment in T-bills, despite the risk from sharp downturns during the period. Hence, the lesson of the past is that risk premiums can translate into vast increases in purchasing power over the long haul.

Figure 5.4
The normal distribution.

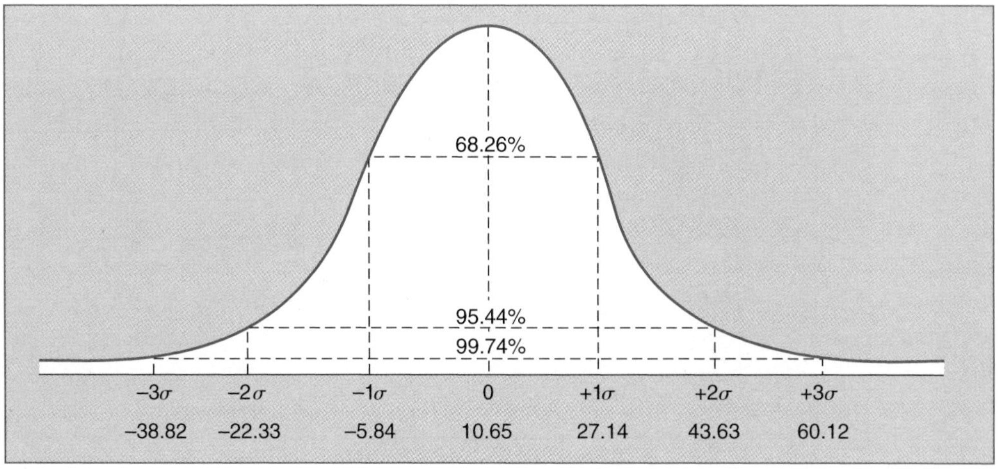

[4]See R. Roll, "Industrial Structure and the Comparative Behavior of International Stock Market Indexes," *Journal of Finance* 47, no. 1 (March 1992).

Figure 5.5a Frequency distributions of the annual HPR on three asset classes: T-bills and long-term bonds.

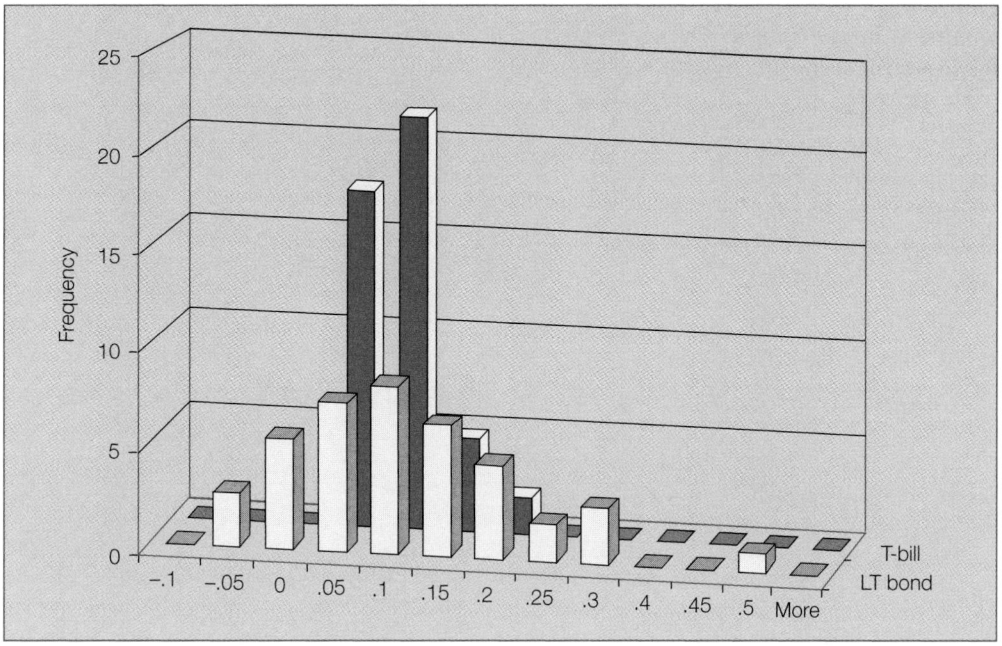

Source: Data from Scotia Capital's "Debt Market Indices," various years. Used by permission of Scotia Capital Markets Fixed Income Research.

We should stress that variability of HPR in the past can be an unreliable guide to risk, at least in the case of the risk-free asset. For an investor with a holding period of one year, for example, a one-year T-bill is risk-free with a σ of zero, despite the fact that the standard deviation of the one-year T-bill rate estimated from historical data is not zero.

The risk of cash flows of real assets reflects both *business risk* (profit fluctuations due to business conditions) and *financial risk* (increased profit fluctuations due to leverage). This reminds

Figure 5.5b Frequency distributions of the annual HPR on three asset classes: stocks and inflation.

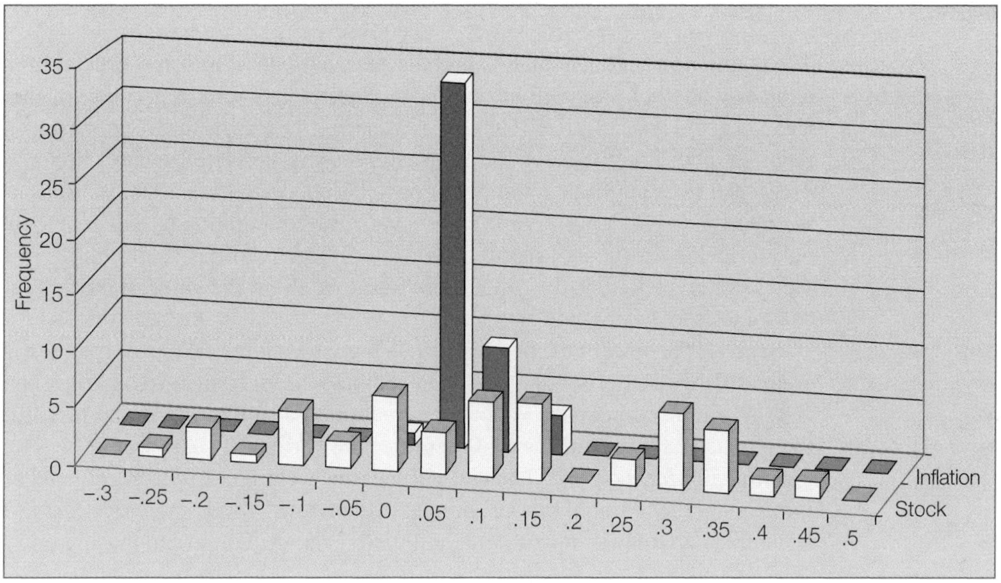

Source: Data from Scotia Capital's "Debt Market Indices," various years. Used by permission of Scotia Capital Markets Fixed Income Research.

Figure 5.6 Wealth indices for investments in three asset classes.

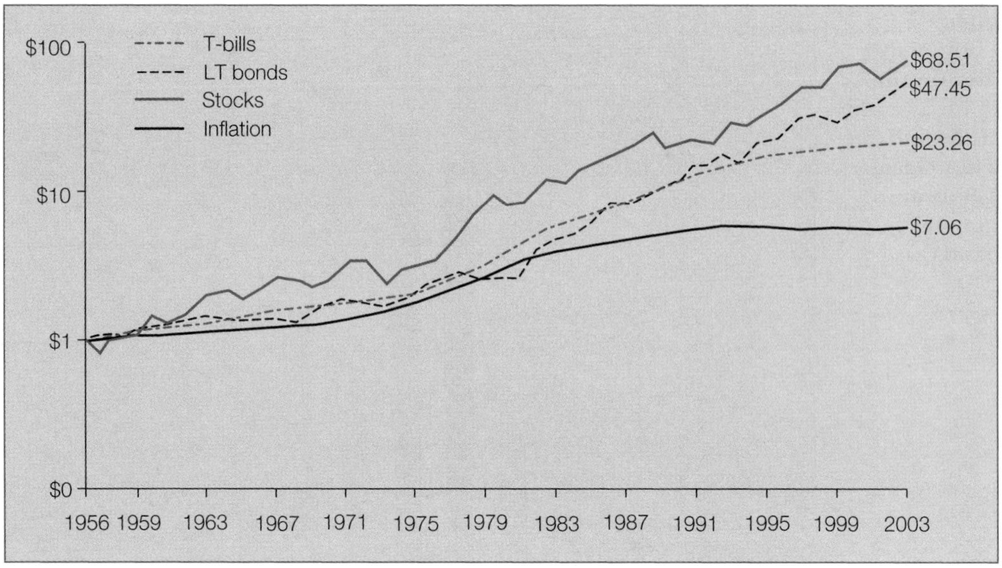

Source: Data from Scotia Capital's "Debt Market Indices," various years. Used by permission of Scotia Capital Markets Fixed Income Research.

us that an all-stock portfolio represents claims on leveraged corporations. Most corporations carry some debt, the service of which is a fixed cost. Greater fixed cost makes profits riskier; thus, leverage increases equity risk.

CONCEPT CHECK

2. Compute the average excess return on stocks (over the T-bill rate) and its standard deviation for the years 1957–1971.

5.4 REAL VERSUS NOMINAL RISK

The distinction between the real and the nominal rate of return is crucial in making investment choices when investors are interested in the future purchasing power of their wealth. Thus, a Canada bond that offers a "risk-free" *nominal* rate of return is not truly a risk-free investment—it does not guarantee the future purchasing power of its cash flow.

An example might be a bond that pays $1,000 on a date 20 years from now but nothing in the interim. While some people see such a zero-coupon bond as a convenient way for individuals to lock in attractive, risk-free, long-term interest rates (particularly in RRSP[5] accounts), the evidence in Table 5.3 is rather discouraging about the value of $1,000 in 20 years in terms of today's purchasing power.

Suppose the price of the bond is $103.67, giving a nominal rate of return of 12 percent per year (since $103.67 \times 1.12^{20} = 1{,}000$). We can compute the real annualized HPR for each inflation rate.

A revealing comparison is at a 12 percent rate of inflation. At that rate, Table 5.3 shows that the purchasing power of the $1,000 to be received in 20 years would be $103.67, or what was paid initially for the bond. The real HPR in these circumstances is zero. When the rate of inflation equals the nominal rate of interest, the price of goods increases just as fast as the money accumulated from the investment, and there is no growth in purchasing power.

[5]Registered retirement savings plan.

Table 5.3 Purchasing Power of $1,000 20 Years from Now and 20-Year Real Annualized HPR

Assumed Annual Rate of Inflation	Number of Dollars Required 20 Years from Now to Buy What $1 Buys Today	Purchasing Power of $1,000 to Be Received in 20 Years	Annualized Real HPR
4%	$2.19	$456.39	7.69%
6	3.21	311.80	5.66
8	4.66	214.55	3.70
10	6.73	148.64	1.82
12	9.65	103.67	

Purchase price of bond is $103.67.
Nominal 20-year annualized HPR is 12% per year.
Purchasing power = $1,000/(1 + Inflation rate)^{20}.
Real HPR, *r*, is computed from the following relationship:

$$r = (1 + R)/(1 + i) - 1$$
$$= 1.12/(1 + i) - 1$$

At an inflation rate of only 4 percent per year, however, the purchasing power of $1,000 will be $456.39 in terms of today's prices; that is, the investment of $103.67 grows to a real value of $456.39, for a real 20-year annualized HPR of 7.69 percent per year.

Again looking at Table 5.3, you can see that an investor expecting an inflation rate of 8 percent per year anticipates a real annualized HPR of 3.70 percent. If the actual rate of inflation turns out to be 10 percent per year, the resulting real HPR is only 1.82 percent per year. These differences show the important distinction between expected and actual inflation rates.

Even professional economic forecasters acknowledge that their inflation forecasts are hardly certain even for the next year, not to mention the next 20.

When you look at an asset from the perspective of its future purchasing power, you can see that an asset that is riskless in nominal terms can be very risky in real terms.[6]

CONCEPT CHECK

3. Suppose the rate of inflation turns out to be 13 percent per year. What will be the real annualized 20-year HPR on the nominally risk-free bond?

5.5 RETURN DISTRIBUTIONS AND VALUE AT RISK

What does history teach us about the risk of a representative portfolio of stocks? The distribution of stock returns over the last 47 years may be a rough guide as to potential losses from future investments in the market. Let's take a brief look at that distribution, focusing particularly on its "left tail," representing investment losses.

The valuation of a stock is based on its (discounted) expected future cash flows, and the equilibrium price is set so as to yield a fair expected return, commensurate with its risk. Deviations of the actual return from its expectation result from forecasting errors concerning the various economic factors that affect future cash flows. It is natural to expect that the net effect of these many potential forecasting errors, and hence rates of return on stocks, will be at least approximately normally distributed.[7]

[6]Since 1991, the Canadian government has been issuing the so-called *real return bonds* or RRBs, which are inflation-indexed; these are dicussed in Chapter 11. Most bonds, however, make payments that are fixed in dollar terms and subject to inflation risk.The Central Limit
[7]Theorem tells us that in many circumstances the combined effect of many random variables will be approximately normally distributed. Since new information about economic factors flows practically continuously, it is more reasonable to describe continuously compounded returns, rather than holding-period returns, using a normal distribution. See Appendix 5A for a refresher on continuous compounding, and Appendix 5B on the lognormal distribution and its applications to continuously compounded returns.

The **normal distribution** has at least two attractive properties. First, it is symmetric and completely described by two parameters, its mean and standard deviation. This property implies that the risk of a normally distributed investment return is fully described by its standard deviation. Second, a weighted average of variables that are normally distributed also will be normally distributed. Therefore, when individual stock returns are normally distributed, the return on any portfolio combining any set of stocks will also be normally distributed and its standard deviation will fully convey its risk. For these reasons, it is useful to know whether the assumption of normality is warranted. Figure 5.5 is derived from raw annual returns and is too crude to make this determination.

Figure 5.7 compares the cumulative probability distributions of continuously compounded monthly returns on stocks with those of a normal distribution with matching mean and standard deviation. While the cumulative distribution roughly matches the normal distribution, we can see that extreme values are more frequent than suggested by the normal. Moreover, these extreme values appear to be more frequent at the negative end of the distribution.

We would like a measure that reveals whether extreme negative values are too large and frequent to be adequately characterized by the normal distribution. One approach is to compute the standard deviation separately for the negative deviations. This statistic is called *lower partial standard deviation* (LPSD). If the LPSD is large relative to the overall standard deviation, it should replace the standard deviation as a measure of risk, since investors presumably think about risk as the possibility of large *negative* outcomes.

Another way to describe the negative extreme values is to quantify the asymmetry of the distribution. This we do by averaging the cubed (instead of squared) deviations from the mean. Just as the variance is called the second moment around the mean, the average cubed deviation is called the *third moment* of the distribution. The cubed deviations preserve sign, which allows us to distinguish good from bad outcomes. Moreover, since cubing exaggerates larger deviations, the sign and magnitude of the average cubed deviation reveal the direction and extent of the asymmetry. To scale the third moment (its unit is percent cubed), we divide it by the cubed standard deviation. The resulting statistic is called the skew of the distribution, and *skewness* is a measure of asymmetry. Table 5.4 compares the lower partial standard deviation to the overall standard deviation. The LPSD is somewhat larger than the overall standard deviation. The next line indicates that the distribution is negatively skewed.

Figure 5.7 Actual versus normal cumulative frequencies of monthly returns for stocks, 1957–2003 (returns are expressed as continuously compounded percentage rates).

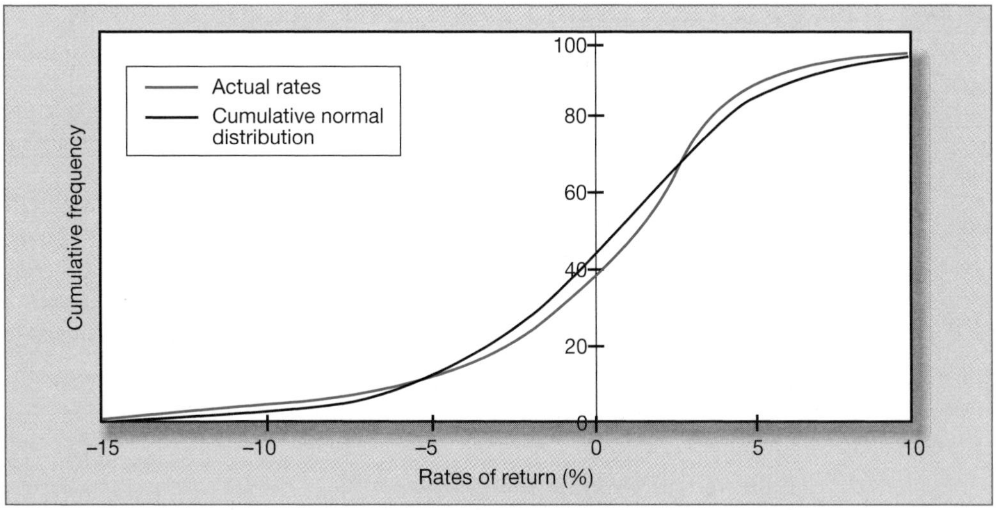

Source: Data from Scotia Capital's "Debt Market Indices," various years. Used by permission of Scotia Capital Markets Fixed Income Research.

Table 5.4
Deviations from Normality and VaR (continuously compounded monthly S&P/TSX returns)

Mean	0.7273%
Standard deviation	4.524%
LPSD	4.7242%
Skew	–0.96188
VaR normal	–6.737%
VaR actual	–6.848%

Professional investors extensively use a risk measure that highlights the potential loss from extreme negative returns, called **value at risk**, denoted by VaR (to distinguish it from VAR or Var, commonly used to denote variance). The VaR is another name for the quantile of a distribution. The quantile (q) of a distribution is the value below which lie q percent of the values. Thus the median of the distribution is the 50 percent quantile. Practitioners commonly call the 5 percent quantile the VaR of the distribution. It tells us that, with a probability of 5 percent, we can expect a loss equal to or greater than the VaR. For a normal distribution, which is completely described by its mean and standard deviation, the VaR always lies 1.65 standard deviations below the mean, and thus, while it may be a convenient benchmark, it adds no information about risk. But if the distribution is not adequately described by the normal, the VaR does give useful information about the magnitude of loss we can expect in a "bad" (i.e., 5 percent quantile) scenario.

Table 5.4 shows the 5 percent VaR based on a normal distribution with the same mean and standard deviation as those of the stocks. Actual VaR based on historic returns show somewhat greater losses (–6.85 percent vs. –6.74 percent). One can compute the VaR corresponding to other quantiles, for example a 1 percent VaR. The VaR has become widely used by portfolio managers and regulators as a measure of potential losses.

5.6 A GLOBAL VIEW OF THE HISTORICAL RECORD

As financial markets around the world grow and become more regulated and transparent, Canadian investors look to improve diversification by investing internationally. Investors in many countries that traditionally used U.S. financial markets as a safe haven to supplement home-country investments also seek international diversification to reduce risk. The question arises as to how historical Canadian and U.S. experience compare with that of stock markets around the world.

Figure 5.8 shows a century-long history (1900–2000) of average nominal and real returns in stock markets of 16 developed countries. We find the United States in fourth place and Canada in fifth place in terms of real, average returns, behind Sweden, Australia, and South Africa. Figure 5.9 shows the standard deviations of real stock and bond returns for these same countries. We find Canada in first place and the United States tied with four other countries for third place in terms of lowest standard deviation of real stock returns. So Canada has done well, but not abnormally so, compared with these countries.

One interesting feature of these figures is that the countries with the worst results, measured by the ratio of average real returns to standard deviation, are Italy, Belgium, Germany, and Japan—the countries most devastated by World War II. The top-performing countries are Australia, Canada, and the United States, the countries least devastated by the wars of the twentieth century. Another, perhaps more telling feature, is the insignificant difference between the real returns in the different countries. The difference between the highest average real rate (Sweden, at 7.6 percent) from the average return across the 16 countries (5.1 percent) is 2.5 percent. Similarly,

Figure 5.8 Nominal and real equity returns around the world, 1900–2000.

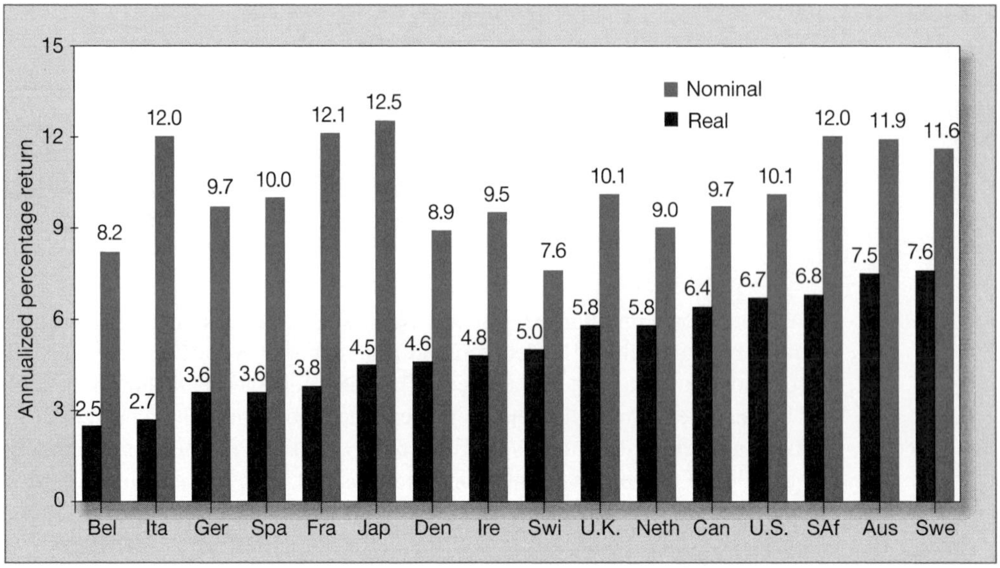

Source: Elroy Dimson, Paul Marsh, and Mike Staunton, *Triumph of the Optimists: 101 Years of Global Investment Returns*. (Princeton University Press, 2002).

Figure 5.9 Standard deviations of real equity and bond returns around the world, 1900–2000.

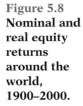

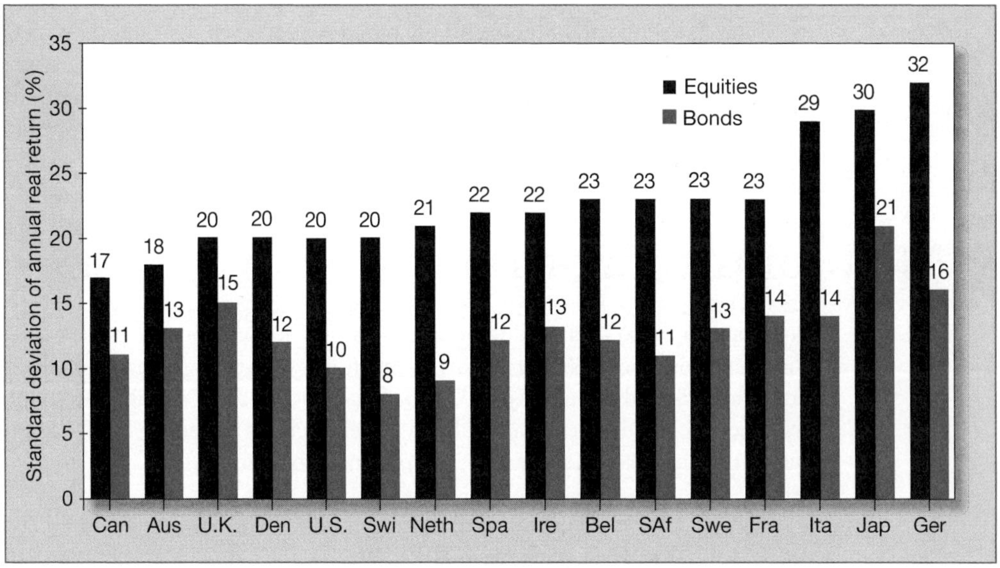

Source: Elroy Dimson, Paul Marsh, and Mike Staunton, *Triumph of the Optimists: 101 Years of Global Investment Returns*. (Princeton University Press, 2002).

the difference between the average and the lowest country return (Belgium, at 2.5 percent) is 2.6 percent. Using the average standard deviation of 23 percent, the *t*-statistic for a difference of 2.6 percent with 100 observations is

$$t\text{-statistic} = \frac{\text{Difference in mean}}{\text{Standard deviation}/\sqrt{n}} = \frac{2.6}{2.6\sqrt{100}} = 1.3$$

which is far below conventional levels of statistical significance. We conclude that neither the Canadian nor the U.S. experience can be dismissed as an outlier case. Hence, using the large U.S. stock market as a yardstick for return characteristics may be reasonable.

5.7 FORECASTS FOR THE LONG HAUL

While portfolio managers struggle daily to adjust their portfolios to changing expectations, individual investors are more concerned with long-term expectations. A middle-aged investor at the age of 40 is typically saving largely for retirement with a horizon of some 25 years. With a \$100,000 investment, a 1 percent increase in the average real rate, from 6 percent to 7 percent, would increase the real retirement fund in 25 years from $100{,}000 \times 1.06^{25} = \$429{,}187$ to $100{,}000 \times 107^{25} = \$542{,}743$, a difference of \$113,556 in real-consumption dollars. You can see why a reliable long-term return forecast is crucial to the determination of how much to save and how much of the savings to invest in risky assets for the risk premium they offer.

The Japanese experience in the 1990s provides another idea of the stakes involved. In 1990, the Nikkei 225 (an index of Japanese stocks akin to the S&P 500 in the United States) stood at just about 40,000. By 2003, that index stood at about 8,000, a nominal loss of 80 percent over 13 years and an even greater loss in real terms. A Japanese investor who invested in stocks at the age 50 in 1990 would have found himself in 2003, only a few years before retirement, with less than 20 percent of his 1990 savings. For such investors, the rosy long-term history of stock market investments is cold comfort.

These days, practitioners and scholars are debating whether the historical U.S. average risk-premium of large stocks over T-bills of 8.22 percent (12.04 percent − 3.82 percent), is a reasonable forecast for the long term.[8] This debate centres around two questions: First, do economic factors that prevailed over that historic period (1926–2002) adequately represent those that may prevail over the forecasting horizon? Second, is the arithmetic average from the available history a good yardstick for long-term forecasts?

Fama and French[9] note that for U.S. stocks the risk premium on equities over the period 1872–1949 was 4.62 percent, much lower than the 8.41 percent premium realized over the period 1950–1999. They argue that returns over the later half of the twentieth century were largely driven by unexpected capital gains that cannot be expected to prevail in the next century.

In fact, the data shows that the large-stock risk premium as measured by geometric averages over the period 1926–2002 is much lower, at 6.23 percent, than the 8.22 percent premium based on the arithmetic average. This difference alone would take away about half of the range of the debate. So which average should we use?

The use of the arithmetic average to forecast future rates of return derives from the statistical property that it is unbiased. This desirable property has made arithmetic averages the norm for estimating expected holding-period rates of return. However, for forecasts of *cumulative returns* over long horizons, the arithmetic average is inadequate. Jacquier, Kane, and Marcus[10] show that the correct forecast of total returns over long horizons requires compounding at a weighted average of the arithmetic and geometric historical averages. The proper weight applied to the geometric average equals the ratio of the length of the forecast horizon to the length of the estimation period. For example, if we wish to forecast the cumulative return for a 25-year horizon from a 77-year history, an unbiased estimate would be to compound at a rate of

$$\text{Geometric average} \times \frac{25}{77} + \text{Arithmetic average} \times \frac{77 - 25}{77}$$

[8]Note that the average risk premium in Canada is much lower at 3.66 percent (10.65 percent – 6.99 percent; see Table 5.2) over the period 1957–2003.

[9]Eugene Fama and Kenneth French, "The Equity Premium," *Journal of Finance* 57 (April 2000), pp. 637–60. Similar evidence appears in Ravi Jagannathan, Ellen R. McGrattan, and Anna Scherbina, "The Declining U.S. Equity Premium," *Federal Reserve Bank of Minneapolis Quarterly Review* 24 (Fall 2000), pp. 3–19.

[10]Eric Jacqier, Alex Kane, and Alan J. Marcus, "Geometric or Arithmetic Means: A Reconsideration," *Financial Analysts Journal*, November/December 2003.

This correction would take about .7 percent off the historical arithmetic average risk premium on large stocks. A forecast for the next 77 years would require compounding at only the geometric average, and for longer horizons at an even lower number. The forecast horizons that are relevant for current middle-aged investors must, however, be resolved primarily on economic rather than statistical grounds.

We now turn to a more detailed exploration of investor risk aversion and the need for a risk premium to induce investors to hold stocks.

5.8 RISK AND RISK AVERSION

Risk with Simple Prospects

The presence of risk means that more than one outcome is possible. A *simple prospect* is an investment opportunity in which a certain initial wealth is placed at risk, and there are only two possible outcomes. For the sake of simplicity, it is useful to begin our analysis and elucidate some basic concepts using simple prospects.

Take as an example initial wealth, W, of \$100,000, and assume two possible results. With a probability, p, of .6, the favourable outcome will occur, leading to final wealth, W_1, of \$150,000. Otherwise, with probability $1 - p = .4$, a less favourable outcome, $W_2 = \$80,000$, will occur. We can represent the simple prospect using an event tree:

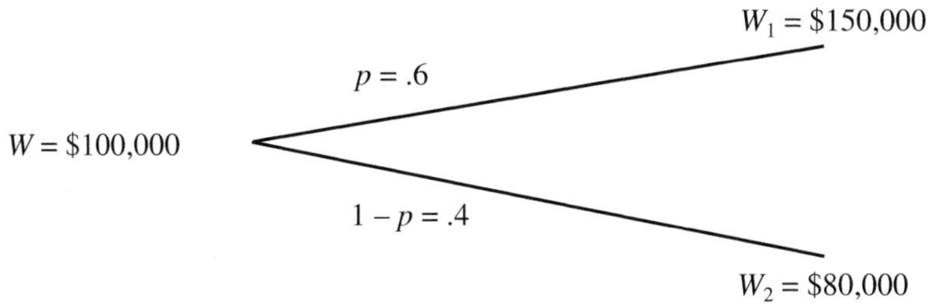

Suppose that an investor, Susan, is offered an investment portfolio with a payoff in one year that is described by such a simple prospect. How can she evaluate this portfolio?

First, she could try to summarize it using descriptive statistics. For instance, her mean or expected end-of-year wealth, denoted $E(W)$, is

$$\begin{aligned} E(W) &= pW_1 + (1 - p)W_2 \\ &= .6 \times 150{,}000 + .4 \times 80{,}000 \\ &= \$122{,}000 \end{aligned}$$

The expected profit on the \$100,000 investment portfolio is \$22,000: 122,000 – 100,000. The variance, σ^2, of the portfolio's payoff is calculated as the expected value of the squared deviations of each possible outcome from the mean:

$$\begin{aligned} \sigma^2 &= p[W_1 - E(W)]^2 + (1 - p)[W_2 - E(W)]^2 \\ &= .6(150{,}000 - 122{,}000)^2 + .4(80{,}000 - 122{,}000)^2 \\ &= 1{,}176{,}000{,}000 \end{aligned}$$

The standard deviation, σ, the square root of the variance, is therefore \$34,292.86.

Clearly, this is risky business: the standard deviation of the payoff is large, much larger than the expected profit of $22,000. Whether the expected profit is large enough to justify such risk depends on the alternative portfolios.

Let us suppose Treasury bills are one alternative to Susan's risky portfolio. Suppose that at the time of the decision, a one-year T-bill offers a rate of return of 5 percent; $100,000 can be invested to yield a sure profit of $5,000. We can now draw Susan's decision tree:

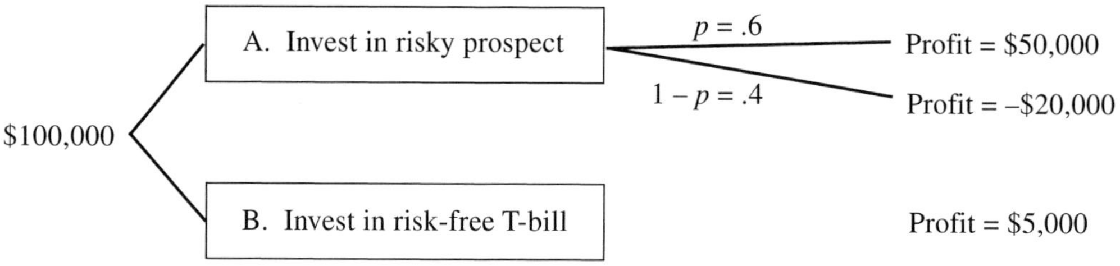

Earlier, we showed the expected profit on the portfolio to be $22,000. Therefore, the expected marginal, or incremental, profit of the risky portfolio over investing in safe T-bills is

$$\$22{,}000 - \$5{,}000 = \$17{,}000$$

meaning that one can earn an expected risk premium of $17,000 as compensation for the risk of the investment.

The question of whether a given risk premium provides adequate compensation for the investment's risk is age-old. Indeed, one of the central concerns of finance theory (and much of this text) is the measurement of risk and the determination of the risk premiums that investors can expect of risky assets in well-functioning capital markets.

CONCEPT CHECK

4. What is the risk premium of Susan's risky portfolio in terms of rate of return rather than dollars?

Risk, Speculation, and Gambling

One definition of *speculation* is "the assumption of considerable business risk in obtaining commensurate gain." Although this definition is fine linguistically, it is useless without first specifying what is meant by "commensurate gain" and "considerable risk."

By *commensurate gain* we mean a positive expected profit beyond the risk-free alternative. This is the risk premium. In our example, the dollar risk premium is the profit net of the alternative, which is the sure T-bill profit. The risk premium is the incremental expected gain from taking on the risk. By *considerable risk* we mean that the risk is sufficient to affect the decision. An individual might reject a prospect that has a positive risk premium because the added gain is insufficient to make up for the risk involved.

To gamble is "to bet or wager on an uncertain outcome." If you compare this definition to that of speculation, you will see that the central difference is the lack of "good profit." Economically speaking, a gamble is the assumption of risk for no purpose but enjoyment of the risk itself, whereas speculation is undertaken because one perceives a favourable risk-return tradeoff. To turn a gamble into a speculative prospect requires an adequate risk premium for compensation to risk-averse investors for the risks that they bear. Hence *risk aversion and speculation are not inconsistent.*

In some cases a gamble may appear to the participants as speculation. Suppose that two investors disagree sharply about the future exchange rate of the Canadian dollar against the

British pound. They may choose to bet on the outcome. Suppose that Paul will pay Mary $100 if the value of one pound exceeds $2 one year from now, whereas Mary will pay Paul if the pound is worth less than $2. There are only two relevant outcomes: (1) the pound will exceed $2, or (2) it will fall below $2. If Paul and Mary agree on the probabilities of the two possible outcomes, and if neither party anticipates a loss, it must be that they assign $p = .5$ to each outcome. In that case the expected profit to both is zero and each has entered one side of a gambling prospect.

What is more likely, however, is that the bet results from differences in the probabilities that Paul and Mary assign to the outcome. Mary assigns it $p > .5$, whereas Paul's assessment is $p < .5$. They perceive, subjectively, two different prospects. Economists call this case of differing belief's *heterogeneous expectations.* In such cases investors on each side of a financial position see themselves as speculating rather than gambling.

Both Paul and Mary should be asking, "Why is the other willing to invest in the side of a risky prospect that I believe offers a negative expected profit?" The ideal way to resolve heterogeneous beliefs is for Paul and Mary to "merge their information," that is, for each party to verify that he or she possesses all relevant information and processes the information properly. Of course, the acquisition of information and the extensive communication that is required to eliminate all heterogeneity in expectations is costly, and thus, up to a point, heterogeneous expectations cannot be taken as irrational. If, however, Paul and Mary enter such contracts frequently, they would recognize the information problem in one of two ways: either they will realize that they are creating gambles when each wins half of the bets, or the consistent loser will admit that he or she has been betting on inferior forecasts.

CONCEPT CHECK

5. Assume that dollar-denominated T-bills in Canada and pound-denominated bills in the United Kingdom offer equal yields to maturity. Both are short-term assets, and both are free of default risk. Neither offers investors a risk premium. However, a Canadian investor who holds U.K. bills is subject to exchange rate risk since the pounds earned on the U.K. bills eventually will be exchanged for dollars at the future exchange rate. Is the Canadian investor engaging in speculation or gambling?

Risk Aversion and Utility Values

We have discussed risk with simple prospects and how risk premiums bear on speculation. A prospect that has a zero-risk premium is called a *fair game.* Investors who are *risk-averse* reject investment portfolios that are fair games or worse. Risk-averse investors are willing to consider only risk-free or speculative prospects. Loosely speaking, a risk-averse investor "penalizes" the expected rate of return of a risky portfolio by a certain percentage (or penalizes the expected profit by a dollar amount) to account for the risk involved. The greater the risk the investor perceives, the larger the penalization. (One might wonder why we assume risk aversion as fundamental. We believe that most investors accept this view from simple introspection, but we discuss the question more fully in Appendix 5C at the end of this chapter.)

We can formalize this notion of a risk-penalty system. To do so, we will assume that each investor can assign a welfare, or **utility**, score to competing investment portfolios based on the expected return and risk of those portfolios. The utility score may be viewed as a means of ranking portfolios. Higher utility values are assigned to portfolios with more attractive risk-return profiles. Portfolios receive higher utility scores for higher expected returns and lower scores for higher volatility. Many particular "scoring" systems are legitimate. One reasonable function that is commonly employed by financial theorists and the CFA Institute assigns a portfolio with expected return $E(r)$ and variance of returns σ^2 the following utility score:

$$U = E(r) - \frac{1}{2}A\sigma^2 \tag{5.4}$$

where U is the utility value and A is an index of the investor's aversion to taking on risk. (The factor of ½ is a scaling convention that will simplify calculations in later chapters. It has no economic significance, and we could eliminate it simply by defining a "new" A with half the value of the A used here.)

Equation 5.4 is consistent with the notion that utility is enhanced by high expected returns and diminished by high risk. (Whether variance is an adequate measure of portfolio risk is discussed in Appendix 5B.) The extent to which variance lowers utility depends on A, the investor's degree of risk aversion. More risk-averse investors (who have the larger A's) penalize risky investments more severely. Investors choosing among competing investment portfolios will select the one providing the highest utility level.

Risk aversion obviously will have a major impact on the investor's appropriate risk-return tradeoff. The box here discusses some techniques that financial advisors use to gauge the risk aversion of their clients.

Notice in equation 5.4 that the utility provided by a risk-free portfolio is simply the rate of return on the portfolio, since there is no penalization for risk. This provides us with a convenient benchmark for evaluating portfolios. For example, recall Susan's investment problem, choosing between a portfolio with expected return .22 (22 percent) and standard deviation $\sigma = .34$, and T-bills, providing a risk-free return of 5 percent. Although the risk premium on the risky portfolio is large, 17 percent, the risk of the project is so great that Susan does not need to be very risk-averse to choose the safe all-bills strategy. Even for A = 3, a moderate risk-aversion parameter, equation 5.4 shows the risky portfolio's utility value as $.22 - ½ \times 3 \times .34^2 = .0466$, or 4.66 percent, which is slightly lower than the risk-free rate. In this case, Susan would reject the portfolio in favour of T-bills.

The downward adjustment of the expected return as a penalty for risk is $½ \times 3 \times .34^2 = .1734$, or 17.34 percent. If Susan were less risk-averse (more risk-tolerant), for example with $A = 2$, she would adjust the expected rate of return downward by only 11.56 percent. In that case, the utility level of the portfolio would be 10.44 percent, higher than the risk-free rate, leading her to accept the prospect.

CONCEPT CHECK

6. A portfolio has an expected rate of return of .20 and standard deviation of .20. Bills offer a sure rate of return of .07. Which investment alternative will be chosen by an investor whose $A = 4$? What if $A = 8$?

Because we can compare utility values to the rate offered on risk-free investments when choosing between a risky portfolio and a safe one, we may interpret a portfolio's utility value as its "certainty equivalent" rate of return to an investor. That is, the **certainty equivalent rate** of a portfolio is the rate that risk-free investments would need to offer with certainty to be considered equally attractive to the risky portfolio.

Now we can say that a portfolio is desirable only if its certainty equivalent return exceeds that of the risk-free alternative. A sufficiently risk-averse investor may assign any risky portfolio, even one with a positive risk premium, a certainty equivalent rate of return that is below the risk-free rate, which will cause the investor to reject the portfolio. At the same time, a less risk-averse (more risk-tolerant) investor will assign the same portfolio a certainty equivalent rate that exceeds the risk-free rate and thus will prefer the portfolio to the risk-free alternative. If the risk premium is zero or negative to begin with, any downward adjustment to utility only makes the portfolio look worse. Its certainty equivalent rate will be below that of the risk-free alternative for all risk-averse investors.

TIME FOR INVESTING'S FOUR-LETTER WORD

What four-letter word should pop into mind when the stock market takes a harrowing nose dive?

No, not those. R-I-S-K.

Risk is the potential for realizing low returns or even losing money, possibly preventing you from meeting important objectives, like sending your kids to the college of their choice or having the retirement lifestyle you crave.

But many financial advisers and other experts say that these days investors aren't taking the idea of risk as seriously as they should, and they are overexposing themselves to stocks.

"The market has been so good for years that investors no longer believe there's risk in investing," says Gary Schatsky, a financial adviser in New York.

So before the market goes down and stays down, be sure that you understand your tolerance for risk and that your portfolio is designed to match it.

Assessing your risk tolerance, however, can be tricky. You must consider not only how much risk you can afford to take but also how much risk you can stand to take.

Determining how much risk you can stand—your temperamental tolerance for risk—is more difficult. It isn't quantifiable.

To that end, many financial advisers, brokerage firms and mutual-fund companies have created risk quizzes to help people determine whether they are conservative, moderate or aggressive investors. Some firms that offer such quizzes include Merrill Lynch, T. Rowe Price Associates Inc., Baltimore, Zurich Group Inc.'s Scudder Kemper Investments Inc., New York, and Vanguard Group in Malvern, Pa.

Typically, risk questionnaires include seven to 10 questions about a person's investing experience, financial security and tendency to make risky or conservative choices.

The benefit of the questionnaires is that they are an objective resource people can use to get at least a rough idea of their risk tolerance. "It's impossible for someone to assess their risk tolerance alone," says Mr. Bernstein. "I may say I don't like risk, yet will take more risk than the average person."

Many experts warn, however, that the questionnaires should be used simply as a first step to assessing risk tolerance. "They are not precise," says Ron Meier, a certified public accountant.

The second step, many experts agree, is to ask yourself some difficult questions, such as: How much you can stand to lose over the long term?

"Most people can stand to lose a heck of a lot temporarily," says Mr. Schatsky. The real acid test, he says, is how much of your portfolio's value you can stand to lose over months or years.

As it turns out, most people rank as middle-of-the-road risk-takers, say several advisers. "Only about 10% to 15% of my clients are aggressive," says Mr. Roge.

What's Your Risk Tolerance?

Circle the letter that corresponds to your answer.

1. Just 60 days after you put money into an investment its price falls 20 percent. Assuming none of the fundamentals have changed, what would you do?
   a. Sell to avoid further worry and try something else
   b. Do nothing and wait for the investment to come back
   c. Buy more. It was a good investment before; now it's a cheap investment too
2. Now look at the previous question another way. Your investment fell 20 percent, but it's part of a portfolio being used to meet investment goals with three different time horizons.

2A. What would you do if the goal were five years away?
   a. Sell
   b. Do nothing
   c. Buy more

In contrast to risk-averse investors, **risk-neutral** investors judge risky prospects solely by their expected rates of return. The level of risk is irrelevant to the risk-neutral investor, meaning that there is no penalization for risk. For this investor, a portfolio's certainty equivalent rate is simply its expected rate of return.

A **risk lover** is willing to engage in fair games and gambles; this investor adjusts the expected return upward to take into account the "fun" of confronting the prospect's risk. Risk lovers always will take a fair game because their upward adjustment of utility for risk gives the fair game a certainty equivalent that exceeds the alternative of the risk-free investment.

We can depict the individual's tradeoff between risk and return by plotting the characteristics of potential investment portfolios that the individual would view as equally attractive on a graph with axes measuring the expected value and standard deviation of portfolio returns. Figure 5.10 plots the characteristics of one portfolio.

Portfolio P, which has expected return $E(r_p)$ and standard deviation σ_p, is preferred by risk-averse investors to any portfolio in quadrant IV because it has an expected return equal to or greater than any portfolio in that quadrant and a standard deviation equal to or smaller than any

2B. What would you do if the goal were 15 years away?
   a. Sell
   b. Do nothing
   c. Buy more

2C. What would you do if the goal were 30 years away?
   a. Sell
   b. Do nothing
   c. Buy more

3. The price of your retirement investment jumps 25% a month after you buy it. Again, the fundamentals haven't changed. After you finish gloating, what do you do?
   a. Sell it and lock in your gains
   b. Stay put and hope for more gain
   c. Buy more; it could go higher

4. You're investing for retirement, which is 15 years away. Which would you rather do?
   a. Invest in a money-market fund or guaranteed investment contract, giving up the possibility of major gains, but virtually assuring the safety of your principal
   b. Invest in a 50-50 mix of bond funds and stock funds, in hopes of getting some growth, but also giving yourself some protection in the form of steady income
   c. Invest in aggressive growth mutual funds whose value will probably fluctuate significantly during the year, but have the potential for impressive gains over five or 10 years

5. You just won a big prize! But which one? It's up to you.
   a. $2,000 in cash
   b. A 50% chance to win $5,000
   c. A 20% chance to win $15,000

6. A good investment opportunity just came along. But you have to borrow money to get in. Would you take out a loan?
   a. Definitely not
   b. Perhaps
   c. Yes

7. Your company is selling stock to its employees. In three years, management plans to take the company public. Until then, you won't be able to sell your shares and you will get no dividends. But your investment could multiply as much as 10 times when the company goes public. How much money would you invest?
   a. None
   b. Two months' salary
   c. Four months' salary

Scoring Your Risk Tolerance

To score the quiz, add up the number of answers you gave in each category *a–c*, then multiply as shown to find your score.

(*a*) answers	______	× 1 =	______	points
(*b*) answers	______	× 2 =	______	points
(*c*) answers	______	× 3 =	______	points

YOUR SCORE ______ points

If you scored . . .	You may be a(n):
9–14 points	Conservative investor
15–21 points	Moderate investor
22–27 points	Aggressive investor

portfolio in that quadrant. Conversely, any portfolio in quadrant I is preferable to portfolio *P* because its expected return is equal to or greater than *P*'s and its standard deviation is equal to or smaller than *P*'s.

This is the mean-standard deviation, or equivalently, **mean-variance (M-V) criterion**. It can be stated as A dominates *B* if

$$E(r_A) \geq E(r_B)$$

and

$$\sigma_A \leq \sigma_B$$

and at least one inequality is strict.

In the expected return–standard deviation graph, the preferred direction is northwest, because in this direction we simultaneously increase the expected return *and* decrease the variance of the rate of return. This means that any portfolio that lies northwest of *P* is superior to *P*.

What can be said about the portfolios in quadrants II and III? Their desirability, compared with *P*, depends on the exact nature of the investor's risk aversion. Suppose an investor identifies all

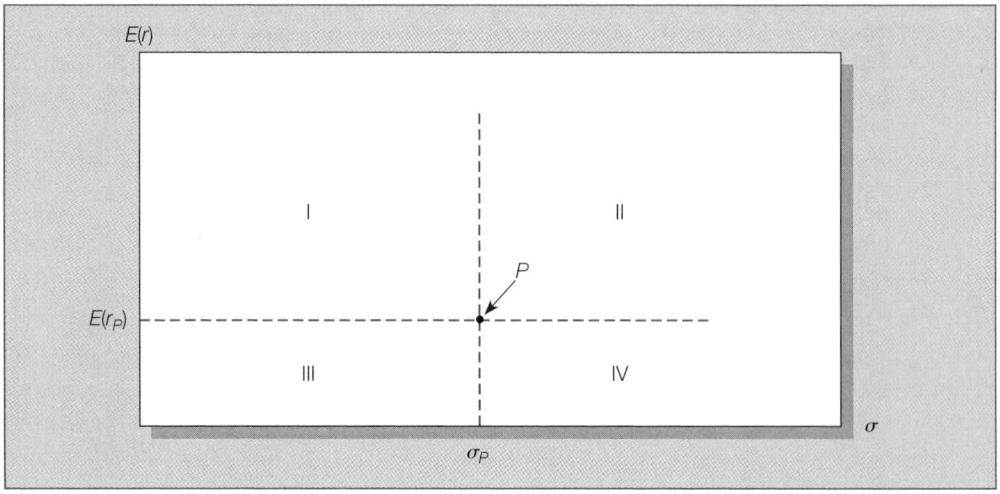

Figure 5.10 The tradeoff between risk and return of a potential investment portfolio.

portfolios that are equally attractive as portfolio *P*. Starting at *P*, an increase in standard deviation lowers utility; it must be compensated for by an increase in expected return. Thus, point *Q* is equally desirable to this investor as *P*. Investors will be equally attracted to portfolios with high risk and high expected returns compared with other portfolios with lower risk but lower expected returns.

These equally preferred portfolios will lie on a curve in the mean-standard deviation graph that connects all portfolio points with the same utility value (Figure 5.11). This is called the **indifference curve**.

To determine some of the points that appear on the indifference curve, examine the utility values of several possible portfolios for an investor with $A = 4$, presented in Table 5.5. Note that each portfolio offers identical utility, since the high-return portfolios also have high risk. Although in practice the exact indifference curves of various investors cannot be known, this analysis can take us a long way in determining appropriate principles for portfolio selection strategy.

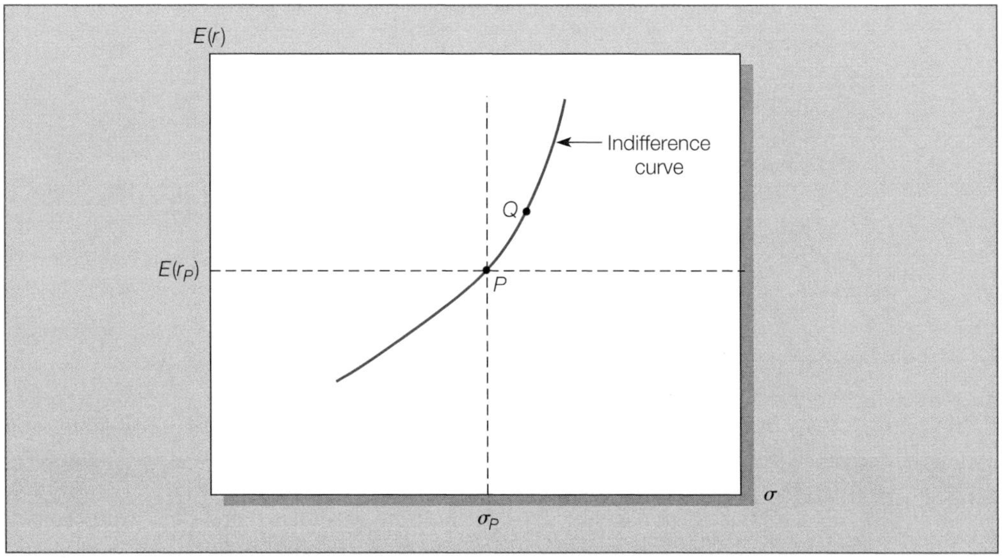

Figure 5.11 The indifference curve.

Table 5.5 Utility Values of Possible Portfolios

Expected Return, $E(r)$	Standard Deviation, σ	Utility = $E(r) - \frac{1}{2}A\sigma^2$
.10	.200	$.10 - .5 \times 4 \times .04 = .02$
.15	.255	$.15 - .5 \times 4 \times .065 = .02$
.20	.300	$.20 - .5 \times 4 \times .09 = .02$
.25	.339	$.25 - .5 \times 4 \times .115 = .02$

CONCEPT CHECK

7. *a.* How will the indifference curve of a less risk-averse investor compare to the indifference curve drawn in Figure 5.11?
   b. Draw both indifference curves passing through point *P*.

5.9 PORTFOLIO RISK

Asset Risk Versus Portfolio Risk

We have focused so far on the return and risk of an individual's overall investment portfolio. Such portfolios are composed of diverse types of assets. In addition to their direct investment in financial markets, investors have stakes in pension funds, life insurance policies with savings components, homes, and, not least, the earning power of their skills (human capital).

Investors must take account of the interplay between asset returns when evaluating the risk of a portfolio. At a most basic level, for example, an insurance contract serves to reduce risk by providing a large payoff when another part of the portfolio is faring poorly. A fire insurance policy pays off when another asset in the portfolio—a house or factory, for example—suffers a big loss in value. The offsetting patterns of returns on these two assets (the house and the insurance policy) stabilizes the risk of the overall portfolio. Investing in an asset with a payoff pattern that offsets our exposure to a particular source of risk is called **hedging.**

Insurance contracts are obvious hedging vehicles. In many contexts financial markets offer similar, although perhaps less direct, hedging opportunities. For example, consider two firms, one producing suntan lotion, the other producing umbrellas. The shareholders of each firm face weather risk of an opposite nature. A rainy summer lowers the return on the suntan-lotion firm but raises it on the umbrella firm. Shares of the umbrella firm act as "weather insurance" for the suntan-lotion firm shareholders in precisely the same way that fire insurance policies insure houses. When the lotion firm does poorly (bad weather), the "insurance" asset (umbrella shares) provides a high payoff that offsets the loss.

Another means to control portfolio risk is **diversification,** by which we mean that investments are made in a wide variety of assets so that the exposure to the risk of any particular security is limited. By putting one's eggs in many baskets, overall portfolio risk actually may be less than the risk of any component security considered in isolation.

To examine these effects more precisely, and to lay a foundation for the mathematical properties that will be used in coming chapters, we will consider an example with less than perfect hedging opportunities, and in the process review the statistics underlying portfolio risk and return characteristics.

A Review of Portfolio Mathematics

Consider the problem of Humanex, a nonprofit organization deriving most of its income from the return of its endowment. Years ago, the founders of Best Candy willed a large block of Best

Candy stock to Humanex with the provision that Humanex may never sell it. This block of shares now makes up 50 percent of Humanex's endowment. Humanex has free choice as to where to invest the remainder of its portfolio.[11]

The value of Best Candy stock is sensitive to the price of sugar. In years when the Caribbean sugar crop fails, the price of sugar rises significantly and Best Candy suffers considerable losses. We can describe the fortunes of Best Candy stock using the following scenario analysis:

	Normal Year for Sugar		Abnormal Year
	Bullish Stock Market	**Bearish Stock Market**	**Sugar Crisis**
Probability	.5	.3	.2
Rate of return	.25	.10	–.25

To summarize these three possible outcomes using conventional statistics, we review some of the key roles governing the properties of risky assets and portfolios.

Rule 1. The mean or *expected return* of an asset is a probability-weighted average of its return in all scenarios. Calling $Pr(s)$ the probability of scenario s and $r(s)$ the return in scenario s, we may write the expected return, $E(r)$, as

$$E(r) = \sum_s Pr(s)r(s) \tag{5.5}$$

Applying this formula to the case at hand, with three possible scenarios, we find that the expected rate of return of Best Candy's stock is

$$\begin{aligned} E(r_{\text{Best}}) &= .5 \times .25 + .3 \times .10 + .2(-.25) \\ &= .105 \\ &= 10.5\% \end{aligned}$$

Rule 2. The *variance* of an asset's returns is the expected value of the squared deviations from the expected return. Symbolically,

$$\sigma^2 = \sum_s Pr(s)[r(s) - E(r)]^2 \tag{5.6}$$

Therefore, in our example

$$\begin{aligned} \sigma^2_{\text{Best}} &= .5(.25 - .105)^2 + .3(.10 - .105)^2 + .2(-.25 - .105)^2 \\ &= .035725 \end{aligned}$$

The *standard deviation* of Best's return, which is the square root of the variance, is $\sqrt{.035725} = .189$, or 18.9 percent.

Humanex has 50 percent of its endowment in Best's stock. To reduce the risk of the overall portfolio, it could invest the remainder in T-bills, which yield a sure rate of return of 5 percent. To derive the return of the overall portfolio, we apply rule 3:

Rule 3. The rate of return on a portfolio is a weighted average of the rates of return of each asset comprising the portfolio, with portfolio proportions as weights. This implies that the *expected* rate of return on a portfolio is a weighted average of the *expected* rate of return on each component asset.

[11]The portfolio restriction is admittedly unusual. We use this example only to illustrate the various strategies that might be used to control risk and to review some useful results from statistics.

In this case, the portfolio proportions in each asset are .5, and the portfolio's expected rate of return is

$$
\begin{aligned}
E(r_{\text{Humanex}}) &= .5E(r_{\text{Best}}) + .5r_{\text{bills}} \\
&= .5 \times .105 + .5 \times .05 \\
&= .0775 \\
&= 7.75\%
\end{aligned}
$$

The standard deviation of the portfolio may be derived from the following:

Rule 4. When a risky asset is combined with a risk-free asset, the portfolio standard deviation equals the risky asset's standard deviation multiplied by the portfolio proportion invested in the asset.

In this case, the Humanex portfolio is 50 percent invested in Best stock and 50 percent invested in risk-free bills. Therefore

$$
\begin{aligned}
\sigma_{\text{Humanex}} &= .5\sigma_{\text{Best}} \\
&= .5 \times .189 \\
&= .0945 \\
&= 9.45\%
\end{aligned}
$$

By reducing its exposure to the risk of Best by half, Humanex reduces its portfolio standard deviation by half. The cost of this risk reduction, however, is a reduction in expected return. The expected rate of return on Best stock is 10.5 percent. The expected return on the one-half T-bill portfolio is 7.75 percent. This makes the risk premiums over the 5 percent rate on risk-free bills 5.5 per-cent for Best stock and 2.75 percent for the half T-bill portfolio. By reducing the share of Best stock in the portfolio by one-half, Humanex reduces its portfolio risk premium by one-half, from 5.5 percent to 2.75 percent.

In an effort to improve the contribution of the endowment to the operating budget, Humanex's trustees hire Sally, a recent MBA, as a consultant. Investigating the sugar and candy industry, Sally discovers, not surprisingly, that during years of sugar crisis in the Caribbean basin, SugarBeet, a Canadian sugar refiner that uses beets as raw material, reaps unusual profits and its stock price soars. A scenario analysis of SugarBeet's stock looks like this:

	Normal Year for Sugar		Abnormal Year
	Bullish Stock Market	Bearish Stock Market	Sugar Crisis
Probability	.5	.3	.2
Rate of return	.01	−.05	.35

The expected rate of return on SugarBeet's stock is 6 percent, and its standard deviation is 14.73 percent. Thus, SugarBeet is almost as volatile as Best, yet its expected return is only a notch better than the T-bill rate. This cursory analysis makes SugarBeet appear to be an unattractive investment. For Humanex, however, the stock holds great promise.

SugarBeet offers excellent hedging potential for holders of Best stock because its return is highest precisely when Best's return is lowest—during a Caribbean sugar crisis. Consider Humanex's portfolio when it splits its investment evenly between Best and SugarBeet. The rate of return for each scenario is the simple average of the rates on Best and SugarBeet because the portfolio is split evenly between the two stocks (see rule 3).

	Normal Year for Sugar		Abnormal Year
	Bullish Stock Market	Bearish Stock Market	Sugar Crisis
Probability	.5	.3	.2
Rate of return	..13	.025	.05

The expected rate of return on Humanex's hedged portfolio is .0825, with a standard deviation of 0.0483, or 4.83 percent.

Sally now summarizes the reward and risk of the three alternatives:

Portfolio	Expected Return	Standard Deviation
All in Best Candy	.105	.1890
Half in T-bills	.0775	.0945
Half in SugarBeet	.0825	.0483

The numbers speak for themselves. The hedge portfolio including SugarBeet clearly dominates the simple risk-reduction strategy of investing in safe T-bills. It has higher expected return *and* lower standard deviation than the one-half T-bill portfolio. The point is that, despite SugarBeet's large standard deviation of return, it is a risk reducer for some investors—in this case, those holding Best stock.

The risk of the individual assets in the portfolio must be measured in the context of the effect of their return on overall portfolio variability. This example demonstrates that assets with returns that are inversely associated with the initial risky position are the most powerful risk reducers.

CONCEPT CHECK

8. Suppose that the stock market offers an expected rate of return of 20 percent, with a standard deviation of 15 percent. Gold has an expected rate of return of 6 percent, with a standard deviation of 17 percent. In view of the market's higher expected return and lower uncertainty, will anyone choose to hold gold in a portfolio?

To quantify the hedging or diversification potential of an asset, we use the concepts of covariance and correlation. The **covariance** measures how much the returns on two risky assets move in tandem. A positive covariance means that asset returns move together. A negative covariance means that they vary inversely, as in the case of Best and SugarBeet.

To measure covariance, we look at return "surprises" or deviations from expected value in each scenario. Consider the product of each stock's deviation from expected return in a particular scenario:

$$[r_{\text{Best}} - E(r_{\text{Best}})][r_{\text{Beet}} - E(r_{\text{Beet}})]$$

This product will be positive if the returns of the two stocks move together across scenarios, that is, if both returns exceed their expectations or both fall short of those expectations in the scenario in question. On the other hand, if one stock's return exceeds its expected value when the other's falls short, the product will be negative. Thus, a good measure of how much the returns move together is the *expected value* of this product across all scenarios, which is defined as the covariance:

$$\text{Cov}(r_{\text{Best}}, r_{\text{Beet}}) = \sum_{s} Pr(s)[r_{\text{Best}}(s) - E(r_{\text{Best}})][r_{\text{Beet}}(s) - E(r_{\text{Beet}})] \tag{5.7}$$

In this example, with $E(r_{\text{Best}}) = .105$ and $E(r_{\text{Beet}}) = .06$ and with returns in each scenario summarized as follows, we find the covariance from a simple application of equation 5.7.

	Normal Year for Sugar		Abnormal Year
	Bullish Stock Market	**Bearish Stock Market**	**Sugar Crisis**
Probability	.5	.3	.2
Stock:			
Best Candy	.25	.10	−.25
SugarBeet	.01	−.05	.35

The covariance between the two stocks is

$$\begin{aligned}\text{Cov}(r_{\text{Best}},r_{\text{Beet}}) &= .5(.25 - .105)(.01 - .06) + .3(.10 - .105)(-.05 - .06)\\ &\quad + .2(-.25 - .105)(.35 - .06)\\ &= -.02405\end{aligned}$$

The negative covariance confirms the hedging quality of SugarBeet stock relative to Best Candy. SugarBeet's returns move inversely with Best's.

An easier statistic to interpret than the covariance is the **correlation coefficient**, which scales the covariance to a value between −1 (perfect negative correlation) and +1 (perfect positive correlation). The correlation coefficient between two variables equals their covariance divided by the product of the standard deviations. Denoting the correlation by the Greek letter ρ, we find that

$$\begin{aligned}\rho(\text{Best, Beet}) &= \frac{\text{Cov}[r_{\text{Best}}, r_{\text{Beet}}]}{\sigma_{\text{Best}}\sigma_{\text{Beet}}}\\ &= \frac{-.02405}{.189 \times .1473} \qquad (5.8)\\ &= -.86\end{aligned}$$

This large negative correlation (close to −1) confirms the strong tendency of Best and Beet stocks to move inversely, or "out of phase" with one another.

The impact of the covariance of asset returns on portfolio risk is apparent in the following formula for portfolio variance.

Rule 5. When two risky assets with variances σ^2_1 and σ^2_2, respectively, are combined into a portfolio with portfolio weights w_1 and w_2, respectively, the portfolio variance σ^2_P is given by

$$\sigma^2_P = w^2_1\sigma^2_1 + w^2_2\sigma^2_2 + 2w_1w_2\text{Cov}(r_1,r_2)$$

In this example, with equal weights in Best and Beet, $w_1 = w_2 = .5$, and with $\sigma_{\text{Best}} = .189$, $\sigma_{\text{Beet}} = .1473$, and $\text{Cov}(r_{\text{Best}}, r_{\text{Beet}}) = -.02405$, we find that

$$\sigma^2_P = .5^2 \times .189^2 + .5^2 \times .1473^2 + 2 \times .5 \times .5\,(-.02405) = .00233$$

or that $\sigma_P = \sqrt{.00233} = .0483$, precisely the same answer for the standard deviation of the returns on the hedged portfolio that we derived directly from the scenario analysis.

Rule 5 for portfolio variance highlights the effect of covariance on portfolio risk. A positive covariance increases portfolio variance, and a negative covariance acts to reduce portfolio variance. This makes sense because returns on negatively correlated assets tend to be offsetting, which stabilizes portfolio returns.

Basically, hedging involves the purchase of a risky asset that is negatively correlated with the existing portfolio. This negative correlation makes the volatility of the hedge asset a risk-reducing feature. A hedge strategy is a powerful alternative to the simple risk-reduction strategy of including a risk-free asset in the portfolio.

In later chapters we will see that, in a rational equilibrium, hedge assets must offer relatively low expected rates of return. The perfect hedge, an insurance contract, is by design perfectly negatively correlated with a specified risk. As one would expect in a "no free lunch" world, the insurance premium reduces the portfolio's expected rate of return.

? CONCEPT CHECK

9. Suppose that the distribution of SugarBeet stock returns is as follows:

Bullish Stock Market	Bearish Stock Market	Sugar Crisis
.07	−.05	.20

a. What would be its correlation with Best?

b. Is SugarBeet stock a useful hedge asset now?

c. Calculate the portfolio rate of return in each scenario and the standard deviation of the portfolio from the scenario returns. Then evaluate σ_P using rule 5.

d. Are the two methods of computing portfolio standard deviation consistent?

SUMMARY

1. The economy's equilibrium level of real interest rates depends on the willingness of households to save (as reflected in the supply curve of funds) and the expected profitability of business investment in plant, equipment, and inventories, as reflected in the demand curve for funds. It also depends on government fiscal and monetary policy.
2. In Canada, investors can invest in securities offering a guaranteed nominal rate of interest. Their real rate of return depends on the actual rate of inflation. There is an issue of Canada bonds that offers a guaranteed real rate of return.
3. The equilibrium expected rate of return on any security is the sum of the risk-free rate and a security-specific risk premium.
4. Investors face a tradeoff between risk and expected return. Historical data confirms our intuition that assets with low degrees of risk provide lower returns on average than do those of higher risk.
5. Assets with guaranteed nominal interest rates are risky in real terms because the future inflation rate is uncertain.
6. Historical returns on stocks exhibit more frequent large negative deviations from the mean than would be predicted from a normal distribution. The lower partial standard deviation (LPSD) and the skewness of the actual distribution quantify the deviation from normality. The LPSD, instead of the standard deviation, is sometimes used by practitioners as a measure of risk.
7. A widely used measure of risk is value at risk (VaR). VaR measures the loss that will be exceeded with a specified probability such as 5 percent. The VaR does not add new information when returns are normally distributed. When negative deviations from the average are larger and more frequent than the normal distribution, the 5 percent VaR will be more than 1.65 standard deviations below the average return.
8. Historical rates of return over the twentieth century in developed capital markets suggest the Canadian history of stock returns is not an outlier compared to other countries.
9. The arithmetic average of the risk premium on U.S. stocks over the period 1926–2002 is arguably too optimistic as a forecast for long-term investments. Some evidence suggests returns

over the latter half of the twentieth century were unexpectedly high, and hence the full-century average is upwardly-biased. In addition, the arithmetic average return may give upwardly-biased estimates of long-term cumulative return. Long-term forecasts require compounding at an average of the geometric and arithmetic historical means, which reduces the forecast.

10. Speculation is the undertaking of a risky investment for its risk premium. The risk premium has to be large enough to compensate a risk-averse investor for the risk of the investment.
11. A fair game is a risky prospect that has a zero-risk premium. It will not be undertaken by a risk-averse investor.
12. Investors' preferences toward the expected return and volatility of a portfolio may be expressed by a utility function that is higher for higher expected returns and lower for higher portfolio variances. More risk-averse investors will apply greater penalties for risk. We can describe these preferences graphically using indifference curves.
13. The desirability of a risky portfolio to a risk-averse investor may be summarized by the certainty equivalent value of the portfolio. The certainty equivalent rate of return is a value that, if it is received with certainty, would yield the same utility as the risky portfolio.
14. Hedging is the purchase of a risky asset to reduce the risk of a portfolio. The negative correlation between the hedge asset and the initial portfolio turns the volatility of the hedge asset into a risk-*reducing* feature. When a hedge asset is perfectly negatively correlated with the initial portfolio, it serves as a perfect hedge and works like an insurance contract on the portfolio.

KEY TERMS

nominal interest rate 146
real interest rate 146
holding-period return (HPR) 150
expected return 150
mean return 150
standard deviation 150
variance 150
risk-free rate 151
risk premium 151
excess return 151
risk aversion 151
normal distribution 158
value at risk 159
utility 164
certainty equivalent rate 165
risk-neutral 166
risk lover 166
mean-variance (M-V) criterion 167
indifference curve 168
hedging 169
diversification 169
covariance 172
correlation coefficient 173

SELECTED READINGS

A classic work on risk and risk aversion is:

Arrow, Kenneth. *Essays in the Theory of Risk Bearing*. Amsterdam: North Holland, 1971.

The classic article on the determination of the level of interest rates is:

Fisher, Irving. *The Theory of Interest: As Determined by Impatience to Spend Income and Opportunity to Invest It*. New York: Augustus M. Kelley, Publishers, 1965 (originally published in 1930).

The first Canadian study on bond returns was:

Khoury, Nabil T. "Historical Return Distributions of Investments in Canadian Bonds: 1950–1976." *Journal of Business Administration* 12, no. 1 (Fall 1980).

Historical returns on a variety of Canadian instruments, updated monthly, are published by Scotia Capital under the title Debt Market Indices.

PROBLEMS

1. You have $5,000 to invest for the next year and are considering the following three alternatives:
   a. A money market fund with an average maturity of 30 days offering a current yield of 6 percent per year
   b. A one-year savings deposit at a bank offering an interest rate of 7.5 percent
   c. A 20-year Canada bond offering a yield to maturity of 9 percent per year

   What role does your forecast of future interest rates play in your decision?

Visit us at www.mcgrawhill.ca/college/bodie

2. Use Figure 5.1 in this chapter to analyze the effect of the following on the level of real interest rates:
   a. Businesses become more optimistic about future demand for their products and decide to increase their capital spending.
   b. Households are induced to save more because of increased uncertainty about their future Canada Pension Plan benefits.
   c. The Bank of Canada undertakes open-market sales of Canada Treasury securities to reduce the supply of money.
3. You are considering the choice between investing $50,000 in a conventional one-year bank GIC offering an interest rate of 7 percent and a one-year inflation-plus GIC offering 3.5 percent per year plus the rate of inflation.
   a. Which is the safer investment?
   b. Which offers the higher expected return?
   c. If you expect the rate of inflation to be 4 percent over the next year, which is the better investment? Why?
   d. If we observe a risk-free nominal interest rate of 7 percent per year and a risk-free real rate of 3.5 percent, can we infer that the market's expected rate of inflation is 3.5 percent per year?
4. Suppose that you revise your expectations regarding the stock market (which were summarized in Table 5.1 in the chapter) as follows:

State of Economy	Probability	Ending Price ($)	HPR (%)
Boom	.35	140	44
Normal growth	.30	110	14
Recession	.35	80	–16

   Use equations 5.1 and 5.2 to compute the mean and standard deviation of the HPR on stocks. Compare your revised parameters with your previous ones.
5. Derive the probability distribution of the one-year holding period return on a 30-year Canada bond with an 8 percent coupon if it is currently selling at par and the probability distribution of its yield to maturity (YTM) a year from now is as follows:

State of Economy	Probability	YTM (%)
Boom	.20	11.0
Normal growth	.50	8.0
Recession	.30	7.0

   For simplicity, assume that the entire 8 percent coupon is paid at the end of the year rather than every six months.
6. Using the historical risk premiums as your guide, if the current risk-free interest rate is 6 percent, what is your estimate of the expected annual HPR on the S&P/TSX Composite stock portfolio?
7. Compute the means and standard deviations of the annual holding period returns listed in Table 5.2 of the chapter using only the last 23 years, 1981–2003. How do they compare with these same statistics computed from data for the period 1957–1980? Which do you think are the most relevant statistics to use for projecting into the future?
8. During a period of severe inflation, a bond offered a nominal HPR of 80 percent per year. The inflation rate was 70 percent per year.

a. What was the real HPR on the bond over the year?

b. Compare this real HPR to the approximation $R = r - i$.

Use the following expectations on stocks *X* and *Y* to answer problems 9 through 11 (round to the nearest percent).

	Bear Market	Normal Market	Bull Market
Probability	0.2	0.5	0.3
Stock *X*	−20%	18%	50%
Stock *Y*	−15%	20%	10%

CFA® PROBLEMS

9. What is the expected return for stocks *X* and *Y*?

	Stock *X*	Stock *Y*
a.	18%	5%
b.	18%	12%
c.	20%	11%
d.	20%	10%

CFA® PROBLEMS

10. What is the standard deviation of returns on stocks *X* and *Y*?

	Stock *X*	Stock *Y*
a.	15%	26%
b.	20%	4%
c.	24%	13%
d.	28%	8%

CFA® PROBLEMS

11. Assume you invest your \$10,000 portfolio in \$9,000 of stock *X* and \$1,000 of stock *Y*. What is the expected return on your portfolio?

a. 18%

b. 19%

c. 20%

d. 23%

CFA® PROBLEMS

12. Given \$100,000 to invest, what is the expected risk premium in dollars of investing in equities versus risk-free T-bills based on the following table?

Action	Probability	Expected Return
Invest in equities	.6	\$50,000
	.4	−\$30,000
Invest in risk-free T-bills	1.0	\$ 5,000

a. \$13,000

b. \$15,000

c. \$18,000

d. \$20,000

CFA® PROBLEMS

13. Judging from the scenarios below, what is the expected return for a portfolio with the following return profile?

	Market Condition		
	Bear	**Normal**	**Bull**
Probability	.2%	.3%	.5%
Rate of return	–25%	10%	24%

a. 4%

b. 10%

c. 20%

d. 25%

CFA® PROBLEMS

14. An analyst estimates that a stock has the following probabilities of return depending on the state of the economy:

State of Economy	Probability	Return
Good	.1	15%
Normal	.6	13%
Poor	.3	7%

The expected return of the stock is

a. 7.8%

b. 11.4%

c. 11.7%

d. 13.0%

CFA® PROBLEMS

15. Probabilities for three states of the economy, and probabilities for the returns on a particular stock in each state, are shown in the table below.

State of Economy	Probability of Economic State	Stock Performance	Probability of Stock Performance in Given Economic State
Good	.3	Good	.6
		Neutral	.3
		Poor	.1
Neutral	.5	Good	.4
		Neutral	.3
		Poor	.3
Poor	.2	Good	.2
		Neutral	.3
		Poor	.5

The probability that the economy will be neutral *and* the stock will experience poor performance is

a. .06

b. .15

c. .50

d. .80

Problems 16–17 represent a greater challenge. You may need to review the definitions of call and put options in Chapter 2.

16. You are faced with the probability distribution of the HPR on the stock market index fund given in Table 5.1 of the text. Suppose the price of a put option on a share of the index fund with exercise price of \$110 and maturity of one year is \$12.
    a. What is the probability distribution of the HPR on the put option?
    b. What is the probability distribution of the HPR on a portfolio consisting of one share of the index fund and a put option?
    c. In what sense does buying the put option constitute a purchase of insurance in this case?
17. Take as given the conditions described in the previous question, and suppose the risk-free interest rate is 6 percent per year. You are contemplating investing \$107.55 in a one-year CD and simultaneously buying a call option on the stock market index fund with an exercise price of \$110 and a maturity of one year. What is the probability distribution of your dollar return at the end of the year?
18. Consider a risky portfolio. The end-of-year cash flow derived from the portfolio will be either \$70,000 or \$200,000 with equal probabilities of .5. The alternative risk-free investment in T-bills pays 6 percent per year.
    a. If you require a risk premium of 8 percent, how much will you be willing to pay for the portfolio?
    b. Suppose that the portfolio can be purchased for the amount you found in (*a*). What will be the expected rate of return on the portfolio?
    c. Now suppose that you require a risk premium of 12 percent. What is the price that you will be willing to pay?
    d. Comparing your answers to (*a*) and (*c*), what do you conclude about the relationship between the required risk premium on a portfolio and the price at which the portfolio will sell?
19. Consider a portfolio that offers an expected rate of return of 12 percent and a standard deviation of 18 percent. T-bills offer a risk-free 7 percent rate of return. What is the maximum level of risk aversion for which the risky portfolio is still preferred to bills?
20. Draw the indifference curve in the expected return–standard deviation plane corresponding to a utility level of .05 for an investor with a risk aversion coefficient of 3. *Hint:* Choose several possible standard deviations, ranging from .05 to .25, and find the expected rates of return providing a utility level of .05. Then plot the expected return–standard deviation points so derived.
21. Now draw the indifference curve corresponding to a utility level of .04 for an investor with risk aversion coefficient $A = 4$. Comparing your answers to problems 19 and 20, what do you conclude?
22. Draw an indifference curve for a risk-neutral investor providing a utility level of .05.
23. What must be true about the sign of the risk aversion coefficient, *A*, for a risk lover? Draw the indifference curve for a utility level of .05 for a risk lover.

Use the following data in answering problems 24, 25, and 26.

Utility Formula Data

Investment	Expected Return $E(r)$	Standard Deviation (σ)
1	12%	30%
2	15	50
3	21	16
4	24	21

$$U = E(r) - \tfrac{1}{2}A\sigma^2 \text{ where } A = 4.0$$

CFA® PROBLEMS

24. On the basis of the utility formula above, which investment would you select if you were risk-averse?
   a. 1
   b. 2
   c. 3
   d. 4

CFA® PROBLEMS

25. On the basis of the utility formula above, which investment would you select if you were risk-neutral?
   a. 1
   b. 2
   c. 3
   d. 4

CFA® PROBLEMS

26. The variable *A* in the utility formula represents the
   a. Investor's return requirement
   b. Investor's aversion to risk
   c. Certainty-equivalent rate of the portfolio
   d. Preference for one unit of return per four units of risk

Consider the historical data of Table 5.2, showing that the average annual rate of return on the S&P/TSX Composite portfolio over the past 47 years has averaged about 3.66 percent more than the Treasury bill return and that the Composite standard deviation has been about 16.49 percent per year. Assume that these values are representative of investors' expectations for future performance and that the current T-bill rate is 5 percent. Use these values to answer problems 27 to 29.

27. Calculate the expected return and standard deviation of portfolios invested in T-bills and the Composite index with weights as follows:

W_{bills}	W_{market}
0	1.0
0.2	0.8
0.4	0.6
0.6	0.4
0.8	0.2
1.0	0

28. Calculate the utility levels of each portfolio of problem 27 for an investor with $A = 3$. What do you conclude?

29. Repeat problem 28 for an investor with $A = 5$. What do you conclude?

Reconsider the Best and SugarBeet stock market hedging example in the text, but assume for problems 30 to 32 that the probability distribution of the rate of return on SugarBeet stock is as follows:

	Bullish Stock Market	Bearish Stock Market	Sugar Crisis
Probability	.5	.3	.2
Rate of return	.10	−.05	.20

30. If Humanex's portfolio is half Best stock and half SugarBeet, what are its expected return and standard deviation? Calculate the standard deviation from the portfolio returns in each scenario.

31. What is the covariance between Best and SugarBeet?

32. Calculate the portfolio standard deviation using rule 5 and show that the result is consistent with your answer to problem 30.

STANDARD &POOR'S

Enter the Market Insight database at **www.mcgrawhill.ca/edumarketinsight** and click on *Educational Version of Marketing Insight*. After logging in, go to the *Company* tab, then click the *Population* button. Select a Canadian company of interest to you and link to the *Company Research* page with a menu of company information reports on the left. Link to the *Excel Analytics* reports and open the *annual income statement* for your company. The report will open using the Excel viewer software. You will note that the Excel Analytic reports provide six years of data, in this case, income statements. To work with the file, for example, to recalculate the income statement as a percent of total sales (percentage composition of sales), save the file to a folder, open Excel, and make any changes desired. The *Excel Analytics* output now is your page to work with as you like. (More on this later in the text.) If you cannot access the *Excel Analytics* pages, you may have to update your Windows and/or MS Office package. Review the various reports for later reference.

E-INVESTMENTS
Analytics Tutorial

Go to **gozips.uakron.edu/~drd/downloadtutorial.html**. Review the step-by-step tutorial providing instructions for downloading economic and financial data in a variety of file formats into Excel. Work through the example provided at the end of the tutorial. Later assignments in this text will ask you to use the data that you have downloaded, so learning how to access it is a first step for later assignments.

APPENDIX 5A: CONTINUOUS COMPOUNDING

Suppose your money earns interest at an annual nominal percentage rate (APR) of 6 percent per year compounded semiannually. What is your *effective* annual rate of return, accounting for compound interest?

We find the answer by first computing the per-(compounding-)period rate, 3 percent per half-year, and then computing the future value (FV) at the end of the year per dollar invested at the beginning of the year. In this example, we get

$$FV = (1.03)^2 = 1.0609$$

The effective annual rate (R_{EFF} is just this number minus 1.0).

$$R_{EFF} = 1.0609 - 1 = .0609 = 6.09\% \text{ per year}$$

The general formula for the effective annual rate is:

$$R_{EFF} = \left(1 + \frac{APR}{n}\right)^n - 1$$

where APR is the annual percentage rate, and n is the number of compounding periods per year. Table 5A.1 presents the effective annual rates corresponding to an annual percentage rate of 6 percent per year for different compounding frequencies.

Table 5A.1 Effective Annual Rates for an APR of 6 Percent

Compounding Frequency	n	R_{EFF}(%)
Annually	1	6.00000
Semiannually	2	6.09000
Quarterly	4	6.13636
Monthly	12	6.16778
Weekly	52	6.17998
Daily	365	6.18313

As the compounding frequency increases, $(1 + \text{APR}/n)^n$ gets closer and closer to e^{APR} where e is the number 2.71828 (rounded off to the fifth decimal place). In our example, $e^{.06} = 1.0618365$. Therefore, if interest is continuously compounded, $R_{EFF} = .0618365$, or 6.18365 percent per year.

Continuously compounded rates are extensively used for two reasons. First, as noted in Section 5.5, since information flows into capital markets continuously, rates of return are best modelled as evolving and compounding continuously. Second, pricing models for derivative assets such as call and put options on stocks often are based on continuously rebalanced portfolios. The need to model stock prices as trading continuously calls for continuously compounded rates of return.

With continuous compounding the effective rate is given by

$$1 + R_{EFF} = e^{\text{APR}}$$

We also can compute the continuously compounded rate from the observed effective holding-period returns as

$$\text{Continuously compounded rate} = \ln(1 + R_{EFF})$$

For short-term (e.g., daily) holding-period returns, the difference between the effective and continuously compounded rate is quite small. But for longer-term rates such as quarterly or annual, the difference is greater.

Using continuously compounded rates simplifies the algebraic relationship between real and nominal rates of return. To see how, let us compute the real rate of return first using annual compounding and then using continuous compounding. Assume the nominal interest rate is 6 percent per year compounded annually and the rate of inflation is 4 percent per year compounded annually. Using the relationship

$$\text{Real rate} = \frac{1 + \text{Nominal rate}}{1 + \text{Inflation rate}} - 1$$

$$r = \frac{(1 + R)}{(1 + i)} - 1 = \frac{R - i}{1 + i}$$

we find that the effective annual real rate is

$$r = 1.06/1.04 - 1 = .01923 = 1.923\% \text{ per year}$$

With continuous compounding, the relationship becomes

$$e^r = e^R/e^i = e^{R-i}$$

Taking the natural logarithm we get

$$r = R - i$$

$$\text{Real rate} = \text{Nominal rate} - \text{Inflation rate}$$

all expressed as annual, continuously compounded percentage rates.

Thus, if we assume a nominal interest rate of 6 percent per year compounded continuously and an inflation rate of 4 percent per year compounded continuously, the real rate is 2 percent per year compounded continuously.

To pay a fair interest rate to a depositor, the compounding frequency must be at least equal to the frequency of deposits and withdrawals. Only when you compound at least as frequently as transactions in an account can you assure that each dollar will earn the full interest due for the exact duration it has been in the account. These days, online computing for deposits is feasible, so one expects the frequency of compounding to grow until the use of continuous or at least daily compounding becomes the norm.

APPENDIX 5B: A DEFENCE OF MEAN-VARIANCE ANALYSIS

Describing Probability Distributions

The axiom of risk aversion needs little defence. So far, however, our treatment of risk has been limiting in that it took the variance (or equivalently, the standard deviation) of portfolio returns as an adequate risk measure. In situations in which variance alone is not adequate to measure risk, this assumption is potentially restrictive. Here, we provide some justification for mean-variance analysis.

The basic question is how one can best describe the uncertainty of portfolio rates of return. In principle, one could list all possible outcomes for the portfolio over a given period. If each outcome results in a payoff such as a dollar profit or rate of return, then this payoff value is the *random variable* in question. A list assigning a probability to all possible values of the random variable is called the probability distribution of the random variable.

The reward for holding a portfolio typically is measured by the expected rate of return across all possible scenarios, which equals

$$E(r) = \sum_{s=1}^{n} Pr(s)r_s$$

where $s = 1, \ldots, n$ are the possible outcomes or scenarios, r_s is the rate of return for outcome s, and $Pr(s)$ is the probability associated with it.

Actually, the expected value or mean is not the only candidate for the central value of a probability distribution. Other candidates are the median and the mode.

The median is defined as the outcome value that exceeds the outcome values for half the population and is exceeded by the other half. Whereas the expected rate of return is a weighted average of the outcomes, the weights being the probabilities, the median is based on the rank order of the outcomes and takes into account only the order of the outcome values.

The median differs significantly from the mean in cases where the expected value is dominated by extreme values. One example is the income (or wealth) distribution in a population. A relatively small number of households command a disproportionate share of total income (and wealth). The mean income is "pulled up" by these extreme values, which makes it nonrepresentative. The median is free of this effect, since it equals the income level that is exceeded by half the population, regardless of by how much.

Finally, a third candidate for the measure of central value is the mode, which is the most likely value of the distribution or the outcome with the highest probability. However, the expected value is by far the most widely used measure of central or average tendency.

We now turn to the characterization of the risk implied by the nature of the probability distribution of returns. In general, it is impossible to quantify risk by a single number. We can, however, describe the probabilities and magnitudes of the possible deviations from the mean, or the "surprises," in a concise fashion, to illuminate the risk-return tradeoff. The easiest way to accomplish this is to answer a set of questions in order of their informational value and to stop at the point where additional questions would not affect our notion of the risk-return tradeoff.

The first question is, "What is a typical deviation from the expected value?" A natural answer would be, "The expected deviation from the expected value is ______________." Unfortunately, this answer is meaningless because it is necessarily zero: positive deviations from the mean are offset exactly by negative deviations.

There are two ways of getting around this problem. The first is to use the expected *absolute* value of the deviation. This is known as MAD (mean absolute deviation), which is given by

$$\sum_{s=1}^{n} Pr(s) \times \text{Absolute value}[r_s - E(r)]$$

The second is to use the expected *squared* deviation from the expected, or mean, value, which is simply the variance of the probability distribution

$$\sigma^2 = \sum_{s=1}^{n} Pr(s)[r_s - E(r)]^2$$

Note that the unit of measurement of the variance is percent squared. To return to our original units, we compute the standard deviation as the square root of the variance, which is measured in percentage terms, as is the expected value.

The variance also is called the *second central moment* around the mean, with the expected return itself being the first moment. Although the variance measures the average squared deviation from the expected value, it does not provide a full description of risk. To see why, consider the two probability distributions for rates of return on a portfolio, in Figure 5B.1.

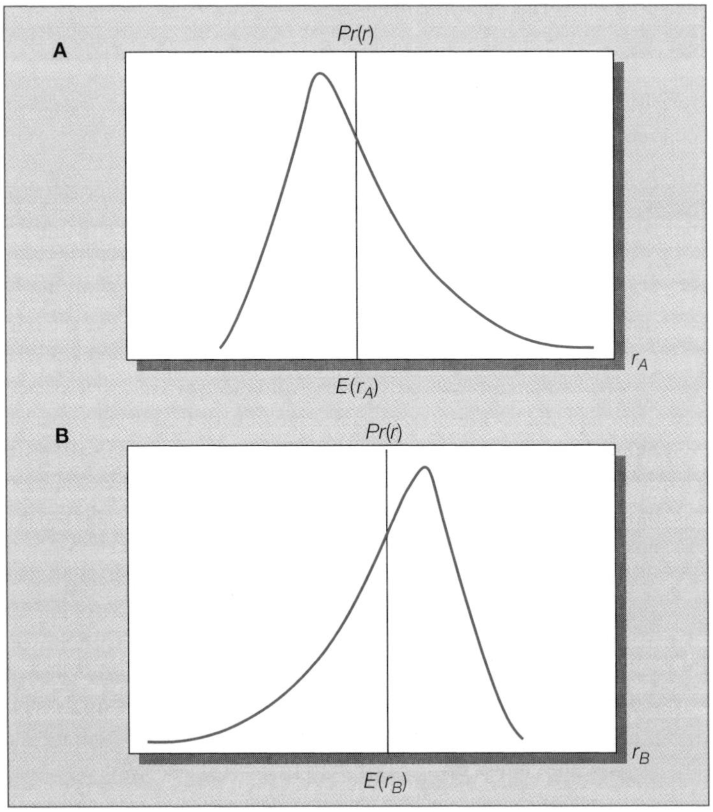

Figure 5B.1 Skewed probability distributions for rates of return on a portfolio.

A and *B* are probability distributions with identical expected values and variances. The graphs show that the variances are identical because probability distribution *B* is the mirror image of *A*.

What is the principal difference between *A* and *B*? *A* is characterized by more likely but small losses and less likely but extreme gains. This pattern is reversed in *B*. The difference is important. When we talk about risk, we really mean "*bad* surprises." The bad surprises in *A*, although they are more likely, are small (and limited) in magnitude. The bad surprises in *B* could be extreme, indeed unbounded. A risk-averse investor will prefer *A* to *B* on these grounds; hence, it is worthwhile to quantify this characteristic. The asymmetry of the distribution is called *skewness,* which we measure by the *third central moment,* given by

$$M_3 = \sum_{s=1}^{n} = Pr(s)[r_s - E(r)]^3$$

Cubing the deviations from expected value preserves their signs, which allows us to distinguish good from bad surprises. Because this procedure gives greater weight to larger deviations, it causes the "long tail" of the distribution to dominate the measure of skewness. Thus, the skewness of the distribution will be positive for a right-skewed distribution such as *A* and negative for a left-skewed distribution such as *B*. The asymmetry is a relevant characteristic, although it is not as important as the magnitude of the standard deviation.

To summarize, the first moment (expected value) represents the expected reward. The second and higher central moments characterize the uncertainty of the reward. All the even moments (variance, M_4, and so on) represent the likelihood of extreme values. Larger values for these moments indicate greater uncertainty. The odd moments (M_3, M_5, and so on) represent measures of asymmetry. Positive numbers are associated with positive skewness and hence are desirable.

We can characterize the risk aversion of any investor by the preference scheme that the investor assigns to the various moments of the distribution. In other words, we can write the utility value derived from the probability distribution as

$$U = E(r) - b_0\sigma^2 + b_1 M_3 - b_2 M_4 + b_3 M_5 - \ldots$$

where the importance of the terms lessens as we proceed to higher moments. Notice that the "good" (odd) moments have positive coefficients, whereas the "bad" (even) moments have minus signs in front of the coefficients.

How many moments are needed to describe the investor's assessment of the probability distribution adequately? Samuelson[12] proves that in many important circumstances

1. The importance of all moments beyond the variance is much smaller than that of the expected value and variance. In other words, disregarding moments higher than the variance will not affect portfolio choice.
2. The variance is as important as the mean to investor welfare.

Samuelson's proof is the major theoretical justification for mean-variance analysis. Under the conditions of this proof, mean and variance are equally important, and we can overlook all other moments without harm.

The major assumption that Samuelson makes to arrive at this conclusion concerns the "compactness" of the distribution of stock returns. The distribution of the rate of return on a portfolio is said to be compact if the risk can be controlled by the investor. Practically speaking, we test for compactness of the distribution by posing a question: Will the risk of my position in the portfolio decline if I hold it for a shorter period, or will the risk approach zero if I hold the risky portfolio for only an instant? If the answer is yes, then the distribution is compact.

[12]Paul A. Samuelson, "The Fundamental Approximation Theorem of Portfolio Analysis in Terms of Means, Variances, and Higher Moments," *Review of Economic Studies* 37 (1970).

In general, compactness may be seen as being equivalent to continuity of stock prices. If stock prices do not take sudden jumps, then the uncertainty of stock returns over smaller and smaller time periods decreases. Under these circumstances, investors who can rebalance their portfolios frequently will act so as to make higher moments of the stock return distribution so small as to be unimportant. It is not that skewness, for example, does not matter in principle. It is, instead, that the actions of investors in frequently revising their portfolios will limit higher moments to negligible levels.

Continuity or compactness is not, however, an innocuous assumption. Portfolio revisions entail transaction costs, meaning that rebalancing must of necessity be somewhat limited and that skewness and other higher moments cannot be ignored entirely. Compactness also rules out such phenomena as the major stock price jumps that occur in response to takeover attempts. It also rules out such dramatic events as the 25 percent one-day decline of the stock market on October 19, 1987. Except for these relatively unusual events, however, mean-variance analysis is adequate. In most cases, if the portfolio may be revised frequently, we need to worry about the mean and variance only.

Portfolio theory, for the most part, is built on the assumption that the conditions for mean-variance (or mean-standard deviation) analysis are satisfied. Accordingly, we typically ignore higher moments.

CONCEPT CHECK

B1. How does the simultaneous popularity of both lotteries and insurance policies confirm the notion that individuals prefer positive to negative skewness of portfolio returns?

Normal and Lognormal Distributions

Modern portfolio theory, for the most part, assumes that asset returns are normally distributed. This is a convenient assumption because the normal distribution can be described completely by its mean and variance, which provides another justification for mean-variance analysis. The argument has been that, even if individual asset returns are not exactly normal, the distribution of returns of a large portfolio will resemble a normal distribution quite closely.

The data support this argument. Table 5B.1 shows summaries of the results of one-year investments in many portfolios selected randomly from NYSE stocks. The portfolios are listed in order of increasing degrees of diversification; that is, the numbers of stocks in each portfolio sample are 1, 8, 32, and 128. The percentiles of the distribution of returns for each portfolio are compared to what one would have expected from portfolios identical in mean and variance but drawn from a normal distribution.

www.nyse.com

Looking first at the single stock portfolios ($N = 1$), the departure of the return distribution from normality is significant. The mean of the sample is 28.2 percent, and the standard deviation is 41.0 percent. In the case of a normal distribution with the same mean and standard deviation, we would expect the fifth percentile stock to lose 39.2 percent, but the fifth percentile stock actually lost 14.4 percent. In addition, while the normal distribution's mean coincides with its median, the actual sample median of the single stock was 19.6 percent, far below the sample mean of 28.2 percent.

In contrast, the returns of the 128-stock portfolios are virtually identical in distribution to the hypothetical normally distributed portfolio. The normal distribution therefore is a pretty good working assumption for well-diversified portfolios. How large a portfolio must be for this result to take hold depends on how far the distribution of the individual stocks is from normality. It appears that a portfolio typically must include at least 32 stocks for the one-year return to be close to normally distributed.

There remain theoretical objections to the assumption that individual stock returns are normally distributed. Given that a stock price cannot be negative, the normal distribution cannot be truly representative of the behaviour of a holding period rate of return because it allows for any outcome, including the whole range of negative prices. Specifically, rates of return lower than –100 percent are

Table 5B.1 Frequency Distributions of Rates of Return from a One-Year Investment in Randomly Selected Portfolios from NYSE-Listed Stocks

	N = 1		*N* = 8		*N* = 32		*N* = 12	
Statistic	**Observed**	**Normal**	**Observed**	**Normal**	**Observed**	**Normal**	**Observed**	**Normal**
Minimum	−71.1	NA	−12.4	NA	6.5	NA	16.4	NA
5th centile	−14.4	−39.2	8.1	4.6	17.4	16.7	22.7	22.6
20th centile	−.5	−6.3	16.3	16.1	22.2	22.3	25.3	25.3
50th centile	19.6	28.2	26.4	28.2	27.8	28.2	28.1	28.2
70th centile	38.7	49.7	33.8	35.7	31.6	32.9	30.0	30.0
95th centile	96.3	95.6	54.3	51.8	40.9	39.9	34.1	33.8
Maximum	442.6	NA	136.7	NA	73.7	NA	43.1	NA
Mean	28.2	28.2	28.2	28.2	28.2	28.2	28.2	28.2
Standard deviation	41.0	41.0	14.4	14.4	7.1	7.1	3.4	3.4
Skewness (M_3)	255.4	0.0	88.7	0.0	44.5	0.0	17.7	0.0
Sample size	1,227	—	131,072	—	32,768	—	16,384	—

Source: Lawrence Fisher and James H. Lorie, "Some Studies of Variability of Returns on Investments in Common Stocks," *Journal of Business* 43 (April 1970); published by the University of Chicago. Reprinted by permission.

theoretically impossible because they imply the possibility of negative security prices. The failure of the normal distribution to rule out such outcomes must be viewed as a shortcoming.

An alternative assumption is that the continuously compounded annual rate of return is normally distributed. If we call this rate r and we call the effective annual rate r_e, then $r_e = e^r - 1$, and since e^r can never be negative, the smallest possible value for r_e is −1 or −100 percent. Thus, this assumption nicely rules out the troublesome possibility of negative prices while still conveying the advantages of working with normal distributions.

Under this assumption, the distribution of r_e will be *lognormal.* This distribution is depicted in Figure 5B.2.

For *short* holding periods, that is, where t is small, the approximation of $r_e(t) = e^{rt} - 1$ by rt is quite accurate and the normal distribution provides a good approximation to the lognormal. With rt normally distributed, the effective annual return over short time periods may be taken as approximately normally distributed.

For short holding periods, therefore, the mean and standard deviation of the effective holding period returns are proportional to the mean and standard deviation of the annual, continuously compounded rate of return on the stock and to the time interval.

Therefore, if the standard deviation of the annual continuously compounded rate of return on a stock is 40 percent ($\sigma = .40$), then the variance of the holding period return for one month, for example, is for all practical purposes

$$\sigma^2(\text{monthly}) = \frac{\sigma^2}{12} = \frac{.16}{12} = .0133$$

and the standard deviation is $\sqrt{.0133} = .1155$.

To illustrate this principle, suppose that the Dow Jones Industrials went up one day by 50 points from 10,000 to 10,050. Is this a "large" move? Looking at annual, continuously compounded rates on the Dow Jones portfolio, we find that the annual standard deviation historically has been about 16 percent. Under the assumption that the return on the Dow Jones portfolio is lognormally distributed and that returns between successive subperiods are uncorrelated, the one-day distribution has a standard

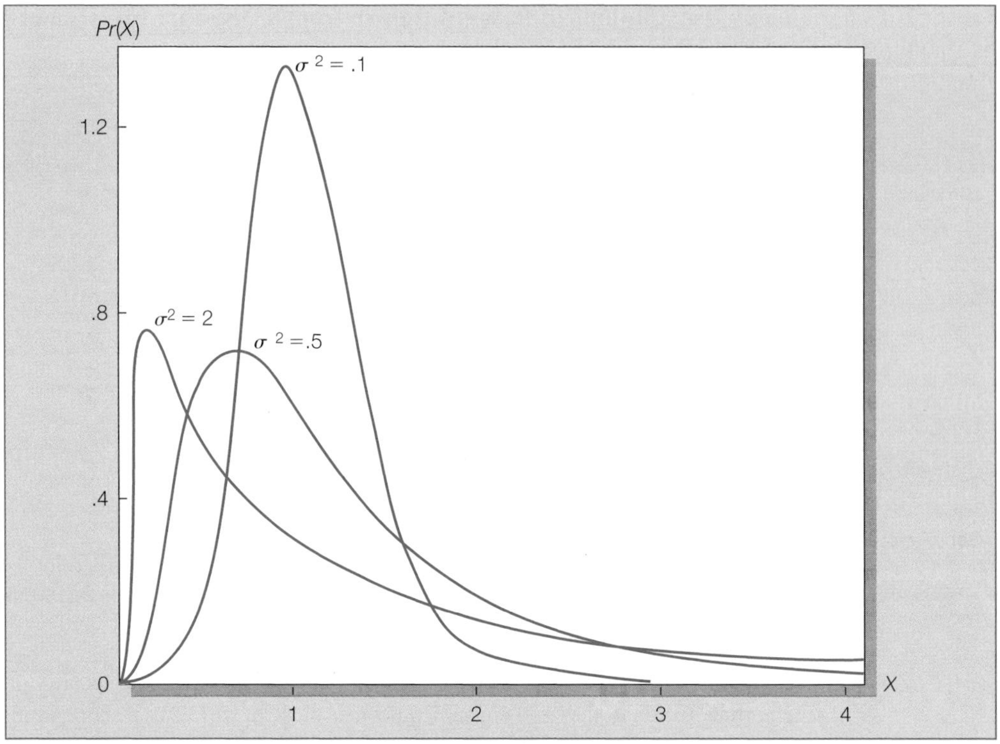

Figure 5B.2 The lognormal distribution for three values of σ^2.

deviation (based on 250 trading days per year) of

$$\sigma(\text{day}) = \sigma(\text{year})\sqrt{1/250}$$
$$= \frac{.16}{\sqrt{250}}$$
$$= .0101$$
$$= 1.01\% \text{ per day}$$

Applying this to the opening level of the Dow Jones on that trading day, 10,000, we find that the daily standard deviation of the Dow Jones index is 10,000 × .0101 = 101 points per day.

Since the daily rate on the Dow Jones portfolio is approximately normal, we know that in one day out of three, the Dow Jones will move by more than 1 percent either way. Thus, a move of 50 points is hardly an unusual event.

CONCEPT CHECK

B2. Look again at Table 5B.1. Are you surprised that the minimum rates of return are less negative for more diversified portfolios? Is your explanation consistent with the behaviour of the sample's maximum rates of return?

SUMMARY: APPENDIX 5B

1. The probability distribution of the rate of return can be characterized by its moments. The reward from taking the risk is measured by the first moment, which is the mean of the return distribution. Higher moments characterize the risk. Even moments provide information on the likelihood of extreme values, and odd moments provide information on the asymmetry of the distribution.
2. Investors' risk preferences can be characterized by their preferences for the various moments of the distribution. The fundamental approximation theorem shows that when portfolios are revised often

enough, and prices are continuous, the desirability of a portfolio can be measured by its mean and variance alone.

3. The rates of return on well-diversified portfolios for holding periods that are not too long can be approximated by a normal distribution. For short holding periods (up to one month), the normal distribution is a good approximation for the lognormal.

PROBLEM: APPENDIX 5B

1. The Smartstock investment consulting group prepared the following scenario analysis for the end-of-year dividend and stock price of Klink Inc., which is selling now at $12 per share:

		End-of-Year	
Scenario	**Probability**	**Dividend ($)**	**Price ($)**
1	.10	0	0
2	.20	.25	2.00
3	.40	.40	14.00
4	.25	.60	20.00
5	.05	.85	30.00

Compute the rate of return for each scenario and

a. The mean, median, and mode

b. The standard deviation and mean absolute deviation

c. The first moment, and the second and third moments around the mean. Is the probability distribution of Klink stock positively skewed?

APPENDIX 5C: RISK AVERSION AND EXPECTED UTILITY

We digress here to examine the rationale behind our contention that investors are risk-averse. Recognition of risk aversion as central in investment decisions goes back at least to 1738. Daniel Bernoulli, one of a famous Swiss family of distinguished mathematicians, spent the years 1725 through 1733 in St. Petersburg, where he analyzed the following coin-toss game. To enter the game one pays an entry fee. Thereafter, a coin is tossed until the *first* head appears. The number of tails, denoted by n, that appear until the first head is tossed is used to compute the payoff, $\$R$, to the participant, as

$$R(n) = 2^n$$

The probability of no tails before the first head ($n = 0$) is ½ and the corresponding payoff is $2^0 = \$1$. The probability of one tail and then heads ($n = 1$) is ½ × ½ with payoff $2^1 = \$2$, the probability of two tails and then heads ($n = 2$) is ½ × ½ × ½, and so forth.

The following table illustrates the probabilities and payoffs for various outcomes:

Tails	Probability	Payoff = $\$R(n)$	Probability × Payoff
0	$\frac{1}{2}$	$1	$1/2
1	$\frac{1}{4}$	$2	$1/2
2	$\frac{1}{8}$	$4	$1/2
3	$\frac{1}{16}$	$8	$1/2
—	—	—	—
—	—	—	—
n	$(\frac{1}{2})^{n+1}$	$\$2^n$	$1/2

The expected payoff is therefore

$$E(R) = \sum_{n=0}^{\infty} Pr(n)R(n)$$
$$= \tfrac{1}{2} + \tfrac{1}{2} + \ldots$$
$$= \infty$$

This game is called the "St. Petersburg Paradox." Although the expected payoff is infinite, participants obviously will be willing to purchase tickets to play the game only at a finite, and possibly quite modest, entry fee.

Bernoulli resolved the paradox by noting that investors do not assign the same value per dollar to all payoffs. Specifically, the greater their wealth, the less their "appreciation" for each extra dollar. We can make this insight mathematically precise by assigning a welfare or utility value to any level of investor wealth. Our utility function should increase as wealth is higher, but each extra dollar of wealth should increase utility by progressively smaller amounts.[13] (Modern economists would say that investors exhibit "decreasing marginal utility" from an additional payoff dollar.) One particular function that assigns a subjective value to the investor from a payoff of $\$R$, which has a smaller value per dollar the greater the payoff, is the function $\log(R)$. If this function measures utility values of wealth, the subjective utility value of the game is indeed finite.[14] The certain wealth level necessary to yield this utility value is \$2, because log (2.00) = .693. Hence the certainty equivalent value of the risky payoff is \$2, which is the maximum amount that this investor will pay to play the game.

Von Neumann and Morgenstern adapted this approach to investment theory in a complete axiomatic system in 1946. Avoiding unnecessary technical detail, we restrict ourselves here to an intuitive exposition of the rationale for risk aversion.

Imagine two individuals who are identical twins, except that one of them is less fortunate than the other. Peter has only \$1,000 to his name while Paul has a net worth of \$200,000. How many hours of work would each twin be willing to offer to earn one extra dollar? It is likely that Peter (the poor twin) has more essential uses for the extra money than does Paul. Therefore, Peter will offer more hours. In other words, Peter derives a greater personal welfare or assigns a greater "utility" value to the 1,001st dollar than Paul does to the 200,001st.

Figure 5C.1 depicts graphically the relationship between wealth and the utility value of wealth that is consistent with this notion of decreasing marginal utility.

Individuals have different rates of decrease in their marginal utility of wealth. What is constant is the *principle* that per-dollar utility decreases with wealth. Functions that exhibit the property of decreasing per-unit value as the number of units grows are called *concave*. A simple example is the log function, familiar from high school mathematics. Of course, a log function will not fit all investors, but it is consistent with the risk aversion that we assume for all investors.

Now consider the following simple prospect:

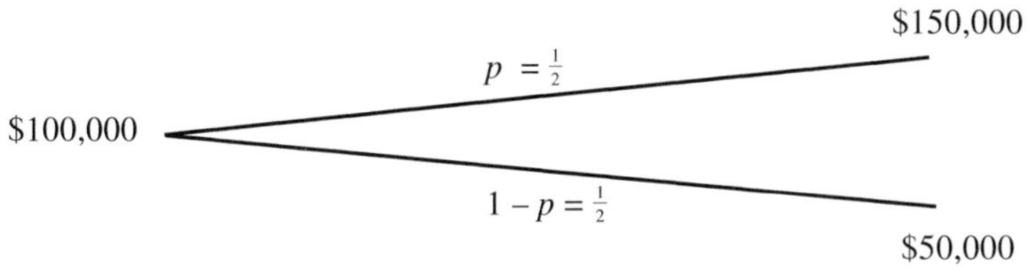

[13]This utility function is similar in spirit to the one that assigns a satisfaction level to portfolios with given risk-and-return attributes. However, the utility function here refers not to investors' satisfaction with alternative portfolio choices but only to the subjective welfare they derive from different levels of wealth.

[14]If we substitute the "utility" value, $\log(R)$, for the dollar payoff, R, to obtain an expected utility value of the game (rather than expected dollar value), we have, calling $V(R)$ the expected utility,

$$V(R) = \sum_{n=0}^{\infty} Pr(n) \log[R(n)] = \sum_{n=0}^{\infty} (\tfrac{1}{2})^{n+1} \log(2^n) = .693$$

Figure 5C.1 Utility of wealth with a log utility function.

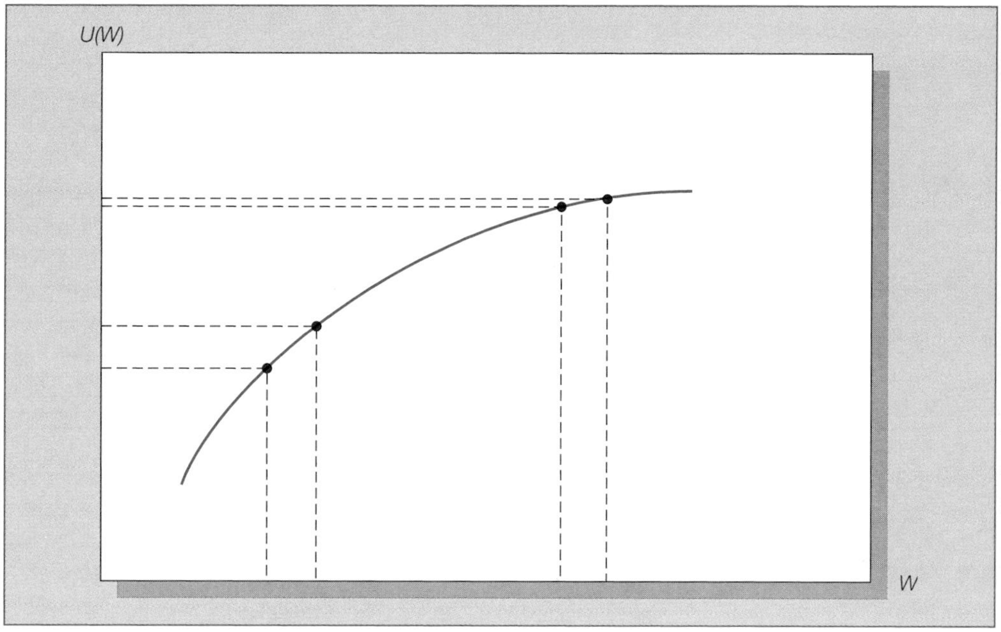

This is a fair game in that the expected profit is zero. Suppose, however, that the curve in Figure 5C.1 represents the investor's utility value of wealth, assuming a log utility function. Figure 5C.2 shows this curve with the numerical values marked.

Figure 5C.2 shows that the loss in utility from losing \$50,000 exceeds the gain from winning \$50,000. Consider the gain first. With probability $p = .5$, wealth goes from \$100,000 to \$150,000. Using the log utility function, utility goes from log(100,000) = 11.51 to log(150,000) = 11.92, the distance G on the graph. This gain is $G = 11.92 - 11.51 = .41$. In expected utility terms, then, the gain is $pG = .5 \times .41 = .21$.

Now consider the possibility of coming up on the short end of the prospect. In that case, wealth goes from \$100,000 to \$50,000. The loss in utility, the distance L on the graph, is L = log(100,000) – log(50.000) = 11.51 – 10.82 = .69. Thus the loss in expected utility terms is $(1 - p)L = .5 \times .69 = .35$, which exceeds the gain in expected utility from the possibility of winning the game.

Figure 5C.2 Fair games and expected utility.

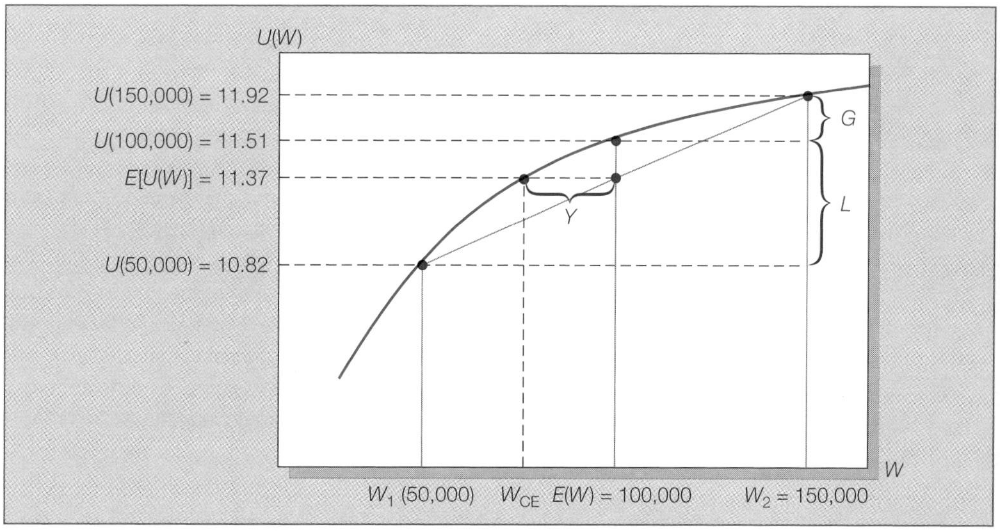

We compute the expected utility from the risky prospect as follows:

$$E[U(W)] = pU(W_1) + (1 - p)U(W_2)$$
$$= \tfrac{1}{2}\log(50{,}000) + \tfrac{1}{2}\log(150{,}000)$$
$$= 11.37$$

If the prospect is rejected, the utility value of the (sure) \$100,000 is log(100,000) = 11.51, which is greater than that of the fair game (11.37). Hence the risk-averse investor will reject the fair game.

Using a specific investor utility function (such as the log utility) allows us to compute the certainty equivalent value of the risky prospect to a given investor. This is the amount that, if received with certainty, the investor would consider equally attractive as the risky prospect.

If log utility describes the investor's preferences toward wealth outcomes, then Figure 5C.2 also can tell us what is, for her, the dollar value of the prospect. We ask: What sure level of wealth has a utility value of 11.37 (which equals the expected utility from the prospect)? A horizontal line drawn at the level 11.37 intersects the utility curve at the level of wealth W_{CE}. This means that

$$\log(W_{CE}) = 11.37$$

which implies that

$$W_{CE} = e^{11.37}$$
$$= \$86{,}681.86$$

W_{CE} is therefore the certainty equivalent of the prospect. The distance Y in Figure 5C.2 is the penalty, or the downward adjustment, to the expected profit that is attributable to the risk of the prospect:

$$Y = E(W) - W_{CE}$$
$$= \$100{,}000 - \$86{,}681.86$$
$$= \$13{,}318.14$$

Smith views \$86,681.86 for certain as being equal in utility value as \$100,000 at risk. Therefore, she would be indifferent between the two.

? CONCEPT CHECK

C1. Suppose the utility function is $U(W) = \sqrt{w}$.

a. What is the utility level at wealth levels \$50,000 and \$150,000?

b. What is expected utility if p still equals .5?

c. What is the certainty equivalent of the risky prospect?

d. Does this utility function also display risk aversion?

e. Does this utility function display more or less risk aversion than the log utility function?

Does revealed behaviour of investors demonstrate risk aversion? Looking at prices and past rates of return in financial markets, we can answer with a resounding yes. With remarkable consistency, riskier bonds are sold at lower prices than safer ones with otherwise similar characteristics. Riskier stocks also have provided higher average rates of return over long periods of time than less risky assets such as T-bills. For example, over the 1957–2003 period, the average rate of return on the S&P/TSX Composite portfolio exceeded the T-bill return by about 3.66 percent per year.

It is abundantly clear from financial data that the average, or representative, investor exhibits substantial risk aversion. For readers who recognize that financial assets are priced to compensate for risk by providing a risk premium and at the same time feel the urge for some gambling, we have a constructive recommendation: Direct your gambling desire to investment in financial markets. As Von Neumann once said, "The stock market is a casino with the odds in your favour." A small risk-seeking investor may provide all the excitement you want with a positive expected return to boot!

PROBLEMS: APPENDIX 5C

1. Suppose that your wealth is $250,000. You buy a $200,000 house and invest the remainder in a risk-free asset paying an annual interest rate of 6 percent. There is a probability of .001 that your house will burn to the ground and its value will be reduced to zero. With a log utility of end-of-year wealth, how much would you be willing to pay for insurance (at the beginning of the year)? (Assume that if the house does not burn down, its end-of-year value still will be $200,000.)
2. If the cost of insuring your house is $1 per $1,000 of value, what will be the certainty equivalent of your end-of-year wealth if you insure your house at
   a. ½ its value?
   b. Its full value?
   c. 1½ times its value?

PORTFOLIO SELECTION

As the boxed article that follows explains in historical perspective, modern portfolio managers seek to achieve the best possible tradeoff between risk and return. A top-down analysis of their strategies starts with the broadest decisions concerning portfolio composition and progresses to ever-finer details about the exact makeup of the portfolio.

For example, the **capital allocation decision** refers to the proportion of the overall portfolio that the investor chooses to place in safe but low-return money market securities versus risky but higher-return securities like stocks. Given the fraction of funds apportioned to risky investments, the investor next makes an **asset allocation decision**, which describes the distribution of risky investments across broad asset classes like stocks, bonds, real estate, foreign assets, and so on. Finally, the **security selection decision** describes the choice of which particular securities to hold within each asset class.

The top-down analysis of portfolio construction has much to recommend it. Most institutional investors follow a top-down approach. Capital allocation and asset allocation decisions will be made at a high organizational level, with the choice of the specific securities to hold within each asset class delegated to particular portfolio managers. Individual investors typically follow a less structured approach to investment management, but they too typically give priority to broader allocation issues. For example, an individual's first decision is usually how much of his or her wealth must be left in a safe bank or money market account.

This chapter starts with the broadest investment decision: capital allocation between **risk-free assets** versus the risky portion of the portfolio, in which the composition of the risky portfolio is taken as given and referred to as "the" **risky asset**. Then we examine how to construct that optimal risky portfolio.

The capital allocation problem is solved in two stages. First we determine the risk-return tradeoff encountered when choosing between the risky and risk-free assets. Then we show how risk aversion determines the optimal mix of the two assets. This analysis leads us to examine so-called passive strategies, which call for allocation of the portfolio between a (risk-free) asset money market fund and an index fund of common stocks.

The discussion of the construction of the optimal risky portfolio begins at the simplest level, with an explanation of how diversification can reduce the variability of portfolio returns. Then we examine efficient diversification strategies at the asset allocation and security selection levels. We start with a simple, restricted example of asset allocation with two risky mutual funds: a long-term debt fund and an equity fund. With this example we investigate the relationship between investment proportions and the resulting portfolio expected return and standard deviation. We then add a risk-free asset (e.g., T-bills) to the menu of assets and determine the optimal asset allocation.

Moving from asset allocation to security selection, we first generalize our discussion of restricted asset allocation (with only two risky assets) to a universe of many risky securities. We show how the best attainable capital allocation line emerges from the efficient portfolio algorithm, so that portfolio optimization can be conducted in two stages, asset allocation and security selection.

Finally, in the appendices to this chapter, we examine common fallacies regarding the power of diversification in the context of the insurance principle.

6.1 CAPITAL ALLOCATION ACROSS RISKY AND RISK-FREE PORTFOLIOS

History shows us that long-term bonds have been riskier investments than investments in Treasury bills and that stock investments have been riskier still. On the other hand, the riskier investments have offered higher average returns. Investors, of course, do not make all-or-nothing choices from these investment classes. They can and do construct their portfolios using securities from all asset classes. Some of the portfolio may be in risk-free Treasury bills, and some in high-risk stocks.

The most straightforward way to control the risk of the portfolio is through the fraction of the portfolio invested in Treasury bills and other safe money market securities versus risky assets. This *capital allocation decision* is an example of an *asset allocation* choice—a choice among broad investment classes, rather than among the specific securities within each asset class. Most investment professionals consider asset allocation to be the most important part of portfolio construction. Therefore, we start our discussion of the risk-return tradeoff available to investors by examining the most basic asset allocation choice: the choice of how much of the portfolio to place in risk-free money market securities versus in other risky asset classes.

We will denote the investor's portfolio of risky assets as P, and the risk-free asset as F. We will assume for the sake of illustration that the risky component of the investor's overall portfolio

PRACTISING PORTFOLIO THEORY: DIVERSIFICATION THE KEY

First presented by Harry S. Markowitz in 1952, modern portfolio theory revolutionized the way investments were managed. Prior to 1952, investments were managed as individual securities, with no thought about what the collection represented. Mr. Markowitz revolutionized the portfolio building process by first advocating that investors look at the portfolio as a whole, rather than at the individual parts. In fact, he suggested that there was a synergy effect: the portfolio was more than just the sum of its parts. A portfolio of securities, he said, will outperform even the best individual security on a risk-adjusted basis.

Second, Mr. Markowitz proved that diversification should be based on a security's return correlation with another security, rather than by function. It no longer mattered what a company did for a living. What mattered was, if one security or asset class experiences poor returns for a time, another security or asset class in the portfolio will be experiencing above-average returns during that same time.

Portfolio investing can make sense if you consider the opposite. History shows that equities outperform all other asset classes over time. If you believe this, then you might consider investing all of your money in equities. But to take it a step further, if one of those equities was the best stock in the world, why not put all of your money into that?

The problem of course is that no investment will provide you with its return without some price volatility. Without proper diversification, fear takes hold and investors are not able to cope with the risk, and tend to sell at exactly the wrong time. Studies have shown that it takes 15 to 20 stocks in a portfolio to virtually eliminate non-systematic risk. That is the risk unique to an individual company.

Even if you can diversify away the non-systematic risk, what remains—systematic risk—is still part of the problem. Systematic risk is defined as the risk of simply being in the stock market. The only way to reduce this risk is to be in different asset classes at the same time with a portfolio that includes cash, fixed-income securities and stocks. And to take this one step further, your equity exposure should be diversified outside your own country, taking other geographic regions into account.

By structuring a portfolio that is diversified by asset mix, geographic region and management style, and then matching that to your personal risk tolerance, you are starting to look at portfolio management the way a professional money manager looks at it.

Source: Richard Croft, Financial Post, *National Post*, April 30, 2001, p. C9.

comprises two mutual funds: one invested in stocks and the other invested in long-term bonds. For now, we take the composition of the risky portfolio as given and focus only on the allocation between it and risk-free securities. In later sections, we turn to asset allocation and security selection across risky assets.

When we shift wealth from the risky portfolio to the risk-free asset, we do not change the relative proportions of the various risky assets within the risky portfolio. Rather, we reduce the relative weight of the risky portfolio as a whole in favour of risk-free assets.

For example, assume that the total market value of an initial portfolio is \$300,000, of which \$90,000 is invested in the Ready Asset money market fund, a risk-free asset for practical purposes. The remaining \$210,000 is invested in risky equity securities—\$113,400 in Brascan (BC) and \$96,600 in Canadian Tire (CT). The BC and CT holding is "the" risky portfolio, 54 percent in BC and 46 percent in CT:

$$\text{BC:} \qquad w_1 = \frac{113{,}400}{210{,}000} = .54$$

$$\text{CT:} \qquad w_2 = \frac{96{,}600}{210{,}000} = .46$$

The weight of the risky portfolio, P, in the **complete portfolio**, including risk-free investments, is denoted by y:

$$y = \frac{210{,}000}{300{,}000} = .7 \text{ (Risky assets)}$$

$$1 - y = \frac{90,000}{300,000} = .3 \text{ (Risk-free assets)}$$

The weights of each stock in the complete portfolio are as follows:

$$\text{BC:} \quad \frac{\$113,400}{\$300,000} = .378$$

$$\text{CT:} \quad \frac{\$96,600}{\$300,000} = .322$$

$$\text{Risky portfolio} \quad = .700$$

The risky portfolio is 70 percent of the complete portfolio.

Suppose that the owner of this portfolio wishes to decrease risk by reducing the allocation to the risky portfolio from $y = .7$ to $y = .56$. The risky portfolio would total only \$168,000 (.56 × \$300,000 = \$168,000), requiring the sale of \$42,000 of the original \$210,000 risky holdings, with the proceeds used to purchase more shares in Ready Asset (the money market fund). Total holdings in the risk-free asset will increase to 300,000 (1 – .56) = \$132,000, or the original holdings plus the new contribution to the money market fund:

$$\$90,000 + \$42,000 = \$132,000$$

The key point, however, is that we leave the proportions of each stock in the risky portfolio unchanged. Because the weights of BC and CT in the risky portfolio are .54 and .46, respectively, we sell .54 × \$42,000 = \$22,680 of BC and .46 × \$42,000 = \$19,320 of CT. After the sale, the proportions of each share in the risky portfolio are in fact unchanged:

$$\text{BC:} \quad w_1 = \frac{113,400 - 22,680}{210,000 - 42,000} = .54$$

$$\text{CT:} \quad w_2 = \frac{96,600 - 19,320}{210,000 - 42,000} = .46$$

Rather than thinking of our risky holdings as BC and CT stock separately, we may view our holdings as if they were in a single fund that holds BC and CT in fixed proportions. In this sense we treat the risky fund as a single risky asset, that asset being a particular bundle of securities. As we shift in and out of safe assets, we simply alter our holdings of that bundle of securities commensurately.

Given this assumption, we now can turn to the desirability of reducing risk by changing the risky/risk-free asset mix, that is, reducing risk by decreasing the proportion y. As long as we do not alter the weights of each stock within the risky portfolio, the probability distribution of the rate of return on the risky portfolio remains unchanged by the asset reallocation. What will change is the probability distribution of the rate of return on the complete portfolio that consists of the risky asset and the risk-free asset.

CONCEPT CHECK

1. What will be the dollar value of your position in BC and its proportion in your overall portfolio if you decide to hold 50 percent of your investment budget in Ready Asset?

6.2 THE RISK-FREE ASSET

By virtue of its power to tax and control the money supply, only the government can issue default-free bonds. Actually, the default-free guarantee by itself is not sufficient to make the bonds risk-free in real terms. The only risk-free asset in real terms would be a perfectly price-indexed bond. Moreover, a default-free perfectly indexed bond offers a guaranteed real rate to an investor only if the maturity of the bond is identical to the investor's desired holding period. Even indexed bonds are subject to interest rate risk, because real interest rates change unpredictably through time. When future real rates are uncertain, so is the future price of perfectly indexed bonds.

Nevertheless, it is common practice to view Treasury bills as "the" risk-free asset. Their short-term nature makes their values insensitive to interest rate fluctuations. Indeed, an investor can lock in a short-term nominal return by buying a bill and holding it to maturity. The inflation uncertainty over the course of a few weeks, or even months, is negligible compared with the uncertainty of stock market returns.

In practice, most investors use a broader range of money market instruments as a risk-free asset. All the money market instruments are virtually free of interest rate risk because of their short maturities and are fairly safe in terms of default or credit risk.

Most money market funds hold, for the most part, three types of securities: Treasury bills, bearer deposit notes (BDNs), and commercial paper (CP), differing slightly in their default risk. The yields to maturity on BDNs and CP for identical maturity, for example, are always slightly higher than those of T-bills. The pattern of this yield spread for short-term high-quality commercial paper is shown in Figure 6.1.

Money market funds have changed their relative holdings of these securities over time, but by and large, T-bills make up only about 15 percent of their portfolios. Nevertheless, the risk of such

Figure 6.1 Yield spread between 3-month high-quality corporate paper and T-bills.

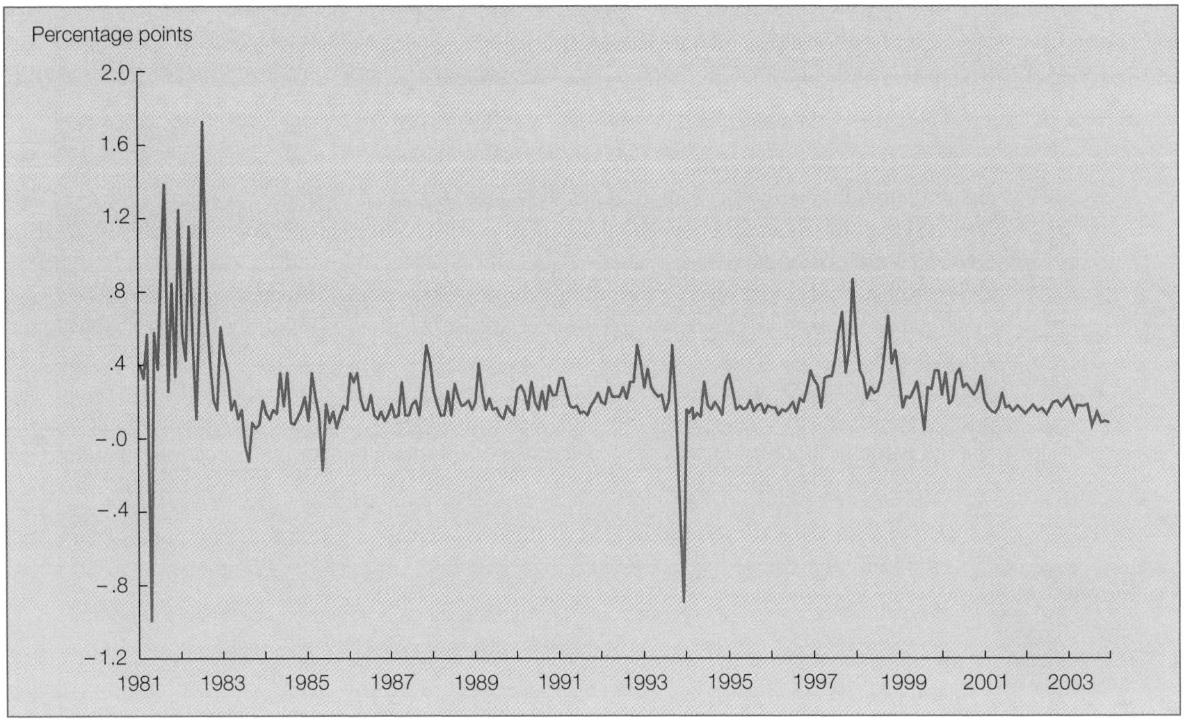

Source: Data from Scotia Capital, *Debt Market Indices*, various years. Available www.scotiacapital.com.

blue-chip short-term investments as BDNs and CP is minuscule compared with that of most other assets, such as long-term corporate bonds, common stocks, or real estate. Hence, we treat money market funds as the most easily accessible risk-free asset for most investors.

6.3 PORTFOLIOS OF ONE RISKY ASSET AND ONE RISK-FREE ASSET

In this section, we examine the risk-return combinations available to investors. This is the "technological" part of asset allocation; it deals with only the opportunities available to investors given the features of the broad asset markets in which they can invest. In the next section, we will address the "personal" part of the problem—the specific individual's choice of the best risk-return combination from the set of feasible combinations.

Suppose that the investor already has decided on the composition of the optimal risky portfolio. The investment proportions in all the available risky assets are known. Now the final concern is with the proportion of the investment budget, y, to be allocated to the risky portfolio, P. The remaining proportion, $1 - y$, is to be invested in the risk-free asset, F.

Denote the risky rate of return by r_P and denote the expected rate of return on P by $E(r_P)$ and its standard deviation by σ_P. The rate of return on the risk-free asset is denoted as r_f. In the numerical example we assume that $E(r_P) = 15$ percent, $\sigma_P = 22$ percent, and the risk-free rate is $r_f = 7$ percent. Thus, the risk premium on the risky asset is $E(r_P) - r_f = 8$ percent.

With a proportion y in the risky portfolio and $1 - y$ in the risk-free asset, the rate of return on the *complete* portfolio, denoted C, is r_C where

$$r_C = yr_P + (1 - y)r_f$$

Taking the expectation of this portfolio's rate of return,

$$\begin{aligned} E(r_C) &= yE(r_P) + (1 - y)r_f \\ &= r_f + y[E(r_P) - r_f] \\ &= .07 + y(.15 - .07) \end{aligned} \tag{6.1}$$

This result is easily interpreted. The base rate of return for any portfolio is the risk-free rate. In addition, the portfolio is *expected* to earn a risk premium that depends on the risk premium of the risky portfolio, $E(r_P) - r_f$, and the investor's exposure to the risky asset, denoted by y. Investors are assumed to be risk-averse and thus unwilling to take on a risky position without a positive risk premium.

As we noted in Chapter 5, when we combine a risky asset and a risk-free asset in a portfolio, the standard deviation of that portfolio is the standard deviation of the risky asset multiplied by the weight of the risky asset in that portfolio. In our case, the complete portfolio consists of the risky asset and the risk-free asset. Since the standard deviation of the risky portfolio is $\sigma_P = .22$,

$$\begin{aligned} \sigma_C &= y\sigma_P \\ &= .22y \end{aligned} \tag{6.2}$$

which makes sense because the standard deviation of the portfolio is proportional to both the standard deviation of the risky asset and the proportion invested in it. In sum, the rate of return of the complete portfolio will have expected return $E(r_C) = r_f + y[E(r_P) - r_f] = .07 + .08y$ and standard deviation $\sigma_C = .22y$.

The next step is to plot the portfolio characteristics (as a function of y) in the expected return–standard deviation plane. This is done in Figure 6.2. The expected return–standard deviation combination for the risk-free asset, F, appears on the vertical axis because the standard

Figure 6.2 Expected return–standard deviation combinations.

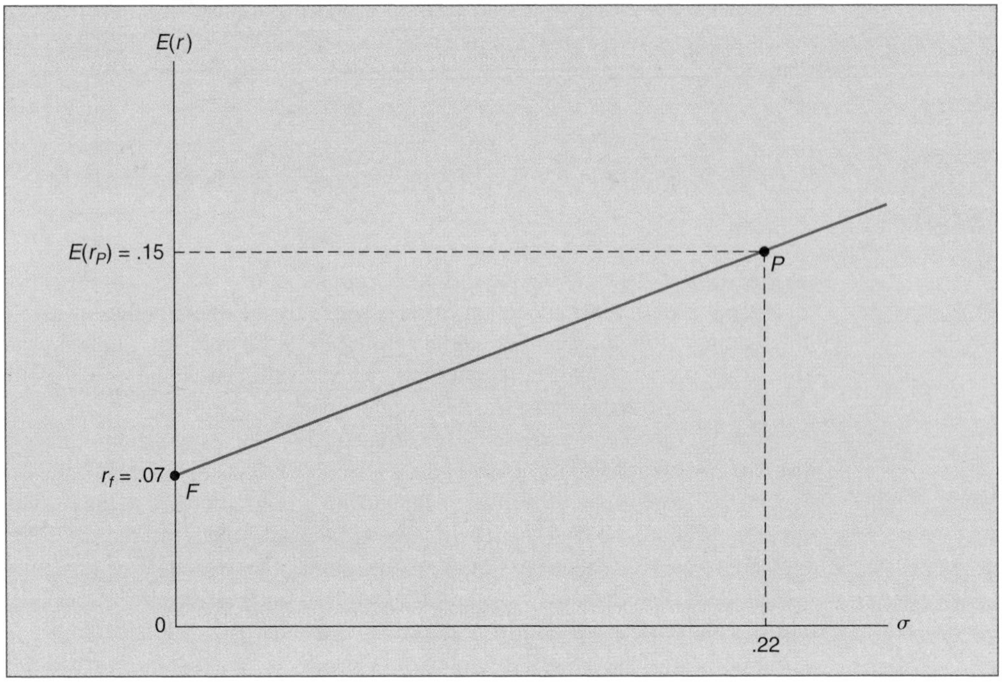

deviation is zero. The risky asset, P, is plotted with a standard deviation, $\sigma_P = .22$, and expected return of .15. If an investor chooses to invest solely in the risky asset, then $y = 1.0$, and the resulting portfolio is P. If the chosen position is $y = 0$, then $1 - y = 1.0$, and the resulting portfolio is the risk-free portfolio F.

What about the more interesting midrange portfolios where y lies between zero and 1? These portfolios will graph on the straight line connecting points F and P. The slope of that line is simply $[E(r_P) - r_f]/\sigma_P$ (or rise/run), in this case .08/.22.

The conclusion is straightforward. Increasing the fraction of the overall portfolio invested in the risky asset increases the expected return by the risk premium of equation 6.1, which is .08. It also increases portfolio standard deviation according to equation 6.2 at the rate of .22. The extra return per extra risk is thus .08/.22 = .36.

To derive the exact equation for the straight line between F and P, we rearrange equation 6.2 to find that $y = \sigma_C/\sigma_P$, and substitute for y in equation 6.1 to describe the expected return–standard deviation tradeoff:

$$E[r_C(y)] = r_f + y[E(r_P) - r_f]$$

$$= r_f + \frac{\sigma_C}{.22}[E(r_P) - r_f]$$

$$= .07 + \frac{.08}{.22}\sigma_C$$

Thus, the expected return of the portfolio as a function of its standard deviation is a straight line, with intercept r_f and slope as follows:

$$S = \frac{E(r_P) - r_f}{\sigma_P}$$

$$= \frac{.08}{.22}$$

Figure 6.3 The investment opportunity set with a risky asset and a risk-free asset.

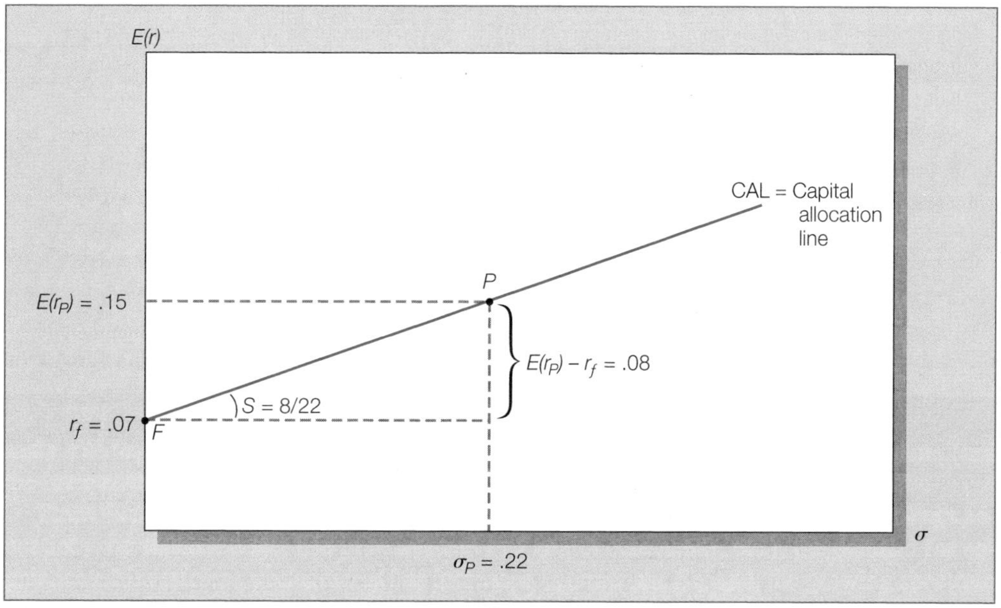

Figure 6.3 graphs the *investment opportunity set,* which is the set of feasible expected return and standard deviation pairs of all portfolios resulting from different values of y. The graph is a straight line originating at r_f and going through the point labelled P.

This straight line is called the **capital allocation line (CAL)**. It depicts all the risk-return combinations available to investors. The slope of the CAL, S, equals the increase in the expected return of the chosen portfolio per unit of additional standard deviation—in other words, the measure of extra return per extra risk. For this reason, the slope also is called the **reward-to-variability ratio.**

A portfolio equally divided between the risky asset and the risk-free asset, that is, where $y = .5$, will have an expected rate of return of $E(r_C) = .07 + .5 \times .08 = .11$, implying a risk premium of 4 percent, and a standard deviation of $\sigma_C = .5 \times .22 = .11$, or 11 percent. It will plot on the line FP midway between F and P. The reward-to-variability ratio will be $S = .04/.11 = .36$, same as that of portfolio P.

CONCEPT CHECK

2. Can the reward-to-variability ratio, $S = [E(r_C) - r_f]/\sigma$, of any combination of the risky asset and the risk-free asset be different from the ratio for the risky asset taken alone, $[E(r_P) - r_f]/\sigma$, which in this case is .36?

What about points on the line to the right of portfolio P in the investment opportunity set? If investors can borrow at the (risk-free) rate of $r_f = 7$ percent, they can construct portfolios that may be plotted on the CAL to the right of P.

Suppose the investment budget is \$300,000, and our investor borrows an additional \$120,000, investing the total available funds in the risky asset. This is a *leveraged* position in the risky asset; it is financed in part by borrowing. In that case

$$y = \frac{420,000}{300,000}$$

$$= 1.4$$

and $1 - y = 1 - 1.4 = -.4$, reflecting a short position in the risk-free asset, which is a borrowing position. Rather than lending at a 7 percent interest rate, the investor borrows at 7 percent. The distribution of the portfolio rate of return still exhibits the same reward-to-variability ratio:

$$E(r_C) = .07 + (1.4 \times .08) = .182$$

$$\sigma_C = 1.4 \times .22 = .308$$

$$S = \frac{E(r_C) - r_f}{\sigma_C}$$

$$= \frac{.182 - .07}{.308} = .36$$

As one might expect, the leveraged portfolio has a higher standard deviation than does an unleveraged position in the risky asset.

Of course, nongovernment investors cannot borrow at the risk-free rate. The risk of a borrower's default causes lenders to demand higher interest rates on loans. Therefore, the nongovernment investor's borrowing cost will exceed the lending rate of $r_f = 7$ percent. Suppose that the borrowing rate is $r^B{}_f = 9$ percent. Then, in the borrowing range the reward-to-variability ratio, the slope of the CAL, will be $[E(r_P) - r^B_f]/\sigma_P = .06/.22 = .27$. The CAL therefore will be "kinked" at point P as shown in Figure 6.4. To the left of P the investor is lending at 7 percent, and the slope of the CAL is .36. To the right of P, where $y > 1$, the investor is borrowing to finance extra investments in the risky asset, and the slope is .27.

In practice, borrowing to invest in the risky portfolio is easy and straightforward if you have a margin account with a broker. All you have to do is tell your broker that you want to buy "on margin." Margin purchases may not exceed 70 percent of the purchase value. Therefore, if your net worth in the account is \$300,000, the broker is allowed to lend you up to \$300,000 to purchase additional stock.[1] You would then have \$600,000 on the asset side of your account and \$300,000 on the liability side, resulting in $y = 2.0$.

Figure 6.4 The opportunity set with differential borrowing and lending rates.

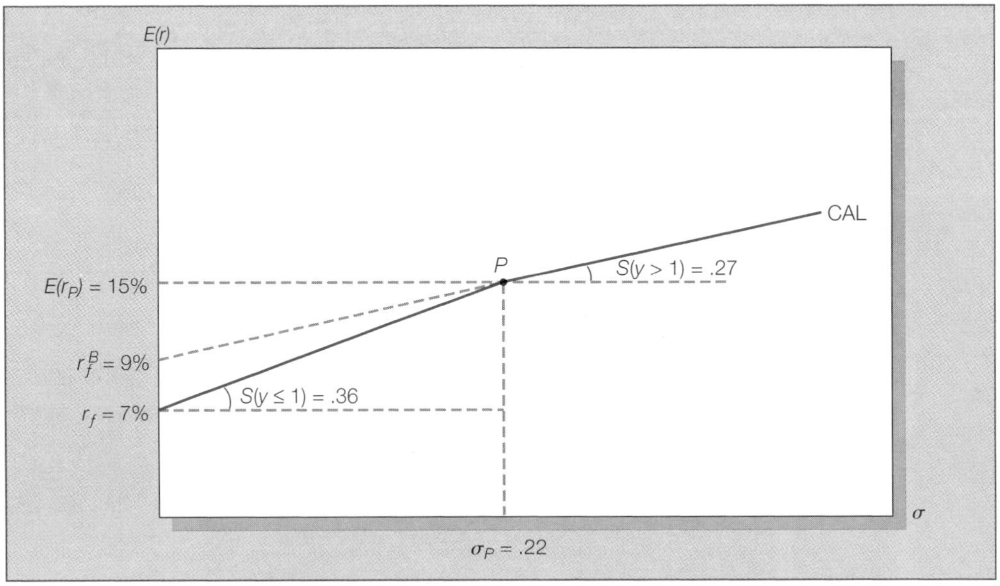

[1]Margin purchases require the investor to maintain the securities in a margin account with the broker. If the value of the securities declines below a maintenance margin, a margin call is sent out, requiring a deposit to bring the net worth of the account up to the appropriate level. If the margin call is not met, regulations mandate that some or all of the securities be sold by the broker and the proceeds used to reestablish the required margin. See Chapter 3, Section 3.4, for a further discussion.

CONCEPT CHECK

3. Suppose that there is a shift upward in the expected rate of return on the risky asset, from 15 percent to 17 percent. If all other parameters remain unchanged, what will be the slope of the CAL for $y \leq 1$ and $y > 1$?

6.4 RISK TOLERANCE AND ASSET ALLOCATION

We have shown how to develop the CAL, the graph of all feasible risk-return combinations available from different asset-allocation choices. The investor confronting the CAL now must choose one optimal combination from the set of feasible choices. This choice entails a tradeoff between risk and return. Individual investor differences in risk aversion imply that, given an identical opportunity set (as described by a risk-free rate and a reward-to-variability ratio), different investors will choose different positions in the risky asset. In particular, the more risk-averse investors will choose to hold less of the risky asset and more of the risk-free asset.

In Chapter 5, we showed that the utility an investor derives from a portfolio with a given probability distribution of rates of return can be described by the expected return and variance of the portfolio rate of return. Specifically, we developed the following representation:

$$U = E(r) - \tfrac{1}{2}A\sigma^2$$

where A is the coefficient of risk aversion. We interpret this expression to say that the utility from a portfolio increases as the expected rate of return increases, and it decreases when the variance increases. The relative magnitude of these changes is governed by the coefficient of risk aversion A. For risk-neutral investors, $A = 0$. Higher levels of risk aversion are reflected in larger values for A.

An investor who faces a risk-free rate, r_f, and a risky portfolio with expected return $E(r_P)$ and standard deviation σ_P will find that, for any choice of y, the expected return of the complete portfolio is given by equation 6.1, part of which we repeat here:

$$E(r_C) = r_f + y[E(r_P) - r_f]$$

From equation 6.2, the variance of the overall portfolio is

$$\sigma^2_C = y^2\sigma^2_P$$

The investor attempts to maximize his or her utility level, U, by choosing the best allocation to the risky asset, y. Typically, we write this problem as follows:

$$\underset{y}{\text{Max}}\ U = E(r_C) - \tfrac{1}{2}A\sigma^2_C = r_f + y[E(r_P) - r_f] - \tfrac{1}{2}y^2A\sigma^2_P$$

where A is the coefficient of risk aversion.

Students of calculus will remember that the maximization problem is solved by setting the derivative of this expression to zero. Doing so and solving for y yields the optimal position for risk-averse investors in the risky asset, y^*, as follows.[2]

$$y^* = \frac{E(r_P) - r_f}{A\sigma^2_P} \qquad (6.3)$$

This solution shows that the optimal position in the risky asset is, as one would expect, *inversely* proportional to the level of risk aversion and the level of risk, as measured by the variance, and directly proportional to the risk premium offered by the risky asset.

[2]The derivative with respect to y equals $E(r_P) - r_f - yA\sigma^2_P$. Setting this expression equal to zero and solving for y yields equation 6.3.

Going back to our numerical example [r_f = 7 percent, $E(r_P)$ = 15 percent, and σ_P = 22 percent], the optimal solution for an investor with a coefficient of risk aversion, $A = 4$, is

$$y^* = \frac{.15 - .07}{4 \times .22^2}$$

$$= .41$$

In other words, this particular investor will invest 41 percent of the investment budget in the risky asset and 59 percent in the risk-free asset. (Note that r_f, $E(r_P)$, and σ_P must be expressed as decimals, or else it is necessary to change the scale of A.)

With 41 percent invested in the risky portfolio, the rate of return of the complete portfolio will have an expected return and standard deviation as follows:

$$E(r_C) = .07 + .41 \times (.15 - .07)$$
$$= .1028$$
$$\sigma_C = .41 \times .22$$
$$= .0902$$

The risk premium of the complete portfolio is $E(r_C) - r_f$ = 3.28 percent, which is obtained by taking on a portfolio with a standard deviation of 9.02 percent. Notice that 3.28/9.02 = .36, which is the reward-to-variability ratio assumed for this problem.

A graphical way of presenting this decision problem is to use indifference curve analysis. Recall from Chapter 5 that the indifference curve is a graph in the expected return–standard deviation plane of all points that result in a given level of utility. The curve then displays the investor's required tradeoff between expected return and standard deviation.

For example, suppose that the initial portfolio under consideration is the risky asset itself, $y = 1$. The coloured curve in Figure 6.5 represents the indifference curve for an investor with a degree of risk aversion, $A = 4$, that passes through the risky asset with $E(r_P)$ = 15 percent and σ_P = 22 percent. The light curve, by contrast, shows an indifference curve going through P with a smaller degree of risk aversion, $A = 2$. The light indifference curve is flatter, that is, the more risk-tolerant (less risk-averse) investor requires a smaller increase in expected return to compensate for a given

Figure 6.5 Two indifference curves through a risky asset.

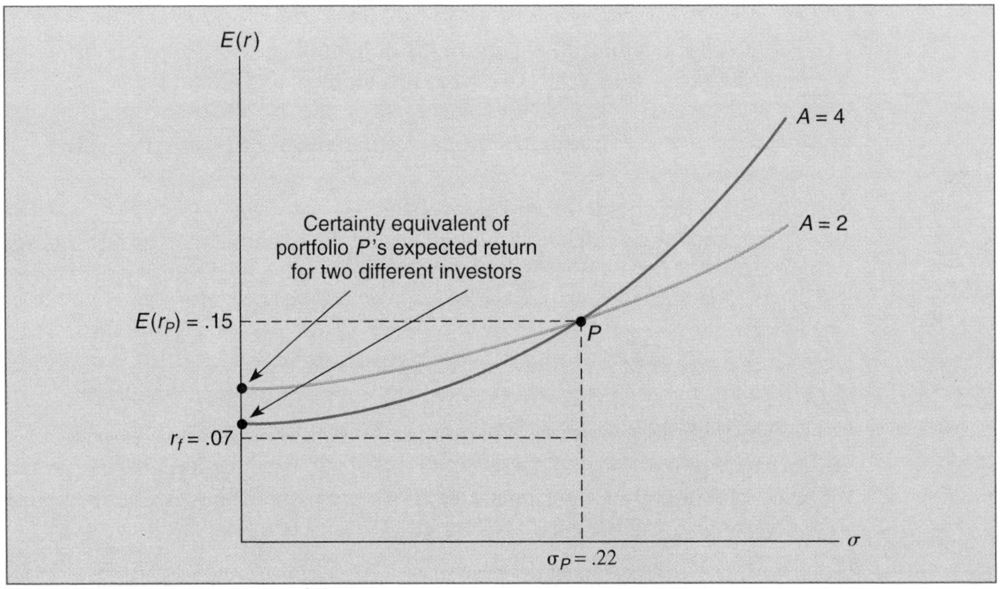

Figure 6.6 A set of indifference curves.

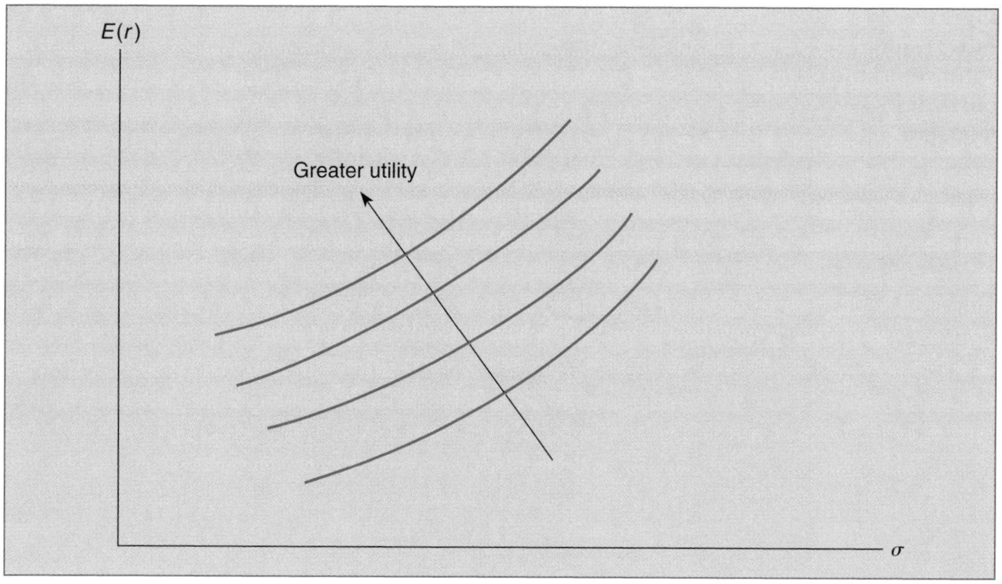

increase in standard deviation. The intercept of the indifference curve with the vertical axis is the *certainty equivalent* of the risky portfolio's expected rate of return because it gives a risk-free return with the same utility as the risky portfolio. Notice in Figure 6.5 that the less risk-averse investor (with $A = 2$) has a higher certainty equivalent for a risky portfolio such as P than the more risk-averse investor ($A = 4$).

The indifference curves of an investor with a given degree of risk aversion can be drawn for many benchmark portfolios, representing various levels of utility. Figure 6.6 shows this set of indifference curves.

To show how to use indifference curve analysis to determine the choice of the optimal portfolio for a specific CAL, Figure 6.7 superimposes the graphs of the indifference curves on the graph of the investment opportunity set, the CAL.

The investor seeks the position with the highest feasible level of utility, represented by the highest possible indifference curve that touches the investment opportunity set. This is the indifference curve tangent to the CAL.

This optimal overall portfolio is represented by point C on the investment opportunity set. Such a graphical approach yields the same solution as the algebraic approach

$$E(r_C) = .1028$$

and

$$\sigma_C = .0902$$

which yields $y^* = .41$.

In summary, the asset allocation process can be broken down into two steps: (1) determine the CAL; and (2) find the point of highest utility along that line.

CONCEPT CHECK

4. *a.* If an investor's coefficient of risk aversion is $A = 3$, how does the optimal asset mix change? What are the new $E(r_C)$ and σ_C?

   b. Suppose that the borrowing rate, $r^B_f = 9$ percent, is greater than the lending rate, $r_f = 7$ percent. Show, graphically, how the optimal portfolio choice of some investors will be affected by the higher borrowing rate. Which investors will not be affected by the borrowing rate?

Figure 6.7 The graphical solution to the portfolio decision.

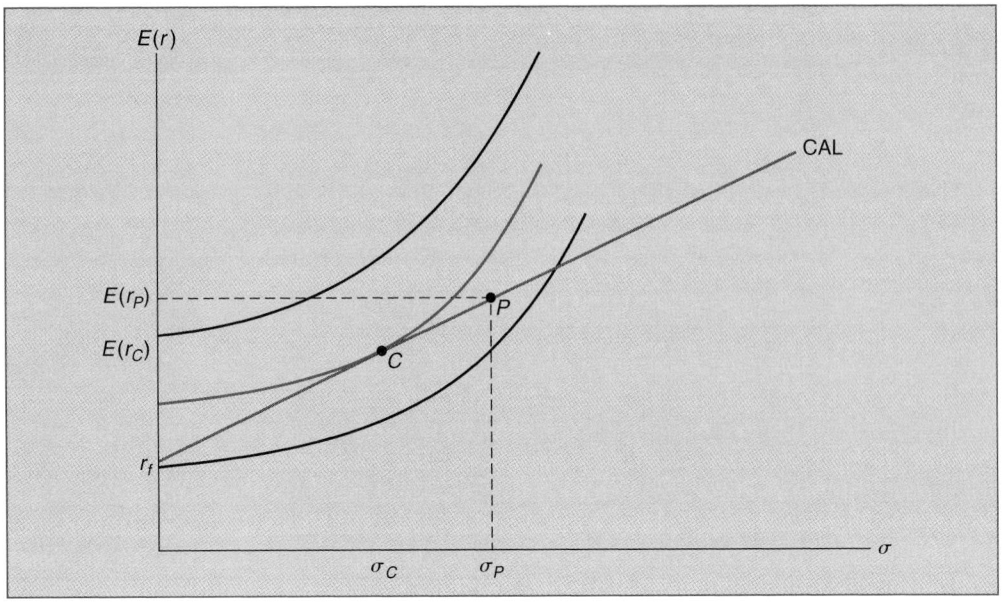

6.5 PASSIVE STRATEGIES: THE CAPITAL MARKET LINE

The CAL is derived with the risk-free asset and "the" risky portfolio *P*. Determination of the assets to include in risky portfolio *P* may result from a passive or an active strategy. A **passive strategy** describes a portfolio decision that avoids *any* direct or indirect security analysis.[3] At first blush, a passive strategy would appear to be naïve. As will become apparent, however, forces of supply and demand in large capital markets may make such a strategy a reasonable choice for many investors.

A natural candidate for a passively held risky asset would be a well-diversified portfolio of common stocks. We already have said that a passive strategy requires that we devote no resources to acquiring information on any individual stock or group of stocks, so we must follow a "neutral" diversification strategy. One way is to select a diversified portfolio of stocks that mirrors the value of the corporate sector of the Canadian economy. This results in a value-weighted portfolio in which, for example, the proportion invested in Nortel's stock will be the ratio of Nortel's total market value to the market value of all listed stocks.

www.tsx.com

The most frequently used value-weighted stock portfolio in Canada is the Toronto Stock Exchange's composite index of the largest capitalization Canadian corporations[4] (TSX Composite). Table 6.1 shows the historical record of this portfolio. The last pair of columns shows the average risk premium over T-bills and its standard deviation. The risk premium of 3.66 percent and standard deviation of 17.03 percent over the entire period correspond to the figures of 8 percent and 22 percent we assumed for the risky portfolio example in Section 6.4.

We call the capital allocation line provided by one-month T-bills and a broad index of common stocks the **capital market line (CML)**. A passive strategy generates an investment opportunity set that is represented by the CML.

How reasonable is it for an investor to pursue a passive strategy? Of course, we cannot answer such a question without comparing the strategy to the costs and benefits accruing to an active portfolio strategy. Some thoughts are relevant at this point, however.

[3]By "indirect security analysis" we mean the delegation of that responsibility to an intermediary, such as a professional money manager.

[4]For a discussion of value-weighted Canadian stock portfolios in asset allocation, see Paul Potvin, "Passive Management, the TSE 300 and the Toronto 35 Stock Indexes," *Canadian Investment Review* 5, no. 1 (Spring 1992).

Table 6.1 Annual Rates of Return for Common Stocks and 3-Month Bills, and the Risk Premium over Bills on Common Stock

	Common Stocks		3-Month T-Bills		Risk Premium over Bills on Common Stocks	
	Mean	Standard Deviation	Mean	Standard Deviation	Mean	Standard Deviation
1957–1972	9.68	15.69	4.37	1.34	5.31	16.24
1973–1988	12.44	13.06	10.26	3.42	2.18	18.57
1989–2003	9.78	16.43	6.28	3.27	3.49	17.19
1957–2003	10.65	16.49	6.99	3.73	3.66	17.03

Source: Modified from Scotia Capital, Inc., *Debt Market Indices*, various years. Available www.scotiacapital.com.

First, the alternative active strategy is not free. Whether you choose to invest the time and cost to acquire the information needed to generate an optimal active portfolio of risky assets, or whether you delegate the task to a professional who will charge a fee, construction of an active portfolio is more expensive than construction of a passive one. The passive portfolio requires only small commissions on purchases of T-bills (or zero commissions if you purchase bills directly from the government) and management fees to a mutual fund company that offers a market index fund to the public. First Canadian's Equity Index Fund, for example, mimics the S&P/TSX Composite index. It purchases shares of the firms constituting the Composite in proportion to the market values of the outstanding equity of each firm, and therefore essentially replicates it. The fund thus duplicates its performance. It has low operating expenses (as a percentage of assets) when compared to other mutual stock funds precisely because it requires minimal managerial effort.

A second reason supporting a passive strategy is the free-rider benefit. If we assume there are many active, knowledgeable investors who quickly bid up prices of undervalued assets and bid down overvalued assets (by selling), we have to conclude that at any time most assets will be fairly priced. Therefore, a well-diversified portfolio of common stock will be a reasonably fair buy, and the passive strategy may not be inferior to that of the average active investor. (We will explain this assumption and provide a more comprehensive analysis of the relative success of passive strategies in later chapters.)

To summarize, however, a passive strategy involves investment in two passive portfolios: virtually risk-free, short-term T-bills (or, alternatively, a money market fund), and a fund of common stocks that mimics a broad market index. The capital allocation line representing such a strategy is called the *capital market line.* Historically, based on data from 1957 to 2003, the passive risky portfolio offered an average risk premium of 3.66 percent and a standard deviation of 17.03 percent, resulting in a reward-to-variability ratio of .21. Passive investors allocate their investment budgets among instruments according to their degree of risk aversion.[5]

6.6 DIVERSIFICATION AND PORTFOLIO RISK

Suppose that your risky portfolio is composed of only one stock, Dominion Computing Corporation (DCC). What would be the sources of risk to this "portfolio"? You might think of two broad sources of uncertainty. First, there is the risk that comes from conditions in the general economy, such as the business cycle, the inflation rate, interest rates, and exchange rates. None

[5]Several studies that take into account the full range of available assets place the degree of risk aversion for the representative investor in the range of 2.0 to 4.0. See, for example, I. Friend and M. Blume, "The Demand for Risky Assets," *American Economic Review* 65 (1975), pp. 900–922.

of these macroeconomic factors can be predicted with certainty, and all affect the rate of return that DCC stock eventually will provide. In addition to these macroeconomic factors there are firm-specific influences, such as DCC's success in research and development, and personnel changes. These factors affect DCC without noticeably affecting other firms in the economy.

Now consider a naïve **diversification** strategy, in which you include additional securities in your risky portfolio. For example, suppose that you place half of your risky portfolio in an oil and minerals firm, Energy Resources Ltd (ERL), leaving the other half in DCC. What should happen to portfolio risk? To the extent that the firm-specific influences on the two stocks differ, we should reduce portfolio risk. For example, when oil prices fall, hurting ERL, computer prices might rise, helping DCC. The two effects are offsetting and stabilize portfolio return.

But why end diversification at only two stocks? If we diversify into many more securities, we continue to spread out our exposure to firm-specific factors, and portfolio volatility should continue to fall. Ultimately, however, even if we include a large number of risky securities in our portfolio, we cannot avoid risk altogether, since virtually all securities are affected by the common macroeconomic factors. For example, if all stocks are affected by the business cycle, we cannot avoid exposure to business cycle risk no matter how many stocks we hold.

When all risk is firm-specific, as in Figure 6.8, panel A, diversification can reduce risk to arbitrarily low levels. The reason is that with all risk sources independent, and with the portfolio spread across many securities, the exposure to any particular source of risk is reduced to a negligible level. The reduction of risk to very low levels in the case of independent risk sources is sometimes called the **insurance principle**, because of the conventional belief that an insurance company depends on the risk reduction achieved through diversification when it writes many policies insuring against many independent sources of risk, with each policy being a small part of the company's overall portfolio. (See Appendix 6B for a discussion of the insurance principle.)

When common sources of risk affect all firms, however, even extensive diversification cannot eliminate risk. In Figure 6.8, panel B, portfolio risk measured by variance or standard deviation, falls as the number of securities increases, but it cannot be reduced to zero.[6] The risk that remains even after extensive diversification is called **market risk**, risk that is attributable to marketwide risk sources. Such risk also is called **systematic risk**, or **nondiversifiable risk.** In contrast, the risk that *can* be eliminated by diversification is called **unique risk, firm-specific risk, nonsystematic risk**, or **diversifiable risk**.

Figure 6.8 Portfolio risk as a function of the number of stocks in the portfolio.

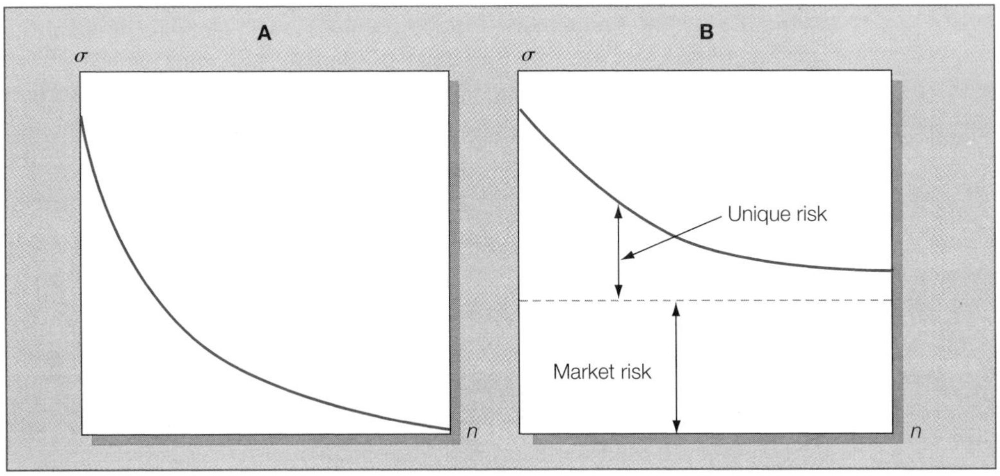

[6]The interested reader can find a more rigorous demonstration of these points in Appendix 6A. That discussion, however, relies on tools developed later in this chapter.

Figure 6.9 Portfolio diversification. The average standard deviation of returns of portfolios composed of only one stock was 49.2 percent. The average portfolio risk fell rapidly as the number of stocks included in the portfolio increased. In the limit, portfolio risk could be reduced to only 19.2 percent.

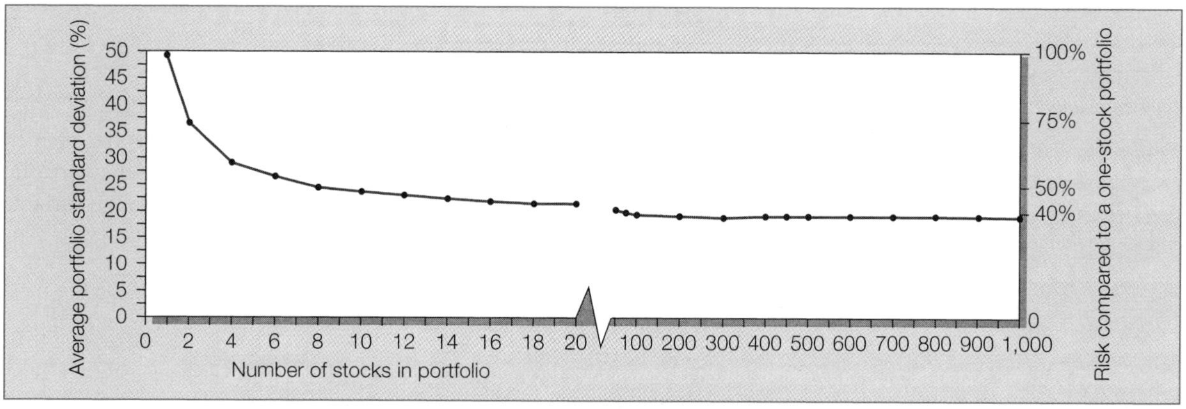

Source: Meir Statman, "How Many Stocks Make a Diversified Portfolio?" *Journal of Financial and Quantitative Analysis* 22 (September 1987). Reprinted by permission.

This analysis is borne out by empirical studies. Figure 6.9 shows the effect of portfolio diversification, using data on NYSE stocks. The figure shows the average standard deviation of equally weighted portfolios constructed by selecting stocks at random as a function of the number of stocks in the portfolio. On average, portfolio risk does fall with diversification, but the power of diversification to reduce risk is limited by systematic or common sources of risk.

6.7 PORTFOLIOS OF TWO RISKY ASSETS

In the last section, we analyzed naïve diversification, examining the risk of equally weighted portfolios composed of several securities. It is time now to study efficient diversification, whereby we construct risky portfolios to provide the lowest possible risk for any given level of expected return.

Portfolios of two risky assets are relatively easy to analyze, and they illustrate the principles and considerations that apply to portfolios of many assets. We will consider a portfolio comprising two mutual funds, a bond portfolio specializing in long-term debt securities, denoted *D*, and a stock fund that specializes in equity securities, *E*. Table 6.2 lists the parameters describing the rate-of-return distribution of these funds. These parameters are representative of those that can be estimated from actual funds.

A proportion denoted by w_D is invested in the bond fund, and the remainder, $1 - w_D$, denoted w_E, is invested in the stock fund. The rate of return on this portfolio will be

$$r_p = w_D r_D + w_E r_E$$

where r_p stands for the rate of return on the portfolio, r_D the return on investment in the debt fund, and r_E the return on investment in the equity fund.

Table 6.2 Descriptive Statistics for Two Assets

	Debt (%)		Equity (%)
Expected return, $E(r)$	8		13
Standard deviation, σ	12		20
Covariance, $\text{Cov}(r_D, r_E)$		72	
Correlation coefficient, ρ_{DE}		.30	

As we noted in Chapter 5, the expected rate of return on the portfolio is a weighted average of expected return on the component securities with portfolio proportions as weights:

$$E(r_P) = w_D E(r_D) + w_E E(r_E) \qquad (6.4)$$

The variance of the two-asset portfolio (rule 5 of Chapter 5) is

$$\sigma^2_p = w^2_D\sigma^2_D + w^2_E\sigma^2_E + 2w_Dw_E\text{Cov}(r_D,r_E) \qquad (6.5)$$

The first observation is that the variance of the portfolio, unlike the expected return, is *not* a weighted average of the individual asset variances. To understand the formula for the portfolio variance more clearly, recall that the covariance of a variable with itself (in this case the variable is the uncertain rate of return) is the variance of that variable; that is,

$$\begin{aligned}\text{Cov}(r_D,r_D) &= \sum_{\text{scenarios}} \Pr(\text{scenario})[r_D - E(r_D)][r_D - E(r_D)] \\ &= \sum_{\text{scenarios}} \Pr(\text{scenario})[r_D - E(r_D)]^2 \\ &= \sigma^2_D\end{aligned}$$

Therefore, another way to write the variance of the portfolio is as follows:

$$\sigma^2_p = w_Dw_D\text{Cov}(r_D,r_D) + w_Ew_E\text{Cov}(r_E,r_E) + 2w_Dw_E\text{Cov}(r_D,r_E)$$

In words, the variance of the portfolio is a weighted sum of covariances, where each weight is the product of the portfolio proportions of the pair of assets in the covariance term.

Why do we double the covariance between the two *different* assets in the last term of equation 6.5? This should become clear in the covariance matrix, Table 6.3, which is bordered by the portfolio weights.

The diagonal (from top left to bottom right) of the covariance matrix is made up of the asset variances. The off-diagonal elements are the covariances. Note that

$$\text{Cov}(r_D,r_E) = \text{Cov}(r_E,r_D)$$

so that the matrix is symmetric. To compute the portfolio variance, we sum over each term in the matrix, first multiplying it by the product of the portfolio proportions from the corresponding row and column. Thus we have *one* term for each asset variance, but twice the term for each covariance pair because each covariance appears twice.

Table 6.3 Bordered Covariance Matrix

	Covariances	
Portfolio Weights	w_D	w_E
w_D	σ^2_D	$\text{Cov}(r_D,r_E)$
w_E	$\text{Cov}(r_E,r_D)$	σ^2_E

CONCEPT CHECK

5. *a.* Confirm that this simple rule for computing portfolio variance from the covariance matrix is consistent with equation 6.5.

b. Consider a portfolio of three funds, *X*, *Y*, and *Z*, with weights w_X, w_Y, and w_Z. Show that the portfolio variance is

$$w^2_X\sigma^2_X + w^2_Y\sigma^2_Y + w^2_Z\sigma^2_Z + 2w_Xw_Y\text{Cov}(r_X,r_Y) + 2w_Xw_Z\text{Cov}(r_X,r_Z) + 2w_Yw_Z\text{Cov}(r_Y,r_Z)$$

Equation 6.5 reveals that variance is reduced if the covariance term is negative. It is important to recognize that, even if the covariance term is positive, the *portfolio* standard deviation still is less than the weighted average of the individual security standard deviations, unless the two securities are perfectly positively correlated.

To see this, recall from Chapter 5, equation 5.8 that the covariance can be written as

$$\text{Cov}(r_D, r_E) = \rho_{DE}\sigma_D\sigma_E$$

Substituting into equation 6.5

$$\sigma^2{}_p = w^2{}_D\sigma^2{}_D + w^2{}_E\sigma^2{}_E + 2w_D w_E \sigma_D \sigma_E \rho_{DE} \tag{6.6}$$

$$\sigma_p = \sqrt{\sigma^2{}_p} \tag{6.7}$$

You can see from this information that the covariance term adds the most to the portfolio variance when the correlation coefficient, ρ_{DE}, is highest, that is, when it equals 1—as it would in the case of perfect positive correlation. In this case, the right-hand side of equation 6.6 is a perfect square, and simplifies to

$$\sigma^2{}_p = (w_D\sigma_D + w_E\sigma_E)^2$$

or

$$\sigma_p = w_D\sigma_D + w_E\sigma_E$$

In other words, the standard deviation of the portfolio with perfect positive correlation is just the weighted average of the component standard deviations. In all other cases, the correlation coefficient is less than 1, making the portfolio standard deviation *less* than the weighted average of the component standard deviations.

We know already from Chapter 5 that a hedge asset reduces the portfolio variance. This algebraic exercise adds the additional insight that the standard deviation of a portfolio of assets is less than the weighted average of the component security standard deviations, even when the assets are positively correlated. Because the portfolio expected return always is the weighted average of its component expected returns, while its standard deviation is less than the weighted average of the component standard deviations, *portfolios of less than perfectly correlated assets always offer better risk-return opportunities than the individual component securities on their own.* The less correlation between assets, the greater the gain in efficiency. The boxed article makes this point, advising you to find "funds that zig when the blue chips zag."

How low can portfolio standard deviation be? The lowest possible value of the correlation coefficient is –1, representing perfect negative correlation, in which case the portfolio variance is as follows:[7]

$$\sigma^2{}_p = (w_D\sigma_D - w_E\sigma_E)^2$$

and the portfolio standard deviation is

$$\sigma_p = \text{Absolute value } (w_D\sigma_D - w_E\sigma_E)$$

Where $\rho = -1$, the investor has the opportunity of creating a perfectly hedged position. If the portfolio proportions are chosen as

$$w_D = \frac{\sigma_E}{\sigma_D + \sigma_E}$$

$$w_E = \frac{\sigma_D}{\sigma_D + \sigma_E} = 1 - w_D$$

the standard deviation of the portfolio will equal zero.[8]

---

[7]This expression can also be derived from equation 6.6. When $\rho_{DE} = -1$, equation 6.6 is a perfect square that can be factored as shown.

[8]It is possible to drive portfolio variance to zero with perfectly positively correlated assets as well, but this would require short sales.

FINDING FUNDS THAT ZIG WHEN THE BLUE CHIPS ZAG

Investors hungry for lower risk are hearing some surprising recommendations from financial advisers:

- Mutual funds investing in less-developed nations that many Americans can't immediately locate on a globe
- Funds specializing in small European companies with unfamiliar names
- Funds investing in commodities

All of these investments are risky by themselves, advisers readily admit. But they also tend to zig when big U.S. stocks zag. And that means that such fare, when added to a portfolio heavy in U.S. blue-chip stocks, actually may damp the portfolio's ups and downs.

Combining types of investments that don't move in lock step "is one of the very few instances in which there is a free lunch—you get something for nothing," says Gary Greenbaum, president of investment counselors Greenbaum & Associates in Oradell, N.J. The right combination of assets can trim the volatility of an investment portfolio, he explains, without reducing the expected return over time.

Getting more variety in one's holdings can be surprisingly tricky. For instance, investors who have shifted dollars into a diversified international-stock fund may not have ventured as far afield as they think, says an article in the most recent issue of *Morningstar Mutual Funds*. Those funds typically load up on European blue-chip stocks that often behave similarly and respond to the same world-wide economic conditions as do U.S. corporate giants. . . .

Many investment professionals use a statistical measure known as a "correlation coefficient" to identify categories of securities that tend to zig when others zag. A figure approaching the maximum 1.0 indicates that two assets have consistently moved in the same direction. A correlation coefficient approaching the minimum, negative 1.0, indicates that the assets have consistently moved in the opposite direction. Assets with a zero correlation have moved independently.

Funds invested in Japan, developing nations, small European companies, and gold stocks have been among those moving opposite to the Vanguard Index 500 over the past several years.

Source: Karen Damato, "Finding Funds That Zig When the Blue Chips Zag," *The Wall Street Journal*, June 17, 1997. Excerpted by permission of The Wall Street Journal,

Let us apply this analysis to the data of the bond and stock funds as presented in Table 6.2. Using these data, the formulas for the expected return, variance, and standard deviation of the portfolio are

$$E(r_p) = 8w_D + 13w_E \tag{6.8}$$

$$\sigma^2_p = 12^2 w^2_D + 20^2 w^2_E + 2 \times 72\, w_D w_E \tag{6.9}$$

$$\sigma_p = \sqrt{\sigma^2_p}$$

Now we are ready to experiment with different portfolio proportions to observe the effect on portfolio expected return and variance. Suppose we change the proportion invested in bonds. The effect on the portfolio's expected return is plotted in Figure 6.10. When the proportion invested in debt varies from zero to one (so that the proportion in equity varies from one to zero), the portfolio expected return goes from 13 percent (the stock fund's expected return) to 8 percent (the expected return on bonds).

What happens to the left of this region, when $w_D > 1$ and $w_E < 0$? In this case, portfolio strategy would be to sell the stock fund short and invest the proceeds of the short sale in bonds. This will decrease the expected return of the portfolio. For example, when $w_D = 2$ and $w_E = -1$, expected portfolio return falls to 3 percent $[2 \times 8 + (-1) \times 13]$. At this point, the value of the bond fund in the portfolio is twice the net worth of the account. This extreme position is financed in part by short-selling stocks equal in value to the portfolio's net worth.

The reverse happens when $w_D < 0$ and $w_E > 1$. This strategy calls for selling the bond fund short and using the proceeds to finance additional purchases of the equity fund.

Of course, varying investment proportions also has an effect on portfolio standard deviation. Table 6.4 presents portfolio standard deviations for different portfolio weights calculated from equations 6.6 and 6.7 for the assumed value of the correlation coefficient, .30, as well as for other values of ρ. Figure 6.11 shows the relationship between standard deviation and portfolio weights. Look first at the curve for $\rho = .30$. The graph shows that as the portfolio weight in the

Figure 6.10 **Portfolio expected return as a function of investment proportions.**

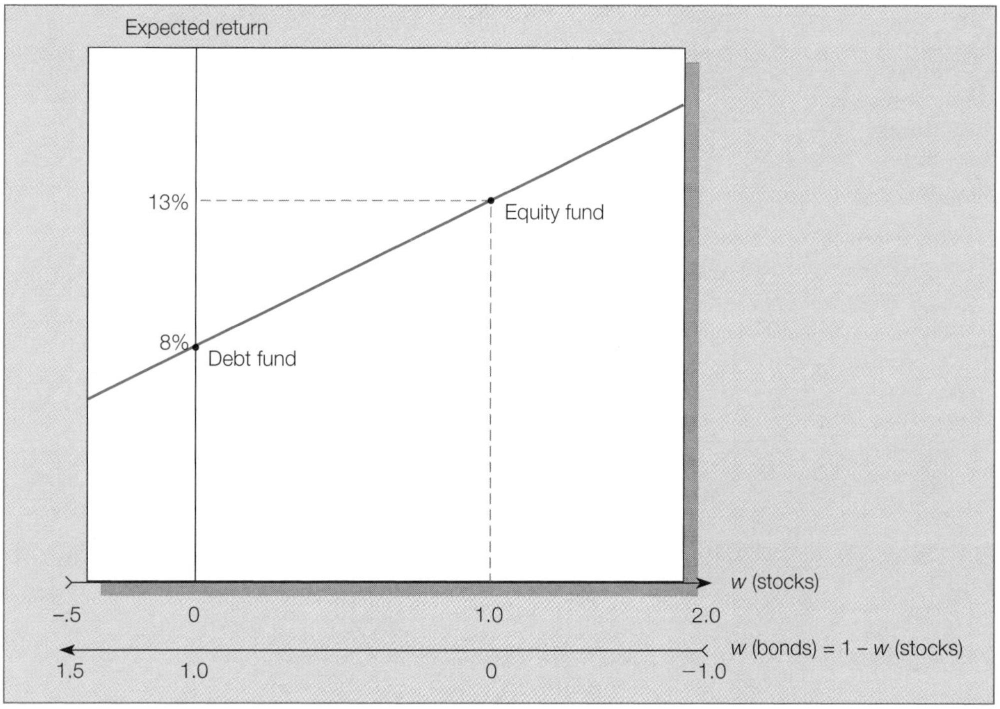

equity fund increases from zero to one, portfolio standard deviation first falls with the initial diversification from bonds into stocks but then rises again as the portfolio becomes heavily concentrated in stocks and again is undiversified.

This pattern generally will hold as long the correlation coefficient between the funds is not too high. For a pair of assets with a large positive correlation of returns, the portfolio standard

Table 6.4 **Expected Return and Standard Deviation with Various Correlation Coefficients**

			Portfolio Standard Deviation for Given Correlation			
w_D	w_E	$E(r_P)$	$\rho = -1$	$\rho = 0$	$\rho = .30$	$\rho = 1$
0.00	1.00	13.00	20.00	20.00	20.00	20.00
0.10	0.90	12.50	16.80	18.04	18.40	19.20
0.20	0.80	12.00	13.60	16.18	16.88	18.40
0.30	0.70	11.50	10.40	14.46	15.47	17.60
0.40	0.60	11.00	7.20	12.92	14.20	16.80
0.50	0.50	10.50	4.00	11.66	13.11	16.00
0.60	0.40	10.00	0.80	10.76	12.26	15.20
0.70	0.30	9.50	2.40	10.32	11.70	14.40
0.80	0.20	9.00	5.60	10.40	11.45	13.60
0.90	0.10	8.50	8.80	10.98	11.56	12.80
1.00	0.00	8.00	12.00	12.00	12.00	12.00

	Minimum Variance Portfolio		
w_D	0.6250	0.7353	0.8200
w_E	0.3750	0.2647	0.1800
$E(r_p)$	9.8750	9.3235	8.9000
σ_p	0.0000	10.2899	11.4473

Figure 6.11 Portfolio standard deviation as a function of investment proportions.

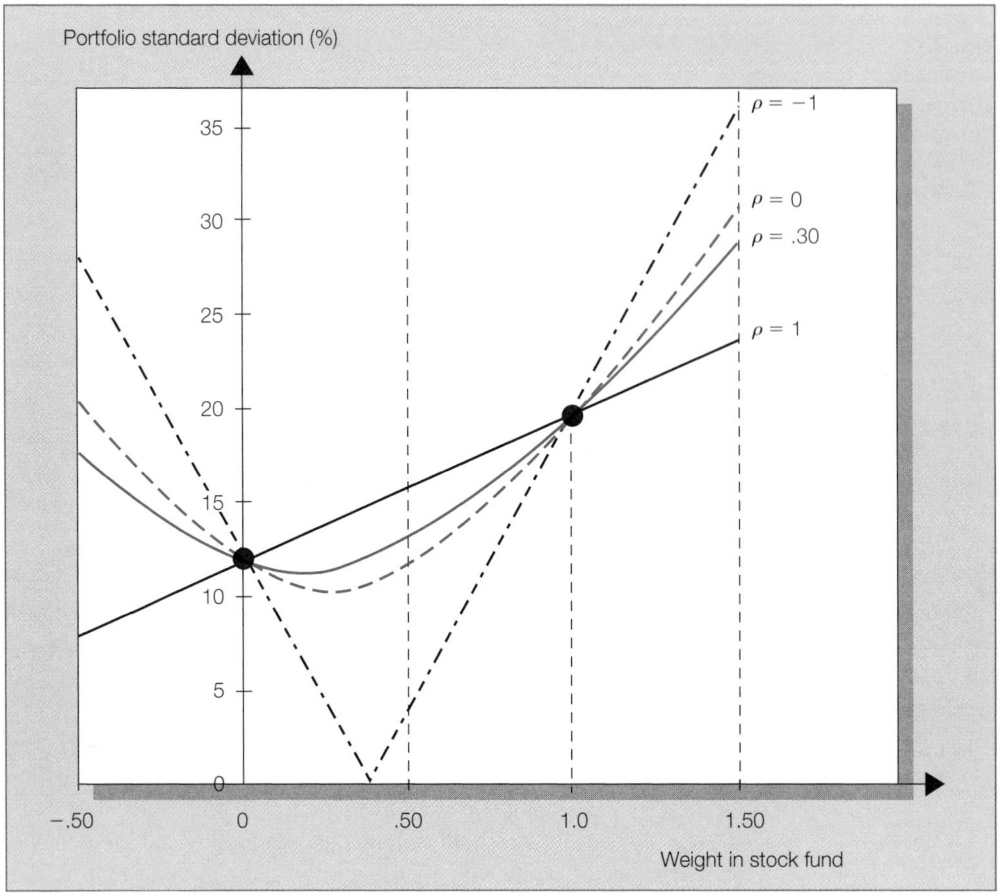

deviation will increase monotonically from the low-risk asset to the high-risk asset. Even in this case, however, there is a positive (if small) value of diversification.

What is the minimum level to which portfolio standard deviation can be held? For the parameter values stipulated in Table 6.2, the portfolio weights that solve this minimization problem turn out to be:[9]

$$w_{\min}(D) = \frac{\sigma^2_E - \text{Cov}(r_D, r_E)}{\sigma^2_D + \sigma^2_E - 2\text{Cov}(r_D, r_E)}$$

$$= \frac{20^2 - 72}{12^2 + 20^2 - 2 \times 72}$$

$$= .82$$

$$w_{\min}(E) = 1 - .82$$

$$= .18$$

This minimum variance portfolio has a standard deviation of

[9]This solution uses the minimization techniques of elementary calculus. Write out the expression for portfolio variance from equation 6.5, substitute $1 - w_D$ for w_E, differentiate the result with respect to w_D, set the derivative equal to zero, and solve for w_D. With a computer spreadsheet, however, you can obtain an accurate solution by generating a fine grid for Table 6.4 and observing the minimum.

$$\sigma_{\min}(P) = [.82^2 \times 12^2 + .18^2 \times 20^2 + 2 \times .82 \times .18 \times 72]^{1/2}$$
$$= 11.45\%$$

as indicated in the last line of Table 6.2 for the column $\rho = .30$.

The curved solid line in Figure 6.11 represents the portfolio standard deviation when $\rho = .30$ as a function of the investment proportions. It passes through the two undiversified portfolios of $w_D = 1$ and $w_E = 1$. Note that the **minimum-variance portfolio** has a standard deviation smaller than that of either of the individual component assets. This highlights the effect of diversification.

The other three lines in Figure 6.11 show how portfolio risk varies for other values of the correlation coefficient, holding the variances of each asset constant. These lines plot the values in the other three columns of Table 6.4.

The straight line connecting the undiversified portfolios of all-bonds or all-stocks, $w_D = 1$ or $w_E = 1$, demonstrates portfolio standard deviation with perfect positive correlation, $\rho = 1$. In this case, there is no advantage from diversification, and the portfolio standard deviation is the simple weighted average of the component asset standard deviations.

The dashed curve depicts portfolio risk for the case of uncorrelated assets, $\rho = 0$. With lower correlation between the two assets, diversification is more effective and portfolio risk is lower (at least when both assets are held in positive amounts). The minimum portfolio standard deviation when $\rho = 0$ is 10.32 percent (see Table 6.4), which again is lower than the standard deviation of either assets.

Finally, the V-shaped broken line illustrates the perfect hedge potential when the two assets are perfectly negatively correlated ($\rho = -1$). In this case, the solution for the minimum-variance portfolio is

$$w_{\min}(D;\rho = -1) = \frac{\sigma_E}{\sigma_D + \sigma_E}$$
$$= \frac{20}{12 + 20}$$
$$= .625$$
$$w_{\min}(E;\rho = -1) = 1 - .625$$
$$= .375$$

and the portfolio variance (and standard deviation) is zero.

We can combine Figures 6.10 and 6.11 to demonstrate the relationship between the portfolio's level of risk (standard deviation) and the expected rate of return on that portfolio—given the parameters of the available assets. This is done in Figure 6.12. For any pair of investment proportions, w_D, w_E, we read the expected return from Figure 6.10 and the standard deviation from Figure 6.11. The resulting pairs of portfolio expected return and standard deviation are plotted in Figure 6.12.

The solid curve in Figure 6.12 shows the **portfolio opportunity set** for $\rho = .30$, so called because it shows the combination of expected return and standard deviation of all the portfolios that can be constructed from the two available assets. The broken and dotted lines show the portfolio opportunity set for other values of the correlation coefficient. The line farthest to the right, which is the straight line connecting the undiversified portfolios, shows that there is no benefit from diversification when the correlation between the two assets is perfectly positive ($\rho = 1$). The opportunity set is not "pushed" to the northwest. The dashed curve shows that there is greater benefit from diversification when the correlation coefficient is zero than when it is positive.

Finally, the $\rho = -1$ lines show the effect of perfect negative correlation. The portfolio opportunity set is linear, but now it offers a perfect hedging opportunity and the maximum advantage from diversification.

Figure 6.12 Portfolio expected return as a function of standard deviation.

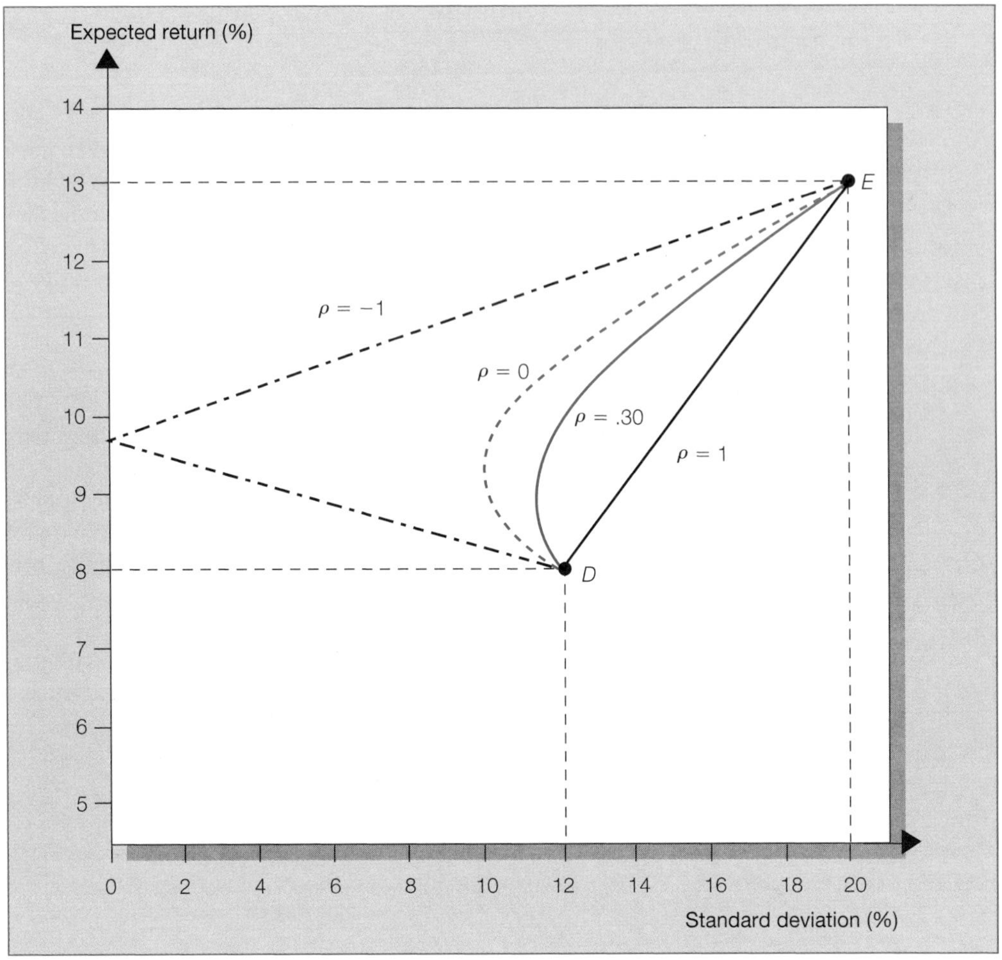

To summarize, although the expected rate of return of any portfolio is simply the weighted average of the asset expected return, this is not true of the portfolio standard deviation. Potential benefits from diversification arise when correlation is less than perfectly positive. The lower the correlation coefficient, the greater the potential benefit of diversification. In the extreme case of perfect negative correlation, we have a perfect hedging opportunity and can construct a zero-variance portfolio.

Suppose now that an investor wishes to select the optimal portfolio from the opportunity set. The best portfolio will depend on risk aversion. Portfolios to the northeast in Figure 6.12 provide higher rates of return, but they impose greater risk. The best tradeoff among these choices is a matter of personal preference. Investors with greater risk aversion will prefer portfolios to the southwest, with lower expected return, but lower risk.[10]

---

[10]Given a level of risk aversion, one can determine the portfolio that provides the highest level of utility. Recall from Chapter 5 that we were able to describe the utility provided by a portfolio as a function of its expected return, $E(r_p)$, and its variance, σ^2_p, according to the relationship $U = E(r_p) - .5A\sigma^2_p$. The portfolio mean and variance are determined by the portfolio weights in the two funds, w_E and w_D, according to equations 6.4 and 6.5. Using those equations, one can show, using elementary calculus, that the optimal investment proportions in the two funds are

$$w_D = \frac{E(r_D) - E(r_E) + A(\sigma^2_E - \sigma_D\sigma_E\rho_{DE})}{A(\sigma^2_D + \sigma^2_E - 2\sigma_D\sigma_E\rho_{DE})}, \quad w_E = 1 - w_D$$

CONCEPT CHECK

6. Compute and draw the portfolio opportunity set for the debt and equity funds when the correlation coefficient between them is $\rho = .25$.

6.8 ASSET ALLOCATION WITH STOCKS, BONDS, AND BILLS

The Optimal Risky Portfolio with Two Risky Assets and a Risk-Free Asset

What if we were still confined to the bond and stock funds, but now could also invest in risk-free T-bills yielding 5 percent? We start with a graphical solution. Figure 6.13 shows the opportunity set generated from the joint probability distribution of the bond and stock funds, using the data from Table 6.2.

Two possible capital allocation lines (CALs) are drawn from the risk-free rate ($r_f = 5$ percent) to two feasible portfolios. The first possible CAL is drawn through the minimum-variance portfolio A, which is invested 82 percent in bonds and 18 percent in stocks (equation 6.10). Portfolio A's expected return is $E(r_A) = 8.90$ percent, and its standard deviation is $\sigma_A = 11.45$ percent. With a T-bill rate of $r_f = 5$ percent, the reward-to-variability ratio, which is the slope of the CAL combining T-bills and the minimum-variance portfolio, is

$$S_A = \frac{E(r_A) - r_f}{\sigma_A}$$

$$= \frac{8.9 - 5}{11.45}$$

$$= .34$$

Figure 6.13 **The opportunity set of the debt and equity funds and two feasible CLAs.**

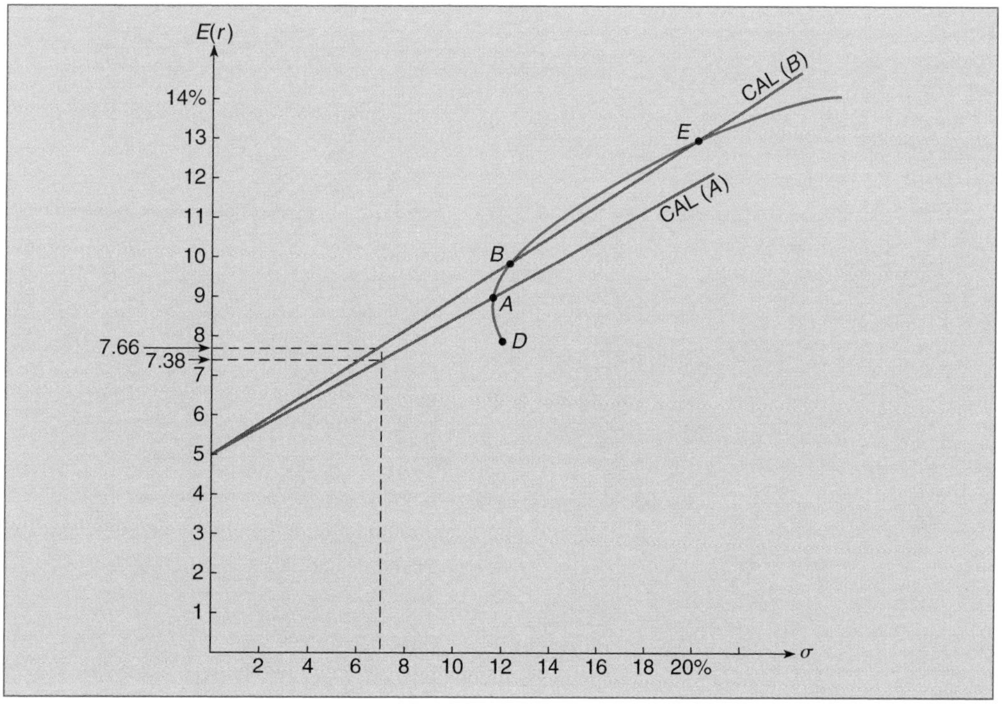

Now consider the CAL that uses portfolio B instead of A. Portfolio B invests 70 percent in bonds and 30 percent in stocks. Its expected return is 9.5 percent (giving it a risk premium of 4.5 percent), and its standard deviation is 11.70 percent. Thus, the reward-to-variability ratio on the CAL that is generated using portfolio B is

$$S_B = \frac{9.5 - 5}{11.7}$$
$$= .38$$

higher than the reward-to-variability ratio of the CAL that we obtained using the minimum-variance portfolio and T-bills. Thus, portfolio B dominates portfolio A.

But why stop at portfolio B? We can continue to ratchet the CAL upward until it ultimately reaches the point of tangency with the investment opportunity set. This must yield the CAL with the highest feasible reward-to-variability ratio. Therefore, the tangency portfolio, P, drawn in Figure 6.14, is the **optimal risky portfolio** to mix with T-bills. We can read the expected return and standard deviation of portfolio P from the graph in Figure 6.14:

$$E(r_p) = 11\%$$
$$\sigma_p = 14.2\%$$

In practice, we obtain an algebraic solution to this problem with a computer program. The spreadsheet we present further on in this chapter can be used to construct efficient portfolios of many assets. Here we describe the process briefly, with only two risky assets.

The objective is to find the weights w_D, w_E that result in the highest slope of the CAL (i.e., the yield of the risky portfolio with the highest reward-to-variability ratio). Therefore, the objective is to maximize the slope of the CAL for any possible portfolio, p. Thus our *objective function* is the slope that we have called S_p:

Figure 6.14
The opportunity set of the stock and bond funds with the optimal CAL and the optimal risky portfolio.

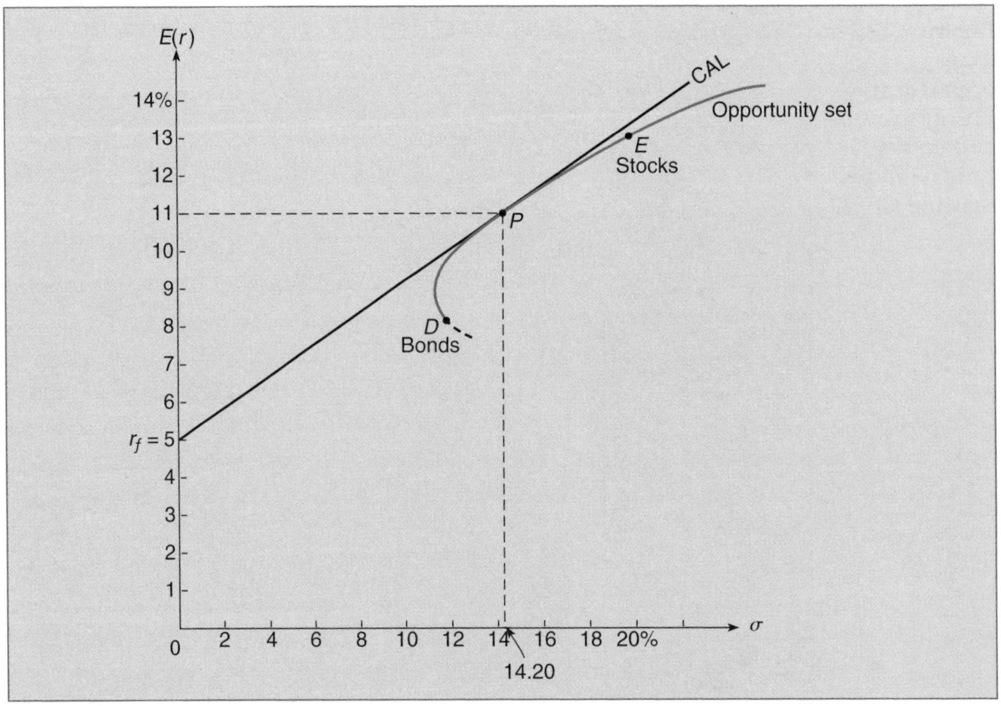

$$S_p = \frac{E(r_p) - r_f}{\sigma_p}$$

For the portfolio with two risky assets, the expected return and standard deviation of portfolio p are

$$E(r_p) = w_D E(r_D) + w_E E(r_E)$$
$$= 8w_D + 13w_E$$
$$\sigma_p = [w^2_D \sigma^2_D + w^2_E \sigma^2_E + 2w_D w_E \text{Cov}(r_D, r_E)]^{1/2}$$
$$= [144w^2_D + 400w^2_E + 2 \times 72 w_D w_E]^{1/2}$$

When we maximize the objective function, S_p, we have to satisfy the constraint that the portfolio weights sum to one (100 percent), that is, $w_D + w_E = 1$. Therefore, we solve a mathematical problem formally written as

$$\underset{w_i}{\text{Max}}\ S_p = \frac{E(r_p) - r_f}{\sigma_p}$$

subject to $\sum w_i = 1$. This is a standard problem in optimization.

In the case of two risky assets, the solution for the weights of the optimal risky portfolio, P, can be shown to be as follows:[11]

$$w_D = \frac{[E(r_D) - r_f]\sigma^2_E - [E(r_E) - r_f]\text{Cov}(r_D, r_E)}{[E(r_D) - r_f]\sigma^2_E + [E(r_E) - r_f]\sigma^2_D - [E(r_D) - r_f + E(r_E) - r_f]\text{Cov}(r_D, r_E)} \tag{6.10}$$

$$w_E = 1 - w_D$$

Substituting our data, the solution is

$$w_D = \frac{(8-5)400 - (13-5)72}{(8-5)400 + (13-5)144 - (8-5+13-5)72}$$
$$= .40$$
$$w_E = 1 - .4$$
$$= .6$$

The expected return on this optimal risky portfolio is 11 percent [$E(r_p) = .4 \times 8 + .6 \times 13$]. The standard deviation is 14.2 percent:

$$\sigma_p = (.4^2 \times 144 + .6^2 \times 400 + 2 \times .4 \times .6 \times 72)^{1/2}$$
$$= 14.2\%$$

The CAL using this optimal portfolio has a slope of

$$S_p = \frac{11 - 5}{14.2} = .42$$

which is the reward-to-variability ratio of portfolio P. Notice that this slope exceeds the slope of any of the other feasible portfolios that we have considered, as it must if it is to be the slope of the best feasible CAL.

In Section 6.4 we found the optimal *complete* portfolio given an optimal risky portfolio and the CAL generated by a combination of this portfolio and T-bills. Now that we have constructed

[11]The solution procedure is as follows. Substitute for $E(r_p)$ from equation 6.4 and for σp from equation 6.5. Substitute $1 - w_D$ for w_E. Differentiate the resulting expression for S_p with respect to w_D, set the derivative equal to zero, and solve for w_D.

the optimal risky portfolio, P, we can use the individual investor's degree of risk aversion, A, to calculate the optimal proportion of the complete portfolio to invest in the risky component.

An investor with a coefficient of risk aversion $A = 4$, would take a position in portfolio P of

$$y = \frac{E(r_P) - r_f}{A\sigma^2_P} \tag{6.11}$$

$$= \frac{.11 - .05}{4 \times .142^2}$$

$$= .7439$$

Thus, the investor will invest 74.39 percent of his or her wealth in portfolio P and 25.61 percent in T-bills. Portfolio P consists of 40 percent in bonds, so the percentage of wealth in bonds will be $yw_D = .4 \times .7439 = .2976$, or 29.76 percent. Similarly, the investment in stocks will be $yw_E = .6 \times .7439 = .4463$, or 44.63 percent. The graphical solution of this problem is presented in Figures 6.15 and 6.16.

Once we have reached this point, generalizing to the case of many risky assets is straightforward. Before we move on, let us briefly summarize the steps we followed to arrive at the complete portfolio.

1. Specify the return characteristics of all securities (expected returns, variances, covariances).

Figure 6.15
Determination of the optimal overall portfolio.

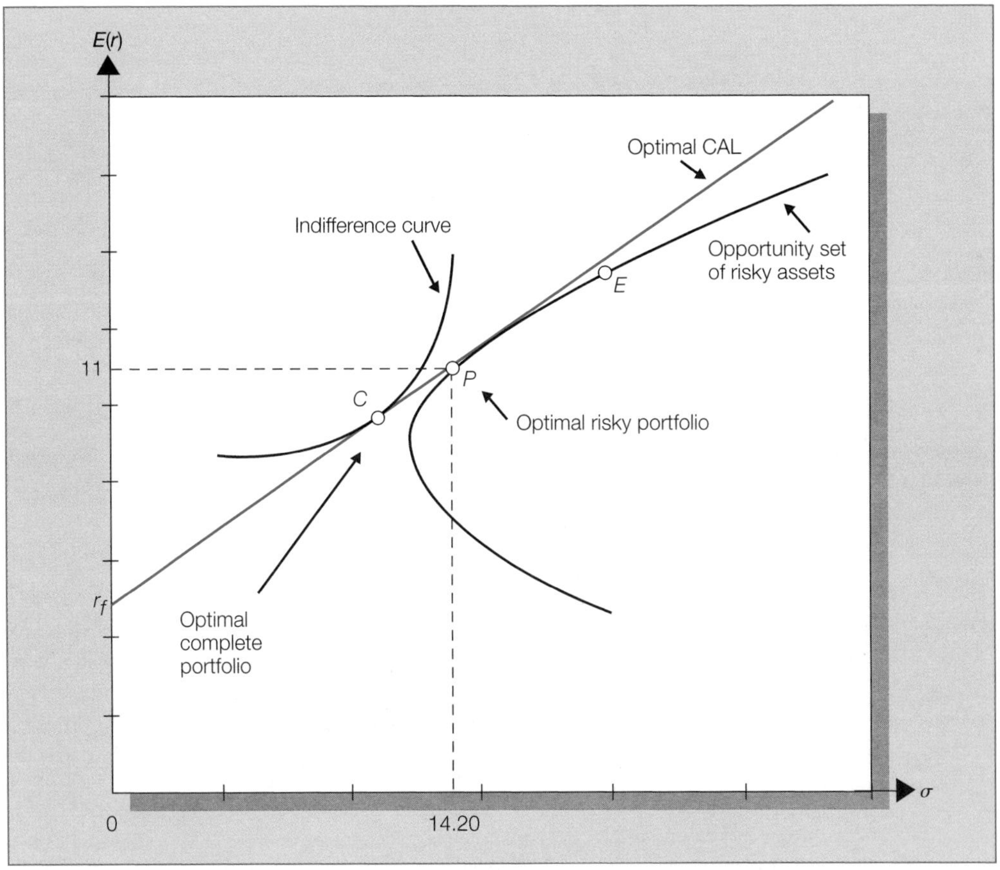

Figure 6.16 The proportions of the optimal overall portfolio.

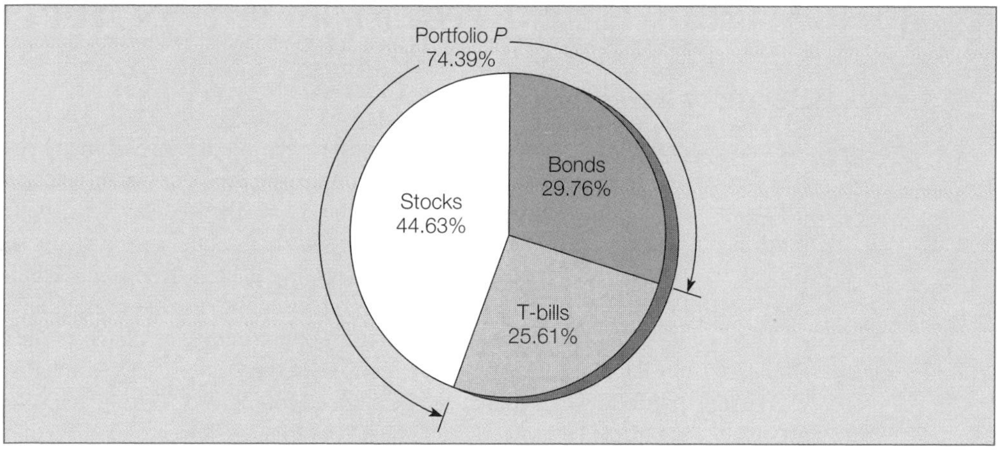

2. Establish the risky portfolio:
   a. Calculate the optimal risky portfolio, *P* (equation 6.10).
   b. Calculate the properties of portfolio *P* using the weights determined in step (*a*) and equations 6.4 and 6.5.
3. Allocate funds between the risky portfolio and the risk-free asset:
   a. Calculate the fraction of the complete portfolio allocated to portfolio *P* (the risky portfolio) and to T-bills (the risk-free asset) (equation 6.11).
   b. Calculate the share of the complete portfolio invested in each asset and in T-bills.

Before moving on, recall that the two assets in the asset allocation problem are already diversified portfolios. The diversification *within* each of these portfolios must be credited for most of the risk reduction, compared to undiversified single securities. For example, the standard deviation of the rate of return on an average stock is about 50 percent. In contrast, the standard deviation of our hypothetical stock index fund is only 20 percent. This is evidence of the importance of diversification within the asset class. Asset allocation between bonds and stocks contributed incrementally to the improvement in the reward-to-volatility ratio of the complete portfolio. The CAL with stocks, bonds, and bills (Figure 6.14) shows that the standard deviation of the complete portfolio can be further reduced to 18 percent, while maintaining the same expected return of 13 percent as the stock portfolio.

? CONCEPT CHECK

7. The universe of available securities includes two risky stock funds, *A* and *B*, and T-bills. The data for the universe are as follows:

	Expected Return	Standard Deviation
A	.10	.20
B	.30	.60
T-bills	.05	0

The correlation coefficient between funds *A* and *B* is –.2.

a. Draw the opportunity set of funds *A* and *B*.

b. Find the optimal risky portfolio *P* and its expected return and standard deviation.

c. Find the slope of the CAL supported by T-bills and portfolio *P*.

d. How much will an investor with *A* = 5 invest in funds *A* and *B* and in T-bills?

6.9 THE MARKOWITZ PORTFOLIO SELECTION MODEL

Security Selection

We can generalize the portfolio construction problem to the case of many risky securities and a risk-free asset. As in the two risky assets example, the problem has three parts. First, we identify the risk-return combinations available from the set of risky assets. Next, we identify the optimal portfolio of risky assets by finding the portfolio that results in the steepest CAL. Finally, we choose an appropriate complete portfolio by mixing the risk-free asset, T-bills, with the optimal risky portfolio. Before describing the process in detail, let us first present an overview.

The first step is to determine the risk-return opportunities available to the investor. These are summarized by the **minimum-variance frontier** of risky assets. This frontier is a graph of the lowest possible portfolio variance that can be attained for a given portfolio expected return. Given the set of data for expected returns, variances, and covariances, we can calculate the minimum-variance portfolio (or equivalently, minimum-standard deviation portfolio) for any targeted expected return. The plot of these expected return–standard deviation pairs is presented in Figure 6.17.

Notice that all the individual assets lie to the right inside of the frontier, at least when we allow short sales in the construction of risky portfolios.[12] This tells us that risky portfolios composed of only a single asset are inefficient. Diversifying investments leads to portfolios with higher expected returns and lower standard deviations.

All the portfolios that lie on the minimum-variance frontier, from the global minimum-variance portfolio and upward, provide the best risk-return combinations and thus are candidates for the optimal portfolio. The part of the frontier that lies above the global minimum-variance portfolio, therefore, is called the **efficient frontier.** For any portfolio on the lower portion of the

Figure 6.17 The minimum-variance frontier of risky assets.

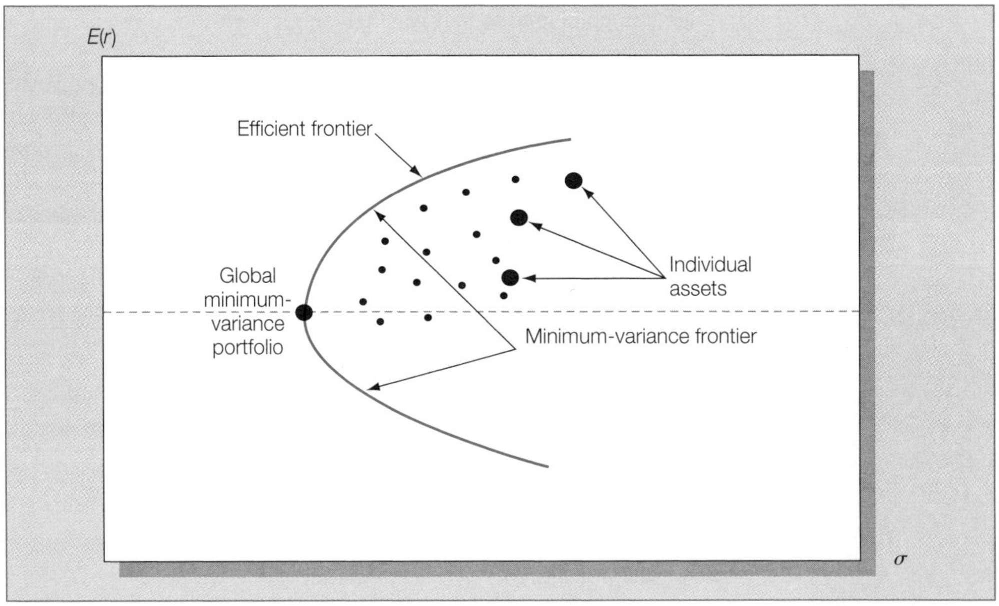

[12]When short sales are prohibited, single securities may lie on the frontier. For example, the security with the highest expected return must lie on the frontier, as that security represents the only way that one can obtain a return that high, and so it also must be the minimum-variance way to obtain that return. When short sales are feasible, however, portfolios can be constructed that offer the same expected return and lower variance. These portfolios typically will have short positions in low-expected-return securities.

minimum-variance frontier, there is a portfolio with the same standard deviation and a greater expected return positioned directly above it. Hence, the bottom part of the minimum-variance frontier is inefficient.

The second part of the optimization plan involves the risk-free asset. As before, we search for the capital allocation line with the highest reward-to-variability ratio (i.e., the steepest slope) as shown in Figure 6.18.

The CAL that is supported by the optimal portfolio, *P*, is, as before, the one that is tangent to the efficient frontier. This CAL dominates all alternative feasible lines that may be drawn through the frontier. Portfolio *P*, therefore, is the optimal risky portfolio.

Finally, in the last part of the problem, the individual investor chooses the appropriate mix between the optimal risky portfolio *P* and T-bills, exactly as in Figure 6.15.

Now let us consider each part of the portfolio construction problem in more detail. In the first part of the problem, risk-return analysis, the portfolio manager needs, as inputs, a set of estimates for the expected returns of each security and a set of estimates for the covariance matrix. (In Part Five, "Equities," we will examine the security valuation techniques and methods of financial analysis that analysts use. For now, we will assume that analysts have already spent the time and resources to prepare the inputs.)

Suppose that the horizon of the portfolio plan is one year. Therefore all estimates pertain to a one-year holding period return. Our security analysts cover n securities. As of now, time zero, we observed these security prices: $P^0{}_1, \ldots, P^0{}_n$. The analysts derive estimates for each security's expected rate of return by forecasting end-of-year (time 1) prices: $E(P^1{}_1), \ldots, E(P^1{}_n)$, and the expected dividends for the period: $E(D_1), \ldots, E(D_n)$. The set of expected rates of return is then computed from

$$E(r_i) = \frac{E(P^1{}_i) + E(D_i) - P^0{}_i}{P^0{}_i}$$

The covariances among the rates of return on the analyzed securities (the covariance matrix) are usually estimated from historical data. Another method is to use a scenario analysis of possible returns from all securities instead of, or as a supplement to, historical analysis.

Figure 6.18 **The efficient frontier of risky assets with the optimal CAL.**

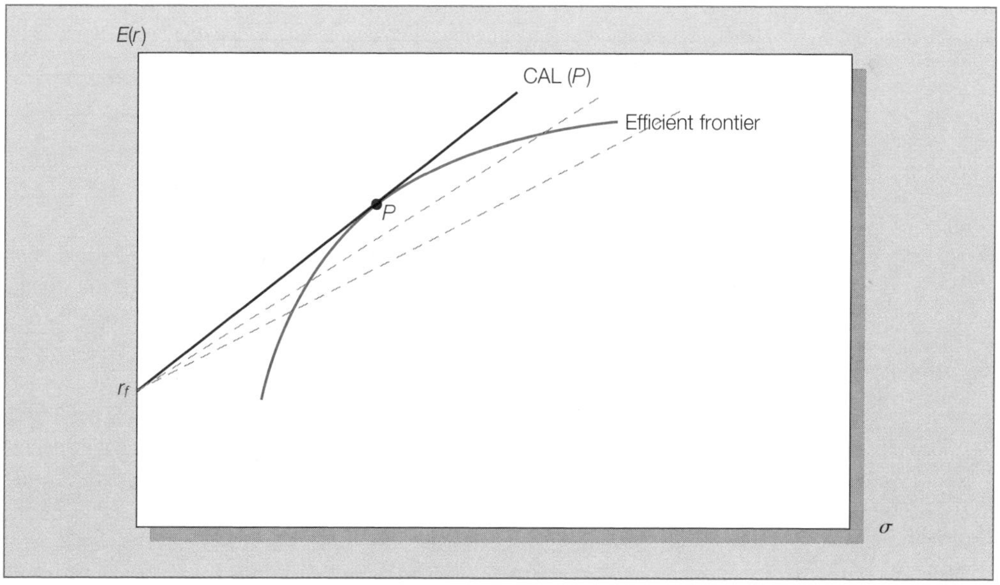

TWO-SECURITY MODEL

The spreadsheet here (constructed with the two-security return data from the text, Table 6.2) can be used to measure the return and risk of a portfolio of two risky assets. The model calculates the return and risk for varying weights of each security along with the optimal risky and minimum-variance portfolio. Graphs are automatically generated for various model inputs. The model allows you to specify a target rate of return and solves for optimal combinations using the risk-free asset and the optimal risky portfolio.

Additional problems using this spreadsheet are available at www.mcgrawhill.ca/college/bodie.

	A	B	C	D	E	F
1	**Asset Allocation Analysis: Risk and Return**					
2		**Expected**	**Standard**	**Corr**		
3		**Return**	**Deviation**	**Coeff s,b**	**Covariance**	
4	Security 1	0.08	0.12	0.3	0.0072	
5	Security 2	0.13	0.2			
6	T-Bill	0.05	0			
7						
8	**Weight**	**Weight**		**Expected**	**Standard**	**Reward to**
9	**Security 1**	**Security 2**		**Return**	**Deviation**	**Variability**
10	1	0		0.08000	0.12000	0.25000
11	0.9	0.1		0.08500	0.11559	0.30281
12	0.8	0.2		0.09000	0.11454	0.34922
13	0.7	0.3		0.09500	0.11696	0.38474
14	0.6	0.4		0.10000	0.12264	0.40771
15	0.5	0.5		0.10500	0.13115	0.41937
16	0.4	0.6		0.11000	0.14199	0.42258
17	0.3	0.7		0.11500	0.15466	0.42027
18	0.2	0.8		0.12000	0.16876	0.41479
19	0.1	0.9		0.12500	0.18396	0.40771
20	0	1		0.13000	0.20000	0.40000
21						

The portfolio manager now is armed with the n estimates of $E(r_i)$ and the $n \times n$ estimates in the covariance matrix in which the n diagonal elements are estimates of the variances, σ^2_i, and the $n^2 - n = n(n-1)$ off-diagonal elements are the estimates of the covariances between each pair of asset returns. (You can verify this from Table 6.3 for the case $n = 2$.) We know that each covariance appears twice in this table, so actually we have $n(n-1)/2$ different covariance estimates. If our portfolio management unit covers 50 securities, our security analysts need to deliver 50 estimates of expected returns, 50 estimates of variances, and $50 \times 49/2 = 1{,}225$ different estimates of covariances. This is a daunting task! (We show later how the number of required estimates can be reduced substantially.)

Once these estimates are compiled, the expected return and variance of any risky portfolio with weights in each security, w_i, can be calculated from the following formulas:

	A	B	C	D	E	F
21	Optimal Risky Portfolio					
22				**Short Sales**	**No Short**	
23				**Allowed**	**Sales**	
24			Weight 1	.40	.40	
25			Weight 2	.60	.60	
26			Return	.11	.11	
27			Std. Dev.	.142	.142	
28						
29						

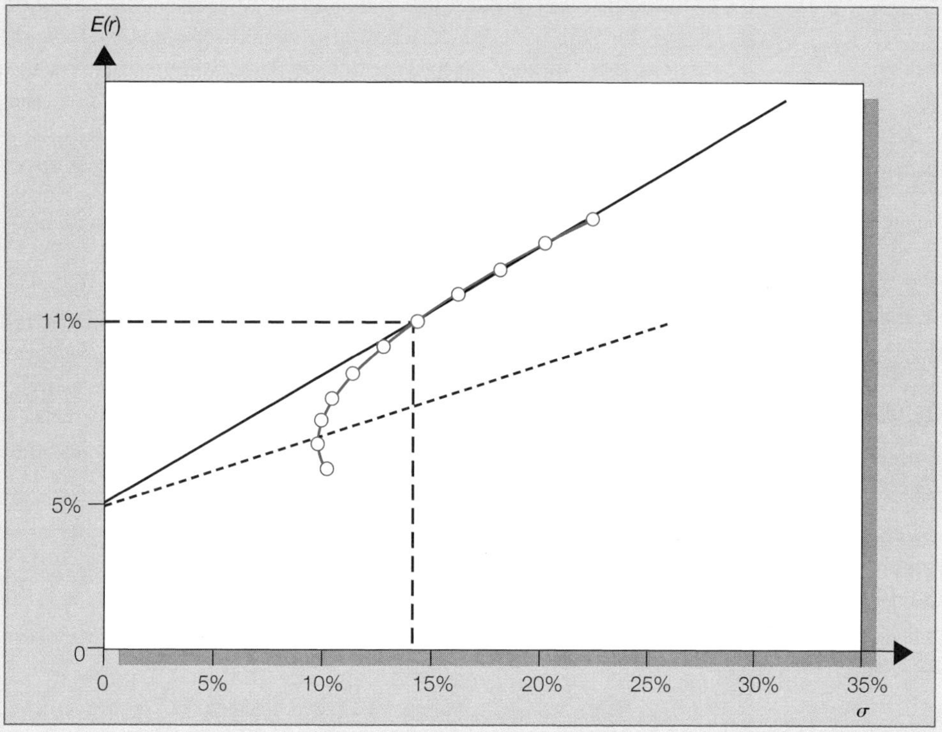

$$E(r_p) = \sum_{i=1}^{n} w_i E(r_i) \tag{6.12}$$

$$\sigma^2_p = \sum_{i=1}^{n} w^2_i \sigma^2_i + \sum_{\substack{i=1 \\ i \neq j}}^{n} \sum_{j=1}^{n} w_i w_j \text{Cov}(r_i, r_j) \tag{6.13}$$

An extended worked example showing you how to do this on a spreadsheet is presented in the next section.

We mentioned earlier that the idea of diversification is age-old. The adage "Don't put all your eggs in one basket" existed long before modern finance theory. It was not until 1952, however, that Harry Markowitz published a formal model of portfolio selection embodying diversification principles, ultimately earning himself the 1990 Nobel prize for economics.[13] His model is precisely step one of portfolio management: the identification of the efficient set of portfolios, or, as it is often called, the efficient frontier of risky assets.

The principal idea behind the frontier set of risky portfolios is that, for any risk level, we are interested only in that portfolio with the highest expected return. Alternatively, the frontier is the set of portfolios that minimizes the variance for any target expected return.

Indeed, the two methods of computing the efficient set of risky portfolios are equivalent. To see this, consider the graphical representation of these procedures. Figure 6.19 shows the minimum-variance frontier.

The points marked by squares are the result of a variance-minimization program. We first draw the constraint, that is, a horizontal line at the level of required expected return. We then look for the portfolio with the lowest standard deviation that plots on this horizontal line—we look for the portfolio that will plot farthest to the left (smallest standard deviation) on that line. When we repeat this for various levels of required expected returns, the shape of the minimum-variance frontier emerges. We then discard the bottom part of the frontier, because it is inefficient.

In the alternative approach, we draw a vertical line that represents the standard deviation constraint. We then consider all portfolios that plot on this line (have the same standard deviation) and choose the one with the highest expected return, that is, that portfolio falling highest on this vertical line. Repeating this procedure for various vertical lines (levels of standard deviation) gives us the points marked by circles that trace the upper portion of the minimum-variance frontier, the efficient frontier.

When this step is completed, we have a list of efficient portfolios, because the solution to the optimization program includes the portfolio proportions, w_i, the expected return, $E(r_p)$, and standard deviation, σ_p.

Let us restate what our portfolio manager has done so far. The estimates generated by the analysts were transformed into a set of expected rates of return and a covariance matrix. This group of estimates we shall call the **input list.** This input list was then fed into the optimization program.

Figure 6.19 **The efficient portfolio set.**

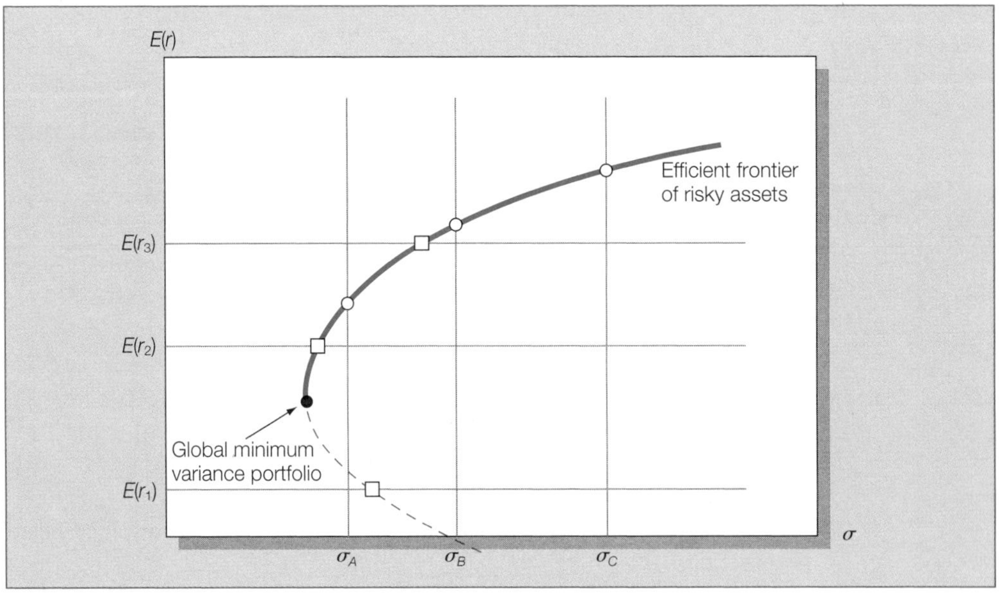

[13]Harry Markowitz, "Portfolio Selection," *Journal of Finance*, March 1952.

Before we proceed to the second step of choosing the optimal risky portfolio from the frontier set, let us consider a practical point. Some clients may be subject to additional constraints. For example, many institutions are prohibited from taking short positions in any asset. For these clients, the portfolio manager will add to the program constraints that rule out negative (short) positions in the search for efficient portfolios. In this special case it is possible that single assets may be, in and of themselves, efficient risky portfolios. For example, the asset with the highest expected return will be a frontier portfolio because, without the opportunity of short sales, the only way to obtain that rate of return is to hold the asset as one's entire risky portfolio.

Short-sale restrictions are by no means the only such constraints. For example, some clients may want to assure a minimal level of expected dividend yield on the optimal portfolio. In this case, the input list will be expanded to include a set of expected dividend yields $d_1, \ldots, d_n$ and the optimization program will include an additional constraint that ensures that the expected dividend yield of the portfolio will equal or exceed the desired level, d.

Portfolio managers can tailor the efficient set to conform to any desire of the client. Of course, any constraint carries a price tag in the sense that an efficient frontier constructed subject to extra constraints will offer a reward-to-variability ratio inferior to that of a less constrained one. The client should be made aware of this cost and should reconsider constraints that are not mandated by law.

Another type of constraint that has become increasingly popular is aimed at ruling out investments in industries or countries considered ethically or politically undesirable. This is referred to as *socially responsible investing*.

6.10 A SPREADSHEET MODEL

Calculation of Expected Return and Variance

www.microsoft.com

Several software packages can be used to generate the efficient frontier. We will demonstrate the method using Microsoft Excel. Excel is far from the best program for this purpose and is limited in the number of assets it can handle, but working through a simple portfolio optimizer in Excel can illustrate concretely the nature of the calculations used in more sophisticated "black-box" programs. You will find that even in Excel, the computation of the efficient frontier is fairly easy.

We will apply the Markowitz portfolio optimizer to the problem of international diversification. Table 6.5 shows average returns, standard deviations, and the correlation matrix for the rates of return on the stock indices of seven countries over the period 1980–1993. Suppose that toward the end of 1979, the analysts of International Capital Management (ICM) had produced an input list that anticipated these results. As portfolio manager of ICM, what set of efficient portfolios would you have considered as investment candidates?

After we input Table 6.5 into our spreadsheet as shown, we create the bordered covariance matrix in panel B using the relationship $\text{Cov}(r_i, r_j) = \rho_{ij}\sigma_i\sigma_j$. The table shows both cell formulas (upper panel) and numerical results (lower panel).

Next we prepare the data for the computation of the efficient frontier. To establish a benchmark against which to evaluate our efficient portfolios, we use an equally weighted portfolio, that is, the weights for each of the seven countries is equal to 1/7 = .1429. To compute the properties of this portfolio, these portfolio weights are entered in the border column A53–A59 and border row B52–H52.[14] We calculate the variance of this portfolio in cell B77 in panel C. The entry in this cell equals the sum of each element in the covariance matrix where each element is first multiplied by

[14]You should not enter the portfolio weights in these rows and columns independently, since if a weight in the row changes, the weight in the corresponding column must change to the same value for consistency. Thus you should *copy* each entry from column A to the corresponding element of row 52.

the portfolio weights given in both the border row and the border column.[15] We also include two cells to compute the standard deviation and expected return of the equally weighted portfolio (formulas in cells B62, B63) and find that they yield an expected return of 16.5 percent with a standard deviation of 17.7 percent (results in cells B78 and B79).

To compute points along the *efficient* frontier we use the Excel Solver in panel D (which you can find in the Tools menu under Add-Ins). Once you bring up Solver, you are asked to enter the cell of the target (objective) function. In our application, the target is the variance of the portfolio, given in cell B93. Solver will minimize this target. You next must input the cell range of the decision variables (in this case, the portfolio weights, contained in cells B85–B91). Finally, you enter all necessary constraints. For an unrestricted efficient frontier that allows short sales, there are two constraints: first, that the sum of the weights equals 1.0 (cell A92 = 1), and second, that the portfolio expected return equals a target mean return. We will choose a target return equal to that of the equally weighted portfolio, 16.5 percent, so our second constraint is that cell B95 = 16.5. Once you have entered the two constraints you ask the Solver to find the optimal portfolio weights.

The Solver beeps when it has found a solution and alters automatically the portfolio weight cells in row 84 and column A to show the makeup of the efficient portfolio. It adjusts the entries in the bordered covariance matrix to reflect the multiplication by these new weights, and it shows the mean and variance of this optimal portfolio—the minimum variance portfolio with mean return of 16.5 percent. These results are shown in panel D, cells B93–B95. The table shows that the standard deviation of the *efficient* portfolio with same mean as the *equally weighted* portfolio is 17.2 percent, a reduction of risk of about one-half percentage point. Observe that the weights of the efficient portfolio differ radically from equal weights.

To generate the entire efficient frontier, keep changing the required mean in the constraint (cell B95) and letting the Solver work for you. If you record a sufficient number of points, you will be able to generate a graph of the quality of Figure 6.20.

The outer frontier in Figure 6.20 is drawn assuming that the investor may maintain negative portfolio weights. If short selling is not allowed, we may impose the additional constraints that each weight (the elements in column A and row 84) must be nonnegative; we would then obtain the restricted efficient frontier curve in Figure 6.20, which lies inside the frontier obtained allowing short sales. The superiority of the unrestricted efficient frontier reminds us that restrictions imposed on portfolio choice may be costly.

The Solver allows you to add short sale and other constraints easily. Once they are entered, you repeat the variance-minimization exercise until you generate the entire restricted frontier. By using macros in Excel or—even better—with specialized software, the entire routine can be accomplished with one push of a button.

Table 6.5 presents a number of points on the two frontiers. The first column gives the required mean and the next two columns show the resultant variance of efficient portfolios with and without short sales. Note that the restricted frontier cannot obtain a mean return less than 10.5 percent (which is the mean in Canada, the country index with the lowest mean return) or more than 21.7 percent (corresponding to Germany, the country with the highest mean return). The last seven columns show the portfolio weights of the seven country stock indexes in the optimal portfolios. You can see that the weights in restricted portfolios are never negative. For mean returns in the range from about 14 percent to 18 percent, the two frontiers overlap since the optimal weights in the unrestricted frontier turn out to be positive (see also Figure 6.20).

[15]We need the sum of each element of the covariance matrix, where each term has first been multiplied by the product of the portfolio weights from its row and column. These values appear in panel C of Table 6.5. We will first sum these elements for each column and then add up the column sums. Row 60 contains the appropriate column sums. Therefore, the sum of cells B60–H60, which appears in cell B61, is the variance of the portfolio formed using the weights appearing in the borders of the covariance matrix.

Table 6.5 Performance of Stock Indices of Seven Countries, 1980–1993

	A	B	C	D	E	F	G	H
1								
2		A. Annualized Standard Deviation, Average Return,						
3		and Correlation Coefficients of International Stocks, 1980–1993						
4								
5		Std. Dev. (%)	Average Ret. (%)					
6	US	21.1	15.7					
7	Germany	25.0	21.7					
8	UK	23.5	18.3					
9	Japan	26.6	17.3					
10	Australia	27.6	14.8					
11	Canada	23.4	10.5					
12	France	26.6	17.2					
13								
14		Correlation Matrix						
15		US	Germany	UK	Japan	Australia	Canada	France
16	US	1.00	0.37	0.53	0.26	0.43	0.73	0.44
17	Germany	0.37	1.00	0.47	0.36	0.29	0.36	0.63
18	UK	0.53	0.47	1.00	0.43	0.50	0.54	0.51
19	Japan	0.26	0.36	0.43	1.00	0.26	0.29	0.42
20	Australia	0.43	0.29	0.50	0.26	1.00	0.56	0.34
21	Canada	0.73	0.36	0.54	0.29	0.56	1.00	0.39
22	France	0.44	0.63	0.51	0.42	0.34	0.39	1.00

	A	B	C	D	E	F	G	H
27		B. Covariance Matrix: Cell Formulas						
28								
29		US	Germany	UK	Japan	Australia	Canada	France
30	US	b6*b6*b16	b7*b6*c16	b8*b6*d16	b9*b6*e16	b10*b6*f16	b11*b6*g16	b12*b6*h16
31	Germany	b6*b7*b17	b7*b7*c17	b8*b7*d17	b9*b7*e17	b10*b7*f17	b11*b7*g17	b12*b7*h17
32	UK	b6*b8*b18	b7*b8*c18	b8*b8*d18	b9*b8*e18	b10*b8*f18	b11*b8*g18	b12*b8*h18
33	Japan	b6*b9*b19	b7*b9*c19	b8*b9*d19	b9*b9*e19	b10*b9*f19	b11*b9*g19	b12*b9*h19
34	Australia	b6*b10*b20	b7*b10*c20	b8*b10*d20	b9*b10*e20	b10*b10*f20	b11*b10*g20	b12*b10*h20
35	Canada	b6*b11*b21	b7*b11*c21	b8*b11*d21	b9*b11*e21	b10*b11*f21	b11*b11*g21	b12*b11*h21
36	France	b6*b12*b22	b7*b12*c22	b8*b12*d22	b9*b12*e22	b10*b12*f22	b11*b12*g22	b12*b12*h22
37								
38		Covariance Matrix: Results						
39								
40		US	Germany	UK	Japan	Australia	Canada	France
41	US	445.21	195.18	262.80	145.93	250.41	360.43	246.95
42	Germany	195.18	625.00	276.13	239.40	200.10	210.60	418.95
43	UK	262.80	276.13	552.25	268.79	324.30	296.95	318.80
44	Japan	145.93	239.40	268.79	707.56	190.88	180.51	297.18
45	Australia	250.41	200.10	324.30	190.88	761.76	361.67	249.61
46	Canada	360.43	210.60	296.95	180.51	361.67	547.56	242.75
47	France	246.95	418.95	318.80	297.18	249.61	242.75	707.56

	A	B	C	D	E	F	G	H
49		C. Border-Multiplied Covariance Matrix for the Equally Weighted Portfolio and Portfolio Variance:						
50		Cell Formulas						
51		US	Germany	UK	Japan	Australia	Canada	France
52	Weights	a53	a54	a55	a56	a57	a58	a59
53	0.1429	a53*b52*b41	a53*c52*c41	a53*d52*d41	a53*e52*e41	a53*f52*f41	a53*g52*g41	a53*h52*h41
54	0.1429	a54*b52*b42	a54*c52*c42	a54*d52*d42	a54*e52*e42	a54*f52*f42	a54*g52*g42	a54*h52*h42
55	0.1429	a55*b52*b43	a55*c52*c43	a55*d52*d43	a55*e52*e43	a55*f52*f43	a55*g52*g43	a55*h52*h43
56	0.1429	a56*b52*b44	a56*c52*c44	a56*d52*d44	a56*e52*e44	a56*f52*f44	a56*g52*g44	a56*h52*h44
57	0.1429	a57*b52*b45	a57*c52*c45	a57*d52*d45	a57*e52*e45	a57*f52*f45	a57*g52*g45	a57*h52*h45
58	0.1429	a58*b52*b46	a58*c52*c46	a58*d52*d46	a58*e52*e46	a58*f52*f46	a58*g52*g46	a58*h52*h46
59	0.1429	a59*b52*b47	a59*c52*c47	a59*d52*d47	a59*e52*e47	a59*f52*f47	a59*g52*g47	a59*h52*h47
60	Sum(a53:a59)	sum(b53:b59)	sum(c53:c59)	sum(d53:d59)	sum(e53:e59)	sum(f53:f59)	sum(g53:g59)	sum(h53:h59)
61	Portfolio variance	sum(b60:h60)						
62	Portfolio SD	b61^.5						
63	Portfolio mean	a53*c6+a54*c7+a55*c8+a56*c9+a57*c10+a58*c11+a59*c12						

Table 6.5 (Continued)

	A	B	C	D	E	F	G	H
64								
65		C. Border-Multiplied Covariance Matrix for the Equally Weighted Portfolio and Portfolio Variance:						
66		Results						
67	Portfolio	US	Germany	UK	Japan	Australia	Canada	France
68	weights	0.1429	0.1429	0.1429	0.1429	0.1429	0.1429	0.1429
69	0.1429	9.09	3.98	5.36	2.98	5.11	7.36	5.04
70	0.1429	3.98	12.76	5.64	4.89	4.08	4.30	8.55
71	0.1429	5.36	5.64	11.27	5.49	6.62	6.06	6.51
72	0.1429	2.98	4.89	5.49	14.44	3.90	3.68	6.06
73	0.1429	5.11	4.08	6.62	3.90	15.55	7.38	5.09
74	0.1429	7.36	4.30	6.06	3.68	7.38	11.17	4.95
75	0.1429	5.04	8.55	6.51	6.06	5.09	4.95	14.44
76	1.0000	38.92	44.19	46.94	41.43	47.73	44.91	50.65
77	Portfolio variance	314.77						
78	Portfolio SD	17.7						
79	Portfolio mean	16.5						

	A	B	C	D	E	F	G	H
80		D. Border-Multiplied Covariance Matrix for the Efficient Frontier Portfolio with Mean of 16.5%						
81		(after change of weights by Solver)						
82								
83	Portfolio	US	Germany	UK	Japan	Australia	Canada	France
84	weights	0.3467	0.1606	0.0520	0.2083	0.1105	0.1068	0.0150
85	0.3467	53.53	10.87	4.74	10.54	9.59	13.35	1.29
86	0.1606	10.87	16.12	2.31	8.01	3.55	3.61	1.01
87	0.0520	4.74	2.31	1.49	2.91	1.86	1.65	0.25
88	0.2083	10.54	8.01	2.91	30.71	4.39	4.02	0.93
89	0.1105	9.59	3.55	1.86	4.39	9.30	4.27	0.41
90	0.1068	13.35	3.61	1.65	4.02	4.27	6.25	0.39
91	0.0150	1.29	1.01	0.25	0.93	0.41	0.39	0.16
92	1.0000	103.91	45.49	15.21	61.51	33.38	33.53	4.44
93	Portfolio variance	297.46						
94	Portfolio SD	17.2						
95	Portfolio mean	16.5						

	A	B	C	D	E	F	G	H	I	J
96		E. The Unrestricted Efficient Frontier and the Restricted Frontier (with no short sales)								
97										
98		Standard Deviation		Country Weights In Efficient Portfolios						
99	Mean	Unrestricted	Restricted	US	Germany	UK	Japan	Australia	Canada	France
100	9.0	24.239	not feasible	−0.0057	−0.2859	−0.1963	0.2205	0.0645	0.9811	0.2216
101	10.5	22.129		0.0648	−0.1966	−0.1466	0.2181	0.0737	0.8063	0.1803
102	10.5		23.388	0.0000	0.0000	0.0000	0.0007	0.0000	0.9993	0.0000
103	11.0	21.483		0.0883	−0.1668	−0.1301	0.2173	0.0768	0.7480	0.1665
104	11.0		22.325	0.0000	0.0000	0.0000	0.0735	0.0000	0.9265	0.0000
105	12.0	20.292		0.1353	−0.1073	−0.0970	0.2157	0.0829	0.6314	0.1390
106	12.0		20.641	0.0000	0.0000	0.0000	0.1572	0.0325	0.7668	0.0435
107	14.0	18.408		0.2293	0.0118	−0.0308	0.2124	0.0952	0.3982	0.0839
108	14.0		18.416	0.2183	0.0028	0.0000	0.2068	0.0884	0.4020	0.0816
109	15.0	17.767	17.767	0.2763	0.0713	0.0023	0.2108	0.1013	0.2817	0.0563
110	16.0	17.358	17.358	0.3233	0.1309	0.0355	0.2091	0.1074	0.1651	0.0288
111	17.0	17.200	17.200	0.3702	0.1904	0.0686	0.2075	0.1135	0.0485	0.0012
112	17.5	17.216		0.3937	0.2202	0.0851	0.2067	0.1166	−0.0098	−0.0125
113	17.5		17.221	0.3777	0.2248	0.0867	0.2021	0.1086	0.0000	0.0000
114	18.0	17.297		0.4172	0.2499	0.1017	0.2059	0.1197	−0.0681	−0.0263
115	18.0		17.405	0.3285	0.2945	0.1157	0.1869	0.0744	0.0000	0.0000
116	18.5	17.441		0.4407	0.2797	0.1182	0.2051	0.1227	−0.1263	−0.0401
117	18.5		17.790	0.2792	0.3642	0.1447	0.1716	0.0402	0.0000	0.0000
118	21.0	19.036		0.5582	0.4285	0.2010	0.2010	0.1380	−0.4178	−0.1090
119	21.0		22.523	0.0000	0.8014	0.1739	0.0247	0.0000	0.0000	0.0000
120	22.0	20.028	not feasible	0.6052	0.4880	0.2341	0.1994	0.1442	−0.5343	−0.1365
121	26.0	25.390	not feasible	0.7931	0.7262	0.3665	0.1929	0.1687	−1.0006	−0.2467

Figure 6.20 Efficient frontier with seven countries.

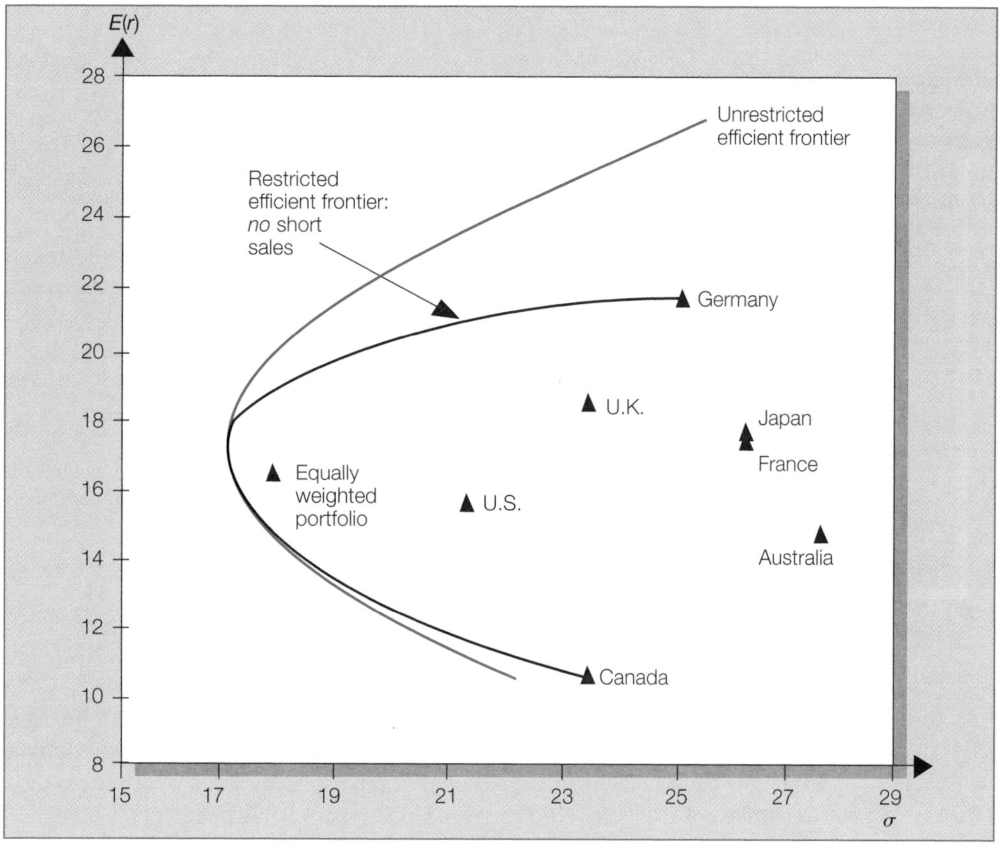

Notice that despite the fact that German stocks offer the highest mean return and even the highest reward-to-variability ratio, the weight of U.S. stocks is generally higher in both restricted and unrestricted portfolios. This is due to the lower correlation of U.S. stocks with stocks of other countries, and it illustrates the importance of diversification attributes when forming efficient portfolios. Figure 6.20 presents points corresponding to means and standard deviations of individual country indices, as well as the equally weighted portfolio. The figure clearly shows the benefits from diversification.

Capital Allocation and Separation Property

Now that we have the efficient frontier, we proceed to step two and introduce the risk-free asset. Figure 6.21 shows the efficient frontier plus three CALs representing various portfolios from the efficient set. As before, we ratchet up the CAL by selecting different portfolios until we reach portfolio *P*, which is the tangency point of a line from *F* to the efficient frontier. Portfolio *P* maximizes the reward-to-variability ratio, the slope of the line from *F* to portfolios on the efficient frontier. At this point, our portfolio manager is done. Portfolio *P* is the optimal risky portfolio for the manager's clients. This is a good time to ponder our results and their implementation.

The most striking conclusion is that a portfolio manager will offer the same risky portfolio, *P*, to all clients regardless of their degree of risk aversion.[16] The degree of risk aversion of the client

[16]Clients who impose special restrictions (constraints) on the manager, such as dividend yield, will obtain another optimal portfolio. Any constraint that is added to an optimization problem leads, in general, to a different and less desirable optimum compared to an unconstrained program.

Figure 6.21 Capital allocation lines with various portfolios from the efficient set.

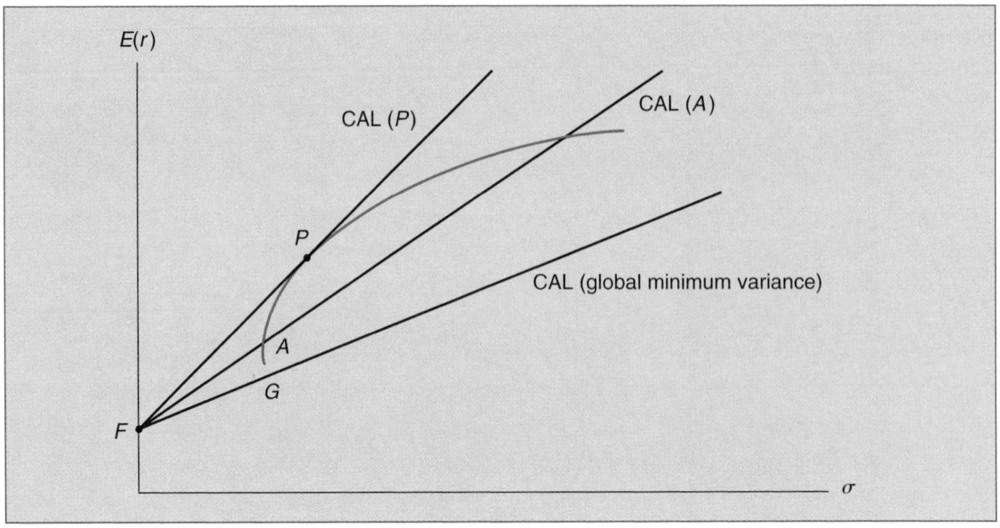

comes into play only in the selection of the desired point on the CAL. Thus, the only difference between clients' choices is that the more risk-averse client will invest more in the risk-free asset and less in the optimal risky portfolio, *P*, than will a less risk-averse client. However, both will use portfolio *P* as their optimal risky investment vehicle.

This result is called a **separation property**; it tells us that the portfolio choice problem may be separated into two independent tasks. The first task, determination of the optimal risky portfolio, *P*, is purely technical. Given the manager's input list, the best risky portfolio is the same for all clients, regardless of risk aversion. The second task, however, allocation of the complete portfolio to T-bills versus the risky portfolio, depends on personal preference. Here the client is the decision maker.

The crucial point is that the optimal portfolio *P* that the manager offers is the same for all clients. This result makes professional management more efficient and hence less costly. One management firm can serve any number of clients with relatively small incremental administrative costs.

In practice, however, different managers will estimate different input lists, thus deriving different efficient frontiers, and offer different "optimal" portfolios to their clients. The source of the disparity lies in the security analysis. It is worth mentioning here that the rule of GIGO (garbage in, garbage out) applies to security analysis, too. If the quality of the security analysis is poor, a passive portfolio such as a market index fund will result in a better CAL than an active portfolio that uses low-quality security analysis to tilt the portfolio weights toward seemingly favourable (seemingly mispriced) securities.

As we have seen, the optimal risky portfolios for different clients also may vary because of portfolio constraints such as dividend-yield requirements, tax considerations, or other client preferences. Nevertheless, this analysis suggests that only a very limited number of portfolios may be sufficient to serve the demands of a wide range of investors. This is the theoretical basis of the mutual fund industry.

The (computerized) optimization technique is the easiest part of the portfolio construction problem. The real arena of competition among portfolio managers is in sophisticated security analysis.

Asset Allocation and Security Selection

As we have seen, the theories of security selection and asset allocation are identical. Both activities call for the construction of an efficient frontier and the choice of a particular portfolio from along that frontier. The determination of the optimal combination of securities proceeds in the

? CONCEPT CHECK

8. Suppose that two portfolio managers who work for competing investment management houses each employ a group of security analysts to prepare the input list for the Markowitz algorithm. When all is completed, it turns out that the efficient frontier obtained by portfolio manager *A* dominates that of manager *B*. By domination we mean that *A*'s optimal risky portfolio lies northwest of *B*'s. Hence, given a choice, investors will always prefer the risky portfolio that lies on the CAL of *A*.
   a. What should be made of this outcome?
   b. Should it be attributed to better security analysis by *A*'s analysts?
   c. Could it be that *A*'s computer program is superior?
   d. If you were advising clients (and had an advance glimpse at the efficient frontiers of various managers), would you tell them to periodically switch their money around to the manager with the most northwesterly portfolio?

same manner as the analysis of the optimal combination of asset classes. Why, then, do we (and the investment community) distinguish between asset allocation and security selection?

Three factors are at work. First, as a result of greater need and ability to save (for college education, recreation, longer life in retirement and health care needs, etc.), the demand for sophisticated investment management has increased enormously. Second, the growing spectrum of financial markets and financial instruments have put sophisticated investment beyond the capacity of most amateur investors. Finally, there are strong economic returns to scale in investment management. The end result is that the size of a competitive investment company has grown with the industry, and efficiency in organization has become an important issue.

A large investment company is likely to invest both in domestic and international markets and in a broad set of asset classes, each of which requires specialized expertise. Hence, the management of each asset-class portfolio needs to be decentralized, and it becomes impossible to simultaneously optimize the entire organization's risky portfolio in one stage (although this would be prescribed as optimal on *theoretical* grounds).

The practice is therefore to optimize the security selection of each asset-class portfolio independently. At the same time, top management continually updates the asset allocation of the organization, adjusting the investment budget of each asset-class portfolio. When changed frequently in response to intensive forecasting activity, the reallocations are called *market timing*. The shortcoming of this two-step approach to portfolio construction versus the theory-based one-step optimization approach is the failure to exploit the covariance of the individual securities in one asset-class portfolio with the individual securities in the other asset classes. Only the covariance matrix of the securities within each asset-class portfolio can be used. However, this loss might be small, due to the depth of diversification of each portfolio and the extra layer of diversification at the asset allocation level.

6.11 OPTIMAL PORTFOLIOS WITH RESTRICTIONS ON THE RISK-FREE ASSET

The availability of a risk-free asset greatly simplifies the portfolio decision. When all investors can borrow and lend at that risk-free rate, we are led to a *unique* optimal risky portfolio that is appropriate for all investors, given a common input list. This portfolio maximizes the reward-to-variability ratio. All investors use the same risky portfolio and differ only in the proportion they invest in it and in the risk-free asset.

What if a risk-free asset is not available? Although T-bills are risk-free assets in nominal terms, their real returns are uncertain. Without a risk-free asset, there is no tangency portfolio that is best

Figure 6.22 Individual portfolio selection without a risk-free asset.

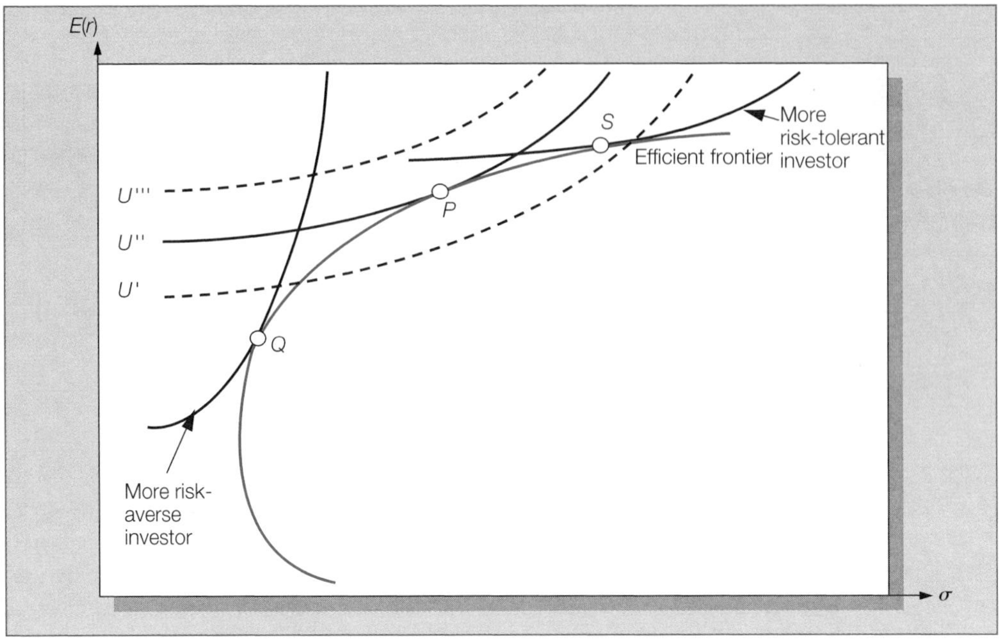

for all investors. In this case, investors have to choose a portfolio from the efficient frontier of risky assets redrawn in Figure 6.22.

Each investor will now choose the optimal risky portfolio by superimposing a particular set of indifference curves on the efficient frontier, as Figure 6.22 shows. The optimal portfolio, *P*, for the investor whose risk aversion is represented by the set of indifference curves in Figure 6.22 is tangent to the highest attainable indifference curve.

Investors who are more risk-averse than the one represented in Figure 6.22 would have steeper indifference curves, meaning that the tangency portfolio would be of smaller standard deviation

Figure 6.23 Individual portfolio selection with risk-free lending only.

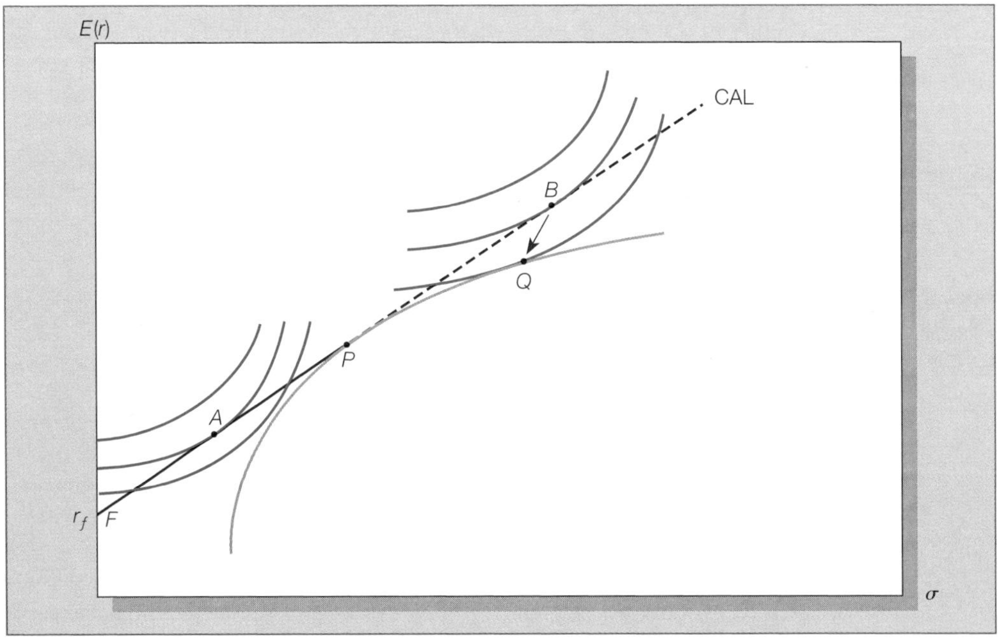

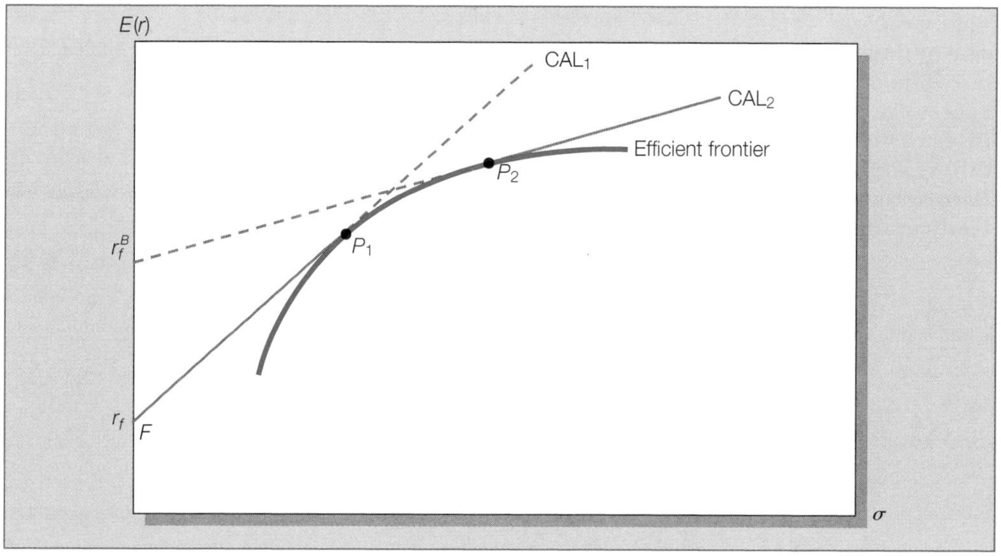

Figure 6.24 The investment opportunity set with differential rates for borrowing and lending.

and expected return than portfolio P, such as portfolio Q. Conversely, investors who are more risk-tolerant than the one represented in Figure 6.22 would be characterized by flatter indifference curves, resulting in a tangency portfolio of higher expected return and standard deviation than portfolio P, such as portfolio S. The common feature of all these rational investors is that they choose portfolios on the efficient frontier; that is, they choose mean-variance efficient portfolios.

Even if virtually risk-free lending opportunities are available, many investors do face borrowing restrictions. They may be unable to borrow altogether, or, more realistically, they may face a borrowing rate that is significantly greater than the lending rate. Let us first consider investors who can lend without risk but are prohibited from borrowing.

When a risk-free investment is available but an investor can take only positive positions in it (he or she can lend at r_f, but cannot borrow), a CAL exists but is limited to the line FP, as in Figure 6.23.

Any investors whose preferences are represented by indifference curves with tangency portfolios on the portion FP of the CAL, such as portfolio A, are unaffected by the borrowing restriction. Such investors are net *lenders* at rate r_f.

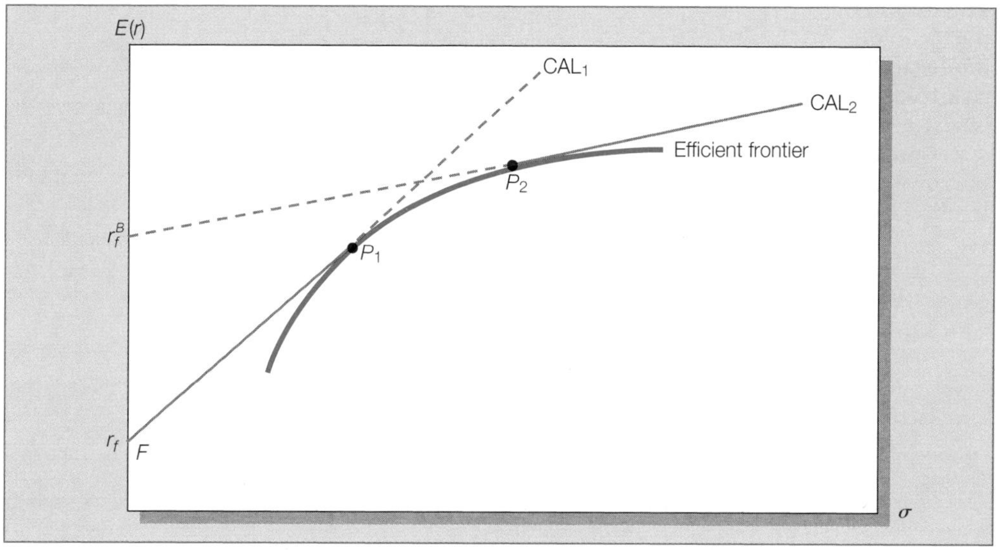

Figure 6.25 The optimal portfolio of defensive investors with differential borrowing and lending rates.

Figure 6.26 The optimal portfolio of aggressive investors with differential borrowing and lending rates.

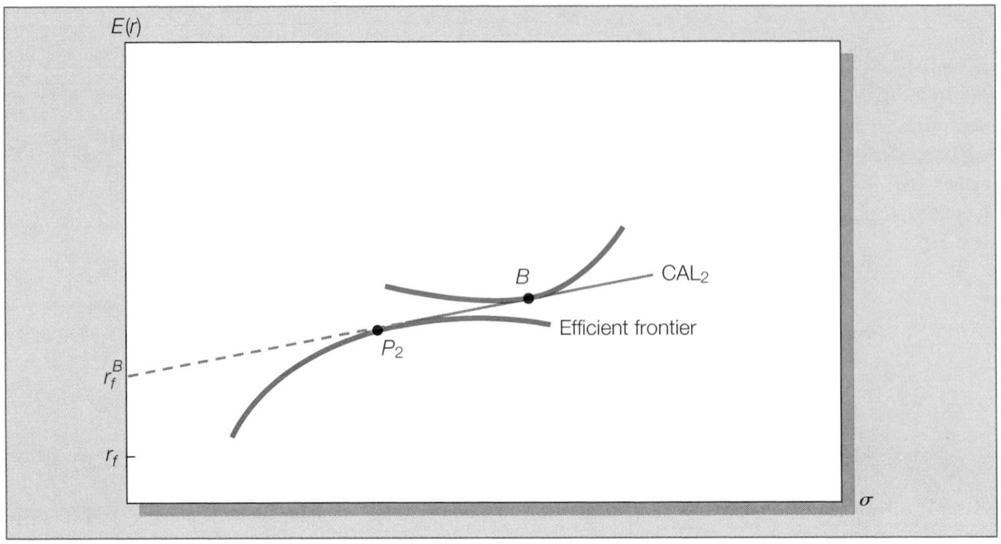

Aggressive or more risk-tolerant investors, who *would* choose portfolio B in the absence of the borrowing restriction, are affected, however. For them, the borrowing restriction is a binding constraint. Such investors will be driven to portfolios on the efficient frontier, such as portfolio Q. Portfolios such as Q represent a zero investment in the risk-free asset.

In more realistic scenarios, individuals who wish to borrow to invest in a risky portfolio will have to pay an interest rate higher than the T-bill rate. For example, the call money rate charged by brokers on margin accounts is higher than the T-bill rate.

Investors who face a borrowing rate greater than the lending rate confront a three-part CAL such as in Figure 6.24. CAL_1, which is relevant in the range FP_1, represents the efficient portfolio set for defensive (risk-averse) investors. These investors invest part of their funds in T-bills at rate r_f. They find that the tangency portfolio is P_1, and they choose a complete portfolio such as portfolio A in Figure 6.25.

Figure 6.27 The optimal portfolio of moderately risk-tolerant investors with differential borrowing and lending rates.

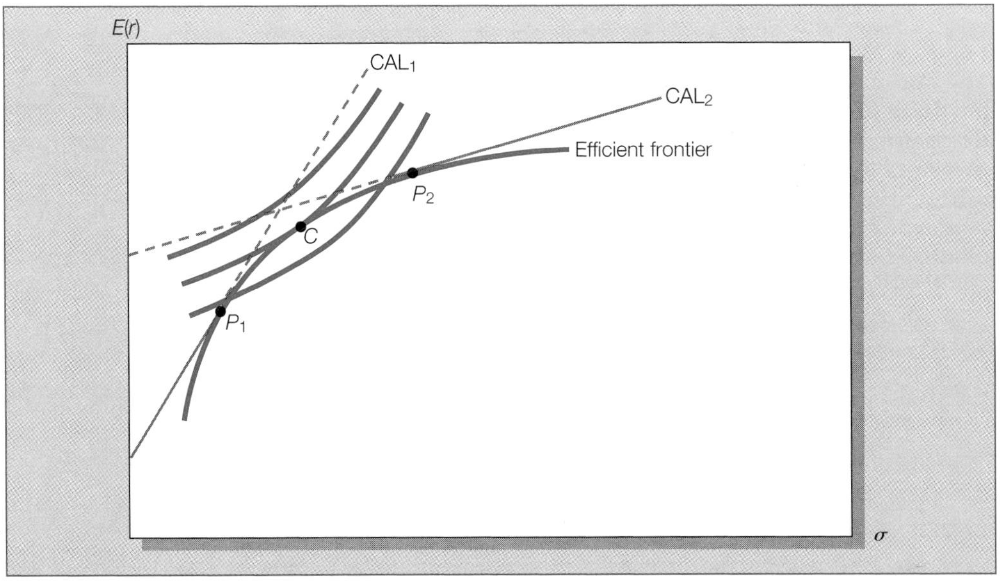

CAL_2, which is relevant in a range to the right of portfolio P_2, represents the efficient portfolio set for more aggressive, or risk-tolerant, investors. This line starts at the borrowing rate, $r^B{}_f$, but it is unavailable in the range $r^B{}_f P_2$, because *lending* (investing in T-bills) is available only at the risk-free rate r_f, less than $r^B{}_f$.

Investors who are willing to *borrow* at the higher rate, $r^B{}_f$, to invest in an optimal risky portfolio will choose portfolio P_2 as their risky investment vehicle. Such a case is described in Figure 6.26, which superimposes a relatively risk-tolerant investor's indifference curve on CAL_2 of Figure 6.24. The investor with the indifference curve in Figure 6.26 chooses portfolio P_2 as the optimal risky portfolio and borrows to invest in it, arriving at overall portfolio *B*.

Investors in the middle range, neither defensive enough to invest in T-bills nor aggressive enough to borrow, choose a risky portfolio from the efficient frontier in the range P_1P_2. This case is described in Figure 6.27. The indifference curve representing the investor in Figure 6.27 leads to a tangency portfolio on the efficient frontier, portfolio *C*.

CONCEPT CHECK

9. With differential lending and borrowing rates, only investors with about average degrees of risk aversion will choose a portfolio in the range P_1P_2 in Figure 6.25. Other investors will choose a portfolio on CAL_1, if they are more risk-averse, or on CAL_2, if they are more risk-tolerant.
   a. Does this mean that investors with average risk aversion are more dependent on the quality of the forecasts that generate the efficient frontier?
   b. Describe the tradeoff between expected return and standard deviation for portfolios between P_1 and P_2 in Figure 6.25, compared with portfolios on CAL_2 beyond P_2.

SUMMARY

1. Shifting funds from the risky portfolio to the risk-free asset is the simplest way to reduce risk. Other methods involve diversification of the risky portfolio and hedging.
2. T-bills provide a perfectly risk-free asset in nominal terms only. Nevertheless, the standard deviation of real rates on short-term T-bills is small compared to that of other assets such as long-term bonds and common stocks, so for the purpose of our analysis we consider T-bills as the risk-free asset. Money market funds hold, in addition to T-bills, short-term and relatively safe obligations such as CP and BDNs. These entail some default risk, but again the additional risk is small relative to most other risky assets. For convenience, we often refer to money market funds as risk-free assets.
3. An investor's risky portfolio (the risky asset) can be characterized by its reward-to-variability ratio, $S = [E(r_P) - r_f]/\sigma_P$. This ratio also is the slope of the CAL, the line that, when graphed, goes from the risk-free asset through the risky asset. All combinations of the risky asset and the risk-free asset lie on this line. Other things equal, an investor would prefer a steeper-sloping CAL, because that means higher expected return for any level of risk. If the borrowing rate is greater than the lending rate, the CAL will be "kinked" at the point of the risky asset.
4. The investor's degree of risk aversion is characterized by the slope of his or her indifference curve. Indifference curves show, at any level of expected return and risk, the required risk premium for taking on one additional percentage of standard deviation. More risk-averse investors have steeper indifference curves; that is, they require a greater risk premium for taking on more risk.
5. The exact optimal position, y^*, in the risky asset is proportional to the risk premium and inversely proportional to the variance and degree of risk aversion:

$$y^* = \frac{E(r_P) - r_f}{A\sigma^2{}_P}$$

   Graphically, this portfolio represents the point at which the indifference curve is tangent to the CAL.

6. A passive investment strategy disregards security analysis, targeting instead the risk-free asset and a broad portfolio of risky assets, such as the S&P/TSX Composite stock portfolio.
7. The expected return of a portfolio is the weighted average of the component assets' expected returns with the investment proportions as weights.
8. The variance of a portfolio is the weighted sum of the elements of the covariance matrix with the product of the investment proportions as the weight. Thus, the variance of each asset is weighted by the square of its investment proportion. Each covariance of any pair of assets appears twice in the covariance matrix, and thus the portfolio variance includes twice each covariance weighted by the product of the investment proportions in each of two assets.
9. Even if the covariances are positive, the portfolio standard deviation is less than the weighted average of the component standard deviations, as long as the assets are not perfectly positively correlated. Thus, portfolio diversification is of value as long as assets are less than perfectly correlated.
10. The greater an asset's *covariance* with the other assets in the portfolio, the more it contributes to portfolio variance. An asset that is perfectly negatively correlated with a portfolio can serve as a perfect hedge. The perfect hedge asset can reduce the portfolio variance to zero.
11. The efficient frontier is the graphical representation of a set of portfolios that maximize expected return for each level of portfolio risk. Rational investors will choose a portfolio on the efficient frontier.
12. A portfolio manager identifies the efficient frontier by first establishing estimates for the asset expected returns and the covariance matrix. This input list then is fed into an optimization program that reports as outputs the investment proportions, expected returns, and standard deviations of the portfolios on the efficient frontier.
13. In general, portfolio managers will arrive at different efficient portfolios due to a difference in methods and quality of security analysis. Managers compete on the quality of their security analysis relative to their management fees.
14. If a risk-free asset is available and input lists are identical, all investors will choose the same portfolio on the efficient frontier of risky assets: the portfolio tangent to the CAL. All investors with identical input lists will hold an identical risky portfolio, differing only in how much each allocates to this optimal portfolio and to the risk-free asset. This result is characterized as the separation principle of portfolio construction.
15. When a risk-free asset is not available, each investor chooses a risky portfolio on the efficient frontier. If a risk-free asset is available but borrowing is restricted, only aggressive investors will be affected. They will choose portfolios on the efficient frontier according to their degree of risk tolerance.

KEY TERMS

capital allocation decision 194
asset allocation decision 194
security selection decision 194
risk-free asset 194
risky asset 194
complete portfolio 196
capital allocation line (CAL) 201
reward-to-variability ratio 201
passive strategy 206
capital market line (CML) 206
diversification 208
insurance principle 208
market risk 208
systematic risk 208
nondiversifiable risk 208
unique risk 208
firm-specific risk 208
nonsystematic risk 208
diversifiable risk 208
minimum-variance portfolio 215
portfolio opportunity set 215
optimal risky portfolio 218
minimum-variance frontier 222
efficient frontier 222
input list 226
separation property 232

SELECTED READINGS

The classic article describing the asset allocation choice, whereby investors choose the optimal fraction of their wealth to place in risk-free assets, is:

Tobin, James. "Liquidity Preference as Behavior Towards Risk." *Review of Economic Studies* 25 (February 1958).

Practitioner-oriented approaches to asset allocation may be found in:

Maginn, John L., and Donald L. Tuttle. *Managing Investment Portfolios: A Dynamic Process*, 2nd ed. New York: Warren, Gorham, & Lamont, Inc., 1990.

Similar practitioner-oriented Canadian contributions include:

Auger, Robert, and Denis Parisien. "Understanding Asset Allocation." *Canadian Investment Review* 4, no. 1 (Spring 1991).

Potvin, Paul. "Passive Management, the TSE 300, and the Toronto 35 Stock Indexes." *Canadian Investment Review* 5, no. 1 (Spring 1992).

Two frequently cited papers on the impact of diversification on portfolio risk are:

Evans, John L., and Stephen H. Archer. "Diversification and the Reduction of Dispersion: An Empirical Analysis." *Journal of Finance*, December 1968.

Wagner, W. H., and S. C. Lau. "The Effect of Diversification on Risk." *Financial Analysts Journal*, November/December 1971.

The seminal works on portfolio selection are:

Markowitz, Harry M. "Portfolio Selection." *Journal of Finance*, March 1952.

Markowitz, Harry M. *Portfolio Selection: Efficient Diversification of Investments*. New York: John Wiley & Sons, Inc., 1959.

Also see:

Samuelson, Paul A. "Risk & Uncertainty: A Fallacy of Large Numbers." *Scientia* 98 (1963).

PROBLEMS

You manage a risky portfolio with an expected rate of return of 18 percent and a standard deviation of 28 percent. The T-bill rate is 8 percent. Use these data for questions 1–10.

1. Your client chooses to invest 70 percent of a portfolio in your fund and 30 percent in a T-bill money market fund. What is the expected value and standard deviation of the rate of return on your client's portfolio?

2. Suppose that your risky portfolio includes the following investments in the given proportions:

   Stock *A:* 27 percent

   Stock *B:* 33 percent

   Stock *C:* 40 percent

   What are the investment proportions of your client's overall portfolio, including the position in T-bills?

3. What is the reward-to-variability ratio (S) of your risky portfolio? Your client's?

4. Draw the CAL of your portfolio on an expected return–standard deviation diagram. What is the slope of the CAL? Show the position of your client on your fund's CAL.

5. Suppose that your client decides to invest in your portfolio a proportion y of the total investment budget so that the overall portfolio will have an expected rate of return of 16 percent.
   a. What is the proportion y?
   b. What are your client's investment proportions in your three stocks and the T-bill fund?
   c. What is the standard deviation of the rate of return on your client's portfolio?

6. Suppose that your client prefers to invest in your fund a proportion y that maximizes the expected return on the overall portfolio subject to the constraint that the overall portfolio's standard deviation will not exceed 18 percent.
   a. What is the investment proportion (y)?
   b. What is the expected rate of return on the overall portfolio?

7. Your client's degree of risk aversion is $A = 3.5$.
   a. What proportion (y) of the total investment should be invested in your fund?
   b. What is the expected value and standard deviation of the rate of return on your client's optimized portfolio?

   You estimate that a passive portfolio (i.e., one invested in a risky portfolio that mimics the S&P/TSX Composite index) yields an expected rate of return of 13 percent with a standard deviation of 25 percent. Continue to assume that $r_f = 8$ percent.

8. Draw the CML and your fund's CAL on an expected return–standard deviation diagram.
   a. What is the slope of the CML?
   b. Characterize in one short paragraph the advantage(s) of your fund over the passive fund.

9. Your client ponders whether to switch the 70 percent that is invested in your fund to the passive portfolio.
   a. Explain to your client the disadvantage(s) of the switch.
   b. Show your client the maximum fee you could charge (as a percentage of the investment in your fund deducted at the end of the year) that would still leave him or her at least as well off investing in your fund as in the passive one. (*Hint*: The fee will lower the slope of your client's CAL by reducing the expected return net of the fee.)

10. Consider the client in problem 7 with $A = 3.5$.
    a. If the client chose to invest in the passive portfolio, what proportion (y) would be selected?
    b. Is the fee (percentage of the investment in your fund, deducted at the end of the year) that you can charge to make the client indifferent between your fund and the passive strategy affected by her capital allocation decision?

Problems 11–14 are based on the following assumptions. Suppose that the lending rate is $r_f = 5$ percent, while the borrowing rate that your client faces is 9 percent. Continue to assume that the S&P/TSX Composite index has an expected return of 13 percent and a standard deviation of 25 percent. Your fund here has $r_p = 11$ percent and $\sigma_p = 15$ percent.

11. Draw a diagram of the CML your client faces with the borrowing constraints. Superimpose on it two sets of indifference curves, one for a client who will choose to borrow, and one for a client who will invest in both the index fund and a money market fund.

12. What is the range of risk aversion for which the client will neither borrow nor lend, that is, for which $y = 1$?

13. Solve problems 11 and 12 for a client who uses your fund rather than an index fund.

14. Amend your solution to problem 10(*b*) for clients in the risk-aversion range that you found in problem 12.

15. Look at the data in Table 6.1 regarding the average risk premium of the S&P/TSX Composite over T-bills and the standard deviation of that risk premium. Suppose that the S&P/TSX Composite is your risky portfolio.
    a. If your risk-aversion coefficient is 2 and you believe that the entire 1957–2003 period is representative of future expected performance, what fraction of your portfolio should be allocated to T-bills and what fraction to equity?
    b. What if you believe that the most recent subperiod period is representative?
    c. What do you conclude upon comparing your answers to (*a*) and (*b*)?

16. What do you think would happen to the expected return on stocks if investors perceived higher volatility in the equity market? Relate your answer to equation 6.3.

CFA® PROBLEMS

17. You manage an equity fund with an expected risk premium of 10 percent and an expected standard deviation of 14 percent. The rate on Treasury bills is 6 percent. Your client chooses to invest $60,000 of her portfolio in your equity fund and $40,000 in a T-bill money market fund. What is the expected return and standard deviation of return on your client's portfolio?

	Expected Return	Standard Deviation of Return
a.	8.4%	8.4%
b.	8.4%	14.0%
c.	12.0%	8.4%
d.	12.0%	14.0%

18. What is the reward-to-variability ratio for the *equity fund* in problem 17?

a. 0.71
b. 1.00
c. 1.19
d. 1.91

CFA® PROBLEMS

19. Given $100,000 to invest, what is the expected risk premium in dollars of investing in equities versus risk-free T-bills based on the following table?

Action	Probability	Expected Return
Invest in equities	.6	50,000
	.4	−$30,000
Invest in risk-free T-bills	1.0	$ 5,000

a. $13,000
b. $15,000
c. $18,000
d. $20,000

CFA® PROBLEMS

20. The change from a straight to a kinked capital allocation line is a result of the

a. Reward-to-variability ratio increasing
b. Borrowing rate exceeding the lending rate
c. Investor's risk tolerance decreasing
d. Increase in the portfolio proportion of the risk-free asset

The following data apply to problems 21–28:

A pension fund manager is considering three mutual funds. The first is a stock fund, the second is a long-term government and corporate bond fund, and the third is a T-bill money market fund that yields a rate of 8 percent. The probability distribution of the risky funds is as follows:

	Expected Return	Standard Deviation
Stock fund (*S*)	.20	.30
Bond fund (*B*)	.12	.15

The correlation between the fund returns is .10.

21. What are the investment proportions of the minimum-variance portfolio of the two risky funds, and what is the expected value and standard deviation of its rate of return?

22. Tabulate and draw the investment opportunity set of the two risky funds. Use investment proportions for the stock fund of zero to 100 percent in increments of 20 percent.

23. Draw a tangent from the risk-free rate to the opportunity set. What does your graph show for the expected return and standard deviation of the optimal portfolio?

24. Solve numerically for the proportions of each asset and for the expected return and standard deviation of the optimal risky portfolio.

25. What is the reward-to-variability ratio of the best feasible CAL?

26. You require that your portfolio yield an expected return of 14 percent and be efficient on the best feasible CAL.

a. What is the standard deviation of your portfolio?

b. What is the proportion invested in the T-bill fund and each of the two risky funds?

27. If you were to use only the two risky funds and will require an expected return of 14 percent, what must be the investment proportions of your portfolio? Compare its standard deviation to that of the optimized portfolio in problem 26. What do you conclude?

28. Suppose that you face the same opportunity set, but you cannot borrow. You wish to construct a portfolio with an expected return of 24 percent. What are the appropriate portfolio proportions and the resulting standard deviation? What reduction in standard deviation could you attain if you were allowed to borrow at the risk-free rate?

29. Stocks offer an expected rate of return of 18 percent, with a standard deviation of 22 percent. Gold offers an expected return of 10 percent with a standard deviation of 30 percent.

a. In the light of the apparent inferiority of gold with respect to both mean return and volatility, would anyone hold gold? If so, demonstrate graphically why one would do so.

b. Given the data above, reanswer problem (*a*) with the additional assumption that the correlation coefficient between gold and stocks equals 1. Draw a graph illustrating why one would or would not hold gold in one's portfolio. Could this set of assumptions for expected returns, standard deviations, and correlation represent an equilibrium for the security market?

30. Suppose that there are many stocks in the market and that the characteristics of stocks *A* and *B* are as follows:

Stock	Expected Return	Standard Deviation
A	.10	.05
B	.15	.10
	Correlation = −1	

Suppose that it is possible to borrow at the risk-free rate, r_f. What must be the value of the risk-free rate? (*Hint*: Think about constructing a risk-free portfolio from stocks *A* and *B*.)

31. Assume that expected returns and standard deviations for all securities (including the risk-free rate for borrowing and lending) are known. "In this case all investors will have the same optimal risky portfolio." True or false?

32. "The standard deviation of the portfolio always is equal to the weighted average of the standard deviations of the assets in the portfolio." True or false?

33. Suppose that you have a project that has a .7 chance of doubling your investment in a year and a .3 chance of halving your investment in a year. What is the standard deviation of the rate of return on this investment?

34. Suppose that you have $1 million and the following two opportunities from which to construct a portfolio:

a. Risk-free asset earning .12 per year

b. Risky asset earning .30 per year with a standard deviation of .40. If you construct a portfolio with a standard deviation of .30, what will be the rate of return?

The following data apply to problems 35–37:

CFA® PROBLEMS

Hennessy & Associates manages a $30 million equity portfolio for the multi-manager Wilstead Pension Fund. Jason Jones, financial vice-president of Wilstead, noted that Hennessy had rather consistently achieved the best record among Wilstead's six equity managers. Performance of the Hennessy portfolio had been clearly superior to that of the S&P 500 in four of the past five years. In the one less favourable year, the shortfall was trivial.

Hennessy is a "bottom-up" manager. The firm largely avoids any attempt to "time the market." It also focuses on selection of individual stocks, rather than the weighting of favoured industries.

There is no apparent conformity of style among the six equity managers. The five managers, other than Hennessy, manage portfolios aggregating $250 million made up of more than 150 individual issues.

Jones is convinced that Hennessy is able to apply superior skill to stock selection, but the favourable results are limited by the high degree of diversification in the portfolio. Over the years, the portfolio generally has held 40–50 stocks, with about 2 percent to 3 percent of total funds committed to each issue. The reason Hennessy seemed to do well most years was because the firm was able to identify each year 10 or 12 issues that registered particularly large gains.

On the basis of this overview, Jones outlined the following plan to the Wilstead pension committee:

"Let's tell Hennessy to limit the portfolio to no more than 20 stocks. Hennessy will double the commitments to the stocks that it really favours and eliminate the remainder. Except for this one new restriction, Hennessy should be free to manage the portfolio exactly as before."

All the members of the pension committee generally supported Jones' proposal, because all agreed that Hennessy had seemed to demonstrate superior skill in selecting stocks. Yet the proposal was a considerable departure from previous practice, and several committee members raised questions. Respond to each of these questions:

35. Answer the following:

a. Will the limitation of 20 stocks likely increase or decrease the risk of the portfolio? Explain.

b. Is there any way Hennessy could reduce the number of issues from 40 to 20 without significantly affecting risk? Explain.

36. One committee member was particularly enthusiastic concerning Jones' proposal. He suggested that Hennessy's performance might benefit further from reduction in the number of issues to 10. If the reduction to 20 could be expected to be advantageous, explain why reduction to 10 might be less likely to be advantageous. (Assume that Wilstead will evaluate the Hennessy portfolio independently of the other portfolios in the fund.)

37. Another committee member suggested that, rather than evaluating each managed portfolio independently of other portfolios, it might be better to consider the effects of a change in the Hennessy portfolio on the total fund. Explain how this broader point of view could affect the committee decision to limit the holdings in the Hennessy portfolio to either 10 or 20 issues.

The following data apply to problems 38–40:

The correlation coefficients between pairs of stocks is as follows:

$$\text{Corr}(A,B) = .85;\ \text{Corr}(A,C) = .60;\ \text{Corr}\ (A,D) = .45$$

Each stock has an expected return of 8 percent and a standard deviation of 20 percent.

CFA® PROBLEMS

38. If your entire portfolio now comprises stock *A* and you can add only one more, which of the following would you choose, and why?

a. *B*

b. *C*

c. *D*

d. Need more data

39. Would your answer to problem 38 change for more risk-averse or risk-tolerant investors? Explain.

40. Suppose that in addition to investing in one more stock you can invest in T-bills as well. Would you change your answers to problems 37 and 38 if the T-bill rate is 8 percent?

CFA® PROBLEMS

41. Which *one* of the following portfolios *cannot* lie on the efficient frontier as described by Markowitz?

	Portfolio	Expected Return	Standard Deviation
a.	*W*	15%	36%
b.	*X*	12%	15%
c.	*Z*	5%	7%
d.	*Y*	9%	21%

CFA® PROBLEMS

42. Which of the following statements about portfolio diversification is *correct*?

a. Proper diversification can reduce or eliminate systematic risk.

b. Diversification reduces the portfolio's expected return because diversification reduces a portfolio's total risk.

c. As more securities are added to a portfolio, total risk typically would be expected to fall at a decreasing rate.

d. The risk-reducing benefits of diversification do not occur meaningfully until at least 30 individual securities are included in the portfolio.

CFA® PROBLEMS

43. Stocks *A, B,* and *C* have the same expected return and standard deviation. The following table shows the correlations between the returns on these stocks.

	Stock *A*	Stock *B*	Stock *C*
Stock *A*	+1.0		
Stock *B*	+0.9	+1.0	
Stock *C*	+0.1	–0.4	+1.0

Given these correlations, the portfolio constructed from these stocks having the lowest risk is a portfolio:

a. Equally invested in stocks *A* and *B*

b. Equally invested in stocks *A* and *C*

c. Equally invested in stocks *B* and *C*

d. Totally invested in stock *C*

CFA® PROBLEMS

44. Statistics for three stocks, *A, B,* and *C*, are shown in the following tables.

Standard Deviations of Returns

	Stock		
	A	*B*	*C*
Standard deviation:	.40	.20	.40

Correlations of Returns

Stock	*A*	*B*	*C*
A	1.00	0.90	0.50
B		1.00	0.10
C			1.00

Only on the basis of the information provided in the tables, and given a choice between a portfolio made up of equal amounts of stocks *A* and *B* *or* a portfolio made up of equal amounts of stocks *B* and *C*, state which portfolio you would recommend. Justify your choice.

The following table of U.S. compound annual returns by decade applies to problems 45 and 46.

	1920s*	1930s	1940s	1950s	1960s	1970s	1980s	1990s
Small company stocks	−3.72%	7.28%	20.63%	19.01%	13.72%	8.75%	12.46%	13.84%
Large company stocks	18.36	−1.25	9.11	19.41	7.84	5.90	17.60	18.20
Long-term government	3.98	4.60	3.59	0.25	1.14	6.63	11.50	8.60
Intermediate-term government	3.77	3.91	1.70	1.11	3.41	6.11	12.01	7.74
Treasury bills	3.56	0.30	0.37	1.87	3.89	6.29	9.00	5.02
Inflation	−1.00	−2.04	5.36	2.22	2.52	7.36	5.10	2.93

*Based on the period 1926–1929.

45. Input the data from the table into a spreadsheet. Compute the serial correlation in decade returns for each asset class and for inflation. Also find the correlation between the returns of various asset classes. What do the data indicate?

46. Convert the asset returns by decade presented in the table into real rates. Repeat the analysis of problem 45 for the real rates of return.

47. Abigail Grace has a $900,000 fully diversified portfolio. She subsequently inherits ABC Company common stock worth $100,000. Her financial advisor provided her with the following forecasted information:

Risk and Return Characteristics

	Expected Monthly Returns	Standard Deviation of Monthly Returns
Original portfolio	0.67%	2.37%
ABC Company	1.25	2.95

The correlation coefficient of ABC stock returns with the original portfolio returns is .40.

a. The inheritance changes Grace's overall portfolio and she is deciding whether to keep the ABC stock. Assuming Grace keeps the ABC stock, calculate the
   i. Expected return of her new portfolio which includes the ABC stock
   ii. Covariance of ABC stock returns with the original portfolio returns
   iii. Standard deviation of her new portfolio which includes the ABC stock

b. If Grace sells the ABC stock, she will invest the proceeds in risk-free government securities yielding .42 percent monthly. Assuming Grace sells the ABC stock and replaces it with the government securities, calculate the
   i. Expected return of her new portfolio which includes the government securities
   ii. Covariance of the government security returns with the original portfolio returns
   iii. Standard deviation of her new portfolio which includes the government securities

c. On the basis of conversations with her husband, Grace is considering selling the $100,000 of ABC stock and acquiring $100,000 of XYZ Company common stock instead. XYZ stock has the same expected return and standard deviation as ABC stock. Her husband comments, "It doesn't matter whether you keep all of the ABC stock or replace it with $100,000 of XYZ stock." State whether her husband's comment is correct or incorrect. Justify your response.

d. In a recent discussion with her financial advisor, Grace commented, "If I just don't lose money in my portfolio, I will be satisfied." She went on to say, "I am more afraid of losing money than I am concerned about achieving high returns."

i. Describe *one* weakness of using standard deviation of returns as a risk measure for Grace.
ii. Identify an alternative risk measure that is more appropriate under the circumstances.

The following questions are adapted from the Canadian Securities Course.

CSI

48. "When securities are combined in a portfolio, the return on the portfolio will be an average of the returns of securities in the portfolio." True or false?

49. A portfolio is equally split between three securities. Security *A* has an expected return of 12 percent. Security *B* has an expected return of 10 percent. Security *C* has an expected return of 6 percent. The expected return on the S&P/TSX is predicted to be 8 percent. What is the portfolio expected return?

50. ______________ risk, also called *specific risk*, is the risk that the price of a specific security or a specific group of securities will change in price.

51. A type of risk that cannot be diversified away in either equities or debt securities is known as ______________ risk.

E-INVESTMENTS
Risk Comparisons

Go to **www.morningstar.com** and select the tab entitled *Funds.* In the dialogue box for selecting a particular fund, type "Fidelity Select" and hit the *Go* button. This will list all of the Fidelity Select funds. Select the Fidelity Select Multimedia Fund. Find the fund's top 25 individual holdings from the displayed information. The top holdings are found in the *Style* section. Identify the top five holdings by using the ticker symbol.

Once you have obtained this information, go to **www.financialengines.com**. From the site menu, select the *Forecast and Analysis* tab and then select the fund's *Scorecard* tab. You will find a dialogue box that allows you to search for funds or individual stocks. You can enter the name or ticker for each of the individual stocks and the fund. Compare the risk rankings of the individual securities with the risk ranking of the fund. What factors are likely leading to the differences in the individual rankings and the overall fund ranking?

APPENDIX 6A: THE POWER OF DIVERSIFICATION

Section 6 introduced the concept of diversification and the limits to the benefits of diversification caused by systematic risk. Given the tools we have developed, we can reconsider this intuition more rigorously and at the same time sharpen our insight regarding the power of diversification.

Recall from equation 6.14 that the general formula for the variance of a portfolio is

$$\sigma^2_p = \sum_{i=1}^{n} w^2_i \sigma^2_i + \sum_{\substack{j=1 \\ j \neq i}}^{n} \sum_{i=1}^{n} w_i w_j \text{Cov}(r_i, r_j) \qquad (6.A1)$$

Consider now the naïve diversification strategy in which an equally weighted portfolio is constructed, meaning that $w_i = 1/n$ for each security. In this case, equation 6A.1 may be rewritten as follows:

$$\sigma^2_p = \frac{1}{n} \sum_{i=1}^{n} \frac{1}{n} \sigma^2_i + \sum_{\substack{j=1 \\ j \neq i}}^{n} \sum_{i=1}^{n} \frac{1}{n^2} \text{Cov}(r_i, r_j) \qquad (6A.2)$$

Note that there are n variance terms and $n(n-1)$ covariance terms in equation 6A.2.

If we define the average variance and average covariance of the securities as

$$\overline{\sigma}^2 = \frac{1}{n} \sum_{i=1}^{n} \sigma^2_i$$

$$\overline{\text{Cov}} = \frac{1}{n(n-1)} \sum_{\substack{i=1 \\ j \neq i}}^{n} \sum_{j=1}^{n} \text{Cov}(r_i, r_j)$$

we can express portfolio variance as

$$\sigma^2_p = \frac{1}{n}\overline{\sigma}^2 + \frac{n-1}{n}\overline{\text{Cov}} \qquad (6A.3)$$

Now examine the effect of diversification. When the average covariance among security returns is zero, as it is when all risk is firm-specific, portfolio variance can be driven to zero. We see this from equation 6A.3: the second term on the right-hand side will be zero in this scenario while the first term approaches zero as n becomes larger. Hence, when security returns are uncorrelated, the power of diversification to limit portfolio risk is unlimited.

However, the more important case is the one in which economywide risk factors impart positive correlation among stock returns. In this case, as the portfolio becomes more highly diversified (n increases), portfolio variance remains positive. While firm-specific risk, represented by the first term in equation 6A.3, still is diversified away, the second term simply approaches $\overline{\text{Cov}}$ as n becomes greater. (Note that $(n - 1)/n = 1 - 1/n$, which approaches 1 for large n.) Thus the irreducible risk of a diversified portfolio depends on the covariance of the returns of the component securities, which in turn is a function of the importance of systematic factors in the economy.

To see further the fundamental relationship between systematic risk and security correlations, suppose for simplicity that all securities have a common standard deviation, σ, and all security pairs have a common correlation coefficient ρ. Then the covariance between all pairs of securities is $\rho\sigma^2$, and equation 6A.3 becomes

$$\sigma^2_p = \frac{1}{n}\sigma^2 + \frac{n-1}{n}\rho\sigma^2 \qquad (6A.4)$$

The effect of correlation is now explicit. When $\rho = 0$, we again obtain the insurance principle, where portfolio variance approaches zero as n becomes greater. For $\rho > 0$, however, portfolio variance remains positive. In fact, for $\rho = 1$, portfolio variance equals σ^2 regardless of n, demonstrating that diversification is of no benefit: in the case of perfect correlation, all risk is systematic. More generally, as n becomes greater, equation 6A.4 shows that systematic risk becomes $\rho\sigma^2$.

Table 6A.1 presents portfolio standard deviation as we include even greater numbers of securities in the portfolio for two cases: $\rho = 0$ and $\rho = .40$. The table takes σ to be 50 percent. As one would expect, portfolio risk is greater when $\rho = .40$. More surprising, perhaps, is that portfolio risk diminishes far less rapidly as n increases in the positive correlation case. The correlation among security returns limits the power of diversification.

Note that, for a 100-security portfolio, the standard deviation is 5 percent in the uncorrelated case—still significant when we consider the potential of zero standard deviation. For $\rho = .40$, the

Table 6A.1 Risk Reduction of Equally Weighted Portfolios in Correlated and Uncorrelated Universes

		$\rho = 0$		$\rho = .4$	
Universe Size n	Optimal Portfolio Proportion $1/n$(%)	Standard Deviation (%)	Reduction in σ	Standard Deviation (%)	Reduction in σ
1	100	50.00	14.64	50.00	8.17
2	50	35.36		41.83	
5	20	22.36	1.95	36.06	.70
6	16.67	20.41		35.36	
10	10	15.81	.73	33.91	.20
11	9.09	15.08		33.71	
20	5	11.18	.27	32.79	.06
21	4.76	10.91		32.73	
100	1	5.00	.02	31.86	.00
101	.99	4.98		31.86	

standard deviation is high, 31.86 percent, yet it is very close to undiversifiable systematic risk in the infinite-sized universe, $\sqrt{\rho\sigma^2} = \sqrt{.4 \times .50} = .3162$, or 31.62 percent. At this point, further diversification is of little value.

We also gain an important insight from this exercise. When we hold diversified portfolios, the contribution to portfolio risk of a particular security will depend on the *covariance* of that security's return with those of other securities, and *not* on the security's variance. As we shall see in Chapter 7, this implies that fair risk premiums also should depend on covariances rather than the total variability of returns.

CONCEPT CHECK

6A.1 Suppose that the universe of available risky securities consists of a large number of stocks, identically distributed with $E(r)$ = 15 percent, σ = 60 percent, and a common correlation coefficient of $\rho = .5$.

a. What is the expected return and standard deviation of an equally weighted risky portfolio of 25 stocks?

b. What is the smallest number of stocks necessary to generate an efficient portfolio with a standard deviation equal to or smaller than 43 percent?

c. What is the systematic risk in this universe?

d. If T-bills are available and yield 10 percent, what is the slope of the CAL?

APPENDIX 6B: THE INSURANCE PRINCIPLE: RISK-SHARING VERSUS RISK-POOLING

Mean-variance analysis has taken a strong hold among investment professionals, and insight into the mechanics of efficient diversification has become quite widespread. Common misconceptions or fallacies about diversification still persist, however, and we will try to put some to rest.

It is commonly believed that a large portfolio of independent insurance policies is a necessary and sufficient condition for an insurance company to shed its risk. The fact is that a multitude of independent insurance policies is neither necessary nor sufficient for a sound insurance portfolio. Actually, an individual insurer who would not insure a single policy also would be unwilling to insure a large portfolio of independent policies.

Consider Paul Samuelson's (1963) story. He once offered a colleague 2-to-1 odds on a $1,000 bet on the toss of a coin. His colleague refused, saying "I won't bet because I would feel the $1,000 loss more than the $2,000 gain. But I'll take you on if you promise to let me make a hundred such bets."

Samuelson's colleague, as many others, might have explained his position, not quite correctly, that "One toss is not enough to make it reasonably sure that the law of averages will turn out in my favour. But with a hundred tosses of a coin, the law of averages will make it a darn good bet."

Another way to rationalize this argument is to think in terms of rates of return. In each bet you put up $1,000 and then get back $3,000 with a probability of one-half, or zero with a probability of one-half. The probability distribution of the rate of return is 200 percent with $p = \frac{1}{2}$ and –100 percent with $p = \frac{1}{2}$.

The bets are all independent and identical and therefore the expected return is $E(r) = \frac{1}{2}(200) + \frac{1}{2}(-100) = 50$ percent, regardless of the number of bets. The standard deviation of the rate of return on the portfolio of independent bets is[17]

$$\sigma(n) = \frac{\sigma}{\sqrt{n}}$$

[17]This follows from equation 6.14, setting $w_i = 1/n$ and all covariances equal to zero because of the independence of the bets.

where σ is the standard deviation of a single bet:

$$\sigma = [\tfrac{1}{2}(200 - 50)^2 + \tfrac{1}{2}(-100 - 50)^2]^{1/2}$$
$$= 150\%$$

The rate of return on a sequence of bets, in other words, has a smaller standard deviation than that of a single bet. By increasing the number of bets we can reduce the standard deviation of the rate of return to any desired level. It seems at first glance that Samuelson's colleague was correct. But he was not.

The fallacy of the argument lies in the use of a rate of return criterion to choose from portfolios *that are not equal in size*. Although the portfolio is equally weighted across bets, each extra bet increases the scale of the investment by \$1,000. Recall from traditional corporate finance that when choosing among mutually exclusive projets you cannot use the internal rate of return (IRR) as your decision criterion when the projects are of different sizes. You have to use the net present value (NPV) rule.

Consider the dollar profit (as opposed to rate of return) distribution of a single bet:

$$E(R) = \tfrac{1}{2} \times 2{,}000 + \tfrac{1}{2} \times (-1{,}000)$$
$$= \$500$$

$$\sigma_R = [\tfrac{1}{2}(2{,}000 - 500)^2 + \tfrac{1}{2}(-1{,}000 - 500)^2]^{1/2}$$
$$= 1{,}500\%$$

These are independent bets where the total profit from n bets is the sum of the profits from the single bets. Therefore, with n bets

$$E[R(n)] = \$500n$$

$$\text{Variance}\left(\sum_{i=1}^{n} R_i\right) = n\sigma^2_R$$

$$\sigma_R(n) = \sqrt{n\sigma^2_R}$$

$$= \sigma_R\sqrt{n}$$

so that the standard deviation of the dollar return *increases* by a factor equal to the square root of the number of bets, n, in contrast to the standard deviation of the rate of return, which *decreases* by a factor of the square root of n.

As further evidence, consider the standard coin-tossing game. Whether one flips a fair coin 10 times or 1,000 times, the expected percentage of heads flipped is 50 percent. One expects the actual proportion of heads in a typical running of 1,000-toss experiment to be closer to 50 percent than in the 10-toss experiment. This is the law of averages.

But the actual number of heads typically will depart from its expected value by a greater amount in the 1,000-toss experiment. For example, 504 heads is close to 50 percent and is 4 more than the expected number. To exceed the expected number of heads by 4 in the 10-toss game would require 9 out of 10 heads, which is a much more extreme departure from the mean. In the many-toss case, there is more volatility of the number of heads and less volatility of the percentage of heads. This is the same when an insurance company takes on more policies: the dollar variance of its portfolio increases while the rate of return variance falls.

The lesson is this: Rate-of-return analysis is appropriate when considering mutually exclusive portfolios of equal size, which is what we did in all the examples so far. We applied a fixed investment budget, and we investigated only the consequences of varying investment proportions in various assets. But if an insurance company takes on more and more insurance policies, it is increasing portfolio dollar investments. The analysis that is called for in that case must be cast in terms of dollar profits, in much the same way that NPV is called for instead of IRR when we compare different-sized projects. This is why risk-pooling (i.e., accumulating independent risky prospects) does not act to eliminate risk.

Samuelson's colleague should have counteroffered: "Let's make 1,000 bets, each with your $2 against my $1." Then he would be holding a portfolio of fixed size, equal to $1,000, which is diversified into 1,000 identical independent prospects. This would make the insurance principle work.

Another way for Samuelson's colleague to get around the riskiness of this tempting bet is to share the large bets with friends. Consider a firm engaging in 1,000 of Paul Samuelson's bets. In each bet the firm puts up $1,000 and receives $3,000 or nothing as before. Each bet is too large for you. Yet if you hold a 1/1,000 share of the firm, your position is exactly the same as if you were to make 1,000 small bets of $2 against $1. A 1/1,000 share of a $1,000 bet is equivalent to a $1 bet. Holding a small share of many large bets essentially allows you to replace a stake in one large bet with a diversified portfolio of manageable bets.

How does this apply to insurance companies? Investors can purchase insurance company shares in the stock market, so they can choose to hold as small a position in the overall risk as they please. No matter how great the risk of the policies, a large group of individual small investors will agree to bear the risk if the expected rate of return exceeds the risk-free rate. Thus, it is the sharing of risk among many shareholders that makes the insurance industry tick.

PART THREE

EQUILIBRIUM IN CAPITAL MARKETS

7 The Capital Asset Pricing Model

8 Index Models and the Arbitrage Pricing Theory

9 Market Efficiency

10 Empirical Evidence on Security Returns

THE CAPITAL ASSET PRICING MODEL

The capital asset pricing model, almost always referred to as the CAPM, is a centrepiece of modern financial economics.

The model gives us a precise prediction of the relationship that we should observe between the risk of an asset and its expected return. This relationship serves two vital functions. First, it provides a benchmark rate of return for evaluating possible investments. For example, if we are analyzing securities, we might be interested in whether the expected return we forecast for a stock is more or less than its "fair" return, given risk. Second, the model helps us to make an educated guess as to the expected return on assets that have not yet been traded in the marketplace. For example, how do we price an initial public offering of stock? How will a major new investment project affect the return investors require on a company's stock? Although the CAPM does not fully withstand empirical tests, it is widely used both because of the insight if offers and because its accuracy suffices for many important applications.

7.1 THE CAPITAL ASSET PRICING MODEL

The **capital asset pricing model (CAPM)** is a set of predictions concerning equilibrium expected returns on risky assets. We intend to explain it in one short chapter, but do not expect this to be easy going. Harry Markowitz laid down the foundation of modern portfolio management in 1952. The CAPM was developed 12 years later in articles by William Sharpe,[1] John Lintner,[2] and Jan Mossin.[3] The time for this gestation indicates that the leap from Markowitz's portfolio selection model to the CAPM is not trivial.

Sharpe Ratio www.stanford.edu/~wfsharpe/art/sr/sr.htm

We will approach the CAPM by posing the question "what if," in which the "if" part refers to a simplified world. Posting an admittedly unrealistic world allows a relatively easy leap to the "then" part. Once we accomplish this, we can add complexity to the hypothesized environment one step at a time and see how the conclusions must be amended. This process allows us to derive a reasonably realistic and comprehensible model.

We can summarize the simplifying assumptions that lead to the basic version of the CAPM in the following list. The thrust of these assumptions is that we try to ensure that individuals are as alike as possible, with the notable exceptions of initial wealth and risk tolerance. We will see that conformity of investor behaviour vastly simplifies our analysis.

1. *There are many investors, each with an endowment (wealth) that is small compared to the total endowment of all investors.* Investors are price takers, in that they act as though security prices are unaffected by their own trades. This is the usual perfect competition assumption of microeconomics.
2. *All investors plan for one identical holding period.* This behaviour sometimes is said to be myopic (short-sighted) in that it ignores everything that might happen after the end of the single-period horizon. Myopic behaviour is, in general, suboptimal.
3. *Investments are limited to a universe of publicly traded financial assets, such as stocks and bonds, and to risk-free borrowing or lending arrangements.* This assumption rules out investment in nontraded assets such as in education (human capital), private enterprises, and governmentally funded assets such as town halls and nuclear submarines. It is assumed also that investors may borrow or lend any amount at a fixed, risk-free rate.
4. *Investors pay no taxes on returns and no transaction costs (commissions and service charges) on trades in securities.* In reality, of course, we know that investors are in different tax brackets and that this may govern the type of assets in which they invest. For example, tax implications may differ depending on whether the income is from interest, dividends, or capital gains. Furthermore, trading is costly, and commissions and fees depend on the size of the trade and the good standing of the individual investor.
5. *All investors are rational mean-variance optimizers, meaning that they all use the Markowitz portfolio selection model.*
6. *All investors analyze securities in the same way and share the same economic view of the world.* The result is identical estimates of the probability distribution of future cash flows from investing in the available securities; that is, for any set of security prices, they all derive the same input list to feed into the Markowitz model. Given a set of security prices and the risk-free interest rate, all investors use the same expected returns and covariance matrix of security returns to generate the efficient frontier and the unique optimal risky portfolio. This assumption often is referred to as **homogeneous expectations** or beliefs.

---

[1]William Sharpe, "Capital Asset Prices: A Theory of Market Equilibrium," *Journal of Finance*, September 1964.

[2]John Lintner, "The Valuation of Risk Assets and the Selection of Risky Investments in Stock Portfolios and Capital Budgets," *Review of Economics and Statistics*, February 1965.

[3]Jan Mossin, "Equilibrium in a Capital Asset Market," *Econometrica*, October 1966.

These assumptions represent the "if" of our "what if" analysis. Obviously, they ignore many real-world complexities. With these assumptions, however, we can gain some powerful insights into the nature of equilibrium in security markets.

We can summarize the equilibrium that will prevail in this hypothetical world of securities and investors briefly. The rest of the chapter explains and elaborates on these implications.

1. All investors will choose to hold a portfolio of risky assets in proportions that duplicate representation of the assets in the **market portfolio** (M), which includes all traded assets. For simplicity, we shall often refer to all risky assets as stocks. The proportion of each stock in the market portfolio equals the market value of the stock (price per share multiplied by the number of shares outstanding) divided by the total market value of all stocks.
2. Not only will the market portfolio be on the efficient frontier, but it also will be the tangency portfolio to the optimal capital allocation line (CAL) derived by each and every investor. As a result, the capital market line (CML), the line from the risk-free rate through the market portfolio, M, is also the best attainable capital allocation line. All investors hold M as their optimal risky portfolio, differing only in the amount invested in it versus in the risk-free asset.
3. The risk premium on the market portfolio will be proportional to the risk of the market portfolio and the market degree of risk aversion. Mathematically,

$$E(r_M) - r_f = \bar{A}\sigma^2_M$$

where σ^2_M is the variance of the market portfolio and $\bar{A}$ is the average degree of risk aversion across investors. Note that because M is the optimal portfolio, which is efficiently diversified across all stocks, σ^2_M is the systematic risk of this universe.
4. The risk premium on individual assets will be proportional to the risk premium on the market portfolio, M, and the *beta coefficient* of the security, relative to the market portfolio. We will see that beta measures the extent to which returns on the stock and the market move together. Formally, beta is defined as

$$\beta_i = \frac{\text{Cov}(r_i, r_M)}{\sigma^2_M}$$

and we can write

$$E(r_i) - r_f = \frac{\text{Cov}(r_i, r_M)}{\sigma^2_M}[E(r_M) - r_f]$$

$$= \beta_i[E(r_M) - r_f]$$

We will elaborate on these results and their implications shortly.

Why Do All Investors Hold the Market Portfolio?

www.nortel networks.com

Given the assumptions of the previous section, it is easy to see that all investors will desire to hold identical risky portfolios. If all investors use identical Markowitz analysis (assumption 5) applied to the same universe of securities (assumption 3) for the same time horizon (assumption 2) and use the same input list (assumption 6), they all must arrive at the same determination of the optimal risky portfolio, the portfolio on the efficient frontier identified by the tangency line from T-bills to that frontier, as in Figure 7.1. This implies that if the weight of Nortel (NT) stock, for example, in each common risky portfolio is 1 percent, then when we sum over all investors' portfolios to obtain the aggregate market portfolio, NT also will make up 1 percent of the market portfolio. The same principle applies to the proportion of any stock in each investor's risky

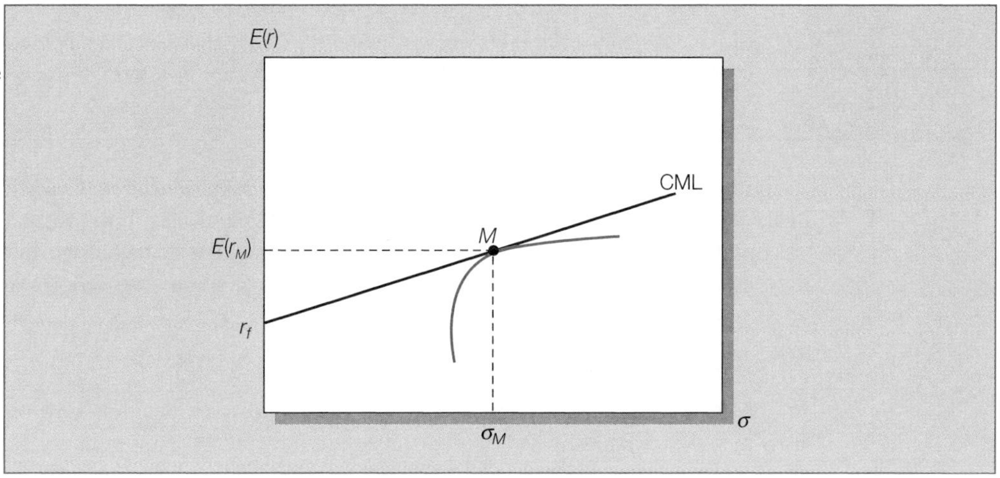

Figure 7.1 The efficient frontier and the capital market line.

portfolio. As a result, the optimal risky portfolio of all investors is simply a share of the market portfolio, which we label *M* in Figure 7.1.

www.canadiantire.ca

Now suppose that the optimal portfolio of our investors does not include the stock of some company such as Canadian Tire (CT). When all investors avoid CT stock, the demand is zero, and CT's price takes a free fall. As CT stock gets progressively cheaper, it becomes ever more attractive as an investment and all other stocks look (relatively) less attractive. Ultimately, CT reaches a price where it is profitable enough to include in the optimal stock portfolio.

Such a price adjustment process guarantees that all stocks will be included in the optimal portfolio. It shows that *all* assets have to be included in the market portfolio. The only issue is the price at which investors will be willing to include a stock in their optimal risky portfolio.

This may seem a roundabout way to derive a simple result: if all investors hold an identical risky portfolio, this portfolio has to be *M,* the market portfolio. Our intention, however, is to demonstrate a connection between this result and its underpinnings, the equilibrating process that is fundamental to security market operation.

The Passive Strategy Is Efficient

Efficient Frontier www.efficientfrontier.com

In Chapter 6 we defined the CML (capital market line) as the CAL (capital allocation line) that is constructed from either a money market account or T-bills and the market portfolio. Perhaps now you can fully appreciate why the CML is an interesting CAL. In the simple world of the CAPM, *M* is the optimal tangency portfolio on the efficient frontier. This is shown in Figure 7.1.

In this scenario, the market portfolio, *M,* that all investors hold is based on the common input list, thereby incorporating all relevant information about the universe of securities. This means an investor can skip the trouble of doing specific analysis and obtain an efficient portfolio simply by holding the market portfolio. (Of course, if everyone were to follow this strategy, no one would perform security analysis, and this result would no longer hold. We discuss this issue in depth in Chapter 9 on market efficiency.)

Thus, the passive strategy of investing in a market index portfolio is efficient. For this reason, we sometimes call this result a **mutual fund theorem.** The mutual fund theorem is another incarnation of the separation property discussed in Chapter 6. Assuming that all investors choose to hold a market index mutual fund, we can separate portfolio selection into two components—a technological problem (creation of mutual funds by professional managers) and a personal problem that depends on an investor's risk aversion (allocation of the complete portfolio between the mutual fund and risk-free assets).

CONCEPT CHECK

1. If there are only a few investors who perform security analysis, and all others hold the market portfolio M, would the CML still be the efficient CAL for investors who do not engage in security analysis? Why or why not?

In reality different investment managers do create risky portfolios that differ from the market index. We attribute this in part to the use of different input lists in the formation of the optimal risky portfolio. Nevertheless, the significance of the mutual fund theorem is that a passive investor may view the market index as a reasonable first approximation of an efficient risky portfolio.

The Risk Premium of the Market Portfolio

In Chapter 6 we discussed how individual investors go about deciding how much to invest in the risky portfolio. Returning now to the decision of how much to invest in portfolio M versus in the risk-free asset, what can we deduce about the equilibrium risk premium of portfolio M?

We asserted earlier that the equilibrium risk premium on the market portfolio, $E(r_M) - r_f$, will be proportional to the average degree of risk aversion of the investor population and the risk of the market portfolio, σ^2_M. Now we can explain this result.

Recall that each individual investor chooses a proportion, y, allocated to the optimal portfolio M, such that

$$y = \frac{E(r_M) - r_f}{A\sigma^2_M} \tag{7.1}$$

In the simplified CAPM economy, risk-free investments involve borrowing and lending among investors. Any borrowing position must be offset by the lending position of the creditor. This means that net borrowing and lending across all investors must be zero and, in consequence, the average position in the risky portfolio is 100 percent, or $y = 1$. Setting $\bar{y} = 1$ in equation 7.1 and rearranging, we find that the risk premium on the market portfolio is related to its variance by the average degree of risk aversion:

$$E(r_M) - r_f = \bar{A}\sigma^2_M \tag{7.2}$$

CONCEPT CHECK

2. Data from the period 1957–2003 for the S&P/TSX Composite index yield the following statistics: average excess return, 3.66 percent; standard deviation, 17.03 percent.
   a. To the extent that these averages approximated investor expectations for the period, what must have been the average coefficient of risk aversion?
   b. If the coefficient of risk aversion were actually 1.5, what risk premium would have been consistent with the market's historical standard deviation?

Expected Returns on Individual Securities

www.inco.com

The CAPM is built on the insight that the appropriate risk premium of an asset will be determined by its contribution to the risk of investors' overall portfolios. Portfolio risk is what matters to investors and governs the risk premiums they demand.

Suppose, for example, that we want to gauge the portfolio risk of Inco stock. We measure the contribution to the risk of the overall portfolio from holding Inco stock by its covariance with the market portfolio. To see why this is so, let us look again at the way the variance of the market portfolio is calculated. To calculate the variance of the market portfolio, we use the covariance matrix bordered by market portfolio weights, as discussed in Chapter 6. We highlight Inco in this depiction of the n stocks in the market portfolio.

Portfolio Weights:	w_1	w_2	...	w_I	...	w_n
w_1	$\mathrm{Cov}(r_1,r_1)$	$\mathrm{Cov}(r_1,r_2)$	...	$\mathrm{Cov}(r_1,r_I)$	...	$\mathrm{Cov}(r_1,r_n)$
w_2	$\mathrm{Cov}(r_2,r_1)$	$\mathrm{Cov}(r_2,r_2)$	...	$\mathrm{Cov}(r_2,r_I)$	...	$\mathrm{Cov}(r_2,r_n)$
.	.	.		.		.
.	.	.		.		.
.	.	.		.		.
w_I	$\mathrm{Cov}(r_I,r_1)$		...	$\mathrm{Cov}(r_I,r_I)$	...	$\mathrm{Cov}(r_I,r_n)$
.	.	.		.		.
.	.	.		.		.
.	.	.		.		.
w_n	$\mathrm{Cov}(r_n,r_1)$	$\mathrm{Cov}(r_n,r_2)$	...	$\mathrm{Cov}(r_n,r_I)$	...	$\mathrm{Cov}(r_n,r_n)$

Recall that we calculate the variance of the portfolio by summing over all the elements of the covariance matrix and multiplying each element by the portfolio weights from the row and the column. The contribution of one stock to portfolio variance therefore can be expressed as the sum of all the covariance terms in the row corresponding to the stock where each covariance is multiplied by both the portfolio weight from its row and the weight from its column.[4]

For example, the contribution of Inco's stock to the variance of the market portfolio is

$$w_I[w_1\mathrm{Cov}(r_1,r_I) + w_2\mathrm{Cov}(r_2,r_I) + \ldots + w_I\mathrm{Cov}(r_I,r_I) + \ldots + w_n\mathrm{Cov}(r_n,r_I)] \quad (7.3)$$

Equation 7.3 provides a clue about the respective roles of variance and covariance in determining asset risk. When there are many stocks in the economy, there will be many more covariance terms than variance terms. Consequently, the covariance of a particular stock with all other stocks will dominate the stock's contribution to total portfolio risk. We may summarize the term in brackets in the equation simply as the covariance of Inco with the market portfolio. In other words, we can best measure the stock's contribution to the risk of the market portfolio by its covariance with that portfolio.

This should not surprise us. For example, if the covariance between Inco and the rest of the market is negative, then Inco makes a "negative contribution" to portfolio risk: by providing returns that move inversely with the rest of the market, Inco stabilizes the return on the overall portfolio. If the covariance is positive, Inco makes a positive contribution to overall portfolio risk because its returns amplify swings in the rest of the portfolio.

To prove this more rigorously, note that the rate of return on the market portfolio may be written as

$$r_M = \sum_{k=1}^{n} w_k r_k$$

Therefore the covariance of the return on Inco with the market portfolio is

$$\mathrm{Cov}(r_I,r_M) = \mathrm{Cov}(r_I, \sum_{k=1}^{n} w_k r_k) = \sum_{k=1}^{n} w_k \mathrm{Cov}(r_I,r_k) \quad (7.4)$$

[4]An alternative and equally valid approach would be to measure Inco's contribution to market variance as the sum of the elements in the row *and* the column corresponding to Inco. In this case, Inco's contribution would be twice the sum in equation 7.3. The approach that we take in the text allocates contributions to portfolio risk among securities in a convenient manner in that the sum of the contributions of each stock equals the total portfolio variance, whereas the alternative measure of contribution would sum to twice the portfolio variance. This results from a type of double-counting, because adding both the rows and the columns for each stock would result in each entry in the matrix being added twice.

Notice that the last term of equation 7.4 is precisely the same as the term in brackets in equation 7.3. Therefore, equation 7.3, which is the contribution of Inco to the variance of the market portfolio, may be simplified to $w_I \mathrm{Cov}(r_I, r_M)$. We also observe that the contribution of our holding of Inco to the risk premium of the market portfolio is $w_I [E(r_M) - r_f]$.

Therefore, the reward-to-risk ratio for investments in Inco can be expressed as

$$\frac{\text{Inco's contribution to risk premium}}{\text{Inco's contribution to variance}} = \frac{w_I[E(r_I) - r_f]}{w_I \mathrm{Cov}(r_I, r_M)} = \frac{E(r_I) - r_f}{\mathrm{Cov}(r_I, r_M)}$$

The market portfolio is the tangency (efficient mean-variance) portfolio. The reward-to-risk ratio for investment in the market portfolio is

$$\frac{\text{Market risk premium}}{\text{Market variance}} = \frac{E(r_M) - r_f}{\sigma^2_M} \tag{7.5}$$

The ratio in equation 7.5 is often called the **market price of risk**[5] because it quantifies the extra return that investors demand to bear portfolio risk. Notice that for *components* of the efficient portfolio, such as shares of Inco, we measure risk as the *contribution* to portfolio variance. In contrast, for the efficient portfolio itself, its variance is the appropriate measure of risk.

A basic principle of equilibrium is that all investments should offer the same reward-to-risk ratio. If the ratio were better for one investment than another, investors would rearrange their portfolios, tilting toward the alternative with the better tradeoff and shying away from the other. Such activity would impart pressure on security prices until the ratios were equalized. Therefore we conclude that the reward-to-risk ratios of Inco and the market portfolio should be equal:

$$\frac{E(r_I) - r_f}{\mathrm{Cov}(r_I, r_M)} = \frac{E(r_M) - r_f}{\sigma^2_M} \tag{7.6}$$

To determine the fair risk premium of Inco stock, we rearrange equation 7.6 slightly to obtain

$$E(r_I) - r_f = \frac{\mathrm{Cov}(r_I, r_M)}{\sigma^2_M}[E(r_M) - r_f] \tag{7.7}$$

The ratio $\mathrm{Cov}(r_I, r_M)/\sigma^2_M$ measures the contribution of Inco stock to the variance of the market portfolio as a fraction of the total variance of the market portfolio. The ratio is called **beta** and is denoted by β. Using this measure, we can restate equation 7.7 as

$$E(r_I) = r_f + \beta_I[E(r_M) - r_f] \tag{7.8}$$

This **expected return–beta relationship** is the most familiar expression of the CAPM to practitioners. We will have a lot more to say about the expected return–beta relationship shortly.

We see now why the assumptions that made individuals act similarly are so useful. If everyone holds an identical risky portfolio, then everyone will find that the beta of each asset with the market portfolio equals the asset's beta with his or her own risky portfolio. Hence, everyone will agree on the appropriate risk premium for each asset.

Does this mean that the fact that few real-life investors actually hold the market portfolio implies that the CAPM is of no practical importance? Not necessarily. Recall from Chapter 6 that reasonably-well-diversified portfolios shed firm-specific risk and are left with only systematic or

[5] We open ourselves up to ambiguity in using this term, because the market portfolio's reward-to-variability ratio

$$\frac{E(r_M) - r_f}{\sigma_M}$$

is sometimes referred to as the market price of risk. Note that since the appropriate risk measure of Inco is its covariance with the market portfolio (its contribution to the variance of the market portfolio), this risk is measured in percent squared. Accordingly, the price of this risk, $[E(r_M) - r_f]/\sigma^2$, is defined as the percentage expected return per percent square of variance.

market risk. Even if one does not hold the precise market portfolio, a well-diversified portfolio will be so very highly correlated with the market that a stock's beta relative to the market will still be a useful risk measure.

In fact, several authors have shown that modified versions of the CAPM will hold true even if we consider differences among individuals leading them to hold different portfolios. For example, Brennan[6] examines the impact of differences in investors' personal tax rates on market equilibrium, and Mayers[7] looks at the impact of nontraded assets, such as human capital (earning power). Both found that, although the market is no longer each investor's optimal risky portfolio, the expected return–beta relationship still should hold in a somewhat modified form.

If the expected return–beta relationship holds for any individual asset, it must hold for any combination of assets. Suppose that some portfolio P has weight w_k for stock k, where k takes on values $1, \ldots, n$. Writing out the CAPM equation 7.7 for each stock and multiplying each equation by the weight of the stock in the portfolio, we obtain these equations, one for each stock:

$$\begin{aligned} w_1E(r_1) &= w_1r_f + w_1\beta_1[E(r_M) - r_f] \\ +\, w_2E(r_2) &= w_2r_f + w_2\beta_2[E(r_M) - r_f] \\ +\quad \ldots &= \ldots \\ +\, w_nE(r_n) &= w_nr_f + w_n\beta_n[E(r_M) - r_f] \\ E(r_P) &= r_f + \beta_P[E(r_M) - r_f] \end{aligned}$$

Summing each column shows that the CAPM holds for the overall portfolio because $E(r_P) = \sum_k w_kE(r_k)$ is the expected return on the portfolio and $\beta_P = \sum_k w_k\beta_k$ is the portfolio beta. Incidentally, this result has to be true for the market portfolio itself.

$$E(r_M) = r_f + \beta_M[E(r_M) - r_f]$$

Indeed, this is a tautology because $\beta_M = 1$, as we can verify by demonstrating that

$$\beta_M = \frac{\text{Cov}(r_M, r_M)}{\sigma^2_M} = \frac{\sigma^2_M}{\sigma^2_M}$$

This also establishes 1 as the weighted average value of beta across all assets. If the market beta is 1, and the market is a portfolio of all assets in the economy, the weighted average beta of all assets must be 1. Hence betas greater than 1 are considered aggressive in that investment in high-beta stocks entails above-average sensitivity to market swings. Betas below 1 can be described as defensive.

CONCEPT CHECK

3. Suppose that the risk premium on the market portfolio is estimated at 8 percent with a standard deviation of 22 percent. What is the risk premium on a portfolio invested 25 percent in Inco and 75 percent in Noranda, if they have betas of 1.10 and 1.25 respectively?

A word of caution: We all are accustomed to hearing that well-managed firms will provide high rates of return. We agree this is true if one measures the *firm's* return on investments in plant and equipment. The CAPM, however, predicts returns on investments in the *securities* of the firm.

---

[6]Michael J. Brennan, "Taxes, Market Valuation, and Corporate Finance Policy," *National Tax Journal*, December 1973.

[7]David Mayers, "Nonmarketable Assets and Capital Market Equilibrium Under Uncertainty," in M. C. Jensen, ed., *Studies in the Theory of Capital Markets* (New York: Praeger, 1972).

Let us say that everyone knows a firm is well run. Its stock price will therefore be bid up and, consequently, returns to shareholders who buy at those high prices will not be excessive. Security prices, in other words, reflect public information about a firm's prospects, but only the risk of the company (as measured by beta in the context of the CAPM) should affect expected returns. In a rational market investors receive high expected returns only if they are willing to bear risk.

Of course, investors do not directly observe or determine expected returns on securities. Rather, they observe security prices and bid those prices up or down. Expected rates of return are determined by the prices investors must pay compared to the cash flows those investments might garner. The connection between security expected returns and the market-price equilibrium process is described in more detail in the appendix to this chapter.

The Security Market Line

We can view the expected return–beta relationship as a reward-risk equation. The beta of a security is the appropriate measure of its risk because beta is proportional to the risk that the security contributes to the optimal risky portfolio.

Risk-averse investors measure the risk of the optimal risky portfolio by its variance. In this world we would expect the reward, or the risk premium on individual assets, to depend on the risk that an individual asset contributes to the portfolio. The beta of a stock measures the stock's contribution to the variance of the market portfolio. Hence we expect, for any asset or portfolio, the required risk premium to be a function of beta. The CAPM confirms this intuition, stating further that the security's risk premium is directly proportional to both the beta and the risk premium of the market portfolio; that is, the risk premium equals

$$\beta[E(r_M) - r_f]$$

The expected return–beta relationship can be portrayed graphically as the **security market line (SML)** in Figure 7.2. Its slope is the risk premium of the market portfolio. At the point where $\beta = 1$ on the horizontal axis (which is the market portfolio's beta), we can read off the vertical axis the expected return on the market portfolio.

It is useful to compare the security market line to the capital market line. The CML graphs the risk premiums of efficient portfolios (i.e., portfolios composed of the market and the risk-free asset) as a function of portfolio standard deviation. This is appropriate because standard deviation is a

Figure 7.2
The security market line.

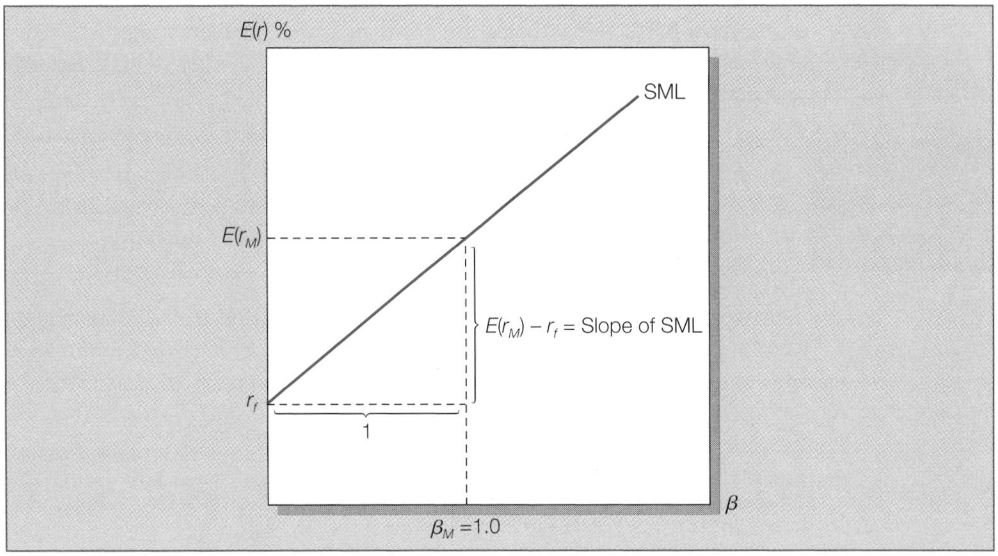

valid measure of risk for efficiently diversified portfolios that are candidates for an investor's overall portfolio. The SML, in contrast, graphs *individual asset* risk premiums as a function of asset risk. The relevant measure of risk for individual assets held as parts of well-diversified portfolios is not the asset's standard deviation or variance; it is, instead, the contribution of the asset to the portfolio variance, which we measure by the asset's beta. The SML is valid for both efficient portfolios and individual assets.

The security market line provides a benchmark for the evaluation of investment performance. Given the risk of an investment, as measured by its beta, the SML provides the required rate of return from that investment to compensate investors for risk, as well as the time value of money.

Because the security market line is the graphic representation of the expected return–beta relationship, "fairly priced" assets plot exactly on the SML; that is, their expected returns are commensurate with their risk. Given the assumptions we made in the beginning of this section, all securities must lie on the SML in market equilibrium. Nevertheless, we see here how the CAPM may be of use in the money-management industry. Suppose that the SML relation is used as a benchmark to assess the fair expected return on a risky asset. Then security analysis is performed to calculate the return actually expected. (Notice that we depart here from the simple CAPM world in that some investors now apply their own unique analysis to derive an "input list" that may differ from their competitors'.) If a stock is perceived to be a good buy, or underpriced, it will provide an expected return in excess of the fair return stipulated by the SML. Underpriced stocks, therefore, plot above the SML: given their betas, their expected returns are greater than dictated by the CAPM. Overpriced stocks plot below the SML.

The difference between the fair and actually expected rates of return on a stock is called the stock's **alpha,** denoted α. For example, if the market is expected to be 14 percent, a stock has a beta of 1.2, and the T-bill rate is 10 percent, the SML would predict an expected return on the stock of $10 + 1.2\,(14 - 10) = 14.8$ percent. If one believed the stock would provide a return of 17 percent, the implied alpha would be 2.2 percent (see Figure 7.3). One could say that security analysis, which we cover in Part Five, is about uncovering securities with nonzero alphas.

Figure 7.3
The SML and a positive-alpha stock.

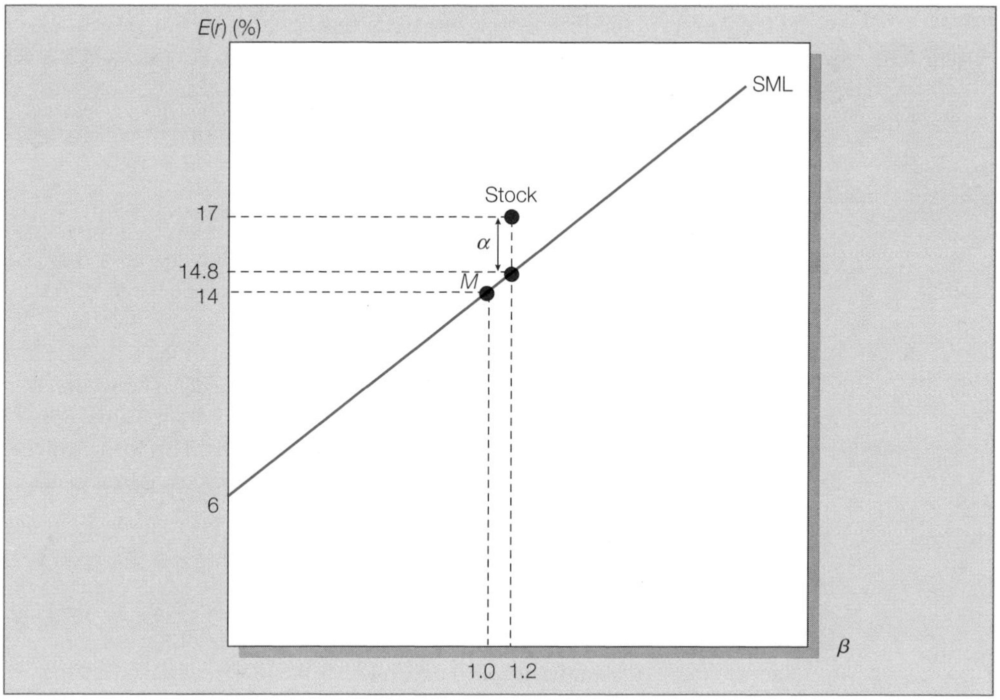

CONCEPT CHECK

4. Stock XYZ has an expected return of 12 percent and risk of $\beta = 1$. Stock ABC has expected return of 13 percent and $\beta = 1.5$. The market's expected return is 11 percent and $r_f = 5$ percent.
   a. According to the CAPM, which stock is a better buy?
   b. What is the alpha of each stock? Plot the SML and each stock's risk return point on one graph. Show the alphas graphically.

The CAPM is also useful in capital budgeting decisions. For a firm considering a new project, the CAPM can provide the return that the project needs to yield, based on its beta, to be acceptable to investors. Managers can use the CAPM to obtain this cutoff internal rate of return (IRR) or "hurdle rate" for the project.

CONCEPT CHECK

5. The risk-free rate is 8 percent and the expected return on the market portfolio is 12 percent. A firm considers a project that is expected to have a beta of 1.3.
   a. What is the required rate of return on the project?
   b. If the expected IRR of the project is 15 percent, should it be accepted?

The boxed article here describes how the CAPM can be used in capital budgeting. It also discusses some empirical anomalies concerning the model, which we address in detail in Chapters 8 and 9. The article asks whether the CAPM is useful for capital budgeting in light of these shortcomings: it concludes that even given the anomalies cited, the model still can be useful to managers who wish to increase the fundamental value of their firms.

Yet another use of the CAPM is in utility rate-making cases. In this case, the issue is the rate of return that a regulated utility should be allowed to earn on its investment in plant and equipment. Suppose that the equityholders have invested \$100 million in the firm and that the beta of the equity is .6. If the T-bill rate is 6 percent and the market risk premium is 4 percent, then the fair profits to the firm would be assessed as $6 + .6(4) = 8.4$ percent of the \$100 million investment, or \$8.4 million. The firm would be allowed to set prices at a level expected to generate these profits.

7.2 EXTENSIONS OF THE CAPM

The assumptions that allowed Sharpe to derive the simple version of the CAPM are admittedly unrealistic. Financial economists have been at work ever since the CAPM was devised to extend the model to more realistic scenarios.

There are two classes of extensions to the simple version of the CAPM. The first attempts to relax the assumptions that we outlined at the outset of the chapter. The second acknowledges the fact that investors worry about sources of risk other than the uncertain value of their securities, such as unexpected changes in the relative prices of consumer goods. This idea involves the introduction of additional risk factors besides security returns, and we will discuss it later in this and the next chapter.

The CAPM with Restricted Borrowing: The Zero-Beta Model

The CAPM is predicated on the assumption that all investors share an identical input list that they feed into the Markowitz algorithm. Thus all investors agree on the location of the efficient (minimum-variance) frontier, where each portfolio has the lowest variance among all feasible portfolios

TALES FROM THE FAR SIDE

Financial markets' evaluation of risk determines the way firms invest. What if the markets are wrong?

Investors are rarely praised for their good sense. But for the past two decades a growing number of firms have based their decisions on a model which assumes that people are perfectly rational. If they are irrational, are businesses making the wrong choices?

The model, known as the "capital-asset pricing model," or CAPM, has come to dominate modern finance. Almost any manager who wants to defend a project—be it a brand, a factory or a corporate merger—must justify his decision partly based on the CAPM. The reason is that the model tells a firm how to calculate the return that its investors demand. If shareholders are to benefit, the returns from any project must clear this "hurdle rate."

Although the CAPM is complicated, it can be reduced to five simple ideas:

- Investors can eliminate some risks—such as the risk that workers will strike, or that a firm's boss will quit—by diversifying across many regions and sectors.
- Some risks, such as that of a global recession, cannot be eliminated though diversification. So even a basket of all of the stocks in a stockmarket will still be risky.
- People must be rewarded for investing in such a risky basket by earning returns above those that they can get on safer assets, such as Treasury bills.
- The rewards on a specific investment depend only on the extent to which it affects the market basket's risk.
- Conveniently, that contribution to the market basket's risk can be captured by a single measure—dubbed "beta"—which expresses the relationship between the investment's risk and the market's.

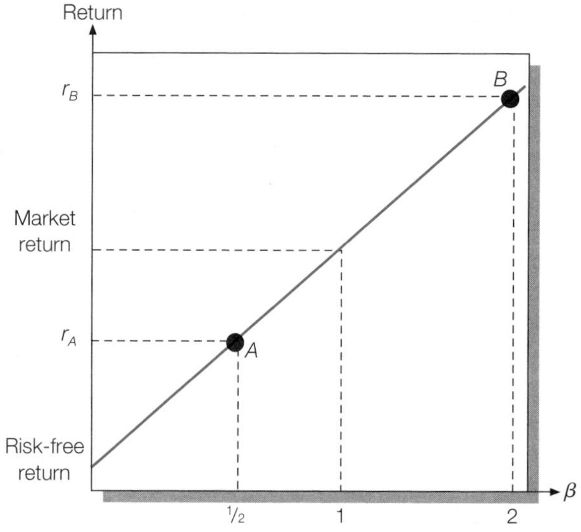

Beta is what makes the CAPM so powerful. Although an investment may face many risks, diversified investors should care only about those that are related to the market basket. Beta not only tells managers how to measure those risks, but it also allows them to translate them directly into a hurdle rate. If the future profits from a project will not exceed that rate, it is not worth shareholders' money.

The diagram shows how the CAPM works. Safe investments, such as Treasury bills, have a beta of zero. Riskier investments should earn a premium over the risk-free rate which increases with beta. Those whose risks roughly match the market's have a beta of one, by definition, and should earn the market return.

(Continued)

at a target expected rate of return. When all investors can borrow and lend at the safe rate, r_f, all agree on the optimal tangency portfolio and choose to hold a share of the market portfolio.

However, when borrowing is restricted, as it is for many financial institutions, or when the borrowing rate is higher than the lending rate because borrowers pay a default premium, the market portfolio is no longer the common optimal portfolio for all investors.

When investors no longer can borrow or lend at a common risk-free rate, they may choose risky portfolios from the entire set of efficient frontier portfolios according to how much risk they choose to bear. The market is no longer the common optimal portfolio. In fact, with investors choosing different portfolios, it is no longer obvious whether the market portfolio, which is the aggregate of all investors' portfolios, will even be on the efficient frontier. If the market portfolio is no longer mean-variance efficient, then the expected return–beta relationship of the CAPM will no longer characterize market equilibrium.

So suppose that a firm is considering two projects, *A* and *B*. Project *A* has a beta of $\frac{1}{2}$: when the market rises or falls by 10%, its returns tend to rise or fall by 5%. So its risk premium is only half that of the market. Project *B*'s risk premium is twice that of the market, so it must earn a higher return to justify the expenditure.

Never Knowingly Underpriced

But there is one small problem with the CAPM: Financial economists have found that beta is not much use for explaining rates of return on firms' shares. Worse, there appears to be another measure which explains these returns quite well.

That measure is the ratio of a firm's book value (the value of its assets at the time they entered the balance sheet) to its market value. Several studies have found that, on average, companies that have high book-to-market ratios tend to earn excess returns over long periods, even after adjusting for the risks that are associated with beta.

The discovery of this book-to-market effect has sparked a fierce debate among financial economists. All of them agree that some risks ought to carry greater rewards. But they are now deeply divided over how risk should be measured. Some argue that since investors are rational, the book-to-market effect must be capturing an extra risk factor. They conclude, therefore, that managers should incorporate the book-to-market effect into their hurdle rates. They have labeled this alternative hurdle rate the "new estimator of expected return," or NEER.

Other financial economists, however, dispute this approach. Since there is no obvious extra risk associated with a high book-to-market ratio, they say, investors must be mistaken. Put simply, they are underpricing high book-to-market stocks, causing them to earn abnormally high returns. If managers of such firms try to exceed those inflated hurdle rates, they will forgo many profitable investments. With economists now at odds, what is a conscientious manager to do?

In a new paper,* Jeremy Stein, an economist at the Massachusetts Institute of Technology's business school, offers a paradoxical answer. If investors are rational, then beta cannot be the only measure of risk, so managers should stop using it. Conversely, if investors are irrational, then beta is still the right measure in many cases. Mr. Stein argues that if beta captures an asset's fundamental risk—that is, its contribution to the market basket's risk—then it will often make sense for managers to pay attention to it, even if investors are somehow failing to.

Often, but not always. At the heart of Mr. Stein's argument lies a crucial distinction—that between (*a*) boosting a firm's long-term value and (*b*) trying to raise its share price. If investors are rational, these are the same thing: any decision that raises long-term value will instantly increase the share price as well. But if investors are making predictable mistakes, a manager must choose.

For instance, if he wants to increase today's share price—perhaps because he wants to sell his shares, or to fend off a takeover attempt—he must usually stick with the NEER approach, accommodating investors' misperceptions. But if he is interested in long-term value, he should usually continue to use beta. Showing a flair for marketing, Mr. Stein labels this far-sighted alternative to NEER the "fundamental asset risk"—or FAR—approach.

Mr. Stein's conclusions will no doubt irritate many company bosses, who are fond of denouncing their investors' myopia. They have resented the way in which CAPM—with its assumption of investor infallibility—has come to play an important role in boardroom decision-making. But it now appears that if they are right, and their investors are wrong, then those same far-sighted managers ought to be the CAPM's biggest fans.

*Jeremy Stein, "Rational Capital Budgeting in an Irrational World," *The Journal of Business*, October 1996.

Source: "Tales from the FAR Side," *The Economist*, November 16, 1996, p. 8.

An equilibrium expected return–beta relationship in the case of restricted risk-free investments has been developed by Fischer Black.[8] Black's model is fairly difficult and requires a good deal of facility with mathematics. Therefore, we will satisfy ourselves with a sketch of Black's argument and spend more time with its implications.

Black's model of the CAPM in the absence of a risk-free asset rests on the three following properties of mean-variance efficient portfolios:

1. Any portfolio constructed by combining efficient portfolios is itself on the efficient frontier.
2. Every portfolio on the efficient frontier has a companion portfolio on the bottom half (the inefficient part) of the minimum-variance frontier with which it is uncorrelated. Because

[8]Fischer Black, "Capital Market Equilibrium with Restricted Borrowing," *Journal of Business*, July 1972.

the portfolios are uncorrelated, the companion portfolio is referred to as the **zero-beta portfolio** of the efficient portfolio.

The expected return of an efficient portfolio's zero-beta companion portfolio can be derived by the following graphical procedure. From any efficient portfolio such as P in Figure 7.4 draw a tangency line to the vertical axis. The intercept will be the expected return on portfolio P's zero-beta companion portfolio, denoted $Z(P)$. The horizontal line from the intercept to the minimum-variance frontier identifies the standard deviation of the zero-beta portfolio. Notice in Figure 7.4 that different efficient portfolios such as P and Q have different zero-beta companions.

These tangency lines are only helpful constructs—they do *not* signify that one can invest in portfolios with expected return–standard deviation pairs along the line. That would be possible only by mixing a risk-free asset with the tangency portfolio. In this case, however, we assume that risk-free assets are not available to investors.

3. The expected return of any asset can be expressed as an exact, linear function of the expected return on any two frontier portfolios. Consider, for example, the minimum-variance frontier portfolios P and Q. Black shows that the expected return on any asset i can be expressed as

$$E(r_i) = E(r_Q) + [E(r_P) - E(r_Q)]\,\frac{\text{Cov}(r_i,r_P) - \text{Cov}(r_P,r_Q)}{\sigma^2_P - \text{Cov}(r_P,r_Q)} \tag{7.9}$$

Note that this last property has nothing to do with the market equilibrium. It is a purely mathematical property relating frontier portfolios and individual securities.

With these three properties, the Black model can be applied to any of several variations: no risk-free asset at all, risk-free lending but no risk-free borrowing, and borrowing at a rate higher than r_f. We show here how the model works for the case with risk-free lending but no borrowing.

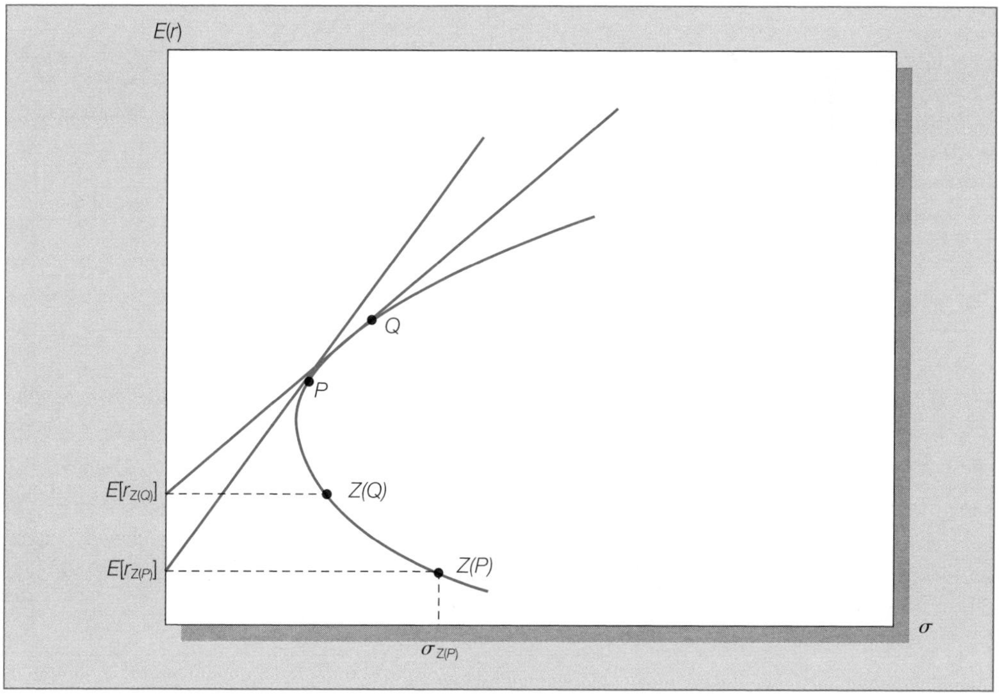

Figure 7.4 Efficient portfolios and their zero-beta companions.

Imagine an economy with only two investors, one relatively risk-averse and one risk-tolerant. The risk-averse investor will choose a portfolio on the CAL supported by portfolio *T* in Figure 7.5, that is, he will mix portfolio *T* with lending at the risk-free rate. *T* is the tangency portfolio on the efficient frontier from the risk-free lending rate, r_f. The risk-tolerant investor is willing to accept more risk to earn a higher-risk premium; she will choose portfolio *S*. This portfolio lies along the efficient frontier with higher risk and return than portfolio *T*. The aggregate risky portfolio (i.e., the market portfolio, *M*) will be a combination of *T* and *S*, with weights determined by the relative wealth and degrees of risk aversion of the two investors. Since *T* and *S* are each on the efficient frontier, so is *M* (from Property 1).

From Property 2, *M* has a companion zero-beta portfolio on the minimum-variance frontier, *Z(M)*, shown in Figure 7.5. Moreover, by Property 3 we can express the return on any security in terms of *M* and *Z(M)* as in equation 7.9. But, since by construction $\text{Cov}[r_M, r_{Z(M)}] = 0$, the expression simplifies to

$$E(r_i) = E[r_{Z(M)}] + E[r_M - r_{Z(M)}] \frac{\text{Cov}(r_i, r_M)}{\sigma^2_M} \tag{7.10}$$

where *P* from equation 7.9 has been replaced by *M* and *Q* has been replaced by *Z(M)*. Equation 7.10 may be interpreted as a variant of the simple CAPM, in which r_f has been replaced with $E[r_{Z(M)}]$.

A more realistic scenario is one in which the investor can lend at the risk-free rate r_f and borrow at a higher rate. This case was considered in Chapter 6. The same arguments that we have just employed also can be used to establish the zero-beta CAPM in this situation. Problem 18 at the end of this chapter asks you to fill in the details of the argument for this situation.

CONCEPT CHECK

6. Suppose that the zero-beta portfolio exhibits returns that are, on average, greater than the rate on T-bills. Is this fact relevant to the question of the validity of the CAPM?

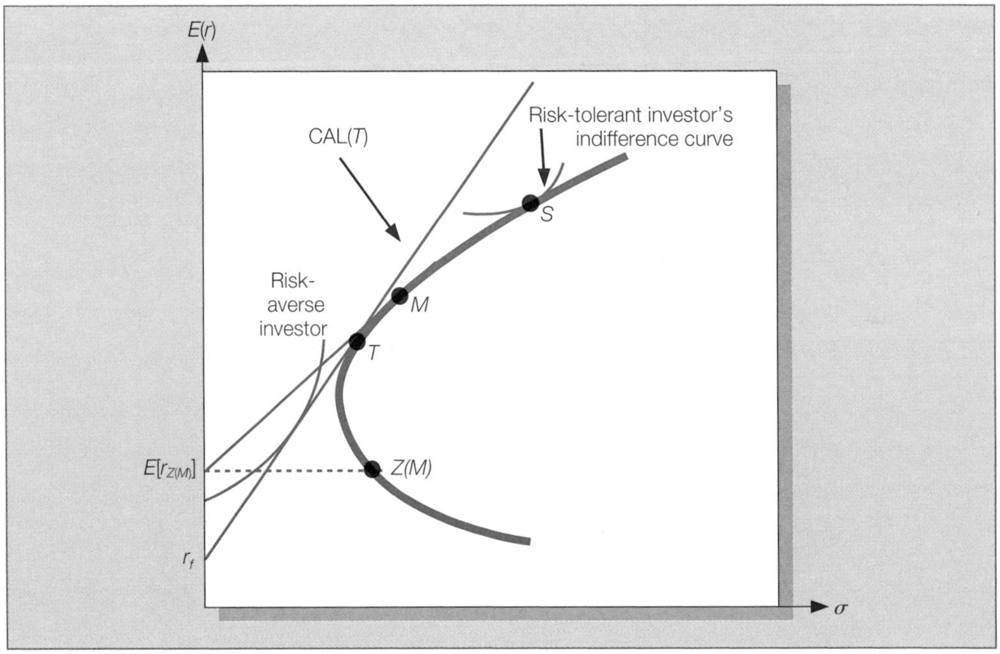

Figure 7.5 Capital market equilibrium with no borrowing.

Lifetime Consumption: The CAPM with Dynamic Programming

One of the restrictive assumptions of the simple version of the CAPM is that investors are myopic—they plan for one common holding period. Investors actually may be concerned with a lifetime consumption plan and a possible desire to leave a bequest to children. Consumption plans that are feasible for them depend on current wealth and future rates of return on the investment portfolio. These investors will want to rebalance their portfolios as often as required by changes in wealth.

However, Eugene Fama[9] shows that, even if we extend our analysis to a multiperiod setting, the single CAPM still may be appropriate. The key assumptions that Fama uses to replace myopic planning horizons are that investor preferences are unchanging over time and that the risk-free interest rate and probability distribution of security returns do not change unpredictably over time. Of course, this latter assumption is itself somewhat unrealistic. Extensions to the CAPM engendered by considering random changes to the so-called "investment opportunity set" are examined in the next chapter.

7.3 THE CAPM AND LIQUIDITY: A THEORY OF ILLIQUIDITY PREMIUMS

Liquidity refers to the cost and ease with which an asset can be converted into cash, that is, sold. Traders have long recognized the importance of liquidity, and some evidence suggests that illiquidity can reduce market prices substantially. For example, one study[10] finds that market discounts on closely held (and therefore nontraded) firms can exceed 30 percent. The boxed article here focuses on the relationship between liquidity and stock returns.

A rigorous treatment of the value of liquidity has been developed by Amihud and Mendelson.[11] Recent studies show that liquidity plays an important role in explaining rates of return on financial assets.[12] For example, Chordia, Roll, and Subrahmanyam[13] find commonality across stocks in the variable costs of liquidity: quoted spreads, quoted depth, and effective spreads covary with the market and industrywide liquidity. Hence, liquidity risk is systematic and therefore difficult to diversify. We believe that liquidity will become an important part of standard valuation and present here a simplified version of their model.

Recall assumption 4 of the CAPM, that all trading is costless. In reality, no security is perfectly liquid, in that all trades involve some transaction cost. Investors prefer more liquid assets with lower transaction costs, so it should not surprise us to find that (all else being equal) relatively illiquid assets trade at lower prices, or equivalently, that the expected rate of return on illiquid assets must be higher. Therefore, an **illiquidity premium** must be impounded into the price of each asset. The impact of liquidity will depend on both the distribution of transaction costs across assets as well as the distribution of investors across investment horizons. We will use very simplified distributions to illustrate the effect of liquidity on equilibrium expected returns. However, these simplifications are expositional only and the predicted effect of liquidity on equilibrium returns is quite general.

We start with the simplest case, in which we ignore systematic risk. Imagine, a world with a large number of uncorrelated securities. Because the securities are uncorrelated, highly diversified

---

[9]Eugene F. Fama, "Multiperiod Consumption-Investment Decisions," *American Economic Review* 60 (1970).

[10]Shannon P. Pratt, *Valuing a Business: The Analysis of Closely Held Companies*, 2nd ed. (Homewood, IL: Dow Jones–Irwin, 1989).

[11]Yakov Amihud and Haim Mendelson, "Asset Pricing and the Bid-Ask Spread," *Journal of Financial Economics* 17 (1986), pp. 223–249.

[12]For example, Venkat Eleswarapu, "Costs of Transacting and Expected Returns in the NASDAQ Market," *Journal of Finance* 2, no. 5 (1993), pp. 2113–27.

[13]Tarun Chordia, Richard Roll, and Avanidhar Subrahmanyam, "Commonality and Liquidity," *Journal of Financial Economics*, April 2000.

STOCK INVESTORS PAY HIGH PRICE FOR LIQUIDITY

Given a choice between liquid and illiquid stocks, most investors, to the extent they think of it at all, opt for issues they know are easy to get in and out of.

But for long-term investors who don't trade often—which includes most individuals—that may be unnecessarily expensive. Recent studies of the performance of listed stocks show that, on average, less-liquid issues generate substantially higher returns—as much as several percentage points a year at the extremes. . . .

Illiquidity Payoff

Among the academic studies that have attempted to quantify this illiquidity payoff is a recent work by two finance professors, Yakov Amihud of New York University and Tel Aviv University, and Haim Mendelson of the University of Rochester. Their study looks at New York Stock Exchange issues over the 1961–1980 period and defines liquidity in terms of bid–asked spreads as a percentage of overall share price.

Market makers use spreads in quoting stocks to define the difference between the price they'll bid to take stock off an investor's hands and the price they'll offer to sell stock to any willing buyer. The bid price is always somewhat lower because of the risk to the broker of tying up precious capital to hold stock in inventory until it can be resold.

If a stock is relatively illiquid, which means there's not a ready flow of orders from customers clamoring to buy it, there's more of a chance the broker will lose money on the trade. To hedge this risk, market makers demand an even bigger discount to service potential sellers, and the spread will widen further.

The study by Profs. Amihud and Mendelson shows that liquidity spreads—measured as a percentage discount from the stock's total price—ranged from less than 0.1%, for widely held International Business Machines Corp., to as much as 4% to 5%. The widest-spread group was dominated by smaller, low-priced stocks.

The study found that, overall, the least-liquid stocks averaged an 8.5 percent-a-year higher return than the most-liquid stocks over the 20-year period. On average, a one percentage point increase in the spread was associated with a 2.5% higher annual return for New York Stock Exchange stocks. The relationship held after results were adjusted for size and other risk factors.

An extension of the study of Big Board stocks done at *The Wall Street Journal's* request produced similar findings. It shows that for the 1980–85 period, a one percentage-point-wider spread was associated with an extra average annual gain of 2.4%. Meanwhile, the least-liquid stocks outperformed the most-liquid stocks by almost six percentage points a year.

Cost of Trading

Since the cost of the spread is incurred each time the stock is traded, illiquid stocks can quickly become prohibitively expensive for investors who trade frequently. On the other hand, long-term investors needn't worry so much about spreads, since they can amortize them over a longer period.

In terms of investment strategy, this suggests "that the small investor should tailor the types of stocks he or she buys to his expected holding period," Prof. Mendelson says. If the investor expects to sell within three months, he says, it's better to pay up for the liquidity and get the lowest spread. If the investor plans to hold the stock for a year or more, it makes sense to aim at stocks with spreads of 3% or more to capture the extra return.

Source: Barbara Donnelly, *The Wall Street Journal*, April 28, 1987, p. 37. Reprinted by permission of The Wall Street Journal.

portfolios of these securities will have standard deviations near zero and the market portfolio will be virtually as safe as the risk-free asset. Moreover, the covariance between any pair of securities also is zero, implying that the beta of any security with the diversified market portfolio is zero. Therefore, according to the CAPM, all assets should have expected rates of return equal to that of the risk-free asset, which we will take to be T-bills.

Assume that investors know in advance for how long they intend to hold their portfolios, and suppose that there are n types of investors, grouped by investment horizon. Type 1 investors intend to liquidate their portfolios in one period, type 2 investors in two periods, and so on, until the longest-horizon investors (type n) intend to hold their portfolios for n periods.

Because we are now dealing with a multiperiod model, we should be careful in our comparison with the single-period CAPM. However, we've seen that Fama's work (see footnote 9) implies that even if investors have multiperiod investment horizons, the simple expected return–beta relationship of the CAPM still might describe equilibrium security returns. To maintain Fama's results, we will assume that as investors liquidate their portfolios, just enough investors of each type enter the market to take the place of those who depart. Thus, in each period, there is identical demand for securities, as Fama requires. However, even with these assumptions, the presence of trading costs *in conjunction with* differing investment horizons will require an adaptation of the CAPM.

We assume that there are only two classes of securities: liquid and illiquid. The liquidation cost of a class L (more liquid) stock to an investor with a horizon of h years (a type h investor) will reduce the per-period rate of return by c_L/h percent. For example, if the combination of commissions and the bid-ask spread on a security resulted in a liquidation cost of 10 percent, then the per-period rate of return for an investor who holds the stock for 5 years would be reduced by approximately 2 percent per year, while the return on a ten-year investment would fall by only 1 percent per year.[14] Class I (illiquid) assets have higher liquidation costs that reduce the per-period return by c_I/h percent, where c_I is greater than c_L. Therefore, if you intend to hold a class L security for h periods, your expected rate of return *net* of transaction costs is $E(r_L) - c_L/h$. There is no liquidation cost on T-bills.

The following table presents the expected rates of return investors would realize from the risk-free asset and class L and class I stock portfolios *assuming* that the simple CAPM is correct and all securities have an expected rate of return of r:

Asset:	**Risk-Free**	**Class L**	**Class I**
Gross rate of return	r	r	r
One-period liquidation cost	0	c_L	c_I
Investor Type		**Net Rate of Return**	
1	r	$r - c_L$	$r - c_I$
2	r	$r - c_L/2$	$r - c_I/2$
. . .	. . .	. . .	. . .
n	r	$r - c_L/n$	$r - c_I/n$

These net rates of return are inconsistent with a market in equilibrium, because with equal gross rates of return of r, all investors would prefer to invest in zero-transaction-cost T-bills. As a result, both class L and class I stock prices must fall, causing their expected rates of return to rise until investors are willing to hold these shares.

Suppose, therefore, that each gross return is higher by some fraction of liquidation cost. Specifically, assume that the gross expected rate of return on class L stocks is $r + xc_L$ and that of class I stocks is $r + yc_I$, where x and y are smaller than 1 (otherwise diversified stock portfolios would dominate the risk-free asset in terms of net returns). The *net* rate of return on class L stocks to an investor with a horizon of h will be $(r + xc_L) - c_L/h = r + c_L(x - 1/h)$. In general, the rates of return to investors will be

Asset:	**Risk-Free**	**Class L**	**Class I**
Gross rate of return	r	$r + xc_L$	$r + yc_I$
One-period liquidation cost	0	c_L	c_I
Investor Type		**Net Rate of Return**	
1	r	$r + c_L(x - 1)$	$r + c_I(y - 1)$
2	r	$r + c_L(x - 1/2)$	$r + c_I(y - 1/2)$
. . .	. . .	. . .	. . .
n	r	$r + c_L(x - 1/n)$	$r + c_I(y - 1/n)$

[14]This simple structure of liquidation costs allows us to derive a correspondingly simple solution for the effect of liquidity on expected returns. Amihud and Mendelson use a more general formulation but then need to rely on complex and more difficult-to-interpret mathematical programming. All that matters for the qualitative results below, however, is that illiquidity costs be less onerous to longer-term investors.

Notice that the liquidation cost has a greater impact on per-period returns for short-term investors. This is because the cost is amortized over fewer periods. As the horizon becomes very large, the per-period impact of the transaction cost approaches zero and the net rate of return approaches the gross rate.

Figure 7.6 graphs the net rate of return on the three asset classes for investors of differing horizons. The more illiquid stock has the lowest net rate of return for very short investment horizons because of its large liquidation costs. However, in equilibrium, the stock must be priced at a level that offers a rate of return high enough to induce some investors to hold it, implying that its gross rate of return must be higher than that of the more liquid stock. Therefore, for long enough investment horizons, the net return on class I stocks will exceed that on class L stocks.

Both stock classes underperform T-bills for very short investment horizons, because the transactions costs then have the largest per-period impact. Ultimately, however, because the *gross* rate of return of stocks exceeds r for a sufficiently long investment horizon, the more liquid stocks in class L will dominate bills. The threshold horizon can be read from Figure 7.6 as h_{rL}. Anyone with a horizon that exceeds h_{rL} will prefer class L stocks to T-bills. Those with horizons below h_{rL} will choose bills. For even longer horizons, because c_I exceeds c_L, the net rate of return on relatively illiquid class I stocks will exceed that on class L stocks. Therefore, investors with horizons greater than h_{LI} will specialize in the most illiquid stocks with the highest gross rate of return. These investors are harmed least by the effect of trading costs.

Now we can determine equilibrium illiquidity premiums. For the marginal investor with horizon h_{LI}, the *net* returns from class I and L stocks is the same. Therefore,

$$r + c_L(x - 1/h_{LI}) = r + c_I(y - 1/h_{LI})$$

Figure 7.6
Net return as a function of investment horizon.

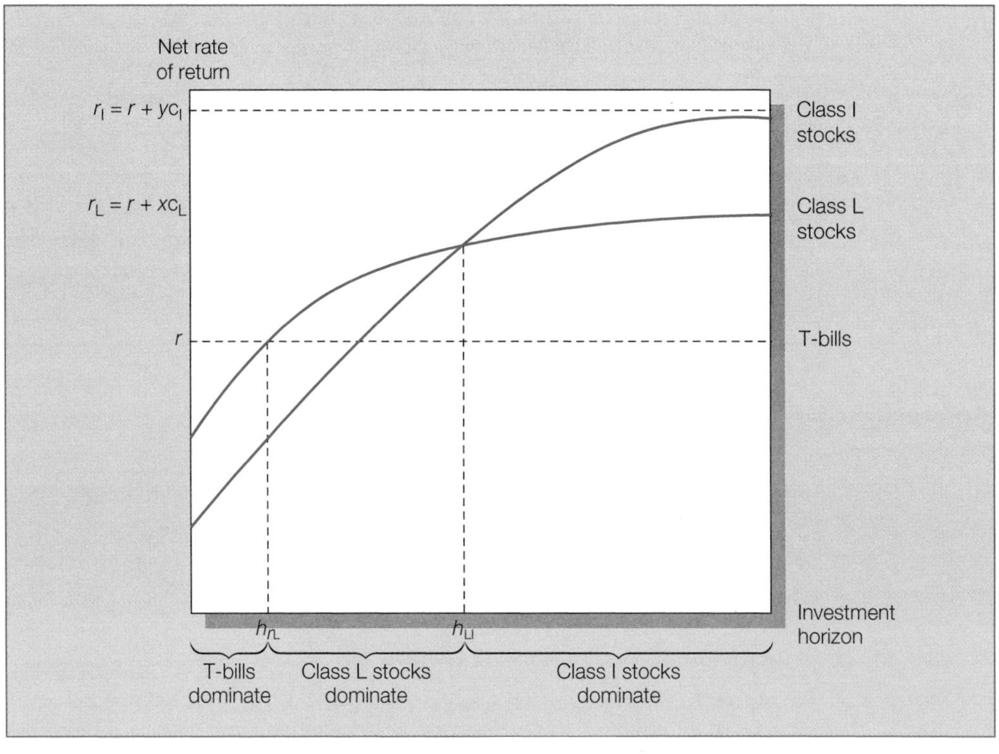

We can use this equation to solve for the relationship between x and y as follows:

$$y = \frac{1}{h_{\mathrm{LI}}} + \frac{c_{\mathrm{L}}}{c_{\mathrm{I}}}(x - \frac{1}{h_{\mathrm{LI}}})$$

The expected gross return on illiquid stocks is then

$$r_{\mathrm{I}} = r + c_{\mathrm{L}}y = r + \frac{c_{\mathrm{I}}}{h_{\mathrm{LI}}} + c_{\mathrm{L}}\left(x - \frac{1}{h_{\mathrm{LI}}}\right) = r + c_{\mathrm{L}}x + \frac{1}{h_{\mathrm{LI}}}(c_{\mathrm{I}} - c_{\mathrm{L}}) \tag{7.11}$$

Recalling that the expected gross return on class L stocks is $r_{\mathrm{L}} = r + c_{\mathrm{L}}x$, we conclude that the illiquidity premium of class I versus class L stocks is

$$r_{\mathrm{I}} - r_{\mathrm{L}} = \frac{1}{h_{\mathrm{LI}}}(c_{\mathrm{I}} - c_{\mathrm{L}}) \tag{7.12}$$

Similarly, we can derive the liquidity premium of class L stocks over T-bills. Here, the marginal investor who is indifferent between bills and class L stocks will have investment horizon $h_{r\mathrm{L}}$ and a net rate of return just equal to r. Therefore, $r + c_{\mathrm{L}}(x - 1/h_{r\mathrm{L}}) = r$, implying that $x = 1/h_{r\mathrm{L}}$ and the liquidity premium of class L stocks must be $xc_{\mathrm{L}} = c_{\mathrm{L}}/h_{r\mathrm{L}}$. Therefore,

$$r_{\mathrm{L}} - r = \frac{1}{h_{r\mathrm{L}}}c_{\mathrm{L}} \tag{7.13}$$

There are two lessons to be learned from this analysis. First, as predicted, equilibrium expected rates of return are bid up to compensate for transaction costs, as demonstrated by equations 7.12 and 7.13. Second, the illiquidity premium is *not* a linear function of transaction costs. In fact, the incremental illiquidity premium steadily declines as transaction costs increase. To see that this is so, suppose that c_{L} is 1 percent and $c_{\mathrm{I}} - c_{\mathrm{L}}$ also is 1 percent. Therefore, the transaction cost increases by 1 percent as you move out of bills into the more liquid stock class and by another 1 percent as you move into the illiquid stock class. Equation 7.13 shows that the illiquidity premium of class L stocks over no-transaction-cost bills is then $1/h_{r\mathrm{L}}$, and equation 7.12 shows that the illiquidity premium of class I over class L stocks is $1/h_{\mathrm{LI}}$. But h_{LI} exceeds $h_{r\mathrm{L}}$ (see Figure 7.6), so we conclude that the incremental effect of illiquidity declines as we move into ever more illiquid assets.

The reason for this last result is simple. Recall that investors will self-select into different asset classes, with longer-term investors holding assets that have the highest gross return and the greatest illiquidity. For these investors, the effect of illiquidity is less costly because trading costs can be amortized over a longer horizon. Therefore, as these costs increase, the investment horizon associated with the holders of these assets also increases, which mitigates the impact on the required gross rate of return.

CONCEPT CHECK

7. Consider a very illiquid asset class of stocks, class V, with $c_{\mathrm{V}} > c_{\mathrm{I}}$. Use a graph like Figure 7.6 to convince yourself that there is an investment horizon, h_{IV}, for which an investor would be indifferent between stocks in illiquidity classes I and V. Analogously to equation 7.12, in equilibrium, the differential in gross returns must be

$$r_{\mathrm{V}} - r_{\mathrm{I}} = \frac{1}{h_{\mathrm{IV}}}(c_{\mathrm{V}} - c_{\mathrm{I}})$$

Our analysis so far has focused on the case of uncorrelated assets, allowing us to ignore issues of systematic risk. This special case turns out to be easy to generalize. If we were to allow for correlation among assets due to common systematic risk factors, we would find that the illiquidity premium is simply additive to the risk premium of the usual CAPM.[15] Therefore, we can generalize the CAPM expected return–beta relationship to include a liquidity effect as follows:

$$E(r_i) - r_f = \beta_i[E(r_M) - r_f] + f(c_i)$$

where $f(c_i)$ is a function of trading costs that measures the effect of the illiquidity premium given the trading costs of security *i*. We have seen that $f(c_i)$ is increasing in c_i but at a decreasing rate. The usual CAPM equation is modified because each investor's optimal portfolio is now affected by liquidation cost as well as risk-return considerations.

The model can be generalized in other ways as well. For example, even if investors do not know their investment horizon for certain, as long as investors do not perceive a connection between unexpected needs to liquidate investments and security returns, the implications of the model are essentially unchanged, with expected horizons replacing actual horizons in equations 7.12 and 7.13.

Amihud and Mendelson provide a considerable amount of empirical evidence that liquidity has a substantial impact on gross stock returns. We will defer our discussion of most of that evidence until Chapter 10. However, for a preview of the quantitative significance of the illiquidity effect, examine Figure 7.7, which is derived from their study. It shows that average monthly returns over the 1961–1980 period rise from 0.35 percent for the group of stocks with the lowest bid-ask spread (the most liquid stocks) to 1.024 percent for the highest-spread stocks. This is an annualized differential of about 8 percent, nearly equal to the historical average risk premium on the S&P 500 index! Moreover, as their model predicts, the effect of the spread on average monthly returns is nonlinear, with a curve that flattens out as spreads increase.

Figure 7.7 The relationship between illiquidity and average returns.

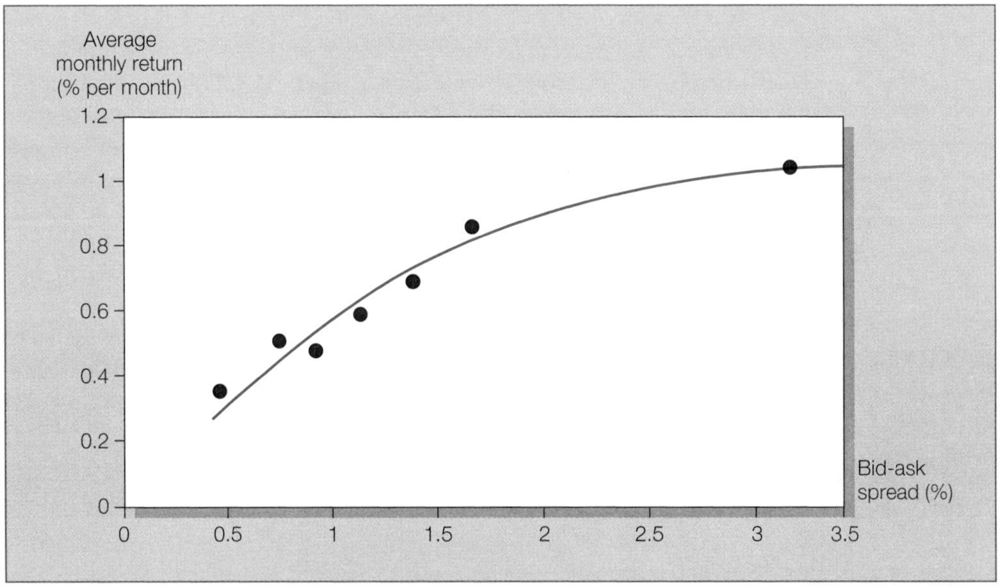

Source: Derived from Yakov Amihud and Haim Mendelson, "Asset Pricing and the Bid-Ask Spread," *Journal of Financial Economics* 17 (1986), pp. 223–249. Reprinted by permission.

[15]The only assumption necessary to obtain this result is that for each level of beta, there are many securities within that risk class, with a variety of transaction costs. (This is essentially the same assumption used by Modigliani and Miller in their famous capital structure irrelevance proposition.) Thus, our earlier analysis could be applied within each risk class, resulting in an illiquidity premium that simply adds on to the systematic risk premium.

SUMMARY

1. The CAPM assumes that investors are single-period planners who agree on a common input list from security analysis and seek mean-variance optimal portfolios.
2. The CAPM assumes that security markets are ideal in the sense that:
   a. They are large, and investors are price-takers.
   b. There are no taxes or transaction costs.
   c. All risky assets are publicly traded.
   d. Investors can borrow and lend any amount at a fixed risk-free rate.
3. With these assumptions, all investors hold identical risky portfolios. The CAPM holds that in equilibrium the market portfolio is the unique mean-variance efficient tangency portfolio. Thus, a passive strategy is efficient.
4. The CAPM market portfolio is a value-weighted portfolio. Each security is held in a proportion equal to its market value divided by the total market value of all securities.
5. If the market portfolio is efficient and the average investor neither borrows nor lends, then the risk premium on the market portfolio is proportional to its variance, σ^2_M, and to the average coefficient of risk aversion across investors $\bar{A}$:

$$E(r_M) - r_f = 1.0 \times \bar{A}\sigma^2_M$$

6. The CAPM implies that the risk premium on any individual asset or portfolio is the product of the risk premium on the market portfolio and the beta coefficient:

$$E(r) - r_f = \beta[E(r_M) - r_f]$$

   where the beta coefficient is the covariance of the asset with the market portfolio as a fraction of the variance of the market portfolio:

$$\beta = \frac{\text{Cov}(r,r_M)}{\sigma^2_M}$$

7. When risk-free investments are restricted but all other CAPM assumptions hold, then the simple version of the CAPM is replaced by its zero-beta version. Accordingly, the risk-free rate in the expected return–beta relationship is replaced by the zero-beta portfolio's expected rate of return:

$$E(r_i) = E[r_{Z(M)}] + \beta_i E[r_M - r_{Z(M)}]$$

8. The simple version of the CAPM assumes that investors are myopic. When investors are assumed to be concerned with lifetime consumption and bequest plans but their tastes and security return distributions are stable over time, the market portfolio remains efficient and the simple version of the expected return–beta relationship holds.
9. The simple version of the CAPM must be modified when investors are concerned with extramarket sources of uncertainty pertaining to future consumption and investment opportunities. These concerns give rise to demands for securities that hedge these risks. With the extra hedging demands, equilibrium security returns will satisfy a multifactor version of the expected return–beta relationship.
10. Liquidity costs can be incorporated into the CAPM relationship. When there is a large number of assets with any combination of beta and liquidity cost c_i, the expected return is bid up to reflect this undesired property according to:

$$E(r_i) - r_f = \beta_i[E(r_M) - r_f] + f(c_i)$$

KEY TERMS

capital asset pricing model (CAPM) 253
homogeneous expectations 253
market portfolio 254
mutual fund theorem 255
market price of risk 258
beta 258
expected return–beta relationship 258
security market line (SML) 260
alpha 261
zero-beta portfolio 265
liquidity 267
illiquidity premium 267

SELECTED READINGS

A good introduction to the intuition of the CAPM is:

Malkiel, Burton G. *A Random Walk Down Wall Street.* New York: W. W. Norton & Company, Inc., 1985.

The four articles that established the CAPM are:

Sharpe, William. "Capital Asset Prices: A Theory of Market Equilibrium." *Journal of Finance,* September 1964.

Lintner, John. "The Valuation of Risk Assets and the Selection of Risky Investments in Stock Portfolios and Capital Budgets." *Review of Economics and Statistics,* February 1965.

Mossin, Jan. "Equilibrium in a Capital Asset Market." *Econometrica,* October 1966.

Treynor, Jack. "Towards a Theory of Market Value of Risky Assets." Unpublished manuscript, 1961.

A review of the simple CAPM and its variants is contained in:

Jensen, Michael C. "The Foundation and Current State of Capital Market Theory." In Michael C. Jensen (ed.), *Studies in the Theory of Capital Markets.* New York: Praeger Publishers, 1972.

The zero-beta version of the CAPM appeared in:

Black, Fischer. "Capital Market Equilibrium with Restricted Borrowing." *Journal of Business,* July 1972.

Excellent practitioner-oriented discussions of the CAPM are:

Mullins, David. "Does the Capital Asset Pricing Model Work?" *Harvard Business Review,* January/February 1982.

Rosenberg, Barr, and Andrew Rudd. "The Corporate Uses of Beta." In J. M. Stern and D. H. Chew, Jr., eds., *The Revolution in Corporate Finance.* New York: Basil Blackwell, 1986.

PROBLEMS

1. What is the beta of a portfolio with $E(r_p) = 18$ percent, if $r_f = 6$ percent and $E(r_M) = 14$ percent?

2. The market price of a security is $50. Its expected rate of return is 14 percent. The risk-free rate is 6 percent and the market risk premium is 8.5 percent. What will be the market price of the security if its covariance with the market portfolio doubles (and all other variables remain unchanged)?

3. You are a consultant to a large manufacturing corporation that is considering a project with the following net after-tax cash flows (in millions of dollars):

Years from Now	After-Tax Cash Flow
0	–40
1–10	15

The project's beta is 1.7. Assuming that $r_f = 8$ percent and $E(r_M) = 16$ percent, what is the net present value of the project? What is the highest possible beta estimate for the project before its NPV becomes negative?

4. Are the following statements true or false?

a. Stocks with a beta of zero offer an expected rate of return of zero.

b. The CAPM implies that investors require a higher return to hold highly volatile securities.

c. You can construct a portfolio with a beta of .75 by investing .75 of the budget in bills and the remainder in the market portfolio.

5. Consider the following table, which gives a security analyst's expected return on two stocks for two particular market returns:

Market Return	Aggressive Stock	Defensive Stock
.05	−.02	.06
.25	.38	.12

a. What are the betas of the two stocks?

b. What is the expected rate of return on each stock if the market return is equally likely to be 5 percent or 25 percent?

c. If the T-bill rate is 6 percent and the market return is equally likely to be 5 percent or 25 percent, draw the SML for this economy.

d. Plot the two securities on the SML graph. What are the alphas of each?

e. What hurdle rate should be used by the management of the aggressive firm for a project with the risk characteristics of the defensive firm's stock?

If the simple CAPM is valid, which of the following situations in problems 6–12 are possible? Explain. Consider each situation independently.

6.

Portfolio	Expected Return	Beta
A	.20	1.4
B	.25	1.2

7.

Portfolio	Expected Return	Standard Deviation
A	.30	.35
B	.40	.25

8.

Portfolio	Expected Return	Standard Deviation
Risk-free	.10	0
Market	.18	.24
A	.16	.12

9.

Portfolio	Expected Return	Standard Deviation
Risk-free	.10	0
Market	.18	.24
A	.20	.22

10.

Portfolio	Expected Return	Beta
Risk-free	.10	0
Market	.18	1.0
A	.16	1.5

11.

Portfolio	Expected Return	Beta
Risk-free	.10	0
Market	.18	1.0
A	.16	.9

12.

Portfolio	Expected Return	Standard Deviation
Risk-free	.10	0
Market	.18	.24
A	.16	.22

In problems 13–15, assume that the risk-free rate of interest is 6 percent and the expected rate of return on the market is 16 percent.

13. A share of stock sells for $50 today. It will pay a dividend of $6 per share at the end of the year. Its beta is 1.2. What do investors expect the stock to sell for at the end of the year?

14. I am buying a firm with an expected cash flow of $1,000 but am unsure of its risk. If I think the beta of the firm is 0.5, when in fact the beta is really 1, how much *more* will I offer for the firm than it is truly worth?

15. A stock has an expected rate of return of 4 percent. What is its beta?

16. Two investment advisors are comparing performance. One averaged a 19 percent rate of return and the other a 16 percent rate of return. However, the beta of the first investor was 1.5, whereas that of the second was 1.

a. Can you tell which investor was a better predictor of individual stocks (aside from the issue of general movements in the market)?

b. If the T-bill rate were 6 percent and the market return during the period were 14 percent, which investor would be the superior stock selector?

c. What if the T-bill rate were 3 percent and the market return were 15 percent?

17. In 1999, the rate of return on short-term government securities (perceived to be risk-free) was about 5 percent. Suppose the expected rate of return required by the market for a portfolio with a beta measure of 1 is 12 percent. According to the capital asset pricing model (security market line),

a. What is the expected rate of return on the market portfolio?

b. What would be the expected rate of return on a stock with $\beta = 0$?

c. Suppose you consider buying a share of stock at $40. The stock is expected to pay $3 in dividends next year and to sell then for $41. The stock risk has been evaluated by $\beta = -.5$. Is the stock overpriced or underpriced?

18. Suppose that you can invest risk-free at rate r_f but can borrow only at a higher rate, r^B_f. This case was first considered in Section 6.11.

a. Draw a minimum-variance frontier. Show on the graph the risky portfolio that will be selected by defensive investors. Show the portfolio that will be selected by aggressive investors.

b. What portfolios will be selected by investors who neither borrow nor lend?

c. Where will the market portfolio lie on the efficient frontier?

d. Will the zero-beta CAPM be valid in this scenario? Explain. Show graphically the expected return on the zero-beta portfolio.

19. Consider an economy with two classes of investors. Tax-exempt investors can borrow or lend at the safe rate, r_f. Taxed investors pay tax rate t on all interest income, so their net-of-tax safe interest rate is $r_f(1 - t)$. Show that the zero-beta CAPM will apply to this economy and that $(1 - t)r_f < E[r_{Z(M)}] < r_f$.

20. Suppose that borrowing is restricted so that the zero-beta version of the CAPM holds. The expected return on the market portfolio is 17 percent, and on the zero-beta portfolio it is 8 percent. What is the expected return on a portfolio with a beta of 0.6?

CFA® PROBLEMS

21. The security market line depicts

a. A security's expected return as a function of its systematic risk

b. The market portfolio as the optimal portfolio of risky securities

c. The relationship between a security's return and the return on an index

d. The complete portfolio as a combination of the market portfolio and the risk-free asset

CFA® PROBLEMS

22. Within the context of the capital asset pricing model (CAPM), assume:

- Expected return on the market = 15 percent
- Risk-free rate = 8 percent
- Expected rate of return on XYZ security = 17 percent
- Beta of XYZ security = 1.25

Which *one* of the following is *correct*?

a. XYZ is overpriced.

b. XYZ is fairly priced.

c. XYZ's alpha is –.25 percent.

d. XYZ's alpha is .25 percent.

CFA® PROBLEMS

23. What is the expected return of a zero-beta security?

a. Market rate of return

b. Zero rate of return

c. Negative rate of return

d. Risk-free rate of return

CFA® PROBLEMS

24. Capital asset pricing theory asserts that portfolio returns are best explained by

a. Economic factors

b. Specific risk

c. Systematic risk

d. Diversification

CFA® PROBLEMS

25. According to CAPM, the expected rate of return of a portfolio with a beta of 1.0 and an alpha of 0 is

a. Between r_M and r_f

b. The risk-free rate, r_f

c. $\beta(r_M - r_f)$

d. The expected return on the market, r_M

The following table shows risk and return measures for two portfolios.

Portfolio	Average Annual Rate of Return	Standard Deviation	Beta
R	11%	10%	0.5
S&P 500	14%	12%	1.0

CFA® PROBLEMS

26. When plotting portfolio R on the preceding table relative to the SML, portfolio R lies

a. On the SML

b. Below the SML

c. Above the SML

d. Insufficient data given

CFA® PROBLEMS

27. When plotting portfolio R relative to the capital market line, portfolio R lies

a. On the CML

b. Below the CML

c. Above the CML

d. Insufficient data given

CFA® PROBLEMS

28. Briefly explain whether investors should expect a higher return from holding portfolio A versus portfolio B under the CAPM. Assume that both portfolios are fully diversified.

	Portfolio A	**Portfolio B**
Systematic risk (beta)	1.0	1.0
Specific risk for each individual security	High	Low

CFA® PROBLEMS

29. Joan McKay is a portfolio manager for a bank trust department. McKay meets with two clients, Kevin Murray and Lisa York, to review their investment objectives. Each client expresses an interest in changing his or her individual investment objectives. Both clients currently hold well-diversified portfolios of risky assets.

a. Murray wants to increase the expected return of his portfolio. State what action McKay should take to achieve Murray's objective. Justify your response in the context of the Capital Market Line.

b. York wants to reduce the risk exposure of her portfolio but does not want to engage in borrowing or lending activities to do so. State what action McKay should take to achieve York's objective. Justify your response in the context of the Security Market Line.

30. *a.* A mutual fund with beta of .8 has an expected rate of return of 14 percent. If r_f 5 percent, and you expect the rate of return on the market portfolio to be 15 percent, should you invest in this fund? What is the fund's alpha?

b. What passive portfolio consisting of a market-index portfolio and a money market account would have the same beta as the fund? Show that the difference between the expected rate of return on this passive portfolio and that of the fund equals the alpha from part (a).

CFA® PROBLEMS

31. Karen Kay, a portfolio manager at Collins Asset Management, is using the capital asset pricing model for making recommendations to her clients. Her research department has developed the information shown in the following exhibit.

Forecast Returns, Standard Deviations, and Betas

	Forecast Return	**Standard Deviation**	**Beta**
Stock X	14.0%	36%	0.8
Stock Y	17.0	25	1.5
Market index	14.0	15	1.0
Risk-free rate	5.0		

a. Calculate expected return and alpha for each stock.

b. Identify and justify which stock would be more appropriate for an investor who wants to

i. Add this stock to a well-diversified equity portfolio

ii. Hold this stock as a single-stock portfolio

STANDARD &POOR'S

Enter the Market Insight database at **www.mhhe.com/business/finance/edumarket insight** and link to *Company,* then *Population.* Select a Canadian company of interest to you and link to the Company Research page with a menu of company information reports on the left. Go to the *Excel Analytics, Valuation Data,* and review the *Profitability* report. Using current risk-free rates (available at **www.bankofcanada.ca**), and the historical risk premiums discussed in Chapter 5, estimate the expected rate of return on your company's stock by using the CAPM.

E-INVESTMENTS

Beta and Security Returns

Fidelity provides data on the risk and return of its funds at **www.fidelity.com**. Find the annual return and beta of one of Fidelity's equity funds over the last year. Click on *Research*, then *Mutual Funds*, then under *Fund Facts* type the name, symbol, etc. of the fund. Then click *Snapshot*. Use the CAPM to estimate the required rate of return and calculate the alpha of the fund over the most recent annual period. You can find recent performance of several market indices at **finance.yahoo.com**. Yahoo! also contains current Treasury rates (click on *Bonds—Rates*). What market risk premium seems reasonable to you? You will want to look back at Chapter 5. How have the Fidelity funds done for their investors?

APPENDIX 7A: DEMAND FOR STOCKS AND EQUILIBRIUM PRICES

We have been concerned with efficient diversification, the optimal risky portfolio and its risk-return profile. We haven't had much to say about how expected returns are determined in a competitive securities market. To understand how market equilibrium is formed we need to connect the determination of optimal portfolios with security analysis and the actual buy/sell transactions of investors. We will show in this section how the quest for efficient diversification leads to a demand schedule for shares. In turn, the supply and demand for shares determine equilibrium prices and expected rates of return.

Imagine a simple world with only two corporations: Bottom Up Inc. (BU) and Top Down Inc. (TD). Stock prices and market values are shown in Table 7A.1. Investors can also invest in a money market fund (MMF) which yields a risk-free interest rate of 5 percent.

Sigma Fund is a new actively managed mutual fund that has raised $220 million to invest in the stock market. The security analysis staff of Sigma believes that neither BU nor TD will grow in the future and therefore, that each firm will pay level annual dividends for the foreseeable future. This is a useful simplifying assumption because, if a stock is expected to pay a stream of level dividends, the income derived from each share is a perpetuity. Therefore, the present value of each share—often called the *intrinsic value* of the share—equals the dividend divided by the appropriate discount rate. A summary of the report of the security analysts appears in Table 7A.2.

The expected returns in Table 7A.2 are based on the assumption that next year's dividends will conform to Sigma's forecasts, and share prices will be equal to intrinsic values at year-end. The standard deviations and the correlation coefficient between the two stocks were estimated by Sigma's security analysts from past returns and assumed to remain at these levels for the coming year.

Table 7A.1 Share Prices and Market Values of Bottom Up (BU) and Top Down (TD)

	BU	TD
Price per share ($)	39.00	39.00
Shares outstanding	5,000,000	4,000,000
Market value ($ millions)	195	156

Table 7A.2 Capital Market Expectations of Portfolio Manager

		BU	TD
Expected annual dividend ($/share)		6.40	3.80
Discount rate = Required return* (%)		16	10
Expected end-of-year price† ($/share)		40	38
Current price		39	39
Expected return (%):	Capital gain	2.56	−2.56
	Dividend yield	16.41	9.74
Total expected return for the year		18.97	7.18
Standard deviation of rate of return		40%	20%
Correlation coefficient between rates of return on BU and TD		.20	

*Based on assessment of risk.
†Obtained by discounting the dividend perpetuity at the required rate of return.

Using these data and assumptions Sigma easily generates the efficient frontier shown in Figure 7A.1 and computes the optimal portfolio proportions corresponding to the tangency portfolio. These proportions, combined with the total investment budget, yield the fund's buy orders. With a budget of \$220 million, Sigma wants a position in BU of \$220,000,000 × .8070 = \$177,540,000, or \$177,540,000/39 = 4,552,308 shares, and a position in TD of \$220,000,000 × .1930 = \$42,460,000, which corresponds to 1,088,718 shares.

Sigma's Demand for Shares

The expected rates of return that Sigma used to derive its demand for shares of BU and TD were computed from the forecast of year-end stock prices and the current prices. If, say, a share of BU could be purchased at a lower price, Sigma's forecast of the rate of return on BU would be higher. Conversely, if BU shares were selling at a higher price, expected returns would be lower. A new expected return would result in a different optimal portfolio and a different demand for shares.

Figure 7A.1 Sigma's efficient frontier and optimal portfolio.

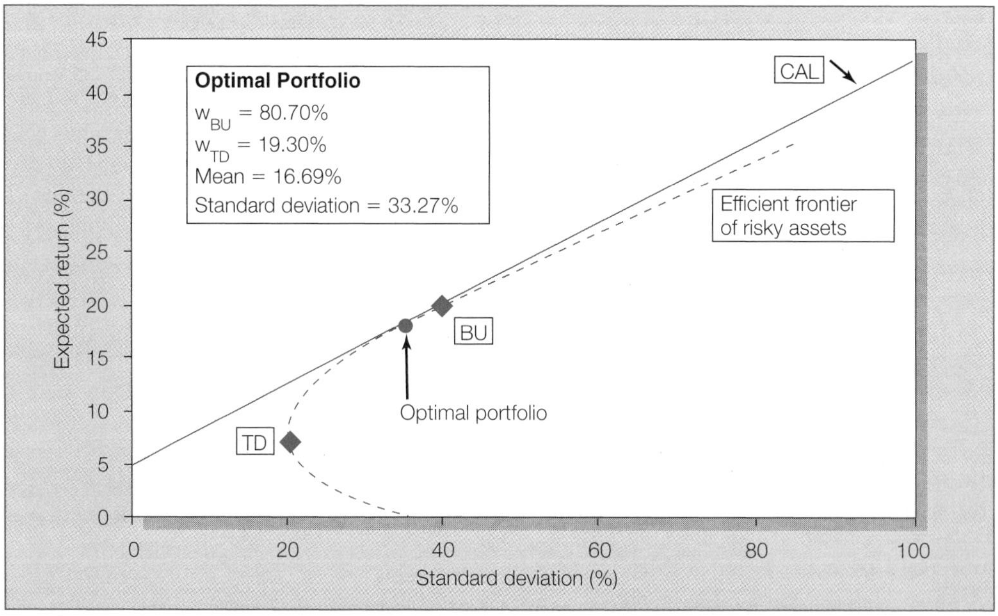

Table 7A.3 Calculation of Sigma's Demand for BU Shares

Current Price ($)	Capital Gain (%)	Dividend Yield (%)	Expected Return (%)	BU Optimal Proportion	Desired BU Shares
45.0	−11.11	14.22	3.11	−.4113	−2,010,582
42.5	−5.88	15.06	9.18	.3192	1,652,482
40.0	0	16.00	16.00	.7011	3,856,053
37.5	6.67	17.07	23.73	.9358	5,490,247
35.0	14.29	18.29	32.58	1.0947	6,881,225

We can think of Sigma's demand schedule for a stock as the number of shares Sigma would want to hold at different share prices. In our simplified world, producing the demand for BU shares is not difficult. First, we revise Table 7A.2 to recompute the expected return on BU at different current prices given the forecasted year-end price. Then, for each price and associated expected return, we construct the optimal portfolio and find the implied position in BU. A few samples of these calculations are shown in Table 7A.3. The first four columns in Table 7A.3 show the expected returns on BU shares given their current price. The optimal proportion (column 5) is calculated using these expected returns. Finally, Sigma's investment budget, the optimal proportion in BU and the current price of a BU share determine the desired number of shares. Note that we compute the demand for BU shares *given* the price and expected return for TD. This means that the entire demand schedule must be revised whenever the price and expected return on TD is changed.

Sigma's demand curve for BU stock is given by the Desired Shares column in Table 7A.3 and is plotted in Figure 7A.2. Notice that the demand curve for the stock slopes downward. When BU's stock price falls, Sigma will desire more shares for two reasons: (1) an income effect—at a lower price Sigma can purchase more shares with the same budget, and (2) a substitution effect—the increased expected return at the lower price will make BU shares more attractive relative to TD shares. Notice that one can desire a negative number of shares, that is, a short position. If the stock price is high enough, its expected return will be so low that the desire to sell will overwhelm diversification

Figure 7A.2 Supply and demand for BU shares.

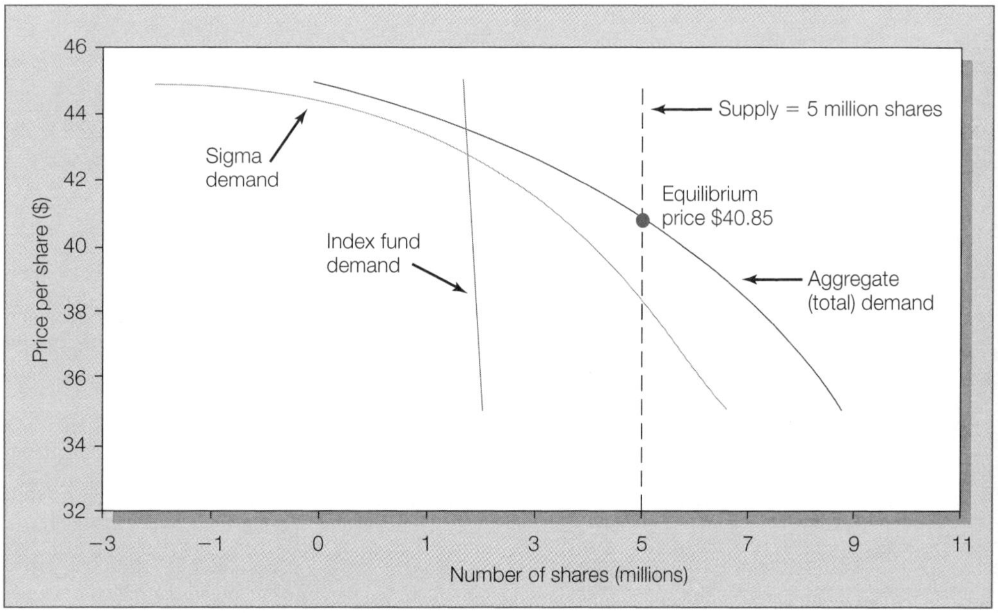

motives and investors will want to take a short position. Figure 7A.2 shows that when the price exceeds \$44, Sigma wants a short position in BU.

The demand curve for BU shares assumes that the price and therefore expected return of TD remain constant. A similar demand curve can be constructed for TD shares given a price for BU shares. As before, we would generate the demand for TD shares by revising Table 7A.2 for various current prices of TD, leaving the price of BU unchanged. We use the revised expected returns to calculate the optimal portfolio for each possible price of TD, ultimately obtaining the demand curve shown in Figure 7A.3.

Index Funds' Demands for Stock

We will see shortly that index funds play an important role in portfolio selection, so let's see how an index fund would derive its demand for shares. Suppose that \$130 million of investor funds in our hypothesized economy are given to an index fund—named Index—to manage. What will it do?

Index is looking for a portfolio that will mimic the market. Suppose current prices and market values are as in Table 7A.1. Then the required proportions to mimic the market portfolio are:

$$w_{BU} = 195/(195 + 156) = .5556\ (55.56\%);\ w_{TD} = 1 - .5556 = .4444\ (44.44\%)$$

With \$130 million to invest, Index will place .5556 × \$130 million = \$72.22 million in BU shares. Table 7A.4 shows a few other points on Index's demand curve for BU shares. The second column of the table shows the proportion of BU in total stock market value at each assumed price. In our two-stock example, this is BU's value as a fraction of the combined value of BU and TD. The third column is Index's desired dollar investment in BU and the last column shows shares demanded. The bold row corresponds to the case we analyzed in Table 7A.1, for which BU is selling at \$39.

Index's demand curve for BU shares is plotted in Figure 7A.2 next to Sigma's demand, and in Figure 7A.3 for TD shares. Index's demand is smaller than Sigma's because its budget is smaller. Moreover, the demand curve of the index fund is very steep, or "inelastic," that is, demand hardly responds to price changes. This is because an index fund's demand for shares does not respond to expected returns. Index funds seek only to replicate market proportions. As the stock price goes up, so does its proportion in the market. This leads the index fund to invest more in the stock. Nevertheless, because each share costs more, the fund will desire fewer shares.

Figure 7A.3 Supply and demand for TD shares.

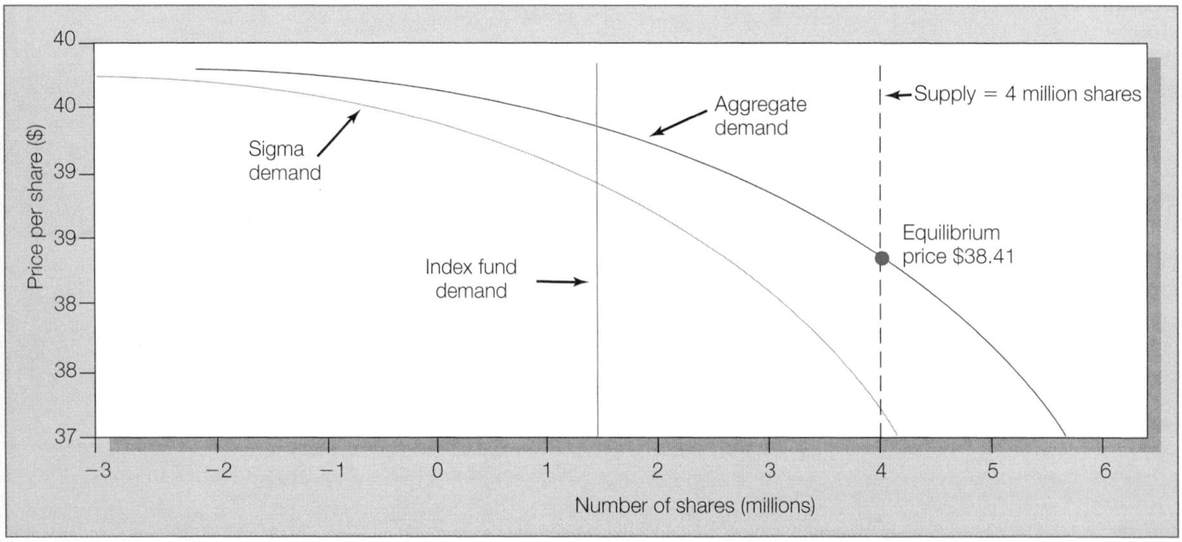

Table 7A.4 Calculation of Index Demand for BU Shares

Current Price	BU Market Value Proportion	Dollar Investment* ($ million)	Shares Desired
$45.00	.5906	76.772	1,706,037
42.50	.5767	74.966	1,763,908
40.00	.5618	73.034	1,825,843
39.00	**.5556**	**72.222**	**1,851,852**
37.50	.5459	70.961	1,892,285
35.00	.5287	68.731	1,963,746

*Dollar investment = BU proportion × $130 million.

Equilibrium Prices and the Capital Asset Pricing Model

Market prices are determined by supply and demand. At any one time, the supply of shares of a stock is fixed, so supply is vertical at 5,000,000 shares of BU in Figure 7A.2 and 4,000,000 shares of TD in Figure 7A.3. Market demand is obtained by "horizontal aggregation," that is, for each price we add up the quantity demanded by all investors. You can examine the horizontal aggregation of the demand curves of Sigma and Index in Figures 7A.2 and 7A.3. The equilibrium prices are at the intersection of supply and demand.

However, the prices shown in Figures 7A.2 and 7A.3 will likely not persist for more than an instant. The reason is that the equilibrium price of BU ($40.85) was generated by demand curves derived by assuming that the price of TD was $39. Similarly, the equilibrium price of TD ($38.41) is an equilibrium price only when BU is at $39, which also is not the case. A full equilibrium would require that the demand curves derived for each stock be consistent with the actual prices of all other stocks. Thus, our model is only a beginning. But it does illustrate the important link between security analysis and the process by which portfolio demands, market prices, and expected returns are jointly determined. The CAPM treats the problem of finding a set of mutually consistent equilibrium prices and expected rates of return across all stocks. The model here illustrates the process that underlies the adjustment of market expected returns to demand pressures.

One might wonder why we originally posited that Sigma expects BU's share price to increase only by year-end when we have just argued that the adjustment to the new equilibrium price ought to be instantaneous. The reason is that when Sigma observes a market price of $39, it must assume that this is an equilibrium price based on investor beliefs *at the time*. Sigma believes that the market will catch up to its (presumably) superior estimate of intrinsic value of the firm by year-end, when its better assessment about the firm becomes widely adopted. In our simple example, Sigma is the only active manager, so its demand for "low-priced" BU stock would move the price immediately. But more realistically, since Sigma would be a small player compared to the entire stock market, the stock price would barely move in response to Sigma's demand, and the price would remain around $39 until Sigma's assessment was adopted by the average investor.

CHAPTER EIGHT

INDEX MODELS AND THE ARBITRAGE PRICING THEORY

The exploitation of security mispricing in such a way that risk-free economic profits may be earned is called **arbitrage**. It involves the simultaneous purchase and sale of equivalent securities in order to profit from discrepancies in their price relationship. The concept of arbitrage is central to the theory of capital markets. This chapter discusses the nature, and illustrates the use, of arbitrage.

Perhaps the most basic principle of capital market theory is that equilibrium market prices are rational: they rule out arbitrage opportunities. If actual security prices allow for arbitrage, the result will be strong pressure on security prices to restore equilibrium. Therefore, security markets ought to satisfy a "no arbitrage condition."

In this chapter, we show how such no-arbitrage conditions allow us to generalize the security market line of the CAPM to gain richer insight into the risk-return relationship.

We show how the decomposition of risk into market versus firm-specific influences introduced in the chapter can be extended to deal with the multifaceted nature of systematic risk. Multifactor models of security returns can be used to measure and manage exposure to each of many economywide factors such as business-cycle risk, interest or inflation rate risk, energy price risk, and so on. These models also lead us to a multifactor version of the security market line in which each factor is a separate source of risk with its own risk premium. This approach to the risk-return tradeoff is called arbitrage pricing theory or APT. We derive the APT and show why it implies a multifactor security market line. We also discuss the relation of the APT to a multifactor version of the CAPM.

A single-factor APT is based on the assumption that only one systematic common factor affects the returns of all securities. This assumption, however, was also at the origin of another class of models, known as *index* or *market models*, that predate the APT by several years. These models are initially introduced in order to simplify the computations of the Markowitz portfolio selection model. Since they also offer significant new insights into the nature of systematic risk versus firm-specific risk and constitute a good introduction to the concept of factor models of security returns, they will be examined in the first sections of this chapter.

8.1 A SINGLE-INDEX SECURITY MARKET

Systematic Risk Versus Firm-Specific Risk

The success of a portfolio selection rule depends on the quality of the input list, that is, the estimates of expected security returns and the covariance matrix. In the long run, efficient portfolios will beat portfolios with less reliable input lists and consequently inferior reward-to-risk tradeoffs.

Suppose your security analysts can thoroughly analyze 50 stocks. This means that your input list will include the following:

$$
\begin{aligned}
n &= \quad 50 \text{ estimates of expected returns} \\
n &= \quad 50 \text{ estimates of variances} \\
(n^2 - n)/2 &= 1{,}225 \text{ estimates of covariances} \\
& \quad\; 1{,}325 \text{ estimates}
\end{aligned}
$$

This is a formidable task, particularly in the light of the fact that a 50-security portfolio is relatively small. Doubling n to 100 will nearly quadruple the number of estimates to 5,150. If n = 1,600, roughly the number of TSX-listed stocks in 1990, we need nearly 1.3 *million* estimates.

Another difficulty in applying the Markowitz model to portfolio optimization is that errors in the assessment or estimation of correlation coefficients can lead to nonsensical results. This can happen because some sets of correlation coefficients are mutually inconsistent, as the following example demonstrates:[1]

		Correlation Matrix		
Asset	**Standard Deviation (%)**	**A**	**B**	**C**
A	20	1.00	0.90	0.90
B	20	0.90	1.00	0.00
C	20	0.90	0.00	1.00

[1]We are grateful to Andy Kaplin for this example.

Suppose that you construct a portfolio with weights: –1.00; 1.00; 1.00, for assets A; B; C, respectively, and calculate the portfolio variance. You will find that the portfolio variance appears to be negative (–200). This of course is not possible because portfolio variances cannot be negative: we conclude that the inputs in the estimated correlation matrix must be mutually inconsistent. Of course, *true* correlation coefficients are always consistent.[2] But we do not know these true correlations and can only estimate them with some imprecision. Unfortunately, it is difficult to determine whether a correlation matrix is inconsistent, providing another motivation to seek a model that is easier to implement.

Covariances between security returns tend to be positive because the same economic forces affect the fortunes of many firms. Some examples of common economic factors are business cycles, inflation, money-supply changes, technological changes, and cost of labour and raw materials. All these (interrelated) factors affect almost all firms. Thus unexpected changes in these variables cause, simultaneously, unexpected changes in the rates of return on the entire stock market.

Suppose that we group all relevant factors into one macroeconomic indicator and assume that it moves the security market as a whole. We further assume that, beyond this common effect, all remaining uncertainty in stock returns is firm-specific; that is, there is no other source of correlation between securities. Firm-specific events would include new inventions, deaths of key employees, and other factors that affect the fortune of the individual firm without affecting the broad economy in a measurable way.

We can summarize the distinction between macroeconomic and firm-specific factors by writing the return, r_i, realized on any security during some holding period as

$$r_i = E(r_i) + m_i + e_i \tag{8.1}$$

where $E(R_i)$ is the expected return on the security as of the beginning of the holding period, m_i is the impact of unanticipated macroevents on the security's return during the period, and e_i is the impact of unanticipated firm-specific events. Both m_i and e_i have zero expected values because each represents the impact of unanticipated events, which by definition must average out to zero.

We can gain further insight by recognizing that different firms have different sensitivities to macroeconomic events. Thus, if we denote the unanticipated component of the macro factor by F, and denote the responsiveness of security i to macroevents by beta, β_i, then equation 8.1 becomes[3]

$$r_i = E(r_i) + \beta_i F + e_i \tag{8.2}$$

Equation 8.2 is known as a **single-factor model** for stock returns. It is easy to imagine that a more realistic decomposition of security returns would require more than one factor in equation 8.2. We treat this issue in subsequent sections. For now, let us examine the easy case with only one macro factor.

Of course, a single-factor model is of little use without specifying a way to measure the factor that is posited to affect security returns. One reasonable approach is to assert that the rate of return on a broad index of securities such as the S&P/TSX Composite is a valid proxy for the common macro factor. This approach leads to an equation similar to the single-factor model, which is called a **single-index model** because it uses the market index to proxy for the common or systematic factor.

According to the index model, we can separate the actual or realized rate of return on a security into macro (systematic) and micro (firm-specific) components in a manner similar to that in equation 8.2. We write the rate of return on each security as a sum of three components:

---

[2]The mathematical term for a correlation matrix that cannot generate negative portfolio variance is *positive definite*.

[3]You may wonder why we choose the notation β for the responsiveness coefficient, since β already has been defined in Chapter 7 in the context of the CAPM. The choice is deliberate, however. Our reason will be obvious shortly.

	Symbol
1. The stock's expected return if the market is neutral, that is, if the market's excess return, $r_M - r_f$, is zero	α_i
2. The component of return due to movements in the overall market; β_i is the security's responsiveness to market movements	$\beta_i(r_M - r_f)$
3. The unexpected component due to unexpected events that are relevant only to this security (firm-specific)	e_i

The holding period excess rate of return on the stock, which measures the stock's relative performance, then can be stated as

$$r_i - r_f = \alpha_i + \beta_i(r_M - r_f) + e_i$$

Let us denote security excess returns over the risk-free rate using capital R and so rewrite this equation as

$$R_i = \alpha_i + \beta_i R_M + e_i \tag{8.3}$$

We write the index model in terms of excess returns over r_f rather than in terms of total returns, because the level of the stock market return represents the state of the macroeconomy only to the extent that it exceeds or falls short of the rate of return on risk-free T-bills. For example, in the 1950s, when T-bills were yielding only a 3 percent or 4 percent rate of return, a return of 8 percent or 9 percent on the stock market would be considered good news. In contrast, in the early 1980s, when bills were yielding over 10 percent, that same 8 percent or 9 percent stock market return would signal disappointing macroeconomic news.[4]

Equation 8.3 says that each security therefore has two sources of risk: *market or "systematic" risk*, attributable to its sensitivity to macroeconomic factors as reflected in R_M, and *firm-specific risk* as reflected in e. If we denote the variance of the excess return on the market, R_M, as σ^2_M, then we can break the variance of the rate of return on each stock into two components:

	Symbol
1. The variance attributable to the uncertainty of the common macroeconomic factors	$\beta^2_i\sigma^2_M$
2. The variance attributable to firm-specific uncertainty	$\sigma^2(e_i)$

The covariance between R_M and e_i is zero because e_i is defined as firm-specific, that is, independent of movements in the market. Hence, the variance of the rate of return on security i, is

$$\sigma^2_i = \beta^2_i\sigma^2_M + \sigma^2(e_i)$$

The covariance between the excess rates of return on two stocks, for example, R_i and R_j, derives only from the common factor, R_M, because e_i and e_j are each firm-specific and therefore presumed to be uncorrelated. Hence, the covariance between two stocks is

$$\text{Cov}(R_i, R_j) = \text{Cov}(\beta_i R_M, \beta_j R_M) = \beta_i\beta_j\sigma^2_M \tag{8.4}$$

These calculations show that if we have

n estimates of the expected returns, $E(R_i)$
n estimates of the sensitivity coefficients, β_i
n estimates of the firm-specific variances, $\sigma^2(e_i)$
1 estimate for the variance of the (common) macroeconomic factor, σ^2_M

[4]In practice, however, a "modified" index model is often used that is similar to equation 8.3 except that it uses total rather than excess returns. This practice is most common when daily data are used. In this case, the rate of return on bills is on the order of only about .02 percent per day, so total and excess returns are almost indistinguishable.

then these $(3n + 1)$ estimates will enable us to prepare the input list for this single-index security universe. Thus for a 50-security portfolio we will need 151 estimates, rather than 1,325, and for a 100-security portfolio we will need only 301 estimates, rather than 5,150.

It is easy to see why the index model is such a useful abstraction. For large universes of securities, the data estimates required for this model are only a small fraction of what otherwise would be needed.

Another advantage is less obvious but equally important. The index model abstraction is crucial for specialization of effort in security analysis. If a covariance term had to be calculated directly for each security pair, then security analysts could not specialize by industry. For example, if one group were to specialize in the retail industry and another in the banking industry, who would have the common background necessary to estimate the covariance *between* Canadian Tire and CIBC? Neither group would have the deep understanding of other industries necessary to make an informed judgment of co-movements among industries. In contrast, the index model suggests a simple way to compute covariances. Covariances among securities are due to the influence of the single common factor, represented by the market index return, and can be easily estimated using equation 8.4.

www.cibc.com

The simplification derived from the index model assumption is, however, not without cost. The "cost" of the model lies in the restrictions it places on the structure of asset return uncertainty. The classification of uncertainty into a simple dichotomy—macro versus micro risk—oversimplifies sources of real-world uncertainty and misses some important sources of dependence in stock returns. For example, this dichotomy rules out industry events, events that may affect many firms within an industry without substantially affecting the broad macroeconomy.

Statistical analysis shows that the firm-specific components of some firms are correlated. Examples are the nonmarket components of stocks in a single industry, such as retail stocks or banking stocks. At the same time, statistical significance does not always correspond to economic significance. Economically speaking, the question that is more relevant to the assumption of a single-index model is whether portfolios constructed using covariances that are estimated on the basis of the single-factor or single-index assumption are significantly different from, and less efficient than, portfolios constructed using covariances that are estimated directly for each pair of stocks. In Part Seven on active portfolio management, we explore this issue further.

CONCEPT CHECK

1. Suppose that the index model for stocks A and B is estimated with the following results:

$$R_A = .01 + .9R_M + e_A$$
$$R_B = -.02 + 1.1R_M + e_B$$
$$\sigma_M = .20$$
$$\sigma(e_A) = .3$$
$$\sigma(e_B) = .1$$

Find the standard deviation of each stock and the covariance between them.

Estimating the Index Model

Equation 8.3 also suggests how we might go about actually measuring market and firm-specific risk. Suppose that we observe the excess return on the market index and a specific asset over a number of holding periods. We use as an example hypothetical monthly excess returns on the S&P/TSX Composite index and X stock. We can summarize the results for a sample period in a **scatter diagram**, as illustrated in Figure 8.1.

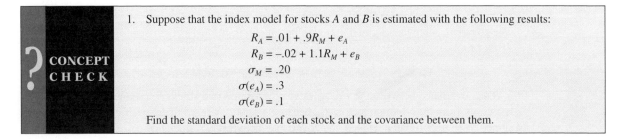

The horizontal axis in Figure 8.1 measures the excess return (over the risk-free rate) on the market index, whereas the vertical axis measures the excess return on the asset in question (X stock in our example). A pair of excess returns (one for the market index, one for X stock) over a holding period constitutes one point on this scatter diagram. The points are numbered 1–12, representing excess returns for the S&P/TSX Composite and X for each month from January to December. The single-index model states that the relationship between the excess returns on X and the Composite is given by

$$R_{Xt} = \alpha_X + \beta_X R_{Mt} + e_X$$

Note the resemblance of this relationship to a **regression equation**.

In a single-variable linear regression equation, the dependent variable plots around a straight line with an intercept α and a slope β. The deviations from the line, e_t, are assumed to be mutually independent and independent of the right-hand variable. Because these assumptions are identical to those of the index model, we can look at the index model as a regression model. The sensitivity of X to the market, measured by β_X, is the slope of the regression line. The intercept of the regression line is α, and deviations of particular observations from the regression line are denoted e. These **residuals** are the parts of stock returns not explained by the independent variable (the market-index return); therefore they measure the impact of firm-specific events during the particular month. The parameters of interest, α, β, and Var(e), can be estimated using standard regression techniques.

Estimating the regression equation of the single-index model gives us the **security characteristic line (SCL)**, which is plotted in Figure 8.1. (The regression results and raw data appear in Table 8.1.) The SCL is a plot of the typical excess return on a security over the risk-free rate as a function of the excess return on the market.

This sample of holding period returns is, of course, too small to yield reliable statistics. We use it only for demonstration. For this sample period we find that the beta coefficient of X stock, as estimated by the slope of the regression line, is 1.1357, and that the intercept for this SCL is –2.59 percent per month.

Figure 8.1 Characteristic line for X.

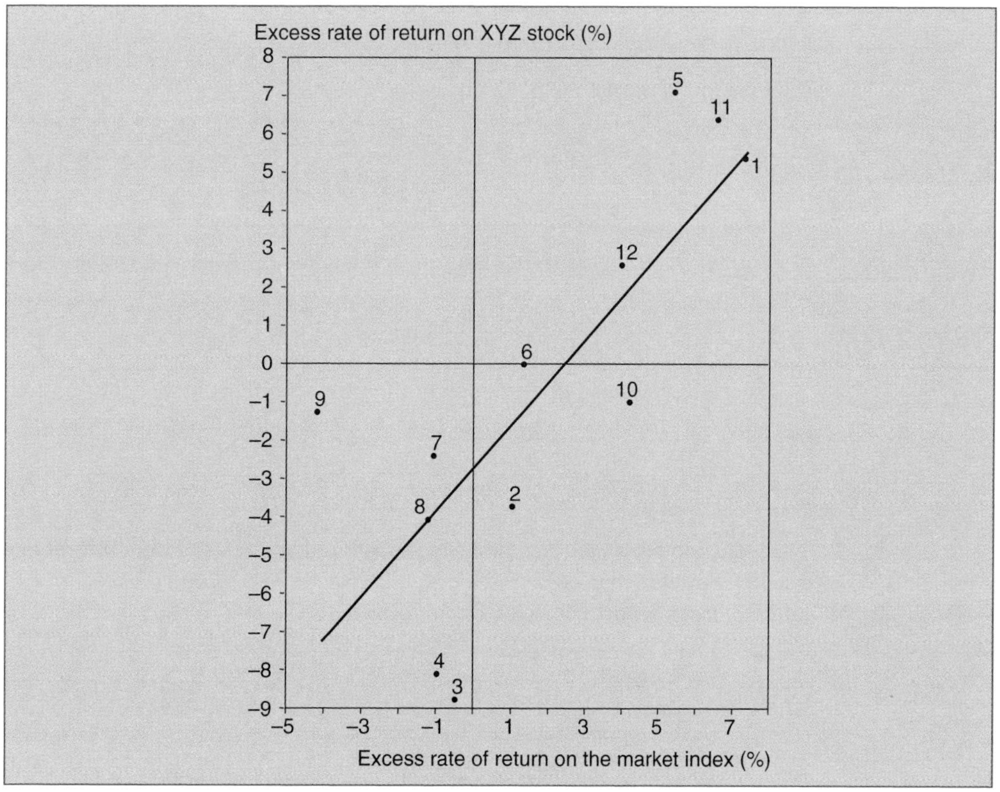

Table 8.1 Characteristic Line for X Stock

Month	X Return	Market Return	Monthly T-Bill Rate	Excess X Return	Excess Market Return
January	6.06	7.89	0.65	5.41	7.24
February	−2.86	1.51	0.58	3.44	0.93
March	−8.18	0.23	0.62	−8.79	−0.38
April	−7.36	−0.29	0.72	−8.08	−1.01
May	7.76	5.58	0.66	7.10	4.92
June	0.52	1.73	0.55	−0.03	1.18
July	−1.74	−0.21	0.62	−2.36	−0.83
August	−3.00	−0.36	0.55	−3.55	−0.91
September	−0.56	−3.58	0.60	−1.16	−4.18
October	−0.37	4.62	0.65	−1.02	3.97
November	6.93	6.85	0.61	6.32	6.25
December	3.08	4.55	0.65	2.43	3.90
Mean	0.02	2.38	0.62	−0.60	1.75
Standard deviation	4.97	3.33	0.05	4.97	3.32
Regression results	$r_X - r_f = \alpha + \beta(r_M - r_f)$				
		α	β		
Estimated coefficient		−2.590	1.1357		
Standard error of estimate		(1.547)	(0.309)		
Variance of residuals = 12.601					
Standard deviation of residuals = 3.550					
R-square = 0.575					

For each month, our estimate of the residual, e, which is the deviation of X's excess return from the prediction of the SCL, equals

$$\text{Deviation} = \text{Actual} - \text{Predicted return}$$

$$e_{Xt} = R_{Xt} - (\beta_X R_{Mt} + \alpha_X)$$

These residuals are estimates of the monthly unexpected *firm-specific* component of the rate of return on XYZ stock. Hence we can estimate the firm-specific variance by[5]

$$\sigma^2(e_{Xt}) = \frac{1}{10}\sum_{t=1}^{12} e^2_t = 12.60$$

Therefore, the standard deviation of the firm-specific component of X's return, $\sigma(e_{Xt})$, equals $\sqrt{12.60} = 3.55$ percent per month, equal to the standard deviation of the regression residual.

The Index Model and Diversification

The index model, which was first suggested by Sharpe,[6] also offers insight into portfolio diversification. Suppose that we choose an equally weighted portfolio of n securities. The excess rate of return on each security is given by

---

[5]Because the mean of e_t is zero, e^2_t is the squared deviation from its mean. The average value of e^2_t is therefore the estimate of the variance of the firm-specific component. We divide the sum of squared residuals by the degrees of freedom of the regression, $n - 2 = 12 - 2 = 10$, to obtain an unbiased estimate of $\sigma^2(e)$.

[6]William F. Sharpe, "A Simplified Model of Portfolio Analysis," *Management Science*, January 1963.

$$R_i = \alpha_i + \beta_i R_M + e_i$$

Similarly, we can write the excess return on the portfolio of stocks as

$$R_P = \alpha_P + \beta_P R_M + e_P \tag{8.5}$$

We now show that, as the number of stocks included in this portfolio increases, the part of the portfolio risk attributable to nonmarket factors becomes ever smaller. This part of the risk is diversified away. In contrast, the market risk remains, regardless of the number of firms combined into the portfolio.

To understand these results, note that the excess rate of return on this equally weighted portfolio, for which $w_i = 1/n$, is

$$R_P = \sum_{i=1}^{n} w_i R_i = \frac{1}{n}\sum_{i=1}^{n} R_i = \frac{1}{n}\sum_{i=1}^{n} (\alpha_i + \beta_i R_M + e_i)$$

$$= \frac{1}{n}\sum_{i=1}^{n} \alpha_i + \left(\frac{1}{n}\sum_{i=1}^{n} \beta_i\right) R_M + \frac{1}{n}\sum_{i=1}^{n} e_i \tag{8.6}$$

Comparing equations 8.5 and 8.6, we see that the portfolio has a sensitivity to the market given by

$$\beta_P = \frac{1}{n}\sum_{i=1}^{n} \beta_i$$

(which is the average of the individual β_is), and it has a nonmarket return component of a constant (intercept)

$$\alpha_P = \frac{1}{n}\sum_{i=1}^{n} \alpha_i$$

(which is the average of the individual alphas), plus the zero mean variable

$$e_P = \frac{1}{n}\sum_{i=1}^{n} e_i$$

which is the average of the firm-specific components. Hence the portfolio's variance is

$$\sigma^2{}_P = \beta^2{}_P \sigma^2{}_M + \sigma^2(e_P) \tag{8.7}$$

The systematic risk component of the portfolio variance, which we defined as the part that depends on marketwide movements, is $\beta^2{}_P\sigma^2{}_M$ and depends on the sensitivity coefficients of the individual securities. This part of the risk depends on portfolio beta and $\sigma^2{}_M$ and will persist regardless of the extent of portfolio diversification. No matter how many stocks are held, their common exposure to the market will be reflected in portfolio systematic risk.[7]

In contrast, the nonsystematic component of the portfolio variance is $\sigma^2(e_P)$ and is attributable to firm-specific components, e_i. Because these e_i's are independent, and all have zero expected value, the law of averages can be applied to conclude that as more and more stocks are added to the portfolio, the firm-specific components tend to cancel out, resulting in ever-smaller nonmarket risk. Such risk is thus termed *diversifiable*. To see this more rigorously, examine the formula for the variance of the equally weighted "portfolio" of firm-specific components. Because the e_i's are all uncorrelated,

[7]Of course, one can always construct a portfolio with zero systematic risk by mixing negative β and positive β assets. The point of our discussion is that the vast majority of securities have a positive β, implying that well-diversified portfolios with small holdings in large numbers of assets will indeed have positive systematic risk.

$$\sigma^2(e_P) = \sum_{i=1}^{n} \left(\frac{1}{n}\right)^2 \sigma^2(e_i) = \frac{1}{n}\,\overline{\sigma}^2(e)$$

where $\overline{\sigma}^2(e)$ is the average of the firm-specific variances. Since this average is independent of n, when n gets large, $\overline{\sigma}^2(e_P)$ becomes negligible.

To summarize, as diversification increases, the total variance of a portfolio approaches the systematic variance, defined as the variance of the market factor multiplied by the square of the portfolio sensitivity coefficient, β_P. This is shown in Figure 8.2.

Figure 8.2 shows that, as more and more securities are combined into a portfolio, the portfolio variance decreases because of the diversification of firm-specific risk. However, the power of diversification is limited. Even for very large n, risk remains because of the exposure of virtually all assets to the common, or market, factor. Therefore this systematic risk is said to be nondiversifiable.

This analysis is borne out by empirical analysis. We saw the effect of portfolio diversification on portfolio standard deviations in Figure 6.9. These empirical results are similar to the theoretical graph presented here in Figure 8.2.

The assumption that all security returns can be represented by equation 8.1 is the main assumption of the index model. It can be combined with other assumptions in order to lead to the CAPM. Alternatively, it can be used as the basis of the single-factor APT, examined in later sections.

CONCEPT CHECK

2. Reconsider the two stocks in Concept Check 1. Suppose we form an equally weighted portfolio of A and B. What will be the nonsystematic standard deviation of that portfolio?

Figure 8.2 The variance of a portfolio with β in the single-factor economy.

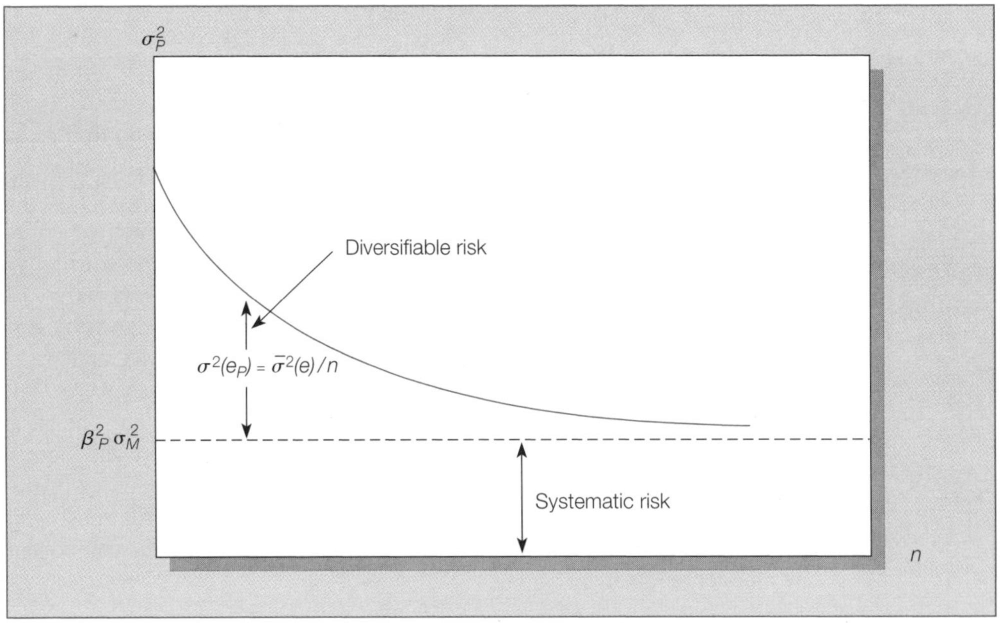

8.2 THE INDUSTRY VERSION OF THE INDEX MODEL

Not surprisingly, the index model has attracted the attention of practitioners. To the extent that it is approximately valid, it provides a convenient benchmark for security analysis. Also, as the boxed article here shows, it can generate instruments that allow investors to invest in the entire market.

A modern practitioner using the CAPM who has no special information about a security or insight that is unavailable to the general public will conclude that the security is "properly" priced. By "properly" priced, the analyst means that the expected return on the security is fair, given its risk, and therefore plots on the security market line. For instance, if one has no private information about Alcan's (AL) stock, then one should expect

$$E(r_{\text{AL}}) = r_f + \beta_{\text{AL}}[E(r_M) - r_f]$$

A portfolio manager who has a forecast for the market index, $E(r_M)$, and observes the risk-free T-bill rate, r_f, can use the model to determine the benchmark expected return for any stock. The beta coefficient, the market risk, $\sigma^2{}_M$, and the firm-specific risk, $\sigma^2(e)$, can be estimated from historical SCLs, that is, from regressions of security excess returns on market index excess returns.

www.bmo.com

There are many sources for such regression results. For instance, the Quantitative Analysis division of BMO Nesbitt Burns Inc. publishes periodic estimates of stock betas. It uses the S&P/TSX Composite index as the proxy for the market portfolio.[8] It relies on the 54 most recent monthly observations to calculate the regression parameters. BMO Nesbitt Burns and most services[9] use total returns, rather than excess returns (deviations from T-bill rates), in their regressions. In this way they estimate a variant of our index model, which is

$$r = a + br_M + e \tag{8.8}$$

instead of

$$r - r_f = \alpha + \beta(r_M - r_f) + e \tag{8.9}$$

To see the effect of this departure, we can rewrite equation 8.9 as

$$r = r_f + \alpha + \beta r_M - \beta r_f + e = \alpha + r_f(1 - \beta) + \beta r_M + e \tag{8.10}$$

Comparing equations 8.8 and 8.10, you can see that if r_f is constant over the sample period both equations have the same independent variable, r_M, and residual, e. Therefore the slope coefficient will be the same in the two regressions.[10]

However, the intercept that BMO Nesbitt Burns calls alpha is really, using the parameters of the CAPM, an estimate of $\alpha + r_f(1 - \beta)$. The apparent justification for this procedure is that, on a monthly basis, $r_f(1 - \beta)$ is small and is apt to be swamped by the volatility of actual stock returns. However, it is worth noting that for $\beta \neq 1$, the regression intercept in equation 8.8 will not equal the CAPM alpha as it does when excess returns are used as in equation 8.9.

Company Beta Estimates

Table 8.2 illustrates some BMO Nesbitt Burns estimates of equation 8.8 for a number of important Canadian firms, for two different non-overlapping periods of 54 months. For each period, after the

---

[8]Although the S&P/TSX Composite is the most easily available and most often used proxy for the market portfolio, it clearly does not include all stocks available for investment to Canadian investors. In addition to many Canadian stocks, it also ignores Canadians' opportunity to invest in foreign stocks. This should be taken into account when interpreting the results.

[9]Merrill Lynch and Value Line are two well-known sources of U.S. betas; Merrill Lynch uses monthly returns and the S&P 500 for the market proxy, while Value Line uses weekly returns and the NYSE index.

[10]Actually, r_f does vary over time and so should not be grouped casually with the constant term in the regression. However, variations in r_f are tiny compared with swings in the market return. The actual volatility in the T-bill rate has only a small impact on the estimated value of beta.

PRAISE FOR INDEX FUNDS

The mutual-fund industry is crowing this RRSP season over the performance of Canadian equity mutual funds, which handily beat the Toronto Stock Exchange's key index in 2001. The TSE 300 [now known as the S&P/TSX] composite index (total return) dropped 12.6 per cent last year while the average Canadian equity fund fell just 4.3 per cent.

But does that underperformance mean investors should turn their backs on funds that passively track market indexes and stick to actively managed funds? Not at all, according to Montreal investment adviser Keith Matthews. Matthews is an expert on exchange-trade funds (ETFs), which trade like stocks but track market indexes. They charge bargain-basement management fees and make low taxable distributions.

Contrary to popular perception, Matthews says index investing actually enjoyed quite a good year in 2001. He notes that the average actively managed mutual fund failed to beat its benchmark index in virtually every asset class except Canadian equity. The index beat average mutual-fund managers in such classes as U.S. equity, European equity, Japanese equity, emerging-markets equity and Canadian bonds. "ETFs are some of the most powerful investment tools available to investors and advisors," said Matthews, a vice-president at fee-based wealth-management firm PWL Capital Inc.

The big reason behind the poor performance of the Canadian equity index vs. actively managed mutual funds last year can be traced to the Nortel Networks effect. During the tech bubble, Nortel ballooned to a weighting of more than 40 per cent of the TSE 300, showering index investors with riches and giving fits to mutual-fund managers forbidden by law from investing more than 10 per cent of their fund in any one stock. The effect was reversed, however, when Nortel plunged. The active mutual funds were rewarded for their underweighting in Nortel and the index funds were punished.

Matthews said the Nortel phenomenon goes to show that index investors need to know what is in the benchmark they're considering and ensure that they're comfortable with its diversification. They should also ensure their portfolio is diversified across asset classes and geographically.

The most popular ETF of 16 available on the Toronto Stock Excange is the i60 fund (ticker XIU), which tracks the S&P/TSE 60 index of Canadian blue-chip stocks. Assets in the i60 now stand at about $4 billion, making it one of the largest Canadian equity funds in the country.

Investors can buy all sorts of other ETFs to track, for example, industrial subindexes or make RRSP-eligible investments in foreign markets for the low management-expense ratio of 0.3 per cent.

The i60 charges a management-expense ratio of just 0.17 per cent. That compares with an average of about 0.9 for index funds offered by the large banks and 2.5 per cent for the average actively managed mutual fund. In that discrepancy lies the secret of the success of ETFs.

A 2.5-per-cent management fee comes right off the top of your capital, and that hurts, especially in the poor markets we're experiencing. It's also a big handicap that an active manager starts with in his battle to beat the index.

The reality of the market is that most mutual-fund managers don't beat the index, and it's impossible to predict which managers will be next year's winners. Index funds are good insurance against poor performance and should be the core of most investors portfolios.

Source: Don Macdonald, "Praise for Index Funds," The Markets, *The Gazette* (Montreal), February 22, 2002, p. C.11.BR.

company name, the next two columns show the beta and alpha coefficients. Remember that BMO Nesbitt Burns' alpha is actually $a + r_f(1 - \beta)$.

The next column, "% Expl. by Market," shows the square of the correlation coefficient, also known as *R*-square, between r_i and r_M. The *R*-square statistic, which is sometimes called the *coefficient* of *determination*, gives the fraction of the variance of the dependent variable (the return on the stock) that is explained by movements in the independent variable (the return on the TSE 300 index). Recall from Section 8.1 that the part of the total variance of the rate of return on an asset, σ^2, that is explained by market returns is the systematic variance $\beta^2\sigma^2_M$. Hence the *R*-square is systematic variance over total variance, which tells us what fraction of a firm's volatility is attributable to market movements:

$$R\text{-square} = \frac{\beta^2\sigma^2_M}{\sigma^2}$$

The firm-specific variance, $\sigma^2(e)$, is the part of the asset variance that is unexplained by the market index. Therefore, because

$$\sigma^2 = \beta^2\sigma^2_M + \sigma^2(e)$$

the coefficient of determination also may be expressed as

$$R\text{-square} = 1 - \frac{\sigma^2(e)}{\sigma^2} \tag{8.11}$$

The American brokerage firm Merrill Lynch provides another estimate of beta, called *adjusted beta.* The motivation for adjusting beta estimates is the observation that, on average, the beta coefficients of stocks seem to move toward 1 over time. One explanation for this phenomenon is intuitive. A business enterprise usually is established to produce a specific product or service, and a new firm may be more unconventional than an older one in many ways, from technology to management style. As it grows, however, a firm diversifies, first expanding to similar products and later to more diverse operations. As the firm becomes more conventional, it starts to resemble the rest of the economy even more. Thus, its beta coefficient will tend to change in the direction of 1.

Another explanation for this phenomenon is statistical. We know that the average beta over all securities is 1. Thus, before estimating the beta of a security our guess would be that it is 1. When we estimate this beta coefficient over a particular sample period, we sustain some unknown sampling error of the estimated beta. The greater the difference between our beta estimate and 1, the greater is the chance that we incurred a large estimation error and that, when we estimate this same beta in a subsequent sample period, the new estimate will be closer to 1.

The sample estimate of the beta coefficient is the best guess for the sample period. Given that beta has a tendency to evolve toward 1, however, a forecast of the future beta coefficient should adjust the sample estimate in that direction.

Table 8.2 Estimates of Stock Total Return Betas

	March 1995–August 1999			September 1999–February 2004		
Company	**Beta**	**Alpha**	**% Expl. by Market**	**Beta**	**Alpha**	**% Expl. by Market**
Abitibi Consolidated	1.54	−1.26	50.1	0.60	−0.64	9.3
Alcan Incorporated	1.13	−0.24	44.5	0.67	0.52	15.2
Bank of Montreal	0.99	0.49	58.2	0.06	1.76	0.3
Bank of Nova Scotia	1.24	0.59	63.3	0.27	1.63	5.2
Barrick Gold	1.29	−1.04	28.6	−0.03	0.36	0.0
BCE Inc.	1.05	1.48	44.5	0.56	1.50	12.7
Biovail Corp	0.61	5.73	3.9	0.76	1.23	5.8
Bombardier B	0.78	1.71	27.7	1.53	−0.76	27.0
CN Railway Co.	1.05	1.68	43.7	0.19	1.21	1.6
Dofasco Inc.	1.25	−0.18	62.3	0.31	1.01	4.4
Imperial Oil	0.43	1.22	10.3	−0.11	1.64	0.9
Magna Intl. B	0.55	0.60	15.0	0.48	0.70	14.2
Nortel Networks	1.38	2.04	35.1	3.53	−0.02	30.1
Petro-Canada	1.12	0.34	36.4	0.03	2.15	0.0
Rogers Communications B	1.38	0.31	15.6	1.24	−0.22	27.2
Suncor Inc.	0.74	1.87	26.1	0.06	1.81	0.2
Thomson Corporation	0.86	1.05	49.3	0.44	0.08	9.4
George Weston	0.59	2.08	14.8	−0.08	1.47	0.5

Sources: Quantitative Analysis division of BMO Nesbitt Burns Inc. Reprinted by permission.

Merrill Lynch adjusts beta estimates in a simple way. It takes the sample estimate of beta and averages it with 1, using the weights of two-thirds and one-third:

$$\text{Adjusted beta} = \tfrac{2}{3}\,(\text{sample beta}) + \tfrac{1}{3}(1)$$

For instance, since Alcan is actively traded on the NYSE, Merrill Lynch will be interested in providing an adjusted beta for it. Assuming it had the same estimate for beta of .67 for the 54 months ending in February 2004, the adjusted beta for Alcan would be .78, taking it one-third of the way toward 1.

www.biovail.com

A comparison of the beta estimates between the two different periods shows that some of them were remarkably stable, even though they were estimated several years apart. For instance, Rogers' beta went from 1.38 to 1.24; Magna Intl. B from .55 to .48; and Biovail from .61 to .76. Most of the betas, though, showed significant variability: Abitibi Consolidated went from 1.54 to .60, and Imperial Oil from .43 to –.11.

The sample period regression beta for Alcan's for 2001 is .67. Since Alcan's beta is less than 1, we know that this means that the index model alpha estimate is somewhat smaller. As we did in equation 8.10, we have to subtract $(1 - \beta)r_f$ from the regression alpha to obtain the index model alpha.

CONCEPT CHECK

3. What was Alcan's CAPM alpha per month during the period covered by BMO Nesbitt Burns' 2004 regression if during this period the average monthly rate of return of T-bills was .3 percent?

By contrast, for 1999, where beta is greater than 1, the index model alpha is larger. More importantly, these alpha estimates are ex post (after the fact) measures. They do not mean that anyone could have forecast these alpha values ex ante (before the fact). In fact, the name of the game in security analysis is to forecast alpha values ahead of time. A well-constructed portfolio that includes long positions in future positive alpha stocks and short positions in future negative alpha stocks will outperform the market index. The key term here is *well constructed,* meaning that the portfolio has to balance concentration on high alpha stocks with the need for risk-reducing diversification. The beta and residual variance estimates from the index model regression make it possible to achieve this goal. (We examine this technique in more detail in Part Seven on active portfolio management.)

In the absence of special information concerning Alcan, if our forecast for the market index is 10 percent and T-bills pay 3 percent, we learn from the BMO Nesbitt Burns' estimates that the CAPM forecast for the rate of return on Alcan stock is

$$\begin{aligned} E(r_{\text{AL}}) &= r_f + \beta \times [E(r_M) - r_f] \\ &= .03 + .67(.10 - .03) \\ &= .0769 = 7.69\% \end{aligned}$$

8.3 INDEX MODELS AND TRACKING PORTFOLIOS

Suppose a portfolio manager believes she has identified an underpriced portfolio. Her security analysis team estimates the index model equation for this portfolio (using the S&P/TSX Composite index) in excess return form and obtains the following estimates:

$$R_P = .04 + 1.4R_{\text{S\&P/TSX}} + e_P \qquad (8.12)$$

ESTIMATING BETA COEFFICIENTS

The spreadsheet Betas, which you will find on the Online Learning Centre at www.mcgrawhill.ca/college/bodie, contains 60 months' returns for ten individual stocks. Returns are calculated over the five years ending in December 2000. The spreadsheet also contains returns for S&P 500 Index and the observed risk-free rates as measured by the one-year Treasury bill. With this data, monthly excess returns for the individual securities and the market as measured by the S&P 500 Index can be used with the regression module in Excel. The spreadsheet also contains returns on an equally weighted portfolio of the individual securities. The regression module is available under Tools Data Analysis. The dependent variable is the security excess return. The independent variable is the market excess return.

A sample of the output from the regression is shown below. The estimated beta coefficient for American Express is 1.21, and 48 percent of the variance in returns for American Express can be explained by the returns on the S&P 500 Index.

	A	B	C	D	E	F
1	**SUMMARY OUTPUT**	**AXP**				
2						
3	*Regression Statistics*					
4	Multiple R	0.69288601				
5	R-Square	0.48009103				
6	Adjusted R-Square	0.47112708				
7	Standard Error	0.05887426				
8	Observations	60				
9						
10	ANOVA					
11		*df*	*SS*	*MS*	*F*	*Significance F*
12	Regression	1	0.185641557	0.1856416	53.55799	8.55186E-10
13	Residual	58	0.201038358	0.0034662		
14	Total	59	0.386679915			
15						
16		*Coefficients*	*Standard*	*t Stat*	*P-value*	*Lower 95%*
17			*Error*			
18	Intercept	0.01181687	0.00776211	1.522379	0.133348	-0.003720666
19	X Variable 1	1.20877413	0.165170705	7.3183324	8.55E-10	0.878149288

Therefore, P has an alpha value of 4 percent (which measures the extent of mispricing) and a beta of 1.4. The manager is confident in the quality of her security analysis but is wary about the performance of the broad market in the near term. If she buys the portfolio, and the market as a whole turns down, she still could lose money on her investment (which has a large positive beta) even if her team is correct that the portfolio is underpriced on a relative basis. She would like a position that takes advantage of her team's analysis but is independent of the performance of the overall market.

To this end, a **tracking portfolio** (T) can be constructed. A tracking portfolio for portfolio P is a portfolio designed to match the systematic component of P's return. The idea is for the portfolio to "track" the market-sensitive component of P's return. This means the tracking portfolio must have the same beta on the index portfolio as P and as little nonsystematic risk as possible.

A tracking portfolio for P will have a levered position in the S&P/TSX to achieve a beta of 1.4. Therefore, T includes positions of 1.4 in the Composite and 20.4 in T-bills. Because T is constructed from the index and bills, it has an alpha value of zero.

Now consider buying portfolio P but at the same time offsetting systematic risk by assuming a short position in the tracking portfolio. The short position in T cancels out the systematic exposure of the long position in P: the overall combined position is thus *market neutral*. Therefore, even if the market does poorly, the combined position should not be affected. But the alpha on portfolio P will remain intact. The combined portfolio, C, provides a return per dollar of

$$R_C = R_P - R_T = (.04 + 1.4R_{S\&P/TSX} + e_P) - 1.4R_{S\&P/TSX} = .04 + e_P \tag{8.13}$$

While this portfolio is still risky (due to the residual risk, e_P), the systematic risk has been eliminated, and if P is reasonably well-diversified, the remaining nonsystematic risk will be small. Thus the objective is achieved: the manager can take advantage of the 4 percent alpha without inadvertently taking on market exposure.

This "long-short strategy" is characteristic of the activity of many *hedge funds*. Hedge fund managers identify an underpriced security and then try to attain a "pure play" on the perceived underpricing. They hedge out all extraneous risk, focusing the bet only on the perceived "alpha." Tracking funds are the vehicle used to hedge the exposures to which they do *not* want exposure. Hedge fund managers use index regressions such as those discussed here, as well as more sophisticated variations, to create the tracking portfolios at the heart of their hedging strategies.

8.4 MULTIFACTOR MODELS

The index model's decomposition of returns into systematic and firm-specific components is compelling, but confining systematic risk to a single factor is not. Indeed, when we introduced the index model, we noted that the systematic or macro factor summarized by the market return arises from a number of sources, for example, uncertainty about the business cycle, interest rates, and inflation. It stands to reason that a more explicit representation of systematic risk, allowing for the possibility that different stocks exhibit different sensitivities to its various components, would constitute a useful refinement of the index model.

To illustrate the approach, let's start with a two-factor model. Suppose the two most important macroeconomic sources of risk are uncertainties surrounding the state of the business cycle, which we will measure by gross domestic product, GDP, and interest rates, denoted IR. The return on any stock will respond to both sources of macro risk as well as to its own firm-specific risks. We therefore can generalize the single-index model into a two-factor model describing the excess rate of return on a stock in some time period as follows:

$$R_t = \alpha + \beta_{GDP}\text{GDP}_t + \beta_{IR}\text{IR}_t + e_t \tag{8.14}$$

The two macro factors on the right-hand side of the equation are the systematic factors in the economy; thus they play the role of the market index in the single-index model. Their coefficients are sometimes called *factor sensitivities*, *factor loadings*, or, equivalently, *factor betas*. As before, e_t reflects firm-specific influences.

Now consider two firms, one a regulated utility, the other an airline. Because its profits are controlled by regulators, the utility is likely to have a low sensitivity to GDP risk, that is, a "low GDP beta." But it may have a relatively high sensitivity to interest rates: When rates rise, its stock price will fall; this will be reflected in a large (negative) interest rate beta. Conversely, the performance of the airline is very sensitive to economic activity, but it is not very sensitive to interest rates. It will have a high GDP beta and a small interest rate beta. Suppose that on a particular day, a news item suggests that the economy will expand. GDP is expected to increase, but so are interest rates. Is the "macro news" on this day good or bad? For the utility this is bad news, since its dominant sensitivity is to rates. But for the airline, which responds more to GDP, this is good news. Clearly a one-factor or single-index model cannot capture such differential responses to varying sources of macroeconomic uncertainty.

Of course the market return reflects macro factors as well as the average sensitivity of firms to those factors. When we estimate a single-index regression, therefore, we implicitly impose an (incorrect) assumption that each stock has the same relative sensitivity to each risk factor. If stocks actually differ in their betas relative to the various macroeconomic factors, then lumping all systematic sources of risk into one variable such as the return on the market index will ignore the nuances that better explain individual-stock returns. Once you see why a two-factor model can better explain stock returns, it is easy to see that models with even more factors—**multifactor models**—can provide even better descriptions of returns.

Another reason that multifactor models can improve on the descriptive power of the index model is that betas seem to vary over the business cycle. Therefore, it makes sense that we can improve the single-index model by including variables that are related to the business cycle.

Suppose we estimate the two-factor model in equation 8.14 for Dominion Airlines and find the following result:

$$r = .10 + 1.8(\text{GDP}) + .7(\text{IR}) + e$$

This tells us that on the basis of currently available information, the expected rate of return for Dominion is 10 percent, but that for every percentage point increase in GDP beyond current expectations, the return on Dominion shares increases on average by 1.8 percent, while for every unanticipated percentage point that interest rates decreases, Dominion's shares rise on average by .7 percent.

The factor betas can provide a framework for a hedging strategy. The idea for an investor who wishes to hedge a source of risk is to establish an opposite factor exposure to offset that particular source of risk. Often, futures contracts can be used to hedge particular factor exposures. We explore this application in Chapter 19.

A Multifactor Security Market Line

As it stands, the multifactor model is no more than a *description* of the factors that affect security returns. There is no "theory" in the equation. The obvious question left unanswered by a factor model like equation 8.14 is where $E(r)$ comes from, in other words, what determines a security's expected rate of return. This is where we need a theoretical model of equilibrium security returns.

In the previous chapter we developed one example of such a model: the security market line of the capital asset pricing model. The CAPM asserts that securities will be priced to give investors an expected return comprising two components: the risk-free rate, which is compensation for the time value of money, and a risk premium, determined by multiplying a benchmark risk premium (i.e., the risk premium offered by the market portfolio) times the relative measure of risk, beta:

$$E(r) = r_f + \beta[E(r_M) - r_f] \qquad (8.15)$$

If we denote the risk premium of the market portfolio by RP_M, then a useful way to rewrite equation 8.15 is as follows:

$$E(r) = r_f + \beta\text{RP}_M \qquad (8.16)$$

We pointed out in Section 8.1 that you can think of beta as measuring the exposure of a stock or portfolio to marketwide or macroeconomic risk factors. Therefore, one interpretation of the SML is that investors are rewarded with a higher expected return for their exposure to macro risk, based on both the sensitivity to that risk (beta) as well as the compensation for bearing each unit of that source of risk (i.e., the risk premium, RP_M), but are *not* rewarded for exposure to firm-specific uncertainty.

How might this single-factor view of the world generalize once we recognize the presence of multiple sources of systematic risk? We will work out the details of the argument in the next section, but before getting lost in the trees, we will start with the lay of the forest, motivating intuitively the results that are to come. Perhaps not surprisingly, a multifactor index model gives rise to a multifactor security market line in which the risk premium is determined by the exposure to *each* systematic risk factor, and by a risk premium associated with each of those factors.

For example, in a two-factor economy in which risk exposures can be measured by equation 8.14, we would conclude that the expected rate of return on a security would be the sum of

1. The risk-free rate of return
2. The sensitivity to GDP risk (i.e., the GDP beta) times the risk premium for GDP risk
3. The sensitivity to interest rate risk (i.e., the interest rate beta) times the risk premium for interest rate risk

This assertion is expressed as follows in equation 8.17. In that equation, for example, β_{GDP} denotes the sensitivity of the security return to unexpected changes in GDP growth, and RP_{GDP} is the risk premium associated with "one unit" of GDP exposure, i.e., the exposure corresponding to a GDP beta of 1.0. Here then is a two-factor security market line.

$$E(r) = r_f + \beta_{GDP}RP_{GDP} + \beta_{IR}RP_{IR} \tag{8.17}$$

If you look back at equation 8.16, you will see that equation 8.17 is a generalization of the simple security market line. In the usual SML, the benchmark risk premium is given by the market portfolio, $RP_M = E(r_M) - r_f$, but once we generalize to multiple risk sources, each with its own risk premium, we see that the insights are highly similar.

We still need to specify how to estimate the risk premium for each factor. Analogously to the simple CAPM, the risk premium associated with each factor can be thought of as the risk premium of a portfolio that has a beta of 1.0 on that particular factor and a beta of zero on all other factors. In other words, it is the risk premium one might expect to earn by taking a "pure play" on that factor. We will return to this below, but for now, let's just take the factor risk premia as given and see how a multifactor SML might be used.

Think about our regression estimates for our earlier example of Dominion Airlines. Dominion has a GDP beta of 1.8 and an interest rate beta of .7. Suppose the risk premium for one unit of exposure to GDP risk is 6 percent, while the risk premium for one unit of exposure to interest rate risk is 3 percent. Then the overall risk premium on the Dominion portfolio should equal the sum of the risk premiums required as compensation for each source of systematic risk.

The risk premium attributable to GDP risk should be the stock's exposure to that risk multiplied by the risk premium of the first factor portfolio, 6 percent. Therefore, the portion of the firm's risk premium that is compensation for its exposure to the first factor is $1.8 \times 6\% = 10.8\%$. Similarly, the risk premium attributable to interest rate risk is $.7 \times 3\% = 2.1\%$. The total risk premium should be $10.8 + 2.1 = 12.9\%$. Therefore, if the risk-free rate is 4 percent, the total return on the portfolio should be

4.0%	Risk-free rate
+ 10.8	+ Risk premium for exposure to GDP risk
+ 2.1	+ Risk premium for exposure to interest rate risk
16.9%	Total expected return

More concisely,

$$E(r) = 4\% + 1.8 \times 6\% + .7 \times 3\% = 16.9\%$$

The multifactor model clearly gives us a much richer way to think about risk exposures and compensation for those exposures than the single-index model or CAPM. Let us now fill in some of the gaps in the argument and more carefully explore the link between multifactor models of security returns and multifactor security market lines.

CONCEPT CHECK

4. Suppose the risk premia in the above example were RP_{GDP} = 4 percent and RP_{IR} = 2 percent. What would be the new value for the equilibrium expected rate of return on Dominion Airlines?

8.5 ARBITRAGE PRICING THEORY

Stephen Ross developed the **arbitrage pricing theory (APT)** in 1976.[11] Like the CAPM, the APT predicts a security market line linking expected returns to risk, but the path it takes to its SML is quite different. Ross's APT relies on three key propositions: (1) security returns can be described by a factor model; (2) there are sufficient securities to diversify away idiosyncratic risk; and (3) well-functioning security markets do not allow for the persistence of arbitrage opportunities. We begin with a simple version of Ross's model, which assumes that only one systematic factor affects security returns. However, the usual discussion of the APT is concerned with the multifactor case, so we treat this more general case as well.

Arbitrage, Risk Arbitrage, and Equilibrium

An arbitrage opportunity arises when an investor can earn riskless profits without making a net investment. A trivial example of an arbitrage opportunity would arise if shares of a stock sold for different prices on two different exchanges. For example, suppose IBM sold for $60 on the NYSE but only $58 on Nasdaq. Then you could buy the shares on Nasdaq and simultaneously sell them on the NYSE, clearing a riskless profit of $2 per share without tying up any of your own capital. The **Law of One Price** states that if two assets are equivalent in all economically relevant respects, then they should have the same market price. The Law of One Price is enforced by arbitrageurs: if they observe a violation of the law, they will engage in *arbitrage activity*—simultaneously buying the asset where it is cheap and selling where it is expensive. In the process, they will bid up the price where it is low and force it down where it is high until the arbitrage opportunity is eliminated.

The idea that market prices will move to rule out arbitrage opportunities is perhaps the most fundamental concept in capital market theory. Violation of this restriction would indicate the grossest form of market irrationality.

The critical property of a risk-free arbitrage portfolio is that any investor, regardless of risk aversion or wealth, will want to take an infinite position in it. Because those large positions will quickly force prices up or down until the opportunity vanishes, security prices should satisfy a "no-arbitrage condition," that is, a condition that rules out the existence of arbitrage opportunities.

There is an important difference between arbitrage and risk-return dominance arguments in support of equilibrium price relationships. A dominance argument holds that when an equilibrium

[11] Stephen A. Ross, "Return, Risk and Arbitrage," in I. Friend and J. Bicksler, eds., *Risk and Return in Finance* (Cambridge, MA: Ballinger, 1976).

price relationship is violated, many investors will make limited portfolio changes, depending on their degree of risk aversion. Aggregation of these limited portfolio changes is required to create a large volume of buying and selling, which in turn restores equilibrium prices. By contrast, when arbitrage opportunities exist each investor wants to take as large a position as possible; hence it will not take many investors to bring about the price pressures necessary to restore equilibrium. Therefore, implications for prices derived from no-arbitrage arguments are stronger than implications derived from a risk-return dominance argument.

The CAPM is an example of a dominance argument, implying that all investors hold mean-variance efficient portfolios. If a security is mispriced, then investors will tilt their portfolios toward the underpriced and away from the overpriced securities. Pressure on equilibrium prices results from many investors shifting their portfolios, each by a relatively small dollar amount. The assumption that a large number of investors are mean-variance sensitive is critical. In contrast, the implication of a no-arbitrage condition is that a few investors who identify an arbitrage opportunity will mobilize large dollar amounts and quickly restore equilibrium.

Practitioners often use the terms "arbitrage" and "arbitrageurs" more loosely than our strict definition. "Arbitrageur" often refers to a professional searching for mispriced securities in specific areas such as merger-target stocks, rather than to one who seeks strict (risk-free) arbitrage opportunities. Such activity is sometimes called **risk arbitrage** to distinguish it from pure arbitrage.

Well-Diversified Portfolios

We start by examining a single-factor model similar in spirit to the index model introduced in Section 8.1. As in that model, uncertainty in asset returns has two sources: a common or macroeconomic factor and a firm-specific or microeconomic cause. The common factor is assumed to have zero expected value, since it measures new information concerning the macroeconomy, which, by definition, has zero expected value. There is no need, however, to assume that the factor can be proxied by the return on a market index portfolio. The return r_i on firm i is given by equation 8.2.

Now we look at the risk of a portfolio of stocks. We first show that if a portfolio is well diversified, its firm-specific or nonfactor risk can be diversified away. Only factor (or systematic) risk remains. If we construct an n-stock portfolio with weights, w_i, $\Sigma w_i = 1$, then the rate of return on this portfolio is as follows:

$$r_P = E(r_P) + \beta_P F + e_P \tag{8.18}$$

where

$$\beta_P = \Sigma w_i \beta_i$$

is the weighted average of the β_i of the n securities. The portfolio nonsystematic component (which is uncorrelated with F) is

$$e_P = \Sigma w_i e_i$$

which similarly is a weighted average of the e_i of the n securities.

We can divide the variance of this portfolio into systematic and nonsystematic sources, as we saw in Section 8.1 (equation 8.7). The portfolio variance is

$$\sigma^2{}_P = \beta^2{}_P \sigma^2{}_F + \sigma^2(e_P)$$

where $\sigma^2{}_F$ is the variance of the factor F, and $\sigma^2(e_P)$ is the nonsystematic risk of the portfolio, which is given by

$$\sigma^2(e_P) = \text{Variance}(\Sigma w_i e_i) = \Sigma w^2{}_i \sigma^2(e_i)$$

Note that, in deriving the nonsystematic variance of the portfolio, we depend on the fact that the firm-specific e_i's are uncorrelated and hence that the variance of the "portfolio" of nonsystematic e_i's is the weighted sum of the individual nonsystematic variances with the square of the investment proportions as weights.

If the portfolio were equally weighted, $w_i = 1/n$, then the nonsystematic variance would be

$$\sigma^2\left(e_P;\, w_i = \frac{1}{n}\right) = \sum\left(\frac{1}{n}\right)^2 \sigma^2(e_i) = \frac{1}{n}\sum\frac{\sigma^2(e_i)}{n} = \frac{1}{n}\overline{\sigma}^2(e_i)$$

In this case, we divide the average nonsystematic variance, $\sigma^2(e_i)$, by n, so that when the portfolio gets large (in the sense that n is large and the portfolio remains equally weighted across all n stocks), the nonsystematic variance approaches zero.

CONCEPT CHECK

5. What will be the nonsystematic standard deviation of the equally weighted portfolio if the average value of $\sigma^2(e_i)$ equals .30, and (*a*) $n = 10$, (*b*) $n = 100$, (*c*) $n = 1{,}000$, and (*d*) $n = 10{,}000$? What do you conclude about the nonsystematic risk of large, diversified portfolios?

The set of portfolios for which the nonsystematic variance approaches zero as n gets large consists of more portfolios than just the equally weighted portfolio. Any portfolio for which each w_i becomes consistently smaller as n gets large (specifically where each $w^2{}_i$ approaches zero as n gets large) will satisfy the condition that the portfolio nonsystematic risk will approach zero as n gets large.

In fact, this property motivates us to define a **well-diversified portfolio** as one that is diversified over a large enough number of securities with proportions, w_i, each small enough that for practical purposes the nonsystematic variance, $\sigma^2(e_P)$, is negligible. Because the expected return of e_P is zero, if its variance also is zero, we can conclude that any realized value of e_P will be virtually zero. Rewriting equation 8.14, we conclude that for a well-diversified portfolio for all practical purposes

$$r_P = E(r_p) + \beta_P F$$

and

$$\sigma^2{}_P = \beta^2{}_P\sigma^2{}_F;\ \sigma_P = \beta_P\sigma_F$$

Large (mostly institutional) investors hold portfolios of hundreds and even thousands of securities; thus the concept of well-diversified portfolios clearly is operational in contemporary financial markets. Well-diversified portfolios, however, are not necessarily equally weighted.

As an illustration, consider a portfolio of 1,000 stocks. Let our position in the first stock be w percent. Let the position in the second stock be $2w$ percent, the position in the third $3w$ percent, and so on. In this way our largest position (in the thousandth stock) is $1{,}000w$ percent. Can this portfolio possibly be well diversified, considering the fact that the largest position is 1,000 times the smallest position? Surprisingly, the answer is yes.

To see this, let us determine the largest weight in any one stock, in this case, the thousandth stock. The sum of the positions in all stocks must be 100 percent; therefore

$$w + 2w + \ldots + 1{,}000w = 100$$

Solving for w, we find that

$$w = .0002\%$$

$$1{,}000w = .2\%$$

Our *largest* position amounts to only .2 of 1 percent. And this is very far from an equally weighted portfolio. Yet, for practical purposes, this still is a well-diversified portfolio.

Betas and Expected Returns

Because nonfactor risk can be diversified away, only factor risk commands a risk premium in market equilibrium. Nonsystematic risk across firms cancels out in well-diversified portfolios, so that only the systematic risk of a security can be related to its expected returns.

The solid line in Figure 8.3, panel A plots the return of a well-diversified portfolio (A) with $\beta_A = 1$ for various realizations of the systematic factor. The expected return of portfolio A is 10 percent: this is where the solid line crosses the vertical axis. At this point, the systematic factor is zero, implying no macro surprises. If the macro factor is positive, the portfolio's return exceeds its expected value; if it is negative, the portfolio's return falls short of its mean. The return on the portfolio is therefore

$$E(r_A) + \beta_A F = .10 + 1.0 \times F$$

Compare panel A with panel B, which is a similar graph for a single stock (S) with $\beta_S = 1$. The undiversified stock is subject to nonsystematic risk, which is seen in a scatter of points around the line. The well-diversified portfolio's return, in contrast, is determined completely by the systematic factor.

Now consider Figure 8.4, where the line B plots the return on another well-diversified portfolio, portfolio B, with an expected return of 8 percent and β_B also equal to 1.0. Could portfolios A and B coexist with the return pattern depicted? Clearly not: no matter what the systematic factor turns out to be, portfolio A outperforms portfolio B, leading to an arbitrage opportunity.

If you sell short \$1 million of B and buy \$1 million of A, a zero net investment strategy, your return would be \$20,000, as follows:

$(.10 + 1.0 \times F) \times \$1$ million	(From long position in A)
$-(.08 + 1.0 \times F) \times \$1$ million	(From short position in B)
$.02 \times \$1$ million = \$20,000	(Net proceeds)

You make a risk-free profit because the factor risk cancels out across the long and short positions. Moreover, the strategy requires zero net investment. You should pursue it on an infinitely large scale until the return discrepancy between the two portfolios disappears. Portfolios with equal betas must have equal expected returns in market equilibrium, or arbitrage opportunities exist.

What about portfolios with different betas? We show now that their risk premiums must be proportional to beta. To see why, consider Figure 8.5. Suppose that the risk-free rate is 4 percent and that well-diversified portfolio C, with a beta of .5, has an expected return of 6 percent. Portfolio C plots below the line from the risk-free asset to portfolio A. Consider therefore a

Figure 8.3 Returns as a function of the systematic factor. Panel A: well-diversified portfolio (A). Panel B: single stock (S).

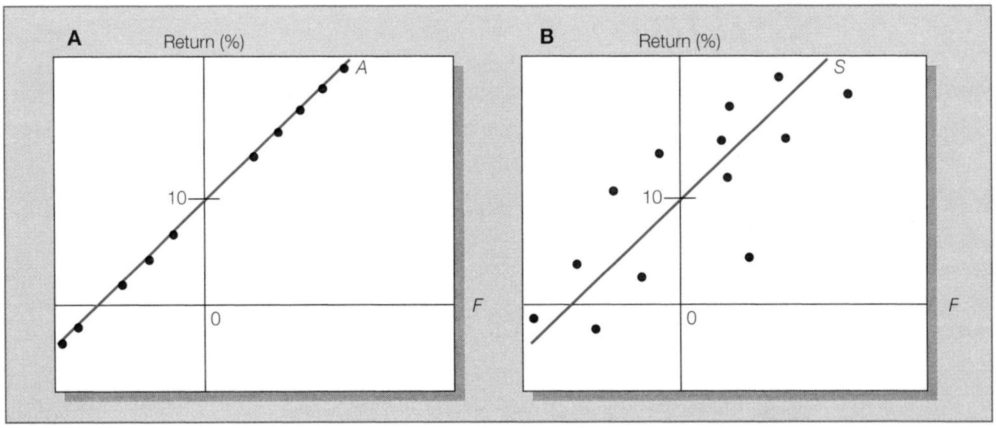

Figure 8.4
Returns as a function of the systematic factor: an arbitrage opportunity.

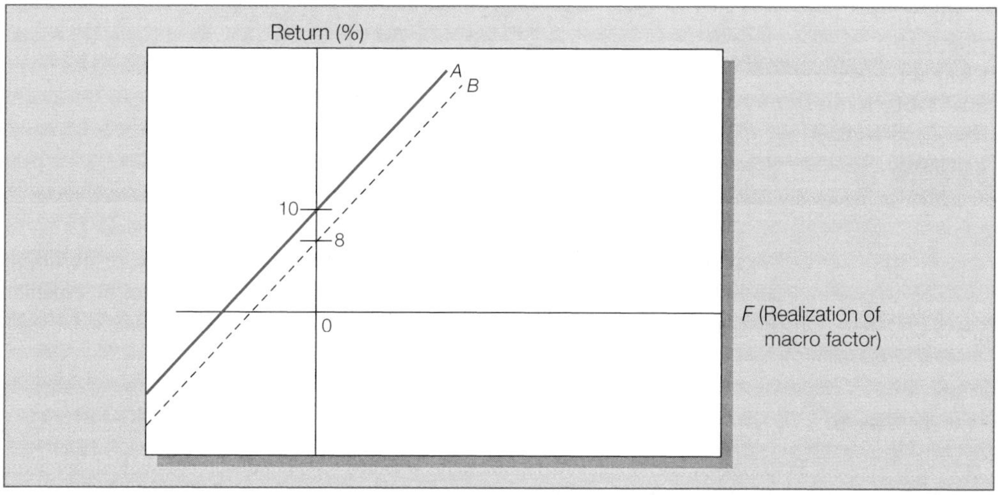

Figure 8.5
An arbitrage opportunity.

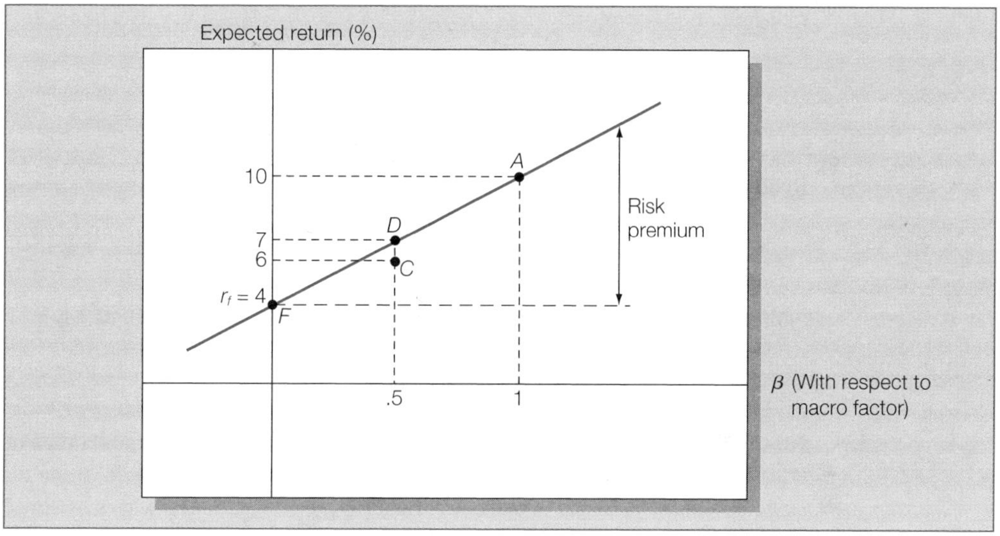

new portfolio, *D*, composed of half of portfolio *A* and half of the risk-free asset. Portfolio *D*'s beta will be $(\frac{1}{2} \times 0 + \frac{1}{2} \times 1.0) = .5$, and its expected return will be $(\frac{1}{2} \times 4 + \frac{1}{2} \times 10) = 7$ percent. Now portfolio *D* has an equal beta but a greater expected return than portfolio *C*. From our analysis in the previous paragraph we know that this constitutes an arbitrage opportunity.

We conclude that, to preclude arbitrage opportunities, the expected return on all well-diversified portfolios must lie on the straight line from the risk-free asset in Figure 8.5. The equation of this line will dictate the expected return on all well-diversified portfolios.

CONCEPT CHECK

6. Suppose that portfolio *E* is well diversified with a beta of $\frac{2}{3}$ and expected return of 9 percent. Would an arbitrage opportunity exist? If so, what would be the arbitrage opportunity?

Notice in Figure 8.5 that risk premiums are indeed proportional to portfolio betas. The risk premium is depicted by the vertical arrow, which measures the distance between the risk-free rate and the expected return on the portfolio. The risk premium is zero for $\beta = 0$, and rises in direct proportion to β.

Table 8.3 Portfolio Characteristics and Weights in the Zero-Beta Portfolio

Portfolio	Expected Return	Beta	Portfolio Weight
U	$E(r_U)$	β_U	$\frac{\beta_V}{\beta_V - \beta_U}$
V	$E(r_V)$	β_V	$\frac{-\beta_U}{\beta_V - \beta_U}$

More formally, suppose that two well-diversified portfolios are combined into a zero-beta portfolio, Z, by choosing the weights shown in Table 8.3. The weights of the two assets in portfolio Z sum to 1, and the portfolio beta is zero:

$$\beta_Z = w_U\beta_U + w_V\beta_V = \frac{\beta_V}{\beta_V - \beta_U}\beta_U + \frac{-\beta_U}{\beta_V - \beta_U}\beta_V = 0$$

Portfolio Z is riskless: It has no diversifiable risk because it is well diversified, and no exposure to the systematic factor because its beta is zero. To rule out arbitrage, then, it must earn only the risk-free rate. Therefore,

$$\begin{aligned} E(r_Z) &= w_U E(r_U) + w_V E(r_V) \\ &= \frac{\beta_V}{\beta_V - \beta_U} E(r_U) + \frac{-\beta_U}{\beta_V - \beta_U} E(r_V) = r_f \end{aligned}$$

Rearranging the last equation, we can conclude that

$$\frac{E(r_U) - r_f}{\beta_U} = \frac{E(r_V) - r_f}{\beta_V} \tag{8.19}$$

which implies that risk premiums be proportional to betas, as in Figure 8.5.

The Security Market Line

Now consider the market portfolio as a well-diversified portfolio, and let us measure the systematic factor as the unexpected return on the market portfolio. The beta of the market portfolio is 1, since that is the beta of the market portfolio with itself. Hence, the market portfolio is at point A on the line in Figure 8.5, and we can use it to determine the equation describing that line. The intercept is r_f, and the slope is $E(r_M) - r_f$[rise $= E(r_M) - r_f$; run = 1], implying that the equation of the line is

$$E(r_P) = r_f + [E(r_M) - r_f]\beta_P \tag{8.20}$$

Hence, Figure 8.5 is identical to the SML relationship of the CAPM.

We have used the no-arbitrage condition to obtain an expected return–beta relationship identical to that of the CAPM, without the restrictive assumptions of the CAPM. This suggests that despite its restrictive assumptions, the main conclusion of the CAPM—namely, the SML expected return–beta relationship—is likely to be at least approximately valid.

It is worth noting that, in contrast to the CAPM, the APT does not require that the benchmark portfolio in the SML relationship be the true market portfolio. Any well-diversified portfolio lying on the SML of Figure 8.5 may serve as the benchmark portfolio. For example, one might define the benchmark portfolio as the well-diversified portfolio most highly correlated with whatever systematic factor is thought to affect stock returns. Accordingly, the APT has more flexibility than does the CAPM because problems associated with an unobservable market portfolio are not a concern.

In addition, the APT provides further justification for use of the index model in the practical implementation of the SML relationship. Even if the index portfolio is not a precise proxy for the true market portfolio, which is a cause of considerable concern in the context of the CAPM, we now know that if the index portfolio is sufficiently well diversified, the SML relationship should still hold true according to the APT.

So far we have demonstrated the APT relationship for well-diversified portfolios only. The CAPM expected return–beta relationship applies to single assets, as well as to portfolio. In the next section, we generalize the APT result one step further.

8.6 INDIVIDUAL ASSETS AND THE APT

We have demonstrated that if arbitrage opportunities are to be ruled out, each well-diversified portfolio's expected excess return must be proportional to its beta. The question is whether this relationship tells us anything about the expected returns on the component stocks. The answer is that if this relationship is to be satisfied by all well-diversified portfolios, it must be satisfied by *almost* all individual securities, although a full proof of this proposition is somewhat difficult. We can illustrate the argument less formally.

Suppose that the expected return–beta relationship is violated for all single assets. Now create a pair of well-diversified portfolios from these assets. What are the chances that in spite of the fact that for any pair of assets the relationship does *not* hold, the relationship *will* hold for both well-diversified portfolios? The chances are small, but it is possible that the relationships among the single securities are violated in offsetting ways so that somehow it holds for the pair of well-diversified portfolios.

Now construct yet a third well-diversified portfolio. What are the chances that the violations of the relationships for single securities are such that the third portfolio also will fulfill the no-arbitrage expected return–beta relationship? Obviously, the chances are smaller still, but the relationship is possible. Continue with a fourth well-diversified portfolio, and so on. If the no-arbitrage expected return–beta relationship has to hold for infinitely many different, well-diversified portfolios, it must be virtually certain that the relationship holds for all but a small number of individual securities.

We use the term *virtually certain* advisedly because we must distinguish this conclusion from the statement that all securities surely fulfill this relationship. The reason we cannot make the latter statement has to do with a property of well-diversified portfolios.

Recall that to qualify as well diversified, a portfolio must have very small positions in all securities. If, for example, only one security violates the expected return–beta relationship, then the effect of this violation on a well-diversified portfolio will be too small to be of importance for any practical purpose, and meaningful arbitrage opportunities will not arise. But if many securities violate the expected return–beta relationship, the relationship will no longer hold for well-diversified portfolios, and arbitrage opportunities will be available. Consequently, we conclude that imposing the no-arbitrage condition on a single-factor security market implies maintenance of the expected return–beta relationship for all well-diversified portfolios and for all but possibly a *small* number of individual securities.

The APT and the CAPM

The APT serves many of the same functions as the CAPM. It gives us a benchmark for rates of return that can be used in capital budgeting, security evaluation, or investment performance evaluation. Moreover, the APT highlights the crucial distinction between nondiversifiable risk (factor risk) that requires a reward in the form of a risk premium and diversifiable risk that does not.

The APT is an extremely appealing model. It depends on the assumption that a rational equilibrium in capital markets precludes arbitrage opportunities. A violation of the APT's pricing relationships will cause extremely strong pressure to restore them even if only a limited number of investors become aware of the disequilibrium. Furthermore, the APT yields an expected return–beta relationship using a well-diversified portfolio that practically can be constructed from a large number of securities.

In contrast, the CAPM is derived assuming an inherently unobservable "market" portfolio. The CAPM argument rests on mean-variance efficiency; that is, if any security violates the expected return–beta relationship, then many investors (each relatively small) will tilt their portfolios so that their combined overall pressure on prices will restore an equilibrium that satisfies the relationship.

In spite of these apparent advantages, the APT does not fully dominate the CAPM. The CAPM provides an unequivocal statement on the expected return–beta relationship for all securities, whereas the APT implies that this relationship holds for all but perhaps a small number of securities. Because it focuses on the no-arbitrage condition, without the further assumptions of the market or index model, the APT cannot rule out a violation of the expected return–beta relationship for any particular asset. For this, we need the CAPM assumptions and its dominance arguments.

8.7 A MULTIFACTOR APT

We have assumed so far that there is only one systematic factor affecting stock returns. This simplifying assumption is in fact too simplistic. We've noted that it is easy to think of several factors driven by the business cycle that might affect stock returns: interest rate fluctuations, inflation rates, oil prices, and so on. Presumably, exposure to any of these factors will affect a stock's risk and hence its expected return. We can derive a multifactor version of the APT to accommodate these multiple sources of risk.

Suppose that we generalize the factor model expressed in equation 8.2 to a two-factor model:

$$r_i = E(r_i) + \beta_{i1}F_1 + \beta_{i2}F_2 + e_i \tag{8.21}$$

In an earlier example factor 1 was the departure of GDP growth from expectations, and factor 2 was the unanticipated decline in interest rates. Each factor has zero expected value because each measures the *surprise* in the systematic variable rather than the level of the variable. Similarly, the firm-specific component of unexpected return, e_i, also has zero expected value. Extending such a two-factor model to any number of factors is straightforward.

Establishing a multifactor APT is similar to the one-factor case. But first we must introduce the concept of a **factor portfolio**, which is a well-diversified portfolio constructed to have a beta of 1 on one of the factors and a beta of 0 on any other factor. We can think of a factor portfolio as a *tracking portfolio*. That is, the returns on such a portfolio track the evolution of particular sources of macroeconomic risk, but are uncorrelated with other sources of risk. It is possible to form such factor portfolios because we have a large number of securities to choose from, and a relatively small number of factors. Factor portfolios will serve as the benchmark portfolios for a multifactor security market line.

Suppose that the two-factor portfolios, Portfolios 1 and 2, have expected returns $E(r_1) = 10\%$ and $E(r_2) = 12\%$. Suppose further that the risk-free rate is 4 percent. The risk premium on the first factor portfolio is $10\% - 4\% = 6\%$, whereas that on the second factor portfolio is $12\% - 4\% = 8\%$.

Now consider a well-diversified portfolio, Portfolio *A*, with beta on the first factor, $\beta_{A1} = .5$, and beta on the second factor, $\beta_{A2} = .75$. The multifactor APT states that the overall risk premium on this portfolio must equal the sum of the risk premiums required as compensation for each source of systematic risk. The risk premium attributable to risk factor 1 should be the portfolio's exposure to factor 1, β_{A1}, multiplied by the risk premium earned on the first factor portfolio, $E(r_1) - r_f$. Therefore, the portion of Portfolio *A*'s risk premium that is compensation for its exposure to the first factor is $\beta_{A1}[E(r_1) - r_f] = .5(10\% - 4\%) = 3\%$, whereas the risk premium attributable to risk factor 2 is $\beta_{A2}[E(r_2) - r_f] = .75(12\% - 4\%) = 6\%$. The total risk premium on the portfolio should be $3 + 6 = 9\%$ and the total return on the portfolio should be $4\% + 9\% = 13\%$.

To generalize the argument in the above example, note that the factor exposures of any portfolio, *P*, are given by its betas, β_{p1} and β_{p2}. A competing portfolio, *Q*, can be formed by investing in factor portfolios with the following weights: β_{p1} in the first factor portfolio, β_{p2} in the second factor portfolio, and $1 - \beta_{p1} - \beta_{p2}$ in T-bills. By construction, portfolio *Q* will have betas equal to those of Portfolio *P* and expected return of

$$\begin{aligned} E(r_Q) &= \beta_{P1}E(r_1) + \beta_{P2}E(r_2) + (1 - \beta_{P1} - \beta_{P2})r_f \\ &= r_f + \beta_{P1}[E(r_1) - r_f] + \beta_{P2}[E(r_2) - r_f] \end{aligned} \tag{8.22}$$

Using the numbers in the example:

$$E(r_Q) = 4 + .5 \times (10 - 4) + .75 \times (12 - 4) = 13\%$$

Because Portfolio *Q* has precisely the same exposures as Portfolio *A* to the two sources of risk, their expected returns also ought to be equal. So Portfolio *A* also ought to have an expected return of 13 percent. If it does not, there will be an arbitrage opportunity.

Suppose that the expected return on Portfolio A were 12 percent rather than 13 percent. This return would give rise to an arbitrage opportunity. Form a portfolio from the factor portfolios with the same betas as Portfolio *A*. This requires weights of .5 on the first factor portfolio, .75 on the second factor portfolio, and −.25 on the risk-free asset. This portfolio has exactly the same factor betas as Portfolio *A*: it has a beta of .5 on the first factor because of its .5 weight on the first factor portfolio, and a beta of .75 on the second factor. (The weight of −.25 on risk-free T-bills does not affect the sensitivity to either factor.)

Now invest \$1 in Portfolio *Q* and sell (short) \$1 in Portfolio *A*. Your net investment is zero, but your expected dollar profit is positive and equal to

$$\$1 \times E(r_Q) - \$1 \times E(r_A) = \$1 \times .13 - \$1 \times .12 = \$.01$$

Moreover, your net position is riskless. Your exposure to each risk factor cancels out because you are long \$1 in Portfolio *Q* and short \$1 in Portfolio *A*, and both of these well-diversified portfolios have exactly the same factor betas. Thus, if Portfolio A's expected return differs from that of Portfolio *Q*'s, you can earn positive risk-free profits on a zero net investment position. This is an arbitrage opportunity.

CONCEPT CHECK ?

7. Using the factor portfolios of the above example, find the equilibrium rate of return on a portfolio with $\beta_1 = .2$ and $\beta_2 = 1.4$.

We conclude that any well-diversified portfolio with betas β_{p1} and β_{p2} must have the return given in equation 8.22 if arbitrage opportunities are to be precluded. If you compare equations 8.20 and 8.22, you will see that equation 8.22 is simply a generalization of the one-factor SML.

Finally, the extension of the multifactor SML of equation 8.22 to individual assets is precisely the same as for the one-factor APT. Equation 8.22 cannot be satisfied by every well-diversified portfolio unless it is satisfied by virtually every security taken individually. Equation 8.22 thus represents the multifactor SML for an economy with multiple sources of risk.

We pointed out earlier that one application of the CAPM is to provide "fair" rates of return for regulated utilities. The multifactor APT can be used to the same ends. The nearby box summarizes a study in which the APT was applied to find the cost of capital for regulated electric companies.

8.8 WHERE SHOULD WE LOOK FOR FACTORS?

One shortcoming of the multifactor APT is that it gives no guidance concerning the determination of the relevant risk factors or their risk premiums. Two principles guide us when we specify a reasonable list of factors. First, we want to limit ourselves to systematic factors with considerable ability to explain security returns. If our model calls for hundreds of explanatory variables, it does little to simplify our description of security returns. Second, we wish to choose factors that seem likely to be important risk factors, that is, factors that concern investors sufficiently that they will demand meaningful risk premiums to bear exposure to those sources of risk.

One example of the multifactor approach is the work of Chen, Roll, and Ross[12] who chose the following set of factors based on the ability of these factors to paint a broad picture of the macroeconomy. Their set is obviously but one of many possible sets that might be considered.

IP = % change in industrial production
EI = % change in expected inflation
UI = % change in unanticipated inflation
CG = excess return of long-term corporate bonds over long-term government bonds
GB = excess return of long-term government bonds over T-bills

This list gives rise to the following five-factor model of security returns during holding period t as a function of the change in the set of macroeconomic indicators:

$$r_{it} = \alpha_i + \beta_{i\,\mathrm{IP}}\mathrm{IP}_t + \beta_{i\,\mathrm{EI}}\mathrm{EI}_t + \beta_{i\,\mathrm{UI}}\mathrm{UI}_t + \beta_{i\,\mathrm{CG}}\mathrm{CG}_t + \beta_{i\,\mathrm{GB}}\mathrm{GB}_t + e_{it} \tag{8.23}$$

Equation 8.23 is a multidimensional security characteristic line (SCL), with five factors. As before, to estimate the betas of a given stock we can use regression analysis. Here, however, because there is more than one factor, we estimate a *multiple* regression of the returns of the stock in each period on the five macroeconomic factors. The residual variance of the regression estimates the firm-specific risk. We discuss the results of this model in the next chapter, which focuses on empirical evidence on security pricing.

An alternative approach to specifying macroeconomic factors as candidates for relevant sources of systematic risk uses firm characteristics that seem on empirical grounds to proxy for exposure to systematic risk. In other words, the factors are chosen as variables that on past evidence seem to predict high average returns and therefore may be capturing risk premiums. One example of this approach is the so-called Fama and French three-factor model,[13]

$$r_{it} = \alpha_i + \beta_{iM}R_{Mt} + \beta_{i\mathrm{SMB}}\mathrm{SMB}_t + \beta_{i\mathrm{HML}}\mathrm{HML}_t + e_{it} \tag{8.24}$$

where

SMB = Small Minus Big, that is, the return of a portfolio of small stocks in excess of the return on a portfolio of large stocks
HML = High Minus Low, that is, the return of a portfolio of stocks with a high book-to-market ratio in excess of the return on a portfolio of stocks with a low book-to-market ratio

Note that in this model the market index does play a role and is expected to capture systematic risk originating from macroeconomic factors.

These two firm-characteristic variables are chosen because of long-standing observations that corporate capitalization (firm size) and book-to-market ratio seem to be predictive of average

[12] N. Chen, R. Roll, and S. Ross, "Economic Forces and the Stock Market," *Journal of Business* 59 (1986), pp. 383–403.

[13] Eugene F. Fama and Kenneth R. French, "Multifactor Explanations of Asset Pricing Anomalies," *The Journal of Finance* 51 (1996), pp. 55–84.

USING THE APT TO FIND COST OF CAPITAL

Elton, Gruber, and Mei* use the APT to derive the cost of capital for electric utilities. They assume that the relevant risk factors are unanticipated developments in the term structure of interest rates, the level of interest rates, inflation rates, the business cycle (measured by GDP), foreign exchange rates, and a summary measure they devise to measure other macro factors.

Their first step is to estimate the risk premium associated with exposure to each risk source. They accomplish this in a two-step strategy ... :

1. *Estimate "factor loadings" (i.e., betas) of a large sample of firms.* Regress returns of 100 randomly selected stocks against the systematic risk factors. They use a time-series regression for each stock (e.g., 60 months of data), therefore estimating 100 regressions, one for each stock.
2. *Estimate the reward earned per unit of exposure to each risk factor.* For each month, regress the return of each stock against the five betas estimated. The coefficient on each beta is the extra average return earned as beta increases, that is, it is an estimate of the risk premium for that risk factor from that month's data. These estimates are of course subject to sampling error. Therefore, average the risk premium estimates across the 12 months in each year. The *average* response of return to risk is less subject to sampling error.

The risk premiums found for 1990 are in the second column of the table at the top of the next column.

Notice that some risk premiums are negative. The interpretation of this result is that risk premium should be positive for risk factors you don't want exposure to, but *negative* for factors you *do* want exposure to. For example, you should desire securities that have higher returns when inflation increases and be willing to accept lower expected returns on such securities; this shows up as a negative risk premium.

Factor	Factor Risk Premium	Factor Betas for Niagra Mohawk
Term structure	.425	1.0615
Interest rates	−.051	−2.4167
Exchange rates	−.049	1.3235
Business cycle	.041	.1292
Inflation	−.069	−.5220
Other macro factors	.530	.3046

Therefore, the expected return on any security should be related to its factor betas as follows:

$$r_f + .425\beta_{\text{term struc}} - .051\beta_{\text{int rate}} - .049\beta_{\text{ex rate}} + .041\beta_{\text{bus cycle}} - .069\beta_{\text{inflation}} + .530\beta_{\text{other}}$$

Finally, to obtain the cost of capital for a particular firm, the authors estimate the firm's betas against each source of risk, multiply each factor beta by the "cost of factor risk" from the table above, sum over all risk sources to obtain the total risk premium, and add the risk-free rate.

For example, the beta estimates for Niagra Mohawk appear in the last column of the table above. Therefore its cost of capital is

$$\begin{aligned}\text{Cost of capital} &= r_f + .425 \times 1.0615 - .051(-2.4167) \\ &\quad - .049(1.3235) + .041(.1292) \\ &\quad - .069(2.5220) + .530(.3046) \\ &= r_f + .72\end{aligned}$$

In other words, the monthly cost of capital for Niagra Mohawk is .72 percent above the monthly risk-free rate. Its annualized risk premium is therefore .72% × 12 = 8.64%.

*Edwin J. Elton, Martin J. Gruber, and Jianping Mei, "Cost of Capital Using Arbitrage Pricing Theory: A Case Study of Nine New York Utilities," *Financial Markets, Institutions, and Instruments* 3 (August 1994), pp. 46–68.

stock returns. Fama and French justify this model on empirical grounds: while SMB and HML are not themselves obvious candidates for relevant risk factors, the hope is that these variables proxy for yet-unknown more-fundamental variables. For example, Fama and French point out that firms with high ratios of book to market value are more likely to be in financial distress and that small stocks may be more sensitive to changes in business conditions. Thus, these variables may capture sensitivity to risk factors in the macroeconomy. Evidence on the Fama-French model also appears in the next chapter.

The problem with empirical approaches such as the Fama-French model, which use proxies for extramarket sources of risk, is that none of the factors in the proposed models can be clearly identified as hedging a significant source of uncertainty. Black[14] points out that when researchers scan and rescan the database of security returns in search of explanatory factors (an activity often

[14]Fischer Black, "Beta and Return," *Journal of Portfolio Management* 20 (1993), pp. 8–18.

called data snooping), they may eventually uncover past "patterns" that are due purely to chance. Black observes that return premiums to factors such as firm size have largely vanished since first discovered. However, Fama and French point out that size and book-to-market ratios have predicted average returns in various time periods and in markets all over the world, thus mitigating potential effects of data snooping.

8.9 A MULTIFACTOR CAPM

The CAPM presupposes that the only relevant source of risk arises from variations in security returns, and therefore a representative (market) portfolio can capture this entire risk. As a result, individual-stock risk can be defined by the contribution to overall portfolio risk; hence, the risk premium on an individual stock is solely determined by its beta on the market portfolio. But is this narrow view of risk warranted?

Consider a relatively young investor whose future wealth is determined in large part by labour income. The stream of future labour income is also risky and may be intimately tied to the fortunes of the company for which the investor works. Such an investor might choose an investment portfolio that will help to diversify labour-income risk. For that purpose, stocks with lower-than-average correlation with future labour income would be favoured, that is, such stocks will receive higher weights in the individual portfolio than their weights in the market portfolio. Put another way, using this broader notion of risk, these investors no longer consider the market portfolio as efficient and the rationale for the CAPM expected return–beta relationship no longer applies.

In principle, the CAPM may still hold if the hedging demands of various investors are equally distributed across different types of securities so that deviations of portfolio weights from those of the market portfolio are offsetting. But if hedging demands are common to many investors, the prices of securities with desirable hedging characteristics will be bid up and the expected return reduced, which will invalidate the CAPM expected return–beta relationship. For example, suppose the prices of energy stocks were driven up by investors who buy such stocks to hedge uncertainty about energy expenditures. At those higher stock prices, expected rates of return will be lower than dictated by the expected return–beta relationship of the CAPM. The simple SML relationship needs to be generalized to account for the effects of extramarket hedging demands on equilibrium rates of return.

Merton[15] has shown that these hedging demands will result in an expanded or multifactor version of the CAPM that recognizes the multidimensional nature of risk. His model is called the multifactor CAPM or, alternatively, the intertemporal CAPM (ICAPM for short). The focal point of Merton's model is not dollar returns per se, but the consumption and investment made possible by the investor's wealth. Each source of risk to consumption or investment opportunities may in principle command its own risk premium.

In the case of energy price risk, for example, Merton's model would imply that the expected return–beta relationship of the single-factor CAPM would be generalized to the following two-factor relationship:

$$E(r_i) = r_f + \beta_{iM}\,[E(r_M) - r_f] + \beta_{ie}\,[E(r_e) - r_f]$$

where β_{iM} is the beta of security i with respect to the market portfolio, and bie is the beta with respect to energy price risk. Similarly, $E(r_e) - r_f$ is the risk premium associated with exposure to energy price uncertainty. The rate of return of the portfolio that best hedges energy price uncertainty is r_e. This equation, therefore, is a two-factor CAPM. More generally, we will have a beta and a risk premium for every significant source of risk that consumers try to hedge.

[15]Robert C. Merton, "An Intertemporal Capital Asset Pricing Model," *Econometrica* 41 (1973), pp. 867–87.

Notice that this expanded version of the CAPM provides a prediction for security returns identical to that of the multifactor APT. Therefore, there is no contradiction between these two theories of the risk premium. The CAPM approach does offer one notable advantage, however. In contrast to the APT, which is silent on the relevant systematic factors, the CAPM provides guidance as to where to look for those factors. The important factors will be those sources of risk that large groups of investors try to offset by establishing extramarket hedge portfolios. By specifying the likely sources of risk against which dominant groups of investors attempt to hedge, we identify the dimensions along which the CAPM needs to be generalized.

When a source of risk has an effect on expected returns, we say that this risk "is priced." While the single-factor CAPM predicts that only market risk will be priced, the ICAPM predicts that other sources of risk also may be priced. Merton suggested a list of possible common sources of uncertainty that might affect expected security returns. Among these are uncertainties in labour income, prices of important consumption goods (e.g., energy prices), or changes in future investment opportunities (e.g., changes in the riskiness of various asset classes). However, it is difficult to predict whether there exists sufficient demand for hedging these sources of uncertainty to affect security returns.

CONCEPT CHECK

8. Consider the following regression results for stock X.

$$r_X = 2\% + 1.2 \text{ (percentage change in oil prices)}$$

a. If I live in Alberta, where the local economy is heavily dependent on oil industry profits, does stock X represent a useful asset to hedge my overall economic well-being?

b. What if I live in Nova Scotia, where most individuals and firms are energy *consumers*?

c. If energy consumers are far more numerous than energy producers, will high oil-beta stocks have higher or lower expected rates of return in market equilibrium than low oil-beta stocks?

SUMMARY

1. A single-factor model of the economy classifies sources of uncertainty as systematic (macroeconomic) factors or firm-specific (microeconomic) factors. The index model assumes that the macro factor can be represented by a broad index of stock returns.
2. The single-index model drastically reduces the necessary inputs into the Markowitz portfolio selection procedure. It also aids in specialization of labour in security analysis.
3. If the index model specification is valid, then the systematic risk of a portfolio or asset equals $\beta^2\sigma^2_M$, and the covariance between two assets equals $\beta_i\beta_j\sigma^2_M$.
4. The index model is estimated by applying regression analysis to excess rates of return. The slope of the regression curve is the beta of an asset, whereas the intercept is the asset's alpha during the sample period. The regression line also is called the security characteristic line. The regression beta is equivalent to the CAPM beta, except that the regression uses actual returns and the CAPM is specified in terms of expected returns. The CAPM predicts that the average value of alphas measured by the index model regression will be zero.
5. Multifactor models seek to improve the explanatory power of single-factor models by explicitly accounting for the various systematic components of security risk. These models use indicators intended to capture a wide range of macroeconomic risk factors.
6. Once we allow for multiple risk factors, we conclude that the security market line also ought to be multidimensional, with exposure to each risk factor contributing to the total risk premium of the security.
7. A risk-free arbitrage opportunity arises when two or more security prices enable investors to construct a zero net investment portfolio that will yield a sure profit. Rational investors will want to take infinitely large positions in arbitrage portfolios regardless of their degree of risk aversion.

Visit us at www.mcgrawhill.ca/college/bodie

8. The presence of arbitrage opportunities and the resulting large volume of trades will create pressure on security prices. This pressure will continue until prices reach levels that preclude arbitrage.
9. When securities are priced so that there are no risk-free arbitrage opportunities, we say that they satisfy the no-arbitrage condition. Price relationships that satisfy the no-arbitrage condition are important because we expect them to hold in real-world markets.
10. Portfolios are called *well diversified* if they include a large number of securities and the investment proportion in each is sufficiently small. The proportion of a security in a well-diversified portfolio is small enough so that, for all practical purposes, a reasonable change in that security's rate of return will have a negligible effect on the portfolio rate of return.
11. In a single-factor security market, all well-diversified portfolios have to satisfy the expected return–beta relationship of the security market line in order to satisfy the no-arbitrage condition. If all well-diversified portfolios satisfy the expected return–beta relationship, then all but a small number of securities also satisfy this relationship.
12. The APT does not require the restrictive assumptions of the CAPM and its (unobservable) market portfolio. The price of this generality is that the APT does not guarantee this relationship for all securities at all times.
13. A multifactor APT generalizes the single-factor model to accommodate several sources of systematic risk. The multidimensional security market line predicts that exposure to each risk factor contributes to the security's total risk premium by an amount equal to the factor beta times the risk premium of the factor portfolio that tracks that source of risk.
14. A multifactor extension of the single-factor CAPM, the ICAPM, is a model of the risk–return tradeoff that predicts the same multidimensional security market line as the APT. The ICAPM suggests that priced risk factors will be those sources of risk that lead to significant hedging demand by a substantial fraction of investors.

KEY TERMS

arbitrage 284
single-factor model 286
single-index model 286
scatter diagram 288
regression equation 289
residuals 289
security characteristic line (SCL) 289
tracking portfolio 298
multifactor models 299
arbitrage pricing theory (APT) 301
Law of One Price 301
risk arbitrage 302
well-diversified portfolio 303
factor portfolio 308

SELECTED READINGS

The seminal paper relating the index model to the portfolio selection problem is:

Sharpe, William F. "A Simplified Model of Portfolio Analysis." *Management Science*, January 1963.

Stephen Ross developed the arbitrage pricing theory in two articles:

Ross, S. A. "Return, Risk and Arbitrage." In I. Friend and J. Bicksler, eds., *Risk and Return in Finance.* Cambridge, MA: Ballinger, 1976.

Ross, S. A. "Arbitrage Theory of Capital Asset Pricing." *Journal of Economic Theory*, December 1976.

Articles exploring the factors that influence common stock returns are:

Bower, D. A., R. S. Bower, and D. E. Logue. "Arbitrage Pricing and Utility Stock Returns." *Journal of Finance,* September 1984.

Chen, N. F., R. Roll, and S. Ross. "Economic Forces and the Stock Market: Testing the APT and Alternative Asset Pricing Theories." *Journal of Business*, July 1986.

Sharpe, W. "Factors in New York Stock Exchange Security Returns, 1931–1979." *Journal of Portfolio Management,* Summer 1982.

Articles exploring the requirement from reference portfolios for testing the expected return–beta relationship are:

Reisman, H. "Reference Variables, Factor Structure, and the Approximate Multibeta Representation." *Journal of Finance,* September 1992.

Shanken, J. "Multivariate Proxies and Asset Pricing Relations: Living with the Roll Critique." *Journal of Financial Economics*, March 1987.

PROBLEMS

1. A portfolio management organization analyzes 60 stocks and constructs a mean-variance efficient portfolio that is constrained to these 60 stocks.
   a. How many estimates of expected returns, variances, and covariances are needed to optimize this portfolio?
   b. If one could safely assume that stock market returns closely resemble a single-index structure, how many estimates would be needed?

2. The following are estimates for two of the stocks in problem 1.

Stock	Expected Return	Beta	Firm-Specific Standard Deviation
A	.13	.8	.30
B	.18	1.2	.40

The market index has a standard deviation of .22 and the riskless rate is .08.

a. What is the standard deviation of stocks *A* and *B*?

b. Suppose that we were to construct a portfolio with the following proportions:

Stock *A*	.30
Stock *B*	.45
T-bills	.25 ($r_f = 8\%$)

Compute the expected return, standard deviation, beta, and nonsystematic standard deviation of the portfolio.

3. Consider the following two regression curves for stocks A and B.

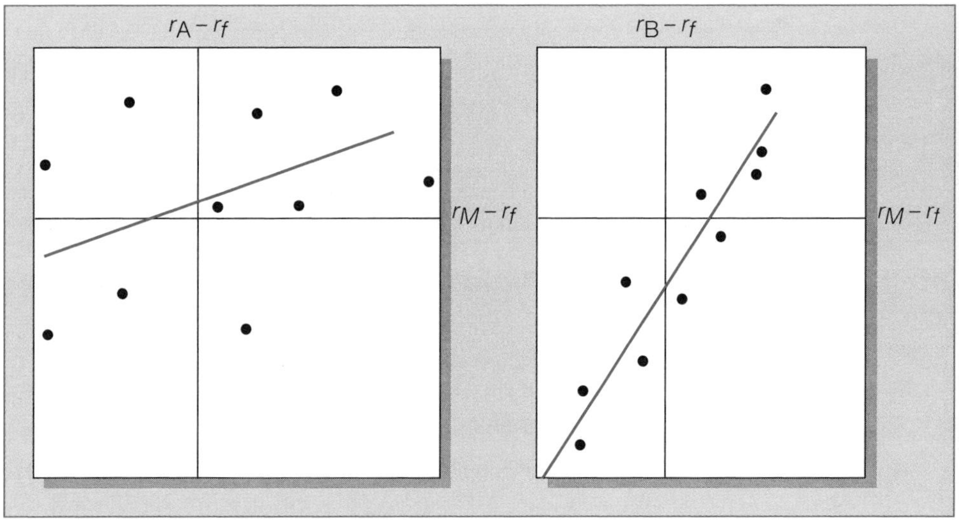

a. Which stock has higher firm-specific risk?
b. Which stock has greater systematic (market) risk?
c. Which stock has higher *R*-square?
d. Which stock has higher alpha?
e. Which stock has higher correlation with the market?

4. Consider the two (excess return) index model regression results for stocks A and B:

$$R_A = .01 + 1.2R_M$$
$$R\text{-square} = .576$$
$$\sigma(e) = 10.3\%$$

$$R_B = -.02 + .8R_M$$
$$R\text{-square} = .436$$
$$\sigma(e) = 9.1\%$$

a. Which stock has more firm-specific risk?
b. Which has greater market risk?
c. For which stock does market movement explain a greater fraction of return variability?
d. Which stock had an average return in excess of that predicted by the CAPM?
e. If r_f were constant at 6 percent and the regression had been run using total rather than excess returns, what would have been the regression intercept for stock A?

Use the following data for problems 5–11. Suppose that the index model for stocks A and B is estimated with the following results:

$$R_A = .03 + .70R_M + e_A$$
$$R_B = -.02 + 1.20R_M + e_B$$
$$\sigma_M = .20;\ R_A\text{-square} = .20;\ R_B\text{-square} = .12$$

5. What is the standard deviation of each stock?

6. Break down the variance of each stock to the systematic and firm-specific components.

7. What is the covariance and correlation coefficient between the two stocks?

8. What is the covariance between each stock and the market index?

9. Are the intercepts of the two regressions consistent with the CAPM? Interpret their values.

10. For portfolio P with investment proportions of .60 in A and .40 in B, rework problems 5, 6, and 8.

11. Rework problem 10 for portfolio Q with investment proportions of .50 in P, .30 in the market index, and .20 in T-bills.

12. In a two-stock capital market, the capitalization of stock A is twice that of B. The standard deviation of the excess return on A is 30 percent and on B is 50 percent. The correlation coefficient between the excess returns is .7.

a. What is the standard deviation of the market index portfolio?
b. What is the beta of each stock?
c. What is the residual variance of each stock?
d. If the index model holds and stock A is expected to earn 11 percent in excess of the risk-free rate, what must be the risk premium on the market portfolio?

CFA® PROBLEMS

13. When the annualized monthly percentage rates of return for a stock market index were regressed against the returns for ABC and XYZ stocks over the period 1992–2001 in an ordinary least squares regression, the following results were obtained:

Statistic	ABC	XYZ
Alpha	−3.20%	7.3%
Beta	0.60	0.97
R-square	0.35	0.17
Residual standard deviation	13.02%	21.45%

Explain what these regression results tell the analyst about risk–return relationships for each stock over the 1992–2001 period. Comment on their implications for future risk–return relationships, assuming both stocks were included in a diversified common stock portfolio, especially in view of the following additional data obtained from two brokerage houses, which are based on two years of weekly data ending in December 2001.

Brokerage House	Beta of ABC	Beta of XYZ
A	.62	1.45
B	.71	1.25

14. Suppose that the following factors have been identified for the Canadian economy: the growth rate of industrial production, IP, and the inflation rate, IR. IP is expected to be 3 percent, and IR 5 percent. A stock with a beta of 1 on IP and .5 on IR currently is expected to provide a rate of return of 12 percent. If industrial production actually grows by 5 percent while the inflation rate turns out to be 8 percent, what is your revised estimate of the expected rate of return on the stock?

15. Suppose that there are two independent economic factors, F_1 and F_2. The risk-free rate is 6 percent, and all stocks have independent firm-specific components with a standard deviation of 45 percent. The following are well-diversified portfolios:

Portfolio	Beta on F_1	Beta on F_2	Expected Return
A	1.5	2.0	31
B	2.2	–0.2	27

What is the expected return–beta relationship in this economy?

16. Consider the following data for a one-factor economy. All portfolios are well diversified.

Portfolio	$E(r)$	Beta
A	12%	1.2
F	6%	0

Suppose that portfolio *B* is well diversified with a beta of .6 and expected return of 8 percent. Would an arbitrage opportunity exist? If so, what would be the arbitrage strategy?

17. The following is a scenario for three stocks constructed by the security analysts of Pf Inc.

		Scenario Rate of Return (%)		
Stock	Price ($)	Recession	Average	Boom
A	10	–15	20	30
B	15	25	10	–10
C	50	12	15	12

Construct an arbitrage portfolio using these stocks.

18. Assume that both portfolios *A* and *B* are well diversified, that $E(r_A) = .12$, and $E(r_B) = .09$. If the economy has only one factor, and $\beta_A = 1.2$ whereas $\beta_B = .8$, what must be the risk-free rate?

19. Assume that stock market returns have the market index as a common factor, and that all stocks in the economy have a beta of 1 on the market index. Firm-specific returns all have a standard deviation of .30.

Suppose that an analyst studies 20 stocks and finds that one-half have an alpha of 2 percent, and the other half an alpha of –2 percent. Suppose the analyst buys $1 million of an equally weighted portfolio of the positive alpha stocks and shorts \$1 million of an equally weighted portfolio of the negative alpha stocks.

a. What is the expected profit (in dollars) and standard deviation of the analyst's profit?

b. How does your answer change if the analyst examines 50 stocks instead of 20 stocks? 100 stocks?

20. Assume that security returns are generated by the single-index model

$$R_i = \alpha_i + \beta_i R_M + e_i$$

where R_i is the excess return for security i, and R_M is the market's excess return. The risk-free rate is 2 percent. Suppose also that there are three securities, A, B, and C, characterized by the following data:

Security	β_i	$E(R_i)$	$\sigma(e_i)$
A	.8	.10	.25
B	1.0	.12	.10
C	1.2	.14	.20

a. If $\sigma_M = .20$, calculate the variance of returns of securities A, B, and C.

b. Now assume that there are an infinite number of assets with return characteristics identical to those of A, B, and C, respectively. If one forms a well-diversified portfolio of type A securities, what will be the mean and variance of the portfolio's excess returns? What about portfolios composed only of type B or C stocks?

c. Is there an arbitrage opportunity in this market? What is it? Analyze the opportunity graphically.

21. The SML relationship states that the expected risk premium on a security in a one-factor model must be directly proportional to the security's beta. Suppose that this were not the case. For example, suppose that expected return rises more than proportionately with beta as in the following figure.

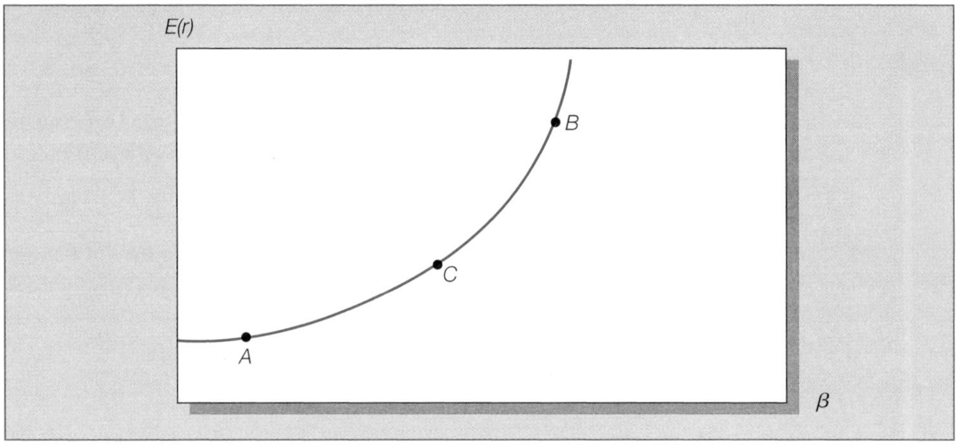

a. How could you construct an arbitrage portfolio? (*Hint:* Consider combinations of portfolios *A* and *B*, and compare the resultant portfolio to *C*.)

b. We will see in Chapter 10 that some researchers have examined the relationship between average return on diversified portfolios and the β and β^2 of those portfolios. What should they have discovered about the effect of β^2 on portfolio return?

22. If the APT is to be a useful theory, the number of systematic factors in the economy must be small. Why?

23. The APT itself does not provide guidance concerning the factors that one might expect to determine risk premiums. How should researchers decide which factors to investigate? Why, for example, is industrial production a reasonable factor to test for a risk premium?

CFA® PROBLEMS

24. Consider the following multifactor (APT) model of security returns for a particular stock:

Factor	Factor Beta	Factor Risk-Premium (%)
Inflation	1.2	6
Industrial production	0.5	8
Oil prices	0.3	3

a. If T-bills currently offer a 6 percent yield, find the expected rate of return on this stock if the market views the stock as fairly priced.

b. Suppose that the market expected the values for the three macro factors given in the middle column below, but that the actual values turn out as given in the last column. Calculate the revised expectations for the rate of return on the stock once the "surprises" become known.

Factor	Expected Rate of Change (%)	Actual Rate of Change (%)
Inflation	5	4
Industrial production	3	6
Oil prices	2	0

CFA® PROBLEMS

25. Suppose that the market can be described by the following three sources of systematic risk with associated risk premiums:

Factor	Risk Premium (%)
Industrial production (*I*)	6
Interest rates (*R*)	2
Consumer confidence (*C*)	4

The return on a particular stock is generated according to the following equation:

$$r = 15\% + 1.0I + .5R + .75C + e$$

Find the equilibrium rate of return on this stock using the APT. The T-bill rate is 6 percent. Is the stock over- or underpriced? Explain.

CFA® PROBLEMS

26. Assume that both *X* and *Y* are well-diversified portfolios and the risk-free rate is 8 percent.

Portfolio	Expected Return (%)	Beta
X	16	1.00
Y	12	0.25

In this situation you would conclude that portfolios *X* and *Y*

a. Are in equilibrium?

b. Offer an arbitrage opportunity?

c. Are both underpriced?

d. Are both fairly priced?

CFA® PROBLEMS

27. According to the theory of arbitrage,
    a. High-beta stocks are consistently overpriced
    b. Low-beta stocks are consistently overpriced
    c. Positive alpha stocks will quickly disappear
    d. Rational investors will arbitrage consistent with their risk tolerance

CFA® PROBLEMS

28. A zero investment portfolio with a positive alpha could arise if
    a. The expected return of the portfolio equals zero
    b. The capital market line is tangent to the opportunity set
    c. The law of one price remains unviolated
    d. A risk-free arbitrage opportunity exists

CFA® PROBLEMS

29. The arbitrage pricing theory (APT) differs from the capital asset pricing model (CAPM) because the APT
    a. Puts more emphasis on market risk
    b. Minimizes the importance of diversification
    c. Recognizes multiple unsystematic risk factors
    d. Recognizes multiple systematic risk factors

CFA® PROBLEMS

30. An investor will take as large a position as possible when an equilibrium price relationship is violated. This is an example of
    a. A dominance argument
    b. The mean-variance efficient frontier
    c. A risk-free arbitrage
    d. The capital asset pricing model

CFA® PROBLEMS

31. The feature of APT that offers the greatest potential advantage over the simple CAPM is the
    a. Identification of anticipated changes in production, inflation, and term structure of interest rates as key factors explaining the risk–return relationship
    b. Superior measurement of the risk-free rate of return over historical time periods
    c. Variability of coefficients of sensitivity to the APT factors for a given asset over time
    d. Use of several factors instead of a single market index to explain the risk–return relationship

CFA® PROBLEMS

32. In contrast to the capital asset pricing model, arbitrage pricing theory
    a. Requires that markets be in equilibrium
    b. Uses risk premiums based on micro variables
    c. Specifies the number and identifies specific factors that determine expected returns
    d. Does not require the restrictive assumptions concerning the market portfolio

STANDARD & POOR'S

Go to **www.mcgrawhill.ca/edumarketinsight** to obtain monthly rates of return on Alcan and the S&P 500 over the last three years. Save these returns in an Excel spreadsheet. Calculate Alcan's beta over this time period using the index model. (You can use the regression feature of Excel to perform the calculation.) What is the intercept of the regression? If your regression specification is in total returns rather than excess returns (see the section in the chapter on the industry version of the index model), what was the CAPM alpha of the stock over the time period? You can find recent interest rates at **www.stls.frb.org**.

E-INVESTMENTS

Comparing Volatilities and Beta Coefficients

Go to Yahoo finance at the following address: **finance.yahoo.com**. Using the *Symbol Lookup* function, find the ticker symbols for Alcan, Nortel Networks, and Canadian Pacific.

Once you have the tickers, return to the home page for Yahoo finance and get quotes for all of the stocks by entering the ticker symbol in the *Get Quote* function dialogue box and use the pull-down menu to the right of the *Get Quotes* box to ask for *Charts.*

When the chart appears, change the period from 1 to 2 years and use the *Compare* function, adding the other two ticker symbols and the S&P index. Hit the *Compare* button and examine your results. You should get a graph that looks similar to the one printed below.

Using the graph for comparison, which of the securities would you predict to have a beta coefficient in excess of 1.0? Which of the companies would you expect to have the highest beta coefficient?

Get the company profile by clicking *Profile,* which appears next to the company name at the top of the chart. Look through the data in the profile report until you find the beta coefficient. When in *Profile,* you can request the profile for the other companies. Are the betas as you predicted?

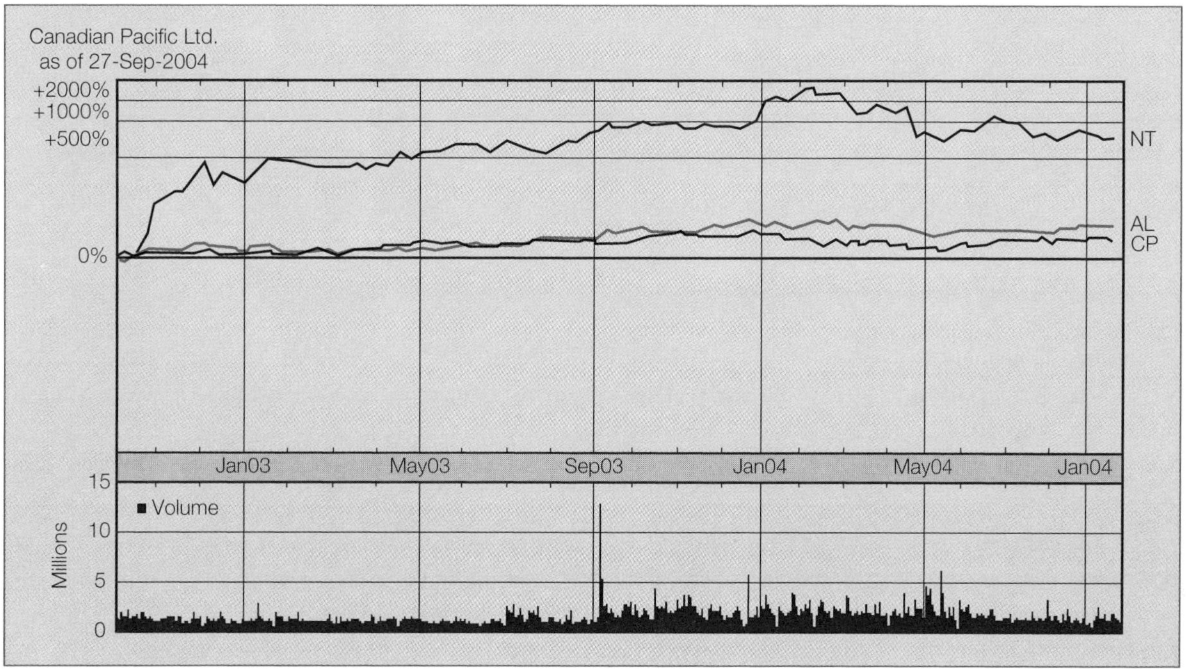

Source: Quotes & Info, Yahoo! Finance site (finance.yahoo.com), accessed September 28, 2004.

STANDARD &POOR'S

Enter the Market Insight database at **www.mcgrawhill.ca/edumarketinsight** and link to *Industry.* From the pull-down menu link to the *Computer Hardware* industry and *GO.* Review the latest S&P Industry Survey on that industry. What are the current major "industry" risk factors pertinent to the Computer Hardware industry? Which of these factors would you expect to be priced, that is, command a significant risk premium?

MARKET EFFICIENCY

In the 1950s, an early application of computers in economics was for analysis of economic time series. Business cycle theorists felt that tracing the evolution of several economic variables over time would clarify and predict the progress of the economy through boom and bust periods. A natural candidate for analysis was the behaviour of stock market prices over time. Assuming that stock prices reflect the prospects of the firm, recurrent patterns of peaks and troughs in economic performance ought to show up in those prices.

Maurice Kendall examined this proposition in 1953.[1] He found to his great surprise that he could identify *no* predictable patterns in stock prices. Prices seemed to evolve randomly. They were as likely to go up as they were to go down on any particular day, regardless of past performance. The data provided no way to predict price movements.

At first blush, Kendall's results were disturbing to some financial economists. They seemed to imply that the stock market is dominated by erratic market psychology, or "animal spirits"—that it follows no logical rules. In short, the results appeared to confirm the irrationality of the market. On further reflection, however, economists came to reverse their interpretation of Kendall's study.

It soon became apparent that random price movements indicated a well-functioning or efficient market, not an irrational one. In this chapter we will explore the reasoning behind what may seem a surprising conclusion. We show how competition among analysts leads naturally to market efficiency, and we examine the implications of the efficient market hypothesis for investment policy. We consider empirical evidence that supports and contradicts the notion of market efficiency.

Last, we examine a critique of efficient markets theory based on investors' behaviour patterns, and evaluate it in the context of evidence on security returns.

[1]Maurice Kendall, "The Analysis of Economic Time Series, Part I: Prices," *Journal of the Royal Statistical Society* 96 (1953).

9.1 RANDOM WALKS AND THE EFFICIENT MARKET HYPOTHESIS

Suppose Kendall had discovered that stock prices are predictable. What a gold mine this would have been for investors! If they could use Kendall's equations to predict stock prices, investors would reap unending profits simply by purchasing stocks that the computer model implied were about to increase in price and by selling those stocks about to fall in price.

A moment's reflection should be enough to convince yourself that this situation could not persist for long. For example, suppose that the model predicts with great confidence that XYZ's stock price, currently at $100 per share, will rise dramatically in three days to $110. What would all investors with access to the model's prediction do today? Obviously, they would place a great wave of immediate buy orders to cash in on the prospective increase in stock price. No one holding XYZ, however, would be willing to sell. The net effect would be an *immediate* jump in the stock price to $110. The forecast of a future price increase will lead instead to an immediate price increase. In other words, the stock price will immediately reflect the "good news" implicit in the model's forecast.

This simple example illustrates why Kendall's attempt to find recurrent patterns in stock price movements was doomed to failure. A forecast about favourable *future* performance leads instead to favourable *current* performance, as market participants all try to get in on the action before the price jump.

More generally, one might say that any information that could be used to predict stock performance must already be reflected in stock prices. As soon as there is any information indicating that a stock is underpriced and therefore offers a profit opportunity, investors flock to buy the stock and immediately bid up its price to a fair level, where only ordinary rates of return can be expected. These "ordinary rates" are simply rates of return commensurate with the risk of the stock.

However, if prices are bid immediately to fair levels, given all available information, it must be that they increase or decrease only in response to new information. New information, by definition, must be unpredictable; if it could be predicted, then the prediction would be part of today's information. Thus stock prices that change in response to new (unpredictable) information also must move unpredictably.

This is the essence of the argument that stock prices should follow a **random walk**, that is, that price changes should be random and unpredictable.[2] Far from a proof of market irrationality, randomly evolving stock prices are the necessary consequence of intelligent investors competing to discover relevant information on which to buy or sell stocks before the rest of the market becomes aware of that information. Indeed, if stock price movements were predictable, that would be damning evidence of stock market inefficiency, because the ability to predict prices would indicate that all available information was not already reflected in stock prices. Therefore, the notion that stocks already reflect all available information is referred to as the **efficient market hypothesis (EMH)**.[3]

Competition as the Source of Efficiency

Why should we expect stock prices to reflect "all available information"? After all, if you are willing to spend time and money gathering information, it might seem reasonable that you could turn

---

[2]Actually, we are being a little loose with terminology here. Strictly speaking, we should characterize stock prices as following a *submartingale*, meaning that the expected change in the price can be positive, presumably as compensation for the time value of money and systematic risk. Moreover, the expected return may change over time as risk factors change. A random walk is more restrictive in that it constrains successive stock returns to be independent *and* identically distributed. Nevertheless, the term *random walk* is commonly used in the looser sense that price changes are essentially unpredictable. We will follow this convention.

[3]Market efficiency should not be confused with the idea of efficient portfolios introduced in Chapter 6. An informationally efficient *market* is one in which information is rapidly disseminated and reflected in prices. An efficient *portfolio* is one with the highest expected return for a given level of risk.

up something that has been overlooked by the rest of the investment community. When information is costly to uncover and analyze, one would expect investment analysis calling for such expenditures to result in an increased expected return. This point has been stressed by Grossman and Stiglitz.[4] They argue that investors will have an incentive to spend time and resources to analyze and uncover new information only if such activity is likely to generate higher investment returns. Thus, in market equilibrium efficient information-gathering activity should be fruitful. Moreover, it would not be surprising to find that the degree of efficiency differs across various markets. For example, emerging markets that are less intensively analyzed than U.S. or Canadian markets and in which accounting disclosure requirements are much less rigorous may be less efficient than U.S. or Canadian markets. Small stocks which receive relatively little coverage by analysts may be less efficiently priced than large ones. Still, while we would not go so far as to say that you absolutely cannot come up with new information, it makes sense to consider and respect your competition.

Consider an investment management fund currently managing a \$5 billion portfolio. Suppose that the fund manager can devise a research program that could increase the portfolio rate of return by one-tenth of one percent per year, a seemingly modest amount. This program would increase the dollar return to the portfolio by \$5 billion × .001, or \$5 million. Therefore, the fund would be willing to spend up to \$5 million per year on research to increase stock returns by a mere one-tenth of one percent per year. With such large rewards for such small increases in investment performance, it should not be surprising that professional portfolio managers are willing to spend large sums on industry analysts, computer support, and research effort and therefore that price changes are, generally speaking, difficult to predict.

With so many well-backed analysts willing to spend considerable resources on research, there will not be many easy pickings in the market. Moreover, the incremental rates of return on research activity are likely to be so small that only managers of the largest portfolios will find them worth pursuing.

Although it may not literally be true that "all" relevant information will be uncovered, it is virtually certain that there are many investigators hot on the trail of any leads that may improve investment performance. Competition among these many well-backed, highly paid, aggressive analysts ensures that, as a general rule, stock prices ought to reflect available information regarding their proper levels.

Versions of the Efficient Market Hypothesis

It is common to distinguish among three versions of the EMH: the weak, semistrong, and strong forms of the hypothesis. These versions differ by their notions of what is meant by the term *all available information.*

The **weak-form** hypothesis asserts that stock prices already reflect all information that can be derived by examining market trading data, such as the history of past prices, trading volume, or short interest. This version of the hypothesis implies that trend analysis is fruitless. Past stock price data are publicly available and virtually costless to obtain. The weak-form hypothesis holds that if such data ever conveyed reliable signals about future performance, all investors would have learned already to exploit the signals. Ultimately, the signals lose their value as they become widely known because a buy signal, for instance, would result in an immediate price increase.

The **semistrong-form** hypothesis states that all publicly available information regarding the prospects of a firm must be reflected already in the stock price. Such information includes, in addition to past prices, fundamental data on the firm's product line, quality of management,

[4]Sanford J. Grossman and Joseph E. Stiglitz, "On the Impossibility of Informationally Efficient Markets," *American Economic Review* 70 (June 1980).

balance sheet composition, patents held, earning forecasts, and accounting practices. Again, if any investor has access to such information from publicly available sources, one would expect it to be reflected in stock prices.

Finally, the **strong-form** version of the efficient market hypothesis states that stock prices reflect all information relevant to the firm, even including information available only to company insiders. This version of the hypothesis is quite extreme. Few would argue with the notion that corporate officers have access to pertinent information long enough before public release to enable them to profit from trading on that information. Indeed, much of the activities of the provincial securities commissions is directed toward preventing insiders from profiting by exploiting their privileged situation. In Ontario, corporate officers, directors, and substantial owners are required to report trades in their firms' shares within ten days of the end of the month in which the trade took place. These insiders, their relatives, and any associates who trade on information supplied by insiders are considered in violation of the law.

Defining insider trading is not always easy, however. After all, stock analysts are in the business of uncovering information not already widely known to market participants. As we saw in Chapter 3, the distinction between private and inside information is sometimes murky.

CONCEPT CHECK

1. If the weak form of the efficient market hypothesis is valid, must the strong form also hold? Conversely, does strong-form efficiency imply weak-form efficiency?

9.2 IMPLICATIONS OF THE EMH FOR INVESTMENT POLICY

Technical Analysis

Technical analysis is essentially the search for recurring and predictable patterns in stock prices. Although technicians recognize the value of information that has to do with future economic prospects of the firm, they believe such information is not necessary for a successful trading strategy. Whatever the fundamental reason for a change in stock price, if the stock price responds slowly enough, the analyst will be able to identify a trend that can be exploited during the adjustment period. Technical analysis assumes a sluggish response of stock prices to fundamental supply and demand factors. This assumption is diametrically opposed to the notion of an efficient market.

Technical analysts sometimes are called *chartists* because they study records or charts of past stock prices, hoping to find patterns they can exploit to make a profit. As an example of technical analysis, consider the *relative strength* approach. The chartist compares stock performance over a recent period to performance of the market or other stocks in the same industry. A simple version of relative strength takes the ratio of the stock price to a market indicator, such as the S&P/TSX Composite index. If the ratio increases over time, the stock is said to exhibit relative strength, because its price performance is better than that of the broad market. Such strength presumably may continue for a long enough period to offer profit opportunities. We will explore this technique as well as several other tools of technical analysis further in Chapter 16.

The efficient market hypothesis predicts that technical analysis is without merit. The past history of prices and trading volume is publicly available at minimal cost. Therefore, any information that was ever available from analyzing past prices has already been reflected in stock prices. As investors compete to exploit their common knowledge of a stock's price history, they necessarily drive stock prices to levels where expected rates of return are commensurate with risk. At those levels, stocks are neither bad nor good buys. They are just fairly priced, meaning one should not expect abnormal returns.

Despite these theoretical considerations, some technically oriented trading strategies would have generated abnormal profits in the past. We will consider these strategies, and technical analysis more generally, in Chapter 16.

Fundamental Analysis

Fundamental analysis uses earnings and dividend prospects of the firm, expectations of future interest rates, and risk evaluation of the firm to determine proper stock prices. Ultimately, it represents an attempt to determine the present discounted value of all the payments a shareholder will receive from each share of stock. If that value exceeds the stock price, the fundamental analyst will recommend purchasing the stock.

Fundamental analysts usually start with a study of past earnings and an examination of company balance sheets. They supplement this analysis with further detailed economic analysis, ordinarily including an evaluation of the quality of the firm's management, the firm's standing within its industry, and the prospects for the industry as a whole. The hope is to attain some insight into the future performance of the firm that is not yet recognized by the rest of the market. Chapters 14–15 provide a detailed discussion of the types of analyses that underlie fundamental analysis.

Once again, the efficient market hypothesis predicts that *most* fundamental analysis adds little value. If analysts rely on publicly available earnings and industry information, one analyst's evaluation of the firm's prospects is not likely to be significantly more accurate than another's. There are many well-informed, well-financed firms conducting such market research, and in the face of such competition, it will be difficult to uncover data not also available to other analysts. Only analysts with a unique insight will be rewarded.

Fundamental analysis is much more difficult than merely identifying well-run firms with good prospects. Discovery of good firms does an investor no good in and of itself if the rest of the market also knows those firms are good: if the knowledge is already public, the investor will be forced to pay a high price for those firms and will not realize a superior rate of return. The trick is not to identify firms that are good, but to find firms that are *better* than everyone else's estimate. Similarly, poorly run firms can be great bargains if they are not quite as bad as their stock prices suggest. This is why fundamental analysis is difficult. It is not enough to do a good analysis of a firm; you can make money only if your analysis is better than that of your competitors, because the market price is expected already to reflect all commonly available information.

Active Versus Passive Portfolio Management

By now it is apparent that casual efforts to pick stocks are not likely to pay off. Competition among investors ensures that any easily implemented stock evaluation technique will be used widely enough so that any insights derived will be reflected in stock prices. Only serious, time-consuming, and expensive techniques are likely to generate the *differential* insight necessary to generate trading profits.

Moreover, these techniques are economically feasible only for managers of large portfolios. If you have only $100,000 to invest, even a 1 percent per year improvement in performance generates only $1,000 per year, hardly enough to justify herculean efforts. The billion-dollar manager, however, reaps extra income of $10 million annually from the same 1 percent increment.

If small investors are not in a favoured position to conduct active portfolio management, what are their choices? The small investor probably is better off placing funds in a mutual fund. By pooling resources in this way, small investors can gain from economies of size.

More difficult decisions remain, though. Can investors be sure that even large mutual funds have the ability or resources to uncover mispriced stocks? Further, will any mispricing be sufficiently large to repay the costs entailed in active portfolio management?

Proponents of the efficient market hypothesis believe that active management is largely wasted effort and unlikely to justify the expenses incurred. Therefore, they advocate a **passive investment strategy** that makes no attempt to outsmart the market. A passive strategy aims only at establishing a well-diversified portfolio of securities without attempting to find under- or overvalued stocks. Passive management usually is characterized by a buy-and-hold strategy. Because the efficient market theory indicates that stock prices are at fair levels, given all available information, it makes no sense to buy and sell securities frequently, which generates large brokerage fees without increasing expected performance.

www.td.com

One common strategy for passive management is to create an **index fund**. Such a fund aims to mirror the performance of a broad-based index of stocks. For example, TD Asset Management sponsors a mutual fund called the TD S&P/TSX Composite Index Fund, which holds stocks in direct proportion to their weight in the S&P/TSX Composite index. The performance of the fund therefore replicates the performance of the Composite. Investors in this fund obtain broad diversification with relatively low management fees. The fees can be kept to a minimum because there is no need to pay analysts for assessing stock prospects or to incur transaction costs from high portfolio turnover.

As the boxed article here shows, indexing has grown considerably in appeal in recent years, especially in the United States. Many institutional investors now hold indexed bond portfolios in addition to indexed stock portfolios. Such bond portfolios aim to replicate the features of well-known bond indices. Managers of large portfolios, such as those of pension funds, often create their own indexed funds rather than paying a mutual fund manager to do so for them. A hybrid strategy also is fairly common, where the fund maintains a *passive core,* which is an indexed position, and augments that position with one or more actively managed portfolios.

CONCEPT CHECK

2. What would happen to market efficiency if *all* investors attempted to follow a passive strategy?

The Role of Portfolio Management in an Efficient Market

If the market is efficient, why not throw darts at *The Globe and Mail*'s stock quotations page instead of trying rationally to choose a stock portfolio? This is a tempting conclusion to draw from the notion that security prices are fairly set, but it is far too facile. There is a role for rational portfolio management, even in perfectly efficient markets.

You have learned that a basic principle in portfolio selection is diversification. Even if all stocks are priced fairly, each still poses firm-specific risks that can be eliminated through diversification. Therefore, rational security selection, even in an efficient market, calls for the selection of a well-diversified portfolio providing the systematic risk level that the investor wants.

Rational investment policy also requires that tax considerations be reflected in security choice. High tax-bracket investors generally will not want the same securities that low-bracket investors find favourable. For instance, high-bracket investors might want to tilt their portfolios in the direction of capital gains as opposed to dividend or interest income, because the option to defer the realization of capital gain income is more valuable the higher the current tax bracket. Hence these investors may prefer stocks that yield lower dividends yet offer greater expected capital gain income. They also will be more attracted to investment opportunities for which returns are sensitive to tax benefits, such as real estate ventures.

A third argument for rational portfolio management relates to the particular risk profile of the investor. For example, an executive for an auto parts firm whose annual bonus depends on his firm's profits generally should not invest additional amounts in auto stocks. To the extent that his

ARE ALL INDEX FUNDS CREATED EQUAL?

The very high rates of return observed, until recently, on many stock markets around the world and their superior performance over managed domestic portfolios has led to increased interest in investment funds whose performance mirrors that of a specific index. This increased interest is seen in the large number of new index funds that have been introduced based on domestic and foreign markets. Of the 63 Canadian-based index funds covering Canadian and foreign indexes (including segregated funds), 63% have been in operation less than three years.

With this increased interest, do investors know exactly what they are purchasing when they buy an index fund? Are there some elements of index funds and their construction that should be understood before purchase?

It is my contention that a careful analysis of index funds is needed, or the investor may have an unexpected surprise.

What Is an Index Fund?

An index fund is a portfolio of securities chosen to replicate the performance of a specific benchmark portfolio, such as a stock market index (either broadly or narrowly defined), or a bond market index. Indexing is a passive strategy in which portfolio rebalancing occurs only when the benchmark composition changes. The divergence of the index fund's performance from that of the benchmark is an indication of how effectively the fund has performed its replication. This divergence is referred to as tracking error and can be the result of a number of factors, including the management expense ratio (MER), uninvested cash, or the replication strategy used by the fund.

It is important to note that performance in the index fund context is not the same as performance for non-index portfolios. For the latter funds, performance is related to observed return over a benchmark relative to the risk incurred. For the index fund, excluding the management expense ratio, perfect replication would result in no excess return over the benchmark, no difference in risk, and complete alignment of movement in index values and rates of return between the replicating fund and the benchmark.

Who Uses Index Funds?

The list of index fund users is large and includes institutional investors, who often manage their own replication strategies, and individual investors who purchase either mutual funds or closed-end investment funds that provide units replicating the composition of the benchmark. These latter portfolios are called Index Participation Units (IPUs).

What Are the Uncertainties?

First, the investor must fully understand the benchmark used. The benchmark can vary from a small subset of available stocks on a domestic market, such as the i60 found on the Toronto Stock Exchange, to a large set of stocks such as SPDRs which replicate the S&P 500 index, to a combination of bond, domestic and foreign stock indexes.

Depending on the investor's rationale for purchasing an index fund, the choice of index can be very important. For example, the investor may want to use the index fund as a base upon which to place an overlay portfolio built on her own expectations concerning certain stocks or sectors. If the index fund does not match the benchmark, the investor may end up with an overall portfolio strategy that is not what was expected.

To further confuse the issue, some funds are not "pure" index funds, but add an overlay equity portfolio; these are often referred to as enhanced index funds. For example, National Bank Mutual Funds has an open-end index fund called Canadian Index Plus that invests between 70% to 80% of its funds in the i60, with the remainder actively managed. The fund has an MER between that of a pure index fund and a non-index fund.

or her compensation already depends on the auto industry's well-being, the executive already is overinvested in that industry and should not exacerbate the lack of diversification.

Investors of varying ages also might warrant different portfolio policies with regard to risk bearing. For example, older investors who are essentially living off savings might choose to avoid long-term bonds whose market values fluctuate dramatically with changes in interest rates (discussed in Part Four). Because these investors are living off accumulated savings, they require conservation of principal. In contrast, younger investors might be more inclined toward long-term bonds. The steady flow of income over long periods of time that is locked in with long-term bonds can be more important than preservation of principal to those with long life expectancies.

In conclusion, there is a role for portfolio management even in an efficient market. Investors' optimal positions will vary according to factors such as age, tax bracket, risk aversion, and employment. The role of the portfolio manager in an efficient market is to tailor the portfolio to these needs, rather than to beat the market.

If an investor believes that mutual fund managers are "closet indexers," then an index fund strategy is sensible. However, purchasing an enhanced index fund will generate a portfolio that due to its lack of correlation with the benchmark does not track it well, and will over- or underperform the benchmark based on the bets taken within the portfolio.

Tracking Error

Tracking uncertainty exists based on the replication methodology. Each replication method has a set of transaction costs. For example, consider the strategy where the fund buys all of the stocks in the benchmark portfolio in their existing proportions. This eliminates tracking error, but increases transaction costs by the purchase of small capitalization stocks in the benchmark, which will increase bid-ask cost and could have an impact on the share price. As well, if the fund is not sufficiently large, this strategy will lead to rounding error as it forces expensive odd lot transactions.

At the other extreme is a partial replication strategy that uses a subset of the stocks in the benchmark. The replicating portfolio usually includes the stocks with the greatest weight and invests a smaller amount, if any, in the small cap stocks in the benchmark. Since the benchmark portfolio is not perfectly replicated, rebalancing will be required as market prices of stocks in the benchmark change. A partial replication strategy reduces the transaction costs of building the portfolio, but increases tracking error.

Provided the investor knows the benchmark that is being used, tracking error is the fundamental source of uncertainty. Up to this point I have left the definition of tracking error vague; it is related to the difference between the return (value) of the replicating portfolio and the return (value) of the benchmark. I consider two general methods to measure tracking error. One is a simple average of the deviations of the returns (values). This approach gives the same weight to all observations. Thus, two index funds based on the same index will have the same tracking error as long as their average returns are the same over the measurement period—their variability could be very different. However, if a large deviation, regardless of direction, is given a larger weight than a small deviation, tracking error can be measured as the average of the squared values of the deviations. This approach is consistent with the measurement of error in forecasting models. It permits decomposition of the error into a number of identifiable components, one of which is the difference in the average returns (values).

The index fund purchaser should have a way to determine ex ante whether the fund is expected to track well and, after the fact, how well it did track. For funds that have been in existence long enough, assuming the replication philosophy will not change, expected tracking error can be assessed using historical data. However, how does a buyer of a new index fund assess its tracking error? The fund's published replication strategy will give some indication. The fund can provide the tracking error components based on a simulation of the performance of the index fund and the benchmark.

Since all index funds are not the same and can differ in fundamental ways, more information should be provided to the investor. Information on a fund's replication philosophy, the method used to construct the portfolio, and a rating system for index funds based on their observed or simulated tracking error and its components would help investors make informed investment decisions.

Source: Paul Halpern, "Are All Index Funds Created Equal?" *Canadian Investment Review* 13, no. 4 (Winter 2000), pp. 57–58. Used by permission.

9.3 EVENT STUDIES

The notion of informationally efficient markets leads to a powerful research methodology. If security prices reflect all currently available information, then price changes must reflect new information. Therefore it seems that one should be able to measure the importance of an event of interest by examining price changes during the period in which the event occurs.

An **event study** describes a technique of empirical financial research that enables an observer to assess the impact of a particular event on a firm's stock price. A stock market analyst might want to study the impact of dividend changes on stock prices, for example. An event study would quantify the relationship between dividend changes and stock returns. Using the results of such a study together with a superior means of predicting dividend changes, the analyst could, in principle, earn superior trading profits.

Analyzing the impact of an announced change in dividends is more difficult than it might first appear. On any particular day stock prices respond to a wide range of economic news, such as updated forecasts for GNP, inflation rates, interest rates, or corporate profitability. Isolating the part of a stock price movement that is attributable to a dividend announcement is not a trivial exercise.

The statistical approach that researchers commonly use to measure the impact of a particular information release, such as the announcement of a dividend change, is a marriage of efficient market theory with the index model discussed in Chapter 8. We want to measure the unexpected return that results from an event. This is the difference between the actual stock return and the return that might have been expected given the performance of the market. This expected return can be calculated using the index model.

Recall that the index model holds that stock returns are determined by a market factor and a firm-specific factor. The stock return, r_t, during a given period, t, would be expressed mathematically as

$$r_t = a + br_{Mt} + e_t \qquad (9.1)$$

where r_{Mt} is the market's excess rate of return during the period and e_t is the part of a security's return resulting from firm-specific events. The parameter b measures sensitivity to the market return, and a is the average rate of return the stock would realize in a period with a zero market return. Equation 9.1 therefore provides a decomposition of r_t into market and firm-specific factors. The firm-specific return may be interpreted as the unexpected return that results from the event.

Determination of the firm-specific return in a given period requires that we obtain an estimate of the term e_t. Therefore, we rewrite equation 9.1

$$e_t = r_t - (a + br_{Mt}) \qquad (9.2)$$

Equation 9.2 has a simple interpretation: to determine the firm-specific component of a stock's return, subtract the return that the stock ordinarily would earn for a given level of market performance from the actual rate of return on the stock. The residual, e_t, is the stock's return over and above what one would predict from broad market movements in that period, given the stock's sensitivity to the market.

For example, suppose that the analyst has estimated that $a = .5\%$ and $b = .8$. On a day that the market goes up by 1 percent, you would predict from equation 9.1 that the stock should rise by an expected value of $.5\% + .8 \times 1\% = 1.3\%$.[5] If the stock actually rises by 2 percent, the analyst would infer that firm-specific news that day caused an additional stock return of $2\% - 1.3\% = .7\%$. We sometimes refer to the term e_t in equation 9.2 as the **abnormal return**—the return beyond what would be predicted from market movements alone.

The general strategy in event studies is to estimate the abnormal return around the date that new information about a stock is released to the market and attribute the abnormal stock performance to the new information. The first step in the study is to estimate parameters a and b for each security in the study. These typically are calculated using index model regressions, as described in Chapter 8, in a period before that in which the event occurs. The prior period is used for estimation so that the impact of the event will not affect the estimates of the parameters. Next, the information release dates for each firm are recorded. For example, in a study of the impact of merger attempts on the stock prices of target firms, the **announcement date** is the date on which the public is informed that a merger is to be attempted. Finally, the abnormal returns of each firm surrounding the announcement date are computed, and the statistical significance and magnitude of the typical abnormal return is assessed to determine the impact of the newly released information.

---

[5]We know from Chapter 7, Section 7.1, that the CAPM implies that the intercept a in equation 9.1 should equal $r_f(1 - b)$. Nevertheless, it is customary to estimate the intercept in this equation empirically rather than imposing the CAPM value. One justification for this practice is the empirically fitted security market lines seem flatter than predicted by the CAPM (see Chapter 10), which would make the intercept implied by the CAPM too small.

One concern that complicates event studies arises from *leakage* of information. Leakage occurs when information regarding a relevant event is released to a small group of investors before official public release. In this case, the stock price might start to increase (in the case of a "good news" announcement) days or weeks before the official announcement date. Any abnormal return on the announcement date is then a poor indicator of the total impact of the information release. A better indicator would be the **cumulative abnormal return**, which is simply the sum of all abnormal returns over the time period of interest. The cumulative abnormal return thus captures the total firm-specific stock movement for an entire period when the market might be responding to new information.

Figure 9.1 presents the results from a fairly typical event study. The authors of this study were interested in leakage of information before minority buyout[6] announcements and constructed a sample of 172 firms that were targets of a minority buyout attempt. In most buyouts, shareholders of the acquired firms sell their shares to the acquirer at substantial premiums over market value. Announcement of a buyout attempt is good news for shareholders of the target firm and therefore should cause stock prices to jump.

Figure 9.1 confirms the good-news nature of the announcements. On the announcement day, called day 0, the average cumulative abnormal return (CAR) for the sample of buyout candidates increases substantially, indicating a large and positive abnormal return on the announcement date. Notice that immediately after the announcement date the CAR no longer increases or decreases significantly. This is in accord with the efficient market hypothesis. Once the new information became public, the stock prices jumped almost immediately in response to the good news. With prices once again fairly set, reflecting the effect of the new information, further abnormal returns on any particular day are equally likely to be positive or negative. In fact, for a sample of many firms, the average abnormal return will be extremely close to zero, and thus the CAR will show neither upward nor downward drift. This is precisely the pattern shown in Figure 9.1.

The pattern of returns for the days preceding the public announcement date yields some interesting evidence about efficient markets and information leakage. If insider trading rules were perfectly obeyed and perfectly enforced, stock prices should show no abnormal returns

Figure 9.1 Cumulative abnormal returns before minority buyout attempts: target companies.

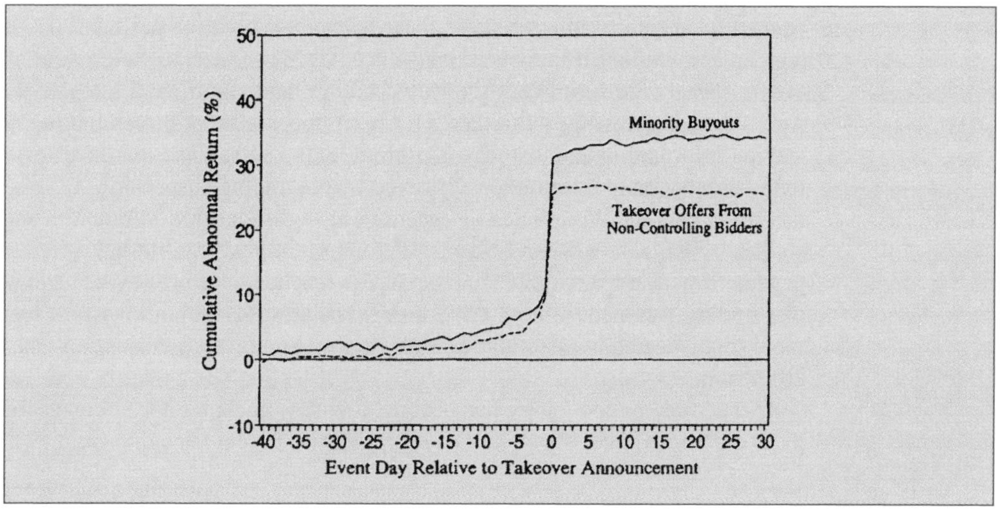

Source: Brian F. Smith and Ben Amoako-Adu, "Minority Buyouts and Ownership Characteristics: Evidence from the Toronto Stock Exchange," *Financial Management*, Summer 1992. Reprinted by permission.

[6] A minority buyout occurs when a controlling shareholder purchases the remaining shares of the firm from the minority shareholders.

on days before the public release of relevant news, because no special firm-specific information would be available to the market before public announcement. Instead, we should observe a clean jump in the stock price only on the announcement day. In fact, the prices of these buyout or, more generally, takeover targets clearly start an upward drift 30 days before the public announcement. There are two possible interpretations of this pattern. One is that information is leaking to some market participants who then purchase the stocks before the public announcement. At least some abuse of insider trading rules is occurring.

Another interpretation is that in the days before a takeover attempt the public becomes suspicious of the attempt as it observes someone buying large blocks of stock. As acquisition intentions become more evident, the probability of an attempted merger is gradually revised upward so that we see a gradual increase in CARs. Although this interpretation is certainly a valid possibility, evidence of leakage appears almost universally in event studies, even in cases where the public's access to information is not gradual. It appears as if insider trading violations do occur.

Actually, securities commissions can take some comfort from patterns such as that in Figure 9.1. If insider trading rules were widely and flagrantly violated, we would expect to see abnormal returns earlier than they appear in these results. The CAR would turn positive as soon as the minority buyout is decided, because insiders would start trading immediately. By the time of the public announcement, the insiders would have bid up the stock price to levels reflecting the buyout attempt, and the abnormal returns on the actual public announcement date would be close to zero. The dramatic increase in the CAR that we see on the announcement date indicates that a good deal of these announcements were indeed news to the market and that stock prices did not already reflect complete knowledge about the buyouts. It would appear, therefore, that securities commission enforcement does have a substantial effect on restricting insider trading, even if some amount of it persists.

Early Canadian studies had painted a less optimistic picture of the contribution of securities trading regulation to market efficiency. For instance, the event studies methodology was applied by Kryzanowski[7] to investigate the effectiveness of trading suspensions in the three major Canadian stock exchanges (TSE, ME, and VSE) in arresting manipulative activities (mostly through dissemination of misleading information) on stock returns. The study identified stocks suspended from floor trading in these three exchanges over the period 1967–1973 because of alleged manipulation. It then examined the CARs in the weeks before and after the suspension event. These were significantly positive before, and significantly negative after, for up to ten weeks around the suspension date. Hence, it appeared that disseminating and exploiting misleading information about stocks is profitable. It also seemed that investors were slow to react to the unfavourable information conveyed by the trading suspension.

Fortunately these inefficiencies seem to have disappeared in more recent years. Two recent studies by Kryzanowski and Nemiroff[8] found that post-trading-halt price adjustments of suspended firms were very quick, and the CARs reached their post-event level within the same day that trading resumed, in both Canadian exchanges. Canadian investors seem to have become more sophisticated in assimulating and reacting to relevant information, thus enhancing market efficiency.

Event study methodology has become a widely accepted tool to measure the economic impact of a wide range of events. For example, two recent Canadian studies have used the event

[7]Lawrence Kyzanowski, "Misinformation and Regulatory Actions in the Canadian Capital Markets: Some Empirical Evidence," *The Bell Journal of Economics* 9, no. 2 (Fall 1978); and "The Efficacy of Trading Suspensions: A Regulatory Action Designed to Prevent the Exploitation of Monopoly Information," *Journal of Finance* 34 (December 1979).

[8]L. Kryzanowski and Howard Nemiroff, "Price Discovery Around Trading Halts on the Montreal Exchange Using Trade Data" and "Market Quote and Spread Component Cost Behaviour Around Trading Halts for Stocks Inter-listed on the Toronto Stock Exchange," both in the *Financial Review*, 1998, pp. 195–212 and 2001, pp. 115–138.

methodology to investigate the impact of banking merger failures and the announcements of business relocation decisions.[9] The U.S. SEC regularly uses event studies to measure illicit gains captured by traders who may have violated insider trading or other securities laws.[10] Event studies are also used in fraud cases, where the courts must assess damages caused by a fraudulent activity.

CONCEPT CHECK

3. Suppose that we see negative abnormal returns (declining CARs) after an announcement date. Is this a violation of efficient markets?

9.4 ARE MARKETS EFFICIENT?

The Issues

Not surprisingly, the efficient market hypothesis does not exactly arouse enthusiasm in the community of professional portfolio managers. It implies that a great deal of the activity of portfolio managers—the search for undervalued securities—is at best wasted effort and quite probably harmful to clients because it costs money and leads to imperfectly diversified portfolios. Consequently, the EMH has never been widely accepted among professionals, and debate continues today on the degree to which security analysis can improve investment performance (see boxed article here). Before discussing empirical tests of the hypothesis, we want to note three factors that together imply that the debate probably never will be settled: the *magnitude issue,* the *selection bias issue,* and the *lucky event issue.*

The Magnitude Issue Consider an investment manager overseeing a $2 billion portfolio. If she can improve performance by only one-tenth of one percent per year, that effort will be worth .001 × $2 billion = $2 million annually. This manager clearly would be worth her salary! Yet can we, as observers, statistically measure her contribution? Probably not: a one-tenth of one percent contribution would be swamped by the yearly volatility of the market. Remember, the annual standard deviation of the well-diversified S&P/TSX Composite index has been more than 16 percent per year. Against these fluctuations, a small increase in performance would be hard to detect. Nevertheless, $2 million remains an extremely valuable improvement in performance.

All might agree that stock prices are very close to fair values, and that only managers of large portfolios can earn enough trading profits to make the exploitation of minor mispricing worth the effort. According to this view, the actions of intelligent investment managers are the driving force behind the constant evolution of market prices to fair levels. Rather than ask the qualitative question, "Are markets efficient?" we ought to instead ask a more quantitative question: "How efficient are markets?"

info.wsj.com

The Selection Bias Issue Suppose that you discover an investment scheme that could really make money. You have two choices: either publish your technique in *The Wall Street Journal* or *The Globe and Mail* to win fleeting fame, or keep your technique secret and use it

[9]Ramon Baltazar and Michael Santos, "The Benefits of Banking Mega-mergers: Event Study Evidence from the 1998 Failed Mega-merger Attempts in Canada," and H. Bhabra, U. Lel, and D. Tirtiroglu, "Stock Market's Reaction to Business Relocations: Canadian Evidence," both in *Canadian Journal of Administrative Sciences*, September 2003 and December 2002.

[10]For a review of SEC applications of this technique, see Mark Mitchell and Jeffry Netter, "The Role of Financial Economics in Securities Fraud Cases: Applications at the Securities and Exchange Commission," School of Business Administration, University of Michigan, Working Paper No. 93-25, October 1993.

SECOND THOUGHTS ABOUT INDEX FUNDS

I am looking at a clipping, sent by a friend, of something I wrote in 1976 about the potential drawbacks of index funds. Even then it was a quixotic argument, easily ignored in the dramatic rise of the "passive" school of investing. And yet the question still bears thinking about: Don't these funds, by their refusal to favour one stock over another, subvert the basic economic purpose of the markets?

Index investors seek merely to match the performance of an index such as the Standard & Poor's 500. By dispensing with the effort and expense of research and minimizing trading costs, index funds gain an edge against the average managed fund. I didn't dispute this compelling rationale then, nor do I now. Only it isn't the whole story.

Good old 1976 was a big year for landmarks, what with the U.S. Bicentennial. It was also the year that indexing was adapted to the mutual fund format by Jack Bogle, founder of what is now the second-largest fund firm, the Vanguard Group.

Back in 1976, John Humbach of the Fordham University School of Law and economist Stephen Dresch lamented that index funds go against a prime function of the markets—steering capital to places where it can be put to the most productive use. "For this to work," they said, "investors in the capital market must pick and choose intelligently among competing investment possibilities." Index investors don't do that; they allocate their money by default according to whatever decisions are made by other investors as a group.

Now consider the proposition that many of the savviest investors are likely to be attracted to indexing, leaving judgments about which company is most promising to less prudent speculators.

By the late 1990s we had a speculative boom in the markets. For a time, the very popularity of indexing helped create demand for the big stocks that dominate the S&P 500. Then, near the peak, money poured into stocks of small companies that had never turned a profit, and in quite a few cases never would. Wouldn't it be interesting to see research on how much indexing might have contributed to the extremes of the late 1990s stock market?

"Excessive indexing can lead to an inefficient market," says Vladimir de Vassal, director of quantitative research at Glenmede Trust Co. in Philadelphia, which manages US$18-billion. "The equity market can only be efficient when active investors continually adjust security prices based on new information." This line of thinking leads to one positive conclusion. The more "inefficiencies" arise in any market, the more money-making opportunities present themselves to investors willing to stake their money on their judgment.

So unless everybody becomes an indexer, there's a self-correcting mechanism in place here. The catch is, it will function only so long as stubborn holdouts remain who refuse to index their money.

Source: Chet Currier, "Second Thoughts About Index Funds: Passive Approach Undermines Market Efficiency," *National Post*, August 18, 2001, p. D.2.

to earn millions of dollars. Most investors would choose the latter option, which presents us with a conundrum. Only investors who find that an investment scheme cannot generate abnormal returns will be willing to report their findings to the whole world. Hence, opponents of the efficient-market view of the world always can use evidence that various techniques do not provide investment rewards as proof that the techniques that do work simply are not being reported to the public. This is a problem in *selection bias:* the outcomes we are able to observe have been preselected in favour of failed attempts. Therefore, we cannot fairly evaluate the true ability of portfolio managers to generate winning stock market strategies.

The Lucky Event Issue In virtually any month it seems we read an article about some investor or investment company with a fantastic investment performance over the recent past. Surely the superior records of such investors disprove the efficient market hypothesis.

Yet this conclusion is far from obvious. As an analogy to the investment game, consider a contest to flip the most number of heads out of 50 trials using a fair coin. The expected outcome for any person is, of course, 50 percent heads and 50 percent tails. If 10,000 people, however, compete in this contest, it would not be surprising if at least one or two contestants flipped more than 75 percent heads. In fact, elementary statistics tells us that the expected number of contestants flipping 75 percent or more heads would be two. It would be silly, though, to crown these people the "head-flipping champions of the world." Obviously, they are simply the contestants who happened to get lucky on the day of the event. (See the boxed article "How to Guarantee a Successful Market Newsletter" here.)

HOW TO GUARANTEE A SUCCESSFUL MARKET NEWSLETTER

Suppose you want to make your fortune publishing a market newsletter. You need first to convince potential subscribers that you have talent worth paying for. Ah, but what if you have no talent? The solution is simple: start eight newsletters.

In year 1, let four of your newsletters predict an up-market and four a down-market. In year 2, let half of the originally optimistic group of newsletters continue to predict an up-market and the other half a down-market. Do the same for the originally pessimistic group. Continue in this manner to obtain the pattern of predictions shown in the table here (U = prediction of an up-market, D = prediction of a down-market).

After three years, no matter what has happened to the market, one of the newsletters would have had a perfect prediction record. This is because after three years there are $2^3 = 8$ outcomes for the market, and we have covered all eight possibilities with the eight newsletters. Now, we simply slough off the seven unsuccessful newsletters, and market the eighth newsletter on its perfect track record. If we want to establish a newsletter with a perfect track record over a four-year period, we need $2^4 = 16$ newsletters. A five-year period requires 32 newsletters, and so on.

After the fact, the one newsletter that was always right will attract attention for your uncanny foresight and investors will rush to pay large fees for its advice. Your fortune is made, and you never even researched the market!

Warning: This scheme is illegal! The point, however, is that with hundreds of market newsletters, you can find one that has stumbled onto an apparently remarkable string of successful predictions without any real degree of skill. After the fact, *someone's* prediction history can seem to imply great forecasting skill. This person is the one we will read about in *The Wall Street Journal* and *The Globe and Mail*; the others will be forgotten.

	Newsletter Predictions							
Year	**1**	**2**	**3**	**4**	**5**	**6**	**7**	**8**
1	U	U	U	U	D	D	D	D
2	U	U	D	D	U	U	D	D
3	U	D	U	D	U	D	U	D

The analogy to efficient markets is clear. Under the hypothesis that any stock is fairly priced given all available information, any bet on a stock is simply a coin toss. There is equal likelihood of winning or losing the bet. However, if many investors using a variety of schemes make fair bets, statistically speaking, *some* of those investors will be lucky and win a great majority of the bets. For every big winner, there may be many big losers, but we never hear of these managers. The winners, though, turn up in the financial press as the latest stock market gurus; then they can make a fortune publishing market newsletters.

Our point is that after the fact there will have been at least one successful investment scheme. A doubter will call the results luck, the successful investor will call it skill. The proper test would be to see whether the successful investors can repeat their performance in another period, yet this approach is rarely taken.

With these caveats in mind, we now turn to some of the empirical tests of the efficient markets hypothesis.

CONCEPT CHECK

4. The Fidelity Magellan Fund managed by Peter Lynch outperformed the S&P 500 in 11 of the 13 years that Lynch managed the fund, resulting in an average annual return more than 10 percent better than that of the index. Is this performance sufficient to dissuade you from a belief in efficient markets? If not, would *any* performance record be sufficient to dissuade you?

Weak-Form Tests: Patterns in Stock Returns

Returns over Short Horizons Early tests of efficient markets were tests of the weak form. Could speculators find trends in past prices that would enable them to earn abnormal profits? This is essentially a test of the efficacy of technical analysis.

One way of discerning trends in stock prices is by measuring the *serial correlation* of stock market returns. Serial correlation refers to the tendency for stock returns to be related to past returns. Positive serial correlation means that positive returns tend to follow positive returns (a momentum type of property). Negative serial correlation means that positive returns tend to be followed by negative returns (a reversal or "correction" property). Both Conrad and Kaul[11] and Lo and MacKinlay[12] examine weekly returns of NYSE stocks and find positive serial correlation over short horizons. However, the correlation coefficients of weekly returns tend to be fairly small, at least for large stocks for which price data are the most reliably up to date. Thus, while these studies demonstrate weak price trends over short periods, the evidence does not clearly suggest the existence of trading opportunities.

A more sophisticated version of trend analysis is a **filter rule**. A filter technique gives a rule for buying or selling a stock depending on past price movements. One rule, for example, might be: "Buy if the last two trades each resulted in a stock price increase." A more conventional one might be: "Buy a security if its price increased by 1 percent, and hold it until its price falls by more than 1 percent from the subsequent high." Alexander[13] and Fama and Blume[14] found that such filter rules generally could not generate trading profits.

These very-short-horizon studies suggest momentum in stock market prices, albeit of a magnitude that may be too small to exploit. However, in an investigation of intermediate-horizon stock price behaviour (using 3-to-12-month holding periods) Jegadeesh and Titman[15] found that stocks exhibit a momentum property in which good or bad recent performance continues. They conclude that while the performance of individual stocks is highly unpredictable, *portfolios* of the best-performing stocks in the recent past appear to outperform other stocks with enough reliability to offer profit opportunities.

The momentum property has also been documented in Canada by several studies, especially Cleary and Inglis.[16] As in the U.S., momentum was found for both good and bad recent performance, but the excess returns that it generated may not have been sufficient to overcome transaction costs of a magnitude of about 100 basis points.

Returns over Long Horizons While studies of short-horizon returns have detected modest positive serial correlation in stock market prices, tests[17,18] of long-horizon returns (i.e., returns over multiyear periods) have found suggestions of pronounced negative long-term serial correlation. The latter result has given rise to a "fads hypothesis," which asserts that stock prices might overreact to relevant news. Such overreaction leads to positive serial correlation (momentum) over short time horizons. Subsequent correction of the overreaction leads to poor performance following good performance and vice versa. The corrections mean that a run of positive returns eventually will tend to be followed by negative returns, leading to negative serial correlation over

[11] Jennifer Conrad and Gautam Kaul, "Time-Variation in Expected Returns." *Journal of Business* 61 (October 1988), pp. 409–425.

[12] Andrew W. Lo and A. Craig MacKinlay, "Stock Market Prices Do Not Follow Random Walks: Evidence from a Simple Specification Test," *Review of Financial Studies* 1 (1988), pp. 41–66.

[13] Sidney Alexander, "Price Movements in Speculative Markets: Trends or Random Walks, No. 2," in Paul Cootner, ed., *The Random Character of Stock Market Prices* (Cambridge, MA: MIT Press, 1964).

[14] Eugene Fama and Marshall Blume, "Filter Rules and Stock Market Trading Profits," *Journal of Business* 39 (Supplement January 1966).

[15] Narasimhan Jegadeesh and Sheridan Titman, "Returns to Buying Winners and Selling Losers: Implications for Stock Market Efficiency," *Journal of Finance* 48 (March 1993), pp. 65–91.

[16] S. Cleary and M. Inglis, "Momentum in Canadian Stock Returns," *Canadian Journal of Administrative Sciences* 10, no. 3 (September 1998), 279–291. See also S. Foerster, "Back to the Future—Again," and R. Kan and G. Kirikos, "Now You See Them, Now You Don't," both in the Fall 1996 issue of the *Canadian Investment Review*, and the survey articles by V. Jog, "Canadian Stock Pricing Anomalies: Revisited," *Canadian Investment Review* (Winter 1998) and G. Athanassakos and S. Foerster, "Canadian Security Market Anomalies," in *Security Market Imperfections in Worldwide Equity Markets*, W. Ziemba and D. Keim, eds. (Cambridge University Press, 1999).

[17] Eugene F. Fama and Kenneth R. French, "Permanent and Temporary Components of Stock Prices," *Journal of Political Economy* 96 (April 1988), pp. 246–273.

[18] James Poterba and Lawrence Summers, "Mean Reversion in Stock Prices: Evidence and Implications," *Journal of Financial Economics* 22 (October 1988), pp. 27–59.

longer horizons. These episodes of apparent overshooting followed by correction give stock prices the appearance of fluctuating around their fair values.

These long-horizon results are dramatic, but the studies offer far from conclusive evidence regarding efficient markets. First, the study results need not be interpreted as evidence for stock market fads. An alternative interpretation of these results holds that they indicate only that market risk premiums vary over time. The response of market prices to variation in the risk premium can lead one to incorrectly infer the presence of mean reversion and excess volatility in prices. For example, when the risk premium and the required return on the market rises, stock prices will fall. When the market then rises (on average) at this higher rate of return, the data convey the impression of a stock price recovery. The impression of overshooting and correction is in fact no more than a rational response of market prices to changes in discount rates.

In addition to studies suggestive of overreaction in overall stock market returns over long horizons, many other studies suggest that over long horizons, extreme performance in particular securities also tends to reverse itself: the stocks that have performed best in the recent past seem to underperform the rest of the market in following periods, while the worst past performers tend to offer above-average future performance. DeBondt and Thaler[19] and Chopra, Lakonishok, and Ritter[20] find strong tendencies for poorly performing stocks in one period to experience sizable reversals over the subsequent period, while the best-performing stocks in a given period tend to follow with poor performance in the following period.

For example, the DeBondt and Thaler study found that if one were to rank order the performance of stocks over a five-year period and then group stocks into portfolios based on investment performance, the base-period "loser" portfolio (defined as the 35 stocks with the worst investment performance) outperformed the "winner" portfolio (the top 35 stocks) by an average of 25 percent (cumulative return) in the following three-year period. This **reversal effect**, in which losers rebound and winners fade back, suggests that the stock market overreacts to relevant news. After the overreaction is recognized, extreme investment performance is reversed. This phenomenon would imply that a *contrarian* investment strategy—investing in recent losers and avoiding recent winners—should be profitable.

It would be hard to explain apparent overreaction in the cross section of stocks by appealing to time-varying risk premiums. Moreover, these returns seem pronounced enough to be exploited profitably.

Thus it appears that there may be short-run momentum but long-run reversal patterns in price behaviour both for the market as a whole and across sectors of the market. One interpretation of this pattern is that short-run overreaction (which causes momentum in prices) may lead to long-term reversals (when the market recognizes its past error). This interpretation is emphasized by Haugen.[21]

Predictors of Broad Market Returns Several studies have documented the ability of easily observed variables to predict market returns. For example, Fama and French[22] show that the return on the aggregate stock market tends to be higher when the dividend/price ratio, the dividend yield, is high. Campbell and Shiller[23] find that the earnings yield can predict market returns. Keim and Stambaugh[24] show that bond market data, such as the spread between yields on high- and low-grade corporate bonds, also help predict broad market returns.

---

[19]Werner F. M. DeBondt and Richard Thaler, "Does the Stock Market Overreact?" *Journal of Finance* 40 (1985), pp. 793–805.

[20]Navin Chopra, Josef Lakonishok, and Jay R. Ritter, "Measuring Abnormal Performance: Do Stocks Overreact?" *Journal of Financial Economics* 31 (1992), pp. 235–68.

[21]Robert A. Haugen, *The New Finance: The Case Against Efficient Markets* (Englewood Cliffs, NJ: Prentice Hall, 1995).

[22]Eugene F. Fama and Kenneth R. French, "Dividend Yields and Expected Stock Returns," *Journal of Financial Economics* 22 (October 1988), pp. 3–25.

[23]John Y. Campbell and Robert Shiller, "Stock Prices, Earnings and Expected Dividends," *Journal of Finance* 43 (July 1988), pp. 661–676.

[24]Donald B. Keim and Robert F. Stambaugh, "Predicting Returns in the Stock and Bond Markets," *Journal of Financial Economics* 17 (1986), pp. 357–390.

Again, the interpretation of these results is difficult. On the one hand, they may imply that stock returns can be predicted, in violation of the efficient market hypothesis. More probably, however, these variables are proxying for variation in the market risk premium. For example, given a level of dividends or earnings, stock prices will be lower and dividend and earnings yields will be higher when the risk premium (and therefore the expected market return) is larger. Thus, a high dividend or earnings yield will be associated with higher market returns. This does not indicate a violation of market efficiency—the predictability of market returns is due to predictability in the risk premium, not in risk-adjusted abnormal returns.

Fama and French[25] show that the yield spread between high- and low-grade bonds has greater predictive power for returns on low-grade bonds than for returns on high-grade bonds and greater predictive power for stock returns than for bond returns, suggesting that the predictability in returns is in fact a risk premium rather than evidence of market inefficiency. Similarly, the fact that the dividend yield on stocks helps to predict bond market returns suggests that the yield captures a risk premium common to both markets rather than mispricing in the equity market.

Semistrong Tests: Market Anomalies

Fundamental analysis calls on a much wider range of information to create portfolios than does technical analysis, and tests of the value of fundamental analysis are thus correspondingly more difficult to evaluate. They have, however, revealed a number of so-called **anomalies**, that is, evidence that seems inconsistent with the efficient market hypothesis. We will review several such anomalies in the following pages.

We must note before starting that one major problem with these tests is that most require risk adjustments to portfolio performance and most use the CAPM to make the risk adjustments. Although beta seems to be a relevant descriptor of stock risk, the empirically measured quantitative tradeoff between risk as measured by beta and expected return differs from the predictions of the CAPM. (We review this evidence in the next chapter.) If we use the CAPM to adjust portfolio returns for risk, inappropriate adjustments may lead to the conclusion that various portfolio strategies can generate superior returns, when in fact it simply is the risk-adjustment procedure that has failed.

Another way to put this is to note that tests of risk-adjusted returns are *joint tests* of the efficient market hypothesis *and* the risk-adjustment procedure. If it appears that a portfolio strategy can generate superior returns, we must then decide whether this is due to a failure of the EMH or to an inappropriate risk-adjustment technique. Usually, the risk-adjustment technique is based on more questionable assumptions than is the EMH; by opting to reject the procedure, we are left with no conclusion about market efficiency.

An example of this issue is the discovery by Basu[26] that portfolios of low price-earnings ratio stocks have higher average returns than do high P/E portfolios. The **P/E effect** holds up even if returns are adjusted for portfolio beta. Is this a confirmation that the market systematically misprices stocks according to P/E ratios? This would be an extremely surprising and, to us, disturbing conclusion, because analysis of P/E ratios is such a simple procedure. Although it may be possible to earn superior returns using hard work and much insight, it hardly seems possible that such a simplistic technique is enough to generate abnormal returns. One possible interpretation

[25]Eugene F. Fama and Kenneth R. French, "Business Conditions and Expected Returns on Stocks and Bonds," *Journal of Financial Economics* 25 (November 1989), pp. 3–22.

[26]Sanjoy Basu, "The Investment Performance of Common Stocks in Relation to Their Price-Earnings Ratios: A Test of the Efficient Market Hypothesis," *Journal of Finance* 32 (June 1977), pp. 663–682; and "The Relationship Between Earnings Yield, Market Value, and Return for NYSE Common Stocks: Further Evidence," *Journal of Financial Economics* 12 (June 1983). See also J. Bourgeois and J. Lussier, "P/E's and Performance in the Canadian Market," *Canadian Investment Review*, Spring 1994.

of these results is that the model of capital market equilibrium is at fault in that the returns are not properly adjusted for risk.

This makes sense, because if two firms have the same expected earnings, then the riskier stock will sell at a lower price and lower P/E ratio. Because of its higher risk, the low P/E stock also will have higher expected returns. Therefore, unless the CAPM beta fully adjusts for risk, P/E will act as a useful additional descriptor of risk, and will be associated with abnormal returns if the CAPM is used to establish benchmark performance.

The Small-Firm-in-January Effect One of the most important anomalies with respect to the efficient market is the so-called size, or **small-firm effect**, originally documented by Banz.[27] Figure 9.2 illustrates the size effect. It shows the historical performance of portfolios formed by dividing the NYSE stocks into ten portfolios each year according to firm size (i.e., the total value of outstanding equity). Average annual returns are consistently higher on the small-firm portfolios. The difference in average annual return between portfolio 10 (with the largest firms) and portfolio 1 (with the smallest firms) is 8.59 percent. Of course, the smaller-firm portfolios tend to be riskier. But even when returns are adjusted for risk using the CAPM, there is still a consistent premium for the smaller-sized portfolios. Even on a risk-adjusted basis, the smallest-size portfolio outperforms the largest-firm portfolio by an average of 4.3 percent annually.

This is a huge premium; imagine earning a premium of this size on a billion-dollar portfolio. Yet it is remarkable that following a simple (even simplistic) rule such as "invest in low capitalization stocks" should enable an investor to earn excess returns. After all, any investor can measure firm size at little cost. One would not expect such minimal effort to yield such large rewards.

Later studies (Keim,[28] Reinganum,[29] and Blume and Stambaugh[30]) showed that the small-firm effect occurs virtually entirely in January, in fact, in the first two weeks of January. The size effect is in fact a "small-firm-in-January" effect.[31]

Some researchers believe that the January effect is tied to tax-loss selling at the end of the year. The hypothesis is that many people sell stocks that have declined in price during the previous

Figure 9.2
Returns in excess of risk-free rate and in excess of the Security Market Line for ten size-based portfolios.

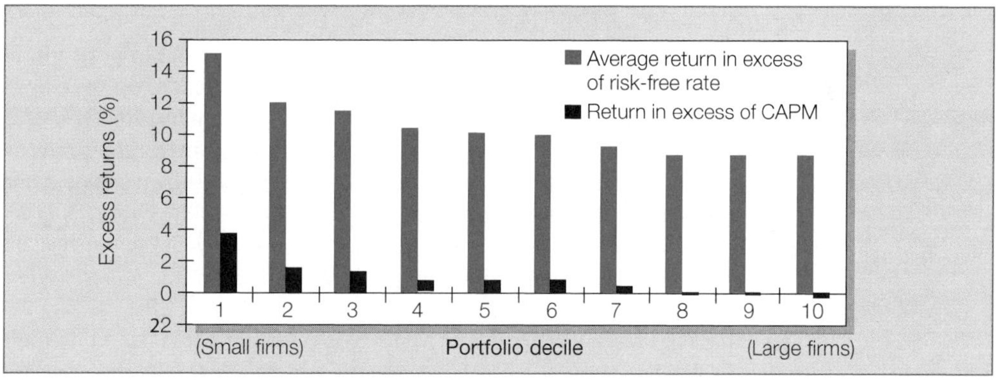

Source: Ibbotson Associates, *Stocks, Bonds, Bills, and Inflation 2000 Yearbook*, 2000.

---

[27]Rolf Banz, "The Relationship Between Return and Market Value of Common Stocks," *Journal of Financial Economics* 9 (March 1981).

[28]Donald B. Keim, "Size Related Anomalies and Stock Return Seasonality: Further Empirical Evidence," *Journal of Financial Economics* 12 (June 1983).

[29]Marc R. Reinganum, "The Anomalous Stock Market Behavior of Small Firms in January: Empirical Tests for Tax-Loss Effects," *Journal of Financial Economics* 12 (June 1983).

[30]Marshall E. Blume and Robert F. Stambaugh, "Biases in Computed Returns: An Application to the Size Effect," *Journal of Financial Economics* 12 (1983), pp. 387–404.

[31]The small-firm-in-January effect appears also in a recent Canadian study by K. Assoé and O. Sy, "Profitability of the Short-Run Contrarian Strategy in Canadian Stock Markets," *Canadian Journal of Administrative Sciences* 20, no. 4 (December 2003).

months to realize their capital losses before the end of the tax year. Such investors do not put the proceeds from these sales back into the stock market until after the turn of the year. At that point the rush of demand for stock puts upward pressure on prices that results in the January effect. Indeed, Ritter[32] shows that the ratio of stock purchases to sales of individual investors reaches an annual low at the end of December and an annual high at the beginning of January. The January effect is said to show up most dramatically for the smallest firms because the small-firm group includes, as an empirical matter, stocks with the greatest variability of prices during the year. The group therefore includes a relatively large number of firms that have declined sufficiently to induce tax-loss selling.

From a theoretical standpoint, this theory has substantial flaws. First, if the positive January effect is a manifestation of buying pressure, it should be matched by a symmetric negative December effect when the tax-loss incentives induce selling pressure. Second, the predictable January effect flies in the face of efficient market theory. If investors who do not already hold these firms know that January will bring abnormal returns to the small-firm group, they should rush to purchase stock in December to capture those returns. This would push buying pressure from January to December. Rational investors should not "allow" such predictable abnormal January returns to persist. However, small firms outperform large ones in January in every year of Keim's study, 1963–1979.

Despite these theoretical objections, some empirical evidence supports the belief that the January effect is connected to tax-loss selling. For example, Reinganum found that, within size class, firms that had declined more severely in price had larger January returns.

Several Canadian studies confirm the ambiguous nature of the conclusions drawn from the U.S. results. Berges, McConnell, and Schlarbaum[33] found a significant January effect in Canadian stock returns, and this effect was more pronounced for firms with smaller values. The abnormally high January returns, however, were present during the entire period covered by the study (1951–1980), even though Canada did not introduce a capital gains tax until 1973. Thus, there is little evidence that tax-loss selling caused the January effect. A subsequent study by Tinic, Barone-Adesi, and West[34] confirmed the fact that tax-loss selling could not be the sole cause for the high January returns. This last study, however, did find some influence of the tax laws on the seasonality of returns, since the introduction of capital gains taxation in 1972 was shown to have some influence for stocks listed solely in Canada.

More recent Canadian work[35] attributes the January effect to portfolio rebalancing by professional portfolio managers in the securities industry. According to its arguments, such portfolio managers are rewarded at the end of the year with bonuses that are determined by the rate of return that they earned during the year. The managers invest the funds allocated to them in risky securities at the beginning of the year. If the securities produce a satisfactory return at some time during the year, the managers tend to lock in their returns (and their bonuses) by moving investments out of the equity market and into low-risk securities. The following January they move back into the equity market, thus producing the abnormal returns.

A 1998 survey article by Jog[36] confirms that the January effect still exists in Canada, albeit in a somewhat reduced form. It is part of a *month-end* effect, in which abnormal returns are found in the last trading day of any month and the first two trading days of the following

---

[32]Jay R. Ritter, "The Buying and Selling Behavior of Individual Investors at the Turn of the Year," *Journal of Finance* 43 (July 1988), pp. 701–717.

[33]Angel Berges, John J. McConnell, and Gary G. Schlarbaum, "The Turn-of-the-Year in Canada," *Journal of Finance* 39, no. 1 (March 1984).

[34]Seha M. Tinic, Giovanni Barone-Adesi, and Richard R. West, "Seasonality in Canadian Stock Prices: A Test of the 'Tax-Loss-Selling' Hypothesis," *Journal of Financial and Quantitative Analysis* 21, no. 1 (March 1986).

[35]G. Athanassakos, "Portfolio Rebalancing and the January Effect in Canada," *Financial Analysts Journal* (November/December 1992); and "The January Effect: Solving the Mystery," *Canadian Investment Review*, Spring 1995. See also G. Athanassakos and L. Ackert, "Institutional Investors, Analyst Following, and the January Anomaly," *Journal of Business Finance and Accounting* 27, nos. 3–4 (April/May 2000).

[36]V. Jog, "Canadian Stock Pricing Anomalies: Revisited," *Canadian Investment Review*, Winter 1998.

month; December and January, however, are not the highest-return months. Further, the January effect is more pronounced in large firms, thus contradicting earlier evidence.

The Neglected-Firm Effect and Liquidity Effects Arbel and Strebel[37] give another interpretation of the small-firm-in-January effect. Because small firms tend to be neglected by large institutional traders, information about such firms is less available. This information deficiency makes smaller firms riskier investments that command higher returns. "Brand-name" firms, after all, are subject to considerable monitoring from institutional investors that assures high-quality information, and presumably investors do not purchase "generic" stocks without the prospect of greater returns.

As evidence for the **neglected-firm effect**, Arbel[38] divided firms into highly researched, moderately researched, and neglected groups based on the number of institutions holding the stock. The January effect was in fact largest for the neglected firms.

Work by Amihud and Mendelson[39] on the effect of liquidity on stock returns might be related to both the small-firm and neglected-firm effects. They argue that investors will demand a rate of return premium to invest in less liquid stocks, which entail higher trading costs (see Chapter 7 for more details). Indeed, spreads for the least liquid stocks easily can be more than 5 percent of stock value. In accord with their hypothesis, Amihud and Mendelson show that these stocks show a strong tendency to exhibit abnormally high risk-adjusted rates of return. Because small and less-analyzed stocks as a rule are less liquid, the liquidity effect might be a partial explanation of their abnormal returns. However, this theory does not explain why the abnormal returns of small firms should be concentrated in January. In any case, exploiting these effects can be more difficult than it would appear. The trading costs on small stocks can easily wipe out any apparent abnormal profit opportunity.

Book-to-Market Ratios Fama, French, and Reinganum[40] show that a very powerful predictor of returns across securities is the ratio of the book value of the firm's equity to the market value of equity. They stratify firms into ten groups according to book-to-market ratios and examine the average monthly rate of return of each of the ten groups during the period July 1963–December 1990. The decile with the highest book-to market ratio had an average monthly return of 1.65 percent, while the lowest-ratio decile averaged only .72 percent per month. Figure 9.3 shows the pattern of returns across deciles. The dramatic dependence of returns on book-to-market ratio is independent of beta, suggesting either that low book-to-market ratio firms are relatively underpriced or that the book-to-market ratio is serving as a proxy for a risk factor that affects equilibrium-expected returns.

In fact, Fama and French found that after controlling for the size and **book-to-market effects**, beta seemed to have no power to explain average security returns.[41] This finding is an important challenge to the notion of rational markets, since it seems to imply that a factor that should affect returns—systematic risk—seems not to matter, while a factor that should not matter—the book-to-market ratio—seems capable of predicting future returns. We will return to the interpretation of this anomaly.

---

[37]Avner Arbel and Paul J. Strebel, "Pay Attention to Neglected Firms," *Journal of Portfolio Management*, Winter 1983.

[38]Avner Arbel, "Generic Stocks: An Old Product in a New Package," *Journal of Portfolio Management*, Summer 1985.

[39]Yakov Amihud and Haim Mendelson, "Asset Pricing and the Bid-Ask Spread," *Journal of Financial Economics* 17 (December 1987), pp. 223–250; and "Liquidity, Asset Prices, and Financial Policy," *Financial Analysts Journal* 47 (November/December 1991), pp. 56–66.

[40]Eugene F. Fama and Kenneth R. French, "The Cross Section of Expected Stock Returns," *Journal of Finance* 47 (1992), pp. 427–465; Marc R. Reinganum, "The Anatomy of a Stock Market Winner," *Financial Analysts Journal*, March/April 1988, pp. 272–284.

[41]However, a study by S. P. Kothari, Jay Shanken, and Richard G. Sloan, "Another Look at the Cross-Section of Expected Stock Returns," *Journal of Finance* 50 (March 1995), pp. 185–224 finds that when betas are estimated using annual rather than monthly returns, securities with high beta values do in fact have higher average returns. Moreover, the authors find a book-to-market effect that is attenuated compared to the results in Fama and French and furthermore is inconsistent across different samples of securities. They conclude that the empirical case for the importance of the book-to-market ratio may be somewhat weaker than the Fama and French study would suggest.

Figure 9.3 Average rate of return as a function of the book-to-market ratio.

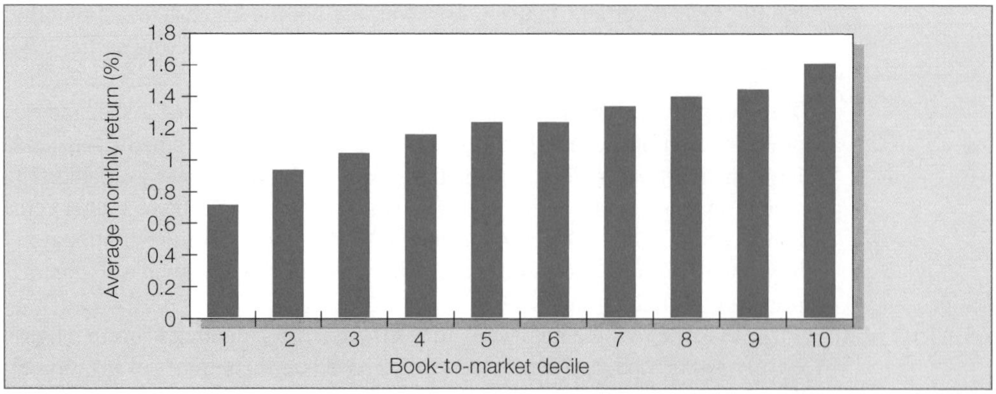

Source: Eugene F. Fama and Kenneth R. French, "The Cross Section of Expected Stock Returns," *Journal of Finance* 47 (1992), pp. 427–65.

Post-Earnings-Announcement Price Drift A puzzling anomaly is the apparently sluggish response of stock prices to firms' earnings announcements. The "news content" of an earnings announcement can be evaluated by comparing the announcement to the value previously expected by market participants. The difference is the "earnings surprise." While firms' stock prices react to earnings surprises immediately upon announcement, there are also significant abnormal returns *after* the announcement date. We shall review the relevant studies in Chapter 15.

Strong-Form Tests: Inside Information

It would not be surprising if insiders were able to make superior profits trading in their firm's stock. The ability of insiders to trade profitably in their own stock has been documented in U.S. studies by Jaffe,[42] Seyhun,[43] Givoly and Palmon,[44] and others. Jaffe's was one of the earlier studies that documented the tendency for stock prices to rise after insiders intensively bought shares and to fall after intensive insider sales.

Similar results also were found in Canadian studies by Masse, Hanrahan, and Kushner[45] and Eckbo,[46] who examined the daily returns to companies targeted for mergers or acquisitions prior to the date of public announcement. They found evidence of significant abnormally high returns, which is consistent with the use of inside information to trade profitably in the market.

To enhance fairness, securities commissions require all insiders to register the changes in their holdings of company stock within ten days of the end of the month in which the changes take place. Once the insiders file the required statements, the knowledge of their trades becomes public information. At that point, if markets are efficient, fully and immediately processing the released information, an investor should no longer be able to profit from following the pattern of those trades.

The U.S. study by Seyhun, which carefully tracked the public release dates of the insider trading information, found that following **insider transactions** would be of no avail. Although there is some tendency for stock prices to increase even after public reports of insider buying, the abnormal returns are not of sufficient magnitude to overcome transaction costs.

[42] Jeffrey F. Jaffe, "Special Information and Insider Trading," *Journal of Business* 47 (July 1974).

[43] H. Nejat Seyhun, "Insiders' Profits, Costs of Trading and Market Efficiency," *Journal of Financial Economics* 16 (1986).

[44] Dan Givoly and Dan Palmon, "Insider Trading and Exploitation of Inside Information: Some Empirical Evidence," *Journal of Business* 58 (1985).

[45] Isidore Masse, Robert Hanrahan, and Joseph Kushner, "Returns to Insider Trading: The Canadian Evidence," *Canadian Journal of Administrative Sciences* 5, no. 3 (September 1988).

[46] B. Espen Eckbo, "Mergers and the Market for Corporate Control: The Canadian Evidence," *Canadian Journal of Economics* 19, no. 2 (May 1986).

The Canadian evidence yields mixed conclusions. Baesel and Stein[47] investigated the performance of two insider groups on the TSX, ordinary insiders and insiders who were bank directors. Although both groups earned significant positive abnormal returns, the second group's such returns were higher. Fowler and Rorke[48] used monthly returns of firms listed on the TSE during the period 1967–1977 to investigate whether an outsider could realize abnormal returns by following insider transactions after they were publicly reported. They found that abnormal returns following "intense" buying or selling activity by insiders persisted for at least 12 months after the official release of the insider trading information. Moreover, the size of the returns indicated that trading profits could have been realized even after paying reasonable transactions costs. Similar results were also found in subsequent studies by Lee and Bishara,[49] for the period 1975–1983, and Suret and Cormier,[50] for the period May 1986–July 1988. These findings seem to indicate a clear violation of market efficiency for the TSX, at least for the periods covered by these studies.

On the other hand, a study by Heinkel and Kraus[51] on the Vancouver Stock Exchange[52] (VSE) found rather weak evidence of the ability of insider trading to generate abnormal returns for insiders. The sample of firms that Heinkel and Kraus examined over the period June 1979–June 1, 1981, was rather atypical. It consisted of small resource companies listed on the VSE, for which insiders are by far the largest shareholders. Thus, although the results could be interpreted as evidence of market efficiency of the strong form, they cannot be extrapolated to other situations.

Interpreting the Evidence

Risk Premiums or Anomalies? The small-firm, market-to-book, and long-term reversal effects are currently among the most puzzling phenomena in empirical finance. There are several interpretations of these effects. First note that to some extent, these three phenomena may be related. The feature that small firms, low market-to-book firms, and recent "losers" seem to have in common is a stock price that has fallen considerably in recent months or years. Indeed, a firm can become a small firm, or a low market-to-book firm by suffering a sharp drop in price. These groups therefore may contain a relatively high proportion of distressed firms that have suffered recent difficulties.

Fama and French[53] argue that these effects can be explained as manifestations of risk premiums. Using an arbitrage pricing type of model, they show that stocks with higher "betas" (also known as factor loadings) on size or market-to-book factors have higher average returns; they interpret these returns as evidence of a risk premium associated with the factor.

Fama and French propose a *three-factor model*, in the spirit of arbitrage pricing theory. Risk is determined by the sensitivity of a stock to three factors: (1) the market portfolio, (2) a portfolio that reflects the relative returns of small versus large firms, and (3) a portfolio that reflects the relative returns of firms with high versus low ratios of book value to market value. This model does a good job in explaining security returns. While size or book-to-market ratios per se are obviously not risk factors, they perhaps might act as proxies for more fundamental determinants of

---

[47]Jerome Baesel and Garry Stein, "The Value of Information Inferences from the Profitability of Insider Trading," *Journal of Financial and Quantitative Analysis* 14 (September 1979).

[48]David J. Fowler and C. Harvey Rorke, "Insider Trading Profits on the Toronto Stock Exchange, 1967–1977," *Canadian Journal of Administrative Sciences* 5, no. 1 (March 1988).

[49]M. H. Lee and H. Bishara, "Recent Canadian Experience on the Profitability of Insider Trades," *The Financial Review* 24, no. 2 (May 1989).

[50]Jean-Marc Suret and Elise Cormier, "Insiders and the Stock Market," *Canadian Investment Review* 3, no. 2 (Fall 1990).

[51]Robert Heinkel and Alan Kraus, "The Effect of Insider Trading on Average Rates of Return," *Canadian Journal of Economics* 20, no. 3 (August 1987).

[52]The VSE is now part of the TSX Venture Exchange.

[53]Eugene F. Fama and Kenneth R. French, "Common Risk Factors in the Returns on Stocks and Bonds," *Journal of Financial Economics* 33 (1993) pp. 3–56.

risk. Fama and French argue that these patterns of returns may therefore be consistent with an efficient market in which expected returns are consistent with risk. We examine this paper in more detail in the next chapter.

The opposite interpretation is offered by Lakonishok, Shleifer, and Vishny[54] who argue that these phenomena are evidence of inefficient markets, more specifically, of systematic errors in the forecasts of stock analysts. They believe that analysts extrapolate past performance too far into the future and therefore overprice firms with recent good performance and underprice firms with recent poor performance. Ultimately, when market participants recognize their errors, prices reverse. This explanation is obviously consistent with the reversal effect and also, to a degree, consistent with the small firm and market-to-book effects because firms with sharp price drops may tend to be small or have low market-to-book ratios.

If Lakonishok, Shleifer, and Vishny are correct, we ought to find that analysts systematically err when forecasting returns of recent "winner" versus "loser" firms. A study by La Porta[55] is consistent with this pattern. He finds that equity of firms for which analysts predict low growth rates of earnings actually perform better than those with high expected earnings growth. Analysts seem overly pessimistic about firms with low growth prospects and overly optimistic about firms with high growth prospects. When these too-extreme expectations are "corrected," the low-expected-growth firms outperform high-expected-growth firms.

Daniel and Titman[56] attempt to test whether these effects can in fact be explained as risk premia. They first classify firms according to size and market-to-book ratio and then further stratify portfolios based on the betas of each stock on size and market-to-book factors. They find that once size and market-to-book ratio are held fixed, the betas on these factors do not add any additional information about expected returns. They conclude that the characteristics per se, and not the betas on the size or market-to-book factors, influence returns. This result is inconsistent with the Fama-French interpretation that the high returns on these portfolios may reflect risk premia.

The Daniel and Titman results do not *necessarily* imply irrational markets. As noted, it might be that these characteristics per se measure a distressed condition that itself commands a return premium. Moreover, as we have noted, a good part of these apparently abnormal returns may be reflective of an illiquidity premium since small and low-priced firms tend to have bigger bid-asked spreads. Nevertheless, a compelling explanation of these results has yet to be offered.

Anomalies or Data Mining? We have covered many of the so-called anomalies cited in the literature, but our list could go on and on. Some wonder whether these anomalies really are unexplained puzzles in financial markets, or whether they instead are an artifact of data mining. After all, if one reruns the computer database of past returns over and over and examines stock returns along enough dimensions, simple chance will cause some criteria to *appear* to predict returns.

In this regard, it is noteworthy that some anomalies have not shown much staying power after being reported in the academic literature. For example, after the small-firm effect was published in the early 1980s, it promptly disappeared for much of the rest of the decade. Similarly, the book-to-market strategy, which commanded considerable attention in the early 1990s, was ineffective for the rest of that decade.

Still, even acknowledging the potential for data mining, a common thread seems to run through many of the anomalies we have considered, lending support to the notion that there is

---

[54]Josef Lakonishok, Andrei Shleifer, and Robert W. Vishny, "Contrarian Investment, Extrapolation, and Risk," *Journal of Finance* 49 (1994), pp. 1541–1578.

[55]Raphael La Porta, "Expectations and the Cross Section of Stock Returns," *Journal of Finance* 51 (December 1996), pp. 1715–1742.

[56]Kent Daniel and Sheridan Titman, "Evidence of the Characteristics of Cross Sectional Variation in Stock Returns," *Journal of Finance* 40 (1995), pp. 383–399.

a real puzzle to explain. Value stocks—defined by low P/E ratio, high book-to-market ratio, or depressed prices relative to historic levels—seem to have provided higher average returns than "glamour" or growth stocks.

One way to address the problem of data mining is to find a data set that has not already been researched and see whether the relationship in question shows up in the new data. Such studies have revealed size, momentum, and book-to-market effects in other security markets around the world. While these phenomena may be a manifestation of a systematic risk premium, the precise nature of that risk is not fully understood.

9.5 A BEHAVIOURAL INTERPRETATION

The premise of **behavioural finance** is that conventional financial theory ignores how real people make decisions and that people make a difference.[57] A growing number of economists have come to interpret the anomalies literature as consistent with several "irrationalities" individuals exhibit when making complicated decisions. These irrationalities stem from two main premises: first, that investors do not always process information correctly and therefore infer incorrect probability distributions about future rates of return; and second, that even given a probability distribution of returns, investors often make inconsistent or systematically suboptimal decisions.

Of course, the existence of irrational investors would not by itself be sufficient to render capital markets inefficient. If such irrationalities did affect prices, sharp-eyed arbitrageurs taking advantage of profit opportunities might be expected to push prices back to their proper values. Thus, the second leg of the behavioural critique is that in practice the actions of such arbitrageurs are limited.

This leg of the argument is important when we interpret tests of market efficiency. Virtually everyone agrees that if prices are right (i.e., price = intrinsic value), there are no easy profit opportunities. But the reverse is not necessarily true. If behaviourists are correct about limits to arbitrage activity, the absence of profit opportunities does not necessarily imply that markets are efficient. Most tests of the efficient market hypothesis have focused on the existence of profit opportunities, often as reflected in the performance of money managers. But their failure to perform well (see Chapter 4 and the next section) need not imply that markets are in fact efficient.

We will examine some of the information-processing and behavioural irrationalities documented by psychologists and show how these tendencies might be consistent with the anomalies discussed earlier in this chapter. We will then briefly consider limits to arbitrage, and finally evaluate the import of the behavioural debate.

Information Processing

Errors in information processing can lead investors to misestimate the true probabilities of possible events or associated rates or return. Several such biases have been catalogued. Here are four of the more important ones.

Forecasting Errors A series of experiments by Kahneman and Tversky[58] indicates that people give too much weight to recent experience compared to prior beliefs when making forecasts (sometimes dubbed a *memory bias*) and tend to make forecasts that are too extreme given

[57]The discussion in this section is based on two excellent survey articles: Nicholas Barberis and Richard Thaler, "A Survey of Behavioral Finance," in *Handbook of the Economics of Finance*, eds. G. Constantinides, M. Harris, and R. Stulz (Amsterdam: Elsevier North-Holland, 2003), Chapter 18; and Werner F. M. DeBondt and R. H. Thaler, "Financial Decision Making in Markets and Firms," in *Handbooks in Operations Research and Management Science, Volume 9: Finance*, eds. R. A. Jarrow, V. Maksimovic, W. T. Ziemba (Amsterdam, Elsevier: 1995).

[58]D. Kahneman and A. Tversky, "On the Psychology of Prediction," *Psychology Review* 80 (1973), pp. 237–51; and "Subjective Probability: A Judgment of Representativeness," *Cognitive Psychology* 3 (1972), pp. 430–54.

the uncertainty inherent in their information. DeBondt and Thaler[59] argue that the P/E effect can be explained by earnings expectations that are too extreme. In this view, when forecasts of a firm's future earnings are high, perhaps due to favourable recent performance, they tend to be *too* high relative to the objective prospects of the firm. This results in a high initial P/E (due to the optimism built into the stock price) and poor subsequent performance when investors recognize their error. Thus, high P/E firms tend to be poor investments.

Overconfidence People tend to overestimate the precision of their beliefs or forecasts, and they tend to overestimate their abilities. In one famous survey, 90 percent of drivers in Sweden ranked themselves as better-than-average drivers. Such overconfidence may be responsible for the prevalence of active versus passive investment management—itself an anomaly to an adherent of the efficient market hypothesis. Despite the recent growth in indexing, less than 10 percent of the equity in the mutual fund industry is held in indexed accounts. The dominance of active management in the face of the typical underperformance of such strategies (consider the disappointing performance of actively managed mutual funds documented in Chapter 4 as well as in the following section) is consistent with a tendency to overestimate ability.

An interesting example of overconfidence in financial markets is provided by Barber and Odean,[60] who compare trading activity and average returns in brokerage accounts of men and women. They find that men (in particular single men) trade far more actively than women, consistent with the greater overconfidence among men well documented in the psychology literature. They also find that high trading activity is highly predictive of poor investment performance. The top 20 percent of accounts ranked by portfolio turnover had average returns 7 percentage points lower than the 20 percent of the accounts with the lowest turnover rates. As they conclude, "Trading [and by implication, overconfidence] is hazardous to your wealth."

Conservatism A conservatism bias means that investors are too slow (too conservative) in updating their beliefs in response to recent evidence. This means that they might initially underreact to news about a firm, so that prices will fully reflect new information only gradually. Such a bias would give rise to momentum in stock market returns.

Sample Size Neglect and Representativeness It seems that people commonly do not take into account the size of a sample, apparently reasoning that a small sample is just as representative of a population as a large one. They may therefore infer a pattern too quickly based on a small sample and extrapolate apparent trends too far into the future. It is easy to see how such a pattern would be consistent with overreaction and correction anomalies. A short-lived run of good earnings reports or high returns on a stock would lead such investors to revise their assessments of likely future performance, and thus generate buying pressure that exaggerates the price run-up. Eventually, the gap between price and intrinsic value becomes glaring and the market corrects its initial error.

Interestingly, there is evidence[61] that stocks with the best recent performance show reversals precisely in the few days surrounding earnings announcements, suggesting that the correction occurs just as investors learn that their initial beliefs were too extreme. Combining the conservatism and representativeness biases, we can obtain a pattern of short-to-middle–term momentum, along with long-term reversals, broadly consistent with much of the literature.

---

[59]Werner F. M. DeBondt and R. H. Thaler, "Do Security Analysts Overreact?" *American Economic Review* 80 (1990), pp. 52–57.

[60]Brad Barber and Terrance Odean, "Boys Will Be Boys: Gender, Overconfidence, and Common Stock Investment," *Quarterly Journal of Economics* 16 (2001), pp. 262–92, and "Trading Is Hazardous to Your Wealth: The Common Stock Investment Performance of Individual Investors," *Journal of Finance* 55 (2000), pp. 773–806.

[61]N. Chopra, J. Lakonishok, and J. Ritter, "Measuring Abnormal Performance: Do Stocks Overreact?" *Journal of Financial Economics* 31 (1992), pp. 235-68.

Behavioural Biases

Even if information processing were perfect, individuals might make less-than-fully rational decisions using that information. These behavioural biases largely affect how investors frame questions of risk versus return and therefore make risk–return tradeoffs.

Framing Decisions seem to be affected by how choices are framed. For example, famous studies by Kahneman and Tversky[62] find an individual may reject a bet when it is posed in terms of the risk surrounding possible gains but may accept that same bet when described in terms of the risk surrounding potential losses. In other words, individuals may act risk-averse in terms of gains but risk-seeking in terms of losses. But in many cases, the choice of how to frame a risky venture—as involving gains or losses—can be arbitrary.

Consider a coin toss with a payoff of $50 for tails. Now consider a gift of $50 that is bundled with a bet that imposes a loss of $50 if the coin comes up heads. In both cases, you end up with zero for heads, and $50 for tails. But the former description frames the coin toss as posing a risky gain while the latter frames the coin toss in terms of risky losses. The difference in framing can lead to different attitudes toward the bet.

Mental Accounting Mental accounting is a specific form of framing in which people segregate certain decisions. For example, an investor may take a lot of risk with one investment account but establish a very conservative position with another account that is dedicated to her child's education. Rationally, it might be better to view both accounts as part of the investor's overall portfolio with the risk-return profiles of each integrated into a unified framework. Statman[63] argues that mental accounting is consistent with some investors' irrational preference for stocks with high cash dividends (they feel free to spend dividend income, but would not "dip into capital" by selling a few shares of another stock with the same total rate of return) and with a tendency to ride losing stock positions for too long (since "behavioural investors" are reluctant to realize losses). Odean[64] documents that investors are more likely to sell stocks with gains than those with losses, precisely contrary to a tax-minimization strategy.

Mental accounting effects also can help explain momentum in stock prices. The "house money effect" refers to gamblers' greater willingness to accept new bets if they are currently ahead. They think of (i.e., frame) the bet as being made with their "winnings account," that is, with the casino's and not with their own money, and thus are more willing to accept risk. Analogously, after a stock market runup, they view investments as largely funded out of a "capital gains account," become more tolerant of risk, discount future cash flows at a lower rate, and thus further push up prices.

Regret Avoidance Psychologists have found that individuals who make decisions that turn out badly have more regret (blame themselves more) when that decision was more unconventional. For example, buying a blue-chip portfolio that turns down is not as painful as experiencing the same losses on an unknown startup firm. Any losses on the blue-chip stocks can be more easily attributed to bad luck rather than bad decision-making and cause less regret. DeBondt and Thaler[65] argue that such regret avoidance is consistent with both the size and book-to-market effect. Higher book-to-market firms tend to have lower stock prices. These firms are "out of favour" and more likely to be in a financially precarious position. Similarly, smaller less-well-known firms are also less conventional investments. Such firms require more "courage" on the part of the

[62] D. Kahneman and A. Tversky, "Prospect Theory: An Analysis of Choice Under Risk," *Econometrica* 47 (March 1979), pp. 263–91.

[63] Meir Statman, "Behavioral Finance," *Contemporary Finance Digest* 1 (Winter 1997), pp. 5–22.

[64] T. Odean, "Are Investors Reluctant to Realize Their Losses?" *Journal of Finance* 53 (1998), pp. 1775–98.

[65] Werner F. M. DeBondt and R. H. Thaler, "Further Evidence on Investor Overreaction and Stock Market Seasonality," *Journal of Finance* 42 (1987), pp. 557–81.

investor, which increases the required rate of return. Mental accounting can add to this effect. If investors focus on the gains or losses of individual stocks, rather than on broad portfolios, then they can become more risk-averse concerning stocks with recent poor performance, discount their cash flows at a higher rate, and thereby create a "value stock risk premium."

Limits to Arbitrage

These behavioural biases would not matter for stock pricing if rational investors could fully profit from the mistakes of behavioural investors. As soon as prices went out of alignment, rational profit-seeking trading would reestablish proper pricing. However, behavioural advocates argue that in practice, several factors limit the ability to profit from mispricing.[66]

Fundamental Risk Suppose that a share of IBM is underpriced. Buying it may present a profit opportunity, but it is hardly risk-free, since the presumed market underpricing can get worse. While price eventually should converge to intrinsic value, this may not happen until after the investor's investment horizon. For example, the investor may be a mutual fund manager who may lose clients (not to mention a job) if short-term performance is poor or a trader who may run through her capital if the market turns against her even temporarily. Risk incurred in exploiting the apparent profit opportunity presumably will limit both the activity and effectiveness of these arbitrage traders.

Implementation Costs Exploiting overpricing can be particularly difficult. Short selling a security entails costs; short-sellers may have to return the borrowed security on little notice, rendering the horizon of the short sale uncertain; and some investors such as pension or mutual fund managers are simply not allowed to short securities. This can limit the ability of arbitrage activity to force prices to fair value. For example, Pontiff[67] demonstrates that deviations of price from net asset value in closed-end funds tend to be higher in funds that are more costly to arbitrage, for example those with high nonsystematic risk, making it difficult to hedge the risk incurred by taking a position in the fund. On the other hand, Ross[68] illustrates that premiums and discounts on closed-end funds can be explained in a "rational framework." Initial expectations of abnormal returns due to skilled management can drive price above net asset value. But management fees that reduce investors' net returns can drive price below the net asset value of the portfolio.

Model Risk One always has to worry that an apparent profit opportunity is more apparent than real. Perhaps you are using a faulty model to value the security, and the price actually is right. This possibility, again, makes the trading activity risky and limits the extent to which it will be pursued.

Evaluating the Behavioural Critique

The efficient market hypothesis implies that prices usually "are right" and *therefore* there are no easy profit opportunities. Behaviourists emphasize that these two implications (correct prices and no profit opportunities) can be severed: prices can be wrong, but still not give rise to easy profit

---

[66]Some of the more influential references on limits to arbitrage are: J. Bradford De Long, Andrei Shleifer, Lawrence H. Summers, and Robert J. Waldmann, "Noise Trader Risk in Financial Markets," *Journal of Political Economy* 98 (August 1990), pp. 704–38; Andrei Schleifer and Robert W. Vishny, "Equilibrium Short Horizons of Investors and Firms," *American Economic Review* 80 (May 1990), pp. 148–53; and Andrei Schleifer and Robert W. Vishny, "The Limits of Arbitrage," *Journal of Finance* 52 (March 1997), pp. 35–55.

[67]Jeffrey Pontiff, "Costly Arbitrage: Evidence from Closed-End Funds," *Quarterly Journal of Economics* 111 (November 1996), pp. 1135–51.

[68]Stephen A. Ross, "Neoclassical Finance, Alternative Finance and the Closed End Fund Puzzle, "Keynote Address, European Financial Management 8 (2002), pp. 129–38.

opportunities. Thus, evidence that profit opportunities are scarce does not necessarily imply that prices are right.

As investors, we are concerned with the existence of profit opportunities. The behavioural explanations of efficient market anomalies do not give guidance as to how to exploit any irrationality. For investors, the question is still whether there is money to be made from mispricing, and the behavioural literature is largely silent on this point.

However, as we pointed out earlier, one of the important implications of the efficient market hypothesis is that security prices serve as reliable guides to the allocation of real capital. If prices are distorted, then capital markets will give misleading signals as to where the resources are best allocated. In this important sense, the behavioural critique of the efficient market hypothesis is potentially important.

There is considerable debate among financial economists concerning the strength of the behavioural critique. Many believe that the behavioural approach is too unstructured, in effect allowing virtually any anomaly to be explained by some combination of irrationalities chosen from a laundry list of behavioural biases.

More fundamentally, others are not convinced that the anomalies literature as a whole is a convincing indictment of the efficient market hypothesis. Fama[69] reviews the anomalies literature and mounts a counterchallenge to the behavioural school. He argues that the anomalies are inconsistent in terms of their support for one type of irrationality versus another. For example, many papers document long-term corrections (consistent with overreaction) while many others document long-term continuations of abnormal returns (consistent with underreaction). Moreover, the statistical significance of many of these results is less than meets the eye. Even small errors in choosing a benchmark against which to compare returns can cumulate to large apparent abnormalities when applied to long-term returns. Therefore, many of the results in these studies are sensitive to small benchmarking errors, and Fama finds that seemingly minor changes in methodology can have big impacts on conclusions. We will return to some of these issues in the next chapter.

Behavioural finance is still in its infancy. Its critique of full rationality in investor decision making is well taken, but the extent to which limited rationality affects asset pricing is controversial. It is probably still too early to pass judgment on the behavioural approach, specifically, which behavioural models will "stick" and become part of the standard tool kit of financial analysts.

9.6 MUTUAL FUND PERFORMANCE

We have documented some of the apparent chinks in the armour of efficient market proponents. Ultimately, however, the issue of market efficiency boils down to whether skilled investors can make consistent abnormal trading profits. The best test is simply to look at the performance of market professionals to see if that performance is superior to that of a passive index fund that buys and holds the market.

Such a test was carried out in Canada by Lawson,[70] who examined filter rules for buying or selling a stock depending on the trading activity of stock market professionals. He constructed a database of all transactions on the TSX over a 30-month period, which identified trades carried out by professional traders. The filter rules prescribed buying or selling a stock when professionals showed a corresponding "unusually high" buying or selling activity. Lawson found

[69]Eugene F. Fama, "Market Efficiency, Long-Term Returns, and Behavioral Finance," *Journal of Financial Economics* 49 (September 1998), pp. 283–306.

[70]William M. Lawson, "Market Efficiency: The Trading of Professionals on the Toronto Stock Exchange," *Journal of Business Administration* 12, no. 1 (Fall 1980).

that his filters could not generate any trading profits and were in fact inferior to a strategy of buying and holding the stock.

As we pointed out in Chapter 4, casual evidence does not support the claim that professionally managed portfolios can consistently beat the market. Between 1972 and 2001 the returns of a passive portfolio indexed to the Wilshire 5000 typically would have been better than those of the average equity fund. On the other hand, there was some (admittedly inconsistent) evidence of persistence in performance, meaning that the better managers in one period tended to be better managers in following periods. Such a pattern would suggest that the better managers can with some consistency outperform their competitors, and it would be inconsistent with the notion that market prices already reflect all relevant information.

The analyses cited in Chapter 4 were based on total returns; they did not properly adjust returns for exposure to systematic risk factors. In this section we revisit the question of mutual fund performance, paying more attention to the benchmark against which performance ought to be evaluated.

As a first pass, we can examine the risk-adjusted returns (i.e., the alpha, or return in excess of required return based on beta and the market return in each period) of a large sample of mutual funds. Malkiel[71] computed these abnormal returns for a large sample of mutual funds between 1972 and 1991. His results, which appear in Figure 9.4, show that the distribution of alphas is roughly bell-shaped, with a mean that is slightly negative but statistically indistinguishable from zero.

One problem in interpreting these alphas is that the S&P 500 may not be an adequate benchmark against which to evaluate mutual fund returns. Because mutual funds tend to maintain considerable holdings in equity of small firms, whereas the S&P 500 exclusively comprises large firms, mutual funds as a whole will tend to outperform the S&P when small firms outperform large ones and underperform when small firms fare worse. Thus a better benchmark for the performance of funds would be an index that incorporates the stock market performance of smaller firms.

The importance of the benchmark can be illustrated by examining the returns on small stocks in various subperiods.[72] In the 20-year period between 1945 and 1964, a small-stock index

Figure 9.4 Estimates of individual mutual fund alphas, 1972 to 1991.

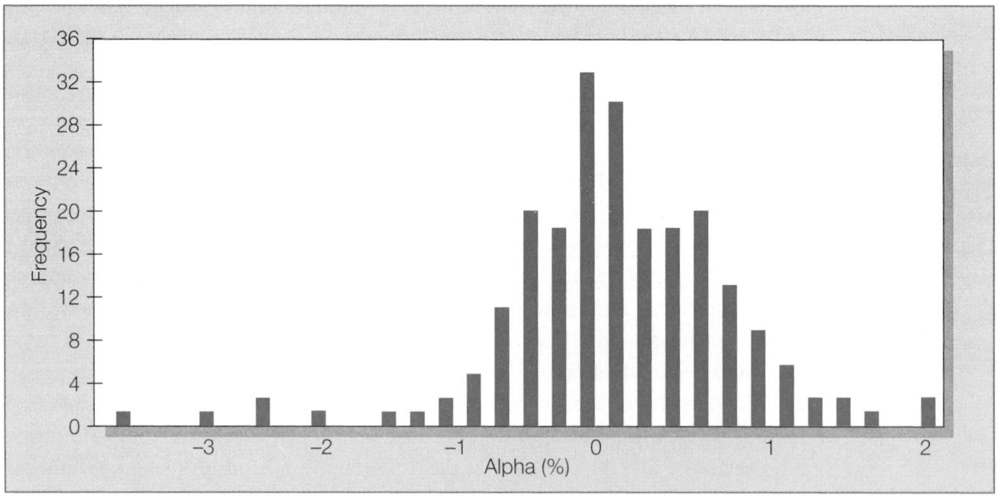

Note: The frequency distribution of estimated alphas for all equity mutual funds with ten-year continuous records.

Source: Burton G. Malkiel, "Returns from Investing in Equity Mutual Funds 1971–1991," *Journal of Finance* 50 (June 1995), pp. 549–572.

[71]Burton G. Malkiel, "Returns from Investing in Equity Mutual Funds 1971–1991," *Journal of Finance* 50 (June 1995), pp. 549–572.

[72]This illustration and the statistics cited are based on E. J. Elton, M. J. Gruber, S. Das, and M. Hlavka, "Efficiency with Costly Information: A Reinterpretation of Evidence from Managed Portfolios," *Review of Financial Studies* 6 (1993), pp. 1–22, which is discussed shortly.

www.
compustat.com

underperformed the S&P 500 by about 4 percent per year (i.e., the alpha of the small-stock index after adjusting for systematic risk was –4 percent). In the more recent 20-year period between 1965 and 1984, small stocks outperformed the S&P index by 10 percent. Thus if one were to examine mutual fund returns in the earlier period, they would tend to look poor, not necessarily because small-fund managers were poor stock pickers, but simply because mutual funds as a group tend to hold more small stocks than are represented in the S&P 500. In the later period, funds would look better on a risk-adjusted basis relative to the S&P 500 because small funds performed better. The "style choice," that is, the exposure to small stocks (which is an asset allocation decision) would dominate the evaluation of performance even though it has little to do with managers' stock-picking ability.[73]

Elton, Gruber, Das, and Hlavka attempted to control for the impact of non-S&P assets on mutual fund performance. They used a multifactor version of the index model of security returns (see equation 8.12) and calculated fund alphas using regressions that include as explanatory variables the excess returns of three benchmark portfolios rather than just one proxy for the market index. Their three factors are the excess return on the S&P 500 index, the excess return on an equity index of non-S&P low capitalization (i.e., small) firms, and the excess return on a bond market index. Some of their results are presented in Table 9.1, which shows that average alphas are negative for each type of equity fund, although generally not of statistically significant magnitude. They concluded that after controlling for the relative performance of these three asset classes—large stocks, small stocks, and bonds—mutual fund managers as a group do not demonstrate an ability to beat passive index strategies that would simply mix index funds from among these asset classes. They also found that mutual fund performance is worse for firms that have higher expense ratios and higher turnover ratios. Thus it appears that funds with higher fees do not increase gross returns by enough to justify those fees.

Carhart[74] reexamined the issue of consistency in mutual fund performance—sometimes called the "hot hands" phenomenon—controlling for non-S&P factors in a manner similar to Elton, Gruber, Das, and Hlavka. Carhart used a four-factor extension of the index model in which the four benchmark portfolios are the S&P 500 index and portfolios based on book-to-market ratio, size, and prior-year stock market return. These portfolios capture the impacts of three anomalies

Table 9.1
Performance of Mutual Funds Based on Three-Index Model

Type of Fund (Wiesenberger Classification)	Number of Funds	Alpha	t-Statistic for Alpha
Equity funds:			
Maximum capital gain	12	–4.59	–1.87
Growth	33	–1.55	–1.23
Growth and income	40	–0.68	–1.65
Balanced funds	31	–1.27	–2.73

Note: The three-index model calculates the alpha of each fund as the intercept of the following regression:

$$r - r_f = \alpha + \beta_M(r_M - r_f) + \beta_S(r_S - r_f) + \beta_D(r_D - r_f) + e$$

where r is the return on the fund, r_f is the risk-free rate, r_M is the return on the S&P 500 index, r_S is the return on a non-S&P small-stock index, r_D is the return on a bond index, e is the fund's residual return, and the betas measure the sensitivity of fund returns to the various indices.

Source: E. J. Elton, M. J. Gruber, S. Das, and M. Hlavka, "Efficiency with Costly Information: A Reinterpretation of Evidence from Managed Portfolios," *Review of Financial Studies* 6 (1993), pp. 1–22.

[73]Remember that the asset allocation decision is usually in the hands of the individual investor. Investors allocate their investment portfolios to funds in asset classes they desire to hold, and they can reasonably expect only that mutual fund portfolio managers will choose stocks advantageously *within* those asset classes.

[74]Mark M. Carhart, "On Persistence in Mutual Fund Performance," *Journal of Finance* 52 (1997), pp. 57–82.

discussed earlier: the small-firm effect, the book-to-market effect, and the intermediate-term price momentum documented by Jegadeesh and Titman.

Carhart found that there is persistence in relative performance across managers. However, much of that persistence seems due to expenses and transactions costs rather than gross investment returns. This last point is important; although there can be no consistently superior performers in a fully efficient market, there *can* be consistently inferior performers. Repeated weak performance would not be due to an ability to pick bad stocks consistently (that would be impossible in an efficient market!) but could result from a consistently high expense ratio and consistently high portfolio turnover with the resulting trading costs. Nevertheless, even allowing for expenses, some amount of performance persistence seems to be due to differences in investment strategy. Carhart found, however, that the evidence of persistence is concentrated at the two extremes. This suggests that there may be a small group of exceptional managers who can with some consistency outperform a passive strategy, but that for the majority of managers, over- or underperformance in any period is largely a matter of chance.

In contrast to the extensive studies of equity fund managers, there have been very few studies on the performance of bond fund managers. Blake, Elton, and Gruber[75] examined the performance of fixed-income mutual funds. They found that, on average, bond funds underperform passive fixed-income indices by an amount roughly equal to expenses, and that there is no evidence that past performance can predict future performance. Their evidence is consistent with the hypothesis that bond managers operate in an efficient market in which performance before expenses is only as good as that of a passive index.

A Canadian study by Jog[76] confirms these findings for a sample of Canadian pension fund managers. The study used several different performance measures, which included the alphas, and four different benchmark portfolios, one of which was the S&P/TSX Composite index. The results, however, were virtually identical for all measures and benchmark portfolios: managers of pension funds included in the sample failed to exhibit any significant or consistent ability to achieve superior risk-adjusted performance of the portfolios that they managed. Pension funds would have achieved a better risk-return combination by using combinations of suitable index funds.

Thus, the evidence on the risk-adjusted performance of professional managers is mixed at best. We conclude that the performance of professional managers is broadly consistent with market efficiency. The amounts by which professional managers as a group beat or are beaten by the market fall within the margin of statistical uncertainty. In any event, it is quite clear that performance superior to passive strategies is far from routine. Studies show either that most managers cannot outperform passive strategies or that if there is a margin of superiority, it is small.

On the other hand, a small number of investment superstars—Peter Lynch (formerly of Fidelity's Magellan Fund), Warren Buffett (of Berkshire Hathaway), John Templeton (of Templeton Funds), and John Neff (of Vanguard's Windsor Fund) among them—have compiled career records that show a consistency of superior performance hard to reconcile with absolutely efficient markets. Nobel prize winner Paul Samuelson[77] reviews this investment hall of fame but points out that the records of the vast majority of professional money managers offer convincing evidence that there are no easy strategies to guarantee success in the securities markets.

---

[75]Christopher R. Blake, Edwin J. Elton, and Martin J. Gruber, "The Performance of Bond Mutual Funds," *Journal of Business* 66 (July 1993), pp. 371–404.

[76]Vijay M. Jog, "Investment Performance of Pension Funds—A Canadian Study," *Canadian Journal of Administrative Sciences* 3, no. 1 (June 1986).

[77]Paul Samuelson, "The Judgment of Economic Science on Rational Portfolio Management," *Journal of Portfolio Management* 16 (Fall 1989), pp. 4–12.

So Are Markets Efficient?

There is a telling joke about two economists walking down the street. They spot a $20 bill on the sidewalk. One starts to pick it up, but the other one says, "Don't bother; if the bill were real someone would have picked it up already."

The lesson is clear. An overly doctrinaire belief in efficient markets can paralyze the investor and make it appear that no research effort can be justified. This extreme view is probably unwarranted. There are enough anomalies in the empirical evidence to justify the search for underpriced securities that clearly goes on.

The bulk of the evidence, however, suggests that any supposedly superior investment strategy should be taken with many grains of salt. The market is competitive *enough* that only differentially superior information or insight will earn money; the easy pickings have been picked. In the end it is likely that the margin of superiority that any professional manager can add is so slight that the statistician will not be able to detect it.

For the United States, we can safely conclude that markets are very efficient, but that rewards to the especially diligent, intelligent, or creative may in fact be waiting. In Canada, the anomalies are stronger and last longer. However, Canadian professional investment managers as a whole have shown no evidence of having exploited such inefficiencies.

SUMMARY

1. Statistical research has shown that stock prices seem to follow a random walk with no discernible predictable patterns that investors can exploit. Such findings are now taken to be evidence of market efficiency, that is, of evidence that market prices reflect all currently available information. Only new information will move stock prices, and this information is equally likely to be good news or bad news.
2. Market participants distinguish among three forms of the efficient market hypothesis. The weak form asserts that all information to be derived from past stock prices already is reflected in stock prices. The semistrong form claims that all publicly available information is already reflected. The strong form, usually taken only as a straw man, asserts that all information, including insider information, is reflected in prices.
3. Technical analysis focuses on stock price patterns and on proxies for buy or sell pressure in the market. Fundamental analysis focuses on the determinants of the underlying value of the firm, such as current profitability and growth prospects. Since both types of analysis are based on public information, neither should generate excess profits if markets are operating efficiently.
4. Proponents of the efficient market hypothesis often advocate passive as opposed to active investment strategies. The policy of passive investors is to buy and hold a broad-based market index. They expend resources neither on market research nor on the frequent purchase and sale of stocks. Passive strategies may be tailored to meet individual investor requirements.
5. Event studies are used to evaluate the economic impact of events of interest, using abnormal stock returns. Such studies usually show that there is some leakage of inside information to some market participants before the public announcement date. Therefore insiders do seem to be able to exploit their access to information to at least a limited extent.
6. Empirical studies of technical analysis do not support the hypothesis that such analysis can generate superior trading profits. One notable exception to this conclusion over intermediate-term horizons is the apparent success of momentum-based strategies over intermediate-term horizons.
7. Several anomalies regarding fundamental analysis have been uncovered. These include the P/E effect, the small-firm-in-January effect, the neglected-firm effect, post-earnings-announcement price drift, the book-to-market effect, and the insider trading effect in Canada. Whether these anomalies represent market inefficiency or poorly understood risk premiums is still a matter of debate.

8. Behavioural finance focuses on systematic irrationalities that characterize investor decision making. These "behavioural shortcomings" may be consistent with some of the efficient market anomalies uncovered by several researchers.
9. By and large, the performance record of professionally managed funds lends little credence to claims that professionals can consistently beat the market.

KEY TERMS

random walk 323
efficient market hypothesis (EMH) 323
weak-form EMH 324
semistrong-form EMH 324
strong-form EMH 325
technical analysis 325
fundamental analysis 326
passive investment strategy 327
index fund 327
event study 329
abnormal return 330
announcement date 330
cumulative abnormal return 331
filter rule 336
reversal effect 337
anomalies 338
P/E effect 338
small-firm effect 339
neglected-firm effect 341
book-to-market effects 341
insider transactions 342
behavioural finance 345

SELECTED READINGS

One of the best treatments of the efficient market hypothesis is this paperback book, which provides an entertaining and insightful treatment of the ideas presented in this chapter as well as fascinating historical examples of securities markets in action:

Malkiel, Burton G. *A Random Walk Down Wall Street*. 6th ed. New York: W. W. Norton & Co., Inc., 1995.

A more rigorous introduction to the theoretical underpinnings of the EMH, as well as a review of early empirical work, may be found in:

Fama, Eugene F. "Efficient Capital Markets: A Review of Theory and Empirical Work." *Journal of Finance* 25 (May 1970).

A more recent survey is:

Fama, Eugene F. "Efficient Capital Markets: II." *Journal of Finance* 46 (December 1991).

PROBLEMS

1. If markets are efficient, what should be the correlation coefficient between stock returns for two nonoverlapping time periods?
2. Which of the following most appears to contradict the proposition that the stock market is *weakly* efficient? Explain.
   a. Over 25 percent of mutual funds outperform the market on average.
   b. Insiders earn abnormal trading profits.
   c. Every January, the stock market earns above-normal returns.
3. Suppose that, after conducting an analysis of past stock prices, you come up with the following observations. Which would appear to *contradict* the *weak* form of the efficient market hypothesis? Explain.
   a. The average rate of return is significantly greater than zero.
   b. The correlation between the return during a given week and the return during the following week is zero.
   c. One could have made superior returns by buying stock after a 10 percent rise in price and selling after a 10 percent fall.
   d. One could have made higher than average capital gains by holding stock with low dividend yields.
4. Which of the following statements are true if the efficient market hypothesis holds?
   a. Future events can be forecast with perfect accuracy.
   b. Prices reflect all available information.

c. Security prices change for no discernible reason.
d. Prices do not fluctuate.

5. Which of the following observations would provide evidence *against* the *semistrong-form* version of the efficient market theory? Explain.
a. Mutual fund managers do not on average make superior returns.
b. You cannot make superior profits by buying (or selling) stocks after the announcement of an abnormal rise in dividends.
c. Low P/E stocks tend to have positive abnormal returns.
d. In any year, approximately 50 percent of pension funds outperform the market.

Problems 6–11 are taken from past CFA exams.

CFA® PROBLEMS

6. The semistrong form of the efficient market hypothesis asserts that stock prices
a. Fully reflect all historical price information
b. Fully reflect all publicly available information
c. Fully reflect all relevant information including insider information
d. May be predictable

7. Assume that a company announces an unexpectedly large cash dividend to its shareholders. In an efficient market *without* information leakage, one might expect
a. An abnormal price change at the announcement
b. An abnormal price increase before the announcement
c. An abnormal price decrease after the announcement
d. No abnormal price change before or after the announcement

8. Which one of the following would provide evidence *against* the *semistrong form* of the efficient market theory?
a. About 50 percent of pension funds outperform the market in any year.
b. All investors have learned to exploit signals about future performance.
c. Trend analysis is worthless in determining stock prices.
d. Low P/E stocks tend to have positive abnormal returns over the long run.

9. According to the efficient market hypothesis,
a. High-beta stocks are consistently overpriced
b. Low-beta stocks are consistently overpriced
c. Positive alphas on stocks will quickly disappear
d. Negative alpha stocks consistently yield low returns for arbitrageurs

10. A "random walk" occurs when
a. Stock price changes are random but predictable
b. Stock prices respond slowly to both new and old information
c. Future price changes are uncorrelated with past price changes
d. Past information is useful in predicting future prices

11. Two basic assumptions of technical analysis are that security prices adjust
a. Gradually to new information, and study of the economic environment provides an indication of future market movements
b. Rapidly to new information, and study of the economic environment provides an indication of future market movements
c. Rapidly to new information, and market prices are determined by the interaction between supply and demand
d. Gradually to new information, and prices are determined by the interaction between supply and demand

12. A successful firm like Alcan has consistently generated large profits for years. Is this a violation of the EMH?

13. Suppose you find that prices of stocks before large dividend increases show on average consistently positive abnormal returns. Is this a violation of the EMH?

14. "If the business cycle is predictable, and a stock has a positive beta, the stock's returns also must be predictable." Respond.

15. Which of the following phenomena would be either consistent with or a violation of the efficient market hypothesis? Explain briefly.

a. Nearly half of all professionally managed mutual funds are able to outperform the S&P/TSX Composite in a typical year.

b. Money managers that outperform the market (on a risk-adjusted basis) in one year are likely to outperform it in the following year.

c. Stock prices tend to be predictably more volatile in January than in other months.

d. Stock prices of companies that announce increased earnings in January tend to outperform the market in February.

e. Stocks that perform well in one week perform poorly in the following week.

16. "If all securities are fairly priced, all must offer equal market rates of return." Comment.

17. An index model regression applied to past monthly excess returns in ABC Corporation's stock price produces the following estimates, which are believed to be stable over time:

$$R_{\text{ABC}} = .10\% + 1.1R_M$$

If the market index subsequently rises by 8 percent and ABC's stock price rises by 7 percent, what is the abnormal change in ABC's stock price? The T-bill return during the month is 1 percent.

18. The monthly rate of return on T-bills is 1 percent. The market went up this month by 1.5 percent. In addition, AmbChaser, Inc., which has an equity beta of 2, surprisingly just won a lawsuit that awards it $1 million immediately.

a. If the original value of AmbChaser equity were $100 million, what would you guess was the rate of return of its stock this month?

b. What is your answer to (*a*) if the market had expected AmbChaser to win $2 million?

19. In a recent, closely contested lawsuit, Apex sued Bpex for patent infringement. The jury came back today with its decision. The rate of return on Apex was $r_A = 3.1$ percent. The rate of return on Bpex was only $r_B = 2.5$ percent. The market today responded to very encouraging news about the unemployment rate, and $r_M = 3$ percent. The historical relationship between returns on these stocks and the market portfolio has been estimated from index model regressions as

$$\text{Apex: } r_A = .2\% + 1.4r_M$$
$$\text{Bpex: } r_B = -.1\% + .6r_M$$

Judging from these data, which company do you think won the lawsuit?

20. Dollar cost averaging means that you buy equal dollar amounts of a stock every period, for example, $500 per month. The strategy is based on the idea that when the stock price is low, your fixed monthly purchase will buy more shares, and when the price is high, it will buy fewer shares. Averaging over time, you will end up buying more shares when the stock is cheaper and fewer when it is relatively expensive. Therefore, by design, you will exhibit good market timing. Evaluate this strategy.

21. Steady Growth Industries has never missed a dividend payment in its 94-year history. Does this make it more attractive to you as a possible purchase for your stock portfolio?

22. We know that the market should respond positively to good news and that good-news events, such as a coming end of a recession, can be predicted with at least some accuracy. Why, then, can we not predict the market will go up as the economy recovers?

23. If prices are as likely to increase as decrease, why do investors earn positive returns from the market on average?

24. You know that firm XYZ is very poorly run. On a scale of 1 (worst) to 10 (best), you would give it a score of 3. The market consensus evaluation is that the management score is only 2. Should you buy or sell the stock?

25. Good News Inc. just announced an increase in its annual earnings, yet its stock price fell. Is there a rational explanation for this phenomenon?

26. Investors *expect* the market rate of return in the coming year to be 12 percent. The T-bill rate is 4 percent. Changing Fortunes Industries' stock has a beta of .5. The market value of its outstanding equity is $100 million.
   a. What is your best guess currently as to the expected rate of return on Changing Fortunes' stock? You believe that the stock is fairly priced.
   b. If the market return in the coming year actually turns out to be 10 percent, what is your best guess as to the rate of return that will be earned on Changing Fortunes' stock?
   c. Suppose now that Changing Fortunes wins a major lawsuit during the year. The settlement is $5 million. Changing Fortunes' stock return during the year turns out to be 10 percent. What is your best guess as to the settlement the market previously *expected* Changing Fortunes to receive from the lawsuit? (Continue to assume that the market return in the year turned out to be 10 percent.) The magnitude of the settlement is the only unexpected firm-specific event during the year.

27. You are a portfolio manager meeting a client. During the conversation that followed your formal review of her account, your client asked the following question:

   My grandson, who is studying investments, tells me that one of the best ways to make money in the stock market is to buy the stocks of small-capitalization firms on a Monday morning late in December and to sell the stocks one month later. What is he talking about?

   a. Identify the apparent market anomalies that would justify the proposed strategy.
   b. Explain why you believe such a strategy might or might not work in the future.

28. Examine the figure[78] on the next page, which presents cumulative abnormal returns both before and after dates on which insiders buy or sell shares in their firms. How do you interpret it? What are we to make of the pattern of CARs before and after the event date?

29. Suppose that during a certain week the Fed in the U.S. announces a new monetary growth policy. Congress surprisingly passes legislation restricting imports of foreign automobiles, and Ford comes out with a new car model that it believes will increase profits substantially. How might you go about measuring the market's assessment of Ford's new model?

CFA® PROBLEMS

30. Your investment client asks for information concerning the benefits of active portfolio management. She is particularly interested in the question of whether or not active managers can be expected to consistently exploit inefficiencies in the capital markets to produce above-average returns without assuming higher risk.

   The semistrong form of the efficient market hypothesis asserts that all publicly available information is rapidly and correctly reflected in securities prices. This implies that investors cannot expect to derive above-average profits from purchases made after information has become public because security prices already reflect the information's full effects.

[78]From Nejat H. Seyhun, "Insiders, Profits, Costs of Trading and Market Efficiency," *Journal of Financial Economics* 16 (1986).

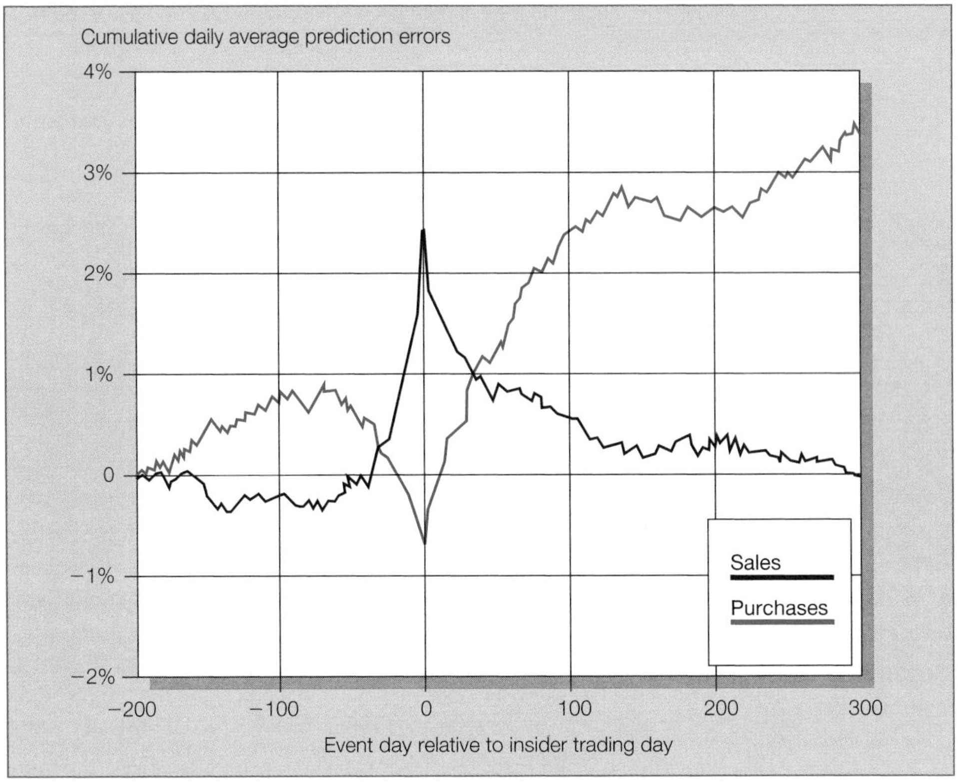

a. Identify and explain two examples of empirical evidence that tend to support the EMH implication stated above.

b. Identify and explain two examples of empirical evidence that tend to refute the EMH implication stated above.

c. Discuss reasons why an investor might choose not to index even if the rnarkets were, in fact, semistrong form efficient.

CFA® PROBLEMS

31. *a.* Briefly explain the concept of the efficient market hypothesis (EMH) and each of its three forms—weak, semistrong, and strong—and briefly discuss the degree to which existing, empirical evidence supports each of the three forms of the EMH.

b. Briefly discuss the implications of the efficient market hypothesis for investment policy as it applies to:

i. Technical analysis in the form of charting

ii. Fundamental analysis

c. Briefly explain the roles or responsibilities of portfolio managers in an efficient market environment.

CFA® PROBLEMS

32. Growth and value can be defined in several ways. "Growth" usually conveys the idea of a portfolio emphasizing or including only issues believed to possess above-average future rates of per-share earnings growth. Low current yield, high price-to-book ratios. and high price-to-earnings ratios are typical characteristics of such portfolios. "Value" usually conveys the idea of portfolios emphasizing or including only issues currently showing low price-to-book ratios, low price-to-earnings ratios, above-average levels of dividend yield, and market prices believed to be below the issues' intrinsic values.

a. Identify and provide reasons why, over an extended period of time, value-stock investing might outperform growth-stock investing.

b. Explain why the outcome suggested in (*a*) should not be possible in a market widely regarded as being highly efficient.

CFA® PROBLEMS

33. Don Sampson begins a meeting with his financial advisor by outlining his investment philosophy as follows:

Statement Number	Statement
1	Investments should offer strong return potential but with very limited risk. I prefer to be conservative and to minimize losses, even if I miss out on substantial growth opportunities.
2	All nongovernmental investments should be in industry-leading and financially strong companies.
3	Income needs should be met entirely through interest income and cash dividends. All equity securities held should pay cash dividends.
4	Investment decisions should be based primarily on consensus forecasts of general economic conditions and company-specific growth.
5	If an investment falls below the purchase price, that security should be retained until it returns to its original cost. Conversely, I prefer to take quick profits on successful investments.
6	I will direct the purchase of investments, including derivative securities, periodically. These aggressive investments result from personal research and may not prove consistent with my investment policy. I have not kept records on the performance of similar past investments, but I have had some "big winners."

Select the statement from the table above that best illustrates each of the following behavioural finance concepts. Justify your selection.

i. Mental accounting
ii. Overconfidence (illusion of control)
iii. Reference dependence (framing)

CFA® PROBLEMS

34. Monty Frost's tax-deferred retirement account is invested entirely in equity securities. Because the international portion of his portfolio has performed poorly in the past, he has reduced his international equity exposure to 2 percent. Frost's investment advisor has recommended an increased international equity exposure. Frost responds with the following comments:

a. In view of past poor performance, I want to sell all my remaining international equity securities once their market prices rise to equal their original cost.

b. Most diversified international portfolios have had disappointing results over the past five years. During that time, however, the market in Country XYZ has outperformed all other markets, even our own. If I do increase my international equity exposure, I would prefer that the entire exposure consist of securities from Country XYZ.

c. International investments are inherently more risky. Therefore, I prefer to purchase any international equity securities in my "speculative" account, my best chance at becoming rich. I do not want them in my retirement account, which has to protect me from poverty in my old age.

Frost's advisor is familiar with behavioural finance concepts but prefers a traditional or standard finance approach (modern portfolio theory) to investments.

Indicate the behavioural finance concept that Frost most directly exhibits in each of his three comments. Explain how each of Frost's comments can be countered with an argument from standard finance.

STANDARD &POOR'S

1. Use data from Market Insight (**www.mcgrawhill.ca/edumarketinsight**) to rank firms by one of these criteria:
   a. Market-to-book ratio
   b. Price-earnings ratio
   c. Market capitalization (size)
   d. Another criterion that interests you

   Divide the firms into five groups based on their ranking for the criterion that you choose, and calculate the average rate of return of the firms in each group. Do you confirm or reject any of the anomalies cited in this chapter? Can you uncover a new anomaly? *Note:* For your test to be valid, you must base your portfolios on criteria observed at the *beginning* of the period when you form the stock groups. Why?
2. Now form stock groups that use more than one criterion simultaneously. For example, form a portfolio of stocks that are both in the lowest quintile of price-earnings ratios and in the lowest quintile of market-to-book ratio. Does selecting stocks by more than one characteristic improve your ability to devise portfolios with abnormal returns?

E-INVESTMENTS
Efficient Markets and Insider Trading

Do restrictions on insider trading limit strong-form market efficiency? Go to Wallpost.com and pull down the *Insiders* and *Insiders-Stock of the Day.* Read the Insiders analysis for the stock of the day. Enter the stock symbol for the Stock-of-the-Day and review a price chart for the time period mentioned in the Stock of the Day article. What do you conclude about the investment timing of the insiders?

EMPIRICAL EVIDENCE ON SECURITY RETURNS

In this chapter, we consider the empirical evidence in support of the CAPM and APT. At the outset, however, it is worth noting that many of the implications of these models already have been accepted in widely varying applications. Consider the following:

1. Many professional portfolio managers use the expected return–beta relationship of security returns. Furthermore, many firms rate the performance of portfolio managers according to the reward-to-variability ratios they maintain and the average rates of return they realize relative to the CML or SML.
2. Regulatory commissions use the expected return–beta relationship along with forecasts of the market index return as one factor in determining the cost of capital for regulated firms.
3. Court rulings on torts cases sometimes use the expected return–beta relationship to determine discount rates to evaluate claims of lost future income.
4. Many firms use the SML to obtain a benchmark hurdle rate for capital budgeting decisions.

These practices show that the financial community has passed a favourable judgment on the CAPM and the APT, if only implicitly.

In this chapter we consider the evidence along more explicit and rigorous lines. The first part of the chapter presents the methodology that has been deployed in testing the single-factor CAPM and APT and assesses the results. The second part of the chapter provides an overview of current efforts to establish the validity of the multifactor versions of the CAPM and APT. In the third part, we discuss recent literature on so-called anomalies in patterns of security returns and some of the responses to these puzzling findings. We briefly discuss evidence on how the volatility of asset returns evolves over time. Finally, we present interesting research on stock returns that examines the size of the equity risk premium. Conventional wisdom has held for a long time that the history of returns on equities is quite puzzling. Recent studies address the puzzle.

Why lump together empirical works on the CAPM and APT? The CAPM is a theoretical construct that predicts *expected* rates of return on assets, relative to a market portfolio of all risky assets. It is difficult to test these predictions empirically because both expected returns and the exact market portfolio are unobservable (see Chapter 7). To overcome this difficulty, a single-factor or multifactor capital market usually is postulated, where a broad-based market index portfolio (such as the S&P 500 or the S&P/TSX Composite) is assumed to represent the factor, or one of the factors. Furthermore, to obtain more reliable statistics, most tests have been conducted with the rates of return on highly diversified portfolios rather than on individual securities. For both of these reasons tests that have been directed at the CAPM actually have been more suitable to establish the validity of the APT. We will see that it is more important to distinguish the empirical work on the basis of the factor structure that is assumed or estimated than to distinguish between tests of the CAPM and the APT.

10.1 THE INDEX MODEL AND THE SINGLE-FACTOR APT

The Expected Return–Beta Relationship

Recall that if the expected return–beta relationship holds with respect to an observable ex ante efficient index, M, the expected rate of return on any security i is

$$E(r_i) = r_f + \beta_i[E(r_M) - r_f] \tag{10.1}$$

where β_i is defined as $\text{Cov}(r_i, r_M)/\sigma^2_M$.

This is the most commonly tested implication of the CAPM. Early simple tests followed three basic steps: establishing sample data, estimating the SCL (security characteristic line), and estimating the SML (security market line).

Setting Up the Sample Data Determine a sample period of, for example, 60 monthly holding periods (five years). For each of the 60 holding periods collect the rates of return on 100 stocks, a market portfolio proxy (e.g., the S&P 500 or the S&P/TSX Composite), and one-month (risk-free) T-bills. Your data thus consist of

r_{it} Returns on the 100 stocks over the 60-month sample period; $i = 1, \ldots, 100$, and $t = 1, \ldots, 60$

r_{Mt} Returns on the S&P 500 index over the sample period

r_{ft} Risk-free rate each month

This constitutes a table of $102 \times 60 = 6{,}120$ rates of return

Estimating the SCL View equation 10.1 as a security characteristic line (SCL), as in Chapter 7. For each stock i, you estimate the beta coefficient as the slope of a **first-pass regression** equation. (The terminology *first-pass* regression is due to the fact that the estimated coefficients will be used as input into a **second-pass regression**.)

$$r_{it} - r_{ft} = a_i + b_i(r_{Mt} - r_{ft}) + e_{it}$$

You will use the following statistics in later analysis:

$\overline{r_i - r_f}$	Sample averages (over the 60 observations) of the excess return on each of the 100 stocks
b_i	Sample estimates of the beta coefficients of each of the 100 stocks
$\overline{r_M - r_f}$	Sample average of the excess return of the market index
$\sigma^2(e_i)$	Estimates of the variance of the residuals for each of the 100 stocks

The sample average excess returns on each stock and the market portfolio are taken as estimates of expected excess returns, and the values of b_i are estimates of the true beta coefficients for the 100 stocks during the sample period. The $\sigma^2(e_i)$ estimates the nonsystematic risk of each of the 100 stocks.

? CONCEPT CHECK

1. *a.* How many regression estimates of the SCL do we have from the sample?
   b. How many observations are there in each of the regressions?
   c. According to the CAPM, what should be the intercept in each of these regressions?

Estimating the SML Now view equation 10.1 as a security market line (SML) with 100 observations for the stocks in your sample. You can estimate γ_0 and γ_1 in the following second-pass regression equation with the estimates b_i from the first pass as the independent variable:

$$\overline{r_i - r_f} = \gamma_0 + \gamma_1 b_i \quad i = 1, \ldots, 100 \qquad (10.2)$$

Compare equations 10.1 and 10.2; you should conclude that if the CAPM is valid, then γ_0 and γ_1 should satisfy

$$\gamma_0 = 0 \quad \gamma_1 = \overline{r_M - r_f}$$

In fact, however, you can go a step further and argue that the key property of the expected return–beta relationship described by the SML is that the expected excess return on securities is determined *only* by the systematic risk (as measured by beta) and should be independent of the nonsystematic risk, as measured by the variance of the residuals, $\sigma^2(e_i)$, which also were estimated from the first-pass regression. These estimates can be added as a variable in equation 10.2 of an expanded SML that now looks like this:

Beta
www.barra.com/Research Resources/NonBarraPub/pocs-j.asp

$$\overline{r_i - r_f} = \gamma_0 + \gamma_1 b_i + \gamma_2 \sigma^2(e_i) \qquad (10.3)$$

This *second-pass* regression is estimated with the hypotheses

$$\gamma_0 = 0 \quad \gamma_1 = \overline{r_M - r_f} \quad \gamma_2 = 0$$

The hypothesis that $\gamma_2 = 0$ is consistent with the notion that nonsystematic risk should not be "priced," that is, that there is no risk premium earned for bearing nonsystematic risk. More generally, according to the CAPM, the risk premium depends only on beta. Therefore, *any* additional right-hand-side variable in equation 10.3 beyond beta should have a coefficient that is insignificantly different from zero in the second-pass regression.

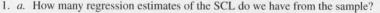

Tests of the CAPM

World CAPM
www.duke.edu/~charvey/Country_risk/ccr/ccrl.htm

Early tests of the CAPM performed by John Lintner,[1] later replicated by Merton Miller and Myron Scholes,[2] used annual data on 631 NYSE stocks for ten years, 1954 to 1963, and produced the following estimates (with returns expressed as decimals rather than percentages):

Coefficient:	$\gamma_0 = .127$	$\gamma_1 = .042$	$\gamma_2 = .310$
Standard error:	.006	.006	.026
Sample average:		$\overline{r_M - r_f} = .165$	

These results are inconsistent with the CAPM. First, the estimated SML is "too flat"; that is, the γ_1 coefficient is too small. The slope should be $\overline{r_M - r_f} = .165$ (16.5 percent per year), but it is estimated at only .042. The difference, .122, is about 20 times the standard error of the estimate, .006, which means that the measured slope of the SML is less than it should be by a statistically significant margin. At the same time, the intercept of the estimated SML, γ_0, which is hypothesized to be zero, in fact equals .127, which is more than 20 times its standard error of .006.

CONCEPT CHECK

2. *a.* What is the implication of the empirical SML being "too flat"?
   b. Do high- or low-beta stocks tend to outperform the predictions of the CAPM?
   c. What is the implication of the estimate of γ_2?

The two-stage procedure employed by these researchers (i.e., first estimate security betas using a time series regression and then use those betas to test the SML relationship between risk and average return) seems straightforward, and the rejection of the CAPM using this approach is disappointing. However, it turns out that there are several difficulties with this approach. First and foremost, stock returns are extremely volatile, which lessens the precision of any tests of average return. For example, the average standard deviation of annual returns of the stocks in the S&P 500 is about 40 percent; the average standard deviation of annual returns of the stocks included in these tests is probably even higher.

In addition, there are fundamental concerns about the validity of the tests. First, the market index used in the tests is surely not the "market portfolio" of the CAPM. Second, in light of asset volatility, the security betas from the first-stage regressions are necessarily estimated with substantial sampling error and therefore cannot readily be used as inputs to the second-stage regression. Finally, investors cannot borrow at the risk-free rate, as assumed by the simple version of the CAPM. We investigate the implications of these problems after examining the empirical studies in the Canadian context.

Estimating Index Models for Canadian Stocks

Relatively few studies on the SML along the lines of the previous section have been done using Canadian data. The availability of data in computerized form was scarce in the early testing years. Furthermore, the Canadian financial markets present certain problems not encountered in the United States.

One of the earlier estimations of the SML in Canada was by Morin,[3] who used monthly return data on 620 securities trading continuously for at least five years on the TSX during the

[1]John Lintner, "Security Prices, Risk and Maximal Gains from Diversification," *Journal of Finance* 20 (December 1965).

[2]Merton H. Miller and Myron Scholes, "Rate of Return in Relation to Risk: A Reexamination of Some Recent Findings," in Michael C. Jensen, ed., *Studies in the Theory of Capital Markets* (New York: Praeger, 1972).

[3]Roger A. Morin, "Market Line Theory and the Canadian Equity Market," *Journal of Business Administration* 12, no. 1 (Fall 1980).

period 1957–1971. The basic methodology was the one developed by Black, Jensen and Scholes,[4] with its extensions by Fama and MacBeth, reviewed further on in this section.[5] The market index was an equally weighted average of the returns of all securities in the databank.

The general flavour of the results can be obtained by quoting from the study's conclusions: "Overall, the empirical results of this study indicate that the capital asset pricing theory, in all its forms, fares poorly in attempting to explain differential returns on Canadian equities." The return–beta relationship turned out to be weak, erratic, and nonlinear, and implied unreasonably high estimates of the returns on low-risk assets.

Several other SML studies using Canadian data[6] reached conclusions that seem to confirm the basic outcome observed in the United States, namely that the single-variable expected return–beta relationship is, at best, only weakly supported by empirical work. For instance, Calvet and Lefoll[7] use monthly TSX security return data and a value-weighted index of all stocks in their databank as a market index. Although a significant linear relationship between systematic risk and portfolio returns was found almost always, the introduction of unsystematic risk and of the squared beta coefficient in the regression, as in the Fama and MacBeth study, showed both to be significant and more important than the beta.

Empirical research in Canadian financial markets is hindered by two effects that are not present to the same extent in the United States. The first is the existence of seasonal abnormal returns that are at variance with market efficiency as documented in the previous chapter. The second is the persistent problem of **thin trading** in a majority of Canadian securities.

Thin Trading

If transactions for many securities listed on the TSX are irregular and infrequent, then the prices quoted as closing by the exchange are unreliable and may also reflect situations that are no longer current. For instance, if a stock did not trade at all during a given month, then its recorded rate of return is zero during that month (in the absence of dividends). If many such securities and months occur in our database, then the statistical estimations of the SML will yield biased results.

Table 10.1 reproduces data from a study by Fowler, Rorke, and Jog[8] on the frequency of trading on the TSX during the period 1970–1979. The database contained 120 monthly returns for each security listed on the TSX during that period. The three categories of trading frequency distinguished by the authors were defined as follows: a "fat" security showed a trade during the closing day of each month; a "moderate" security was one that traded every month, but not necessarily on the last day; and an "infrequent" security was one that showed entire months without any trade. As the data show, this last category was by far the largest, accounting for 42–59 percent of the total, depending on the type of securities considered.

In addition to biases in the estimated coefficients, thinness of trading also causes heteroskedasticity,[9] that is, different variances of the residuals in the regressions. There are a number of procedures for correcting the biases arising out of thinness of trading, of which the one

[4]Fischer Black, Michael C. Jensen, and Myron Scholes, "The Capital Asset Pricing Model: Some Empirical Tests," in Michael C. Jensen, ed., *Studies in the Theory of Capital Markets* (New York: Praeger, 1972).

[5]Eugene Fama and James MacBeth, "Risk, Return, and Equilibrium: Empirical Tests," *Journal of Political Economy* 81 (March 1973).

[6]For instance, J. D. Jobson and R. M. Korkie, "Some Tests of Linear Asset Pricing with Multivariate Normality," *Canadian Journal of Administrative Sciences* 2, no. 1 (June 1985). See also M. J. Robinson, "Univariate Canadian CAPM Tests," in M. J. Robinson and B. F. Smith, eds., *Canadian Capital Markets* (London, ON: 1993).

[7]A. L. Calvet and J. Lefoll, "Risk and Return on Canadian Capital Markets," *Canadian Journal of Administrative Sciences* 5, no. 1 (March 1988).

[8]David J. Fowler, C. Harvey Rorke, and V. M. Jog, "Thin Trading and Beta Estimation Problems on the Toronto Stock Exchange," *Journal of Business Administration* 12, no. 1 (Fall 1980).

[9]David J. Fowler, C. Harvey Rorke, and V. M. Jog, "Heteroscedasticity, R^2 and Thin Trading on the Toronto Stock Exchange," *Journal of Finance* 34, no. 5 (December 1979).

Table 10.1 Thin Trading Breakdown on TSE Listings, January 1970–December 1979

	All Securities		Securities Listed at Least 12 Months*		Securities Listed for Whole 10-Year Period		Broader "Fat" Category for 10-Year Group†	
	Number	%	Number	%	Number	%	Number	%
Fat	112	5.3	78	4.3	38	6.0	156	24.6
Moderate	744	35.3	679	37.7	328	51.7	210	33.1
Infrequent	1251	59.4	1043	58.0	268	42.3	268	42.3
Total	**2107**	**100.0**	**1800**	**100.0**	**634**	**100.0**	**634**	**100.0**

*The prime difference between the all-securities and the 12-month groups is that warrants and rights are largely eliminated from the latter.

†This category includes any security for which a trade could always be found in the last five days of the month.

Source: D. J. Fowler, C. H. Rorke, and V. M. Jog, "Thin Trading and Beta Estimation Problems on the Toronto Stock Exchange," *Journal of Business Administration* 12, no. 1 (Fall 1980). Reprinted by permission.

developed by Dimson[10] is perhaps the most popular. The Dimson method augments the single simultaneous market index term in the regression by two other terms, one with a lagged and one with a leading value of the index, each one with its own beta; an unbiased estimate of the "true" beta is equal to the sum of three estimated betas. Another bias-correcting method also was developed by Scholes and Williams,[11] but the small-sample properties of both methods are somewhat questionable.[12]

The Market Index

In what has become known as *Roll's critique*, Richard Roll[13] pointed out that:

The CAPM and the Market Model
www.barra.com/Research Resources/NonBarraPub/tcap-j.asp

1. There is a single testable hypothesis associated with the CAPM: the market portfolio is mean-variance efficient.
2. All the other implications of the model, the best-known being the linear relation between expected return and beta, follow from the market portfolio's efficiency and therefore are not independently testable. There is an "if and only if" relation between the expected return–beta relationship and the efficiency of the market portfolio.
3. In any sample of observations of individual returns there will be an infinite number of ex post (i.e., after-the-fact) mean-variance efficient portfolios using the sample period returns and covariances (as opposed to the ex ante expected returns and covariances). Sample betas calculated between each such portfolio and individual assets will be exactly linearly related to sample average returns. In other words, if betas are calculated against such portfolios, they will satisfy the SML relation exactly whether or not the true market portfolio is mean-variance efficient in an ex ante sense.
4. The CAPM is not testable unless we know the exact composition of the true market portfolio and use it in the tests. This implies that the theory is not testable unless *all* individual assets are included in the sample.
5. Using a proxy such as the S&P 500 for the market portfolio is subject to two difficulties. First, the proxy itself might be mean-variance efficient even when the true market

[10] E. Dimson, "Risk Measurement When Shares Are Subject to Infrequent Trading," *Journal of Financial Economics* 7 (1979).

[11] M. Scholes and J. Williams, "Estimating Betas from Nonsynchronous Data," *Journal of Financial Economics* 5 (1977).

[12] See Fowler, Rorke, and Jog, "Thin Trading and Beta Estimation Problems," 1980.

[13] Richard Roll, "A Critique of the Asset Pricing Theory's Tests: Part I: On Past and Potential Testability of the Theory," *Journal of Financial Economics* 4 (1977).

portfolio is not. Conversely, the proxy may turn out to be inefficient, but obviously this alone implies nothing about the true market portfolio's efficiency. Furthermore, most reasonable market proxies will be very highly correlated with each other and with the true market portfolio whether or not they are mean-variance efficient. Such a high degree of correlation will make it seem that the exact composition of the market portfolio is unimportant, whereas the use of different proxies can lead to quite different conclusions. This problem is referred to as **benchmark error**, because it refers to the use of an incorrect benchmark (market proxy) portfolio in the tests of the theory.

Roll and Ross[14] and Kandel and Stambaugh[15] expanded Roll's critique. Essentially, they argued that tests that reject a positive relationship between average return and beta point to inefficiency of the market proxy used in those tests, rather than refuting the theoretical expected return–beta relationship. Their work demonstrates that it is plausible that even highly diversified portfolios, such as the value- or equally weighted portfolios of all stocks in the sample, will fail to produce a significant average return–beta relationship.

Roll and Ross (RR) derived an analytical characterization of market indices (proxies for the market portfolio) that produce an *arbitrary* cross-sectional slope coefficient in the regression of average asset returns on beta. Their derivation applies to any universe of assets and requires only that the market proxy be constructed from that universe or one of its subsets. They show that the set of indices that produce a zero second-pass slope lies within a parabola that is tangent to the efficient frontier at the point corresponding to the global minimum variance portfolio.

Figure 10.1 shows one such configuration. In this plausible universe, where "plausible" is taken to mean that the return distribution is not extraordinary, the set of portfolios with zero slope coefficient in the return–beta regression lies near the efficient frontier. Thus even portfolios that are "nearly efficient" do not necessarily support the expected return–beta relationship.

RR concluded that the slope coefficient in the average return–beta regression cannot be relied on to test the theoretical expected return–beta relationship. It can only indicate that the market proxy that produces this result is inefficient in the second-pass regression.

Many studies use the more sophisticated regression procedure called *generalized least squares* (GLS) to improve on statistical reliability. Can the use of GLS overcome the problems raised by Roll and Ross?

Kandel and Stambaugh (KS) extended this analysis and considered whether the use of generalized least squares regressions can overcome some of the problems identified by RR. They found that GLS does help, but only to the extent that the researcher can obtain a nearly efficient market index.

KS considered the properties of the usual two-pass test of the CAPM in an environment in which borrowing is restricted but the zero-beta version of the CAPM holds. In this case, you will recall that the expected return–beta relationship describes the expected returns on a stock, a portfolio E on the efficient frontier, and that portfolio's zero-beta companion, Z (see equation 7.9):

$$E(r_i) - E(r_Z) = \beta_i[E(r_E) - E(r_Z)] \tag{10.4}$$

where β_i denotes the beta of security i on efficient portfolio E.

We cannot construct or observe the efficient portfolio E (since we do not know expected returns and covariances of all assets), and so we cannot estimate equation 10.4 directly. KS asked what would happen if we followed the common procedure of using a market proxy portfolio M

[14]Richard Roll and Stephen A. Ross, "On the Cross-Sectional Relation Between Expected Return and Betas," *Journal of Finance* 49 (1994), pp. 101–121.

[15]Schmuel Kandel and Robert F. Stambaugh, "Portfolio Inefficiency and the Cross-Section of Expected Returns," *Journal of Finance* 50 (1995), pp. 185–224; "A Mean-Variance Framework for Tests of Asset Pricing Models," *Review of Financial Studies* 2 (1989), pp. 125–156; "On Correlations and Inferences About Mean-Variance Efficiency," *Journal of Financial Economics* 18 (1987), pp. 61–90.

Figure 10.1 Market index proxies that produce betas having no relation to expected returns.

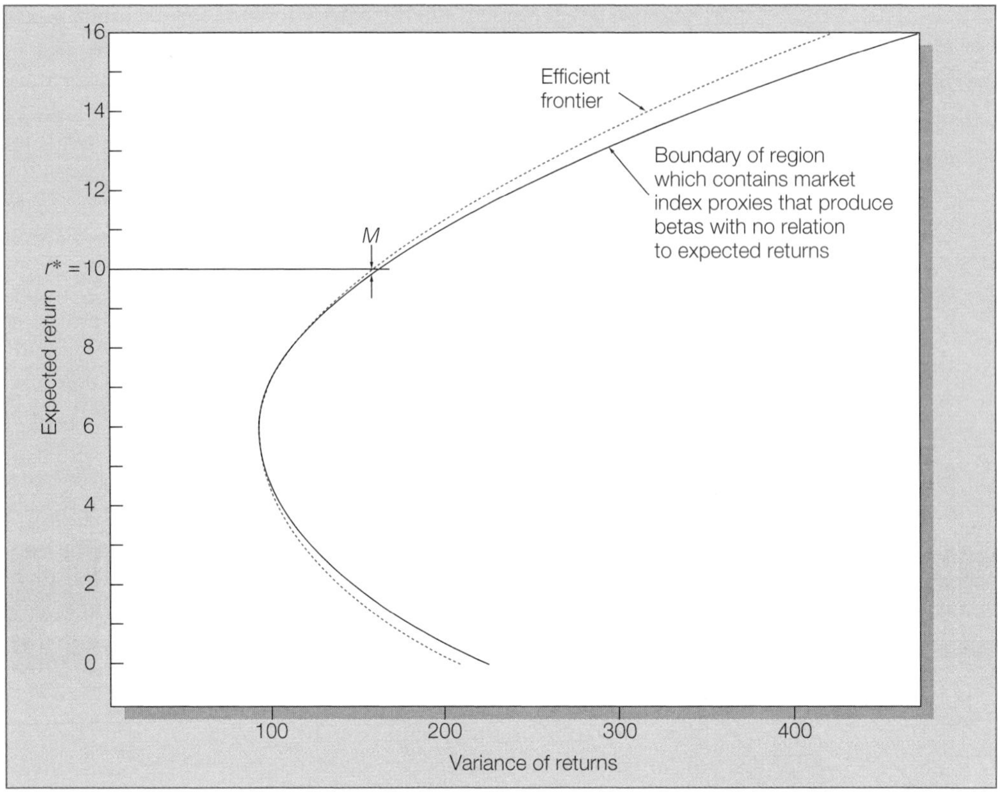

These proxies are located within a restricted region of the mean-variance space, a region bounded by a parabola that lies inside the efficient frontier except for a tangency at the global minimum variance point. The market proxy is located on the boundary at a distance of $M = 22$ basis points below the efficient frontier. While betas against this market proxy have zero cross-sectional correlation with expected returns, a market proxy on the efficient frontier just 22 basis points above it would produce betas that are perfectly positively collinear with expected returns.

Source: Richard Roll and Stephen A. Ross, "On the Cross-Sectional Relation Between Expected Return and Betas," *Journal of Finance* 49 (1994), pp. 101–121.

in place of E, and used as well the more efficient GLS regression procedure in estimating the second-pass regression for the zero-beta version of the CAPM, that is,

$$r_i - r_Z = \gamma_0 + \gamma_1 \times (\text{Estimated } \beta_i)$$

They showed that the estimated values of γ_0 and γ_1 will be biased by a term proportional to the relative efficiency of the market proxy. If the market index used in the regression is fully efficient, the test will be well specified. But the second-pass regression will provide a poor test of the CAPM if the proxy for the market portfolio is not efficient. Thus, while GLS regressions may not give totally arbitrary results, as RR argue may occur using standard OLS regressions, we still cannot test the model in a meaningful way without a reasonably efficient market proxy. Unfortunately, it is difficult to tell how efficient our market index is relative to the theoretical true market portfolio, so we cannot tell how good our tests are.

Measurement Error in Beta

Roll's critique tells us that CAPM tests are handicapped from the outset. But suppose that we could get past Roll's problem by obtaining data on the returns of the true market portfolio. We still would have to deal with the statistical problems caused by measurement error in the estimates of beta from the first-stage regressions.

It is well known in statistics that if the right-hand-side variable of a regression equation is measured with error (in our case, beta is measured with error and is the right-hand-side variable in the second-pass regression), then the slope coefficient of the regression equation will be biased downward and the intercept biased upward. This is consistent with the findings cited above, which found that the estimate of γ_0 was higher than predicted by the CAPM and that the estimate of γ_1 was lower than predicted.

Indeed, a well-controlled simulation test by Miller and Scholes[16] confirms these arguments. In this test a random-number generator simulated rates of return with covariances similar to observed ones. The average returns were made to agree exactly with the CAPM expected return–beta relationship. Miller and Scholes then used these randomly generated rates of return in the tests we have described as if they were observed from a sample of stock returns. The results of this "simulated" test were virtually identical to those reached using real data, despite the fact that the simulated returns were *constructed* to obey the SML, that is, the true γ coefficients were $\gamma_0 = 0$, $\gamma_1 = \overline{r_M - r_f}$, and $\gamma_2 = 0$.

This post mortem of the early test gets us back to square one. We can explain away the disappointing test results, but we have no positive results to support the CAPM-APT implications.

The next wave of tests was designed to overcome the measurement error problem that led to biased estimates of the SML. The innovation in these tests, pioneered by Black, Jensen, and Scholes (BJS),[17] was to use portfolios rather than individual securities. Combining securities into portfolios diversifies away most of the firm-specific part of returns, thereby enhancing the precision of the estimates of beta and the expected rate of return of the portfolio of securities. This mitigates the statistical problems that arise from measurement error in the beta estimates.

Obviously, however, combining stocks into portfolios reduces the number of observations left for the second-pass regression. For example, suppose that we group our sample of 100 stocks into five portfolios of 20 stocks each. If the assumption of a single-factor market is reasonably accurate, then the residuals of the 20 stocks in each portfolio will be practically uncorrelated and, hence, the variance of the portfolio residual will be about one-twentieth the residual variance of the average stock. Thus the portfolio beta in the first-pass regression will be estimated with far better accuracy. However, now consider the second-pass regression. With individual securities we had 100 observations to estimate the second-pass coefficients. With portfolios of 20 stocks each we are left with only five observations for the second-pass regression.

To get the best of this tradeoff, we need to construct portfolios with the largest possible dispersion of beta coefficients. Other things being equal, a sample yields more accurate regression estimates the more widely spaced are the observations of the independent variables. Consider the first-pass regressions where we estimate the SCL, that is, the relationship between the excess return on each stock and the market's excess return. If we have a sample with a great dispersion of market returns, we have a greater chance of accurately estimating the effect of a change in the market return on the return of the stock. In our case, however, we have no control over the range of the market returns. But we can control the range of the independent variable of the second-pass regression, the portfolio betas. Rather than allocate 20 stocks to each portfolio randomly, we can rank portfolios by betas. Portfolio 1 will include the 20 highest-beta stocks and portfolio 5 the 20 lowest-beta stocks. In that case a set of portfolios with small nonsystematic components, e_P, and widely spaced betas will yield reasonably powerful tests of the SML.

Fama and MacBeth[18] used this methodology to verify that the observed relationship between average excess returns and beta is indeed linear and that nonsystematic risk does not explain

[16]Merton H. Miller and Myron Scholes, "Rate of Return in Relation to Risk: A Reexamination of Some Recent Findings," in Michael C. Jensen, ed., *Studies in the Theory of Capital Markets* (New York: Praeger, 1972).

[17]Fischer Black, Michael C. Jensen, and Myron Scholes, "The Capital Asset Pricing Model: Some Empirical Tests," in Michael C. Jensen, ed., *Studies in the Theory of Capital Markets* (New York: Praeger, 1972).

[18]Eugene Fama and James MacBeth, "Risk, Return, and Equilibrium: Empirical Tests," *Journal of Political Economy* 81 (March 1973).

average excess returns. Using 20 portfolios constructed according to the BJS methodology, Fama and MacBeth expanded the estimation of the SML equation to include the square of the beta coefficient (to test for linearity of the relationship between returns and betas) and the estimated standard deviation of the residual (to test for the explanatory power of nonsystematic risk). For a sequence of many subperiods they estimated for each subperiod, the equation

$$r_i = \gamma_0 + \gamma_1\beta_i + \gamma_2\beta_i^2 + \gamma_3\sigma(e_i) \qquad (10.5)$$

The term γ_2 measures potential nonlinearity of return, and γ_3 measures the explanatory power of nonsystematic risk, $\sigma(e_i)$. According to the CAPM, both γ_2 and γ_3 should have coefficients of zero in the second-pass regression.

Fama and MacBeth estimated equation 10.5 for every month of the period January 1935 through June 1968. The results are summarized in Table 10.2, which shows average coefficients and *t*-statistics for the overall period as well as for three subperiods. Fama and MacBeth observed that the coefficients on residual standard deviation (nonsystematic risk), denoted by γ_3, fluctuate greatly from month to month and were insignificant, consistent with the hypothesis that nonsystematic risk is not rewarded by higher average returns. Likewise, the coefficients on the square of beta, denoted by γ_2, were insignificant, consistent with the hypothesis that the expected return–beta relationship is linear.

With respect to the expected return–beta relationship, however, the picture is mixed. The estimated SML is too flat, consistent with previous studies, as can be seen from the fact that $\gamma_0 - r_f$ is positive, and that γ_1 is, on average, less than $r_M - r_f$. On the positive side, the difference does not appear to be significant, so that the CAPM is not clearly rejected.

CONCEPT CHECK

3. According to the CAPM, what are the predicted values of γ_0, γ_1, γ_2, and γ_3 in the Fama and MacBeth regressions for the period 1946–1955?

In conclusion, these tests of the CAPM provide mixed evidence on the validity of the theory. We can summarize the results as follows:

1. The insights that are supported by the single-factor CAPM and APT are as follows:
   a. Expected rates of return are linear and increase with beta, the measure of systematic risk.
   b. Expected rates of return are not affected by nonsystematic risk.

Table 10.2 Summary of Fama and MacBeth (1973) Study (all rates in basis points per month)

Period	1935/6–1968	1935–1945	1946–1955	1956/6–1968
Av. r_f	13	2	9	26
Av. $\gamma_0 - r_f$	8	10	8	5
Av. $t(\gamma_0 - r_f)$	0.20	0.11	0.20	0.10
Av. $r_M - r_f$	130	195	103	95
Av. γ_1	114	118	209	34
Av. $t(\gamma_1)$	1.85	0.94	2.39	0.34
Av. γ_2	−26	−9	−76	0
Av. $t(\gamma_2)$	−0.86	−0.14	−2.16	0
Av. γ_3	516	817	−378	960
Av. $t(\gamma_3)$	1.11	0.94	−0.67	1.11
Av. R-square	0.31	0.31	0.32	0.29

2. The single-variable expected return–beta relationship predicted by either the risk-free rate or the zero-beta version of the CAPM is not fully consistent with empirical observation.

Thus, although the CAPM seems *qualitatively* correct in that β matters and $\sigma(e_i)$ does not, empirical tests do not validate its *quantitative* predictions.

CONCEPT CHECK

4. What would you conclude if you performed the Fama and MacBeth tests and found that the coefficients on β^2 and $\sigma(e)$ were positive?

The EMH and the CAPM

Roll's critique also provides a positive avenue to view the empirical content of the CAPM and APT. Recall, as Roll pointed out, that the CAPM and the expected return–beta relationship follow directly from the efficiency of the market portfolio. This means that if we can establish that the market portfolio is efficient, we would have no need to further test the expected return–beta relationship.

As demonstrated in Chapter 9 on the efficient market hypothesis, proxies for the market portfolio such as the S&P 500 and the NYSE index have proven hard to beat by professional investors. This is perhaps the strongest evidence for the empirical content of the CAPM and APT.

Accounting for Human Capital and Cyclical Variations in Asset Betas

We are reminded of two important deficiencies of the tests of the single-index models:

1. Only a fraction of the value of assets in the United States is traded in capital markets; perhaps the most important nontraded asset is human capital.
2. There is ample evidence that asset betas are cyclical and that accounting for this cyclicality may improve the predictive power of the CAPM.

One of the CAPM assumptions is that all assets are traded and accessible to all investors. Mayers[19] proposed a version of the CAPM that accounts for a violation of this assumption; this requires an additional term in the expected return–beta relationship.

An important nontraded asset that may partly account for the deficiency of standard market proxies such as the S&P 500 is human capital. The value of future wages and compensation for expert services is a significant component of the wealth of investors who expect years of productive careers prior to retirement. Moreover, it is reasonable to expect that changes in human capital are far less than perfectly correlated with asset returns, and hence they diversify the risk of investor portfolios.

Jaganathan and Wang (JW)[20] used a proxy for changes in the value of human capital based on the rate of change in aggregate labour income. In addition to the standard security betas estimated using the value-weighted stock market index, which we denote β^{vw}, JW also estimated the betas of assets with respect to labour income growth, which we denote β^{labour}. Finally, they considered the possibility that business cycles affect asset betas, an issue that has been examined in a number of other studies.[21] They used the difference between the yields on low- and

[19]David Mayers, "Nonmarketable Assets and Capital Market Equilibrium Under Uncertainty," in Michael C. Jensen, ed., *Studies in the Theory of Capital Markets* (New York: Praeger, 1972), pp. 223–48.

[20]Ravi Jaganathan and Zhenyu Wang, "The Conditional CAPM and the Cross-Section of Expected Returns," *Journal of Finance* 51 (March 1996), pp. 3–54.

[21]For example, Campbell Harvey, "Time-Varying Conditional Covariances in Tests of Asset Pricing Models," *Journal of Financial Economics* 24 (October 1989), pp. 289–317; Wayne Ferson and Campbell Harvey, "The Variation of Economic Risk Premiums," *Journal of Political Economy* 99 (April 1991), pp. 385–415; and Wayne Ferson and Robert Korajczyk, "Do Arbitrage Pricing Models Explain the Predictability of Stock Returns?" *Journal of Business* 68 (July 1995), pp. 309–49.

high-grade corporate bonds as a proxy for the state of the business cycle and estimate asset betas relative to this business cycle variable; we denote this beta as β^{prem}.

With the estimates of these three betas for several stock portfolios, JW estimated a second-pass regression which includes firm size (market value of equity, denoted ME):

$$E(R_i) = c_0 + c_{size}\log(\text{ME}) + c_{vw}\beta^{vw} + c_{prem}\beta^{prem} + c_{labour}\beta^{labour} \tag{10.6}$$

Table 10.3 shows the results of various versions of the second-pass estimates. These results are far more supportive of the CAPM than earlier tests. The explanatory power of the equations that include JW's expanded set of explanatory variables (which they call a "conditional" CAPM because beta is conditional on the state of the economy) is much greater than in earlier tests, and the significance of the size variable disappears.

Figure 10.2 shows the improvements of these tests more dramatically. Figure 10.2A shows that the conventional CAPM indeed works poorly. The figure compares predicted security returns fitted using the firm's beta versus actual returns. There is obviously almost no relationship between the two. This is indicative of the weak performance of the conventional CAPM in empirical tests. But if we use the conditional CAPM to compare fitted to actual returns, as in Figure 10.2B, we get a dramatically improved fit. Moreover, adding firm size to this model turns out to do nothing to improve the fit. We conclude that firm size does not improve return predictions once we account for the variables addressed in the conditional CAPM.

JW also compare the conditional CAPM to the Fama and French three-factor model and find that the significance of the book-to-market and size factors disappears once we account for human capital and cyclical variation of the single-index betas.

Table 10.3 Evaluation of Various CAPM Specifications

This table gives the estimates for the cross-sectional regression model

$$E(R_{it}) = c_0 + c_{size}\log(\text{ME}_i) + c_{vw}\beta_i^{vw} + c_{prem}\beta_i^{prem} + c_{labour}\beta_i^{labour}$$

with either a subset or all of the variables. Here, R_{it} is the return on portfolio i (i = 1, 2, . . . , 100) in month t (July 1963–December 1990), R_t^{vw} is the return on the value-weighted index of stocks, R_{t-1}^{prem} is the yield spread between low- and high-grade corporate bonds, and R_t^{labour} is the growth rate in per capita labour income. The β_i^{vw} is the slope coefficient in the OLS regression of R_{it} on a constant and R_t^{vw}. The other betas are estimated in a similar way. The portfolio size, log(ME$_i$), is calculated as the equally weighted average of the logarithm of the market value (in millions of dollars) of the stocks in portfolio i. The regression models are estimated by using the Fama-MacBeth procedure. The "corrected t-values" take sampling errors in the estimated betas into account. All R^2s are reported as percentages.

Coefficient	c_0	c_{vw}	c_{prem}	c_{labour}	c_{size}	R^2
A. The Static CAPM Without Human Capital						
Estimate	1.24	−0.10				1.35
t-value	5.17	−0.28				
Estimate	2.08	−0.32			−0.11	57.56
t-value	5.79	−0.94			−2.30	
B. The Conditional CAPM with Human Capital						
Estimate	1.24	−0.40	0.34	0.22		55.21
t-value	5.51	−1.18	3.31	2.31		
Estimate	1.70	−0.40	0.20	0.10	−0.07	64.73
t-value	4.61	−1.18	3.00	2.09	−1.45	

Figure 10.2 Fitted expected returns versus realized average returns.

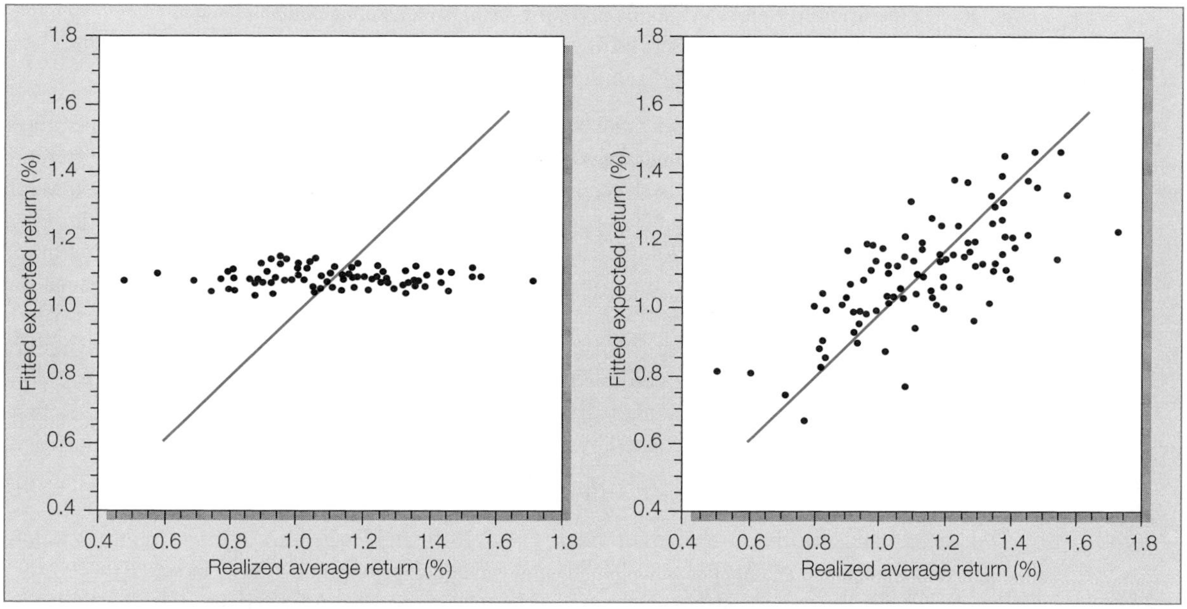

Each scatter point in the graph represents a portfolio, with the realized average return as the horizontal axis and the fitted expected return as the vertical axis. For each portfolio *i*, the realized average return is the time-series average of the portfolio return, and the fitted expected return is the fitted value for the expected return, $E(R_i)$, in the following regression model:

$$E(R_i) = c_0 + c_{vw}\beta_i^{vw}$$

where β_i^{vw} is the slope coefficient in the OLS regression of the portfolio return on a constant and the return on the value-weighted index portfolio of stocks. The straight line in the graph is the 45° line from the origin.

Each scatter point in the graph represents a portfolio, with the realized average return as the horizontal axis and the fitted expected return as the vertical axis. For each portfolio *i*, the realized average return is the time-series average of the portfolio return, and the fitted expected return is the fitted value for the expected return, $E(R_i)$, in the following regression model:

$$E(R_i) = c_0 + c_{vw}\beta_i^{vw} + c_{prem}\beta_i^{prem} + c_{labour}\beta_i^{labour}$$

where β_i^{vw} is the slope coefficient in the OLS regression of the portfolio return on a constant and the return on the value-weighted index portfolio of stocks, β_i^{prem} is the slope coeficient in the OLS regression of the portfolio return on a constant and the yield spread between low- and high-grade corporate bonds, and β_i^{labour} is the slope coefficient in the OLS regression of the portfolio return on a constant and the growth rate in per capita labour income. The straight line in the graph is the 45° line from the origin.

10.2 TESTS OF MULTIFACTOR CAPM AND APT

The multifactor CAPM and APT are elegant theories of how exposure to systematic risk factors should influence expected returns, but they provide little guidance concerning which factors (sources of risk) ought to result in risk premiums. A test of this hypothesis would require three stages:

1. Specification of risk factors.
2. Identification of portfolios that hedge these fundamental risk factors.
3. Test of the explanatory power and risk premiums of the hedge portfolios.

A Macro Factor Model

Chen, Roll, and Ross,[22] identify several possible variables that might proxy for systematic factors:

IP = Growth rate in industrial production
EI = Changes in expected inflation measured by changes in short-term (T-bill) interest rates
UI = Unexpected inflation defined as the difference between actual and expected inflation

[22] Nai-Fu Chen, Richard Roll, and Stephen Ross, "Economic Forces and the Stock Market," *Journal of Business* 59 (1986).

CG = Unexpected changes in risk premiums measured by the difference between the returns on corporate Baa-rated bonds and long-term government bonds

GB = Unexpected changes in the term premium measured by the difference between the returns on long- and short-term government bonds

With the identification of these potential economic factors, Chen, Roll, and Ross skipped the procedure of identifying factor portfolios (the portfolios that have the highest correlation with the factors). Instead, by using the factors themselves, they implicitly assumed that factor portfolios exist that can proxy for the factors. The factors are now used in a test similar to that of Fama and MacBeth.

A critical part of the methodology is the grouping of stocks into portfolios. Recall that in the single-factor tests, portfolios were constructed to span a wide range of betas to enhance the power of the test. In a multifactor framework the efficient criterion for grouping is less obvious. Chen, Roll, and Ross chose to group the sample stocks into 20 portfolios by size (market value of outstanding equity), a variable that is known to be associated with stock returns.

They first used five years of monthly data to estimate the factor betas of the 20 portfolios in a first-pass regression. This is accomplished by estimating the following regressions for each portfolio:

$$r = a + \beta_M r_M + \beta_{\text{IP}}\text{IP} + \beta_{\text{EI}}\text{EI} + \beta_{\text{UI}}\text{UI} + \beta_{\text{CG}}\text{CG} + \beta_{\text{GB}}\text{GB} + e \qquad (10.7\text{a})$$

where M stands for the stock market index. Chen, Roll, and Ross used as the market index both the value-weighted NYSE index (VWNY) and the equally weighted NYSE index (EWNY).

Using the 20 sets of first-pass estimates of factor betas as the independent variables, they now estimated the second-pass regression (with 20 observations, one for each portfolio):

$$r = \gamma_0 + \gamma_M\beta_M + \gamma_{\text{IP}}\beta_{\text{IP}} + \gamma_{\text{EI}}\beta_{\text{EI}} + \gamma_{\text{UI}}\beta_{\text{UI}} + \gamma_{\text{CG}}\beta_{\text{CG}} + \gamma_{\text{GB}}\beta_{\text{GB}} + e \qquad (10.7\text{b})$$

where the gammas become estimates of the risk premiums on the factors.

Chen, Roll, and Ross ran this second-pass regression for every month of their sample period, reestimating the first-pass factor betas once every 12 months. They ran the second-pass tests in four variations. First (Table 10.4, panels A and B), they excluded the market index altogether and

Table 10.4 Economic Variables and Pricing (percent per month × 10), Multivariate Approach

A	YP	IP	EI	UI	CG	GB	Constant
	4.341	13.984	−0.111	−0.672	7.941	−5.8	4.112
	(0.538)	(3.727)	(−1.499)	(−2.052)	(2.807)	(−1.844)	(1.334)
B	**IP**	**EI**	**UI**	**CG**	**GB**	**Constant**	
	13.589	−0.125	−6.29	7.205	−5.211	4.124	
	(3.561)	(−1.640)	(−1.979)	(2.590)	(−1.690)	(1.361)	
C	**EWNY**	**IP**	**EI**	**UI**	**CG**	**GB**	**Constant**
	5.021	14.009	−0.128	−0.848	0.130	−5.017	6.409
	(1.218)	(3.774)	(−1.666)	(−2.541)	(2.855)	(−1.576)	(1.848)
D	**VWNY**	**IP**	**EI**	**UI**	**CG**	**GB**	**Constant**
	−2.403	11.756	−0.123	−0.795	8.274	−5.905	10.713
	(−0.633)	(3.054)	(−1.600)	(−2.376)	(2.972)	(−1.879)	(2.755)

VWNY = Return on the value-weighted NYSE index; EWNY = Return on the equally weighted NYSE index; IP = Monthly growth rate in industrial production; EI = Change in expected inflation; UI = Unanticipated inflation; CG = Unanticipated change in the risk premium (Baa and under return − Long-term government bond return); GB = Unanticipated change in the term structure (Long-term government bond return − Treasury-bill rate); and YP = Yearly growth rate in industrial production. Note that *t*-statistics are in parentheses.

Source: Modified from Nai-Fu Chen, Richard Roll, and Stephen Ross, "Economic Forces and the Stock Market," *Journal of Business* 59 (1986); published by the University of Chicago.

used two alternative measures of industrial production (YP based on annual growth of industrial production and IP based on monthly growth). Finding that IP is a more effective measure, they next included the two versions of the market index, EWNY and VWNY, one at a time (panels C and D). The estimated risk premiums (the values for the parameters, γ) were averaged over all the second-pass regressions.

Note in panels C and D that the two market indexes EWNY (equally weighted index of NYSE) and VWNY (value-weighted NYSE index) are not significant (their t-statistics of 1.218 and –.633 are less than 2). Note also that the VWNY factor has the wrong sign in that it seems to imply a negative market-risk premium. Industrial production (IP), the risk premium on corporate bonds (CG), and unanticipated inflation (UI) are the factors that appear to have significant explanatory power.

A variant of the Chen, Roll, and Ross study was replicated with Canadian data by Otuteye,[23] but the results were not as satisfactory. While the exogenous variables were more or less similar to the ones used by Chen, Roll, and Ross, the market index (the return on a value-weighted portfolio of Canadian stocks) turned out to be highly significant, in contrast to the U.S. results.

These results must be treated as only preliminary in this line of inquiry, but they indicate that it may be possible to hedge some economic factors that affect future consumption risk with appropriate portfolios. A CAPM or APT multifactor equilibrium expected return–beta relationship may one day supersede the now widely used single-factor model.

10.3 THE FAMA-FRENCH THREE-FACTOR MODEL

The multifactor model that occupies centre stage these days is the three-factor model introduced by Fama and French, briefly discussed in Chapters 8 and 9. The systematic factors in the Fama-French model are firm size and book-to-market ratio as well as the market index. These additional factors are empirically motivated by the observations that historical-average returns on stocks of small firms and on stocks with high ratios of book equity to market equity (B/M) are higher than predicted by the security market line of the CAPM. These observations suggest that size or the book-to-market ratio may be proxies for exposures to sources of systematic risk not captured by the CAPM beta and thus result in the return premiums we see associated with these factors.

To create portfolios that track the firm size and book-to-market factors, Davis, Fama, and French[24] (DFF) sorted industrial firms annually by size (market capitalization) and by book-to-market (B/M) ratio. The small-firm group (group S) includes all firms with capitalization below the median, while big (group B) firms have above-median capitalization. Similarly, firms are annually sorted into three groups based on book-to-market ratio: a low-ratio group (group L) with the 33 percent lowest B/M ratio, a medium-ratio group (group M), and a high-ratio group (group H). The high-ratio firms often are called *value firms*, since they appear to be "good values," selling at low multiples of book value. The intersections of the two size groups with the three value groups results in six groups of firms. Six such portfolios (S/L, S/M, S/H, B/L, B/M, B/H) were constructed each year throughout the period, and the monthly returns of each were recorded. This procedure generated six time series of monthly returns for the years 1929 to 1997.

For each year, the size premium is constructed as the difference in returns between small and large firms. Specifically, the difference in returns of an equally weighted long position in the three small-firm portfolios and an equally weighted short position in the three big-firm portfolios

---

[23] E. Otuteye, "How Economic Forces Explain Canadian Stock Returns," *Canadian Investment Review* 4 (Spring 1991), pp. 93–99; and "The Arbitrage Pricing Dichotomy," *Canadian Investment Review,* Winter 1998.

[24] James L. Davis, Eugene F. Fama, and Kenneth R. French, "Characteristics, Covariances, and Average Returns, 1929 to 1997," *Journal of Finance* 55, no. 1 (2000), pp. 389–406.

are computed. SMB (for small minus big) is the return difference. Thus, SMB is calculated from the monthly returns of the six portfolios as

$$SMB = \tfrac{1}{3}(S/L + S/M + S/H) - \tfrac{1}{3}(B/L + B/M + B/H) \qquad (10.8a)$$

Similarly, the book-to-market effect is calculated from the difference in returns between high B/M ratio and low B/M ratio firms. HML (for high minus low ratio) is constructed as the difference in returns between an equally weighted long position in the high B/M portfolios and an equally weighted short position in the low B/M portfolios. The monthly values of HML were calculated from the monthly returns on the low and high B/M portfolios as

$$HML = \tfrac{1}{2}(S/H + B/H) - \tfrac{1}{2}(S/L + B/L) \qquad (10.8b)$$

The monthly returns on the market portfolio were calculated from the value-weighted portfolio of all firms listed on the NYSE, AMEX, and Nasdaq. The risk-free rate was the return on 1-month T-bills.

The Fama-French three-factor asset pricing model equation is

$$E(r_i) - r_f = a_i + b_i[E(r_M) - r_f] + s_i E(SMB) + h_i E(HML) \qquad (10.9a)$$

The coefficients b_i, s_i, and h_i, are the factor loadings (equivalently, factor betas) on the three relevant risk factors. According to the APT, the intercept a_i should be zero, since a portfolio with zero loading on all three factors should have an expected excess return of zero. This equation is estimated as a first-pass regression for each portfolio over the 816 months between 1929 and 1997 using the regression model

$$r_i - r_f = a_i + b_i(r_M - r_f) + s_i\, SMB + h_i HML + e_i \qquad (10.9b)$$

Summary statistics for the market excess return, the factor portfolio returns, and the six size-value portfolios are shown in Table 10.5. The data clearly indicate that the small firms and high book-to-market firms have significantly higher average returns. SMB and HML are both reliably positive. Portfolios of small firm (S) and value firms (H) earned significantly higher average returns.

Table 10.5 Summary Statistics for Monthly Percent Three-Factor Explanatory Returns

	$R_M - R_f$	SMB	HML	S/L	S/M	S/H	B/L	B/M	B/H
7/29–6/97: 816 months									
Ave	0.67	0.20	0.46	1.05	1.30	1.53	0.89	1.04	1.34
Std	5.75	3.26	3.11	7.89	7.49	8.38	5.65	6.19	7.41
t(Ave)	3.34	1.78	4.24	3.80	4.96	5.21	4.52	4.78	5.16
7/29–6/63: 408 months									
Ave	0.82	0.19	0.50	1.09	1.22	1.49	0.81	1.01	1.40
Std	6.89	3.65	3.59	9.01	9.13	10.57	6.50	7.73	9.52
t(Ave)	2.41	1.07	2.80	2.44	2.71	2.85	2.52	2.64	2.98
7/63–6/97: 408 months									
Ave	0.52	0.21	0.43	1.01	1.38	1.57	0.98	1.06	1.27
Std	4.32	2.83	2.54	6.60	5.38	5.37	4.65	4.12	4.38
t(Ave)	2.44	1.53	3.38	3.10	5.17	5.88	4.24	5.20	5.87
7/73–12/93: 246 months									
Ave	0.51	0.33	0.50	1.23	1.60	1.76	0.96	1.20	1.44
Std	4.79	2.75	2.74	6.88	5.64	5.68	5.22	4.53	4.67
t(Ave)	1.68	1.88	2.87	2.81	4.46	4.87	2.90	4.17	4.83

Source: James L. Davis, Eugene F. Fama, and Kenneth R. French, "Characteristics, Covariances, and Average Returns, 1929 to 1999," *Journal of Finance* 55, no. 1 (2000), pp. 393.

To estimate the regressions (10.9b) for a somewhat larger number of portfolios (nine) and secure an equal number of stocks in each group to equalize diversification, DFF repeat the sorts on both size and B/M, but this time they allocate a third of the sample to small, medium, and large firms in the size sort, as well as to low, medium, and high B/M ratio firms in an independent sort. The intersections of these groups lead to nine portfolios containing equal numbers of stocks.

The estimation results of the nine regressions (equation 10.9b) for the overall sample period and for the early and late half-periods are presented in Table 10.6. The *R*-square statistics, all in excess of 0.91, show that returns are well explained by the three factor portfolios, and the t-statistics of the loadings on the size and value factors show that these factors contribute significantly to explanatory power. Moreover, for the full sample period, only one of the nine portfolios has an economically and statistically significant intercept.

Table 10.6 Three-Factor Regressions for Portfolios Formed from Independent Sorts on Size and BE/ME

	BE/ME	Size	Ex. Ret.	*a*	*b*	*s*	*h*	*t*(*a*)	*t*(*b*)	*t*(*s*)	*t*(*h*)	R^2
7/29–6/97												
S/L	0.55	22.39	0.61	−0.42	1.06	1.39	0.09	−4.34	30.78	19.23	1.73	0.91
S/M	1.11	22.15	1.05	−0.01	0.97	1.16	0.37	−0.18	53.55	19.49	9.96	0.96
S/H	2.83	19.05	1.24	−0.03	1.03	1.12	0.77	−0.73	67.32	39.21	26.97	0.98
M/L	0.53	55.85	0.70	−0.06	1.04	0.59	−0.12	−1.29	55.83	18.01	−4.30	0.96
M/M	1.07	55.06	0.95	−0.01	1.05	0.47	0.34	−0.15	32.98	17.50	9.50	0.96
M/H	2.18	53.21	1.13	−0.04	1.08	0.53	0.73	−0.90	47.85	8.99	11.12	0.97
B/L	0.43	94.65	0.58	0.02	1.02	−0.10	−0.23	0.88	148.09	−6.88	−13.52	0.98
B/M	1.04	92.06	0.72	−0.09	1.01	−0.14	0.34	−1.76	61.61	−4.96	13.66	0.95
B/H	1.87	89.53	1.00	−0.09	1.06	−0.07	0.84	−1.40	52.12	−0.86	21.02	0.93
7/29–6/63												
S/L	0.68	23.83	0.69	−0.53	1.01	1.47	0.23	−3.04	18.66	15.72	2.82	0.90
S/M	1.35	23.63	1.21	−0.01	0.96	1.24	0.38	−0.07	34.72	15.60	6.21	0.95
S/H	3.96	20.23	1.44	−0.03	1.02	1.17	0.83	−0.40	44.71	28.80	17.76	0.98
M/L	0.64	55.20	0.84	−0.08	0.98	0.56	0.01	−1.14	37.44	12.26	0.39	0.96
M/M	1.28	54.20	1.13	0.00	1.07	0.47	0.33	0.07	26.38	11.77	7.73	0.97
M/H	2.83	51.59	1.30	−0.07	1.07	0.50	0.79	−0.92	52.49	5.44	7.74	0.97
B/L	0.48	94.92	0.72	−0.01	1.02	−0.08	−0.20	−0.20	131.66	−4.89	−8.09	0.99
B/M	1.21	91.97	0.89	−0.09	1.00	−0.12	0.37	−1.20	43.96	−2.90	10.08	0.96
B/H	2.33	88.91	1.30	0.00	1.02	−0.12	0.97	−0.01	34.28	−0.96	17.99	0.94
7/63–6/97												
S/L	0.42	20.94	0.54	−0.22	1.06	1.22	−0.14	−3.31	60.47	39.87	−4.51	0.96
S/M	0.87	20.68	0.89	0.03	0.97	1.02	0.31	0.71	74.53	52.41	13.82	0.98
S/H	1.71	17.88	1.04	0.04	0.99	1.03	0.62	1.27	75.12	64.49	25.86	0.98
M/L	0.42	56.51	0.56	−0.02	1.07	0.58	−0.24	−0.33	71.73	27.08	−9.73	0.96
M/M	0.87	55.93	0.77	0.02	1.00	0.48	0.30	0.31	64.36	22.60	11.22	0.95
M/H	1.54	54.83	0.96	0.03	1.05	0.55	0.63	0.53	69.16	28.08	24.23	0.96
B/L	0.38	94.38	0.45	0.10	0.99	−0.15	−0.32	2.89	91.73	−8.92	−16.53	0.98
B/M	0.86	92.14	0.54	−0.04	0.99	−0.19	0.25	−0.70	55.19	−6.91	8.53	0.91
B/H	1.41	90.16	0.70	−0.13	1.04	−0.01	0.69	−2.59	76.64	−0.36	28.53	0.94

Source: James L. Davis, Eugene F. Fama, and Kenneth R. French, "Characteristics, Covariances, and Average Returns, 1929–1997," *Journal of Finance* 55, no. 1 (2000) pp. 396.

How should we interpret these results? One argument is that size and relative value (as measured by the B/M ratio) proxy for risk not captured by the CAPM beta alone.[25] This explanation is consistent with the APT in that it implies that size and value are priced risk factors and, hence, that these premiums do not represent mispricing. Another explanation attributes these premiums to irrational investor preferences for large size or low B/M firms, which drives up their prices and drives down the returns on these firms. This question may be more relevant for the B/M or "value" factor in the light of evidence that the size premium has largely vanished in recent years.

The question about the source of the value premium must be resolved by testing whether, within each group, portfolios with larger loadings on the value factor (larger h coefficient on the HML portfolio) do indeed earn a higher average return. If they do not, then it appears that firms with these *characteristics* (i.e., a higher ratio of B/M) earn higher returns but that a greater *exposure* to the B/M factor per se does not itself predict higher returns. This would be evidence of mispricing.[26]

To address this issue, DFF sort each of the portfolios into three subgroups according to their h value over the previous three years and show that higher h portfolios (with greater exposure to HML) earned a higher average return over the full sample period. But DFF also found that this was not the case in the 20-year period between 1973 and 1993. Thus, the important question of whether the model is consistent with a three-factor version of the APT, or instead suggests irrational investor behaviour, is not categorically resolved. See the boxed article here for further recent approaches to the risk-return tradeoff.

10.4 TIME-VARYING VOLATILITY

We may associate the variance of the rate of return on the stock with the rate of arrival of new information, because new information may lead investors to revise their assessment of intrinsic value. As a casual survey of the media would indicate, the rate of revision in predictions of business cycles, industry ascents or descents, and the fortunes of individual enterprises fluctuates regularly; in other words, the rate of arrival of new information is time-varying. Consequently, we should expect the variances of the rates of return on stocks (as well as the covariances among them) to be time-varying.

In an exploratory study of the volatility of NYSE stocks over more than 150 years (using monthly returns over 1835–1987), Pagan and Schwert[27] computed estimates of the variance of monthly returns. Their results, depicted in Figure 10.3, show just how important it may be to consider time variation in stock variance. The centrality of the risk-return tradeoff suggests that once we make sufficient progress in the modelling, estimation, and prediction of the time variation in return variances and covariances, we should expect a significant refinement in understanding expected returns as well.

In 1982 Robert F. Engle published a study[28] of U.K. inflation rates that measured their time-varying volatility. His model, named ARCH (autoregressive conditional heteroskedasticity), is

---

[25]Maria Vassalou and Yuhang Xing, "Default Risk and Equity Returns," *Journal of Finance* (forthcoming), show that these factors contain information on return beyond default risk.

[26]This point is emphasized in Kent Daniel and Sheridan Titman, "Evidence on the Characteristics of Cross Sectional Variation in Common Stock Returns," *Journal of Finance* 40 (1995), pp. 383–99.

[27]Adrian Pagan and G. William Schwert, "Alternative Models for Conditional Stock Volatility," *Journal of Econometrics* 45 (1990), pp. 267–290.

[28]Robert F. Engle, "Autoregressive Conditional Heteroskedasticity with Estimates of the Variance of U.K. Inflation," *Econometrica* 50 (1982), pp. 987–1008.

TAKING STOCK

Since the stock market bubble burst more than 3 years ago, investors have had ample time to ponder where to put the remains of their money. Economists and analysts too have been revisiting old ideas. None has been dearer to them than the capital asset pricing model (CAPM), a formula linking movements in a single share price to those of the market as a whole. The key statistic there is "beta."

However, many investors and managers have given up on beta. Although it is useful for working out overall correlation with the market, it tells you little about share-price performance in absolute terms. In fact, the CAPM's obituary was already being written more than a decade ago when a paper by Eugene Fama and Kenneth French showed that the shares of small companies and "value stocks" do much better over time than their betas would predict.

Another new paper, by John Campbell and Tuomo Vuolteenaho of Harvard University, tries to resuscitate beta by splitting it into two.* The authors start from first principles. In essence, the value of a company depends on two things; its expected profits and the interest rate used to discount these profits. Changes in share prices therefore stem from changes in one of these factors.

From this observation, they propose two types of beta: one to gauge shares' responses to changes in profits; the other to pick up the effects of changes in the interest rate. Allowing for separate cash flow versus interest rate betas helps better explain the performance of small and value companies. Shares of such companies are more sensitive than the average to news about profits, in part because they are bets on future growth. Shares with high price–earnings ratios vary more with the discount rate. In all cases, above-average returns compensate investors for above-average risks.

Equity's Allure

Beta is a tool for comparing shares with each other. Recently, however, investors have been worried about equity as an asset class. The crash has left investors asking what became of the fabled equity premium, the amount by which they can expect returns on shares to exceed those from government bonds.

History says that shareholders have a lot to be optimistic about. Over the past 100 years, investors in American shares have enjoyed a premium, relative to Treasury bonds, of around seven percentage points. Similar effects have been seen in other countries. Some studies have reached less optimistic conclusions, suggesting a premium of four or five points. But even this premium seems generous.

Many answers have been put forward to explain the premium. One is that workers cannot hedge against many risks, such as losing their jobs, which tend to hit at the same time as stock market crashes; this means that buying shares would increase the volatility of their income, so that investors require a premium to be persuaded to hold them. Another is that shares, especially in small companies, are much less liquid than government debt. It is also sometimes argued that in extreme times—in depression or war, or after bubbles—equities fare much worse than bonds, so that equity investors demand higher returns to compensate them for the risk of catastrophe.

Yes, over long periods equities have done better than bonds. But the equity "premium" is unpredictable. Searching for a consistent, God-given premium is a fool's errand.

*John Y. Campbell and Tuomo Vuolteenaho, "Bad Beta, Good Beta," Harvard University mimeo, 2003.

Source:

based on the idea that a natural way to update a variance forecast is to average it with the most recent squared "surprise" (i.e., the squared deviation of the rate of return from its mean).

When we consider a time-varying return distribution, we must refer to the *conditional* mean, variance, and covariance, that is, the mean, variance, or covariance conditional on currently available information. The "conditions" that vary over time are the values of variables that determine the level of these parameters. In contrast, the usual estimate of return variance, the average of squared deviations over the sample period, provides an *unconditional* estimate, because it treats the variance as constant over time.

Today, the most widely used model to estimate the conditional (hence time-varying) variance of stocks and stock index returns is the generalized autoregressive conditional heteroskedasticity (GARCH) model, also pioneered by Robert F. Engle.[29] (The generalized ARCH model allows greater flexibility in the specification of how volatility evolves over time.)

[29]Robert F. Engle, "Autoregressive Conditional Heteroskedasticity with Estimates of the Variance of U.K. Inflation."

Figure 10.3 Estimates of the monthly stock return variance, 1835–1987.

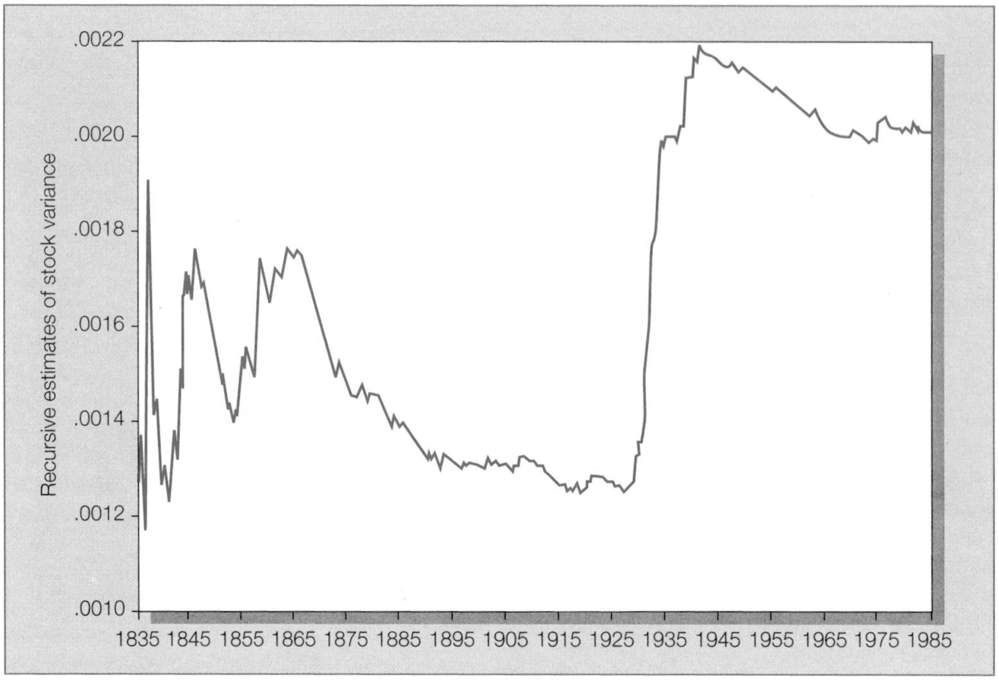

Source: Adrian R. Pagan and G. William Schwert, "Alternative Models for Conditional Stock Volatility," *Journal of Econometrics* 45 (1990), pp. 267–290.

The GARCH model uses rate of return history as the information set used to form our estimates of variance. The model posits that the forecast of market volatility evolves relatively smoothly each period in response to new observations on market returns. The updated estimate of market-return variance in each period depends on both the previous estimate and the most recent squared residual return on the market. The squared residual is an unbiased estimate of variance, so this technique essentially mixes in a statistically efficient manner the previous volatility estimate with an unbiased estimate based on the new observation of market return. The updating formula is

$$\sigma_t^2 = a_0 + a_1\epsilon^2_{t-1} + a_2\sigma^2_{t-1} \tag{10.10}$$

As noted, equation 10.10 asserts that the updated forecast of variance is a function of the most recent variance forecast σ^2_{t-1}, and the most recent squared prediction error in market return, ϵ^2_{t-1}. The parameters a_0, a_1, and a_2 are estimated from past data.

Evidence on the relationship between mean and variance has been mixed. Whitelaw[30] found that average returns and volatility are negatively related, but Kane, Marcus, and Noh[31] found a positive relationship.

The GARCH model was also applied to Canadian stock index return data in a study by Calvet and Rahman,[32] who examined the effects on model specification of shifting U.S. monetary regimes and exogenous events over the period 1975–1991. U.S. regime shifts are expected to affect Canadian stock returns, given the close linkages between the U.S. and

[30]Robert F. Whitelaw, "Time Variation and Covariations in the Expectation and Volatility of Stock Returns," *Journal of Finance* 49 (1994), pp. 515–542.

[31]Alex Kane, Alan J. Marcus, and Jaesun Noh, "The P/E Multiple and Market Volatility," *Financial Analysts Journal* 52 (July/August 1996), pp. 16–24.

[32]A. Louis Calvet and Abdul Rahman, "Persistence of Stock Return Volatility in Canada," *Canadian Journal of Administrative Sciences* 12 (1995), 224–237.

Figure 10.4 **Implied versus estimated volatility. Implied volatility is derived from options on the S&P 100 index. Estimated volatility is derived from an ARCH-M model.**

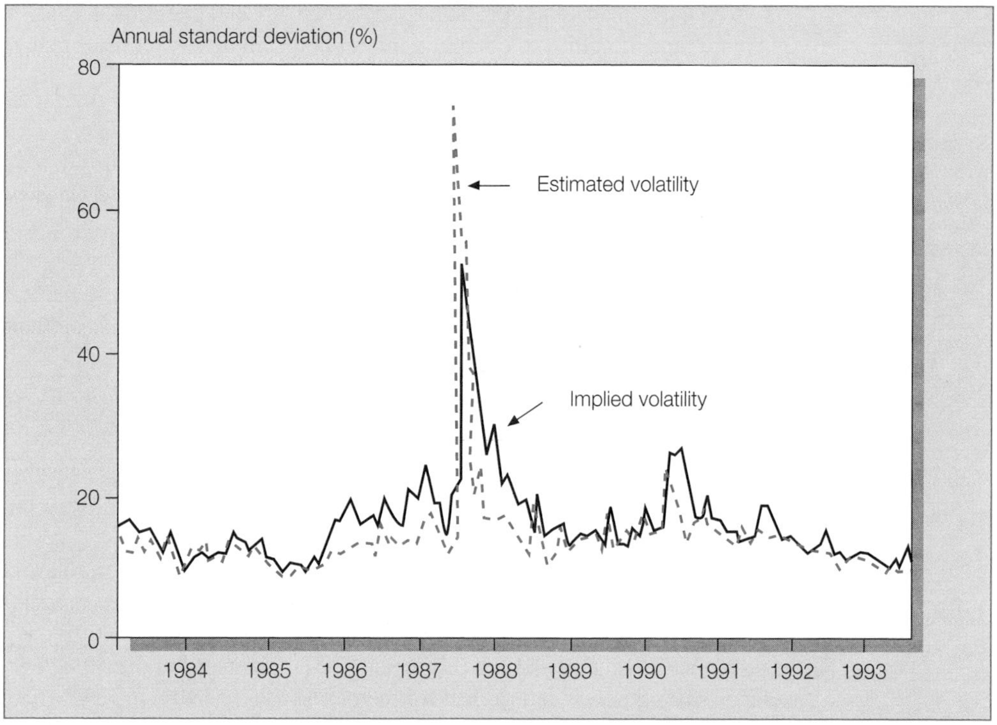

Canadian financial markets.[33] The study shows that taking into account the changes in monetary regimes results in a reduction of the excess price volatility observed over the entire period. Similar reductions are also observed when "extraordinary" events (corresponding to the release of business and economic news) are introduced into the GARCH model as dummy variables.

ARCH-type models clearly capture much of the variation in stock market volatility. Figure 10.4 compares volatility estimates derived from an ARCH model to volatility estimates derived from prices on market-index options.[34] The variation in volatility, as well as the close agreement between the estimates, is evident.

10.5 THE EQUITY PREMIUM PUZZLE

In an intriguing article[35] Mehra and Prescott examined the excess returns earned on equity portfolios over the risk-free rate during the period 1889–1978. They concluded that the historical-average excess return has been too large to be consistent with reasonable levels of risk aversion. In other words, it appears that the reward investors have received for bearing risk has been so generous that it is hard to reconcile with rational security pricing. This research has since engendered a large body of literature attempting to explain this puzzle.[36]

[33]Several studies have documented these linkages. See, for instance, Usha R. Mittoo, "Additional Evidence on Integration in the Canadian Stock Market," *Journal of Finance* 47 (1992), 2035–2054.

[34]We will show you how such estimates can be derived from option prices in Chapter 18.

[35]Jarnish Mehra and Edward Prescott, "The Equity Premium: A Puzzle," *Journal of Monetary Economics*, March 1985.

[36]For Canadian evidence on the same topic see Laurence Booth, "Canadian Equities and Why They Won't Outperform Bonds as in the Past," *Canadian Investment Review*, Spring 1995, pp. 9–15. Booth, however, focuses on the changes in the premium of Canadian stocks over long-term bonds, which he attributes to the high volatility of bond returns.

Two recent explanations for the puzzle deserve special attention, as they utilize important insights into the difficulties of obtaining inferences from observations of realized returns.

Equity Premium Puzzle
www.slate.com/Features/Stocks/Stocks.asp

Expected Versus Realized Returns

Fama and French[37] offer one possible interpretation of the puzzle. They work with an expanded sample period, 1872–1999, and report the average risk-free rates, average return on equity (represented by the S&P 500 index), and the resultant risk premium for the overall period and subperiods:

Period	Risk-Free Rate	S&P 500 Return	Equity Premium
1872–1999	4.87	10.97	6.10
1872–1949	4.05	8.67	4.62
1950–1999	6.15	14.56	8.41

The difference in results before and after 1949 suggests that the equity premium puzzle is really a creature of modern times.

Fama and French (FF) suspect that estimating the risk premium from average realized returns may be the problem. They use the constant growth dividend discount model (see an introductory finance text or Chapter 14) to estimate expected returns and find that for the period 1872–1949, the dividend discount model (DDM) yields similar estimates of the *expected* risk premium as the average *realized* excess return. But for the period 1950–1999, the DDM yields a much smaller risk premium, which suggests that the high average excess return in this period may have exceeded the returns investors actually expected to earn at the time.

In the constant growth DDM, the expected capital gains rate on the stock will equal the growth rate of dividends. As a result, the expected total return on the firm's stock will be the sum of dividend yield (dividend/price) plus the expected dividend growth rate, g:

$$E(r) = \frac{D_1}{P_0} + g \tag{10.11}$$

where D_1 is end-of-year dividends and P_0 is the current price of the stock. FF treat the S&P 500 as representative of the average firm, and use equation 10.11 to produce estimates of $E(r)$.

For any sample period, $t = 1, \ldots, T$, Fama and French estimate expected return from the arithmetic average of the dividend yield (D_t/P_{t-1}) plus the dividend growth rate ($g_t = D_t/D_{t-1}$). In contrast, the *realized* return is the dividend yield plus the rate of capital gains ($P_t/P_{t-1} - 1$). Because the dividend yield is common to both estimates, the difference between the expected and realized return equals the difference between the dividend growth and capital gains rates. While dividend growth and capital gains were similar in the earlier period, capital gains significantly exceeded the dividend growth rate in modern times. Hence, FF conclude that the equity premium puzzle may be due at least in part to unanticipated capital gains in the latter period.

FF argue that dividend growth rates produce more reliable estimates of expected capital gains than the average of realized capital gains. They give three reasons:

1. Average realized returns over 1950–1999 exceeded the internal rate of return on corporate investments. If those returns were representative of expectations, we would have to conclude that firms were willingly engaging in negative NPV investments.
2. The statistical precision of estimates from the DDM are far higher than those using average historical returns. The standard error of the estimates of the risk premium from

[37] Eugene Fama and Kenneth French, "The Equity Premium," *Journal of Finance* 57, no. 2 (2002).

realized returns is about 2.5 times the standard error from the dividend discount model (see table below).

3. The reward-to-variability (Sharpe) ratio derived from the DDM is far more stable than that derived from realized returns. If risk aversion remains the same over time, we would expect the Sharpe ratio to be stable.

The evidence for the second and third points is shown in the table below, where estimates from the dividend model ("DDM") and from realized returns ("Realized") are shown side by side.

	Mean Return		Standard Error		*t*-statistic		Sharpe Ratio	
Period	DDM	Realized	DDM	Realized	DDM	Realized	DDM	Realized
1872–1999	4.03	6.10	1.14	1.65	3.52	3.70	.22	.34
1872–1949	4.35	4.62	1.76	2.20	2.47	2.10	.23	.24
1950–1999	3.54	8.41	1.03	2.45	3.42	3.43	.21	.51

FF's innovative study thus provides an explanation of the equity premium puzzle. Another implication from the study may be even more important for today's investor: the study predicts that future excess returns will be significantly lower than those experienced in recent decades.

Survivorship Bias

The equity premium puzzle emerged from long-term averages of U.S. stock returns. There are reasons to suspect that these estimates of the risk premium are subject to **survivorship bias**, as the United States has arguably been the most successful capitalist system in the world, an outcome that probably would not have been anticipated several decades ago. Jurion and Goetzmann[38] assembled a database of capital appreciation indexes for the stock markets of 39 countries over the period 1926–1996. Figure 10.5 shows that U.S. equities had the highest real return of all countries, at 4.3 percent annually, versus a median of 0.8 percent for other countries. Moreover, unlike the United States, many other countries have had equity markets that actually closed, either permanently, or for extended periods of time.

The implication of these results is that using average U.S. data may induce a form of survivorship bias to our estimate of expected returns, since unlike many other countries, the United States has never been a victim of such extreme problems. Estimating risk premiums from the experience of the most successful country and ignoring the evidence from stock markets that did not survive for the full sample period will impart an upward bias in estimates of expected returns. The high realized equity premium obtained for the United States may not be indicative of required returns.

As an analogy, think of the effect of survivorship bias in the mutual fund industry. We know that some companies regularly close down their worst-performing mutual funds. If performance studies include only mutual funds for which returns are available during an entire sample period, the average returns of the funds that make it into the sample will be reflective of the performance of long-term survivors only. With the failed funds excluded from the sample, the average measured performance of mutual fund managers will be better than one could reasonably expect from the full sample of managers. Think back to the boxed article in Chapter 9, "How to Guarantee a Successful Market Newsletter." If one starts many newsletters with a range of forecasts, and continues only the newsletters that turned out to have successful advice, then it will *appear* from the sample of survivors that the average newsletter had forecasting skill.

[38]Philippe Jurion and William N. Goetzmann, "Global Stock Markets in the Twentieth Century," *Journal of Finance* 54, no. 3 (June 1999).

Figure 10.5 **Real returns on global stock markets. The figure displays average real returns for 39 markets over the period 1921 to 1996. Markets are sorted by years of existence. The graph shows that markets with long histories typically have higher returns. An asterisk indicates that the market suffered a long-term break.**

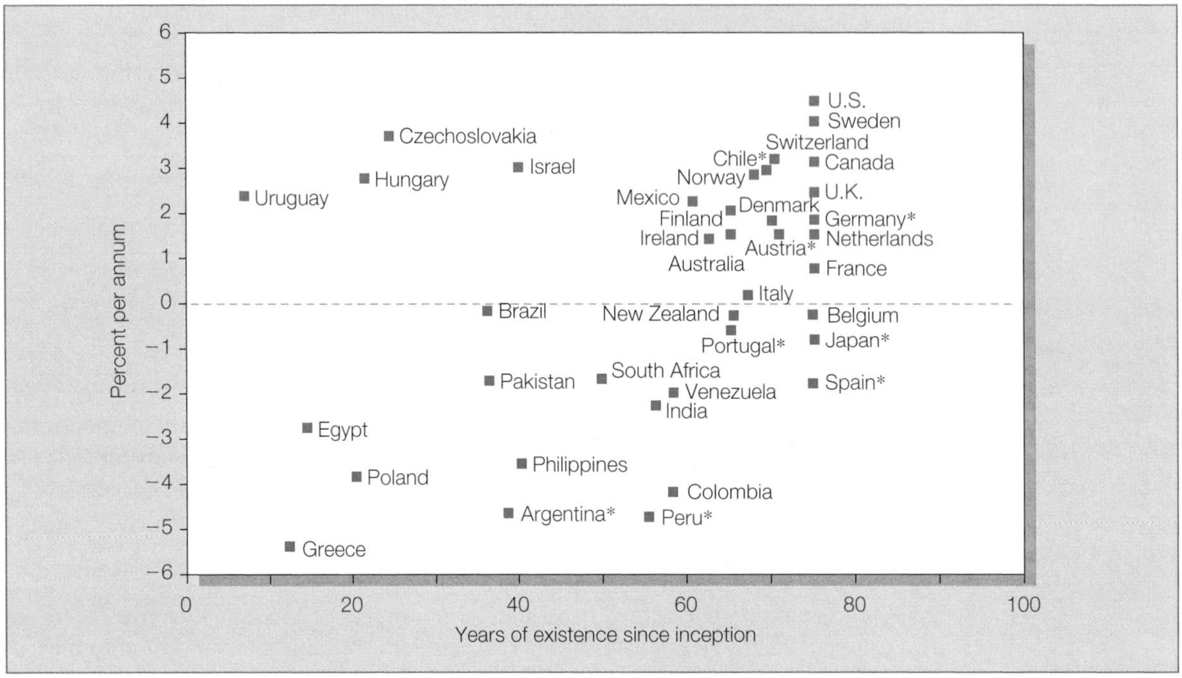

10.6 SURVIVORSHIP BIAS AND TESTS OF MARKET EFFICIENCY

We've seen that survivorship bias might be one source of the equity premium puzzle. It turns out that survivorship bias also can affect our measurement of *persistence* in stock market returns, an issue that is crucial for tests of market efficiency. For a demonstration of the potential impact of survivorship bias, imagine that a new group of mutual funds is set up. Half the funds are managed aggressively and the other half conservatively; however, none of the managers are able to beat the market in expectation. The probability distribution of alpha values is given by:

	Probability	
Alpha Value (%)	Conservative Manager	Aggressive Manager
3	0	.5
1	.5	0
−1	.5	0
−3	0	.5

Because there are an equal number of aggressive and conservative managers, the frequency distribution of alphas in a given period is:

Alpha Value (%)	Relative Frequency of Funds	
	Conservative Manager	Aggressive Manager
3	0	.25
1	.25	0
−1	.25	0
−3	0	.25
Total	.5	.5

Define a "winner" fund as one in the top half of the distribution of returns in a given period; a "loser" is one in the bottom half of the sample. Manager alphas are assumed to be serially uncorrelated. Therefore, the probability of being a winner or a loser in the second quarter is the same regardless of first-quarter performance. A 2 × 2 tabulation of performance in two consecutive periods, such as in the following table, will show absence of any persistence in performance.

Distribution of Two-Period Performance: Full Sample

First Period	Second Period	
	Winners	Losers
Winners	.25	.25
Losers	.25	.25

But now assume that in each quarter funds are ranked by returns and the bottom 5 percent are closed down. A researcher obtains a sample of four quarters of fund returns and ranks the semiannual performance of funds that survived the entire sample. The following table, based only on surviving funds, seems to show that first-period winners are far more likely to be second period winners as well. Despite lack of true persistence in performance, the loss of just a few funds each period induces an appearance of significant persistence.

Distribution of Two-Period Performance: Surviving Sample

First Period	Second Period		
	Winners	Losers	Row Total
Winners	.3893	.1401	.5294
Losers	.1107	.4706	.4706
Column total	.5001	.4999	1.0000

The degree of survivorship bias depends first and foremost on how aggressively poorly performing funds are shut down. (In this example, the worst 5 percent of performers were shut down.) The bias increases enormously with the cut-off rate. Other factors affecting bias are correlation across manager portfolios, serial correlation of returns, the dispersion of style across managers, and the strategic response of managers to the possibility of cutoff.

To assess the potential effect of actual survivorship bias, Brown, Goetzmann, Ibbotson, and Ross[39] conducted a simulation using observed characteristics of mutual fund returns. Their results demonstrate that actual survivorship bias could be strong enough to create apparent persistence in the performance of portfolio managers. They simulate annual returns over a four-year period for 600 mutual fund managers, drawing from distributions that are constructed to mimic observed

[39]Stephen J. Brown, William Goetzmann, Roger G. Ibbotson, and Stephen A. Ross, "Survivorship Bias in Performance Studies," *Review of Financial Studies* 5, no. 4 (1992).

equity returns in the United States over the period 1926–1989,[40] and mutual fund returns reported in a performance study by Goetzmann and Ibbotson.[41] Four annual returns for each manager are generated independently so that relative performance over the first two-year period does not persist in the following two-year period. The simulated returns of the funds and the market index are used to compute four risk-adjusted annual returns (alphas) for each of the 600 managers. Winners (losers) are identified by positive (negative) alphas.

Two-by-two tabulations of the frequency of first-period/second-period winners and losers are shown in Table 10.7. When all 600 managers are included in the four-year sample, no persistence in performance can be detected. But when the poor performers in each year are eliminated from the sample, performance persistence shows up. Elimination of even a small number of poor performers can generate a significant level of apparent persistence.

Table 10.7
Two-Way Table of Managers Classified by Risk-Adjusted Returns over Successive Intervals, a Summary of 20,000 Simulations Assuming 0, 5, 10, and 20 Percent Cutoffs

	Second-Period Winners	Second-Period Losers
	No cutoff ($n = 600$)	
First-period winners	150.09	149.51
First-period losers	149.51	150.09
		Average cross-section t-value = −.004
		Average annual excess return = .0%
		Average β = .950
	5% cutoff ($n = 494$)	
First-period winners	127.49	119.51
First-period losers	119.51	127.49
		Average cross-section t-value = 2.046
		Average annual excess return = .44%
		Average β = .977
	10% cutoff ($n = 398$)	
First-period winners	106.58	92.42
First-period losers	92.42	106.58
		Average cross-section t-value = 3.356
		Average annual excess return = .61%
		Average β = .994
	20% cutoff ($n = 249$)	
First-period winners	71.69	53.31
First-period losers	53.31	70.69
		Average cross-section t-value = 4.679
		Average annual excess return = .80%
		Average β = 1.018

In each of the four years, managers who experience returns in the lowest percentile indicated by the cutoff value are excluded from the sample, and this experiment is repeated 20,000 times. Thus, the numbers in the first 2 × 2 table give the average frequency with which the 600 managers fall into the respective classifications. The second panel shows the average frequencies for the 494 managers who survive the performance cut, while the third and fourth panels give corresponding results for 398 and 249 managers. For each simulation, the winners are defined as those managers whose average two-year Jensen's α measure was greater than or equal to that of the median manager in that sample.

[40]They draw market risk premiums from a normal distribution with mean 8.6 percent and standard deviation 20.8 percent. The 600 manager betas are drawn from a normal distribution with mean .95 and standard deviation .25. The residual standard deviation for each manager is estimated from actual data.

[41]William Goetzmann and Roger Ibbotson, "Do Winners Repeat? Predicting Mutual Fund Performance," *Journal of Portfolio Management* 20 (1994).

The results for a 5 percent cut-off rate in Table 10.7 are not as strong as in the "clean" example we presented above; apparently, other factors mitigate the effect somewhat. Still, survivorship bias is sufficient to create an appearance of significant performance persistence even when actual returns are consistent with efficient markets.

SUMMARY

1. Although the single-factor expected return–beta relationship has not yet been confirmed by scientific standards, its use is already commonplace in economic life.
2. Early tests of the single-factor CAPM rejected the SML, finding that nonsystematic risk did explain average security returns.
3. Later tests controlling for the measurement error in beta found that nonsystematic risk does not explain portfolio returns but also that the estimated SML is too flat compared with what the CAPM would predict.
4. Roll's critique implied that the usual CAPM test is a test only of the mean-variance efficiency of a prespecified market proxy and therefore that tests of the linearity of the expected return–beta relationship do not bear on the validity of the model.
5. Tests of the mean-variance efficiency of professionally managed portfolios against the benchmark of a prespecified market index conform with Roll's critique in that they provide evidence of the efficiency of the prespecific market index.
6. Empirical evidence suggests that most professionally managed portfolios are outperformed by market indices, which lends weight to acceptance of the efficiency of those indices and hence the CAPM.
7. Work with economic factors suggests that factors such as unanticipated inflation do play a role in the expected return–beta relationship of security returns.
8. Recent tests of the single-index model, accounting for human capital and cyclical variations in asset betas, are far more consistent with the single-index CAPM and APT. These tests suggest that macroeconomic variables are not necessary to explain expected returns. Moreover, anomalies such as effects of size and book-to-market ratios disappear once these variables are accounted for.
9. Volatility of stock returns is constantly changing. Empirical evidence on stock returns must account for this phenomenon. Contemporary researchers use the variations of the ARCH algorithm to estimate the level of volatility and its effect on mean returns.
10. The equity premium puzzle originates from the observation that equity returns exceeded the risk-free rate to an extent that is inconsistent with reasonable levels of risk aversion—at least when average rates of return are taken to represent expectations. Fama and French show that the puzzle emerges from excess returns over the last 50 years. Alternative estimates of expected returns using the dividend growth model instead of average returns suggest that excess returns on stocks were high because of unexpected large capital gains. The study implies that future excess returns will be lower than realized in recent decades.

KEY TERMS

first-pass regression 363
second-pass regression 363
thin trading 365
benchmark error 367
survivorship bias 383

SELECTED READINGS

The key readings concerning tests of the CAPM are still:

Black, Fischer, Michael C. Jensen, and Myron Scholes. "The Capital Asset Pricing Model: Some Empirical Tests." In *Studies in the Theory of Capital Markets*, ed. Michael C. Jensen. New York: Praeger, 1972.

Fama, Eugene, and James MacBeth. "Risk, Return, and Equilibrium: Empirical Tests." *Journal of Political Economy* 81 (1973), pp. 607–636.

Roll, Richard. "A Critique of the Asset Pricing Theory's Tests." *Journal of Financial Economics* 4 (1977).

A test of the model using more recent econometric tools is:

Gibbons, Michael. "Multivariate Tests of Financial Models." *Journal of Financial Economics* 10 (1982).

The factor analysis approach to testing multivariate models is treated in:

Roll, Richard, and Stephen Ross. "An Empirical Investigation of the Arbitrage Pricing Theory." *Journal of Finance* 20 (1980).

Kryzanowski, Laurence, and Minla Chau To, "General Factor Models and the Structure of Security Returns," *Journal of Financial and Quantitative Analysis* 18, no. 1 (March 1982).

Lehman, Bruce, and David Modest. "The Empirical Foundation of the Arbitrage Pricing Theory." *Journal of Financial Economics* 21 (1988).

A good paper that tests the APT with prespecified factors is:

Chen, Nai-Fu, Richard Roll, and Stephen A. Ross. "Economic Forces and the Stock Market." *Journal of Business* 59 (1986).

PROBLEMS

The following annual excess rates of return (%) were obtained for nine individual stocks and a market index:

		Stocks								
Year	Market Index	*A*	*B*	*C*	*D*	*E*	*F*	*G*	*H*	*I*
1	29.65	33.88	−25.20	36.48	42.89	−39.89	39.67	74.57	40.22	90.19
2	−11.91	−49.87	24.70	−25.11	−54.39	44.92	−54.33	−79.76	−71.58	−26.64
3	14.73	65.14	−25.04	18.91	−39.86	−3.91	−5.69	26.73	14.49	18.14
4	27.68	14.46	−38.64	−23.31	−0.72	−3.21	92.39	−3.82	13.74	0.09
5	5.18	15.67	61.93	63.95	−32.82	44.26	−42.96	101.67	24.24	8.98
6	25.97	−32.17	44.94	−19.56	69.42	90.43	76.72	1.72	77.22	72.38
7	10.64	−31.55	−74.65	50.18	74.52	15.38	21.95	−43.95	−13.40	28.95
8	1.02	−23.79	47.02	−42.28	28.61	−17.64	28.83	98.01	28.12	39.41
9	18.82	−4.59	28.69	−0.54	2.32	42.36	18.93	−2.45	37.65	94.67
10	23.92	−8.03	48.61	23.65	26.26	−3.65	23.31	15.36	80.59	52.51
11	−41.61	78.22	−85.02	−0.79	−68.70	−85.71	−45.64	2.27	−72.47	−80.26
12	−6.64	4.75	42.95	−48.60	26.27	13.24	−34.34	−54.47	−1.50	−24.46

1. Perform the first-pass regressions and tabulate the summary statistics.
2. Specify the hypotheses for a test of the second-pass regression for the SML.
3. Perform the second-pass SML regression by regressing the average excess return of each portfolio on its beta.
4. Summarize your test results and compare them to the reported results in the text.
5. Group the nine stocks into three portfolios, maximizing the dispersion of the betas of the three resultant portfolios. Repeat the test and explain any changes in the results.
6. Explain Roll's critique as it applies to the tests performed in problems 1 to 5.
7. Plot the capital market line (CML), the nine stocks, and the three portfolios on a graph of average returns versus standard deviation. Compare the mean-variance efficiency of the three portfolios and the market index. Does the comparison support the CAPM?

Suppose that, in addition to the market factor that has been considered in problems 1 to 7, a second factor is considered. The values of this factor for years 1 to 12 were as follows:

Year	% Change in Factor Value
1	−9.84
2	6.46
3	16.12
4	−16.51
5	17.82
6	−13.31
7	−3.52
8	8.43
9	8.23
10	7.06
11	−15.74
12	2.03

8. Perform the first-pass regressions as Chen, Roll, and Ross did and tabulate the relevant summary statistics. (*Hint*: Use a multiple regression as in a standard spreadsheet package. Estimate the betas of the 12 stocks on the two factors.)
9. Specify the hypothesis for a test of a second-pass regression for the two-factor SML.
10. Do the data suggest a two-factor economy?
11. Can you identify a factor portfolio for the second factor?
12. Identify and briefly discuss three criticisms of beta as used in the capital asset pricing model. CFA® PROBLEMS
13. Richard Roll, in an article on using the CAPM to evaluate portfolio performance, indicated that it may not be possible to evaluate portfolio management ability if there is an error in the benchmark used. CFA® PROBLEMS
    a. In evaluating portfolio performance, describe the general procedure, with emphasis on the benchmark employed.
    b. Explain what Roll meant by the benchmark error and identify the specific problem with this benchmark.
    c. Draw a graph that shows how a portfolio that has been judged as superior relative to a "measured" security market line (SML) can be inferior relative to the "true" SML.
    d. Assume that you are informed that a given portfolio manager has been evaluated as superior when compared to the Dow Jones Industrial Average, the S&P 500, and the NYSE Composite Index. Explain whether this consensus would make you feel more comfortable regarding the portfolio manager's true ability.
    e. Although conceding the possible problem with benchmark errors as set forth by Roll, some contend this does not mean the CAPM is incorrect, but only that there is a measurement problem when implementing the theory. Others contend that because of benchmark errors the whole technique should be scrapped. Take and defend one of these positions.
14. Bart Campbell, CFA is a portfolio manager who has recently met with a prospective client, Jane Black. After conducting a survey market line (SML) performance analysis using the Dow Jones Industrial Average as her market proxy, Black claims that her portfolio has experienced superior performance. Campbell uses the capital asset pricing model as an investment performance measure and finds that Black's portfolio plots below the SML. Campbell concludes that Black's apparent superior performance is a function of an incorrectly specified market proxy, not superior investment management. Justify Campbell's conclusion, by addressing the likely effects of an incorrectly specified market proxy on both beta and the slope of the SML. CFA® PROBLEMS

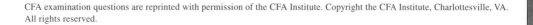

STANDARD &POOR'S

First obtain monthly returns for a sample of 10 Canadian firms and the S&P 500 from the Market Insight database at **www.mcgrawhill.ca/edumarketinsight**. Then obtain the corresponding returns on the HML (high minus low book value) and SMB (small minus big) portfolios from Ken French's Web site at **mba.tuck.dartmouth.edu/pages/faculty/ken.french/data_library.html**. Finally, obtain monthly interest rates from the Fed's site at **www.federalreserve.gov/releases/h15/data.htm**. Evaluate the alphas of each firm over the past three years as the intercept in a first-pass regression using excess returns in a single-index model. Then evaluate the alphas using a first-pass Fama-French three-factor multiple regression. Under which model is alpha more variable across firms? What do you conclude?

E-INVESTMENTS
Portfolio Theory

The History of Economic Thought Web site presents a concise history of portfolio theory development and the research contributors at **cepa.newschool.edu/het** (click on *Schools of Thought, Themes, Finance Theory*). Who would you list as major contributors to the development of modern portfolio theory? Why?

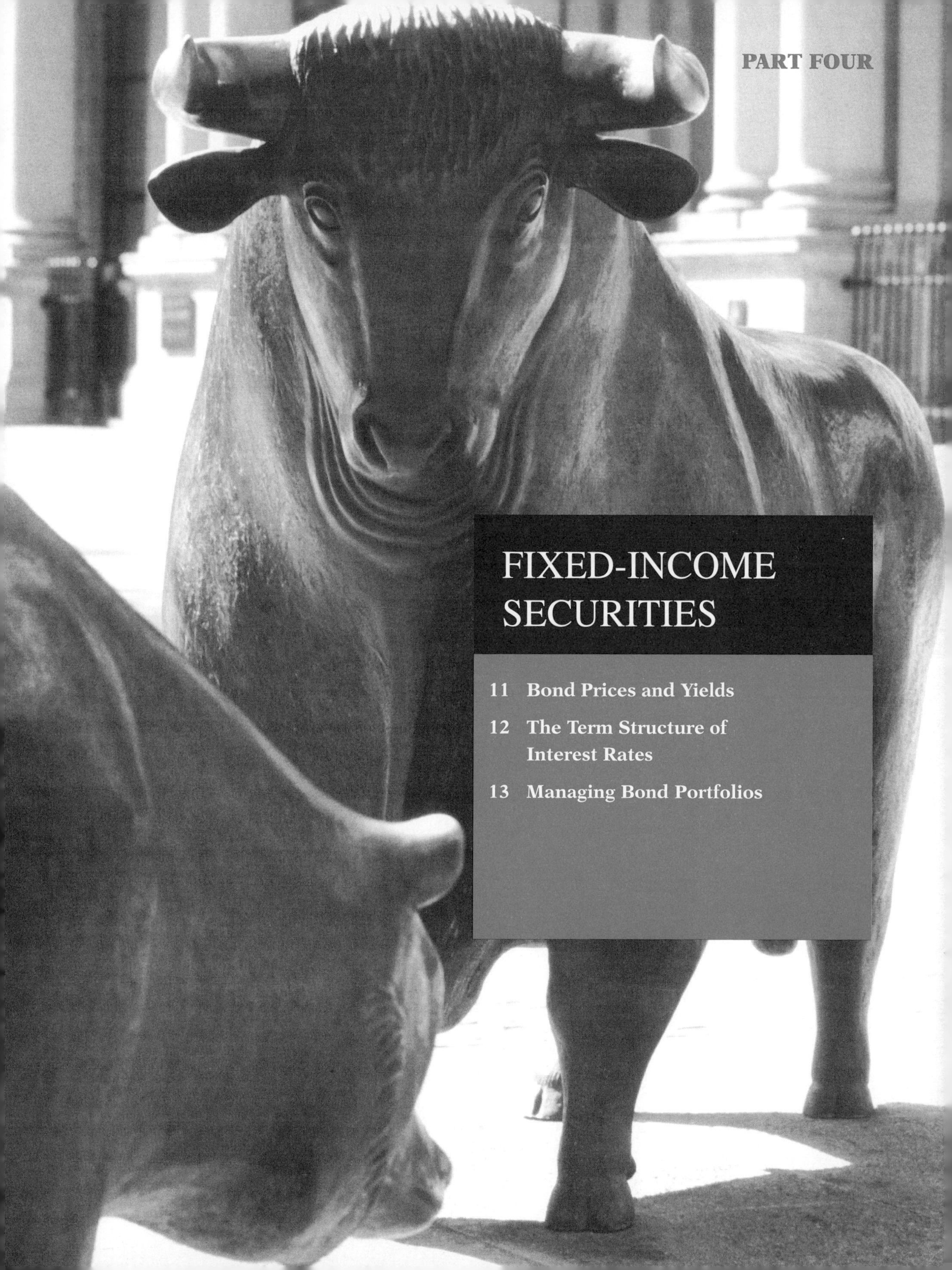

PART FOUR

FIXED-INCOME SECURITIES

11 Bond Prices and Yields
12 The Term Structure of Interest Rates
13 Managing Bond Portfolios

BOND PRICES AND YIELDS

In the previous chapters on risk and return relationships, we have treated securities at a high level of abstraction.

We have assumed implicitly that a prior, detailed analysis of each security already has been performed, and that its risk and return features have been assessed.

We turn now to specific analyses of particular security markets. We examine valuation principles, determinants of risk and return, and portfolio strategies commonly used within and across the various markets.

We begin by analyzing **fixed-income securities**, also known as *debt securities*. A fixed-income security is a claim on a specified periodic stream of income. Fixed-income securities have the advantage of being relatively easy to understand because the level of payments is fixed in advance. Risk considerations are minimal as long as the issuer of the security is sufficiently creditworthy. That makes these securities a convenient starting point for our analysis of the universe of potential investment vehicles. The bond is the basic fixed-income security, and this chapter reviews the principles of bond pricing. We show how bond prices are set in accordance with market interest rates, and why bond prices change with those rates. After examining the Canada bond market, where default risk may be ignored, we move to the corporate bond sector. We examine the impact of call and convertibility provisions on prices and yields. We discuss certain tax rules that apply to fixed-income investments and show how to calculate after-tax returns. Finally, we look at the determinants of credit risk and the default premium built into bond yields.

11.1 BOND CHARACTERISTICS

A **bond** is a borrowing arrangement in which the borrower issues (sells) an IOU to the investor. The arrangement obligates the issuer to make specified payments to the bondholder on specified dates. A typical *coupon bond* obligates the issuer to make semiannual payments of interest, called coupon payments, to the bondholder for the life of the bond, and then to pay in addition the bond's **par value** (equivalently, **face value**) at the bond's maturity date. The **coupon rate** of the bond is the coupon payment divided by the bond's par value. The coupon rate, maturity date, and par value of the bond are part of the **bond indenture** contract between the issuer and the bondholder.

To illustrate, a bond with a par value of $1,000 and a coupon rate of 8 percent might be sold to a buyer for $1,000. The bondholder is then entitled to a payment of 8 percent of $1,000, or $80 per year, for the stated life of the bond, say 30 years. The $80 payment typically comes in two semiannual installments of $40 each. At the end of the 30-year life of the bond, the issuer also pays the $1,000 par value to the bondholder.

Bonds usually are issued with coupon rates set high enough to induce investors to pay par value to buy the bond. Sometimes, however, **zero-coupon bonds** are issued that make no coupon payments. In this case, investors receive par value at the maturity date, but they receive no interest payments until then: the bond has a coupon rate of zero. These bonds are issued at prices considerably below par value, and the investor's return comes solely from the difference between the issue price and the payment of par value at maturity. We will return to these bonds below.

Canada Bonds

www.globeandmail.ca

Bond Market Canada www.bondcan.com

Figure 11.1 is an excerpt from the listing of bond issues in *The Globe and Mail.* Canada bond maturities range up to 30 years. The bonds are issued in denominations of $1,000 or more and make semiannual coupon payments.

Some bonds are callable. They are easily identified in a listing such as Figure 11.1 because of a range of years appearing in the maturity date column. The first date is the time at which the bond is first callable. The second date is the maturity date of the bond. The bond may be called by the issuer at any coupon date in the call period, but it must be retired by the maturity date. No such bonds appear in Figure 11.1.

The bond in Figure 11.1 (*highlighted*) matures in June 2011. Its coupon rate is 6 percent. Par value is $1,000; thus, the bond pays interest of $60 per year in two semiannual payments of $30. Payments are made in June and December of each year. Both bid and ask prices are quoted.[1]

Although bonds are sold in denominations of $1,000 par value, the prices are quoted as a percentage of par value. Therefore, the bid price of the bond is 111.80 percent of par value or $1,118, and the ask price 111.88 or $$1,118.80.

The columns labelled "Yield" show the yield to maturity on the bond. The yield to maturity is a measure of the average rate of return to an investor who purchases the bond for the quoted price and holds it until its maturity date. We will have much to say about yield to maturity below.

Bonds generally are traded over the counter, meaning that the market for the bonds is a loosely organized network of bond dealers linked by a computer quotation system. (See Chapter 3 for a comparison of exchange and OTC trading.) In practice, the bond market can be quite "thin," in that there are few investors interested in trading a particular bond at any particular time. On any day it might be difficult to find a buyer or seller for a particular issue, which introduces some "liquidity risk" into the bond market. It may be difficult to sell one's holdings quickly if the need arises.

[1]Recall that the bid price is the price at which you can sell the bond to a dealer. The asked price, which is slightly higher, is the price at which you can buy the bond from a dealer.

Figure 11.1 Listings of Canadian bonds.

CANADIAN BONDS

Bond quotations supplied by CBID Markets Inc. Closing prices and yields as of 4:00 PM yesterday. Most active based on volume traded. Yields are semi-annual compound to maturity. "Yield Chg" is the change in ask yield from the previous close.

Issuer	Coupon	Maturity Date	Bid Price	Ask Price	Bid Yld	Ask Yld	Yield Chg
GOVERNMENT OF CANADA BENCHMARKS							
2 Year	3.000	2005-Dec-01	101.02	101.09	2.40	2.36	+0.018
5 Year	4.250	2008-Sep-01	103.38	103.45	3.43	3.41	-0.020
10 Year	5.250	2013-Jun-01	106.68	106.80	4.36	4.35	-0.047
20 Year	8.000	2023-Jun-01	137.46	137.64	4.96	4.94	-0.046
30 Year	5.750	2029-Jun-01	109.75	109.90	5.06	5.05	-0.046
ACTIVE PROVINCIALS AND AGENCIES							
Ontario	5.850	2033-Mar-08	105.62	105.82	5.46	5.45	-0.041
Ontario	3.500	2006-Sep-08	101.69	101.70	2.80	2.79	+0.015
Ontario	4.750	2013-Jun-02	100.89	101.01	4.63	4.61	-0.045
Quebec	6.000	2029-Oct-01	106.43	106.62	5.53	5.51	-0.040
Ontario	4.400	2008-Nov-19	103.32	103.41	3.63	3.61	-0.024
ACTIVE CORPORATES							
BNS	4.295	2008-Aug-22	102.42	102.59	3.70	3.66	-0.005
Telus Corp	7.500	2006-Jun-01	108.83	108.94	3.38	3.33	-0.007
Bombard Cap	6.600	2004-Nov-29	101.80	102.25	4.09	3.48	-0.011
GE Cap Cda	5.150	2013-Jun-06	102.83	103.09	4.77	4.73	-0.041
Bell CDA	6.250	2012-Apr-12	109.48	109.83	4.82	4.77	-0.051
ACTIVE STRIPS (COUPONS AND RESIDUALS)							
Canada	0.000	2007-Oct-01	89.08	89.39	3.26	3.16	-0.033
Canada	0.000	2008-Dec-01	84.02	84.42	3.70	3.60	-0.033
Canada	0.000	2011-Dec-01	70.86	71.40	4.50	4.40	-0.048
Ontario	0.000	2006-Jun-02	93.93	94.12	2.80	2.71	+0.049
Ontario	0.000	2009-Jun-02	81.03	82.06	4.05	3.80	-0.035
GOVERNMENT OF CANADA AND AGENCIES							
CMHC	6.250	2005-Dec-01	106.53	106.54	2.41	2.40	-0.004
CMHC	5.300	2007-Dec-03	107.17	107.20	3.25	3.24	-0.033
Canada	3.500	2004-Jun-01	100.33	100.36	2.15	2.02	+0.043
Canada	6.500	2004-Jun-01	101.06	101.10	2.13	1.99	+0.018
Canada	5.000	2004-Sep-01	101.39	101.41	2.15	2.12	+0.115
Canada	4.250	2004-Dec-01	101.57	101.63	2.13	2.05	+0.024
Canada	9.000	2004-Dec-01	105.09	105.12	2.10	2.07	-0.006
Canada	3.500	2005-Jun-01	101.59	101.62	2.20	2.17	+0.034
Canada	6.000	2005-Sep-01	105.39	105.46	2.32	2.27	-0.006
Canada	8.750	2005-Dec-01	110.82	110.88	2.39	2.36	-0.002
Canada	3.000	2006-Jun-01	100.98	101.08	2.55	2.50	-0.006
Canada	5.750	2006-Sep-01	107.38	107.43	2.68	2.66	+0.004
Canada	7.000	2006-Dec-01	111.09	111.15	2.78	2.76	-0.010
Canada	7.250	2007-Jun-01	113.13	113.15	2.98	2.97	-0.007
Canada	4.500	2007-Sep-01	104.66	104.73	3.08	3.06	-0.019
Canada	10.000	2008-Jun-01	126.27	126.43	3.31	3.28	-0.033
Canada	6.000	2008-Jun-01	110.39	110.49	3.35	3.33	-0.024
Canada	4.250	2008-Sep-01	103.38	103.45	3.43	3.41	-0.020
Canada	5.500	2009-Jun-01	108.72	108.74	3.66	3.65	-0.010
Canada	10.750	2009-Oct-01	135.24	135.40	3.70	3.67	-0.035
Canada	5.500	2010-Jun-01	108.75	108.76	3.91	3.90	-0.020
Canada	9.500	2010-Jun-01	130.95	130.98	3.87	3.87	-0.020
Canada	6.000	2011-Jun-01	111.80	111.88	4.10	4.09	-0.048
Canada	5.250	2012-Jun-01	106.89	106.96	4.25	4.24	-0.049
Canada	5.250	2013-Jun-01	106.68	106.80	4.36	4.35	-0.047
Canada	8.000	2023-Jun-01	137.46	137.64	4.96	4.94	-0.046
Canada	8.000	2027-Jun-01	140.07	140.22	5.05	5.04	-0.046
Canada	5.750	2029-Jun-01	109.75	109.90	5.06	5.05	-0.046
Canada	5.750	2033-Jun-01	110.83	110.92	5.04	5.03	-0.046
Cda House Tr	5.527	2006-Jun-15	106.36	106.42	2.64	2.61	-0.004
Cda House Tr	4.750	2007-Mar-15	105.12	105.19	2.97	2.95	-0.012
Cda House Tr	5.100	2007-Sep-15	106.38	106.46	3.18	3.15	-0.029
Cda House Tr	4.400	2008-Mar-15	103.86	103.93	3.37	3.35	-0.033
Cda House Tr	4.100	2008-Dec-15	102.06	102.10	3.63	3.62	-0.035
Farm Cr Cda	3.700	2005-Mar-15		101.39		2.33	+0.006
PROVINCIALS AND AGENCIES							
Alberta	6.375	2004-Jun-01		101.06		1.97	-0.012
Alberta	5.750	2004-Dec-01	102.65	102.70	2.14	2.07	+0.011
Alberta	7.500	2005-Dec-01	108.62	108.68	2.43	2.39	0.000
Alberta	5.650	2007-Oct-01		108.36		3.16	-0.033
AltaCapFinAu	5.850	2012-Jun-01		109.86		4.41	-0.049
BC	8.000	2005-Aug-23	108.11	108.20	2.37	2.31	+0.034
BC	6.000	2008-Jun-09	109.88	109.93	3.49	3.47	-0.011
BC	5.700	2009-Jun-01	108.88	108.91	3.81	3.81	-0.001
BC	6.250	2009-Dec-01	111.77	111.82	3.94	3.93	-0.023
BC	6.375	2010-Aug-23	112.71	112.82	4.12	4.10	-0.059
BC	5.750	2012-Jan-09	109.01	109.04	4.38	4.38	-0.033
BC	8.500	2013-Aug-23	129.64	130.14	4.60	4.55	-0.049
BC	8.000	2023-Sep-08		133.75		5.22	-0.037
BC	6.150	2027-Nov-19		110.97		5.33	-0.047
BC	5.700	2029-Jun-18	104.15	104.33	5.40	5.38	-0.040
BC	6.350	2031-Jun-18	113.52	113.74	5.40	5.38	-0.040
BC MFA	8.500	2005-Apr-12		106.86		2.20	+0.006
BC MFA	5.500	2007-Mar-24		107.05		3.07	-0.012
BC MFA	6.750	2007-Apr-24		110.92		3.07	-0.031
Hydro-Quebec	8.500	2005-Aug-15	108.75	108.82	2.34	2.29	-0.008
Hydro-Quebec	6.000	2010-Feb-15		110.21		4.05	-0.041
Hydro-Quebec	6.500	2011-Feb-15	113.26	113.35	4.27	4.26	-0.011
Hydro-Quebec	10.000	2011-Sep-26		136.14		4.34	-0.037
Hydro-Quebec	6.500	2035-Feb-15	113.97	114.70	5.55	5.51	-0.040
Manitoba	5.650	2004-Jul-15	101.25	101.29	2.22	2.10	-0.010
Manitoba	9.375	2004-Nov-15	104.89	104.94	2.29	2.22	+0.085
Manitoba	6.250	2005-Jun-22	105.06	105.14	2.28	2.22	+0.006
Manitoba	6.625	2007-May-16		110.69		3.09	-0.033
Manitoba	5.750	2008-Jun-02	108.87	109.05	3.48	3.44	-0.033
Manitoba	4.450	2008-Dec-01		103.64		3.61	+0.013
Manitoba	5.250	2009-Mar-02	106.96	106.96	3.71	3.71	-0.035
Manitoba	5.250	2012-Dec-03	105.05	105.40	4.54	4.50	-0.049
NB MFA	5.625	2004-Aug-25		101.67		2.12	-0.026
NB MFA	6.250	2005-Aug-10		105.31		2.47	-0.008
NS MFC	8.000	2004-Nov-14		103.96		2.24	+0.006
NewBrunswick	5.400	2004-Jun-09		100.92		1.91	-0.013
NewBrunswick	7.100	2006-Oct-16		110.78		2.80	-0.012
NewBrunswick	5.250	2009-Jun-02		106.70		3.83	-0.035
NewBrunswick	10.000	2009-Nov-23		130.68		3.95	-0.035
NewBrunswick	5.800	2011-Jul-12	109.01	109.12	4.36	4.34	-0.066
NewBrunswick	5.850	2011-Dec-01	109.39	109.43	4.41	4.40	-0.048
NewBrunswick	5.875	2012-Dec-06	109.21	109.32	4.59	4.57	-0.039
NewBrunswick	5.650	2028-Dec-27		102.38		5.47	-0.015
NewBrunswick	5.500	2034-Jan-27		100.63		5.46	-0.025
Nfld MFC	10.000	2004-Dec-15		105.97		2.27	+0.007
Nfld MFC	8.000	2005-Jan-10		104.75		2.35	+0.008
Nfld MFC	10.875	2008-Dec-01		131.10		3.67	-0.033
Nfld MFC	6.000	2009-Sep-20		110.25		3.93	-0.035
NfldLabHydro	5.050	2006-Dec-01		105.54		2.93	-0.012
Nova Scotia	6.250	2004-Dec-01	102.88	102.95	2.32	2.23	+0.116
Nova Scotia	6.400	2005-Jun-01	105.02	105.07	2.28	2.25	-0.006
Nova Scotia	6.400	2010-Sep-01	112.35	112.43	4.21	4.19	-0.014
Ont Elec Fin	7.750	2005-Nov-03	108.64	108.70	2.43	2.39	-0.008
Ont Elec Fin	5.600	2008-Jun-02	108.25	108.28	3.49	3.48	-0.015
Ont Elec Fin	10.750	2021-Aug-06		162.71		5.22	-0.037
Ont Elec Fin	10.125	2021-Oct-15		156.00		5.22	-0.037
Ontario	4.875	2004-Jun-02	100.67	100.68	2.12	2.07	+0.041
Ontario	9.000	2004-Sep-15	103.58	103.64	2.21	2.10	+0.046
Ontario	6.250	2005-Mar-08	104.03	104.04	2.21	2.20	+0.032
Ontario	8.250	2005-Dec-01	109.84	109.85	2.45	2.45	-0.004
Ontario	7.500	2006-Jan-19	109.08	109.13	2.52	2.50	-0.002
Ontario	5.900	2006-Mar-08	106.48	106.53	2.58	2.55	-0.003
Ontario	5.200	2007-Mar-08	106.28	106.33	3.00	2.99	-0.007
Ontario	6.125	2007-Sep-12	109.65	109.74	3.21	3.18	-0.033
Ontario	5.700	2008-Dec-01	108.91	108.97	3.64	3.62	-0.026
Ontario	6.200	2009-Nov-19	111.43	111.44	3.94	3.94	-0.014
Ontario	6.100	2010-Nov-19	111.14	111.25	4.18	4.16	-0.050
Ontario	6.100	2011-Dec-02	111.19	111.22	4.38	4.38	-0.035
Ontario	5.375	2012-Dec-02	105.87	105.97	4.55	4.54	-0.040
Ontario	5.000	2014-Mar-08	102.01	102.31	4.75	4.71	-0.039
Ontario	8.100	2023-Sep-08	133.47	134.02	5.32	5.28	-0.037
Ontario	7.600	2027-Jun-02	128.85	129.08	5.40	5.39	-0.041
Ontario	6.500	2029-Mar-08	114.24	114.33	5.45	5.44	-0.040
Ontario	6.200	2031-Jun-02	110.65	110.81	5.44	5.43	-0.039
Quebec	6.500	2005-Dec-01	106.82	106.90	2.48	2.43	-0.007
Quebec	7.750	2006-Mar-30	110.37	110.43	2.58	2.55	-0.007
Quebec	9.500	2006-May-01		114.51		2.56	-0.004
Quebec	6.500	2007-Oct-01	110.99	111.03	3.22	3.21	-0.025
Quebec	5.550	2009-Apr-01		108.03		3.80	-0.035
Quebec	5.500	2009-Jun-01	107.79	107.84	3.84	3.83	-0.014
Quebec	10.000	2010-Jun-28		132.75		4.07	-0.041
Quebec	6.250	2010-Dec-01	111.81	111.92	4.22	4.20	-0.049
Quebec	6.000	2012-Oct-01	109.96	110.06	4.58	4.57	-0.041
Quebec	9.375	2023-Jan-16		148.00		5.31	-0.034
Quebec	6.000	2029-Oct-01	106.43	106.62	5.53	5.51	-0.040
Quebec	6.250	2032-Jun-01	110.39	110.49	5.52	5.51	-0.040
Quebec	5.750	2036-Dec-01	103.23	104.52	5.53	5.45	-0.044
Saskatchewan	7.500	2005-Dec-19		108.82		2.44	-0.004
Saskatchewan	4.750	2006-Dec-01		105.11		2.80	-0.012
Saskatchewan	6.650	2007-May-15		110.72		3.10	-0.033
Saskatchewan	5.000	2007-Sep-06		105.97		3.19	-0.025
Saskatchewan	5.500	2008-Jun-02	107.88	108.00	3.49	3.46	-0.033
Saskatchewan	6.150	2010-Sep-01		111.41		4.13	-0.041
Saskatchewan	5.250	2012-Dec-03	105.03	105.05	4.55	4.54	-0.049
Saskatchewan	10.250	2014-Apr-10		144.63		4.66	-0.049
Saskatchewan	6.400	2031-Sep-05		113.79		5.43	-0.034
CORPORATES							
407 Intl	6.050	2009-Jul-27		109.39		4.09	-0.035
BCE Inc.	7.350	2009-Oct-30		115.68		4.20	-0.003
BMO Cap Tr	6.685	2011-Dec-31	112.58	112.89	4.74	4.70	-0.049
Bell CDA	6.500	2005-May-09		104.81		2.36	+0.005
Bell CDA	6.700	2007-Jun-28	110.67	110.81	3.28	3.24	-0.033
Bell CDA	6.250	2008-Jan-18		109.80		3.52	+0.001
Bell CDA	6.150	2009-Jun-15	109.58	109.81	4.11	4.07	-0.013
Bell CDA	5.500	2010-Aug-12		106.42		4.35	-0.041
Bell CDA	6.250	2012-Apr-12	109.48	109.83	4.82	4.77	-0.051
Bombard Cap	6.600	2004-Nov-29	101.80	102.25	4.09	3.48	-0.011
Bombard Cap	6.350	2006-Jul-19	103.75	104.75	4.66	4.23	-0.002
Bombardier	6.400	2006-Dec-22	103.78	104.50	4.93	4.67	+0.094
CIBC	7.400	2006-Jan-31		108.80		2.65	+0.003
CdnTire Corp	5.650	2006-Jan-16		105.16		2.80	-0.003
Coca-ColaCda	5.650	2004-Mar-17		100.18		1.25	-0.094
ConsumersGas	11.150	2009-Mar-31		132.04		4.09	-0.035
DPL Tr	4.667	2005-Jul-05		102.96		2.41	-0.008
DaimChry Fin	6.600	2004-Jun-21		101.19		2.56	-0.013
Duke Energy	9.700	2004-Nov-15		105.06		2.36	+0.022
GMAC Cda	5.500	2005-Jun-09		103.32		2.82	-0.007
Hudson's Bay	7.100	2004-May-13		100.75		3.20	-0.052
Hydro One	6.940	2005-Jun-03		105.68		2.31	-0.007
Hydro One	7.150	2010-Jun-03	115.77	116.16	4.25	4.18	-0.049
Hydro One	6.400	2011-Dec-01	111.81	112.17	4.57	4.52	-0.036
LaurentianBk	6.000	2006-Oct-02		106.74		3.25	+0.010
LaurentianBk	5.750	2004-Jun-01		100.78		2.51	+0.293
LaurentianBk	7.000	2004-Dec-15		103.41		2.57	+0.054
LaurentianBk	8.900	2005-Oct-18		109.46		2.90	-0.004
LaurentianBk	6.500	2006-Jun-01		106.98		3.25	-0.004
ManuF Cap Tr	6.700	2012-Jun-30	112.45	112.77	4.86	4.82	-0.050
Manulife Fin	6.240	2011-Feb-16		110.75		4.43	-0.048
Molson Brew	6.000	2008-Jun-02		108.18		3.89	-0.033
MutLifeAssur	5.800	2008-May-15		108.28		3.65	-0.002
NAV Cda	4.250	2006-Feb-13	102.64	102.94	2.85	2.69	-0.004
NAV Cda	6.600	2006-Dec-01		109.27		3.05	-0.012
Provigo Inc.	6.350	2004-Dec-01		103.02		2.24	+0.013
Royal Bank	5.100	2004-Jun-11		100.79		2.15	-0.011
Royal Bank	7.100	2010-Jan-25		115.60		4.09	-0.035
Royal Bank	6.300	2011-Apr-12	110.90	111.03	4.49	4.47	-0.024
TD Bank	6.000	2006-Jul-26		107.22		2.86	+0.028
Telus Corp	7.500	2006-Jun-01	108.83	108.94	3.38	3.33	-0.007
STRIPS (COUPONS AND RESIDUALS)							
BC	0.000	2007-Jun-09	90.15	90.53	3.20	3.07	-0.033
BC	0.000	2007-Sep-05		89.63		3.15	-0.033
BC	0.000	2008-Jun-09		86.12		3.53	-0.033
Canada	0.000	2006-Mar-01	94.92	95.11	2.63	2.53	-0.004
Canada	0.000	2006-Dec-01	91.99	92.24	3.06	2.96	-0.012
Canada	0.000	2007-Oct-01	89.08	89.39	3.26	3.16	-0.033
Canada	0.000	2008-Dec-01	84.02	84.42	3.70	3.60	-0.033
Canada	0.000	2010-Dec-01	75.02	75.46	4.31	4.22	-0.030
Canada	0.000	2011-Jun-01	72.71	73.23	4.45	4.35	-0.048
Canada	0.000	2011-Dec-01	70.86	71.40	4.50	4.40	-0.048
Canada	0.000	2012-Jun-01	68.46	69.02	4.65	4.55	-0.049
Canada	0.000	2012-Dec-01	66.80	67.37	4.67	4.57	-0.049
Canada	0.000	2025-Jun-01	32.24	32.91	5.40	5.30	-0.044
Hydro-Quebec	0.000	2005-Jul-15		96.86		2.35	-0.004
Hydro-Quebec	0.000	2012-Feb-15		69.88		4.56	-0.048
Hydro-Quebec	0.000	2017-Jan-15		49.88		5.48	-0.044
Hydro-Quebec	0.000	2019-Feb-26		43.40		5.65	-0.044
Hydro-Quebec	0.000	2021-Aug-15		37.31		5.73	-0.044
Hydro-Quebec	0.000	2022-Jan-16		36.06		5.79	-0.044
Hydro-Quebec	0.000	2022-Feb-15		36.21		5.74	-0.045
Hydro-Quebec	0.000	2022-Aug-15		35.20		5.74	-0.044
Newfoundland	0.000	2016-Jul-07		52.87		5.23	-0.044
Newfoundland	0.000	2027-Oct-17		25.56		5.86	-0.045
NfldLabHydro	0.000	2014-Jun-15		61.05		4.86	-0.048
Ont Elec Fin	0.000	2005-Apr-15		97.52		2.26	-0.002
Ontario	0.000	2005-Dec-01		95.76		2.50	+0.033
Quebec	0.000	2013-Jun-01		64.05		4.88	-0.049
Quebec	0.000	2013-Dec-01		62.22		4.93	-0.049

Source: *The Globe and Mail*, February 28, 2004.

This lack of liquidity may be a partial explanation for the inefficiencies that some studies claim to have uncovered in the Canadian bond market. These inefficiencies imply that some Canada bonds are traded below or above their "correct" values, where the latter are estimated from the entire universe of Canada bonds and T-bills. This, in turn, may give rise to arbitrage profits. Such mispricings were quite frequent in earlier years, but they have been much less so more recently.[2]

Investing in Bonds
www.investinginbonds.com

Accrued Interest and Quoted Bond Prices The bond prices that you see quoted in the financial pages are not actually the prices that investors pay for the bond. This is because the quoted price does not include the interest that accrues between coupon payment dates.

If a bond is purchased between coupon payments, the buyer must pay the seller for accrued interest, the prorated share of the upcoming semiannual coupon. For example, if 40 days have passed since the last coupon payment, the seller is entitled to a payment of accrued interest of 40/365 of the annual coupon.[3] The sale, or *invoice price,* of the bond would equal the stated price plus the accrued interest.

To illustrate, suppose that the coupon rate is 8 percent. Then the annual coupon payment is \$80. Because 40 days have passed since the last coupon payment, the accrued interest on the bond is \$80 × (40/365) = \$8.76. If the quoted price of the bond is \$990, then the invoice price will be \$990 + \$8.76 = \$998.76.

The practice of quoting bond prices net of accrued interest explains why the price of a maturing bond is listed at \$1,000 rather than \$1,000 plus one coupon payment. A purchaser of an 8 percent coupon bond one day before the bond's maturity would receive \$1,040 on the following day and so should be willing to pay a total price of \$1,040 for the bond. In fact, \$40 of that total payment constitutes the accrued interest for the preceding half-year period. The bond price is quoted net of accrued interest in the financial pages and thus appears as \$1,000.

Corporate Bonds

www.scotiabank.ca

Like the government, corporations borrow money by issuing bonds. Figure 11.1 also shows corporate bond listings from *The Globe and Mail.* The data presented follow the same format as Government of Canada and provincial bond listings. For example, the Royal Bank 6.30 bond (*highlighted*) pays a coupon rate of 6.30 percent and matures in 2011. Like government bonds, corporate bond listings quote the bid and ask prices as well as the APR or bond equivalent yields. By contrast, U.S. corporate bond listings quote the *current yield,* which is simply the annual coupon payment divided by the bond price. Unlike yield to maturity, the current yield ignores any prospective capital gains or losses based on the bond's price relative to par value. The last column shows the change in yield from the previous day. Like government bonds, corporate bonds sell in units of \$1,000 par value but are quoted as a percentage of par value.

Bonds issued in Canada today can be either *registered bonds* or *bearer bonds.* For registered bonds, the issuing firm keeps records of the owner of the bond and can mail interest cheques to him or her. Registration of bonds is clearly helpful to tax authorities in the enforcement of tax collection. In contrast, bearer bonds are traded without any record of ownership. The investor's physical possession of the bond certificate is the only evidence of ownership.

Call Provisions on Corporate Bonds Many corporate bonds are issued with call provisions. The call provision allows the issuer to repurchase the bond at a specified *call price* before

---

[2]See Tim Appelt and Ramaswamy Krishnan, "Valuation, Mispricing and Change in the Canadian Bond Market," and John Rumsey, "Same Maturity, Different Yields?" both in *Canadian Investment Review*, Spring 1994.

[3]Alternatively, the accrued interest may be estimated by the formula

$$\text{Accrued interest} = \frac{\text{Annual coupon payment}}{2} \times \frac{\text{Days since last coupon payment}}{\text{Days separating coupon payments}}$$

the maturity date. For example, if a company issues a bond with a high coupon rate when market interest rates are high and interest rates later fall, the firm might like to retire the high coupon debt and issue new bonds at a lower coupon rate to reduce interest payments. This is called *refunding.*

The call price of a bond is commonly set at an initial level near par value plus one annual coupon payment. The call price falls as time passes, gradually approaching par value.

Callable bonds typically come with a period of call protection, an initial time during which the bonds are not callable. Such bonds are referred to as *deferred* callable bonds.

The option to call the bond is valuable to the firm, allowing it to buy back the bonds and refinance at a lower interest rate when market rates fall. Of course, the firm's benefit is the bondholder's burden. Holders of called bonds forfeit their bonds for the call price, thereby giving up the prospect of an attractive rate of interest on their original investment. To compensate investors for this risk, callable bonds are issued with higher coupons and promised yields to maturity than noncallable bonds.

CONCEPT CHECK

1. Suppose that a corporation issues two bonds with identical coupon rates and maturity dates. One bond is callable, however, whereas the other is not. Which bond will sell at a higher price?

Convertible Bonds **Convertible bonds** give bondholders an option to exchange each bond for a specified number of shares of common stock of the firm. The *conversion ratio* gives the number of shares for which each bond may be exchanged. To see the value of this right, suppose a convertible bond that is issued at par value of $1,000 is convertible into 40 shares of a firm's stock. The current stock price is $20 per share, so the option to convert is not profitable now. Should the stock price later rise to $30, however, each bond may be converted profitably into $1,200 worth of stock. The *market conversion value* is the current value of the shares for which the bonds may be exchanged. At the $20 stock price, for example, the bond's conversion value is $800. The *conversion premium* is the excess of the bond value over its conversion value. If the bond were selling currently for $950, its premium would be $150.

Convertible bonds give their holders the ability to share in the price appreciation of the company's stock. Again, this benefit comes at a price; convertible bonds offer lower coupon rates and stated or promised yields to maturity than do nonconvertible bonds. At the same time, the actual return on the convertible bond may exceed the stated yield to maturity if the option to convert becomes profitable.

We discuss convertible and callable bonds further in Chapter 17.

Retractable and Extendible Bonds Whereas the callable bond gives the issuer the option to retire the bond at the call date or to continue to the maturity date, the **retractable bond** gives the option to the bondholder. Thus, if the bond's coupon rate is below current market yields, the bondholder will choose to redeem the bond early, through retraction. An **extendible bond,** on the other hand, allows the bondholder to retain the bond for an additional period beyond maturity, which he or she will do if the coupon exceeds current rates. Retractable and extendible bonds are known as *puttable bonds* in the United States. These additional privileges granted to the bondholders are paid for by a slightly lower coupon.

There have also been retractable and extendible bond issues where the option to extend or retract rests with the issuer. In such a case it would be excercised in the diametrically opposite scenario from the case where the option lies with the investor.

Floating-Rate Bonds **Floating-rate bonds** make interest payments that are tied to some measure of current market rates. For example, the rate might be adjusted annually to the current T-bill rate plus 2 percent. If the one-year T-bill rate at the adjustment date is 4 percent, the bond's coupon rate over the next year would then be 6 percent. This arrangement means that the bond always pays approximately current market rates.

The major risk involved in floaters has to do with changes in the firm's financial strength. The yield spread is fixed over the life of the security, which may be many years. If the financial health of the firm deteriorates, then a greater yield premium would be required than is offered by the security. In this case, the price of the bond would fall. Although the coupon rate on floaters adjusts to changes in the general level of market interest rates, it does not adjust to changes in the financial condition of the firm.

Preferred Stock

Although preferred stock strictly speaking is considered to be equity, it often is included in the fixed-income universe. This is because, like bonds, preferred stock promises to pay a specified stream of dividends. However, unlike bonds, the failure to pay the promised dividend does not result in corporate bankruptcy. Instead, the dividends owed simply cumulate, and the common shareholders may not receive any dividends until the preferred shareholders have been paid in full. In the event of bankruptcy, the claims of preferred shareholders to the firm's assets have lower priority than those of bondholders, but higher priority than those of common shareholders.

Most preferred stock pays a fixed dividend. Therefore, it is in effect a perpetuity, providing a level cash flow indefinitely. In the last few years, however, adjustable or floating-rate preferred stock has become popular. Floating-rate preferred stock is much like floating-rate bonds. The dividend rate is linked to a measure of current market interest rates and is adjusted at regular intervals.

Other Issuers

There are, of course, several issuers of bonds in addition to the federal government and private corporations. For example, provinces, Crown corporations, and local governments issue bonds. They also appear in the listings of Figure 11.1.

International Bonds

International bonds are commonly divided into two categories, *foreign bonds* and *Eurobonds*. Foreign bonds are issued by a borrower from a country other than the one in which the bond is sold. The bond is denominated in the currency of the country in which it is marketed. For example, if a German firm sells a dollar-denominated bond in the United States, the bond is considered a foreign bond. These bonds are given colourful names based on the countries in which they are marketed. For example, foreign bonds sold in the United States are called *Yankee bonds*. Like other bonds sold in the United States, they are registered with the Securities and Exchange Commission. Yen-denominated bonds sold in Japan by non-Japanese issuers are called *Samurai bonds*. British pound-denominated foreign bonds sold in the United Kingdom are called *bulldog bonds*.

www.sec.gov

In contrast to foreign bonds, Eurobonds are bonds issued in the currency of one country but sold in other national markets. For example, the Eurodollar market refers to dollar-denominated bonds sold outside the United States (not just in Europe), although London is the largest market for Eurodollar bonds. Because the Eurodollar market falls outside U.S. jurisdiction, these bonds are not regulated by U.S. federal agencies. Similarly, Euroyen bonds are yen-denominated bonds selling outside of Japan. Eurosterling bonds are pound-denominated Eurobonds selling outside the United Kingdom, Euro-Canadian dollar bonds are $Canadian-denominated bonds selling outside Canada, and so on.

Innovation in the Bond Market

Issuers constantly develop innovative bonds with unusual features; these issues illustrate that bond design can be extremely flexible.

Here are examples of some novel bonds. They should give you a sense of the potential variety in security design.

Reverse Floaters These are similar to the floating-rate bonds we described earlier, except that the coupon rate on these bonds *falls* when the general level of interest rates rises. Investors in these bonds suffer doubly when rates rise. Not only does the present value of each dollar of cash flow from the bond fall as the discount rate rises, but the level of those cash flows falls as well. Of course, investors in these bonds benefit doubly when rates fall.

Asset-Backed Bonds Walt Disney has issued bonds with coupon rates tied to the financial performance of several of its films. Similarly, "David Bowie bonds" have been issued with payments that will be tied to royalties on some of his albums. These are examples of asset-backed securities. The income from a specified group of assets is used to service the debt. More conventional asset-backed securities are mortgage-backed securities or securities backed by auto or credit card loans, as we discussed in Chapter 2.

Catastrophe Bonds Electrolux once issued a bond with a final payment that depended on whether there had been an earthquake in Japan. Winterthur has issued a bond whose payments depend on whether there has been a severe hailstorm in Switzerland. These bonds are a way to transfer "catastrophe risk" from the firm to the capital markets. They represent a novel way of obtaining insurance from the capital markets against specified disasters. Investors in these bonds receive compensation for taking on the risk in the form of higher coupon rates.

Indexed Bonds Indexed bonds make payments that are tied to a general price index or the price of a particular commodity. For example, Mexico has issued 20-year bonds with payments that depend on the price of oil. Some bonds are tied to the general price level. The United States Treasury started issuing such inflation-indexed bonds in January 1997. They are called Treasury Inflation Protected Securities (TIPS). In Canada such bonds are known as Real Return Bonds (RRBs). Four such bonds are quoted in Figure 11.1. By tying the par value of the bond to the general level of prices, coupon payments as well as the final repayment of par value on these bonds will increase in direct proportion to the consumer price index. Therefore, the interest rate on these bonds is a risk-free real rate.

To illustrate how RRBs work, consider a newly issued bond with a three-year maturity, par value of $1,000, and a coupon rate of 4 percent. For simplicity, we will assume the bond makes annual coupon payments. Assume that inflation turns out to be 2 percent, 3 percent, and 1 percent in the next three years. Table 11.1 shows how the bond cash flows will be calculated. The first payment comes at the end of the first year, at $t = 1$. Because inflation over the year was 2 percent, the par value of the bond is increased from $1,000 to $1,020; since the coupon rate is 4 percent, the coupon payment is 4 percent of this amount, or $40.80. Notice that principal value increases in tandem with inflation, and because the coupon payments are 4 percent of principal, they too increase in proportion to the general price level. Therefore, the cash flows paid by the bond are fixed in *real* terms. When the bond matures, the investor receives a final coupon payment of $42.44 plus the (price-level-indexed) repayment of principal, $1,061.11.[4]

---

[4]By the way, total nominal income (i.e., coupon plus that year's increase in principal) is treated as taxable income in each year.

Table 11.1 Principal and Interest Payments for a Real Return Bond

Time	Inflation in Year Just Ended	Par Value	Coupon Payment	+	Principal Repayment	=	Total Payment
0		$1,000.00					
1	2%	1,020.00	$40.80		$0		$ 40.80
2	3	1,050.60	42.02		0		42.02
3	1	1,061.11	42.44		1,061.11		1,103.55

The *nominal* rate of return on the bond in the first year is

$$\text{Nominal return} = \frac{\text{Interest} + \text{Price appreciation}}{\text{Initial price}} = \frac{40.80 + 20}{1000} = 6.08\%$$

The real rate of return is precisely the 4 percent real yield on the bond:

$$\text{Real return} = \frac{1 + \text{Nominal return}}{1 + \text{Inflation}} - 1 = \frac{1.0608}{1.02} - 1 = .04, \text{ or } 4\%$$

One can show in a similar manner (see problem 16 in the end-of-chapter problems) that the rate of return in each of the three years is 4 percent as long as the real yield on the bond remains constant. If real yields do change, then there will be capital gains or losses on the bond.

11.2 BOND PRICING

Review of the Present Value Relationship

Because a bond's coupon payments and principal repayment all occur months or years in the future, the price an investor would be willing to pay for a claim to those payments depends on the value of dollars to be received in the future compared to dollars in hand today.

This "present value" calculation depends in turn on market interest rates. As we saw in Chapter 5, the nominal risk-free interest rate equals the sum of (1) a real risk-free rate of return and (2) a premium above the real rate to compensate for expected inflation. In addition, because most bonds are not riskless, the discount rate will embody an additional premium that reflects bond-specific characteristics such as default risk, liquidity, tax attributes, call risk, and so on.

We simplify for now by assuming there is one interest rate that is appropriate for discounting cash flows of any maturity, but we can relax this assumption easily. In practice, there may be different discount rates for cash flows accruing in different periods. For the time being, however, we ignore this refinement.

To value a security, we discount its expected cash flows by the appropriate discount rate. The cash flows from a bond consist of coupon payments until the maturity date plus the final payment of par value. Therefore

$$\text{Bond value} = \text{Present value of coupons} + \text{Present value of par value}$$

If we call the maturity date T and the interest rate r, the bond value can be written as

$$\text{Bond value} = \sum_{t=1}^{T} \frac{\text{Coupon}}{(1+r)^t} + \frac{\text{Par value}}{(1+r)^T} \tag{11.1}$$

The summation sign in equation 11.1 directs us to add the present value of each coupon payment; each coupon is discounted based on the time until it will be paid. The first term on the right-hand side of equation 11.1 is the present value of an annuity. The second term is the present value of a single amount, the final payment of the bond's par value.

You may recall from an introductory finance class that the present value of a $1 annuity that lasts for T periods when the interest rate equals r is $\frac{1}{r}\left(1-\frac{1}{(1+r)^T}\right)$. We call this expression the T-period *annuity factor* for an interest rate of r.[5] Similarly,we call $\frac{1}{(1+r)^T}$ the *PV factor*, that is the present value of a single payment of $1 to be received in T periods. Therefore, we can write the price of the bond as

$$\text{Price} = \text{Coupon} \times \frac{1}{r}\left(1-\frac{1}{(1+r)^T}\right) + \text{Par value} \times \frac{1}{(1+r)^T} \tag{11.2}$$

$$= \text{Coupon} \times \text{Annuity factor}(r, T) + \text{Par value} \times \text{PV factor}(r, T)$$

An Example: Bond Pricing

We discussed earlier an 8 percent coupon, 30-year maturity bond with par value of $1,000 paying 60 semiannual coupon payments of $40 each. Suppose that the interest rate is 8 percent annually, or 4 percent per six-month period. Then the value of the bond can be written as

$$\text{Price} = \sum_{t=1}^{60} \frac{\$40}{(1.04)^t} + \frac{\$1{,}000}{(1.04)^{60}} \tag{11.3}$$

For notational simplicity, we can write equation 11.3 as

$$\text{Price} = \$40 \times \text{PA}(4\%, 60) + \$1{,}000 \times \text{PF}(4\%, 60)$$

where PA(4%, 60) represents the present value of an annuity of $1 when the interest rate is 4 percent and the annuity lasts for 60 six-month periods, and PF(4%, 60) is the present value of a single payment of $1 to be received in 60 periods.

It is easy to confirm that the present value of the bond's 60 semiannual coupon payments of $40 each is $904.94, whereas the $1,000 final payment of par value has a present value of $95.06, for a total bond value of $1,000. You can perform these calculations on any financial calculator or use a set of present value tables.

In this example, the coupon rate equals yield to maturity, and the bond price equals par value. If the interest rate were not equal to the bond's coupon rate, the bond would not sell at par value. For example, if the interest rate were to rise to 10 percent (5 percent per six months), the bond's price would fall by $189.29, to $810.71, as follows

$$\begin{aligned} &\$40 \times \text{PA}(5\%, 60) + \$1{,}000 \times \text{PF}(5\%, 60) \\ &= \$757.17 + \$53.54 \\ &= \$810.71 \end{aligned}$$

At a higher interest rate, the present value of the payments to be received by the bondholder is lower. Therefore, the bond price will fall as market interest rates rise. This illustrates a crucial general rule in bond valuation. When interest rates rise, bond prices must fall because the present values of the bond's payments are obtained by discounting at a higher interest rate.

Figure 11.2 shows the price of the 30-year, 8 percent coupon bond for a range of interest rates. The negative slope illustrates the inverse relationship between prices and yields. Note also from the

---

[5]Here is a quick derivation of the formula for the present value of an annuity. An annuity lasting T periods can be viewed as equivalent to a perpetuity whose first payment comes at the end of the current period *less* another perpetuity whose first payment comes at the end of the $(T + 1)$st period. The immediate perpetuity net of the delayed perpetuity provides exactly T payments. We know that the value of a $1 per period perpetuity is $\$1/r$. Therefore, the present value of the delayed perpetuity is $\$1/r$ discounted for T additional periods, or $\frac{1}{r} \times \frac{1}{(1+r)^T}$. The present value of the annuity is the present value of the first perpetuity minus the present value of the delayed perpetuity, or $\frac{1}{r}\left(1-\frac{1}{(1+r)^T}\right)$.

figure (and from Table 11.2) that the shape of the curve implies that an increase in the interest rate results in a price decline that is smaller than the price gain resulting from a decrease of equal magnitude in the interest rate. This property of bond prices is called *convexity* because of the convex shape of the bond price curve. This curvature reflects the fact that progressive increases in the interest rate result in progressively smaller reductions in the bond price.[6] Therefore, the price curve becomes flatter at higher interest rates. We return to the issue of convexity in Chapter 13.

CONCEPT CHECK

2. Calculate the price of the bond for a market interest rate of 3 percent per half-year. Compare the capital gains for the interest rate decline to the losses incurred when the rate increases to 5 percent.

Corporate bonds typically are issued at par value. This means that the underwriters of the bond issue (the firms that market the bonds to the public for the issuing corporation) must choose a coupon rate that very closely approximates market yields. In a primary issue of bonds, the underwriters attempt to sell the newly issued bonds directly to their customers. If the coupon rate is inadequate, investors will not pay par value for the bonds.

After the bonds are issued, bondholders may buy or sell bonds in secondary markets, such as the over-the-counter market, where many U.S. and all Canadian bonds trade. In these secondary markets, bond prices move in accordance with market forces. The bond prices fluctuate inversely with the market interest rate.

The inverse relationship between price and yield is a central feature of fixed-income securities. Interest rate fluctuations represent the main source of risk in the fixed-income market, and we devote considerable attention in Chapter 13 to assessing the sensitivity of bond prices to market yields. For now, however, it is sufficient to highlight one key factor that determines that sensitivity, namely, the maturity of the bond.

A general rule in evaluating bond price risk is that, keeping all other factors the same, the longer the maturity of the bond, the greater the sensitivity of price to fluctuations in the interest rate. For example, consider Table 11.2, which presents the price of an 8 percent coupon bond at different market yields and times to maturity. For any departure of the interest rate from 8 percent (the rate at which the bond sells at par value), the change in the bond price is smaller for shorter times to maturity.

This makes sense. If you buy the bond at par with an 8 percent coupon rate, and market rates subsequently rise, then you suffer a loss: you have tied up your money earning 8 percent when

Figure 11.2
The inverse relationship between bond prices and yields.

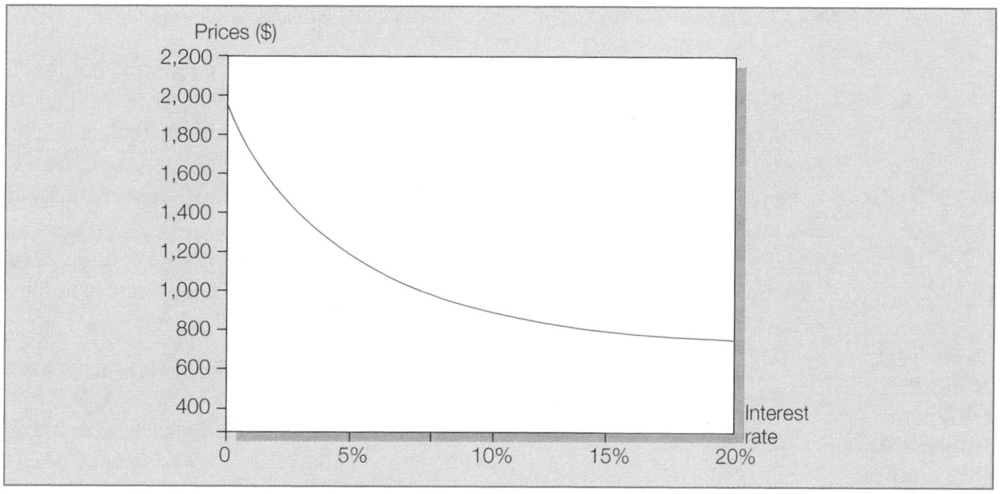

[6]The progressively smaller impact of interest increases results from the fact that at higher rates the bond is worth less. Therefore, an additional increase in rates operates on a smaller initial base, resulting in a smaller price reduction.

BOND PRICING

Excel and most other spreadsheet programs provide built-in functions to compute bond prices and yields. They typically ask you to input both the date you buy the bond (called the *settlement date*) and the maturity date of the bond. The Excel function for bond price is

=PRICE(settlement date, maturity date, annual coupon rate, yield to maturity, redemption value as percent of par value, number of coupon payments per year)

As a first example, consider a 4.875 percent coupon bond maturing on 2/15/2012, purchased on 2/15/2003 at a price of 107.655 corresponding to a yield of 3.86 percent. We might enter the values in the following spreadsheet. Alternatively, we might simply enter the following function in Excel:

=PRICE(DATE(2003,02,15), DATE(2012,02,15), .04875, .0386, 100, 2)

	A	B	C	D	E	F
1						
2						
3						
4		**4.875% coupon**		**6% coupon**		**8% coupon**
5		**maturing**		**maturing**		**30-year**
6		**Feb 2012**		**June 2011**		**maturity**
7						
8	Settlement date	2/15/2003		2/27/2004		1/1/2000
9	Maturity date	2/15/2012		06/01/2004		1/1/2030
10	Annual coupon rate	0.04875		0.06		0.08
11	Yield to maturity	0.0386		0.0410		0.1
12	Redemption value (% of par value)	100		100		100
13	Coupon payments per year	2		2		2
14						
15			**Formula in column B**			
16	**Flat price (% of par)**	**107.655**	**=PRICE(B8,B9,B10,B11,B12,B13)**	**111.80**		**81.071**
17	Days since last coupon	0	=COUPDAYBS(B8,B9,2,1)	88		0
18	Days in coupon period	181	=COUPDAYS(B8,B9,2,1)	182		182
19	Accrued interest	0	=(B17/B18)*B10*100/2	1.451		0
20	**Invoice price**	**107.655**	**=B16+B19**	**113.251**		**81.071**

alternative investments offer higher returns. This is reflected in a capital loss on the bond—a fall in its market price. The longer the period for which your money is tied up, the greater the loss, and, correspondingly, the greater the drop in the bond price. In Table 11.2, the row for one-year maturity bonds shows little price sensitivity—that is, with only one year's earnings at stake, changes in interest rates are not too threatening. But for 30-year maturity bonds, interest rate swings have a large impact on bond prices.

This is why short-term government securities such as T-bills are considered to be the safest. They are free not only of default risk, but also largely of price risk attributable to interest rate volatility.

Table 11.2 Bond Prices at Different Interest Rates (8% coupon bond, coupons paid semiannually)

	Bond Price at Given Market Interest Rate				
Time to Maturity	**4%**	**6%**	**8%**	**10%**	**12%**
1 year	1,038.83	1,019.13	1,000.00	981.41	963.33
10 years	1,327.03	1,148.77	1,000.00	875.35	770.60
20 years	1,547.11	1,231.15	1,000.00	828.41	699.07
30 years	1,695.22	1,276.76	1,000.00	810.71	676.77

The DATE function in Excel, which we use for both the settlement and maturity date, uses the format DATE(year,month,day). The first date is February 15, 2003, when the bond is purchased, and the second is February 15, 2012, when it matures. Most bonds pay coupons on the 15th of the month.

Notice that the coupon rate and yield to maturity are expressed as decimals, not percentages. In most cases, redemption value is 100 (i.e., 100 percent of par value), and the resulting price similarly is expressed as a percent of par value. Occasionally, however, you may encounter bonds that pay off at a premium or discount to par value. One example would be callable bonds, discussed shortly.

The value of the bond returned by the pricing function is 107.655 (cell B16), which matches the sales price to the nearest 32nd of a point. This bond has just paid a coupon. In other words, the settlement date is precisely at the beginning of the coupon period, so no adjustment for accrued interest is necessary.

To illustrate the procedure for bonds between coupon payments, let us apply the spreadsheet to the 6 percent coupon June 2011 bond highlighted in Figure 11.1 and valued on 2/27/2004. Using the entries in column D of the spreadsheet, we find in cell D16 that the (flat) price of the bond is 111.80, which matches the actual price of the bond except for a few cents' rounding error.

What about the bond's invoice price? Rows 17 through 20 make the necessary adjustments. The function described in cell C17 counts the days since the last coupon. This day count is based on the bond's settlement date, maturity date, coupon period (1 = annual; 2 = semiannual), and day count convention (choice 1 uses actual days). The function described in cell C18 counts the total days in each coupon payment period. Therefore, the entries in row 19 are the semiannual coupon multiplied by the fraction of a coupon period that has elapsed since the last payment. Finally, the invoice prices in row 20 are the sum of flat price plus accrued interest.

As a final example, suppose you wish to find the price of the bond discussed in the previous section under "An Example: Bond Pricing." It is a 30-year maturity bond with a coupon rate of 8 percent (paid semiannually). The market interest rate given in the latter part of the example is 10 percent. However, you are not given a specific settlement or maturity date. You can still use the PRICE function to value the bond. Simply choose an *arbitrary* settlement date (January 1, 2000, is convenient) and let the maturity date be 30 years hence. The appropriate inputs appear in column F of the spreadsheet, with the resulting price, 81.071 percent of face value, appearing in cell F20.

Bond Pricing Between Coupon Dates

Equation 11.2 for bond prices assumes that the next coupon payment is in precisely one payment period, either a year for an annual payment bond or six months for a semiannual payment bond. But you probably want to be able to price bonds all 365 days of the year, not just on the one or two dates each year that it makes a coupon payment!

We apply the same principles to pricing regardless of the date: we simply compute the present value of the remaining payments. However, if we are between coupon dates, there will be fractional periods remaining until each payment. Even if the principles are no more complicated, this certainly complicates the arithmetic computations.

Fortunately, bond pricing functions are included in most spreadsheet programs such as Excel. The spreadsheet allows you to enter today's date as well as the maturity date of the bond, and so can provide prices for bonds at any date. The Excel Application box here shows you how.

As we pointed out earlier, bond prices are typically quoted net of accrued interest. These prices, which appear in the financial press, are called *flat prices*. The actual *invoice price* that a buyer pays for the bond includes accrued interest. Thus,

$$\text{Invoice price} = \text{Flat price} + \text{Accrued interest}$$

When a bond pays its coupon, flat price equals invoice price, since at that moment accrued interest reverts to zero. However, this will be the exceptional case, not the rule.

The Excel pricing function provides the flat price of the bond. To find the invoice price, we need to add accrued interest. Fortunately, Excel also provides functions that count the days since the last coupon payment date and thus can be used to compute accrued interest. The Excel box also illustrates how to use these functions. It provides examples using bonds that have just paid a coupon and so have zero accrued interest, as well as a bond that is between coupon dates.

11.3 BOND YIELDS

We have noted that the current yield of a bond measures only the cash income provided by the bond as a percentage of bond price and ignores any prospective capital gains or losses. We would like a measure of rate of return that accounts for both current income as well as the price increase or decrease over the bond's life. The yield to maturity is the standard measure of the total rate of return of the bond over its life. However, it is far from a perfect measure, and we will explore several variations of this statistic.

Yield to Maturity

Government of Canada Bond Yields www.bankofcanada.ca/en/bonds.htm

In practice, an investor considering the purchase of a bond is not quoted a promised rate of return. Instead, the investor must use the bond price, maturity date, and coupon payments to infer the return offered by the bond over its life. The **yield to maturity (YTM)** is a measure of the average rate of return that will be earned on a bond if it is bought now and held until maturity. To calculate the yield to maturity, we solve the bond price equation for the interest rate given the bond's price.

For example, suppose an 8 percent coupon, 30-year bond is selling at $1,276.76. What average rate of return would be earned by an investor purchasing the bond at this price? To answer this question, we find the interest rate at which the present value of the remaining bond payments equals the bond price. This is the rate that is consistent with the observed price of the bond. Therefore, we solve for r in the following equation.

$$\$1{,}276.76 = \sum_{t=1}^{60} \frac{\$40}{(1+r)^t} + \frac{\$1{,}000}{(1+r)^{60}}$$

or, equivalently

$$1{,}276.76 = 40 \times \text{PA}(r,\, 60) + 1{,}000 \times \text{PF}(r,\, 60)$$

These equations have only one unknown variable, the interest rate, r. You can use a financial calculator to confirm that the solution to the equation is $r = .03$, or 3 percent per half year.[7] This is considered the bond's yield to maturity.

The financial press reports yields on an annualized basis and annualizes the bond's semiannual yield using simple interest techniques, resulting in an annual percentage rate, or APR. Yields annualized using simple interest are also called "bond equivalent yields." Therefore, the semiannual yield would be doubled and reported in the newspaper as a bond equivalent yield of 6 percent. The *effective* annual yield of the bond, however, accounts for compound interest. If one earns 3 percent interest every six months, then after one year, each dollar invested grows with interest to $\$1 \times (1.03)^2 = 1.0609$, and the effective annual interest rate on the bond is 6.09 percent.

The bond's yield to maturity is the internal rate of return on an investment in the bond. The yield to maturity can be interpreted as the compound rate of return over the life of the bond under the assumption that all bond coupons can be reinvested at an interest rate equal to the bond's yield to maturity.[8] Yield to maturity is widely accepted as a proxy for average return.

---

[7]Without a financial calculator, you still could solve the equation, but you would need to use a trial-and-error approach.

[8]If the reinvestment rate does not equal the bond's yield to maturity, the compound rate will differ from YTM. This is illustrated later.

Yield to maturity is different from the *current yield* of a bond, which is the bond's annual coupon payment divided by the bond price. For example, for the 8 percent, 30-year bond currently selling at $1,276.76, the current yield would be $80/$1,276.76 = .0627, or 6.27 percent per year. In contrast, recall that the effective annual yield to maturity is 6.09 percent. For this bond, which is selling at a premium over par value ($1,276 rather than $1,000), the coupon rate (8 percent) exceeds the current yield (6.27 percent), which exceeds the yield to maturity (6.09 percent). The coupon rate exceeds current yield because the coupon rate divides the coupon payments by par value ($1,000) rather than by the bond price ($1,276). In turn, the current yield exceeds yield to maturity because the yield to maturity accounts for the built-in capital loss on the bond; the bond bought today for $1,276 will eventually fall in value to $1,000 at maturity.

It is common to hear people talking loosely about the yield on a bond. In these cases, it is almost always the case that they are referring to the yield to maturity.

CONCEPT CHECK

3. What will be the relationship among coupon rate, current yield, and yield to maturity for bonds selling at discounts from par? Illustrate using the 8 percent (semiannual payment) coupon bond assuming it is selling at a yield to maturity of 10 percent.

Excel also provides a function for yield to maturity. It is

=YIELD(settlement date, maturity date, annual coupon rate, bond price, redemption value as percent of par value, number of coupon payments per year)

The bond price used in the function should be the reported flat price, without accrued interest. For example, to find the yield to maturity of the 30-year 8 percent bond, we would use column E of Spreadsheet 11.1. If the coupons were paid only annually, we would change the entry for payments per year to 1 (see cell G12), and the yield would fall slightly to 5.99 percent.

Spreadsheet 11.1

	A	B	C	D	E	F	G	H
1								
2								
3								
4					Semiannual		Annual	
5					coupons		coupons	
6								
7	Settlement date				1/1/2000		1/1/2000	
8	Maturity date				1/1/2030		1/1/2030	
9	Annual coupon rate				0.08		0.08	
10	Bond price				127.676		127.676	
11	Redemption value (% of face value)				100		100	
12	Coupon payments per year				2		1	
13								
14	**Yield to maturity (decimal)**				**0.0600**		**0.0599**	
15								
16								
17		The formula entered here is: =YIELD(E7,E8,E9,E10,E11,E12)						

Yield to Call

Yield to maturity is calculated on the assumption that the bond will be held until maturity. What if the bond is callable, however, and may be retired prior to the maturity date? How should we measure average rate of return for bonds subject to a call provision?

Figure 11.3 illustrates the risk of call to the bondholder. The upper line is the value at various market interest rates of a "straight" (i.e., noncallable) bond with par value $1,000, an 8 percent coupon rate, and a 30-year time to maturity. If interest rates fall, the bond price, which equals the present value of the promised payments, can rise substantially.

Figure 11.3 The inverse relationship between bond prices and yields for a callable bond.

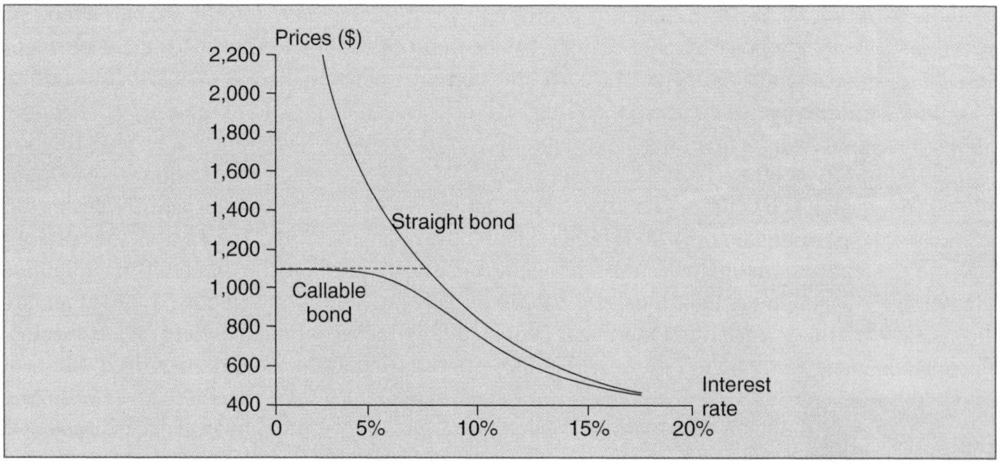

Now consider a bond that has the same coupon rate and maturity date but is callable at 110 percent of par value, or $1,100. When interest rates fall, the present value of the bond's *scheduled* payments rises, but the call provision allows the issuer to repurchase the bond at the call price. If the call price is less than the present value of the scheduled payments, the issuer can call the bond at the expense of the bondholder.

The lower line in Figure 11.3 is the value of the callable bond. At high interest rates, the risk of call is negligible, and the values of the straight and callable bonds converge. At lower rates, however, the values of the bonds begin to diverge, with the difference reflecting the value of the firm's opinion to reclaim the callable bond at the call price. At very low rates, the bond is called, and its value is simply the call price, $1,100.

This analysis suggests that bond market analysts might be more interested in a bond's yield to call rather than yield to maturity if the bond is especially vulnerable to being called. The yield to call is calculated just like the yield to maturity except that the time until call replaces the time until maturity, and the call price replaces the par value.

For example, suppose the 8 percent coupon, 30-year maturity bonds sells for $1,150 and is callable in 10 years at a call price of $1,100. Its yield to maturity and yield to call would be calculated using the following inputs:

	Yield to Call	Yield to Maturity
Coupon payment	$40	$40
Number of semiannual periods	20 periods	60 periods
Final payment	$1,100	$1,000
Price	$1,150	$1,150

The yield to call is then 6.64 percent, whereas yield to maturity is 6.82 percent.

We have noted that most callable bonds are issued with an initial period of call protection. In addition, an implicit form of call protection operates for bonds selling at deep discounts from their call prices. Even if interest rates fall a bit, deep-discount bonds still will sell below the call price and thus will not be subject to a call.

Premium bonds that might be selling near their call prices, however, are especially apt to be called if rates fall further. If interest rates fall, a callable premium bond is likely to provide a lower return than could be earned on a discount bond whose potential price appreciation is not limited by the likelihood of a call. As a consequence, investors in premium bonds often are more interested in the bond's yield to call than its yield to maturity, because it may appear to them that the bond will be retired at the call date.

CONCEPT CHECK

4. The yield to maturity on two 10-year maturity bonds currently is 7 percent. Each bond has a call price of $1,100. One bond has a coupon rate of 6 percent, the other 8 percent. Assume for simplicity that bonds are called as soon as the present value of their remaining payments exceeds their call price. What will be the capital gain on each bond if the market interest rate suddenly falls to 6 percent?

CONCEPT CHECK

5. A 20-year maturity 9 percent coupon bond paying coupons semiannually is callable in five years at a call price of $1,050. The bond currently sells at a yield to maturity of 8 percent. What is the yield to call?

Realized Compound Yield Versus Yield to Maturity

We have noted that yield to maturity will equal the rate of return realized over the life of the bond if all coupons are reinvested at an interest rate equal to the bond's yield to maturity. Consider, for example, a two-year bond selling at par value paying a 10 percent coupon once a year. The yield to maturity is 10 percent. If the $100 coupon payment is reinvested at an interest rate of 10 percent, the $1,000 investment in the bond will grow after two years to $1,210, as illustrated in Figure 11.4, panel A. The coupon paid in the first year is reinvested and grows with interest to a second-year value of $110, which, together with the second coupon payment and payment of par value in the second year, results in a total value of $1,210. The compound growth rate of invested funds, therefore, is calculated from

$$\$1{,}000\,(1 + y_{\text{realized}})^2 = \$1{,}210$$
$$y_{\text{realized}} = .10 = 10\%$$

Figure 11.4 Growth of invested funds.

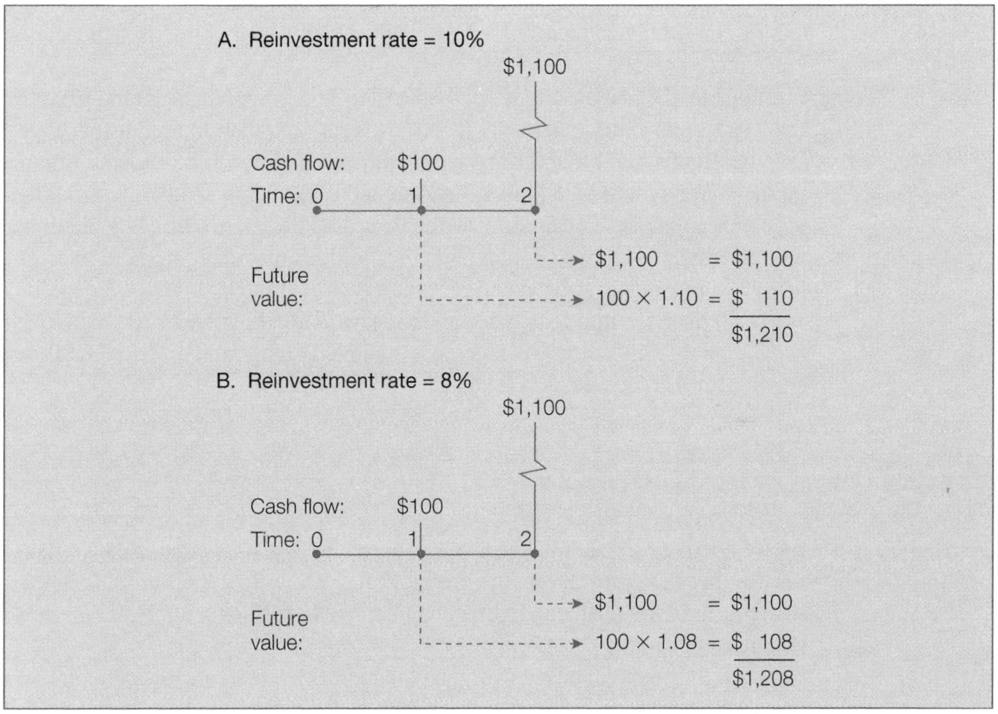

With a reinvestment rate equal to the 10 percent yield to maturity, the *realized* compound yield equals yield to maturity.

But what if the reinvestment rate is not 10 percent? If the coupon can be invested at more than 10 percent, funds will grow to more than $1,210, and the realized compound return will exceed 10 percent. If the reinvestment rate is less than 10 percent, so will be the realized compound return.

Suppose, for example, that the interest rate at which the coupon can be invested equals 8 percent. The following calculations are illustrated in panel B of Figure 11.4:

Future value of first coupon payment with interest earnings	$\$100 \times 1.08 = \$\ \ 108$
Cash payment in second year (final coupon plus par value)	$1,100
Total value of investment with reinvested coupons	$1,208

The realized compound yield is computed by calculating the compound rate of growth of invested funds, assuming that all coupon payments are reinvested. The investor purchased the bond for par at $1,000, and this investment grew to $1,208.

$$\$1{,}000\,(1 + y_{\text{realized}})^2 = \$1{,}208$$

$$y_{\text{realized}} = .0991 = 9.91\%$$

This example highlights the problem with conventional yield to maturity when reinvestment rates can change over time. Conventional yield to maturity will not equal realized compound return. However, in an economy with future interest rate uncertainty, the rates at which interim coupons will be reinvested are not yet known. Therefore, although realized compound yield can be computed *after* the investment period ends, it cannot be computed in advance without a forecast of future reinvestment rates. This reduces much of the attraction of the realized yield measure.

Forecasting the realized compound yield over various holding periods or investment horizons is called **horizon analysis**. The forecast of total return depends on your forecasts of *both* the price of the bond when you sell it at the end of your horizon *and* the rate at which you are able to reinvest coupon income. The sales price depends in turn on the yield to maturity at the horizon date. With a longer investment horizon, however, reinvested coupons will be a larger component of your final proceeds.

Suppose, for instance, that you buy a 30-year, 7.5 percent (annual payment) coupon bond for $980 (when its yield to maturity is 7.67 percent) and plan to hold it for 20 years. Your forecast is that the bond's yield to maturity will be 8 percent when it is sold and that the reinvestment rate on the coupons will be 6 percent. At the end of your investment horizon, the bond will have 10 years remaining until expiration, so the forecast sales price (using a yield to maturity of 8 percent) will be $966.45. The 20 coupon payments will grow with compound interest to $2,758.92. (This is the future value of a 20-year $75 annuity with an interest rate of 6 percent.)

Based on these forecasts, your $980 investment will grow in 20 years to $966.45 + $2,758.92 = $3,725.37. This corresponds to an annualized compound return of 6.90 percent, calculated by solving for r in the equation $\$980(1 + r)^{20}$ 5 $3,725.37.

11.4 BOND PRICES OVER TIME

As we noted earlier, a bond will sell at par value when its coupon rate equals the market interest rate. In these circumstances, the investor receives fair compensation for the time value of money in the form of the recurring interest payments. No further capital gain is necessary to provide fair compensation.

When the coupon rate is lower than the market interest rate, the coupon payments alone will not provide investors as high a return as they could earn elsewhere in the market. To receive a fair return on such an investment, investors also need to earn price appreciation on their bonds. The bonds, therefore, would have to sell below par value to provide a "built-in" capital gain on the investment.

To illustrate this point, suppose a bond was issued several years ago when the interest rate was 7 percent. The bond's annual coupon rate was thus set at 7 percent. (We will suppose for simplicity that the bond pays its coupon annually.) Now, with three years left in the bond's life, the interest rate is 8 percent per year. The bond's fair market price is the present value of the remaining annual coupons plus payment of par value. That present value is

$$\$70 \times PA(8\%, 3) + \$1{,}000 \times PF(8\%, 3) = \$974.23$$

which is less than par value.

In another year, after the next coupon is paid, the bond would sell at

$$\$70 \times PA(8\%, 2) + \$1{,}000 \times PF(8\%, 2) = \$982.17$$

thereby yielding a capital gain over the year of $7.94. If an investor had purchased the bond at $974.23, the total return over the year would equal the coupon payment plus capital gain, or $70 + $7.94 = $77.94. This represents a rate of return of $77.94/$974.23, or 8 percent, exactly the current rate of return available elsewhere in the market.

CONCEPT CHECK

6. What will the bond price be in yet another year, when only one year remains until maturity? What is the rate of return to an investor who purchases the bond at $982.17 and sells it one year hence?

When bond prices are set according to the present value formula, any discount from par value provides an anticipated capital gain that will augment a below-market coupon rate just sufficiently to provide a fair total rate of return. Conversely, if the coupon rate exceeds the market interest rate, the interest income by itself is greater than that available elsewhere in the market. Investors will bid up the price of these bonds above their par values. As the bonds approach maturity, they will fall in value because fewer of these above-market coupon payments remain. The resulting capital losses offset the large coupon payments so that the bondholder again receives only a fair rate of return.

Problem 8 at the end of the chapter asks you to work through the case of the high coupon bond. Figure 11.5 traces out the price paths of high and low coupon bonds (net of accrued interest) as time

Figure 11.5 Price paths of coupon bonds.

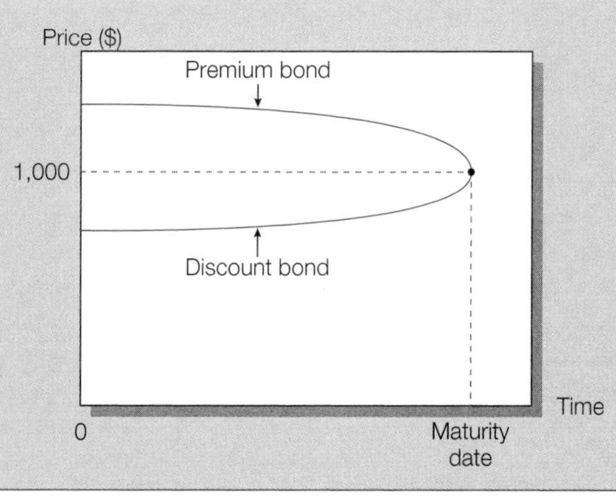

to maturity approaches. The low coupon bond enjoys capital gains, whereas the high coupon bond suffers capital losses.[9]

We use these examples to show that each bond offers investors the same total rate of return. Although the capital gain versus income components differ, the price of each bond is set to provide competitive rates, as we should expect in well-functioning capital markets. Security returns all should be comparable on an after-tax risk-adjusted basis. If they are not, investors will try to sell low-return securities, thereby driving down the prices until the total return at the now-lower price is competitive with other securities. Prices should continue to adjust until all securities are fairly priced, in that expected returns are appropriate (given necessary risk and tax adjustments).

Yield to Maturity Versus Holding Period Return

We just considered an example in which the holding period return and the yield to maturity were equal. In our example, the bond yield started and ended the year at 8 percent, and the bond's holding period return also equalled 8 percent. This turns out to be a general result. When the yield to maturity is unchanged over the period, the rate of return on the bond will equal that yield. As we noted, this should not be a surprising result: the bond must offer a rate of return competitive with those available on other securities.

However, when yields fluctuate, so will a bond's rate of return. Unanticipated changes in market rates will result in unanticipated changes in bond returns, and after the fact, a bond's holding period return can be better or worse than the yield at which it initially sells. An increase in the bond's yield acts to reduce its price, which means that the holding period return will be less than the initial yield. Conversely, a decline in yield will result in a holding period return greater than the initial yield.

Consider as example a 30-year bond paying an annual coupon of \$80 and selling at par value of \$1,000. The bond's initial yield to maturity is 8 percent. If the yield remains at 8 percent over the year, the bond price will remain at par, so the holding period return also will be 8 percent. But if the yield falls below 8 percent, the bond price will increase. Suppose the price increases to \$1,050. Then the holding period return is greater than 8 percent:

$$\text{Holding period return} = \frac{\$80 + (\$1{,}050 - \$1{,}000)}{\$1{,}000} = .13 \text{ or } 13\%$$

Here is another way to think about the difference between yield to maturity and holding period return. Yield to maturity depends only on the bond's coupon, *current* price, and par value at maturity. All of these values are observable today, so yield to maturity can be easily calculated. Yield to maturity can be interpreted as a measure of the *average* rate of return if the investment in the bond is held until the bond matures. In contrast, holding period return is the rate of return over a particular investment period, and depends on the market price of the bond at the end of that holding period; of course this price is *not* known today. Since bond prices over the holding period will respond to unanticipated changes in interest rates, holding period return can at most be forecasted.

Zero-Coupon Bonds

Original issue discount bonds are less common than coupon bonds issued at par. These are bonds that are issued intentionally with low coupon rates that cause the bond to sell at a discount from par value. An extreme example of this type of bond is the *zero-coupon bond,* which carries no coupons and must provide all its return in the form of price appreciation. Zeroes provide only one cash flow to their owners, and that is on the maturity date of the bond.

---

[9]If interest rates are volatile, the price path will oscillate around the path shown in Figure 11.5, reflecting capital gains or losses as interest rates fall or rise. Ultimately, however, the price path must reach par value at the maturity date, implying that the price of the premium bond will fall over time while that of the discount bond will rise.

Figure 11.6 The price of a 30-year zero-coupon bond over time. Price equals $1{,}000/(1.10)^T$ where T is time until maturity.

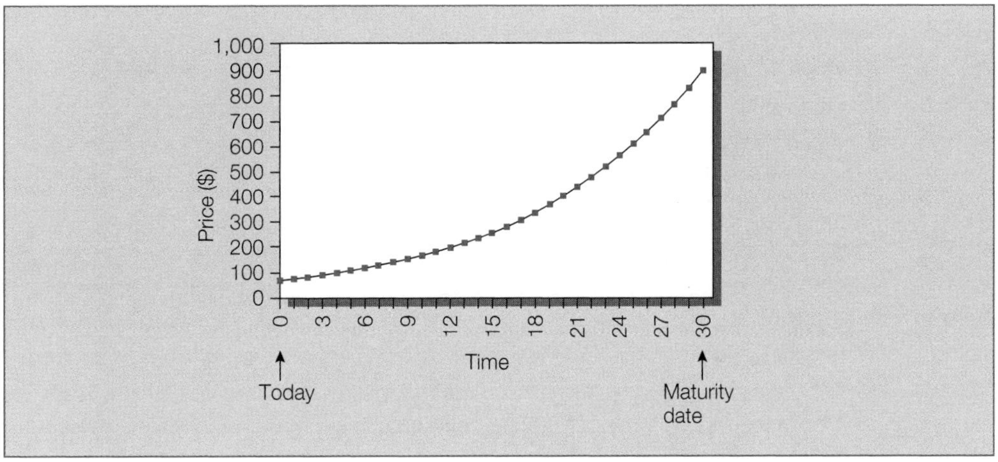

www.bankofcanada.ca

Government of Canada Treasury bills are examples of short-term zero-coupon instruments. The Bank of Canada issues or sells a bill for some amount ranging from $1,000 to $1 million, agreeing to repay that amount at the bill's maturity. All of the investor's return comes in the form of price appreciation over time.

Longer-term zero-coupon bonds are commonly created synthetically. Several investment banking firms buy coupon-paying Government of Canada or provincial bonds and sell rights to single payments backed by the bonds. These bonds are said to be *stripped* of coupons, and often are called *strips.* The single payments are, in essence, zero-coupon bonds collateralized by the original securities and so are virtually free of default risk. Several such strips are shown in Figure 11.1.

What should happen to prices of zeroes as time passes? On their maturity date, zeroes must sell for par value. Before maturity, however, they should sell at discounts from par, because of the time value of money. As time passes, price should approach par value. In fact, if the interest rate is constant, a zero's price will increase at exactly the rate of interest.

To illustrate this property, consider a zero with 30 years until maturity, and suppose the market interest rate is 10 percent per year. The price of the bond today will be $\$1{,}000/(1.10)^{30} = \$57.31$. Next year, with only 29 years until maturity, the price will be $\$1{,}000/(1.10)^{29} = \$63.04$, a 10 percent increase over its previous-year value. Because the par value of the bond is now discounted for one fewer year, its price has increased by the one-year discount factor.

Figure 11.6 presents the price path of a 10-year zero-coupon bond until its maturity date for an annual market interest rate of 10 percent. The bond's price rises exponentially, not linearly, until its maturity.

After-Tax Returns

www.cra-arc.gc.ca

The tax authorities recognize that the "built-in" price appreciation on original issue discount (OID) bonds such as zero-coupon bonds represents an implicit interest payment to the holder of the security. The Canada Revenue Agency (CRA), therefore, calculates a price appreciation schedule to impute taxable interest income for the built-in appreciation during a tax year, even if the asset is not sold or does not mature until a future year. Any additional gains or losses that arise from changes in market interest rates are treated as capital gains or losses if the OID bond is sold during the tax year.

Let's consider an example. If the interest rate originally is 10 percent, the 30-year zero would be issued at a price of $\$1{,}000/(1.10)^{30} = \$57.31$. The following year, CCRA calculates what the bond price would be if the yield remains at 10 percent. This is $\$1{,}000/(1.10)^{29} = \$63.04$. Therefore, the tax authorities impute interest income of $\$63.04 - \$57.31 = \$5.73$. This amount is subject to tax. Notice that the imputed interest income is based on a "constant-yield method" that ignores any changes in market interest rates.

If interest rates actually fall, let's say to 9.9 percent, the bond price actually will be $\$1{,}000/(1.099)^{29} = \$64.72$. If the bond is sold, then the difference between \$64.72 and \$63.04 will be treated as capital gains income and taxed at the capital gains tax rate. If the bond is not sold, then the price difference is an unrealized capital gain and does not result in taxes in that year. In either case, the investor must pay taxes on the \$5.73 of imputed interest at the rate of ordinary income.

The same reasoning is applied to the taxation of other original issue discount bonds, even if they are not zero-coupon bonds. Consider, as an example, a 30-year maturity bond that is issued with a coupon rate of 4 percent and a yield to maturity of 8 percent. For simplicity, we will assume that the bond pays coupons once annually. Because of the low coupon rate, the bond will be issued at a price far below par value, specifically at a price of \$549.69. If the bond's yield to maturity remains at 8 percent, then its price in one year will rise to \$553.66. (Confirm this for yourself.) This provides a pretax holding period return of exactly 8 percent.

$$\text{HPR} = \frac{\$40 + (\$553.66 - \$549.69)}{\$549.69} = .08$$

The increase in the bond price based on a constant yield, however, is treated as interest income, so the investor is required to pay taxes on imputed interest income of \$553.66 – \$549.69 = \$3.97. If the bond's yield actually changes during the year, the difference between the bond's price and the "constant-yield value" of \$553.66 will be treated as capital gains income if the bond is sold.

CONCEPT CHECK

7. Suppose that the yield to maturity of the 4 percent coupon, 30-year maturity bond actually falls to 7 percent by the end of the first year, and that the investor sells the bond after the first year. If the investor's tax rate on interest income is 36 percent and the tax rate on capital gains is 20 percent, what is the investor's after-tax rate of return?

11.5 DEFAULT RISK

Although bonds generally *promise* a fixed flow of income, that income stream is not riskless unless the investor can be sure the issuer will not default on the obligation. While government bonds may be treated as free of default risk, this is not true of corporate bonds. If the company goes bankrupt, the bondholders will not receive all the payments they have been promised. Therefore, the actual payments on these bonds are uncertain, for they depend to some degree on the ultimate financial status of the firm.

www.dbrs.com

Bond default risk is measured by both Moody's and Standard & Poor's in the United States and Dominion Bond Rating Service (DBRS) in Canada; the two U.S. rating services also rate several Canadian issues. All rating agencies assign letter grades to the bonds of corporations and municipalities to reflect their assessment of the safety of the bond issue. The top rating is AAA (Standard & Poor's and DBRS) and Aaa (Moody's). Moody's modifies each rating class with a 1, 2, or 3 suffix (e.g., Aaa1, Aaa2, Aaa3) to provide a finer gradation of ratings. S&P uses a + or – modification, and the Canadian service uses the terms "(high)" and "(low)" as modifiers.

Bonds rated BBB or above (S&P and DBRS) and Baa or above (Moody's), are considered **investment-grade bonds,** whereas lower-rated bonds are classified as **speculative-grade** or **junk bonds.** Certain regulated institutional investors such as insurance companies have not always been allowed to invest in speculative-grade bonds.

Figure 11.7 provides the definitions of each bond rating classification.

Figure 11.7 Definitions of each bond rating class.

BOND RATINGS

	Very High Quality	High Quality	Speculative	Very Poor
DBRS	AAA AA	A BBB	BB B	CCC D
Standard & Poor's	AAA AA	A BBB	BB B	CCC D
Moody's	Aaa Aa	A Baa	Ba B	Caa C

At times all services have used adjustments to these ratings. S&P uses plus and minus signs: A+ is the strongest A rating and A– the weakest. Moody's uses a 1, 2, or 3 designation—with 1 indicating the strongest. DBRS uses a (high) for the strongest and a (low) for the weakest designations.

DBRS	Moody's	S&P	
AAA	Aaa	AAA	Debt rated Aaa and AAA has the highest rating. Capacity to pay interest and principal is extremely strong.
AA	Aa	A	Debt rated Aa and AA has a very strong capacity to pay interest and repay principal. Together with the highest rating, this group makes up the high-grade bond class.
A	A	A	Debt rated A has a strong capacity to pay interest and repay principal, although it is somewhat more susceptible to the adverse effects of changes in circumstances and economic conditions than debt in higher-rated categories.
BBB	Baa	BBB	Debt rated Baa and BBB is regarded as having an adequate capacity to pay interest and repay principal. Whereas it normally exhibits adequate protection parameters, adverse economic conditions or changing circumstances are more likely to lead to a weakened capacity to pay interest and repay principal for debt in this category than in higher-rated categories. These bonds are medium-grade obligations.
BB B CCC CC	Ba B Caa Ca	BB B CCC CC	Debt rated in these categories is regarded, on balance, as predominantly speculative with respect to capacity to pay interest and repay principal in accordance with the terms of the obligation. BB and Ba indicate the lowest degree of speculation, and CC and Ca the highest degree of speculation. Although such debt will likely have some quality and protective characteristics, these are outweighed by large uncertainties or major risk exposures to adverse conditions. Some issues may be in default.
C	C	C	This rating is reserved for income bonds on which no interest is being paid.
D	D	D	Debt rated D is in default, and payment of interest and/or repayment of principal is in arrears.

Source: Various editions of *Standard & Poor's Bond Guide, Moody's Bond Guide,* and *DBRS Bond Rating.*

Junk Bonds

Junk Bonds
www.efmoody.com/investments/junk

Junk bonds, also known as *high-yield bonds,* are nothing more than speculative-grade (low-rated or unrated) bonds. Before 1977, almost all junk bonds were "fallen angels," that is, firm-issued bonds that originally had investment grade ratings but that had since been downgraded. In 1977, however, firms began to issue "original-issue junk."

Much of the credit for this innovation is given to Drexel Burnham Lambert and especially its trader, Michael Milken. Drexel had long enjoyed a niche as a junk bond trader and had established a network of potential investors in junk bonds. Its reasoning for marketing original-issue junk, so-called emerging credits, lay in the belief that default rates on these bonds did not justify the large yield spreads commonly exhibited in the marketplace. Firms not able to muster an investment-grade rating were happy to have Drexel (and other investment bankers) market their bonds directly to the public, as this opened up a new source of financing. Junk issues were a lower-cost financing alternative than borrowing from banks.

High-yield bonds gained considerable notoriety in the 1980s when they were used as financing vehicles in leveraged buyouts and hostile takeover attempts. Shortly thereafter, however, the junk bond market suffered. The legal difficulties of Drexel and Michael Milken in connection with Wall Street's insider trading scandals of the late 1980s tainted the junk bond market.

JUNK CAN BE TREASURE FOR INVESTORS

Equity investors looking for a little more stability in the wake of last year's volatile markets may want to consider adding some "junk" to their portfolios. So-called junk bonds offer the higher returns more in keeping with stocks than bonds, but with less volatility than is usually associated with stocks.

"From a risk point of view, junk bonds are between government bonds and equities," says Dan Hallett, an analyst with Toronto-based FundMonitor.com.

Junk bond dealers and investment managers prefer to use the term "high-yield debt" to describe these non-investment-grade corporate bonds, which carry ratings of BB at the high end and go lower for more speculative holdings.

Lower ratings are associated with more volatility, but they also reflect a junk bond's potential to outperform more highly rated debt over the long term. Indeed, junk bonds usually outperform plain-vanilla bonds by an annual two percentage points over the average three- to five-year period, says Ben Cheng, manager of the $7.8-million BPI Corporate Bond Fund.

This long-term outperformance potential prompts many financial advisers to suggest that investors comfortable with buying a company's stock should feel even safer buying its debt through a high-yield bond fund.

After all, debt-holders rank ahead of common shareholders when a bankrupt company's assets are being distributed. During volatile markets, junk-bond investors can rely on interest payments and not just capital gains for growth, making them less susceptible than stocks to general market downturns.

For those reasons, equity investors whose impulse is to jump into government bonds at the first sign of stock market volatility might be wiser to cast their eye on higher-yielding junk bonds instead.

Though over the long term, junk bonds tend to beat their more traditional brethren, a flight to quality last year in the wake of Russia's default on some of its debt and the ensuing market turmoil took some of the shine off junk bond prices. The Scotia McLeod High Yield Index posted a one-year return of 6.09 per cent, underperforming the benchmark Scotia McLeod Universe Bond Index's 9.2 per cent.

But the High Yield Index's perfomance was far better than the 3.2-per-cent loss posted by the Toronto Stock Exchange 300 composite index. In the four years to last Dec. 31, the Scotia McLeod index posted a 13.8-per-cent return versus the TSE 300's 13.5 per cent.

But fallen junk bond prices—they're about 8 per cent lower than they were in June, producing current yields of about 11 per cent—represent a buying opportunity, says Levi Folk, an analyst with the Fund Counsel in Toronto. He says the dip means "good valuations" are now available.

One of the main factors affecting junk bonds prices is an issuing company's financial strength as reflected in its stock price. When picking a junk-bond fund, "it's important to go with a professional manager who can find the better bond issues from companies that don't risk [credit] downgrades or earnings disappointments," Mr. Hallett says.

The second major component that drives junk bond prices is interest rates. Rising interest rates hurt all bonds. But many analysts are pointing to a bond-friendly interest-rate climate in 1999.

"We see the Fed moving rates downward during the next three months, with the Bank of Canada following," Mr. Folk says.

Even if interest rates don't stay low, junk bonds could still be a good bet. High interest payouts from junk bonds often cushion them from some of the worst effects of interest rate rises.

At the height of Drexel's difficulties, the high-yield bond market nearly dried up. Since then, the market has rebounded dramatically. However, it is worth noting that the average credit quality of high-yield debt issued today is higher than the average quality in the boom years of the 1980s.

Determinants of Bond Safety

Bond rating agencies base their quality ratings largely on an analysis of the level and trend of some of the issuer's financial ratios. The key ratios used to evaluate safety are:

1. *Coverage ratios*. Ratios of company earnings to fixed costs. For example, the *times-interest-earned ratio* is the ratio of earnings before interest payments and taxes to interest obligations. The *fixed-charge coverage ratio* adds lease payments and sinking fund payments to interest obligations to arrive at the ratio of earnings to all fixed cash obligations. Low or falling coverage ratios signal possible cash flow difficulties.
2. *Leverage ratio*. Debt-to-equity ratio. A too-high leverage ratio indicates excessive indebtedness, signalling the possibility the firm will be unable to earn enough to satisfy the obligations on its bonds.
3. *Liquidity ratios*. The two common liquidity ratios are the *current ratio* (current assets/current liabilities) and the *quick ratio* (current assets excluding inventories/current

"On average, high-yield bonds have coupons that are 300 to 500 basis points higher than government bonds. They also typically mature in under 10 years, which makes them less sensitive to changes in long rates," says Mr. Cheng.

Mr. Cheng's fund, which returned 4.3 per cent in the year ended Dec. 31, underperformed the average Canadian bond fund's 6.7 per cent, but was nevertheless, among the dozen junk bond funds that are available.

How did he get there? Mr. Cheng credits a well-diversified portfolio of about 50 companies, with no single holding accounting for more than 3 per cent.

He also likes to move up the credit spectrum, taking advantage of more stable bonds during volatile markets. A-rated Bell Canada and BBB-rated names like waste management giant Laidlaw Inc. helped support the BPI fund last year.

This year, Mr. Cheng believes that junk bonds should regain the upper hand, based on his positive view of interest rates and a bullish outlook for stocks.

Another reason that junk bonds should shine is because of a continued government aversion to deficit financing, Mr. Hallett says. As government bond issues become scarcer, investors are forced to look further down the credit spectrum, boosting the popularity of junk bonds, he says.

Among other junk bond funds, Mr. Hallett likes the $806-million Trimark Advantage Bond Fund, the No. 2 performer among such funds last year, with a return of 3.9 per cent.

The Trimark fund minimizes volatility by offering a blend of high-quality government bonds and junk bonds. It is managed by Patrick Farmer, Toronto-based vice-president at Trimark Investment Management Inc.

"I'm comfortable with Pat Farmer's investment style. During the big market meltdown in September and October, his fund really held in well for my clients," says Geoffrey Belisle, a senior investment adviser and Toronto-based branch manager with Toronto-Dominion Bank's TD Evergreen wealth management services.

While both the BPI and Trimark funds are not shy about moving into investment-grade bonds when markets are volatile, investors willing to take bigger risks may want to focus on funds that invest exclusively in higher-yielding, lower-grade credits.

Mr. Folk likes the more aggressive $360.5-million O'Donnell High Income Fund, managed by Doug Knight, a partner at Vancouver-based Deans Knight Capital Management Ltd., which returned 0.9 per cent last year. It is typically invested fully in higher-yielding bonds. Top holdings include forest products company Avenor Inc., cable giant Rogers Communications Inc. and banking conglomerate Hees International Bancorp Inc.

"Knight has been doing a good job for years. He hates highly rated debt because he can't get the extra yield he's looking for," says Mr. Folk. "The O'Donnell High Income Fund can give equity-like returns without all of the equity risk."

If you do invest in a junk-bond fund, analysts caution that, like stock holdings, they should be kept for the long term. "High-yield bond funds are a three-to-four-year commitment," Mr. Hallett says.

Source: Matthew Bonsall, "Junk Can Be Treasure for Investors," *The Globe and Mail*, January 21, 1999, p. C6. Reprinted by permission of the author.

liabilities). These ratios measure the firm's ability to pay bills coming due with cash currently being collected.

4. *Profitability ratio*. Measures of rates of return on assets or equity. Profitability ratios are indicators of a firm's overall financial health. The *return on assets* (earnings before interest and taxes divided by total assets) is the most popular of these measures. Firms with higher return on assets should be better able to raise money in security markets because they offer prospects for better returns on the firm's investments.
5. *Cash-flow-to-debt ratio*. This is the ratio of total cash flow to outstanding debt.

Standard & Poor's periodically computes median values of selected ratios for firms in several rating classes, which we present in Table 11.3. Of course, ratios must be evaluated in the context of industry standards, and analysts differ in the weights they place on particular ratios. Nevertheless, Table 11.3 demonstrates the tendency of ratios to improve along with the firm's rating class.

Direct statistical tests of the ability of financial ratios to predict bond ratings in the five top rating classes of the Canadian Bond Rating Service[10] (CBRS) were conducted in a study by Barnes and Byng.[11] The study examined 27 financial variables that included ratios similar to those in

[10]CBRS was bought up by Standard & Poor's in 2000.

[11]Tom Barnes and Tom Byng, "The Prediction of Corporate Bond Ratings: The Canadian Case," *Canadian Journal of Administrative Sciences* 5, no. 3 (September 1988).

Table 11.3 Financial Ratios by Rating Class

3-Year (1998 to 2000) Medians	AAA	AA	A	BBB	BB	B	CCC
EBIT interest coverage ratio	21.4	10.1	6.1	3.7	2.1	0.8	0.1
EBITDA interest coverage	26.5	12.9	9.1	5.8	3.4	1.8	1.3
Funds flow/total debt (%)	84.2	25.2	15.0	8.5	2.6	−3.2	−12.9
Free operating cash flow/total debt (%)	128.8	55.4	43.2	30.8	18.8	7.8	1.6
Return on capital (%)	34.9	21.7	19.4	13.6	11.6	6.6	1.0
Operating income/sales (%)	27.0	22.1	18.6	15.4	15.9	11.9	11.9
Long-term debt/capital (%)	13.3	28.2	33.9	42.5	57.2	69.7	68.8
Total debt/capital (incl. STD) (%)	22.9	37.7	42.5	48.2	62.6	74.8	87.7

Note: EBITDA, earnings before interest, taxes, depreciation, and amortization; STD, short-term debt.

Source: Standard & Poor's *Credit Week*, July 28, 2001. Used by permission of Standard & Poor's.

Table 11.3, as well as variables representing the size and earnings stability of the firm. The results showed that the observed ratings assigned by CBRS in the years 1972, 1978, and 1983 could be predicted fairly accurately by an appropriate set of weights applied to the 27 variables for each year. These weights, though, tended to change from year to year, and the accuracy of one year's predictors tended to deteriorate with time.

Many studies have tested whether financial ratios can in fact be used to predict default risk. One of the best-known series of tests has been conducted by Edward Altman, who has used discriminant analysis to predict bankruptcy. With this technique, a firm is assigned a score based on its financial characteristics. If its score exceeds a cutoff value, the firm is deemed creditworthy. A score below the cutoff value indicates significant bankruptcy risk in the near future.

To illustrate the technique, suppose that we were to collect data on the return on equity (ROE) and coverage ratios of a sample of firms and then keep records of any corporate bankruptcies. In Figure 11.8 we plot the ROE and coverage ratios for each firm using *X* for firms that eventually went bankrupt and *O* for those who remained solvent. Clearly, the *X* and *O* firms show different patterns of data, with the solvent firms typically showing higher values for the two ratios.

The discriminant analysis determines the equation of the line that best separates the *X* and *O* observations. Suppose that the equation of the line is $.75 = .9 \times \text{ROE} + .4 \times \text{Coverage}$. Each firm is assigned a "Z-score" equal to $.9 \times \text{ROE} + .4 \times \text{Coverage}$ using the firm's ROE and coverage ratios. If the Z-score exceeds .75, the firm plots above the line and is considered a safe bet; Z-scores below .75 foretell financial difficulty.

The discriminant analysis method was applied to a sample of Canadian firms in a study by Altman and Lavallee,[12] who found the following equation to best separate failing and nonfailing firms:

$$
\begin{aligned}
Z = 0.234 \frac{\text{Sales}}{\text{Total assets}} &+ 0.972 \frac{\text{Net after-tax profits}}{\text{Total debt}} \\
&+ 1.002 \frac{\text{Current assets}}{\text{Current liabilities}} - 0.531 \frac{\text{Total debt}}{\text{Total assets}} \\
&+ 0.612\,(\text{Rate of equity growth} - \text{Rate of asset growth})
\end{aligned}
$$

Firms with Z-scores above 1.626 were deemed safe; 81.5 percent of these were still in business in the next year. In contrast, 85.2 percent of bankrupt firms had Z-scores below 1.626 the year before they failed.

[12]Edward I. Altman and Marion Y. Lavallee, "Business Failure Classification in Canada," *Journal of Business Administration* 12, no. 1 (Fall 1980).

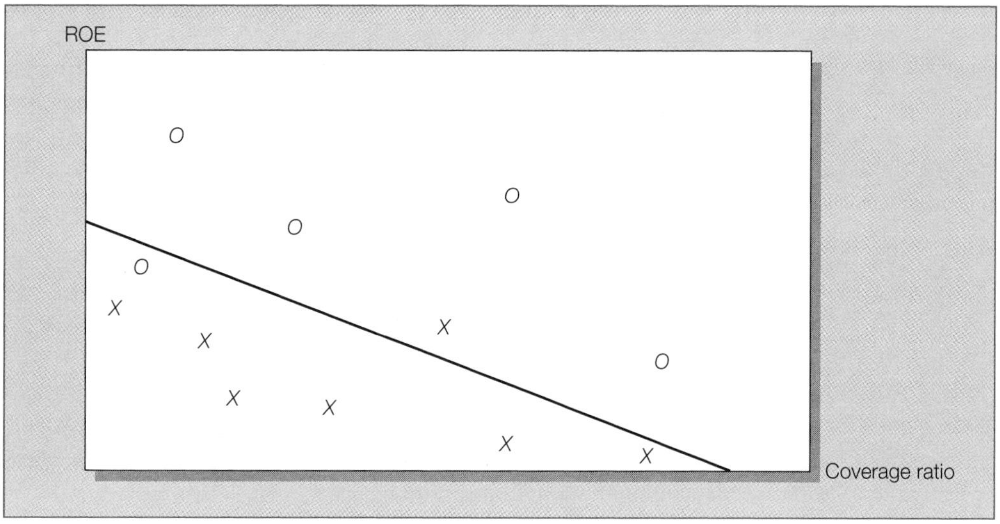

Figure 11.8 Discriminant analysis.

A rather more skeptical view of the ability of financial ratios to predict default risk emerges from a Canadian study of *small-business* debt (mainly bank loans) by Kryzanowski and To.[13] They found that default risk depended on variables such as the firm's size and age, the type of loan, and the project performance assessment made by the lending institution. Several important financial ratios were examined, and none of them were found to be a significant determinant of default risk. It seems, therefore, that financial ratios are not good indicators of such risk for small businesses.

CONCEPT CHECK

8. Suppose we add to the Altman-Lavallee equation a new variable equal to market value of equity/book value of debt. Would you expect this variable to receive a positive or negative coefficient?

Bond Indentures

A bond is issued with an **indenture,** which is the contract between the issuer and the bondholder. Part of the indenture is a set of restrictions on the firm issuing the bond to protect the rights of the bondholders. Such restrictions include provisions relating to collateral, sinking funds, dividend policy, and further borrowing. The issuing firm agrees to these so-called *protective covenants* in order to market its bonds to investors concerned about the safety of the bond issue.

Sinking Funds Bonds call for the payment of par value at the end of the bond's life. This payment constitutes a large cash commitment for the issuer. To help ensure the commitment does not create a cash flow crisis, the firm agrees to establish a **sinking fund** to spread the payment burden over several years. The fund may operate in one of two ways:

1. The firm may repurchase a fraction of the outstanding bonds in the open market each year.
2. The firm may purchase a fraction of outstanding bonds at a special call price associated with the sinking fund provision. The firm has an option to purchase the bonds at either the market price or the sinking fund price, whichever is lower. To allocate the burden of

[13]Lawrence Kryzanowski and Minh Chau To, "Small-Business Debt Financing: An Empirical Investigation of Default Risk," *Canadian Journal of Administrative Sciences* 2, no. 1 (June 1985).

the sinking fund call fairly among bondholders, the bonds chosen for the call are selected at random on the basis of serial numbers.[14]

The sinking fund call differs from a conventional bond call in two important ways. First, the firm can repurchase only a limited fraction of the bond issue at the sinking fund call price. At best, some indentures allow firms to use a *doubling option,* which allows repurchase of double the required number of bonds at the sinking fund call price. Second, the sinking fund call price generally is lower than the call price established by other call provisions in the indenture. The sinking fund call price usually is set at the bond's par value.

Although sinking funds ostensibly protect bondholders by making principal repayment more likely, they can hurt the investor. If interest rates fall and bond prices rise, firms will benefit from the sinking fund provision that enables them to repurchase their bonds at below-market prices. In these circumstances, the firm's gain is the bondholder's loss.

One bond issue that does not require a sinking fund is a *serial bond issue.* In a serial bond issue, the firm sells bonds with staggered maturity dates. As bonds mature sequentially, the principal repayment burden for the firm is spread over time just as it is with a sinking fund. Serial bonds do not include call provisions.

Subordination of Further Debt One of the factors determining bond safety is total outstanding debt of the issuer. If you bought a bond today, you would be understandably distressed to see the firm tripling its outstanding debt tomorrow. Your bond would be of lower quality than it appeared when you bought it. To prevent firms from harming bondholders in this manner, **subordination clauses** restrict the amount of additional borrowing. Additional debt might be required to be subordinated in priority to existing debt; that is, in the event of bankruptcy, *subordinated* or *junior* debtholders will not be paid unless and until the prior senior debt is fully paid off. For this reason, subordination is sometimes called a "me-first rule," meaning the senior (earlier) bondholders are to be paid first in the event of bankruptcy.

Dividend Restrictions Covenants also limit firms in the amount of dividends they are allowed to pay. These limitations protect the bondholders because they force the firm to retain assets rather than paying them out to shareholders. A typical restriction disallows payments of dividends if cumulative dividends paid since the firm's inception exceed cumulative net income plus proceeds from sales of stock.

Collateral Some bonds are issued with specific collateral behind them. **Collateral** can take several forms, but it represents a particular asset of the firm that the bondholders receive if the firm defaults on the bond. If the collateral is property, the bond is called a *mortgage bond.* If the collateral takes the form of other securities held by the firm, the bond is a *collateral trust bond.* In the case of equipment, the bond is known as an *equipment obligation bond.* This last form of collateral is used most commonly by firms such as railroads, where the equipment is fairly standard and can be easily sold to another firm should the firm default and the bondholders acquire the collateral.

Because of the specific collateral that backs them, collateralized bonds generally are considered the safest variety of corporate bonds. General **debenture** bonds by contrast do not provide for specific collateral; they are *unsecured* bonds. The bondholder relies solely on the general earning power of the firm for the bond's safety. If the firm defaults, debenture owners become general creditors of the firm. Because they are safer, collateralized bonds generally offer lower yields than general debentures.

---

[14]Although it is uncommon, the sinking fund provision also may call for periodic payments to a trustee, with the payments invested so that the accumulated sum can be used for retirement of the entire issue at maturity.

Figure 11.9
Callable bond issued by Mobil.

& Mobil Corp. debenture 8s, due 2032:
Rating — Aa2

AUTH — $250,000,000.
OUTSTG — Dec. 31, 1993, $250,000,000.
DATED — Oct. 30, 1991.
INTEREST — F&A 12.
TRUSTEE — Chemical Bank.
DENOMINATION — Fully registered, $1,000 and integral multiples thereof. Transferable and exchangeable without service charge.
CALLABLE — As a whole or in part, at any time, on or after Aug. 12, 2002, at the option of Co. on at least 30 but not more than 60 days' notice to each Aug. 11 as follows:

2003.......105.007	2004.......104.756	2005.......104.506
2006.......104.256	2007.......104.005	2008.......103.755
2009.......103.505	2010.......103.254	2011.......103.004
2012.......102.754	2013.......102.503	2014.......102.253
2015.......102.003	2016.......101.752	2017.......101.502
2018.......101.252	2019.......101.001	2020.......100.751
2021.......100.501	2022.......100.250	

and thereafter at 100 plus accrued interest.
SECURITY — Not secured. Ranks equally with all other unsecured and unsubordinated indebtedness of Co. Co. nor any Affiliate will not incurr any indebtedness; provided that Co. will not create as security for any indebtedness for borrowed money, any mortgage, pledge, security interest or lien on any stock or indebtedness is directly owned by Co., without effectively providing that the debt securities shall be secured equally and ratably with such indebtedness, so long as such indebtedness shall be so secured.
INDENTURE MODIFICATION — Indenture may be modified, except as provided with, consent of 66⅔% of debs. outstg.
RIGHTS ON DEFAULT — Trustee, or 25% of debs. outstg., may declare principal dua nad payable (30 days' grace for payment of interest).
LISTED — On New York Stock Exchange.
PURPOSE — Proceeds used for general corporate purposes.
OFFERED — ($250,000,000) at 99.51 plus accrued interest (proceeds to Co., 99.11) on Aug. 5 1992 thru Merrill Lynch & Co., Donaldson, Lufkin & Jenerette Securities Corp., PaineWebber Inc., Prudential Securities Inc., Smith Barney, Harris Upham & Co. Inc. and associates.

Source: *Moody's Industrial Manual*, Moody's Investor Services, 1994.

Figure 11.9 shows the terms of a bond issued by Mobil as described in *Moody's Industrial Manual*. The terms of the bond are typical and illustrate many of the indenture provisions we have mentioned. The bond is registered and listed on the NYSE. Although it was issued in 1991, it was not callable until 2002. Although the call price started at 105.007 percent of par value, it falls gradually until it reaches par after 2020.

Yield to Maturity and Default Risk

Because corporate bonds are subject to default risk, we must distinguish between the bond's promised yield to maturity and its expected yield. The promised or stated yield will be realized only if the firm meets the obligations of the bond issue. Therefore, the stated yield is the *maximum possible* yield to maturity of the bond. The expected yield to maturity must take into account the possibility of a default.

For example, in April 1999, Service Merchandise was in bankruptcy proceedings, and its bonds due in 2004 were selling at about 23 percent of par value, resulting in a yield to maturity of over 60 percent. Investors did not really expect these bonds to provide a 60 percent rate of return. They recognized that bondholders were very unlikely to receive all the payments promised in the bond contract, and that the yield based on *expected* cash flows was far less than the yield based on *promised* cash flows.

To illustrate the difference between expected and promised yield to maturity, suppose a firm issued a 9 percent coupon bond 20 years ago. The bond now has 10 years left until its maturity date but the firm is having financial difficulties. Investors believe that the firm will be able to make good on the remaining interest payments, but that at the maturity date, the firm will be forced into bankruptcy, and bondholders will receive only 70 percent of par value. The bond is selling at $750.

Yield to maturity (YTM) would then be calculated using the following inputs:

	Expected YTM	Stated YTM
Coupon payment	$45	$45
Number of semiannual periods	20 periods	20 periods
Final payment	$700	$1,000
Price	$750	$750

The yield to maturity based on promised payments is 13.7 percent. Based on the expected payment of $700 at maturity, however, the yield to maturity would be only 11.6 percent. The stated yield to maturity is greater than the yield investors actually expect to receive.

CONCEPT CHECK

9. What is the expected yield to maturity if the firm is in even worse condition and investors expect a final payment of only $600?

To compensate for the possibility of default, corporate bonds must offer a **default premium**. The default premium is the difference between the promised yield on a corporate bond and the yield of an otherwise-identical government bond that is riskless in terms of default. If the firm remains solvent and actually pays the investor all of the promised cash flows, the investor will realize a higher yield to maturity than would be realized from the government bond. If, however, the firm goes bankrupt, the corporate bond is likely to provide a lower return than the government bond. The corporate bond has the potential for both better and worse performance than the default-free Treasury bond. In other words, it is riskier.

The pattern of default premiums offered on risky bonds is sometimes called the *risk structure of interest rates*. The greater the default risk, the higher the default premium. Figure 11.10 shows

Figure 11.10 Yields on long-term bonds.

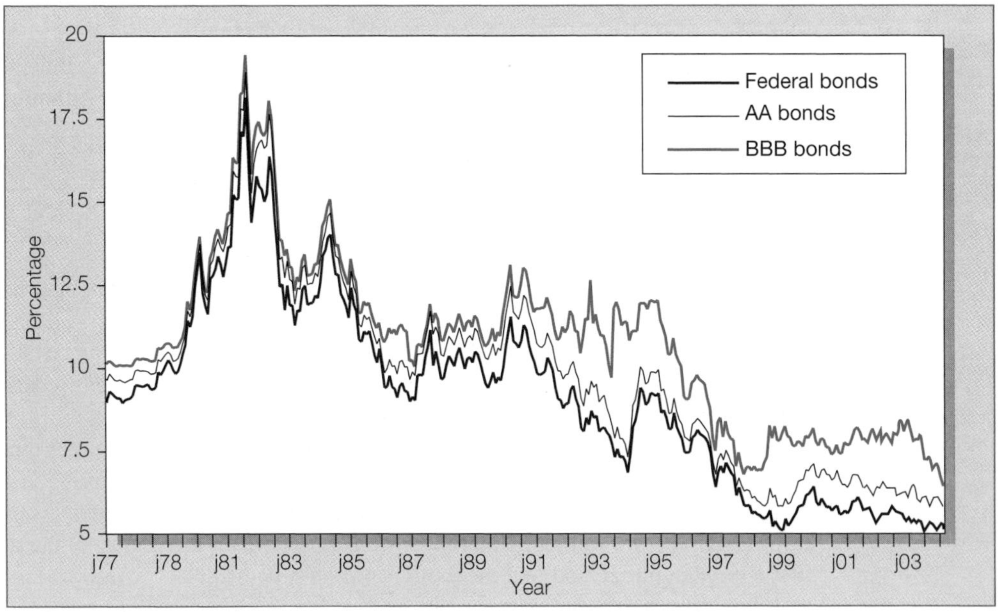

Source: Scotia Capital, *Debt Market Indices*, various years.

yield to maturity of bonds of different risk classes since 1977. You can see here clear evidence of credit-risk premiums on promised yields.

One particular manner in which yield spreads seem to vary over time is related to the business cycle. Yield spreads tend to be wider when the economy is in a recession. Apparently, investors perceive a higher probability of bankruptcy when the economy is faltering, even holding bond ratings constant. They require a commensurately higher default premium. This is sometimes termed a *flight to quality*, meaning that investors move their funds into safer bonds unless they can obtain larger premiums on lower-rated securities.

SUMMARY

1. Fixed-income securities are distinguished by their promise to pay a fixed or specified stream of income to their holders. The coupon bond is a typical fixed-income security.
2. Government bonds have original maturities greater than one year. They are issued at or near par value, with their prices quoted net of accrued interest.
3. Callable bonds should offer higher promised yields to maturity to compensate investors for the fact that they will not realize full capital gains should the interest rate fall and the bonds be called away from them at the stipulated call price. Bonds often are issued with a period of call protection. In addition, discount bonds selling significantly below their call price offer implicit call protection.
4. Retractable and extendible bonds give the bondholder rather than the issuer the option to terminate or extend the life of the bond.
5. Convertible bonds may be exchanged, at the bondholder's discretion, for a specified number of shares of stock. Convertible bondholders "pay" for this option by accepting a lower coupon rate on the security.
6. Floating-rate bonds pay a fixed premium over a reference short-term interest rate. Risk is limited because the rate paid is tied to current market conditions.
7. The yield to maturity is the single interest rate that equates the present value of a security's cash flows to its price. Bond prices and yields are inversely related. For premium bonds, the coupon rate is greater than the current yield, which is greater than the yield to maturity. The order of these inequalities is reversed for discount bonds.
8. The yield to maturity often is interpreted as an estimate of the average rate of return to an investor who purchases a bond and holds it until maturity. This interpretation is subject to error, however. Related measures are yield to call, realized compound yield, and expected (versus promised) yield to maturity.
9. Prices of zero-coupon bonds rise exponentially over time, providing a rate of appreciation equal to the interest rate. CRA treats this price appreciation as imputed taxable interest income to the investor.
10. When bonds are subject to default, the stated yield to maturity is the maximum possible yield to maturity that can be realized by the bondholder. In the event of default, however, that promised yield will not be realized. To compensate bond investors for default risk, bonds must offer default premiums, that is, promised yields in excess of those offered by default-free government securities. If the firm remains healthy, its bonds will provide higher returns than government bonds. Otherwise the returns may be lower.
11. Bond safety is often measured using financial ratio analysis. Bond indentures are another safeguard to protect the claims of bondholders. Common indentures specify sinking fund requirements, collateralization of the loan, dividend restrictions, and subordination of future debt.

KEY TERMS

fixed-income securities 392
bond 393
par value 393
face value 393
coupon rate 393
bond indenture 393
zero-coupon bonds 393
convertible bonds 396
retractable bond 396
extendible bond 396
floating-rate bonds 396
yield to maturity (YTM) 404
horizon analysis 408
investment-grade bonds 412
speculative-grade bonds 412

junk bonds 412
indenture 417
sinking fund 417
subordination clauses 418
collateral 418
debenture 418
default premium 420

SELECTED READINGS

A comprehensive treatment of price issues related to fixed-income securities is given in:

Fabozzi, Frank J. *Bond Markets, Analysis, and Strategies*, 4th ed. Englewood Cliffs, NJ: Prentice Hall, 2000.

Surveys of fixed-income instruments and investment characteristics are contained in:

Fabozzi, Frank J., and T. Dessa Fabozzi. *The Handbook of Fixed Income Securities*. Homewood, IL: Business One Irwin, 1995.

Stigum, Marcia, and Frank J. Fabozzi. *The Dow-Jones Guide to Bond and Money Market Investments*. Homewood, IL: Dow Jones–Irwin, 1987.

Surveys of Canadian fixed-income instruments can be found in:

Hunter, W. T. *Canadian Financial Markets*. Peterborough, ON: Broadview, 1988.

Canadian Securities Institute. *The Canadian Securities Course* (annual).

Canadian references on retractable and extendible bonds include:

Ananthanarayanan, A. L., and Eduardo Schwartz. "Retractable and Extendible Bonds: The Canadian Experience." *Journal of Finance* 35, no. 1 (March 1980).

Dipchand, Cecil R., and Robert J. Hanrahan. "Exit and Exchange Option Values on Government of Canada Retractable Bonds." *Financial Management* 8, no. 3 (Autumn 1979).

PROBLEMS

1. Which security has a higher *effective* annual interest rate?

a. A three-month T-bill selling at $97,645 with par value $100,000

b. A coupon bond selling at par and paying a 10 percent coupon semiannually

2. Treasury bonds paying an 8 percent coupon rate with *semiannual* payments currently sell at par value. What coupon rate would they have to pay in order to sell at par if they paid their coupons *annually*?

3. Two bonds have identical times to maturity and coupon rates. One is callable at 105, the other at 110. Which should have the higher yield to maturity? Why?

4. Consider a bond with a 10 percent coupon and with yield to maturity = 8 percent. If the bond's yield to maturity remains constant, then in one year, will the bond price be higher, lower, or unchanged? Why?

5. Consider an 8 percent coupon bond selling for $953.10 with three years until maturity making *annual* coupon payments. The interest rates in the next three years will be, with certainty, $r_1 = 8\%$, $r_2 = 10\%$, and $r_3 = 12\%$. Calculate the yield to maturity and realized compound yield of the bond.

CFA® PROBLEMS

6. Bonds of Zello Corporation with a par value of $1,000 sell for $960, mature in five years, and have a 7 percent annual coupon rate paid semiannually.

a. Calculate the

i. Current yield

ii. Yield to maturity (to the nearest whole percent, i.e., 3 percent, 4 percent, 5 percent, etc.)

iii. Realized compound yield for an investor with a three-year holding period and a reinvestment rate of 6 percent over the period; at the end of three years the 7 percent coupon bonds with two years remaining will sell to yield 7 percent

b. Cite one major shortcoming for each of the following fixed-income yield measures:

i. Current yield

ii. Yield to maturity

iii. Realized compound yield

7. Assume you have a one-year investment horizon and are trying to choose among three bonds. All have the same degree of default risk and mature in 10 years. The first is a zero-coupon bond that pays $1,000 at maturity. The second has an 8 percent coupon rate and pays the $80 coupon once per year. The third has a 10 percent coupon rate and pays the $100 coupon once per year.
   a. If all three bonds are now priced to yield 8 percent to maturity, what are their prices?
   b. If you expect their yields to maturity to be 8 percent at the beginning of next year, what will their prices be then? What is your before-tax holding period return on each bond? If your tax bracket is 30 percent on ordinary income and 20 percent on capital gains income, what will your after-tax rate of return be on each?
   c. Recalculate your answer to (*b*) under the assumption that you expect the yields to maturity on each bond to be 7 percent at the beginning of next year.
8. Consider a bond paying a coupon rate of 10 percent per year semiannually when the market interest rate is only 4 percent per half year. The bond has three years until maturity.
   a. Find the bond's price today and six months from now after the next coupon is paid.
   b. What is the total rate of return on the bond?
9. A 20-year maturity bond with par value of $1,000 makes semiannual coupon payments at a coupon rate of 8 percent. Find the bond equivalent and effective annual yield to maturity of the bond if the bond price is:
   a. $950
   b. $1,000
   c. $1,050
10. Repeat problem 9 using the same data, but assuming that the bond makes its coupon payments annually. Why are the yields you compute lower in this case?
11. Fill in the table below for the following zero-coupon bonds, all of which have par values of $1,000.

Price ($)	Maturity (years)	Bond-Equivalent Yield to Maturity (%)
400	20	___
500	20	___
500	10	___
___	10	10
___	10	8
400	___	8

12. A newly issued bond pays its coupons once annually. Its coupon rate is 5 percent, its maturity is 20 years, and its yield to maturity is 8 percent.
   a. Find the holding period return for a one-year investment period if the bond is selling at a yield to maturity of 7 percent by the end of the year.
   b. If you sell the bond after one year, what taxes will you owe if the tax rate on interest income is 40 percent and the tax rate on capital gains income is 30 percent? The bond is subject to original issue discount tax treatment.
   c. What is the after-tax holding period return on the bond?
   d. Find the realized compound yield *before taxes* for a two-year holding period, assuming that (1) you sell the bond after two years; (2) the bond yield is 7 percent at the end of the second year; and (3) the coupon can be reinvested for one year at a 3 percent interest rate.
   e. Use the tax rates in part (*b*) to compute the *after-tax* two-year realized compound yield. Remember to take account of OID tax rules.

13. A bond with a coupon rate of 7 percent makes semiannual coupon payments on January 15 and July 15 of each year. *The Globe and Mail* reports the price for the bond on January 30 at 100.02. What is the invoice price of the bond? The coupon period has 182 days.

14. A bond has a current yield of 9 percent and a yield to maturity of 10 percent. Is the bond selling above or below par value? Explain.

15. Is the coupon rate of the bond in problem 14 more or less than 9 percent?

16. Return to Table 11.1 and calculate the real and nominal rates of return on the RRB bond in the second and third years.

17. A newly issued 20-year maturity, zero-coupon bond is issued with a yield to maturity of 8 percent and a face value of $1,000. Find the imputed interest income in the first, second, and last year of the bond's life.

18. A newly issued 10-year maturity, 4 percent coupon bond making *annual* coupon payments is sold to the public at a price of $800. What will be an investor's taxable income from the bond over the coming year? The bond will not be sold at the end of the year. The bond is treated as an original issue discount bond.

19. A 30-year maturity, 8 percent coupon bond paying coupons semiannually is callable in five years at a call price of $1,100. The bond currently sells at a yield to maturity of 7 percent (3.5 percent per half-year).

a. What is the yield to call?

b. What is the yield to call if the call price is only $1,050?

c. What is the yield to call if the call price is $1,100, but the bond can be called in two years instead of five years?

20. A 10-year bond of a firm in severe financial distress has a coupon rate of 14 percent and sells for $900. The firm is currently renegotiating the debt, and it appears that the lenders will allow the firm to reduce coupon payments on the bond to one-half the originally contracted amount. The firm can handle these lower payments. What is the stated and expected yield to maturity of the bonds? The bond makes its coupon payments annually.

21. A two-year bond with a par value of $1,000 making annual coupon payments of $100 is priced at $1,000. What is the yield to maturity of the bond? What will be the realized compound yield to maturity if the one-year interest rate next year turns out to be (*a*) 8 percent, (*b*) 10 percent, (*c*) 12 percent?

22. The stated yield to maturity and realized compound yield to maturity of a (default-free) zero-coupon bond always will be equal. Why?

23. Suppose that today's date is April 15. A bond with a 10 percent coupon paid semiannually every January 15 and July 15 is listed as selling at an ask price of 101.125. If you buy the bond from a dealer today, what price will you pay for it?

CFA® PROBLEMS

24. In June 1982, when the yield to maturity (YTM) on long-term bonds was about 14 percent, many observers were projecting an eventual decline in these rates. It was not unusual to hear of customers urging portfolio managers to "lock in" these high rates by buying some new issues with these high coupons. You recognize that it is not possible to really lock in such returns for coupon bonds because of the potential reinvestment rate problem if rates decline. Assuming the following expectations for a five-year bond bought at par, compute the total realized compound yield (without taxes) for the bond below.

Coupon: 14% (assume annual interest payments at end of each year)
Maturity: Five years
One-year reinvestment rates during:
Year 2, 3: 10%
Year 4, 5: 8%

25. Assume that two firms issue bonds with the following characteristics. Both bonds are issued at par.

	ABC Bonds	XYZ Bonds
Issue size	$1.2 billion	$150 million
Maturity	10 years*	20 years
Coupon	9%	10%
Collateral	First mortgage	General debenture
Callable	Not callable	In 10 years
Call price	None	110
Sinking fund	None	Starting in 5 years

*Bond is extendible at the discretion of the bondholder for an additional 10 years.

Ignoring credit quality, identify four features of these issues that might account for the lower coupon on the ABC debt. Explain.

26. A large corporation issued both fixed- and floating-rate notes five years ago, with terms given in the following table:

	9% Coupon Notes	Floating-Rate Note
Issue size	$250 million	$280 million
Maturity	20 years	10 years
Current price (% of par)	93	98
Current coupon	9%	8%
Coupon adjusts	Fixed coupon	Every year
Coupon reset rule	—	1-year T-bill rate +2%
Callable	10 years after issue	10 years after issue
Call price	106	102
Sinking fund	None	None
Yield to maturity	9.9%	—
Price range since issued	$85 1/8–$112	$97–$102

a. Why is the price range greater for the 9 percent coupon bond than the floating-rate note?

b. What factors could explain why the floating-rate note is not always sold at par value?

c. Why is the call price for the floating-rate note not of great importance to investors?

d. Is the probability of call for the fixed-rate note high or low?

e. If the firm were to issue a fixed-rate note with a 15-year maturity, what coupon rate would it need to offer to issue the bond at par value?

f. Why is an entry for yield to maturity for the floating-rate note not appropriate?

CFA® PROBLEMS

27. On May 30, 1999, Janice Kerr is considering one of the newly issued 10-year AAA corporate bonds:

Description	Coupon	Price	Callable	Call Price
Sentinel, due May 30, 2009	6.00%	100	Noncallable	NA
Colina, due May 30, 2009	6.20%	100	Currently callable	102

a. Suppose that market interest rates decline by 100 basis points (i.e., 1 percent). Contrast the effect of this decline on the price of each bond.

Visit us at www.mcgrawhill.ca/college/bodie

b. Should Kerr prefer the Colina over the Sentinel bond when rates are expected to rise or to fall?

c. What would be the effect, if any, of an increase in the *volatility* of interest rates on the prices of each bond?

28. Masters Corp. issues two bonds with 20-year maturities. Both bonds are callable at $1,050. The first bond is issued at a deep discount with a coupon rate of 4 percent and a price of $580 to yield 8.4 percent. The second bond is issued at par value with a coupon rate of 8¾ percent.

a. What is the yield to maturity of the par bond? Why is it higher than the yield of the discount bond?

b. If you expect rates to fall substantially in the next two years, which bond would you prefer to hold?

c. In what sense does the discount bond offer "implicit call protection"?

CFA® PROBLEMS

29. A convertible bond has the following features:

Coupon	5.25%
Maturity	June 15, 2027
Market price of bond	$77.50
Market price of underlying common stock	$28.00
Annual dividend	$1.20
Conversion ratio	20.83 shares

Calculate the conversion premium for this bond.

CFA® PROBLEMS

30. *a.* In terms of option theory, explain the impact on the offering yield of adding a call feature to a proposed bond issue.

b. Explain the impact on the bond's expected life of adding a call feature to a proposed bond issue.

c. Describe *one* advantage and *one* disadvantage of including callable bonds in a portfolio.

CFA® PROBLEMS

31. The multiple-choice problems following are based on questions that appeared in past CFA examinations.

a. The spread between Treasury and BAA corporate bond yields widens when
   i. Interest rates are low
   ii. There is economic uncertainty
   iii. There is a "flight from quality"
   iv. All of the above

b. The market risk of an AAA-rated preferred stock relative to an AAA-rated bond is
   i. Lower
   ii. Higher
   iii. Equal
   iv. Unknown

c. A bond with a call feature
   i. Is attractive because the immediate receipt of principal plus premium produces a high return
   ii. Is more apt to be called when interest rates are high because the interest saving will be greater
   iii. Will usually have a higher yield than a similar noncallable bond
   iv. None of the above

d. The yield to maturity on a bond is
   i. Below the coupon rate when the bond sells at a discount, and above the coupon rate when the bond sells at a premium
   ii. The discount rate that will set the present value of the payments equal to the bond price

iii. The current yield plus the average annual capital gains rate
iv. Based on the assumption that any payments received are reinvested at the coupon rate

e. A particular bond has a yield to maturity on an APR basis of 12.00 percent but makes equal quarterly payments. What is the effective annual yield to maturity?
i. 11.45 percent
ii. 12.00 percent
iii. 12.55 percent
iv. 37.35 percent

f. In which *one* of the following cases is the bond selling at a discount?
i. Coupon rate is greater than current yield, which is greater than yield to maturity.
ii. Coupon rate, current yield, and yield to maturity are all the same.
iii. Coupon rate is less than current yield, which is less than yield to maturity.
iv. Coupon rate is less than current yield, which is greater than yield to maturity.

g. Consider a five-year bond with a 10 percent coupon that has a present yield to maturity of 8 percent. If interest rates remain constant, one year from now the price of this bond will be:
i. Higher
ii. Lower
iii. The same
iv. Par

h. Which *one* of the following is *not* an advantage of convertible bonds for the investor?
i. The yield on the convertible will typically be higher than the yield on the underlying common stock.
ii. The convertible bond will likely participate in a major upward move in the price of the underlying common stock.
iii. Convertible bonds typically are secured by specific assets of the issuing company.
iv. Investors normally may convert to the underlying common stock.

i. The call feature of a bond means the
i. Investor can call for payment on demand
ii. Investor can only call if the firm defaults on an interest payment
iii. Issuer can call the bond issue before the maturity date
iv. Issuer can call the issue during the first three years

j. The annual interest paid on a bond relative to its prevailing market price is called its
i. Promised yield
ii. Yield to maturity
iii. Coupon rate
iv. Current yield

k. Which *one* of the following statements about convertible bonds is *false*?
i. The yield on the convertible typically will be higher than the yield on the underlying common stock.
ii. The convertible bond will likely participate in a major upward movement in the price of the underlying common stock.
iii. Convertible bonds typically are secured by specific assets of the issuing company.
iv. A convertible bond can be valued as a straight bond with an attached option.

l. All else being equal, which *one* of the following bonds would be *most likely* to sell at the highest yield?
i. Callable debenture
ii. Puttable mortgage bond
iii. Callable mortgage bond
iv. Puttable debentures

m. Yields on nonconvertible preferred stock usually are lower than yields on bonds of the same company because of differences in
   i. Marketability
   ii. Risk
   iii. Taxation
   iv. Call protection

n. The yield to maturity on a bond is
   i. Below the coupon rate when the bond sells at a discount and above the coupon rate when the bond sells at a premium
   ii. The interest rate that makes the present value of the payments equal to the bond price
   iii. Based on the assumption that all future payments received are reinvested at the coupon rate
   iv. Based on the assumption that all future payments received are reinvested at future market rates

The following questions are adapted from the Canadian Securities Course.

CSI

32. Which of the following statements regarding long-term debt is correct?
a. Bonds are usually secured by real assets.
b. Subordinated debentures rank behind some other long-term debt security.
c. A collateral trust bond is usually secured by financial assets.
d. A unit is a package of two or more corporate securities for sale at an overall price.

33. Which of the following bond theorems is/are correct?
a. Bond prices move inversely to interest rates.
b. The longer the term to maturity the greater the interest-rate risk.
c. Bonds with low coupon rates have more price volatility than bonds with high coupon rates.
d. Bond prices are more volatile when interest rates are high.

34. "Bond ratings are an excellent indication of the quality of bond issues. Other things being equal, the lower the rating the higher the coupon rate and the higher the interest cost to the firm." True or false?

35. The yield on short-term and long-term bonds tends to vary. When the return on bonds with different maturity dates is plotted on a graph, the plot is called a(n) ______________.

36. "If two bonds, issued on the same day, had the same maturity dates and the same market prices, then a higher coupon rate on one would imply that it has a higher risk." True or false?

37. A 10-year bond was issued three years ago at par. The coupon rate on the bond was 10 percent and its par value or face value is $1,000. If the bond's current market price is $1,000 and it is rated as A++, which of the following statements regarding this issue is/are correct?
a. The term to maturity is 7 years.
b. The annual interest payment would be $100.
c. At its current market price, the average purchase/redemption yield would be 10 percent.
d. The bond is investment-grade.

38. A bond is quoted in the newspaper as follows:

Coupon	3.5%
Maturity date	1 July 08/98
Bid	99.25
Ask	99.75

Which of the following statements would be correct?
a. The bond pays $35 in interest on a $1,000 par value bond.

b. On July 1, 1998, an investor could receive the face value of the bond and an interest payment, but then no further payments would be made to the bondholder.

c. An investor would pay $992.50 plus any accrued interest per $1,000 par value.

d. This is an example of an extendible bond.

39. "The real rate of return is the actual dollar amount received from an investment rather than its expected return." True or false?

40. High-yield bonds that are not investment-grade are often called ______________ bonds.

STANDARD &POOR'S

Go to **www.mcgrawhill.ca/edumarketinsight**. Find the bond ratings of Abitibi Consolidated Inc. (ABY) and Bell Canada Enterprises (BCE) in the *Financial Highlights* section. Which has higher-rated bonds? Now compare the financial ratios of the two firms. Are the relative bond ratings of the two firms consistent with their financial ratios?

E-INVESTMENTS
Credit Spreads

At **www.bondsonline.com** review the *Industrial Spreads* for various ratings (at the menu under *Corporate/Agency Bonds*). These are spreads above U.S. Treasuries of comparable maturity. What factors tend to explain the yield differences? How might these yield spreads differ during an economic boom versus a recession? From the home page, analyze and summarize the historic bond spreads and current yield curves (see *Today's Bond News at* **www.bondsonline.com/bpfaq.html**).

THE TERM STRUCTURE OF INTEREST RATES

In Chapter 11 we assumed for the sake of simplicity that the same constant interest rate is used to discount cash flows of any maturity. In the real world this is rarely the case. We have seen, for example, that in early 2004 short-term bonds and notes carried yields to maturity of about 2.20 percent while the longest-term bonds offered yields of over 5 percent. At the time when these bond prices were quoted, anyway, the longer-term securities had higher yields. This, in fact, is a common empirical pattern, but as we shall see below, the relationship between time to maturity and yield to maturity can vary dramatically from one period to another.

In this chapter we explore the pattern of interest rates for different-term assets. We attempt to identify the factors that account for that pattern and determine what information may be derived from an analysis of the so-called **term structure of interest rates,** the structure of interest rates for discounting cash flows of different maturities.

We show how traders can use the term structure to compute forward rates that represent interest rates on "forward" or deferred loans, and consider the relationship between forward rates and future interest rates. Finally, we give an overview of some issues involved in measuring the term structure.

12.1 THE TERM STRUCTURE UNDER CERTAINTY

What do you conclude from the observation that longer-term bonds offer higher yields to maturity? One possibility is that longer-term bonds are riskier and that the higher yields are evidence of a risk premium that compensates for interest rate risk. Another possibility is that investors expect interest rates to rise and that the higher average yields on long-term bonds reflect the anticipation of high interest rates in the latter years of the bond's life. We will start our analysis of these possibilities with the easiest case: a world with no uncertainty where investors already know the path of future interest rates.

Bond Pricing

The interest rate for a given time interval is called the **short interest rate** for that period. Suppose that all participants in the bond market are convinced that the short rates for the next four years will follow the pattern in Table 12.1.

Table 12.1 Interest Rates on One-Year Bonds in Coming Years

Year	Interest Rate
0 (Today)	8%
1	10
2	11
3	11

Of course, market participants cannot look up such a sequence of short rates in the financial press. All they observe there are prices and yields of bonds of various maturities. Nevertheless, we can think of the short-rate sequence of Table 12.1 as the series of interest rates that investors keep in the back of their minds when they evaluate the prices of different bonds. Given this pattern of rates, what prices might we observe on various maturity bonds? To keep the algebra simple, for now we will treat only a zero-coupon bond.

A bond paying \$1,000 in one year would sell today for \$1,000/1.08 = \$925.93. Similarly, a two-year maturity bond would sell today at price

$$P = \frac{\$1{,}000}{(1.08)(1.10)} = \$841.75 \qquad (12.1)$$

This is the present value of the future \$1,000 cash flow, because \$841.75 would need to be set aside now to provide a \$1,000 payment in two years. After one year, the \$841.75 set aside would grow to \$841.75(1.08) = \$909.09 and after the second year to \$909.09(1.10) = \$1,000.

In general, we may write the present value of \$1 to be received after n periods as

$$\text{PV of \$1 in } n \text{ periods} = \frac{1}{(1 + r_1)(1 + r_2) \ldots (1 + r_n)}$$

where r_i is the one-year interest rate that will prevail in year i. Continuing in this manner, we find the values of the three- and four-year bonds as shown in the middle column of Table 12.2.

Table 12.2 Prices and Yields of Zero-Coupon Bonds

Time to Maturity	Price	Yield to Maturity
1	\$925.93	8.000%
2	841.75	8.995
3	758.33	9.660
4	683.18	9.993

Term Structure of Interest Rates
www.finpipe.com/termstru.htm

From the bond prices we can calculate the yield to maturity on each bond. Recall that the yield is the *single* interest rate that equates the present value of the bond's payments to the bond's price. Although interest rates may vary over time, the yield to maturity is calculated as one "average" rate that is applied to discount all of the bond's payments. For example, the yield on the two-year zero-coupon bond, which we will call y_2, is the interest rate that satisfies

$$841.75 = 1{,}000/(1 + y_2)^2 \tag{12.2}$$

which we solve for $y_2 = .08995$. We repeat the process for the two other bonds, with results as reported in the table. For example, we find y_3 by solving

$$758.33 = 1{,}000/(1 + y_3)^3$$

Now we can make a graph of the yield to maturity on the four bonds as a function of time to maturity. This graph, which is called the **yield curve,** appears in Figure 12.1.

While the yield curve in Figure 12.1 rises smoothly, a wide range of curves may be observed in practice. Figure 12.2 presents three such curves. Panel A is a hump-shaped curve, first falling and then rising. The yield curve in panel B is essentially flat. In panel C the yield curve is flat for short maturities and then rising for maturities beyond six months.

The yield to maturity on zero-coupon bonds is sometimes called the **spot rate** that prevails today for a period corresponding to the maturity of the zero. The yield curve, or equivalently, the last column of Table 12.2, thus presents the spot rates for four maturities. Note that the spot rates or yields do *not* equal the one-year interest rates for each year.

To emphasize the differences between the sequence of *short* rates for each future year, and *spot* rates for different maturity dates, examine Figure 12.3. The first line of data presents the short rate for each annual period. The lower lines present the spot rates or equivalently, the yields to maturity, for different holding periods that extend from the present to each relevant maturity date.

The yield on the two-year bond is close to the average of the short rates for years one and two. This makes sense because if interest rates of 8 percent and 10 percent will prevail in the next two years, then (ignoring compound interest) a sequence of two one-year investments will provide a cumulative return of 18 percent. Therefore, we would expect a two-year bond to provide a competitive total return of about 18 percent, which translates into an annualized yield to maturity of 9 percent, just about equal to the 8.995 percent yield we derived in Table 12.2. Because the yield

Figure 12.1
Yield curve.

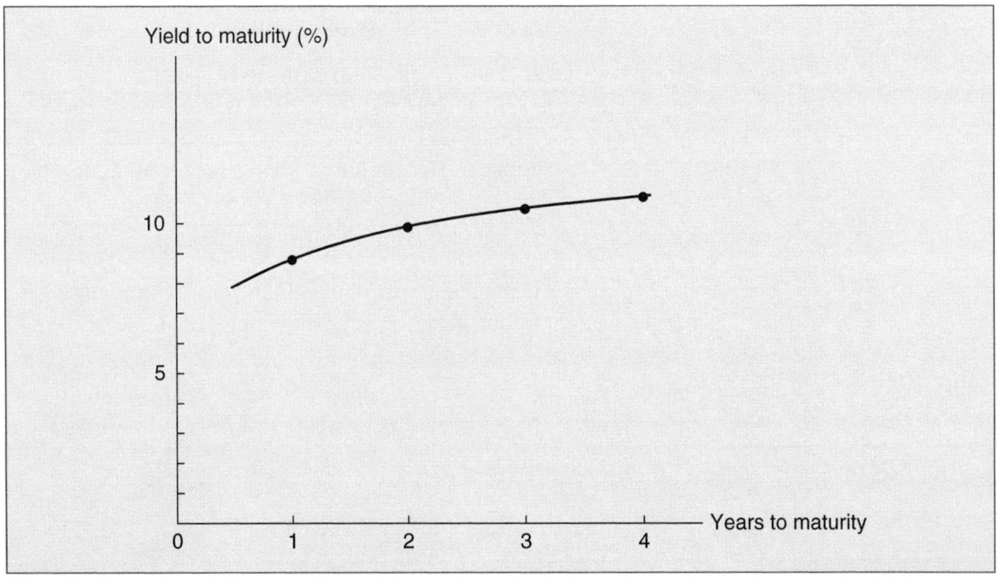

Figure 12.2
Treasury yield curves.

canada.gc.ca

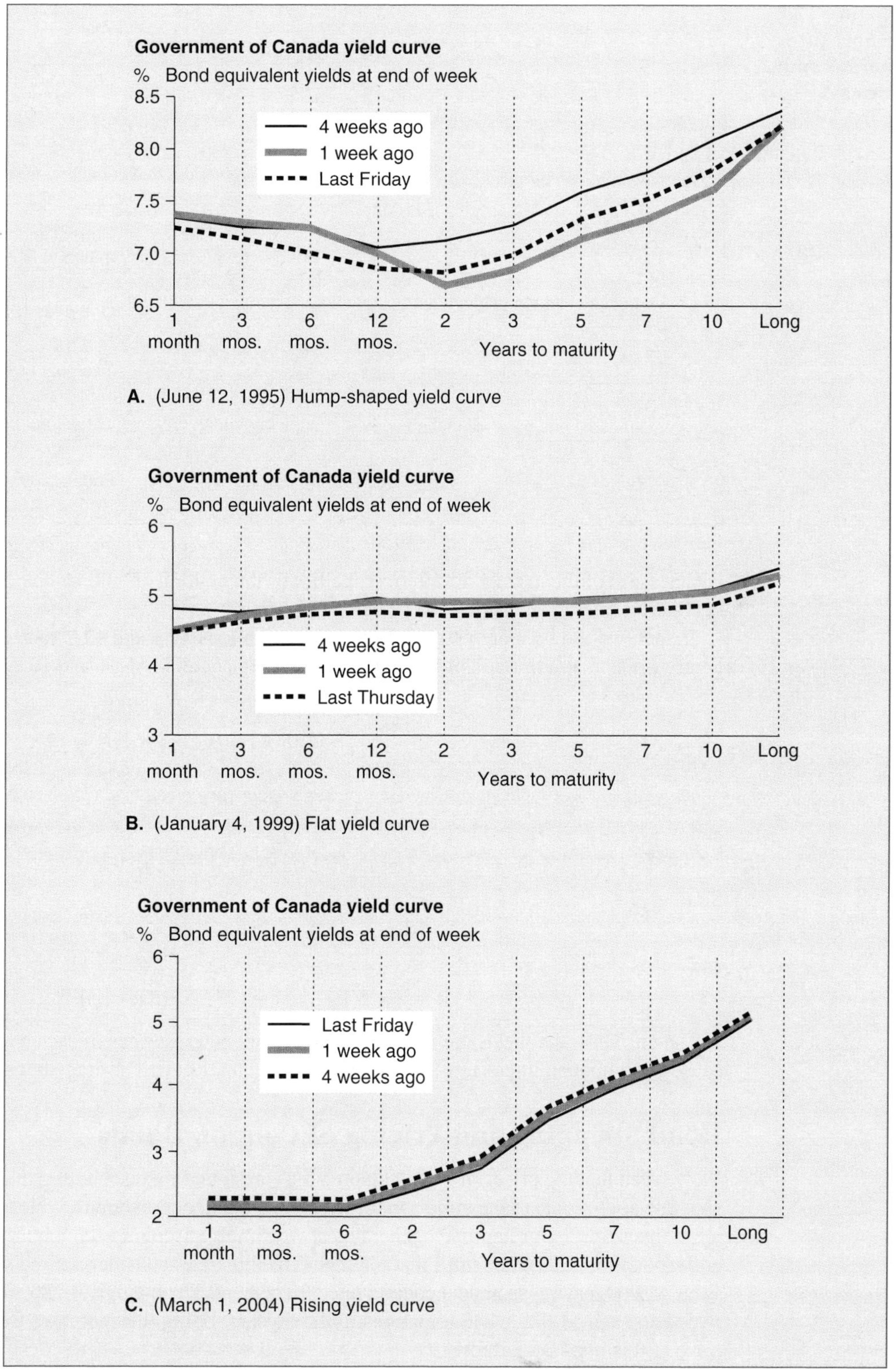

A. (June 12, 1995) Hump-shaped yield curve

B. (January 4, 1999) Flat yield curve

C. (March 1, 2004) Rising yield curve

Source: Royal Bank of Canada. Data from Datastream. Reprinted with permission of The Globe and Mail.

Figure 12.3 Short rates versus spot rates.

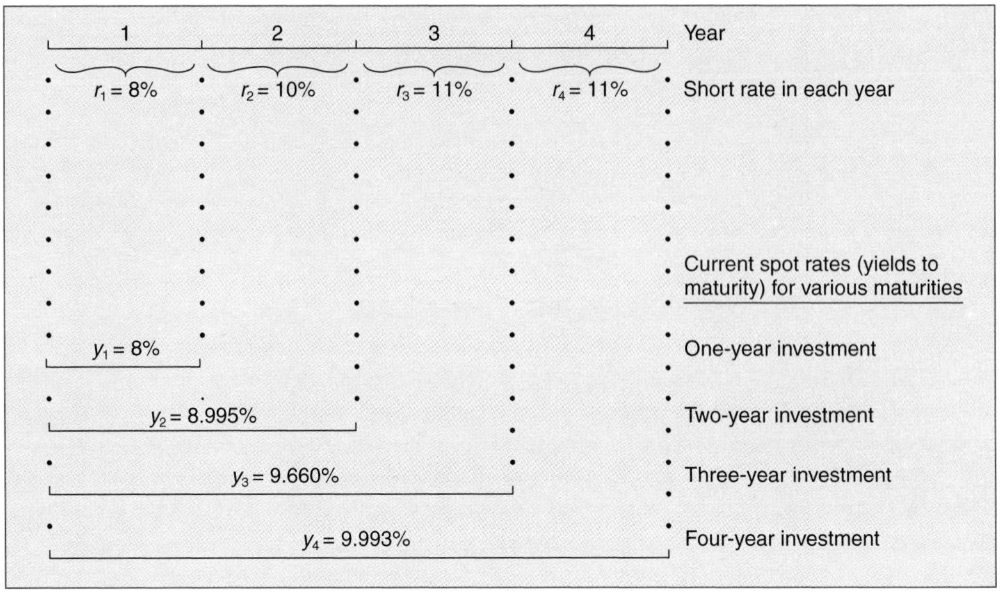

is a measure of the average return over the life of the bond, it should be determined by the market interest rates available in both years one and two.

In fact, we can be more precise. Notice that equations 12.1 and 12.2 each relate the two-year bond's price to appropriate interest rates. Combining equations 12.1 and 12.2, we find

$$841.75 = \frac{1{,}000}{(1.08)(1.10)} = \frac{1{,}000}{(1 + y_2)^2}$$

so that

$$(1 + y_2)^2 = (1.08)(1.10)$$

and

$$1 + y_2 = [(1.08)(1.10)]^{1/2} = 1.08995$$

Similarly,

$$1 + y_3 = [(1 + r_1)(1 + r_2)(1 + r_3)]^{1/3}$$

and

$$1 + y_4 = [(1 + r_1)(1 + r_2)(1 + r_3)(1 + r_4)]^{1/4} \tag{12.3}$$

and so on. Thus, the yields are in fact averages of the interest rates in each period. However, because of compound interest, the relationship is not an arithmetic average but a geometric one.

Bond Stripping and Pricing of Coupon Bonds

We've seen that the prices of zero-coupon bonds are found by discounting their face value at the spot rate appropriate to the bond's maturity. What about coupon bonds, which make several payments over time? Our approach generalizes: we simply discount each payment by the spot rate corresponding to the time until that payment. To illustrate, consider a three-year bond with par value $1,000, paying an annual coupon rate of 8 percent. The bond pays $80 at the end of the next two years, and $1,080 when it matures in three years. Using the spot rates from Table 12.2, the price of this bond is therefore

$$P = \frac{80}{1.08} + \frac{80}{1.08995^2} + \frac{1{,}080}{1.09660^3} = \$960.41$$

In other words, we can treat each of the bond's payments as in effect a stand-alone zero-coupon security that can be valued independently. The total value of the bond is just the sum of the values of each of its cash flows.

Notice that the yield to maturity of this three-year coupon bond is 9.58 percent, a bit less than that of the three-year zero-coupon bond. This makes sense: if we think of the coupon bond as a "portfolio" of three zeros (corresponding to each of its three coupon payments), then its yield should be a weighted average of the three spot rates for years 1–3. Of course, the yield on the last payment will dominate, since it accounts for the overwhelming proportion of the value of the bond. But as a general rule, we conclude that yields to maturity can differ for bonds of the same maturity if their coupon rates differ.

CONCEPT CHECK

1. Find the price and yield to maturity on a four-year maturity bond with a coupon rate of 8 percent also making annual payments. How does its yield to maturity compare to the spot rate on the four-year zero-coupon bond in Table 12.2?

Bond traders often distinguish between the yield curve for zero-coupon bonds and that for coupon-paying bonds. The **pure yield curve** refers to the relationship between yield to maturity and time to maturity for zero-coupon bonds. The coupon-paying curve portrays this relationship for coupon bonds, as in Figure 12.2. The most recently issued Treasuries are said to be **on the run**. On-the-run Treasuries have the greatest liquidity, so traders have keen interest in the on-the-run yield curve.

Turn back to Figure 11.1 in the previous chapter, and you will see the difference between the pure and coupon-paying yield curves. The latter part of the figure shows prices and yields of Canada strips. As discussed in that chapter, strips are created by breaking down a Canada bond's coupons and ultimate repayment of par value into a series of independent zero-coupon bonds. Thus, you can plot the pure yield curve by using the data on Canada strips. You can see from Figure 11.1 that yields on zeros and coupon-paying bonds can differ considerably.

Holding-Period Returns

What is the rate of return on each of the four bonds in Table 12.2 over a one-year holding period? You might think at first that higher-yielding bonds would provide higher one-year rates of return, but this is not the case. In our simple world with no uncertainty all bonds must offer identical rates of return over any holding period. Otherwise, at least one bond would be dominated by the others in the sense that it would offer a lower rate of return than would combinations of other bonds; no one would be willing to hold the bond, and its price would fall. In fact, despite their different yields to maturity, each bond will provide a rate of return over the coming year equal to this year's short interest rate.

To confirm this point, we can compute the rates of return on each bond. The one-year bond is bought today for $925.93 and matures in one year to its par value of $1,000. Because the bond pays no coupon, total income is $1,000 – $925.93 = $74.07, and the rate of return is $74.07/$925.93 = .08, or 8 percent. The two-year bond is bought today for $841.75. Next year the interest rate will be 10 percent, and the bond will have one year left until maturity. It will sell for $1,000/1.10 = $909.09. Thus, the *holding-period return* is ($909.09 – $841.75)/$841.75 = .08, again implying an 8 percent rate of return. Similarly, the three-year bond will be purchased for $758.33 and will be sold at year-end for $1,000/(1.10)(1.11) = $819.00, for a rate of return of ($819.00 – $758.33)/$758.33 = .08, again, an 8 percent return.

CONCEPT CHECK

2. Confirm that the return on the four-year bond also will be 8 percent.

Therefore we conclude that, when interest rate movements are known with certainty, if all bonds are fairly priced, all will provide equal one-year rates of return. The higher yields on the longer-term bonds merely reflect the fact that future interest rates are higher than current rates, and that the longer bonds are still alive during the higher-rate period. Owners of the short-term bonds receive lower yields to maturity, but they can reinvest or "roll over" their proceeds for higher yields in later years when rates are higher. In the end, both long-term bonds and short-term rollover strategies provide equal returns over the holding period, at least in a world of interest-rate certainty.

Forward Rates

Unfortunately, investors do not have access to short-term interest-rate quotations for coming years. What they do have are newspaper quotations of bond prices and yields to maturity. Can they infer future short rates from the available data?

Suppose we are interested in the interest rate that will prevail during year three, and we have access only to the data reported in Table 12.2. We start by comparing two alternatives, illustrated in Figure 12.4.

1. Invest in a three-year zero-coupon bond.
2. Invest in a two-year zero-coupon bond. After two years, reinvest the proceeds in a one-year bond.

Assuming an investment of \$100, under strategy 1, with a yield to maturity of 9.660 percent on three-year zero-coupon bonds, our investment would grow to $\$100(1.0966)^3 = \$131.87$. Under strategy 2, the \$100 investment in the two-year bond would grow after two years to $\$100(1.08995)^2 = \$118.80$. Then in the third year it would grow by an additional factor of $1 + r_3$.

In a world of certainty both of these strategies must yield exactly the same final payoff. If strategy 1 were to dominate strategy 2, no one would hold two-year bonds; their prices would fall and their yields would rise. Likewise if strategy 2 dominated strategy 1, no one would hold three-year bonds. Therefore, we can conclude that $\$131.87 = \$118.80(1 + r_3)$, which implies that

Figure 12.4 Two three-year investment programs.

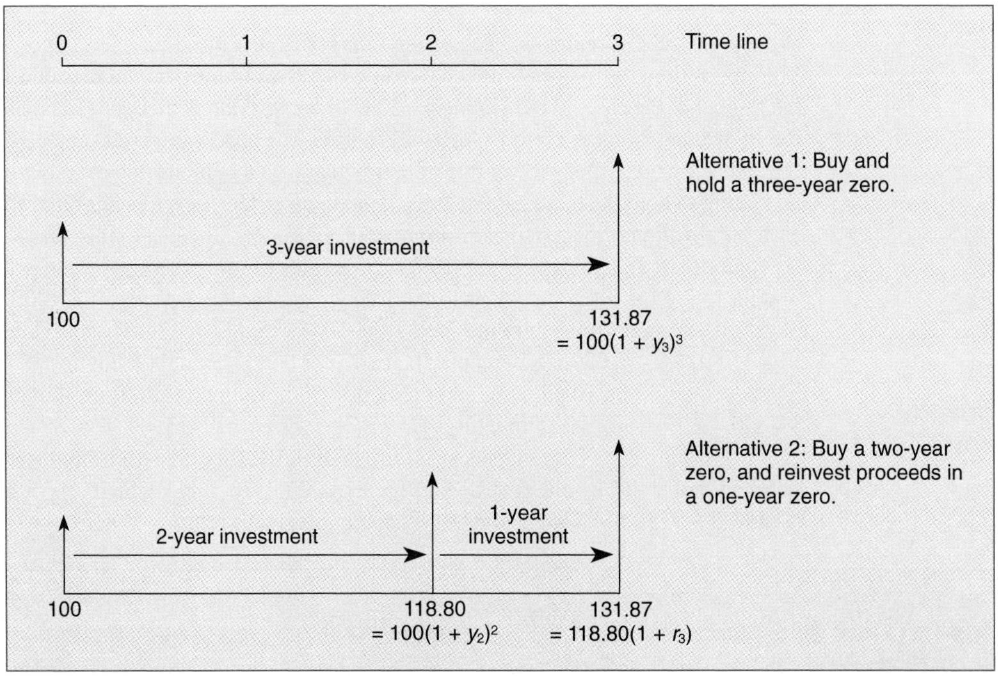

$(1 + r_3) = 1.11$, or $r_3 = 11$ percent. This is in fact the rate that will prevail in year 3, as Table 12.1 indicates. Thus, our method of obtaining the third-period interest rate does provide the correct solution in the certainty case.

More generally, the comparison of the two strategies establishes that the return on a three-year bond equals that on a two-year bond and rollover strategy:

$$100(1 + y_3)^3 = 100(1 + y_2)^2(1 + r_3)$$

so that $1 + r_3 = (1 + y_3)^3/(1 + y_2)^2$. Generalizing for the certainty case, a simple rule for inferring a future short interest rate from the yield curve of zero-coupon bonds is to use the following formula:

$$(1 + r_n) = (1 + y_n)^n/(1 + y_{n-1})^{n-1} \qquad (12.4)$$

where n denotes the period in question and y_n is the yield to maturity of a zero-coupon bond with an n-period maturity.

Equation 12.4 has a simple interpretation. The numerator on the right-hand side is the total growth factor of an investment in an n-year zero held until maturity. Similarly, the denominator is the growth factor of an investment in an $(n - 1)$-year zero. Because the former investment lasts for one more year than the latter, the difference in these growth factors must be the rate of return available in year n when the $(n - 1)$-year zero can be rolled over into a one-year investment.

Interpretation of Forward Rates and Term Structure www.e-analytics.com/fued11.htm

Of course, when future interest rates are uncertain, as they are in reality, there is no meaning to inferring "the" future short rate. No one knows today what the future interest rate will be. At best, we can speculate as to its expected value and associated uncertainty. Nevertheless, it still is common to use equation 12.4 to investigate the implications of the yield curve for future interest rates. In recognition of the fact that future interest rates are uncertain, we call the interest rate that we infer in this matter the **forward interest rate** rather than the *future short rate,* because it need not be the interest rate that actually will prevail at the future date.

If the forward rate for period n is f_n, we define f_n by the equation

$$1 + f_n = (1 + y_n)^n/(1 + y_{n-1})^{n-1}$$

Equivalently, we may rewrite the equation as

$$(1 + y_n)^n = (1 + y_{n-1})^{n-1}(1 + f_n) \qquad (12.5)$$

In this formulation, the forward rate is *defined* as the "breakeven" interest rate that equates the return on an n-period zero-coupon bond to that of a $(n - 1)$-period zero-coupon bond rolled over into a one-year bond in year n. The actual total returns on the two n-year strategies will be equal if the spot interest rate in year n turns out to equal f_n.

We emphasize that the interest rate that actually will prevail in the future need not equal the forward rate, which is calculated from today's data. Indeed, it is not even necessarily the case that the forward rate equals the expected value of the future short interest rate. This is an issue that we address in much detail shortly. For now, however, we note that forward rates do equal future short rates in the special case of interest rate certainty.

12.2 INTEREST RATE UNCERTAINTY AND FORWARD RATES

Let us turn now to the more difficult analysis of the term structure when future interest rates are uncertain. We have argued so far that, in a certain world, different investment strategies with common terminal dates must provide equal rates of return. For example, two consecutive one-year investments in zeroes would need to offer the same total return as an equal-sized investment in a two-year zero. Therefore, under certainty,

$$(1 + r_1)(1 + r_2) = (1 + y_2)^2$$

What can we say when r_2 is not known today?

For example, referring once again to Table 12.1, suppose that today's rate, $r_1 = 8\%$, and that the expected rate next year is $E(r_2) = 10\%$. If bonds were priced based only on the expected value of the interest rate, then a one-year zero would sell for \$1,000/1.08 = \$925.93, and a two-year zero would sell for \$1,000/[(1.08)(1.10)] = \$841.75, just as in Table 12.1.

But now consider a short-term investor who wishes to invest only for one year. She can purchase the one-year zero and lock in a riskless 8 percent return because she knows that at the end of the year, the bond will be worth its maturity value of \$1,000. She also can purchase the two-year zero. Its *expected* rate of return also is 8 percent: Next year, the bond will have one year to maturity, and we expect that the one-year interest rate will be 10 percent, implying a price of \$909.09 and a holding-period return of 8 percent. But the rate of return on the two-year bond is risky. If next year's interest rate turns out to be above expectations, that is, greater than 10 percent, the bond price will be below \$909.09, and conversely, if r_2 turns out to be less than 10 percent, the bond price will exceed \$909.09. Why should this short-term investor buy the risky two-year bond when its expected return is 8 percent, no better than that of the risk-free one-year bond? Clearly, she would not hold the two-year bond unless it offered an expected rate of return greater than the riskless 8 percent return available on the competing one-year bond. This requires that the two-year bond sell at a price lower than the \$841.75 value we derived when we ignored risk.

Suppose, for example, that most investors have short-term horizons and are willing to hold the two-year bond only if its price falls to \$819. At this price, the expected holding-period return on the two-year bond is 11 percent (because 909.09/819 = 1.11). The risk premium of the two-year bond, therefore, is 3 percent; it offers an expected rate of return of 11 percent versus the 8 percent risk-free return on the one-year bond. At this risk premium, investors are willing to bear the price risk associated with interest rate uncertainty.

In this environment, the forward rate, f_2, no longer equals the expected short rate, $E(r_2)$. Although we have assumed that $E(r_2) = 10\%$, it is easy to confirm that $f_2 = 13\%$. The yield to maturity on the two-year zero selling at \$819 is 10.5 percent, and

$$1 + f_2 = \frac{(1 + y_2)^2}{1 + y_1} = \frac{1.105^2}{1.08} = 1.13$$

This result—that the forward rate exceeds the expected short rate—should not surprise us. We defined the forward rate as the interest rate that would need to prevail in the second year to make the long- and short-term investments equally attractive, ignoring risk. When we account for risk, it is clear that short-term investors will shy away from the long-term bond unless it offers an expected return greater than that offered by the one-year bond. Another way of putting this is to say that investors will require a risk premium to hold the longer-term bond. The risk-averse investor would be willing to hold the long-term bond only if $E(r_2)$ is less than the breakeven value, f_2, because the lower the expectation of r_2, the greater the anticipated return on the long-term bond.

Therefore, if most individuals are short-term investors, bonds must have prices that make f_2 greater than $E(r_2)$. The forward rate will embody a premium compared with the expected future short-interest rate. This **liquidity premium** compensates short-term investors for the uncertainty about the price at which they will be able to sell their long-term bonds at the end of the year.[1]

CONCEPT CHECK

3. Suppose that the required liquidity premium for the short-term investor is 1 percent. What must $E(r_2)$ be if f_2 is 10 percent?

[1] *Liquidity* refers to the ability to sell an asset easily at a predictable price. Because long-term bonds have greater price risk, they are considered less liquid in this context and thus must offer a premium.

Perhaps surprisingly, we also can imagine scenarios in which long-term bonds can be perceived by investors to be *safer* than short-term bonds. To see how, we now consider a "long-term" investor, who wishes to invest for a full two-year period. Suppose that the investor can purchase a two-year $1,000 par value zero-coupon bond for $841.75 and lock in a guaranteed yield to maturity of $y_2 = 9\%$. Alternatively, the investor can roll over two one-year investments. In this case an investment of 841.75 would grow in two years to $841.75 \times (1.08)(1 + r_2)$, which is an uncertain amount today because r_2 is not yet known. The breakeven year 2 interest rate is, once again, the forward rate, 10 percent, because the forward rate is defined as the rate that equates the terminal value of the two investment strategies.

The expected value of the payoff of the rollover strategy is $841.75(1.08)[1 + E(r_2)]$. If $E(r_2)$ equals the forward rate, f_2, then the expected value of the payoff from the rollover strategy will equal the *known* payoff from the two-year maturity bond strategy.

Is this a reasonable presumption? Once again, it is only if the investor does not care about the uncertainty surrounding the final value of the rollover strategy. Whenever that risk is important, the long-term investor will not be willing to engage in the rollover strategy unless its expected return exceeds that of the two-year bond. In this case, the investor would require that

$$(1.08)[1 + E(r_2)] > (1.09)^2 = (1.08)(1 + f_2)$$

which implies that $E(r_2)$ exceeds f_2. The investor would require that the expected period two interest rate exceed the breakeven value of 10 percent, which is the forward rate.

Therefore, if all investors were long-term investors, no one would be willing to hold short-term bonds unless those bonds offered a reward for bearing interest rate risk. In this situation, bond prices would be set at levels such that rolling over short bonds would result in greater expected returns than holding long bonds. This would cause the forward rate to be less than the expected future spot rate.

For example, suppose that in fact $E(r_2) = 11\%$. The liquidity premium therefore is negative: $f_2 - E(r_2) = 10\% - 11\% = -1\%$. This is exactly opposite from the conclusion that we drew in the first case of the short-term investor. Clearly, whether forward rates will equal expected future short rates depends on investors' readiness to bear interest rate risk, as well as their willingness to hold bonds that do not correspond to their investment horizons.

12.3 THEORIES OF THE TERM STRUCTURE

The Expectations Hypothesis

The simplest theory of the term structure is the **expectations hypothesis.** A common version of this hypothesis states that the forward rate equals the market consensus expectation of the future short interest rate; in other words, that $f_2 = E(r_2)$, and that liquidity premiums are zero. Because $f_2 = E(r_2)$, we may relate yields on long-term bonds to expectations of future interest rates. In addition, we can use the forward rates derived from the yield curve to infer market expectations of future short rates. For example, with $(1 + y_2)^2 = (1 + r_1)(1 + f_2)$ from equation 12.5, we may also write that $(1 + y_2)^2 = (1 + r_1)[1 + E(r_2)]$ if the expectations hypothesis is correct. The yield to maturity would thus be determined solely by current and expected future one-period interest rates. An upward-sloping yield curve would be clear evidence that investors anticipate increases in interest rates.

CONCEPT CHECK

4. If the expectations hypothesis is valid, what can we conclude about the premiums necessary to induce investors to hold bonds of different maturities from their investment horizons?

Liquidity Preference

We noted in our discussion of long- and short-term investors that short-term investors will be unwilling to hold long-term bonds unless the forward rate exceeds the expected short interest rate, $f_2 > E(r_2)$, whereas long-term investors will be unwilling to hold short bonds unless $E(r_2)$ exceeds f_2. In other words, both groups of investors require a premium to induce them to hold bonds with maturities different from their investment horizons. Advocates of the **liquidity preference theory** of the term structure believe that short-term investors dominate the market so that, generally speaking, the forward rate exceeds the expected short rate. The excess of f_2 over $E(r_2)$, the liquidity premium, is predicted to be positive.

CONCEPT CHECK

5. The liquidity premium hypothesis also holds that *issuers* of bonds prefer to issue long-term bonds. How would this preference contribute to a positive liquidity premium?

To illustrate the differing implications of these theories for the term structure of interest rates, consider a situation in which the short interest rate is expected to be constant indefinitely. Suppose that $r_1 = 10$ percent and that $E(r_2) = 10$ percent, $E(r_3) = 10$ percent, and so on. Under the expectations hypothesis, the two-year yield to maturity could be derived from the following:

$$\begin{aligned}(1 + y_2)^2 &= (1 + r_1)[1 + E(r_2)] \\ &= (1.10)(1.10)\end{aligned}$$

so that y_2 equals 10 percent. Similarly, yields on all-maturity bonds would equal 10 percent.

In contrast, under the liquidity preference theory, f_2 would exceed $E(r_2)$. For the sake of illustration, suppose that f_2 is 11 percent, implying a 1 percent liquidity premium. Then, for two-year bonds,

$$\begin{aligned}(1 + y_2)^2 &= (1 + r_1)(1 + f_2) \\ &= (1.10)(1.11) = 1.221\end{aligned}$$

implying that $1 + y_2 = 1.105$. Similarly, if f_3 also equals 11 percent, then the yield on three-year bonds would be determined by

$$\begin{aligned}(1 + y_3)^3 &= (1 + r_1)(1 + f_2)(1 + f_3) \\ &= (1.10)(1.11)(1.11) = 1.35531\end{aligned}$$

implying that $1 + y_3 = 1.1067$. The plot of the yield curve in this situation would be given as in Figure 12.5, panel A. Such an upward-sloping yield curve is commonly observed in practice.

If interest rates are expected to change over time, then the liquidity premium may be overlaid on the path of expected spot rates to determine the forward interest rate. Then the yield to maturity for each date will be an average of the single-period forward rates. Several such possibilities for increasing and declining interest rates appear in panels B to D.

12.4 INTERPRETING THE TERM STRUCTURE

We have seen that under certainty, one plus the yield to maturity on a zero-coupon bond is simply the geometric average of one plus the future short rates that will prevail over the life of the bond. This is the meaning of equation 12.3, which we repeat here in a more general form:

$$1 + y_n = [(1 + r_1)(1 + r_2) \ldots (1 + r_n)]^{1/n}$$

Figure 12.5 Yield curves. Panel A: Constant expected short rate. Liquidity premium of 1 percent. Result is a rising yield curve. Panel B: Declining expected short rates. Increasing liquidity premiums. Result is a rising yield curve despite falling expected interest rates.

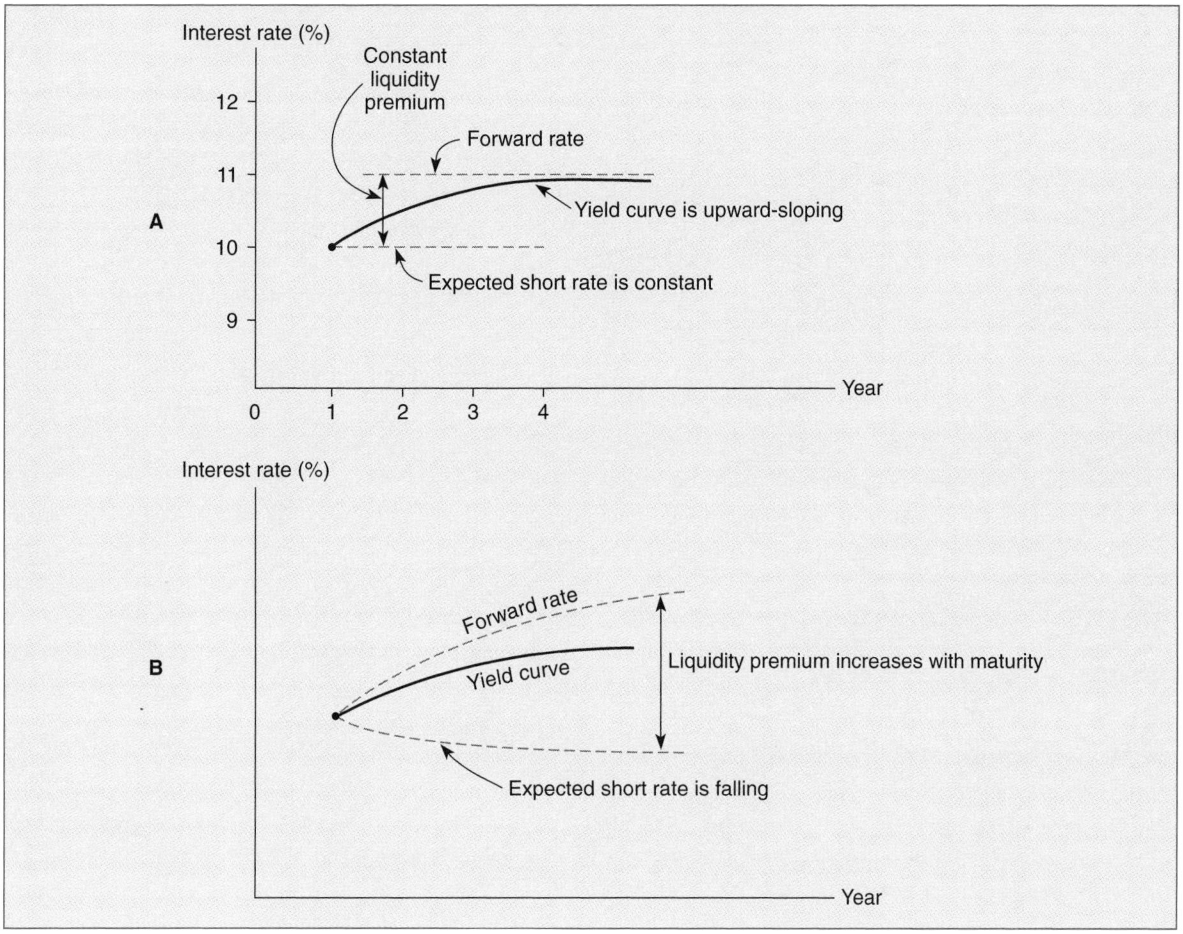

When future rates are uncertain, we modify equation 12.3 by replacing future short rates with forward rates:

$$1 + y_n = [(1 + r_1)(1 + f_2)(1 + f_3) \ldots (1 + f_n)]^{1/n} \quad (12.6)$$

Thus, there is a direct relationship between yields on various maturity bonds and forward interest rates. This relationship is the source of the information that can be gleaned from an analysis of the yield curve.

First, we ask what factors can account for a rising yield curve. Mathematically, if the yield curve is rising, f_{n+1} must exceed y_n. In words, the yield curve is upward-sloping at any maturity date, n, for which the forward rate for the coming period is greater than the yield at that maturity. This rule follows from the notion of the yield to maturity as an average (albeit a geometric average) of forward rates.

If the yield curve is to rise as one moves to longer maturities, it must be the case that extension to a longer maturity results in the inclusion of a "new" forward rate that is higher than the average of the previously observed rates. This is analogous to the observation that if a new student's test score is to increase the class average, that student's score must exceed the class's average without

Figure 12.5 ***(Continued)*** **Panel C: Declining expected short rates. Constant liquidity premiums. Result is a hump-shaped yield curve, panel D. Panel D: Increasing expected short rates. Increasing liquidity premiums. Result is a sharply increasing yield curve.**

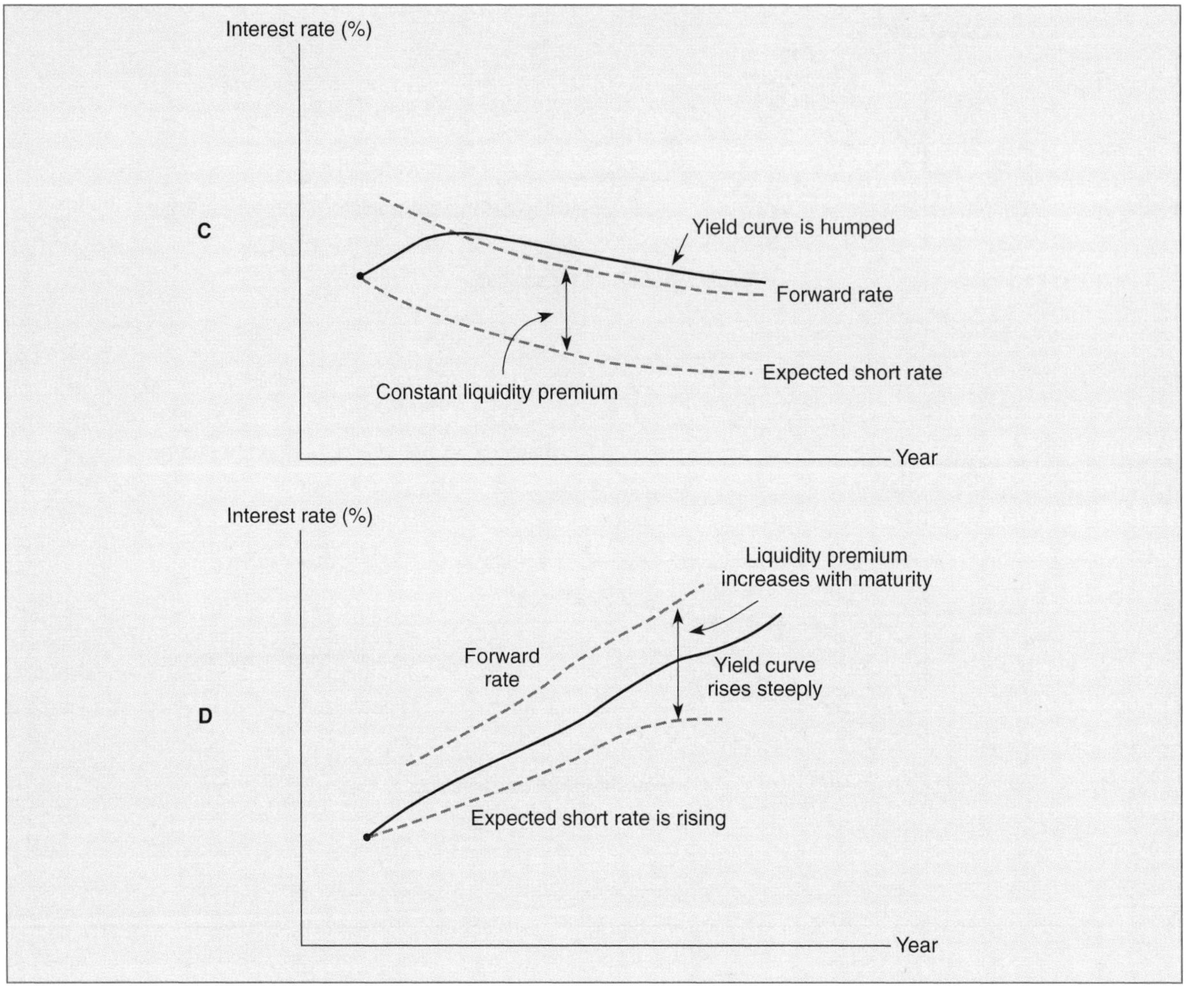

her score. To raise the yield to maturity, an above-average forward rate must be added to the other rates in the averaging computation.

For example, if the yield to maturity on three-year bonds is 9 percent, then the yield on four-year bonds will satisfy the following equation:

$$(1 + y_4)^4 = (1.09)^3(1 + f_4)$$

If $f_4 = .09$, then y_4 also will equal .09. (Confirm this!) If f_4 is greater than 9 percent, y_4 will exceed 9 percent, and the yield curve will slope upward.

CONCEPT CHECK

6. Look back at Tables 12.1 and 12.2. Show that y_4 would exceed y_3 if and only if the interest rate for period 4 had been greater than 9.66 percent, which was the yield to maturity on the three-year bond, y_3.

Given that an upward-sloping yield curve is always associated with a forward rate higher than the spot, or current, yield, we need to ask next what can account for that higher forward rate. Unfortunately, there always are two possible answers to this question. Recall that the forward rate can be related to the expected future short rate according to the equation

$$f_n = E(r_n) + \text{Liquidity premium}$$

where the liquidity premium might be necessary to induce investors to hold bonds of maturities that do not correspond to their preferred investment horizons.

By the way, the liquidity premium need not be positive, although that is the position generally taken by advocates of the liquidity premium hypothesis. We showed previously that if most investors have long-term horizons, the liquidity premium could be negative.

In any case, the equation shows that there are two reasons that the forward rate could be high. Either investors expect rising interest rates, meaning that $E(r_n)$ is high, or they require a large premium for holding longer-term bonds. Although it is tempting to infer from a rising yield curve that investors believe that interest rates will eventually increase, this is not a valid inference. Indeed, Figure 12.5, panel A provides a simple counterexample to this line of reasoning. There, the spot rate is expected to stay at 10 percent forever. Yet there is a constant 1 percent liquidity premium so that all forward rates are 11 percent. The result is that the yield curve continually rises, starting at a level of 10 percent for one-year bonds, but eventually approaching 11 percent for long-term bonds as more and more forward rates at 11 percent are averaged into the yields to maturity.

Therefore, although it is true that expectations of increases in future interest rates can result in a rising yield curve, the converse is not true: a rising yield curve does not in and of itself imply expectations of higher future interest rates. This is the heart of the difficulty in drawing conclusions from the yield curve. The effects of possible liquidity premiums confound any simple attempt to extract expectations from the term structure. But estimating the market's expectations is a crucial task, because only by comparing your own expectations to those reflected in market prices can you determine whether you are relatively bullish or bearish on interest rates.

One very rough approach to deriving expected future spot rates is to assume that liquidity premiums are constant. An estimate of that premium can be subtracted from the forward rate to obtain the market's expected interest rate. For example, again making use of the example plotted in Figure 12.5, panel A, the researcher would estimate from historical data that a typical liquidity premium in this economy is 1 percent. After calculating the forward rate from the yield curve to be 11 percent, the expectation of the future spot rate would be determined to be 10 percent.

This approach has little to recommend it for two reasons. First, it is next to impossible to obtain precise estimates of a liquidity premium. The general approach to doing so would be to compare forward rates and eventually realized future short rates and to calculate the average difference between the two. However, the deviations between the two values can be quite large and unpredictable because of unanticipated economic events that affect the realized short rate. The data do not contain enough information to calculate a reliable estimate of the expected premium. Second, there is no reason to believe that the liquidity premium should be constant. Figure 12.6 shows the rate of return variability of Canada long-term bonds since 1977. Interest rate risk fluctuated dramatically during the period. So might we expect risk premiums on various maturity bonds to fluctuate, and empirical evidence suggests that term premiums do in fact fluctuate over time.

Still, very steep yield curves are interpreted by many market professionals as warning signs of impending rate increases. In fact, the yield curve is a good predictor of the business cycle as a whole, since long-term rates tend to rise in anticipation of an expansion in the economy. When the curve is steep, there is a far lower probability of a recession in the next year than when it is inverted or falling. For this reason, the yield curve has been added to the index of leading economic indicators.

Figure 12.6 Yield volatility of long-term bonds, 1977–2003.

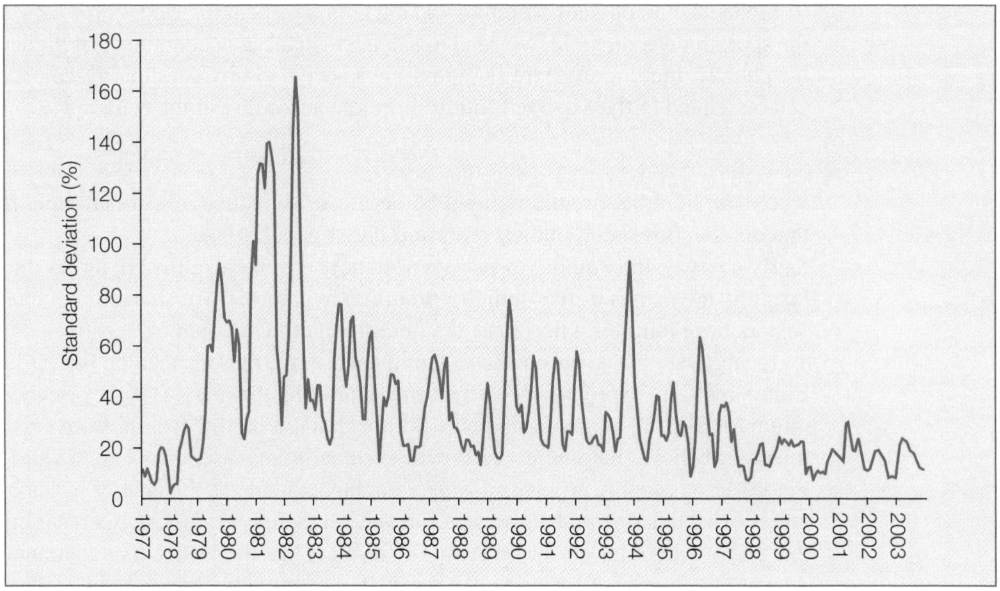

Source: Scotia Capital, *Debt Market Indices*, various years.

The usually observed upward slope of the yield curve, especially for short maturities, is the empirical basis for the liquidity premium doctrine that long-term bonds offer a positive liquidity premium. In the face of this empirical regularity, perhaps it is valid to interpret a downward-sloping yield curve as evidence that interest rates are expected to decline. If **term premiums,** the spread between yields on long- and short-term bonds, are generally positive, then anticipated declines in rates could account for a downward-sloping yield curve.

Figure 12.7 presents a history of yields on short-term and long-term Canada bonds. Yields on the longer-term bonds *generally* exceed those on the short-term bonds, meaning that the yield curve generally slopes upward. Moreover, the exceptions to this rule seem to precede episodes of falling short rates, which, if anticipated, would induce a downward-sloping yield curve. For example, 1989–1990 were years in which short-term yields exceeded long-term yields. These years preceded a drastic drop in the general level of rates.

Figure 12.7 Yields on long-term versus short-term government securities: term spread, 1980–2004.

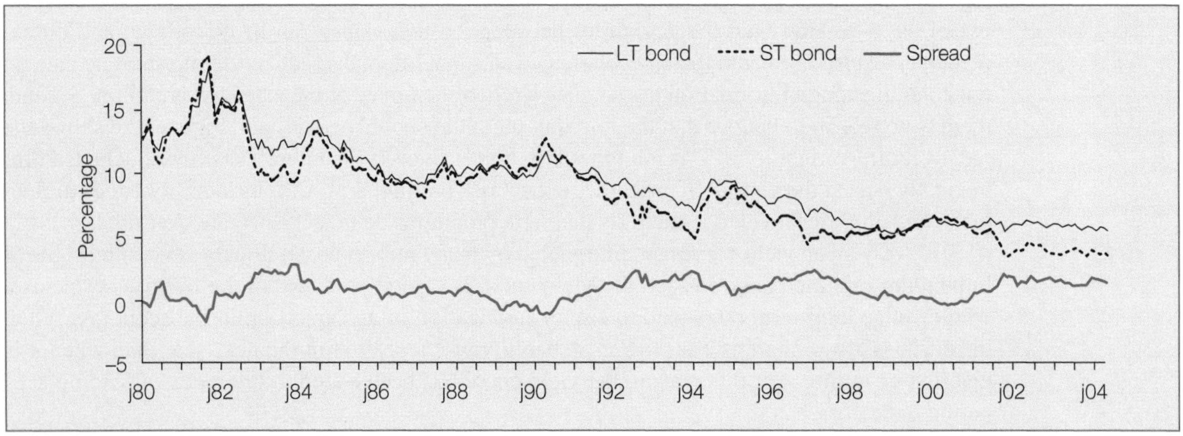

Source: Scotia Capital, *Debt Market Indices*, various years.

Why might interest rates fall? There are two factors to consider: the real rate and the inflation premium. Recall that the nominal interest rate is composed of the real rate plus a factor to compensate for the effect of inflation:

$$1 + \text{Nominal rate} = (1 + \text{Real rate})(1 + \text{Inflation rate})$$

or approximately,

$$\text{Nominal rate} = \text{Real rate} + \text{Inflation rate}$$

Therefore, an expected change in interest rates can be due to changes either in expected real rates or expected inflation rates. Usually, it is important to distinguish between these two possibilities because the economic environments associated with them may vary substantially. High real rates may indicate a rapidly expanding economy, high budget deficits, and tight monetary policy. Although high inflation rates also can arise out of a rapidly expanding economy, inflation also may be caused by rapid expansion of the money supply or supply-side shocks to the economy, such as interruptions in oil supplies. These factors have very different implications for investments. Even if we conclude from an analysis of the yield curve that rates will fall, we need to analyze the macroeconomic factors that might cause such a decline.

12.5 FORWARD RATES AS FORWARD CONTRACTS

We have seen that forward rates may be derived from the yield curve, using equation 12.5. In general, forward rates will not equal the eventually realized short rate, or even today's expectation of what that short rate will be. But there is still an important sense in which the forward rate is a market interest rate. Suppose that you wanted to arrange *now* to make a loan at some future date. You would agree today on the interest rate that will be charged, but the loan would not commence until some time in the future. How would the interest rate on such a "forward loan" be determined? Perhaps not surprisingly, it would be the forward rate of interest for the period of the loan. Let's use an example to see how this might work.

Suppose the price of one-year maturity zero-coupon bonds with face value \$1,000 is 925.93 and the price of two-year zeros with \$1,000 face value is \$841.68. The yield to maturity on the one year bond is therefore 8 percent, while that on the two-year bond is 9 percent. The forward rate for the second year is thus

$$f_2 = \frac{(1 + y_2)^2}{(1 + y_1)} - 1 = \frac{1.09^2}{1.08} - 1 = .1001, \text{ or } 10.01\%$$

Now consider the strategy laid in out the following table. In the first column we present data for this example, and in the last column we generalize. We denote by $B_0(T)$, today's price of a zero maturing at time T.

	Initial Cash Flow	In General
Buy a 1-year zero coupon bond	−925.93	$-B_0(1)$
Sell 1.1001 2-year zeros	+841.68 × 1.1001 = 925.93	$+B_0(2) \times (1 + f_2)$
	0	0

The initial cash flow (at time 0) is zero. You pay \$925.93, or in general $B_0(1)$, for a zero maturing in one year, and you receive \$841.68, or in general $B_0(2)$, for each zero you sell maturing in two years. By selling 1.1001 of these bonds, you set your initial cash flow to zero.[2]

[2]Of course, in reality one cannot sell a fraction of a bond, but you can think of this part of the transaction as follows. If you sold one of these bonds, you would effectively be borrowing \$841.68 for a two-year period. Selling 1.1001 of these bonds means simply that you are borrowing \$841.68 × 1.1001 = \$925.93.

At time 1, the one-year bond matures and you receive \$1,000. At time 2, the two-year maturity zero-coupon bonds that you sold mature, and you have to pay $1.1001 \times \$1{,}000 = \$1{,}100.10$. Your cash flow stream is shown in Figure 12.8, panel A. Notice that you have created a "synthetic" forward loan: you effectively *will* borrow \$1,000 a year from now, and repay \$1,100.10 a year later. The rate on this forward loan is therefore 10.01 percent, precisely equal to the forward rate for the second year.

In general, to construct the synthetic forward loan, you sell $1 + f_2$ two-year zeros for every one-year zero that you buy. This makes your initial cash flow zero because the prices of the one- and two-year zeros differ by the factor $(1 + f_2)$; notice that

$$B_0(1) = \frac{\$1{,}000}{(1 + y_1)} \qquad \text{while} \qquad B_0(2) = \frac{\$1{,}000}{(1 + y_2)^2} = \frac{\$1{,}000}{(1 + y_1)(1 + f_2)}$$

Therefore, when you sell $(1 + f_2)$ two-year zeros you generate just enough cash to buy one one-year zero. Both zeros mature to a face value of \$1,000, so the difference between the cash inflow at time 1 and the cash outflow at time 2 is the same factor, $1 + f_2$, as illustrated in panel B. As a result, f_2 is the rate on the forward loan.

Obviously, you can construct a synthetic forward loan for periods beyond the second year, and you can construct such loans for multiple periods. Problems 19 and 20 at the end of the chapter lead you through some of these variants.

CONCEPT CHECK

7. Suppose that the price of three-year zero coupon bonds is \$761.65. What is the forward rate for the third year? How would you construct a synthetic one-year forward loan that commences at $t = 2$ and matures at $t = 3$?

Figure 12.8 Engineering a synthetic forward loan.

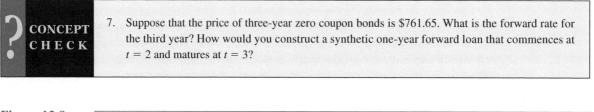

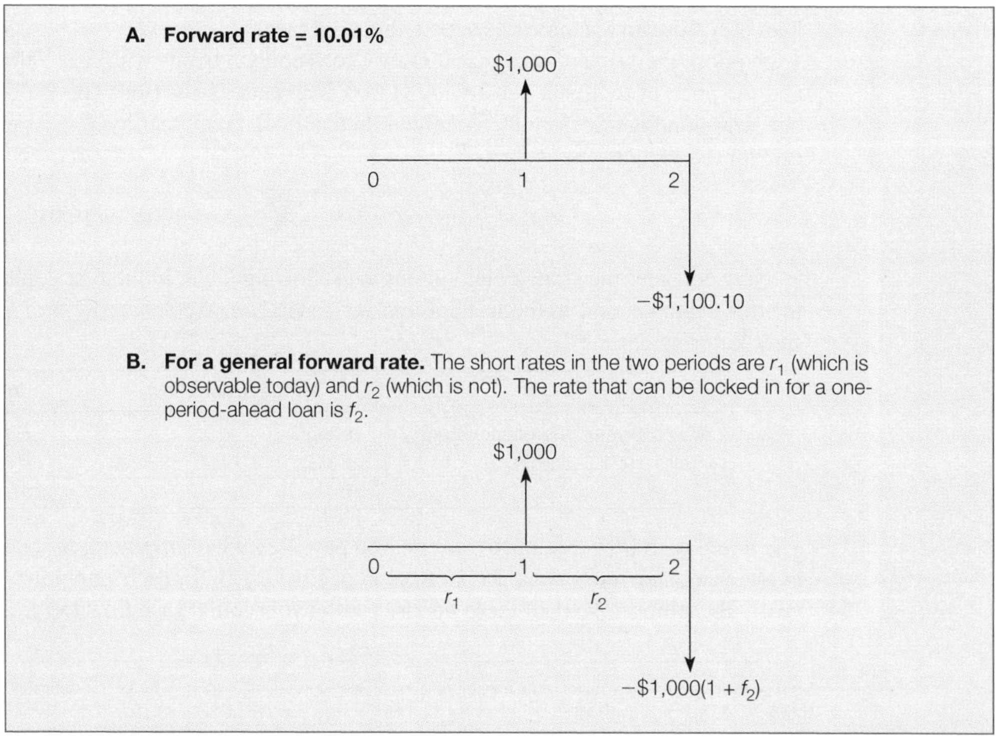

12.6 MEASURING THE TERM STRUCTURE

Thus far spot and forward rates have been determined from default-free zero-coupon bonds. These bonds are easiest to analyze because their maturity is given by their single payment. In practice, however, the great majority of bonds pay coupons, and most available data pertain to coupon bonds, so we must develop a general approach to calculate spot and forward rates from prices of coupon bonds.

Equations 12.4 and 12.5 for the determination of the forward rate from available yields apply only to zero-coupon bonds. They were derived by equating the returns to competing investment strategies that both used zeros. If coupon bonds had been used in those strategies, we would have had to deal with the issue of coupons paid and reinvested during the investment period, which complicates the analysis.

A further complication arises from the fact that bonds with different coupon rates can have different yields even if their maturities are equal. For example, consider two bonds, each with a two-year time to maturity and annual coupon payments. Bond A has a 3 percent coupon; bond B a 12 percent coupon. Using the interest rates of Table 12.1, we see that bond A will sell for

$$\frac{\$30}{1.08} + \frac{\$1{,}030}{(1.08)(1.10)} = \$894.78$$

At this price its yield to maturity is 8.98 percent. Bond B will sell for

$$\frac{\$120}{1.08} + \frac{\$1{,}120}{(1.08)(1.10)} = \$1{,}053.87$$

at which price its yield to maturity is 8.94 percent. Because bond B makes a greater share of its payments in the first year when the interest rate is lower, its yield to maturity is slightly lower. Because bonds with the same maturity can have different yields, we conclude that a single yield curve relating yields and times to maturity cannot be appropriate for all bonds.

The solution to this ambiguity is to perform all of our analysis using the yield curve for zero-coupon bonds, the pure yield curve mentioned earlier in this chapter. Our goal, therefore, is to calculate the pure yield curve even if we have to use data on more common coupon-paying bonds.

The pure yield curve is a very useful instrument for valuing *any* fixed-income security, including mortgages and bonds with arbitrary coupons. Each individual cash flow of such instruments is discounted by the yield corresponding to its time of receipt, as given by the pure yield curve. It may also be used to identify mispriced bonds.

The trick we use to infer the yield curve from data on coupon bonds is to treat each coupon payment as a separate "mini" zero-coupon bond. A coupon bond then becomes just a "portfolio" of many zeros. Indeed, we saw in the previous chapter that most zero-coupon bonds are created by stripping coupon payments from coupon bonds and repackaging the separate payments from many bonds into portfolios with common maturity dates. By determining the price of each of these "zeroes," we can calculate the yield to that maturity date for a single-payment security and thereby construct the pure yield curve.

CONCEPT CHECK ?

8. A T-bill with six-month maturity and $10,000 face value sells for $9,700. A one-year maturity T-bond paying semiannual coupons of $40 sells for $1,000. Find the current six-month short rate and the forward rate for the following six-month period.

The simplest way to apply this technique is by successive estimations of the implied spot rates from the observed prices of coupon bonds of increasing maturities. This method is known as **bootstrapping**. As a specific example, suppose that you observe in the money market yields of 4 percent and 5 percent, respectively for six-month and one-year T-bills (all yields are bond equivalent yields). You also observe a 5 percent coupon bond maturing in one-and-a-half-year trading at 99, and a 6 percent coupon bond maturing in two years trading at par. We shall use the bootstrapping method to estimate the implied spot rates y_3 and y_4 for 1.5 and two years from now.

The first bond pays a coupon of \$25 every six months on a \$1,000 face value and trades at \$990. The second bond pays \$30 every six months and trades at \$1,000. Hence, the two spot rates y_3 and y_4 must satisfy the following equations, with time measured in semesters:

$$990 = 25/1.02 + 25/1.05 + 1{,}025/(1 + y_3)^3$$

$$1{,}000 = 30/1.02 + 30/1.05 + 30/(1 + y_3)^3 + 1{,}030/(1 + y_4)^4$$

Solving the first equation yields $y_3 = 0.028664$, which gives us an implied spot rate of 5.73 percent annually for the period 1.5 years from now. Substituting into the second equation and solving for y_4 gives us similarly $y_4 = 0.0302$ and an implied spot rate of 6.04 percent annually for two years from now.

In practice the use of bootstrapping from quoted bond prices is more complicated, because it must take into account the fact that part of the first coupon must be paid to the seller and is not reflected in the quoted price of the bond. Also, the times the quoted bonds mature are not spaced in equal one-semester increments. Consider, for instance, the bonds quoted in Figure 11.1. On the day of the quotes, February 27, 2004, the six-month and one-year T-bill yields were 2.18 and 2.17 percent. To find the spot rate for June 1, 2005 we use the 3.5 percent Canada bond maturing on that day and quoted at 101.62. This bond pays \$17.5 coupons on \$1,000 face value at June 1, 2004, at December 1, 2004, and at expiration. The quoted price of the bond, though, does not reflect the value of the cash flows accruing to its owner; the part of it that goes to the seller has been subtracted and must be added back for the bootstrapping. This part is approximately equal to $3 \times 17.5/6 = \$8.75$, since between August 17 and December 1 there are approximately three months. Hence, the invoice price of the bond is \$1,016.20 + \$8.75 = \$1,024.95, and the equation for finding the spot rate y_3 for June 1, 2005 is[3]

$$1{,}024.95 = \frac{17.5}{(1.0218)^{3/12}} + \frac{17.5}{(1.0217)^{9/12}} + \frac{1{,}024.95}{(1 + y_3)^{15/12}}$$

Solving this equation, we find $y_3 = .0279$, corresponding to a spot rate of 2.79 percent annually.

When we analyze many bonds, such an inference procedure is more difficult, in part because of the greater number of bonds and time periods, but also because not all bonds give rise to identical estimates for the discounted value of a future \$1 payment. In other words, there seem to be error terms in the pricing relationship.[4] Nevertheless, treating these errors as random aberrations, we can use a statistical approach to infer the pattern of forward rates embedded in the yield curve.

To see how the statistical procedure would operate, suppose that we observe many coupon bonds, indexed by *i*, selling at prices P_i. The coupon and/or principal payment (the cash flow) of bond *i* at time *t* is denoted CF_{it}, and the present value of a \$1 payment at time *t*, which is the implied price of a zero-coupon bond that we are trying to determine, is denoted d_t. Then for each bond we may write the following:

---

[3]We use the six-month and one-year spot rates to discount the first two coupons

[4]We will consider later some of the reasons for the appearance of these error terms.

$$
\begin{aligned}
P_1 &= d_1\text{CF}_{11} + d_2\text{CF}_{12} + d_3\text{CF}_{13} + \ldots + e_1 \\
P_2 &= d_1\text{CF}_{21} + d_2\text{CF}_{22} + d_3\text{CF}_{23} + \ldots + e_2 \\
P_3 &= d_1\text{CF}_{31} + d_2\text{CF}_{32} + d_3\text{CF}_{33} + \ldots + e_3 \\
&\;\;\vdots \\
P_n &= d_1\text{CF}_{n1} + d_2\text{CF}_{n2} + d_3\text{CF}_{n3} + \ldots + e_n
\end{aligned}
\qquad (12.7)
$$

Each line of equation system 12.7 equates the price of the bond to the sum of its cash flows, discounted according to time until payment. The last term in each equation, e_i, represents the error term that accounts for the deviations of a bond's price from the prediction of the equation.

Students of statistics will recognize that equation 12.7 is a simple system of equations that can be estimated by regression analysis. The dependent variables are the bond prices, the independent variables are the cash flows, and the coefficients d_t are to be estimated from the observed data.[5] The estimates of d_t are our inferences of the present value of $1 to be paid at time t. The pattern of d_t for various times to payment is called the *discount function,* because it gives the discounted value of $1 as a function of time until payment. From the discount function, which is equivalent to a list of zero-coupon bond prices for various maturity dates, we can calculate the yields on pure zero-coupon bonds. We would use government securities in this procedure to avoid complications arising from default risk.

Before leaving the issue of the measurement of the yield curve, it is worth pausing briefly to discuss the error terms. Why is it that all bond prices do not conform exactly to a common discount function that sets price equal to present value? Two reasons relate to factors not accounted for in the regression analysis of equation 12.7: taxes and options associated with the bond.

www.cra-arc.gc.ca

Taxes affect bond prices because investors care about their after-tax return on investment. Therefore, the coupon payments should be treated as net of taxes. Similarly, if a bond is not selling at par value, the Canada Revenue Agency requires that a "built-in" interest payment be imputed by amortizing the difference between the price and the par value of the bond. These considerations are difficult to capture in a mathematical formulation because different individuals are in different tax brackets, meaning that the net-of-tax cash flows from a given bond depend on the identity of the owner. Moreover, the specification of equation 12.7 implicitly assumes that the bond is held until maturity: it discounts *all* the bond's coupon and principal payments. This, of course, ignores the investor's option to sell the bond before maturity and so to realize a different stream of income from that described by equation 12.7. Moreover, it ignores the investor's ability to engage in *tax-timing options.* For example, an investor whose tax bracket is expected to change over time may benefit by realizing capital gains during the period when the tax rate is the lowest.

Another feature affecting bond pricing is the call provision. First, if the bond is callable, how do we know whether to include in equation 12.7 coupon payments in years following the first call date? Similarly, the date of the principal repayment becomes uncertain. More importantly, one must realize that the issuer of the callable bond will exercise the option to call only when it is profitable to do so. Conversely, the call provision is a transfer of value away from the bondholder who has "sold" the option to call to the bond issuer. The call feature therefore will affect the bond's price and introduce further error terms in the simple specification of equation 12.7.

Finally, we must recognize that the yield curve is based on price quotes that often are somewhat inaccurate. Price quotes used in the financial press may be stale (i.e., out of date), even if only by a few hours. Moreover, they may not represent prices at which dealers actually are willing to trade.

---

[5] In practice, variations of regression analysis called "splining techniques" are usually used to estimate the coefficients. This method was first suggested by McCulloch in the following two articles: J. Huston McCulloch, "Measuring the Term Structure of Interest Rates," *Journal of Business* 44 (January 1971); and "The Tax Adjusted Yield Curve," *Journal of Finance* 30 (June 1975).

SPOT AND FORWARD YIELDS

The spreadsheet below (available at www.mcgrawhill.ca/college/bodie) can be used to estimate spot rates from coupon bonds and to calculate the forward rates for both single-year and multiyear periods. The model sequentially solves for the spot rates that are associated with each of the periods. The methodology is similar to but slightly different from the regression methodology described in Section 12.6. Spot yields are derived from the yield curve of bonds that are selling at their par value, also referred to as the current coupon or "on-the-run" bond yield curve.

The spot rates for each maturity date are used to calculate the present value of each period's cash flow. The sum of these cash flows is the price of the bond. Given its price, the bond's yield to maturity can then be computed. If you were to err and use the yield to maturity of the on-the-run bond to discount each of the bond's coupon payments, you could find a significantly different price. That difference is calculated in the worksheet.

	A	B	C	D	E	F	G	H
56		Forward Rate Calculations						
57								
58		Spot Rate	1-yr. for.	2-yr. for.	3-yr. for.	4-yr. for.	5-yr. for.	6-yr. for.
59	Period	Rate						
60	1	8.0000%	7.9792%	7.6770%	7.2723%	6.9709%	6.8849%	6.7441%
61	2	7.9896%	7.3757%	6.9205%	6.6369%	6.6131%	6.4988%	6.5520%
62	3	7.7846%	6.4673%	6.2695%	6.3600%	6.2807%	6.3880%	6.1505%
63	4	7.4537%	6.0720%	6.3065%	6.2186%	6.3682%	6.0872%	6.0442%
64	5	7.1760%	6.5414%	6.2920%	6.4671%	6.0910%	6.0387%	5.8579%
65	6	7.0699%	6.0432%	6.4299%	5.9413%	5.9134%	5.7217%	5.6224%
66	7	6.9227%	6.8181%	5.8904%	5.8701%	5.6414%	5.5384%	5.3969%
67	8	6.9096%	4.9707%	5.3993%	5.2521%	5.2209%	5.1149%	5.1988%

SUMMARY

1. The term structure of interest rates refers to the interest rates for various terms to maturity embodied in the prices of default-free zero-coupon bonds.
2. In a world of certainty all investments must provide equal total returns for any investment period. Short-term holding-period returns on all bonds would be equal in a risk-free economy, and all would be equal to the rate available on short-term bonds. Similarly, total returns from rolling over short-term bonds over longer periods would equal the total returns available from long-maturity bonds.
3. The forward rate of interest is the breakeven future interest rate that would equate the total return from a rollover strategy to that of a longer-term zero-coupon bond. It is defined by the equation

$$(1 + y_n)^n(1 + f_{n+1}) = (1 + y_{n+1})^{n+1}$$

where n is a given number of periods from today. This equation can be used to show that yields to maturity and forward rates are related by the equation

$$(1 + y_n)^n = (1 + r_1)(1 + f_2)(1 + f_3) \ldots (1 + f_n)$$

4. A common version of the expectations hypothesis holds that forward interest rates are unbiased estimates of expected future interest rates. However, there are good reasons to believe that forward rates differ from expected short rates by a risk premium known as a *liquidity premium.* A liquidity premium can cause the yield curve to slope upward even if no increase in short rates is anticipated.
5. The existence of liquidity premiums makes it extremely difficult to infer expected future interest rates from the yield curve. Such an inference would be made easier if we could assume the liquidity

premium remained reasonably stable over time. However, both empirical and theoretical insights cast doubt on the constancy of that premium.

6. Forward rates are market interest rates in the important sense that commitments to forward (i.e., deferred) borrowing or lending arrangements can be made at these rates.
7. A pure yield curve could be plotted easily from a complete set of zero-coupon bonds. In practice, however, most bonds carry coupons, payable at different future times, so that yield-curve estimates usually must be inferred from prices of coupon bonds. Measurement of the term structure is complicated by tax issues such as tax timing options and the different tax brackets of different investors.

KEY TERMS

term structure of interest rates 430
short interest rate 431
yield curve 432
spot rate 432
pure yield curve 435
on the run 435
forward interest rate 437
liquidity premium 438
expectations hypothesis 439
liquidity preference theory 440
term premiums 444
bootstrapping 448

SELECTED READINGS

A detailed presentation of yield-curve analytics and relationships among spot rates, yields to maturity, and realized compound yields is contained in:

Homer, Sidney, and Martin Liebowitz. *Inside the Yield Book: New Tools for Bond Market Strategy.* Englewood Cliffs, NJ: Prentice Hall, 1972.

A discussion of the various versions of the expectations hypothesis is:

Cox, John, Jonathan Ingersoll, and Stephen Ross. "A Reexamination of Traditional Hypotheses About the Term Structure of Interest Rates." *Journal of Finance* 36 (September 1981).

Evidence on liquidity premiums may be found in:

Fama, Eugene. "The Information in the Term Structure." *Journal of Financial Economics* 13 (1984).
Mankiw, N. Gregory. "The Term Structure of Interest Rates Revisited." *Brookings Papers on Economic Activity* 61 (1986).

Problems in the measurement of the yield curve are treated in:

McCulloch, J. Houston. "The Tax-Adjusted Yield Curve." *Journal of Finance* 30 (June 1975).

E-INVESTMENTS
The Yield Curve

Go to **www.smartmoney.com**. Click the *Economy* tab to access the *Living Yield Curve*, a moving picture of the yield curve. Is the yield curve usually upward- or downward-sloping? What about today's yield curve? How much does the slope of the curve vary? Which varies more: short-term or long-term rates? Can you explain why this might be the case?

PROBLEMS

CFA® PROBLEMS

1. Briefly explain why bonds of different maturities have different yields in terms of the expectations and liquidity preferences hypotheses.

   Briefly describe the implications of each hypothesis when the yield curve is (i) upward-sloping and (ii) downward-sloping.

CFA® PROBLEMS

2. Which one of the following statements about the term structure of interest rates is true?
   a. The expectations hypothesis indicates a flat yield curve if anticipated future short-term rates exceed current short-term rates.
   b. The expectations hypothesis contends that the long-term rate is equal to the anticipated short-term rate.

c. The liquidity premium theory indicates that, all else being equal, longer maturities will have lower yields.

d. The liquidity preference theory contends that lenders prefer to buy securities at the short end of the yield curve.

3. What is the relationship between forward rates and the market's expectation of future short rates? Explain in the context of both the expectations and liquidity preference theories of the term structure of interest rates.

4. "Under the expectations hypothesis, if the yield curve is upward-sloping, the market must expect an increase in short-term interest rates." Is this statement true, false, or uncertain? Why?

5. "Under the liquidity preference theory, if inflation is expected to be falling over the next few years, long-term interest rates will be higher than short-term rates." Is this statement true, false, or uncertain? Why?

6. The following is a list of prices for zero-coupon bonds of various maturities. Calculate the yields to maturity of each bond and the implied sequence of forward rates.

Maturity (years)	Price of Bond ($)
1	943.40
2	898.47
3	847.62
4	792.16

7. Assuming that the expectations hypothesis is valid, compute the expected price path of the four-year bond in problem 6 as time passes. What is the rate of return of the bond in each year? Show that the expected return equals the forward rate for each year.

CFA® PROBLEMS

8. Suppose the following table shows yields to maturity of U.S. Treasury securities as of January 1, 1996:

Term to Maturity (in years)	Yield to Maturity
1	3.50%
2	4.50
3	5.00
4	5.50
5	6.00
10	6.60

a. Using the data in the table, calculate the implied forward one-year rate of interest at January 1, 1999.

b. Describe the conditions under which the calculated forward rate would be an unbiased estimate of the one-year spot rate of interest at January 1, 1999.

Assume that one year earlier, on January 1, 1995, the prevailing term structure for U.S. Treasury securities was such that the implied forward one-year rate of interest on January 1, 1999 was significantly higher than the corresponding rate implied by the term structure on January 1, 1996.

c. On the basis of the pure expectations theory of the term structure, briefly discuss *two* factors that could account for such a decline in the implied forward rate.

9. Would you expect the yield on a callable bond to lie above or below a yield curve fitted from non-callable bonds?

CFA® PROBLEMS

10. The tables below show, respectively, the characteristics of two annual-pay bonds from the same issuer with the same priority in the event of default, and spot interest rates. Neither bond's price is consistent with the spot rates. Using the information in these tables, recommend either bond *A* or bond *B* for purchase. Justify your choice.

Bond Characteristics

	Bond *A*	Bond *B*
Coupons	Annual	Annual
Maturity	3 years	3 years
Coupon rate	10%	6%
Yield to maturity	10.65%	10.75%
Price	98.40	88.34

Spot Interest Rates

Term (years)	Spot Rates (zero coupon)
1	5%
2	8
3	11

11. The current yield curve for default-free zero-coupon bonds is as follows:

Maturity (years)	YTM
1	10%
2	11
3	12

a. What are the implied one-year forward rates?

b. Assume that the pure expectations hypothesis of the term structure is correct. If market expectations are accurate, what will the pure yield curve, that is, the yields to maturity on one- and two-year zero-coupon bonds, be next year?

c. If you purchase a two-year zero-coupon bond now, what is the expected total rate of return over the next year? What if it were a three-year zero-coupon bond? (*Hint*: Compute the current and expected future prices.) Ignore taxes.

d. What should be the current price of a three-year maturity bond with a 12 percent coupon rate paid annually? If you purchased it at that price, what would your total expected rate of return be over the next year (coupon plus price change)? Ignore taxes.

12. The term structure for zero-coupon bonds is currently:

Maturity (years)	YTM
1	4%
2	5
3	6

Next year at this time, *you* expect it to be:

Maturity (years)	YTM
1	5%
2	6
3	7

a. What do *you* expect the rate of return to be over the coming year on a three-year zero-coupon bond?

b. Under the expectations theory, what yield to maturity does the market expect to observe on one- and two-year zeroes next year? Is the market's expectation of the return on the three-year bond more or less than yours?

13. The yield to maturity on one-year zero-coupon bonds is currently 7 percent; the YTM on two-year zeroes is 8 percent. The federal government plans to issue a two-year maturity *coupon* bond, paying coupons once per year with a coupon rate of 9 percent. The face value of the bond is $100.

a. At what price will the bond sell?

b. What will be the yield to maturity on the bond?

c. If the expectations theory of the yield curve is correct, what is the market expectation of the price that the bond will sell for next year?

d. Recalculate your answer to (*c*) if you believe in the liquidity preference theory and you believe that the liquidity premium is 1 percent.

14. Below is a list of prices for zero-coupon bonds of various maturities.

Maturity (years)	Price of $1,000 Par Bond (zero coupon)
1	943.40
2	873.52
3	816.37

a. An 8.5 percent coupon $1,000 par bond pays an annual coupon and will mature in three years. What should be the yield to maturity on the bond?

b. If at the end of the first year the yield curve flattens out at 8 percent, what will be the one-year holding-period return on the coupon bond?

15. Prices of zero-coupon bonds reveal the following pattern of forward rates:

Year	Forward Rate
1	5%
2	7
3	8

In addition to the zero-coupon bond, investors also may purchase a three-year bond making annual payments of $60 with a par value of $1,000.

a. What is the price of the coupon bond?

b. What is the yield to maturity of the coupon bond?

c. Under the expectations hypothesis, what is the expected realized compound yield of the coupon bond?

d. If you forecast that the yield curve in one year will be flat at 7 percent, what is your forecast for the expected rate of return on the coupon bond for the one-year holding period?

16. You observe the following term structure:

	Effective Annual YTM
1-year zero-coupon bond	6.1%
2-year zero-coupon bond	6.2
3-year zero-coupon bond	6.3
4-year zero-coupon bond	6.4

a. If you believe that the term structure next year will be the same as today's, will the one-year or the four-year zeroes provide a greater expected one-year return?

b. What if you believe in the expectations hypothesis?

CFA® PROBLEMS

17. Canada bonds represent a significant holding in many pension portfolios. You decide to analyze the yield curve for Canada bonds.

a. Using the data in the table below, calculate the five-year spot and forward rates assuming annual compounding. Show your calculations.

Canada Bond Yield Curve Data

Years to Maturity	Par Coupon Yield to Maturity	Calculated Spot Rates	Calculated Forward Rates
1	5.00	5.00	5.00
2	5.20	5.21	5.42
3	6.00	6.05	7.75
4	7.00	7.16	10.56
5	7.00	—	—
4	7.00	7.16	10.56
5	7.00	—	—

b. Define and describe each of the following three concepts:

- Yield to maturity
- Spot rate
- Forward rate

Explain how these *three* concepts are related.

You are considering the purchase of a zero-coupon Canada bond with four years to maturity.

c. On the basis of above yield curve analysis, calculate both the expected yield to maturity and the price for the security. Show your calculations.

18. The yield to maturity (YTM) on one-year maturity zero-coupon bonds is 5 percent and the YTM on two-year maturity zero-coupon bonds is 6 percent. The yield to maturity on two-year maturity coupon bonds with coupon rates of 12 percent (paid annually) is 5.8 percent. What arbitrage opportunity is available for an investment banking firm? What is the profit on the activity?

19. Suppose that a one-year zero-coupon bond with a face value of $100 currently sells at $94.34, while a two-year zero sells at $84.99. You are considering the purchase of a two-year maturity bond making *annual* coupon payments. The face value of the bond is $100, and the coupon rate is 12 percent per year.

a. What is the yield to maturity of the two-year zero? The two-year coupon bond?

b. What is the forward rate for the second year?

c. If the expectations hypothesis is accepted, what are (i) the expected price of the coupon bond at the end of the first year and (ii) the expected holding period return on the coupon bond over the first year?

d. Will the expected rate of return be higher or lower if you accept the liquidity preference hypothesis?

20. Suppose that the prices of zero-coupon bonds with various maturities are given in the following table. The face value of each bond is $1,000.

Maturity (years)	Price
1	925.93
2	853.39
3	782.92
4	715.00
5	650.00

a. Calculate the forward rate of interest for each year.

b. How could you construct a one-year forward loan beginning in year 3? Confirm that the rate on that loan equals the forward rate.

c. Repeat (*b*) for a one-year forward loan beginning in year 4.

21. Continue to use the data in the preceding problem. Suppose that you want to construct a *two-year* maturity forward loan commencing in *three* years.

a. Suppose that you buy *today* one three-year maturity zero-coupon bond. How many five-year maturity zeros would you have to sell to make your initial cash flow equal to zero?

b. What are the cash flows on this strategy in each year?

c. What is the effective two-year interest rate on the effective three-year-ahead forward loan?

d. Confirm that the effective two-year interest rate equals $(1 + f_4) \times (1 + f_5) - 1$. You therefore can interpret the two-year loan rate as a two-year forward rate for the last two years. Alternatively, show that the effective two-year forward rate equals

$$\frac{(1 + y_5)^5}{(1 + y_3)^3} - 1$$

22. The following are the current coupon yields to maturity and spot rates of interest for six U.S. Treasury securities. Assume all securities pay interest annually.

Yields to Maturity and Spot Rates of Interest

Term to Maturity	Current Coupon Yield to Maturity	Spot Rate of Interest
1-year Treasury	5.25%	5.25%
2-year Treasury	5.75	5.79
3-year Treasury	6.15	6.19
5-year Treasury	6.45	6.51
10-year Treasury	6.95	7.10
30-year Treasury	7.25	7.67

Compute, under the expectations theory, the two-year implied forward rate three years from now, given the information provided in the preceding table. State the assumption underlying the calculation of the implied forward rate.

CSI

23. The ______________ theory posits that the yield curve is said to reflect a market consensus of expected future interest rates.

24. The spot rates of interest for five U.S. Treasury securities are shown in the following table. Assume all securities pay interest annually.

Spot Rates of Interest

Term to Maturity (years)	Spot Rate of Interest
1	13.00%
2	12.00
3	11.00
4	10.00
5	9.00

a. i. Compute the two-year implied forward rate for a deferred loan beginning in three years.
ii. Explain your answer by using the expectations theory.

b. Compute the price of a five-year annual-pay Treasury security with a coupon rate of 9 percent by using the information in the table.

E-INVESTMENTS
Expectations and Term Spreads

Go to the St. Louis Fed's FRED database at **research.stlouisfed.org/fred2**. Examine the spread between short- and long-term yields in the early 1980s when rates were generally high but the slope of the yield curve turned steeply negative. What happened to yields in the next several years? How does this square with the expectations hypothesis?

Visit us at www.mcgrawhill.ca/college/bodie

MANAGING BOND PORTFOLIOS

In this chapter we turn to various strategies that bond portfolio managers can pursue, making a distinction between passive and active strategies. A *passive investment strategy* takes market prices of securities as fairly set. Rather than attempting to beat the market by exploiting superior information or insight, passive managers act to maintain an appropriate risk–return balance given market opportunities. One special case of passive management is an immunization strategy that attempts to insulate or immunize the portfolio from interest rate risk. In contrast, an *active investment strategy* attempts to achieve returns greater than those commensurate with the risk borne. In the context of bond management this style of management can take two forms. Active managers either use interest rate forecasts to predict movements in the entire fixed-income market, or they employ some form of intramarket analysis to identify particular sectors of the fixed-income market or particular bonds that are relatively mispriced.

Because interest-rate risk is crucial to formulating both active and passive strategies, we begin our discussion with an analysis of the sensitivity of bond prices to interest rate fluctuations. This sensitivity is measured by the duration of the bond, and we devote considerable attention to what determines bond duration. We discuss several passive investment strategies, and show how duration-matching techniques can be used to immunize the holding-period return of a portfolio from interest-rate risk. After examining the broad range of applications of the duration measure, we consider refinements in the way that interest rate sensitivity is measured, focusing on the concept of bond convexity. Duration is important in formulating active investment strategies as well, and we next explore several of these strategies. We consider strategies based on intramarket analysis as well as on interest rate forecasting. We also show how interest rate swaps may be used in bond portfolio management. We conclude the chapter with a discussion of financial engineering and derivatives in the bond market, and the novel risk profiles that can be achieved through such techniques.

13.1 INTEREST RATE RISK

We have seen already that an inverse relationship exists between bond prices and yields, and we know that interest rates can fluctuate substantially. As interest rates rise and fall, bondholders experience capital losses and gains. These gains or losses make fixed-income investments risky, even if the coupon and principal payments are guaranteed, as in the case of Treasury obligations.

Why do bond prices respond to interest rate fluctuations? Remember that in a competitive market all securities must offer investors fair expected rates of return. If a bond is issued with an 8 percent coupon when competitive yields are 8 percent, then it will sell at par value. If the market rate rises to 9 percent, however, who would purchase an 8 percent coupon bond at par value? The bond price must fall until its expected return increases to the competitive level of 9 percent. Conversely, if the market rate falls to 7 percent, the 8 percent coupon on the bond is attractive compared to yields on alternative investments. In response, investors eager for that return would bid the bond price above its par value until the total rate of return falls to the market rate.

Interest Rate Sensitivity

Interest Rate Risk
www.investinginbonds.com/info/igcorp/risk.htm

The sensitivity of bond prices to changes in market interest rates is obviously of great concern to investors. To gain some insight into the determinants of interest rate risk, turn to Figure 13.1, which presents the percentage change in price corresponding to changes in yield to maturity for four bonds that differ according to coupon rate, initial yield to maturity, and time to maturity. All four bonds illustrate that bond prices decrease when yields rise, and that the price curve is convex, meaning that decreases in yields have bigger impacts on price than increases in yields of equal magnitude. We summarize these observations in the following two propositions:

1. *Bond prices and yields are inversely related: as yields increase, bond prices fall; as yields fall, bond prices rise.*
2. *An increase in a bond's yield to maturity results in a smaller price decline than the price gain associated with a decrease of equal magnitude in yield.*

Now compare the interest rate sensitivity of bonds *A* and *B,* which are identical except for maturity. Figure 13.1 shows that bond *B,* which has a longer maturity than bond *A,* exhibits greater sensitivity to interest rate changes. This illustrates another general property:

3. *Prices of long-term bonds tend to be more sensitive to interest rate changes than prices of short-term bonds.*

Although bond *B* has six times the maturity of bond *A,* it has less than six times the interest rate sensitivity. Although interest rate sensitivity seems to increase with maturity, it does so less than proportionally as bond maturity increases. Therefore, our fourth property is that:

4. *The sensitivity of bond prices to changes in yields increases at a decreasing rate as maturity increases. In other words, interest rate risk is less than proportional to bond maturity.*

Bonds *B* and *C,* which are alike in all respects except for coupon rate, illustrate another point. The lower-coupon bond exhibits greater sensitivity to changes in interest rates. This turns out to be a general property of bond prices:

5. *Interest rate risk is inversely related to the bond's coupon rate. Prices of high-coupon bonds are less sensitive to changes in interest rates than prices of low-coupon bonds.*

Finally, bonds *C* and *D* are identical except for the yield to maturity at which the bonds currently sell. Yet bond *C,* with a higher yield to maturity, is less sensitive to changes in yields. This illustrates our final property:

6. *The sensitivity of a bond's price to a change in its yield is inversely related to the yield to maturity at which the bond currently is selling.*

The first five of these general properties were described by Malkiel[1] and are sometimes known as Malkiel's bond-pricing relationships. The last property was demonstrated by Homer and Liebowitz.[2]

These six propositions confirm that maturity is a major determinant of interest rate risk (see also the boxed article here). However, they also show that maturity alone is not sufficient to measure interest rate sensitivity. For example, bonds *B* and *C* in Figure 13.1 have the same maturity, but the higher-coupon bond has less price sensitivity to interest rate changes. Obviously, we need to know more than a bond's maturity to quantify its interest rate risk.

To see why bond characteristics such as coupon rate or yield to maturity affect interest rate sensitivity, let's start with a simple numerical example. Table 13.1 gives bond prices for 8 percent semiannual coupon bonds at different yields to maturity and times to maturity, *T.* (The interest rates are expressed as annual percentage rates [APRs], meaning that the true six-month yield is doubled to obtain the stated annual yield.) The shortest-term bond falls in value by less than 1 percent when the interest rate increases from 8 percent to 9 percent. The 10-year bond falls by 6.5 percent, and the 20-year bond by over 9 percent.

Let us now look at a similar computation using a zero-coupon bond rather than the 8 percent coupon bond. The results are shown in Table 13.2. Notice that for each maturity, the price of the

Figure 13.1
Change in bond price as a function of change in yield to maturity.

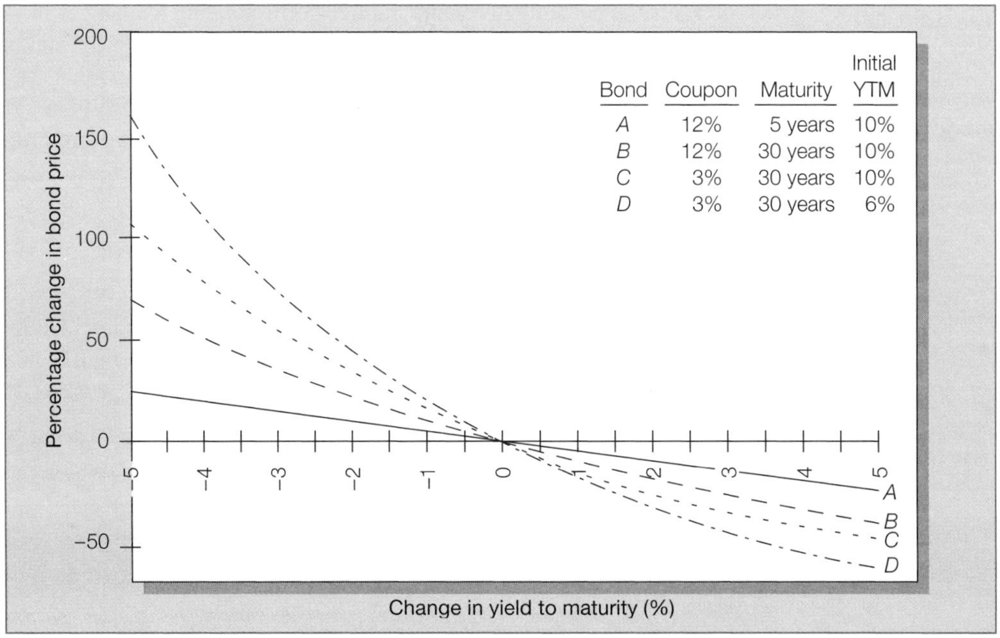

[1]Burton G. Malkiel, "Expectations, Bond Prices, and the Term Structure of Interest Rates," *Quarterly Journal of Economics* 76 (May 1962), pp. 197–218.

[2]Sidney Homer and Martin L. Liebowitz, *Inside the Yield Book: New Tools for Bond Market Strategy* (Englewood Cliffs, NJ: Prentice Hall, 1972).

BUY SHORTER-TERM DEBT: INFLATION WARNING

Bill Gross, who runs the world's biggest bond fund at Pacific Investment Management Co., recommends investors buy shorter-term debt to protect against the likelihood inflation will accelerate. "While total return is the name of the game, one must always be cognizant of what constitutes the majority of that return over long periods of time—interest payments," Mr. Gross wrote in a monthly commentary published on Newport Beach, Calif.-based Pimco's Web site.

Specifically, Mr. Gross recommends investors holding U.S. or Japanese debt reduce the so-called duration of their portfolios, and increase durations in European debt. Duration measures a bond's price sensitivity to changes in interest rates over time. An investor can cut duration by buying shorter-term debt, which typically carries lower yields. "Investment managers in order to succeed against their bogies and peers must take what I consider to be measured risk," said Mr. Gross, who manages the US$74-billion Total Return Fund. Pimco is owned by Allianz AG, Europe's biggest insurer.

In the Total Return Fund, Mr. Gross has reduced his holdings of debt maturing in more than eight years to 8% as of Jan. 31—as measured by duration—from 56% as of June, 2003. At the same time, he has increased his allocation of treasury notes maturing between five and eight years to 44% from 15%; and boosted his holdings of notes between three and five years to 22% from 8%. Mr. Gross has held his holdings of notes maturing from one to three years at 13%.

The Federal Reserve has kept its target interest rate at a 45-year low of 1% since June to ward off a threat that inflation will slow too much. In such an environment, firms can't raise prices, leading to stagnant profit margins and keeping them from hiring more workers.

Last month, the U.S. Labor Department said consumer prices rose 0.5% in January, the most in almost a year. Inflation erodes the value of fixed-income payments over time.

Mr. Gross also recommends investors buy U.S. municipal securities, which would benefit from higher tax rates, and Treasury Inflation-Protected Securities, or TIPS. Pimco purchased about US$3-billion of TIPS at the government's last auction of the securities in January.

Source: Monee Fields-White, "Buy Shorter-Term Debt, Pimco's Gross Advises: Inflation Warning," Financial Post Investing, *National Post*, March 5, 2004, p. IN.03.

Table 13.1 Prices of 8 Percent Coupon Bond (coupons paid semiannually)

Yield to Maturity (APR)	T = 1 Year	T = 10 Years	T = 20 Years
8%	1,000.00	1,000.00	1,000.00
9%	990.64	934.96	907.99
Change in price (%)*	0.94%	6.50%	9.20%

*Equals value of bond at a 9 percent yield to maturity divided by value of bond at (the original) 8 percent yield, minus 1.

zero-coupon bond falls by a greater proportional amount than the price of the 8 percent coupon bond. Because we know that long-term bonds are more sensitive to interest rate movements than are short-term bonds, this observation suggests that in some sense a zero-coupon bond represents a longer-term bond than an equal-time-to-maturity coupon bond. In fact, this insight about effective maturity is a useful one that we can make mathematically precise.

To start, note that the times to maturity of the two bonds in this example are not perfect measures of the long- or short-term nature of the bonds. The 20-year 8 percent bond makes many coupon payments, most of which come years before the bond's maturity date. Each of these payments may be considered to have its own "maturity date," and the effective maturity of the bond is therefore some sort of average of the maturities of *all* the cash flows paid out by the bond. The zero-coupon bond, by contrast, makes only one payment at maturity. Its time to maturity is, therefore, a well-defined concept.

Table 13.2 Prices of Zero-Coupon Bond (semiannual compounding)

Yield to Maturity (APR)	T = 1 Year	T = 10 Years	T = 20 Years
8%	924.56	456.39	208.29
9%	915.73	414.64	171.93
Change in price (%)*	0.96%	9.15%	17.46%

*Equals value of bond at a 9 percent yield to maturity divided by value of bond at (the original) 8 percent yield, minus 1.

Duration

To deal with the ambiguity of the "maturity" of a bond making many payments, we need a measure of the average maturity of the bond's promised cash flows to serve as a useful summary statistic of the effective maturity of the bond. We would like also to use the measure as a guide to the sensitivity of a bond to interest rate changes, because we have noted that price sensitivity tends to increase with time to maturity.

Frederick Macaulay[3] termed the effective maturity concept the **duration** of the bond and suggested that duration be computed as the weighted average of the times to each coupon or principal payment made by the bond. He recommended that the weight associated with each payment time be related to the "importance" of that payment to the value of the bond; specifically, that the weight applied to each payment time be the proportion of the total value of the bond accounted for by that payment. This proportion is just the present value of the payment divided by the bond price.

Figure 13.2 can help us interpret Macaulay's duration. The figure shows the cash flows made by an eight-year maturity annual payment bond with a coupon rate of 9 percent, selling at a yield to maturity of 10 percent. In the first seven years, cash flow is simply the $90 coupon payment; in the last year, cash flow is the sum of coupon plus par value, or $1,090. The height of each bar is the size of the cash flow; the lower part of each bar is the *present value* of that cash flow using a discount rate of 10 percent. If you view the cash flow diagram as a balancing scale, like a seesaw, the duration of the bond is the fulcrum point where the scale would be balanced using present values of each cash flow as weights. The balancing point in Figure 13.2 is at 5.97 years, which in fact is the weighted average of the times until each payment, with weights proportional to the present value of each cash flow. The coupon payments made prior to maturity make the effective (i.e., weighted average) maturity of the bond less than its actual time to maturity.

To calculate the weighted average directly, we define the weight, w_t, associated with the cash flow made at time t (denoted CF_t) as

$$w_t = \frac{\text{CF}_t/(1+y)^t}{\text{Bond price}}$$

Figure 13.2 **Cash flows paid by 9 percent coupon, annual payment bond with 8-year maturity.**

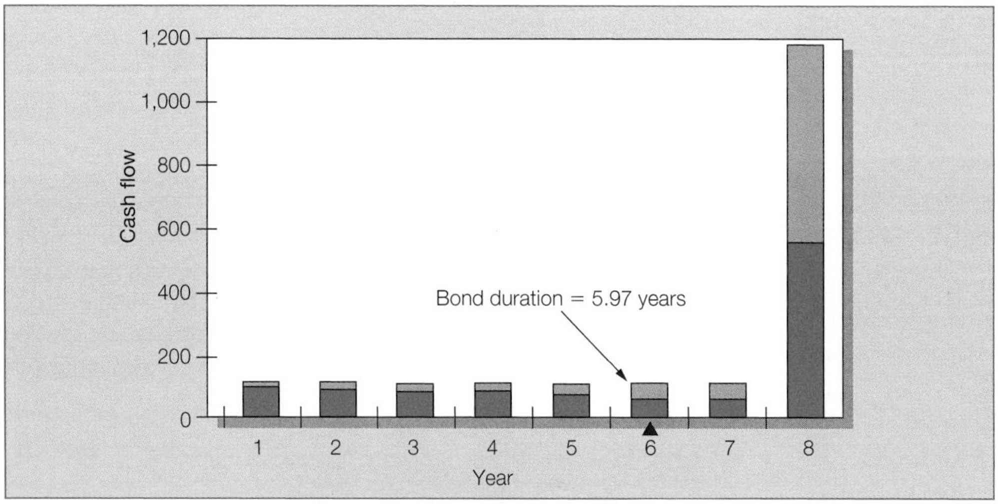

The height of each bar is the total of interest and principal. The lower portion of each bar is the present value of that total cash flow. The fulcrum point is Macaulay's duration, the weighted average of the time until each payment.

[3]Frederick Macaulay, *Some Theoretical Problems Suggested by the Movements of Interest Rates, Bond Yields, and Stock Prices in the United States Since 1856* (New York: National Bureau of Economic Research, 1938).

where y is the bond's yield to maturity. The numerator on the right-hand side of this equation is the present value of the cash flow occurring at time t while the denominator is the value of all the payments forthcoming from the bond. These weights sum to 1.0 because the sum of the cash flows discounted at the yield to maturity equals the bond price.

Using these values to calculate the weighted average of the times until the receipt of each of the bond's payments, we obtain Macaulay's duration formula:

$$D = \sum_{t=1}^{T} t \times w_t \tag{13.1}$$

As an example of the application of equation 13.1, we derive in Table 13.3 the durations of an 8 percent coupon and zero-coupon bond, each with two years to maturity. We assume that the yield to maturity on each bond is 10 percent, or 5 percent per half-year.

The numbers in column 5 are the products of time to payment and payment weight. Each of these products corresponds to one of the terms in equation 13.1. According to that equation, we can calculate the duration of each bond by adding the numbers in column 5.

The duration of the zero-coupon bond is exactly equal to its time to maturity, two years. This makes sense, because with only one payment, the average time until payment must be the bond's maturity. In contrast, the two-year coupon bond has a shorter duration of 1.8853 years.

Figure 13.3 shows the spreadsheet formulas used to produce the entries in Table 13.3. The inputs in the spreadsheet—specifying the cash flows the bond will pay—are given in columns B–D. In column E we calculate the present value of each cash flow using the assumed yield to maturity, in column F we calculate the weights for equation 13.1, and in column G we compute the product of time to payment and payment weight. Each of these terms corresponds to one of the values that are summed in equation 13.1. The sums computed in cells G8 and G14 are therefore the durations of each bond. Using the spreadsheet, you can easily answer several "what if" questions such as the one in Concept Check 1.

Duration is a key concept in fixed-income portfolio management for at least three reasons. First, it is a simple summary statistic of the effective average maturity of the portfolio. Second,

CONCEPT CHECK

1. Suppose the interest rate decreases to 9 percent at an annual percentage rate. What will happen to the prices and durations of the two bonds in Table 13.3?

Table 13.3 Calculating the Duration of Two Bonds

	(1) Time Until Payment (years)	(2) Payment	(3) Payment Discounted at 5% Semiannually	(4) Weight*	(5) Column 1 Multiplied by Column 4
Bond *A*					
8% bond	0.5	$ 40	$ 38.095	0.0395	0.0198
	1.0	40	36.281	0.0376	0.0376
	1.5	40	34.553	0.0358	0.0537
	2.0	1,040	855.611	0.8871	1.7742
Sum			$964.540	1.0000	1.8853
Bond *B*					
Zero-coupon bond	0.5–1.5	$ 0	$ 0	0	0
	2.0	1,000	822.70	1.0	2
Sum			$ 822.70	1.0	2

*Weight = Present value of each payment (column 3) divided by the bond price, $964.54 for bond *A* and $822.70 for bond *B*.

Figure 13.3 Spreadsheet formulas for calculating duration.

	A	B	C	D	E	F	G
1			Time Until		PV of CF		Column (C)
2			Payment		(discount rate =		Times
3		Period	(years)	Cash Flow	5% per period)	Weight	Column (F)
4	**A.** 8% coupon bond	1	0.5	40	=D4/(1+$B$16)^B4	=E4/E$8	=F4*C4
5		2	1	40	=D5/(1+$B$16)^B5	=E5/E$8	=F5*C5
6		3	1.5	40	=D6/(1+$B$16)^B6	=E6/E$8	=F6*C6
7		4	2	1040	=D7/(1+$B$16)^B7	=E7/E$8	=F7*C7
8	Sum:				=SUM(E4:E7)	=SUM(F4:F7)	=SUM(G4:G7)
9							
10	**B.** Zero-coupon	1	0.5	0	=D10/(1+$B$16)^B10	=E10/E$14	=F10*C10
11		2	1	0	=D11/(1+$B$16)^B11	=E11/E$14	=F11*C11
12		3	1.5	0	=D12/(1+$B$16)^B12	=E12/E$14	=F12*C12
13		4	2	1000	=D13/(1+$B$16)^B13	=E13/E$14	=F13*C13
14	Sum:				=SUM(E10:E13)	=SUM(F10:F13)	=SUM(G10:G13)
15							
16	Semiannual int rate:	0.05					

it turns out to be an essential tool in immunizing portfolios from interest rate risk. We explore this application in Section 13.3. Third, duration is a measure of the interest rate sensitivity of a portfolio, which we explore here.

We have seen that long-term bonds are more sensitive to interest rate movements than are short-term bonds. The duration measure enables us to quantify this relationship. Specifically, it can be shown that when interest rates change, the proportional change in a bond's price can be related to the change in its yield to maturity, y, according to the rule

$$\frac{\Delta P}{P} = -D \times \left[\frac{\Delta(1+y)}{1+y}\right] \tag{13.2}$$

The proportional price change equals the proportional change in 1 plus the bond's yield times the bond's duration. Therefore, bond price volatility is proportional to the bond's duration, and duration becomes a natural measure of interest rate exposure.

Practitioners commonly use equation 13.2 in a slightly different form. They define **modified duration** as $D^* = D/(1+y)$, note that $\Delta(1+y) = \Delta y$, and rewrite equation 13.2 as

$$\frac{\Delta P}{p} = -D^*\Delta y \tag{13.3}$$

The percentage change in bond price is just the product of modified duration and the change in the bond's yield to maturity. Because the percentage change in the bond price is proportional to modified duration, modified duration is a natural measure of the bond's exposure to changes in interest rates.[4]

To confirm the relationship between duration and the sensitivity of bond price to interest rate changes, let's compare the price sensitivity of the two-year coupon bond in Table 13.3, which has a duration of 1.8853 years, to the sensitivity of a zero-coupon bond with maturity *and* duration of 1.8853 years. Both should have equal price sensitivity if duration is a useful measure of interest rate exposure.

[4]Actually, equation 13.2, or equivalently 13.3, is only approximately valid for large changes in the bond's yield. The approximation becomes exact as one considers smaller, or localized, changes in yields. Students of calculus will recognize that modified duration is proportional to the derivative of the bond's price with respect to changes in the bond's yield:

$$D^* = -\frac{1}{P}\frac{dP}{dy}$$

As such, it gives a measure of the slope of the bond price curve only in the neighbourhood of the current price.

The coupon bond sells for \$964.5405 at the initial semiannual interest rate of 5 percent. If the bond's semiannual yield increases by 1 basis point (i.e., .01 percent) to 5.01 percent, its price will fall to \$964.1942, a percentage decline of .0359 percent. The zero-coupon bond has a maturity of $1.8853 \times 2 = 3.7706$ half-year periods. (Because we use a half-year interest rate of 5 percent, we also need to define duration in terms of a number of half-year periods to maintain consistency of units.) At the initial half-year interest rate of 5 percent, it sells at a price of \$831.9623 ($\$1{,}000/1.05^{3.7706}$). Its price falls to \$831.6636 ($\$1{,}000/1.0501^{3.7706}$) when the interest rate increases, for an identical .0359 percent capital loss. We conclude, therefore, that equal-duration assets are in fact equally sensitive to interest rate movements.

Incidentally, this example confirms the validity of equation 13.2. Note that the equation predicts that the proportional price change of the two bonds should have been $3.7706 \times .0001/1.05 = .000359$, or .0359 percent, exactly as we found from direct computation.

CONCEPT CHECK ?

2. *a.* In Concept Check 1, you calculated the price and duration of a two-year maturity, 8 percent coupon bond making semiannual coupon payments when the market interest rate is 9 percent. Now suppose the interest rate increases to 9.05 percent. Calculate the new value of the bond and the percentage change in the bond's price.

   b. Calculate the percentage change in the bond's price predicted by the duration formula in equation 13.2 or 13.3. Compare this value to your answer for (*a*).

What Determines Duration? Malkiel's bond price relations, which we laid out in the previous section, characterize the determinants of interest rate sensitivity. Duration allows us to quantify that sensitivity, which greatly enhances our ability to formulate investment strategies. For example, if we wish to speculate on interest rates, duration tells us how strong a bet we are making. Conversely, if we wish to remain "neutral" on rates, and simply match the interest rate sensitivity of a chosen bond-market index, duration allows us to measure that sensitivity and mimic it in our own portfolio. For these reasons, it is crucial to understand the determinants of duration, and convenient to have formulas to calculate the duration of some commonly encountered securities. Therefore, in this section, we present several "rules" that summarize most of the important properties of duration.

Duration Properties The sensitivity of a bond's price to changes in market interest rates is influenced by three key factors: time to maturity, coupon rate, and yield to maturity. These determinants of price sensitivity are important to fixed-income portfolio management. Therefore, we summarize some of the important relationships in the following eight rules. These rules are also illustrated in Figure 13.4, where durations of bonds of various coupon rates, yields to maturity, and times to maturity are plotted.

We have already established:

Rule 1 for Duration The duration of a zero-coupon bond equals its time to maturity.

We have also seen that the two-year coupon bond has a lower duration than the two-year zero because coupons early in the bond's life lower the bond's weighted average time until payments. This illustrates another general property:

Rule 2 for Duration Holding maturity constant, a bond's duration is higher when the coupon rate is lower.

This property corresponds to Malkiel's fifth relationship and is attributable to the impact of early coupon payments on the average maturity of a bond's payments. The higher these coupons, the higher the weights on the early payments and the lower the weighted average maturity of the payments. Compare the plots in Figure 13.4 of the durations of the 3 percent coupon and 15 percent coupon bonds, each with identical yields of 15 percent. The plot of the duration of the 15 percent coupon bond lies below the corresponding plot for the 3 percent coupon bond.

Rule 3 for Duration Holding the coupon rate constant, a bond's duration generally increases with its time to maturity. Duration always increases with maturity for bonds selling at par or at a premium to par.

This property of duration corresponds to Malkiel's third relationship, and it is fairly intuitive. What is surprising is that duration need not always increase with time to maturity. It turns out that for some deep-discount bonds, duration may fall with increases in maturity. However, for virtually all traded bonds it is safe to assume that duration increases with maturity.

Notice in Figure 13.4 that for the zero-coupon bond, maturity and duration are equal. However, for coupon bonds duration increases by less than a year with a year's increase in maturity. The slope of the duration graph is less than 1.

Although long-maturity bonds generally will be high-duration bonds, duration is a better measure of the long-term nature of the bond because it also accounts for coupon payments. Time to maturity is an adequate statistic only when the bond pays no coupons; then, maturity and duration are equal.

Notice also in Figure 13.4 that the two 15 percent coupon bonds have different durations when they sell at different yields to maturity. The lower-yield bond has greater duration. This makes sense, because at lower yields the more distant payments made by the bond have relatively greater present values and account for a greater share of the bond's total value. Thus in the weighted-average calculation of duration the distant payments receive greater weights, which results in a higher duration measure. This establishes rule 4:

Figure 13.4
Bond duration versus bond maturity.

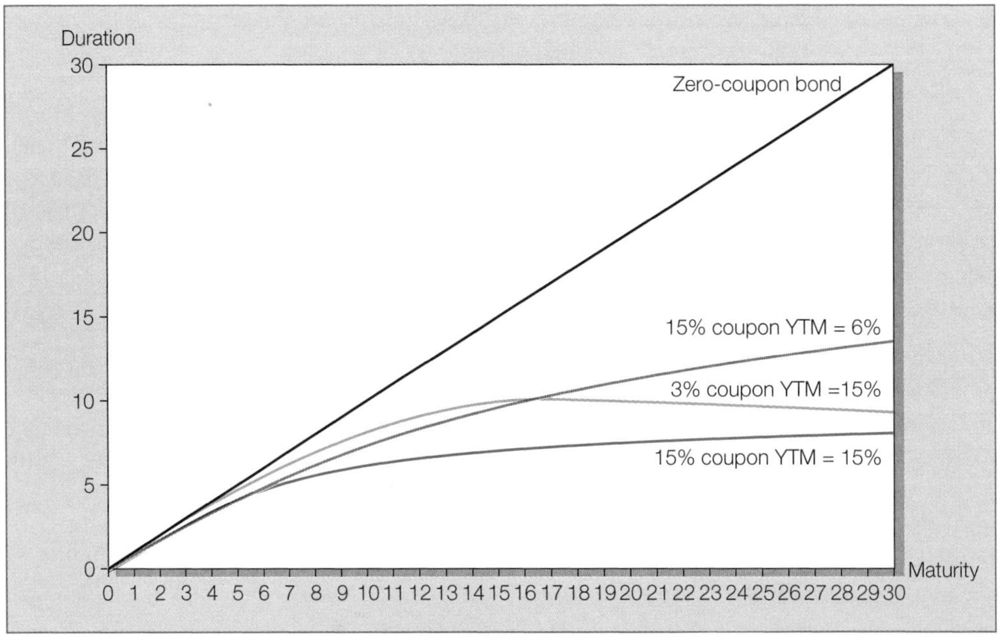

BOND PRICING AND DURATION

Bond pricing and duration calculations can be cumbersome. The calculations are set up in a spreadsheet that is available on the Online Learning Centre at www.mcgrawhill.ca/college/bodie. The models allow you to calculate the price and duration for bonds of different maturities. The models also allow you to examine the sensitivity of the calculations to changes in coupon rate and yield to maturity.

	A	B	C	D	E
1	Duration Example: Using Data Tables				
2					
3	Bond				
4	Coupon Rate	0.08			
5	Par Value	1000			
6	Years Mat	10			
7	YTM	0.06			
8					
9	Bond Price	Years	Cash Flow	PVCF	PVCF×t
10		1	80	75.4717	75.4717
11		2	80	71.19972	142.3994
12		3	80	67.16954	201.5086
13		4	80	63.36749	253.47
14		5	80	59.78065	298.9033
15		6	80	56.39684	338.3811
16		7	80	53.20457	372.432
17		8	80	50.19299	401.5439
18		9	80	47.35188	426.1669
19		10	1080	603.0664	6030.664
20					
21	Sum			1147.202	8540.94
22					
23	Price	1147.202			
24	Duration	7.44502			

Rule 4 for Duration Holding other factors constant, the duration of a coupon bond is higher when the bond's yield to maturity is lower.

Rule 4, which is the sixth bond-pricing relationship above, applies to coupon bonds. For zeros, of course, duration equals time to maturity, regardless of the yield to maturity.

Finally, we develop some algebraic rules for the duration of securities of special interest. These rules are derived from and consistent with the formula for duration given in equation 13.1 but may be easier to use for long-term bonds.

Rule 5 for Duration The duration of a level perpetuity is $(1 + y)/y$. For example, at a 10 percent yield, the duration of a perpetuity that pays \$100 once a year forever will equal 1.10/.10 = 11 years, but at an 8 percent yield it will equal 1.08/.08 = 13.5 years.

Rule 5 makes it obvious that maturity and duration can differ substantially. The maturity of the perpetuity is infinite, whereas the duration of the instrument at a 10 percent yield is only 11 years. The present-value-weighted cash flows early on in the life of the perpetuity dominate the computation of duration.

Notice from Figure 13.4 that as their maturities become ever longer, the durations of the two coupon bonds with yields of 15 percent converge to the duration of the perpetuity with the same yield, 7.67 years.

> **CONCEPT CHECK**
> 3. Show that the duration of the perpetuity increases as the interest rate decreases in accordance with rule 4.

Rule 6 for Duration The duration of a level annuity is equal to

$$\frac{1+y}{y} - \frac{T}{(1+y)^T - 1} \tag{13.4}$$

where T is the number of payments and y is the annuity's yield per payment period. For example, a 10-year annual annuity with a yield of 8 percent will have duration

$$\frac{1.08}{.08} - \frac{10}{1.08^{10} - 1} = 4.87 \text{ years} \tag{13.5}$$

Rule 7 for Duration The duration of a coupon bond equals

$$\frac{1+y}{y} - \frac{(1+y) + T(c-y)}{c[(1+y)^T - 1] + y}$$

where c is the coupon rate per payment period, T is the number of payment periods, and y is the bond's yield per payment period. For example, a 10 percent coupon bond with 20 years until maturity, paying coupons semiannually, would have a 5 percent semiannual coupon and 40 payment periods. If the yield to maturity were 4 percent per half-year period, the bond's duration would be

$$\frac{1.04}{.04} - \frac{1.04 + 40(.05 - .04)}{.05[1.04^{40} - 1] + .04} = 19.74 \text{ half-years} = 9.87 \text{ years}$$

This calculation reminds us again of the importance of maintaining consistency between the time units of the payment period and interest rate. When the bond pays a coupon semiannually, we must use the effective semiannual interest rate and semiannual coupon rate in all calculations. This unit of time (one half-year) is then carried into the duration measure, when we calculate duration to be 19.74 half-year periods.

Rule 8 for Duration For coupon bonds selling at par value, rule 7 simplifies to the following formula for duration:

$$\frac{1+y}{y}\left[1 - \frac{1}{(1+y)^T}\right] \tag{13.6}$$

The equations for the durations of coupon bonds are somewhat tedious. Moreover, they assume that the bond is at the beginning of a coupon payment period. Fortunately, spreadsheet programs such as Excel come with generalizations of these equations that can accommodate bonds between coupon payment dates. Figure 13.5 illustrates how to use Excel to compute duration. The spreadsheet uses many of the same conventions as the bond-pricing spreadsheets described in Chapter 11.

The settlement date (i.e., today's date) and maturity date are entered in cells B4 and B5 using Excel's date function, DATE(year, month, day). The coupon and maturity rates are entered as decimals in cells B6 and B7, and the payment periods per year are entered in cell B8. Macaulay and modified duration appear in cells B11 and B12. The spreadsheet shows that the duration of the bond in Figure 13.2 is indeed 5.97 years. For this eight-year maturity bond, we don't have a

Figure 13.5 Using Excel to compute duration.

	A	B	C
1	**Using Excel to compute duration**		
2			
3	**Inputs**		**Formula in column B**
4	Settlement date	1/1/2000	=DATE(2000,1,1)
5	Maturity date	1/1/2008	=DATE(2008,1,1)
6	Coupon rate	0.09	0.09
7	Yield to maturity	0.1	0.1
8	Coupons per year	1	1
9			
10	**Outputs**		
11	Macaulay Duration	5.9735	=DURATION(B4,B5,B6,B7,B8)
12	Modified Duration	5.4304	=MDURATION(B4,B5,B6,B7,B8)

specific settlement date. We arbitrarily set the settlement date to January 1, 2000, and use a maturity date precisely eight years later.

Durations can vary widely among traded bonds. Table 13.4 presents durations computed from rule 7 for several bonds all assumed to pay semiannual coupons and to yield 4 percent per half-year. Notice that duration decreases as coupon rates increase, and duration generally increases with time to maturity. According to Table 13.4 and equation 13.2, if the interest rate were to increase from 8 percent to 8.1 percent, the 6 percent coupon 20-year bond would fall in value by about 1.01 percent (10.922 × .1%/1.08), whereas the 10 percent coupon one-year bond would fall by only .090 percent. Notice also from Table 13.4 that duration is independent of coupon rate only for the perpetual bond.

Table 13.4 Bond Durations (initial bond yield = 8 percent APR)

	Coupon Rates (per year)			
Years to Maturity	**6%**	**8%**	**10%**	**12%**
1	0.985	0.980	0.976	0.972
5	4.361	4.218	4.095	3.990
10	7.454	7.067	6.772	6.541
20	10.922	10.292	9.870	9.568
Infinite (perpetuity)	13.000	13.000	13.000	13.000

13.2 CONVEXITY

Duration clearly is a key tool in fixed-income portfolio management. Yet the duration rule for the impact of interest rates on bond prices is only an approximation. Equation 13.2, or its equivalent, 13.3, which we repeat here, states that the percentage change in the value of a bond approximately equals the product of modified duration times the change in the bond's yield:

$$\frac{\Delta P}{P} = -D^*\Delta y \qquad (13.3)$$

This rule asserts that the percentage price change is directly proportional to the change in the bond's yield. If this were *exactly* so, however, a graph of the percentage change in bond price as a function of the change in its yield would plot as a straight line, with slope equal to $-D^*$. Yet we know from Figure 13.1, and more generally from Malkiel's five rules (specifically rule 2), that the relationship between bond prices and yields is *not* linear. The duration rule is a good approximation for small changes in bond yield, but it is less accurate for larger changes.

Figure 13.6 illustrates this point. Like Figure 13.1, the figure presents the percentage change in bond price in response to a change in the bond's yield to maturity. The curved line is the percentage price change for a 30-year maturity, 8 percent coupon bond, selling at an initial yield to maturity of 8 percent. The straight line is the percentage price change predicted by the duration rule: the modified duration of the bond at its initial yield is 11.26 years, so the straight line is a plot of $-D^*\Delta y = -11.26 \times \Delta y$. Notice that the two plots are tangent at the initial yield. Thus for small changes in the bond's yield to maturity, the duration rule is quite accurate. However, for larger changes in yield, there is progressively more "daylight" between the two plots, demonstrating that the duration rule becomes progressively less accurate.

Notice from Figure 13.6 that the duration approximation (the straight line) always understates the value of the bond; it underestimates the increase in bond price when the yield falls, and it overestimates the decline in price when the yield rises. This is due to the curvature of the true price-yield relationship. Curves with shapes such as that of the price-yield relationship are said to be *convex*, and the curvature of the price-yield curve is called the **convexity** of the bond.

We can quantify convexity as the rate of change of the slope of the price-yield curve, expressed as a fraction of the bond price.[5] As a practical rule, you can view bonds with higher convexity as exhibiting higher curvature in the price-yield relationship. The convexity of noncallable bonds such as that in Figure 13.6 is positive: the slope increases (i.e., becomes less negative) at higher yields.

Figure 13.6 Bond price convexity.

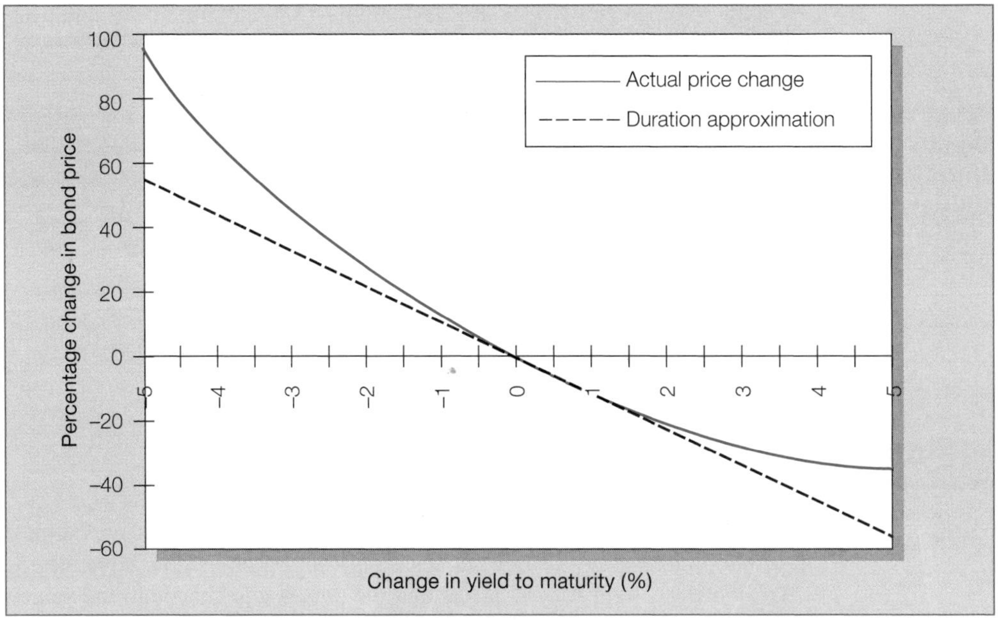

[5]We pointed out in footnote 4 that equation 13.2 for modified duration can be written as $dP/P = -D^*dy$. Thus $D^* = -1/P \times dP/dy$ is the slope of the price-yield curve expressed as a fraction of the bond price. Similarly, the convexity of a bond equals the second derivative (the rate of change of the slope) of the price-yield curve divided by bond price: $1/P \times d^2P/dy^2$. The formula for the convexity of a bond with a maturity of n years making annual coupon payments is

$$\text{Convexity} = \frac{1}{P \times (1+y)^2} \sum_{t=1}^{n} \left[\frac{CF_t}{(1+y)^t} (t^2 + t) \right]$$

where CF_t is the cash flow paid to the bondholder at date t; CF_t represents either a coupon payment before maturity or final coupon plus par value at the maturity date.

Convexity allows us to improve the duration approximation for bond price changes. Accounting for convexity, equation 13.2 can be modified as follows:[6]

$$\frac{\Delta P}{P} = -D^*\Delta y + \frac{1}{2} \times \text{Convexity} \times (\Delta y)^2 \qquad (13.7)$$

The first term on the right-hand side is the same as the duration rule, equation 13.2. The second term is the modification for convexity. Notice that for a bond with positive convexity, the second term is positive, regardless of whether the yield rises or falls. This insight corresponds to the fact noted just above that the duration rule always underestimates the new value of a bond following a change in its yield. The more accurate equation 13.3, which accounts for convexity, always predicts a higher bond price than equation 13.2. Of course, if the change in yield is small, the convexity term, which is multiplied by $(\Delta y)^2$ in equation 13.3, will be extremely small and will add little to the approximation. In this case, the linear approximation given by the duration rule will be sufficiently accurate. Thus convexity is more important as a practical matter when potential interest rate changes are large.

Let's use a numerical example to examine the impact of convexity. The bond in Figure 13.6 has a 30-year maturity, an 8 percent coupon, and sells at an initial yield to maturity of 8 percent. Because the coupon rate equals yield to maturity, the bond sells at par value, or $1,000. The modified duration of the bond at its initial yield is 11.26 years, and its convexity is 212.4 (which can be verified using the formula in footnote 5). If the bond's yield increases from 8 percent to 10 percent, the bond price will fall to $811.46, a decline of 18.85 percent. The duration rule, equation 13.3, would predict a price decline of

$$\frac{\Delta P}{P} = -D^*\Delta y = -11.26 \times .02 = -.2252, \text{ or } -22.52\%$$

which is considerably more than the bond price actually falls. The duration-with-convexity rule, equation 13.3, is more accurate:[7]

$$\begin{aligned}\frac{\Delta P}{P} &= -D^*\Delta y + \frac{1}{2} \times \text{Convexity} \times (\Delta y)^2 \\ &= -11.26 \times .02 + \frac{1}{2} \times 212.4 \times (.02)^2 = -.1827, \text{ or } -18.27\%\end{aligned}$$

which is far closer to the exact change in bond price.

Notice that if the change in yield were smaller, say .1 percent, convexity would matter less. The price of the bond actually would fall to $988.85, a decline of 1.115 percent. Without accounting for convexity, we would predict a price decline of

$$\frac{\Delta P}{P} = -D^*\Delta y = -11.26 \times .001 = .01126, \text{ or } 1.126\%$$

Accounting for convexity, we get almost the precisely correct answer:

$$\frac{\Delta P}{P} = -11.26 \times .001 + \frac{1}{2} \times 212.4 \times (.001)^2 = .01115, \text{ or } 1.115\%$$

Nevertheless, the duration rule is quite accurate in this case, even without accounting for convexity.

Why Do Investors Like Convexity?

Convexity is generally considered a desirable trait. Bonds with greater curvature gain more in price when yields fall than they lose when yields rise. For example in Figure 13.7 bonds *A* and *B*

---

[6]To use the convexity rule, you must express interest rates as decimals rather than percentages.

[7]Notice that when we use equation 13.3, we express interest rates as decimals rather than percentages. The change in rates from 8 percent to 10 percent is represented as $\Delta y = .02$.

Figure 13.7 Convexity of two bonds.

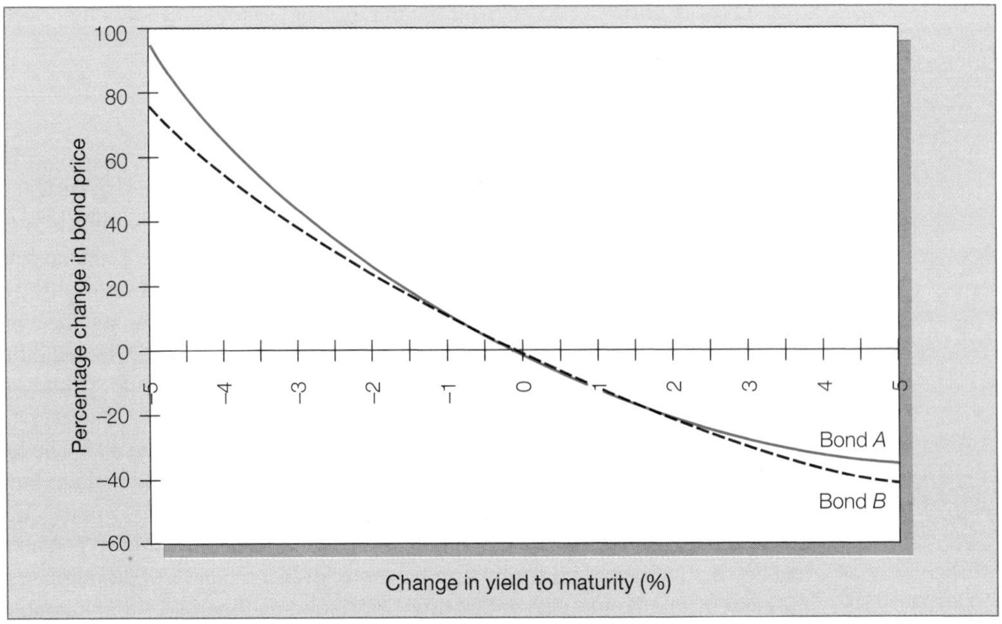

have the same duration at the initial yield. The plots of their proportional price changes as a function of interest-rate changes are tangent, meaning that their sensitivities to changes in yields at that point are equal. However, bond A is more convex than bond B. It enjoys greater price increases and smaller price decreases when interest rates fluctuate by larger amounts. If interest rates are volatile, this is an attractive asymmetry that increases the expected return on the bond, since bond A will benefit more from rate decreases and suffer less from rate increases. Of course, if convexity is desirable, it will not be available for free: investors will have to pay more and accept lower yields on bonds with greater convexity.

Duration and Convexity of Callable Bonds

Look at Figure 13.8, which depicts the price-yield curve for a callable bond. When interest rates are high, the curve is convex, as it would be for a straight bond. For example, at an interest rate of 10 percent, the price-yield curve lies above its tangency line. But as rates fall, there is a ceiling on the possible price: the bond cannot be worth more than its call price. So as rates fall, we sometimes say that the bond is subject to price compression—its value is "compressed" to the call price. In this region, for example at an interest rate of 5 percent, the price-yield curve lies *below* its tangency line, and the curve is said to have *negative convexity.*[8]

Notice that in the region of negative convexity, the price-yield curve exhibits an *unattractive* asymmetry. Interest rate increases result in a larger price decline than the price gain corresponding to an interest rate decrease of equal magnitude. The asymmetry arises from the fact that the bond issuer has retained an option to call back the bond. If rates rise, the bondholder loses, as would be the case for a straight bond. But if rates fall, rather than reaping a large capital gain, the investor may have the bond called back from her. The bondholder is thus in a "Heads I lose, tails I don't win" position. Of course, she was compensated for this unattractive situation when she purchased the bond. Callable bonds sell at lower initial prices (higher initial yields) than otherwise comparable straight bonds.

---

[8]If you've ever taken a calculus course, you will recognize that the curve is *concave* in this region. However, rather than saying that these bonds exhibit "concavity," bond traders prefer to say "negative convexity."

Figure 13.8 Price-yield curve for a callable bond.

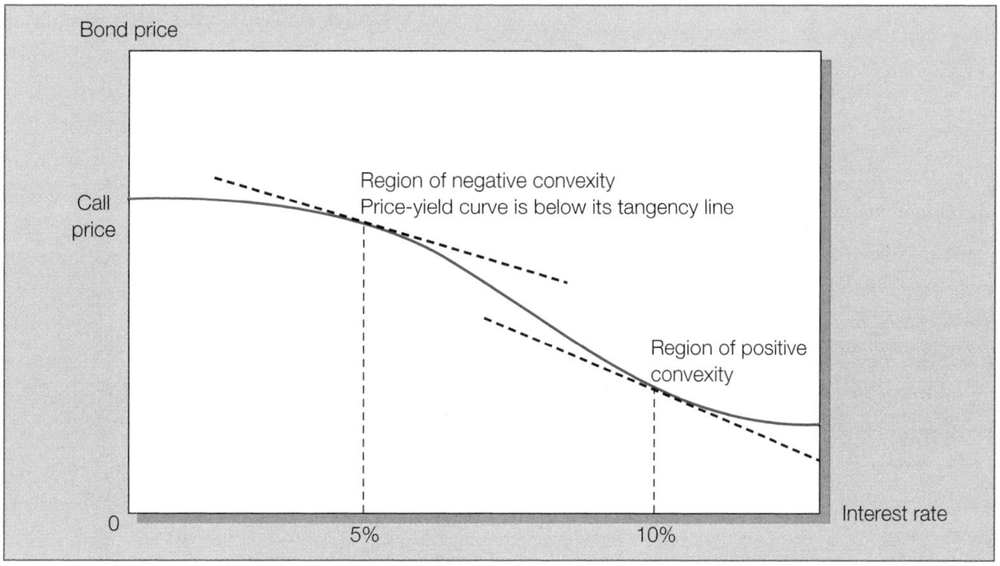

The effect of negative convexity is highlighted in equation 13.7. When convexity is negative, the second term on the right-hand side is necessarily negative, meaning that bond price performance will be worse than would be predicted by the duration approximation. However, callable bonds, or more generally, bonds with "embedded options," are difficult to analyze in terms of Macaulay's duration. This is because in the presence of such options, the future cash flows provided by the bonds are no longer known. If the bond may be called, for example, its cash flow stream may be terminated and its principal repaid earlier than was initially anticipated. Because cash flows are random, we can hardly take a weighted average of times until each future cash flow, as would be necessary to compute Macaulay's duration.

The convention on Wall Street is to compute the **effective duration** of bonds with embedded options. Effective duration cannot be computed with a simple formula such as equation 13.1 for Macaulay's duration. Instead, more complex bond valuation approaches that account for the embedded options are used, and effective duration is *defined* as the proportional change in the bond price per unit change in market interest rates:

$$\text{Effective duration} = -\frac{\Delta P/P}{\Delta r} \tag{13.8}$$

This equation *seems* merely like a slight manipulation of the modified duration formula 13.3. However, there are important differences. First, note that we do not compute effective duration relative to a change in the bond's own yield to maturity. (The denominator is Δr, not Δy.) This is because for bonds with embedded options, which may be called early, the yield to maturity is often not a relevant statistic. Instead, we calculate price change relative to a shift in the level of the term structure of interest rates. Second, the effective duration formula relies on a pricing methodology that accounts for embedded options. In contrast, modified or Macaulay duration can be computed directly from the promised bond cash flows and yield to maturity.

To illustrate, suppose that a callable bond with a call price of $1,050 is selling today for $980. If the yield curve shifts up by .5 percent, the bond price will fall to $930. If it shifts down by .5 percent, the bond price will rise to $1,010. To compute effective duration, we compute:

$$\Delta r = \text{Assumed increase in rates} - \text{Assumed decrease in rates}$$
$$= .5\% - (-.5\%) = 1\% = .01$$

$$\Delta P = \text{Price at .5\% increase in rates} - \text{Price at .5\% decrease in rates}$$
$$= \$930 - \$1,010 = -\$80$$

Then the effective duration of the bond is

$$\text{Effective duration} = -\frac{\Delta P/P}{\Delta r} = -\frac{-\$80/\$980}{.01} = 8.16 \text{ years}$$

In other words, the bond price changes by 8.16 percent for a 1 percentage point swing in rates around current values.

CONCEPT CHECK

4. What are the differences between Macaulay duration, modified duration, and effective duration?

13.3 PASSIVE BOND MANAGEMENT

Passive managers take bond prices as fairly set and seek to control only the risk of their fixed-income portfolio. Two broad classes of passive management are pursued in the fixed-income market. The first is an indexing strategy that attempts to replicate the performance of a given bond index. The second broad class of passive strategies are known as **immunization** techniques and are used widely by financial institutions such as insurance companies and pension funds. These are designed to shield the overall financial status of the institution from exposure to interest rate fluctuations. While both indexing and immunization strategies are alike in that they accept market prices as correctly set, they are very different in terms of risk exposure. A **bond index portfolio** will have the same risk-reward profile as the bond market index to which it is tied. In contrast, immunization strategies seek to establish a virtually zero-risk profile, in which interest rate movements have no impact on the value of the firm.

Bond Index Funds

www.tse.com

In principle, bond market indexing is similar to stock market indexing. The idea is to create a portfolio that mirrors the composition of an index that measures the broad market. Thus, stock index funds will purchase shares of each firm in the S&P/TSX Composite or S&P 500 in proportion to the market value of outstanding equity, to create index portfolios. A similar strategy is used for bond index funds, but as we shall see shortly, several modifications are required because of difficulties unique to the bond market and its indices.

The major indices of the Canadian bond market are compiled by Scotia Capital, its Universe Index being the relevant one. In the United States, there are three: the Salomon Brothers Broad Investment Grade (BIG) Index, the Lehman Brothers Aggregate Index, and the Merrill Lynch Domestic Master Index. These bond indices are market value-weighted indices of total returns on (U.S.) government, corporate, mortgage-backed, and Yankee (foreign issuer, U.S.-dollar-denominated) bonds with maturities greater than one year; as time passes and the maturity of a bond falls below one year, the bond is dropped from the indices.

The Scotia Capital bond indices actually are based only on those bonds that are considered to be available for public investment. Those bonds that are held by the Bank of Canada in particular and other institutions that buy on issue to hold to maturity are not included in calculating the value weighting. This realization points to the well-known illiquidity of the Canadian

Figure 13.9 Stratification of bonds into cells.

Sector / Term to Maturity	Treasury	Agency	Mortgage-Backed	Industrial	Finance	Utility	Yankee
<1 year	12.1%						
1–3 years	5.4%						
3–5 years			4.1%				
5–7 years							
7–10 years		0.1%					
10–15 years							
15–30 years			9.2%			3.4%	
30+ years							

www.scotiacapital.com

bond market, which has a bearing on the subject of index funds. In the late 1980s, ScotiaMcLeod created a Canadian bond index fund but was disappointed with the results. The same problems that make an index portfolio difficult to maintain in the U.S. market were exaggerated in Canada, such that the fund became infeasible. There also proved to be very little interest for the fund from Canadian institutional and professional investors.

The first problem that arises in the formation of a bond index portfolio is that the index includes a vast number of securities (the U.S. indices include more than 5,000); hence, it is quite difficult to purchase each security in the index in proportion to its market value. Moreover, many bonds are very thinly traded, especially in Canada.

Bond index funds also present more difficult rebalancing problems than do stock index funds. Bonds are continually dropped from the index as their maturities fall below one year. Moreover, as new bonds are issued, they are added to the index. Therefore, in contrast to equity indices, the securities used to compute bond indices constantly change. As they do, the manager must update or rebalance the portfolio to ensure a close match between the composition of the portfolio and the bonds included in the index. The fact that bonds generate considerable interest income that must be reinvested further complicates the job of the index fund manager.

In practice, it is deemed infeasible to precisely replicate the broad bond indices. Instead, a stratified sampling or *cellular* approach is often pursued. Figure 13.9 illustrates the idea behind the cellular approach. First, the bond market is stratified into several subclasses. Figure 13.9 shows a simple two-way breakdown by maturity and issuer; in practice, however, criteria such as the bond's coupon rate or the credit risk of the issuer also would be used to form cells. Bonds falling within each cell are then considered reasonably homogeneous. Next, the percentages of the entire universe (i.e., the bonds included in the index that is to be matched) falling within each cell are computed and reported, as we have done for a few cells in Figure 13.9. Finally, the portfolio manager establishes a bond portfolio with representation for each cell that matches the representation of that cell in the bond universe. In this way, the characteristics of the portfolio in terms of maturity, coupon rate, credit risk, industrial representation, and so on, will match the characteristics of the index, and the performance of the portfolio likewise should match the index.

Immunization

In contrast to indexing strategies, many institutions try to insulate their portfolios from interest rate risk altogether. Generally, there are two ways of viewing this risk, depending on the circumstances of the particular investor. Some institutions, such as banks, are concerned with protecting the current net worth or net market value of the firm against interest rate fluctuations. Other investors, such as pension funds, may face an obligation to make payments after a given number of years. These investors are more concerned with protecting the future values of their portfolios.

What is common to the bank and the pension fund, however, is interest rate risk. The net worth of the firm or the ability to meet future obligations fluctuates with interest rates. These institutions presumably might be interested in methods to control that risk. We will see that, by properly adjusting the maturity structure of their portfolios, these institutions can shed their interest rate risk. Immunization techniques refer to strategies used by such investors to shield their overall financial status from exposure to interest rate fluctuations.

Many banks and thrift institutions have a natural mismatch between asset and liability maturity structures. Bank liabilities are primarily the deposits owed to customers, most of which are very short-term in nature and, consequently, of low duration. Bank assets by contrast are composed largely of outstanding commercial and consumer loans or mortgages. These assets are of longer duration than are deposits, and their values are correspondingly more sensitive to interest rate fluctuations. In periods when interest rates increase unexpectedly, banks can suffer serious decreases in net worth—their assets fall in value by more than their liabilities.

The watchword in bank portfolio strategy has become asset and liability management. Techniques called *gap management* were developed to limit the "gap" between asset and liability durations. Adjustable-rate mortgages are one way to reduce the duration of bank asset portfolios. Unlike conventional mortgages, adjustable-rate mortgages do not fall in value when market interest rates rise, because the rates they pay are tied to an index of the current market rate. Even if the indexing is imperfect or entails lags, indexing greatly diminishes sensitivity to interest rate fluctuations. On the other side of the balance sheet, the introduction of bank certificates of deposit with fixed terms to maturity serves to lengthen the duration of bank liabilities, also reducing the duration gap.

One way to view gap management is that the bank is attempting to equate the durations of assets and liabilities to effectively immunize its overall position from interest rate movements. Because bank assets and liabilities are roughly equal in size, if their durations also are equal, any change in interest rates will affect the values of assets and liabilities equally. Interest rates would have no effect on net worth, in other words. Therefore, net worth immunization requires a portfolio duration of zero. This will result if assets and liabilities are equal in both magnitude and duration.

CONCEPT CHECK

5. If assets and liabilities are not equal, then immunization requires that $D_A A = D_L L$ where D denotes duration and A and L denote assets and liabilities, respectively. Explain why the simpler condition, $D_A = D_L$, is no longer valid in this case.

In contrast to banks, pension funds think more in terms of future commitments than current net worth. Pension funds have an obligation to provide workers with a flow of income upon their retirement, and they must have sufficient funds available to meet these commitments. As interest rates fluctuate, both the value of the assets held by the fund and the rate at which those assets generate income fluctuate. The pension fund manager, therefore, may want to protect, or "immunize," the future accumulated value of the fund at some target date against interest rate movements. (See the boxed article "How Pension Funds Lost in the Boom.")

Pension funds are not alone in this concern. Any institution with a future fixed obligation might consider immunization a reasonable risk management policy. Insurance companies, for example, also pursue immunization strategies. Indeed, the notion of immunization was introduced by F. M. Redington,[9] an actuary for a life insurance company. The idea behind immunization is that duration-matched assets and liabilities let the asset portfolio meet the firm's obligations despite interest rate movements. Consider, for example, an insurance company that issues a guaranteed investment contract, or GIC, for \$10,000. (Essentially, GICs are zero-coupon bonds issued by the insurance company to its customers. They are popular products for individuals' retirement-saving accounts.) If the GIC has a five-year maturity and a guaranteed interest rate of 8 percent, the insurance company is obligated to pay $\$10{,}000 \times (1.08)^5 = \$14{,}693.28$ in five years.

Suppose that the insurance company chooses to fund its obligation with \$10,000 of 8 percent *annual* coupon bonds, selling at par value, with six years to maturity. As long as the market interest rate stays at 8 percent, the company has fully funded the obligation, as the present value of the obligation exactly equals the value of the bonds.

Table 13.5, panel A shows that if interest rates remain at 8 percent, the accumulated funds from the bond will grow to exactly the \$14,693.28 obligation. Over the five-year period, the year-end coupon income of \$800 is reinvested at the prevailing 8 percent market interest rate. At the end of the period, the bonds can be sold for \$10,000; they still will sell at par value because the coupon rate still equals the market interest rate. Total income after five years from reinvested coupons and the sale of the bond is precisely \$14,693.28.

Table 13.5 Terminal Value of a Bond Portfolio After Five Years (all proceeds reinvested)

Payment Number	Years Remaining Until Obligation	Accumulated Value of Invested Payment		
A. Rates remain at 8%				
1	4	$800 \times (1.08)^4$	=	1,088.39
2	3	$800 \times (1.08)^3$	=	1,007.77
3	2	$800 \times (1.08)^2$	=	933.12
4	1	$800 \times (1.08)^1$	=	864.00
5	0	$800 \times (1.08)^0$	=	800.00
Sale of bond	0	10,800/1.08	=	10,000.00
				14,693.28
B. Rates fall to 7%				
1	4	$800 \times (1.07)^4$	=	1,048.64
2	3	$800 \times (1.07)^3$	=	980.03
3	2	$800 \times (1.07)^2$	=	915.92
4	1	$800 \times (1.07)^1$	=	856.00
5	0	$800 \times (1.07)^0$	=	800.00
Sale of bond	0	10,800/1.07	=	10,093.46
				14,694.05
C. Rates increase to 9%				
1	4	$800 \times (1.09)^4$	=	1,129.27
2	3	$800 \times (1.09)^3$	=	1,036.02
3	2	$800 \times (1.09)^2$	=	950.48
4	1	$800 \times (1.09)^1$	=	872.00
5	0	$800 \times (1.09)^0$	=	800.00
Sale of bond	0	10,800/1.09	=	9,908.26
				14,696.02

Note: The sale price of the bond portfolio equals the portfolio's final payment (\$10,800) divided by $1 + r$, because the time to maturity of the bonds will be one year at the time of sale.

[9] F. M. Redington, "Review of the Principle of Life-Office Valuations," *Journal of the Institute of Actuaries* 78 (1952).

If interest rates change, however, two offsetting influences will affect the ability of the fund to grow to the targeted value of $14,693.28. If interest rates rise, the fund will suffer a capital loss, impairing its ability to satisfy the obligation. The bonds will be worth less in five years than if interest rates had remained at 8 percent. However, at a higher interest rate, reinvested coupons will grow at a faster rate, offsetting the capital loss. In other words, fixed-income investors face two offsetting types of interest rate risk: *price risk* and *reinvestment rate risk*. Increases in interest rates cause capital losses but at the same time increase the rate at which reinvested income will grow. If the portfolio duration is chosen appropriately, these two effects will cancel out exactly. When the portfolio duration is set equal to the investor's horizon date, the accumulated value of the investment fund at the horizon date will be unaffected by interest rate fluctuations. *For a horizon equal to the portfolio's duration, price risk and reinvestment risk exactly cancel out.*

In the example we are discussing, the duration of the six-year maturity bonds used to fund the GIC is five years. You can confirm this using equation 13.6. Because the fully funded plan has equal duration for its assets and liabilities, the insurance company should be immunized against interest rate fluctuations. To confirm that this is the case, let us now investigate whether the bond can generate enough income to pay off the obligation five years from now regardless of interest rate movements.

Panels B and C in Table 13.5 consider two possible interest rate scenarios: rates either fall to 7 percent, or increase to 9 percent. In both cases, the annual coupon payments from the bond are reinvested at the new interest rate, which is assumed to change before the first coupon payment, and the bond is sold in year 5 to help satisfy the obligation of the GIC.

Panel B shows that if interest rates fall to 7 percent, the total funds will accumulate to $14,694.05, providing a small surplus of $.77. If rates increase to 9 percent as in panel C, the fund accumulates to $14,696.02, providing a small surplus of $2.74.

Several points are worth highlighting. First, duration matching balances the difference between the accumulated value of the coupon payments (reinvestment rate risk) and the sale value of the bond (price risk). That is, when interest rates fall, the coupons grow less than in the base case, but the gain on the sale of the bond offsets this. When interest rates rise, the resale value of the bond falls, but the coupons more than make up for this loss because they are reinvested at the

Figure 13.10 Growth of invested funds.

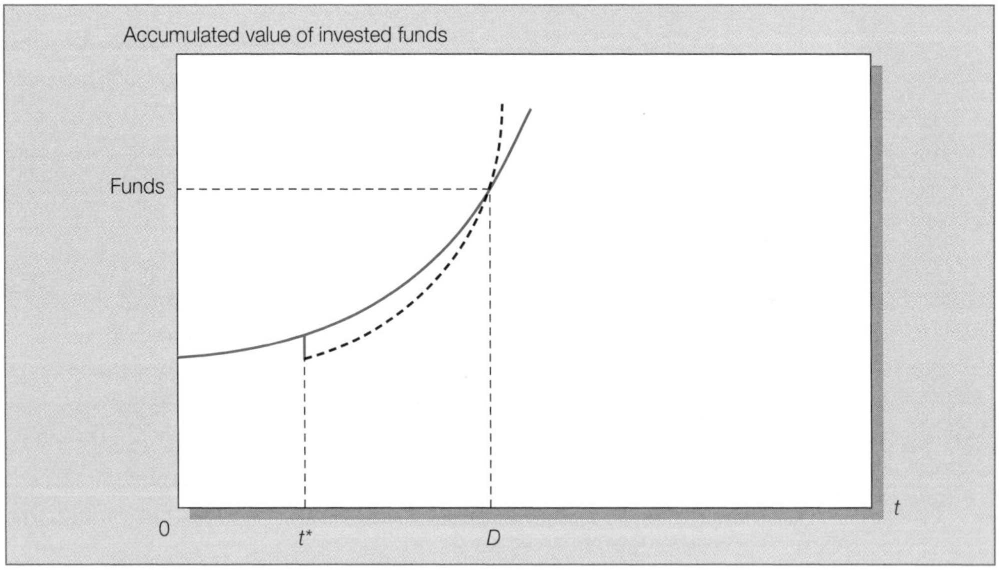

The solid coloured curve represents the growth of portfolio value at the original interest rate. If interest rates increase at time t^*, the portfolio value initially falls but increases thereafter at the faster rate represented by the broken curve. At time D (duration) the curves cross.

HOW PENSION FUNDS LOST IN THE BOOM

In one of the happiest reports to come out of Detroit lately, General Motors proclaimed Tuesday that its U.S. pension funds are now "fully funded on an economic basis." Less noticed was GM's admission that, in accounting terms, it is still a few cents—well, $3 billion—shy of the mark.

Wait a minute. If GM's pension plans were $9.3 billion in the hole when the year began, and if the company, to its credit, shoveled in $10.4 billion more during the year, how come its pension deficit wasn't wiped out in full?

We'll get to that, but the real news here is broader than GM. According to experts, most pension funds actually lost ground, ... even though, as you may recall, it was a rather good year for stocks and bonds.

True, pension-fund assets did have a banner year. But as is sometimes overlooked, pension funds also have liabilities (their obligations to retirees). And at most funds, liabilities grew at a rate that put asset growth to shame. At the margin, that means more companies' pension plans will be "underfunded." And down the road, assuming no reversal in the trend, more companies will have to pony up more cash.

What's to blame? The sharp decline in interest rates that brought joy to everyone else. As rates fall, pension funds have to set aside more money today to pay off a fixed obligation tomorrow. In accounting-speak, this "discounted present value" of their liabilities rises.

By now, maybe you sense that pension liabilities swing more, in either direction, than assets. How come? In a phrase, most funds are "mismatched," meaning their liabilities are longer-lived than their investments. The longer an obligation, the more its present value reacts to changes in rates. And at a typical pension fund, even though the average obligation is 15 years away, the average duration of its bond portfolio is roughly five years.

If this seems to defy common sense, it does. No sensible family puts its grocery money (a short-term obligation) into common stocks (a long-term asset). Ordinary Joes and Janes grasp the principle of "matching" without even thinking about it.

But fund managers—the pros—insist on shorter, unmatching bond portfolios for a simple, stupefying reason. They are graded—usually by consultants—according to how they perform against standard (and shorter-term) bond indexes. Thus, rather than invest to keep up with liabilities, managers are investing so as to avoid lagging behind the popular index in any year.

Source: Roger Lowenstein, "How Pension Funds Lost in Market Boom," *The Wall Street Journal*, February 1, 1996. Excerpted by permission of The Wall Street Journal,

higher rate. Figure 13.10 illustrates this case. The solid curve traces out the accumulated value of the bonds if interest rates remain at 8 percent. The dashed curve shows that value if interest rates happen to increase. The initial impact is a capital loss, but this loss eventually is offset by the now-faster growth rate of reinvested funds. At the five-year horizon date, the two effects just cancel each other out, leaving the company able to satisfy its obligation with the accumulated proceeds from the bond. The boxed article here discusses this tradeoff between price and reinvestment rate risk, suggesting how duration can be used to tailor a fixed-income portfolio to the horizon of the investor.

We can also analyze immunization in terms of present as opposed to future values. Table 13.6, panel A shows the initial balance sheet for the insurance company's GIC account. Both assets and the obligation have market values of $10,000, so that the plan is just fully funded. Panels B and

Table 13.6 Market Value Balance Sheet

Assets		Liabilities	
A. Interest rate = 8%			
Bonds	$10,000	Obligation	$10,000
B. Interest rate = 7%			
Bonds	$10,476.65	Obligation	$10,476.11
C. Interest rate = 9%			
Bonds	$ 9,551.41	Obligation	$ 9,549.62

Notes:

$$\text{Value of bonds} = 800 \times \text{Annuity factor}(r, 6) + 10{,}000 \times \text{PV factor}(r, 6)$$

$$\text{Value of obligation} = \frac{14{,}693.28}{(1+r)^5} = 14{,}693.28 \times \text{PV factor}(r, 5)$$

C show that whether the interest rate increases or decreases, the value of the bonds funding the GIC and the present value of the company's obligation change by virtually identical amounts. Regardless of the interest rate change, the plan remains fully funded, with the surplus in panels B and C just about zero. The duration-matching strategy has ensured that both assets and liabilities react equally to interest rate fluctuations.

Figure 13.11 is a graph of the present values of the bond and the single-payment obligation as a function of the interest rate. At the current rate of 8 percent, the values are equal, and the obligation is fully funded by the bond. Moreover, the two present value curves are tangent at $y = 8$ percent. As interest rates change, the change in value of both the asset and the obligation is equal, so the obligation remains fully funded. For greater changes in the interest rate, however, the present value curves diverge. This reflects the fact that the fund actually shows a small surplus at market interest rates other than 8 percent.

If the obligation was immunized, why is there any surplus in the fund? The answer is convexity. Figure 13.11 shows that the coupon bond has greater convexity than the obligation it funds. Hence, when rates move substantially, the bond value exceeds the present value of the obligation by a noticeable amount. Another way to think about it is that although the duration of the bond is indeed equal to 5 years at a yield to maturity of 8 percent, it rises to 5.02 years when its yield falls to 7 percent and drops to 4.97 years at $y = 9$ percent; that is, the bond and the obligation were not duration-matched *across* the interest rate shift.

This example highlights the importance of **rebalancing** immunized portfolios. As interest rates and asset durations change, a manager must rebalance the portfolio of fixed-income assets continually to realign its duration with the duration of the obligation. Moreover, even if interest rates do not change, asset durations *will* change solely because of the passage of time. Recall from Figure 13.4 that duration generally decreases less rapidly than does maturity. Thus, even if an obligation is immunized at the outset, as time passes the durations of the asset and liability will

Figure 13.11
Immunization.

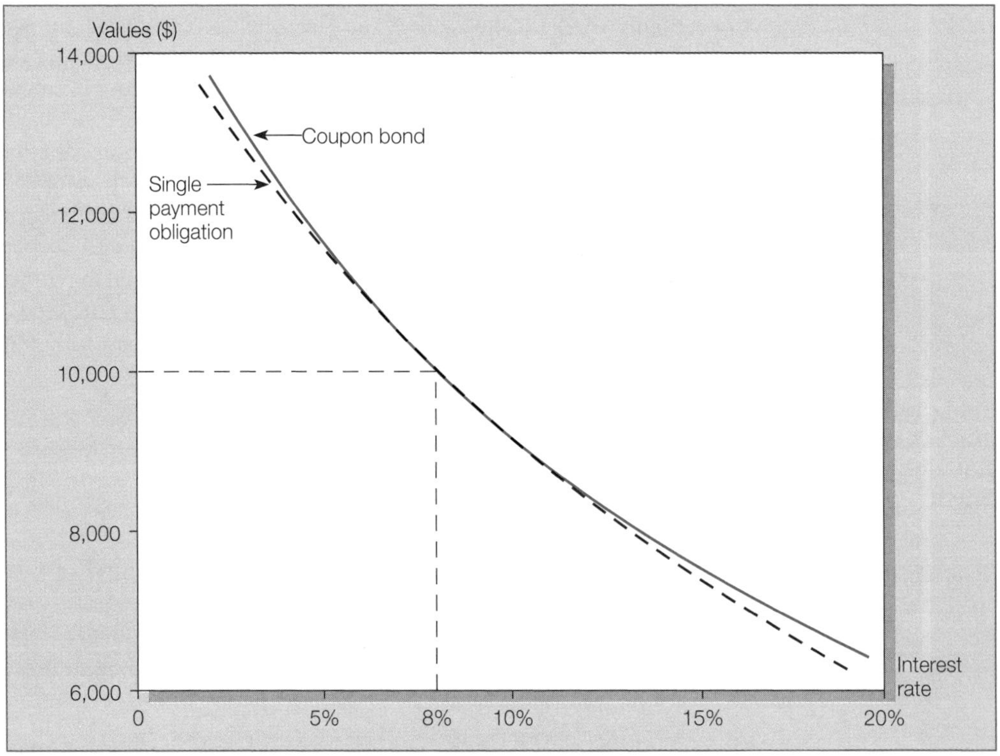

EXCEL APPLICATION

HOLDING-PERIOD IMMUNIZATION

The Online Learning Centre, at www.mcgrawhill.ca/college/bodie, contains a spreadsheet that is useful in understanding the concept of holding-period immunization. The spreadsheet calculates duration and holding-period returns on bonds of any maturity. The spreadsheet shows how price risk and reinvestment risk offset if a bond is sold at its duration.

	A	B	C	D	E	F
1	**Holding Period Immunization**					
2	**Example:**					
3	YTM	0.1158	Mar Price	1111.929		
4	Coupon R	0.14				
5	Maturity	7				
6	Par Value	1000				
7	Holding P	5				
8	Duration	5.000251				
9						
10						
11	If Rates Increase by 200 Basis Points				If Rates Increase by 100 Basis Points	
12	Rate	0.1358			Rate	0.1258
13	FV of CPS	917.739			FV of CPS	899.7046
14	SalesP	1006.954			SalesP	1023.817
15	Total	1924.693			Total	1923.522
16	IRR	0.115981			IRR	0.115845
17						
18						
19						
20	If Rates Decrease by 200 Basis Points				If Rates Decrease by 100 Basis Points	
21	Rate	0.0958			Rate	0.1058
22	FV of CPS	847.5959			FV of CPS	864.6376
23	SalesP	1077.145			SalesP	1058.897
24	Total	1924.741			Total	1923.534
25	IRR	0.115987			IRR	0.115847

fall at different rates. Without portfolio rebalancing, durations will become unmatched and the goals of immunization will not be realized. Obviously, immunization is a passive strategy only in the sense that it does not involve attempts to identify undervalued securities. Immunization managers still actively update and monitor their positions.

As another example of the need for rebalancing, consider a portfolio manager facing an obligation of \$19,487 in seven years, which, at a current market interest rate of 10 percent, has a present value of \$10,000. Right now, suppose that the manager wishes to immunize the obligation by holding only three-year zero-coupon bonds and perpetuities paying annual coupons. (Our focus on zeros and perpetuities helps keep the algebra simple.) At current interest rates, the perpetuities have a duration of 1.10/.10 = 11 years. The duration of the zero is simply three years.

For assets with equal yields, the duration of a portfolio is the weighted average of the durations of the assets making up the portfolio. To achieve the desired portfolio duration of seven years, the manager would have to choose appropriate values for the weights of the zero and the perpetuity in the overall portfolio. Call w the zero's weight and $(1 - w)$ the perpetuity's weight. Then w must be chosen to satisfy the equation

$$w \times 3 \text{ years} + (1 - w) \times 11 \text{ years} = 7 \text{ years}$$

which implies that $w = \frac{1}{2}$. The manager invests \$5,000 in the zero-coupon bond[10] and \$5,000 in the perpetuity, providing annual coupon payments of \$500 per year indefinitely. The portfolio duration is then seven years, and the position is immunized.

Next year, even if interest rates do not change, rebalancing will be necessary. The present value of the obligation has grown to \$11,000, because it is one year closer to maturity. The manager's funds also have grown to \$11,000: the zero-coupon bonds have increased in value from \$5,000 to \$5,500 with the passage of time, while the perpetuity has paid its annual \$500 coupon and is still worth \$5,000. However, the portfolio weights must be changed. The zero-coupon bond now will have duration of 2 years, while the perpetuity remains at 11 years. The obligation is now due in 6 years. The weights must now satisfy the equation

$$w \times 2 + (1 - w) \times 11 = 6$$

which implies that $w = \frac{5}{9}$. Now, the manager must invest a total of $\$11,000 \times \frac{5}{9} = \$6,111.11$ in the zero. This requires that the entire \$500 coupon payment be invested in the zero and that an additional \$111.11 of the perpetuity be sold and invested in the zero in order to maintain an immunized position.

Of course, rebalancing of the portfolio entails transaction costs as assets are bought or sold, so one cannot rebalance continuously. In practice, an appropriate compromise must be established between the desire for perfect immunization, which requires continual rebalancing, and the need to control trading costs, which dictates less frequent rebalancing.

CONCEPT CHECK

6. What would be the immunizing weights in the second year if the interest rate had fallen to 8 percent?

Cash Flow Matching and Dedication

The problems associated with immunization seem to have a simple solution. Why not simply buy a zero-coupon bond that provides a payment in an amount exactly sufficient to cover the projected cash outlay? If we follow the principle of **cash flow matching** we automatically immunize the portfolio from interest rate movement because the cash flow from the bond and the obligation exactly offset each other.

Cash flow matching on a multiperiod basis is referred to as a **dedication strategy**. In this case, the manager selects either zero-coupon or coupon bonds that provide total cash flows in each period that match a series of obligations. The advantage of dedication is that it is a once-and-for-all approach to eliminating interest rate risk. Once the cash flows are matched, there is no need for rebalancing. The dedicated portfolio provides the cash necessary to pay the firm's liabilities regardless of the eventual path of interest rates.

Cash flow matching is not more widely pursued probably because of the constraints that it imposes on bond selection. Immunization-dedication strategies are appealing to firms that do not wish to bet on general movements in interest rates, but these firms may want to immunize using bonds that they perceive are undervalued. Cash flow matching, however, places so many more constraints on the bond selection process that it can be impossible to pursue a dedication strategy using only "underpriced" bonds. Firms looking for underpriced bonds give up exact and easy dedication for the possibility of achieving superior returns from the bond portfolio.

Sometimes, cash flow matching is not possible. To cash-flow-match for a pension fund that is obligated to pay out a perpetual flow of income to current and future retirees, the pension fund

[10]Note that the *face value* of the zero will be $\$5,000 \times (1.10)^3 = \$6,655$.

would need to purchase fixed-income securities with maturities ranging up to hundreds of years. Such securities do not exist, making exact dedication infeasible.

CONCEPT CHECK

7. How would an increase in trading costs affect the attractiveness of dedication versus immunization?

Other Problems with Conventional Immunization

If you look back at the definition of duration in equation 13.1, you note that it uses the bond's yield to maturity to calculate the weight applied to the time until each coupon payment. Given this definition and limitations on the proper use of yield to maturity, it is perhaps not surprising that this notion of duration is strictly valid only for a flat yield curve for which all payments are discounted at a common interest rate.

If the yield curve is not flat, the definition of duration must be modified and $CF_t/(1 + y)^t$ replaced with the present value of CF_t, where the present value of each cash flow is calculated by discounting with the appropriate interest rate from the yield curve corresponding to the date of the *particular* cash flow, instead of by discounting with the *bond's* yield to maturity. Moreover, even with this modification, duration matching will immunize portfolios only for parallel shifts in the yield curve. Clearly, this sort of restriction is unrealistic. As a result, much work has been devoted to generalizing the notion of duration. Multifactor duration models have been developed to allow for tilts and other distortions in the shape of the yield curve, in addition to shifts in its level. (We refer to some of this work in the suggested readings at the end of this chapter.) However, it does not appear that the added complexity of such models pays off in terms of substantially greater effectiveness.[11]

There is an extensive literature on the design and testing of immunization strategies. Gagnon and Johnson[12] investigated the success of duration- versus convexity-based strategies for asset-liability matching to solve the problem of fluctuating interest rates, finding the duration-based approach to be more effective. Bierwag, Fooladi, and Roberts[13] analyzed a sophisticated strategy known as M-squared minimization and found it to perform less well than anticipated, while Fooladi and Roberts[14] also conducted an empirical study of Canadian bond portfolio management. These analyses point up the complexity of bond trading and the difficulties in attaining the objectives stated for various types of portfolios.

Risk and Return in the Canadian Bond Market www.barra.com/Research Resources/BarraPub/randr-p2-n.asp

Finally, immunization can be an inappropriate goal in an inflationary environment. Immunization is essentially a nominal notion and makes sense only for nominal liabilities. It makes no sense to immunize a projected obligation that will grow with the price level using nominal assets, such as bonds. For example, if your child will attend college in 15 years and if the annual cost of tuition is expected to be \$15,000 at that time, immunizing your portfolio at a locked-in terminal value of \$15,000 is not necessarily a risk-reducing strategy. The tuition obligation will vary with the realized inflation rate, whereas the asset portfolio's final value will not. In the end, the tuition obligation will not necessarily be matched by the value of the portfolio.

---

[11] G. O. Bierwag, G. C. Kaufman, and A. Toevs (eds.), *Innovations in Bond Portfolio Management: Duration Analysis and Immunization* (Greenwich, CT: JAI Press, 1983). See also G. O. Bierwag and G. S. Roberts, "Single-Factor Duration Models," *The Journal of Financial Research* 13, no. 1 (Spring 1990), pp. 23–38.

[12] Louis Gagnon and Lewis D. Johnson, "Dynamic Immunization Under Stochastic Interest Rates," *Journal of Portfolio Management* 20, no. 3 (Spring 1994), pp. 48–54. Johnson also has written a series of articles on extending the notion of duration to equity portfolios, which appeared in *Financial Analysts Journal* in 1989, 1990, and 1992 and in *Canadian Journal of Administrative Sciences* in March 1991.

[13] G. O. Bierwag, I. Fooladi, and G. S. Roberts, "Designing an Immunized Portfolio—Is M-Squared the Key," *Journal of Banking and Finance* 17 (December 1993), pp. 1147–1170.

[14] I. Fooladi and G. S. Roberts, "Bond Portfolio Immunization: Canadian Tests," *Journal of Economics and Business* 44 (February 1992), pp. 3–17.

13.4 ACTIVE BOND MANAGEMENT

Sources of Potential Profit

Broadly speaking, there are two sources of potential value in active bond management. The first is interest rate forecasting, which tries to anticipate movements across the entire spectrum of the fixed-income market. If interest rate declines are anticipated, managers will increase portfolio duration (and vice versa). The second source of potential profit is identification of relative mispricing within the fixed-income market. An analyst, for example, might believe that the default premium on one particular bond is unnecessarily large and therefore that the bond is underpriced.

These techniques will generate abnormal returns only if the analyst's information or insight is superior to that of the market. You cannot profit from knowledge that rates are about to fall if everyone else in the market is aware of this. You know this from our discussion of market efficiency.

Valuable information is differential information. In this context it is worth noting that interest rate forecasters have a notoriously poor track record. If you consider this record, you will approach attempts to time the bond market with caution. The boxed article here offers some thoughts on bond portfolio management in Canada.

Homer and Liebowitz coined a popular taxonomy of active bond portfolio strategies. They characterize portfolio rebalancing activities as one of four types of *bond swaps*. In the first two swaps the investor typically believes that the yield relationship between bonds or sectors is only temporarily out of alignment. When the aberration is eliminated, gains can be realized on the underpriced bond. The period of realignment is called the *workout period.*

1. The **substitution swap** is an exchange of one bond for a nearly identical substitute. The substituted bonds should be of essentially equal coupon, maturity, quality, call features, sinking fund provisions, and so on. This swap would be motivated by a belief that the market has temporarily mispriced the two bonds, and that the discrepancy between the prices of the bonds represents a profit opportunity.

   An example of a substitution swap would be a sale of a 20-year maturity, 9 percent coupon Weston bond callable after five years at $1,050 that is priced to provide a yield to maturity of 9.05 percent, coupled with a purchase of a 9 percent coupon Loblaw bond with the same call provisions and time to maturity that yields 9.15 percent. If the bonds have about the same credit rating, there is no apparent reason for the Loblaw bonds to provide a higher yield. Therefore, the higher yield actually available in the market makes the Loblaw bond seem relatively attractive. Of course, the equality of credit risk is an important condition. If the Loblaw bond is in fact riskier, then its higher yield does not represent a bargain.

www.loblaw.com

2. The **intermarket spread swap** is pursued when an investor believes that the yield spread between two sectors of the bond market is temporarily out of line. For example, if the current spread between corporate and government bonds is considered too wide and is expected to narrow, the investor will shift from government bonds into corporate bonds. If the yield spread does in fact narrow, corporates will outperform governments. For example, if the yield spread between 20-year Canada bonds and 20-year Baa-rated corporate bonds is now 3 percent, and the historical spread has been only 2 percent, an investor might consider selling holdings of Canada bonds and replacing them with corporates. If the yield spread eventually narrows, the Baa-rated corporate bonds will outperform the Canadas.

   Of course, the investor must consider carefully whether there is a good reason that the yield spread seems out of alignment. For example, the default premium on corporate bonds might have increased because the market is expecting a severe recession. In this case, the wider spread would not represent attractive pricing of corporates relative to Canadas, but would simply be an adjustment for a perceived increase in credit risk.

HISTORICALLY LOW INTEREST RATES

Historically low interest rates call for a new, and more active, approach to managing fixed income risk.

A number of structural changes are transforming the Canadian fixed income market. The biggest change is the shift in relative market weight from government to corporate bonds. It is altering the risk, return and liquidity characteristics available to passive bond investors, as well as the strategies to add value from active bond management. This is expected to boost the anticipated return of the bond portfolio given an increase in credit risk and decrease in potential diversification resulting from higher expected correlations between lower-grade bonds and equities for same issuers.

The return correlations arc above 0.9 for five of the nine pairings of the Scotia Capital (SC) universe fixed income series. They are highest for Corp BBB and the TSE 300 [S&P/TSX] Composite Index (0.440) over the 15-year period from 1987 to 2001. These changes make it more difficult for Canadian fixed income portfolio managers and investors to fully diversify their portfolios, decrease liquidity and increase the associated trade costs of bond investing. At the same time, this shift also increases the need for effective credit analysis.

In this environment it is important that securities regulators implement changes to restore investor confidence in the veracity of corporate accounting by eliminating corporate malfeasance. Credit risk premiums will increase in the absence of such changes, and bond raters are likely to exhibit rating overreaction due to a lowered tolerance to possible downward credit risk jumps for lower-rated borrowers.

Previously, when government bonds dominated the fixed income market, investors and plan sponsors embraced the case for indexing or passively managing at least the core portion of a fixed income portfolio. Gains from active management were not easily obtained from assets with low levels of credit risk, especially from those that were both widely held and recognized by investors, and traded in sufficient volume to ensure reasonably low trade costs and high liquidity.

That period of low credit risk coincided with high and volatile interest rates. Active Canadian institutional bond investors essentially used rate or rate-curve anticipation strategies to add net value. Between 1987 and 2001, all nine SC indexes outperformed the TSE 300 Composite Index mean annual return of 9 per cent. However, when the level and volatility of interest rates are low as they are today, these active strategics offer much poorer prospects of adding value compared to yield or yield-spread anticipation strategies that are based on effective credit analysis.

The importance of tracking credit rating transition patterns and conducting effective credit risk analysis for both passive and active fixed income portfolio management is higher for yield spread strategics. Historical evidence suggests that the likelihood of a credit quality rating movement is correlated across issuers and increases for the same issue with an increasing tracking horizon.

Recent Canadian estimates are 13 per cent and 53 per cent for a corporate bond currently rated as AAA after one and five years, respectively. An assessment of the risk-mitigation protection offered by covenants (which requires a thorough understanding of the wording of debt covenants) is another important component of credit analysis.

Future fixed income portfolio management will require greater risk management and control, as well as varying degrees of active management as investors strive to deal with the greater credit risk of the average fixed income security investment. Institutional investors and sponsors will need to shift towards a more focused credit management strategy to achieve their required returns in an environment of historically low interest rates.

Source: Lawrence Kryzanowski, "Historically Low Interest Rates," *Canadian Investment Review* 15, no. 4 (Winter 2002), p. 40. Reprinted by permission of the *Canadian Investment Review*.

3. The **rate anticipation swap** is pegged to interest rate forecasting. In this case if investors believe that rates will fall, they will swap into bonds of longer duration. Conversely, when rates are expected to rise, they will swap into shorter duration bonds. For example, the investor might sell a 5-year maturity Canada bond, replacing it with a 25-year maturity Canada bond. The new bond has the same lack of credit risk as the old one, but has longer duration.
4. The **pure yield pickup swap** is pursued not in response to perceived mispricing, but as a means of increasing return by holding higher-yield bonds. This must be viewed as an attempt to earn an expected term premium in higher-yield bonds. The investor is willing to bear the interest rate risk that this strategy entails.

   A yield pickup swap can be illustrated using the Canada bond listings in Figure 11.1. You can see from that figure that a Canada bond maturing in two years yields about 3.0 percent, whereas one maturing in 20 years yields about 5 percent. The investor who swaps the shorter-term bond for the longer one will earn a higher rate of return as long as the yield curve does not shift up during the holding period. Of course if it does, the longer-duration bond will suffer a greater capital loss.

We can add a fifth swap, called a **tax swap**, to this list. This simply refers to a swap to exploit some tax advantage. For example, an investor may swap from one bond that has decreased in price to another if realization of capital losses is advantageous for tax purposes.

Horizon Analysis

One form of interest rate forecasting is called **horizon analysis**. The analyst using this approach selects a particular holding period and predicts the yield curve at the end of that period. Given a bond's time to maturity at the end of the holding period, its yield can be read from the predicted yield curve and its end-of-period price calculated. Then the analyst adds the coupon income and prospective capital gain of the bond to obtain the total return on the bond over the holding period.

For example, suppose a 20-year maturity bond with a 10 percent coupon rate (paid annually) currently sells at a yield to maturity of 9 percent. A portfolio manager with a two-year horizon needs to forecast the total return on the bond over the coming two years. In two years, the bond will have an 18-year maturity. The analyst forecasts that two years from now, 18-year bonds will sell at yields to maturity of 8 percent, and that coupon payments can be reinvested in short-term securities over the coming two years at a rate of 7 percent.

To calculate the two-year return on the bond, the analyst would perform the following calculations:

1. Current price = \$100 × Annuity factor(9%, 20 years) + \$1,000 × PV factor (9%, 20 years)
   = \$1,091.29
2. Forecast price = \$100 × Annuity factor(8%, 18 years) + \$1,000 × PV factor (8%, 18 years)
   = \$1,187.44
3. The future value of reinvested coupons will be (\$100 × 1.07) + \$100 = \$207
4. The two-year return is $\frac{\$207 + (\$1{,}187.44 - \$1{,}091.29)}{\$1{,}091.29} = 0.278$, or 27.8%

The annualized rate of return over the two-year period would then be $(1.278)^{1/2} - 1 = .13$, or 13 percent.

CONCEPT CHECK

8. Consider a 30-year, annual pay 8 percent coupon bond currently selling at \$925. The analyst believes that in two years the yield on 28-year bonds will be 8.3 percent. Should she purchase the 20-year bond of the above example or the 30-year bond?

Contingent Immunization

Contingent immunization is a mixed passive-active strategy suggested by Liebowitz and Weinberger.[15] To illustrate, suppose that interest rates currently are 10 percent and that a manager's portfolio is worth \$10 million right now. At current rates the manager could lock in, via conventional immunization techniques, a future portfolio value of \$12.1 million after two years. Now suppose that the manager wishes to pursue active management but is willing to risk losses only to the extent that the terminal value of the portfolio would not drop lower than \$11 million. Because only \$9.09 million (\$11 million/1.10^2) is required to achieve this minimum acceptable terminal value,

[15]Martin L. Liebowitz and Alfred Weinberger, "Contingent Immunization—Part I: Risk Control Procedures," *Financial Analysts Journal* 38 (November/December 1982).

and the portfolio currently is worth $10 million, the manager can afford to risk some losses at the outset and might start off with an active strategy rather than immediately immunizing.

The key is to calculate the funds required to lock in via immunization a future value of $11 million at current rates. If T denotes the time left until the horizon date, and r is the market interest rate at any particular time, then the value of the fund necessary to guarantee an ability to reach the minimum acceptable terminal value is $11 million/$(1 + r)^T$, because this size portfolio, if immunized, will grow risk-free to $11 million by the horizon date. This value becomes the trigger point: If and when the actual portfolio value dips to the trigger point, active management will cease. *Contingent* upon reaching the trigger, an immunization strategy is initiated instead, guaranteeing that the minimal acceptable performance can be realized.

Figure 13.12 illustrates two possible outcomes in a contingent immunization strategy. In panel A, the portfolio falls in value and hits the trigger at time t^*. At that point, immunization is pursued and the portfolio rises smoothly to the $11 million terminal value. In panel B, the portfolio does well, never reaches the trigger point, and is worth more than $11 million at the horizon date.

CONCEPT CHECK

9. What would be the trigger point with a three-year horizon, an interest rate of 12 percent, and a minimum acceptable terminal value of $10 million?

Figure 13.12 Contingent immunization.

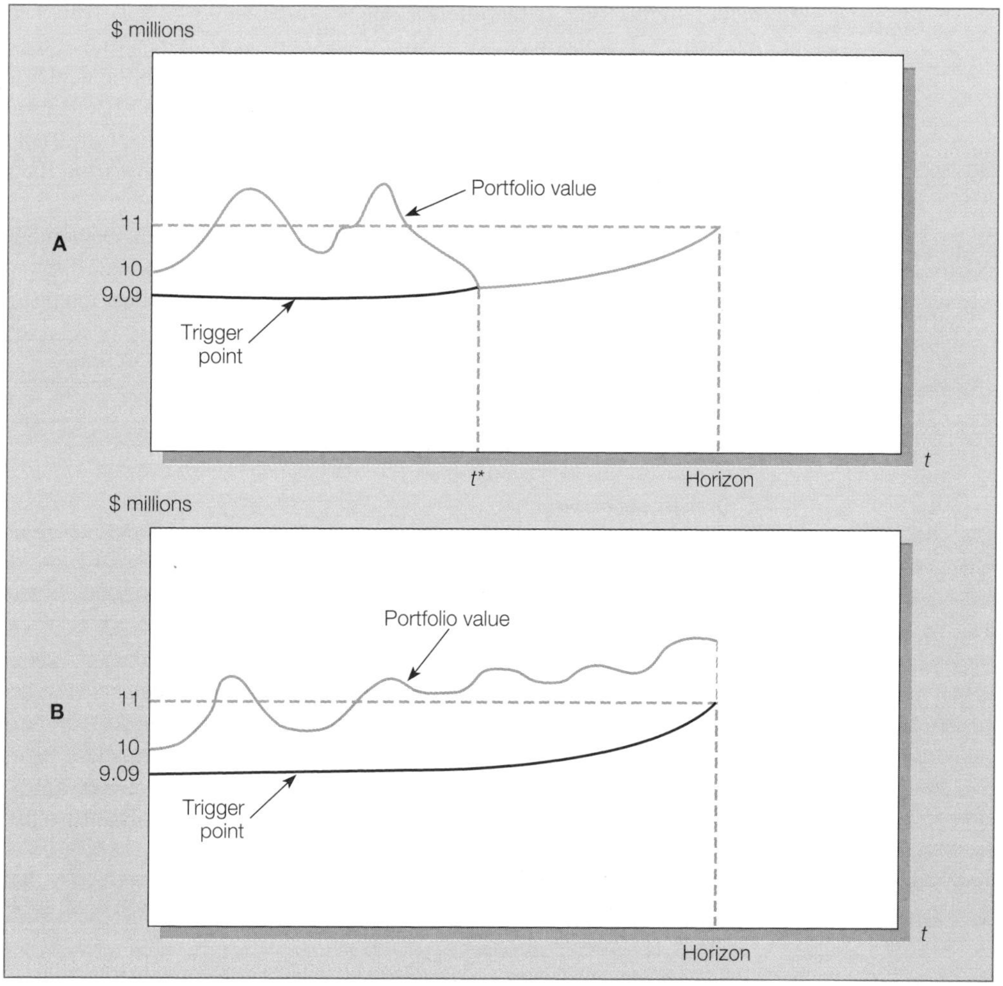

13.6 INTEREST RATE SWAPS

Interest rate swaps have emerged recently as a major fixed-income tool. An interest rate swap is a contract between two parties to exchange a series of cash flows similar to those that would result if the parties instead were to exchange equal dollar values of different types of bonds. Swaps arose originally as a means of managing interest rate risk. The volume of swaps has increased from virtually zero in 1980 to over $60 trillion today. (Interest rate swaps do not have anything to do with the Homer-Liebowitz bond swap taxonomy set out earlier.)

Interest Rate Swaps www.atrading.com/adt3/begin3.htm

To illustrate how swaps work, consider the manager of a large portfolio that currently includes $100 million dollars par value of long-term bonds paying an average coupon rate of 7 percent. The manager believes that interest rates are about to rise. As a result, he would like to sell the bonds and replace them with either short-term or floating-rate issues. However, it would be exceedingly expensive in terms of transaction costs to replace the portfolio every time the forecast for interest rates is updated. A cheaper and more flexible way to modify the portfolio is for the managers to "swap" the $7 million a year in interest income the portfolio currently generates for an amount of money that is tied to the short-term interest rate. That way, if rates do rise, so will the portfolio's interest income.

A swap dealer might advertise its willingness to exchange, or "swap," a cash flow based on the six-month LIBOR rate for one based on a fixed rate of 7 percent. (The LIBOR, or London Interbank Offered Rate, is the interest rate at which banks borrow from each other in the Eurodollar market. It is the most commonly used short-term interest rate in the swap market.) The portfolio manager would then enter into a swap agreement with the dealer to *pay* 7 percent on **notional principal** of $100 million and *receive* payment of the LIBOR rate on that amount of notional principal.[16] In other words, the manager swaps a payment of .07 × $100 million for a payment of LIBOR × $100 million. The manager's *net* cash flow from the swap agreement is therefore (LIBOR – .07) × $100 million.

Note that the swap arrangement does not mean that a loan has been made. The participants have agreed only to exchange a fixed cash flow for a variable one.

Now consider the net cash flow to the manager's portfolio in three interest rate scenarios:

	LIBOR Rate		
	6.5%	7.0%	7.5%
Interest income from bond portfolio (= 7% of $100 million bond portfolio)	$7,000,000	$7,000,000	$7,000,000
Cash flow from swap [= (LIBOR – 7%) × notional principal of $100 million]	(500,000)	0	500,000
Total (= LIBOR × $100 million)	$6,500,000	$7,000,000	$7,500,000

Notice that the total income on the overall position—bonds plus swap agreement—is now equal to the LIBOR rate in each scenario times $100 million. The manager has, in effect, converted a fixed-rate bond portfolio into a synthetic floating-rate portfolio.

You can see now that swaps can be immensely useful for firms in a variety of applications. For example, a corporation that has issued fixed-rate debt can convert it into synthetic floating-rate debt by entering a swap to receive a fixed interest rate (offsetting its fixed-rate coupon

[16]The participants to the swap do not loan each other money. They agree only to exchange a fixed cash flow for a variable cash flow that depends on the short-term interest rate. This is why the principal is described as notional. The notional principal is simply a way to describe the size of the swap agreement. In this example, the parties to the swap exchange a 7 percent fixed rate for the LIBOR rate; the difference between LIBOR and 7 percent is multiplied by notional principal to determine the cash flow exchanged by the parties.

obligation) and pay a floating rate. Or a bank that pays current market interest rates to its depositors might enter a swap to receive a floating rate and pay a fixed rate on some amount of notional principal. This swap position, added to its floating-rate deposit liability, would result in a net liability of a fixed stream of cash. The bank might then be able to invest in long-term fixed-rate loans without encountering interest rate risk.

What about the swap dealer? Why is the dealer, which is typically a financial intermediary such as a bank, willing to take on the opposite side of the swaps desired by these participants?

Consider a dealer who takes on one side of a swap, let's say paying LIBOR and receiving a fixed rate. The dealer will search for another trader in the swap market who wishes to receive a fixed rate and pay LIBOR. For example, company A may have issued a 7 percent coupon fixed-rate bond that it wishes to convert into synthetic floating-rate debt, while company B may have issued a floating-rate bond tied to LIBOR that it wishes to convert into synthetic fixed-rate debt. The dealer will enter a swap with company A in which it pays a fixed rate and receives LIBOR, and will enter another swap with company B in which it pays LIBOR and receives a fixed rate. When the two swaps are combined, the dealer's position is effectively neutral on interest rates, paying LIBOR on one swap and receiving it on another. Similarly, the dealer pays a fixed rate on one swap and receives it on another. The dealer becomes little more than an intermediary, funnelling payments from one party to the other.[17] The dealer finds this activity profitable because he or she will charge a bid-asked spread on the transaction.

This rearrangement is illustrated in Figure 13.13. Company A has issued 7 percent fixed-rate debt (*leftmost arrow*), but enters a swap to pay the dealer LIBOR and receive a 6.95 percent fixed rate. Therefore, the company's net payment is 7% + (LIBOR – 6.95%) = LIBOR + .05%. It has thus transformed its fixed-rate debt into synthetic floating-rate debt. Conversely, company B has issued floating-rate debt paying LIBOR (*rightmost arrow*), but enters a swap to pay a 7.05 percent fixed rate in return for LIBOR. Therefore, its net payment is LIBOR + (7.05% – LIBOR) = 7.05%. It has thus transformed its floating-rate debt into synthetic fixed-rate debt. The bid-asked spread in the example illustrated in Figure 13.13 is .10 percent of notional principal each year.

CONCEPT CHECK

10. A pension fund holds a portfolio of money market securities that the manager believes are paying excellent yields compared to other comparable-risk short-term securities. However, the manager believes that interest rates are about to fall. What type of swap will allow the fund to continue to hold its portfolio of short-term securities while at the same time benefiting from a decline in rates?

Figure 13.13 Interest rate swap.

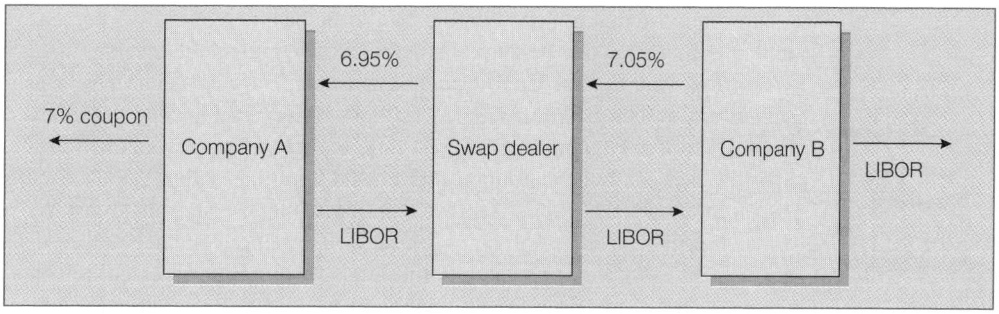

Company B pays a fixed rate of 7.05 percent to the swap dealer in return for LIBOR. Company A receives 6.95 percent from the dealer in return for LIBOR. The swap dealer realizes a cash flow each period equal to .10 percent of notional principal.

[17] Actually, things are a bit more complicated. The dealer is more than just an intermediary because he or she bears the credit risk that one or the other of the parties to the swap might default on the obligation. Referring to Figure 13.13, if company A defaults on its obligation, for example, the swap dealer still must maintain its commitment to company B. In this sense, the dealer does more than simply pass through cash flows to the other swap participants.

13.7 FINANCIAL ENGINEERING AND INTEREST RATE DERIVATIVES

New financial instruments created through financial engineering can have highly unusual risk and return characteristics that offer both opportunities and challenges for fixed-income portfolio managers. To illustrate the possibilities opened up by financial engineering, consider the inverse floater, which is a bond that pays a *lower* coupon payment when a reference interest rate rises. For example, an inverse floater may pay a coupon rate equal to 10 percent *minus* the rate on one-year Treasury bills. Therefore, if the T-bill rate is 4 percent, the bond will pay interest income equal to 10% – 4% = 6% of par value. You can see that such a bond will have an interest rate sensitivity much greater than that of a fixed-rate bond with comparable maturity. If the T-bill rate rises, say to 7 percent, the inverse floater's coupon payments fall to 3 percent of par value; in addition, as other interest rates rise along with the T-bill rate, the bond price falls as well for the usual reason that future cash flows are discounted at higher rates. Therefore, there is a dual impact on value and these securities perform especially poorly when interest rates rise. Conversely, inverse floaters perform especially well when rates fall: coupon payments rise, even as the discount rate falls.

While firms do not commonly issue inverse floaters, they may be created synthetically by allocating the cash flows from a fixed-rate security into two *derivative* securities. An investment banking firm can buy a bond issue and carve the original security into a floating-rate note and an inverse floater. The floater will receive interest payments that rise when the T-bill rate rises; the inverse floater will receive interest payments that fall when the T-bill rate rises. The sum of the interest payments due to the two classes of securities is fixed and equal to the interest from the original bond, the primary asset.

As a concrete example, consider a $100 million par value, 20-year maturity bond with a coupon rate of 8 percent. The bond issue therefore pays total interest of $8 million annually. An investment banking firm might arrange to use the cash flows from the underlying bond to support issues of a floating-rate note and an inverse floater. The floating-rate notes might be issued with aggregate par value of $60 million and a coupon level equal to the T-bill rate plus 1 percent. If the T-bill rate currently is 6 percent, therefore, the coupon rate on the floater would be 7 percent and total interest payments would be .07 × $60 million = $4.2 million. This leaves $8 million – $4.2 million = $3.8 million available to pay interest on the interest floater. The coupon rate on the inverse floater might be set at 18.5% – 1.5 × (T-bill rate), which at the current T-bill rate equals 9.5 percent. Therefore, the coupon income flowing to the inverse floater is 9.5 percent of $40 million, or $3.8 million, which just absorbs the remaining interest flowing from the original bond.

Now suppose that in one year, the T-bill rate has increased by 1 percent. The coupon rate on the floater increases to 8 percent, while the coupon rate on the inverse floater falls to 18.5% – 1.5 × 7% = 8%. Again, total interest paid on the two derivative securities sums to $8 million: .08 × $60 million + .08 × $40 million = $8 million. However, the value of the inverse floater falls precipitously: not only are market interest rates higher (which makes the present value of any future cash flow lower), but the coupon rate on the bond has fallen from 9.5 percent to 8 percent.[18] Therefore, the inverse floater will have extreme interest rate sensitivity. When rates fall, its performance will be spectacular, but when rates rise, its performance will be disastrous. The inverse floater is an example of an interest rate derivative product created by financial engineering in which the cash flows from the original bond are unbundled and reallocated to the floater and inverse floater. Because of the impact of interest rates on its coupon rate, the inverse floater will

---

[18]If the T-bill rate increases beyond 12.33 percent, the formula for the inverse floater's coupon would call for a negative coupon rate. However, in practice, the inverse floater provides that the coupon rate may never fall below zero. This floor on the coupon rate of the inverse floater necessitates a ceiling on the coupon rate of the floater. The total interest paid by the two securities is constrained to equal the interest provided by the underlying bond.

have a very large effective duration,[19] in fact much longer than the maturity of the bond. This property can be useful to investors who wish to immunize very-long-duration liabilities; it is also obviously useful to investors who wish to speculate on decreases in interest rates.

Inverse floaters are not the only financially engineered products with dramatic dependence on interest rates. In Chapters 1 and 2, we introduced you to derivative securities created by allocating the cash flows from mortgage-backed securities into various CMO (collateralized mortgage obligation) tranches. Some of the more popular mortgage derivative products are interest-only (IO) and principal-only (PO) strips. The IO strip gets all the interest payments from the mortgage pool and the PO strip gets all the principal payments. Both have extreme and interesting interest rate exposures. In both cases, the sensitivity is due to the effect of mortgage prepayments on the cash flows accruing to the security holder.

PO securities, like inverse floaters, exhibit very long effective durations, that is, their values are very sensitive to interest rate fluctuations. When interest rates fall and mortgage holders prepay their mortgages, PO holders receive their principal payments much earlier than initially anticipated. Therefore, the payments are discounted for fewer years than expected and have much higher present value. Hence PO strips perform extremely well when rates fall. Conversely, interest rate increases slow mortgage prepayments and reduce the value of PO strips.

The prices of interest-only strips, on the other hand, fall when interest rates fall. This is because mortgage prepayments abruptly end the flow of interest payments accruing to IO security holders. Because rising rates discourage prepayments, they increase the value of IO strips. Thus IOs have effective *negative* durations. They are good investments for an investor who wishes to bet on an increase in rates, or they can be useful for hedging the value of a conventional fixed-income portfolio.

www.pg.com

There are still other ways to make highly sensitive bets on the direction of interest rates. Some of these are custom-designed swaps in which the cash flow paid by one party to the swap varies dramatically with the level of some reference interest rate. Such swaps made news in 1994 when Procter & Gamble lost more than $100 million in an interest rate swap that obligated it to make payments that exploded when interest rates increased. In the wake of its losses, P&G sued Bankers Trust, which sold it the swap, claiming that it was misled about the risks of the swap.

Interest rate derivatives are not necessarily bad, or even dangerous, investments. The dramatic sensitivity of their prices to interest rate fluctuations can be useful for hedging as well as for speculation. They can be potent risk management as well as risk-increasing tools. One Wall Street observer has compared them to power tools: when used well by a trained expert, they can serve a valuable function, but in untrained hands, they can lead to severe damage.

SUMMARY

1. Even default-free bonds such as Treasury issues are subject to interest rate risk. Longer-term bonds generally are more sensitive to interest rate shifts than are short-term bonds. A measure of the average life of a bond is Macaulay's duration, defined as the weighted average of the times until each payment made by the security, with weights proportional to the present value of the payment.
2. Duration is a direct measure of the sensitivity of a bond's price to a change in its yield. The proportional change in a bond's price equals the negative of duration multiplied by the proportional change in $1 + y$.

[19]Strictly speaking, the Macaulay duration (i.e., the weighted average of the times until payment of each cash flow) of an inverse floater is not well defined, since the cash flows accruing from the bond are not fixed but instead vary with the level of interest rates. The *effective* duration of a security therefore does not have the interpretation of an average maturity; it is defined instead as the percentage change in the price of a security given a one-percentage-point increase in yield. Therefore, effective duration, like Macaulay duration, measures interest rate sensitivity.

3. Convexity refers to the curvature of a bond's price-yield relationship. Accounting for convexity can substantially improve on the accuracy of the duration approximation for bond price sensitivity to changes in yields.
4. Immunization strategies are characteristic of passive fixed-income portfolio management. Such strategies attempt to render the individual or firm immune from movements in interest rates. This may take the form of immunizing net worth or, instead, immunizing the future accumulated value of a fixed-income portfolio.
5. Immunization of a fully funded plan is accomplished by matching the durations of assets and liabilities. To maintain an immunized position as time passes and interest rates change, the portfolio must be periodically rebalanced. Classic immunization also depends on parallel shifts in a flat yield curve. Given that this assumption is unrealistic, immunization generally will be less than complete. To mitigate the problem, multifactor duration models can be used to allow for variation in the shape of the yield curve.
6. A more direct form of immunization is dedication, or cash flow matching. If a portfolio is perfectly matched in cash flow with projected liabilities, rebalancing will be unnecessary.
7. Active bond management consists of interest rate forecasting techniques and intermarket spread analysis. One popular taxonomy classifies active strategies as substitution swaps, intermarket spread swaps, rate anticipation swaps, or pure yield pickup swaps.
8. Horizon analysis is a type of interest rate forecasting. In this procedure the analyst forecasts the position of the yield curve at the end of some holding period, and from that yield curve predicts corresponding bond prices. Bonds then can be ranked according to expected total returns (coupon plus capital gain) over the holding period.
9. Interest rate swaps are major recent developments in the fixed-income market. In these arrangements parties trade the cash flows of different securities without actually exchanging any securities directly. This is a useful tool to manage the duration of a portfolio. It also has been used by corporations to borrow at advantageous interest rates in foreign credit markets that are viewed as more hospitable than are domestic credit markets.
10. Financial engineering has created many new fixed-income derivative assets with novel risk characteristics.

KEY TERMS

duration 462
modified duration 464
convexity 470
effective duration 473
immunization 474
bond index portfolio 474
rebalancing 480
cash flow matching 482
dedication strategy 482
substitution swap 484
intermarket spread swap 484
rate anticipation swap 485
pure yield pickup swap 485
tax swap 486
horizon analysis 486
contingent immunization 486
interest rate swaps 488
notional principal 488

PROBLEMS

1. A nine-year bond has a yield of 10 percent and a duration of 7.194 years. If the market yield changes by 50 basis points, what is the percentage change in the bond's price?
2. Find the duration of a 6 percent coupon bond making *annual* coupon payments if it has three years until maturity and has a yield to maturity of 6 percent. What is the duration if the yield to maturity is 10 percent?
3. Find the duration of the bond in problem 2 if the coupons are paid semiannually.
4. Rank the durations of the following pairs of bonds:
   a. Bond *A* is an 8 percent coupon bond, with a 20-year time to maturity selling at par value. Bond *B* is an 8 percent coupon bond, with a 20-year maturity time selling below par value.

b. Bond *A* is a 20-year noncallable coupon bond with a coupon rate of 8 percent, selling at par. Bond *B* is a 20-year callable bond with a coupon rate of 9 percent, also selling at par.

5. An insurance company must make payments to a customer of $10 million in one year and $4 million in five years. The yield curve is flat at 10 percent.

a. If it wants to fully fund and immunize its obligation to this customer with a *single* issue of a zero-coupon bond, what maturity bond must it purchase?

b. What must be the face value and market value of that zero-coupon bond?

CFA® PROBLEMS

6. *a.* Explain the impact on the offering yield of adding a call feature to a proposed bond issue.

b. Explain the impact on *both* bond duration and convexity of adding a call feature to a proposed bond issue.

7. Long-term Canada bonds currently are selling at yields to maturity of nearly 8 percent. You expect interest rates to fall. The rest of the market thinks that they will remain unchanged over the coming year. In each question below, choose the bond that will provide the higher holding-period return over the next year if you are correct. Briefly explain your answer.

a. i. A Baa-rated bond with coupon rate 8 percent and time to maturity 20 years
ii. An Aaa-rated bond with coupon rate of 8 percent and time to maturity 20 years

b. i. An A-rated bond with coupon rate 4 percent and maturity 20 years, callable at 105
ii. An A-rated bond with coupon rate 8 percent and maturity 20 years, callable at 105

c. i. A 6 percent coupon noncallable T-bond with maturity 20 years and YTM = 8 percent
ii. A 9 percent coupon noncallable T-bond with maturity 20 years and YTM = 8 percent

CFA® PROBLEMS

8. The following questions are from past CFA examinations.

a. A 6 percent coupon bond paying interest annually has a modified duration of 10 years, sells for $800, and is priced at a yield to maturity of 8 percent. If the YTM increases to 9 percent, the predicted change in price, using the duration concept, decreases by

i. $76.56
ii. $76.92
iii. $77.67
iv. $80.00

b. A 6 percent coupon bond with semiannual coupons has a convexity (in years) of 120, sells for 80 percent of par, and is priced at a yield to maturity of 8 percent. If the YTM increases to 9.5 percent, the predicted contribution to the percentage change in price, due to convexity, would be

i. 1.08%
ii. 1.35%
iii. 2.48%
iv. 7.35%

c. Which statement is true for the Macaulay duration of a zero-coupon bond? The Macaulay duration of a zero-coupon bond

i. Is equal to the bond's maturity in years
ii. Is equal to one-half the bond's maturity in years
iii. Is equal to the bond's maturity in years divided by its yield to maturity
iv. Cannot be calculated because of the lack of coupons

d. A bond with annual coupon payments has a coupon rate of 8 percent, yield to maturity of 10 percent, and Macaulay duration of 9. The bond's modified duration is

i. 8.18
ii. 8.33
iii. 9.78
iv. 10.00

---

e. The interest rate risk of a bond normally is
   i. Greater for shorter maturities
   ii. Lower for longer duration
   iii. Lower for higher coupons
   iv. None of the above

f. When interest rates decline, the duration of a 30-year bond selling at a premium
   i. Increases
   ii. Decreases
   iii. Remains the same
   iv. Increases at first, then declines

g. If a bond manager swaps a bond for one that is identical in terms of coupon rate, maturity, and credit quality but offers a higher yield to maturity, the swap is
   i. A substitution swap
   ii. An interest rate anticipation swap
   iii. A tax swap
   iv. An intermarket spread swap

h. Which bond has the longest duration?
   i. 8-year maturity, 6 percent coupon
   ii. 8-year maturity, 11 percent coupon
   iii. 15-year maturity, 6 percent coupon
   iv. 15-year maturity, 11 percent coupon

9. Currently, the term structure is as follows: one-year bonds yield 7 percent, two-year bonds yield 8 percent, three-year bonds and greater maturity bonds all yield 9 percent. An investor is choosing between one-, two-, and three-year maturity bonds all paying annual coupons of 8 percent, once a year. Which bond should you buy if you strongly believe that at year-end the yield curve will be flat at 9 percent?

CFA® PROBLEMS

10. Philip Morris has issued bonds that pay semiannually with the following characteristics:

Coupon	Yield to Maturity	Maturity	Macaulay Duration
8%	8%	15 years	10 years

a. Calculate modified duration using the information above.

b. Explain why modified duration is a better measure than maturity when calculating the bond's sensitivity to changes in interest rates.

c. Identify the direction of change in modified duration if:
   i. The coupon of the bond were 4 percent, not 8 percent
   ii. The maturity of the bond were 7 years, not 15 years

d. Define convexity and explain how modified duration and convexity are used to approximate the bond's percentage change in price, given a change in interest rates.

11. You will be paying $10,000 a year in education expenses at the end of the next two years. Bonds currently yield 8 percent.

a. What is the present value and duration of your obligation?

b. What maturity zero-coupon bond would immunize your obligation?

c. Suppose you buy a zero-coupon bond with value and duration equal to your obligation. Now suppose that rates immediately increase to 9 percent. What happens to your net position, that is, to the difference between the value of the bond and that of your education obligation? What if rates fall to 7 percent?

CFA® PROBLEMS

12. Several Investment Committee members have asked about interest rate swap agreements and how are they used in the management of domestic fixed-income portfolios.

a. Define an interest rate swap and briefly describe the obligation of each party involved.
b. Cite and explain two examples of how interest rate swaps could be used by a fixed-income portfolio manager to control risk or improve return.

13. What type of interest rate swap would be appropriate for a corporation holding long-term assets that it funded with floating-rate bonds?

14. A corporation has issued a $10 million issue of floating-rate bonds on which it pays an interest rate 1 percent over the LIBOR rate. The bonds are selling at par value. The firm is worried that rates are about to rise, and it would like to lock in a fixed interest rate on its borrowings. The firm sees that dealers in the swap market are offering swaps of LIBOR for 7 percent. What interest rate swap will convert the firm's interest obligation into one resembling a synthetic fixed-rate loan? What interest rate will it pay on that loan?

15. Pension funds pay lifetime annuities to recipients. If a firm will remain in business indefinitely, the pension obligation will resemble a perpetuity. Suppose, therefore, that you are managing a pension fund with obligations to make perpetual payments of $2 million per year to beneficiaries. The yield to maturity on all bonds is 16 percent.
a. If the duration of 5-year maturity bonds with coupon rates of 12 percent (paid annually) is 4 years and the duration of 20-year maturity bonds with coupon rates of 6 percent (paid annually) is 11 years, how much of each of these coupon bonds (in market value) will you want to hold to both fully fund and immunize your obligation?
b. What will be the par value of your holdings in the 20-year coupon bond?

16. You are managing a portfolio of $1 million. Your target duration is 10 years, and you can choose from two bonds: a zero-coupon bond with maturity of 5 years, and a perpetuity, each currently yielding 5 percent.
a. How much of each bond will you hold in your portfolio?
b. How will these fractions change *next year* if target duration is now nine years?

17. My pension plan will pay me $10,000 once a year for a 10-year period. The first payment will come in exactly five years. The pension fund wants to immunize its position.
a. What is the duration of its obligation to me? The current interest rate is 10 percent per year.
b. If the plan uses 5-year and 20-year zero-coupon bonds to construct the immunized position, how much money ought to be placed in each bond? What will be the *face value* of the holdings in each zero?

18. A 30-year maturity bond making annual coupon payments with a coupon rate of 12 percent has duration of 11.54 years and convexity of 192.4. The bond currently sells at a yield to maturity of 8 percent. Use a financial calculator to find the price of the bond if its yield to maturity falls to 7 percent or rises to 9 percent. What prices for the bond at these new yields would be predicted by the duration rule and the duration-with-convexity rule? What is the percentage error for each rule? What do you conclude about the accuracy of the two rules?

19. A 12.75-year maturity zero-coupon bond selling at a yield to maturity of 8 percent (effective annual yield) has convexity of 150.3 and modified duration of 11.81 years. A 30-year maturity 6 percent coupon bond making annual coupon payments also selling at a yield to maturity of 8 percent has nearly identical duration—11.79 years—but considerably higher convexity of 231.2.
a. Suppose the yield to maturity on both bonds increases to 9 percent. What will be the actual percentage capital loss on each bond? What percentage capital loss would be predicted by the duration-with-convexity rule?
b. Repeat part (*a*), but this time assume the yield to maturity decreases to 7 percent.
c. Compare the performance of the two bonds in the two scenarios, one involving an increase in rates, the other a decrease. Based on the comparative investment performance, explain the attraction of convexity.

d. In view of your answer to (*c*), do you think it would be possible for two bonds with equal duration but different convexity to be priced initially at the same yield to maturity if the yields on both bonds always increased or decreased by equal amounts, as in this example? Would anyone be willing to buy the bond with lower convexity under these circumstances?

20. A newly issued bond has a maturity of 10 years and pays a 7 percent coupon rate (with coupon payments coming once annually). The bond sells at par value.

a. What are the convexity and the duration of the bond? Use the formula for convexity in footnote 5.

b. Find the actual price of the bond assuming that its yield to maturity immediately increases from 7 percent to 8 percent (with maturity still 10 years).

c. What price would be predicted by the duration rule (equation 13.2)? What is the percentage error of that rule?

d. What price would be predicted by the duration-with-convexity rule (equation 13.7)? What is the percentage error of that rule?

CFA® PROBLEMS

21. One common goal among fixed-income portfolio managers is to earn high incremental returns on corporate bonds versus government bonds of comparable durations. The approach of some corporate-bond portfolio managers is to find and purchase those corporate bonds having the largest initial spreads over comparable-duration government bonds. John Ames, HFS's fixed-income manager, believes that a more rigorous approach is required if incremental returns are to be maximized.

The following table presents data relating to one set of corporate/government spread relationships present in the market at a given date:

Current and Expected Spreads and Durations of High-Grade Corporate Bonds (one-year horizon)

Bond Rating	Initial Spread over Governments	Expected Horizon Spread	Initial Duration	Expected Duration One Year from Now
Aaa	31 b.p.	31 b.p.	4 years	3.1 years
Aa	40 b.p.	50 b.p.	4 years	3.1 years

Note: 1 b.p. means 1 basis point, or .01 percent.

a. Recommend purchase of *either* Aaa or Aa bonds for a one-year investment horizon given a goal of maximizing incremental returns.

Ames chooses not to rely *solely* on initial spread relationships. His analytical framework considers a full range of other key variables likely to impact realized incremental returns, including call provisions and potential changes in interest rates.

b. Describe variables, *in addition to those identified* above, that Ames should include in his analysis *and* explain how *each* of these could cause realized incremental returns to differ from those indicated by initial spread relationships.

CFA® PROBLEMS

22. Patrick Wall is considering the purchase of one of the two bonds described in the following table. Wall realizes his decision will depend primarily on effective duration, and he believes that interest rates will decline by 50 basis points at all maturities over the next six months.

Characteristic	CIC	PTR
Market price	101.75	101.75
Maturity date	June 1, 2008	June 1, 2008
Call date	Noncallable	June 1, 2003
Annual coupon	6.25%	7.35%
Interest payment	Semiannual	Semiannual
Effective duration	7.35	5.40
Yield to maturity	6.02%	7.10%
Credit rating	A	A

a. Calculate the percentage price change forecasted by effective duration for *both* the CIC and PTR bonds if interest rates decline by 50 basis points over the next six months.

b. Calculate the six-month horizon return (in percent) for *each* bond, if the actual CIC bond price equals 105.55 and the actual PTR bond price equals 104.15 at the end of six months. Assume you purchased the bonds to settle on June 1, 1998.

Wall is surprised by the fact that although interest rates fell by 50 basis points, the actual price change for the CIC bond was greater than the price change forecasted by effective duration, whereas the actual price change for the PTR bond was less than the price change forecasted by effective duration.

c. Explain why the actual price change would be greater for the CIC bond and the actual price change would be less for the PTR bond.

CFA® PROBLEMS

23. You are the manager for the bond portfolio of a pension fund. The policies of the fund allow for the use of active strategies in managing the bond portfolio.

It appears that the economic cycle is beginning to mature, inflation is expected to accelerate, and in an effort to contain the economic expansion, central bank policy is moving toward constraint. For each of the situations below, state which one of the two bonds you would prefer. Briefly justify your answer in each case.

a. Government of Canada (Canadian pay) 7 percent due in 2007 and priced at 98.75 to yield 10.50 percent to maturity

or

Government of Canada (Canadian pay) 7 percent due in 2015 and priced at 91.75 to yield 11.19 percent to maturity

b. Texas Power and Light Co., $6\frac{1}{2}$ due in 2007, rated AAA, and priced at 95 to yield 8.02 percent to maturity

or

Arizona Public Service Co. 6.45 due in 2007, rated A–, and priced at 85 to yield 9.05 percent to maturity

c. Commonwealth Edison $2\frac{3}{4}$ due in 2007, rated Baa, and priced at 81 to yield 9.2 percent to maturity

or

Commonwealth Edison $12\frac{3}{8}$ due in 2007, rated Baa, and priced at 114.40 to yield 9.2 percent to maturity

d. Shell Oil Co. $7\frac{1}{2}$ sinking fund debentures due in 2020, rated AAA (sinking fund begins September 2004 at par), and priced at 78 to yield 10.91 percent to maturity

or

Warner-Lambert $7\frac{7}{8}$ sinking fund debentures due in 2020, rated AAA (sinking fund begins April 2009 at par), and priced at 84 to yield 10.31 percent to maturity.

e. Bank of Montreal (Canadian pay) 5 percent certificates of deposit due in 2007, rated AAA, and priced at 100 to yield 5 percent to maturity

or

Bank of Montreal (Canadian pay) floating-rate note due in 2012, rated AAA. Coupon currently set at 4.1 percent and priced at 100 (coupon adjusted semiannually to .5 percent above the three-month Government of Canada Treasury bill rate)

CFA® PROBLEMS

24. A member of a firm's investment committee is very interested in learning about the management of fixed-income portfolios. He would like to know how fixed-income managers position portfolios to capitalize on their expectations concerning three factors that influence interest rates:

a. Changes in the level of interest rates

b. Changes in yield spreads across/between sectors

c. Changes in yield spreads as to a particular instrument

Assuming that no investment policy limitations apply, formulate and describe a fixed-income portfolio management strategy for each of these factors that could be used to exploit a portfolio manager's expectations about that factor. (*Note:* Three strategies are required, one for each of the listed factors.)

25. Prices of long-term bonds are more volatile than prices of short-term bonds. However, yields to maturity of short-term bonds fluctuate more than yields of long-term bonds. How do you reconcile these two empirical observations?

26. A fixed-income portfolio manager is unwilling to realize a rate of return of less than 3 percent annually over a five-year investment period on a portfolio currently valued at $1 million. Three years later, the interest rate is 8 percent. What is the trigger point of the portfolio at this time, that is, how low can the value of the portfolio fall before the manager will be forced to immunize to be assured of achieving the minimum acceptable return?

27. A 30-year maturity bond has a 7 percent coupon rate, paid annually. It sells today for $867.42. A 20-year maturity bond has 6.5 percent coupon rate, also paid annually. It sells today for $879.50. A bond market analyst forecasts that in 5 years, 25-year maturity bonds will sell at yields to maturity of 8 percent and 15-year maturity bonds will sell at yields of 7.5 percent. Because the yield curve is upward-sloping, the analyst believes that coupons will be invested in short-term securities at a rate of 6 percent. Which bond offers the higher expected rate of return over the five-year period?

CFA® PROBLEMS

28. Your firm, TMP, is to be interviewed as a possible manager for the $100 million indexed fixed-income portfolio being considered by the investment committee of a large endowment fund. Because the committee has not yet decided which of three indices to use as their benchmark portfolio, the interview will focus on this issue. Information regarding each of the three indices to be discussed is presented in the following table. By way of background, TMP is told that the committee has adopted an aggressive overall investment policy with a long-term horizon and an above-average risk tolerance.

Sector Mix Information

	Index 1	Index 2	Index 3
U.S. Treasuries	50%	50%	80%
U.S. agencies	10	10	10
Corporates:			
Investment-grade	10	10	5
Below-investment-grade	5	5	0
Residential mortgages	20	25	5
Yankee bonds	5	0	0
Total	100%	100%	100%
Index modified duration	5.0	8.0	8.0
Index yield to maturity	7.50%	8.05%	8.00%

Both the level and the volatility of interest rates have been declining for the past several years. The committee believes these trends are unlikely to continue, and is seeking insight as to how the indexed portfolio might perform under a variety of alternative interest-rate scenarios. Two such scenarios are:

i. A cycle over which interest rates generally decline, but are accompanied by generally rising volatility

ii. A cycle over which interest rates are generally flat from beginning to end, but in which volatility is high throughout

a. Using only the data from the table, rank the three indices in order of relative attractiveness under each of the two scenarios above, and justify your rankings by citing the factors that support your conclusions.

b. Recommend and justify one index to the committee for use as its benchmark portfolio. Take into account your answer to part (*a*) and the information which you have been provided about the committee's investment policy.

c. Assume that the committee has selected an index to use as its benchmark and that TMP has been hired to construct and manage the indexed portfolio. Explain the practical problems associated with construction of an indexed fixed-income portfolio. Identify and briefly discuss two methods of such construction, including in your discussion one strength and one weakness of each method.

CFA® PROBLEMS

29. As part of your analysis of debt issued by Monticello Corporation, you are asked to evaluate two specific bond issues, shown in the table below.

Monticello Corporation Bond Information

	Bond A (callable)	Bond B (noncallable)
Maturity	2005	2005
Coupon	11.50%	7.25%
Current price	125.75	100.00
Yield to maturity	7.70%	7.25%
Modified duration to maturity	6.20	6.80
Call date	1999	—
Call price	105	—
Yield to call	5.10%	—
Modified duration to call	3.10	—

a. Using the duration and yield information in the table, compare the price and yield behaviour of the two bonds under each of the following two scenarios:
   i. Strong economic recovery with rising inflation expectations
   ii. Economic recession with reduced inflation expectations

b. Using the information in the table, calculate the projected price change for bond *B* if the yield to maturity for this bond falls by 75 basis points.

c. Describe the shortcoming of analyzing bond *A* strictly to call or to maturity.

CSI

30. For developing the fixed-income component for an asset mix, which of the following would you include?

a. All long- and short-term bonds and debentures
b. Strip and zero-coupon bonds
c. Convertible bonds
d. Preferred shares

CFA® PROBLEMS

31. Fran Arseneault manages investment assets and liabilities for Allied Corporation. Allied's portfolio currently has the following characteristics:

- $300 million of the assets must be invested short term. These assets currently earn a six-month LIBOR rate of 5 percent.
- $300 million in debt is outstanding; $100 million is seven-year-term fixed at a 6.5 percent rate and $200 million is short-term at the six-month LIBOR rate.

a. Describe Arseneault's asset/liability exposure to declining interest rates.

b. Allied has been unable to issue additional variable rate debt at reasonable fees. Hogan Stanfield Investment Bank stands ready to swap intermediate-term 6.5 percent fixed for six-month LIBOR. Devise an appropriate interest rate swap to hedge the firm's interest rate exposure.

CFA® PROBLEMS

32. Acree Corporation issued a floating-rate note that pays one-year LIBOR + 1% annually. The note has a par value of $100 million and a remaining term of five years.

a. Describe the interest rate risk that Acree faces.

b. Explain how a plain vanilla interest rate swap can eliminate Acree's interest rate risk.

CFA® PROBLEMS

33. Noah Kramer, a fixed-income portfolio manager based in the country of Sevista, is considering the purchase of a Sevista government bond. Kramer decides to evaluate two strategies for implementing his investment in Sevista bonds. Table 13.7 gives the details of the two strategies, and Table 13.8 contains the assumptions that apply to both strategies.

Table 13.7 Investment Strategies (amounts are market-value-invested)

Strategy	5-Year Maturity (modified duration = 4.83)	15-Year Maturity (modified duration = 14.35)	25-Year Maturity (modified duration = 23.81)
I	$5 million	0	$5 million
II	0	$10 million	0

Table 13.8 Investment Strategy Assumptions

Market value of bonds	$10 million
Bond maturities	5 and 25 years or 15 years
Bond coupon rates	0.00%
Target modified duration	15 years

Before choosing one of the two bond investment strategies, Kramer wants to analyze how the market value of the bonds will change if an instantaneous interest rate shift occurs immediately after his investment. The details of the interest rate shift are shown in Table 13.9. Calculate, for the instantaneous interest rate shift shown in Table 13.9, the percent change in the market value of the bonds that will occur under each strategy.

Table 13.9 Instantaneous Interest Rate Shift Immediately After Investment

Maturity	Interest Rate Change
5 years	Down 75 basis points (b.p.)
15 years	Up 25 b.p.
25 years	Up 50 b.p.

34. *a.* Use a spreadsheet to calculate the durations of the two bonds in Table 13.3 if the annual interest rate increases to 12 percent. Why does the duration of the coupon bond fall while that of the zero remains unchanged? (*Hint:* Examine what happens to the weights computed in column F.)

b. Use the same spreadsheet to calculate the duration of the coupon bond if the coupon were 12 percent instead of 8 percent and the semiannual interest rate is again 5 percent. Explain why duration is lower than in Table 13.3. (Again, start by looking at column F.)

35. *a.* Footnote 5 presents the formula for the convexity of a bond. Build a spreadsheet to calculate the convexity of a five-year, 8 percent coupon bond making annual payments at the initial yield to maturity of 10 percent.

b. What is the convexity of a five-year zero-coupon bond?

E-INVESTMENTS
Bond Calculations

Go to **www.derivativesmodels.com**. Choose the link for the classic page. You can also experiment with the enhanced page, which requires you first to establish a (free) user account. This site has a wealth of calculators. Scroll down to find *Bond Calculator.* The calculator provides yield to maturity, modified duration, and bond convexity as the bond's price changes. Experiment by trying different inputs. What happens to duration and convexity as coupon increases? As maturity increases? As price increases (holding coupon fixed)?

STANDARD & POOR'S

Go to **www.mcgrawhill.ca/edumarketinsight**. At the Market Insight Company page, enter the stock ticker symbol, "*T*," for AT&T and review the recent *Industry Outlook* report for the telecom industry. Review the variety of AT&T bonds outstanding by reviewing the latest *EDGAR 10K* report for AT&T. (Bonds are listed in the first few pages.) Then go to **www.bondsonline.com**, and search AT&T (enter under *Issue*) at the *Bond Search/Quote Center* link under *Corporate.* What is the current rating and yield to maturity for AT&T debt securities? What explains the yield level? For what type of investor or bond portfolio would AT&T bonds be most interesting?

PART FIVE

EQUITIES

14 Security Analysis

15 Financial Statement Analysis

16 Technical Analysis

SECURITY ANALYSIS

The dilemma for the portfolio manager and the investor is whether to follow the implication of the empirical evidence and the theory of market efficiency or to ignore it. Should one accept a passive investment strategy of an index fund or will the effort and expense of active management provide a superior portfolio? You saw in our discussion of market efficiency that finding undervalued securities is hardly easy. At the same time, there are enough doubts about the accuracy of the efficient market hypothesis that the search for such securities should not be dismissed out of hand. Moreover, it is the continuing search for mispriced securities that maintains a nearly efficient market. Even infrequent discoveries of minor mispricing justify the salary of a stock market analyst.

The area of security analysis can be divided into fundamental analysis and technical analysis. **Fundamental analysis** refers to the search for information concerning the current and prospective profitability of a company in order to discover its fair market value. **Technical analysis** embraces the use of information contained in stock market data to identify trends that will uncover trading opportunities. Empirical evidence suggests that neither of these approaches, especially the latter, is fruitful on the whole, but both are widely practised and must be understood.

Fundamental analysis has various aspects to it, including an economic analysis of how the firm will react to potential future conditions that will affect earnings; alternatively, the analyst can examine the recent financial results of the firm in the hope of finding unrecognized value. In this chapter, we see how valuation based on cash flow can be estimated from earnings; earnings themselves are predicted by examining economic conditions. In the following two chapters, we examine financial statement analysis and technical analysis.

We start with a discussion of alternative measures of the value of a company. From there, we review *dividend discount models*, from the simple growth model to compound variants; this leads to an examination of how earnings and dividend payouts are related to growth. Next, we turn to price-earnings (or P/E) ratios, which are employed widely by analysts but must be used carefully. We explain how P/E ratios are indicative of growth potential for the firm, and thus of dividends. At this point, we discuss two alternative strategies, growth investing and value investing. Finally, we examine the broader issue of how economic conditions affect the prospects of the firm. First, we analyze the effect of inflation, and then we identify key macroeconomic variables and discuss business cycles; from there we consider industry analysis and the sensitivity of the firm to the general environment.

14.1 VALUATION BY COMPARABLES

The purpose of fundamental analysis is to identify securities that are mispriced in the market relative to some measure of "true" value that can be derived from observable financial and company specific data. The Law of One Price mentioned in Chapter 8 notes that two assets paying the same cash flow in the future must trade at the same price; more generally, any two assets promising the same expected cash flows with the same risks should also trade at the same price. Fundamental analysis works to estimate the predictable cash flows and determine a discount factor by comparison with other known asset values. Part of this process involves examining various items in the financial statements, together with market price and perceptions of growth; these are combined in simple ratios to compare against benchmarks for similar companies.

CFA Institute
www.cfainstitute.org

Financial data for publicly traded companies is available in increasingly complete form by the Internet. One source is Standard & Poor's Market Insight service, including COMPUSTAT.[1] Table 14.1 shows some COMPUSTAT output of financial data for one of the world's best-known corporations, Microsoft, as of February 14, 2003. We use this to assess some of Microsoft's financial ratios.

The market price of a share of Microsoft is shown as \$46.99, and the total market capitalization of \$251.443 billion results from multiplying the share price times the 5,351 million shares outstanding. The **book value** of equity is calculated as the net value of total assets less total liabilities and preferred shares, divided by the number of common shares outstanding. Under the heading "Valuation," Table 14.1 reports the ratios of Microsoft's stock price to four different items taken from its latest financial statements (each divided by the number of outstanding shares): operating earnings, book value, sales revenue, and cash flow. Microsoft's price-to-earnings (P/E) ratio is 29.4, the price-to-book-value is 4.5, and price-to-sales is 8.2. Such comparative valuation ratios are used to assess the valuation of one firm versus others in the same industry. In the column to the right in Table 14.1 are comparable ratios for the average firm in the PC software industry.

[1]A free subscription to the educational version of S&P's Market Insight is included with this textbook. Extensive research on Canadian companies is provided by the Financial Post Databank.

Table 14.1 Financial Highlights for Microsoft Corporation, February 14, 2003

Current Quarter Ended:	December 2002	Current Year Ended:	June 2002
Miscellaneous			
Current price	46.990000	Common shareholders (actual)	117,730
Common shares outstanding (mil)	5,351.000	Employees (actual)	50,500
Market capitalization (mil)	251,443.490	S&P issuer credit rating	AA
Latest 12 Months	**Company**	**1 Year Change (%)**	
Sales (mil)	30,785.000	14.7	
EBITDA (mil)	14,580.000	5.9	
Net income (mil)	9,541.000	56.9	
EPS from ops	1.60	32.2	
Dividends/share	0.000000		
Valuation	**Company**	**Industry Average**	
Price/EPS from ops	29.4	34.6	
Price/book	4.5	4.9	
Price/sales	8.2	7.1	
Price/cash flow	23.6		
Profitability (%)			
Return on equity	17.1	14.9	
Return on assets	13.2	10.2	
Oper profit margin	43.8		
Net profit margin	31.0	21.5	
Financial Risk			
Debt/equity	0.0	6.2	

Source: COMPUSTAT company profiles.

We can see that for this date the market price was 4.5 times its book value at the end of December 2002; this compares favourably with the software industry average P/E of 4.9, suggesting undervaluation. The other ratios compare price to a company's ability to generate revenues and profits. For example, an analyst might compare the P/E ratio for Microsoft, 29.4, to the industry average ratio of 34.6. By comparison with this standard, Microsoft appears to be relatively underpriced. The price-to-sales ratio is useful for firms and industries that are in a start-up phase. Earnings figures for start-up firms are often negative and not reported, so analysts shift their focus from earnings per share to sales revenue per share.

The Balance Sheet Approach

Underlying all valuation approaches, there must be an appeal to the fundamental accounting relationship between total assets and liabilities. This would suggest that the book value of equity should approximate market value; yet Microsoft's example shows market value at 4.5 times book value. Does book value represent a floor at least for market value? Apparently not, as December 31, 2000 financial statements for Brascan showed a book value per share of $24.11, while the market price was only $22 that day.

The book value is established by applying a set of arbitrary accounting rules to spread the acquisition cost of assets over a specified number of years, whereas the market price of a stock takes account of the firm's value as a going concern. In other words, the market price reflects the present value of its expected future cash flows. It would be unusual if the market price of Brascan stock were exactly equal to its book value.

A better measure of a floor for the stock price is the **liquidation value** per share of the firm. This represents the amount of money that could be realized by breaking up the firm, selling its assets, repaying its debt, and distributing the remainder to the shareholders. The reasoning behind this concept is that if the market price of equity drops below the liquidation value of the firm, the firm becomes attractive as a takeover target. A corporate raider would find it profitable to buy enough shares to gain control and then actually to liquidate, because the liquidation value exceeds the value of the business as a going concern.

Another balance sheet concept that is of interest in valuing a firm is the **replacement cost** of its assets less its liabilities. Some analysts believe the market value of the firm cannot remain for long too far above its replacement cost because if it did, competitors would try to replicate the firm. The competitive pressure of other similar firms entering the same industry would drive down the market value of all firms until they come into equality with replacement cost.

This idea is popular among economists, and the ratio of market price to replacement cost is known as **Tobin's *q***, after the Nobel Prize–winning economist James Tobin. In the long run, according to this view, the ratio of market price to replacement cost will tend toward 1, but the evidence is that this ratio can differ significantly from 1 for very long periods of time.

A market valuation model accepts the accounting relationship as implicitly recognized by investors. They can proceed from the balance sheet and calculate the market value of equity as the present value of net operating revenues (after tax), less the market value of any debt claims; the latter value is itself a discounted valuation of the cash flows to the liabilities. Or they can find equity value by discounting net cash flows available to equityholders, after subtracting debt payments from operating revenues. (We have ignored noncash items such as depreciation in talking about revenues and cash flows.)

Assessment of the value of the equity of a going concern is based on the return that a stockholder expects to receive, namely cash dividends and capital gains or losses. Assume that an investor will hold one share of ABC stock for a year, at the end of which is expected a dividend $E(D_1)$ of \$4; suppose also that the forecast price at that time will be $E(P_1) = \$52$, with the current price being $P_0 = \$48$. The *expected* holding-period return is $E(D_1)$ plus the expected price appreciation, $E(P_1) - P_0$, all divided by the current price, P_0:

$$\text{Expected HPR} = E(r) = \frac{E(D_1) + [E(P_1) - P_0]}{P_0}$$

$$= \frac{4 + (52 - 48)}{48} = .167, \text{ or } 16.7\%$$

Thus, the stock's expected holding-period return is the sum of the expected dividend yield, $E(D_1)/P_0$, and the expected rate of price appreciation, the capital gains yield, $[E(P_1) - P_0]/P_0$.

But what is the required rate of return for ABC stock? We know from the CAPM that when stock market prices are at equilibrium levels, the rate of return that investors can expect to earn on a security is $r_f + \beta[E(r_M) - r_f]$. Thus, the CAPM may be viewed as providing the rate of return an investor can expect to earn on a security given its risk as measured by beta. This is the return that investors will require of any other investment with equivalent risk. We will denote this required rate of return as k. If a stock is priced "correctly," its *expected* return will equal the *required* return. Of course, the goal of a security analyst is to find stocks that are mispriced. For example, an underpriced stock will provide an expected return greater than the "fair," or required, return.

Suppose that $r_f = 6\%$, $E(r_M) - r_f = 5\%$, and the beta of ABC is 1.2. Then the value of k is

$$k = 6\% + 1.2 \times 5\% = 12\%$$

The rate of return the investor expects exceeds the required rate based on ABC's risk by a margin of 4.7 percent. Naturally, the investor will want to include more of ABC stock in the portfolio than a passive strategy would indicate.

Intrinsic Value Versus Market Price

Another way to see this is to compare the intrinsic value of a share of stock to its market price. The **intrinsic value**, denoted V_0, of a share of stock is defined as the present value of all cash payments to the investor in the stock, including dividends as well as the proceeds from the ultimate sale of the stock, discounted at the appropriate risk-adjusted interest rate, k. Whenever the intrinsic value, or the investor's own estimate of what the stock is really worth, exceeds the market price, the stock is considered undervalued and a good investment. In the case of ABC, using a one-year investment horizon and a forecast that the stock can be sold at the end of the year at price $P_1 = \$52$, the intrinsic value is

$$V_0 = \frac{E(D_1) + E(P_1)}{1 + k} = \frac{\$4 + \$52}{1.12} = \$50$$

Because intrinsic value, \$50, exceeds current price, \$48, we conclude the stock is undervalued in the market. We again conclude investors will want to buy more ABC than they would following a passive strategy. If the intrinsic value turns out to be lower than the current market price, investors should buy less of it than under the passive strategy.

In market equilibrium, the current market price will reflect the intrinsic value estimates of all market participants. This means the individual investor whose V_0 estimate differs from the market price, P_0, in effect must disagree with some or all of the market consensus estimates of $E(D_1)$, $E(P_1)$, or k. A common term for the market consensus value of the required rate of return, k, is the **market capitalization rate**, which we use often throughout this chapter.

The aggregate equity value is the product of the number of shares times the price determined in the market. The total of dividends paid to shareholders comes from the cash flows earned by the firm, after the payment of interest and retained earnings for future growth. In the balance sheet, the sum of the equity value and the liabilities must be the value of total assets, which is the present value of the cash flows derived from the firm's operation of its assets.

To extend the preceding example to the firm level, let's assume that there are one million shares of ABC stock trading at \$50 per share and \$25 million (B) of 10 percent coupon perpetual debt, with no income tax and no depreciation. ABC is a no-growth firm and investors want a 12 percent rate of return on investment. The dividend per share of D each year must be $k = 12\%$ times the share price ($P = \$50$). Total dividend payments ($n \times D$) are the residual of operating income (OI) less interest payments ($I = 10\% \times \$25$ million); hence, reversing the process, we can conclude that operating income in millions is

$$\text{OI} = I + n \times D = \$2.5 + 1 \times .12 \times \$50 = \$8.5 \text{ (million)}$$

Therefore, \$8.5 million of earnings are generated by the assets of the firm, which must be worth \$75 million; we recognize this by observing the share price and using the balance sheet equation:

$$V = B + S = B + n \times P = \$25 + 1 \times \$50 = \$75 \text{ (million)}$$

In arriving at the price $P = \$50$, the market must have predicted operating earnings of \$8.5 million and subtracted interest payments to get net income of \$6 million, or \$6 per share. Alternatively, we can capitalize operating income, estimated as \$8.5 million, at an overall cost of $11\frac{1}{3}$ percent (the weighted average cost of capital) to find asset value of \$75 million. Subtracting the debt of \$25 million and dividing by the number of shares, we derive the share price of \$50. In a simplified way, this is what analysts must do: estimate earnings, determine cash flows to equity, and capitalize them. As we shall see, a more realistic case would also require an estimate of growth in earnings.

In a perfect and simple economic setting, we might expect all of these accounting-based and market values to be about the same. Realistic depreciation rules applied to assets bought at competitive prices should yield values that equate to replacement values; and in a competitive environment, this also would equal capitalized values of earnings from those assets. Reality, however, is far different, as we saw in the Brascan and Nortel examples. Understanding why these differences occur is part of the analyst's job.

? CONCEPT CHECK

1. You expect the price of IBX stock to be \$59.77 per share a year from now. Its current market price is \$50, and you expect it to pay a dividend one year from now of \$2.15 a share.
   a. What is the stock's expected dividend yield, rate of price appreciation, and holding period return?
   b. If the stock has a beta of 1.15, the risk-free rate is 6 percent per year, and the expected rate of return on the market portfolio is 14 percent per year, what is the required rate of return on IBX stock?
   c. What is the intrinsic value of IBX stock, and how does it compare to the current market price?
   d. If there are one million shares and debt is \$20 million paying 8 percent, what are the operating earnings and the value

14.2 DIVIDEND DISCOUNT MODELS

Elementary financial mathematics provides us with some simple formulas for the value of the share price based on cash flows.[2] Under the **dividend discount model (DDM),** we can consider the infinite flow of dividends or the payment of a dividend and sale of the share at the end of a single period; these can be shown to be consistent. Thus, for a stream of dividends D_t, a discount rate *k,* and future price P_1, we see that

$$V_0 = \frac{D_1}{1+k} + \frac{D_2}{(1+k)^2} + \frac{D_3}{(1+k)^3} + \ldots = \frac{D_1 + P_1}{1+k} \tag{14.1}$$

This model appears to give problems in the case of a company paying no dividends; but either the company will eventually decide to pay dividends—even a single liquidating dividend—or it never will and its value will be zero. Predicting an infinite stream of dividends could be challenging, and that is still needed in order to calculate P_1 recursively from future dividends; consequently, we usually move to a model for some growth pattern in dividends.

The basic model is known as the **constant-growth DDM** or the *Gordon model,* after its formulator, Myron J. Gordon. A constant growth rate in dividends, *g,* leads to the simple formula for the *intrinsic value*

$$V_0 = \frac{D_1}{k-g} \tag{14.2}$$

When the market price, P_0, is presumed to be the value, this can be inverted to yield the intuitive result

$$E(r) = k = \frac{D_1}{P_0} + g \tag{14.3}$$

which states that the required return equals the current dividend yield plus the capital gain (the growth in the price). This model also predicts that, for any time *t*, $P_t = (1 + g)\,P_{t-1}$; furthermore, $P_t + D_t = (1 + k)P_{t-1}$ (i.e., the return is always expected to be *k*).

[2]These elementary results are derived in standard corporation finance texts; for those not familiar with them or those needing a review, Appendix 14A to this chapter gives the details.

The analyst or investor using this formula again must escape the circularity trap if an investment opportunity is to be found. Given the market price and a consensus on k, we infer the presumed growth rate. Analysis of financial results and market conditions may lead to the conclusion of a higher growth rate than implied by price. If the assumed k is accepted, then 14.2 will lead to a higher price estimate and a buy recommendation. By contrast, acceptance of the growth rate, combined with a feeling that the risk assessment implied by the discount rate k is too low, would imply that the price is too high, with sale recommended.

Estimation of a higher value is not the end of the process. If the market persists in its view of growth and risk, yet you feel the price should be higher, you may never see the fruits of your analysis, even if you're right. How quickly the market recognizes what you see determines how quickly the price will converge to true value. If in one year the stock is correctly priced, there will be a substantial holding period return (HPR).

EXAMPLE 14.1 Price Changes and HPR

For example, if $g = 10\%$ and $k = 15\%$ for an anticipated dividend of \$1, equation 14.2 gives a price of \$1/(.15 – .10) = \$20. If the market currently sees only \$18 of value but corrects in one year, then at that time, P_1 will be based on D_2 of \$1.10, or \$22. Your HPR will be

$$r = (D_1 + P_1 - P_0)/P_0 = (1.10 + 22 - 18)/18 = .2833$$

The $28\frac{1}{3}$ percent return for one year is well above the required return of 15 percent. If the market never catches on, the return from equation 14.3 is calculated as (1/18) + .10, or 15.5 percent; this is higher than the supposed requirement for a return of 15 percent.

CONCEPT CHECK

2. *a.* IBX's stock dividend at the end of this year is expected to be \$2.15, and it is expected to grow at 11.2 percent per year forever. If the required rate of return on IBX stock is 15.2 percent per year, what is its intrinsic value?
   b. If IBX's current market price is equal to this intrinsic value, what is next year's expected price?
   c. If an investor were to buy IBX stock now and sell it after receiving the \$2.15 dividend a year from now, what is the expected capital gain (i.e., price appreciation) in percentage terms? What is the dividend yield, and what would be the holding period return?

Stock Prices and Investment Opportunities

The major practical issue in evaluating stocks is forecasting the cash flows. Generally firms expand, leading to growth in sales, earnings, and dividends. As we develop this issue, let us start with a simple case that illustrates the growth issue.

Consider two companies, Cash Cow and Prospects, each with expected earnings in the coming year of \$5 per share. Both companies could in principle pay out all of these earnings as dividends, maintaining a perpetual dividend flow of \$5 per share. If the market capitalization rate were $k =$ 12.5 percent, both companies would then be valued at D_1/k = \$5/.125 = \$40 per share. Neither firm would grow in value, because with all earnings paid out as dividends, and no earnings reinvested in the firm, both companies' capital stock and earnings capacity would remain unchanged over time; earnings and dividends would not grow.

Actually, we are referring here to earnings net of the funds necessary to maintain the productivity of the firm's capital, that is, earnings net of "economic depreciation." In other words, the earnings figure should be interpreted as the maximum amount of money the firm could pay out each year in perpetuity without depleting its productive capacity. For this reason, the net earnings number may be quite different from the accounting earnings figure that the firm reports in its financial statements. (We explore this further in the next chapter.)

Now suppose one of the firms, Prospects, engages in projects that generate a return on investment of 15 percent, which is greater than the required rate of return, $k = 12.5\%$. It would be foolish for such a company to pay out all of its earnings as dividends. If Prospects retains or plows back some of its earnings into its highly profitable projects, it can earn a 15 percent rate of return for its shareholders, whereas if it pays out all earnings as dividends, it forgoes the projects, leaving shareholders to invest the dividends in other opportunities at a fair market rate of only 12.5 percent. Suppose, therefore, that Prospects lowers its **dividend payout ratio** (the fraction of earnings paid out as dividends) from 100 percent to 40 percent, maintaining a **plowback ratio** (the fraction of earnings reinvested in the firm) at 60 percent. The plowback ratio is also referred to as the **earnings retention ratio**.

The dividend of the company, therefore, will be \$2 (40 percent of \$5 earnings) instead of \$5. Will share price fall? No—it will rise! Although dividends initially fall under the earnings reinvestment policy, subsequent growth in the assets of the firm because of reinvested profits will generate growth in future dividends, which will be reflected in today's share price.

Figure 14.1 illustrates the dividend streams generated by Prospects under two dividend policies. A low-investment-rate plan allows the firm to pay higher initial dividends, but results in a lower dividend growth rate. Eventually, a high-reinvestment-rate plan will provide higher dividends. If the dividend growth generated by the reinvested earnings is high enough, the stock will be worth more under the high-reinvestment strategy.

How much growth will be generated? Suppose Prospects starts with plant and equipment of \$100 million and is all equity financed. With a return on investment or equity (ROE) of 15 percent, total earnings are ROE × \$100 million = .15 × \$100 million = \$15 million. There are 3 million shares of stock outstanding, so earnings per share are \$5, as posited above. If 60 percent of the \$15 million in this year's earnings is reinvested, then the value of the firm's capital stock will increase by .60 × \$15 million = \$9 million, or by 9 percent. The percentage increase in the capital stock is the rate at which income was generated (ROE) times the plowback ratio (the fraction of earnings reinvested in more capital), which we will denote as b.

Now endowed with 9 percent more capital, the company earns 9 percent more income, and pays out 9 percent higher dividends. The growth rate of the dividends, therefore, is

$$g = \text{ROE} \times b = .15 \times .60 = .09$$

If the stock price equals its intrinsic value, it should sell at

Figure 14.1 Dividend growth for two earnings reinvestment policies.

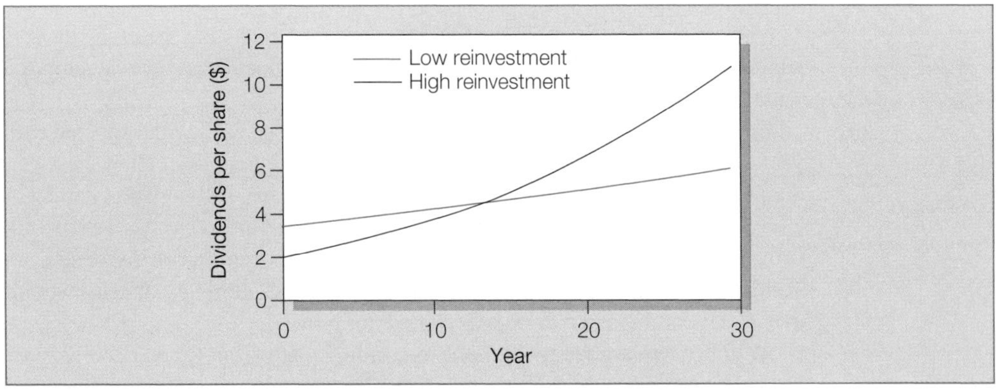

$$P_0 = \frac{D_1}{k-g} = \frac{\$2}{.125-.09} = \$57.14$$

When Prospects pursued a no-growth policy and paid out all earnings as dividends, the stock price was only \$40. Therefore, you can think of \$40 as the value per share of the assets the company already has in place.

When Prospects decided to reduce current dividends and reinvest some of its earnings in new investments, its stock price increased. The increase in the stock price reflects the fact that the planned investments provide an expected rate of return greater than the required rate. In other words, the investment opportunities have positive net present value. The value of the firm rises by the NPV of these investment opportunities. This net present value is also called the *present value of growth opportunities*, or ***PVGO.***

Therefore, we can think of the value of the firm as the sum of the value of assets already in place, or the no-growth value of the firm, plus the net present value of the future investments the firm will make, which is the PVGO. For Prospects, PVGO = \$17.14 per share:

$$\begin{aligned} \text{Price} &= \text{No-growth value per share} + \text{PVGO} \qquad (14.4) \\ P_0 &= \frac{E_1}{k} + \text{PVGO} \\ 57.14 &= 40 + 17.14 \end{aligned}$$

We know that in reality, dividend cuts almost always are accompanied by steep drops in stock prices. Does this contradict our analysis? Not necessarily: Dividend cuts are usually taken as bad news about the future prospects of the firm, and it is the *new information* about the firm—not the reduced dividend yield per se—that is responsible for the stock price decline. The stock price history of Microsoft (which until recently paid no dividends) proves that investors do not demand generous dividends if they are convinced that the funds are better deployed to new investments in the firm.

It is important to recognize that growth per se is not what investors desire. Growth enhances company value only if it is achieved by investment in projects with attractive profit opportunities (i.e., with ROE $> k$). To see why, let's now consider Prospects' unfortunate sister company, Cash Cow, Inc. Cash Cow's ROE is only 12.5 percent, just equal to the required rate of return, k. The net present value of its investment opportunities is zero. We've seen that following a zero-growth strategy with $b = 0$ and $g = 0$, the value of Cash Cow will be $E_1/k = \$5/.125 = \$40$ per share. Now suppose Cash Cow chooses a plowback ratio of $b = .60$, the same as Prospects' plowback. Then g would increase to

$$g = \text{ROE} \times b = .125 \times .60 = .075$$

but the stock price is still

$$P_0 = \frac{D_1}{k-g} = \frac{\$2}{.125-.075} = \$40$$

which is no different from the no-growth strategy.

In the case of Cash Cow, the dividend reduction used to free funds for reinvestment in the firm generates only enough growth to maintain the stock price at the current level. This is as it should be: If the firm's projects yield only what investors can earn on their own, shareholders cannot be made better off by a high-reinvestment-rate policy. This demonstrates that "growth" is not the same as growth opportunities. To justify reinvestment, the firm must engage in projects with better prospective returns than those shareholders can find elsewhere. Notice also that the PVGO of Cash Cow is zero: PVGO $= P_0 - E_1/k = 40 - 40 = 0$. With ROE $= k$, there is no advantage to plowing funds back into the firm; this shows up as PVGO of zero. In fact, this is why firms with considerable cash flow but limited investment prospects are called "cash cows." The cash these firms generate is best taken out of, or "milked" from, the firm.

EXAMPLE 14.2 Growth Opportunities

Takeover Target is run by entrenched management that insists on reinvesting 60 percent of its earnings in projects that provide an ROE of 10 percent, despite the fact that the firm's capitalization rate is $k = 15$ percent. The firm's year-end dividend will be \$2 per share, paid out of earnings of \$5 per share. At what price will the stock sell? What is the present value of growth opportunities? Why would such a firm be a takeover target for another firm?

Given current management's investment policy, the dividend growth rate will be

$$g = \text{ROE} \times b = 10\% \times 0.6 = 6\%$$

and the stock price should be

$$P_0 = \frac{\$2}{0.15 - 0.06} = \$22.22$$

The present value of growth opportunities is

$$\begin{aligned}\text{PVGO} &= \text{Price per share} - \text{No-growth value per share} \\ &= \$22.22 - E_1/k = \$22.22 - \$5/0.15 = -\$11.11\end{aligned}$$

PVGO is *negative.* This is because the net present value of the firm's projects is negative: The rate of return on those assets is less than the opportunity cost of capital.

Such a firm would be subject to takeover, because another firm could buy the firm for the market price of \$22.22 per share and increase the value of the firm by changing its investment policy. For example, if the new management simply paid out all earnings as dividends, the value of the firm would increase to its no-growth value, $E_1/k = \$5/0.15 = \$33.33$.

CONCEPT CHECK

3. *a.* Calculate the price of a firm with a plowback ratio of .60 if its ROE is 20 percent. Current earnings, E_1, will be \$5 per share, and $k = 12.5$ percent. Find the PVGO for this firm. Why is PVGO so high?

   b. Suppose ROE is only 10 percent and the capitalization rate is $k = 15$ percent. At what price will the stock sell? What is the PVGO? Why would such a firm be a target for a takeover by another firm?

Life Cycles and Multistage Growth Models

As useful as the constant-growth DDM formula is, you need to remember that it is based on a simplifying assumption, namely, that the dividend growth rate will be constant forever. In fact, firms typically pass through life cycles with very different dividend profiles in different phases. In early years, there are ample opportunities for profitable reinvestment in the company. Payout ratios are low, and growth is correspondingly rapid. In later years, the firm matures, production capacity is sufficient to meet market demand, competitors enter the market, and attractive opportunities for reinvestment may become harder to find. In this mature phase, the firm may choose to increase the dividend payout ratio, rather than retain earnings. The dividend level increases, but thereafter it grows at a slower rate because of fewer growth opportunities.

Table 14.2 illustrates this pattern. It gives Value Line's forecasts of return on assets, dividend payout ratio, and four-year growth rate in earnings per share of a sample of the firms included in the semiconductor industry versus those in the electric utility group. (We compare return on

Table 14.2 Financial Ratios in Two Industries

	Return on Assets	Payout Ratio	Growth Rate* (2003–2006)
Semiconductors			
Analog Devices	15.5%	0.0%	21.7%
Cirrus Logic	11.0	0.0	11.5
Intel	20.0	8.0	20.1
LSI Logic Corp.	18.0	0.0	23.0
Micron Technologies	12.5	0.0	22.5
National Semiconductor	15.5	0.0	18.5
NVIDIA	20.0	0.0	21.5
Semtech	17.0	0.0	18.5
Texas Instruments	11.0	9.0	24.6
Average	15.6%	1.9%	20.2%
Electric Utilities			
Allegheny Energy	6.0%	78.0%	5.0%
Central Vermont	8.0	48.0	11.2
Consolidated Edison	7.5	68.0	2.0
Energy East	6.5	51.0	5.8
Green Mountain Power	7.5	35.0	5.0
Northeast Utilities	6.0	39.0	18.6
Nstar	8.0	62.0	3.8
Public Services Enter.	8.5	50.0	2.4
United Illuminating	6.5	69.0	4.4
Average	7.2%	55.6%	6.5%

*Year 2003 earnings for some semiconductor firms were negative, which would make growth rates meaningless. In these cases, we used longer-term growth estimates from Value Line.

Source: *Value Line Investment Survey*, 2003.

assets rather than return on equity because the latter is affected by leverage, which tends to be far greater in the electric utility industry than in the semiconductor industry. Return on assets measures operating income per dollar of total assets, regardless of whether the source of the capital supplied is debt or equity. We will return to this issue in the next chapter.)

The semiconductor firms as a group have had attractive investment opportunities. The average return on assets of these firms is forecast to be 15.6 percent, and the firms have responded with high plowback ratios. Many of these firms pay no dividends at all. The high return on assets and high plowback result in rapid growth. The average growth rate of earnings per share in this group is projected at 20.2 percent.

In contrast, the electric utilities are more representative of mature firms. Their return on assets is lower, 7.2 percent; dividend payout is higher, 55.6 percent; and average growth is lower, 6.5 percent.

To value companies with temporarily high growth, analysts use a multistage version of the dividend discount model. Dividends in the early high-growth period are forecast and their combined present value is calculated. Then, once the firm is projected to settle down to a steady-growth phase, the constant-growth DDM is applied to value the remaining stream of dividends.

We can illustrate this with a current example. Figure 14.2 shows a Value Line Investment Survey report on the Bank of Montreal. Some of the relevant information in early 2004 is highlighted.

BMO Financial Group
www.bmo.com

BMO's beta appears at the circled A, the recent stock price at the B, the per-share dividend payments at the C, the ROE at the D, and the dividend payout ratio (referred to as percent of all dividends to net profits) at the E. The rows ending at C, D, and E are historical time series. Each

Figure 14.2 Value Line Investment Survey report on Bank of Montreal.

(B)

BANK OF MONTREAL TSE-BMO.TO [E F]

RECENT PRICE	P/E RATIO	RELATIVE P/E RATIO	DIV'D YLD	VALUE LINE
56.53	14.0 (Trailing: 15.7, Median: 11.0)	0.71	2.5%	1571

(A)

TIMELINESS 3 Raised 10/11/02
SAFETY 2 Raised 8/11/00
TECHNICAL 3 Raised 11/7/03
BETA .80 (1.00 = Market)

2006-08 PROJECTIONS

	Price	Gain	Ann'l Total Return
High	65	(+15%)	*6%*
Low	50	(-10%)	*Nil*

Insider Decisions

NOT REPORTED

U.S. Institutional Decisions

	1Q2003	2Q2003	3Q2003
to Buy	28	33	30
to Sell	21	19	27
Hld's(000)	86479	87284	110723

	1992	1993	1994	1995	1996	1997	1998	1999	2000	2001	2002	2003
High:	12.1	14.0	15.4	15.8	22.8	33.7	43.5	34.7	40.0	44.4	42.2	55.1
Low:	10.4	10.7	11.0	12.2	15.2	21.3	25.9	24.4	21.0	32.8	31.0	39.3

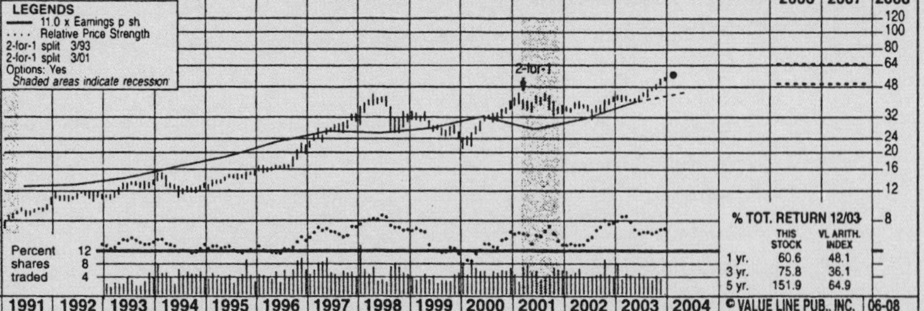

1987	1988	1989	1990	1991	1992	1993	1994	1995	1996	1997	1998	1999	2000	2001	2002	2003	2004	© VALUE LINE PUB., INC.	06-08
d1.11	1.22	.01	1.05	1.16	1.19	1.30	1.51	1.73	2.11	2.43	2.36	2.51	2.94	2.48	2.86	3.59	*4.10*	Earnings per sh [A B F]	*5.20*
.50	.50	.53	.53	.53	.53	.56	.60	.66	.74	.82	.88	.94	1.00	1.12	1.20	1.34	*1.44*	Div'ds Decl'd per sh [C ■]	*2.00*
7.38	7.81	6.99	7.50	8.03	8.85	9.70	10.69	11.71	12.94	14.59	16.36	17.44	19.63	19.69	21.07	22.09	*23.85*	Book Value per sh	*30.00*
408.36	427.05	443.04	459.98	477.54	489.64	498.19	530.91	527.37	519.87	522.87	528.87	534.06	522.58	489.08	492.50	499.63	*499.00*	Common Shs Outst'g [D]	*500.00*
--	5.5	NMF	6.8	7.4	9.3	9.5	8.6	8.0	7.8	10.6	15.0	11.7	9.6	15.6	12.7	11.9		Avg Ann'l P/E Ratio	*11.0*
--	.46	NMF	.51	.47	.56	.56	.56	.54	.49	.61	.78	.67	.62	.80	.69	.68		Relative P/E Ratio	*.73*
6.0%	7.4%	7.0%	7.4%	6.2%	4.8%	4.6%	4.6%	4.8%	4.5%	3.2%	2.5%	3.2%	3.6%	2.9%	3.3%	3.1%		Avg Ann'l Div'd Yield	*3.5%*

(C)

1993	1994	1995	1996	1997	1998	1999	2000	2001	2002	2003	2004		06-08
116869	138175	151834	169832	210128	222590	230615	233396	239409	252864	256494	*260000*	Total Assets ($mill)	*275000*
74028	88634	88442	98413	116063	130857	138001	133817	136829	142695	140545	*146000*	Loans ($mill) [A]	*156000*
3212.0	3380.0	3607.0	3790.0	4077.0	4024.0	4279.0	4204.0	4499.0	4829.0	4899.0	*5200*	Net Interest Inc ($mill)	*6100*
675.0	510.0	275.0	225.0	275.0	130.0	320.0	358.0	980.0	820.0	455.0	*400*	Loan Loss Prov'n ($mill)	*600*
1581.0	1749.0	1975.0	2329.0	2981.0	3118.0	3511.0	4326.0	4222.0	3924.0	4220.0	*4550*	Noninterest Inc ($mill)	*5300*
2916.0	3223.0	3646.0	3949.0	4539.0	4833.0	5201.0	5322.0	5917.0	6019.0	6087.0	*6300*	Noninterest Exp ($mill)	*6350*
709.0	825.0	986.0	1168.0	1346.0	1350.0	1469.0	1672.0	1376.0	1428.0	1825.0	*2100*	Net Profit ($mill)	*2980*
40.5%	40.1%	39.9%	38.9%	38.9%	36.9%	34.3%	36.5%	26.1%	22.2%	26.7%	*32.0%*	Income Tax Rate	*32.0%*
.61%	.60%	.65%	.69%	.64%	.61%	.64%	.72%	.57%	.56%	.71%	*.80%*	Return on Total Assets	*1.10%*
2363.0	2218.0	2595.0	3314.0	3831.0	4791.0	4712.0	4911.0	4674.0	3794.0	2856.0	*2800*	Long-Term Debt ($mill)	*2900*
5686.0	6538.0	7032.0	7586.0	8903.0	10608	10981	11941	10682	11894	12482	*13300*	Shr. Equity ($mill)	*16400*
4.9%	4.7%	4.6%	4.5%	4.2%	4.8%	4.8%	5.1%	4.5%	4.7%	4.9%	*5.0%*	Shr. Eq. to Total Assets	*6.0%*
63.3%	64.1%	58.2%	57.9%	55.2%	58.8%	59.8%	57.3%	57.2%	56.4%	54.8%	*56.0%*	Loans to Tot Assets	*57.0%*
12.5%	12.6%	14.0%	15.4%	15.1%	12.7%	13.4%	14.0%	12.9%	12.0%	14.6%	*16.0%*	Return on Shr. Equity	*18.0%*
7.5%	7.9%	9.2%	10.6%	11.0%	9.0%	9.1%	10.1%	7.6%	7.3%	9.8%	*11.0%*	Retained to Com Eq	*12.0%*
49%	45%	42%	39%	38%	43%	42%	38%	47%	47%	41%	*38%*	All Div'ds to Net Prof	*40%*

(D)

(E)

CAPITAL STRUCTURE as of 10/31/03

LT Debt $2856.0 mill. **LT Interest** $200.0 mill.

Leases, Uncapitalized Annual rentals $142.0 mill.
Pension Assets-10/02 $3.19 bill. **Oblig.** $3.3 bill.

Pfd Stock $1446.0 mill. **Pfd Div'd** $82.0 mill.

Common Stock 499,632,368 shares

MARKET CAP: $28.2 billion (Large Cap) [F]

ASSETS($mill.)	2001	2002	10/31/03
Loans	136829	142695	140545
Securities	37676	43715	54790
Other Earning	47248	47149	41299
Other	17656	19305	19860
LIABILITIES($mill.)			
Deposits	154290	161838	171551
Long-Term Debt	4674	3794	2856
Shr. Equity	10682	11894	12482
Other	69763	75338	69605
Total	239409	252864	256494
Loan Loss Resrv.	1949	1949	1785

ANNUAL RATES of change (per sh)	Past 10 Yrs.	Past 5 Yrs.	Est'd '01-'03 to '06-'08
Loans	7.5%	5.5%	*2.5%*
Earnings	9.5%	5.5%	*11.0%*
Dividends	8.5%	8.5%	*7.5%*
Book Value	9.0%	7.5%	*9.0%*
Total Assets	8.5%	5.5%	*2.5%*

Fiscal Year Ends	LOANS ($ mill.) [A] Jan.31	Apr.30	Jul.31	Oct.31	
2000	133148	136697	137134	133817	
2001	139270	136405	136693	136829	
2002	136067	138149	138643	142695	
2003	142498	144261	140815	140545	
2004	*142500*	*144000*	*145000*	*146000*	

Fiscal Year Ends	EARNINGS PER SHARE [A B] Jan.31	Apr.30	Jul.31	Oct.31	Full Fiscal Year
2000	.7171	.77	.69	.77	2.94
2001	.70	.76	.83	.19	2.48
2002	.75	.59	.72	.80	2.86
2003	.79	.81	.99	1.00	3.59
2004	*1.00*	*1.00*	*1.05*	*1.05*	*4.10*

Cal-endar	QUARTERLY DIVIDENDS PAID [C ■] Mar.31	Jun.30	Sep.30	Dec.31	Full Year
2000	.25	.25	.25	.25	1.00
2001	.28	.28	.28	.28	1.12
2002	.30	.30	.30	.30	1.20
2003	.33	.33	.33	.35	1.34
2004	.35				

BUSINESS: Bank of Montreal is one of the largest banks in Canada (by assets), with 1,134 branches (2,000 ATMs). Also operates in the U.S. and about 17 foreign countries. Owns Harris Bankcorp (Chicago, IL), and Nesbitt Burns, a full-service investment broker-dealer. Acquired Gerard Klauer Mattison, '03; CSFBdirect, '02; Suburban Bancorp, '94. Loans at 10/31/03: residential mortgages, 37%; consumer, 16%; business/gov't loans, 36%; repos, 11%. Net loan losses, 1.01% of average loans in 2003. As of 10/31/03, loan loss reserves, 0.4% of loans; problem assets, 1.3% of loans. Has about 33,912 employees. Chairman/CEO: Anthony Comper. Inc.: Canada. Addr.: P.O. Box 6002, Place d'Armes, Montreal, Quebec, Canada H2Y 3S8. Tel.: 514-877-7110. Internet: www.bmo.com.

Bank of Montreal posted strong results for 2003 on the back of operational improvements, leading us to raise our earnings outlook for 2004 to $4.10 a share. We have factored improvements in the bank's U.S. operations into our forecasts. Structural charges, relating to BMO's recent acquisitions in below-the-border wealth management and investment banking, were $8 million in the fourth quarter. We expect the number associated with this cost to trend downward.
Late last month, the Bank of Canada cut interest rates from 2.75% to 2.5%, lending credence to forecasts of capital market growth, including increased merger & acquisition and issuance activity, for the coming year. In such an environment, BMO's acquisitions leave the bank poised for strong revenue growth in the wealth management and investment banking groups. These segments accounted for 9% and 39%, respectively, of total income in the fourth quarter, but their absolute and relative contributions will likely grow significantly in 2004.
Nonlending income growth is vital to BMO's bottom line, considering that income from retail banking, 53% of net profits in the October period, will likely be relatively flat in 2004. The bank's home markets of Canada and the Chicago area remain competitive environments, and, despite the rate cut in Canada, we expect broadly flat overall American and Canadian consumer spending.
Bank of Montreal's loan loss provision retains little exposure to high-risk industries compared to its peers. The Bank's consumer portfolio represents 55% of total loans, with a low delinquency ratio of 0.27%. Total provisions were down to $455 million in 2003, a number we expect to be moderately lower in 2004 as the corporate default rate continues to decline, offset by increased risk in consumer credit.
This stock's 3- to 5-year capital appreciation is below average, as the share price seems to be benefiting from possibilities for a merger at present. This issue is thus ranked average (3) for Timeliness. Nonetheless, solid dividend growth is a strong point here. The stock still has some suitability for conservative, income-oriented investors.

Andrew Umans *February 6, 2004*

(A) Fiscal year ends October 31st.
(B) Diluted egs., primary before 1999; based on Cdn GAAP. Excl. unusual items: '99, $.42; '00, $.19; '01, $.18; '02, ($0.18); '03: $.15. Next egs. rpt. early Mar.
(C) Div'ds subject to 15% nonres. withholding tax. Dividends historically paid in late Feb., late May, late Aug., late Nov. ■ Div'd reinvestment plan available.
(D) In millions, adjusted for stock splits.
(E) Also trades on NYSE.
(F) All figures are in Canadian dollars.

Company's Financial Strength	B++
Stock's Price Stability	100
Price Growth Persistence	95
Earnings Predictability	75

boldfaced, italicized entry under 2004 is an estimate for the year. Similarly, the entries in the far right column (labelled 06–08) are forecasts for some time between 2006 and 2008, which we will take to be 2007.

Note that dividends have increased fairly steadily, with a slightly larger than usual increase recently. Value Line appears to estimate the 2007 dividend to be in line with the previous pattern. If we interpolate between 2004 and 2007, we obtain dividend forecasts as follows:

2004	$1.44
2005	$1.61
2006	$1.80
2007	$2.00

Now let us assume the dividend growth rate levels off in 2007. What is a good guess for that steady-state growth rate? Value Line forecasts a dividend payout ratio of .40 and an ROE of 18 percent, but the 11-year average ROE has been 13.56 percent. We shall assume future ROE of 13.5 percent, implying that long-term growth will be

$$g = \text{ROE} \times b = 13.5\% \times (1 - .4) = 8.1\%$$

Our estimate of BMO's intrinsic value using an investment horizon of 2007 is therefore obtained from equation 14.1, which we restate here:

$$V_{2003} = \frac{D_{2004}}{(1+k)} + \frac{D_{2005}}{(1+k)^2} + \frac{D_{2006}}{(1+k)^3} + \frac{D_{2007} + P_{2007}}{(1+k)^4}$$

$$= \frac{1.44}{(1+k)} + \frac{1.61}{(1+k)^2} + \frac{1.80}{(1+k)^3} + \frac{2.00 + P_{2007}}{(1+k)^4}$$

Here, P_{2007} represents the forecasted price at which we can sell our shares of BMO at the end of 2007, when dividends enter their constant-growth phase. That price, according to the constant-growth DDM, should be

$$P_{2007} = \frac{D_{2008}}{k - g} = \frac{D_{2007}(1 + g)}{k - g} = \frac{\$2 \times (1.081)}{k - .081}$$

The only variable remaining to be determined in order to calculate intrinsic value is the market capitalization rate, k.

One way to estimate k is through the CAPM. Note the Value Line estimate of BMO's beta as .80 and their reference to the Bank of Canada interest rate of 2.5 percent. Suppose that the current forecast of the market risk premium is 8.0 percent, corresponding to a forecast market return of 10.5 percent. We then solve for the market capitalization rate for BMO as

$$k = r_f + \beta[E(r_M) - r_f] = 2.5\% + .80(8.0\%) = 8.9\%$$

Our estimate of the 2007 stock price is thus

$$P_{2007} = \frac{\$2(1.081)}{.089 - .081} = \$270.25$$

and the current estimate of intrinsic value is

$$V_{2003} = \frac{\$1.44}{(1.089)} + \frac{\$1.61}{(1.089)^2} + \frac{\$1.80}{(1.089)^3} + \frac{\$2 + \$270.25}{(1.089)^4} = \$197.65$$

We know from the Value Line report that BMO's actual price was $56.53 (at the circled B). Our intrinsic value analysis indicates BMO was underpriced. Should we buy BMO?

Perhaps. But before betting the farm, stop to consider how firm our estimate is. We've had to guess at dividends in the near future, the ultimate growth rate of those dividends, and the appropriate discount rate. Moreover, we've assumed BMO will follow a relatively simple two-stage growth process. In practice, the growth of dividends can follow more complicated patterns. Even small errors in these approximations could upset a conclusion.

The vastly higher value calculated should cause us to question the result of the retained earnings approach to estimating dividend growth. For example, if we look at the compound annual growth rate in dividends over the last 10 years (9.11 percent) or a number of other key factors (EPS, 10.69 percent; Book Value, 8.58 percent; Net Interest + Noninterest Income, 6.64 percent; Total Assets, 8.18 percent), the assumption of a growth of 8.1 percent does not appear wildly optimistic. The average payout ratio of dividends for the past 11 years has been about 43 percent. Yet if we use this in place of Value Line's 40 percent, we arrive at a growth estimate of only 7.7 percent, which is also in line with the growth of the company from the other factors. Reworking the exercise using this number yields a value of V_{2003} = \$133.12, far lower than the first estimate but still well above the current price. One last adjustment would be to lower Value Line's dividend estimate for the next four years from the 10.53 percent rate their estimates imply to the 9.11 percent we observed; this would yield estimates for the next four years of \$1.46, \$1.60, \$1.74, and \$1.90, slightly below their estimates. The result of substituting these values is a future price of P_{2007} = \$170.52 and V_{2003} = \$126.64; perhaps BMO *is* a good investment, as the market does not seem to be discounting these values.

This exercise shows that finding bargains is not as easy as it seems. Although the DDM is easy to apply, establishing its inputs is more of a challenge. This should not be surprising. In even a moderately efficient market, finding profit opportunities has to be more involved than sitting down with Value Line for a half hour.

The exercise also highlights the importance of performing sensitivity analysis when you attempt to value stocks. Your estimates of stock values are no better than your assumptions. Sensitivity analysis will highlight the inputs that need to be most carefully examined. For example, we just found that small changes in the estimated dividend retention ratio for the post-2004 period would result in big changes in intrinsic value. Similarly, small changes in the assumed capitalization rate would change intrinsic value substantially. On the other hand, reasonable changes in the dividends forecast between 2004 and 2007 would have a small impact on intrinsic value.

CONCEPT CHECK

4. Confirm that the intrinsic value of BMO using g = 7.7 percent is \$133.12. (*Hint:* First calculate the stock price in 2007. Then calculate the present value of the difference between that value and the given \$270.25 price.)

14.3 EARNINGS, GROWTH, AND PRICE-EARNINGS RATIOS

Much of the real-world discussion of stock market valuation concentrates on the firm's **price-earnings multiple**, the ratio of price per share to earnings per share, commonly called the P/E ratio.

Our discussion of growth opportunities shows why stock market analysts focus on the P/E ratio. Both companies considered, Cash Cow and Prospects, had earnings per share (EPS) of \$5, but Prospects reinvested 60 percent of earnings in prospects with an ROE of 15 percent, whereas Cash Cow paid out all earnings as dividends. Cash Cow had a price of \$40, giving it a P/E multiple of 40/5 = 8.0, whereas Prospects sold for \$57.14, giving it a multiple of 57.14/5 = 11.4. This observation suggests the P/E ratio might serve as a useful indicator of expectations of growth opportunities. We can see this explicitly by rearranging equation 14.4 to

$$\frac{P_0}{E_1} = \frac{1}{k}\left(1 + \frac{\text{PVGO}}{E/k}\right) \tag{14.5}$$

When PVGO = 0, equation 14.5 shows that $P_0 = E_1/k$. The stock is valued like a nongrowing perpetuity of EPS_1. The P/E ratio is just $1/k$. However, as PVGO becomes an increasingly dominant contributor to price, the P/E ratio can rise dramatically.

The ratio of PVGO to E/k has a simple interpretation. It is the ratio of the component of firm value due to growth opportunities to the component of value due to assets already in place (i.e., the no-growth value of the firm, E/k). When future growth opportunities dominate the estimate of total value, the firm will command a high price relative to current earnings. Thus a high P/E multiple appears to indicate a firm is endowed with ample growth opportunities.

Let's see if P/E multiples do vary with growth prospects; consider Intel and AEP from Table 14.2. Between 1992 and 2001, Intel's P/E ratio averaged about 35 while AEP's (an electric utility) average P/E was only about half of that. These numbers do not necessarily imply that Intel was overpriced compared to AEP. If investors believed Intel would grow faster than AEP, the higher price per dollar of earnings would be justified. That is, an investor might well pay a higher price per dollar of *current* earnings if he or she expects that earnings stream to grow more rapidly. In fact, Intel's growth rate has been consistent with its higher P/E multiple. In the decade ending 2000, its earnings per share grew more than eight-fold (before turning down sharply in 2001, which was a difficult year for the entire high-tech sector), while AEP's earnings were essentially unchanged. Figure 14.3 shows the EPS history of the two companies.

Clearly, it is differences in expected growth opportunities that justify particular differentials in P/E ratios across firms. The P/E ratio actually is a reflection of the market's optimism concerning a firm's growth prospects. In their use of a P/E ratio, analysts must decide whether they are more or less optimistic than the market. If they are more optimistic, they will recommend buying the stock.

There is a way to make these insights more precise. Look again at the constant-growth DDM formula, $P_0 = D_1/(k - g)$. Now recall that dividends equal the earnings that are *not* reinvested in the firm: $D_1 = E_1(1 - b)$. Recall also that $g = \text{ROE} \times b$. Hence, substituting for D_1 and g, we find that

$$P_0 = \frac{E_1(1-b)}{k - \text{ROE} \times b}$$

implying the P/E ratio is

$$\frac{P_0}{E_1} = \frac{1-b}{k - \text{ROE} \times b} \qquad (14.6)$$

Figure 14.3 **Earnings growth for two companies.**

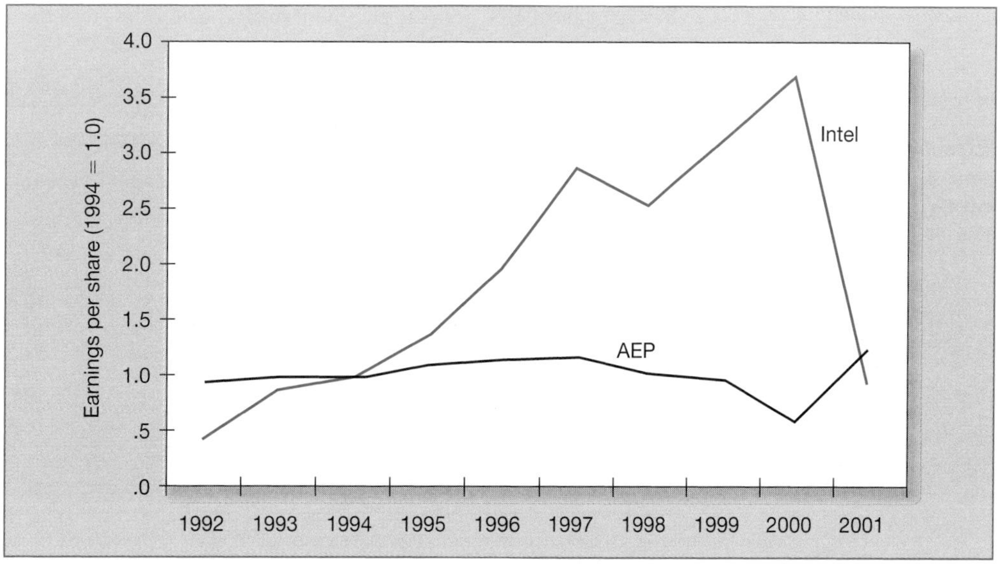

It is easy to verify that the P/E ratio increases with ROE. This makes sense, because high-ROE projects give the firm good opportunities for growth.[3] We also can verify that the P/E ratio increases for higher b as long as ROE exceeds k. This too makes sense. When a firm has good investment opportunities, the market will reward it with a higher P/E multiple if it exploits those opportunities more aggressively by plowing back more earnings into those opportunities.

Remember we noted, however, that growth is not desirable for its own sake. Examine Table 14.3 where we use equation 14.6 to compute both growth rates and P/E ratios for different combinations of ROE and b. Although growth always increases with the plowback rate (move across the rows in Table 14.3, panel A), the P/E ratio does not (move across the rows in panel B). In the top row of panel B, the P/E falls as the plowback rate increases. In the middle row, it is unaffected by plowback. In the third row, it increases.

This pattern has a simple interpretation. When the expected ROE is less than the required return, k, investors prefer that the firm pay out earnings as dividends rather than reinvest earnings in the firm at an inadequate rate of return. That is, for ROE lower than k, the value of the firm falls as plowback increases. Conversely, when ROE exceeds k, the firm offers attractive investment opportunities, so the value of the firm is enhanced as those opportunities are more fully exploited by increasing the plowback rate.

Finally, where ROE just equals k, the firm offers "breakeven" investment opportunities with a fair rate of return. In this case, investors are indifferent between reinvestment of earnings in the firm or elsewhere at the market capitalization rate, because the rate of return in either case is 12 percent. Therefore, the stock price is unaffected by the plowback rate.

One way to summarize these relationships is to say the higher the plowback rate, the higher the growth rate, but a higher plowback rate does not necessarily mean a higher P/E ratio. A higher plowback rate increases P/E only if investments undertaken by the firm offer an expected rate of return higher than the market capitalization rate. Otherwise, higher plowback hurts investors because it means more money is sunk into projects with inadequate rates of return.

Notwithstanding these fine points, P/E ratios commonly are taken as proxies for the expected growth in dividends or earnings. In fact, a common Wall Street rule of thumb is that the growth rate ought to be roughly equal to the P/E ratio. Peter Lynch, the famous portfolio manager, puts it this way in his book *One Up on Wall Street*:

> The P/E ratio of any company that's fairly priced will equal its growth rate. I'm talking here about growth rate of earnings here. . . . If the P/E ratio of Coca Cola is 15, you'd expect the company to be growing at about 15% per year, etc. But if the P/E ratio is less than the growth rate, you may have found yourself a bargain. [p. 198]

Table 14.3 Effect of ROE and Plowback on Growth and the P/E Ratio

	Plowback Rate (*b*)			
ROE	0	.25	.50	.75
	A. Growth rate, *g*			
10%	0	2.5%	5.0%	7.5%
12	0	3.0	6.0	9.0
14	0	3.5	7.0	10.5
	B. P/E ratio			
10%	8.33	7.89	7.14	5.56
12	8.33	8.33	8.33	8.33
14	8.33	8.82	10.00	16.67

Assumption: k = 12% per year.

[3]Note that equation 14.6 is a simple rearrangement of the DDM formula, with ROE × $b = g$. Because that formula requires that $g < k$, equation 14.6 is valid only when ROE × $b < k$.

EXAMPLE 14.3 P/E Ratio Versus Growth Rate

Let's try Lynch's rule of thumb. Assume

$r_f = 8\%$ (Roughly the value when Peter Lynch was writing)

$r_M - r_f = 8\%$ (About the historical average market risk premium)

$b = .4$ (A typical value for the plowback ratio in the United States)

Therefore, $r_M = r_f +$ Market risk premium $= 8\% + 8\% = 16$ percent, and $k = 16$ percent for an average ($\beta = 1$) company. If we also accept as reasonable that ROE = 16 percent (the same value as the expected return on the stock), we conclude that

$$g = \text{ROE} \times b = 16\% \times .4 = 6.4\%$$

and

$$\frac{P}{E} = \frac{1 - .4}{.16 - .064} = 6.25$$

Thus the P/E ratio and g are about equal using these assumptions, which obeys the rule of thumb.

However, note that this rule of thumb, like almost all others, will not work in all circumstances; most of them assume an interest rate environment. For example, the value of r_f today is more like 3 percent, so a comparable forecast of r_M today would be

$$r_f + \text{Market risk premium} = 3\% + 8\% = 11\%$$

If we continue to focus on a firm with $\beta = 1$, and if ROE still is about the same as k, then

$$g = 11\% \times .4 = 4.4\%$$

while

$$\frac{P}{E} = \frac{1 - .4}{.11 - .044} = 9.09$$

The P/E ratio and g now diverge. Nevertheless, it still is the case that high P/E stocks are almost invariably expected to show rapid earnings growth, even if the expected growth rate does not equal the P/E ratio.

www.priceline.com

The importance of growth opportunities is nowhere more evident than in the valuation of Internet firms. Many companies that had yet to turn profit were valued by the market in the late 1990s at billions of dollars. The perceived value of these companies was *exclusively* as growth opportunities. Of course, when company valuation is determined primarily by growth opportunities, those values can be very sensitive to reassessments of such prospects. For example, on September 27, 2000, Priceline.com announced that its third-quarter revenue would fall short of expectations by about 8 percent, and that instead of breaking even for the quarter, it would have a loss of one cent per share. Its stock price fell 42 percent in one day. By April 2001, the stock price of the struggling company was about \$3.50 per share, down from \$20 in September 2000 (and nearly \$100 earlier that year). Priceline has had plenty of company: the stock prices of most Internet retail firms have fallen dramatically since 1999, as the market has become more skeptical of their growth opportunities.

A recent assessment tool is the so-called PEG ratio. PEG is simply the ratio of the P/E ratio to the growth rate. High-tech firms are routinely assessed by comparative PEG ratios. A high PEG means the market is willing to pay more for growth than the price implied by a low PEG. In the example above, the Lynch rule corresponds to a PEG of 6.25/6.4 = .98. Under the alternative assumption, PEG = 9.09/4.4 = 2.06; the higher PEG is a more risky situation.

? CONCEPT CHECK

5. ABC stock has an expected ROE of 12 percent per year, expected earnings per share of \$2, and expected dividends of \$1.50 per share. Its market capitalization rate is 10 percent per year.
   a. What are its expected growth rate, its price, and its P/E ratio?
   b. If the plowback rate were .4, what would be the expected dividend per share, the growth rate, price, and the P/E ratio?

P/E Ratios and Stock Risk

One important implication of any stock valuation model is that (holding all else equal) riskier stocks will have lower P/E multiples. We can see this quite easily in the context of the constant-growth model by examining the formula for the P/E ratio (equation 14.6):

$$\frac{P}{E} = \frac{1 - b}{k - g}$$

Riskier firms will have higher required rates of return, that is, higher values of k. Therefore, the P/E multiple will be lower. This is true even outside the context of the constant-growth model. For *any* expected earnings and dividend stream, the present value of those cash flows will be lower when the stream is perceived to be riskier. Hence the stock price and the ratio of price to earnings will be lower.

Of course, if you scan the financial pages, you will observe many small, risky, start-up companies with very high P/E multiples. This does not contradict our claim that P/E multiples should fall with risk; instead it is evidence of the market's expectations of high growth rates for those companies. This is why we said that high-risk firms will have lower P/E ratios *holding all else equal.* Holding the projection of growth fixed, the P/E multiple will be lower when risk is perceived to be higher.

Pitfalls in P/E Analysis

No description of P/E analysis is complete without mentioning some of its pitfalls. First, consider that the denominator in the P/E ratio is accounting earnings, which are influenced by somewhat arbitrary accounting rules such as the use of historical cost in depreciation and inventory valuation. In times of high inflation, historic cost depreciation and inventory costs will tend to underrepresent true economic values, because the replacement cost of both goods and capital equipment will rise with the general level of prices. As Figure 14.4 demonstrates, P/E ratios have tended to be lower when inflation has been higher. This reflects the market's assessment that earnings in these periods are of "lower quality," artificially distorted by inflation, and warranting lower P/E ratios.

Earnings management is the practice of using flexibility in accounting rules to improve the apparent profitability of the firm. We will have much to say on this topic in the next chapter on interpreting financial statements. A version of earnings management that became common in the 1990s was the reporting of "pro forma earnings" measures. These measures are sometimes called *operating earnings,* a term with no generally accepted definition.

Pro forma earnings are calculated ignoring certain expenses, for example, restructuring charges, stock-option expenses, or write-downs of assets from continuing operations. Firms argue that ignoring these expenses gives a clearer picture of the underlying profitability of the firm. Comparisons with earlier periods probably would make more sense if those costs were excluded.

But there is so much leeway for choosing what to exclude that it becomes hard for investors or analysts to interpret the numbers or to compare them across firms. The lack of standards gives firms considerable leeway to manage earnings. One analyst calculated that in the first three quarters of

Figure 14.4
P/E ratios and inflation.

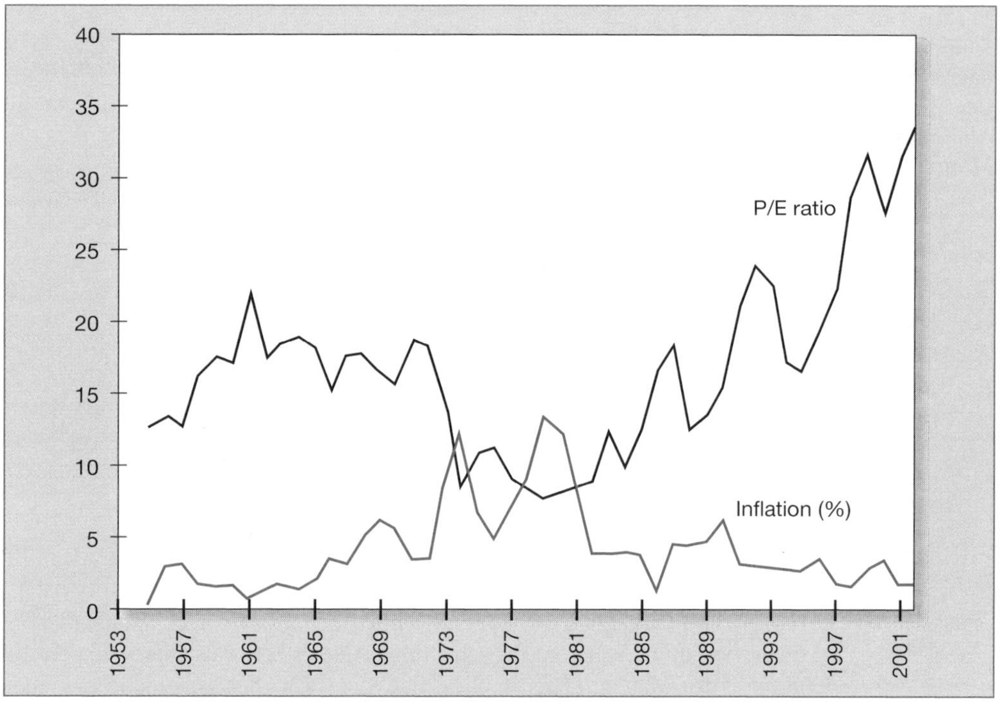

2001, the companies that comprise the Nasdaq 100 index reported collective pro forma earnings of \$82.3 billion, but GAAP losses of \$19.1 billion, a difference of over \$100 billion—for only these 100 firms![4]

Even GAAP allow firms considerable discretion to manage earnings. For example, in the late 1990s, Kellogg took restructuring charges, which are supposed to be one-time events, nine quarters in a row. Were these really one-time events, or were they more appropriately treated as ordinary expenses? Given the available leeway in managing earnings, the justified P/E multiple becomes difficult to gauge.

Another confounding factor in the use of P/E ratios is related to the business cycle. We were careful in deriving the DDM to define earnings as being net of *economic* depreciation, that is, the maximum flow of income that the firm could pay out without depleting its productive capacity. Reported earnings, as we note above, are computed in accordance with generally accepted accounting principles and need not correspond to economic earnings. Beyond this, however, notions of a normal or justified P/E ratio, as in equations 14.5 or 14.6, assume implicitly that earnings rise at a constant rate, or, put another way, on a smooth trend line. In contrast, reported earnings can fluctuate dramatically around a trend line over the course of the business cycle.

Another way to make this point is to note that the "normal" P/E ratio predicted by equation 14.6 is the ratio of today's price to the trend value of future earnings, E_1. The P/E ratio reported in the financial pages of the newspaper, by contrast, is the ratio of price to the most recent *past* accounting earnings. Current accounting earnings can differ considerably from future economic earnings. Because ownership of stock conveys the right to future as well as current earnings, the ratio of price to most recent earnings can vary substantially over the business cycle, as accounting earnings and the trend value of economic earnings diverge by greater and lesser amounts.

As an example, Figure 14.5 graphs the normalized earnings per share of Alcan and Magna International; normalization is the result of dividing the EPS before extraordinary items by the

[4]Reported in *The Economist*, February 23, 2002, p. 77.

Figure 14.5 Normalized earnings per share for Alcan and Magna.

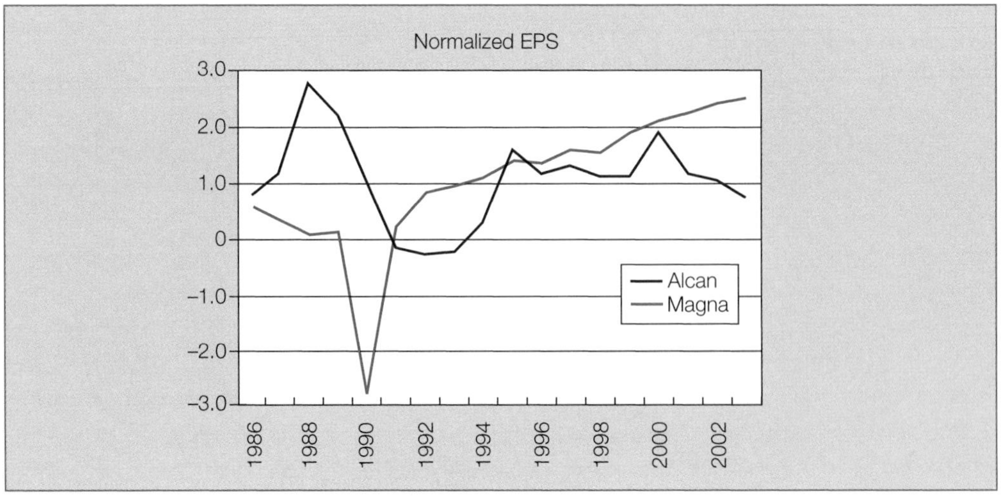

average EPS over the 18-year period. This enables us to see that the Alcan EPS varies considerably more than that of Magna (other than 1990), with Magna's steadily rising over the period. In fact, Alcan's earnings show no trend, while Magna's rose at an annual rate of 9.24 percent to 4.5 times their initial value. At the same time, Alcan's beta was approximately 1.3, in contrast to the lower .5 for Magna. (This implies that Alcan's higher systematic risk should have yielded a higher average gain in earnings.)

Figure 14.6 graphs for each company three ratios that should move in conjunction. As shown by equation 14.6, ROE varies directly with the P/E ratio, which is highly correlated with the P/CF (price-to-cash-flow) ratio discussed below. Note that P/CF is less variable than P/E, reflecting that a major decrease in earnings is not parallelled by an extreme drop in cash flow; we see that Magna's ratios are much more stable than Alcan's. In 1988–1989, a drastic reduction in earnings causes the P/E ratio to soar for Magna, followed by non-meaningful values in 1990 on negative earnings. We see the same general pattern followed by Alcan, with the elevated P/E in 1990 followed by four years of negative earnings and undefined P/E (and in 2003 P/E again soared). Cash flow remained positive but low for Alcan at this time, with higher P/CF, while Magna's cash flow

Figure 14.6 ROE, P/E, and P/CF for Alcan and Magna.

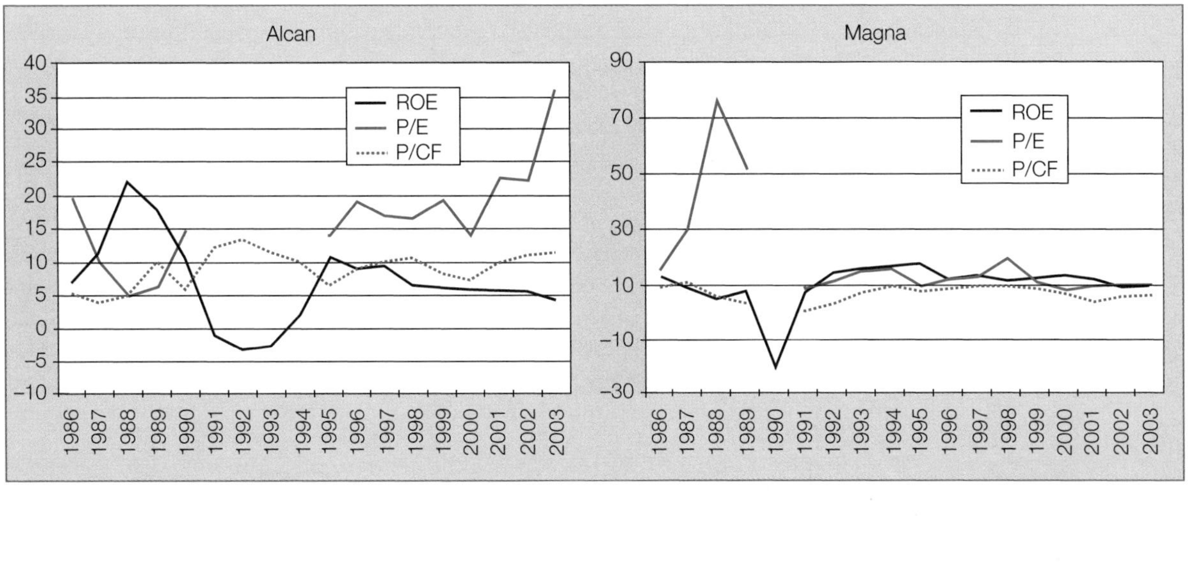

WILL THE REAL P/E STAND UP?

As investors scramble to make sense of volatile markets, they're not getting any help from that old yardstick of value, the price-to-earnings ratio. Shortly before Thanksgiving, one method for calculating the P/E of the S&P 500 showed it was trading at a level of just 14. Things looked cheap, and the rally that followed saw the S&P gain more than 100 points in just a few days, settling at a P/E ratio of 16 the day after the holiday. But wait a minute. Near the end of the rally, data from Standard and Poor's, the tenders of the S&P indexes, reported the P/E ratio of the S&P 500 to be 31. Meanwhile, if you'd glanced at a Bloomberg terminal that week, you would have also found the P/E ratio for the TSX listed there as 37, a number that suggested markets were way overvalued.

How can it be that two wildly divergent measures of the same index exist? For investors looking for a solid indicator on which to base investment decisions, the answer is not comforting: calculating P/E ratios is as much an art as it is an objective math exercise.

A P/E ratio is, of course, the price of a stock (or stock index) divided by the earnings of the company (or companies in the index). It's used to gauge the relative value of a stock or the market as a whole. According to Martin Barnes, managing editor of the Montreal-based *Bank Credit Analyst* journal, the first part of the equation is easy; it's the other side that's difficult. "We always know what P is," says Barnes. "The E is the problem. You have to make a lot of decisions."

One factor is whether to use reported earnings—which include writeoffs and one-time charges—or operating earnings, which reflect the underlying profits. "Generally, if you use the operating earnings, it makes the P/Es look lower because operating earnings are higher than reported," says Barnes.

There is also the matter of whether to use trailing earnings—the earnings that companies actually made over the past year—or forward-looking earnings, the number that analysts think corporations are going to make over the next four quarters. It's the difference between trailing and forward-looking earnings that accounts for the difference in the P/E ratios during the early-October rally. There's a particularly large gap between the numbers right now because the P/E ratio using trailing numbers is still picking up the last recession, when earnings plunged, says Craig Alexander, a senior economist with TD Bank Financial Group. Because he expects corporate earnings to pick up in the quarters ahead, Alexander suggests using forward-looking P/E ratios. "I think at this point you need to look at forward earnings rather than trailing earnings for a sense of what the market is doing," he says.

But keep in mind that forward-looking earnings are culled from the opinions of analysts who—to put it mildly—have a tendency to be optimistic in their assumptions. Although some companies have surprised investors with better-than-expected earnings this season, Chuck Hill, director of research at Thomson First Call, is doubtful about the S&P 500's forward earnings estimate of $54.67. "That's just ridiculous," he says. "The estimates, especially for tech, are still too high. I would have hoped to have seen some more downgrades this earnings season." Confused investors might look to historical P/E levels for guidance. Most market watchers peg the average P/E for the S&P 500 at between 15 and 16—anything below that is, by definition, undervalued. But according to Barnes, that figure can be misleading, too. "The problem is that different kinds of economic environments justify different kinds of predictions," he says. If inflation and interest rates are low, as they are now, then the point at which stocks become undervalued is slightly higher than the historical mean, which takes in periods of high inflation and high interest rates. With that in mind, Barnes suggests using a P/E of 18 when looking for value.

So are we safe to assume that with markets trading well below 18—and low inflation balancing inflated earnings—it's safe to get back into equities? Don't be hasty. As if conflicting P/Es aren't enough, investor psychology is driving the markets right now, not rational adherence to numbers. "Even if 18 is a reasonable number, that doesn't mean you should be buying the stock market now," says Barnes. "The market got away into the high 20s on the upside. So you can't assume it's going right back to the historical mean. Typically, in a bear market, the P/E overshoots on the downside and that hasn't happened yet. Stocks could still be risky."

Source: Jeff Sanford, *Canadian Business* 75, no. 21 (November 11, 2002), p. 20.

was negative, as the economic downturn resulted in depressed earnings and cash flow also, with non-meaningful values for 1992.

Magna's P/Es of 77 and 53 in 1988 and 1989 illustrate that the market did not lower the share price as much as earnings dropped, in recognition of the anticipated recovery, which was delayed until 1991. Because the market values the entire stream of future dividends generated by the company, when earnings are temporarily depressed the P/E ratio should tend to be high—that is, the denominator responds more sensitively to the business cycle than the numerator. This pattern indicated by Alcan's P/E of 36 in 2003 again demonstrates the market's expectation of earnings recovery in 2004. The link between the ratios over time is difficult to follow, with the lag effects of P/Es based on trailing earnings and prices pointing to the future prospects; adding instability, no

VALUATION OF STOCKS WITH SHIFTING GROWTH RATES

The constant growth model may not apply to most stocks. Firms are often expected to experience different rates of growth in earnings and dividends. For example, a firm may be expecting a high rate of growth for the next 5 to 10 years followed by lower or more normal growth.

ShiftingGrowth.xls, which is available on the Online Learning Centre at www.mcgrawhill.ca/college/bodie, allows you to estimate value for firms that do not fit the constant growth model. The model is set up to allow you to specify one or two shifts in growth rates to be followed by

	A	B	C	D	E	F	G	H	I	J
1	**Two-Stage Growth Model**									
2					**Stock Price**					
3	Initial Earnings	4.00						**First Stage Growth Rate**		
4	Initial Dividend	2.00								
5	Stage 1 Growth	0.13			44.08	0.1	0.11	0.12	0.13	0.14
6	Duration of Growth 1	10			5	33.48	34.85	36.28	37.76	39.28
7	Estimated Constant Growth	0.08			10	35.57	38.20	41.03	44.08	47.34
8	Beta Coefficient	1.25		**Duration**	15	37.25	41.01	45.20	49.86	55.06
9	T-Bill Rate	0.05		**of Growth**	20	38.60	43.36	48.85	55.17	62.45
10	Market Risk Premium	0.08			25	39.67	45.33	52.04	60.02	69.53
11					30	40.54	46.98	54.84	64.47	76.30
12	Required Return	0.15			35	41.23	48.36	57.30	68.55	82.78
13	Ratio of (1 + g)/(1 + k)	0.9826			40	41.78	49.52	59.45	72.28	88.99
14	Closed End	9.09								
15	PValue of the Stage 1 Dividends	18.18								
16	PValue of the Constant Growth Dividends	25.89			**Price to Next Year's Expected Earnings**					
17	Value of the Stock	44.08								
18								**First Stage Growth Rate**		
19	Analysis of Growth Opportunities				9.75	0.1	0.11	0.12	0.13	0.14
20	Value of NoGrowth Firm	26.67			5	7.6083	7.85021	8.09843	8.3531	8.6142
21	Present Value of Growth Opportunities	17.41		**Duration**	10	8.0849	8.6045	9.15922	9.7511	10.383
22				**of Growth**	15	8.4666	9.2365	10.0887	11.032	12.075
23	Price to Earnings Ratios				20	8.7722	9.7659	10.9031	12.205	13.696
24	Price/Current Earnings	11.02			25	9.0169	10.2095	11.6166	13.279	15.247
25	Price/Next Year's Expected Earnings	9.75			30	9.2128	10.5811	12.2418	14.264	16.732
26					35	9.3697	10.8924	12.7897	15.165	18.154
27					40	9.4953	11.1532	13.2696	15.991	

pattern can be discerned. Yet the period 1991–2003 for Magna paints a clear picture. All three ratios rise until 1994–1995, and then slowly decline until the present.

This example indicates why analysts must be careful in using P/E ratios. There is no way to say that the P/E ratio is overly high or low without referring to the company's long-run growth prospects, as well as to current earnings per share relative to the long-run trend line. (See the boxed article here for comment on the significance of P/E and earnings.)

This analysis suggests that P/E ratios should vary across industries, and in fact they do. Figure 14.7 shows P/E ratios in early 2003 for a sample of industries. P/E ratios for each industry are computed in two ways: by taking the ratio of price to previous year (i.e., 2002) earnings, and to projected next-year earnings. Notice that although the ratios based on 2002 earnings appear quite high, the ratios are far more moderate when prices are compared to forecasted earnings. This should not surprise you, because stock market prices are based on firms' earnings prospects.

normal or constant growth. The models are built to allow you to use any growth rate and duration of growth for the early stages of growth. The models can help you understand how growth affects value. The models also solve for price-to-earnings ratios to assess the impact of differential growth on P/E ratios.

	A	B
1	**Three-Stage Growth Model**	
2		
3	Initial Earnings	4.00
4	Initial Dividend	2.00
5	Stage 1 Growth	0.35
6	Duration of Growth 1	10
7	Stage 2 Growth	0.15
8	Duration of Growth 2	10
9	Estimated Constant Growth	0.08
10	Beta Coefficient	1.25
11	T-Bill Rate	0.05
12	Market Risk Premium	0.08
13		
14	Required Return	0.15
15	Ratio of (1 + g1)/(1 + k)	1.173913
16	Ratio of (1 + g2)/(1 + k)	1
17	Closed End Ratio 1	26.80
18	Closed End Ratio 2	10.00
19		
20	PValue of the Stage 1 Dividends	53.60
21	PValue of the Stage 2 Dividends	99.40
22	PValue of the Constant Growth Dividends	153.36
23	Value of the Stock	306.36
24		
25	Analysis of Growth Opportunities	
26	Value of NoGrowth Firm	26.67
27	Present Value of Growth Opportunities	279.69
28		
29	Price to Earnings Ratios	
30	Price/Current Earnings	76.59
31	Price/Next Year's Expected Earnings	56.73

Combining P/E Analysis and the DDM

www.edgar-online.com

Some analysts use P/E ratios in conjunction with earnings forecasts to estimate the price of a stock at an investor's horizon date. The BMO analysis in Figure 14.2 shows that Value Line forecasted a P/E ratio for 2007 of 11.0. EPS for 2007 were forecast at \$5.20, implying a price in 2007 of 11 × \$5.20 = \$57.20. Given an estimate of \$57.20 for the 2007 sales price, we would compute BMO's intrinsic value as

$$V_{2003} = \frac{\$1.44}{(1.089)} + \frac{\$1.61}{(1.089)^2} + \frac{\$1.80}{(1.089)^3} + \frac{\$2 + \$57.20}{(1.089)^4} = \$46.17$$

which turns out to be lower than the \$56.53 market price.

Figure 14.7
P/E ratios.

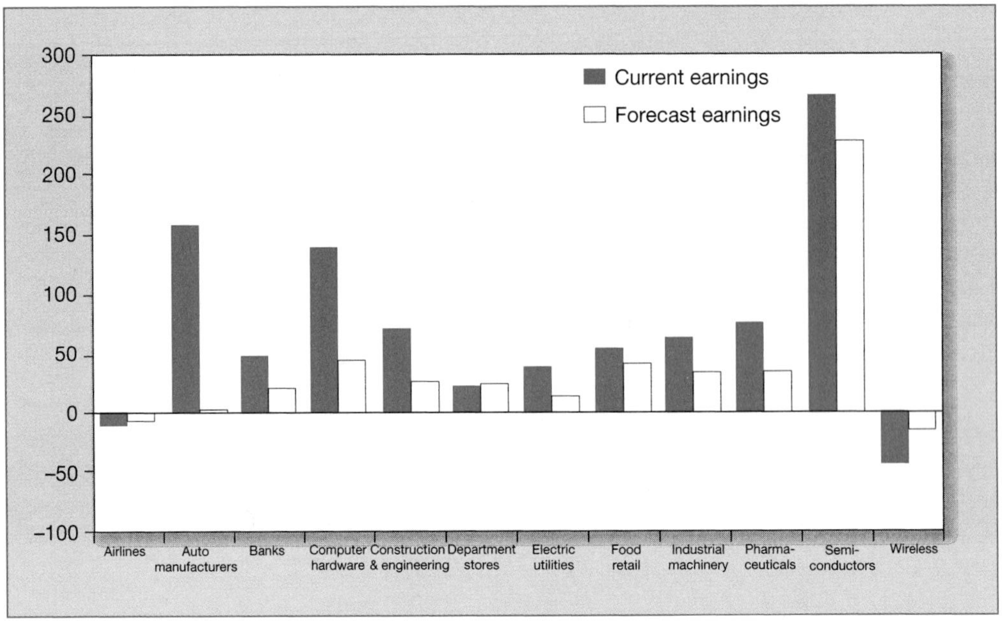

Other Comparative Valuation Ratios

The price-earnings ratio is an example of a comparative valuation ratio. Such ratios are used to assess the valuation of one firm versus another based on a fundamental indicator such as earnings. For example, an analyst might compare the P/E ratios of two firms in the same industry to test whether the market is valuing one firm "more aggressively" than the other. Other such comparative ratios are commonly used:

Price-to-Book Ratio This is the ratio of price per share divided by book value per share. As we noted earlier in this chapter, some analysts view book value as a useful measure of value and therefore treat the ratio of price to book value as an indicator of how aggressively the market values the firm.

Price-to-Cash-Flow Ratio Earnings as reported on the income statement can be affected by the company's choice of accounting practices, and thus are commonly viewed as subject to some imprecision and even manipulation. In contrast, cash flow—which tracks cash actually flowing into or out of the firm—is less affected by accounting decisions. As a result, some analysts prefer to use the ratio of price to cash flow per share rather than price to earnings per share. Some analysts use operating cash flow when calculating this ratio; others prefer "free cash flow," that is, operating cash flow net of new investment.

Price-to-Sales Ratio Many start-up firms have no earnings. As a result, the price-earnings ratio for these firms is meaningless. The price-to-sales ratio (the ratio of stock price to the annual sales per share) has recently become a popular valuation benchmark for these firms. Of course, price-to-sales ratios can vary markedly across industries, since profit margins vary widely.

Figure 14.8 presents the behaviour of these valuation measures since 1955 for the broad market. While the levels of these ratios differ considerably, for the most part they track each other fairly closely, with upturns and downturns at the same times.

Figure 14.8 Market valuation statistics.

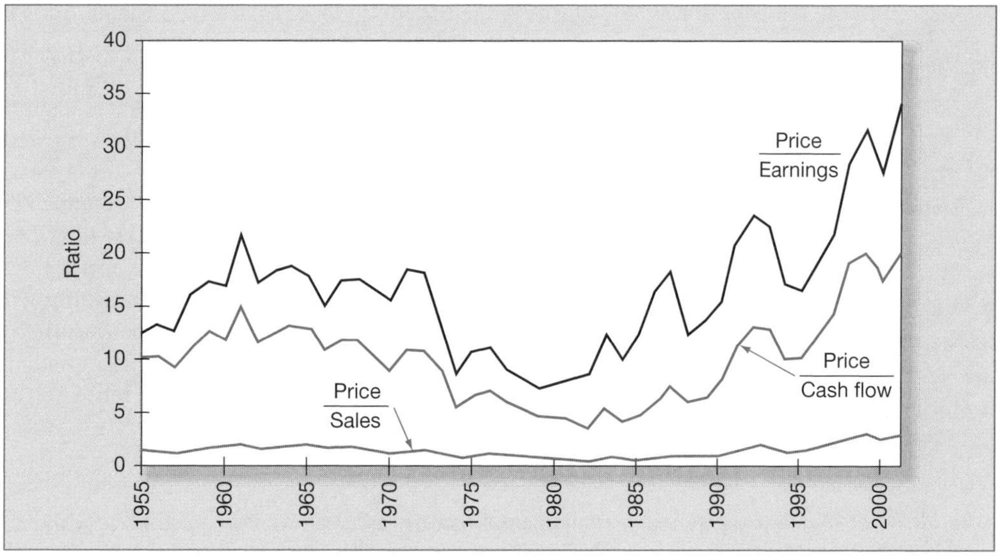

E-INVESTMENTS Stock Screening Tools

Stock screening tools allow one to sort through thousands of companies, based on predetermined criteria such as revenue and earnings growth, debt-equity maximums, profitability minimums, etc. Go to Yahoo's stock screening page at **screen.yahoo.com/stocks.html**. Select firms from any industry with P/E ratios below 20 and one-year growth estimates more than 5 percent. Review the ranked list of companies provided from the screen and the variables listed. What are the top five companies? Modify your list one variable at a time and observe the changes in the ranking. Next, select a stock category and an industry of interest to you. Using these screen variables, what companies are listed? (*Hint:* Do not make large changes in the range and/or the number of screening variables until you have a feel for the screening ranges, or you may find zero companies in your screen!)

14.4 GROWTH OR VALUE INVESTING

Many investment advisors express their approach to portfolio building as either "value investing" or "growth investing." The former is considered to be more conservative and the latter more rewarding, as it entails more risk. Others insist that all investing must be value-based, and that when growth opportunities are undervalued they become value opportunities. The two terms are generally accepted as implying a choice between companies for which there are superior growth prospects and those where fundamental analysis reveals unrecognized value. A more formal definition states that a **growth company** is one for which the growth rate is greater than the market average due to the opportunity to reinvest earnings at a rate greater than the market's required rate of return. (Note that this definition fits with the three stages of company life cycles.) Value is found in companies that can invest only at the market capitalization rate; the value is there because investors overlook these firms as they bid up the price of growth companies.

In fact, value investors rely upon misperceptions as to the real growth prospects of so-called growth companies, leaving true value in stable companies. There is considerable evidence to justify this approach. Growth investing assumes that there is a degree of persistence in growth trends such that superior returns can be generated from investing in companies with a record of growth; this return must justify the risk that actively growing firms often experience financial setbacks during downturns in the economy. More established, stable firms have greater financial resources to weather these difficulties. A famous study by I.M.D. Little in 1962 showed that, for British firms, those identified as growth companies in the first period were no more likely than other firms to be so identified in the second period; that is, there was no persistence of the growth characteristic. Subsequent studies of American firms showed the same results; growth could be identified only ex post.

Investors pay a premium price for future earnings of growth companies, captured by the high P/E ratio; should that growth fail to materialize, they will have inferior returns. Therefore, value investing in companies whose future earnings are much easier to predict will have a higher payoff. On the other hand, surely companies in growing industries with unique products to sell—the Microsofts and Cisco Systems of tomorrow—can be identified as growth companies. Ex post, they are easy to spot; the skill of being an analyst lies in finding them before their success occurs. (See the boxed article here for comment on P/E ratios.)

The Graham Technique

No presentation of fundamental security analysis would be complete without a discussion of the ideas of Benjamin Graham, the greatest of the investment "gurus." Until the evolution of modern portfolio theory in the latter half of this century, Graham was the single most important thinker, writer, and teacher in the field of investment analysis. His influence on investment professionals remains very strong.

Graham's magnum opus is *Security Analysis,* written with Columbia Professor David Dodd in 1934. By analyzing a firm's financial statements carefully, Graham felt one could identify bargain stocks. Over the years, he developed many different rules for determining the most important financial ratios and the critical values for judging a stock to be undervalued. Through its many editions, his book has had a profound influence on investment professionals. It has been so influential and successful, in fact, that widespread adoption of Graham's techniques has led to the elimination of the very bargains they are designed to identify.

In a 1976 seminar, Graham said

> I am no longer an advocate of elaborate techniques of security analysis in order to find superior value opportunities. This was a rewarding activity, say 40 years ago, when our textbook "Graham and Dodd" was first published; but the situation has changed a good deal since then. In the old days any well-trained security analyst could do a good professional job of selecting undervalued issues through detailed studies; but in the light of the enormous amount of research now being carried on, I doubt whether in most cases such extensive efforts will generate sufficiently superior selections to justify their cost. To that very limited extent I'm on the side of the "efficient market" school of thought now generally accepted by the professors.[5]

Standard & Poor's Institutional Market Services www.compustat.com

Nonetheless, in that same seminar Graham suggested a simplified approach to identify bargain stocks:

> My first, more limited, technique confines itself to the purchase of common stocks at less than their working-capital value, or net current-asset value, giving no weight to the plant and other fixed assets, and deducting all liabilities in full from the current assets. We used this approach extensively in managing investment funds, and over a 30-odd-year period we must have earned an average of some 20 percent per year from this source. For a while, however, after the mid-1950s, this brand of buying opportunity became very scarce because of the pervasive bull market. But it has returned in quantity since the 1973–1974 decline. In January 1976 we counted over 100 such issues in the

[5]As cited by John Train in *Money Masters* (New York: Harper & Row, Publishers, Inc., 1987). Graham is reported to have attributed his success in investing to the purchase of growth stocks rather than to reliance on fundamental analysis.

PICKING WINNERS REMAINS A CHALLENGE

Among the lingering hangovers from the stock market bubble of the 1990s are stock high valuations. Time and dismal market conditions have reduced the phenomenon, but some analysts say there are still many stocks that just aren't worth the money they still cost. Investors are left wondering what's unrealistically high-priced and what's a bargain.

There are tools you can use, one of which is the price-earnings ratio, also known as the P/E ratio or P/E multiple. This key ratio—a company's stock price divided by its annual profit per share—owes its popularity to Benjamin Graham, author of the investment classic *Security Analysis*, published in 1934. "Stocks were not really looked at as investments in the sense that we understand until after the 1920s," says Brendan Caldwell, president of Caldwell Securities in Toronto. Graham "came up with ways to evaluate whether a stock was good value, and one of the ratios he would have looked at was price relative to a company's earnings."

During the 1990s bubble, P/E calculations fell into some disrepute as the connection between share prices and profits became hazy or faded entirely—many highly regarded dot-coms had no earnings. At the time, this wasn't supposed to matter because exponents of so-called New Economy declared such quaint ratios obsolete. "They were right but not in the right way," said Caldwell. "Because ... the E part of the equation was made up. Pulled out of the air."

One of Graham's stock-selection criteria was that a P/E ratio should be less than 40 per cent of the highest P/E ratio the stock had attained over the past five years. Generally speaking, the higher the P/E ratio, the higher the risk. But buying stocks at reduced multiples doesn't necessarily represent astute investing. "Yahoo likely had an infinite P/E, now down to 30 and that's low compared to history," observed Brian Acker, president of Acker Finley Inc. "But it doesn't tell us it's a good buy at today's prices. However, running out and buying stocks at, say, 20 doesn't necessarily represent smart stock shopping."

Finding out the stock price is the easy part. Defining earnings is more challenging—only partly because of the accounting flexibility that came to light with the collapse of Enron and WorldCom.

"Is it the price as compared to past earnings, which have the benefit of being, hopefully, carved in stone?" said Caldwell. "Or do we mean the price opposed to projected earnings, which are more ephemeral of course but the consensus of what will happen in the future based upon analysts throwing up the chicken bones and the company's projections?" Another issue is whether to include non-recurring items, such as asset write-downs, in totting up earnings.

"And for every analyst you've got a different opinion," said Acker. "Some stocks have huge variance in terms of earnings because they're cyclical."

Overall, he isn't a big fan of the P/E ratio. "It's a very simple ratio, not really indicative of much." His analysis works through the balance sheet, where a swarm of other computations such as debt coverage ratios and return on equity come into play to assess assets against liabilities, and both of those against cash flowing in and out. "This is more art than science," Acker said. "Unfortunately, the tools out there—present tools—won't give the individual investor much of any indication of where a stock is headed."

In any event, 2003 is shaping up as yet another year in which picking winning stocks is a real challenge. In the overall market, "I think both bonds and equities will have mid-single-digit returns this year," said Acker.

"Get used to it, because we're going to be here for a while."

Source: *Leader Post* (Regina), April 25, 2003, p. B.4.

> Standard & Poor's *Stock Guide*—about 10 percent of the total. I consider it a foolproof method of systematic investment—once again, not on the basis of individual results but in terms of the expectable group outcome.

There are two convenient sources of information for those interested in trying out the Graham technique, which is still influential, as the boxed article suggests. Both Standard & Poor's *Outlook* and the *Value Line Investment Survey* carry lists of stocks selling below net working capital.

14.5 CORPORATE FINANCE AND THE FREE CASH FLOW APPROACH

In both the discounted dividend and capitalized earnings approaches to equity valuation we made the assumption that the only source of financing of new equity investment in the firm was retained earnings. How would our results be affected if we allowed external equity financing of new investments? How would they be affected if we assumed debt financing of new investments? In other words, how do dividend policy and capital structure affect the value of a firm's shares?

The classic answer to these questions was provided by Modigliani and Miller (MM) in a series of articles that have become the foundation for the modern theory of corporate finance,[6] and we will briefly explain their theory.[7]

MM claim that if we take as given a firm's future investments, then the value of its existing common stock is not affected by how those investments are financed. Therefore, neither the firm's dividend policy nor its capital structure should affect the value of a share of its equity.

The reasoning underlying the MM theory is that the intrinsic value of the equity in a firm is the present value of the net cash flows to shareholders that can be produced by the firm's existing assets plus the net present value of any investments to be made in the future. Given those existing and expected future investments, the firm's dividend and financing decisions will affect only the form in which existing shareholders will receive their future returns, that is, as dividends or capital gains, but not their present value.

As a byproduct of their proof of these propositions, MM show the equivalence of three seemingly different approaches to valuing the equity in a firm. The first two are the discounted dividend and capitalized earnings approaches presented in the earlier parts of this chapter. The third is the free cash flow approach.

This third approach starts with an estimate of the value of the firm as a whole and derives the value of the equity by subtracting the market value of all nonequity claims. The estimate of the value of the firm is found as the present value of cash flows, assuming all-equity financing plus the net present value of tax shields created by using debt. This approach is similar to that used by the firm's own management in capital budgeting, or the valuation approach that another firm would use in assessing the firm as a possible acquisition target.

EXAMPLE 14.4 Free Cash Flow Valuation

Consider the MiMo Corporation. Its cash flow from operations before interest and taxes was \$1 million in the year just ended, and it expects that this will grow by 6 percent per year forever. To make this happen, the firm will have to invest an amount equal to 15 percent of pretax cash flow each year. The tax rate is 30 percent. Depreciation was \$100,000 in the year just ended and is expected to grow at the same rate as the operating cash flow. The appropriate market capitalization rate for the unleveraged cash flow is 10 percent per year, and the firm currently has debt of \$2 million outstanding.

MiMo's projected free cash flow for the coming year is

Before-tax cash flow from operations	\$1,060,000
Depreciation	106,000
Taxable income	954,000
Taxes (at 30%)	286,200
After-tax unleveraged income	667,800
After-tax cash flow from operations (after-tax unleveraged income plus depreciation)	773,800
New investment (15% of cash flow from operations)	159,000
Free cash flow (after-tax cash flow from operations minus new investment)	614,800

[6]The original two papers are M. Miller and F. Modigliani, "Dividend Policy, Growth and the Valuation of Shares," *Journal of Business*, October 1961; and F. Modigliani and M. Miller, "The Cost of Capital, Corporation Finance, and the Theory of Investment," *American Economic Review*, June 1958. Miller revised his views in "Debt and Taxes," *Journal of Finance*, May 1976, and Modigliani his in "Debt, Dividend Policy, Taxes, Inflation and Market Valuation," *Journal of Finance*, May 1982.

[7]For a more complete treatment see Stephen A. Ross, Randolph W. Westerfield, Jeffrey F. Jaffe, and Gordon Roberts, *Corporate Finance*, 3rd ed. (Toronto: McGraw-Hill, 1999), Chapters 15 and 16; or Richard A. Brealey and Stewart C. Myers, *Principles of Corporate Finance*, 7th ed. (New York: McGraw-Hill, 1996), Chapters 17 and 18.

It is important to realize that this projected free cash flow is what the firm's cash flow would be under all-equity financing. It ignores the interest expense on the debt, as well as any tax savings resulting from the deductibility of the interest expense.

The present value of all future free cash flows is

$$V_0 = \frac{C_1}{k - g} = \frac{\$614{,}800}{.10 - .06} = \$15{,}370{,}000$$

Thus the value of the whole firm, debt plus equity, is \$15,370,000. Because the value of the debt is \$2 million, the value of the equity is \$13,370,000.

If we believe that the use of financial leverage enhances the total value of the firm, then we should add to the \$15,370,000 estimate of the firm's unleveraged value the gain from leverage. Thus if in our example we believe that the tax shield provided by the deductibility of interest payments on the debt increases the firm's total value by \$.5 million, the value of the firm would be \$15,870,000 and the value of the equity \$13,870,000.

In reconciling this free cash flow approach with either the discounted dividend or the capitalized earnings approach, it is important to realize that the capitalization rate to be used in the present value calculation is different. In the free cash flow approach it is the rate appropriate for unleveraged equity, whereas in the other two approaches, it is the rate appropriate for leveraged equity. Because leverage affects the stock's beta, these two capitalization rates will be different.

14.6 INFLATION AND EQUITY VALUATION

What about the effects of inflation on stock prices? We start with an "inflation-neutral" case in which all *real* variables, and therefore the stock price, are unaffected by inflation. We then explore the ways in which reality might differ.

Consider the case of Inflatotrend, a firm that in the absence of inflation pays out all earnings as dividends. Earnings and dividends per share are \$1, and there is no growth. We will use asterisked (*) letters to denote variables in the no-inflation case, or what represents the real value of variables. We consider an equilibrium real capitalization rate, k^*, of 10 percent per year. The price per share of this stock should be \$10:

$$P_0 = \frac{\$1}{.10} = \$10$$

Now imagine that inflation, i, is 6 percent per year, but that the values of the other economic variables adjust so as to leave their real values unchanged. Specifically, the *nominal* capitalization rate, k, becomes $(1 + k^*)(1 + i) - 1 = 1.10 \times 1.06 - 1 = .166$, or 16.6 percent, and the expected nominal growth rate of dividends, g, is now 6 percent, which is necessary to maintain a constant level of real dividends. The *nominal* dividend expected at the end of this year is therefore \$1.06 per share.

If we apply the constant-growth DDM to these nominal variables we get the same price as in the no-inflation case:

$$P_0 = \frac{D_1}{k - g} = \frac{\$1.06}{.166 - .060} = \$10$$

Thus as long as real values are unaffected, the stock's current price is unaffected by inflation.

Note that the expected nominal dividend yield, D_1/P_0, is 10.6 percent and the expected nominal capital gains rate, $(P_1 - P_0)/P_0$, is 6 percent. Almost the entire 6.6 percent increase in nominal return comes in the form of expected capital gains. A capital gain is necessary if the real value of the stock is to remain unaffected by inflation.

Let us see how these assumptions affect the other variables: earnings and the plowback ratio. To illuminate what otherwise may be confusing implications, we can explore a simplified story behind the examples above.

Inflatotrend produces a product that requires purchase of inventory at the beginning of each year, and sells the finished product at the end of the year. Last year there was no inflation. The inventory cost $10 million. Labour, rent, and other processing costs (paid at year-end) were $1 million, and revenue was $12 million. Assuming no taxes, earnings were $1 million:

Revenue	$12 million
– Labour and rent	1 million
– Cost of goods sold	10 million
Earnings	$ 1 million

All earnings are distributed as dividends to the 1 million shareholders. Because the only invested capital is the $10 million in inventory, the ROE is 10 percent.

This year, inflation of 6 percent is expected, and all prices are expected to rise at that rate. Because inventory is paid for at the beginning of the year, it will still cost $10 million. However, revenue will be $12.72 million instead of $12 million, and other costs will be $1.06 million.

Nominal Earnings

Revenue	$12.72 million
– Labour and rent	1.06 million
– Cost of goods sold	10.00 million
Earnings	$ 1.66 million
ROE	16.6%

Note that the amount required to *replace* inventory at year's end is $10.6 million, rather than the beginning *cost* of $10 million, so the amount of cash available to distribute as dividends is $1.06 million, not the reported earnings of $1.66 million.

A dividend of $1.06 million would be just enough to keep the real value of dividends unchanged and at the same time allow for maintenance of the same real value of inventory. The reported earnings of $1.66 million overstate true economic earnings, in other words.

We thus have the following set of relationships:

	No Inflation	6% Inflation
Dividends	$1 million	$1.06 million
Reported earnings	$1 million	$1.66 million
ROE	10%	16.6%
Plowback ratio	0	.36145
Price of a share	$10	$10
P/E ratio	10	6.0241

There are some surprising findings in this case of "neutral" inflation, that is, inflation that leaves the real interest rate and real earnings unaffected. Although nominal dividends rise at the rate of inflation, 6 percent, reported earnings increase initially by 66 percent. In subsequent years, as long as inflation remains at a constant rate of 6 percent, earnings will grow at 6 percent.

Note also that the plowback ratio rises from 0 to .36145. Although plowback in the no-inflation case was zero, positive plowback of reported earnings now becomes necessary to maintain the level of inventory at a constant real value. Inventory must rise from a nominal level of $10 million to a level of $10.6 million to maintain its real value. This inventory investment requires reinvested earnings of $.6 million.

Thus the proportion of reported income that must be retained and reinvested to keep the real growth rate of earnings at zero is .36145 if inflation is 6 percent per year. Multiplying this plowback ratio by the nominal ROE of 16.6 percent produces a nominal growth rate of dividends of 6 percent, which is equal to the inflation rate:

$$g = b \times \text{ROE}$$
$$= .36145 \times 16.6\% = 6\% \text{ per year}$$

More generally, the relationship between nominal and real variables is:

Variable	Real	Nominal
Growth rate	g^*	$g = (1 + g^*)(1 + i) - 1$
Capitalization rate	k^*	$k = (1 + k^*)(1 + i) - 1$
Return on equity	ROE*	$\text{ROE} = (1 + \text{ROE}^*)(1 + i) - 1$
Expected dividend	D_1^*	$D_1 = (1 + i)D_1^*$
Plowback ratio	b^*	$b = \dfrac{(1 + b^* \times \text{ROE}^*)(1 + i) - 1}{(1 + \text{ROE}^*)(1 + i) - 1}$

Note that it is not true that $E_1 = (1 + i)E_1^*$. That is, expected reported earnings do not, in general, equal expected real earnings times one plus the inflation rate. The reason, as you have seen, is that stated earnings do not accurately measure the cost of replenishing assets.

For example, cost of goods sold is treated as if it were $10 million, even though it now costs $10.6 million to replace the inventory. Historical cost accounting in this case distorts the measured cost of goods sold, which in turn distorts the reported earnings figures. We will return to this point in Chapter 15.

Note also the effect of inflation on the P/E ratio. In our example the P/E ratio drops from 10 in the no-inflation scenario to 6.0241 in the 6 percent inflation scenario. This is entirely a result of the fact that the reported earnings figure gets distorted by inflation and overstates true economic earnings.

This is true in the real world too, not just in our simplified example. Look back at Figure 14.4 and you will see that P/E ratios fall dramatically when the inflation rate increases. Many companies show gains in reported earnings during inflationary periods, even though real earnings may be unaffected. This is one reason analysts must interpret data on the past behaviour of P/E ratios over time with great care.

CONCEPT CHECK

6. Assume that Inflatotrend has a 4 percent annual expected constant growth rate of earnings if there is no inflation. $E_1^* = \$1$ per share; ROE* = 10 percent per year; $b^* = .4$; and $k^* = 10$ percent per year.
   a. What is the current price of a share?
   b. What are the expected real dividend yield and rate of capital appreciation?
   c. If the firm's real revenues and dividends are unaffected by inflation, and expected inflation is 6 percent per year, what should be the nominal growth rate of dividends, the expected nominal dividend yield, the expected ROE, and the nominal plowback ratio?

For many years economists thought that stocks ought to be an inflation-neutral investment in the sense that we have described. They believed, and many of them still believe, that changes in the rate of inflation, whether expected or unexpected, ought to have no effect on the expected real rate of return on common stocks.

Recent empirical research, however, seems to indicate that real rates of return are negatively correlated with inflation. In terms of the simple constant-growth-rate DDM, this would mean that an increase in inflation is associated with a decrease in D_1, an increase in k, a decrease in g, or some combination of all three.

One school of thought[8] believes that economic "shocks" such as oil price hikes can cause a simultaneous increase in the inflation rate and decline of expected real earnings (and dividends). This would result in a negative correlation between inflation and real stock returns.

A second view[9] is that the higher the rate of inflation, the riskier real stock returns are perceived to be. The reasoning here is that higher inflation is associated with greater uncertainty about the economy, which tends to induce a higher required rate of return on equity. In addition, a higher k implies a lower level of stock prices.

A third perspective[10] is that higher inflation results in lower real dividends because our tax system results in lower after-tax real earnings as the inflation rate rises.

Finally, there is the view[11] that many investors in the stock market suffer from a form of "money illusion." Investors mistake the rise in nominal rate of interest for a rise in the real rate. As a result, they undervalue stocks in a period of higher inflation.

14.7 MACROECONOMIC ANALYSIS

In order to forecast a firm's earnings, an analyst must consider the business environment in which it operates. For many firms, macroeconomic and industry circumstances have a greater influence on profits than does the firm's relative performance within its industry. Many portfolio managers attempt to identify superior firms based on their specific advantages, looking at past performance and financial statements, as we shall consider in the next chapter; others prefer to do a "top-down" analysis, examining the state of the economy and its implications for the industry in which the firm operates.

We present here a brief review of macroeconomics, mentioning the kind of factors that economists, working with the analysts, would examine in order to identify the current stage of the business cycle and predict the direction of economic variables. This information is then used by analysts to consider its effect on the industries that they cover in looking for particular companies that excel. This approach to investing is closely tied to the notion of timing the market. We illustrate a means of estimating the market response to the business cycle, especially using the level of interest rates in discounting predicted earnings, and we discuss some of the factors relevant to the sensitivity of the various industry classifications.

Bureau of Economic Analysis www.bea.doc.gov

The Global Economy

A top-down analysis of a firm's prospects must start with the global economy. The international economy might affect a firm's export prospects, the price competition it faces from competitors, or the profits it makes on investments abroad. Certainly, despite the fact that the economies of most countries are linked in a global macroeconomy, there is considerable variation in the economic performance across countries at any time. Consider, for example, Table 14.4, which presents data on several so-called emerging economies. The table documents striking variation in growth rates of economic output in 2003. For while the Chinese economy grew by 9.1 percent in

[8]See Eugene F. Fama, "Stock Returns, Real Activity, Inflation, and Money," *American Economic Review*, September 1981.
[9]See Burton Malkiel, *A Random Walk Down Wall Street*, 6th ed. (New York: W. W. Norton, 1996).
[10]See Martin Feldstein, "Inflation and the Stock Market," *American Economic Review*, December 1980.
[11]See Franco Modigliani and Richard Cohn, "Inflation, Rational Valuation, and the Market," *Financial Analysts Journal*, March/April 1979.

Table 14.4 Economic Performance in Selected Emerging Markets

		Stock Market Return (%)	
Country	% Growth in Real GDP	Local Currency	US$ Change
China	9.1	10.5	10.5
Hong Kong	4.0	33.7	34.3
India	5.7	71.7	80.4
Indonesia	3.9	63.1	72.4
Malaysia	3.5	21.9	21.9
Philippines	4.4	42.4	36.8
Singapore	1.7	29.8	32.4
South Korea	2.3	26.3	25.0
Taiwan	4.2	30.4	33.3
Thailand	6.5	109.5	127.9
Argentina	7.6	105.3	134.0
Brazil	−1.5	95.6	140.9
Chile	3.0	45.8	75.9
Colombia	4.0	44.9	49.6
Mexico	0.4	42.5	32.7
Venezuela	−7.1	175.8	139.3
South Africa	1.6	11.3	42.2
Turkey	4.8	73.3	103.9
Czech Republic	3.4	42.6	64.5
Hungary	2.9	21.4	30.9
Poland	3.8	45.2	48.1
Russia	7.2	46.1	58.7

Source: *The Economist,* January 3–9, 2004.

2003, Venezuela's output fell by 7.1 percent. Similarly, there was considerable variation in stock market returns in these countries in 2003, ranging from a 10.5 percent gain in China (in dollar terms) to a 140.9 percent gain in Brazil.

These data illustrate that the national economic environment can be a crucial determinant of industry performance. It is far harder for businesses to succeed in a contracting economy than in an expanding one; yet annual performance reflects the prior-year basis.

In addition, the global environment presents political risks of far greater magnitude than are typically encountered in Canadian or U.S.-based investments. In the last decade, we have seen several instances where political developments had major impacts on economic prospects. For example, in 1992 and 1993, the Mexican stock market responded dramatically to changing assessments regarding the prospect of the passage of the North American Free Trade Association by the U.S. Congress. In 1997, the Hong Kong stock market was extremely sensitive to political developments leading up to the transfer of governance to China. The biggest international economic story in late 1997 and 1998 was the turmoil in several Asian economies, notably Thailand, Indonesia, and South Korea. The close interplay between politics and economics was also highlighted by these episodes, as both currency and stock values swung with enormous volatility in response to developments concerning the prospects for aid from the International Monetary Fund. In August 1998, the shock waves following Russia's devaluation of the ruble and its default on some of its debt created havoc in world security markets, ultimately requiring a rescue of the giant hedge fund Long Term Capital Management to avoid further major disruptions. The collapse of the Argentinian economy, after the peg of its peso to the dollar was abandoned in 2001, had a huge impact on South American economies and markets. In the immediate future, the degree to which the European Monetary Union is successful will again illustrate the important interaction between the political and economic arenas.

Other political issues that are less sensational but still extremely important to economic growth and investment returns include issues of protectionism and trade policy, the free flow of capital, and the status of a nation's work force.

One obvious factor that affects the international competitiveness of a country's industries is the exchange rate between that country's currency and other currencies. The **exchange rate** is the rate at which domestic currency can be converted into foreign currency. For example, in mid-2004, it took about 80 Japanese yen to purchase one Canadian dollar. We would say that the exchange rate is ¥80 per dollar or, equivalently, \$.0125 per yen.

As exchange rates fluctuate, the dollar value of goods priced in foreign currency similarly fluctuates. For example, in 1980, the dollar-yen exchange rate was about \$.005 per yen. Because the exchange rate today is \$.0125 per yen, a Canadian would need two-and-a-half times as many dollars in 2004 to buy a product selling for ¥10,000 than would have been required in 1980. If the Japanese producer were to maintain a fixed yen price for its product, the price expressed in Canadian dollars would more than double. This would make Japanese products more expensive to Canadian consumers, however, and result in lost sales. Obviously, appreciation of the yen creates a problem for Japanese producers that must compete with Canadian producers.

Figure 14.9 shows the change in the purchasing power of the Canadian dollar relative to the purchasing power of the currencies of several major industrial countries in the period between 1986 and 2002. The ratio of purchasing powers is called the "real," or inflation-adjusted, exchange rate. The change in the real exchange rate measures how much more or less expensive foreign goods have become to Canadians, accounting for both exchange rate fluctuations and inflation differentials across countries. A negative value in Figure 14.9 means that the dollar has lost purchasing power relative to another currency. Therefore, the figure shows that goods priced in terms of British pounds have become far more expensive to Canadian consumers. Conversely, goods priced in Canadian dollars have become more affordable to British consumers.

The Macro Economy

Some of the key variables that analysts use to assess the state of the macro economy include the *gross domestic product* (GDP), the *unemployment rate, inflation, interest rates,* the *budget deficit*, and *sentiment.* The GDP measures the total production of goods and services and allows the

Figure 14.9 Change in real exchange rate: dollar versus major currencies, 1986–2002.

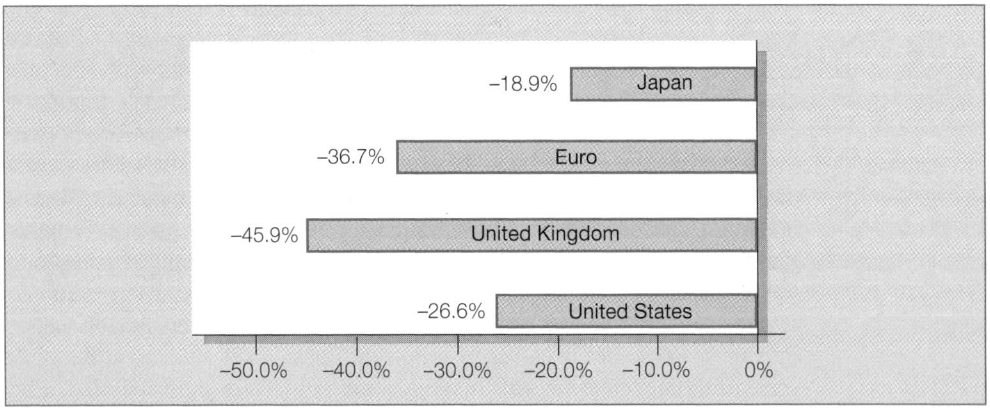

Source: Adapted from *Economic Report of the President*, 2003.

tracking of the rate of growth in the economy; this can be more narrowly focused on industrial production. Employment statistics and capacity utilization rates help analysts determine whether the economy may be overheating. This is closely related to the inflation rate, where various precise measures are used to identify the cause and probable course of inflationary pressures. The perceived tradeoff between inflation and unemployment is at the heart of many macroeconomic policy disputes. Interest rates generally respond to inflation, but they are managed by the central bank policy as well. They also follow from the budget deficit, which is the difference between government spending and revenues. Government borrowing as a result of deficits puts upward pressure on interest rates; excessive borrowing will "crowd out" private borrowing by forcing up interest rates. Sentiment reflects how consumers and producers display optimism or pessimism. Higher optimism leads to increased demand and investment in capital goods.

In an export-dependent economy, such as Canada's, the international variables of the *exchange rate* and the *current account* are crucial. Exchange rates, primarily against the U.S. dollar, determine the balance between exports and imports; they also affect inflation through the domestic cost of imported goods. The current account is determined by the difference between the value of imports and exports and by international transfers of investment funds; these transfers depend greatly on the investment decisions of foreigners holding Canadian assets and Canadians holding foreign assets. Persistent trade deficits and payments to foreign-held debt will cause the dollar to depreciate. Thus, we have a complex interplay of forces affecting interest rates, inflation, and exchange rates resulting from government policies and private investment and production decisions.

CONCEPT CHECK

7. Consider an economy where the dominant industry is automobile production for domestic consumption as well as export. Now suppose the auto market is hurt by an increase in the length of time people use their cars before replacing them. Describe the probable effects of this change on (*a*) GDP, (*b*) unemployment, (*c*) the government budget deficit, and (*d*) interest rates.

Demand and Supply Shocks and Government Policy

A useful way to organize the analysis of the factors that might influence the macro economy is to classify any impact as a demand or supply shock. A **demand shock** is an event that affects the demand for goods and services. Examples of positive demand shocks are reductions in tax rates, increases in the money supply, increases in government spending, or increases in foreign export demand. A **supply shock** is an event that influences production capacity and costs. Examples of supply shocks are changes in the price of imported oil; freezes, floods, or droughts that might destroy large quantities of agricultural crops; changes in the educational level of an economy's work force; or changes in the wage rates at which the labour force is willing to work.

Demand shocks usually are characterized by aggregate output moving in the same direction as interest rates and inflation. Thus, an increase in government spending will stimulate the economy and increase GDP, with a likely increase in borrowing, interest rates, and even inflation. A supply shock has the opposite effect—aggregate output usually moves counter to interest rates and inflation. Increases in world prices of oil increase production costs and prices of finished goods; the inflationary pressure results in higher interest rates and lower production as individuals are less able to purchase more expensive goods.

The federal government has two broad classes of macroeconomic tools with which it attempts to regulate the economy—those that affect demand and those affecting supply. **Fiscal policy** includes taxation and government spending, and has a pronounced effect on demand. Increases in taxes directly restrict consumption and rapidly rein in the economy. An increase in government spending, on the other hand, fuels demand and can cause a prompt increase in production. An increase in one without a corresponding increase in the other changes the deficit; thus a stimulative or restrictive shock can be given to the economy.

The other tool of demand-side policy is **monetary policy**, which refers to the manipulation of the money supply and works mainly through its impact on interest rates. The money supply is increased or decreased by the purchase or sale of securities by the Bank of Canada; the money paid for a security by the bank is a direct increase to the money supply. The bank also can raise or lower the bank rate to make borrowing more or less costly, thereby affecting investment. These tools are easier to implement but less effective than fiscal policy. Many economists believe that an increased money supply leads only to inflation in the long run. The boxed article here indicates how monetary policy obsesses analysts.

The 1970s and 1980s, were characterized by high inflation, high deficits, and high unemployment. These were taken as being the result of poor economic policy. The 1990s, by contrast, witnessed falling inflation and unemployment, and an unprecedented economic expansion. These were credited to low taxes, astute monetary policy, and a technology windfall. Yet this almost perfect scenario led to the market slide and the recession of 2001.

Fiscal and monetary policy are demand-oriented tools that affect the economy by stimulating the total demand for goods and services. The implicit belief is that the economy will not by itself arrive at a full-employment equilibrium, and that macroeconomic policy can push the economy toward this goal. In contrast, supply-side policies treat the issue of the productive capacity of the economy. The goal is to create an environment in which workers and owners of capital have the maximum incentive and ability to produce and develop goods.

Supply-side economists also pay considerable attention to tax policy. Whereas demand-siders look at the effect of taxes on consumption demand, supply-siders focus on incentives and marginal tax rates. They argue that lowering tax rates will elicit more investment and improve incentives to work, thereby enhancing economic growth. Some go so far as to claim that reductions in tax rates can lead to increases in tax revenues because the lower tax rates will cause the economy and the revenue tax base to grow by more than the tax rate is reduced.

? CONCEPT CHECK

8. Large tax cuts in the 1980s were followed by rapid growth in GDP. How would demand-side and supply-side economists differ in their interpretations of this phenomenon?

The Business Cycle

The economy recurrently experiences periods of expansion and contraction, although the length and depth of those cycles can be irregular. This recurring pattern of recession and recovery is called the **business cycle**. The transition points across cycles are called *peaks* and *troughs*. A *peak* is the transition from the end of an expansion to the start of a contraction. A *trough* occurs at the bottom of a recession just as the economy enters a recovery.

As the economy passes through different stages of the business cycle, the relative performance of different industry groups might be expected to vary. For example, at a trough, just before the economy begins to recover from a recession, one would expect that *cyclical industries*, those with above-average sensitivity to the state of the economy, would tend to outperform other industries. Examples of cyclical industries are producers of durable goods such as automobiles or washing machines. Because purchases of these goods can be deferred during a recession, sales are particularly sensitive to macroeconomic conditions. Other cyclical industries are producers of capital goods, that is, goods used by other firms to produce their own products. When demand is slack, few companies will be expanding and purchasing capital goods. Therefore, the capital goods industry bears the brunt of a slowdown but does well in an expansion.

In contrast to cyclical firms, *defensive industries* have little sensitivity to the business cycle. These are industries that produce goods for which sales and profits are least sensitive to the state of the economy. Defensive industries include food producers and processors and pharmaceutical firms. These industries will outperform others when the economy enters a recession.

AS THE U.S. ROARS AHEAD, CANADA STUMBLES

The Canadian economy appears to have hit another soft spot as the effects of this year's record strengthening in the Canadian dollar show through. The trade surplus has diminished, manufacturing shipments and new orders have fallen and employment appears to be poised for a slowdown after a surprising jump in the fall. Even the red-hot housing market might be slipping a bit as evidenced by the recent decline in existing home sales, housing starts and building permits. Auto sales, too, have eased and the latest read on retail sales, though dated, was somewhat disappointing.

The Bank of Canada is targeting a growth rate of at least 4% in the current quarter. With the weakness in the incoming data, additional central bank easing has now become a very real possibility, especially so given that fiscal policy has of late taken on a decidedly contractionary tone. Ontario is now beset with enormous red ink, engorged by the recently divulged losses at Ontario Power Generation and a near 10% surge in program spending this year. Quebec, too, is facing significant cutbacks as the current tensions with the public sector unions attest. Moreover, the swift response of the new administration in Ottawa to clamp down on spending also adds to the negative effects of fiscal policy on the economy in coming quarters.

Very soon, monetary easing may well be necessary to offset fiscal tightening. This is the mirror image of the situation at the start of 2003. The February federal budget presented a meaningful increase in government spending while, at the same time, the Bank of Canada was attempting to cool things down with its early-spring rate hikes. The combination of easy-fiscal/tight-monetary policies is generally quite bullish for a domestic currency, as we saw in the U.S. with the early-1980s Reagan stimulus and Volcker tightening. This was certainly the case for the loonie this year.

Now the tables have turned. We are seeing fiscal policy tighten in Ottawa, Ontario and Quebec just as the Bank of Canada is concerned that growth might be too weak and is itching to cut rates. This combination of tighter-fiscal/easier-monetary policy would be negative for the Canadian dollar as long as it lasts. The big surprise for 2004 might well be a weaker loonie, as most now predict a currency approaching, if not exceeding, 80 cents.

A weaker currency would be welcomed by the hard-hit manufacturing and industrial sectors, still reeling from a marked decline in competitiveness. But the significant rebound in global economic growth might well mitigate the need for rate cuts next year. World GDP growth surged to its strongest level in 20 years last quarter, boosting commodity prices and global trade flows.

This benefits the metals, steel, gold, energy, fertilizer and chemicals sectors in Canada. The lone exception to the materials-sector boost has been the forest products industry, which is inordinately vulnerable to a rise in the Canadian dollar.

But the surge in third quarter growth was led by the United States, where the 8.2% pace is unlikely to be repeated anytime soon. A more sustainable 4% to 5% rate, however, is likely—especially given the extraordinary stimulus coming from U.S. monetary and fiscal policy as well as the weakening U.S. dollar. The Bush administration, earlier this year, threw all the fuel possible at the smoldering U.S. economy. The Federal Reserve cut overnight interest rates to an emergency-low 1%, compared to $2\frac{3}{4}$% in Canada. And the Fed continues to insist that it will leave rates at this level for a considerable period. Many interpret this to mean no rate hikes in the United States until 2005, despite strong growth. The U.S. federal budget has swung from enormous surplus to enormous deficit, thanks to huge spending increases and dramatic tax cuts. And the Treasury, along with the Fed, tacitly approved a weak-dollar policy without really saying so.

All of this assures that election year 2004 will be a strong one in the U.S., which undoubtedly bodes well for Canada.

But, gone are the days when Canada will lead the G-7 growth performance and the economic risks now appear to be firmly on the downside. While the U.S. economy is exhibiting significant positive momentum, the situation is just the opposite in Canada. This means two things: the Bank of Canada may well be forced to lower interest rates again in early 2004; and, the loonie might not be as strong as many have suggested next year.

Source: Sherry Cooper, "As the U.S. Roars Ahead, Canada Stumbles," *National Post*, December 19, 2003, p. FP.11. Reprinted by permission of the author.

If your assessments of the state of the business cycle were reliably more accurate than those of other investors, you would simply choose cyclical industries when you are relatively more optimistic about the economy and defensive firms when you are relatively more pessimistic. Unfortunately, it is not so easy to determine when the economy is passing through a peak or a trough. If it were, choosing between cyclical and defensive industries would be easy. As we know from our discussion of efficient markets, however, attractive investment choices will rarely be obvious. It usually is not apparent that a recession or expansion has started or ended until several months after the fact. With hindsight, the transitions from expansion to recession and back might be apparent, but it is often quite difficult to say whether the economy is heating up or slowing down at any moment.

The cyclical/defensive classification corresponds well to the notion of systematic or market risk introduced in our discussion of portfolio theory. When perceptions about the health of the economy become more optimistic, for example, the prices of most stocks will increase as forecasts of profitability rise. Because the cyclical firms are most sensitive to such developments, their stock prices will rise the most. Thus firms in cyclical industries will tend to have high-beta stocks. In general, then, stocks of cyclical firms will show the best results when economic news is positive but the worst results when that news is bad. Conversely, defensive firms will have low betas and performance that is relatively unaffected by overall market conditions.

It is not surprising that the cycle can be predicted. Statistics Canada has developed a set of cyclical indicators to help forecast and measure short-term fluctuations in economic activity. **Leading economic indicators** are those economic series that tend to rise or fall in advance of the rest of the economy.

Ten series are grouped into a widely followed composite index of leading economic indicators, as specified in Table 14.5. Figure 14.10 graphs percent changes in the composite leading indicator series against changes in the GDP for the years 1962–2003. The leading indicator series appears to anticipate major changes of direction in GDP quite well.

The stock market price index is a leading indicator.[12] Unfortunately, this makes the series of leading indicators much less useful for investment policy—by the time the series predicts an upturn, the market already has made its move. While the business cycle may be somewhat predictable, the stock market may not be. This is one more manifestation of the efficient market hypothesis. Various industries, however, respond early or late in the cycle, while others are more insensitive. Forest products encompass two subsectors: lumber, which responds to home construction as interest rates fall, and pulp and paper, which follows business activity as advertising and packaging increase. Since interest rates fall as a recession deepens, lumber company profits pick up earlier than do pulp and paper; the efficient market anticipates the increased profits by raising the equity prices. You might miss the gains in forest product companies specializing in lumber operations, but still have time to invest in the pulp and paper companies.

Figure 14.10 Composite leading indicator and GDP for Canada.

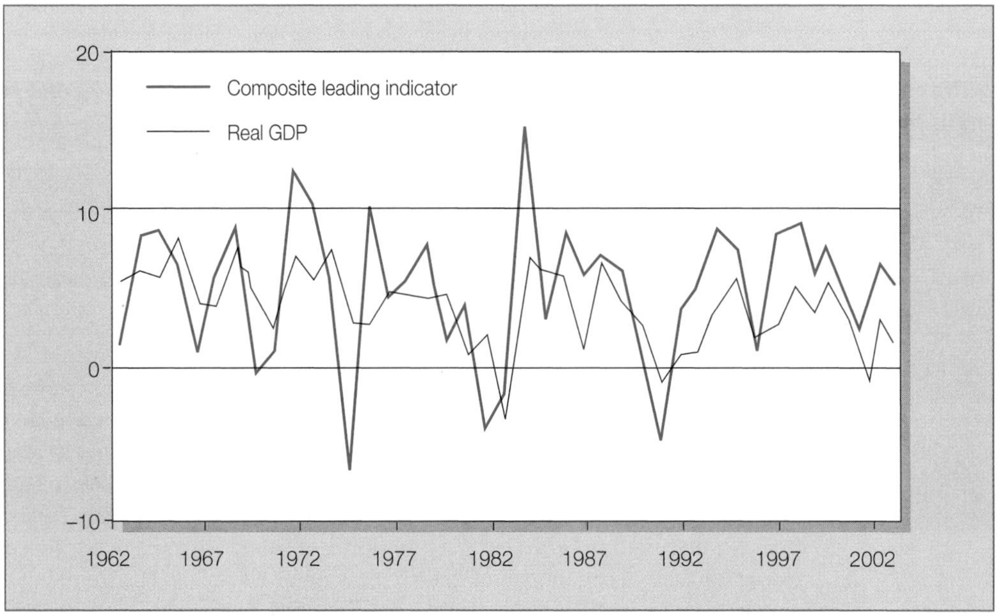

Source: Statistics Canada, Series D100052, D15721.

[12]See, for example, Stanley Fischer and Robert C. Merton, "Macroeconomics and Finance: The Role of the Stock Market," *Carnegie-Rochester Conference Series on Public Policy* 21 (1984).

Table 14.5 Components of Leading Economic Indicators' Composite Index

Retail Sales	Manufacturing
Furniture and appliances	New orders—durables
Other durable sales	Ratio of shipments to stocks
	Average work week
Financial	Business and personnel services employment
Real money supply	
Toronto stock market (S&P/TSX Composite Index)	**House Spending**
U.S. Leading Index	Residential construction

14.8 THE AGGREGATE STOCK MARKET

Explaining Past Behaviour

Most scholars and serious analysts would agree that, although the stock market appears to have a substantial life of its own, responding perhaps to bouts of mass euphoria and then panic, economic events and the anticipation of such events do have a substantial effect on stock prices. Perhaps the two factors with the greatest impact are interest rates and corporate profits.

Figure 14.11 shows the behaviour of the earnings-to-price ratio (i.e., the earnings yield) of the TSE 300 stock index (now known as the S&P/TSX Composite Index) versus the yield to maturity on long-term Canada bonds since 1956. Clearly, the two series track each other quite closely. This is to be expected: the two variables that affect a firm's value are earnings (and implicitly the dividends they can support) and the discount rate, which "translates" future income into present value. Thus, it should not be surprising that the ratio of earnings to stock price (the inverse of the P/E ratio) varies with the interest rate.

CBS MarketWatch www.cbs.marketwatch.com

Forecasting the Stock Market

What can we learn from all of this about the future rate of return on stocks? First, a note of optimism. Although timing the stock market is a very difficult and risky game, it may not be impossible. For example, we saw in Chapter 9 that some variables such as the market dividend yield seem to predict market returns.

Figure 14.11 Long-term bond and TSX earnings yields.

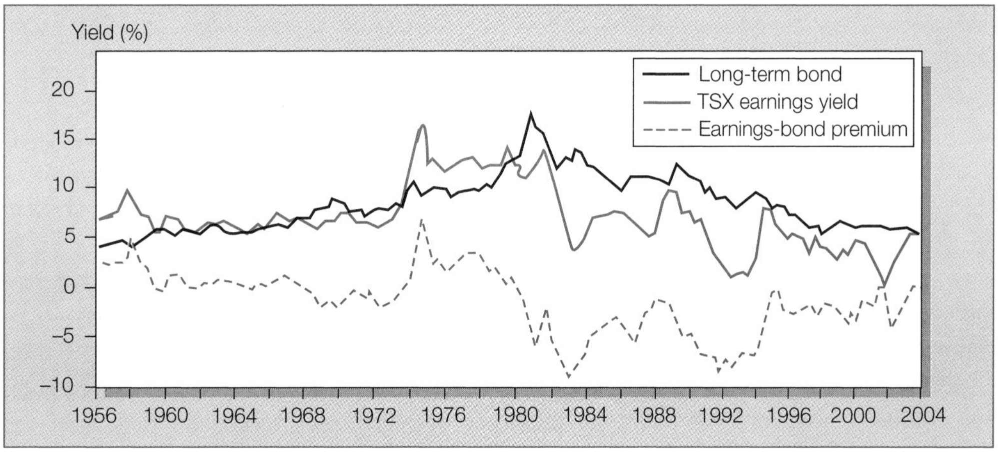

Source: Statistics Canada, CANSIM2, Series V122487, V122629.

However, if market history teaches us anything at all, it is that the market has great variability. Thus, although we can use a variety of methods to derive a best forecast of the expected holding-period return on the market, the uncertainty surrounding that forecast will always be high.

The most popular approach to forecasting the overall stock market is the earnings multiplier approach applied at the aggregate level. The first step is to forecast corporate profits for the coming period. Then we derive an estimate of the earnings multiplier, the aggregate P/E ratio, on the basis of long-term interest rates. The product of the two forecasts is the estimate of the end-of-period level of the market.

The forecast of the P/E ratio of the market is sometimes derived from a graph similar to that in Figure 14.11, which plots the *earnings yield* (earnings per share divided by price per share, the reciprocal of the P/E ratio) of the S&P/TSX Composite and the yield to maturity on 10-year Canada Bonds. This graph is the subject of the boxed article here on the Fed Model.

One might use this relationship and the current yield on 10-year Canada bonds to forecast the earnings yield on the S&P/TSX Composite. Given that earnings yield, a forecast of earnings could be used to predict the level of the TSX in some future period. Let's consider a simple example of this procedure.

The mid-2004 forecast for 2005 earnings per share for the TSX portfolio was about $420. The 10-year bond yield was about 4.95 percent. Because the earnings yield on the Composite has been about one percentage point below the 10-year bond yield, a first guess for the earnings yield on the Composite might be 4.0 percent. This would imply a P/E ratio of $1/.04 = 25$. Our forecast for the index would then be $25 \times 420 = 10{,}500$.

Of course, there is uncertainty regarding all three inputs into this analysis: the actual earnings on the S&P/TSX Composite stocks, the level of bond yields at year-end, and the spread between the bond yield and the earnings yield. One would wish to perform sensitivity or scenario analysis to examine the impact of changes in all of these variables. To illustrate, consider Table 14.6, which shows a simple scenario analysis treating possible effects of variation in the Canada bond yield and EPS forecast. The scenario analysis shows that forecasted level of the stock market varies with dramatic sensitivity to both estimates.

Table 14.6 S&P/TSX Composite Price Targets Under Various Scenarios

Scenarios	Most Likely	Pessimistic	Optimistic
Long-bond yield	5.0%	6.5%	4.8%
Earnings yield	4.0%	5.5%	3.8%
Resulting P/E	25.00	20.00	26.32
EPS forecast	$420	$410	$450
Forecast S&P/TSX Composite	10,500	8,200	11,842

Note: Forecast for the earnings yield on the S&P/TSX Composite equals the long-bond rate minus 1 percent. The P/E ratio is the reciprocal of the forecast earnings yield.

Other analysts use an aggregate version of the discounted dividend model rather than an earnings multiplier approach. All of these models, however, rely heavily on forecasts of such macroeconomic variables as GDP, interest rates, and the rate of inflation, which are themselves very difficult to predict accurately.

14.9 INDUSTRY ANALYSIS

Industry analysis is important for the same reason as macroeconomic analysis is. Just as it is difficult for an industry to perform well when the macroeconomy is ailing, it is unusual for a firm in a troubled industry to perform well. Similarly, just as we have seen that economic performance

RECENT RESEARCH SETS FED MODEL ON ITS EAR

Recent academic study seriously undermines a popular reason for not worrying about the high price-to-earnings ratio of the stock market today: the idea that the ratios should be high when interest rates are low. The theoretical basis for this claim is the so-called Fed Model, which compares the interest rate on the U.S. government's 10-year treasury note with the inverse of the stock market's P/E ratio—known as the market's earnings yield. The stock market is considered undervalued when its earnings yield is greater than the treasury note rate.

According to this model, the stock market is significantly undervalued right now. The P/E ratio of the Standard & Poor's 500-stock index is 18.2, based on companies' estimated operating earnings for 2004. That translates into an earnings yield of 5.5%, much higher than the current yield of 4.09% for the 10-year treasury note.

The Fed Model was constructed by Edward E. Yardeni, now the chief investment strategist at the Prudential Equity Group, who based it on comments in the Fed's Monetary Policy Report to Congress in July, 1997. The Federal Reserve has not endorsed the model.

If the Fed Model held true, earnings growth should be slower when treasury note rates are high and faster when those rates are low. Historically, however, that has not been the case, according to the new study, "Inflation Illusion and Stock Prices," by the Harvard finance professors John Y. Campbell and Tuomo Vuolteenaho. The study has circulated this month as a National Bureau of Economic Research working paper and is at www.nber.org/papers.

A similar conclusion was reached in a study by the finance professors Jay R. Ritter of the University of Florida and Richard S. Warr, now at North Carolina State. That study, published in 2002, covered 1978 to 1999, but the new one covered a much longer period: 1927 through 2002. The government's 10-year treasury note has not traded during all those 75 years, but according to the professors, interest and inflation rates are highly correlated. And during those 75 years, earnings growth has tended to be higher during periods of high inflation and lower when inflation is low.

Put another way, the professors conclude that stocks are a good long-term hedge against inflation. They found that the growth rate of real, or inflation-adjusted, earnings is relatively constant when measured over several-year periods. That means the growth rate of nominal earnings tends to rise and fall with inflation.

Many investors overlook that point, because they assume that changes in inflation will not affect nominal earnings growth. Economists call that assumption an "inflation illusion." If it were true, real earnings growth should be faster in periods of low inflation, justifying higher P/E ratios. But the assumption has not been true over time, according to Messrs. Campbell and Vuolteenaho. As a result, they found that the stock market has tended to become significantly undervalued in times of high inflation and overvalued in times of low inflation.

Consider equity valuations during the late 1970s and early 1980s, when interest rates and inflation were high. Investors used the equivalent of the Fed Model to justify a low P/E ratio for the overall market. The late Franco Modigliani, who was a finance professor at the Massachusetts Institute of Technology during that time and in 1985 would be the Nobel laureate in economics, recognized the inflation illusion that was implicit in this argument. In a 1979 article, he argued that stocks were significantly undervalued—a view that was vindicated in the 1980s and '90s by the strong bull market in stocks.

The situation today is the mirror opposite of what prevailed in the late 1970s, suggesting that stocks may be as overvalued today as they were undervalued then.

Source: Mark Hulbert, "A Time-Tested Sign of an Overvalued Market: Recent Research Sets Fed Model on Its Ear," *National Post*, February 24, 2004, p. IN.01.

can vary widely across countries, performance also can vary widely across industries. Figure 14.12 illustrates the dispersion of industry performance. It shows projected growth in earnings per share in 2001 and 2002 for several major industry groups. The forecasts for 2002, which come from a survey of industry analysts, range from –10.5 percent for natural resources to 69.6 percent for information technology.

Not surprisingly, industry groups exhibit considerable dispersion in their stock market performance. Figure 14.13 illustrates the performance of the 10 best- and the 10 worst-performing industries in 2002. The spread in performance is remarkable, ranging from a 40.5 percent return for the precious metals industry to a 60.0 percent loss in the wireless communications industry.

Even small investors can easily take positions in industry performance by using mutual funds with an industry focus. For example, Fidelity offers about 40 Select Funds, each of which is invested in a particular industry.

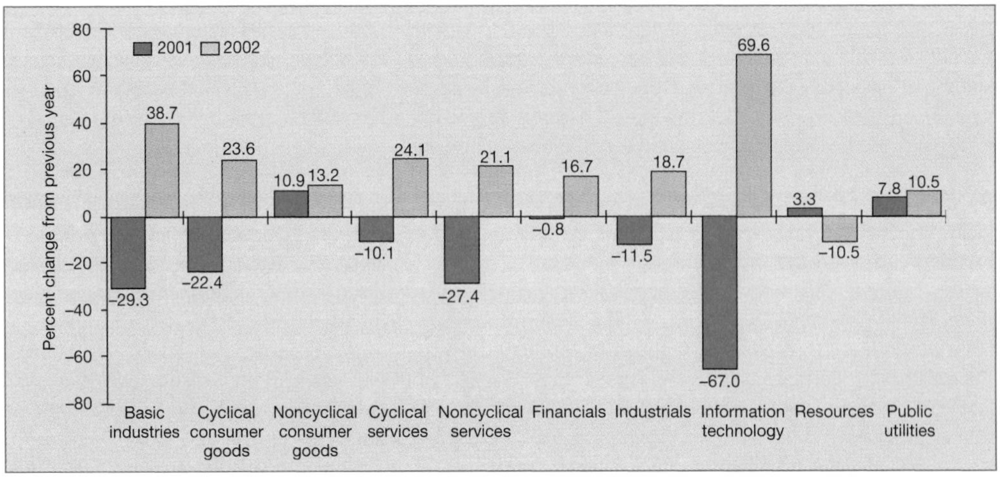

Figure 14.12 Estimates of earnings growth rates in several industries, 2001 and 2002.

Source: Thomson Financial.

Defining an Industry

Although we know what we mean by an "industry," it can be difficult in practice to decide where to draw the line between one industry and another. Consider, for example, the financial industry. Figure 14.12 shows that the forecast for 2002 growth in industry earnings per share was 16.7 percent. But the financial "industry" contains firms with widely differing products and prospects. Figure 14.14 breaks down the industry into six subgroups. The forecasted performance on these

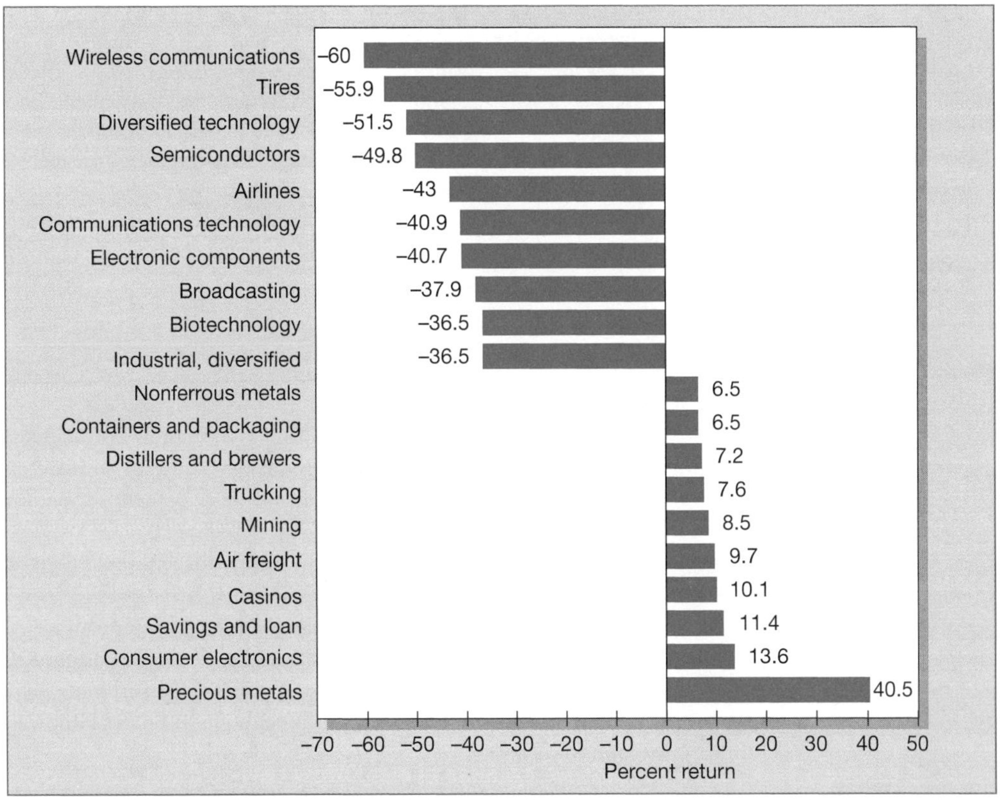

Figure 14.13 Industry stock price performance, 2002.

Source: Data appearing in *The Wall Street Journal*, January 3, 2003.

Figure 14.14 Estimates of earnings growth for finance firms, 2002.

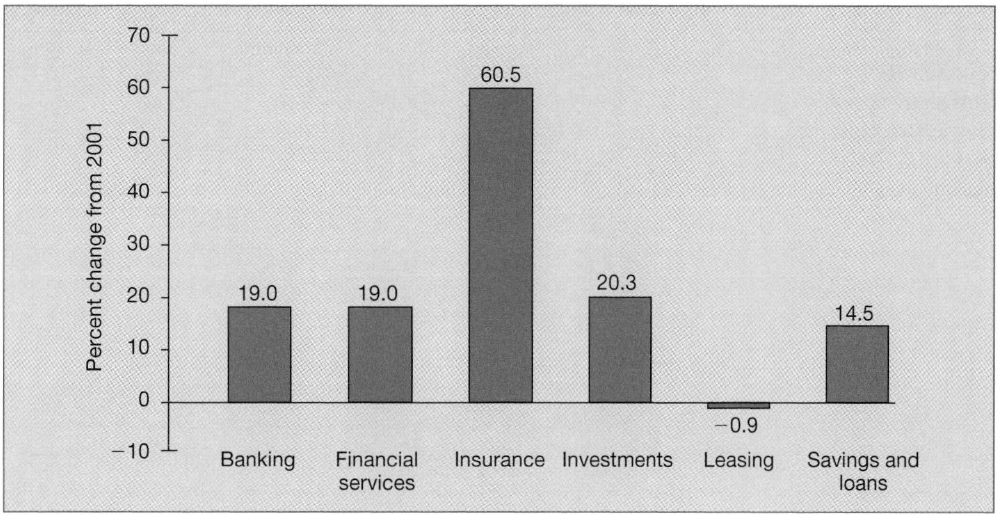

Source: Thomson Financial.

more narrowly defined groups differs widely, from –0.9 percent to 60.5 percent, suggesting that they are not members of a homogeneous industry. Similarly, most of these subgroups in Figure 14.14 might be divided into even smaller and more homogeneous groups.

A useful way to define industry groups in practice is given by the **Global Industry Classification Standard (GICS)** developed by Morgan Stanley Capital International (MSCI), noted earlier in connection with global indices and benchmark-related products and services, and by Standard & Poor's, which provides international financial data as well as global equity indices.

The GICS classifications were specifically designed to enhance the investment research and asset management process for financial professionals, following discussions with international portfolio managers and investment analysts. They were created to respond to the global financial community's need for an accurate, complete, and standard industry definition. The GICS structure consists of 10 sectors, 24 industry groups, 62 industries, and 132 sub-industries. (For specific information and updates to the classifications on the GICS, consult www.msci.com under the GICS section.)

Several other industry classifications are provided by other analysts; for example, Standard & Poor's reports on the performance of about 100 industry groups. S&P computes stock price indices for each group, which is useful in assessing past investment performance. The Value Line Investment Survey reports on the conditions and prospects of about 1,700 firms, grouped into about 90 industries. Value Line's analysts prepare forecasts of the performance of industry groups as well as of each firm.

Sensitivity to the Business Cycle

Once the analyst forecasts the state of the macroeconomy, it is necessary to determine the implication of that forecast for specific industries. Not all industries are equally sensitive to the business cycle. For example, consider Figure 14.15, which is a graph of automobile production and shipments of cigarettes, both scaled so that 1963 has a value of 100.

Clearly, the cigarette industry is largely independent of the business cycle. Demand for cigarettes does not seem affected by the state of the macro economy in any meaningful way. This is not surprising. Cigarette consumption is determined largely by habit and is a small enough part of most budgets that it will not be given up in hard times.

Auto production, by contrast, is highly volatile. In recessions, consumers can try to prolong the lives of their cars until their income is higher. For example, the worst year for auto production,

Figure 14.15 Industry cyclicality: industry sales, scaled so that sales in 1963 equal 100.

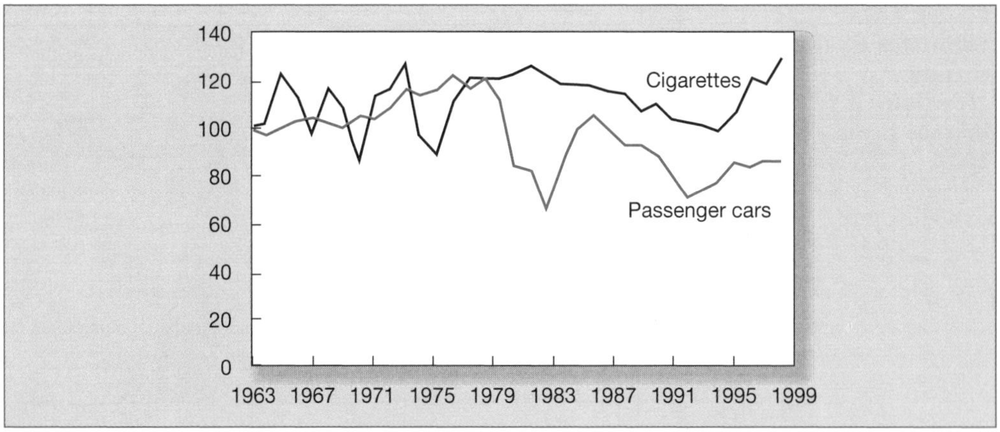

Source: *Passenger car sales: Ward's Automobile Yearbook,* 1994 and www.nada.org. *Cigarette sales:* Department of Alcohol, Tobacco, and Firearms Statistical Releases and Statistical Abstract of the U.S.

according to Figure 14.15, was 1982. This was also a year of deep recession, with the unemployment rate at 9.5 percent.

Three factors will determine the sensitivity of a firm's earnings to the business cycle. First is the sensitivity of sales. Necessities such as food, drugs, and medical services will show little sensitivity to business conditions. Other industries with low sensitivity would be those for which income is not a crucial determinant of demand, such as tobacco products. In contrast, firms in industries such as machine tools, steel, autos, and transportation are highly sensitive to the state of the economy.

The second factor determining business cycle sensitivity is operating leverage, which refers to the division between fixed and variable costs. (Fixed costs are those the firm incurs regardless of its production levels. Variable costs are those that rise or fall as the firm produces more or less product.) Firms with variable as opposed to fixed costs will be less sensitive to business conditions, because in economic downturns these firms can reduce costs as output falls in response to falling sales. Profits for firms with high fixed costs will swing more widely with sales because costs do not move to offset revenue variability. Firms with high fixed costs are said to have high operating leverage, as small swings in business conditions can have large impacts on profitability.

EXAMPLE 14.5 Operating Leverage

Consider two firms operating in the same industry with identical revenues in all phases of the business cycle: recession, normal, and expansion. Firm A has short-term leases on most of its equipment and can reduce its lease expenditures when production slackens. It has fixed costs of \$5 million and variable costs of \$1 per unit of output. Firm B has long-term leases on most of its equipment and must make lease payments regardless of economic conditions. Its fixed costs are higher, \$8 million, but its variable costs are only \$.50 per unit. Table 14.7 shows that firm A will do better in recessions than firm B, but not as well in expansions. A's costs move in conjunction with its revenues to help performance in downturns and impede performance in upturns.

The third factor influencing business cycle sensitivity is financial leverage, which is the use of borrowing. Interest payments on debt must be paid regardless of sales. They are fixed costs that also increase the sensitivity of profits to business conditions. We will have more to say about financial leverage in Chapter 15.

Investors should not always prefer industries with lower sensitivity to the business cycle. Firms in sensitive industries will have high-beta stocks and are riskier. But while they swing

Table 14.7 Operating Leverage

	Recession Scenario		Normal Scenario		Expansion Scenario	
	Firm A	Firm B	Firm A	Firm B	Firm A	Firm B
Sales (million units)	5	5	6	6	7	7
Price per unit	$ 2	$ 2	$ 2	$ 2	$ 2	$ 2
Revenue ($ million)	10	10	12	12	14	14
Fixed costs ($ million)	5	8	5	8	5	8
Variable costs ($ million)	5	2.5	6	3	7	3.5
Total costs ($ million)	$10	$ 10.5	$11	$11	$12	$11.5
Profits	$ 0	$ (0.5)	$ 1	$ 1	$ 2	$ 2.5

lower in downturns, they also swing higher in upturns. As always, the issue you need to address is whether the expected return on the investment is fair compensation for the risks borne.

Sector Rotation

One way that many analysts think about the relationship between industry analysis and the business cycle is the notion of **sector rotation**. The idea is to shift the portfolio more heavily into industry or sector groups that are expected to outperform based on one's assessment of the state of the business cycle.

Figure 14.16 is a stylized depiction of the business cycle. Near the peak of the business cycle, the economy might be overheated with high inflation and interest rates, and price pressures on basic commodities. This might be a good time to invest in firms engaged in natural resource extraction and processing such as minerals or petroleum.

Following a peak, when the economy enters a contraction or recession, one would expect defensive industries that are less sensitive to economic conditions—for example, pharmaceuticals, food, and other necessities—to be the best performers. At the height of the contraction, financial firms will be hurt by shrinking loan volume and higher default rates. Toward the end of the recession, however, contractions induce lower inflation and interest rates, which favour financial firms.

At the trough of a recession, the economy is poised for recovery and subsequent expansion. Firms might thus be spending on purchases of new equipment to meet anticipated increases in demand. This, then, would be a good time to invest in capital goods industries, such as equipment, transportation, or construction.

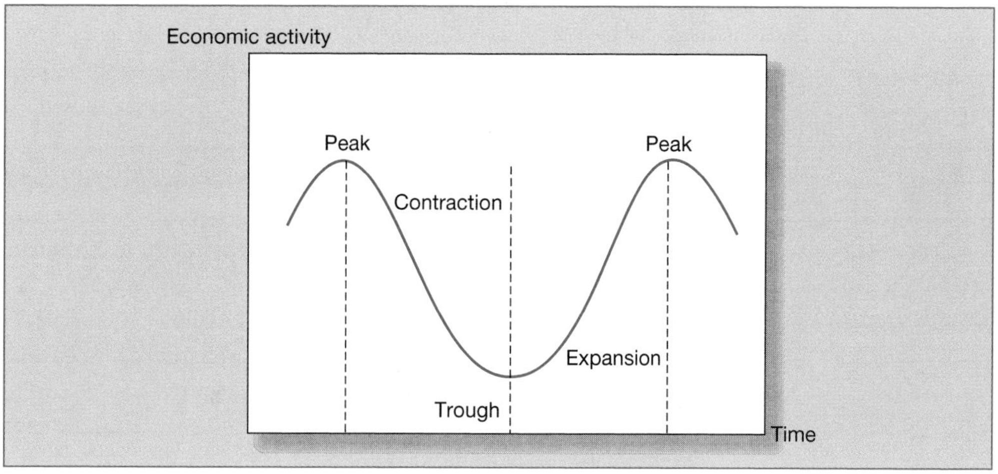

Figure 14.16 A stylized depiction of the business cycle.

Finally, in an expansion, the economy is growing rapidly. Cyclical industries such as consumer durables and luxury items will be most profitable in this stage of the cycle. Banks might also do well in expansions, since loan volume will be high and default exposure low when the economy is growing rapidly.

Let us emphasize again that sector rotation, like any other form of market timing, will be successful only if one anticipates the next stage of the business cycle better than other investors. The business cycle depicted in Figure 14.16 is highly stylized. In real life, it is never as clear how long each phase of the cycle will last, nor how extreme it will be. These forecasts are where analysts need to earn their keep.

CONCEPT CHECK ?

9. In which phase of the business cycle would you expect the following industries to enjoy their best performance?
   a. Newspapers
   b. Machine tools
   c. Beverages
   d. Timber

Industry Life Cycles

Just as there is a life cycle for firms, there is a corresponding **industry life cycle**; in fact, to a great extent the individual firm's life cycle depends upon the stages of its industry's cycle. When the industry is in its earlier stages, we expect to see high rates of return on high investment and low dividends; late in the cycle, during maturity, there will be predictable cash flows and corresponding dividends. Typically, there will be a start-up stage characterized by rapid growth, a consolidation stage with slower growth that still exceeds that of the general economy, a maturity stage that matches average growth, and a stage of relative decline encompassing relatively slow growth or shrinkage.

During the start-up stage, the novelty of the major products leads to extremely rapid sales and earnings growth, as we have seen in the high-technology area; identification of the eventual industry leaders is difficult at first. During the consolidation phase, those leaders become apparent and their performance will parallel that of the industry. During maturity, the dominant firms will produce stable cash flows and may in fact have great appeal to value investors, as their P/E multiples will be much lower. In the stage of decline, competition from newer products or lower-cost suppliers makes it difficult to generate profits.

A different approach to classification is taken by Peter Lynch, who had amazing success as a portfolio manager by avoiding many growth companies, especially if unknown. He characterized companies on the basis of their source of value, rather than the nature of their business, and labelled them as:

- *Slow growers.* Large, mature companies with excess cash flows
- *Stalwarts.* Large, noncyclical companies with well-recognized brand names (probably international), such as Coca-Cola
- *Fast growers.* Small, aggressive new firms, growing at 20 to 25 percent annually, due to industry growth or increasing market share
- *Cyclicals.* Firms with predictable sales and profit cycles
- *Turnarounds.* Distressed firms that have a good probability of recovery (Chrysler being a well-known example)
- *Asset plays.* Firms whose assets are not reflected in the stock price, being hidden in real estate, tax-loss carryforwards, or intangible assets not yielding immediate cash flows

www.coca-cola.com

Another factor is the relationship between industry structure and profitability. Returns are limited in a competitive structure, which can be characterized by the following:

- *Threat of entry*. Barriers to entry deter new entrants who put pressure on price and profits.
- *Rivalry between existing competitors*. Slow industry growth, high fixed costs, and homogeneous products all lead to price pressure (such as in the airline industry).
- *Pressure from substitute products*. Newer industries will generally be able to set higher prices.
- *Bargaining power of buyers*. Industries such as auto parts manufacturing have limited outlets for their products and little opportunity to demand higher profit margins.
- *Bargaining power of suppliers*. Profits also can be squeezed when there is little competition or substitutability among suppliers, as in the case of a unionized labour force.

Analysts seeking unrecognized value must be familiar with the response of industries to the business cycle and with the relative strengths of firms within the different industries. Experience and intelligent appraisal of the economic factors and financial statements can be combined in the process of investing based on timing and security selection. The auto industry is notoriously cyclical as both industry and consumers postpone decisions to replace existing vehicles during recessions. A vehicle that is one year older is a little bit rustier and less reliable than before and more needful of replacement. Therefore the pressure to purchase increases, leading to relatively high auto sales following the low sales due to postponement. *When* the inevitable purchasing will start is a timing decision. Whether Japanese cars or the Big Three—and which of them—will get more of those sales is a question of selectivity; and whether perhaps the leading Canadian parts supplier, Magna International, will have more leverage to increased sales is a further question. The analyst is paid to resolve these questions.

www.magna.com

CONCEPT CHECK

10. In Table 14.7, what will be profits in the three scenarios for a firm C with fixed costs of \$2 million and variable costs of \$1.50 per unit? What are your conclusions regarding operating leverage and business risk?

SUMMARY

1. One approach to estimating intrinsic value is to focus on the firm's book value, either as it appears on the balance sheet or as adjusted to reflect current replacement cost of assets or liquidation value. Another approach is to focus on the present value of expected future dividends, earnings, or free cash flow.
2. The constant growth version of the DDM asserts that if dividends are expected to grow at a constant rate forever, then the intrinsic value of a share is determined by the formula

$$V_0 = D_1/(k - g)$$

The more realistic DDMs allow for several stages of earnings growth. Usually there is an initial stage of rapid growth, followed by a final stage of constant growth at a lower sustainable rate.
3. The expected growth rate of earnings is related both to the firm's ROE and to its dividend policy. The relationship can be expressed as

$$g = \text{ROE on new investment} \times \text{Retention ratio}$$

4. Stock market analysts devote considerable attention to a company's price to earnings ratio. The P/E ratio is a useful measure of the market's assessment of the firm's growth opportunities. Firms with no growth opportunities should have a P/E ratio that is just the reciprocal of the capitalization rate, k. As growth opportunities become a progressively more important component of the value of the firm, the P/E ratio will increase.

5. You can relate any DDM to a simple capitalized earnings model by comparing the expected ROE on future investments to the market capitalization rate, *k*. If the two rates are equal, then the stock's intrinsic value reduces to expected earnings per share (EPS) divided by *k*.
6. Many analysts form their estimate of a stock's value by multiplying their forecast of next year's EPS by a P/E multiple derived from some empirical rule. This rule can be consistent with some version of the DDM, although often it is not.
7. Two approaches to portfolio building are value and growth investing. The first looks for value in slow-growth firms that are overlooked; the second searches for firms growing faster than average, with earnings reinvested at greater than the required return on equity.
8. The free cash flow approach is the one used most often in corporate finance. The analyst first estimates the value of the entire firm as the present value of expected future free cash flows, assuming all-equity financing, then adds the value of tax shields arising from debt financing, and finally subtracts the value of all claims other than equity. This approach will be consistent with the DDM and capitalized earnings approaches as long as the capitalization rate is adjusted to reflect financial leverage.
9. We explored the effects of inflation on stock prices in the context of the constant-growth DDM. Although traditional theory has held that inflation has a neutral effect on real stock returns, recent historical evidence shows a striking negative correlation between inflation and real stock market returns. Four different explanations may account for this negative correlation:
   a. Economic "shocks" that simultaneously produce high inflation and lower real earnings
   b. Increased riskiness of stocks in a more inflationary environment.
   c. Lower real after-tax earnings and dividends attributable to inflation-induced distortions in the tax system
   d. Money "illusion"
10. Macroeconomic analysis plays a major role in fundamental analysis; economists identify supply and demand shocks to the macro economy and the business cycle and use these in predicting future returns in the markets.
11. The models presented in this chapter can be used to explain and to forecast the behaviour of the aggregate stock market. The key macroeconomic variables that determine the level of stock prices in the aggregate are interest rates and corporate profits.
12. The business cycle is the economy's recurring pattern of expansions and recessions. Industries differ in their sensitivity to the business cycle, both in the degree and timing of their response.
13. Industry analysis examines aspects of performance, such as cyclical sensitivity, stages within an industry's life cycle, and competitive pressures.

KEY TERMS

fundamental analysis 503
technical analysis 503
book value 504
liquidation value 506
replacement cost 506
Tobin's *q* 506
intrinsic value 507
market capitalization rate 507
dividend discount model (DDM) 508
constant-growth DDM 508
dividend payout ratio 510
plowback ratio 510
earnings retention ratio 510
price-earnings multiple 516
earnings management 520
growth company 527
exchange rate 536
demand shock 537
supply shock 537
fiscal policy 537
monetary policy 538
business cycle 538
leading economic indicators 540
Global Industry Classification Standard (GICS) 545
sector rotation 547
industry life cycle 548

SELECTED READINGS

For the key issues in the debate about the link between fundamentals and stock prices see:

Merton, Robert C. "On the Current State of the Stock Market Rationality Hypothesis." In *Macroeconomics and Finance, Essays in Honor of Franco Modigliani*, ed. Rudiger Dornbusch, Stanley Fischer, and John Bossons. Cambridge, MA: MIT Press, 1986.

Cutler, David M., James M. Poterba, and Lawrence H. Summers. "What Moves Stock Prices?" *Journal of Portfolio Management* 15 (Spring 1989), pp. 4–12.

West, Kenneth D. "Bubbles, Fads, and Stock Price Volatility Tests: A Partial Evaluation." *Journal of Finance* 43 (July 1988), pp. 639–655.

PROBLEMS

1. *a.* Computer stocks currently provide an expected rate of return of 16 percent. MBI, a large computer company, will pay a year-end dividend of $2 per share. If the stock is selling at $50 per share, what must be the market's expectation of the growth rate of MBI dividends?

b. If dividend growth forecasts for MBI are revised downward to 5 percent per year, what will happen to the price of MBI stock? What will happen to the company's price-earnings ratio?

2. *a.* MF Corp. has an ROE of 16 percent and a plowback ratio of 50 percent. If the coming year's earnings are expected to be $2 per share, at what price will the stock sell? The market capitalization rate is 12 percent.

b. What price do you expect MF shares to sell for in three years?

CFA® PROBLEMS

3. At Litchfield Chemical Corp. (LCC), a director of the company said that the use of dividend discount models by investors is "proof" that the higher the dividend, the higher the stock price.

a. Using a constant-growth dividend discount model as a basis of reference, evaluate the director's statement.

b. Explain how an increase in dividend payout would affect each of the following (holding all other factors constant):

i. Sustainable growth rate

ii. Growth in book value

4. The market consensus is that Analog Electronic Corporation has an ROE of 9 percent, a beta of 1.25, and it plans to maintain indefinitely its traditional plowback ratio of 2/3. This year's earnings were $3 per share. The annual dividend was just paid. The consensus estimate of the coming year's market return is 14 percent, and T-bills currently offer a 6 percent return.

a. Find the price at which Analog stock should sell.

b. Calculate the P/E ratio.

c. Calculate the present value of growth opportunities.

d. Suppose your research convinces you Analog will announce momentarily that it will immediately reduce its plowback ratio to 1/3. Find the intrinsic value of the stock. The market is still unaware of this decision. Explain why V_0 no longer equals P_0 and why V_0 is greater or less than P_0.

5. If the expected rate of return of the market portfolio is 15 percent and a stock with a beta of 1.0 pays a dividend yield of 4 percent, what must the market believe is the expected rate of price appreciation on that stock?

6. The FI Corporation's dividends per share are expected to grow indefinitely by 5 percent per year.

a. If this year's year-end dividend is $8 and the market capitalization rate is 10 percent per year, what must the current stock price be according to the DDM?

b. If the expected earnings per share are $12, what is the implied value of the ROE on future investment opportunities?

c. How much is the market paying per share for growth opportunities (i.e., for an ROE on future investments that exceeds the market capitalization rate)?

7. The risk-free rate of return is 10 percent, the required rate of return on the market is 15 percent, and High-Flyer stock has a beta coefficient of 1.5. If the dividend per share expected during the coming year, D_1, is \$2.50 and $g = 5\%$, at what price should a share sell?

8. Your preliminary analysis of two stocks has yielded the information set forth below. The market capitalization rate for both stock *A* and stock *B* is 10 percent per year.

	Stock *A*	Stock *B*
Expected return on equity, ROE	14%	12%
Estimated earnings per share, E_1	\$ 2.00	\$ 1.65
Estimated dividends per share, D_1	\$ 1.00	\$ 1.00
Current market price per share, P_0	\$27.00	\$25.00

a. What are the expected dividend payout ratios for the two stocks?

b. What are the expected dividend growth rates of each?

c. What is the intrinsic value of each stock?

d. In which, if either, of the two stocks would you choose to invest?

CFA® PROBLEMS

9. Phoebe Black's investment club wants to buy the stock of either NewSoft Inc. or Capital Corp. In this connection, Black prepared the following table. You have been asked to help her interpret the data, based on your forecast for a healthy economy and a strong stock market over the next 12 months.

	NewSoft Inc.	Capital Corp.	S&P/TSX Composite Index
Current price	\$30	\$32	
Industry	Computer software	Capital goods	
P/E ratio (current)	25	14	16
P/E ratio (5-year average)	27	16	16
P/B ratio (current)	10	3	3
P/B ratio (5-year average)	12	4	2
Beta	1.5	1.1	1.0
Dividend yield	.3%	2.7%	2.8%

a. NewSoft's shares have higher price-earnings (P/E) and price-book value (P/B) ratios than those of Capital Corp. (The price-book ratio is the ratio of market value to book value.) Briefly discuss why the disparity in ratios may not indicate that NewSoft's shares are overvalued relative to the shares of Capital Corp. Answer the question in terms of the two ratios, and assume that there have been no extraordinary events affecting either company.

b. Using a constant-growth dividend discount model, Black estimated the value of NewSoft to be \$28 per share and the value of Capital Corp. to be \$34 per share. Briefly discuss weaknesses of this dividend discount model and explain why this model may be less suitable for valuing NewSoft than for valuing Capital Corp.

c. Recommend and justify a more appropriate dividend discount model for valuing NewSoft's common stock.

10. The stock of Nogro Corporation is currently selling for \$10 per share. Earnings per share in the coming year are expected to be \$2. The company has a policy of paying out 50 percent of its earnings each year in dividends. The rest is retained and invested in projects that earn a 20 percent rate of return per year. This situation is expected to continue indefinitely.

a. Assuming the current market price of the stock reflects its intrinsic value as computed using the constant growth rate DDM, what rate of return do Nogro's investors require?

b. By how much does its value exceed what it would be if all earnings were paid as dividends and nothing were reinvested?

c. If Nogro were to cut its dividend payout ratio to 25 percent, what would happen to its stock price? What if Nogro eliminated the dividend?

11. Chiptech, Inc. is an established computer chip firm with several profitable existing products as well as some promising new products in development. The company earned $1 a share last year and just paid out a dividend of $.50 per share. Investors believe the company plans to maintain its dividend payout ratio at 50 percent. ROE equals 20 percent. Everyone in the market expects this situation to persist indefinitely.

a. What is the market price of Chiptech stock? The required return for the computer chip industry is 15 percent, and the company has just gone ex-dividend (i.e., the next dividend will be paid a year from now, at $t = 1$).

b. Suppose you discover that Chiptech's competitor has developed a new chip that will eliminate Chiptech's current technological advantage in this market. This new product, which will be ready to come to the market in two years, will force Chiptech to reduce the prices of its chips to remain competitive. This will decrease ROE to 15 percent and, because of falling demand for its product, Chiptech will decrease the plowback ratio to .40. The plowback ratio will be decreased at the end of the second year, at $t = 2$; the annual year-end dividend for the second year (paid at $t = 2$) will be 60 percent of that year's earnings. What is your estimate of Chiptech's intrinsic value per share? (*Hint*: Carefully prepare a table of Chiptech's earnings and dividends for each of the next three years. Pay close attention to the change in the payout ratio in $t = 2$.)

c. No one else in the market perceives the threat to Chiptech's market. In fact, you are confident that no one else will become aware of the change in Chiptech's competitive status until the competitor firm publicly announces its discovery near the end of year two. What will be the rate of return on Chiptech stock in the coming year (i.e., between $t = 0$ and $t = 1$)? In the second year (between $t = 1$ and $t = 2$)? In the third year (between $t = 2$ and $t = 3$)? (*Hint*: Pay attention to when the *market* catches on to the new situation. A table of dividends and market prices over time might help.)

12. "Growth" and "value" can be defined in several ways, but "growth" usually conveys the idea of a portfolio emphasizing or including only issues believed to possess above-average future rates of per-share earnings growth. Low current yield, high price-to-book ratios, and high price-to-earnings ratios are typical characteristics of such portfolios.

"Value" usually conveys the idea of portfolios emphasizing or including only issues currently showing low price-to-book ratios, low price-to-earnings ratios, above-average levels of dividend yield, and market prices believed to be below the issues' intrinsic values.

a. Identify and explain three reasons why, over an extended period of time, value stock investing might outperform growth stock investing.

b. Explain why the outcome suggested in part (*a*) above should *not* be possible in a market widely regarded as being highly efficient.

CFA® PROBLEMS

13. Janet Ludlow's firm requires all its analysts to use a two-stage dividend discount model (DDM) and the capital asset pricing model (CAPM) to value stocks. Using the CAPM and DDM, Ludlow has valued QuickBrush Company at $63 per share. She now must value SmileWhite Corporation.

a. Calculate the required rate of return for SmileWhite using the information in the following table:

	QuickBrush	SmileWhite
Beta	1.35	1.15
Market price	$45.00	$30.00
Intrinsic value	$63.00	?

Notes:
Risk-free rate: 4.50%.
Expected market return: 14.50%.

b. Ludlow estimates the following EPS and dividend growth rates for SmileWhite:

First three years:	12% per year
Years thereafter:	9% per year

Estimate the 1999 intrinsic value of SmileWhite using the data above, and the two-stage DDM. Dividends per share in 1999 were $1.72.

c. Recommend QuickBrush or SmileWhite stock for purchase by comparing each company's intrinsic value with its current market price.

d. Describe one strength of the two-stage DDM in comparison with the constant-growth DDM. Describe one weakness inherent in all DDMs.

14. The risk-free rate of return is 8 percent, the expected rate of return on the market portfolio is 15 percent, and the stock of Xyrong Corporation has a beta coefficient of 1.2. Xyrong pays out 40 percent of its earnings in dividends, and the latest earnings announced were $10 per share. Dividends were just paid and are expected to be paid annually. You expect that Xyrong will earn an ROE of 20 percent per year on all reinvested earnings forever.

a. What is the intrinsic value of a share of Xyrong stock?

b. If the market price of a share is currently $100, and you expect the market price to be equal to the intrinsic value one year from now, what is your expected one-year holding-period return on Xyrong stock?

15. The Digital Electronic Quotation System (DEQS) Corporation pays no cash dividends currently and is not expected to for the next five years. Its latest EPS was $10, all of which was reinvested in the company. The firm's expected ROE for the next five years is 20 percent per year, and during this time it is expected to continue to reinvest all of its earnings. Starting six years from now, the firm's ROE on new investments is expected to fall to 15 percent, and the company is expected to start paying out 40 percent of its earnings in cash dividends, which it will continue to do forever after. DEQS's market capitalization rate is 15 percent per year.

a. What is your estimate of DEQS's intrinsic value per share?

b. Assuming its current market price is equal to its intrinsic value, what do you expect to happen to its price over the next year? The year after?

c. What effect would it have on your estimate of DEQS's intrinsic value if you expected DEQS to pay out only 20 percent of earnings starting in year six?

CFA® PROBLEMS

16. Peninsular Research is initiating coverage of a mature manufacturing industry. John Jones, CFA, head of the research department, gathered the following fundamental industry and market data to help in his analysis:

Forecast industry earnings retention rate	40%
Forecast industry return on equity	25%
Industry beta	1.2
Government bond yield	6%
Equity risk premium	5%

a. Compute the price-to-earnings (P0/E1) ratio for the industry using this fundamental data.

b. Jones wants to analyze how fundamental P/E ratios might differ among countries. He gathered the following economic and market data:

Fundamental Factors	Country A	Country B
Forecast growth in real GDP	5%	2%
Government bond yield	10%	6%
Equity risk premium	5%	4%

Determine whether each of these fundamental factors would cause P/E ratios to be generally higher for Country A or higher for Country B.

CFA® PROBLEMS

17. At year-end 1991, the Wall Street consensus was that Philip Morris' earnings and dividends would grow at 20 percent for five years, after which growth would fall to a market-like 7 percent. Analysts also projected a required rate of return of 10 percent for the U.S. equity market. You are provided with the following information:

Philip Morris Corporation
Selected Financial Data
Years Ending December 31
($ millions except per-share data)

	1991	1981
Earnings per share	$4.24	$0.66
Dividends per share	1.19	0.25
Shareholders' equity	12,512	3,234
Total liabilities and shareholders' equity	$47,384	$9,180
Other Data		
Philip Morris		
Common shares outstanding (millions)	920	1,003
Closing price common stock	$80.250	$6.125
S&P/TSX Composite Index		
Closing price	$417.09	$122.55
Earnings per share	16.29	15.36
Book value per share	161.08	109.43

a. Using the data in the table and the multistage dividend discount model, calculate the intrinsic value of Philip Morris stock at year-end 1991. Assume a similar level of risk for Philip Morris stock as for the typical U.S. stock. Show all work.

b. Using the data in the table, calculate Philip Morris' P/E ratio and the P/E ratio relative to the S&P/TSX Composite index as of December 31, 1991.

c. Using the data in the table, calculate Philip Morris' P/B ratio and the P/B ratio relative to the S&P/TSX Composite index as of December 31, 1991.

CFA® PROBLEMS

18. *a.* State *one* major advantage and *one* major disadvantage of *each* of the *three* valuation methodologies you used to value Philip Morris stock in the previous problem.

b. State whether Philip Morris stock is undervalued or overvalued as of December 31, 1991. Support your conclusion using your answers to the previous problem and any data provided. (The past 10-year average S&P/TSX Composite index relative P/E and P/B ratios for Philip Morris were 0.80 and 1.61, respectively.)

19. The Duo Growth Company just paid a dividend of $1 per share. The dividend is expected to grow at a rate of 25 percent per year for the next three years and then to level off to 5 percent per year forever. You think the appropriate market capitalization rate is 20 percent per year.

a. What is your estimate of the intrinsic value of a share of the stock?

b. If the market price of a share is equal to this intrinsic value, what is the expected dividend yield?

c. What do you expect its price to be one year from now? Is the implied capital gain consistent with your estimate of the dividend yield and the market capitalization rate?

20. The Generic Genetic (GG) corporation pays no cash dividends currently and is not expected to for the next four years. Its latest EPS was $5, all of which was reinvested in the company. The firm's expected ROE for the next four years is 20 percent per year, during which time it is expected to continue to reinvest all of its earnings. Starting five years from now, the firm's ROE on new investments is expected to fall to 15 percent per year. GG's market capitalization rate is 15 percent per year.

a. What is your estimate of GG's intrinsic value per share?

b. Assuming its current market price is equal to its intrinsic value, what do you expect to happen to its price over the next year?

CFA® PROBLEMS

21. Helen Morgan, CFA, has been asked to use the DDM to determine the value of Sundanci, Inc. Morgan anticipates that Sundanci's earnings and dividends will grow at 32 percent for two years and 13 percent thereafter.

Calculate the current value of a share of Sundanci stock by using a two-stage dividend discount model and the data from Tables 14A and 14B.

CFA® PROBLEMS

22. Abbey Naylor, CFA, has been directed to determine the value of Sundanci's stock using the Free Cash Flow to Equity (FCFE) model. Naylor believes that Sundanci's FCFE will grow at 27 percent for two years and 13 percent thereafter. Capital expenditures, depreciation, and working capital are all expected to increase proportionately with FCFE.

a. Calculate the amount of FCFE per share for the year 2000, using the data from Table 14A.

b. Calculate the current value of a share of Sundanci stock based on the two-stage FCFE model.

c. i. Describe one limitation of the two-stage DDM model that is addressed by using the two-stage FCFE model.

ii. Describe one limitation of the two-stage DDM model that is *not* addressed by using the two-stage FCFE model.

CFA® PROBLEMS

23. Christie Johnson, CFA, has been assigned to analyze Sundanci using the constant dividend growth price/earnings (P/E) ratio model. Johnson assumes that Sundanci's earnings and dividends will grow at a constant rate of 13 percent.

a. Calculate the P/E ratio from information in Tables 14A and 14B and from Johnson's assumptions for Sundanci.

b. Identify, within the context of the constant dividend growth model, how each of the following factors would affect the P/E ratio:

- Risk (beta) of Sundanci
- Estimated growth rate of earnings and dividends
- Market risk premium

24. The MoMi Corporation's cash flow from operations before interest and taxes was $2 million in the year just ended, and its expects that this will grow by 5 percent per year forever. To make this happen, the firm will have to invest an amount equal to 20 percent of pretax cash flow each year. The tax rate is 34 percent. Depreciation was $200,000 in the year just ended and is expected to grow at the same rate as the operating cash flow. The appropriate market capitalization rate for the unleveraged cash flow is 12 percent per year, and the firm currently has debt of $4 million outstanding. Use the free cash flow approach to value the firm's equity.

Table 14A Sundanci Actual 1999 and 2000 Financial Statements for Fiscal Years Ending May 31 ($ million, except per-share data)

Income Statement	1999	2000
Revenue	$474	$598
Depreciation	20	23
Other operating costs	368	460
Income before taxes	86	115
Taxes	26	35
Net income	60	80
Dividends	18	24
Earnings per share	$0.714	$0.952
Dividend per share	$0.214	$0.286
Common shares outstanding (millions)	84.0	84.0
Balance Sheet	**1999**	**2000**
Current assets	$201	$326
Net property, plant, and equipment	474	489
Total assets	675	815
Current liabilities	57	141
Long-term debt	0	0
Total liabilities	57	141
Shareholders' equity	618	674
Total liabilities and equity	675	815
Capital expenditures	34	38

Table 14B Selected Financial Information

Required rate of return on equity	14%
Growth rate of industry	13%
Industry P/E ratio	26

25. The CPI Corporation is expected to pay a real dividend of $1 per share this year. Its expected growth rate of real dividends is 4 percent per year, and its current market price per share is $20.

a. Assuming the constant-growth DDM is applicable, what must be the real market capitalization rate for CPI?

b. If the expected rate of inflation is 6 percent per year, what must be the nominal capitalization rate, the nominal dividend yield, and the growth rate of nominal dividends?

c. If the expected real earnings per share are $1.80, what would be your estimate of intrinsic value if you used a simple capitalized earnings model?

CFA® PROBLEMS

26. The following questions are from past CFA examinations.

a. The constant-growth DDM will not produce a finite value if the dividend growth rate is

i. Above its historical average
ii. Above the market capitalization rate
iii. Below its historical average
iv. Below the market capitalization rate

b. In theory, a firm wanting to maximize share value should pay out as much of its earnings in dividends as possible if it believes that

i. Investors are indifferent to the form of their return
ii. The company's future growth rate will be below its historical average
iii. The company will still have positive cash flow
iv. The company's future return on equity will be below its market capitalization rate

c. According to the constant-growth DDM, a fall in the market capitalization rate will cause a stock's intrinsic value to
   i. Decrease
   ii. Increase
   iii. Remain unchanged
   iv. Decrease or increase, depending on other factors

d. You plan to buy a common stock and hold it for one year. You expect to receive both $1.50 in dividends and $26 from the sale of stock at the end of the year. If you wanted to earn a 15 percent return, the maximum price you would pay for the stock today is
   i. $22.61
   ii. $23.91
   iii. $24.50
   iv. $27.50

e. In the dividend discount model, a factor *not* affecting the discount rate, k, is the
   i. Real risk-free rate
   ii. Risk premium for stocks
   iii. Return on assets
   iv. Expected inflation rate

f. If the return on equity of a firm is 15 percent and the retention ratio is 40 percent, the sustainable growth rate of the firm's earnings and dividends should be
   i. 6 percent
   ii. 9 percent
   iii. 15 percent
   iv. 40 percent

g. A share of stock is expected to pay a dividend of $1 one year from now and grow at 5 percent thereafter. In the context of a dividend discount model, the stock is correctly priced today at $10. According to the single-stage, constant-growth DDM, if the required return is 15 percent, the value of the stock two years from now should be
   i. $11.03
   ii. $12.10
   iii. $13.23
   iv. $14.40

h. After selling its common stock for $20 per share, a company has 5 million shares issued and outstanding. The firm's balance sheet after the sale of the stock is as follows:

Assets ($ millions)		**Liabilities and Equity ($ millions)**	
Current assets	$20	Current liabilities	$12
Net plant and equipment	42	Long-term debt	5
Total	$62	Common equity	45
		Total	$62

The book value per share is
   i. $5.63
   ii. $7.75
   iii. $9
   iv. $12.40

i. A stock is not expected to pay dividends until three years from now. The dividend is then expected to be $2 per share, the dividend payout ratio is expected to be 40 percent, and the return on equity is expected to be 15 percent. If the required rate of return is 12 percent, the value of the stock today is closest to

i. $27
ii. $33
iii. $53
iv. $67

j. In its latest annual report, a company reported the following:

Net income	$1,000,000
Total equity	$5,000,000
Total assets	$10,000,000
Dividend payout ratio	40%

On the basis of the sustainable growth model, the most likely forecast of the company's future earnings growth rate is
i. 4 percent
ii. 6 percent
iii. 8 percent
iv. 12 percent

k. The constant-growth DDM would typically be most appropriate in valuing the stock of a
i. New venture expected to retain all earnings for several years
ii. Rapidly growing company
iii. Moderate-growth, mature company
iv. Company with valuable assets not yet generating profits

l. A stock has a required return of 15 percent, a constant-growth rate of 10 percent, and a dividend payout ratio of 45 percent. The stock's P/E ratio should be
i. 3
ii. 4.5
iii. 9
iv. 11

27. You are trying to forecast the expected level of the aggregate Toronto stock market for the next year. Suppose the current three-month Treasury bill rate is 8 percent, the yield to maturity on 10+-year Canada bonds is 10 percent per year, the expected rate of inflation is 5 percent per year, and the expected EPS for the S&P/TSX Composite is $450. What is your forecast, and why?

28. Consider two firms producing videocassette recorders. One uses a highly automated robotics process, while the other uses human workers on an assembly line and pays overtime when there is heavy production demand.
a. Which firm will have higher profits in a recession? In a boom?
b. Which firm's stock will have a higher beta?

29. Here are four industries and four forecasts for the macro economy. Choose the industry that you would expect to perform best in each scenario.

Industries
Housing construction
Health care
Gold mining
Steel production
Economic Forecasts
Deep recession: Falling inflation, falling interest rates, falling GDP
Superheated economy: Rapidly rising GDP, increasing inflation and interest rates
Healthy expansion: Rising GDP, mild inflation, low unemployment
Stagflation: Falling GDP, high inflation

30. What monetary and fiscal policies might be prescribed for an economy in a deep recession?

CFA® PROBLEMS

31. Briefly discuss what actions the U.S. Federal Reserve would likely take in pursuing an *expansionary* monetary policy using each of the following three monetary tools:

a. Reserve requirements

b. Open market operations

c. Discount rate

CFA® PROBLEMS

32. An unanticipated expansionary monetary policy has been implemented. Indicate the impact of this policy on each of the following four variables:

a. Inflation rate

b. Real output and employment

c. Real interest rate

d. Nominal interest rate

33. If you believe the U.S. dollar will depreciate more dramatically than other investors believe it will, what will be your stance on investments in U.S. auto producers?

34. According to supply-side economists, what will be the long-run impact on prices of a reduction in income tax rates?

35. Unlike other investors, you believe the Bank of Canada is going to loosen monetary policy. What would be your recommendations about investments in the following industries?

a. Gold mining

b. Construction

36. In which stage of the industry life cycle would you place the following industries? (*Warning*: There is often considerable room for disagreement concerning the "correct" answers to this question.)

a. Oil well equipment

b. Computer hardware

c. Computer software

d. Genetic engineering

e. Railroads

37. For each pair of firms, choose the one that you think would be more sensitive to the business cycle.

a. General Autos or General Pharmaceuticals

b. Friendly Airlines or Happy Cinemas

38. Choose an industry and identify the factors that will determine its performance in the next three years. What is your forecast for performance in that time period?

CFA® PROBLEMS

39. Universal Auto is a large multinational corporation headquartered in the United States. For segment reporting purposes, the company is engaged in two businesses: production of motor vehicles and information processing services.

The motor vehicle business is by far the larger of Universal's two segments. It consists mainly of domestic U.S. passenger car production, but it also includes small truck manufacturing operations in the United States and passenger car production in other countries. This segment of Universal has had weak operating results for the past several years, including a large loss in 1996. Although the company does not reveal the operating results of its domestic passenger car segments, that part of Universal's business is generally believed to be primarily responsible for the weak performance of its motor vehicle segment.

Idata, the information processing services segment of Universal, was started by Universal about 15 years ago. This business has shown strong, steady growth that has been entirely internal; no acquisitions have been made.

An excerpt from a research report on Universal prepared by Paul Adams, a CFA candidate, states: "On our assumption that Universal will be able to increase prices significantly on U.S. passenger cars in 1997, we project a multibillion-dollar profit improvement."

a. Discuss the concept of an industrial life cycle by describing each of its four phases.

b. Identify where each of Universal's two primary businesses—passenger cars and information processing—is in such a cycle.

c. Discuss how product pricing should differ between Universal's two businesses, on the basis of the location of each in the industrial life cycle.

CFA® PROBLEMS

40. Adams' research report (see the preceding problem) continued as follows: "With a business recovery already under way, the expected profit surge should lead to a much higher price for Universal Auto stock. We strongly recommend purchase."

a. Discuss the business cycle approach to investment timing. (Your answer should describe actions to be taken on both stocks and bonds at different points over a typical business cycle.)

b. Assuming Adams' assertion is correct (that a business recovery is already under way), evaluate the timeliness of his recommendation to purchase Universal Auto, a cyclical stock, based on the business cycle approach to investment timing.

41. General Weedkillers dominates the chemical weed control market with its patented product Weed-ex. The patent is about to expire, however. What are your forecasts for changes in the industry? Specifically, what will happen to industry prices, sales, the profit prospects of General Weedkillers, and the profit prospects of its competitors? What stage of the industry life cycle do you think is relevant for the analysis of this market?

42. As a securities analyst you have been asked to review a valuation of a closely held business, Wigwam Autoparts Heaven, Inc. (WAH), prepared by the Red Rocks Group (RRG). You are to give an opinion on the valuation and to support your opinion by analyzing each part of the valuation. WAH's sole business is automotive parts retailing. The RRG valuation includes a section called "Analysis of the Retail Autoparts Industry," based completely on the data in Table 14C and the following additional information:

- WAH and its principal competitors each operated more than 150 stores at year-end 2004.
- The average number of stores operated per company engaged in the retail autoparts industry is 5.3.
- The major customer base for auto parts sold in retail stores consists of young owners of old vehicles. These owners do their own automotive maintenance out of economic necessity.

a. One of RRG's conclusions is that the retail autoparts industry as a whole is in the maturity stage of the industry life cycle. Discuss three relevant items of data from Table 14C that support this conclusion.

b. Another RRG conclusion is that WAH and its principal competitors are in the consolidation stage of their life cycle.

  i. Cite three relevant items of data from Table 14C that support this conclusion.

  ii. Explain how WAH and its principal competitors can be in a consolidation stage while their industry as a whole is in the maturity stage.

CFA® PROBLEMS

43. The following questions appeared on recent CFA examinations.

a. Which one of the following statements *best* expresses the central idea of countercyclical fiscal policy?

  i. Planned government deficits are appropriate during economic booms, and planned surpluses are appropriate during economic recessions.

  ii. The balanced budget approach is the proper criterion for determining annual budget policy.

  iii. Actual deficits should equal actual surpluses during a period of deflation.

  iv. Government deficits are planned during economic recessions, and surpluses are utilized to restrain inflationary booms.

Table 14C Selected Retail Autoparts Industry Data

	2004	2003	2002	2001	2000	1999	1998	1997	1996	1995
Population 18–29 years old (percentage change)	−1.8%	−2.0%	−2.1%	−1.4%	−0.8%	−0.9%	−1.1%	−0.9%	−0.7%	−0.3%
Number of households with income more than $35,000 (percentage change)	6.0%	4.0%	8.0%	4.5%	2.7%	3.1%	1.6%	3.6%	4.2%	2.2%
Number of households with income less than $35,000 (percentage change)	3.0%	−1.0%	4.9%	2.3%	−1.4%	2.5%	1.4%	−1.3%	0.6%	0.1%
Number of cars 5–15 years old (percentage change)	0.9%	−1.3%	−6.0%	1.9%	3.3%	2.4%	−2.3%	−2.2%	−8.0%	1.6%
Automotive aftermarket industry retail sales (percentage change)	5.7%	1.9%	3.1%	3.7%	4.3%	2.6%	1.3%	0.2%	3.7%	2.4%
Consumer expenditures on automotive parts and accessories (percentage change)	2.4%	1.8%	2.1%	6.5%	3.6%	9.2%	1.3%	6.2%	6.7%	6.5%
Sales growth of retail autoparts companies with 100 or more stores	17.0%	16.0%	16.5%	14.0%	15.5%	16.8%	12.0%	15.7%	19.0%	16.0%
Market share of retail autoparts companies with 100 or more stores	19.0%	18.5%	18.3%	18.1%	17.0%	17.2%	17.0%	16.9%	15.0%	14.0%
Average operating margin of retail autoparts companies with 100 or more stores	12.0%	11.8%	11.2%	11.5%	10.6%	10.6%	10.0%	10.4%	9.8%	9.0%
Average operating margin of all retail autoparts companies	5.5%	5.7%	5.6%	5.8%	6.0%	6.5%	7.0%	7.2%	7.1%	7.2%

b. The supply-side view stresses that
   i. Aggregate demand is the major determinant of real output and aggregate employment
   ii. An increase in government expenditures and tax rates will cause real income to rise
   iii. Tax rates are a major determinant of real output and aggregate employment
   iv. Expansionary monetary policy will cause real output to expand without causing the rate of inflation to accelerate

c. In macroeconomics, the crowding-out effect refers to
   i. The impact of government deficit spending on inflation
   ii. Increasing population pressures and associated movements toward zero population growth
   iii. A situation where the unemployment rate is below its natural rate
   iv. The impact of government borrowing on interest rates and private investment

d. If the exchange rate value of the British pound goes from US$1.80 to US$1.60, then the pound has
   i. Appreciated and the British will find U.S. goods cheaper
   ii. Appreciated and the British will find U.S. goods more expensive
   iii. Depreciated and the British will find U.S. goods more expensive
   iv. Depreciated and the British will find U.S. goods cheaper

e. The consumer price index is
   i. A measure of the increase in the prices of the goods that are included in the calculation of GDP
   ii. The ratio of the average price of a typical market basket of goods compared to the cost of producing those goods during the previous year

iii. A comparison of the cost of a typical bundle of goods during a given period with the cost of the same bundle during a prior base period
iv. Computed in the same manner as the GDP deflator

f. Changes in which of the following are likely to affect interest rates?
I. Inflation expectations
II. Size of the federal deficit
III. Money supply
i. I and II only
ii. II and III only
iii. I and III only
iv. I, II, and III

g. According to the supply-side view of fiscal policy, if the impact of tax revenues is the same, does it make any difference whether the government cuts taxes by either reducing marginal tax rates or increasing the personal exemption allowance?
i. No, both methods of cutting taxes will exert the same impact on aggregate supply.
ii. No, people in both cases will increase their saving expecting higher future taxes and thereby offset the stimulus effect of lower current taxes.
iii. Yes, the lower marginal tax rates alone will increase the incentive to earn marginal income and thereby stimulate aggregate supply.
iv. Yes, interest rates will increase if marginal tax rates are lowered, whereas they will tend to decrease if the personal exemption allowance is raised.

h. If the Federal Reserve wanted to reduce the supply of money as part of an anti-inflation policy, it might
i. Increase the reserve requirements
ii. Buy U.S. securities on the open market
iii. Lower the discount rate
iv. Buy U.S. securities directly from the Treasury

CSI

44. The following questions are adapted from the Canadian Securities Course.

a. "When the actual inflation rate is greater than was anticipated, debtors gain at the expense of creditors. Conversely, when the inflation rate is less than was anticipated, creditors gain at the expense of debtors." True or false?

b. Which of the following are leading indicators of the progress of the Canadian business cycle?
i. Retail sales
ii. Business loans
iii. The S&P/TSX Composite index
iv. Housing starts

c. "If two companies of equal status in the same industry have similar prospects but different P/E ratios, the company with the lower P/E ratio is usually the better buy." True or false?

d. A(n) ______________ industry is one in which sales and earnings are consistently expanding at a faster rate than most industries.

e. A decline in a growth company's earnings would usually mean ______________ in the company's P/E ratio.

f. The use of interest rates, the exchange rate and the rate of money supply growth to influence demand and inflation is known as ______________ policy.

g. If there were a mild recession, one would expect the ROE of defensive industries to be ______________ previous levels of ROE.

h. When analyzing financial statements, a rising operating margin but a falling pretax profit margin may indicate a proportionately ______________ amount of interest and/or depreciation charges.

i. The earnings of leveraged companies would be ______________ during upswings in the business cycle, relative to unlevered companies.

j. ______________ levels of sales tax or personal income tax have a tendency to stimulate the economy.

k. The expected dividend per share is $1 and expected to grow at 4 percent. The market capitalization rate, or the required rate of return on investments of similar risk is 10 percent. What should be the current intrinsic value of the stock?

APPENDIX 14A: DERIVATION OF THE DIVIDEND DISCOUNT MODEL

Consider an investor who buys a share of Steady State Electronics stock, planning to hold it for one year. The intrinsic value of the share is the present value of the dividend to be received at the end of the first year, D_1, and the expected sales price, P_1. We will henceforth use the simplest notation P_1 instead of $E(P_1)$ to avoid clutter. Keep in mind, though, future prices and dividends are unknown, and we are dealing with expected values, not certain values. Discounting at the cost of equity, *k*,

$$V_0 = \frac{D_1 + P_1}{1 + k} \tag{14A.1}$$

While dividends are fairly predictable given a company's history, you might ask how we can estimate P_1, the year-end price. According to equation 14A.1, V_1 (the year-end value) will be

$$V_1 = \frac{D_2 + P_2}{1 + k}$$

If we assume the stock will be selling for its intrinsic value next year, then $V_1 = P_1$, and we can substitute this value for P_1 into equation 14A.1 to find

$$V_0 = \frac{D_1}{1 + k} + \frac{D_2 + P_2}{(1 + k)^2}$$

This equation may be interpreted as the present value of dividends plus sales price for a two-year holding period. Of course, now we need to come up with a forecast of P_2. Continuing in the same way, we can replace P_2 by $(D_3 + P_3)/(1 + k)$, which relates P_0 to the value of dividends plus the expected sales price for a three-year holding period.

More generally, for a holding period of *H* years, we can write the stock value as the present value of dividends over the *H* years, plus the ultimate sale price, P_H:

$$V_0 = \frac{D_1}{1 + k} + \frac{D_2}{(1 + k)^2} + \cdots + \frac{D_H + P_H}{(1 + k)^H} \tag{14A.2}$$

Note the similarity between this formula and the bond valuation formula developed in Chapter 11. Each relates price to the present value of a stream of payments (coupons in the case of bonds, dividends in the case of stocks) and a final payment (the face value of the bond, or the sales price of the stock). The key differences in the case of stocks are the uncertainty of dividends, the lack of a fixed maturity date, and the unknown sales price at the horizon date. Indeed, one can continue to substitute for price indefinitely to conclude

$$V_0 = \frac{D_1}{1 + k} + \frac{D_2}{(1 + k)^2} + \frac{D_3}{(1 + k)^3} + \cdots \tag{14A.3}$$

Equation 14A.3 states that the stock price should equal the present value of all expected future dividends into perpetuity. As discussed in Section 14.2, this formula is called the *dividend discount model (DDM)* of stock prices.

It is tempting, but incorrect, to conclude from equation 14A.3 that the DDM focuses exclusively on dividends and ignores capital gains as a motive for investing in stock. Indeed, we assume explicitly in equation 14A.1 that capital gains (as reflected in the expected sales price, P_1) are part of the stock's value. At the same time, the price at which you can sell a stock in the future depends on dividend forecasts at that time.

The reason only dividends appear in equation 14A.3 is not that investors ignore capital gains. It is instead that those capital gains will be determined by dividend forecasts at the time the stock is sold. That is why in equation 14A.2 we can write the stock price as the present value of dividends plus sales price for *any* horizon date. P_H is the present value at time H of all dividends expected to be paid after the horizon date. That value is then discounted back to today, time 0. The DDM asserts that stock prices are determined ultimately by the cash flows accruing to shareholders, and those are dividends.[13]

The Constant-Growth DDM

Equation 14A.3 as it stands is still not very useful in valuing a stock, because it requires dividend forecasts for every year into the indefinite future. For a more structured valuation approach, we need to introduce some simplifying assumptions. A useful first pass at the problem is to assume that Steady State Electronics dividends are trending upward at a stable growth rate, which we will call g. Then if $g = .05$, and the most recently paid dividend was $D_0 = 3.81$, expected future dividends would be

$$D_1 = D_0(1+g) = 3.81 \times 1.05 = 4.00$$
$$D_2 = D_0(1+g)^2 = 3.81 \times (1.05)^2 = 4.20$$
$$D_3 = D_0(1+g)^3 = 3.81 \times (1.05)^3 = 4.41$$

and so on.

Using these dividend forecasts in equation 14A.3, we solve for intrinsic value as

$$V_0 = \frac{D_0(1+g)}{1+k} + \frac{D_0(1+g)^2}{(1+k)^2} + \frac{D_0(1+g)^3}{(1+k)^3} + \cdots$$

This equation can be simplified to

$$V_0 = \frac{D_0(1+g)}{k-g} = \frac{D_1}{k-g} \qquad (14A.4)$$

Note in equation 14A.4 that we divide D_1 (not D_0) by $k - g$ to calculate intrinsic value. If the market capitalization rate for Steady State is 12 percent, now we can use equation 14A.4 to show that the intrinsic value of a share of Steady State stock is

$$\frac{\$4}{.12 - .05} = \$57.14$$

Equation 14A.4 is called the *constant-growth DDM* or the *Gordon model,* after Myron J. Gordon, who popularized the model. It should remind you of the formula for the present value of a perpetuity. If dividends were expected not to grow, then the dividend stream would be a simple perpetuity, and the valuation formula would be $P_0 = D_1/k$. Equation 14A.4 is a generalization of the

[13]If investors never expected a dividend to be paid, then this model implies that the stock would have no value. To reconcile the fact that non-dividend-paying stocks do have a market value with this model, one must assume that investors expect that some day it may pay out some cash, even if only a liquidating dividend.

perpetuity formula to cover the case of a *growing* perpetuity. As g increases, the stock price also rises.[14]

The constant-growth DDM is valid only when g is less than k. If dividends were expected to grow forever at a rate faster than k, the value of the stock would be infinite. If an analyst derives an estimate of g that is greater than k, that growth rate must be unsustainable in the long run. The appropriate valuation model to use in this case is a multistage DDM such as that discussed in Section 14.2.

The constant-growth DDM is so widely used by stock market analysts that it is worth exploring some of its implications and limitations. It implies that a stock's value will be greater

1. The larger its expected dividend per share
2. The lower the market capitalization rate, k
3. The higher the expected growth rate of dividends

Another implication of the model is that the stock price is expected to grow at the same rate as dividends. To see this, suppose Steady State stock is selling at its intrinsic value of \$57.14, so that $V_0 = P_0$. Then

$$P_0 = \frac{D_1}{k - g}$$

Note that price is proportional to dividends. Therefore, next year, when the dividends paid to Steady State shareholders are expected to be higher by g = 5 percent, price also should increase by 5 percent. To confirm this, note

$$D_2 = \$4(1.05) = \$4.20$$
$$P_1 = D_2/(k - g) = \$4.20/(.12 - .05) = \$60$$

which is 5 percent higher than the current price of \$57.14. To generalize,

$$P_1 = \frac{D_2}{k - g} = \frac{D_1(1 + g)}{k - g} = \frac{D_1}{k - g}(1 + g)$$
$$= P_0(1 + g)$$

Therefore, the DDM implies that in the case of constant growth of dividends, the rate of price appreciation in any year will equal that constant growth rate, g.

---

[14]Here is a proof that the intrinsic value, V_0, of a stream of cash dividends growing at a constant rate, g, is equal to $\frac{D_1}{k - g}$. By definition,

$$V_0 = \frac{D_1}{1 + k} + \frac{D_1(1 + g)}{(1 + k)^2} + \frac{D_1(1 + g)^2}{(1 + k)^3} + \cdots$$

Multiplying through by $(1 + k)/(1 + g)$, we obtain

$$\frac{(1 + k)}{(1 + g)}V_0 = \frac{D_1}{(1 + g)} + \frac{D_1}{(1 + k)} + \frac{D_1(1 + g)}{(1 + k)^2} + \cdots$$

Subtracting the first equation from the second, we find that

$$\frac{(1 + k)}{(1 + g)}V_0 - V_0 = \frac{D_1}{(1 + g)}$$

which implies

$$\frac{(k - g)V_0}{(1 + g)} = \frac{D_1}{(1 + g)}$$

$$V_0 = \frac{D_1}{k - g}$$

APPENDIX 14B: CONTINGENT CLAIMS APPROACH TO EQUITY VALUATION

In recent years, the theory of contingent claims pricing has been applied to common stocks.[15] This approach can be a useful adjunct to the valuation models presented earlier—especially the free cash flow model—if a firm has substantial debt in its capital structure. In this approach, common stock is viewed as a call option on the assets of the firm, with an exercise price equal to the face value of the debt.

For example, suppose the Hidett Corporation has assets worth \$100 million and debt with a face value of \$100 million. Although the book value of the equity may be zero, the common stock may still have a substantial market value. The equity is a call option in the sense that if the shareholders pay off the debt at its face value at maturity, then they can keep the firm's assets; otherwise assets will belong to the creditors.

Viewing the equity of Hidett Corporation as a call option on the assets of the firm gives considerable insight into the determinants of its value, as well as a well-known methodology for estimating it. A detailed exposition of the techniques used is contained in Part Six, but one insight is worth mentioning now.

How will the value of Hidett's common stock be affected if the riskiness of the firm's assets (as measured by the standard deviation of their market value) increases? The answer is that the value of the common stock will increase, just as the price of an option increases when the standard deviation of the underlying security increases.

[15]See Scott Mason and Robert C. Merton, "The Role of Contingent Claims Analysis in Corporate Finance," in Altman and Subramanyam, eds., *Recent Advances in Corporate Finance* (Homewood, IL: Richard D. Irwin, Inc., 1985).

FINANCIAL STATEMENT ANALYSIS

In the previous chapter, we explored equity valuation techniques. These techniques take as inputs the firm's dividends and earnings prospects. While the valuation analyst is interested in economic earnings streams, only financial accounting data are readily available. What can we learn from a company's accounting data that can help us estimate the intrinsic value of its common stock?

In this chapter, we are not trying to develop the art of financial statement analysis, but rather to show how it relates to stock valuation analysis. We present much more complicated financial statements than are often seen in elementary corporate finance texts; this is to show the complexity and the potential variety of statements. In addition to discussing how to analyze the statements, we also show the importance of analysts' appraisals of sales and accounting information in fore-casting economic earnings and the difficulties they have in formulating those appraisals. The market reaction to the combination of accounting releases and forecasts is important to understand.

We start by reviewing the basic sources of such data—the income statement, the balance sheet, and the statement of cash flows. We next discuss the difference between economic and accounting earnings. While economic earnings are more important for issues of valuation, we examine evidence suggesting that, whatever their shortcomings, accounting data still are useful in assessing the economic prospects of the firm. We show how analysts use financial ratios to explore the sources of a firm's profitability and evaluate the "quality" of its earnings in a systematic fashion. We also examine the impact of debt policy on various financial ratios. Finally, we conclude with a discussion of the limitations of financial statement analysis as a tool in uncovering mispriced securities. Some of these limitations are due to differences in firms' accounting procedures, while others arise from inflation-induced distortions in accounting numbers.

15.1 THE MAJOR FINANCIAL STATEMENTS

The Income Statement

The **income statement** is a summary of the profitability of the firm over a period of time, such as a year. It presents revenues generated during the operating period, the expenses incurred during that same period, and the company's net income, which is simply the difference between revenues and expenses.

Annual Report Gallery www.reportgallery.com

It is useful to distinguish four broad classes of expenses: cost of goods sold (COGS), which is the direct cost attributable to producing the product sold by the firm; salaries, advertising, and other costs of operating the firm that are not directly attributable to production; interest expense on the firm's debt; and taxes on earnings owed to federal and local governments. Typically, this simple breakdown of expenses is not immediately recognizable in the income statements of larger firms.

Table 15.1 presents a 2003 income statement for Teck Corporation. In addition to direct operating expense (COGS), which is about 80 percent of revenues, Teck recognizes depreciation and amortization associated with mineral properties to arrive at operating profit. Subtracting other general expenses, exploration and R&D expense, plus other expense or income not directly associated with operations, leads to EBIT. Teck, however, includes interest on long-term debt with these expenses to arrive at earnings before taxes (EBT) and before other special items of $200 million. (We can reconstruct EBIT of $269 from $200 million + $69 million of interest. This is what the firm would have earned if not for its obligations to its creditors and the income tax authorities, and it is a measure of the profitability of the firm's operations ignoring the cost of debt financing.) Finally, the effect of income and resource taxes and payments to or from investments in other firms leads to net income ($149 million), the "bottom line" of the income statement.

The Balance Sheet

While the income statement provides a measure of the profitability over a period of time, the **balance sheet** provides a snapshot of the financial condition of the firm at a particular point in time. The balance sheet is a list of the firm's assets and liabilities at that moment. The difference in assets and liabilities is the net worth of the firm, also called *shareholders' equity*. Like income statements, balance sheets are reasonably standardized in presentation. Table 15.2 is the balance sheet of Teck for year-end 2003.

The first section of the balance sheet gives a listing of the assets of the firm. Current assets are presented first. These are cash and other items such as accounts receivable or inventories that will be converted into cash within one year; Teck recognizes supplies and prepaid expenses separately from production inventories. Teck next lists the value of investments and other assets, in addition to the usual entry of the company's property, plant, and equipment. The sum of current and long-term assets, plus other adjustments, gives total assets, the last line of the assets side of the balance sheet.

The liability and shareholders' equity side is similarly arranged. First come short-term or current liabilities, such as accounts payable, accrued taxes, and debts due within one year. Following

Table 15.1 Income Statement for Teck Cominco, 2003

Teck Cominco
Consolidated Statements of Earnings
Years Ended December 31
($ in millions, except per-share data)

	2003	2002
Revenues	$ 2,410	$ 2,187
Operating expenses	(1,887)	(1,805)
Depreciation and amortization	(218)	(199)
Operating profit	305	183
Other expenses:		
General, administration, and marketing	(54)	(53)
Interest on long-term debt	(69)	(67)
Mineral exploration	(30)	(34)
Research and development	(14)	(19)
Other income (Note 10)	4	8
Gain on disposition of Los Filos property (Note 2(c))	58	—
	200	18
Provision for income and resource taxes (Note 11):		
Earnings from operations	(44)	(5)
Los Filos property disposition (Note 2(c))	(17)	—
Minority interests	—	—
Equity earnings (loss) (Note 2(b))	10	17
Net earnings (Loss)	$ 149	$ 30
Basic earnings (loss) per share	$ .79	$ .15
Diluted earnings (loss) per share	$ .76	$ .15
Weighted average shares outstanding (000s)	184,823	184,526
Shares outstanding at the end of the year (000s)	186,492	184,537

Consolidated Statement of Retained Earnings
Years Ended December 31
($ in millions)

	2003	2002
Balance as at the beginning of the year	$ 472	$ 502
Adjustment on adoption of new accounting standard for translation of foreign currencies (Note 1)	—	(20)
Balance as at the beginning of the year as restated	472	482
Net earnings (loss)	149	30
Dividends	(37)	(37)
Interest on exchangeable debutures, net of taxes (Note 9(a))	(3)	(3)
Balance as at the end of Year	$ 581	$ 472

Source: Teck Cominco annual report, 2003.

this is long-term debt and other liabilities due in more than a year, as well as other adjustments. Note that deferred income and resource taxes are a substantial liability, as is the case for resource companies receiving favourable tax treatment. Also, Teck has issued debentures allowing the holder the right to convert these into shares of Inco that Teck holds. The difference between total assets and total liabilities is shareholders' equity. This is the net worth or book value of the firm. Shareholders' equity is divided between preferred and common shareholders. The latter section

Table 15.2
Balance Sheet for Teck Cominco, 2003

Teck Cominco
Consolidated Balance Sheets
As at December 31
($ in millions)

	2003	2003 as Percent of Total Assets	2002	2002 as Percent of Total Assets
Current assets:				
Cash (Note 6(c))	$ 96	1.8	$ 91	1.8
Accounts and settlements receivable	315	6.0	235	4.7
Production inventories	387	7.3	495	10.0
Supplies and prepaid expenses	135	2.6	134	2.7
	933	17.7	955	19.3
Investments (Note 3)	478	9.1	414	8.4
Property, plant, and equipment (Note 4)	3,615	68.6	3,393	68.4
Other assets (Note 5)	241	4.6	196	4.0
	$5,267	100.0	$4,958	100.0
Current liabilities:				
Accounts payable and accrued liabilities	$ 334	6.3	$ 294	5.9
Current portion of long-term debt (Note 6)	58	1.1	26	.5
	392	7.4	320	6.4
Long-term debt (Note 6)	1,045	19.8	933	18.8
Other liabilities (Note 7)	408	7.7	381	7.7
Future income and resource taxes (Note 11)	669	12.7	556	11.2
Debentures exchangeable for Inco Shares (Note 8)	248	4.7	248	5.0
Shareholders' equity (Note 9)	2,505	47.6	2,520	50.8
	5,267	100.0	4,958	100.0

Source: Teck Cominco annual report, 2003.

usually is divided into value of common shares, contributed surplus (additional paid-in capital), and retained earnings; the first two of these represent the proceeds realized from the sale of shares to the public, while retained earnings derive from the buildup of equity from profits plowed back into the firm. (This breakdown is provided in Note 9.)

To make it easier to compare firms of different sizes, analysts often present each item on the balance sheet as a percentage of total assets. This is called a *common-size balance sheet*; figures are presented this way in the second and fourth columns of Table 15.2 (added to the official statements).

The Statement of Changes in Financial Position

CCNMatthews (Canadian corporate news) www.cdn-news.com

The **statement of changes in financial position** is also referred to as a *statement of cash flows* or *flow of funds statement.* It is a report of the cash flow generated by the firm's operations, investments, and financial activities. The income statement and balance sheet are based on accrual methods of accounting, which means revenues and expenses are recognized when incurred, even if no cash has yet been exchanged; this third statement, however, recognizes only the results of transactions in which cash changes hands. For example, if goods are sold now, with payment due in 60 days, the income statement will treat the revenue as generated when the sale occurs, and the balance sheet will be immediately augmented by accounts receivable less inventory; but the statement of changes in financial position will not recognize the transaction until the bill is paid and the cash is in hand.

Table 15.3 shows the 2003 consolidated statements of changes in financial position for Teck. The first item under cash from operating activities is net income. The next entries modify that figure by components of income that have been recognized, but for which cash has not yet been exchanged. An increase in accounts receivable, for example, means income has been claimed on the income statement, but cash has not yet been collected. Hence, increases in accounts receivable reduce the cash flows realized from operations in this period. Similarly, increases in accounts

Table 15.3 Consolidated Statements of Changes in Financial Position for Teck Cominco

Teck Cominco
Consolidated Statements of Cash Flows
As at December 31
($ in millions)

	2003	2002
Operating Activities		
Net earnings (loss)	$ 149	$ 30
Items not affecting cash:		
Depreciation and amortization	218	199
Future income and resource taxes	17	(22)
Equity (earnings) loss	(10)	(17)
Gain on disposition of Los Filos, net of current taxes	(45)	—
Other	9	11
	338	201
Net change in non-cash working capital items (Note 13)	62	51
	400	252
Financing Activities		
Short-term bank loans	—	(80)
Long-term debt	259	345
Repayment of long-term debt	(277)	(439)
Decrease in funds held on deposit	—	157
Reduction of long-term liabilities	(55)	(27)
Interest on exchangeable debentures (Note 9(a))	(5)	(5)
Issuance (purchase and cancellation) of Class B Subordinate Voting shares	24	1
Dividends paid	(37)	(37)
	(91)	(85)
Investing Activities		
Property, plant, and equipment	(162)	(187)
Investment in coal partnership and income trust	(275)	—
Deferred payment received from Aur Resources Inc.	48	—
Investments	(22)	(18)
Proceeds from sale of assets	24	28
Proceeds from disposition of Los Filos, net of current taxes	49	—
Cash recognized upon consolidation of Antamina (Note 29(b))	41	—
	(297)	(177)
Effect of exchange rate changes on cash	(7)	—
Increase (Decrease) in cash	5	(10)
Cash at the beginning of the year	91	101
Cash at the end of the year	$ 96	$ 91

The accompanying notes are an integral part of these financial statements.

Source: Teck Cominco annual report, 2003.

payable mean expenses have been incurred, but cash has not yet left the firm. Any payment delay increases the company's net cash flows in this period.

Another major difference between the income statement and the statement of changes in financial position involves depreciation, which is a major addition to income in the adjustment section of cash provided in Table 15.3. The income statement attempts to "smooth" large capital expenditures over time to reflect a measure of profitability not distorted by large infrequent expenditures. The depreciation expense on the income statement is a way of doing this by recognizing capital expenditures over a period of many years rather than at the specific time of those expenditures.

The statement of cash flows, however, recognizes the cash implication of a capital expenditure when it occurs. It will ignore the depreciation "expense" over time, but will account for the full capital expenditure when it is paid in the second section, entitled cash flows from investing activities.

Rather than smooth or allocate expenses over time, as in the income statement, the statement of cash flows reports cash flows separately for operations, investing, and financing activities. This way, any large cash flows (such as those for big investments) can be recognized explicitly as nonrecurring, without affecting the measure of cash flow generated by operating activities.

The second section of the statement of cash flows is the accounting of cash flows from financing activities. Issuance of securities will contribute positive cash flows, while repurchasing or redeeming securities will consume cash. Note that Teck spent $277 million in repaying long-term debt versus the $259 million that it issued. Notice that while dividends paid are included in the cash flows from the financing, interest payments on debt are included with operating activities, because, unlike dividends, interest payments are not discretionary.

Finally, the last section of the statement lists the cash flows resulting from investing activities. These entries are investments in the capital stock necessary for the firm to maintain or enhance its productive capacity, and other financial investments. For example, in 2003 Teck invested $162 million in fixed assets; additionally, its transactions in shares of other companies netted a significant amount ($97 million) of cash. The final cash position increased by $5 million in 2003.

The statement of cash flows provides evidence on the well-being of a firm. If a company cannot pay its dividends and maintain the productivity of its capital stock out of cash flow from operations, for example, and it must resort to borrowing to meet these demands, this is a serious warning that the firm cannot maintain dividend payout at its current level in the long run. The statement of cash flows will reveal this developing problem, when it shows that cash flow from operations is inadequate and that borrowing is being used to maintain dividend payments at unsustainable levels.

15.2 ACCOUNTING VERSUS ECONOMIC EARNINGS

We've seen that stock valuation models require a measure of economic earnings or sustainable cash flow that can be paid out to shareholders without impairing the productive capacity of the firm. In contrast, **accounting earnings** are affected by several conventions regarding the valuation of assets, such as inventories (e.g., LIFO versus FIFO treatment), and by the way some expenditures, such as capital investments, are recognized over time (as depreciation expenses). We will discuss problems with some of these accounting conventions in greater detail later in the chapter. In addition to these accounting issues, as the firm makes its way through the business cycle, its earnings will rise above or fall below the trend line that might more accurately reflect sustainable economic earnings. This introduces an added complication in interpreting net income figures. One might wonder how closely accounting earnings approximate economic earnings and, correspondingly, how useful accounting data might be to investors attempting to value the firm.[1]

[1]In "The Trouble with Earnings," *Financial Analysts Journal*, September/October 1972, Jack Treynor points out some important difficulties with the accounting concept of earnings. In particular, he argues that the trouble stems from accountants' attempts to measure the value of assets.

In fact, the net income figure on the firm's income statement does convey considerable information concerning a firm's prospects. We see this in the fact that stock prices tend to increase when firms announce earnings greater than market analysts or investors anticipate. There are several studies to this effect.

In one well-known study, Foster, Olsen, and Shevlin[2] used time series of earnings for many firms to forecast the coming quarter's earnings announcement. They estimated an equation for more than 2,000 firms between 1974 and 1981:

$$E_{i,t} = E_{i,t-4} + a_i(E_{i,t-1} - E_{i,t-5}) + g_i$$

where

$E_{i,t}$ = Earnings of firm i in quarter t

a_i = Adjustment factor for firm i

g_i = Growth factor for firm i

The rationale is that this quarter's earnings, $E_{i,t}$, will equal last year's earnings for the same quarter, $E_{i,t-4}$, plus a factor representing recent above-trend earnings performance as measured by the difference between last quarter's earnings and the corresponding quarter's earnings a year earlier, plus another factor that represents steady earnings growth over time. Regression techniques are used to estimate a_i and g_i. Given these estimates, the equation is used together with past earnings to forecast future earnings.

Now it is easy to determine earnings surprises. Simply take the difference between actual earnings and forecasted or expected earnings, and see whether earnings surprises correlate with subsequent stock price movements.

Before doing so, however, these researchers introduced an extra refinement (first suggested by Latane and Jones[3]). Instead of using the earnings forecast error itself as the variable of interest, they first divided the forecast errors for each period by the standard deviation of forecast errors calculated from earlier periods; they effectively deflated the earnings surprise in a particular quarter by a measure of the typical surprise in an average quarter. This discounts forecast errors for firms with historically very unpredictable earnings. A large error for such firms might not be as significant as for a firm with typically very predictable earnings. The resulting "normalized" forecast error commonly is called the "standardized unexpected earnings" (SUE) measure. SUE is the variable that was correlated with stock price movements.

Each earnings announcement was placed in 1 of 10 deciles ranked by the magnitude of SUE, and the abnormal returns of the stock in each decile were calculated. The abnormal return in a period is the portfolio return after adjusting for both the market return in that period and the portfolio beta. It measures return over and above what would be expected given market conditions in that period. Figure 15.1 is a graph of the cumulative abnormal returns.

The results of this study are dramatic. The correlation between SUE ranking and abnormal returns across deciles is as predicted. There is a large abnormal return (a large increase in cumulative abnormal return) on the earnings announcement day (time 0). The abnormal return is positive for high-SUE and negative for low-SUE (actually negative-SUE) firms.

The more remarkable, and disturbing, results of the study concerns stock price movements *after* the announcement date. The cumulative abnormal returns of high-SUE stocks continue to grow even after the earnings information becomes public, while the low-SUE firms continue to suffer negative abnormal returns. The market appears to adjust to the earnings information only gradually, resulting in a sustained period of abnormal returns.

---

[2]George Foster, Chris Olsen, and Terry Shevlin, "Earnings Releases, Anomalies, and the Behavior of Security Returns," *The Accounting Review* 59, no. 4 (October 1984).

[3]H. A. Latane and C. P. Jones, "Standardized Unexpected Earnings—1971–1977," *Journal of Finance*, June 1979.

Figure 15.1 Cumulative abnormal returns in response to earnings announcements.

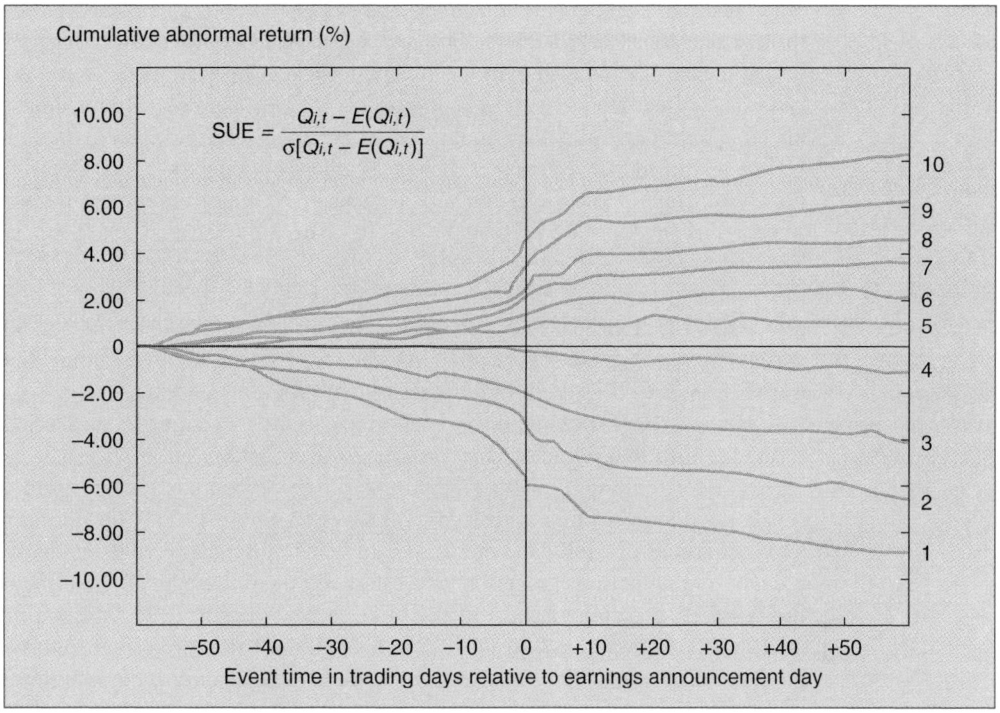

Source: George Foster, Chris Olsen, and Terry Shevlin, "Earnings Releases, Anomalies, and the Behavior of Security Returns," *Accounting Review* 59 (October 1984).

Evidently, one can earn abnormal profits simply by waiting for earnings announcements and purchasing a stock portfolio of high-SUE companies. These are precisely the types of predictable continuing trends that ought to be impossible in an efficient market. This finding is not unique.

Some research suggests that the post-announcement drift in security prices might be related in part to trading costs. Bernard and Thomas[4] find that post-announcement abnormal returns increase with the magnitude of SUE until the earnings surprise becomes fairly large. Beyond this point, they speculate, the change in the perceived value of the firm due to the earnings announcement is so large that transaction costs no longer impede trading. They also point out that post-announcement abnormal returns are larger for smaller firms, for which trading costs are higher. Still, these results do not satisfactorily explain the post-announcement drift anomaly. First, while trading costs may explain the existence of post-announcement drift, they do not explain why the total *post-announcement* abnormal return is higher for high-SUE firms. Second, Bernard and Thomas show that firms with positive earnings surprises in one quarter exhibit positive abnormal returns at the earnings announcement in the *following* quarter, suggesting that the market does not fully account for the implications of current earnings announcements when it revises its expectations for future earnings. This suggests informational inefficiency, leaving this phenomenon a topic for future research.

Analysts' Forecasts and Stock Returns

You might wonder whether security analysts can predict earnings more accurately than can mechanical time series equations. After all, analysts have access to these statistical equations and to

[4]Victor L. Bernard and Jacob K. Thomas, "Post-Earnings-Announcement Drift: Delayed Price Response or Risk Premium?" *Journal of Accounting Research* 27 (1989), pp. 1–36.

other qualitative and quantitative data. The evidence seems to be that analysts in fact do outperform such mechanical forecasts. Two recent Canadian studies analyzed the effect on stock prices of the release of estimated earnings by analysts and of revisions to forecasts announced by analysts. Their findings were consistent with earlier U.S. studies.[5] Both studies used the data contained in publicly available summary reports of analysts' forecasts.

In a test of market efficiency, Brown, Richardson, and Trzcinka[6] determined that there is a positive correlation between analysts' forecasts and abnormal returns in individual stocks. The forecasts of stock prices, presumably based on earnings estimates, are reported in the Research Evaluation Service of *The Financial Post Information Service*. The authors found that use of the service in a trading strategy led to significant excess returns, net of transactions costs. They also tested the significance of the benchmark for risk adjustment and concluded that the result was independent of the choice of a CAPM or APT approach; hence, they demonstrated that use of the simpler CAPM methodology was justified in this context.

Financial Post www.nationalpost.com/financialpost

L'Her and Suret[7] examined the reaction to earnings revisions by measuring abnormal returns. Using the information in the *Institutional Brokers Estimate System* (IBES), they divided earnings revisions into quintiles by magnitude of the percentage change from greatest downward revision (quintile 1) to greatest upward revision (quintile 5). The findings were remarkably similar to those in the Latane and Jones study. Cumulative average residuals were recorded for the nine-month periods preceding and following the release by IBES of the revisions, as shown in Figure 15.2. Although most of the price reaction occurred in anticipation of the announcement, the extreme cases (quintiles 5 and 1) showed that abnormal returns persisted for nine months following release for upward revisions, but for only three months for downward revisions. (On the other hand, the reaction to unfavourable revisions was much more pronounced over the 18-month period.) Findings such as these may lead one to suspect the causality; it is possible that analysts revise their forecasts in response to price changes, which they interpret as inside information.

In an interesting observation, L'Her and Suret note that segregating the data by industrial sector gave varied results. Using a three-sector classification, they found that the primary sector, with unpredictable commodity prices determining earnings, did not react to earnings revisions, while the other two sectors did; the secondary sector had a major reaction, such that purchase or sale of stock, including commissions, after an announced revision yielded significant gains. They also noted that if the revision occurs close to the end of the fiscal year, the signal is more reliable.

The *Value Line Investment Survey* is an influential service that provides reports of most of the recognized publicly traded stocks in the United States, including many large Canadian firms. Brown and Rozeff[8] compared earnings forecasts from Value Line with those made using a sophisticated statistical technique called a Box-Jenkins model. The Value Line forecasts generally were more accurate. Whereas 54 percent of the Box-Jenkins forecasts were within 25 percent of the realized values, and 26.5 percent were within 10 percent, 63.5 percent of the Value Line forecasts were within 25 percent and 23 percent were within 10 percent. Apparently, the qualitative data and firm-specific fundamental analysis that analysts bring to bear are of value.[9]

www.valueline.com

---

[5]A good survey of American studies is given in D. Givoly and J. Lakonishok, "Properties of Analysts' Forecasts of Earnings: A Review and Analysis of the Research," *Journal of Accounting Literature*, 1984.

[6]Lawrence Brown, Gordon Richardson, and Charles Trzcinka, "Strong-Form Efficiency on the Toronto Stock Exchange: An Analysis of Analyst Price Forecasts," *Contemporary Accounting Research*, Spring 1991.

[7]Jean-François L'Her and Jean-Marc Suret, "The Reaction of Canadian Securities to Revisions of Earnings," *Contemporary Accounting Research*, Spring 1991.

[8]Lawrence D. Brown and Michael Rozeff, "The Superiority of Analysts' Forecasts as Measures of Expectations: Evidence from Earnings," *Journal of Finance*, March 1978.

[9]See Section 16.5 for more on Value Line.

Figure 15.2 Cumulative average residuals in response to forecast revisions.

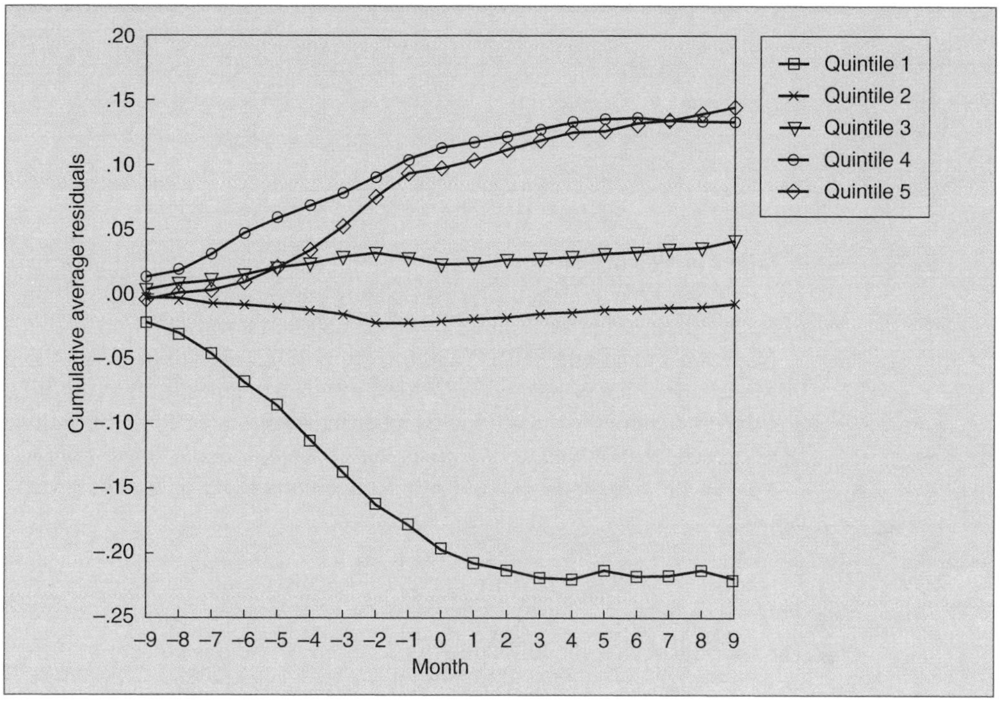

15.3 RETURN ON EQUITY

Past Versus Future ROE

We noted in Chapter 14 that **return on equity** (ROE) is one of the two basic factors in determining a firm's growth rate of earnings. There are two sides to using ROE. Sometimes it is reasonable to assume that future ROE will approximate its past value, but a high ROE in the past does not necessarily imply a firm's future ROE will be high. A declining ROE, on the other hand, is evidence that the firm's new investments have offered a lower ROE than its past investments. The best forecast of future ROE in this case may be lower than the most recent ROE. The vital point for an analyst is not to accept historical values as indicators of future values. Data from the recent past may provide information regarding future performance, but the analyst should always keep an eye on the future. It is expectations of future dividends and earnings that determine the intrinsic value of the company's stock.

Financial Leverage and ROE

An analyst interpreting the past behaviour of a firm's ROE or forecasting its future value must pay careful attention to the firm's debt-equity mix and to the interest rate on its debt. An example will show why. Suppose Nodett is a firm that is all equity financed and has total assets of $100 million. Assume it pays corporate taxes at the rate of 40 percent of taxable earnings.

Table 15.4 shows the behaviour of sales, earnings before interest and taxes, and net profits under three scenarios representing phases of the business cycle. It also shows the behaviour of two of the most commonly used profitability measures: operating **return on assets** (ROA), which equals EBIT/assets, and ROE, which equals net profits/equity.

Table 15.4 Nodett's Profitability over the Business Cycle

Scenario	Sales ($ millions)	EBIT ($ millions)	ROA (% per year)	Net Profit ($ millions)	ROE ($ per year)
Bad year	80	5	5	3	3
Normal year	100	10	10	6	6
Good year	120	15	15	9	9

Somdett is an otherwise identical firm to Nodett, but $40 million of its $100 million of assets are financed with debt bearing an interest rate of 8 percent. It pays annual interest expense of $3.2 million. Table 15.5 shows how Somdett's ROE differs from Nodett's.

Note that annual sales, EBIT, and therefore ROA for both firms are the same in each of the three scenarios, that is, business risk for the two companies is identical. It is their financial risk that differs. Although Nodett and Somdett have the same ROA in each scenario, Somdett's ROE exceeds that of Nodett in normal and good years and is lower in bad years.

We can summarize the exact relationship among ROE, ROA, and leverage in the following equation:[10]

$$\text{ROE} = (1 - \text{Tax rate})\left[\text{ROA} + (\text{ROA} - \text{Interest rate})\frac{\text{Debt}}{\text{Equity}}\right] \tag{15.1}$$

The relationship has the following implications. If there is no debt or if the firm's ROA equals the interest rate on its debt, its ROE will simply equal (1 – Tax rate) × ROA. If its ROA exceeds the interest rate, then its ROE will exceed (1 – Tax rate) × ROA by an amount that will be greater the higher the debt-to-equity ratio.

Table 15.5 Impact of Financial Leverage on ROE

		Nodett		Somdett	
Scenario	EBIT ($ millions)	Net Profits ($ millions)	ROE (%)	Net Profits* ($ millions)	ROE† (%)
Bad year	5	3	3	1.08	1.8
Normal year	10	6	6	4.08	6.8
Good year	15	9	9	7.08	11.8

*Somdett's after-tax profits are given by .6(EBIT – $3.2 million).

†Somdett's equity is only $60 million.

[10]The derivation of equation 15.1 is as follows:

$$\begin{aligned}
\text{ROE} &= \frac{\text{Net profit}}{\text{Equity}} \\
&= \frac{\text{EBIT} - \text{Interest} - \text{Taxes}}{\text{Equity}} \\
&= \frac{(1 - \text{Tax rate})(\text{EBIT} - \text{Interest})}{\text{Equity}} \\
&= (1 - \text{Tax rate})\frac{(\text{ROA} \times \text{Assets} - \text{Interest rate} \times \text{Debt})}{\text{Equity}} \\
&= (1 - \text{Tax rate})\left[\text{ROA} \times \frac{(\text{Equity} + \text{Debt})}{\text{Equity}} - \text{Interest rate} \times \frac{\text{Debt}}{\text{Equity}}\right] \\
&= (1 - \text{Tax rate})\left[\text{ROA} + (\text{ROA} - \text{Interest rate})\frac{\text{Debt}}{\text{Equity}}\right]
\end{aligned}$$

This result makes intuitive sense. If ROA exceeds the borrowing rate, the firm earns more on its money than it pays out to creditors. The surplus earnings are available to the firm's owners, the equityholders, which raises ROE. If, on the other hand, ROA is less than the interest rate, then ROE will decline by an amount that depends on the debt-to-equity ratio.

EXAMPLE 15.1 Leverage and ROE

To illustrate the application of equation 15.1, we can use the numerical example in Table 15.5. In a normal year, Nodett has an ROE of 6 percent, which is .6(1 – Tax rate) × its ROA of 10 percent. However, Somdett, which borrows at an interest rate of 8 percent and maintains a debt/equity ratio of $\frac{2}{3}$, has an ROE of 6.8 percent. The calculation using equation 15.1 is

$$\begin{aligned} ROE &= .6[10\% + (10\% - 8\%)\tfrac{2}{3}] \\ &= .6[10\% + \tfrac{4}{3}\%] \\ &= 6.8\% \end{aligned}$$

The important point to remember is that increased debt will make a positive contribution to a firm's ROE only if the firm's ROA exceeds the interest rate on the debt.

Note also that financial leverage increases the risk of the equityholder returns. Table 15.5 shows that ROE on Somdett is worse than that of Nodett in bad years. Conversely, in good years, Somdett outperforms Nodett because the excess of ROA over ROE provides additional funds for equityholders. The presence of debt makes Somdett more sensitive to the business cycle than Nodett. Even though the two companies have equal business risk (reflected in their identical EBITs in all three scenarios), Somdett carries greater financial risk than Nodett.

Even if financial leverage increases the expected ROE of Somdett relative to Nodett (as it seems to in Table 15.5), this does not imply the market value of Somdett's equity will be higher.[11] Financial leverage increases the risk of the firm's equity as surely as it raises the expected ROE.

Increased operating leverage has a similar effect in magnifying the results of increased sales into greater percentage increases in EBIT. Higher fixed costs work as do fixed financial charges; until sales reach a certain level, lower operating leverage will be superior in terms of EBIT. Given the Principle of matching the financing of fixed assets with long-term capital, high-operating-leverage companies will probably have higher debt loads and interest charges. Thus total leverage, a product of financial and operating leverage, will be even higher, indicating a greater sensitivity to the sales cycle. Conceivably, lower operating leverage combined with higher financial leverage could make one firm equally sensitive to sales changes as another with the reverse leverage position; practically, it is unlikely to happen. Risk and cyclical response tend to be high or low by the nature of the particular industry, where optimal operating structures will suggest roughly equal degrees of operating leverage, financed with similar debt ratios.

CONCEPT CHECK

1. Mordett is a company with the same assets as Nodett and Somdett but a debt-to-equity ratio of 1.0 and an interest rate of 9 percent. What would its net profit and ROE be in a bad year, a normal year, and a good year?

[11] This is the essence of the debate on the Modigliani-Miller theorems regarding the effect of financial leverage on the value of the firm. For a discussion of the issues and evidence, see footnote 7.

15.4 RATIO ANALYSIS

Decomposition of ROE

To understand the factors affecting a firm's ROE, including its trend over time and its performance relative to competitors, analysts often "decompose" ROE into the product of a series of ratios. Each component ratio is in itself meaningful, and the process serves to focus the analyst's attention on the separate factors influencing performance.[12]

One useful decomposition of ROE is

$$\text{ROE} = \frac{\text{Net profits}}{\text{Pretax profits}} \times \frac{\text{Pretax profits}}{\text{EBIT}} \times \frac{\text{EBIT}}{\text{Sales}} \times \frac{\text{Sales}}{\text{Assets}} \times \frac{\text{Assets}}{\text{Equity}}$$

$$(1) \quad \times \quad (2) \quad \times \quad (3) \quad \times \quad (4) \quad \times \quad (5)$$

Table 15.6 shows all these ratios for Nodett and Somdett Corporations under the three different economic scenarios. Let us first focus on factors 3 and 4. Notice that their product, EBIT/Assets, gives us the firm's ROA.

Factor 3 is known as the firm's operating **profit margin** or **return on sales** (ROS). ROS shows operating profit per dollar of sales. In a normal year, ROS is .10, or 10 percent; in a bad year, it is .0625, or 6.25 percent, and in a good year, .125, or 12.5 percent.

Factor 4, the ratio of sales to assets, is known as **asset turnover** (ATO). It indicates the efficiency of the firm's use of assets in the sense that it measures the annual sales generated by each dollar of assets. In a normal year, Nodett's ATO is 1.0 per year, meaning that sales of $1 per year were generated per dollar of assets. In a bad year, this ratio declines to .8 per year, and in a good year, it rises to 1.2 per year.

Comparing Nodett and Somdett, we see that factors 3 and 4 do not depend on a firm's financial leverage. The firms' ratios are equal to each other in all three scenarios.

Similarly, factor 1, the ratio of net income after taxes to pretax profit, is the same for both firms. We call this the *tax-burden ratio*. Its value reflects both the government's tax code and the policies pursued by the firm in trying to minimize its tax burden. In our example it does not change over the business cycle, remaining a constant .6.

Although factors 1, 3, and 4 are not affected by a firm's capital structure, factors 2 and 5 are. Factor 2 is the ratio of pretax profits to EBIT. The firm's pretax profits will be greatest when there are no interest payments to be made to debtholders. In fact, another way to express this ratio is

Table 15.6 Ratio Decomposition Analysis for Nodett and Somdett

	ROE	(1) Net Profit/ Pretax Profit	(2) Pretax Profit/ EBIT	(3) EBIT/ Sales (ROS)	(4) Sales/ Assets (ATO)	(5) Assets/ Equity	(6) Compound Leverage Factor (2) × (5)
Bad Year							
Nodett	.030	.6	1.000	.0625	0.800	1.000	1.000
Somdett	.018	.6	.360	.0625	0.800	1.667	0.600
Normal Year							
Nodett	.060	.6	1.000	.1000	1.000	1.000	1.000
Somdett	.068	.6	.680	.1000	1.000	1.667	1.134
Good Year							
Nodett	.090	.6	1.000	.1250	1.200	1.000	1.000
Somdett	.118	.6	.787	.1250	1.200	1.667	1.311

[12]This kind of decomposition of ROE is often called the *Du Pont system*.

$$\frac{\text{Pretax profits}}{\text{EBIT}} = \frac{\text{EBIT} - \text{Interest expense}}{\text{EBIT}}$$

We will call this factor the *interest-burden ratio (IB)*. It takes on its highest possible value, 1, for Nodett, which has no financial leverage. The higher the degree of financial leverage, the lower the IB ratio. Nodett's IB ratio does not vary over the business cycle. It is fixed at 1.0, reflecting the total absence of interest payments. For Somdett, however, because interest expense is fixed in a dollar amount while EBIT varies, the IB ratio varies from a low of .36 in a bad year to a high of .787 in a good year.

Factor 5, the ratio of assets to equity, is a measure of the firm's degree of financial leverage. It is called the **leverage ratio** and is equal to 1 plus the debt-to-equity ratio.[13] In our numerical example in Table 15.6, Nodett has a leverage ratio of 1, while Somdett's is 1.667.

From our discussion in Section 15.2, we know that financial leverage helps boost ROE only if ROA is greater than the interest rate on the firm's debt. How is this fact reflected in the ratios of Table 15.6?

The answer is that to measure the full impact of leverage in this framework, the analyst must take the product of the IB and leverage ratios (i.e., factors 2 and 5, shown in Table 15.6 as column 6). For Nodett, factor 6, which we call the *compound leverage factor*, remains a constant 1.0 under all three scenarios. But for Somdett, we see that the compound leverage factor is greater than 1 in normal years (1.134) and in good years (1.311), indicating the positive contribution of financial leverage to ROE. It is less than 1 in bad years, reflecting the fact that when ROA falls below the interest rate, ROE falls with increased use of debt.

We can summarize all of these relationships as follows:

$$\text{ROE} = \text{Tax burden} \times \text{Interest burden} \times \text{Margin} \times \text{Turnover} \times \text{Leverage}$$

Because

$$\text{ROA} = \text{Margin} \times \text{Turnover}$$

and

$$\text{Compound leverage factor} = \text{Interest burden} \times \text{Leverage}$$

we can decompose ROE equivalently as follows:

$$\text{ROE} = \text{Tax burden} \times \text{ROA} \times \text{Compound leverage factor}$$

Comparison of ROS and ATO usually is meaningful only in evaluating firms in the same industry. Cross-industry comparisons of these two ratios are often meaningless and can even be misleading.

Example 15.2 Margin Versus Turnover

Consider two firms with the same ROA of 10 percent per year. The first is a supermarket chain, the second is a gas and electric utility.

As Table 15.7 shows, the supermarket chain has a "low" ROS of 2 percent and achieves a 10 percent ROA by "turning over" its assets five times per year. The capital-intensive utility, on the other hand, has a "low" ATO of only .5 times per year and achieves its 10 percent ROA by having an ROS of 20 percent. The point here is that a "low" ROS or ATO ratio need not indicate a troubled firm. Each ratio must be interpreted in light of industry norms.

Even within an industry, ROS and ATO sometimes can differ markedly among firms pursuing different marketing strategies. In the retailing industry, for example, Holt Renfrew pursues a high-margin, low-ATO policy compared to Zellers, which pursues a low-margin, high-ATO policy.

---

[13] $\frac{\text{Assets}}{\text{Equity}} = \frac{\text{Equity + Debt}}{\text{Equity}} = 1 + \frac{\text{Debt}}{\text{Equity}}$

Table 15.7 Differences Between ROS and ATO Across Industries

	ROS	×	ATO	=	ROA
Supermarket chain	2%		5.0		10%
Gas utility	20%		.5		10%

CONCEPT CHECK

2. Do a ratio decomposition analysis for Mordett of question 1, preparing a table similar to Table 15.6.

Turnover and Other Asset Utilization Ratios

It is often helpful in understanding a firm's ratio of sales to assets to compute comparable efficiency-of-utilization, or turnover, ratios for subcategories of assets. For example, *fixed-asset turnover* would be

$$\frac{\text{Sales}}{\text{Fixed assets}}$$

This ratio measures sales per dollar of the firm's money tied up in fixed assets.

To illustrate how you can compute this and other ratios from a firm's financial statements, consider Growth Industries, Inc. (GI). GI's income statement and opening and closing balance sheets for the years 2005, 2006, and 2007 appear in Table 15.8.

GI's total asset turnover in 2007 was .303, which was below the industry average of .4. To understand better why GI underperformed, we can compute asset utilization ratios separately for fixed assets, inventories, and accounts receivable.

GI's sales in 2007 were $144 million. Its only fixed assets were plant and equipment, which were $216 million at the beginning of the year and $259.2 million at year's end. Average fixed assets for the year were, therefore, $237.6 million [($216 million + $259.2 million)/2]. GI's fixed-asset turnover for 2007 therefore was $144 million per year/$237.6 million = .606 per year. In other words, for every dollar of fixed assets, there were $.606 in sales during the year 2007.

Comparable figures for the fixed-asset turnover ratio for 2005 and 2006 and the 2007 industry average are

2005	2006	2007	2007 Industry Average
.606	.606	.606	.700

GI's fixed asset turnover has been stable over time and below the industry average.

Whenever a financial ratio includes one item from the income statement, which covers a period of time, and another from a balance sheet, which is a snapshot at a particular time, the practice is to take the average of the beginning and end-of-year balance sheet figures. Thus in computing the fixed-asset turnover ratio we divided sales (from the income statement) by average fixed assets (from the balance sheet).

Another widely followed turnover ratio is the inventory turnover ratio, which is the ratio of cost of goods sold per dollar of average inventory. The numerator is cost of goods sold instead of sales revenue because inventory is valued at cost. This ratio measures the speed with which inventory is turned over.

In 2005, GI's cost of goods sold (excluding depreciation) was $40 million, and its average inventory was $82.5 million [($75 million + $90 million)/2]. Its inventory turnover was .485 per year ($40 million/$82.5 million). In 2006 and 2007, inventory turnover remained the same, which was below the industry average of .5 per year.

Another measure of efficiency is the ratio of accounts receivable to sales. The accounts receivable ratio usually is computed as average accounts receivable/sales × 365. The result is a

Table 15.8 Growth Industries Financial Statements, 2004–2007 ($ thousands)

	2004	2005	2006	2007
Income Statements				
Sales revenue		$100,000	$120,000	$144,000
Cost of goods sold (including depreciation)		55,000	66,000	79,200
Depreciation		15,000	18,000	21,600
Selling and administrative expenses		15,000	18,000	21,600
Operating income		30,000	36,000	43,200
Interest expense		10,500	19,095	34,391
Taxable income		19,500	16,905	8,809
Income tax (40% rate)		7,800	6,762	3,524
Net income		$ 11,700	$ 10,143	$ 5,285
Balance Sheets (end of year)				
Cash and marketable securities	$ 50,000	$ 60,000	$ 72,000	$ 86,400
Accounts receivable	25,000	30,000	36,000	43,200
Inventories	75,000	90,000	108,000	129,600
Net plant and equipment	150,000	180,000	216,000	259,200
Total assets	$300,000	$360,000	$432,000	$518,400
Accounts payable	$ 30,000	$ 36,000	$ 43,200	$ 51,840
Short-term debt	45,000	87,300	141,957	214,432
Long-term debt (8% bonds maturing in 2025)	75,000	75,000	75,000	75,000
Total liabilities	$150,000	$198,300	$260,157	$341,272
Shareholders' equity (1 million shares outstanding)	$150,000	$161,700	$171,843	$177,128
Other Data				
Market price per common share at year-end		$93.60	$61.00	$21.00

number called the **average collection period**, or **days' receivables**, which equals the total credit extended to customers per dollar of daily sales. It is the number of days' worth of sales tied up in accounts receivable. You can also think of it as the average lag between the date of sale and the date payment is received.

For GI in 2007 this number was 100.4 days:

$$\frac{(\$36 \text{ million} + \$43.2 \text{ million})/2}{\$144 \text{ million}} \times 365 = 100.4 \text{ days}$$

The industry average was 60 days.

In summary, these ratios show us that GI's poor total asset turnover relative to the industry is in part caused by lower-than-average fixed-asset turnover and inventory turnover and higher-than-average days receivables. This suggests GI may be having problems with excess plant capacity along with poor inventory and receivables management procedures.

Liquidity and Coverage Ratios

Liquidity and interest coverage ratios are of great importance in evaluating the riskiness of a firm's securities. They aid in assessing the financial strength of the firm. Liquidity ratios include the current ratio, quick ratio, and interest coverage ratio.

1. *Current ratio*. Current assets/Current liabilities. **Current ratio** measures the ability of the firm to pay off its current liabilities by liquidating its current assets (i.e., turning them into

cash). It indicates the firm's ability to avoid insolvency in the short run. GI's current ratio in 2005, for example, was (60 + 30 + 90)/(36 + 87.3) = 1.46. In other years, it was

2005	2006	2007	2007 Industry Average
1.46	1.17	.97	2.0

This represents an unfavourable time trend and poor standing relative to the industry.

2. *Quick ratio.* (Cash + Receivables)/Current liabilities. The **quick ratio** is also called the **acid test ratio**. It has the same denominator as the current ratio, but its numerator includes only cash, cash equivalents, and receivables. The quick ratio is a better measure of liquidity than the current ratio for firms whose inventory is not readily convertible into cash. GI's quick ratio shows the same disturbing trends as its current ratio:

2005	2006	2007	2007 Industry Average
.73	.58	.49	1.0

3. *Interest coverage ratio.* EBIT/Interest expense. The **interest coverage ratio** is often called **times interest earned**. It is closely related to the interest-burden ratio discussed in the previous section. A high coverage ratio tells the firm's shareholders and lenders that the likelihood of bankruptcy is low because annual earnings are significantly greater than annual interest obligations. It is widely used by both lenders and borrowers in determining the firm's debt capacity and is a major determinant of the firm's bond rating. GI's interest coverage ratios are

2005	2006	2007	2007 Industry Average
2.86	1.89	1.26	5

GI's interest coverage ratio has fallen dramatically over this three-year period, and by 2007 it is far below the industry average. Probably its credit rating has been declining as well, and no doubt GI is considered a relatively poor credit risk in 2007.

Market Price Ratios

Two important market price ratios are the market-to-book-value ratio and the price-to-earnings ratio.

The **market-to-book-value ratio** (P/B) equals the market price of a share of the firm's common stock divided by its *book value*, that is, shareholders' equity per share. Analysts sometimes consider the stock of a firm with a low market-to-book-value to be a "safer" investment, seeing the book value as a "floor" supporting the market price.

Analysts presumably view book value as the level below which market price will not fall because the firm always has the option to liquidate, or sell, its assets for their book values. However, this view is questionable. In fact, some firms sell for less than book value. Nevertheless, low market-to-book-value ratio is seen by some as providing a "margin of safety," and some analysts will screen out or reject high P/B firms in their stock selection process.

Proponents of the P/B screen would argue that if all other relevant attributes are the same for two stocks, the one with the lower P/B ratio is safer. Although there may be firms for which this approach has some validity, book value does not necessarily represent liquidation value, which renders the margin of safety notion unreliable.

The theory of equity valuation offers some insight into the significance of the P/B ratio. A high P/B ratio is an indication that investors think a firm has opportunities of earning a rate of return on their investment in excess of the market capitalization rate, k.

Example 15.3 Price-to-Book Ratio and Investment Opportunities

Return to the numerical example in Chapter 14, Table 14.3. That example assumes the market capitalization rate is 12 percent per year. Now add the assumptions that the book value per share is \$8.33 and that the coming year's expected EPS is \$1, so that in the case for which the expected ROE on future investments also is 12 percent, the stock would sell at \$1/.12 = \$8.33, and the P/B ratio would be 1.

Table 15.9 shows the P/B ratio for alternative assumptions about future ROE and plowback ratio. Reading down any column, you can see how the P/B ratio changes with ROE. The numbers reveal that for a given plowback ratio, the P/B ratio is higher, the higher the expected ROE. This makes sense, because the greater the expected profitability of the firm's future investment opportunities, the greater its market value as an ongoing enterprise compared with the cost of acquiring its assets.

Table 15.9 Effect of ROE and Plowback Ration on P/B

	Plowback Ratio, *b*			
ROE	0	25%	50%	75%
10%	1.00	.95	.86	.67
12%	1.00	1.00	1.00	1.00
14%	1.00	1.06	1.20	2.00

Note: The assumptions and formulas underlying this table are: E_1 = \$1; book value per share = \$8.33; k = 12% per year; and

$g = b \times \text{ROE}$ $\qquad P_0 = \frac{(1-b)E}{k-g}$ $\qquad \text{P/B} = P_0/\$8.33$

We've noted that the **price-earnings ratio** that is based on the firm's financial statements and reported in newspaper stock listings is not the same as the price-earnings multiple that emerges from a dividend discount model. The numerator is the same (the market price of the stock), but the denominator is different. The reported P/E ratio uses the most recent past accountings earnings, whereas the P/E multiple predicted by valuation models uses expected future economic earnings.

Many security analysts pay careful attention to the accounting P/E ratio in the belief that among low P/E stocks they are more likely to find bargains than with high P/E stocks. The idea is that you can acquire a claim on a dollar of earnings more cheaply if the P/E ratio is low. For example, if the P/E ratio is 8, you pay \$8 per share per \$1 of *current* earnings, whereas if P/E is 12, you must pay \$12 for a claim on \$1 of current earnings.

Note, however, that current earnings may differ substantially from future earnings. The higher P/E stock still may be a bargain relative to the low P/E stock if its earnings and dividends are expected to grow at a faster rate. Our point is that ownership of the stock conveys the right to future earnings, as well as to current earnings. An exclusive focus on the commonly reported accounting P/E ratio can be shortsighted, because by its nature it ignores future growth in earnings.

An efficient markets adherent will be skeptical of the notion that a strategy of investment in low P/E stocks would result in an expected rate of return greater than that of investing in high or medium P/E stocks having the same risk. The empirical evidence on this question is mixed, but even if the strategy has worked in the past, it still should not work in the future because too many investors would be following it. This is the lesson of market efficiency.

Before leaving the P/B and P/E ratios, it is worth pointing out the relationship among these ratios and ROE:

$$\begin{aligned}\text{ROE} &= \frac{\text{Earnings}}{\text{Book value}}\\ &= \frac{\text{Market price}}{\text{Book value}} \div \frac{\text{Market price}}{\text{Earnings}}\\ &= \text{P/B ratio} \div \text{P/E ratio}\end{aligned}$$

By rearranging the terms, we find that a firm's **earnings yield**, the ratio of earnings to price, is equal to its ROE divided by the market-to-book-value ratio:

$$\frac{E}{P} = \frac{\text{ROE}}{\text{P/B}}$$

Thus a company with a high ROE can have a relatively low earnings yield because its P/B ratio is high. This indicates that a high ROE does not in and of itself imply the stock is a good buy: the price of the stock already may be bid up to reflect an attractive ROE. If so, the P/B ratio will be above 1.0, and the earnings yield to stockholders will be below the ROE, as the equation demonstrates. The relationship shows that a strategy of investing in the stock of high ROE firms may produce a lower holding-period return than investing in those with a low ROE.

Clayman[14] found that investing in the stocks of 29 "excellent" companies, with mean reported ROE of 19.05 percent during the period of 1976 to 1980, produced results much inferior to investing in 39 "unexcellent" companies, those with a mean ROE of 7.09 percent during the period. An investor putting equal dollar amounts in the stocks of unexcellent companies would have earned a portfolio rate of return over the 1981 to 1985 period that was 11.3 percent higher per year than the rate of return on a comparable portfolio of excellent company stocks.

CONCEPT CHECK

3. What were GI's ROE, P/E, and P/B ratios in the year 2007? How do they compare to the industry average ratios, which were

ROE = 8.64% P/E = 8 P/B = .69

How does GI's earnings yield in 2007 compare to the industry's average?

Choosing a Benchmark

We have discussed how to calculate the principal financial ratios. To evaluate the performance of a given firm, however, you need a benchmark to which you can compare its ratios. One obvious benchmark is the set of ratios for the same company in earlier years. For example, Figure 15.3 shows Teck's asset turnover, profit margin, and return on assets for the past ten years. You can see a general correspondence between ROA and the margin over that period, with a fairly trendless asset turnover. The ROA decrease from 1995 to the present is largely attributable to the decline in margin, but also to a slowing turnover.

Figure 15.3 Teck Cominco financial ratios.

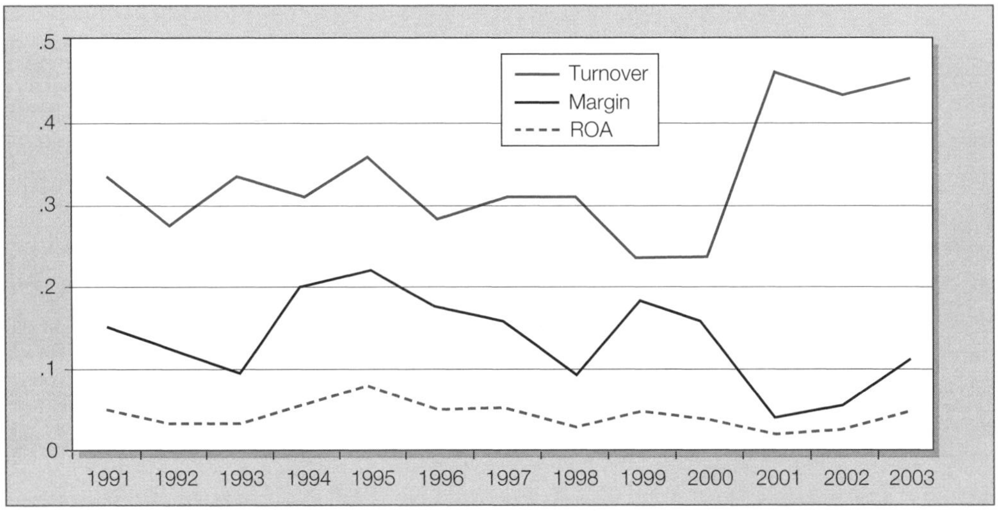

[14]Michelle Clayman, "In Search of Excellence: The Investor's Viewpoint," *Financial Analysts Journal*, May/June 1987.

Table 15.10 Financial Ratios for Paper and Forest Industry, 1997–2003

Latest Quarterly Results (updated May 21, 2004)

Companies Ranked by Annual Revenue	Quarter Ended	Latest Close	P/E Ratio	Dividend Yield	Revenue ($000s)	Net Inc. ($000s)	Earns. per Sh.	Assets ($000s)	Book Value
Abitibi-Consolidated Inc.	Q1: 3/31	9.78	NM	1.00	1,355,000	(106,000)	(0.24)	10,185,000	6.520
Domtar Inc.	Q1: 3/31	16.28	NM	1.50	1,225,000	(44,000)	(0.19)	5,855,000	9.303
Cascades Inc.	Q1: 3/31	13.80	35.4	1.20	870,000	(6,000)	(0.08)	2,927,000	12.920
Tembec Inc.	Q2: 3/27	10.65	NM	NA	756,000	(93,100)	(1.09)	3,818,800	13.510
Nexfor Inc. (US$)	Q1: 3/27	14.88	8.6	2.70	569,000	81,000	0.54	2,042,000	5.790
Norske Skog Canada Ltd.	Q1: 3/31	4.17	NM	NA	399,200	(46,300)	(0.22)	2,816,200	4.982
West Fraser Yimber Co. Ltd.	Q1: 3/31	42.15	26.3	1.30	541,100	26,500	0.72	2,087,730	35.656
International Forest Products Ltd.	Q1: 3/31	6.80	NM	NA	170,194	903	0.02	466,842	7.102
Ainsworth Lumber Co. Ltd.	Q1: 3/31	25.29	4.7	NA	174,700	(19,796)	(1.36)	627,721	11.708
Riverside Forest Products Ltd.	Q2: 3/31	21.75	7.6	0.60	140,850	9,527	1.08	348,753	19.505

Industry Data Bank

Fiscal Year:	2003	2002	2001	2000	1999	1998	1997	7-Year Average
Screens								
Earnings growth—1-yr. growth	205.93	38.22	(83.92)	111.36	133.38	146.79	(67.15)	69.23
Dividend yield %	1.13	1.63	9.50	2.33	2.03	1.98	0.91	2.79
Avg. price/Earnings	20.88	17.96	22.90	7.66	12.26	24.72	27.86	19.18
Avg. price/Book value	1.00	1.04	1.02	1.03	0.95	0.88	1.07	1.00
Avg. price/Sales	0.50	0.58	0.56	0.59	0.61	0.61	1.34	0.68
Avg. price/Cash flow	17.64	7.52	4.83	5.09	4.86	5.50	13.17	8.37
Earnings yield %	40.73	10.93	7.08	16.78	13.78	7.06	6.86	14.75
Estim. payback (yrs.)	10.96	12.73	14.14	5.80	8.86	17.48	8.70	11.24
Safety								
Cash flow/Total debt, %	17.09	34.27	22.51	17.97	33.06	29.85	14.16	24.13
Current ratio	2.13	1.63	1.65	1.95	2.16	2.08	2.16	1.96
Acid test (quick ratio)	1.09	0.76	0.81	1.05	1.15	1.11	1.14	1.02
Acct rec./Acct. pay.	0.69	0.68	0.65	0.77	0.77	0.78	0.83	0.74
Working Cap./Total assets, %	15.03	8.81	9.16	11.91	16.87	15.18	17.03	13.43
Debt—Long-term/Common equity	1.16	1.17	1.06	25.38	(1.47)	1.06	1.01	4.20
Debt—Total/Common equity	1.31	1.27	1.18	28.85	(1.71)	1.12	1.11	4.73
Cash flow/Net bef. disc.	1.94	3.77	4.40	0.87	2.75	7.05	38.02	8.40
Interest coverage	3.65	4.22	2.02	4.41	4.08	2.81	1.85	3.29
ROE/ROA	(14.21)	0.42	0.08	(1.53)	1.85	0.55	0.73	(1.73)
Earnings quality								
EBIT margin, %	15.69	6.58	2.50	13.73	8.32	6.92	0.03	7.68
Asset turnover	0.88	0.85	0.77	0.87	0.90	0.83	0.73	0.83
Interest burden %	3.41	3.78	4.48	3.01	3.62	3.58	2.81	3.53
Retention %	123.75	32.05	51.95	79.66	62.29	60.13	72.92	68.96
After-tax items/Assets %	0.10	0.14	0.02	0.07	0.05	0.00	(0.02)	0.05
Leverage	2.97	2.83	2.76	43.87	(0.95)	2.77	2.75	8.14
Apparent tax rate %	(23.75)	67.95	48.05	20.34	37.71	39.87	27.08	31.04
Profitability and efficiency %								
Operating margin %	9.16	13.70	14.06	17.71	18.36	13.57	6.24	13.26
Pre-tax margin %	11.44	1.23	(4.02)	9.45	3.98	2.18	(4.23)	2.86
Net profit margin %	9.82	0.53	(4.06)	8.50	1.19	0.97	(3.37)	1.94
Return on equity %	11.60	1.46	1.70	(13.25)	11.40	0.16	(2.61)	1.49
Return on assets %	12.19	3.43	(0.38)	7.96	3.86	2.87	2.09	4.58
Return on invested capital %	16.80	5.03	(0.71)	10.31	5.28	3.76	2.73	6.17
Other ratios								
Sales/Receivables	11.62	12.41	11.14	10.79	10.17	9.01	8.18	10.47
Sales/Inventory	6.28	6.27	5.99	6.61	6.47	5.86	4.95	6.06
Sales/Fixed assets	1.53	1.53	1.45	1.69	1.66	1.64	1.55	1.58
Sales/Cash & equiv.	37.09	38.16	42.09	62.36	119.78	28.78	24.97	50.46

Companies included: Abitibi-Consolidated Inc., Ainsworth Lumber Co. Ltd., Cascades Inc., Domtar Inc., International Forest Products Limited, Nexfor Inc., Norske Skog Canada Limited, Riverside Forest Products Limited, Stella-Jones Inc., Tembec Inc., TimberWest Forest Corp., Uniforêt Inc., West Fraser Timber Co. Ltd.

Source: "Paper & Forest," *FP Industry Reports,* FPinfomart.ca site, www.fpinfomart.ca.

Dun & Bradstreet
www.dnb.ca

It is also helpful to compare financial ratios to those of other firms in the same industry. Financial ratios for industries are published by Dun & Bradstreet, particularly as an aid to managerial decisions. They are also published by the *Financial Post*; industry reports are issued for 23 sectors. Table 15.10 shows a historical set of ratios for the paper and forest industry. The report also gives selected recent ratios for all of the major companies in the industry.

15.5 ECONOMIC VALUE ADDED

One common use of financial ratios is to evaluate the performance of the firm. While profitability is typically used to measure that performance, profitability is really not enough. A firm should be viewed as successful only if the return on its projects is better than the rate investors could expect to earn for themselves (on a risk-adjusted basis) in the capital market. Think back to Table 15.9, where we showed that plowing back funds into the firm increases stock price *only* if the firm earns a higher rate of return on the reinvested funds than the opportunity cost of capital, that is, the market capitalization rate. To account for this opportunity cost, we might measure the success of the firm using the *difference* between the return on assets, ROA, and the opportunity cost of capital, *k*. **Economic value added** is the spread between ROA and *k* multiplied by the capital invested in the firm. It therefore measures the dollar value of the firm's return in excess of its opportunity cost.

Table 15.11 shows EVA for a small sample of firms drawn from a larger study of 1,000 firms by Stern Stewart, a consulting firm that has done much to develop and promote the concept of EVA. Another term for EVA (the term coined by Stern Stewart) is **residual income**.

Example 15.4 Economic Value Added

Microsoft had one of the highest returns on assets, at 39.1 percent. Since the cost of capital for Microsoft was only about 14.3 percent, each dollar invested by Microsoft was earning about 24.8 cents more than the return that investors could have expected by investing in equivalent-risk stocks. Applying this 24.8 percent margin of superiority to Microsoft's capital base of $23.89 billion, we calculate economic value added in 2000 as $5.92 billion. GE's EVA was slightly larger than Microsoft's, despite a far smaller margin between ROA and cost of capital. This is because GE applied this margin to a larger capital base. At the other extreme, AT&T earned less than its opportunity cost on a very large capital base, which resulted in a large negative EVA.

Table 15.11 Measures of Company Performance, 2000

	Market-to-Book Ratio	Return on Assets, %	Economic Value Added (billions of dollars)
General Electric	6.6	20.4	$5.94
Microsoft	8.8	39.1	5.92
Wal-Mart Stores	4.4	12.8	1.60
Merck & Co	7.1	24.0	4.84
Philip Morris	2.1	17.4	6.08
ExxonMobil	1.9	10.5	5.36
Viacom	1.3	2.0	−4.37
General Motors	0.7	5.7	−1.07
WorldCom	0.7	6.3	−5.39
AT&T	0.6	4.5	−9.97

Source: Stern Stewart & Co.

Notice that even the EVA "losers" in Table 15.11 generally had positive profits. For example, AT&T's ROA was 4.5 percent. The problem is that its profits were not high enough to compensate for the opportunity cost of funds. EVA treats the opportunity cost of capital as a real cost that, like other costs, should be deducted from revenues to arrive at a more meaningful "bottom line." A firm that is earning profits but is not covering its opportunity cost might be able to redeploy its capital to better uses. Therefore, a growing number of firms now calculate EVA and tie managers' compensation to it.

15.6 AN ILLUSTRATION OF FINANCIAL STATEMENT ANALYSIS

In her 2007 annual report to the shareholders of Growth Industries, Inc., the president wrote: "2007 was another successful year for Growth Industries. As in 2006, sales, assets, and operating income all continued to grow at a rate of 20%."

Is she right?

We can evaluate her statement by conducting a full-scale ratio analysis of Growth Industries. Our purpose is to assess GI's performance in the recent past, to evaluate its future prospects, and to determine whether its market price reflects its intrinsic value.

Table 15.12 shows the key financial ratios we can compute from GI's financial statements. The president is certainly right about the growth rate in sales, assets, and operating income. Inspection of GI's key financial ratios, however, contradicts her first sentence: 2007 was not another successful year for GI—it appears to have been another miserable one.

ROE has been declining steadily from 7.51 percent in 2005 to 3.03 percent in 2007. A comparison of GI's 2007 ROE to the 2007 industry average of 8.64 percent makes the deteriorating time trend appear especially alarming. The low and falling market-to-book-value ratio and the falling price-earnings ratio indicate investors are less and less optimistic about the firm's future profitability.

The fact that ROA has not been declining, however, tells us that the source of the declining time trend in GI's ROE must be inappropriate use of financial leverage. And we see that as GI's leverage ratio climbed from 2.117 in 2005 to 2.723 in 2007, its interest-burden ratio (column 2) fell from .650 to .204—with the net result that the compound leverage factor fell from 1.376 to .556.

The rapid increase in short-term debt from year to year and the concurrent increase in interest expense make it clear that to finance its 20 percent growth rate in sales, GI has incurred sizable amounts of short-term debt at high interest rates. The firm is paying rates of interest greater than the ROA it is earning on the investment financed with the new borrowing. As the firm has expanded, its situation has become ever more precarious.

In 2007, for example, the average interest rate on short-term debt was 20 percent versus an ROA of 9.09 percent. We compute the average interest rate on short-term debt by taking the total

Table 15.12 Key Financial Ratios of Growth Industries, Inc.

Year	ROE	(1) Net Profit/ Pretax Profit	(2) Pretax Profit/ EBIT	(3) EBIT/ Sales (ROS)	(4) Sales/ Assets (ATO)	(5) Assets/ Equity	(6) Compound Leverage Factor (2) × (5)	(7) ROA (3) × (4)	P/E	P/B
2005	7.51%	.6	.650	30%	.303	2.117	1.376	9.09%	8	.58
2006	6.08	.6	.470	30	.303	2.375	1.116	9.09	6	.35
2007	3.03	.6	.204	30	.303	2.723	.556	9.09	4	.12
Industry average	8.64	.6	.800	30	.400	1.500	1.200	12.00	8	.69

Table 15.13 Growth Industries Statement of Cash Flows ($ thousands)

	2005	2006	2007
Cash Flow from Operating Activities			
Net income	$ 11,700	$ 10,143	$ 5,285
+ Depreciation	15,000	18,000	21,600
+ Decrease (increase) in accounts receivable	(5,000)	(6,000)	(7,200)
+ Decrease (increase) in inventories	(15,000)	(18,000)	(21,600)
+ Increase in accounts payable	6,000	7,200	8,640
	$ 12,700	$ 11,343	$ 6,725
Cash Flow from Investing Activities			
Investment in plant and equipment*	$(45,000)	$(54,000)	$(64,800)
Cash Flow from Financing Activities			
Dividends paid†	$ 0	$ 0	$ 0
Short-term debt issued	42,300	54,657	72,475
Change in cash and marketable securities‡	$ 10,000	$ 12,000	$ 14,400

*Gross investment equals increase in net plant and equipment plus depreciation.

†We can conclude that no dividends are paid, because stockholders' equity increases each year by the full amount of net income, implying a plowback ratio of 1.0.

‡Equals cash flow from operations plus cash flow from investment activities plus cash flow from financing activities. Note that this equals the yearly change in cash and marketable securities on the balance sheet.

interest expense of $34,391,000, subtracting the $6 million in interest on the long-term bonds, and dividing by the beginning-of-year short-term debt of $141,957,000. (See Table 15.8.)

GI's problems become clear when we examine its statement of cash flows in Table 15.13. The statement is derived from the income statement and balance sheet in Table 15.8. GI's cash flow from operations is falling steadily, from $12,700,000 in 2005 to $6,725,000 in 2007. The firm's investment in plant and equipment, by contrast, has increased greatly. Net plant and equipment (i.e., net of depreciation) rose from $150,000,000 in 2004 to $259,200,000 in 2007. This near-doubling of the capital assets makes the decrease in cash flow from operations all the more troubling.

The source of the difficulty is GI's enormous amount of short-term borrowing. In a sense, the company is being run as a pyramid scheme. It borrows more and more each year to maintain its 20 percent growth rate in assets and income. However, the new assets are not generating enough cash flow to support the extra interest burden of the debt, as the falling cash flow from operations indicates. Eventually, when the firm loses its ability to borrow further, its growth will be at an end.

At this point GI stock might be an attractive investment. Its market price is only 12 percent of its book value, and with a P/E ratio of 4 its earnings yield is 25 percent per year. GI is a likely candidate for a takeover by another firm that might replace GI's management and build shareholder value through a radical change in policy.

CONCEPT CHECK

4. You have the following information for IBX Corporation for the years 2005 and 2007 (all figures are in $ millions):

	2005	2007
Net income	$ 253.7	$ 239.0
Pretax income	411.9	375.6
EBIT	517.6	403.1
Average assets	4,857.9	3,459.7
Sales	6,679.3	4,537.0
Shareholders' equity	2,233.3	2,347.3

What is the trend in IBX's ROE, and how can you account for it in terms of tax burden, margin, turnover, and financial leverage?

15.7 COMPARABILITY PROBLEMS

Financial statement analysis gives us a good amount of ammunition for evaluating a company's performance and future prospects. But comparing financial results of different companies is not so simple. There is more than one acceptable way to represent various items of revenue and expense according to generally accepted accounting principles (GAAP). This means two firms may have exactly the same economic income yet very different accounting incomes.

Furthermore, interpreting a single firm's performance over time is complicated when inflation distorts the dollar measuring rod. Comparability problems are especially acute in this case because the impact of inflation on reported results often depends on the particular method the firm adopts to account for inventories and depreciation. The security analyst must adjust the earnings and the financial ratio figures to a uniform standard before attempting to compare financial results across firms and over time.

Comparability problems can arise out of the flexibility of GAAP guidelines in accounting for inventories and depreciation and in adjusting for the effects of inflation. Other important potential sources of noncomparability include the capitalization of leases and other expenses and the treatment of pension costs, but they are beyond the scope of this book.

Inventory Valuation

There are two commonly used ways to value inventories: **LIFO** (last-in, first-out), and **FIFO** (first-in, first-out). The difference is best explained using a numerical example. Suppose Generic Products Inc. (GPI) has a constant inventory of 1 million units of generic goods. The inventory turns over once per year, meaning that the ratio of cost of goods sold to inventory is 1.

The LIFO system calls for valuing the million units used up during the year at the current cost of production, so that the last goods produced are considered the first ones to be sold. They are valued at today's cost. The FIFO system assures that the units used up or sold are the ones that were added to inventory first, and therefore that goods sold should be valued at original cost. If the price of generic goods were constant, for example, at the level of $1, the book value of inventory and the cost of goods sold would be the same $1 million under both systems. But suppose the price of generic goods rises by 10 cents during the year as a result of general inflation. LIFO accounting would result in a cost of goods sold of $1.1 million, while the end-of-year balance sheet value of the one million units in inventory remains $1 million. The balance sheet value of inventories is measured as the cost of the goods still in inventory. Under LIFO, the last goods produced are assumed to be sold at the current cost of $1.10; the goods remaining are thus the previously produced goods, at a cost of only $1. You can see that although LIFO accounting accurately measures the cost of goods sold, it understates the current value of the remaining inventory in an inflationary environment.

In contrast, under FIFO accounting the cost of goods sold would be $1 million, and the end-of-year balance sheet value of the inventory would be $1.1 million. The result is that the LIFO firm has both a lower profit and a lower balance sheet of inventories than the FIFO firm.

LIFO is to be preferred to FIFO in computing economic earnings (i.e., real sustainable cash flow), because it uses up-to-date prices to evaluate the cost of goods sold. However, LIFO accounting induces balance sheet distortions when it values investment in inventories at original cost. This practice results in an upward bias in ROE, since the investment base on which return is earned is undervalued.

Canadian tax law requires that firms use FIFO accounting in determining their taxable income, but they are free to use LIFO in their internal or annual reporting. In the case of a discrepancy between accounting methods used, an adjustment must be made for the deferred tax credit or liability that is created with respect to the reported financial statements.

Depreciation

Another source of problems is the measurement of depreciation, which is a key factor in computing true earnings. The accounting and economic measures of depreciation can differ markedly. According to the *economic* definition, depreciation is the amount of a firm's operating cash flow that must be reinvested in the firm to sustain its real productive capacity at the current level.

The *accounting* measurement is quite different. Accounting depreciation or *amortization* is the amount of the original acquisition cost of an asset that is allocated to each accounting period over an arbitrarily specified life of the asset. This is the figure reported in financial statements.

Assume, for example, that a firm buys machines with a useful economic life of 20 years at $100,000 apiece. In its financial statement, however, the firm can depreciate the machines over 10 years using the straight-line method, for $10,000 per year in depreciation. Thus after 10 years a machine will be fully depreciated on the books, even though it remains a productive asset that will not need replacement for another 10 years.

In computing accounting earnings, this firm will overestimate depreciation in the first 10 years of the machine's economic life and underestimate it in the last 10 years. This will cause reported earnings to be understated compared with economic earnings in the first 10 years and overstated in the last 10 years.

If the management of the firm had a zero-plowback policy and distributed as cash dividends only its accounting earnings, it would pay out too little in the first 10 years relative to the sustainable cash flow. Similarly, a security analyst who relied on the (unadjusted) reported earnings figure during the first few years would see understated economic earnings and would underestimate the firm's intrinsic value.

Depreciation comparability problems include one more wrinkle. A firm can use different depreciation methods for tax purposes than for other reporting purposes. Canadian firms must use an accelerated depreciation method (declining balance for most depreciable assets) to calculate the capital cost allowance (CCA) for tax purposes; they are free, however, to use straight-line CCA in published financial statements. There are also differences across firms in their estimates of the depreciable life of plant, equipment, and other depreciable assets.

The major problem related to depreciation, however, is caused by inflation. Because conventional depreciation is based on historical costs rather than on the current replacement cost of assets, measured depreciation in periods of inflation is understated relative to replacement cost, and *real* economic income (sustainable cash flow) is correspondingly overstated.

The situation is similar to what happens in FIFO inventory accounting. Conventional depreciation and FIFO both result in an inflation-induced overstatement of real income, because both use original cost instead of current cost to calculate net income. For example, suppose Generic Products Inc. has a machine with a three-year useful life that originally cost $3 million. Annual straight-line depreciation is $1 million, regardless of what happens to the replacement cost of the machine. Suppose inflation in the first year turns out to be 10 percent. Then the true annual depreciation expense is $1.1 million in current terms, while conventionally measured depreciation remains fixed at $1 million per year. Accounting income therefore overstates *real* economic income by the inflation factor, $100,000. Again, if firms use straight-line depreciation for reported statements while using declining balance for tax purposes, a discrepancy with respect to tax liability is created; consequently, the appropriate adjustment must be noted in the statements.

Inflation and Interest Expense

If inflation can cause distortions in the measurement of a firm's inventory and depreciation costs, it has perhaps an even greater effect on the calculation of *real* interest expense. Nominal interest rates include an inflation premium that compensates the lender for inflation-induced erosion in the *real* value of principal. From the perspective of both lender and borrower, part of what is conventionally measured as interest expense should be treated more properly as repayment of principal.

For example, suppose Generic Products has debt outstanding with a face value of $10 million, paying 10 percent per year. Interest expense, as conventionally measured, is therefore $1 million per year. However, suppose inflation during the year is 6 percent, so that the real interest rate is 4 percent. Then $600,000 of what appears as interest expense on the income statement is really an inflation premium, or compensation for the anticipated reduction in the real value of the $10 million principal; only $400,000 is *real* interest expense. The $600,000 reduction in the purchasing power of the outstanding principal may be thought of as repayment of principal, rather than as an interest expense. Real income of the firm is therefore understated by $600,000. Mismeasurement of real interest means that inflation deflates the statement of real income. The effects of inflation on the reported values of inventories and depreciation that we have discussed work in the opposite direction.

www.cica.ca

In both Canada and the United States, the responsible accounting bodies (in Canada, the Canadian Institute of Chartered Accountants, or CICA) have tried to impose a requirement for inflation-adjusted accounting reports as supplements to regular statements. Reportedly, however, security analysts by and large ignore the inflation-adjusted data, particularly since this adds another element of noncomparability. Consequently, the requirement has been dropped in both jurisdictions.

CONCEPT CHECK

5. In a period of rapid inflation, companies ABC and XYZ have the same *reported* earnings. ABC uses LIFO inventory accounting, has relatively fewer depreciable assets, and has more debt than XYZ. XYZ uses FIFO inventory accounting. Which company has the higher *real* income, and why?

Quality of Earnings

Many firms will make accounting choices that present their financial statements in the best possible light. The different choices that firms can make give rise to the comparability problems we have discussed. As a result, earnings statements for different companies may be more or less rosy presentations of true economic earnings—sustainable cash flow that can be paid to shareholders without impairing the firm's productive capacity. Analysts commonly evaluate the **quality of earnings** reported by a firm. This concept refers to the realism and conservatism of the earnings number, in other words, the extent to which we might expect the reported level of earnings to be sustained.

Examples of the types of factors that influence quality of earnings are:

- *Allowance for bad debt.* Most firms sell goods using trade credit and must make an allowance for bad debt. An unrealistically low allowance reduces the quality of reported earnings.
- *Nonrecurring items.* Some items that affect earnings should not be expected to recur regularly. These include asset sales, effects of accounting changes, effects of exchange rate movements, or unusual investment income. For example, in 1999, which was a banner year for equity returns, some firms enjoyed large investment returns on securities held. These contributed to that year's earnings, but should not be expected to repeat regularly. They would be considered a "low-quality" component of 1999 earnings. Similarly, investment gains in corporate pension plans generated large but one-off contributions to reported earnings.
- *Stock options.* Many firms compensate employees in large part with stock options. To the extent that these options replace cash salary that otherwise would need to be paid, the value

of the options should be considered as one component of the firm's labour expense. But GAAP accounting rules do not require such treatment. Therefore, all else equal, earnings of firms with large employee stock option programs should be considered of lower quality.

- *Revenue recognition.* Under GAAP accounting, a firm is allowed to recognize a sale before it is paid. This is why firms have accounts receivable. But sometimes it can be hard to know when to recognize sales. For example, suppose a computer firm signs a contract to provide products and services over a five-year period. Should the revenue be booked immediately or spread out over five years? A more extreme version of this problem is called "channel stuffing," in which firms "sell" large quantities of goods to customers, but give them the right to later either refuse delivery or return the product. The revenue from the "sale" is booked now, but the likely returns are not recognized until they occur (in a future accounting period). According to the SEC, Sunbeam, which filed for bankruptcy in 2001, generated $60 million in fraudulent profits in 1999 using this technique. If you see accounts receivable increasing far faster than sales, or becoming a larger percentage of total assets, beware of these practices. Global Crossing, which filed for bankruptcy in 2002, illustrates a similar problem in revenue recognition. It swapped capacity on its network for capacity of other companies for periods of up to 20 years. But while it seems to have booked the *sale* of its capacity as immediate revenue, it treated the *acquired* capacity as capital assets that could be expensed over time. Given the wide latitude firms have to manipulate revenue, many analysts choose instead to concentrate on cash flow, which is far harder for a company to manipulate.
- *Off-balance-sheet assets and liabilities.* Suppose that one firm guarantees the outstanding debt of another firm, perhaps a firm in which it has an ownership stake. That obligation ought to be disclosed as a *contingent liability*, since it may require payments down the road. But these obligations may not be reported as part of the firm's outstanding debt. Similarly, leasing may be used to manage off-balance-sheet assets and liabilities. Airlines, for example, may show no aircraft on their balance sheets but have long-term leases that are virtually equivalent to debt-financed ownership. However, if the leases are treated as operating rather than capital leases, they may appear only as footnotes to the financial statements.

The boxed article here discusses proposals to make financial statements more informative.

International Accounting Conventions

The examples cited above illustrate some of the problems that analysts can encounter when attempting to interpret financial data. Even greater problems arise in the interpretation of the financial statements of foreign firms. This is because these firms do not follow U.S. GAAP guidelines. Accounting practices in various countries differ to greater or lesser extents from U.S. standards. (As with currencies, the standard for comparison is U.S. practice.) Here are some of the major issues that you should be aware of when using the financial statements of foreign firms:

- *Reserving practices.* Many countries allow firms considerably more discretion in setting aside reserves for future contingencies than is typical in the United States. Because additions to reserves result in a charge against income, reported earnings are far more subject to managerial discretion than in the United States.

  Germany is a country that allows particularly wide discretion in reserve practice. When Daimler-Benz AG (producer of the Mercedes-Benz) decided to issue shares on the New York Stock Exchange in 1993, it had to revise its accounting statements in accordance with U.S. standards. The revisions transformed a small profit for the first half of 1993 using German accounting rules into a *loss* of a $592 million under more stringent U.S. rules.
- *Depreciation.* In the United States, firms typically maintain separate sets of accounts for tax and reporting purposes. For example, accelerated depreciation is typically used for tax

TRUE AND FAIR IS NOT HARD AND FAST

The procession of companies admitting to having lied in their reported accounts has undermined faith in corporate numbers. The first priority for those who set accounting rules has been to try to choke off the most obvious loopholes.

Looking further into the future, however, some see the crisis in accounting as an opportunity to change the shape and content of accounts more fundamentally. The growing use of market values for assets and liabilities (instead of the accidental "historic cost" at which they were obtained) is going to make shareholders' equity and profits swing around far more than in the past. Under such circumstances, profits may come to be stated as a range of figures, each of them arrived at by using different accounting assumptions.

For the moment though, the efforts of regulators and standard-setters are focused on five main areas:

- *Pro-forma accounts*. These are the first sets of results produced by companies in America: they are unaudited and do not follow America's GAAP (Generally Accepted Accounting Principles). In the years of the stockmarket bubble they were shamelessly abused. Companies regularly reported huge profits in their pro-forma earnings statements, only to register even larger losses in their official filings.
- *Off-balance-sheet vehicles*. These include the "special-purpose entities" made famous by Enron. They allowed the Houston oil trader to hide hundreds of millions of dollars of liabilities from investors' eyes.
- *Stock options*. Most significant of all, perhaps, is the attempt to force companies to account for stock options granted to their employees. This week, FASB agreed that the cost of employee stock options should be treated as an expense. The question is, how to value them.
- *Pension funds*. Another controversial aim is to make companies change the way they account for their employee pension schemes. In March, FASB said it would start examining ways to improve accounting for employee pension plans.
- *Revenue recognition*. This is the vexed issue of when precisely to include revenue in the accounts—for example, when an order is made, when it is shipped, or when payment is received.

Future Standards

Yet another goal is to shift the world's body of accounting standards away from rules (the approach favored in America) towards principles (more influential in Britain). The hard rules embedded in America's GAAP have helped devious financiers to design structures that obey the letter of the law but ignore the spirit.

The way to make accounts more relevant (and to stop executives from fiddling them) is, standard-setters believe, to force companies to value more of their assets and liabilities at market prices, to "mark them to market." Instead of holding assets and liabilities at historic cost, and depreciating assets by a set amount each year, they maintain that companies should be required to mark them to market at the end of each reporting period. The slow march to market value is probably unstoppable in the long run, because so many accountants now believe that it is the most intellectually valid way to value assets.

Some accountants, however, would like to see a far more radical rethink of accounts. To start with the basics, what are accounts for? Most accountants would probably reply that they are there to give a true picture of a company's performance during a particular period of time. Investors, however, want far more than that: they want a sense of the company's future prospects.

Regulators also believe that companies should be obliged to give out new sorts of information. There should be new sections in annual reports on companies' intangible assets and on "key performance indicators"—such as employee turnover, customer acquisition cost, or inventory turnover.

None of this, however, will address the deepest flaw in accounts, says Baruch Lev, a professor of accounting and finance at the New York University Stern School of Business. This is the reality that most of the numbers in accounts are not facts but estimates.

Mr. Lev's remedy is to separate company accounts into two pieces: one "core" and one "satellite." The core part would have the most reliable numbers, or the ones that rely the least on estimates—cash flow would go here, for instance, and perhaps property. The satellite part would contain fair-value numbers and intangible assets, as well as other items.

Although companies and their auditors pretend that they can work out a single profit figure and a single net-assets number, the truth is that accountants do not know exactly how much money a company has made, nor exactly how much it is worth at any one moment. Realistically, the best they can hope for is a range—"X corporation made somewhere between $600m and $800m"—depending on, for instance, what assumption is made about the likelihood that its customers will pay all the money that they owe.

Source: *The Economist*, April 24, 2003. © 2003 The Economist Newspaper Group, Inc. Reprinted with permission. Further reproduction prohibited. www.economist.com.

purposes, whereas straight-line depreciation is used for reporting purposes. In contrast, most other countries do not allow dual sets of accounts, and most firms in foreign countries use accelerated depreciation to minimize taxes despite the fact that it results in lower reported earnings. This makes reported earnings of foreign firms lower than they would be if the firms were allowed to use the U.S. practice.

- *Intangibles.* Treatment of intangibles such as goodwill can vary widely. Are they amortized or expensed? If amortized, over what period? Such issues can have a large impact on reported profits.

Figure 15.4 summarizes some of the major differences in accounting rules in various countries. Note that Canadian and U.S. rules agree on these details. The effect of different accounting practices can be substantial. In a similar vein, a study by Speidell and Bavishi[15] recalculated the financial statements of firms in several countries using common accounting rules. Figure 15.5, from their study, compares P/E ratios as reported and restated on a common basis. The variation is considerable.

Such differences in international accounting standards become more of a problem as the drive to globally integrated capital markets progresses. For example, many foreign firms would like to list their shares on the New York Stock Exchange in order to more easily tap U.S. equity markets, and the NYSE would like to have those firms listed. But the SEC will not allow such shares to be listed unless the firms prepare their financial statements in accordance with U.S. GAAP standards. This has limited listing of non-U.S. companies dramatically.

In contrast to the United States, most other large national stock exchanges allow foreign firms to be listed if their financial statements conform to International Accounting Standards (IAS) rules. IAS disclosure requirements tend to be far more rigorous than those of most countries, and these standards impose greater uniformity in accounting practices. Its advocates argue that IAS rules are already fairly similar to GAAP rules, providing nearly the same quality

Figure 15.4 Comparative accounting rules.

Accounting rules vary worldwide. All Company Financial Reports Include:	Australia	Austria	Britain	Canada	France	Hong Kong	Japan	Netherlands	Singapore	Spain	Switzerland	W. Germany	U.S.
Quarterly data[1]				●									●
Accruals for deferred taxes	●		●	●	●	●		●	●				●
Consolidation of parent and majority-owned subsidiaries[2]	●		●	●	●	●		●	●	●	●		●
Discretionary or hidden reserves		●			●					●	●	●	
Immediate deduction of research and development costs[3]	●		●	●	●		●	●			●	●	●

1 In Austria companies issue only annual data. Other countries besides the U.S. and Canada issue semiannual data. In the Netherlands, companies issue quarterly or semiannual data.
2 In Austria, Japan, Hong Kong, and West Germany, the minority of companies fully consolidate.
3 In Austria. Hong Kong, Singapore, and Spain, the accounting treatment for R&D costs—whether they are immediately deducted or capitalized and deducted over later years—isn't disclosed in financial reports.

Source: Center for International Financial Analysis and Research, Princeton, NJ; and Frederick D. S. Choi and Gerhard G. Mueller, *International Accounting,* 2nd ed. (Englewood Cliffs, NJ: Prentice Hall), 1992.

[15] Lawrence S. Speidell and Vinod Bavishi, "GAAP Arbitrage: Valuation Opportunities in International Accounting Standards," *Financial Analysts Journal*, November/December 1992, pp. 58–66.

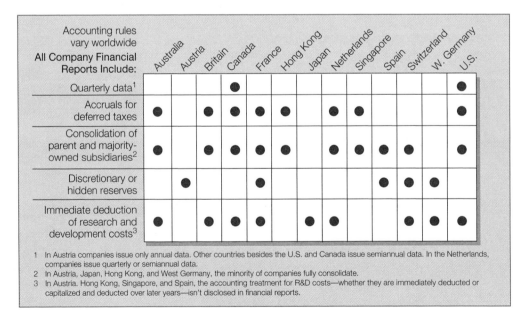

Figure 15.5 Adjusted versus reported price-earnings ratios.

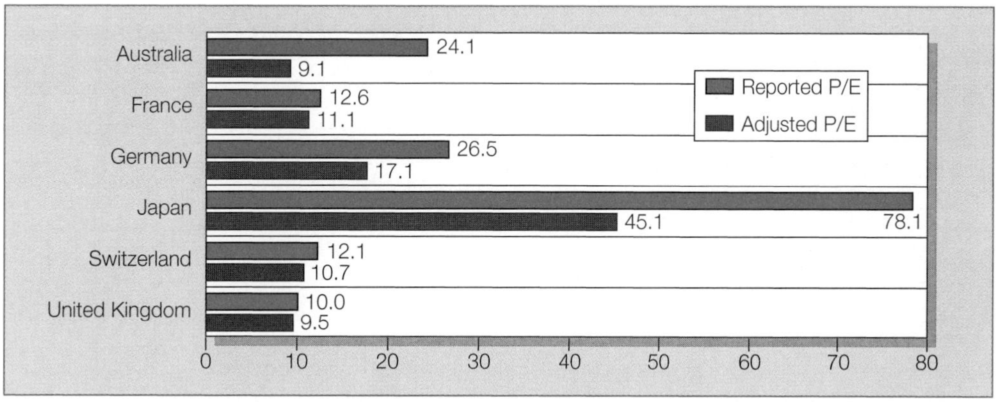

Source: Lawrence S. Speidell and Vinod Bavishi, "GAAP Arbitrage: Valuation Opportunities in International Accounting Standards," *Financial Analysts Journal,* November/December 1992, pp. 58–66.

of financial information about the firm. While the SEC does not yet deem IAS standards acceptable for listing in U.S. markets, negotiations are currently under way to change that situation.

Limitations

The efficient market hypothesis (EMH) refutes the possibility of gleaning additional information of value from the published financial statements of a company. Yet, analysis must be valuable in order to justify the efforts of well-paid analysts in looking for mispriced assets; active management depends upon the identification of opportunities for investment. Financial theory has been slow to accept the possibility that financial statement analysis may have more than the smallest and shortest-lived effect in making extraordinary gains; instead it suggests that the practice of analysis adds to market information, which leads to efficient pricing. Accounting theorists have been more inclined to look for the value in their products and their analyses.

Michael Brennan[16] discusses two aspects of accounting information and its relation to stock prices in a review article. He presents the results of research on market reactions to the release of new information and on the use of accounting information in the determination of value and of stock prices. He suggests that the definition and presentation of accounting data must be carefully controlled when academic studies of the significance of accounting information are conducted.

Ou and Penman,[17] in two articles, demonstrate that accounting information presented in annual statements is not only retrospective but prospective in revealing future results. They claim that financial statements capture fundamentals that are not reflected in prices, contrary to the assertions of the semistrong form of efficiency; in fact, financial statements contain information that can predict future stock returns. Furthermore, they define an accounting measure from the released information that they assert is relevant to future earnings rather than the current earnings revealed in the income statement. The stock returns predicted by their measure are shown to be negatively correlated with the returns predicted by P/E ratios. Brockman, Mossman and Olson[18] report also that use of accounting data and ratios to identify good and bad prospects can yield significant excess returns on long and short portfolios.

---

[16]Michael J. Brennan, "A Perspective on Accounting and Stock Prices," *The Accounting Review* 66, no. 1 (January 1991), pp. 67–79.

[17]Jane A. Ou and Stephen H. Penman, "Financial Statement Analysis and the Prediction of Stock Returns," *Journal of Accounting and Economics* 11 (1985), pp. 295–329; and "Accounting Measurement, Price-Earnings Ratio, and the Information Content of Security Prices," *Journal of Accounting Research* 27 (Spring 1989), pp. 111–144.

[18]Paul Brockman, Charles Mossman, and Dennis Olson, "What's the Value of Fundamental Analysis," *Canadian Investment Review*, Fall 1997, pp. 10–15.

E-INVESTMENTS
Web Sites

Financial statement data is available at the Web sites listed below. Enter the stock symbol and look for ratios.

www.nasdaq.com
moneycentral.msn.com/investor/home.asp
yahoo.marketguide.com
www.edgar-online.com
www.hoovers.com
www.freeedgar.com
www.smartmoney.com
www.executivelibrary.com/Research.asp

Go to **edgarscan.pwcglobal.com/servlets/edgarscan**. Examine financial ratios for time trend and cross-company comparisons. Compare a company's financials with an industry or a company of choice. Use EdgarScan and the Benchmarking Assistant.

Visit **gozips.uakron.edu/~drd/cs4.html** for general industry information.

The site **gozips.uakron.edu/~drd/cs5.html** offers stock performance updates and charting services.

SUMMARY

1. The primary focus of the security analyst should be the firm's real economic earnings rather than its reported earnings. Accounting earnings as reported in financial statements can be a biased estimate of real economic earnings, although empirical studies reveal that reported earnings convey considerable information concerning a firm's prospects.
2. A firm's ROE is a key determinant of the growth rate of its earnings. ROE is affected profoundly by the firm's degree of financial leverage. An increase in a firm's debt-to-equity ratio will raise its ROE and hence its growth rate only if the interest rate on the debt is less than the firm's return on assets.
3. It is often helpful to the analyst to decompose a firm's ROE ratio into the product of several accounting ratios and to analyze their separate behaviour over time and across companies within an industry. A useful breakdown is

$$\text{ROE} = \frac{\text{Net profits}}{\text{Pretax profits}} \times \frac{\text{Pretax profits}}{\text{EBIT}} \times \frac{\text{EBIT}}{\text{Sales}} \times \frac{\text{Sales}}{\text{Assets}} \times \frac{\text{Assets}}{\text{Equity}}$$

4. Other accounting ratios that have a bearing on a firm's profitability and/or risk are fixed asset turnover, inventory turnover, days receivables, and current, quick, and interest coverage ratios.
5. Two ratios that make use of the market price of the firm's common stock in addition to its financial statements are the market-to-book-value ratio and the price-earnings ratio. Analysts sometimes take low values for these ratios as a margin of safety or a sign that the stock is a bargain.
6. A strategy of investing in stocks with high-reported ROE seems to produce a lower rate of return to the investor than investing in low-ROE stocks. This implies that high-reported-ROE stocks are overpriced compared with low-ROE stocks.
7. A major problem in the use of data obtained from a firm's financial statements is comparability. Firms have a great deal of latitude in how they choose to compute various items of revenue and expense. It is therefore necessary for the security analyst to adjust accounting earnings and financial ratios to a uniform standard before attempting to compare financial results across firms.
8. Comparability problems can be acute in a period of inflation. Inflation can create distortions in accounting for inventories, depreciation, and interest expense. Comparability is also an international issue.

KEY TERMS

- income statement 569
- balance sheet 569
- statement of changes in financial position 571
- accounting earnings 573
- return on equity 577
- return on assets 577
- profit margin (return on sales) 580
- asset turnover 580
- leverage ratio 581
- average collection period (days' receivables) 583
- current ratio 583
- quick ratio (acid test ratio) 584
- interest coverage ratio (times interest earned) 584
- market-to-book-value ratio 584
- price-earnings ratio 585
- earnings yield 586
- economic value added 588
- residual income 588
- LIFO 591
- FIFO 591
- quality of earnings 593

SELECTED READINGS

A classic on ratio analysis is:

Lev, Baruch. *Financial Statement Analysis: A New Approach.* Upper Saddle River, NJ: Prentice Hall, Inc., 1974.

PROBLEMS

CFA® PROBLEMS

1. An analyst applies the Du Pont system of financial analysis to the following data for a company:
   - Leverage ratio (assets/equity) 2.2
   - Total asset turnover 2.0
   - Net profit margin 5.5%
   - Dividend payout ratio 31.8%

   What is the company's return on equity?
2. The Crusty Pie Co., which specializes in apple turnovers, has a return on sales higher than the industry average, yet its ROA is the same as the industry average. How can you explain this?
3. The ABC Corporation has a profit margin on sales below the industry average, yet its ROA is above the industry average. What does this imply about its asset turnover?
4. Firm A and firm B have the same ROA, yet firm A's ROE is higher. How can you explain this?

Problems 5 through 21 are from past CFA examinations.

CFA® PROBLEMS

5. The information in the following exhibit comes from the financial statements of QuickBrush Company and SmileWhite Corporation:

	QuickBrush	SmileWhite
Goodwill	The company amortizes goodwill over 20 years.	The company amortizes goodwill over 5 years.
Property, plant, and equipment	The company uses a straight-line depreciation method over the economic lives of the assets, which range from 5 to 20 years for buildings.	The company uses an accelerated depreciation method over the economic lives of the assets, which range from 5 to 20 years for buildings.
Accounts receivable	The company uses a bad debt allowance of 2% of accounts receivable.	The company uses a bad debt allowance of 5% of accounts receivable.

Determine which company has the higher quality of earnings by discussing each of the three notes.

CFA® PROBLEMS

6. Scott Kelly is reviewing MasterToy's financial statements in order to estimate its sustainable growth rate. Using the information presented in the following exhibit.
   a. Identify and calculate the components of the Du Pont formula.
   b. Calculate the ROE for 2005 using the components of the Du Pont formula.
   c. Calculate the sustainable growth rate for 2005 from the firm's ROE and plowback ratios.

MasterToy, Inc.: Actual 1998 and Estimated 1999 Financial Statements for Fiscal Year Ending December 31 ($ millions, except per-share data)

	1998	1999 (est.)	Change (%)
Income Statement			
Revenue	$4,750	$5,140	7.6
Cost of goods sold	2,400	2,540	
Selling, general, and administrative	1,400	1,550	
Depreciation	180	210	
Goodwill amortization	10	10	
Operating income	$ 760	$ 830	8.4
Interest expense	20	25	
Income before taxes	$ 740	$ 805	
Income taxes	265	295	
Net income	$ 475	$ 510	
Earnings per share	$1.79	$1.96	8.6
Average shares outstanding (millions)	265	260	
Balance Sheet			
Cash	$ 400	$ 400	
Accounts receivable	680	700	
Inventories	570	600	
Net property, plant, and equipment	800	870	
Intangibles	500	530	
Total assets	$2,950	$3,100	
Current liabilities	550	600	
Long-term debt	300	300	
Total liabilities	$ 850	$ 900	
Stockholders' equity	2,100	2,200	
Total liabilities and equity	$2,950	$3,100	
Book value per share	$7.92	$8.46	
Annual dividend per share	$0.55	$0.60	

CFA® PROBLEMS

7. The cash flow data of Palomba Pizza Stores for the year ended December 31, 2004, are as follows:

Cash payment of dividends	$ 35,000
Purchase of land	14,000
Cash payments for interest	10,000
Cash payments for salaries	45,000
Sale of equipment	38,000
Retirement of common stock	25,000
Purchase of equipment	30,000
Cash payments to suppliers	85,000
Cash collections from customers	250,000
Cash at beginning of year	50,000

a. Prepare a statement of cash flows for Palomba showing
  - Net cash provided by operating activities
  - Net cash provided by or used in investing activities
  - Net cash provided by or used in financing activities

CFA® PROBLEMS

b. Discuss, from an analyst's viewpoint, the purpose of classifying cash flows into the three categories listed above.

8. This problem should be solved using the following data:

Cash payments for interest	$(12)
Retirement of common stock	(32)
Cash payments to merchandise suppliers	(85)
Purchase of land	(8)
Sale of equipment	30
Payments of dividends	(37)
Cash payment for salaries	(35)
Cash collection from customers	260
Purchase of equipment	(40)

CFA® PROBLEMS

a. What are cash flows from operating activities?
b. Using the data above, calculate cash flows from investing activities.
c. Using the data above, calculate cash flows from financing activities.

9. Janet Ludlow is a recently hired analyst. After describing the electric toothbrush industry, her first report focuses on two companies, QuickBrush Company and SmileWhite Corporation, and concludes:

> QuickBrush is a more profitable company than SmileWhite, as indicated by the 40% sales growth and substantially higher margins it has produced over the last few years. SmileWhite's sales and earnings are growing at a 10% rate and produce much lower margins. We do not think SmileWhite is capable of growing faster than its recent growth rate of 10% whereas QuickBrush can sustain a 30% long-term growth rate.

a. Criticize Ludlow's analysis and conclusion that QuickBrush is more profitable, as defined by return on equity (ROE), than SmileWhite and that it has a higher sustainable growth rate. Use only the information provided in Tables 15A and 15B. Support your criticism by calculating and analyzing
  - The five components that determine ROE
  - The two ratios that determine sustainable growth: ROE and plowback

CFA® PROBLEMS

b. Explain how QuickBrush has produced an average annual earnings per share (EPS) growth rate of 40 percent over the last two years with an ROE that has been declining. Use only the information provided in Table 15A.

The following case should be used to solve problems 10–13.

10. Eastover Company (EO) is a large, diversified forest products company. Approximately 75 percent of its sales are from paper and forest products, with the remainder from financial services and real estate. The company owns 5.6 million acres of timberland, which is carried at very low historical cost on the balance sheet.

Peggy Mulroney, CFA, is an analyst at the investment counselling firm of Centurion Investments. She is assigned the task of assessing the outlook for Eastover, which is being considered for purchase, and comparing it to another forest products company in Centurion's portfolios, Southampton Corporation (SHC). SHC is a major producer of lumber products in the United States. Building products, primarily lumber and plywood, account for 89 percent of SHC's sales, with pulp accounting for the remainder. SHC owns 1.4 million acres of timberland, which is also carried at historical cost on the balance sheet. In SHC's case, however, that cost is not as far below current market as Eastover's.

Table 15A

QuickBrush Company
Financial Statements: Yearly Data
($000 except per-share data)

Income Statement	**December 2002**	**December 2003**	**December 2004**
Revenue	$3,480	$5,400	$7,760
Cost of goods sold	2,700	4,270	6,050
Selling, general, and administrative expense	500	690	1,000
Depreciation and amortization	30	40	50
Operating income (EBIT)	$ 250	$ 400	$ 660
Interest expense	0	0	0
Income before taxes	$ 250	$ 400	$ 660
Income taxes	60	110	215
Income after taxes	$ 190	$ 290	$ 445
Diluted EPS	$0.60	$0.84	$1.18
Average shares outstanding (000)	317	346	376

Financial Statistics	**December 2002**	**December 2003**	**December 2004**	**3-Year Average**
COGS as percent of sales	77.59%	79.07%	77.96%	78.24%
General and administrative expense as % of sales	14.37	12.78	12.89	13.16
Operating margin	7.18	7.41	8.51	
Pretax income/EBIT	100.00	100.00	100.00	
Tax rate	24.00	27.50	32.58	

Balance Sheet	**December 2002**	**December 2003**	**December 2004**
Cash and cash equivalents	$ 460	$ 50	$ 480
Accounts receivable	540	720	950
Inventories	300	430	590
Net property, plant, and equipment	760	1,830	3,450
Total assets	$2,060	$3,030	$5,470
Current liabilities	$ 860	$1,110	$1,750
Total liabilities	$ 860	$1,110	$1,750
Stockholders' equity	1,200	1,920	3,720
Total liabilities and equity	$2,060	$3,030	$5,470
Market price per share	$21.00	$30.00	$45.00
Book value per share	$3.79	$5.55	$9.89
Annual dividend per share	$0.00	$0.00	$0.00

Mulroney began her examination of Eastover and Southampton by looking at the five components of return on equity (ROE) for each company. For her analysis, Mulroney elected to define equity as total shareholders' equity, including preferred stock. She also elected to use year-end data rather than averages for the balance sheet items.

a. Based on the data shown in Tables 15C and 15D, calculate each of the five ROE components for Eastover and Southampton in 2004. Using the five components, calculate ROE for both companies in 2004.

b. Referring to the components calculated in part (*b*), explain the difference in ROE for Eastover and Southampton in 2004.

Table 15B

SmileWhite Corporation
Financial Statements: Yearly Data
($000 except per-share data)

Income Statement	**December 2002**	**December 2003**	**December 2004**	
Revenue	$104,000	$110,400	$119,200	
Cost of goods sold	72,800	75,100	79,300	
Selling, general, and administrative expense	20,300	22,800	23,900	
Depreciation and amortization	4,200	5,600	8,300	
Operating income	$ 6,700	$ 6,900	$ 7,700	
Interest expense	600	350	350	
Income before taxes	$ 6,100	$ 6,550	$ 7,350	
Income taxes	2,100	2,200	2,500	
Income after taxes	$ 4,000	$ 4,350	$ 4,850	
Diluted EPS	$2.16	$2.35	$2.62	
Average shares outstanding (000)	1,850	1,850	1,850	
Financial Statistics	**December 2002**	**December 2003**	**December 2004**	**3-Year Average**
COGS as percent of sales	70.00%	68.00%	66.53%	68.10%
General and administrative expense as % of sales	19.52	20.64	20.05	20.08
Operating margin	6.44	6.25	6.46	
Pretax income/EBIT	91.04	94.93	95.45	
Tax rate	34.43	33.59	34.01	
Balance Sheet	**December 2002**	**December 2003**	**December 2004**	
Cash and cash equivalents	$ 7,900	$ 3,300	$ 1,700	
Accounts receivable	7,500	8,000	9,000	
Inventories	6,300	6,300	5,900	
Net property, plant, and equipment	12,000	14,500	17,000	
Total assets	$33,700	$32,100	$33,600	
Current liabilities	$ 6,200	$ 7,800	$ 6,600	
Long-term debt	9,000	4,300	4,300	
Total liabilities	$15,200	$12,100	$10,900	
Stockholders' equity	18,500	20,000	22,700	
Total liabilities and equity	$33,700	$32,100	$33,600	
Market price per share	$23.00	$26.00	$30.00	
Book value per share	$10.00	$10.81	$12.27	
Annual dividend per share	$1.42	$1.53	$1.72	

c. Using 2004 data, calculate the sustainable growth rate for both Eastover and Southampton. Discuss the appropriateness of using these calculations as a basis for estimating future growth.

CFA® PROBLEMS

11. *a.* Mulroney (see the previous problem) recalled from her CFA studies that the constant-growth discounted dividend model was one way to arrive at a valuation for a company's common stock. She collected current dividend and stock price data for Eastover and Southampton, shown in Table 15E. Using 11 percent as the required rate of return (i.e., discount rate) and a projected growth rate of 8 percent, compute a constant-growth DDM value for Eastover's stock and compare the computed value for Eastover to its stock price indicated in Table 15F.

Table 15C Eastover Company ($ millions, except shares outstanding)

	2000	2001	2002	2003	2004
Income Statement Summary					
Sales	$5,652	$6,990	$7,863	$8,281	$7,406
Earnings before interest and taxes (EBIT)	$ 568	$ 901	$1,037	$ 708	$ 795
Interest expense (net)	(147)	(188)	(186)	(194)	(195)
Income before taxes	$ 421	$ 713	$ 851	$ 514	$ 600
Income taxes	(144)	(266)	(286)	(173)	(206)
Tax rate	34%	37%	33%	34%	34%
Net income	$ 277	$ 447	$ 565	$ 341	$ 394
Preferred dividends	(28)	(17)	(17)	(17)	(0)
Net income to common	$ 249	$ 430	$ 548	$ 324	$ 394
Common shares outstanding (millions)	196	204	204	205	201
Balance Sheet Summary					
Current assets	$1,235	$1,491	$1,702	$1,585	$1,367
Timberland assets	649	625	621	612	615
Property, plant, and equipment	4,370	4,571	5,056	5,430	5,854
Other assets	360	555	473	472	429
Total assets	$6,614	$7,242	$7,852	$8,099	$8,265
Current liabilities	$1,226	$1,186	$1,206	$1,606	$1,816
Long-term debt	1,120	1,340	1,585	1,346	1,585
Deferred taxes	1,000	1,000	1,016	1,000	1,000
Equity—preferred	364	350	350	400	0
Equity—common	2,904	3,366	3,695	3,747	3,864
Total liabilities and equity	$6,614	$7,242	$7,852	$8,099	$8,265

b. Mulroney's supervisor commented that a two-stage DDM may be more appropriate for companies such as Eastover and Southampton. Mulroney believes that Eastover and Southampton could grow more rapidly over the next three years and then settle in at a lower but sustainable rate of growth beyond 2008. Her estimates are indicated in Table 15G. Using 11 percent as the required rate of return, compute the two-stage DDM value of Eastover's stock and compare that value to its stock price indicated in Table 15F.

c. Discuss advantages and disadvantages of using a constant-growth DDM. Briefly discuss how the two-stage DDM improves upon the constant-growth DDM.

CFA® PROBLEMS

12. In addition to the discounted dividendmodel approach, Mulroney (see previous problem) decided to look at the price-earnings ratio and price-book ratio, relative to the S&P 500, for both Eastover and Southampton. Mulroney elected to perform this analysis using 2001–2005 and current data.

a. Using the data in Tables 15E and 15F, compute both the current and the five-year (1999–2003) average relative price-earnings ratios and relative price-book ratios for Eastover and Southampton (i.e., ratios relative to those for the S&P 500). Discuss each company's current relative price-earnings ratio compared to its five-year average relative price-earnings ratio and each company's current relative price-book ratio as compared to its five-year average relative price-book ratio.

b. Briefly discuss one disadvantage for each of the relative price-earnings and relative price-book approaches to valuation.

Table 15D
Southampton Corporation ($ millions, except shares outstanding)

	2000	2001	2002	2003	2004
Income Statement Summary					
Sales	$1,306	$1,654	$1,799	$2,010	$1,793
Earnings before interest and taxes (EBIT)	$ 120	$ 230	$ 221	$ 304	$ 145
Interest expense (net)	(13)	(36)	(7)	(12)	(8)
Income before taxes	$ 107	$ 194	$ 214	$ 292	$ 137
Income taxes	(44)	(75)	(79)	(99)	(46)
Tax rate	41%	39%	37%	34%	34%
Net income	$ 63	$ 119	$ 135	$ 193	$ 91
Common shares outstanding (millions)	38	38	38	38	38
Balance Sheet Summary					
Current assets	$ 487	$ 504	$ 536	$ 654	$ 509
Timberland assets	512	513	508	513	518
Property, plant, and equipment	648	681	718	827	1,037
Other assets	141	151	34	38	40
Total assets	$1,788	$1,849	$1,796	$2,032	$2,104
Current liabilities	$ 185	$ 176	$ 162	$ 180	$ 195
Long-term debt	536	493	370	530	589
Deferred taxes	123	136	127	146	153
Equity	944	1,044	1,137	1,176	1,167
Total liabilities and equity	$1,788	$1,849	$1,796	$2,032	$2,104

Table 15E
Valuation of Eastover Company and Southampton Corporation Compared to S&P 500

	2000	2001	2002	2003	2004	2005	5-Year Average (2001–2005)
Eastover Company							
Earnings per share	$ 1.27	$ 2.12	$ 2.68	$ 1.56	$ 1.87	$ 0.90	
Dividends per share	0.87	0.90	1.15	1.20	1.20	1.20	
Book value per share	14.82	16.54	18.14	18.55	19.21	17.21	
Stock price:							
High	28	40	30	33	28	30	
Low	20	20	23	25	18	20	
Close	25	26	25	28	22	27	
Average P/E	18.9	14.2	9.9	18.6	12.3	27.8	
Average P/B	1.6	1.8	1.5	1.6	1.2	1.5	
Southampton Corporation							
Earnings per share	$ 1.66	$ 3.13	$ 3.55	$ 5.08	$ 2.46	$ 1.75	
Dividends per share	.77	.79	.89	.98	1.04	1.08	
Book value per share	24.84	27.47	29.92	30.95	31.54	32.21	
Stock price:							
High	34	40	38	43	45	46	
Low	21	22	26	28	20	26	
Close	31	27	28	39	27	44	
Average P/E	16.6	9.9	9.0	7.0	13.2	20.6	
Average P/B	1.1	1.1	1.1	1.2	1.0	1.1	
S&P 500							
Average P/E	15.8	16.0	11.1	13.9	15.6	19.2	15.2
Average P/B	1.8	2.1	1.9	2.2	2.1	2.3	2.1

Table 15F Current Information

	Current Share Price	Current Dividends per Share	2006 EPS Estimate	Current Book Value per Share
Eastover	$ 28	$ 1.20	$ 1.60	$ 17.32
Southampton	48	1.08	3.00	32.21
S&P 500	830	24.00	41.08	319.66

Table 15G Projected Growth Rates as of 2003

	Next Three Years (2006, 2007, 2008)	Growth Beyond 2008
Eastover	12%	8%
Southampton	13%	7%

CFA® PROBLEMS

13. Mulroney (see problems 10–12) previously calculated a valuation for Southampton for both the constant-growth and the two-stage DDM as shown below:

Constant-Growth Approach	Two-Stage Approach
$29	$35.50

Using only the information provided and your answers to problems 10–12, select the stock (EO or SHC) that Mulroney should recommend as the better value, and justify your selection.

CFA® PROBLEMS

14. In reviewing the financial statements of the Graceland Rock Company, you note that net income increased while cash flow from operations decreased from 2003 to 2004.

a. Explain how net income could increase for Graceland Rock Company while cash flow from operations decreased. Give some illustrative examples.

b. Explain why cash flow from operations may be a good indicator of a firm's "quality of earnings."

CFA® PROBLEMS

15. A firm has net sales of $3,000, cash expenses (including taxes) of $1,400, and depreciation of $500. If accounts receivable increase over the period by $400, what would be cash flow from operations?

CFA® PROBLEMS

16. A company's current ratio is 2.0. If the company uses cash to retire notes payable due within one year, would this transaction increase or decrease the current ratio and asset turnover ratio?

	Current Ratio	Asset Turnover Ratio
a.	Increase	Increase
b.	Increase	Decrease
c.	Decrease	Increase
d.	Decrease	Decrease

CFA® PROBLEMS

17. During a period of rising prices, the financial statements of a firm using FIFO reporting instead of LIFO reporting would show

a. Higher total assets and higher net income

b. Higher total assets and lower net income

c. Lower total assets and higher net income

d. Lower total assets and lower net income

CFA® PROBLEMS

18. In an inflationary period, the use of FIFO will make which one of the following more realistic than the use of LIFO?

a. Balance sheet

b. Income statement

c. Cash flow statement

d. None of the above

CFA® PROBLEMS

19. All other things being equal, what effect will the payment of a cash dividend have on the following ratios?

	Times Interest Earned	Debt/Equity Ratio
a.	Increase	Increase
b.	No effect	Increase
c.	No effect	No effect
d.	Decrease	Decrease

CFA® PROBLEMS

20. The Du Pont formula defines the net return on shareholders' equity as a function of the following components:

- Operating margin
- Asset turnover
- Interest burden
- Financial leverage
- Income tax rate

Using only the data in Table 15H,

a. Calculate each of the five components listed above for 2005 and 2009, and calculate the return on equity (ROE) for 2005 and 2009, using all of the five components.

b. Briefly discuss the impact of the changes in asset turnover and financial leverage on the change in ROE from 2005 to 2009.

Table 15H Income Statements and Balance Sheets

	2005	2009
Income Statement Data		
Revenues	$542	$979
Operating income	38	76
Depreciation and amortization	3	9
Interest expense	3	0
Pretax income	32	67
Income taxes	13	37
Net income after tax	19	30
Balance Sheet Data		
Fixed assets	$ 41	$ 70
Total assets	245	291
Working capital	123	157
Total debt	16	0
Total shareholders' equity	159	220

CSI

21. Use the financial statements in Table 15I to answer the following questions adapted from the Canadian Securities Course. Calculate for Dominion Fabrics for both years 2002/03 the following ratios and statistics, indicating whether each is improving or not (where relevant).

a. Fully diluted earnings

b. EPS

c. The dividend payout ratio

d. The inventory turnover ratio

e. Gross, operating, and net profit margins
f. Cash-flow-to-total-debt ratio
g. The interest coverage ratio
h. Total debt and D/E ratios

Table 15I Dominion Fabrics Inc. Financial Statements ($ thousands)

Consolidated Balance Sheets as at June 30	2003	2002
Assets		
Current assets:		
Cash and cash equivalents	$ 105,313	$ 156,674
Receivables:		
Trade, less allowance for doubtful accounts of $16,121 in 2003 and $13,416 in 2002	288,788	246,650
Other	23,126	17,512
Inventories	187,298	160,782
Prepaid expenses and other current assets	15,148	16,529
	619,673	598,147
Investments and advancements	17,102	19,979
Property, plant, and equipment, net	603,145	556,358
Intangible assets	127,803	119,486
Other assets	44,860	35,142
Total assets	$1,412,583	$1,329,112
Liabilities and Shareholders' Equity		
Current liabilities:		
Short-term borrowings	$ 62,369	$ 40,041
Accounts payable and accrued liabilities	222,083	197,234
Dividends payable	1,252	1,260
Income taxes payable	13,327	15,154
Long-term debt due within one year	7,504	122,519
	306,535	376,208
Long-term debt	501,833	361,616
Other noncurrent liabilities	44,397	41,637
Deferred income taxes	55,397	41,009
Minority interest	173	61,684
Shareholders' equity		
Capital stock:*		
Preferred shares	69,841	71,441
Common shares	465,668	463,897
	535,509	535,338
Deficit	(49,232)	(77,848)
Cumulative translation adjustment	18,039	(10,532)
Total shareholders' equity	504,316	446,958
Total liabilities and shareholders' equity	$1,412,583	$1,329,112

Table 15I
(Continued)

	2003	2002
Consolidated Statements of Income for the Years Ended 30 June		
Sales	$1,332,848	$1,335,203
Cost of sales	1,012,306	996,549
Selling and administrative expenses	145,032	144,688
Income from operations	175,510	193,966
Depreciation and amortization	(69,786)	(65,733)
Interest expense:		
Long-term debt	(58,815)	(55,701)
Other debt, net	(744)	(5,875)
Share in net income of associated companies	6,625	6,900
Restructuring and other nonrecurring charges	—	—
Other income (expense), net	4,430	(4,868)
Income (loss) before income taxes	57,220	68,689
Current income taxes	(11,866)	(18,843)
Deferred income taxes	(10,651)	(16,477)
Minority interest	(1,168)	(3,035)
Net income (loss)	$ 33,535	$ 30,334
Consolidated Statements of Retained Earnings (Deficit) for the Years Ended 30 June		
Balance at beginning	$ (77,848)	$ (100,715)
Net income (loss)	33,535	30,334
	(44,313)	(70,381)
Dividends:		
Cumulative first preferred	4	4
Second preferred—Series C	204	302
Second preferred—Series D	3,624	3,617
Second preferred—Series E	1,087	1,088
	4,919	5,011
Share issue expenses	—	2,456
Balance at end	$ (49,232)	$ (77,848)

*The company had 2,792,118 preferred shares outstanding in 2003 (2,856,118 in 2002) and 41,037,308 common shares outstanding in 2003 (40,863,402 in 2002).

Visit us at www.mcgrawhill.ca/college/bodie

STANDARD &POOR'S

Enter the Market Insight database at **www.mcgrawhill.ca/edumarket insight** and link to *Company*, then *Population*. Select a company of interest to you and link to the *Company Research* page with a menu of company information reports on the left. Link to the *Excel Analytics Reports*, then, under *Annual*, the *Ratios Report*. What is the five-year trend in the ROE? Look over the trends of the net margin, asset turnover, and leverage, the primary ROE decomposition ratios. Which of these ratios had the greatest impact on ROE changes? What might explain these trends?

TECHNICAL ANALYSIS

In the two previous chapters, we examined fundamental analysis of equity, considering how the general macroeconomic environment and the specific prospects of the firm or industry might affect the present value of the dividend stream the firm can be expected to generate. In this chapter, we examine technical analysis. Technical analysis focuses more on past price movements of a company than on the underlying fundamental determinants of future profitability. Technicians believe that past price and volume data signal future price movements.

Such a view is diametrically opposed to that of the efficient market hypothesis, which holds that all historical data must be reflected in stock prices already. As we lay out the basics of technical analysis in this chapter, we will point out the contradiction between the assumptions on which these strategies are based and the notion of well-functioning capital markets with rational and informed traders.

16.1 TECHNICAL ANALYSIS

Technical analysis is, in most instances, an attempt to exploit recurring and predictable patterns in stock prices to generate abnormal trading profits. In the words of one of its leading practitioners,

> the technical approach to investment is essentially a reflection of the idea that the stock market moves in trends which are determined by the changing attitudes of investors to a variety of economic, monetary, political and psychological forces. The art of technical analysis, for it is an art, is to identify changes in trends at an early stage and to maintain an investment posture until a reversal of that trend is indicated.[1]

Technical Analysis traders.com

Technicians do not necessarily deny the value of fundamental information such as we have discussed in the past two chapters. Many technical analysts believe stock prices eventually "close in" on their fundamental values. Technicians believe, nevertheless, that shifts in market fundamentals can be discerned before the impact of those shifts is fully reflected in prices. As the market adjusts to a new equilibrium, astute traders can exploit these price trends.

Technicians also believe that market fundamentals can be perturbed by irrational factors. More or less random fluctuations in price will accompany any underlying trend. If these fluctuations dissipate slowly, they can be taken advantage of for abnormal profits.

These presumptions, of course, clash head-on with those of the efficient market hypothesis (EMH) and with the logic of well-functioning capital markets. According to the EMH, a shift in market fundamentals should be reflected in prices immediately. According to technicians, though, that shift will lead to a gradual price change that can be recognized as a trend. Such easily exploited trends in stock market prices would be damning evidence against the EMH, as they would indicate profit opportunities that market participants had left unexploited.

The essence of the conflict between the EMH and technical analysis lies in the weak-form statement given in Section 9.1—that the price reflects all information that can be extracted from trading data. Hence, all statistics about price and volume, all trends, all charts must be useless in predicting future movements. Similarly the semi-strong form claims that all publicly available fundamental information is equally useless; this in particular includes economic data that would affect the entire market, an industry or certain companies in an industry. This is not to say that interpreting data in a particular way may not lead to correct forecasts; rather, the balance of interpretations of information has led to the current price levels, and no randomly selected forecast is expected to be better than another.

The line between fundamental analysis and some technical analysis is hard to draw. If certain economic signals suggest that the market will rise (or fall), then the EMH states that the market index should already reflect that view. Betting on that signal should yield no expectable profit. As we saw in Chapter 14, there are leading indicators for the economy, but the market index itself is one of them. As an example of economic predictors, consider Figure 16.1, which shows a smoothed graph of the U.S. GDP growth and of the spread between 10-year Treasuries and 3-month T-bills; note that this is a proxy for the spread between 10-year bonds and the Fed funds rate, itself one of the official leading indicators for the U.S. GDP. In the graph, each series is calculated quarterly from a four-quarter moving average; then the series of term spreads is lagged four quarters and placed concurrently with the GDP series. There is a clear coincidence of the rise and fall of the two series, most obviously at major turning points. A low or negative term spread is associated with the negative growth periods in the GDP (recessions). The lagging of the term spread was used to dramatize the pattern; the four-quarter lag implies that the bond data predicts the economic performance by one year. The obvious interpretation is that when the spread falls to almost nothing, one should be selling the market before it too anticipates the recession. This response very much agrees with the street maxim "Don't fight the Fed"—the time to buy is not

[1] Martin J. Pring, *Technical Analysis Explained*, 2nd ed. (New York: McGraw-Hill Book Company, 1985), p. 2.

BOND MARKET SIGNALLING COMING STOCK RALLY

Market forecasters have been reading bond markets like tea leaves and, so far, they are predicting a bright future for an earnings recovery and a stock market rally. Strategists are pointing to steepening bond yield curves—the widening gap between short- and long-term bond yields—as evidence of a coming stock rally and economic recovery.

With the U.S. 10-year benchmark yield pushed to a recent high of 5.28%, analysts say it can only point to better days. "When you see a steepening of the yield curve, usually it signals a recovery in the economy," said Vincent Lepine, a senior economist at National Bank Financial. "This time, the steepening is really pronounced. Having a signal of such magnitude is pretty solid evidence [of a recovery] in my books."

Mr. Lepine said it is now "payback time" for equity investors, who watched bonds rally as investors fled from stocks to park their money in fixed income. The bond market has been retreating of late as stocks bounce back. As prices drop, yields have risen, steepening the yield curve. "If bonds are telling you the economy is going to recover, earnings—which drive the stock market—are going to recover," Mr. Lepine said.

David Rosenberg, chief Canadian strategist and economist at Merrill Lynch, said the bond yield curve is a bellwether for earnings growth, with a nine-month lead time. He thinks the recovery will come in the fourth quarter after further interest rate cuts. "I'm not expecting any spring during the summer." He said the trends in the bond market will cause major shifts in the equity market. "This is the classic late-cycle, curve-steepening environment that I have found in the past has carried some important equity sector rotation attributes." Cyclical stocks such as metals and transportation should excel in coming months. Bond-sensitive stocks such as real estate and utilities will lag.

Doug Porter, senior economist at BMO Nesbitt Burns, is less optimistic. He concedes the bond yield curve is a "tremendous" signal, but thinks the earnings recovery will not happen until much later. "Growth is going to remain pretty lacklustre for the rest of this year," he said, adding he sees more rate cuts in May and June.

Source: Jason Chow, "Bond Market Signalling Coming Stock Rally: Pretty Solid Evidence,"*Financial Post (National Post)*, April 25, 2001, pp. D1, D2.

when the Federal Reserve is raising interest rates to restrain the economy, but when it is loosening the strings to stimulate growth. An economic graph such as Figure 16.1 would be part of the arsenal of some technicians. (See the boxed article here, in which economists are interpreting the data.)

In Section 16.5, we discuss the Value Line methodology and its success. Much of its analysis is fundamental, referring to financial data; but ultimately, it produces an index as a function of observable, realized data, and recommends purchase or not on this basis. Similarly, new, rigorously tested filters have been devised to identify firms that should yield superior risk-adjusted returns. These might include the Fama-French identification of ratios that offer further explanatory power for returns than given by traditional beta, or patterns of return persistence or price reversal that lead to trading rules. Economic rationalization of the plausibility of these rules makes them appear acceptable strategies. Even if the pricing defies the CAPM, the EMH would argue that investors should react and reprice these securities so that the pattern no longer prevails. If not, then this is technical analysis that works.

A more subtle version of technical analysis holds that there are patterns in stock prices that can be exploited, but that once investors identify and attempt to profit from these patterns their trading activity affects prices, thereby altering price patterns. This means the patterns that characterize market prices will be constantly evolving, and only the best analysts who can identify new patterns earliest will be rewarded. We call this phenomenon *self-destructing* patterns and explore it further later in the chapter.

The notion of evolving patterns is consistent with almost but not quite efficient markets. It allows for the possibility of temporarily unexploited profit opportunities, but it also views market participants as aggressively exploiting those opportunities once they are uncovered. The market is continually groping toward full efficiency, but it is never quite there.

This is in some ways an appealing middle position in the ongoing debate between technicians and proponents of the EMH. Ultimately, however, it is an untestable hypothesis. Technicians will

Figure 16.1 **U.S. GDP growth and the term spread between 10-year Treasuries and 3-month T-bills; smoothed data (4-quarter moving average), lagged term spread (4 quarters).**

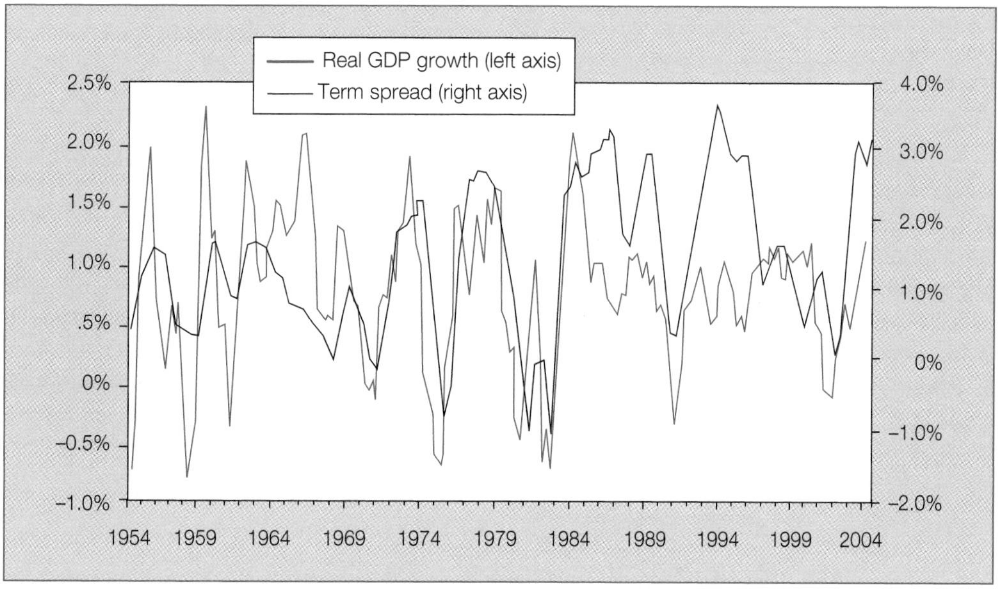

always be able to identify trading rules that would have worked in the past but need not work any longer. Is this evidence of a once-viable trading rule that has not been eliminated by competition? Perhaps. But it is far more likely that the trading rule could have been identified only after the fact.

Until technicians can prove rigorous evidence that their trading rules provide *consistent* trading profits, we must doubt the viability of those rules. As you saw in the chapter on the efficient market hypothesis, the evidence on the performance of professionally managed funds does not support the efficacy of technical analysis.

16.2 CHARTING

Technical analysts are sometimes called *chartists* because they study records or charts of past stock prices and trading volume, hoping to find patterns they can exploit to make a profit. In this section, we examine several specific charting strategies.

The Dow Theory

www.wsj.com

The **Dow theory**, named after its creator Charles Dow (who established *The Wall Street Journal*), is the most famous of technical analyses. The aim of the Dow theory is to identify long-term trends in stock market prices. The two indicators used are the Dow Jones Industrial Average (DJIA) and the Dow Jones Transportation Average (DJTA). The DJIA is the key indicator of underlying trends, while the DJTA usually serves as a check to confirm or reject that signal.

The Dow theory posits three forces simultaneously affecting stock prices:

1. The *primary trend* is the long-term movement of prices, lasting from several months to several years.
2. *Secondary* or *intermediate trends* are caused by short-term deviations of prices from the underlying trend line. These deviations are eliminated via *corrections* when prices revert back to trend values.
3. *Tertiary* or *minor trends* are daily fluctuations of little importance.

Figure 16.2 Dow theory trends.

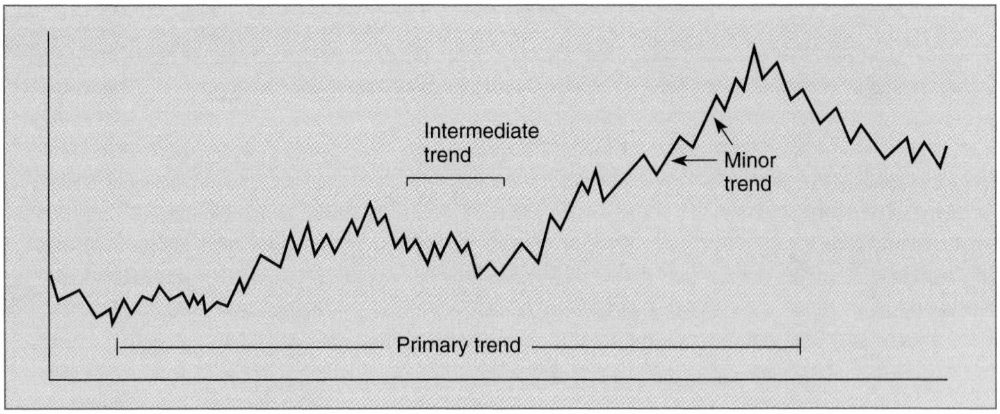

Note: The primary trend is typically measured in years and the intermediate trend is measured in weeks to months, while the minor trend will last from days to weeks.

Source: Melanie F. Bowman and Thom Hartle, "Dow Theory," *Technical Analysis of Stocks and Commodities,* September 1990, p. 690. Reprinted by permission.

Figure 16.2 represents these three components of stock price movements. In this figure, the primary trend is upward, but intermediate trends result in short-lived market declines lasting a few weeks. The intraday minor trends have no long-run impact on price.

Figure 16.3 depicts the course of the DJIA during 1988. The primary trend is upward, as evidenced by the fact that each market peak is higher than the previous peak (point F versus D versus B). Similarly, each low is higher than the previous low (E versus C versus A). This pattern of upward-moving "tops" and "bottoms" is one of the key ways to identify the underlying primary trend. Notice in Figure 16.3 that, despite the upward primary trend, intermediate trends still can lead to short periods of declining prices (points B through C, or D through E).

The Dow theory incorporates notions of support and resistance levels in stock prices. A **support level** is a value below which the market is relatively unlikely to fall. A **resistance level** is a value above which it is difficult to rise. Support and resistance levels are determined by the recent history of prices. In Figure 16.4, the price at point C would be viewed as a resistance level because the recent intermediate-trend high price was unable to rise above C. Hence, piercing the resistance

Figure 16.3 Dow Jones Industrial Average, January–November 1988.

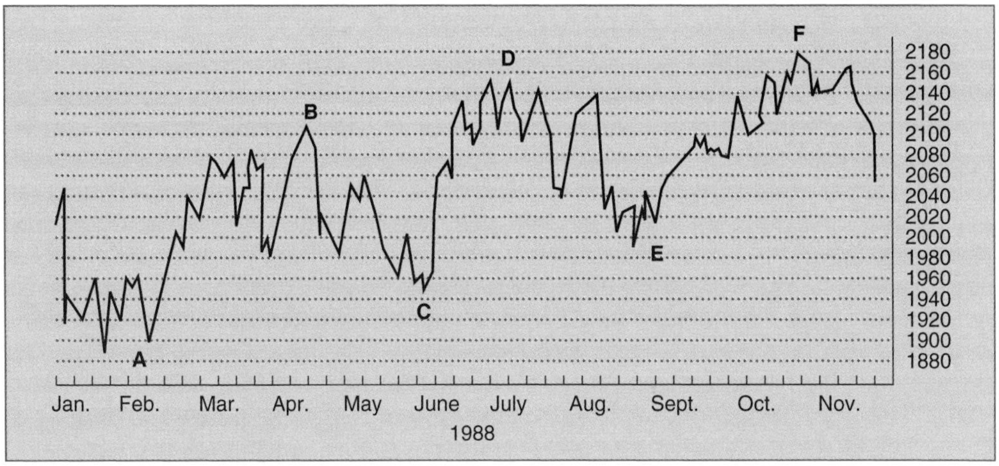

Note: During 1988 the DJIA was bullish as points B, D, and F and points A, C, and E were a series of higher highs and higher lows, respectively.

Source: Melanie F. Bowman and Thom Hartle, "Dow Theory," *Technical Analysis of Stocks and Commodities,* September 1990, p. 690. Reprinted by permission.

CONCEPT CHECK

1. Describe how technicians might explain support levels.

point is a bullish signal. The fact that the transportation index also pierces its resistance level at point D confirms the bull market signal.

Technicians see resistance and support levels as resulting from common psychological investor traits. Consider, for example, stock XYZ, which traded for several months at a price of $72 and then declined to $65. If the stock eventually begins to increase in price, $72 is a natural resistance level because the many investors who bought originally at $72 will be eager to sell their shares as soon as they can break even on their investment. Whenever prices near $72, a wave of selling pressure will develop. Such activity imparts to the market a type of "memory" that allows past price history to influence current stock prospects.

At point G, the DJIA fails to move to a higher high when the DJTA reaches a higher high at point H. This contradictory signal, called a *nonconfirmation,* is a warning sign. At points I and J, both indices fall below the low points of the previous trading range, which is taken as a signal of the end of the primary bull market.

In evaluating the Dow theory, don't forget the lessons of the efficient market hypothesis. The Dow theory is based on a notion of predictably recurring price patterns. Yet the EMH holds that if any pattern is exploitable, many investors would attempt to profit from such predictability, which would ultimately move stock prices and cause the trading strategy to self-destruct. While Figure 16.3 certainly appears to describe a classic upward primary trend, one always must wonder whether we can see that trend only *after* the fact. Recognizing patterns as they emerge is far more difficult.

Recent variations on the Dow theory are the Elliott wave theory and the theory of Kondratieff waves. Like the Dow theory, the idea behind Elliott waves is that stock prices can be described by a set of wave patterns. Long-term and short-term wave cycles are superimposed and result in a complicated pattern of price movements, but by interpreting the cycles, one can, according to

Figure 16.4 Dow theory signals—confirmation simulation.

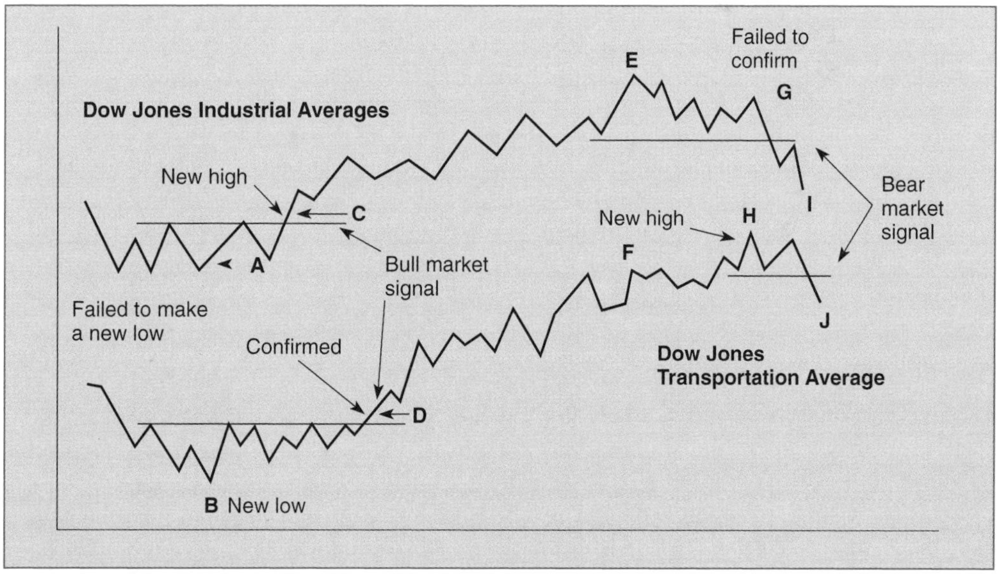

Note: A simulated example of confirmation and nonconfirmation by the DJIA and the DJTA.

Source: Melanie F. Bowman and Thomas Hartle, "Dow Theory," *Technical Analysis of Stocks and Commodities,* September 1990, p. 690. Reprinted by permission.

the theory, predict broad movements. Similarly, Kondratieff waves are named after a Russian economist who asserted that the macroeconomy (and therefore the stock market) moves in broad waves lasting between 48 and 60 years. The Kondratieff waves are therefore analogous to Dow's primary trend, although they are of far longer duration. Kondratieff's assertion is hard to evaluate empirically, however, because cycles that last about 50 years provide only two full data points per century, which is hardly enough data to test the predictive power of the theory.

Other Charting Techniques

The Dow theory posits a particular, and fairly simple, type of pattern in stock market prices: long-lasting trends with short-run deviations around those trends. Not surprisingly, several more involved patterns have been identified in stock market prices. Figure 16.5 illustrates several of these patterns. If stock prices actually follow any of these patterns, profit opportunities result. The patterns are reasonably straightforward to discern, meaning future prices can be extrapolated from current prices.

A variant on pure trend analysis is the **point and figure chart** depicted in Figure 16.6. This figure has no time dimension. It simply traces significant upward or downward moves in stock prices without regard to their timing. The data for Figure 16.6 come from Table 16.1.

Suppose, as in Table 16.1, that a stock's price is currently $40. If the price rises by at least $2, you put an X in the first column at $42 in Figure 16.5. Another increase of at least $2 calls for placement of another X in the first column, this time at the $44 level. If the stock then falls by at least $2, you start a new column and put an O next to $42. Each subsequent $2 price fall results

Table 16.1 Stock Price History

Date	Price	Date	Price
January 2	40	February 1	40*
January 3	$40\frac{1}{2}$	February 2	41
January 4	41	February 5	$40\frac{1}{2}$
January 5	42*	February 6	42*
January 8	$41\frac{1}{2}$	February 7	45*
January 9	$42\frac{1}{2}$	February 8	$44\frac{1}{2}$
January 10	43	February 9	46*
January 11	$43\frac{3}{4}$	February 12	47
January 12	44*	February 13	48*
January 15	45	February 14	$47\frac{1}{2}$
January 16	44	February 15	46†
January 17	$41\frac{1}{2}$†	February 16	45
January 18	41	February 19	44*
January 19	40*	February 20	42*
January 22	39	February 21	41
January 23	$39\frac{1}{2}$	February 22	40*
January 24	$39\frac{3}{4}$	February 23	41
January 25	38*	February 26	$40\frac{1}{2}$
January 26	35*	February 27	38*
January 29	36	February 28	39
January 30	37†	March 1	36*
January 31	39*	March 2	34*

Figure 16.5 Chart representation of market bottoms and tops.

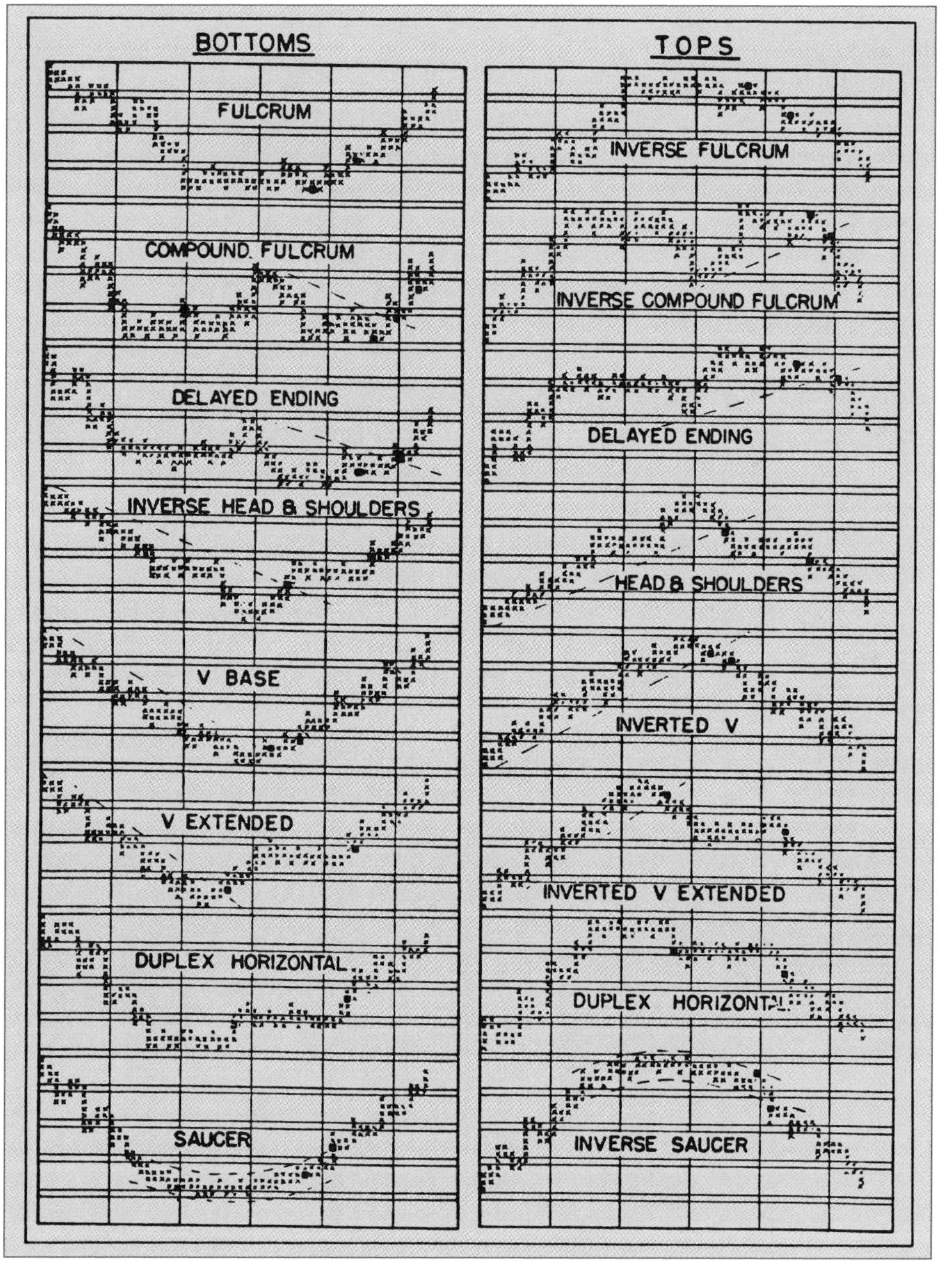

Source: Irwin Shishko, "Techniques of Forecasting Commodity Prices," *Commodity Yearbook* (New York: Commodity Research Bureau, 1965), p. 4. Reprinted by permission.

in another O in the second column. When prices reverse yet again and head upward, you begin the third column with an X denoting each consecutive $2 price increase.

The asterisks in Table 16.1 mark an event resulting in the placement of a new X or O in the chart. The daggers denote price movements that result in the start of a new column of Xs or Os.

CONCEPT CHECK

2. Draw a point and figure chart using the history in Table 16.1 with price increments of $3.

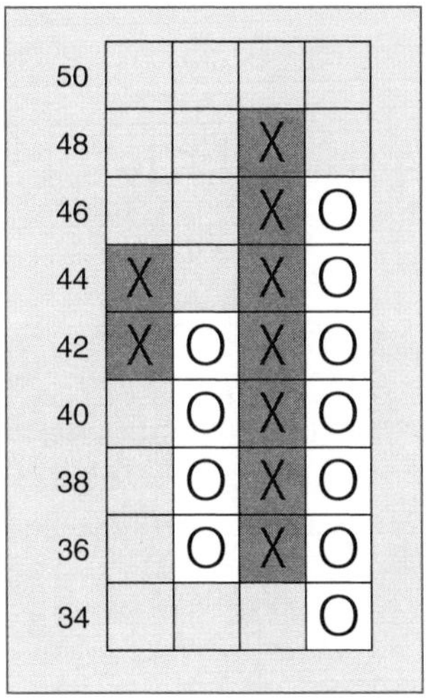

Figure 16.6 **Point and figure chart for Table 16.1.**

Sell signals are generated when the stock price *penetrates* previous lows, and buy signals occur when previous high prices are penetrated. A *congestion area* is a horizontal band of Xs and Os created by several price reversals. These three regions are indicated in Figure 16.7.

One can devise point and figure charts using price increments other than $2, but it is customary in setting up a chart to require reasonably substantial price changes before marking pluses or minuses.

Another graphical technique used to summarize price data and aid in the identification of trends is the so-called **candlestick chart**, illustrated in Figure 16.8. The box with the vertical line

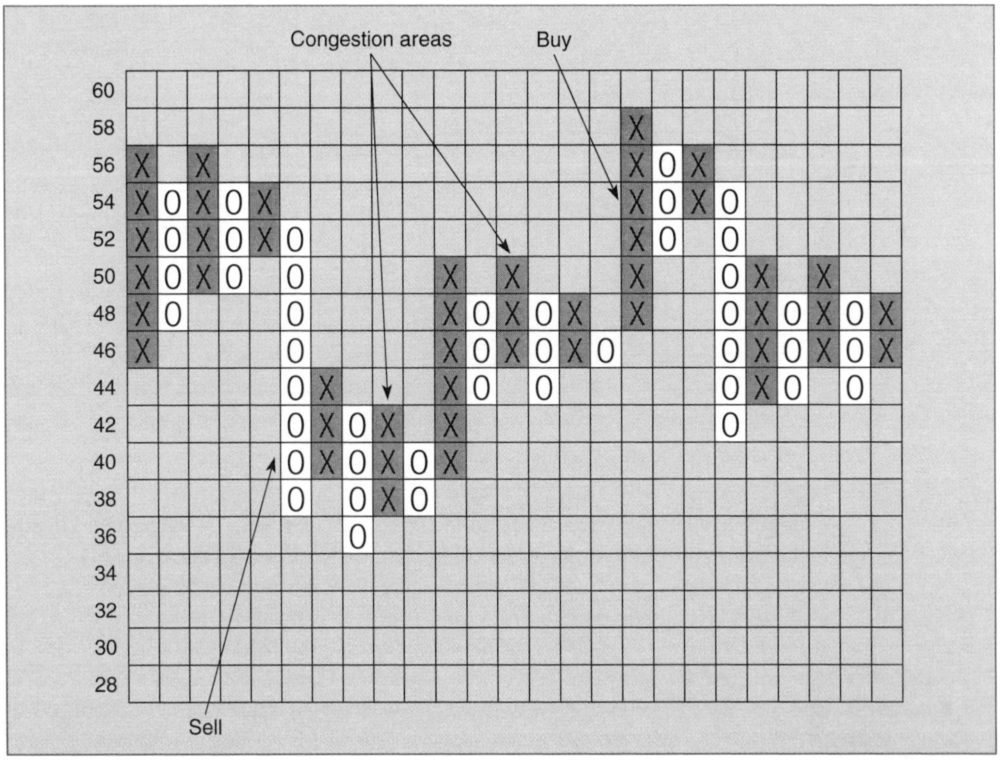

Figure 16.7 **Point and figure chart with sell signal, buy signal, and congestion areas.**

Figure 16.8
Candlestick chart.

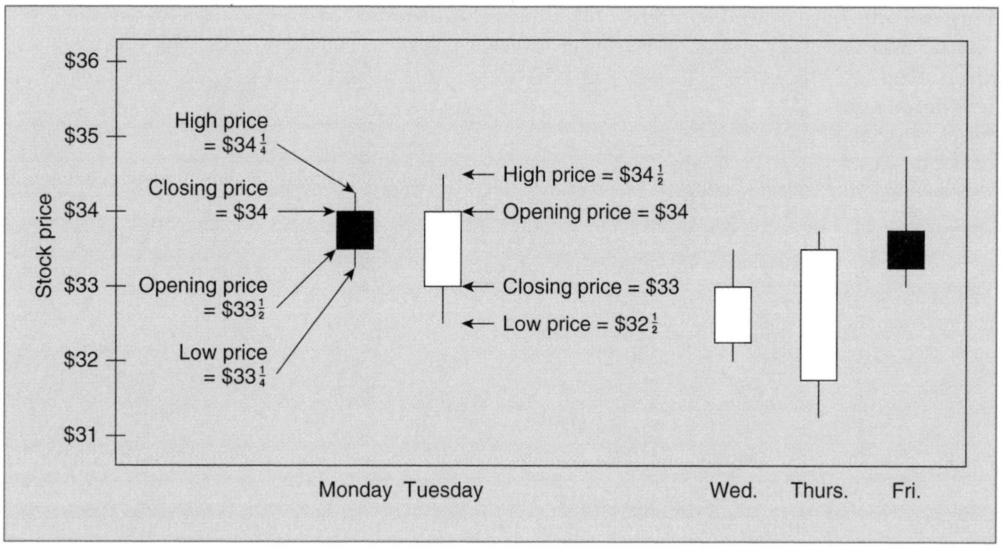

drawn through it allows the chartist to ascertain the open and close price for the day, as well as the high and low price. The top and bottom of each vertical line represent the high and low price, respectively. If the price increases during the day (e.g., Monday in Figure 16.8), the box is shaded, so the analyst knows that the closing price is at the top of the box and the opening price is at the bottom. If the box is left unshaded (e.g., Tuesday), the stock price is understood to have fallen, and the closing price is at the bottom of the box. The vertical lines extend from the daily high to the daily low price. The chart thus conveys a considerable amount of information about recent price history. Obviously, candlestick charts can be drawn using either shorter or longer time periods than one-day returns, for example, using intraday or weekly prices.

A Warning

The search for patterns in stock market prices is nearly irresistible, and the ability of the human eye to discern apparent patterns is remarkable. Unfortunately, it is possible to perceive patterns that really don't exist. Consider Figure 16.9, which presents simulated and actual values of the Dow Jones Industrial Average during 1956 taken from a famous study by Harry Roberts.[2] In panel B, it appears as though the market presents a classic head-and-shoulders pattern where the middle hump (the head) is flanked by two shoulders. When the price index "pierces the right shoulder"—a technical trigger point—it is believed to be heading lower, and it is time to sell your stocks. Panel A also looks like a "typical" stock market pattern. Can you tell which of the two graphs is constructed from the real value of the Dow and which from the simulated data? Panel A is based on the real data. The graph in B was generated using "returns" created by a random number generator. These returns *by construction* were patternless, but the simulated price path that is plotted appears to follow a pattern much like that of A.

Figure 16.10 shows the weekly price changes behind the two panels in Figure 16.9. Here the randomness in both series—the stock price as well as the simulated sequence—is obvious.

A problem related to the tendency to perceive patterns where they don't exist is data mining. After the fact, you can always find patterns and trading rules that would have generated enormous

---

[2]Harry Roberts, "Stock Market 'Patterns' and Financial Analysis: Methodological Suggestions," *Journal of Finance* 14 (March 1959), pp. 701–717.

Figure 16.9 Actual and simulated levels for stock market prices of 52 weeks.

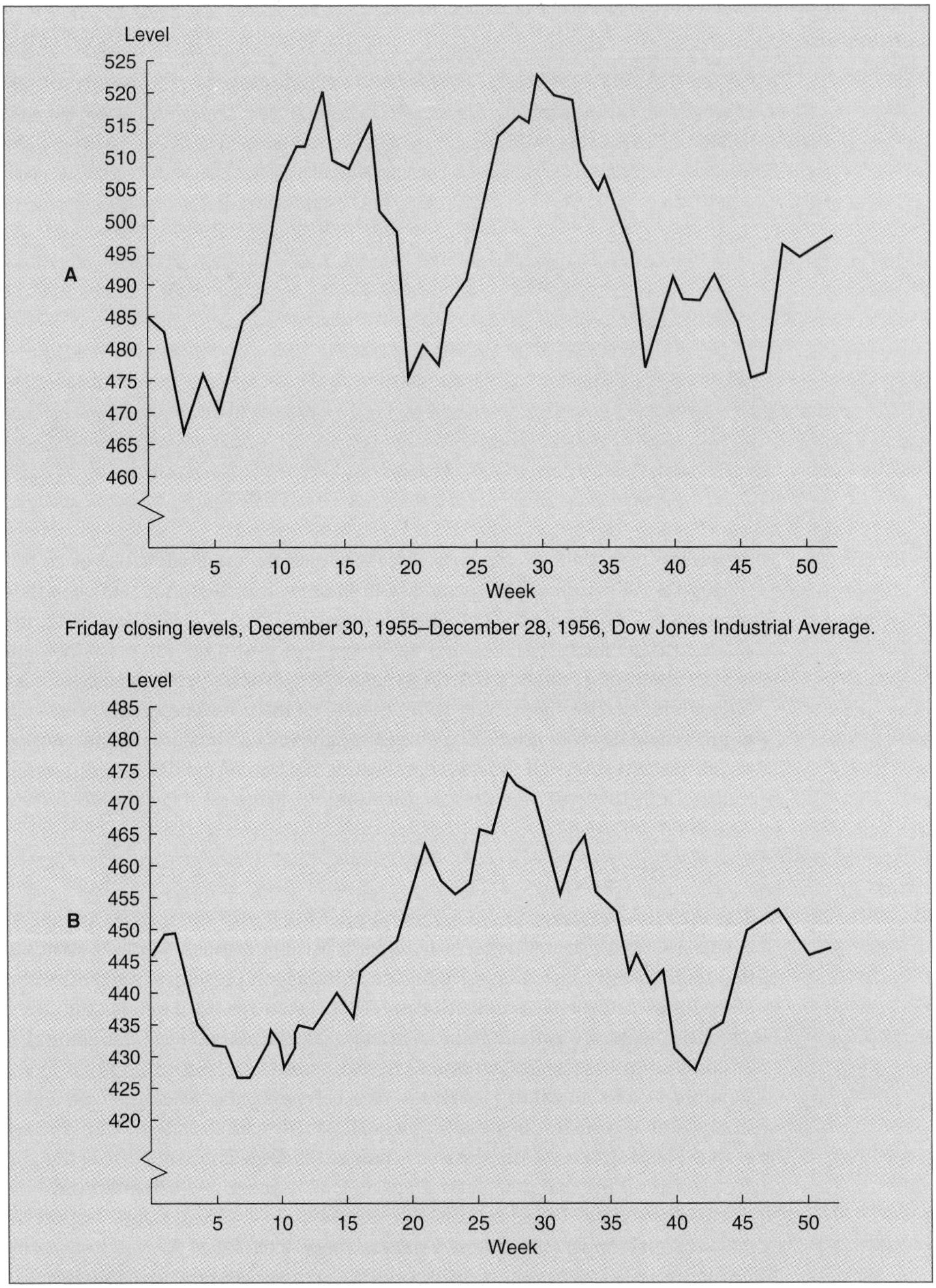

Source: Harry Roberts, "Stock Market 'Patterns' and Financial Analysis: Methodological Suggestions," *Journal of Finance*, March 1959, pp. 5–6. Reprinted by permission.

profits. If you test enough rules, some will have worked in the past. Unfortunately, picking a theory that would have worked after the fact carries no guarantee of future success.

In this regard, consider a curious investment rule that has worked with uncanny precision since 1967. In years that an original National Football League team wins the Superbowl

Figure 16.10 Actual and simulated changes in weekly stock prices for 52 weeks.

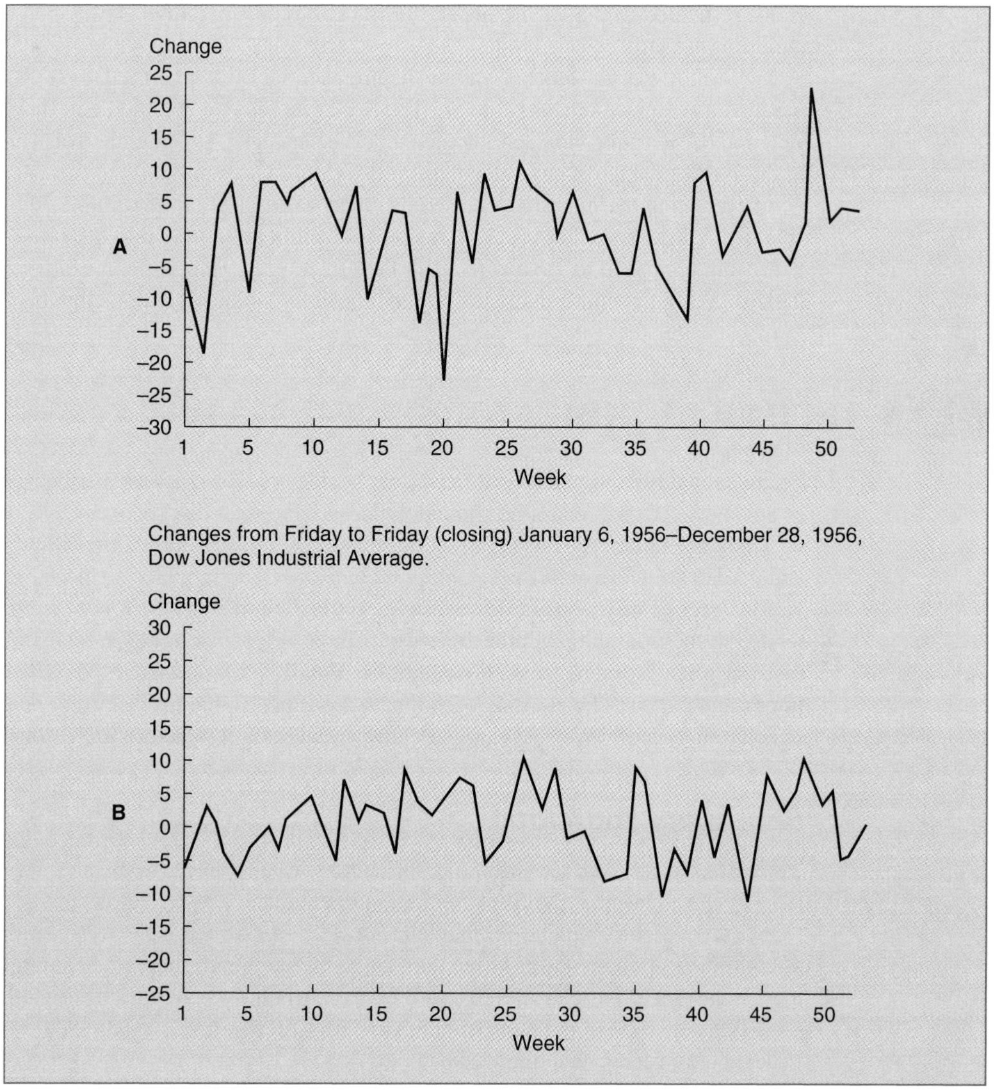

Source: Harry Roberts, "Stock Market 'Patterns' and Financial Analysis: Methodological Suggestions," *Journal of Finance,* March 1959, pp. 5–6. Reprinted by permission.

www.nyse.com

(played in January), bet on the stock market rising for the rest of the year. In years that a team from the American Football Conference that was not originally an NFL team wins, bet on a market decline. Between 1967 and 1990, the NYSE index rose in the year following the Superbowl 15 of the 17 times that an NFC or original NFL team won. The market fell in six out of seven years that an AFC team won.

Besides the Superbowl rule, there is another indicator with more credible economic rationale behind it, based on the presidential cycle. Statistically, it has been amply verified that the stock market performs significantly worse in the second year of the U.S. president's term and better in the third year. It is explained that government economic policy is manipulated to deliver bitter and necessary medicine early in the term to effect improvements later. In the third year, policy is eased to suggest that a healthy economy has resulted from good administration. The market apparently responds in kind. Surprisingly, there is evidence that the phenomenon is not restricted to the U.S. market, but is visible in most other developed markets, obviously including Canada's.

In 1998, it was the second year of the presidential cycle and the Denver Broncos won the Superbowl, two strong omens of doom. The S&P 500 rose by 26.7 percent. In 1999, it was the third year and the Broncos won again to give conflicting signs. Despite the overwhelming past success of these rules, which if any would you follow?

In evaluating trading rules, you should always ask whether the rule would have seemed reasonable *before* you looked at the data. If not, you might be buying into the one arbitrary rule among many that happened to have worked in the recent past. The hard but crucial question is whether there is reason to believe that what worked in the past should continue to work in the future.

16.3 TECHNICAL INDICATORS

Technical analysts use technical indicators besides charts to assess prospects for market declines or advances. We will examine some popular indicators in this section.

There are three types of technical indicators: sentiment indicators, flow of funds indicators, and market structure indicators. *Sentiment indicators* are intended to measure the expectations of various groups of investors, for example, mutual fund issues. *Flow of funds* indicators are intended to measure the potential for various investor groups to buy or sell stocks in order to predict the price pressure from those actions. Finally, *market structure indicators* monitor price trends and cycles. The charting techniques described in the last section are examples of market structure indicators. We will examine a few more market structure indicators in this section.

Sentiment Indicators

Trin Statistic Market volume is sometimes used to measure the strength of a market rise or fall. Increased investor participation in a market advance or retreat is viewed as a measure of the significance of the moment. Technicians consider market advances to be a more favourable omen of continued price increases when they are associated with increased trading volume. Similarly, market reversals are considered more bearish when associated with higher volume. The **trin statistic** is the ratio of the number of advancing to declining issues divided by the ratio of volume in advancing versus declining issues:

$$\text{Trin} = \frac{\text{Number advancing/Number declining}}{\text{Volume advancing/Volume declining}}$$

This expression can be rearranged as

$$\text{Trin} = \frac{\text{Volume declining/Number declining}}{\text{Volume advancing/Number advancing}}$$

Therefore, trin is the ratio of average volume in declining issues to average volume in advancing issues. Ratios above 1.0 are considered bearish because the falling stocks would then have higher average volume than the advancing stocks, indicating net selling pressure. Trin can be calculated from data in the *Financial Post* reports of the market diary section, as in Figure 16.13.

Note, however, for every buyer, there must a seller of stock. Rising volume in a rising market should not necessarily indicate a larger imbalance of buyers versus sellers. For example, a trin statistic above 1.0, which is considered bearish, could equally well be interpreted as indicating that there is more *buying* activity in declining issues.

Odd-Lot Trading Just as short-sellers tend to be larger institutional traders, odd-lot traders are almost always small individual traders. (An odd lot is a transaction of fewer than 100 shares; 100 shares is one board lot.) The **odd-lot theory** holds that these small investors tend to miss key market turning points, typically buying stock after a bull market has already run its course and selling too late into a bear market. Therefore, the theory suggests that when odd-lot traders are widely buying, you should sell, and vice versa.

The Wall Street Journal publishes odd-lot trading data every day. You can construct an index of odd-lot trading by computing the ratio of odd-lot purchases to sales. A ratio substantially above 1.0 is bearish because it implies small traders are net buyers.

www.barrons.com

Confidence Index *Barron's* computes a confidence index using data from the bond market. The presumption is that actions of bond traders reveal trends that will emerge soon in the stock market.

The **confidence index** is the ratio of the average yield on 10 top-rated corporate bonds divided by the average yield on 10 intermediate-grade corporate bonds. The ratio will always be below 100 percent because higher-rated bonds will offer lower promised yields to maturity. When bond trades are optimistic about the economy, however, they might require smaller default premiums on lower-rated debt. Hence, the yield spread will narrow, and the confidence index will approach 100 percent. Therefore, higher values of the confidence index are bullish signals.

CONCEPT CHECK

3. Yields on lower-rated debt will rise after fears of recession have spread through the economy. This will reduce the confidence index. Should the stock market now be expected to fall or will it already have fallen?

Put/Call Ratio Call options give investors the right to buy a stock at a fixed "exercise" price and therefore are a way of betting on stock price increases. Put options give the right to sell a stock at a fixed price and therefore are a way of betting on stock price decreases.[3] The ratio of outstanding put options to outstanding call options is called the **put/call ratio**. Typically, the put/call ratio hovers around 65 percent. Because put options do well in falling markets while call options do well in rising markets, deviations of the ratio from historical norms are considered to be a signal of market sentiment and therefore predictive of market movements.

Interestingly, however, a change in the ratio can be given a bullish or a bearish interpretation. Many technicians see an increase in the ratio as bearish, as it indicates growing interest in put options as a hedge against market declines. Thus, a rising ratio is taken as a sign of broad investor pessimism and a coming market decline. Contrarian investors, however, believe that a good time to buy is when the rest of the market is bearish because stock prices are then unduly depressed. Therefore, they would take an increase in the put/call ratio as a signal of a buy opportunity.

Mutual Fund Cash Positions Technical traders view mutual fund investors as being poor market timers. Specifically, the belief is that mutual fund investors become more bullish after a market advance has already run its course. In this view, investor optimism peaks as the market is nearing its peak. Given the belief that the consensus opinion is incorrect at market turning points, a technical trader will use an indicator of market sentiment to form a contrary trading strategy. The percentage of cash held in mutual fund portfolios is one common measure of sentiment. This percentage is viewed as moving in the opposite direction of the stock market, since funds will tend to hold high cash positions when they are concerned about a falling market and the threat that investors will redeem shares.

[3] Puts and calls are defined in Chapter 2, Section 2.5.

Flow of Funds

Short Interest **Short interest** is the total number of shares of stock currently sold short in the market. Some technicians interpret high levels of short interest as bullish, some as bearish. The bullish perspective is that, because all short sales must be covered (i.e., short-sellers eventually must purchase shares to return the ones they have borrowed), short interest represents latent future demand for the stocks. As short sales are covered, the demand created by the share purchase will force prices up.

The bearish interpretation of short interest is based on the fact that short-sellers tend to be larger, more sophisticated investors. Accordingly, increased short interest reflects bearish sentiment by those investors "in the know," which would be a negative signal of the market's prospects.

Credit Balances in Brokerage Accounts Investors with brokerage accounts will often leave credit balances in those accounts when they plan to invest in the near future. Thus, credit balances may be viewed as measuring the potential for new stock purchases. As a result, a buildup of balances is viewed as a bullish indicator for the market.

Market Structure

Moving Averages The **moving average** of a stock index is the average level of the index over a given interval of time. For example, a 52-week moving average tracks the average index value over the most recent 52 weeks. Each week, the moving average is recomputed by dropping the oldest observation and adding the latest. After a period in which prices have generally been falling, the moving average will be above the current price (because the moving average "averages in" the older and higher prices). When prices have been rising, the moving average will be below the current price.

When the market price breaks through the moving average line from below, it is taken as a bullish signal because it signifies a shift from a falling trend (with prices below the moving average) to a rising trend (with prices above the moving average). Conversely, when prices fall below the moving average, it's considered time to sell.

There is some variation in the length of the moving average considered most predictive of market movements. Two popular measures are 200-day and 50-day moving averages. When the shorter moving average breaks through the longer one, this is a stronger signal than the original price action. Thus, if the 50-day moving average crosses the 200-day moving average from below, it's a buy signal.

Consider the price data in Table 16.2. Each observation represents the closing level of the S&P/TSX Composite on the last trading day of the week. The five-week moving average for

Table 16.2
Price Data

Week	TSX	5-Week Moving Average	Week	TSX	5-Week Moving Average
1	6,290		11	6,590	6,555
2	6,380		12	6,652	6,586
3	6,399		13	6,625	6,598
4	6,379		14	6,657	6,624
5	6,450	6,380	15	6,699	6,645
6	6,513	6,424	16	6,647	6,656
7	6,500	6,448	17	6,610	6,648
8	6,565	6,481	18	6,595	6,642
9	6,524	6,510	19	6,499	6,610
10	6,597	6,540	20	6,466	6,563

each week is the average of the index over the previous five weeks. For example, the first entry, for week 5, is the average of the index value between weeks 1 and 5: 6,290, 6,380, 6,399, 6,379, and 6,450. The next entry is the average of the index values between weeks 2 and 6, and so on.

Figure 16.11 plots the level of the index and the five-week moving average. Notice that while the index itself moves up and down rather abruptly, the moving average is a relatively smooth series, since the impact of each week's price movement is averaged with that of the previous weeks. Week 16 is a bearish point according to the moving average rule. The price series crosses from above the moving average to below it, signifying the beginning of a downward trend in stock prices.

A study by Brock, Lakonishok, and LeBaron[4] actually supports the efficacy of moving-average strategies. They find that stock returns following buy signals from the moving-average rule are higher and less volatile than those after sell signals. However, a more recent paper by Ready,[5] which uses intraday price data, finds that the moving-average rule would not be able to provide profits in practice because of trading costs and the fact that stock prices would already have moved adversely by the time the trader could act on the signal.

Many online sources offer charting services, with a variety of associated charts based on the primary price charts. Volume analyses, price envelopes, and moving averages are all available as desired. Almost any time period can be graphed. Simple high-low-close and open charts are shown, or the candlesticks of Figure 16.8 are produced on demand. The scale can be modified to show logarithmic price, in order to produce a linear rather than exponential trend. Virtually any analysis is now available.

Online services will provide charts that can be tailored to suit individual preferences with popular indicators such as 50-day and 200-day moving averages, Bollinger bands, the stochastic, MACD, and volume. Moving averages, associated with the MACD, indicate the trend over shorter or longer periods. The MACD (moving average convergence-divergence) chart helps one to visualize the difference between and the change in two short-term moving averages; when the two are historically high and turning down, a change from a bullish to a bearish pattern emerges (and vice versa). Bollinger bands indicate a range within which the price trades, rather like a confidence interval. The bands bracket the trend, adding and subtracting from the average price an amount based on the recent volatility, measured by standard deviation. Chartists look at the stochastic as a sign of an overbought or oversold condition in the market trading; extreme high (low) levels are associated with local peaks (troughs) in the price, although both high and low levels can persist with the market continuing to rise (fall) while the stochastic is high (low).[6]

Figure 16.11 Moving averages.

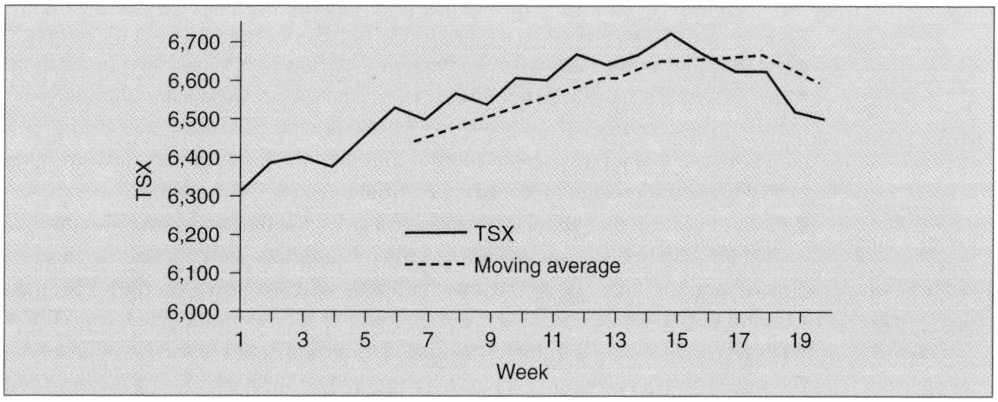

[4]William Brock, Josef Lakonishok, and Blake LeBaron, "Simple Technical Trading Rules and the Stochastic Properties of Stock Returns," *The Journal of Finance* 47 (December 1992), pp. 1731–1764.

[5]M. J. Ready, "Profits from Technical Trading Rules," University of Wisconsin working paper.

[6]We would have like to have given a sample chart, but the preferred source does not authorize reproduction.

Table 16.3
Market Breadth

Day	Advances	Declines	Net Advances	Cumulative Breadth
1	802	748	54	54
2	917	640	277	331
3	703	772	−69	262
4	512	1,122	−610	−348
5	633	1,004	−371	−719

Note: The sum of advances plus declines varies across days because some stock prices are unchanged.

Breadth The **breadth** of the market is a measure of the extent to which movement in a market index is reflected widely in the price movements of all the stocks in the market. The most common measure of breadth is the spread between the number of stocks that advance and decline in price. If advances outnumber declines by a wide margin, then the market is viewed as being stronger because the rally is widespread. These breadth numbers also are reported daily in *The Wall Street Journal.*

Some analysts cumulate breadth data each day as in Table 16.3. The cumulative breadth for each day is obtained by adding that day's net advances (or declines) to the previous day's total. The direction of the cumulated series is then used to discern broad market trends. Analysts might use a moving average of cumulative breadth to gauge broad trends.

Relative Strength **Relative strength** measures the extent to which a security has outperformed or underperformed either the market as a whole or its particular industry. Relative strength is computed by calculating the ratio of the price of the security to a price index for the industry. For example, the relative strength of Ford versus the auto industry would be measured by movements in the ratio of the price of Ford divided by the level of an auto industry index. A rising ratio implies Ford has been outperforming the rest of the industry. If relative strength can be assumed to persist over time, then this would be a signal to buy Ford.

www.ford.ca

Similarly, the relative strength of an industry relative to the whole market can be computed by tracking the ratio of the industry price index to the market price index.

Some evidence in support of the relative strength strategy is provided in a study by Jegadeesh and Titman (1993).[7] They ranked firms according to stock market performance in a six-month base period and then examined returns in various follow-up periods ranging from 1 to 36 months. They found that the best performers in the base period continued to outperform other stocks for several months. This pattern is consistent with the notion of persistent relative strength. Ultimately, however, the pattern reverses, with the best base-period performers giving up their initial superior returns. Figure 16.12 illustrates this pattern. The graph shows the cumulative difference in return between the 10 percent of the sample of stocks with the best base-period returns and the 10 percent with the worst base-period returns. Initially, the curve trends upward, indicating that the best performers continue to outperform the initial laggards. After about a year, however, the curve turns down, suggesting that abnormal returns on stocks with momentum are ultimately reversed.

The middle two columns of Table 16.4 present data on the levels of an auto industry index and a broad market index. Does the auto industry exhibit relative strength? That can be determined by examining the last column, showing the ratio of the two indices. Despite the fact that the auto industry as a whole has exhibited positive returns, reflected in the rising level of the industry index, the industry has *not* shown relative strength. The market ratio of the auto industry index to the market index shows that the auto industry has underperformed the broad market.

[7]Narasimham Jegadeesh and Sheridan Titman, "Returns to Buying Winners and Selling Losers: Implications for Stock Market Efficiency," *Journal of Finance* 48 (March 1993).

Figure 16.12 Cumulative difference in returns of previously best-performing and worst-performing stocks in subsequent months.

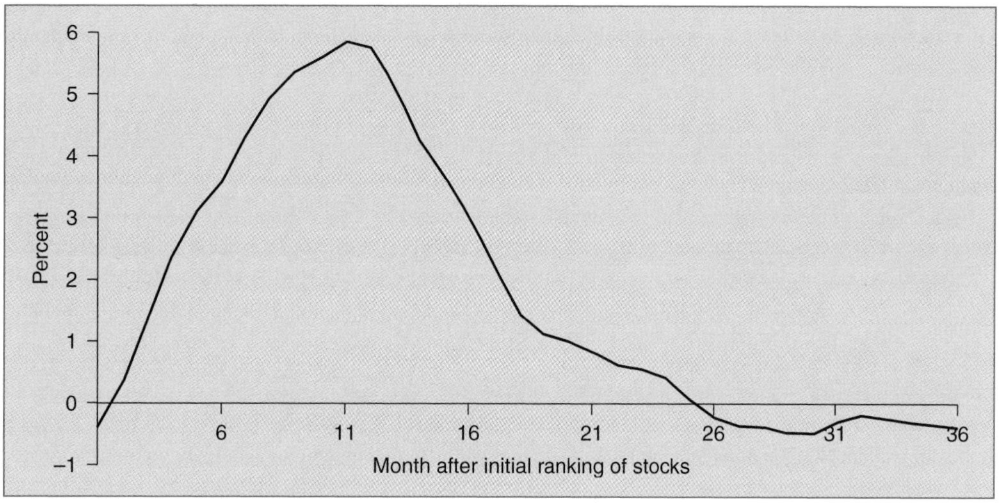

Source: Narasimham Jegadeesh and Sheridan Titman, "Returns to Buying Winners and Selling Losers: Implications for Stock Market Efficiency," *Journal of Finance* 48 (March 1993).

Table 16.4 Relative Strength Assessment

Week	Auto Industry	Market Index	Ratio
1	165.6	447.0	0.370
2	166.7	450.1	0.370
3	168.0	455.0	0.369
4	166.9	459.9	0.363
5	170.2	459.1	0.371
6	169.2	463.0	0.365
7	171.0	469.0	0.365
8	174.1	473.2	0.368
9	173.9	478.8	0.363
10	174.2	481.0	0.362

Some final thoughts on the practice of technical analysis are given in the boxed article that follows.

16.4 TECHNICAL ANALYSIS FOR CANADIAN INVESTORS

The subject of technical analysis followed in Canada can be dividend along macro and micro lines. Broadly, the market in Canada can be viewed as following that in the United States, as evidenced by the high degree of correlation between them. In response to this, a brokerage house can predict the direction of the market by performing technical analysis on the S&P 500 or by following the Dow theory. If market timing is the objective, then either an in-house analysis can be pursued or predictions can be obtained from U.S. affiliates or other sources.

At the level of the individual company, there is an important dichotomy. For those companies that are actively traded on the NYSE, such as Northern Telecom or Alcan, information is likely to be available from U.S. sources; the relevant price behaviour to follow is that on the NYSE, at least as much as that on the TSX. For smaller companies, however, Canadian investment advisors must perform their own technical analysis. This will be done using the same

THE MARKETS STILL DEFY TECHNICAL ANALYSIS

The stock market's recent wiggles and wobbles have many people rethinking their views. For example, not long ago Peter Bernstein, a sober and respected researcher and money manager, criticized buy-and-hold investing and said positive things about market timing. That was a shocker, so what's next, legitimate technical analysis?

Academics and others proponents of orthodox stock market theory say that technical analysis doesn't work. There is no incremental investment information in the behaviour of share prices, so no system that attempts to systematically exploit price behaviour will earn investors any money. Resistance levels, Bollinger Bands, moving averages, stochastics ... the whole bestiary of technical analysis greeblies are all worthless.

Followers of technical analysis disagree, of course. They point to traders that have made a great deal of money using technical analysis, and they say that it works for them. There are patterns in how stocks behave, and understanding those patterns can make you money.

Who Is Right?

In its purest form, efficient market theory says that all available public and private information is reflected in stock prices. In other words, research is useless because as quickly as new information comes out—whether changing stock prices, or information about markets and earnings—that data is assimilated into stocks. You can't make money from technical analysis (or fundamental analysis, for that matter) and you are wasting time trying. This has become known as the "strong" form of efficient market theory. And it doesn't work. For example, studies have shown disproportionate gains from tracking insider (executives, directors, etc.) buying behaviour. There is information out there that works, much of it private.

But violating strong-form efficiency doesn't mean that technical analysts get a free pass. If markets successfully assimilate all public information, from prices to earnings data, then we have what is called "semi-strong" efficiency. Academics tests of semi-strong efficiency have had much success. For example, repeated studies have shown that traditional technical analysis price patterns (e.g., head-and-shoulders, break-outs, etc.) don't work in any consistent, systematic way that can be tested repeatedly with data.

It is, of course, possible that markets are not even semi-strong efficient. This would be a full-employment act for technical analysts, and for pretty much anyone else who wanted to hang out a shingle and call themselves money managers. You could make money from everything from price patterns to earnings releases, and it would be happy days indeed.

The problem is, it is clearly not the case. We all know from our own experience, if not from many credible studies, that most money managers can't consistently make money; and left to our own devices we are no better, at least not consistently. So the market is efficient, it is just a question of how efficient it us. And that is the slim post where technical analysts hang their collective hats. The less sophisticated among them argue that simple patterns like candlesticks and so on work and can make money. More sophisticated technical analysts argue that simple charts and models are over-used, so they don't work, but more sophisticated models do make money.

Generally speaking, most work in the area shows that successful technical investors don't follow their own rules, and they lose money if they do. Instead, they seemingly use their indicators as guides, signposts along the way, and then make buy/sell decisions through some other process that has little do with what they say they are doing.

But these naive and ill-explained processes aside, is it possible that more sophisticated models can detect complex, systematic patterns in the market? Sure, and billions of dollars are being managed that way as I type these words. But those models are exceedingly costly, using a myriad of indicators, and require many PhDs skulking about at hot-houses in New York and Chicago. Their relationship to what passes for technical analysis in everyday chatter is akin to an aeronautics debate that mixes talk of jumbo jets with leaping off a cliff with paper taped to your arms.

So who is right? Strangely enough, it partly comes down to what people believe and how they act. To the extent that many people invest following technical analysis's charts and patterns, then some stocks will sometimes behave as if technical analysis works. So if technical analysts convert the rest of us to their creed, they win. But they haven't done that so far. And that leaves one twig left for technical analysts to grasp at. To the extent that market participants believe the market is highly efficient, and act accordingly, the market is likely somewhat inefficient and there will be opportunities to make money.

But most of the money in the market is invested as if markets aren't efficient. Mutual funds, technical analysts and others all think they can make money from public information. To the extent that the bulk of people believe the market is inefficient then, perversely enough, there is a darn good chance that the market is at least semi-strong efficient. It augurs ill for technical analysis.

Source: Paul Kedrosky, *National Post*, September 10, 2003, p. FP.19.

Figure 16.13 Market breadth.

MARKET DIARIES

	Volume 00s	Previous day 00s	Adv.	Adv. vol 00s	Dec.	Dec. vol 00s	Unch.	Issues traded	New highs	New lows
Toronto	2871480	2135798	700	1730789	599	1036788	198	1497	19	15
TSX Venture	506649	543343	390	238055	382	151055	335	1107	7	24
New York	14478236	13688706	2270	10251363	1057	3985067	137	3464	81	18
American	615534	597354	663	431140	295	167123	81	1039	27	11
Nasdaq	7585587	7380929	1666	4666815	1399	2554623	166	3231	73	21

Source: *Financial Post* (*National Post*), May 28, 2004, p. IN4. Reprinted by permission.

measures as are used in the United States, such as relative strength and charts displaying patterns and trends.

The information on Canadian stocks available to investors is somewhat more limited. Brokers may have displayed on their screens the technical indicators such as the trin and tick for the NYSE; more recently, trin and tick have also been available for TSX stocks. This will enable traders (if they so believe) to speculate on short-run movements in the market, for either Canadian or U.S. securities. Other U.S. indicators like odd-lot trading and the confidence index are not computed, although short interest figures are available.

www.canoe.ca

The Financial Post gives a daily report of market breadth for Canadian markets as well as the three major U.S. markets, as illustrated in Figure 16.13. Investors can also consult the *Graphoscope,* available by subscription or at libraries. This document presents charts on Canadian stocks, commodities, indices, and foreign markets and currencies, giving the advance-decline line and the moving average. The *Independent Survey Co.* gives similar information, including relative strength.

Printed sources of charts are probably becoming obsolete with the availability of online data sources through the Internet. A variety of charts can be called up, either free of charge or as part of a complete investing advisory service. Any online trading system will enable traders to call up charts and other technical analyses as well as fundamental data. The charts allow the viewer to choose periods from intraday and monthly to five or more years of history. They also will permit superposition of comparable stocks or of one or more moving averages, and may have linear or logarithmic scales for the price or return. A list of these sources would include www.canada.bigcharts.com, www.quicken.com, and www.investor.msn.com.

One area where academics are less inclined to reject technical analysis is in commodity trading. For whatever reasons, chart patterns seem to offer information about future prices.[8] In Figure 16.14, the chart pattern for the relative performance of the TSX gold index versus gold illustrates how the analysis may be applied.

16.5 THE VALUE LINE SYSTEM

The Value Line ranking system may be the most celebrated and well-documented example of successful stock analysis. Value Line is the largest investment advisory service in the world. Besides publishing the *Value Line Investment Survey,* which provides information on investment fundamentals for approximately 1,700 publicly traded companies, Value Line also ranks each of these stocks according to their anticipated price appreciation over the next 12 months. Stocks ranked in group 1 are expected to perform the best, while those in group 5 are expected to perform the worst. Value Line calls this "ranking for timeliness."

[8]See, for example, Stephen J. Taylor, "Trading Futures Using a Channel Rule," *Journal of Futures Markets* 14, no. 2 (April 1994), pp. 215–236.

Figure 16.14 TSX gold index versus gold (daily relative performance).

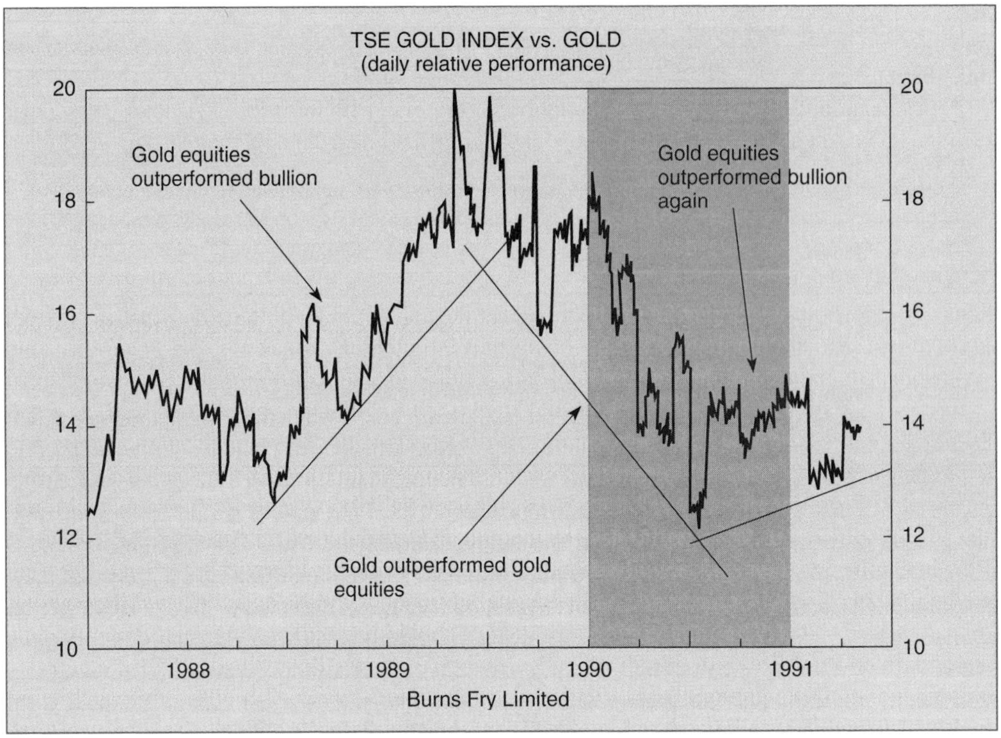

Source: Burns Fry Investment Research, *Gold Chart Book,* December 1991. Reprinted by permission of Nesbitt Burns Fry Ltd.

Figure 16.15 shows the performance of the Value Line ranking system over the 25 years from 1965 to March 1990. Over the total period, the different groups performed just as the rankings would predict, and the differences were quite large. The total 25-year price appreciation for the group 1 stocks was 3,083 percent (or 14.8 percent per year) compared to 15 percent (or 0.5 percent per year) for group 5.

How does the Value Line ranking system work? As Bernhard[9] explains, the ranking procedure has three components: (1) relative earnings momentum, (2) earnings surprise, and (3) a value index. Most (though not all) of the Value Line criteria are technically oriented, relying on either price momentum or relative strength. Points assigned for each factor determine the stock's overall ranking.

The relative earnings momentum factor is calculated as each company's year-to-year change in quarterly earnings divided by the average change for all stocks.

The earnings surprise factor has to do with the difference between actual reported quarterly earnings and Value Line's estimate. The points assigned to each stock increase with the percentage difference between reported and estimated earnings.

The value index is calculated from the following regression equation:

$$V = a + b_1x_1 + b_2x_2 + b_3x_3$$

whee

x_1 = A score from 1 to 10 depending on the relative earnings momentum ranking, compared with the company's rank for the last 10 years

x_2 = A score from 1 to 10 based on the stock's relative price, with ratios calculated in a similar way to the earnings ratio

[9]Arnold Bernhard, *Value Line Methods of Evaluating Common Stocks* (New York: Arnold Bernhard and Co., 1979).

Figure 16.15 Record of Value Line ranking for timeliness (without allowing for changes in rank, 1965–1990).

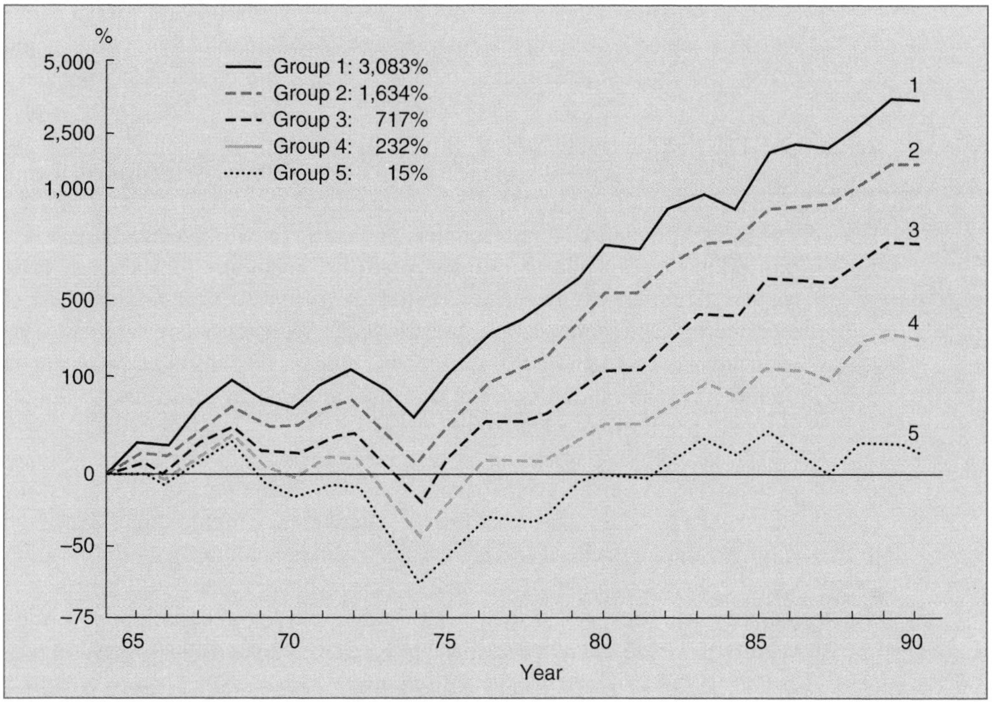

Source: *Value Line Selection & Opinion,* April 20, 1990. Reprinted by permission.

x_3 = The ratio of the stock's latest 10-week average relative price (stock price divided by the average price for all stocks) to its 52-week average relative price

and a, b_1, b_2, and b_3 are the coefficients from the regression estimated on 12 years of data.

Finally, the points for each of the three factors are added, and the stocks are classified into five groups according to the total score.

Investing according to this system does seem to produce superior results on paper, as Figure 16.15 shows. Yet inclusion of transactions costs and implementation of a trading strategy using market prices lead to a drastic reduction in profits.

16.6 CAN TECHNICAL ANALYSIS WORK IN EFFICIENT MARKETS?

Self-Destructing Patterns

It should be abundantly clear from our presentation that most of technical analysis is based on ideas totally at odds with the foundations of the efficient market hypothesis. The EMH follows from the idea that rational profit-seeking investors will act on new information so quickly that prices will nearly always reflect all publicly available information. Technical analysis, on the other hand, posits the existence of long-lived trends that play out slowly and predictably. Such patterns, if they exist, would violate the EMH notion of essentially unpredictable stock price changes.

An interesting question is whether a technical rule that seems to work will continue to work in the future once it becomes widely recognized. A clever analyst may occasionally uncover a profitable trading rule, but the real test of efficient markets is whether the rule itself becomes reflected in stock prices once its value is discovered.

Suppose, for example, the Dow theory predicts an upward primary trend. If the theory is widely accepted, it follows that many investors will attempt to buy stocks immediately in anticipation of the price increase; the effect would be to bid up prices sharply and immediately rather than at the gradual, long-lived pace initially expected. The Dow theory's predicted trend would be replaced by a sharp jump in prices. It is in this sense that price patterns ought to be *self-destructing.* Once a useful technical rule (or price pattern) is discovered, it ought to be invalidated once the mass of traders attempts to exploit it.

For the prediction of a technical indicator to work, enough believers must trade correspondingly to bring about the anticipated price behaviour. In this sense, the trading rule may become self-fulfilling. If everyone were to believe, however, the necessary anticipation of the price movement would eliminate any potential gain. Technicians are happy to admit that they rely on enough believers to produce the effect, but enough skeptics to allow it to continue; alternatively, smaller investors can follow the rules, but institutional investors moving large blocks of stock are unable to profit from technical strategies.

The case of self-destruction for technical analysis requires that the techniques must be practicable by large numbers; if the analysis were available only to a few, then trading opportunities would exist for them. This would be the situation for a highly sophisticated technique such as the *chaos theory* approach. Chaos is the name given to nonlinear patterns in variables that are not observable by conventional (especially mean-variance) analysis. There are a few analysts with mathematical backgrounds who use this approach in forecasting prices. Additionally, the use of *neural networks*—advanced artificial intelligence programs that search for possible patterns—has become popular. There is not yet any reliable evidence on the success of these recent techniques.[10]

An instructive example is the evidence by Jegadeesh[11] and Lehmann[12] that stock prices seem to obey a reversal effect; specifically, the best-performing stocks in one week or month tend to fare poorly in the following period, while the worst performers follow up with good performance. Such a phenomenon can be used to form a straightforward technically based trading strategy: Buy shares that recently have done poorly and sell shares that recently have done well. Lehmann shows such a strategy would have been extremely profitable in the past. Lehmann notes that Rosenberg Institutional Equity Management and the College Retirement Equity Fund now use return reversal strategies in their actively managed portfolios. These activities presumably should eliminate existing profit opportunities by forcing prices to their "correct" levels.

On the other hand, Foerster, Prihar, and Schmitz[13] report evidence of testing for return persistence in Canadian equities. Identifying superior returns in previous quarters, they show that the top performing decile of the data set continues to outperform the market on a risk-adjusted basis. Both before and after transaction costs, a policy of investing in a portfolio of that top decile (revised quarterly) yields extremely high returns—approximately three times those of the TSX. The results of quarterly persistence in Canada appear to contradict the above-mentioned monthly reversals in the United States.[14] They find, however, that the bottom decile has quite average returns, which might indicate reversal for poor performers.

Under the area of market microstructure studies, Blume, Easley, and O'Hara[15] have investigated the importance of analyzing trading volume in determining the underlying pressure on

[10]For an analysis that notes some success and a warning, see Vijay Jog, Wojtek Michalowski, Atul Srivastava and Roland Thomas, "Are Artificial Neural Networks Worth Considering?" *Canadian Investment Review* XI, no. 2 (Spring 1998); also, L. Kryzanowski, M. Galler, and D. W. Wright, "Using Artificial Neural Networks to Pick Stocks," *Financial Analysts Journal* 49 (1993), pp. 21–27.

[11]Narasimhan Jegadeesh, "Evidence of Predictable Behavior of Security Prices," *Journal of Finance* 45 (September 1990), pp. 881–898.

[12]Bruce Lehmann, "Fads, Martingales and Market Efficiency," *Quarterly Journal of Economics* 105 (February 1990), pp. 1–28.

[13]Steven Foerster, Anoop Prihar, and John Schmitz, "Price Momentum Models and How They Beat the Canadian Equity Markets," *Canadian Investment Review* VII, no. 4 (Winter 1995), pp. 9–13.

[14]N. Jegadeesh and S. Titman, "Returns to Buying Winners and Selling Losers: Implications for Stock Market Efficiency," *The Journal of Finance* 48 (March 1993), pp. 65–91.

[15]Marshall Blume, David Easley, and Maureen O'Hara, "Market Statistics and Technical Analysis: The Role of Volume, " *The Journal of Finance* 49 (March 1994), pp. 153–182.

price. Increased volume is likely to be an indication of superior information possessed by some investors. This information as to the true equilibrium value of the stock will cause an increase in buying or selling by insiders. Uninformed investors must take account of the volume information in order to restore strong-form efficiency. Recognition of the volume may allow technical traders to trade and profit before the equilibrium value is identified.

Yet another study[16] offers conclusive evidence that even the simplest of technical trading strategies can be profitable, especially before transaction costs. The charting practices discussed earlier in the chapter, such as determining moving averages and price breakouts, were subjected to more sophisticated statistical analyses (including the GARCH technique) and shown to offer significantly better returns than trading on the basis of no technical signals. These effects are at odds with market efficiency and at the same time, consistent with the viability of technical analysis. The real test of these trading rules will come now that the potential of the strategies has been uncovered.

Thus, technical analysis is a continual search for profitable trading rules, followed by destruction by overuse of those rules found to be successful, followed by more search for yet-undiscovered rules.

A New View of Technical Analysis

Brown and Jennings[17] offer a rigorous foundation for the potential efficacy of technical analysis. They envision an economy where many investors have private information regarding the ultimate value of a stock. Moreover, as time passes, each investor acquires additional information. Each investor can infer something of the information possessed by other traders by observing the price at which securities trade. The entire sequence of past prices can turn out to be useful in the inference of the information held by other traders. In this sense, technical analysis can be useful to traders even if all traders rationally use all information available to them.

Most discussions of the EMH envision public information commonly available to all traders and ask only if prices reflect that information. In this sense, the Brown and Jennings framework is more complex. Here, different individuals receive different private signals regarding the value of a firm. As prices unfold, each trader infers the good-news or bad-news nature of the signals received by other traders and updates assessments of the firm accordingly. Prices *reveal* as well as *reflect* information and become useful data to traders. Without addressing specific technical trading rules, the Brown and Jennings model is an interesting and innovative attempt to reconcile technical analysis with the usual assumption of rational traders participating in efficient markets.

SUMMARY

1. Technical analysis is the search for recurring patterns in stock market prices. It is based essentially on the notion that market prices adjust slowly to new information and, thus, is at odds with the efficient market hypothesis.
2. The Dow theory is the earliest chart-based version of technical analysis. The theory posits the existence of primary, intermediate, and minor trends that can be identified on a chart and acted on by an analyst before the trends fully dissipate. Other trend-based theories are based on relative strength and the point and figures chart.
3. Technicians believe high volume and market breadth accompanying market trends add weight to the significance of a trend.
4. Odd-lot traders are viewed as uninformed, which suggests informed traders should pursue trading strategies in opposition to their activity. In contrast, short-sellers are viewed as informed traders, lending credence to their activity.
5. Relative strength measures performance of a stock against its industry or the market; anomalies based on momentum or reversals support or refute use of this measure.

[16]William Brock, Josef Lakonishok, and Blake LeBaron, "Simple Technical Trading Rules and the Stochastic Properties of Stock Returns," *The Journal of Finance* 47 (December 1992), pp. 1731–1764.

[17]David Brown and Robert H. Jennings, "On Technical Analysis," *Review of Financial Studies* 2 (1989), pp. 527–552.

6. Value Line's ranking system uses technically based data and has shown great ability to discriminate between stocks with good and poor prospects, but the Value Line mutual fund that uses this system most closely has been only a mediocre performer, suggesting that implementation of the Value Line timing system is difficult.
7. New theories of information dissemination in the market suggest there may be a role for the examination of past prices in formulating investment strategies. They do not, however, support the specific charting patterns currently relied on by technical analysts.

KEY TERMS

Dow theory 613
support level 614
resistance level 614
point and figure chart 616
candlestick shart 618
trin statistic 622
odd-lot theory 623
confidence index 623
put/call ratio 623
short interest 624
moving average 624
breadth 626
relative strength 626

SELECTED READINGS

A magazine devoted to technical analysis is:
Technical Analysis of Stocks and Commodities.
The Value Line method is described in:
Bernhard, Arnold. *Value Line Methods of Evaluating Common Stocks.* New York: Arnold Bernhard and Co., 1979.
For an extensive bibliography of technical analysis articles, see:
Spyros Skouras. "Technical Analysis Bibliography." Personal site, www.santafe.edu/~spyros/tabiblio.htm, 1998, accessed October 18, 2004.

PROBLEMS

1. Consider the graph of stock prices over a two-year period in Figure 16.16. Identify likely support and resistance levels.
2. Use the data from *The Financial Post* in Figure 16.13 to construct the trin ratio for the market. Is the trin ratio bullish or bearish?
3. Calculate market breadth using the same data as in problem 2. Is the signal bullish or bearish?

Figure 16.16 Simulated stock prices over time.

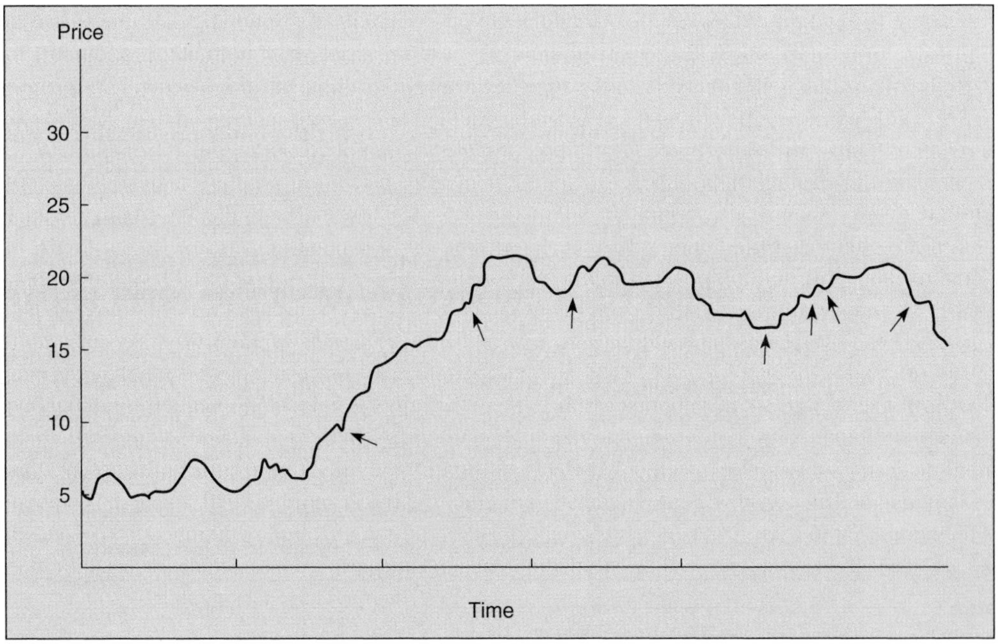

4. Collect data on the TSX 300 for a period covering a few months. Try to identify primary trends. Can you tell whether the market currently is in an upward or downward trend?
5. Go to CBSmarketwatch.com and obtain a chart for CA:XIU. Add 50- and 200-day moving averages, Bollinger bands, MACD, and slow stochastic. What direction would you predict for the XIU? (Assess your prediction one month later.)
6. The ratio of put to call options outstanding is viewed by some as a technical indicator. Do you think a high ratio is viewed as bullish or bearish? Should it be?
7. Table 16.5 presents price data for Computers, Inc. and a computer industry index. Does Computers, Inc. show relative strength over this period?
8. Use the data in Table 16.5 to compute a five-day moving average for Computers, Inc. Can you identify any buy or sell signals?
9. Construct a point and figure chart for Computers, Inc. using the data in Table 16.5. Use $2 increments for your chart. Do the buy or sell signals derived from your chart correspond to those derived from the moving-average rule (see problem 8)?
10. Table 16.6 contains data on market advances and declines. Calculate cumulative breadth and decide whether this technical signal is bullish or bearish.
11. If the trading volume in advancing shares on day 1 in the previous problem was 330 million shares, while the volume in declining issues was 240 million shares, what was the trin statistic for that day? Was trin bullish or bearish?
12. Yesterday, the S&P/TSX 60 gained 54 points. However, 580 issues declined in price while 436 advanced. Why might a technical analyst be concerned even though the market index rose on this day?
13. Baa-rated bonds currently yield 9 percent, while Aa-rated bonds yield 8 percent. Suppose that due to an increase in the expected inflation rate, the yields on both bonds increase, by 1 percent. What would happen to the confidence index? Would this be interpreted as bullish or bearish by a technical analyst? Does this make sense to you?
14. Using Figure 16.17 from *The Wall Street Journal*, determine whether market price movements and volume patterns were bullish or bearish around the following dates: September 17, November 5, and January 5. In each instance, compare your prediction to the subsequent behaviour of the DJIA in the following few weeks.
15. Is the confidence index rising or falling, given the following information?

	This Year (%)	Last Year (%)
Yield on top-rated corporate bonds	8	9
Yield on intermediate-grade corporate bonds	9	10

The following questions are adapted from the Canadian Securities Course.

CSI

16. Which of the following would represent a buy signal, using technical analysis?
    a. The stock's price breaks through the moving-average line from below on heavy volume.
    b. The stock's price breaks through the right shoulder, on heavy volume, on a bottom head-and-shoulders formation.
    c. A high short interest ratio.
    d. The total of odd-lot sales is high on a rally.
17. "A breakthrough above the neckline of an inverted head-and-shoulders formation is a buy signal." True or false?

Figure 16.17 **Dow Jones Industrial Average and market volume.**

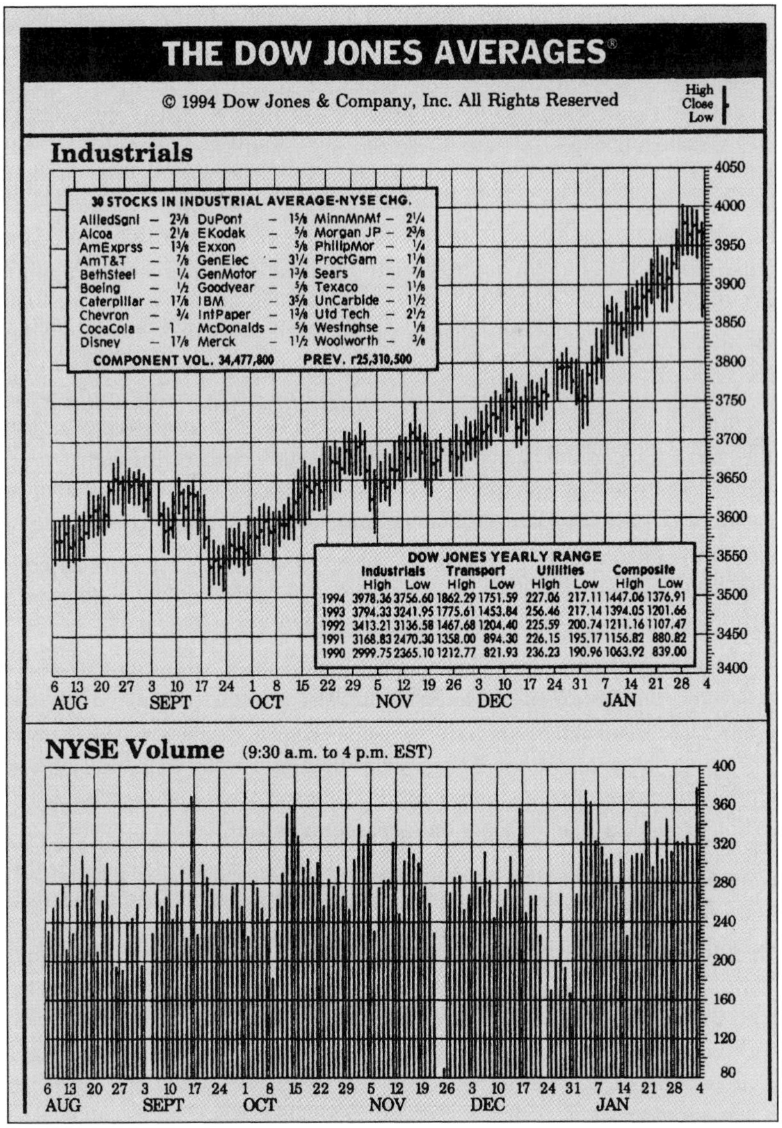

Source: *The Wall Street Journal*, February 7, 1994, p. C3. Reprinted by permission of Dow Jones & Company, Inc. via Copyright Clearance Center, Inc. 1994 Dow Jones & Company, Inc. All rights reserved worldwide.

Table 16.5 Computers, Inc. Stock Price History

Trading Day	Computers, Inc.	Industry Index
1	$19\frac{5}{8}$	50.0
2	20	50.1
3	$20\frac{1}{2}$	50.5
4	22	50.4
5	$21\frac{1}{8}$	51.0
6	22	50.7
7	$21\frac{7}{8}$	50.5
8	$22\frac{1}{2}$	51.1
9	$23\frac{1}{8}$	51.5
10	$23\frac{7}{8}$	51.7
11	$24\frac{1}{2}$	51.4
12	$23\frac{1}{4}$	51.7
13	$22\frac{1}{8}$	52.2
14	22	52.0
15	$20\frac{5}{8}$	53.1
16	$20\frac{1}{4}$	53.5
17	$19\frac{3}{4}$	53.9
18	$18\frac{3}{4}$	53.6
19	$17\frac{1}{2}$	52.9
20	19	53.4
21	$19\frac{5}{8}$	54.1
22	$21\frac{1}{2}$	54.0
23	22	53.9
24	$23\frac{1}{8}$	53.7
25	24	54.8
26	$25\frac{1}{4}$	54.5
27	$26\frac{1}{4}$	54.6
28	27	54.1
29	$27\frac{1}{2}$	54.2
30	28	54.8
31	$28\frac{1}{2}$	54.2
32	28	54.8
33	$27\frac{1}{2}$	54.9
34	29	55.2
35	$29\frac{1}{4}$	55.7
36	$29\frac{1}{2}$	56.1
37	30	56.7
38	$28\frac{1}{2}$	56.7
39	$27\frac{3}{4}$	56.5
40	28	56.1

Table 16.6 Market Advances and Declines

Day	Advances	Declines
1	906	704
2	653	986
3	721	789
4	503	968
5	497	1,095
6	970	702
7	1,002	609
8	903	722
9	850	748
10	766	766

PART SIX

DERIVATIVE ASSETS

17 Options and Other Derivatives: Introduction

18 Option Valuation

19 Futures and Forward Markets

CHAPTER SEVENTEEN

OPTIONS AND OTHER DERIVATIVES: INTRODUCTION

A relatively recent, but extremely important class of financial assets is derivative securities, or simply derivatives. These are securities whose prices are determined by, or "derive from," the prices of other securities. These assets also are called *contingent claims* because their payoffs are contingent on the prices of other securities.

Options and futures contracts are both derivative securities. We will see that their payoffs depend on the value of other securities. Swaps, which we discussed in Chapter 13, also are derivatives. Because the value of derivatives depends on the value of other securities, they can be powerful tools for both hedging and speculation. We will investigate these applications in the next three chapters, starting in this chapter with options.

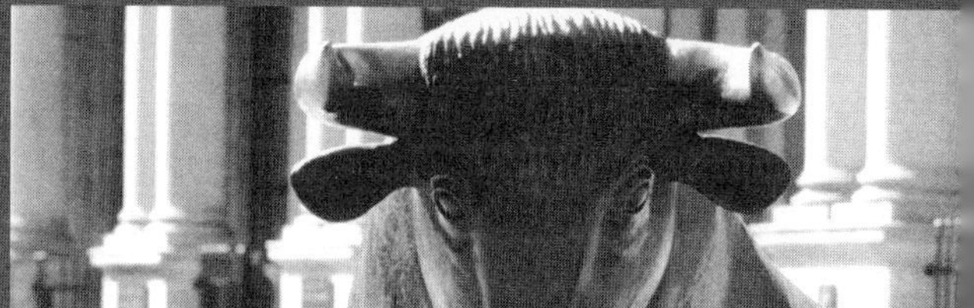

Trading of standardized options contracts on a national exchange started in the United States in 1973 when the Chicago Board Options Exchange (CBOE) began listing call options. These contracts were almost immediately a great success, crowding out the previously existing over-the-counter trading in stock options.

Options contracts are traded now on several U.S. exchanges. They are written on common stock, stock indices, foreign exchange, agricultural commodities, precious metals, and interest rate futures. In addition, the over-the-counter market also has enjoyed a tremendous resurgence in recent years as trading in custom-tailored options has exploded. Popular and potent tools in modifying portfolio characteristics, options have become essential tools a portfolio manager must understand.

In Canada, organized exchange trading of standardized option contracts began in 1975–1976 in Montreal and Toronto. The following year the two exchanges merged their options-clearing corporations, forming TransCanada Options Inc. (TCO). The Vancouver Stock Exchange joined TCO in 1984. Finally, in the year 1999 all derivatives trading in Canada (with the exception of agricultural futures) was transferred to the Montreal Exchange.

Derivatives have received some bad press in recent years, principally because they have been involved in several high-profile financial scandals, like the 1995 failure of the Barings Investment Bank in the United Kingdom. Most, if not all, such scandals have stemmed from fraudulent actions coupled with an insufficient understanding of the instruments. In fact, derivatives are simply tools to hedge or manage risk, and they don't deserve their bad name. While it is true that they are relatively difficult to master, it is also true, as we shall see, that the rewards from their use will largely repay the effort.

This chapter is an introduction to options markets. It explains how puts and calls work and examines their investment characteristics. Popular option strategies are considered next. Finally, the chapter provides a brief overview of securities with embedded options, such as callable or convertible bonds, as well as on some so-called exotic options.

17.1 THE OPTION CONTRACT

A **call option** gives its holder the right to purchase an asset for a specified price, called the **exercise** or **strike price**, on or before some specified expiration date. For example, a March call option on Alcan stock with exercise price $60 entitles its owner to purchase Alcan stock for a price of $60 at any time up to and including the expiration date in March. The holder of the call is not required to exercise the option. The holder will choose to exercise only if the market value of the asset to be purchased exceeds the exercise price. When the market price does exceed the exercise price, the optionholder may "call away" the asset for the exercise price. Otherwise, the option may be left unexercised. If it is not exercised before the expiration date of the contract, a call option simply expires and no longer has value. Therefore, if the stock price is greater than the exercise price on the expiration date, the value of the call option equals the difference between the stock price and the exercise price; but if the stock price is less than the exercise price at expiration, the call will be worthless. The *net profit* on the call is the value of the option minus the price originally paid to purchase it.

The purchase price of the option is called the *premium*. It represents the compensation the purchaser of the call must pay for the right to exercise the option if exercise becomes profitable. Sellers of call options, who are said to *write* calls, receive premium income now as payment against the possibility they will be required at some later date to deliver the asset in return for an exercise price lower than the market value of the asset. If the option is left to expire worthless because the exercise price remains above the market price of the asset, then the writer of the call clears a profit equal to the premium income derived from the sale of the option.

But if the call is exercised, the profit to the option writer is the premium income derived when the option was initially sold minus the difference between the value of the stock that must be delivered and the exercise price that is paid for those shares. If that difference is larger than the initial premium, the writer will incur a loss.

EXAMPLE 17.1 Profits and Losses on a Call Option

Consider April 2004 maturity call options on Alcan stock with an exercise price of \$65 per share, which were selling on February 27, 2004, for \$1.90. Exchange-traded stock options expire on the third Friday of the expiration month, which for this option was April 16, 2004. Until the expiration day, the purchaser of the calls was entitled to buy shares of Alcan for \$65. Because the stock price on February 27, 2004 was only \$63.17, it clearly would not have made sense at that moment to exercise the option to buy at \$65. Indeed, if Alcan stock remained below \$65 by the expiration date, the call would be left to expire worthless. If, on the other hand, Alcan were selling above \$65 at expiration, the call holder would find it optimal to exercise. For example, if Alcan sold for \$67 on April 16, the option would have been exercised since it would have given its holder the right to pay \$65 for a stock worth \$67. The value of the option on the expiration date would then be

$$\text{Value at expiration} = \text{Stock price} - \text{Exercise price} = \$67 - \$65 = \$2$$

Despite the \$2 payoff at maturity, the call holder realizes a gain of only \$.10 on his investment because the initial purchase price was \$1.90:

$$\text{Profit} = \text{Final value} - \text{Original investment} = \$2 - \$1.90 = \$.10$$

Even if the profit were negative, exercise of the call will be optimal at maturity if the stock price is above the exercise price because the exercise proceeds will offset at least part of the investment in the option. The investor in the call will clear a profit if Alcan is selling above \$66.90 at the maturity date. At that stock price, the proceeds from exercise will just cover the original cost of the call.

A **put option** gives its holder the right to *sell* an asset for a specified exercise or strike price on or before some expiration date. An October 2004 put on Alcan with exercise price \$65 entitles its owner to sell Alcan stock to the put writer at a price of \$65 at any time before expiration in October even if the market price of Alcan is less than \$65. While profits on call options increase when the asset increases in value, profits on put options increase when the asset value falls. A put will be exercised only if the exercise price is greater than the price of the underlying asset, that is, only if its holder can deliver for the exercise price an asset with market value less than the exercise price. (One doesn't need to own the shares of Alcan to exercise the Alcan put option. Upon exercise, the investor's broker purchases the necessary shares of Alcan at the market price and immediately delivers, or "puts" them, to an option writer for the exercise price. The owner of the put profits by the difference between the exercise price and market price.)

EXAMPLE 17.2 Profits and Losses on a Put Option

Consider the October 2004 maturity put option on Alcan with an exercise price of \$65 selling on February 27, 2004 for \$6.30. It entitles its owner to sell a share of Alcan for \$65 at any time until October 15, the third Friday. If the holder of the put option bought a share of Alcan and immediately exercised the right to sell at \$65, net proceeds would be \$65 − \$63.17 = \$1.83. Obviously, an investor who paid \$6.30 for the put had no intention of exercising it immediately. If, on the other hand, Alcan sold for \$55 at expiration, the put would turn out to be a profitable investment. The value of the put on the expiration date would be

$$\text{Value at expiration} = \text{Exercise price} - \text{Stock price} = \$65 - \$55 = \$10$$

and the investor's profit would be $10 − $6.30 = $3.70. This is a holding-period return of 3.70/6.30 = .5873, or 58.73 percent—over less than eight months! Obviously, put option sellers (who are on the other side of the transaction) did not consider this outcome very likely.

An option is described as **in the money** when its exercise would produce profits for its holder. An option is **out of the money** when exercise would be unprofitable. Therefore, a call option is in the money when the exercise price is below the asset's value. It is out of the money when the exercise price exceeds the asset value; no one would exercise the right to purchase for the strike price an asset worth less than that price. Conversely, put options are in the money when the exercise price exceeds the asset's value, because delivery of the lower-valued asset in exchange for the exercise price is profitable for the holder. Options are **at the money** when the exercise price and asset price are equal.

Options Trading

Some options trade on over-the-counter (OTC) markets. An OTC market offers the advantage that the terms of the option contract—the exercise price, maturity date, and number of shares committed—can be tailored to the needs of the traders. The costs of establishing an OTC option contract, however, are higher than for exchange-traded options. Today, most option trading takes place on organized exchanges but the OTC market in customized options is also thriving.

Options contracts traded on exchanges are standardized by allowable maturity dates and exercise prices for each listed option. Each stock option contract provides for the right to buy or sell 100 shares of stock. (If stock splits occur after the contract is listed, adjustments are required. We discuss adjustments in option contract terms later in this section.)

Standardization of the terms of listed option contracts means that all market participants trade in a limited and uniform set of securities. This increases the depth of trading in any particular option, which lowers trading costs and results in a more competitive market. Exchanges therefore, offer three important benefits: ease of trading, which flows from a central marketplace where buyers and sellers or their representatives congregate; a liquid secondary market, where buyers and sellers of options can transact quickly and cheaply; and a guarantee by the exchange that both parties to the contract will fulfill their obligations.

www.me.com

Figure 17.1 is a reproduction of a part of listed stock option quotations from *The Globe and Mail*; only the options that traded that day are quoted. Note the option listed (*highlight*) for shares of Alcan. In the first line, following the company name, it is indicated that the last recorded price on the Toronto Stock Exchange for Alcan stock was $63.17 per share. Options are traded on Alcan at exercise prices varying in $2.5 increments. These values are also called *strike prices* and are given in the first column of numbers, next to the expiration month.

The exchanges offer options on stocks with exercise prices that bracket the stock price. Exercise prices generally are set at intervals of either $2.5 or $5, depending on whether the price of the stock is below or above $35; however, tighter intervals also can be set for low stock prices. If the stock price moves outside the range of exercise prices of the existing set of options, new options with appropriate exercise prices may be offered. Therefore, at any time both in-the-money and out-of-the-money options will be listed, as in the Alcan example.

The next four groups or rows of numbers provide the bid, asked, and closing prices of call and put options on Alcan shares that traded that day, with expiration dates of March, April, July, and October. The contracts expire on the Saturday following the third Friday of the month. Notice that the prices of Alcan call options decrease as one moves down each column, toward progressively higher exercise prices. This makes sense, because the right to purchase a share at a given exercise price is worth less as that exercise price increases. At an exercise price of $60, the April Alcan call had a closing price of $4.50, whereas the option to purchase for an exercise price of $65 sold for only $2.

Many options may go an entire day without trading. Because trading is infrequent (especially in Canada), it is not unusual to find option prices that appear out of line with other prices. You might find, for example, two calls with different exercise prices that seem to sell for equal prices. This discrepancy arises because the last trades for these options may have occurred at different times during the day. At any moment the call with the lower exercise price must be worth more than an otherwise-identical call with a higher exercise price.

Several rows, distinguished by a P, report prices of put options with various strike prices and times to maturity. Notice that, in contrast to call options, put prices increase with the exercise price. The right to sell a share of Alcan at a price of $60 obviously is less valuable than the right to sell it at $65.

Figure 17.1 illustrates that the maturities of most exchange-traded options tend to be fairly short, ranging up to only several months. For larger firms, however, longer-term options are traded with maturities ranging up to several years. These options are called LEAPS (for *long-term equity anticipation securities*).

CONCEPT CHECK

1. *a.* What will be the proceeds and net profits to an investor who purchases the July maturity Alcan calls with exercise price $57.50 if the stock price at maturity is $50? What if the stock price at maturity is $65?
   b. Now answer part (*a*) for an investor who purchases a July maturity Alcan put option with exercise price $57.50.

American and European Options

An **American option** allows its holder to exercise the right to purchase (call) or sell (put) the underlying asset on *or before* the expiration date. A **European option** allows for exercise of the option only on the expiration date. American options, because they allow more leeway than do their European counterparts, generally will be more valuable. Virtually all traded options in Canada and the United States are American. Foreign currency options and stock index options traded on the Chicago Board Options Exchange in the United States, and stock index options traded on the Canadian Derivatives Exchange in Canada, are notable exceptions to this rule, however.

www.cboe.com

Adjustments in Option Contract Terms

Because options convey the right to buy or sell shares at a stated price, stock splits would radically alter their value if the terms of the option contract were not adjusted to account for the stock split. For example, reconsider the call options in Figure 17.1.

If Alcan were to announce a ten-for-one split, its share price would fall from $63.17 to about $6.32. A call option with exercise price $65 would be just about worthless, with virtually no possibility that the stock would sell at more than $65 before the option expired.

To account for a stock split, the exercise price is reduced by the factor of the split, and the number of options held is increased by that factor. For example, the original Alcan call option with exercise price of $65 would be altered after a ten-for-one split to 10 new options, with each option carrying an exercise price of $6.5. A similar adjustment is made for stock dividends of more than 10 percent; the number of shares covered by each option is increased in proportion to the stock dividend, and the exercise price is reduced by that proportion.

In contrast to stock dividends, cash dividends do not affect the terms of an option contract. Because payment of a cash dividend reduces the selling price of the stock without inducing offsetting adjustments in the option contract, the value of the option is affected by dividend policy. Other things being equal, call option values are lower for high-dividend-payout policies, because

Figure 17.1 Stock option quotations.

EQUITY OPTIONS

Trading in Canadian equity options on the Montreal Exchange. P is a put.

FIVE MOST ACTIVE

	Volume	Op Int
Nortel Netwk	7407	216898
Royal Bank	2892	26380
Barrick	2386	51815
TransCanad	2049	10603
TD Bank	1478	31981

TRADES

stock series		bid	close ask	tot vol last	vol	tot o.I. op int
ATI Tech			**20.80**	**497**		**7332**
Mar04	18.00	2.90	3.00	3.00	5	2
	19.00	2.00	2.15	2.50	50	6
	20.00	1.25	1.45	1.40	21	83
	20.00p	0.50	0.65	0.35	70	73
	22.00	0.40	0.50	0.50	150	1753
	22.00p	1.60	1.70	1.30	50	193
Apr04	22.00	0.80	0.95	0.85	119	701
Jul04	22.00	1.80	1.95	2.00	9	256
	24.00	1.10	1.30	1.25	23	275
Abitibi Consl			**10.60**	**1072**		**8003**
Mar04	8.00	2.50	2.70	2.60	25	226
	10.00	0.70	0.80	0.65	20	679
	11.00	0.06	0.25	0.10	25	358
Apr04	11.00	0.20	0.40	0.25	1000	0
Jun04	8.00	2.60	2.80	2.60	2	465
Agnico-Ea			**18.24**	**93**		**6878**
Mar04	15.00	3.25	3.45	3.30	10	175
	19.00	0.40	0.45	0.50	40	217
Jun04	15.00	3.65	3.90	4.00	10	396
	18.00p	1.30	1.50	1.35	8	45
	20.00	0.90	1.10	1.00	25	178
Alcan			**63.17**	**613**		**19188**
Mar04	60.00	3.80	4.00	4.25	55	1200
	60.00p	0.40	0.55	0.40	170	274
	67.50	0.25	0.40	0.25	13	220
	70.00	0.04	0.15	0.04	40	0
Apr04	50.00	13.45	13.65	14.00	10	172
	60.00	4.50	4.70	4.50	30	934
	62.50	2.95	3.10	3.20	3	440
	65.00	1.75	1.90	2.00	60	486
	67.50	0.95	1.10	1.00	10	389
Jul04	57.50	7.85	8.05	7.90	10	140
	57.50p	1.70	1.90	1.90	1	315
	65.00	3.55	3.80	3.55	6	255
	67.50	2.55	2.80	2.75	201	716
Oct04	65.00p	6.05	6.30	6.00	4	0
BCE Emer			**6.14**	**279**		**2941**
Mar04	7.00	0.06	0.15	0.15	20	248
Apr04	6.00p	0.25	0.45	0.25	70	0
May04	7.00	0.20	0.35	0.20	20	453
Aug04	5.00p	0.20	0.40	0.25	100	38
	6.00p	0.60	0.80	0.60	69	87
BCE Inc			**29.29**	**255**		**35437**
[illegible]	[illegible]	1.25	1.40	[illegible]	[illegible]	380
	54.00p	2.65	2.85	2.75	11	15
Jan05	30.00	24.30	24.90	24.00	32	214
	45.00	9.90	10.35	10.30	10	502
	50.00p	1.70	1.95	1.80	30	202
	55.00	2.95	3.40	3.30	8	896
Jan06	45.00	10.80	11.50	11.15	10	119
	50.00p	3.35	3.80	3.45	20	57
Bank of NS			**68.65**	**297**		**28057**
Mar04	65.00	3.65	3.70	3.55	20	70
Apr04	62.50p	0.07	0.10	0.07	10	419
	65.00	3.80	3.85	3.50	5	621
	67.50	1.80	1.90	1.85	10	4016
	70.00	0.60	0.70	0.50	10	1755
	72.50p	4.40	4.40	4.75	20	80
	75.00p	5.70	6.75	7.15	10	40
Jul04	65.00	4.20	4.45	4.35	5	355
	67.50	2.55	2.75	2.55	6	335
	70.00	1.40	1.55	1.30	150	6364
Oct04	62.50	6.70	7.00	6.60	10	40
	75.00p	7.35	7.55	8.00	10	10
Jan05	60.00	9.10	9.45	9.40	10	657
Jan06	60.00p	2.75	3.00	3.05	1	160
	65.00	7.70	8.10	8.00	10	154
	65.00p	4.50	4.75	4.85	10	307
Barrick			**27.23**	**2386**		**51815**
Mar04	27.50	0.70	0.70	0.80	174	1745
	27.50p	0.85	0.95	0.90	100	504
Apr04	25.00	2.80	2.80	2.85	60	1256
	25.00p	0.40	0.45	0.45	490	2404
	27.50	1.20	1.25	1.10	110	3384
	27.50p	1.30	1.40	1.25	313	2332
	30.00	0.40	0.50	0.45	110	2932
	30.00p	3.00	3.10	2.95	20	299
Jul04	25.00p	1.05	1.15	1.05	12	5628
	27.50	2.10	2.15	2.20	228	2185
	27.50p	2.20	2.30	2.20	5	898
	30.00	1.20	1.20	1.20	249	5905
	32.50	0.60	0.70	0.65	155	1761
Oct04	22.50p	0.70	0.80	0.75	100	100
	25.00	4.00	4.15	4.10	5	15
	27.50	2.70	2.80	2.80	5	55
	30.00	1.75	1.85	1.70	20	70
	32.50	1.15	1.20	1.15	10	62
Jan05	22.50	6.00	6.15	6.25	50	592
	25.00	4.40	4.55	4.60	60	4839
	25.00p	1.90	2.00	1.90	50	527
Jan06	22.50	7.30	7.50	7.55	50	155
	22.50p	2.05	2.20	2.00	10	163
Biovail			**27.37**	**568**		**10828**
Mar04	25.00p	0.65	0.80	0.65	15	524
	27.50	1.45	1.70	1.50	8	369
	27.50p	1.60	1.80	1.95	9	66
	30.00	0.60	0.85	0.85	108	367
	32.50	0.25	0.50	0.30	30	152
Apr04	20.00p	0.30	0.45	0.40	20	230
	25.00p	1.25	1.35	1.20	20	272
	27.50	2.10	2.40	2.30	34	283
	30.00	1.20	1.50	1.30	115	688
	32.50	0.65	0.90	0.85	52	435
	35.00	0.30	0.55	0.55	10	478
Jul04	25.00	[illegible]	5.30	5.10	15	57
Mar04	45.00	4.60	5.35	4.70	5	13
	50.00	0.70	1.05	0.80	70	106
Apr04	47.50p	0.30	0.70	0.65	1	0
Jun04	50.00	1.95	2.35	2.00	15	82
Sep04	47.50	4.00	4.50	4.00	4	45
	50.00	2.65	3.10	2.75	10	44
CAE Inc			**6.40**	**63**		**13162**
Mar04	6.00	0.40	0.50	0.40	13	2587
Jun04	7.00	0.20	0.30	0.30	10	1048
Sep04	4.00	2.30	2.50	2.40	10	150
	7.00	0.40	0.50	0.45	30	578
CGI			**8.70**	**96**		**7157**
Apr04	7.00	1.65	1.80	1.75	10	0
Aug04	8.00	1.10	1.20	1.15	60	347
	9.00	0.55	0.60	0.55	22	616
	10.00	0.25	0.35	0.25	1	1395
	11.00	0.10	0.20	0.08	3	50
CI Fund Ma			**15.05**	**42**		**1042**
Apr04	16.00	0.15	0.35	0.25	20	625
Jul04	16.00	0.35	0.60	0.45	22	110
CIBC			**68.64**	**1184**		**25129**
Mar04	62.50	6.15	6.40	5.95	20	90
	62.50p	0.02	0.05	0.03	50	98
	65.00p	0.05	0.15	0.09	60	459
	67.50	1.70	1.90	1.65	181	3328
	67.50p	0.45	0.65	0.60	40	158
	70.00	0.50	0.60	0.40	159	1327
	70.00p	1.70	1.90	1.90	212	40
	72.50p	3.75	4.00	3.80	20	10
Apr04	55.00	13.65	13.90	13.00	10	860
	60.00	8.70	8.90	8.75	10	114
	65.00	4.00	4.20	3.95	42	310
	65.00p	0.40	0.60	0.60	50	159
	67.50	2.15	2.35	2.25	45	405
	67.50p	1.15	1.40	1.45	10	74
	70.00	0.95	1.10	0.95	33	608
	70.00p	2.50	2.75	2.65	20	37
	72.50	0.25	0.45	0.35	10	120
	75.00p	6.65	6.95	6.95	40	30
Jul04	65.00	4.85	5.10	5.00	20	132
	67.50	3.30	3.55	3.25	52	323
	70.00	2.05	2.20	2.00	13	250
	72.50	1.20	1.45	1.15	10	2115
	75.00	0.65	0.85	0.65	10	12
Oct04	70.00	2.95	3.25	3.00	15	0
	70.00p	4.65	4.95	4.70	10	0
Jan05	45.00	23.60	23.90	23.75	10	294
	60.00	9.80	10.30	10.05	10	386
	70.00	3.70	4.10	3.65	5	110
	70.00p	5.45	5.90	5.65	15	46
	75.00	1.95	2.15	1.95	2	240
CN Rail			**52.67**	**13**		**4595**
Mar04	53.375	0.50	0.70	0.70	10	150
Apr04	56.00	0.25	0.50	0.35	3	17
Cdn Naturl			**73.25**	**454**		**4993**
Mar04	70.00	4.15	4.40	4.05	52	704
	70.00p	0.60	0.75	0.90	28	109
	75.00	1.30	1.45	1.30	79	81
	75.00p	2.75	2.90	4.30	1	10
[illegible]	[illegible]	[illegible]	[illegible]	[illegible]	[illegible]	[illegible]
Mar04	24.00	0.75	0.95	0.75	25	50
	26.00p	1.80	1.90	1.90	20	15
Apr04	26.00	0.35	0.50	0.40	10	1361
Oct04	24.00p	1.80	1.95	1.85	4	30
Celestica			**23.00**	**470**		**14040**
Mar04	20.00	3.95	4.05	4.00	63	250
	22.50	1.80	2.00	1.60	58	601
	22.50p	0.45	0.50	0.50	55	119
	25.00	0.50	0.65	0.50	50	3727
	25.00p	1.70	1.70	2.20	3	104
	27.50	0.10	0.20	0.15	21	631
Apr04	25.00	1.15	1.25	1.20	23	231
	27.50	0.45	0.65	0.40	2	30
Jun04	20.00p	0.75	0.85	0.85	50	205
	22.50	3.20	3.35	2.70	43	300
	25.00	2.00	2.15	1.70	6	586
	27.50	1.15	1.35	1.15	41	465
Sep04	20.00p	1.35	1.50	1.50	5	20
	27.50	2.05	2.20	2.00	50	176
Cognos			**41.72**	**197**		**3076**
Mar04	45.00	0.15	0.30	0.15	10	160
Apr04	40.00	3.10	3.25	3.00	15	7
	42.50	1.80	1.95	1.85	66	134
	42.50p	2.50	2.70	2.60	5	17
	45.00	0.90	1.05	1.00	71	100
May04	37.50p	1.00	1.25	1.05	5	50
	40.00	3.60	3.90	3.50	5	43
	42.50	2.40	2.65	2.10	15	189
	45.00	1.50	1.65	1.35	5	239
Dofasco Inc			**35.15**	**133**		**3552**
Mar04	34.00	0.95	1.15	1.30	100	1372
Jun04	38.00	0.60	0.80	0.60	12	56
	40.00p	5.80	6.00	5.55	6	26
Sep04	34.00	2.55	2.80	2.90	15	67
EnCana Crp			**57.84**	**1241**		**37241**
Mar04	62.50p	4.70	4.70	4.50	11	0
	50.00	8.00	8.15	8.00	30	162
	52.50	5.55	5.60	5.75	30	228
	52.50p		0.10	0.10	15	222
	55.00	3.25	3.35	3.40	108	4946
	55.00p	0.20	0.30	0.30	20	171
	57.50	1.40	1.50	1.50	25	2066
	60.00	0.45	0.55	0.50	5	68
	60.00p	2.45	2.50	2.55	30	110
Apr04	62.50	0.40	0.50	0.45	6	0
	62.50p	4.95	5.00	5.10	1	0
	47.50	10.50	10.75	10.65	48	603
	50.00	8.10	8.25	8.00	9	881
	52.50	5.80	5.95	6.00	43	863
	55.00	3.70	3.90	3.95	73	1130
	55.00p	0.60	0.70	0.65	35	202
	57.50	2.10	2.20	2.05	33	1285
	60.00	1.00	1.10	1.10	219	191
Jul04	62.50	1.50	1.65	1.50	17	0
	62.50p	5.65	5.80	6.20	1	0
	47.50	10.90	11.10	10.70	5	84
	50.00	8.75	8.95	9.00	76	12085
	52.50	6.70	6.80	6.70	90	488
	52.50p	0.85	1.00	0.90	31	190
	55.00	4.95	5.00	5.05	135	2849
	55.00p	1.65	1.75	1.75	35	1111
	60.00	2.30	2.40	2.30	18	681
Oct04	62.50	2.30	2.50	2.35	16	0
	62.50p	6.25	6.50	6.70	1	0
	50.00	9.30	9.60	9.20	2	10
	55.00	5.70	6.00	5.65	13	10
	55.00p	2.25	2.45	2.40	10	10
	57.50	4.35	4.60	4.40	5	100
	60.00	[illegible]	3.40	[illegible]	45	77

Source: *The Globe and Mail*, February 28, 2004. Reprinted with permission from The Globe and Mail.

such policies slow the rate of increase of stock prices; conversely, put values are higher for high dividend payouts. (Of course, the option values do not rise or fall on the dividend payment or ex-dividend dates. Dividend payments are anticipated, so the effect of the payment already is built into the original option price.)

CONCEPT CHECK

2. Suppose that Alcan stock price at the exercise date is \$60, and the exercise price of the call is \$57.50. What is the profit on one option contract? After a ten-for-one split, the stock price is \$6, the exercise price is \$5.75, and the option holder now can purchase 1,000 shares. Show that the split leaves option profits unaffected.

stock			close	tot vol		tot o.i.
series		**bid**	**ask**	**last**	**vol**	**op int**
	20.00	1.10	1.20	1.15	12	911
Oct04	22.00	1.00	1.15	1.00	5	7
Great Wst			**50.70**	**10**		**1705**
Mar04	48.00p		0.35	0.20	10	5
iUnits Ind			**49.39**	**384**		**27567**
Mar04	46.00	3.35	3.50	3.00	2	164
	48.00	1.50	1.65	1.30	120	1317
	49.00	0.75	0.90	0.70	71	304
	50.00p	0.85	0.95	0.95	55	14
Apr04	47.00p	0.15	0.25	0.30	10	10
	48.00	1.65	1.80	1.65	5	68
	49.00	1.00	1.15	1.00	50	173
	50.00	0.50	0.65	0.50	3	109
	50.00p	1.20	1.40	1.35	10	4
May04	49.00	1.30	1.50	1.20	11	0
Sep04	44.00	5.80	6.05	5.80	7	50
	44.00p	0.35	0.50	0.50	30	132
Mar06	45.00p	1.95	2.45	2.30	10	50
iUnits Enr			**42.05**	**133**		**5821**
Mar04	40.00	2.05	2.40	2.00	33	111
	42.00	0.50	0.75	0.70	50	691
Apr04	38.00	4.05	4.35	4.05	20	20
May04	40.00	2.65	3.10	2.90	10	0
Sep04	43.00p	2.40	3.00	2.95	20	0
iUnits Fin			**35.50**	**100**		**8117**
Jun04	34.00p	0.30	0.60	0.40	100	50
iUnits Gold			**53.00**	**211**		**6884**
Mar04	52.00p	1.05	1.25	1.15	50	1654
	53.00p	1.50	1.70	1.70	10	49
	54.00	1.05	1.30	1.20	50	426
	55.00	0.70	0.90	0.70	41	55
	56.00	0.45	0.70	0.65	10	153
Sep04	54.00	4.40	4.85	4.40	50	0
Iamgold			**9.03**	**115**		**6359**
Apr04	10.00	0.25	0.35	0.25	40	0
May04	9.00	0.75	0.85	0.85	25	157
	9.00p	0.65	0.80	0.70	50	70
Imperial Oil			**61.05**	**12**		**3403**
May04	60.00	2.95	3.20	3.10	10	174
Aug04	67.50	1.10	1.35	1.15	2	217
Inco			**49.52**	**924**		**10959**
Mar04	42.50	7.20	7.45	7.10	20	127
	45.00	4.90	5.10	4.60	20	45
	47.50	2.95	3.10	3.30	94	226
	50.00	1.50	1.60	1.75	86	1342
	50.00p	1.75	1.80	1.60	15	332
	52.50	0.60	0.70	0.70	35	1125
	52.50p	3.35	3.50	3.25	5	34
Apr04	45.00	5.60	5.70	5.45	1	40
	47.50p	1.45	1.55	1.45	10	11
	52.50	1.40	1.55	1.35	460	123
May04	40.00	10.20	10.40	10.00	20	240
	45.00	6.20	6.35	6.10	10	205
	47.50	4.60	4.75	4.45	10	306
	47.50p	2.10	2.30	2.00	30	185
	50.00	3.25	3.40	3.40	35	303
	52.50p	4.75	4.90	5.10	10	64
	55.00	1.50	1.60	1.45	25	1269
	55.00p	6.45	6.60	6.80	3	28
Aug04	45.00p	2.40	2.50	2.45	15	263
	52.50p	6.10	6.20	6.35	20	32
JDS Uniph			**6.56**	**275**		**10659**
May04	5.00	1.70	1.85	1.80	10	468
	6.00	0.95	1.05	1.10	50	446
	6.00p	0.40	0.55	0.40	10	404
	7.00	0.50	0.65	0.60	100	413
Mar04	45.00	2.95	3.00	3.20	20	45
Apr04	47.50	1.40	1.50	1.45	10	1912
Jul04	40.00	8.10	8.40	8.15	20	118
	45.00p	0.75	0.85	0.80	5	153
	47.50	2.25	2.35	2.10	7	401
	50.00	1.20	1.30	1.20	6	279
Oct04	45.00	4.35	4.60	4.60	5	5
	47.50p	2.25	2.55	2.40	10	15
	50.00	1.80	1.90	1.70	3	10
MeridinGl			**16.91**	**81**		**5314**
Mar04	17.50	0.50	0.65	0.55	50	74
Apr04	12.50	4.55	4.80	5.00	5	30
	22.50		0.20	0.10	1	261
Oct04	15.00p	1.05	1.35	1.10	25	0
Molson			**30.50**	**39**		**3222**
Mar04	30.00	0.70	1.00	1.05	10	180
Apr04	30.00	1.00	1.30	1.10	20	0
Aug04	30.00p	1.40	1.70	1.45	5	307
	35.00	0.30	0.50	0.50	1	170
	37.50		0.40	0.10	3	40
NationalBk			**45.65**	**380**		**16928**
Mar04	44.00	1.70	1.85	1.55	20	100
	46.00	0.40	0.50	0.40	20	877
	50.00p	4.30	4.60	4.65	15	0
Apr04	42.00	3.55	3.75	3.15	20	331
	44.00	1.85	2.00	1.90	165	1135
	46.00	0.65	0.80	0.60	3	266
Jul04	42.00	3.95	4.10	3.85	50	138
	44.00	2.40	2.60	2.35	30	304
Oct04	48.00	1.15	1.35	1.10	7	0
Jan05	50.00	0.95	1.25	1.00	50	13
Neuroch			**26.90**	**5**		**461**
Mar04	28.00	1.00	1.25	0.70	5	14
Nexen			**49.95**	**40**		**4839**
Mar04	46.00	3.90	4.30	3.45	1	10
	48.00	2.40	2.70	2.30	30	62
May04	38.00	11.85	12.30	12.10	4	99
	48.00	4.00	4.25	4.05	4	159
Aug04	50.00	4.40	4.75	4.35	1	201
Noranda			**21.91**	**161**		**12279**
Mar04	18.00	3.80	4.00	3.60	15	65
	20.00	1.85	2.05	1.85	11	451
Apr04	20.00	2.10	2.30	2.10	5	0
	22.00	0.90	0.95	0.85	10	14
May04	18.00	3.95	4.25	4.00	20	540
	22.00	1.25	1.30	1.25	1	836
	24.00	0.50	0.60	0.50	50	266
Aug04	16.00	5.95	6.05	5.95	15	65
	18.00	4.30	4.50	4.20	14	141
	22.00	1.75	2.00	1.80	20	649
Nortel Netwk			**10.70**	**7407**		**216898**
Mar04	5.00	5.60	5.70	5.50	15	942
	6.00	4.60	4.70	4.45	500	17124
	6.50	4.10	4.20	4.00	15	4309
	8.00	2.60	2.70	2.60	20	1985
	8.50	2.15	2.20	2.10	15	4129
	9.00	1.65	1.70	1.70	305	5628
	9.50	1.25	1.30	1.15	81	4034
	10.00	0.85	0.90	0.85	270	7147
	10.00p	0.20	0.25	0.25	55	3215
	11.00	0.30	0.35	0.35	653	13576
	11.00p	0.65	0.75	0.70	8	1220
	12.00	0.10	0.15	0.10	113	10228
	13.00	0.02	0.06	0.05	20	2181
	15.00p	4.30	4.40	4.50	4	24
Apr04	9.50p	0.25	0.35	0.30	100	90
	10.00	1.15	1.20	1.10	236	96
	6.00	5.60	5.70	5.70	10	943
	10.00	3.55	3.65	3.50	28	797
	10.00p	2.35	2.55	2.40	5	429
	11.00	3.15	3.30	3.20	27	842
	12.00	2.80	2.95	2.85	80	1325
	15.00	2.00	2.20	2.05	25	1076
Nova Ch			**36.72**	**41**		**817**
Aug04	34.00p	1.35	1.60	1.60	10	45
	36.00	2.85	3.30	3.00	30	51
	38.00	1.90	2.30	2.10	1	28
Open Text			**39.83**	**55**		**1055**
Apr04	40.00	2.55	2.80	2.80	4	164
	42.00	1.80	1.95	1.90	27	68
May04	40.00	3.50	3.75	4.00	20	104
	42.00	2.65	2.90	2.80	4	40
PanAm Si			**23.64**	**44**		**810**
Mar04	20.00p	0.20	0.35	0.25	4	30
	24.00	1.10	1.30	1.10	35	54
	26.00	0.50	0.65	0.60	5	60
Petro-Cda			**60.32**	**343**		**10064**
Mar04	50.00	10.10	10.30	10.20	50	114
	56.00p	0.15	0.30	0.30	13	187
	58.00	2.55	2.80	2.70	44	341
	60.00	1.35	1.50	1.45	10	387
	60.00p	1.20	1.35	1.30	50	89
	62.00p	2.40	2.60	2.55	5	14
Apr04	64.00p	4.40	4.65	4.75	10	0
	58.00p	1.10	1.25	1.25	33	23
	60.00	2.20	2.30	2.20	2	62
	62.00	1.30	1.45	1.35	12	30
	62.00p	3.05	3.20	3.30	10	0
Jun04	54.00p	0.90	1.10	1.00	10	142
	58.00	4.55	4.70	4.60	20	453
	60.00	3.45	3.60	3.55	14	1535
	62.00	2.45	2.60	2.60	22	889
	64.00	1.75	1.95	1.75	25	172
Sep04	64.00	2.95	3.20	2.90	10	110
	68.00	1.75	2.05	1.90	3	11
Placer Do			**22.58**	**973**		**22183**
Mar04	20.00	2.60	2.75	2.65	30	137
	21.00	1.75	1.90	2.15	10	151
	22.00	1.10	1.25	1.45	12	1376
	22.00p	0.55	0.70	0.60	10	500
	23.00	0.60	0.70	0.60	61	459
	23.00p	1.10	1.20	0.80	10	187
Apr04	17.00	5.50	5.65	5.80	10	110
	18.00	4.60	4.70	5.10	20	359
	19.00	3.70	3.85	4.30	30	146
	20.00	2.90	3.00	3.30	10	557
	20.00p	0.40	0.45	0.40	100	435
	22.00	1.55	1.70	1.55	35	967
	22.00p	1.00	1.15	1.00	40	179
	23.00	1.10	1.20	1.05	185	1088
	23.00p	1.55	1.65	1.30	100	165
	24.00	0.70	0.85	0.70	43	560
	25.00	0.40	0.55	0.45	7	331
Jul04	18.00	5.00	5.20	5.40	15	40
	20.00p	1.00	1.10	1.05	10	518
	23.00	2.00	2.20	2.00	180	359
Jan05	20.00p	1.90	2.05	1.65	5	164
Jan06	18.00p	2.00	2.30	2.20	50	56
Precision			**64.10**	**125**		**2667**
Mar04	62.50	2.25	2.55	2.70	5	111
	65.00	0.95	1.15	1.10	3	127
	65.00p	1.80	2.00	1.90	17	20
Apr04	62.50	3.00	3.30	3.30	10	54
	65.00	1.70	1.95	1.75	50	122
	67.50	0.85	[illegible]	[illegible]	[illegible]	[illegible]
Jun04	150.00	6.75	7.75	6.30	10	0
	60.00p	0.40	0.75	0.50	5	113
	95.00	39.25	40.25	40.05	3	27
	110.00	27.15	28.85	25.25	10	122
	110.00p	5.20	6.20	5.40	40	41
	130.00	14.85	16.00	14.45	3	36
	130.00p	12.00	13.60	13.20	2	3
	140.00	10.35	11.45	11.00	21	49
Sep04	95.00p	5.05	6.05	6.05	10	111
	110.00p	8.95	9.95	10.00	5	19
	120.00	24.85	26.65	25.85	1	32
	130.00	19.50	21.10	20.90	3	8
	130.00p	16.90	18.50	18.60	15	2
RgrC			**25.23**	**100**		**3016**
Mar04	25.00	0.55	0.85	0.45	100	350
Royal Bank			**63.45**	**2892**		**26380**
Mar04	60.00	3.55	3.85	3.80	39	25
	62.00	1.75	2.00	1.95	35	91
	64.00	0.60	0.75	0.70	1347	1739
	64.00p	0.90	1.15	0.85	91	77
	66.00	0.05	0.20	0.15	40	316
	66.00p	2.45	2.70	2.10	6	60
Apr04	60.00	3.85	4.10	4.10	2	2243
	62.00	2.35	2.50	2.60	2	489
	62.00p	0.55	0.75	0.60	15	293
	64.00	1.15	1.25	1.15	147	2265
	64.00p	1.30	1.55	1.35	29	150
	66.00	0.40	0.55	0.45	22	1865
Jul04	58.00	6.00	6.50	6.50	10	99
	60.00	4.50	4.80	4.80	200	261
	60.00p	0.80	0.95	0.85	120	349
	62.00	2.95	3.25	3.25	26	155
	62.00p	1.45	1.75	1.55	25	139
	64.00	1.85	2.15	2.05	114	407
	66.00	1.05	1.30	1.25	245	1923
	66.00p	3.65	3.95	3.70	22	425
	68.00	0.65	0.80	0.75	25	394
	70.00	0.20	0.40	0.45	2	61
Oct04	60.00	4.90	5.30	5.25	3	0
	60.00p	1.55	1.65	1.55	13	15
	62.00p	2.30	2.60	2.25	20	0
	64.00	2.70	2.85	2.80	19	10
	64.00p	3.20	3.55	3.30	20	5
Jan05	50.00	13.70	14.30	13.70	2	198
	55.00	9.20	9.80	9.70	36	638
	60.00	5.50	6.00	5.90	10	433
	60.00p	2.25	2.65	2.25	24	264
	62.50	3.90	4.40	4.00	10	380
	67.50	1.80	2.10	2.15	7	612
	67.50p	6.00	6.60	6.00	30	12
	70.00	1.10	1.45	1.35	30	18
	70.00p	7.80	8.40	7.70	10	10
Jan06	55.00	10.70	11.30	11.30	12	335
	60.00	7.30	8.00	7.90	10	131
	62.50p	5.30	5.90	5.40	10	113
	67.50	3.75	4.30	4.10	10	131
	67.50p	8.00	8.70	7.90	10	182
	70.00	2.90	3.50	3.25	29	10
	70.00p	9.60	10.35	9.60	13	0
S&P/TSX 60				**281**		**2662**
Mar04	380.00	109.70	111.10	109.80	40	5
	400.00	89.70	91.10	89.80	22	25
	460.00p		0.55	0.50	2	0
	480.00	11.50	12.90	11.50	45	356
	490.00	4.40	4.75	5.15	8	618
	490.00p	3.90	4.25	4.35	5	75
	500.00	1.00	1.35	1.30	50	58
	500.00p	10.10	11.50	11.90	5	10
	510.00	0.05	[illegible]	0.60	100	0

The Option Clearing Corporation

The Option Clearing Corporation (OCC) is jointly owned by the U.S. exchanges on which stock options are traded. It is the clearinghouse for options trading in the U.S. In Canada, it is called Canadian Derivatives Clearing Corporation (CDCC), and is a subsidiary of the Canadian Derivatives Exchange, the English name of the Montreal Exchange (still called *Bourse de Montréal* in French).

Buyers and sellers of options who agree on a price will consummate the sale of the option. At this point the CDCC steps in, by placing itself between the two traders and becoming the effective buyer of the option from the writer and the effective writer of the option to the buyer. All individuals, therefore, deal only with the CDCC, which effectively guarantees contract performance.

When an option holder exercises an option, the CDCC arranges for a member firm with clients who have written that option to make good on the option obligation. The member firm, in turn, selects from its clients who have written that option to fulfill the contract. The selected client must deliver 100 shares of stock at a price equal to the exercise price for each call option contract written, or purchase 100 shares at the exercise price for each put option contract written.

Because the CDCC guarantees contract performances, option writers are required to post margin amounts to guarantee that they can fulfill their contract obligations. The margin required is determined, in part, by the amount by which the option is in the money, because that value is an indicator of the potential obligation of the option writer upon exercise of the option. When the required margin exceeds the posted margin, the writer will receive a margin call. The holder of the option need not post margin, because the holder will exercise the option only if it is profitable to do so. After purchasing the option, no further money is at risk.

Margin requirements are determined, in part, by the other securities held in the investor's portfolio. For example, a call option writer owning the stock against which the option is written can satisfy the margin requirement simply by allowing a broker to hold that stock in the brokerage account. The stock is then guaranteed to be available for delivery should the call option be exercised. If the underlying security is not owned, however, the margin requirement is determined by both the value of the underlying security and the amount by which the option is in or out of the money. Out-of-the-money options require less margin from the writer, because expected payouts are lower.

Other Listed Options

Options on assets other than stocks also are widely traded, especially in the United States. These include options on market and industry indices; foreign currency; and even the future prices of agricultural products, gold, silver, fixed-income securities, and stock indices. We will discuss these in turn.

Index Options An index option is a call or put based on a stock market index such as the S&P/TSX 60 or the New York Stock Exchange Index. Index options are traded on several broad-based indices, as well as on a few industry-specific indices. We discussed many of these indices in Chapter 2.

The construction of the indices can vary across contracts or exchanges. For example, the S&P/TSX 60 index is a value-weighted average of 60 major Canadian stocks in the S&P/TSX Composite stock group. The weights are proportional to the market value of outstanding equity for each stock. The Dow Jones Industrial Index by contrast, is a price-weighted average of 30 U.S. stocks.

In contrast to stock options, index options do not require that the call writer actually "deliver the index" upon exercise, or that the put writer "purchase the index." Instead, a cash settlement procedure is used. The profits that would accrue upon exercise of the option are calculated, and the option writer simply pays that amount to the option holder. The profits are equal to the difference between the exercise price of the option and the value of the index. For example, if the S&P/TSX 60 index is at $460 when a call option on the index with exercise price $440 is exercised, the holder of the call receives a cash payment of $20 multiplied by the contract multiplier of 100, or $2,000 per contract. The S&P/TSX 60–traded options are listed at the end of Figure 17.1. Figure 17.2 is a sample listing of various index options from *The Financial Post.* These include options on several foreign stock indices.

Foreign Currency Options A currency option offers the right to buy or sell a quantity of foreign currency for a specified amount of domestic currency.

Currency option contracts on U.S. exchanges call for purchase or sale of the currency in exchange for a specified number of U.S. dollars. Contracts are quoted in cents or fractions of a cent per unit of foreign currency. The size of each option contract is specified for each listing. Foreign currency options trade over the counter in Canada. The boxed article here documents their use as part of foreign exchange market activity.

THE CANADIAN FOREIGN EXCHANGE AND DERIVATIVES MARKET

Summary results of a survey of activity in Canadian foreign exchange and derivatives markets conducted by the Bank of Canada in April 2004 are now available. Similar surveys were undertaken in 51 other countries during the same month, and the central banks of many of those countries are also releasing their results today. This worldwide effort was coordinated by the Bank for International Settlements (BIS), which is issuing a press release today that summarizes highlights of the aggregated global turnover.[1] Surveys have been conducted by the Bank of Canada every three years since 1983, and the results of those surveys are shown in the tables included with this release.

All financial institutions in Canada that are active in the wholesale foreign exchange and derivatives markets were surveyed. These consisted of 18 financial institutions, representing approximately 99 per cent of these markets in Canada. With respect to foreign exchange, the survey covered spot transactions, outright forwards, foreign exchange swaps, currency swaps,[2] and over-the-counter (OTC) options. The interest rate products covered were forward rate agreements, interest rate swaps, and OTC options. Participants were also asked to identify transactions by currency and type of counterparty.

Highlights of the 2004 Survey

- The *turnover of traditional foreign exchange transactions* (spot, outright forwards, and foreign exchange swaps) showed the highest growth rate since the 1995 survey. In April 2004, foreign exchange transactions totalled US$1,133 billion, compared with US$833 billion in April 2001, yielding an average daily turnover in 2004 of US$53.9 billion (over 21 business days), compared with an average of US$41.6 billion per day (over 20 business days) in 2001, an increase of close to 30 per cent. ...
- The average turnover for *currency swaps and OTC foreign exchange options* more than doubled to US$5.4 billion per day from the relatively small base of US$2.6 billion in April 2001. With respect to *single-currency interest rate derivatives*, including forward rate agreements, interest rate swaps, and OTC options, average daily turnover in April 2004 totalled US$12.1 billion, compared with US$9.9 billion in April 2001, an increase of 22 per cent (see Table 1 for details on the individual products). ...
- Table 2 shows the composition of foreign exchange business by *type of transaction*. The trend for spot transactions to fall over time and for foreign exchange swaps to rise (with the exception of the 1995 survey) was reversed in 2004. Spot transactions rose from 25 per cent in 2001 to 34 per cent in 2004, while foreign exchange swaps fell from 70 per cent to 59 per cent over the same period. Outright forwards were relatively more stable, increasing from 5 per cent in 2001 to 7 per cent in 2004.
- Table 2 also provides data on the composition of foreign exchange business by *counterparty*. In April 2004, interbank trading accounted for 62 per cent of foreign exchange transactions in Canada and customer business for 38 per cent (compared with 64 per cent and 36 per cent, respectively, in April 2001). ...

Table 1 Derivatives Market Activity: Summary of Surveys (average daily turnover in billions of U.S. dollars)

	Foreign Exchange Derivitives		Single-Currency Interest Rate Derivatives		
	Currency Swaps	OTC Options	Forward Rate Agreements	Interest Rate Swaps	OTC Options
1995	—	.8	3.0	1.0	.3
1998	.3	.8	2.4	2.9	1.1
2001	.3	2.3	2.9	6.1	.9
2004	.6	4.8	3.4	7.3	1.4

Table 2 Composition of Foreign Exchange Market Activity by Type of Transaction and Counterparty: Summary of Surveys (percentage share)

	By Type of Transaction			By Counterparty	
	Spot	Outright Forwards	Foreign Exchange Swaps	Interbank	Customer
1983	43	5	52	74	26
1986	43	5	52	69	31
1989	41	5	54	73	27
1992	33	4	63	76	24
1995	38	9	53	61	39
1998	28	4	68	72	28
2001	25	5	70	64	36
2004	34	7	59	62	38

[1]The highlights of the global results, which have been aggregated by the BIS, along with direct links to other national press releases can be found at www.bis.org/publ/rpfx04.htm [accessed October 25, 2004].

[2]Currency swaps involve the exchange of streams of interest payments and principal amounts, whereas foreign exchange swaps involve the exchange of principal amounts only.

Source: Bank of Canada press release, September 28, 2004, available at www.bankofcanada.ca/en/press/2004/pr04-20.htm.

Figure 17.2
Index options.

INDEX OPTIONS 05.18.04

Figures supplied by CGI.

DJ Inds Avg (CBOE) Index close 9968.51

Strike	Calls May	Calls June	Calls July	Puts May	Puts June	Puts July
70	s	r	s	s	0.20	s
88	11.70	r	r	r	0.15	r
90	r	r	r	r	0.25	0.55
92	r	r	r	r	0.35	r
94	r	6.10	r	r	0.65	0.90
95	s	r	s	s	0.70	s
96	r	r	r	r	0.80	1.60
97	2.75	r	r	0.10	1.10	1.95
98	1.85	3.00	r	0.15	1.35	r
99	1.05	2.30	r	0.35	1.70	r
100	0.45	1.80	2.60	0.80	2.00	2.85
101	0.15	1.25	r	1.45	2.70	r
102	0.10	0.85	r	2.40	3.50	4.00
103	0.05	0.50	1.25	3.30	4.10	4.50
104	0.05	0.30	r	4.40	4.50	r
105	r	0.20	r	r	r	r
106	0.05	0.15	r	6.40	r	r
107	r	0.05	0.25	r	r	r
109	r	0.10	r	r	r	r
112	r	0.05	r	r	r	r
116	r	r	r	r	16.10	r

Total call vol. 20,414 Total put vol. 26,537
Prev. open int. 334,134 Prev. open int. 370,852

Japan Index (AMEX) Index close 112.70

Strike	Calls May	Calls June	Calls July	Puts May	Puts June	Puts July
115	r	r	r	r	4.40	r

Total call vol. 76 Total put vol. 3
Prev. open int. 4,558 Prev. open int. 3,276

Nasdaq 100 (CBOE) Index close 1397.47

Strike	Calls May	Calls June	Calls July	Puts May	Puts June	Puts July
800	597.00	r	r	r	r	r
995	r	r	r	r	0.40	r
1025	r	r	r	r	0.50	r
1050	r	r	r	r	0.60	r
1100	r	r	r	r	0.90	3.70
1125	r	r	r	r	1.25	r
1150	r	r	r	r	r	5.70
1175	r	r	r	r	2.75	8.00
1200	r	r	r	r	3.30	10.20
1225	r	r	r	0.10	4.90	r
1250	r	r	r	0.20	6.30	r
1275	r	r	r	0.10	9.20	20.00
1300	100.00	r	r	0.30	13.00	r
1325	78.00	r	r	0.50	17.50	r
1350	51.00	r	r	1.55	23.00	r
1375	29.40	56.00	r	5.20	33.00	47.50
1400	11.10	42.00	r	12.50	43.50	r
1425	3.00	29.00	r	28.00	60.00	r
1450	0.60	20.00	r	51.10	r	r
1475	0.20	12.50	r	78.00	r	r
1500	0.10	7.30	18.20	100.00	112.00	r
1525	0.10	4.20	r	125.50	r	r
1550	0.10	2.50	r	r	r	r
1575	0.10	1.10	6.00	r	r	r
1600	0.05	r	r	r	r	r
1650	r	0.40	r	r	r	r
1700	0.05	r	r	303.00	r	r

Total call vol. 4,623 Total put vol. 8,771
Prev. open int. 107,295 Prev. open int. 202,923

Russell 2000 (CBOE) Index close 542.56

Strike	Calls May	Calls June	Calls July	Puts May	Puts June	Puts July
490	r	r	s	r	5.00	s
500	r	r	r	0.10	6.70	11.50
510	r	r	r	0.30	8.30	r
520	r	r	r	1.00	11.50	r
530	11.70	r	r	1.70	16.00	r
540	6.90	16.70	r	4.80	17.00	25.00
550	2.30	12.30	r	9.90	25.70	r
560	0.75	9.10	r	r	r	r
570	0.35	r	r	r	39.20	r
580	0.10	r	7.60	38.00	44.70	r
590	0.10	r	r	r	r	r

Total call vol. 405 Total put vol. 3,252
Prev. open int. 17,581 Prev. open int. 41,749

S&P/TSX 60 (ME) Index close 451.84

Strike	Calls May	Calls June	Calls July	Puts May	Puts June	Puts July
460	r	r	r	12.10	r	r
470	0.20	r	r	r	r	r

Total call vol. 1 Total put vol. 3
Prev. open int. 2,334 Prev. open int. 2,438

S&P 100 (CBOE) Index close 533.82

Strike	Calls May	Calls June	Calls July	Puts May	Puts June	Puts July
380	r	r	r	r	0.05	r
430	r	s	r	r	s	0.75
440	r	r	r	r	r	0.80
450	r	r	r	r	0.40	r
460	r	75.50	76.00	r	0.60	r
475	r	r	s	r	1.00	s
480	r	r	r	0.05	1.05	3.10
485	r	r	s	0.05	1.30	s
490	r	r	r	0.10	1.65	4.30
495	r	r	s	0.15	2.10	s
500	r	r	r	0.15	2.70	5.70
505	r	r	s	0.20	3.20	s
510	r	r	r	0.25	4.10	7.80
515	19.70	r	s	0.30	4.90	s
520	15.00	20.80	24.00	0.60	6.20	10.60
525	10.50	16.50	s	0.95	8.00	s
530	5.80	13.60	r	2.05	9.20	14.10
535	2.90	10.20	r	4.20	11.60	16.00
540	1.05	7.50	12.10	7.70	14.00	19.00
545	0.40	5.20	s	12.00	17.00	s
550	0.15	3.90	7.80	17.20	19.50	r
555	0.05	2.35	s	21.50	24.30	s
560	0.05	1.65	4.20	27.00	r	r
565	0.05	0.95	s	r	r	s
570	0.05	0.60	2.10	r	38.20	r
575	0.05	0.35	s	r	r	s
580	0.05	0.20	0.90	r	47.50	r
590	0.05	r	r	r	r	r

Total call vol. 35,393 Total put vol. 66,475
Prev. open int. 246,897 Prev. open int. 247,931

S&P 500 Comp (CBOE) Index close 1091.49

Strike	Calls May	Calls June	Calls July	Puts May	Puts June	Puts July
775	s	r	r	s	r	0.25
800	r	r	r	r	0.15	r
850	r	r	r	r	0.30	r
875	r	r	r	r	0.40	r
900	r	192.90	r	r	0.55	1.85
925	r	r	r	0.05	0.80	3.10
950	r	143.00	r	0.05	1.30	4.00
975	r	r	r	0.10	2.10	5.50
995	r	r	r	0.15	3.40	r
1005	r	91.00	r	0.15	3.80	8.50
1010	s	86.50	s	s	r	s
1025	66.50	71.90	r	0.25	5.60	12.00
1035	r	s	s	0.30	s	s
1040	r	s	s	0.35	s	s
1050	42.20	50.00	58.00	0.45	9.50	16.50
1060	r	s	s	0.90	s	s
1065	r	r	r	1.40	13.60	r
1070	22.00	s	s	1.35	s	s
1075	19.00	33.00	41.10	2.35	15.50	24.00
1080	14.40	29.00	s	3.20	17.50	s
1085	s	25.50	s	s	19.50	s
1090	8.00	22.00	s	6.50	21.00	s
1095	s	20.30	s	s	23.50	s
1100	3.90	16.20	25.50	11.80	26.30	34.50
1110	1.00	12.80	s	18.50	31.00	s
1115	0.60	11.50	s	23.30	32.90	s
1120	0.35	8.60	s	28.30	38.00	s
1125	0.15	7.50	15.00	34.40	40.50	47.50
1130	0.15	6.20	s	38.10	44.30	s
1135	0.10	5.10	s	r	r	s
1140	0.10	4.00	9.80	46.90	53.00	r
1145	0.05	s	s	r	s	s
1150	0.05	2.60	7.00	58.00	61.20	65.80
1155	r	2.00	s	r	r	s
1160	r	1.45	r	67.20	r	r
1165	r	s	4.00	r	s	r
1170	r	1.10	s	r	r	s
1175	0.05	0.90	2.80	r	r	r
1180	0.10	s	s	r	s	s
1190	0.05	s	s	r	s	s
1200	r	0.30	1.00	r	106.50	r
1225	r	r	r	r	137.00	r
1500	s	r	s	s	407.60	s

Total call vol. 38,389 Total put vol. 105,481
Prev. open int. 1,292,848 Prev. open int. 2,196,934

Source: *The Financial Post (National Post)*, May 19, 2004. Reprinted by permission.

Futures Options Futures options give their holders the right to buy or sell a specified futures contract, using as a future price the exercise price of the option. Although the delivery process is slightly complicated, the terms of futures options contracts are designed, in effect, to allow the option to be written on the futures price itself. The option holder receives upon exercise a profit equal to the difference between the current futures price on the specified asset and the exercise price of the option. Thus, if the futures price is, for example, $37, and the call has an exercise price of $35, the holder who exercises the call option on the futures gets a payoff of $2.

Interest Rate Options Options on Canada bonds are traded on the Canadian Derivatives Exchange, although no such options traded that particular day. There also are options on Canada Bond futures and bankers' acceptances futures.

Options on particular U.S. Treasury notes and bonds are listed on the American Exchange and the CBOE. Options also are traded on Treasury bills, certificates of deposit, GNMA pass-through certificates, and yields on Treasury securities. Options on several interest rate futures, such as Treasury bonds, Treasury notes, municipal bonds, and LIBOR also trade on various U.S. exchanges.

17.2 VALUES OF OPTIONS AT EXPIRATION

Call Options

Recall that a call option gives the right to purchase a security at the exercise price. If you hold a call option on Alcan stock with an exercise price of $60 and Alcan currently sells at $70, you can exercise your option to purchase the stock at $60 and simultaneously sell the shares at the market price of $70, clearing $10 per share. On the other hand, if the shares sell below $60, you can sit on the option and do nothing, realizing no further gain or loss. The value of the call option at expiration equals:

$$\text{Payoff to call holder} = \begin{cases} S_T - X & \text{if } S_T > X \\ 0 & \text{if } S_T \le X \end{cases}$$

where S_T is the value of the stock at expiration and X is the exercise price. This formula emphasizes the option property, because the payoff cannot be negative. That is, the option is exercised only if S_T exceeds X. If S_T is less than X, exercise does not occur and the option expires with zero value. The loss to the option holder in this case equals the price originally paid for the right to buy at the exercise price.

The value at expiration of the call on Alcan with exercise price $60 is given by the following schedule:

Alcan value:	$40	$50	$60	$70	$80
Option value:	0	0	$0	$10	$20

For Alcan prices at or below $60, the option is worthless. Above $60, the option is worth the excess of Alcan price over $70. The option's value increases by $1 for each dollar increase in the Alcan stock price. This relationship can be depicted graphically, as in the solid (top) line of Figure 17.3.

The solid line depicts the value of the call at maturity. The net *profit* to the holder of the call equals the gross payoff less the initial investment in the call. Suppose the call cost $10. Then the profit to the call holder would be as given in the broken (bottom) line of the figure. At option expiration, the investor has suffered a loss of $10 if the stock price is less than $60. Profits do not become positive unless the stock price at expiration exceeds $70. The breakeven point is

Figure 17.3 Payoff and profit to call option at expiration.

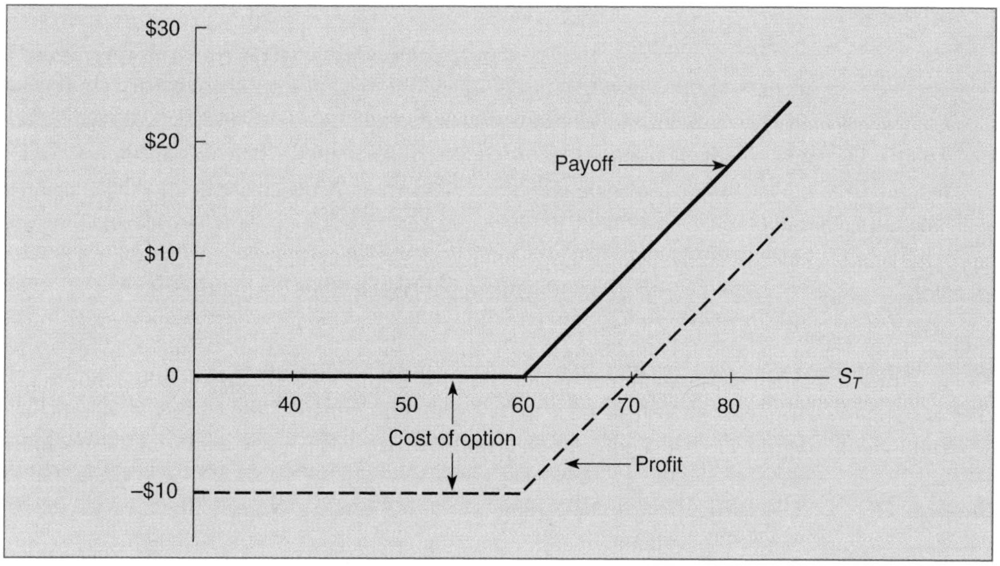

Figure 17.4 Payoff and profit to call writers at expiration.

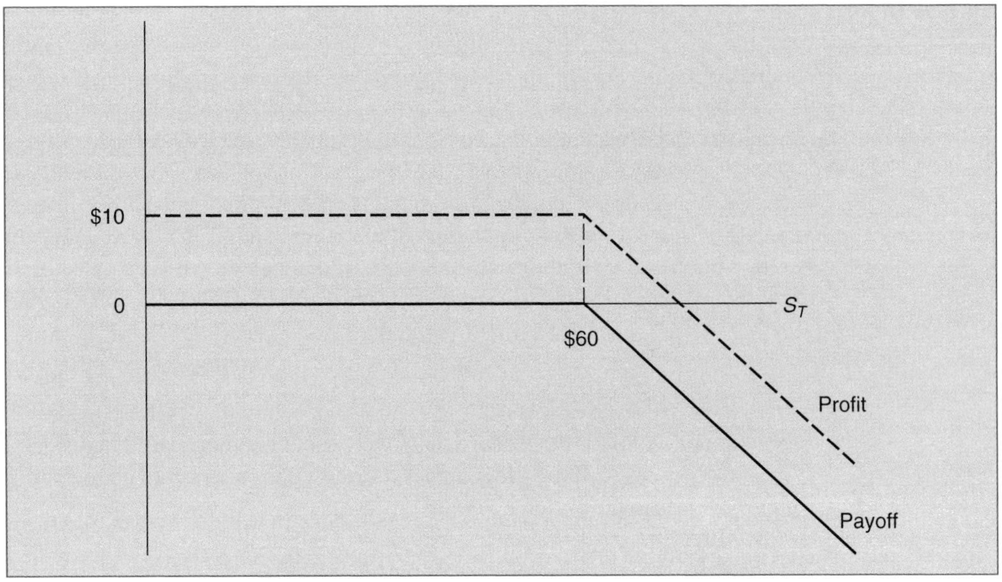

\$70, because at that point the payoff to the call, $S_T - X = \$70 - \$60 = \$10$, equals the cost paid to acquire the call. Hence, the call holder profits only if the stock price is higher.

Conversely, the writer of the call incurs losses if the stock price is high. In that scenario, the writer will receive a call and will be obligated to deliver a stock worth S_T for only X dollars:

$$\text{Payoff to call writer} = \begin{cases} -(S_T - X) & \text{if } S_T \geq X \\ 0 & \text{if } S_T < X \end{cases}$$

The call writer, who is exposed to losses if Alcan stock increases in price, is willing to bear this risk in return for the option premium. Figure 17.4 depicts the payoff and profit diagrams for the call writer. Notice that these are just the mirror images of the corresponding diagrams for call holders. The breakeven point for the option writer also is \$70. The (negative) payoff at that point just offsets the premium originally received when the option was written.

Put Options

A put option conveys the right to sell an asset at the exercise price. In this case, the holder will not exercise the option unless the asset sells for *less* than the exercise price. For example, if Alcan shares were to fall to \$50, a put option with exercise price \$60 could be exercised to give a \$10 profit to its holder. The holder would purchase a share of Alcan for \$50 and simultaneously deliver it to the put option writer for the exercise price of \$60.

The value of a put option at expiration is

$$\text{Payoff to put holder} = \begin{cases} X - S_T & \text{if } S_T \leq X \\ 0 & \text{if } X_T > X \end{cases}$$

The solid (top) line in Figure 17.5 illustrates the payoff at maturity to the holder of a put option on Alcan stock with an exercise price of \$60. If the stock price at option maturity is above \$60, the put has no value, because the right to sell the shares at \$60 would not be exercised. Below a price of \$60, the put value at expiration increases by \$1 for each dollar that the stock price falls. The dashed (bottom) line in the figure is a graph of the put option owner's profit at expiration, net of the initial cost of the put.

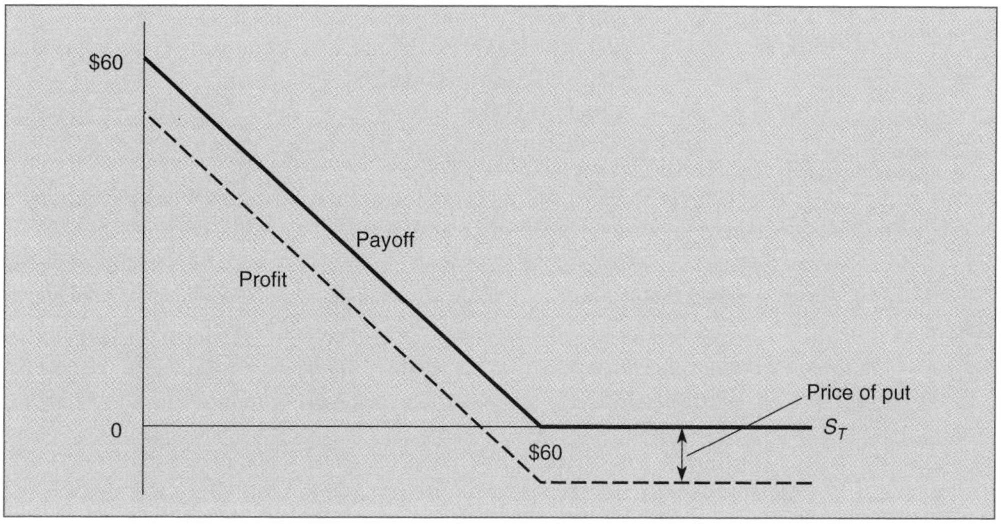

Figure 17.5 Payoff and profit to put option at expiration.

CONCEPT CHECK

3. Analyze the strategy of put writing.
   a. What is the payoff to a put writer as a function of the stock price?
   b. What is the profit?
   c. Draw the payoff and profit graphs.
   d. When do put writers do well? When do they do poorly?

Writing puts *naked* (i.e., writing a put without an offsetting position in the stock for hedging purposes) exposes the writer to losses if the market falls. Writing naked out-of-the-money puts was once considered an attractive way to generate income, since it was believed that, as long as the market did not fall sharply before the option expiration, the option premium could be collected without the put holder ever exercising the option against the writer. Because only sharp drops in the market could result in losses to the writer of the put, the strategy was not viewed as overly risky. However, in the wake of the market crash of October 1987, such put writers suffered huge losses. Participants now perceive much greater risk to this strategy.

Options Versus Stock Investments

Call options are bullish investments; that is, they provide profits when stock prices increase. Puts, in contrast, are bearish investments. Symmetrically, writing calls is bearish and writing puts is bullish. Because option values depend on market movements, purchase of options may be viewed as a substitute for direct purchase or sale of a stock. Why might an option strategy be preferable to direct stock transactions?

For example, why would you purchase a call option rather than buy Alcan's stock directly? Maybe you have some information that leads you to believe that Alcan's stock will increase in value from its current level, which in our examples we will take to be $50. You know your analysis could be incorrect, and that Alcan also could fall in price. Suppose that a six-month maturity call option with exercise price $50 currently sells for $5, and that the six-month interest rate is 3 percent. Consider these three strategies for investing a sum of money, for example, $10,000. For simplicity, suppose that Alcan will not pay any dividends until after the six-month period.

Strategy *A:* Purchase 200 shares of Alcan stock.

Strategy *B:* Purchase 2,000 call options on Alcan with exercise price \$50. (This would require 20 contracts, each for 100 shares.)

Strategy *C:* Purchase 200 call options for \$1,000. Invest the remaining \$9,000 in six-month T-bills, to earn 3 percent interest. The bills will grow to 9,000 × 1.03 = \$9,270.

Let us trace the possible values of these three portfolios when the options expire in six months as a function of Alcan stock price at that time.

Alcan Price	\$45	\$50	\$55	\$60	\$65
Value of portfolio *A:*	\$9,000	\$10,000	\$11,000	\$12,000	\$13,000
Value of portfolio *B:*	0	0	10,000	20,000	30,000
Value of portfolio *C:*	9,270	9,270	10,270	11,270	12,270

Portfolio *A* will be worth 200 times the share value of Alcan. Portfolio *B* is worthless unless Alcan sells for more than the exercise price of the call. Once that point is reached, the portfolio is worth 2,000 times the excess of the stock price over the exercise price. Finally, portfolio *C* is worth \$9,270 from the investment in T-bills plus any profits from the 100 call options. Remember that each of these portfolios involves the same \$10,000 initial investment. The rates of return on these three portfolios are as follows:

Alcan Price	\$45	\$50	\$55	\$60	\$65
A (all stock)	−10.0%	0%	10.0%	20.0%	30.0%
B (all options)	−100.0%	−100.0%	0%	100.0%	200.0%
C (options plus bills)	−7.3%	−7.3%	2.7%	12.7%	27.7%

These rates of return are illustrated in Figure 17.6.

Comparing the returns to portfolios *B* and *C* to those of the simple investment in Alcan stock represented by portfolio *A,* we see that options offer two interesting features. First, an option offers leverage. Compare the returns of portfolio *B* and *A.* When Alcan stock falls in price to \$50, the value of portfolio *B* falls precipitously to zero, a rate of return of −100 percent. Conversely, if the stock price increases from \$50 to \$60, the all-option portfolio jumps in value by a disproportionate

Figure 17.6 Rates of return to three strategies.

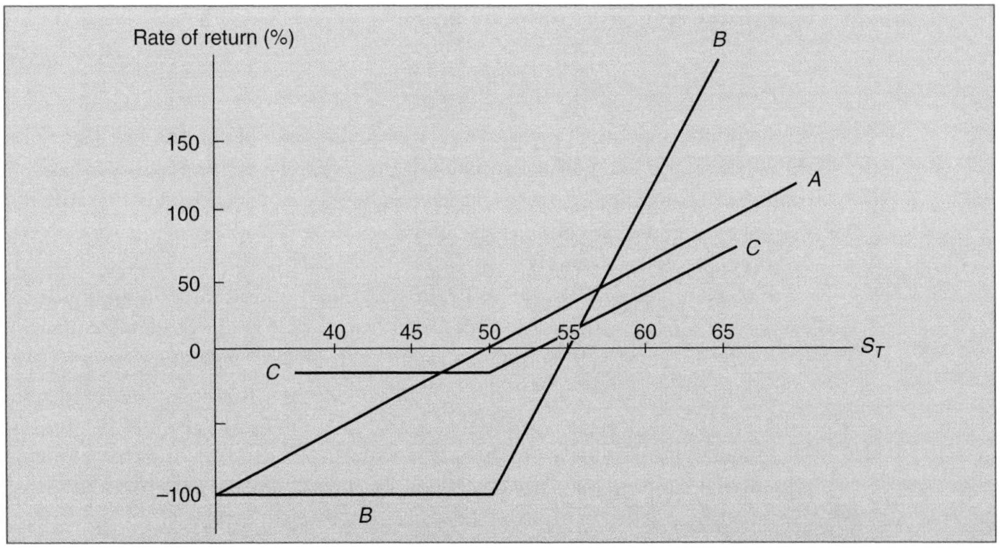

EXCEL APPLICATION

STOCK, OPTIONS, AND COMBINED LENDING AND OPTIONS

The Options, Stock, and Lending spreadsheet extends the analysis presented in this section. The model facilitates comparison of alternative investment strategies involving options, stock, and lending. The spreadsheet allows you to use various combinations of options, stock, and T-bills to explore the flexibility made possible by options. It is built using the data table function so that it allows comparison of investment values and rates of return on investments over a range of ending stock prices.

The full spreadsheet model can be found on the Online Learning Center at www.mcgrawhill.ca/college/bodie.

	A	B	C	D	E	F	G	H	I	J	K
1	**Chapter 17 Solution to Problems**						**LEGEND:**				
2	**Comparison of Options, Equity and Combined Bills and Options**						**Enter data**				
3							**Value calculated**				
4	Current stock price (S_0)	$150.00					**See comment**				
5	Option premium	$20.00									
6	Exercise price(X)	$150.00									
7	Risk-free interest rate (annual)(r_f)	4.00%		**One-Way Data Table**		Value of stock at expiration					
8	Value of stock at expiration (S_T)	$170.00		**Options Only Strategy**		$120	$130	$140	$150	$160	$170
9	Option premium at expiration	$20.00		Total value at expiration	$30,000	$0	$0	$0	$0	$16,000	$30,000
10	Investment amount	$30,000.00									
11				**One-Way Data Table**		Value of stock at expiration					
12	**Options Only Strategy**			**Stock Only Strategy**		$120	$130	$140	$150	$160	$170
13	Number of options purchased	$500.00		Total value at expiration	$34,000	$24,000	$26,000	$28,000	$30,000	$32,000	$34,000
14	Option premium at expiration	$20.00									
15	Total value at expiration	$30,000.00		**One-Way Data Table**		Value of stock at expiration					
16	Total profit	$0.00		**Bills and Options Strategy**		$120	$130	$140	$150	$160	$170
17	Return on Investment	0.00%		Total value at expiration	$31,040	$27,040	$27,040	$27,040	$27,040	$29,040	$31,040
18											
19											

200 percent. In this sense, calls are a leveraged investment on the stock. Their values respond more than proportionately to changes in the stock value. Figure 17.6 vividly illustrates this point. The slope of the all-option portfolio is far steeper than the all-stock portfolio, reflecting its greater proportional sensitivity to the value of the underlying security. The leverage factor is the reason that investors (illegally) exploiting inside information commonly choose options as their investment vehicle.

The potential insurance value of options is the second interesting feature, as portfolio *C* shows. The T-bill plus option portfolio cannot be worth less than $9,270 after six months, since the option can always be left to expire worthless. The worst possible rate of return on portfolio *C* is –7.3 percent, compared to a (theoretically) worst possible rate of return on Alcan stock of –100 percent if the company were to go bankrupt. Of course, this insurance comes at a price: when Alcan does well, portfolio *C* does not perform quite as well as portfolio *A*.

17.3 OPTION STRATEGIES

An unlimited variety of payoff patterns can be achieved by combining puts and calls with various exercise prices. The following subsections explain the motivation and structure of some of the more popular methods.

Protective Put

Imagine that you would like to invest in a stock, for example, Alcan's, but that you are unwilling to bear potential losses beyond some given level. Investing in the stock alone is quite risky, because in

Table 17.1 Payoff to Protective Put Strategy

	$S_T \leq X$	$S_T > X$
Stock	S_T	S_T
Put	$X - S_T$	0
Total	X	S_T

principle you could lose all the money you invest. Instead you might consider investing in stock together with a put option on the stock. Table 17.1 illustrates the total value of your portfolio at option expiration.

Whatever happens to the stock price, you are guaranteed a payoff equal to the put option's exercise price because the put gives you the right to sell Alcan for the exercise price even if the stock price is below that value.

Figure 17.7, illustrates the payoff and profit to this **protective put** strategy. The solid line in Figure 17.7, panel C is the total payoff; the dashed line is displaced downward by the cost of establishing the position, $S_0 + P$. Notice that potential losses are indeed limited.

Figure 17.7 Value of a protective put position at expiration.

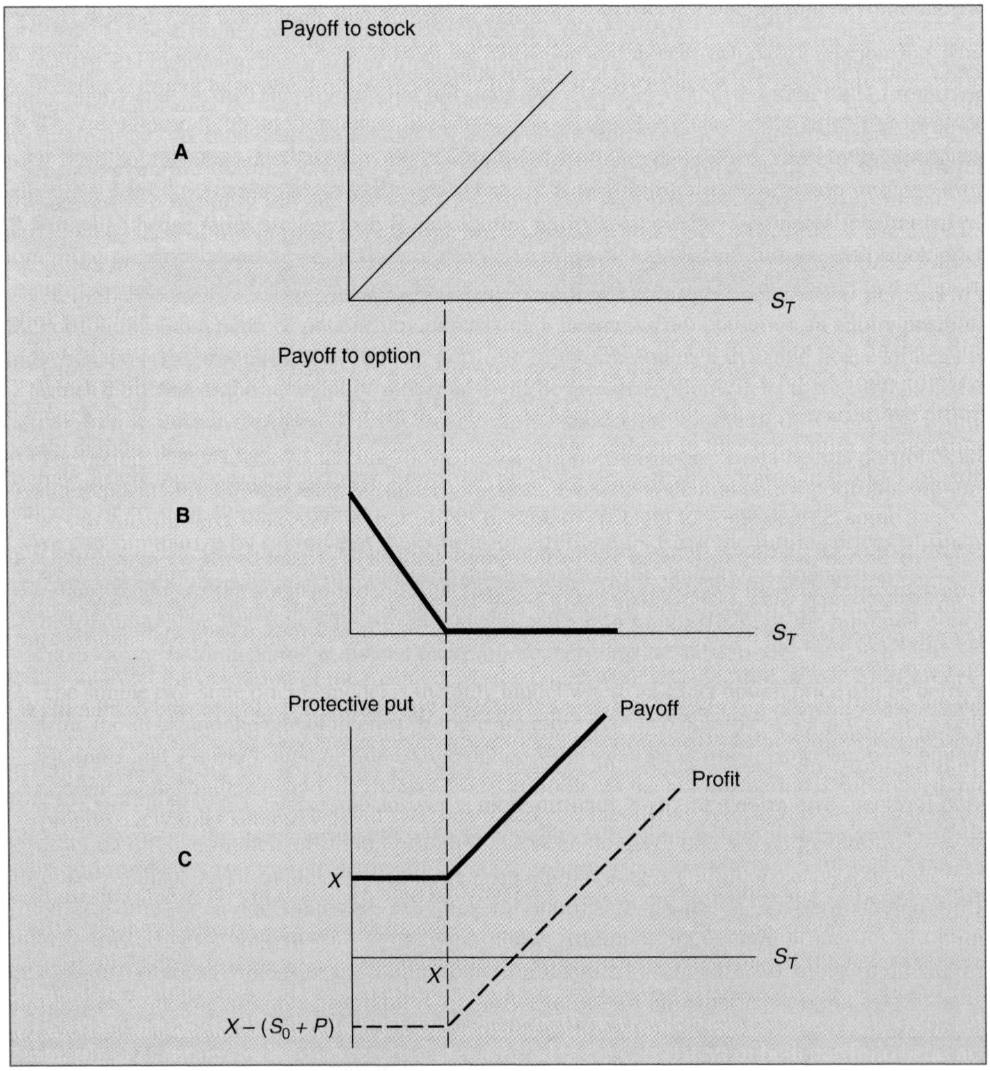

It is instructive to compare the profit to the protective put strategy with that of the stock investment. For simplicity, consider an at-the-money protective put, so that $X = S_0$. Figure 17.8 compares the profits for the two strategies. The profit on the stock is zero if the stock price remains unchanged, and $S_T = S_0$. It rises or falls by $1 for every $1 swing in the ultimate stock price. The profit on the stock plus put portfolio is negative and equal to the cost of the put if S_T is below S_0. The profit on the overall protective put position increases one for one with increases in the stock price, once S_T exceeds S_0.

Figure 17.8 makes it clear that the protective put offers some insurance against stock price declines in that it limits losses. Indeed, protective put strategies provide a form of *portfolio insurance.* The cost of the protection is that, in the case of stock price increases, your profit is reduced by the cost of the put, which turned out to be unneeded.

This example also shows that despite the common perception that derivatives mean risk, derivative securities can be used effectively for *risk management.* In fact, such risk management is becoming accepted as part of the fiduciary responsibility of financial managers. Indeed, in a recent U.S. court case, *Brane v. Roth,* a company's board of directors was successfully sued for failing to use derivatives to hedge the price risk of grain held in storage. Such hedging might have been accomplished using protective puts. Some observers believe that this case will soon lead to a broad legal obligation for firms to use derivatives and other techniques to manage risk.

Covered Call

A **covered call** position is the purchase of a share of stock with a simultaneous sale of a call on that stock. The position is "covered" because the obligation to deliver the stock is covered by the stock held in the portfolio. Writing an option without an offsetting stock position is called, by contrast, *naked option writing.* The payoff to a covered call, presented in Table 17.2, equals the stock value

Figure 17.8 Protective put versus stock investment.

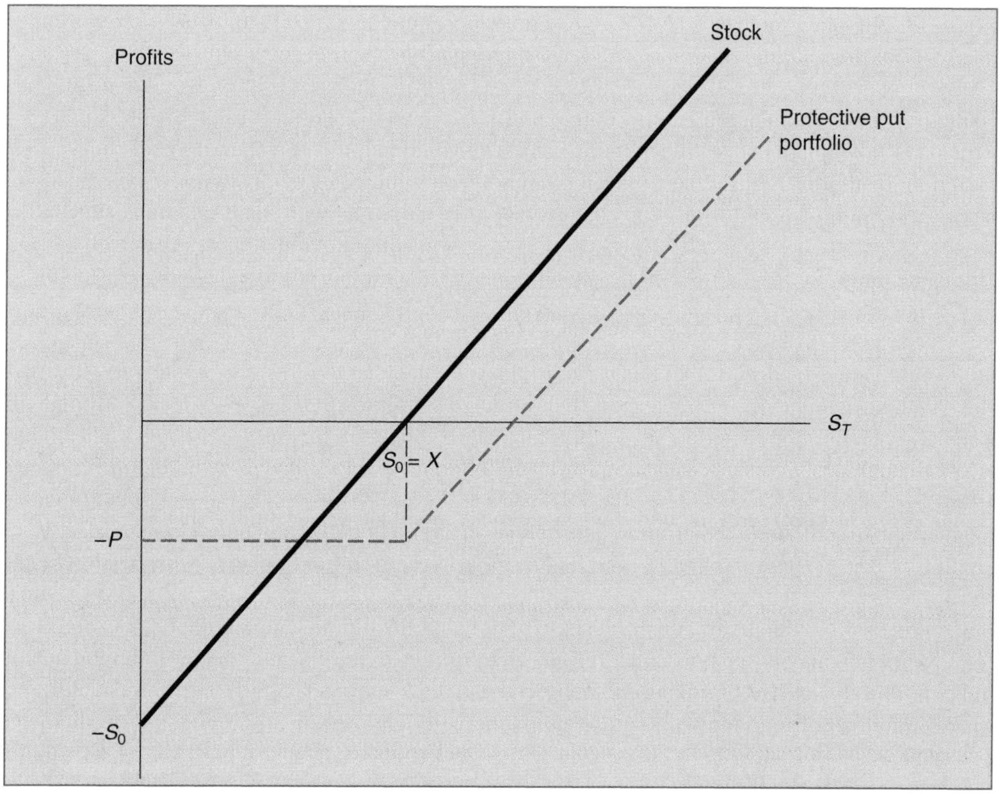

Table 17.2
Payoff to a Covered Call

	$S_T \le X$	$S_T > X$
Payoff of stock	S_T	S_T
–Payoff of call	-0	$-(S_T - X)$
Total	S_T	X

minus the payoff of the call. The call payoff is subtracted because the covered call position involves issuing a call to another investor who can choose to exercise it to profit at your expense.

The solid line in Figure 17.9, panel C illustrates the payoff pattern. We see that the total position is worth S_T when the stock price at time T is below X, and rises to a maximum of X when S_T exceeds X. In essence, the sale of the call option means that the call writer has sold the claim to any stock value above X in return for the initial premium (the call price). Therefore, at expiration the position is worth, at most X. The dashed line of panel C is the net profit to the covered call.

Writing covered call options has been a popular investment strategy among institutional investors. Consider the managers of a fund invested largely in stocks. They might find it appealing

Figure 17.9
Value of a covered call position at expiration.

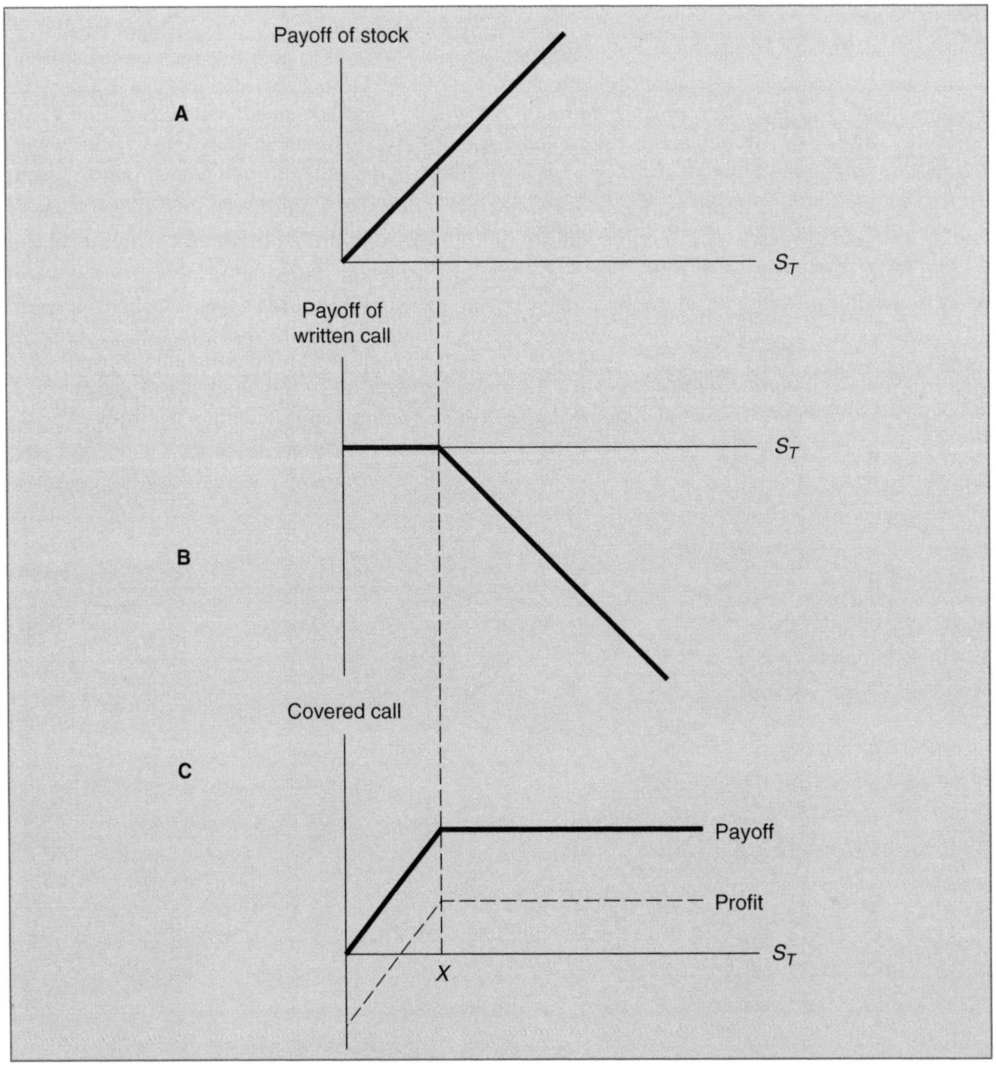

to write calls on some or all of the stock in order to boost income by the premiums collected. Although they thereby forfeit potential capital gains should the stock price rise above the exercise price, if they view X as the price at which they plan to sell the stock anyway, then the call may be viewed as enforcing a kind of "sell discipline." The written call guarantees that the stock sale will take place as planned.

EXAMPLE 17.3 Covered Call

Assume a pension fund is holding 1,000 shares of Alcan stock, with a current price of \$50 per share. Suppose that management intends to sell all 1,000 shares if the share price hits \$55 and that a call expiring in 90 days with an exercise price of \$55 is currently selling for \$5. By writing 10 Alcan call contracts (100 shares each) the fund can pick up \$5,000 in extra income. The fund would lose its share of profits from any movement of Alcan stock above \$55 per share, but given that it would have sold its shares at \$55, it would not have realized those profits anyway.

Straddle

A long **straddle** is established by buying both a call and a put on a stock, each with the same exercise price, X, and the same expiration date, T. Straddles are useful strategies for investors who believe that a stock will move a lot in price, but who are uncertain about the direction of the move. For example, suppose you believe that an important court case that will make or break a company is about to be settled, and the market is not yet aware of the situation. The stock will either double in value if the case is settled favourably, or it will drop by half if the settlement goes against the company. The straddle position will do well regardless of the outcome, because its value is highest when the stock price makes extreme upward or downward moves from X.

The worst-case scenario for a straddle is no movement in the stock price. If S_T equals X, both the call and the put expire worthless, and the investor's outlay for the purchase of the two positions is lost. Straddle positions, in other words, are bets on volatility. An investor who establishes a straddle must view the stock as more volatile than the market does. The payoff to straddle is presented in Table 17.3.

The solid line in panel C of Figure 17.10 illustrates this payoff. Notice that the portfolio payoff is always positive, except at the one point where the portfolio has zero value, $S_T = X$. You might wonder why all investors do not pursue such a no-lose strategy. Remember, however, that the straddle requires that both the put and call be purchased. The value of the portfolio at expiration, although never negative, still must exceed the initial cash outlay for the investor to clear a profit.

The broken line in Figure 17.10, panel C is the profit to the straddle. The profit line lies below the payoff line by the cost of purchasing the straddle, $P + C$. It is clear from the diagram that the straddle position generates a loss unless the stock price deviates substantially from X. The stock price must depart from X by the total amount expended to purchase the call and the put for the purchaser of the straddle to clear a profit.

Strips and *straps* are variations of straddles. A strip is two puts and one call on a security with the same exercise price and maturity date. A strap is two calls and one put.

Table 17.3 Payoff to a Straddle

	$S_T \le X$	$S_T > X$
Payoff of call	0	$S_T - X$
+Payoff of put	$+(X - S_T)$	+0
Total	$X - S_T$	$S_T - X$

Figure 17.10 **Payoff and profit to a straddle at expiration.**

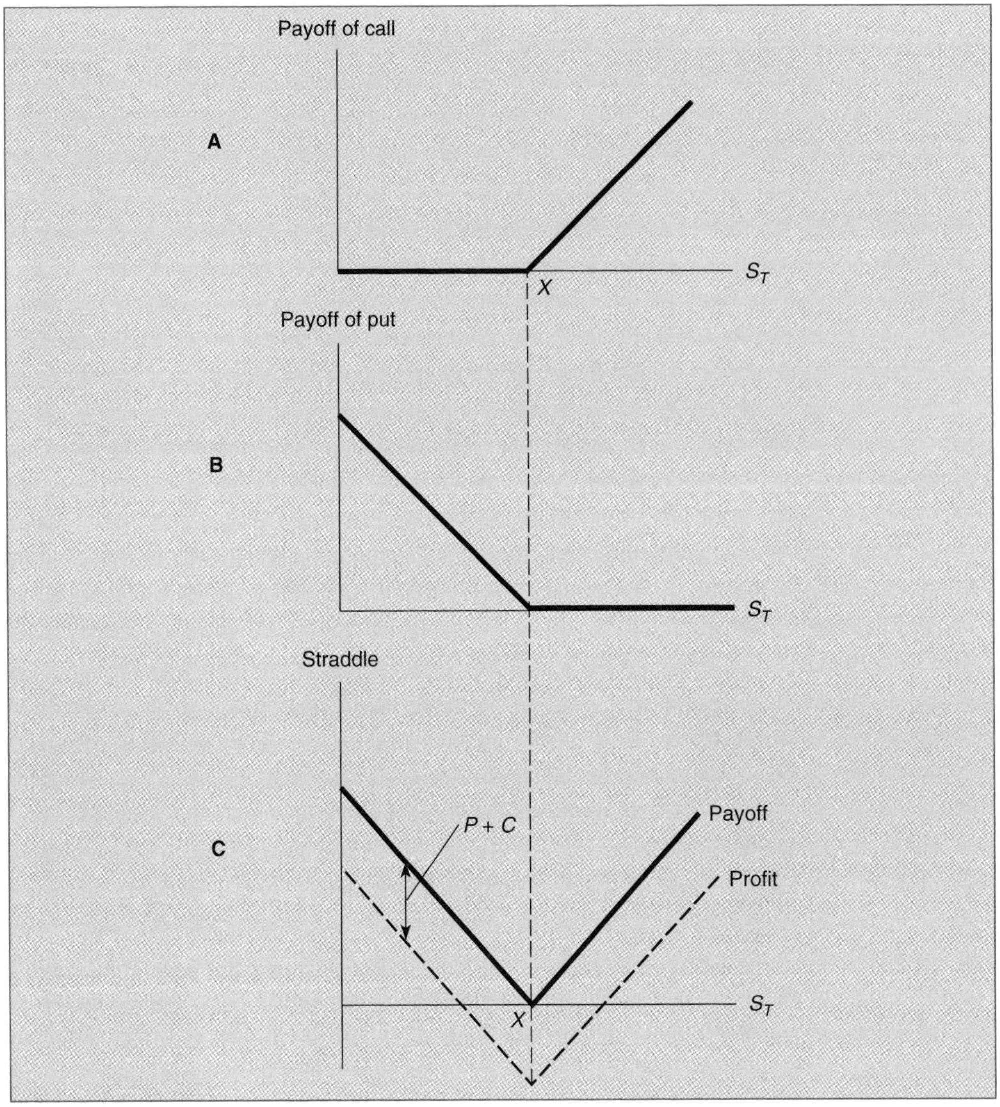

CONCEPT CHECK

4. Graph the profit and payoff diagrams for strips and straps.

Spreads

A **spread** is a combination of two or more call options (or two or more puts) on the same stock with differing exercise prices or times to maturity. Some options will be held long, while others are written. A *money spread* involves the purchase of one option and the simultaneous sale of another with a different exercise price. A *time spread* refers to the sale and purchase of options with differing expiration dates.

Consider a money spread in which one call option is bought with an exercise price X_1, while another call with an identical expiration date but higher exercise price, X_2, is written. The payoff to this position will be the difference in the value of the call held and the value of the call written, as shown in Table 17.4.

Table 17.4 Payoff to a Bullish Vertical Spread

	$S_T \le X_1$	$X_1 < S_T \le X_2$	$S_T > X_2$
Payoff of call, exercise price = X_1	0	$S_T - X_1$	$S_T - X_1$
–Payoff of call, exercise price = X_2	–0	–0	$-(S_T - X_2)$
Total	0	$S_T - X_1$	$X_2 - X_1$

There are now three instead of two outcomes to distinguish: the lowest-price region where S_T is below both exercise prices, a middle region where S_T is between the two exercise prices, and a high-price region where S_T exceeds both exercise prices. Figure 17.11 illustrates the payoff and profit to this strategy, which is called a *bullish spread* because the payoff either increases or is unaffected by stock price increases. Holders of bullish spreads benefit from stock price increases.

One motivation for a bullish spread might be that the investor believes that one option is overpriced relative to another. For example, if the investor believes that an $X = \$135$ call is cheap compared to an $X = \$150$ call, he or she might establish the spread, even without a strong desire to take a bullish position in the stock.

Figure 17.11 Value of a bullish spread position at expiration.

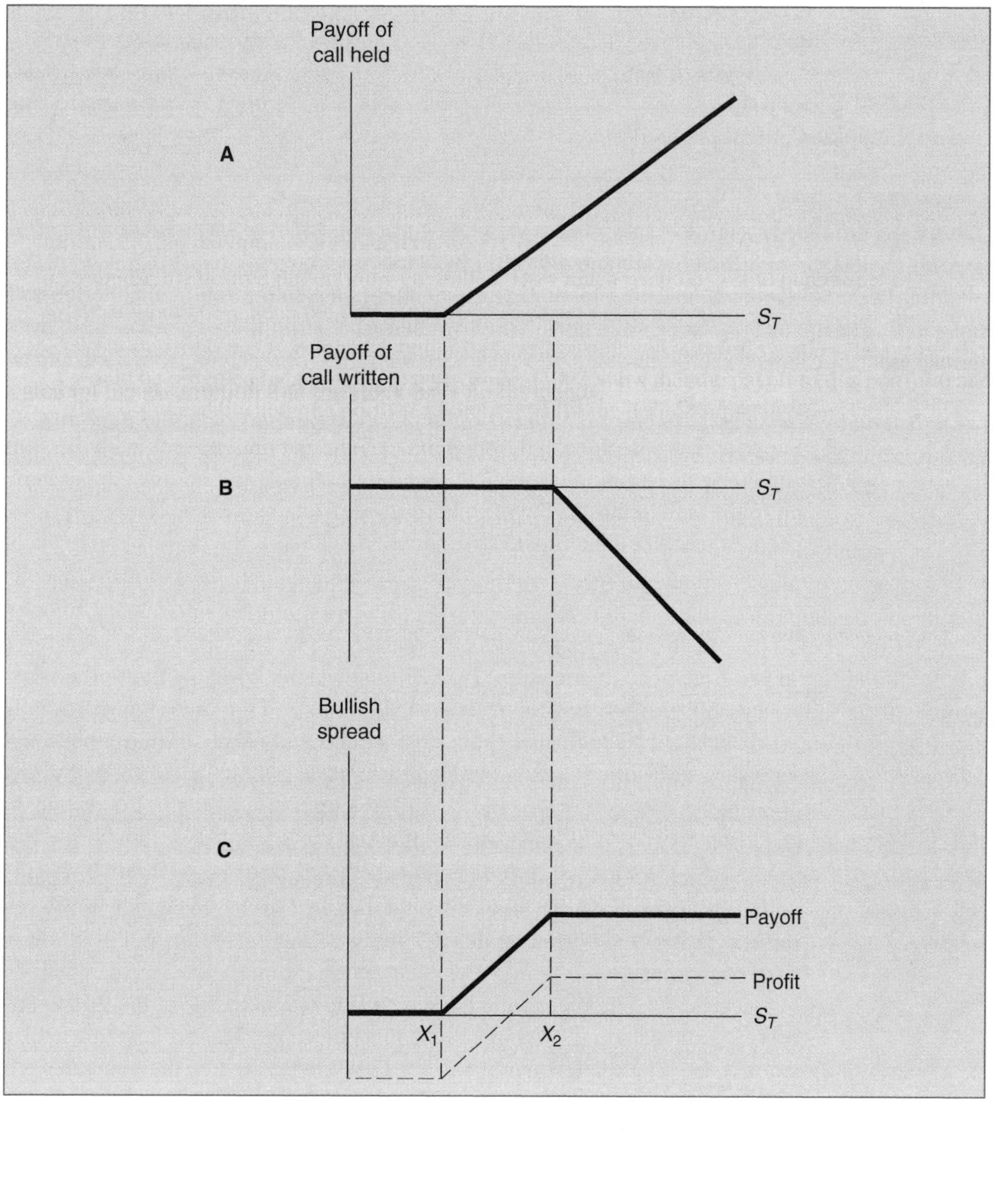

Collars

www.ibm.com

A **collar** is an options strategy that brackets the value of a portfolio between two bounds. Suppose that an investor currently is holding a large position in IBM, which is currently selling at \$100 per share. A lower bound of \$90 can be placed on the value of the portfolio by buying a protective put with exercise price \$90. This protection, however, requires that the investor pay the put premium. To raise the money to pay for the put, the investor might write a call option, say with exercise price \$110. The call might sell for roughly the same price as the put, meaning that the net outlay for the two options positions is approximately zero. Writing the call limits the portfolio's upside potential. Even if the stock price moves above \$110, the investor will do no better than \$110, because at a higher price the stock will be called away. Thus the investor obtains the downside protection represented by the exercise price of the put by selling her claim to any upside potential beyond the exercise price of the call.

A collar would be appropriate for an investor who has a target wealth goal in mind but is unwilling to risk losses beyond a certain level. If you are contemplating buying a house for \$220,000, for example, you might set this figure as your goal. Your current wealth may be \$200,000, and you are unwilling to risk losing more than \$20,000. A collar established by (1) purchasing 2,000 shares of stock currently selling at \$100 per share, (2) purchasing 2,000 put options (20 option contracts) with exercise price \$90, and (3) writing 2,000 calls with exercise price \$110 would give you a good chance to realize the \$20,000 capital gain without risking a loss of more than \$20,000.

CONCEPT CHECK ?

5. Graph the payoff diagram for the collar just described with exercise price of the put equal to \$90, and exercise price of the call equal to \$110.

17.4 THE PUT-CALL PARITY RELATIONSHIP

Suppose that you buy a call option and write a put option, each with the same exercise price, X, and the same expiration date, T. At expiration, the payoff on your investment will equal the payoff to the call, minus the payoff that must be made on the put. The payoff for each option will depend on whether the ultimate stock price, S_T, exceeds the exercise price at contract expiration.

	$S_T \le X$	$S_T > X$
Payoff of call held	0	$S_T - X$
Payoff of put written	$-(X - S_T)$	0
Total	$S_T - X$	$S_T - X$

Figure 17.12 illustrates this payoff pattern. Compare the payoff to that of a portfolio made up of the stock plus a borrowing position, where the money to be paid back will grow, with interest, to X dollars at the maturity of the loan. Such a position, in fact, is a *leveraged* equity position in which $X/(1 + r_f)^T$ dollars is borrowed today (so that X will be repaid at maturity) and S_0 dollars are invested in the stock. The total payoff of the leveraged equity position is $S_T - X$, the same as that of the option strategy. Thus the long call–short put position replicates the leveraged equity position. Again, we see that option trading allows us to construct artificial leverage.

Because the option portfolio has a payoff identical to that of the leveraged equity position, the costs of establishing the two positions must be equal. The net cost of establishing the option position is $C - P$; the call is purchased for C, while the written put generates premium income of P.

Figure 17.12 The payoff pattern of a long call–short put position.

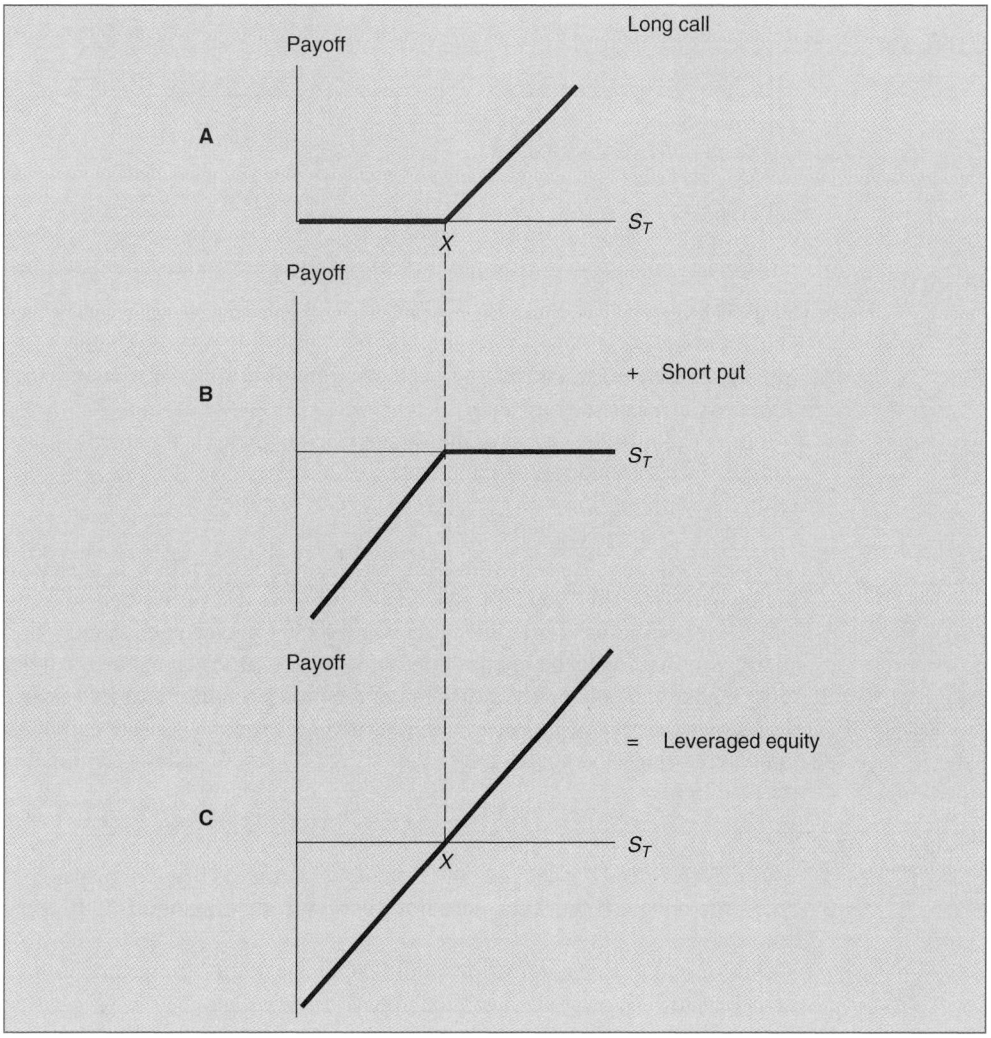

Likewise, the leveraged equity position requires a net cash outlay of $S_0 - X/(1 + r_f)^T$, the cost of the stock less the proceeds from borrowing. Equating these costs, we conclude that

$$C - P = S_0 - X/(1 + r_f)^T \tag{17.1}$$

Equation 17.1 is called the **put-call parity theorem** because it represents the proper relationship between put and call prices. If the parity relationship is ever violated, an arbitrage opportunity arises. For example, suppose that you confront these data for a certain stock:

Stock price	\$110
Call price (6-month maturity, X = \$105)	\$ 17
Put price (6-month maturity, X = \$105)	\$ 5
Risk-free interest rate	10.25 percent annual yield, or 5 percent per 6 months

We use these data in the put-call parity theorem to see if parity is violated:

$$C - P \stackrel{?}{=} S_0 - X/(1 + r_f)^T$$
$$17 - 5 \stackrel{?}{=} 110 - 105/1.05$$
$$12 \stackrel{?}{=} 10$$

Table 17.5 Arbitrage Strategy

Position	Immediate Cash Flow	Cash Flow in 6 Months	
		$S_T \leq 105$	$S_T > 105$
Buy stock	−110	S_T	S_T
Borrow $X/(1 + r_f)^T$ = \$100	+100	−105	−105
Sell call	+ 17	0	$-(S_T - 105)$
Buy put	− 5	$105 - S_T$	0
Total	2	0	0

Parity is violated. To exploit the mispricing, you can buy the relatively cheap portfolio (the stock plus borrowing position represented on the right-hand side of equation 17.1) and sell the relatively expensive portfolio (the long call–short put position corresponding to the left-hand side—that is, write a call and buy a put).

Let us examine the payoff to this strategy. In six months, the stock will be worth S_T. The \$100 borrowed will be paid back with interest, resulting in a cash outflow of \$105. The written call will result in a cash outflow of S_T − \$105 if S_T exceeds \$105.

Table 17.5 summarizes the outcome. The immediate cash inflow is \$2. In six months, the various positions provide exactly offsetting cash flows: the \$2 inflow is thus realized without any offsetting outflows. This is an arbitrage opportunity that will be pursued on a large scale until buying and selling pressures restore the parity condition expressed in equation 17.1.

Equation 17.1 actually applies only to options on stocks that pay no dividends before the maturity date of the option. The extension of the parity condition for European call options on dividend-paying stocks is, however, straightforward. Problem 4 at the end of the chapter leads you through the extension of the parity relationship. The more general formulation of the put-call parity condition is:

$$P = C - S_0 + \text{PV}(X) + \text{PV}(\text{dividends}) \qquad (17.2)$$

where PV(dividends) is the present value of the dividends that will be paid by the stock during the life of the option. If the stock does not pay dividends, equation 17.2 becomes identical to equation 17.1.

Notice that this generalization would apply as well to European options on assets other than stocks. Instead of using dividend income per se in equation 17.2, we would let any income paid only by the underlying asset play the role of the stock dividends. For example, European put and call options on bonds would satisfy the same parity relationship, except that the bond's coupon income would replace the stock's dividend payments in the parity formula.

Even this generalization, however, applies only to European options, as the cash flow stream from the two portfolios represented by the two sides of equation 17.2 will match only if each position is held until maturity. If a call and a put may be optimally exercised at different times before their common expiration date, then the equality of payoffs cannot be assured, or even expected, and the portfolio will have different values.

EXAMPLE 17.4 Put-Call Parity

www.cibc.com

Let's see how well parity works with real data from Figure 17.1, using CIBC options. The April call on CIBC with exercise price \$67.50 and time to expiration of 49 days has an ask price of \$2.35, while the put bid price was \$1.15, CIBC was selling for \$68.54, and the annualized interest rate on this date for 49-day T-bills was 2.20 percent. According to parity, we should find that

$$\$2.35 - \$1.15 = \$68.54 - \frac{67.50}{(1.022)^{49/365}}$$

$$\$1.20 = \$1.24$$

In this case, parity is violated by 4 cents per share. Does this amount outweigh the brokerage fees involved in attempting to exploit the mispricing? Probably not. Moreover, given the infrequent trading of options that we have noted, this discrepancy from parity could be due to "stale" prices, quotes at which you cannot actually trade.

17.5 OPTION-LIKE SECURITIES

Even if you never trade an option directly, you still need to appreciate the properties of options in formulating any investment plan. Why? Many other financial instruments and agreements have features that convey implicit or explicit options to one or more parties. If you are to value and use these securities correctly, you must understand these option attributes.

Callable Bonds

You know from Chapter 11 that many corporate bonds are issued with call provisions entitling the issuer to buy bonds back from bondholders at some time in the future at a specified call price. This provision conveys a call option to the issuer, where the exercise price is equal to the price at which the bond can be repurchased. A callable bond arrangement is essentially a sale of a *straight bond* (a bond with no option features such as callability or convertibility) to the investor and the concurrent issuance of a call option by the investor to the bond-issuing firm.

There must be some compensation for offering this implicit call option to the firm. If the callable bond were issued with the same coupon rate as a straight bond, we would expect it to sell at a discount to the straight bond equal to the value of the call. To sell callable bonds at par, firms must issue them with coupon rates higher than the coupons on straight debt. The higher coupons are the investor's compensation for the call option retained by the issuer. Coupon rates usually are selected so that the newly issued bond will sell at par value.

Figure 17.13 illustrates the option-like property of a callable bond. The horizontal axis is the value of a straight bond with terms otherwise identical to the callable bond. The 45-degree dashed line represents the value of straight debt. The solid line is the value of the callable bond, and the dotted line is the value of the call option retained by the firm. A callable bond's potential for capital gains is limited by the firm's option to repurchase at the call price.

Figure 17.13 Values of callable bonds compared with straight bonds.

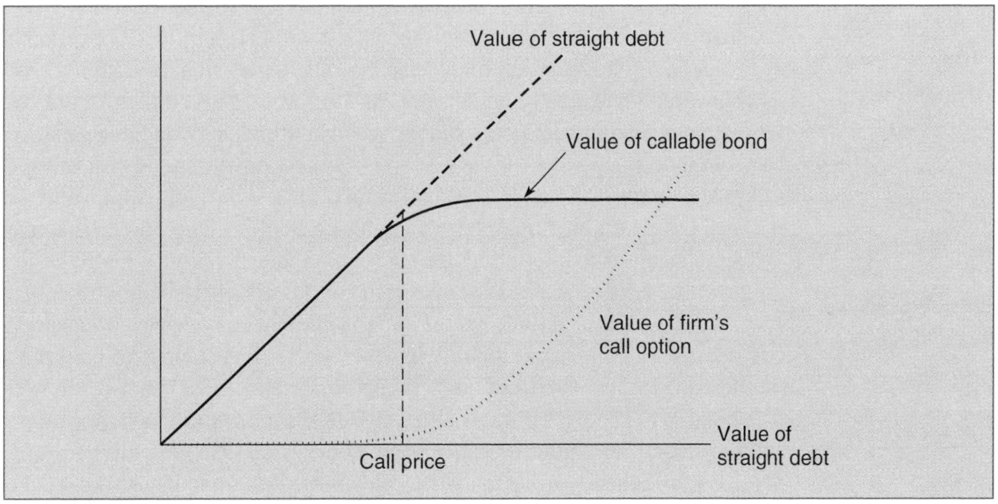

CONCEPT CHECK

6. How is a callable bond similar to a covered call strategy on a straight bond?

The option inherent in callable bonds is actually more complex than an ordinary call option, because usually it may be exercised only after some initial period of call protection. Also, the price at which the bond is callable may change over time. Unlike exchange-listed options, these features are defined in the initial bond offering and will depend on the needs of the issuing firm and its perception of the market's tastes.

CONCEPT CHECK

7. Suppose that the period of call protection is extended. How will the coupon rate that is required for the bond to sell at par value change?

Convertible Securities

Convertible bonds and convertible preferred stock convey options to the holder of the security rather than to the issuing firm. The convertible security typically gives its holder the right to exchange each bond or share of preferred stock for a fixed number of shares of common stock, regardless of the market prices of the securities at the time.

CONCEPT CHECK

8. Should a convertible bond issued at par value have a higher or lower coupon rate than a nonconvertible bond issued at par?

For example, a bond with a conversion ratio of 10 allows its holder to convert one bond of par value $1,000 into 10 shares of common stock. Alternatively, the conversion price in this case is $100: To receive 10 shares of stock, the investor sacrifices bonds with face value $1,000, or $100 of face value per share. If the present value of the bond's scheduled payments is less than 10 times the value of one share of stock, it may pay to convert; that is, the conversion option is in the money. A bond worth $950 with a conversion ratio of 10 could be converted profitably if the stock were selling above $95, since the value of the 10 shares received for each bond surrendered would exceed $950. Most convertible bonds are issued "deep out of the money"; that is, the issuer sets the conversion ratio so that conversion will not be profitable unless there is a substantial increase in stock prices and/or decrease in bond prices from the time of issue.

A bond's conversion value equals the value it would have if you converted it into stock immediately. Clearly, a bond must sell for at least its conversion value. If it did not, you could purchase the bond, convert it immediately, and clear a risk-free profit. This condition could never persist, because all investors would pursue such a strategy, which ultimately would bid up the price of the bond.

The straight bond value or "bond floor" is the value the bond would have if it were not convertible into stock. The bond must sell for more than its straight bond value because a convertible bond is in fact a straight bond plus a valuable call option. Therefore the convertible bond has two lower bounds on its market price: the conversion value and the straight bond value.

Figure 17.14, panel A illustrates the value of the straight debt as a function of the stock price of the issuing firm. For healthy firms the straight debt value is almost independent of the value of the stock because default risk is small. However, if the firm is close to bankruptcy (stock prices are low), default risk increases, and the straight bond value falls. Panel B shows the conversion value of the bond, and panel C compares the value of the convertible bond to these two lower bounds.

When stock prices are low, the straight bond value is the effective lower bound, and the conversion option is nearly irrelevant. The convertible will trade like straight debt. When stock prices

Figure 17.14 **Value of a convertible bond as a function of stock price. Panel A: Straight debt value, or bond floor. Panel B: Conversion value of the bond. Panel C: Total value of convertible bond.**

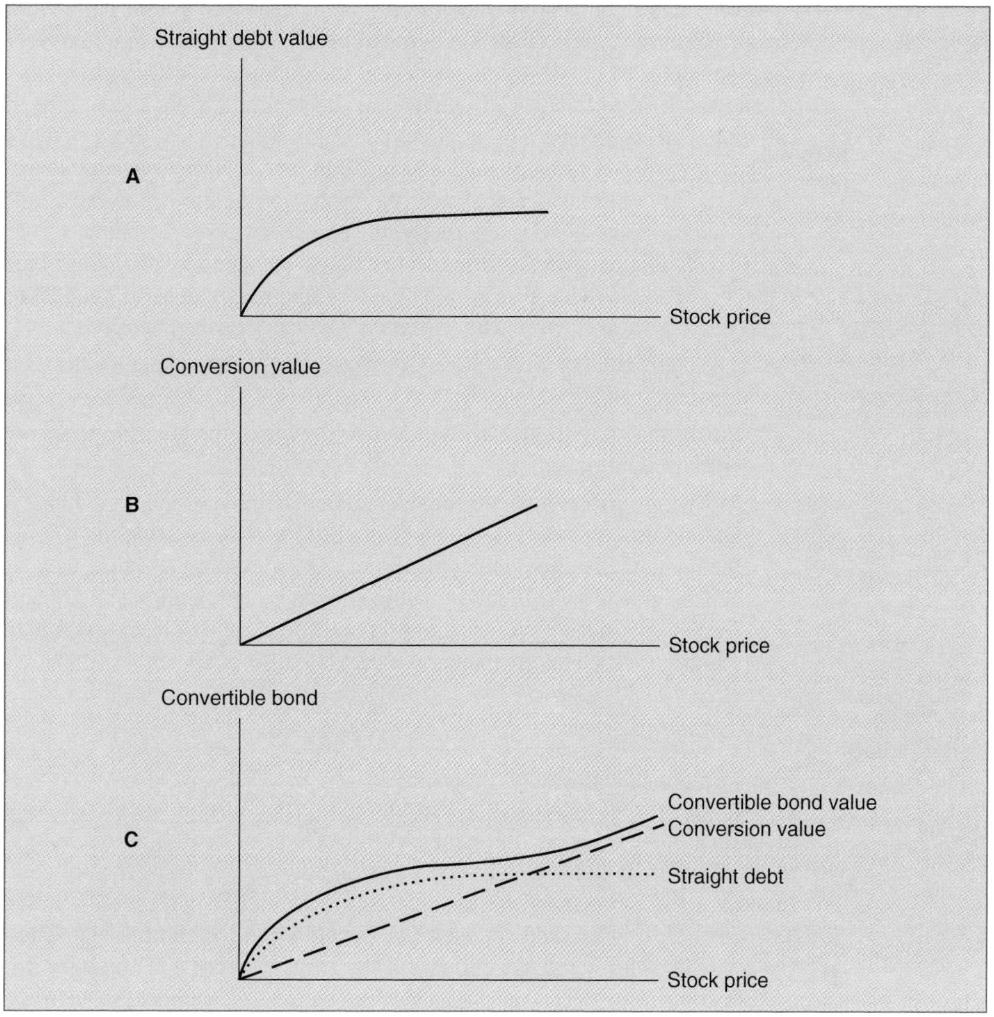

are high, the bond's price is determined by its conversion value. With conversion all but guaranteed, the bond is essentially equity in disguise.

We can illustrate with two examples:

	Bond A	Bond B
Annual coupon	$80	$80
Maturity date	10 years	10 years
Quality rating	Baa	Baa
Conversion ratio	20	25
Stock price	$30	$50
Conversion value	$600	$1,250
Market yield on 10-year Baa-rated bonds	8.5%	8.5%
Value as straight debt	$967	$967
Actual bond price	$972	$1,255
Reported yield to maturity	8.42%	4.76%

Bond A has a conversion value of only $600. Its value as straight debt, in contrast, is $967. This is the present value of the coupon and principal payments at a market rate for straight debt of 8.5 percent. The bond's price is $972, so the premium over straight bond value is only $5, reflecting the low probability of conversion. Its reported yield to maturity based on scheduled coupon payments and the market price of $972 is 8.42 percent, close to that of straight debt.

The conversion option on Bond B is in the money. Conversion value is $1,250, and the bond's price, $1,255, reflects its value as equity (plus $5 for the protection the bond offers against stock price declines). The bond's reported yield is 4.76 percent, far below the comparable yield on straight debt. The big yield sacrifice is attributable to the far greater value of the conversion option. In theory, we could value convertible bonds by treating them as straight debt plus call options. In practice, however, this approach is often impractical for several reasons:

1. The conversion price frequently increases over time, which means the exercise price for the option changes.
2. Stocks may pay several dividends over the life of the bond, further complicating the option valuation analysis.
3. Most convertibles also are callable at the discretion of the firm. In essence, the investor and the firm hold options on each other. If the firm exercises its call option to repurchase the bond, the bondholders typically have a month during which they still can convert. When firms use a call option, while knowing that bondholders will choose to convert, the firm is said to have *forced a conversion.* These conditions together mean that the actual maturity of the bond is indeterminate.

Warrants

Warrants are essentially call options issued by the firm. One important difference between calls and warrants is that exercise of a warrant requires the firm to issue a new share of stock—the total number of shares outstanding increases. Exercise of a call option requires only that the writer of the call deliver an already-issued share of stock to discharge the obligation. In that case, the number of shares outstanding remains fixed. Also unlike call options, warrants result in a cash flow to the firm when the exercise price is paid by the warrant holder. These differences mean that warrant values will differ somewhat from the values of call options with identical terms.

Like convertible debt, warrant terms may be tailored to meet the needs of the firm. Also like convertible debt, warrants generally are protected against stock splits and dividends in that the exercise price and the number of warrants held are adjusted to offset the effects of the split.

Warrants often are issued in conjunction with another security. Bonds, for example, may be packaged together with a warrant "sweetener," frequently a warrant that may be sold separately. This is called a *detachable warrant.*

The issue of warrants and convertible securities creates the potential for an increase in outstanding shares of stock if exercise occurs. Exercise obviously would affect financial statistics that are computed on a per-share basis, so annual reports must provide earnings-per-share (EPS) figures under the assumption that all convertible securities and warrants are exercised. These figures are called *fully diluted* earnings per share.[1]

The executive and employee stock options that became so popular in the past decade were actually warrants. Some of these grants were huge, with payoffs to top executives in excess of $100 million. Yet firms almost uniformly chose not to acknowledge these grants as expenses on their income statements. This dubious practice finally may be changing. The boxed article here makes the case for recognizing employee option grants as an expense, just as it does other components of compensation such as salary or promised pension benefits.

[1]We should note that the exercise of a convertible bond need not reduce EPS. Diluted EPS will be less than undiluted EPS only if interest saved (per share) on the converted bonds is less than the prior EPS.

OPTIONS SHOULD BE REFLECTED IN THE BOTTOM LINE

There are some issues on which accounting and finance professors disagree, but the expensing of employee stock options is not one of them. We believe there is near unanimity of opinion that the value of employee stock options should be expensed on a firm's income statement at the time they are granted.

Stock options have a market price, so when a company grants options to employees, the company has given up something that has considerable value. This is the amount the company would have received had these options been underwritten and sold for cash in a competitive options market. Yet many executives, venture capitalists, politicians, journalists, and even some professional economists have voiced their opposition to proposals that companies reflect the cost of employee stock options on their income statements. We think their arguments make one or more errors in reasoning.

First, some argue that grants of stock options do not involve cash outlays, and therefore no expense should be recorded. This reasoning violates the basic accrual principle of accounting. Not every cash outflow is recorded as an expense in the period in which it occurs, nor does every expense recognized in a period involve a cash outflow. For example, when a company compensates employees by making outright grants of stock, no cash outflows occur. Yet the company would record, as compensation expense, the value of the stock granted. Stock-option grants should receive comparable treatment.

A second error is to argue that the expensing of stock options would be double counting because the diluting effect of granting the options is recognized by an increase in the number of shares in the denominator of a fully diluted earnings-per-share calculation. But this erroneous argument would also enable a company to issue stock options to, say, a supplier of materials, and not record the materials as an expense because the effect would show up in the higher number of shares in an earnings-per-share calculation. Curious reasoning.

Some opponents of expensing employee stock options make two arguments that actually conflict with each other. First, they claim that it is enough to disclose the information in the footnotes to corporate financial statements as is done now. And second, they claim that requiring options to be expensed would hurt companies. But if deducting the expenses of options that are already disclosed in footnotes would drive a company's stock price down, then we have proof that the disclosure alone was inadequate to capture the underlying economic reality.

The accounting for employee stock options on a firm's income statement should be decided according to economic and accounting principles, not by dubious rationalizations. If the following true-or-false question appeared on an accounting exam, the answer is quite clear: Employee stock options should be expensed on a firm's income statement. True.

Source: Zvi Bodie, Robert S. Kaplan, and Robert C. Merton, "Options Should Be Reflected in the Bottom Line," *The Wall Street Journal*, August 1, 2002.

Collateralized Loans

Many loan arrangements require that the borrower put up collateral to guarantee that the loan will be paid back. In the event of default, the lender takes possession of the collateral. A non-recourse loan gives the lender no recourse beyond the right to the collateral; that is, the lender may not sue the borrower for further payment if the collateral turns out not to be valuable enough to repay the loan.

This arrangement, it turns out, gives an implicit call option to the borrower. The borrower, for example, is obligated to pay back L dollars at the maturity of the loan. The collateral will be worth S_T dollars at maturity. (Its value today is S_0.) The borrower has the option to wait until loan maturity and repay the loan only if the collateral is worth more than the L dollars he or she borrowed. If the collateral is worth less than L, the borrower can default on the loan,[2] discharging the obligation by forfeiting the collateral, which is worth only S_T.

Another way of describing such a loan is to view the borrower as, in effect, turning over the collateral to the lender but retaining the right to reclaim it by paying off the loan. The transfer of the collateral with the right to claim it is equivalent to a payment of S_0 dollars, less a future recovery of a sum that resembles a call option with exercise price L. Basically, the borrower turns over collateral and keeps an option to "repurchase" it for L dollars at the maturity of the loan if L turns out to be less than S_T. This is, of course, a call option.

A third way to look at a collateralized loan is to assume the borrower will repay the L dollars with certainty but also retain the option to sell the collateral to the lender for L dollars, even if S_T

[2]In reality, of course, defaulting on a loan is not so simple. There are losses of reputation involved as well as considerations of ethical behaviour. This is a description of a pure non-recourse loan where both parties agree from the outset that only the collateral backs the loan and that default is not to be taken as a sign of bad faith if the collateral is insufficient to repay the loan.

is less than L. In this case, the sale of the collateral would generate the cash necessary to satisfy the loan. The ability to "sell" the collateral for a price of L dollars represents a put option, which guarantees that the borrower can raise enough money to satisfy the loan by turning over the collateral.

It is strange to think that we can describe the same loan as involving either a put option or a call option, since the payoffs to calls and puts are so different. Yet the equivalence of the two approaches is nothing more than a reflection of the put-call parity relationship. In our call option description of the loan, the value of the borrower's liability is $S_0 - C$: The borrower turns over the asset, which is a transfer of S_0 dollars, but retains a call, which is worth C dollars. In the put-option description the borrower is obligated to pay L dollars but retains the put, which is worth P: the present value of this net obligation is $L/(1 + r_f)^T - P$. Because these alternative descriptions are equivalent ways of viewing the same loan, the value of the obligations must be equal:

$$S_0 - C = L/(1 + r_f)^T - P \qquad (17.3)$$

Treating L as the exercise price of the option, equation 17.3 is simply the put-call parity relationship.

Figure 17.15, panel A illustrates the value of the payment to be received by the lender, which equals the minimum of S_T or L. Panel B shows that this amount can be expressed as S_T minus the

Figure 17.15 Collateralized loan.

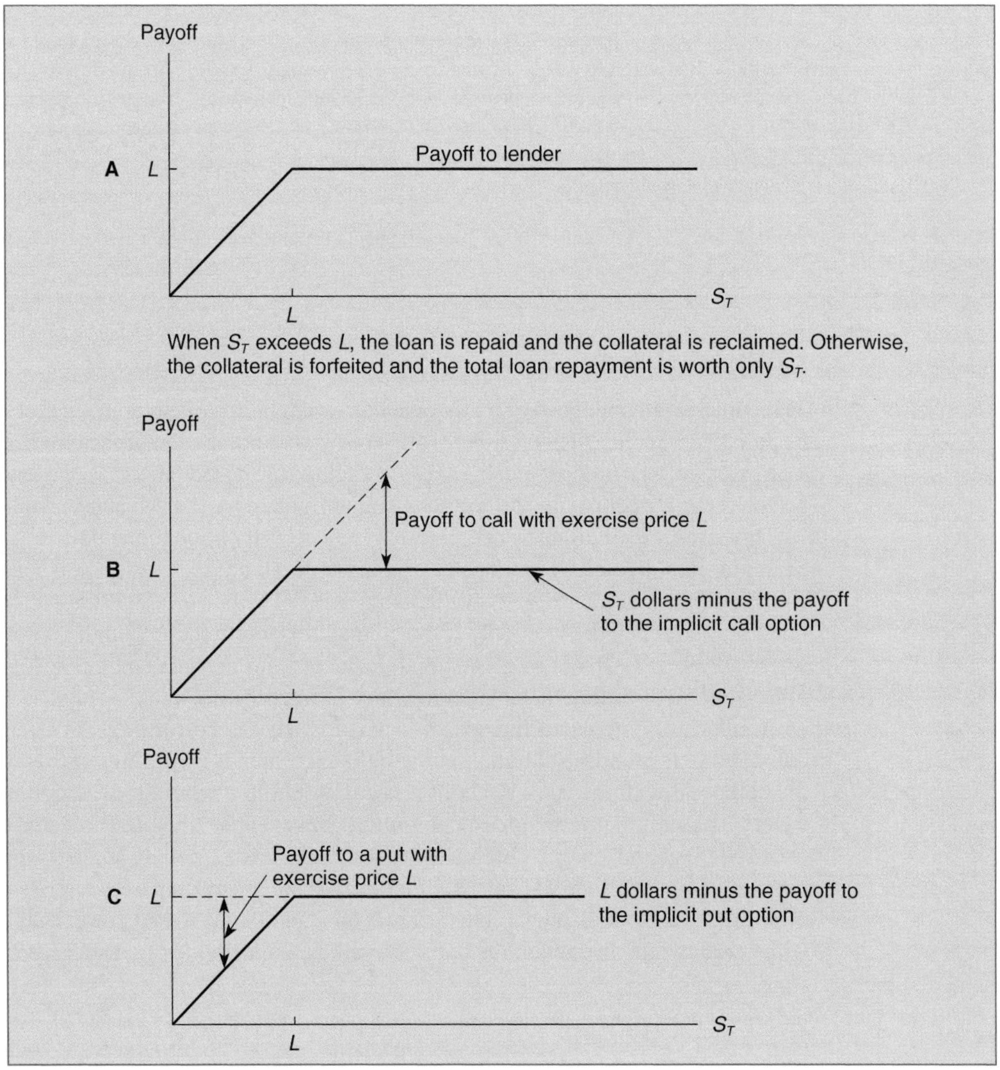

payoff of the call implicitly written by the lender and held by the borrower. Panel C shows that it also can be viewed as a receipt of L dollars minus the proceeds of the put option.

Levered Equity and Risky Debt

Investors holding stock in incorporated firms are protected by limited liability, which means that if the firm cannot pay its debts, the firm's creditors may attach only the firm's assets and may not sue the corporation's equityholders for further payment. In effect, any time the corporation borrows money, the maximum possible collateral for the loan is the total of the firm's assets. If the firm declares bankruptcy, we can interpret this as an admission that the assets of the firm are insufficient to satisfy the claims against it. The corporation may discharge its obligations by transferring ownership of the firm's assets to the creditors.

Just as with non-recourse collateralized loans, the required payment to the creditors represents the exercise price of the implicit option, while the value of the firm is the underlying asset. The equityholders have a put option to transfer their ownership claims on the firm to the creditors in return for the face value of the firm's debt.

Alternatively, we may view the equityholders as retaining a call option. They have, in effect, already transferred their ownership claim on the firm to the creditors but have retained the right to reacquire the ownership claims on the firm by paying off the loan. Hence, the equityholders have the option to "buy back" the firm for a specified price—they have a call option.

The significance of this observation is that the values of corporate bonds can be estimated using option pricing techniques. The default premium required of risky debt, in principle, can be estimated using option valuation models. These will be considered in the next chapter.

17.6 FINANCIAL ENGINEERING

One of the attractions of options is the ability they provide to create investment positions with payoffs that depend in a variety of ways on the values of other securities. We have seen evidence of this capability in the various options strategies examined in Section 17.3. Options also can be used to custom design new securities or portfolios with desired patterns of exposure to the price of an underlying security. In this sense, options (and futures contracts, to be discussed in Chapter 19) provide the ability to engage in *financial engineering,* the creation of portfolios with specified payoff patterns.

Most financial engineering takes place for institutional investors. However, some applications have been designed for the retail market. One innovation is the bond, note, or certificate of deposit that allows its holder to participate in an equity index growth, an *index-linked CD.* Unlike conventional CDs, which pay a fixed rate of interest, index-linked CDs pay depositors a specified fraction of the increase in the rate of return on a market index such as the S&P 500, while guaranteeing a minimum rate of return should the market fall.

The *protected index notes* (PINs) are a Canadian variant of index-linked CDs. They were discount notes issued by the Export Development Corporation (EDC) and denominated in U.S. dollars, which matured in early 1997. Unlike conventional notes, the PINs were redeemable at any time prior to maturity at the larger of the following prices: the original par price, or the par price multiplied by the ratio of the S&P 500 index at redemption time to 1.05 times the value of the index at the time of issuance.

This arrangement is clearly a type of call option. If the market rises, the investor profits according to the relative rise in the index; if the market falls, the investor is guaranteed to receive at least the par value. The return to the prospective investor is at least equal to the ratio of par value to purchase value, and it can increase in proportion to the rise of the S&P index. Just as clearly, the issuer offering these notes is in effect writing call options and can hedge its position by buying index calls in the U.S. options market. Figure 17.16 shows the nature of the issuer's obligation to its depositors.

Index-linked CDs are similar to PINs, except that the holder may receive only a fraction (say 70 percent) of the growth in the index; this fraction is known as the *participation rate* or *multiplier,* and it is set by the issuer. The PIN is essentially an index-linked CD with a multiplier equal to 1/1.05. In valuing PINs we are especially interested in the *inverse multiplier,* equal in this example to 1.05.

How can one value a PIN or index-linked CD at any time prior to expiration? To answer this, note various features of the option:

1. At exercise the PIN holder receives the par value, or (1/1.05) times (par value) times the realized return on the S&P 500 index, whichever is greater. If the PIN sells at par at issuance, then the payoff at exercise time per dollar invested is equal to the larger of 1, and (1/1.05) times (1 plus the market rate of return r_M as measured by the index).
2. Suppose that we want to replicate this pattern of payments, by using call options on the index and a riskless investment (say a T-bill or a conventional CD) with rate of return r_f. If C is the value of a call option on one unit of the index, with exercise price equal to 1.05 times the value S_0 of the index at issuance, then the ratio $C/(1.05S_0)$ is the value of a contingent claim that pays at exercise time the larger of 0, and/or (1/1.05) times $(1 + r_M)$ minus 1. Hence, a portfolio of this contingent claim plus an amount $1/(r_f + 1)$ invested in the riskless investment pays the larger of 1, or (1/1.05) times $(1 + r_M)$, the same as the PIN. To avoid arbitrage, this portfolio must, therefore, have a value equal to that of the PIN at issuance, divided by the par value.
3. To determine whether the PIN should sell at par at issuance it suffices, therefore, to evaluate the quantity $C/(1.05S_0) + 1/(r_f + 1)$: If it is equal to 1, then the PIN should sell at par; it should sell above or below par if the above quantity is respectively greater or smaller than 1.

Figure 17.16 Index-linked CD.

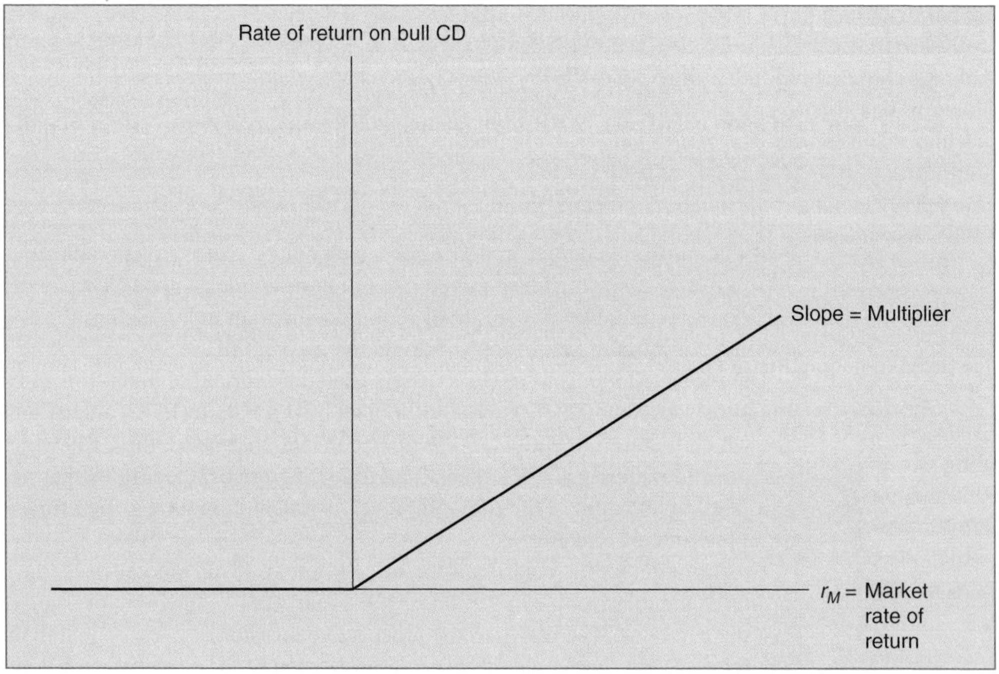

EXAMPLE 17.5 Index-Linked CDs

Suppose that $r_f = 6$ percent per year (3 percent for six months), and that the index is currently at \$240, implying that $1.05S_0 = 252$. The six-month maturity calls on the market index with an exercise price of \$252 are currently valued at \$10. Then the test quantity is equal to \$10/\$252 + 1/1.03 = 1.011 per dollar of par value. Therefore, the PIN should sell at slightly above par.

This PIN was an index-linked CD with a multiplier equal to 1/1.05. Such versions of the index-linked CD have several variants, generally trading over the counter. Investors can purchase index-linked CDs that guarantee a positive minimum return, perhaps in combination with a smaller multiplier. In this case, the index-linked CD per unit par value is replicated by an index call option (with value C) plus a riskless investment portfolio. The call option has an exercise price equal to the inverse multiplier times ($r_{\min} + 1$) times the value of the index at issuance, where $r_{\min}$ is the guaranteed minimum return; the riskless investment is $(1 + r_{\min})/(1 + r_f)$. The test quantity, the riskless investment plus C divided by the inverse multiplier times the index at issuance, is again compared to 1 to determine whether the instrument should be sold at par. Another variant of the "bullish" index-linked CD is the *bear CD,* which pays depositors a fraction of any *fall* in the market index. For example, a bear CD might offer a rate of return of .6 times any percentage decline in the S&P 500. The boxed article that follows argues that most such instruments are not a good value.

CONCEPT CHECK

9. Continue to assume that $r_f = 6$ percent, the appropriate calls sell for \$10, the multiplier is still 1/1.05, and the market index is at 240. What would be the value of index-linked CDs per unit at par value if they offer a guaranteed minimum return of 1 percent on a six-month deposit?

17.7 EXOTIC OPTIONS

Options markets have been tremendously successful. Investors clearly value the portfolio strategies made possible by trading options; this is reflected in the heavy trading volume in these markets. Success breeds imitation, and in recent years we have witnessed considerable innovation in the range of option instruments available to investors. Part of this innovation has occurred in the market for customized options, which now trade in active over-the-counter markets. Many of these options have terms that would have been highly unusual even a few years ago; they are therefore called "exotic options." In this section, we will survey some of the more interesting variants of these new instruments.

Asian Options

You already have been introduced to American and European options. *Asian options* are options with payoffs that depend on the *average* price of the underlying asset during at least some portion of the life of the option. For example, an Asian call option may have a payoff equal to the average stock price over the last three months minus the strike price if that value is positive, and zero otherwise. These options may be of interest, for example to firms that wish to hedge a profit stream that depends on the average price of a commodity over some period of time.

NOTES FOR RISK-AVERSE OFFER SMALL PAYOFF

A fear of stocks afflicts a lot of Canadian investors these days. Even before the equity markets hit the skids last month, many people were shying away from exposure to stocks and equity funds in their investing. In driving terms, it's almost as if they've decided to stay off the highway because it's too scary.

You can see this in the news this week—conservative, income-oriented mutual funds remain more popular than straight equity funds, and also in the fast-growing popularity of a security called a principal protected note. With a principal protected note, you can get the benefit of returns from a grouping of mutual funds, hedge funds, stocks or stock indexes along with a guarantee from a major financial institution, usually a bank, that your capital will be returned to you on maturity. Arguably, they're the dream investment for the pathologically risk-averse.

However you describe principal protected notes, they're obviously a minor hit in the investing world. Consulting firm Investor Economics says there were 120 different issues in the market as of last June 30, more than double the 51 available at the end of 2001. Total assets as of June 30 were $3.4-billion, up from virtually zero in 1999.

Recent additions to the genre include NBC Blue Chip Notes, which are based on a portfolio of 20 blue-chip Canadian stocks and guaranteed by National Bank of Canada, and One Financial All-Star Portfolio Notes, which are based on the returns of five all-star mutual funds and guaranteed by the French bank BNP Paribas.

Some of the most popular principal protected notes have been issued by Canadian Imperial Bank of Commerce under the name FULPaY. These are based on returns of mutual-funds baskets from such families as AGF, CI, Mackenzie and Franklin Templeton.

Would you classify yourself as a long-term investor with a prudently diversified portfolio? If the answer is yes, then cross off principal protected notes from your list of investment possibilities, with the possible exception of notes that offer exposure to hedge funds.

While the promise of capital protection and equity market returns is tempting, the costs and restrictions just aren't a good value.

There are four or so structures used by principal protected notes, but the general idea is the same in most cases. Part of the portfolio is invested in a bond to fund the capital guarantee, while the remainder is invested in various assets to generate gains. When the notes mature, you get your capital back, as well as any profits, which are treated as income for tax purposes in non-registered accounts.

Dundee Securities analyst James Gauthier recently issued a report on principal protected notes in which he outlined drawbacks like potentially high fees and a lack of liquidity. He said the secondary market for these notes is limited or non-existent, which is to say you may not be able to sell at your convenience prior to maturity. These notes are generally redeemable at set intervals, but there is no guarantee of capital until maturity.

Anyone who has experience with index-linked guaranteed investment certificates will know that one of their big limitations is that one's gains from the underlying index are limited through what's known as a "participation rate." The same concept often applies to principal protected notes, although the actual mechanics vary. Suffice it to say that the cost of your guarantee and the need for the notes sponsor to make money will give you significantly lower returns than if you invested in an asset directly.

Mr. Gauthier looked at a FULPaY issue based on three underlying mutual funds from a major fund family and found a cumulative two-year return of 24.5 per cent, which compared to 44 per cent for the funds themselves.

"We've reviewed dozens upon dozens of notes to date and one thing is clear to us: these tools are not the magic solution to anything," Mr. Gauthier concludes in his report. "Yes, they encourage peace of mind; however, our fear is that the cost of obtaining that peace of mind is lost on most investors and many advisers."

Let's go a little further than that and say the cost flat out isn't worth it unless you're traumatized by risk and can't bring yourself to invest the normal way.

Source: Rob Carrick, "Notes for Risk-Averse Offer Small Payoff," Report on Business, *The Globe and Mail*, May 22, 2004, p. B2. Reprinted by permission of The Globe and Mail.

Barrier Options

Barrier options have payoffs that depend not only on some asset price at option expiration, but also on whether the underlying asset price has crossed through some "barrier." For example, a down-and-out option is one type of barrier option that automatically expires worthless if and when the stock price falls below some barrier price. Similarly, down-and-in options will not provide a payoff unless the stock price *does* fall below some barrier at least once during the life of the option. These options also are referred to as knock-out and knock-in options.

Lookback Options

Lookback options have payoffs that depend in part on the minimum or maximum price of the underlying asset during the life of the option. For example, a lookback call option might provide a payoff equal to the *maximum* stock price minus the exercise price. Such an option provides (for a fee, of course) a form of perfect market timing, providing the call holder with a payoff equal to the one that would accrue if the asset were purchased for X dollars and later sold at what turns out to be its high price.

Currency-Translated Options

Currency-translated options have either asset or exercise prices denominated in a foreign currency. A good example of such an option is the *quanto,* which allows an investor to fix in advance the exchange rate at which an investment in a foreign currency can be converted back into dollars. The right to translate a fixed amount of foreign currency into dollars at a given exchange rate is a simple foreign exchange option. Quantos are more interesting, however, because, the amount of currency that will be translated into dollars depends on the investment performance of the foreign security. Therefore, a quanto in effect provides a *random number* of options.

Binary Options

Binary of "bet" options have fixed payoffs that depend on whether a condition is satisfied by the price of the underlying asset. For example, a binary call option might pay off a fixed amount of $100 if the stock price at maturity exceeds the exercise price.

SUMMARY

1. A call option is the right to buy an asset at an agreed-upon exercise price. A put option is the right to sell an asset at a given exercise price.
2. American options allow exercise on or before the expiration date. European options allow exercise only on the expiration date. Most traded options are American in nature.
3. Options are traded on stocks, stock indices, foreign currencies, fixed-income securities, and several futures contracts.
4. Options can be used either to increase an investor's exposure to an asset price or to provide insurance against volatility of asset prices. Popular option strategies include covered calls, protective puts, straddles, spreads, and collars.
5. The put-call parity theorem relates the prices of put and call options. If the relationship is violated, arbitrage opportunities result. Specifically, the relationship that must be satisfied is that

$$P = C - S_0 + \text{PV}(X) + \text{PV(dividends)}$$

   where X is the exercise price of both the call and the put options; PV(X) is the present value of a claim to X dollars to be paid at the expiration date of the options; and PV(dividends) is the present value of dividends to be paid before option expiration.
6. Many commonly traded securities embody option characteristics. Examples include callable bonds, convertible bonds and warrants. Other arrangements, such as collateralized loans and limited-liability borrowing can be analyzed as conveying implicit options to one or more parties.
7. Trading in so-called exotic options now takes place in an active over-the-counter market.

KEY TERMS

call option 640
exercise price (strike price) 640
put option 641
in the money 642
out of the money 642
at the money 642
American option 643
European option 643
protective put 654
covered call 655
straddle 657
spread 658
collar 660
put-call parity theorem 661
warrants 666

SELECTED READINGS

Good treatments of the institutional organization of option markets in the United States and Canada can be found in the following:

Chicago Board Options Exchange. *Reference Manual.* (The CBOE also publishes a *Margin Manual* that provides an overview of margin requirements on many option positions.)

Montreal Exchange. *The Profitable Option: Guide to the Stock Options Market*, August 1992; *LEAPS Options: An Investor's Guide*, May 1995; and *Interest Rate Options: An Investor's Guide*, June 1995.

An excellent discussion of option trading strategies is:

Black, Fischer. "Fact and Fantasy in the Use of Options." *Financial Analysts Journal,* July/August 1975.

The Winter 1992 issue of the Journal of Applied Corporate Finance *highlights financial innovation. The issue contains several articles on the use of futures and options in new security design and risk management.*

RISK Magazine *is an excellent source of material on current developments in option pricing, applications of derivative instruments, and new developments in the derivatives markets. It has assembled a collection of articles that have appeared in its previous issues on option pricing generally and exotic options in particular in:*

From Black-Scholes to Black Holes: Frontiers in Options. London: RISK Magazine, 1992.

A description and empirical evaluation of several characteristics of Canadian option markets is in:

Mandron, Alix. "Some Empirical Evidence About Canadian Stock Options, Part I: Valuation; Part II: Market Structure." *Canadian Journal of Administrative Sciences* 5, no. 2 (June 1988).

An overview of derivative instruments traded in Canadian financial markets is in:

Gagnon, Louis. "Exchange-Traded Financial Derivatives in Canada: Finally off the Launching Pad." *Canadian Investment Review*, Fall 1990.

For more on protected index notes (PINs), see:

Perrakis, Stylianos, Sylvain Brisebois, Carl Pelland, and Carole Larson. "Decoding the PIN Numbers." *Canadian Investment Review,* Winter 1995/96.

PROBLEMS

1. Suppose you think ABC stock is going to appreciate substantially in value in the next six months. Also suppose that the stock's current price, S_0, is \$100, and the call option expiring in six months has an exercise price, X, of \$100 and is selling at a price, C, of \$10. With \$10,000 to invest, you are considering three alternatives.

a. Invest all \$10,000 in the stock, buying 100 shares.

b. Invest all \$10,000 in 1,000 options (10 contracts).

c. Buy 100 options (one contract) for \$1,000, and invest the remaining \$9,000 in a money market fund paying 4 percent in interest over six months (8 percent per year).

What is your rate of return for each alternative for four stock prices six months from now? Summarize your results in the table and diagram that appear next.

2. The common stock of the PUTT Corporation has been trading in a narrow price range for the past month, and you are convinced that it is going to break far out of that range in the next three months. You do not know whether it will go up or down, however. The current price of the stock is \$100 per share, and the price of a three-month call option at an exercise price of \$100 is \$10. The stock will pay no dividends for the next three months.

a. If the risk-free interest rate is 10 percent per year, what must be the price of a three-month put option on PUTT stock at an exercise price of \$100?

b. What would be a simple options strategy to exploit your conviction about the stock price's future movement? How far would it have to move in either direction for you to make a profit on your initial investment?

Rate of Return on Investment

	Price of Stock 6 Months from Now			
Stock Price:	**80**	**100**	**110**	**120**
a. All stocks (100 shares)				
b. All options (1,000 shares)				
c. Bills + 100 options				

3. The common stock of the CALL Corporation has been trading in a narrow range around $50 per share for months, and you are convinced that it is going to stay in that range for the next three months. The price of a three-month put option with an exercise price of $50 is $4. The stock will pay no dividends for the next three months.

a. If the risk-free interest rate is 10 percent per year, what must be the price of a three-month call option on CALL stock at an exercise price of $50 if it is at the money?

b. What would be a simple options strategy using a put and a call to explain your conviction about the stock price's future movement? What is the most money you can make on this position? How far can the stock price move in either direction before you lose money?

c. How can you create a position involving a put, a call, and risk-free lending that would have the same payoff structure as the stock at expiration? What is the net cost of establishing that position now?

4. In this problem, we derive the put-call parity relationship for European options on stocks that pay dividends before option expiration. For simplicity, assume that the stock makes one dividend payment of $\$D$ per share at the expiration date of the option.

a. What is the value of a stock-plus-put position on the expiration date of the option?

b. Now consider a portfolio comprising a call option and a zero-coupon bond with the same maturity date as the option and with face value $(X + D)$. What is the value of this portfolio on the option expiration date? You should find that its value equals that of the stock-plus-put portfolio regardless of the stock price.

c. What is the cost of establishing the two portfolios in parts (*a*) and (*b*)? Equate the costs of these portfolio, and you will derive the put-call parity relationship, equation 17.2.

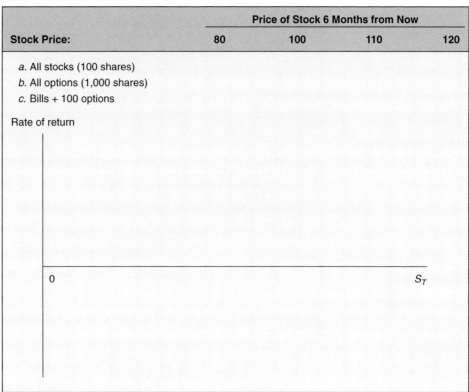

5. *a.* A butterfly spread is the purchase of one call at exercise price X_1, the sale of two calls at exercise price X_2, and the purchase of one call at exercise price X_3. X_1 is less than X_2, and X_2 is less than X_3 by equal amounts, and all calls have the same expiration date. Graph the payoff diagram to this strategy.

   b. A vertical combination is the purchase of a call with exercise price X_2 and a put with exercise price X_1, with X_2 greater than X_1. Graph the payoff to this strategy.

6. A bearish spread is the purchase of a call with exercise price X_2 and the sale of a call with exercise price X_1, with X_2 greater than X_1. Graph the payoff to this strategy and compare it to Figure 17.11.

7. Joseph Jones, a manager at Computer Science, Inc. (CSI), received 10,000 shares of company stock as part of his compensation package. The stock currently sells at $40 a share. Joseph would like to defer selling the stock until the next tax year. In January, however, he will need to sell all his holdings to provide for a down payment on his new house. Joseph is worried about the price risk involved in keeping his shares. At current prices, he would receive $40,000 for the stock. If the value of his stock holdings falls below $35,000, his ability to come up with the necessary down payment would be jeopardized. On the other hand, if the stock value rises to $45,000 he would be able to maintain a small cash reserve even after making the down payment. Joseph considers three investment strategies:

   a. Strategy A is to write January call options on the CSI shares with strike price $45. These calls are currently selling for $3 each.

   b. Strategy B is to buy January put options on CSI with strike price $35. These options also sell for $3 each.

   c. Strategy C is to establish a zero-cost collar by writing the January calls and buying the January puts.

   Evaluate each of these strategies with respect to Joseph's investment goals. What are the advantages and disadvantages of each? Which would you recommend?

8. You are attempting to formulate an investment strategy. On the one hand, you think there is great upward potential in the stock market and would like to participate in the upward move if it materializes. However, you are not able to afford substantial stock market losses and so cannot run the risk of a stock market collapse, which you also think is a possibility. Your investment advisor suggests a protective put position: Buy both shares in a market index stock fund and put options on those shares with three-month maturity and exercise price of $780. The stock index is currently selling for $900. However, your uncle suggests you instead buy a three-month call option on the index fund with exercise price $840 and buy three-month T-bills with face value $840.

   a. On the same graph, draw the *payoffs* to each of these strategies as a function of the stock fund value in three months. (*Hint:* Think of the options as being on one "share" of the stock index fund, with the current price of each share of the index equal to $900.)

   b. Which portfolio must require a greater initial outlay to establish? (*Hint:* Does either portfolio provide a final payoff that is always at least as great as the payoff of the other portfolio?)

   c. Suppose the market prices of the securities are as follows:

Stock fund	$900
T-bills (face value $840)	$810
Call (exercise price $840)	$120
Put (exercise price $780)	$ 6

   Make a table of the profits realized for each portfolio for the following values of the stock price in three months: S_T = $700, $840, $900, $960.

   Graph the profits to each portfolio as a function of S_T on a single graph.

   d. Which strategy is riskier? Which should have a higher beta?

e. Explain why the data for the securities given in part (*c*) do *not* violate the put-call parity relationship.

CFA® PROBLEMS

9. Donna Donie, CFA has a client who believes the common stock price of TRT Materials (currently \$58 per share) could move substantially in either direction in reaction to an expected court decision involving the company. The client currently owns no TRT shares, but asks Donie for advice about implementing a strangle strategy to capitalize on the possible stock price movement. A strangle is a portfolio of a put and a call with different exercise prices but the same expiration date. Donie gathers the TRT option pricing data shown on the following page:

Characteristic	Call Option	Put Option
Price	\$ 5	\$ 4
Strike price	\$60	\$55
Time to expiration	90 days from now	90 days from now

a. Recommend whether Donie should choose a long strangle strategy or a short strangle strategy to achieve the client's objective.

b. Calculate, at expiration for the appropriate strangle strategy in part (*a*), the
   i. Maximum possible loss per share
   ii. Maximum possible gain per share
   iii. Breakeven stock price(s)

10. The agricultural price support system guarantees farmers a minimum price for their output. Describe the program provisions as an option. What is the asset? The exercise price?

11. In what ways is owning a corporate bond similar to writing a put option? A call option?

12. An executive compensation scheme might provide a manager a bonus of \$1,000 for every dollar by which the company's stock price exceeds some cutoff level. In what way is this arrangement equivalent to issuing the manager call options on the firm's stock?

13. Consider the following options portfolio. You write an April maturity call option on CIBC with exercise price 70. You write an April CIBC put option with exercise price 65.

a. Graph the payoff of this portfolio at option expiration as a function of CIBC's stock price at that time.

b. What will be the profit/loss on this position if CIBC is selling at 57 on the option maturity date? What if CIBC is selling at 65? Use the *Globe and Mail* listing from Figure 17.1 to answer this question.

c. At what two stock prices will you just break even on your investment?

d. What kind of "bet" is this investor making—that is, what must this investor believe about the CIBC stock price in order to justify this position?

14. Consider the following portfolio. You write a put option with exercise price 90 and buy a put option on the same stock with the same maturity date with exercise price 95.

a. Plot the value of the portfolio at the maturity date of the options.

b. On the same graph, plot the profit of the portfolio. Which option must cost more?

15. A Ford put option with strike price 60 trading on the Acme options exchange sells for \$2. To your amazement, Ford put with the same maturity selling on the Apex options exchange, but with strike price 62, also sells for \$2. If you plan to hold the options positions to maturity, devise a zero-net-investment arbitrage strategy to exploit the pricing anomaly. Draw the profit diagram at maturity for your position.

---

16. You buy a share of stock, write a one-year call option with $X = \$10$, and buy a one-year put option with $X = \$10$. Your net outlay to establish the entire portfolio is \$9.50. What is the risk-free interest rate? The stock pays no dividends.

17. Demonstrate that an at-the-money call option on a given stock must cost more than an at-the-money put option with the same maturity. (*Hint*: Use put-call parity.)

18. You write a put option with $X = 100$ and buy a put with $X = 110$. The puts are on the same stock and have the same maturity date.

a. Draw the payoff graph for this strategy.

b. Draw the profit graph for this strategy.

c. If the underlying stock has positive beta, does this portfolio have positive or negative beta?

19. Joe Finance has just purchased an indexed stock fund, currently selling at \$400 per share. To protect against losses, Joe also purchased an at-the-money European put option on the fund for \$20, with exercise price \$400, and three-month time to expiration. Sally Calm, Joe's financial advisor, points out that Joe is spending a lot of money on the put. She notes that three-month puts with strike prices of \$390 cost only \$15 and suggests that Joe use the cheaper put.

a. Analyze the strategies of Joe and Sally by drawing the *profit* diagrams for the stock-plus-put positions for various values of the stock fund in three months.

b. When does Sally's strategy do better? When does it do worse?

c. Which strategy entails greater systematic risk?

20. You write a call option with $X = 50$ and buy a call with $X = 60$. The options are on the same stock and have the same maturity date. One of the calls sells for \$3; the other sells for \$9.

a. Draw the payoff graph for this strategy at the option maturity date.

b. Draw the profit graph for this strategy.

c. What is the breakeven point for this strategy? Is the investor bullish or bearish on the stock?

21. Devise a portfolio using only call options and shares of stock with the following value (payoff) at the option maturity date. If the stock price currently is 53, what kind of bet is the investor making?

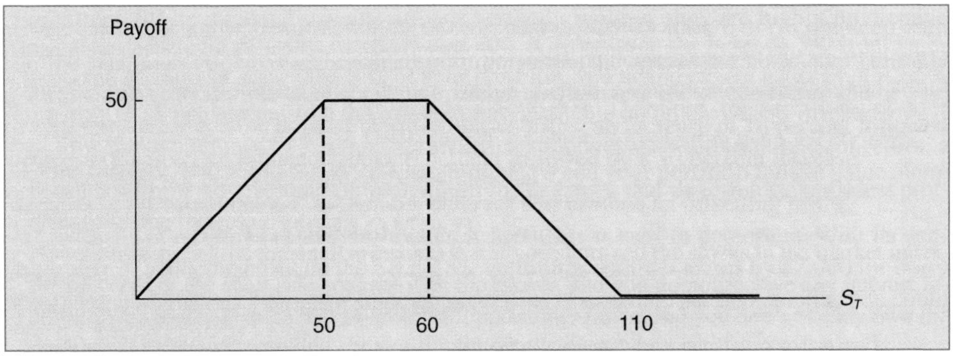

CFA® PROBLEMS

www.gm.com

22. On the death of his grandmother several years ago, Bill Melody received as a bequest from her estate 2,000 shares of General Motors common stock. The price of the stock at time of distribution from the estate was \$75 a share, and this became the cost basis of Melody's holding. Late in 1990, Melody agreed to purchase a new condominium for his parents at a total cost of \$160,000, payable in full upon its completion in March 1991. Melody planned to sell the General Motors stock in order to raise funds to purchase the condominium.

At year-end 1990, GM's market price was around \$75 a share, but it looked to be weakening. This concerned Melody, for if the price of the stock were to drop by a significant amount before he sold, the proceeds would not be sufficient to cover the purchase of the condominium in March 1991.

Melody visited with three investment counselling firms to seek advice in developing a strategy that, at a minimum, would protect the value of his principal at or near $150,000 ($75 a share). Ideally, the strategy would enhance the value to $160,000 so Melody would have the total cost of the condominium. Four alternatives were discussed:

a. Melody's own opinion was to sell the General Motors stock at $75 a share and invest the proceeds in a 10 percent certificate of deposit maturing in three months.

b. Anderson Investment Advisors suggested Melody write a March 1991 call option on his General Motors stock holding at a strike price of $80. The March 1991 calls were quoted at $2.

c. Cole Capital Management suggested Melody purchase March 1991 at-the-money put contracts on General Motors, now quoted at $2.

d. MBA Associates suggested Melody keep the stock, purchase March 1991 at-the-money put contracts on GM, and finance the purchase by selling March calls with a strike price of $80.

Disregarding transaction costs, dividend income, and margin requirements, rank-order the four alternatives in terms of their fulfilling the strategy of at least preserving the value of Melody's principal at $150,000 and preferably increasing the value to $160,000 by March 1991. Support your conclusions by showing the payoff structure of each alternative.

CFA® PROBLEMS

23. Suresh Singh, CFA is analyzing a convertible bond. The characteristics of the bond and the underlying common stock are given in the following exhibit:

Convertible Bond Characteristics	
Par value	$1.000
Annual coupon rate (annual pay)	6.5%
Conversion ratio	22
Market price	105% of par value
Straight value	99% of par value
Underlying Stock Characteristics	
Current market price	$40 per share
Annual cash dividend	$1.20 per share

Compute the bond's

i. Conversion value

ii. Market conversion price

CFA® PROBLEMS

24. Rich Macdonald, CFA is evaluating his investment alternatives in Ytel Incorporated by analyzing a Ytel convertible bond and Ytel common equity. Characteristics of the two securities are given in the following exhibit:

Characteristics	Convertible Bond	Common Equity
Par value	$1.000	—
Coupon (annual payment)	4%	—
Current market price	$980	$35 per share
Straight bond value	$925	—
Conversion ratio	25	—
Conversion option	At any time	—
Dividend	—	$0
Expected market price in 1 year	$1,125	$45 per share

a. Calculate from the exhibit the

i. Current market conversion price for the Ytel convertible bond

ii. Expected one-year rate of return for the Ytel convertible bond

iii. Expected one-year rate of return for the Ytel common equity

One year has passed and Ytel's common equity price has increased to $51 per share. Also, over the year, the interest rate on Ytel's nonconvertible bonds of the same maturity increased, while credit spreads remained unchanged.

b. Name the two components of the convertible bond's value. Indicate whether the value of each component should decrease, stay the same, or increase in response to the
i. Increase in Ytel's common equity price
ii. Increase in interest rates

CFA® PROBLEMS

25. The following questions appeared in past CFA Level I examinations.

a. Which one of the following comparative statements about common stock call options and warrants is correct?

		Call Option	Warrant
i.	Issued by the company	No	Yes
ii.	Sometimes attached to bonds	Yes	Yes
iii.	Maturity greater than one year	Yes	No
iv.	Convertible into the stock	Yes	No

b. Consider a bullish spread option strategy using a call option with a $25 exercise price priced at $4 and a call option with a $40 exercise price priced at $2.50. If the price of the stock increases to $50 at expiration and the option is exercised on the expiration date, the net profit per share at expiration (ignoring transaction costs) is
i. $8.50
ii. $13.50
iii. $16.50
iv. $23.50

c. A convertible bond sells at $1,000 par with a conversion ratio of 40 and an accompanying stock price of $20 per share. The conversion premium and (percentage) conversion premium, respectively, are
i. $200 and 20%
ii. $200 and 25%
iii. $250 and 20%
iv. $250 and 25%

d. A put on XYZ stock with a strike price of $40 is priced at $2 per share, while a call with a strike price of $40 is priced at $3.50. What is the maximum per-share loss to the writer of the uncovered put and the maximum per-share gain to the writer of the uncovered call?

	Maximum Loss to Put Writer	Maximum Gain to Call Writer
i.	$38	$ 3.50
ii.	$38	$36.50
iii.	$40	$ 3.50
iv.	$40	$40.00

e. You create a strap by buying two calls and one put on ABC stock, all with a strike price of $45. The calls cost $5 each, and the put costs $4. If you close your position when ABC is priced at $55, your per share gain or loss is
i. $4 loss
ii. $6 gain
iii. $10 gain
iv. $20 gain

f. In the options markets, the purpose of the clearinghouse is to

Choice A: Issue certificates of ownership

Choice B: Ensure contract performance

Choice C: Match up the option buyer who exercises with the original option writer

i. B only
ii. B and C only
iii. C only
iv. A, B, and C

The following questions are adapted from the Canadian Securities Course.

26. Which of the following statements regarding standardized option contracts is/are true?

a. Both calls and puts trade in cycles with 3-, 6-, or 9-month expiry dates.

b. Option contracts expire on the Saturday following the third Friday of the expiration month.

c. Exercise prices move in structured increments as the stock prices move.

d. All equity put and call option contracts represent 100 shares.

27. The ________________ in a CDCC option quotation is the total number of option contracts in the series that are outstanding and have not been closed out or exercised.

28. A writer of a call option contract who actually owns the underlying shares is known as a(n) ________________ writer.

29. In January, when ABC Co. common trades at $30 per share, an investor buys one ABC July 30 call at $2.50. Which of the following statements is/are correct?

a. The investor breaks even if ABC Co.'s shares reach $32.50.

b. If the share price declines in value, the investor will suffer, excluding commissions, a $250 loss.

c. The strike price is $30.

d. The investor breaks even if ABC Co.'s shares stay at $30.

30. The name of a type of individual that uses futures and forwards to protect an existing portfolio is ________________.

31. In January, when XYZ common trades at $30, an investor buys one XYZ July 30 put at $2. Which of the following statements is/are correct?

a. The investor must accept delivery of the shares if they are put to him.

b. The investor will exercise the option contract if the shares decline below $30.

c. The investor has no contractual obligations to act.

d The investor's losses are limited to the premium.

32. Which of the following statements regarding the rights and obligations associated with options is/are correct?

a. The writer of a call option receives a premium for the contract but has an obligation to sell if called.

b. The holder of a call option pays a premium for the contract but has an obligation to buy at the strike price.

c. The holder of a put pays a premium and has the right to purchase the underlying stock at a lower price.

d. The writer of a put expects the share price to remain the same or possibly increase, but has an obligation to buy the underlying stock at the prescribed strike price if put to her.

E-INVESTMENTS
Options and Straddles

Go to **www.m-x.ca** and enter AL in the quote section. You will be able to access the prices and market characteristics for all put and call options for Alcan. Select the two expiration months that follow the closest expiration month and obtain the prices for the calls and puts that are closest to being at the money. For example, if you are in September and there are AL options expiring in September, you would select the October and January expirations. If the price of AL was $56.40, you would choose the options with the 57.50 strike or exercise price. Answer the following questions.

1. What are the prices for the put and call with the nearest expiration date?
2. What would be the cost of a straddle using the above options?
3. At expiration, what would be the break-even stock prices for the above straddle?
4. What would be the percentage increase or decrease in the stock price required to break even?
5. What are the prices for the put and call with a later expiration date?
6. What would be the cost of a straddle using the later expiration date?
7. At expiration, what would be the break-even stock prices for the above straddle?
8. What would be the percentage increase or decrease in the stock price required to break even?

OPTION VALUATION

In the previous chapter, we examined option markets and strategies. We noted that many securities contain embedded options that affect both their values and their risk-return characteristics. In this chapter, we turn our attention to option valuation issues. To understand most option-valuation models requires considerable mathematical and statistical background. Still, many of the ideas and insights of these models can be demonstrated in simple examples, and we will concentrate on these.

We start with a discussion of the factors that ought to affect option prices. After this discussion, we present several bounds within which option prices must lie. Next, we turn to quantitative models. First, we examine one particular valuation formula, the famous Black-Scholes model, one of the most significant breakthroughs in finance theory in the past three decades. Next, we look at some of the more important applications of option-pricing theory in portfolio management and control. Finally, we examine an alternative option valuation approach, called "two-state" or "binomial" option pricing, and its extensions.

18.1 OPTION VALUATION: INTRODUCTION

Intrinsic and Time Values

Consider a call option that is out of the money at the moment, with the stock price below the exercise price. This does not mean the option is valueless. Even though immediate exercise today would be unprofitable, the call retains a positive value because there is always a chance the stock price will increase sufficiently by the expiration date to allow for profitable exercise. If not, the worst that can happen is that the option will expire with zero value.

The value $S_0 - X$ sometimes is called the **intrinsic value** of in-the-money call options because it gives the payoff that could be obtained by immediate exercise. Intrinsic value is set equal to zero for out-of-the-money or at-the-money options. The difference between the actual call price and the intrinsic value commonly is called the *time value* of the option.

"Time value" is an unfortunate choice of terminology because it may confuse the option's time value with the time value of money. Time value in the options context refers simply to the difference between the option's price and the value the option would have if it were expiring immediately. It is the part of the option's value that may be attributed to the fact that it still has positive time to expiration.

Most of an option's time value typically is a type of "volatility value." As long as the option holder can choose not to exercise, the payoff cannot be worse than zero. Even if a call option is out of the money now, it still will sell for a positive price because it offers the potential for a profit if the stock price increases, while imposing no risk of additional loss should the stock price fall. The volatility value lies in the value of the right not to exercise the call if that action would be unprofitable. The option to exercise, as opposed to the obligation to exercise, provides insurance against poor stock price performance.

As the stock price increases substantially, it becomes more likely that the call option will be exercised by expiration. In this case, with exercise all but assured, the volatility value becomes minimal. As the stock price gets ever larger, the option value approaches the "adjusted" intrinsic value, the stock price minus the present value of the exercise price, $S_0 - PV(X)$.

Why should this be? If you are virtually certain the option will be exercised and the stock purchased for X dollars, it is as though you own the stock already. The stock certificate, with a value today of S_0, might as well be sitting in your safe-deposit box now, as it will be there in only a few months. You just haven't paid for it yet. The present value of your obligation is the present value of X, so the net value of the call option is $S_0 - PV(X)$.[1]

Figure 18.1 illustrates the call option valuation function. The value curve shows that when the stock price is very low, the option is nearly worthless because there is almost no chance that it will be exercised. When the stock price is very high, the option value approaches adjusted intrinsic value. In the midrange case, where the option is approximately at the money, the option curve diverges from the straight lines corresponding to adjusted intrinsic value. This is because although exercise today would have a negligible (or negative) payoff, the volatility value of the option is quite high in this region.

The option always increases in value with the stock price. The slope is greatest, however, when the option is deep in the money. In this case exercise is all but assured and the option increases in price one for one with the stock price.

[1]This discussion presumes the stock pays no dividends until after option expiration. If the stock does pay dividends before maturity, then there is a reason you would care about getting the stock now rather than at expiration—getting it now entitles you to the interim dividend payments. In this case, the adjusted intrinsic value of the option must subtract the value of the dividends the stock will pay out before the call is exercised. Adjusted intrinsic value would more generally be defined as $S_0 - PV(X) - PV(D)$, where D is the dividend to be paid before option expiration.

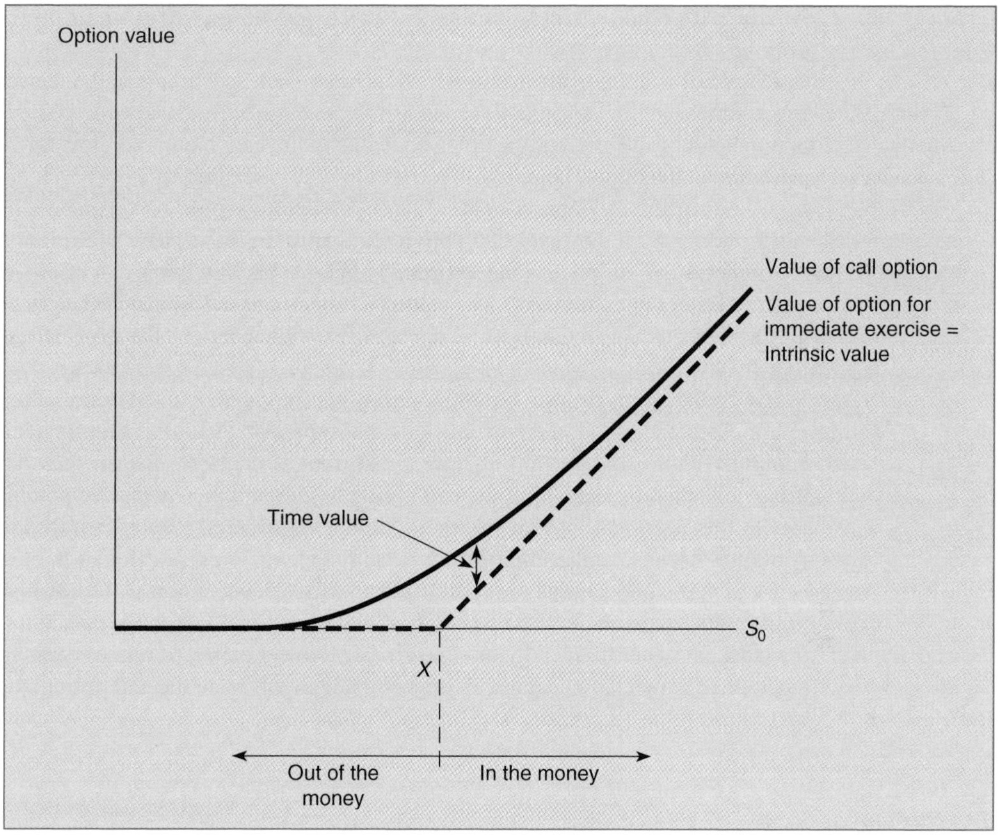

Figure 18.1 Call option value before expiration.

Determinants of Option Values

We can identify at least six factors that should affect the value of a call option: the stock price, the exercise price, the volatility of the stock price, the time to expiration, the interest rate, and the dividend rate of the stock. The call option should increase in value with the stock price and decrease in value with the exercise price because the payoff to a call, if exercised, equals $S_T - X$. The magnitude of the expected payoff from the call increases with the difference of $S_0 - X$.

Call option values also increase with the volatility of the underlying stock price. To see why, consider circumstances where possible stock prices at expiration may range from \$10 to \$50 compared with a situation where stock prices may range only from \$20 to \$40. In both cases the expected stock price will be \$30. Suppose that the exercise price on a call option is also \$30. What are the option payoffs?

High-Volatility Scenario

Stock price	\$10	\$20	\$30	\$40	\$50
Option payoff	0	0	0	\$10	\$20

If each outcome is equally likely, with probability .2, the expected payoff to the option under high-volatility conditions will be \$6.

Low-Volatility Scenario

Stock price	\$20	\$25	\$30	\$35	\$40
Option payoff	0	0	0	\$ 5	\$10

Again, with equally likely outcomes, the expected payoff to the option is half as much, only \$3.

Despite the fact that the average stock price in each scenario is \$30, the average option payoff is greater in the high-volatility scenario. The source of this extra value is the limited loss that an option holder can suffer, or the volatility value of the call. No matter how far below \$30 the stock price drops, the option holder will get \$0. Obviously, extremely poor stock price performance is no worse for the call option holder than is moderately poor performance. In the case of good stock performance, however, the option will expire in the money, and it will be more profitable the higher the stock price. Thus, extremely good stock outcomes can improve the option payoff without limit, but extremely poor outcomes cannot worsen the payoff below zero. This asymmetry means that volatility in the underlying stock price increases the expected payoff to the option, thereby enhancing its value.

Similarly, longer time to expiration increases the value of a call option. For more distant expiration dates, the range of likely stock prices expands, which has an effect similar to that of increased volatility. Moreover, as time to expiration increases, the present value of the exercise price falls, thereby benefiting the call option holder and increasing the option value. As a corollary to this issue, call option values are higher when interest rates rise (holding the stock price constant), because higher interest rates also reduce the present value of the exercise price.

Finally, the dividend payout policy of the firm affects option values. A high-dividend-payout policy puts a drag on the rate of growth of the stock price. For any expected total rate of return on the stock, a higher dividend yield must imply a lower expected rate of capital gain. This drag on stock price appreciation decreases the potential payoff from the call option, thereby lowering the call value. Table 18.1 summarizes these relationships.

Table 18.1
Determinants of Call Option Values

Variable Increases	Value of a Call Option
Stock price, S	Increases
Exercise price, X	Decreases
Volatility, σ	Increases
Time to expiration, T	Increases
Interest rate, r_f	Increases
Cash dividend payouts	Decreases

CONCEPT CHECK

1. Prepare a table like Table 18.1 for the determinants of put option values. How should American put values respond to increases in S, X, σ, T, r_f, and dividend payouts?

18.2 RESTRICTIONS ON OPTION VALUES

Several quantitative models of option pricing have been devised, and we will examine some of these in this chapter. All models, however, rely on simplifying assumptions. You might wonder which properties of option values are truly general and which depend on the particular simplifications. To start with, we will consider some of the more important general properties of option prices. Some of these properties have important implications for the effect of stock dividends on option values and the possible profitability of early exercise of an American option.

Restrictions on the Value of a Call Option

The most obvious restriction on the value of a call option is that its value must be zero or positive. Because the option need not be exercised, it cannot impose any liability on its holder; moreover, as long as there is any possibility that at some point the option can be exercised profitably, the option will command a positive price. Its payoff must be zero at worst, and possibly positive, so that investors are willing to pay some amount to purchase it.

We can place another lower bound on the value of a call option. Suppose that the stock will pay a dividend of D dollars just before the expiration date of the option, denoted by T (where today is time zero). Now compare two portfolios, one consisting of a call option on one share of stock and the other a leveraged equity position consisting of that share and borrowing of $(X + D)/(1 + r_f)^T$ dollars. The loan repayment is $X + D$ dollars, due on the expiration date of the option. For example, for a half-year maturity option with exercise price \$70, dividends to be paid of \$5, and effective annual interest of 10 percent, you would purchase one share of stock and borrow $\$75/(1.10)^{1/2} = \$71.51$. In six months, when the loan matures, the payment due is \$75.

At that time, the payoff to the leveraged equity position would be

	In General	Our Numbers
Stock value	$S_T + D$	$S_T + 5$
–Payback of loan	$-(X + D)$	-75
Total	$S_T - X$	$S_T - 70$

where S_T denotes the stock price at the option expiration date. Notice that the payoff to the stock is the ex-dividend stock value plus dividends received. Whether the total payoff to the stock-plus-borrowing position is positive or negative depends on whether S_T exceeds X. The net cash outlay required to establish this leveraged equity position is $S_0 - \$71.51$, or, more generally, $S_0 - (X + D)/(1 + r_f)^T$, that is, the current price of the purchased stock, S_0, less the initial cash inflow from the borrowing position.

The payoff to the call option will be $S_T - X$ if the option expires in the money and zero otherwise. Thus, the option payoff is equal to the leveraged equity payoff when that payoff is positive and is greater when the leveraged equity position has a negative payoff. Because the option payoff always is greater than or equal to that of the leveraged equity position, the option price must exceed the cost of establishing that position.

In our case the value of the call must be greater than $S_0 - (X + D)/(1 + r_f)^T$, or, more generally,

$$C \geq S_0 - \text{PV}(X) - \text{PV}(D)$$

where PV(X) denotes the present value of the exercise price and PV(D) is the present value of the dividends the stock will pay at the option's expiration. More generally, we can interpret PV(D) as the present value of any and all dividends to be paid prior to the option expiration date. Because we know already that the value of a call option must be non-negative, we may conclude that C is greater than the *maximum* of either 0 or $S_0 - \text{PV}(X) - \text{PV}(D)$.

We also can place an upper bound on the possible value of the call: simply the stock price. No one would pay more than S_0 dollars for the right to purchase a stock currently worth S_0 dollars. Thus, $C \leq S_0$.

Figure 18.2 demonstrates graphically the range of prices that is ruled out by these upper and lower bounds for the value of a call option. Any option value outside the shaded area is not possible according to the restrictions we have derived. Before expiration, the call option value normally will be *within* the allowable range, touching neither the upper nor lower bound, as in Figure 18.3.

Figure 18.2
Range of possible call option values.

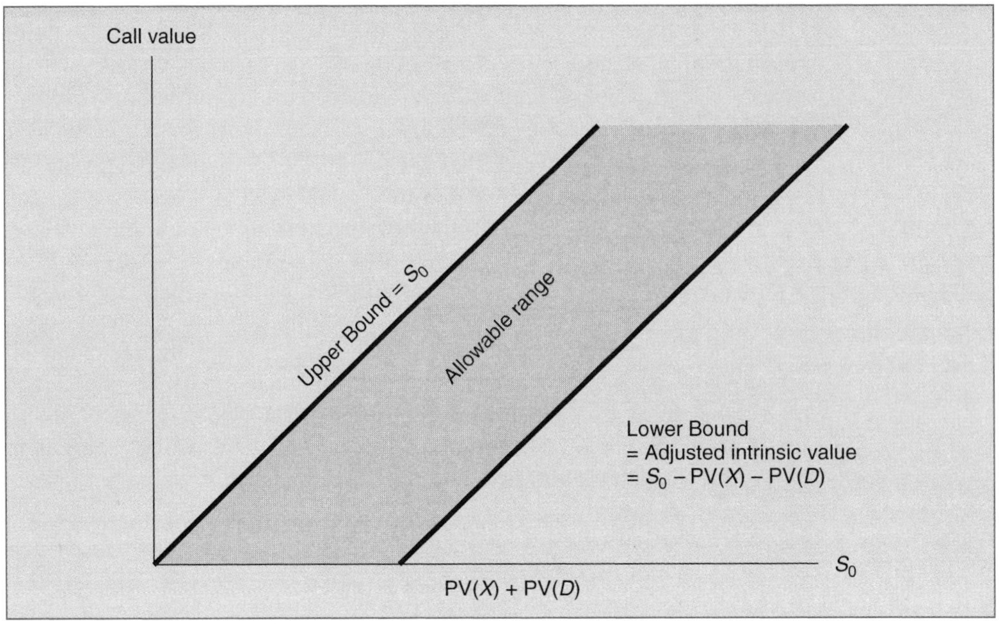

Early Exercise and Dividends

A call option holder who wants to close out that position has two choices: exercise the call or sell it. If the holder exercises at time t, the call will provide a profit of $S_t - X$, assuming, of course, that the option is in the money. We have just seen that the option can be sold for at least S_t – PV(X) – PV(D). Therefore, for an option on a nondividend-paying stock, C is greater than S_t – PV(X). Because the present value of X is less than X itself, it follows that

$$C \geq S_t - \text{PV}(X) \geq S_t - X$$

Figure 18.3
Call option value as a function of the stock price.

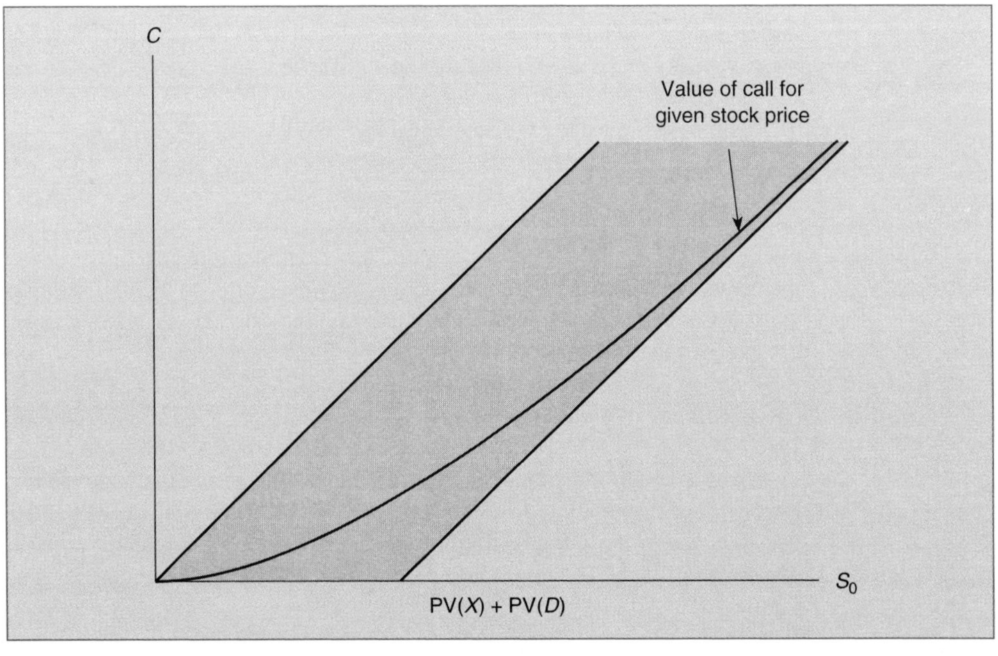

The implication here is that the proceeds from a sale of the option (at price C) must exceed the proceeds from an exercise ($S_t - X$). It is economically more attractive to keep the call option "alive" rather than "killing" it through early exercise. In other words, calls on non-dividend-paying stocks are worth more alive than dead.

If it never pays to exercise a call option before maturity, the right to exercise early actually must be valueless. The right to exercise early an American call is irrelevant because it will never pay to exercise early. We have to conclude that the values of otherwise-identical American and European call options on stocks paying no dividends are equal. If we can find the value for the European call, we also will have found the value of the American call. Therefore, any valuation formula for European call options will apply as well to American calls on non-dividend-paying stocks.

As most stocks do pay dividends, you may wonder whether this result is just a theoretical curiosity. It is not; reconsider our argument and you will see that all that we really require is that the stock pay no dividends *until the option expires.* This condition will be true for many real-world options.

Early Exercise of American Puts

For American *put options,* however, the optimality of early exercise is most definitely a possibility. To see why, consider a simple example. Suppose that you purchase a put option on a stock. Soon the firm goes bankrupt, and the stock price falls to zero. Of course you want to exercise now, because the stock price can fall no lower. Immediate exercise gives you immediate receipt of the exercise price, which can be invested to start generating income. Delay in exercise means a time-value-of-money cost. The right to early exercise of a put option before maturity must have value.

Now suppose instead that the firm is only nearly bankrupt, with the stock selling at just a few cents. Immediate exercise may still be optimal. After all, the stock price can fall by only a very small amount, meaning that the proceeds from future exercise cannot be more than a few cents greater than the proceeds from immediate exercise. Against this possibility of a tiny increase in proceeds must be weighed the time-value-of-money cost of deferring exercise. Clearly, there is some stock price below which early exercise is optimal.

This argument also proves that the American put must be worth more than its European counterpart. The American put allows you to exercise anytime before maturity. Because the right to exercise early may be useful in some circumstances, it will command a positive price in the capital market. The American put therefore will sell for a higher price than a European put with otherwise identical terms.

Figure 18.4, panel A illustrates the value of an American put option as a function of the current stock price, S_0. Once the stock price drops below a critical value, denoted S^* in the figure, exercise becomes optimal. At that point the option-pricing curve is tangent to the straight line depicting the

Figure 18.4 Put option values as a function of the current stock price.

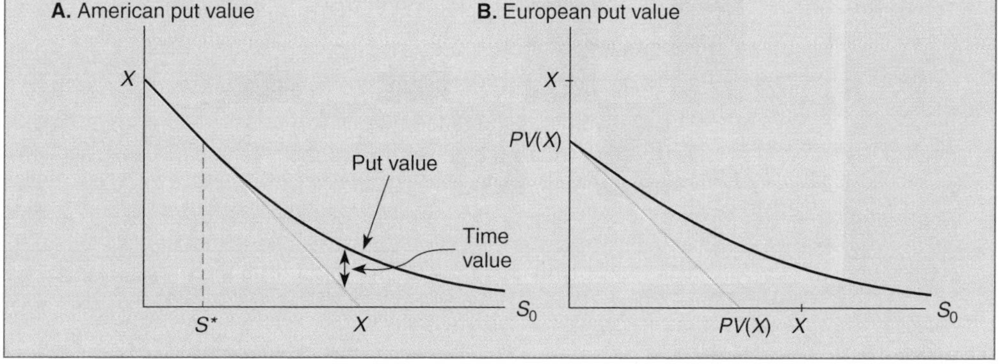

intrinsic value of the option. If and when the stock price reaches S^*, the put option is exercised and its payoff equals its intrinsic value.

In contrast, the value of the European put, which is graphed in panel B, is not asymptotic to the intrinsic value line. Because early exercise is prohibited, the maximum value of the European put is PV(X), which occurs at the point $S_0 = 0$. Obviously, for a long enough horizon, PV(X) can be made arbitrarily small.

CONCEPT CHECK ?

2. In the light of this discussion, explain why the put-call parity relationship is valid only for European options on non-dividend-paying stocks. If the stock pays no dividends, what *inequality* for American options would correspond to the parity theorem?

18.3 BLACK-SCHOLES OPTION VALUATION

Financial economists searched for years for a workable option-pricing model before Black and Scholes[2] and Merton[3] derived a formula for the value of a call option. Scholes and Merton shared the 1997 Nobel prize in economics for their accomplishment.[4] Now widely used by option-market participants, the **Black-Scholes pricing formula** is

$$C_0 = S_0 N(d_1) - Xe^{-rT} N(d_2) \tag{18.1}$$

where

$$d_1 = \frac{\ln(S_0/X) + (r + \sigma^2/2)T}{\sigma\sqrt{T}}$$

$$d_2 = d_1 - \sigma\sqrt{T}$$

and where

C_0 = Current option value

S_0 = Current stock price

X = Exercise price

r = Risk-free interest rate (the annualized continuously compounded rate on a safe asset with the same maturity as the expiration of the option, which is to be distinguished from r_f, the discrete period interest rate)

T = Time to maturity of options in years

σ = Standard deviation of the annualized continuously compounded rate of return of the stock

ln = Natural logarithm function

e = 2.71828, the base of the natural log function

$N(d)$ = The probability that a random draw from a standard normal distribution will be less than d (this equals the percentage of the area under the normal curve up to d, as shown in Figure 18.5)

---

[2]Fischer Black and Myron Scholes, "The Pricing of Options and Corporate Liabilities," *Journal of Political Economy* 81 (May/June 1973).

[3]Robert C. Merton, "Theory of Rational Option Pricing," *Bell Journal of Economics and Management Science* 4 (Spring 1973).

[4]Fischer Black died in 1995.

Figure 18.5 A standard normal curve.

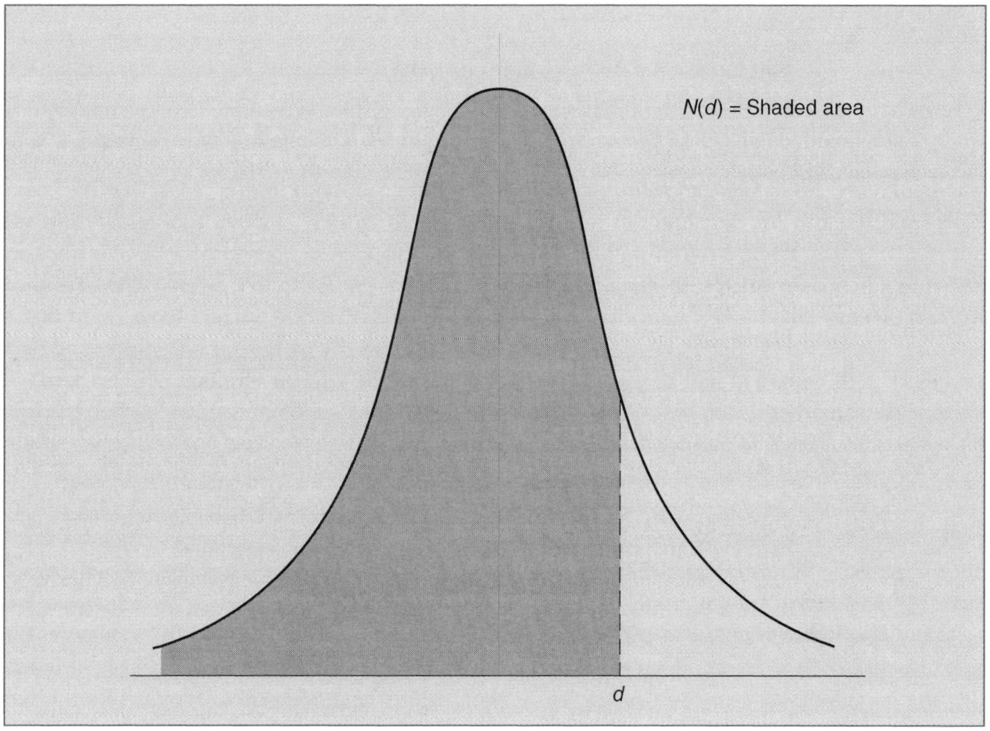

The option value does not depend on the expected rate of return on the stock. In a sense this information is already built into the formula with inclusion of the stock price, which itself depends on the stock's risk-and-return characteristics. This version of the Black-Scholes formula is predicated on the assumption that the stock pays no dividends.

Although you may find the Black-Scholes formula intimidating, we can explain it first at a somewhat intuitive level. The trick is to view the $N(d)$ terms (loosely) as risk-adjusted probabilities that the call option will expire in the money. First, look at equation 18.1 when both $N(d)$ terms are close to 1, indicating a very high probability that the option will be exercised. Then the call option value is equal to $S_0 - Xe^{-rT}$, which is what we called earlier the adjusted intrinsic value, $S_0 - \text{PV}(X)$. This makes sense: if exercise is certain, we have a claim on a stock with current value S_0 and an obligation with present value PV(X), or, with continuous compounding, Xe^{-rT}.

Now look at equation 18.1 when the $N(d)$ terms are close to zero, meaning that the option almost certainly will not be exercised. Then the equation confirms that the call is worth nothing. For middle-range values of $N(d)$ between 0 and 1, equation 18.1 tells us that the call value can be viewed as the present value of the call's potential payoff adjusting for the probability of in-the-money expiration.

How do the $N(d)$ terms serve as risk-adjusted probabilities? This question quickly leads us into advanced statistics. Notice, however, that d_1 and d_2 both increase as the stock price increases. Therefore, $N(d_1)$ and $N(d_2)$ also increase with higher stock prices. This is the property we would desire of our "probabilities." For higher stock prices relative to exercise prices, future exercise is more likely.

EXAMPLE 18.1 Black-Scholes Valuation

You can use the Black-Scholes formula fairly easily. Suppose that you want to value a call option under the following circumstances:

Stock price	$S_0 = 100$
Exercise price	$X = 95$
Interest rate	$r = .10$
Time to expiration	$T = .25$ (one-fourth year)
Standard deviation	$\sigma = .5$

First calculate

$$d_1 = \frac{\ln(100/95) + (.10 + .5^2/2) \times .25}{.5\sqrt{.25}} = .43$$

$$d_2 = .43 - .5\sqrt{.25} = .18$$

Next find $N(d_1)$ and $N(d_2)$. The values of the normal distribution are tabulated and may be found in many statistics textbooks. A table of $N(d)$ is provided here as Table 18.2. The normal distribution function, $n(d)$, is also provided in any spreadsheet program. In Microsoft Excel, for example, the function name is NORMSDIST. Table 18.2 reveals (using interpolation) that

$$N(.43) = .6664$$
$$N(.18) = .5714$$

Thus, the value of the call option is

$$C = 100 \times .6664 - (95e^{-.10 \times .25}) \times .5714$$
$$= 66.64 - 52.94 = \$13.70$$

CONCEPT CHECK

3. Calculate the call option value if the standard deviation on the stock were .6 instead of .5. Confirm that the option is worth more using this higher volatility.

What if the option price in our example were in fact \$15? Is the option mispriced? Maybe, but before betting your fortune on that, you may want to reconsider the valuation analysis. First, like all models, the Black-Scholes formula is based on some simplifying abstractions that make the formula only approximately valid. Some of the important assumptions underlying the formula are the following:

1. The stock will pay no dividends until after the option expiration date.
2. Both the interest rate, r, and variance rate, σ^2, of the stock are constant (or in slightly more general versions of the formula, both are *known* functions of time—any changes are perfectly predictable).
3. Stock prices are continuous, meaning that sudden extreme jumps such as those in the aftermath of an announcement of a takeover attempt are ruled out.

Variants of the Black-Scholes formula have been developed to deal with some of these limitations.

Second, even within the context of the model, you must be sure of the accuracy of the parameters used in the formula. Four of these—S_0, X, T, and r—are straightforward. The stock price, exercise

Table 18.2 Cumulative Normal Distribution

d	*N*(*d*)	*d*	*N*(*d*)	*d*	*N*(*d*)	*d*	*N*(*d*)	*d*	*N*(*d*)
−3.00	.0013	−1.42	.0778	−0.44	.3300	0.54	.7054	1.52	.9357
−2.95	.0016	−1.40	.0808	−0.42	.3373	0.56	.7123	1.54	.9382
−2.90	.0019	−1.38	.0838	−0.40	.3446	0.58	.7191	1.56	.9406
−2.85	.0022	−1.36	.0869	−0.38	.3520	0.60	.7258	1.58	.9429
−2.80	.0026	−1.34	.0901	−0.36	.3594	0.62	.7324	1.60	.9452
−2.75	.0030	−1.32	.0934	−0.34	.3669	0.64	.7389	1.62	.9474
−2.70	.0035	−1.30	.0968	−0.32	.3745	0.66	.7454	1.64	.9495
−2.65	.0040	−1.28	.1003	−0.30	.3821	0.68	.7518	1.66	.9515
−2.60	.0047	−1.26	.1038	−0.28	.3897	0.70	.7580	1.68	.9535
−2.55	.0054	−1.24	.1075	−0.26	.3974	0.72	.7642	1.70	.9554
−2.50	.0062	−1.22	.1112	−0.24	.4052	0.74	.7704	1.72	.9573
−2.45	.0071	−1.20	.1151	−0.22	.4129	0.76	.7764	1.74	.9591
−2.40	.0082	−1.18	.1190	−0.20	.4207	0.78	.7823	1.76	.9608
−2.35	.0094	−1.16	.1230	−0.18	.4286	0.80	.7882	1.78	.9625
−2.30	.0107	−1.14	.1271	−0.16	.4365	0.82	.7939	1.80	.9641
−2.25	.0122	−1.12	.1314	−0.14	.4443	0.84	.7996	1.82	.9556
−2.20	.0139	−1.10	.1357	−0.12	.4523	0.86	.8051	1.84	.9671
−2.15	.0158	−1.08	.1401	−0.10	.4602	0.88	.8106	1.86	.9686
−2.10	.0179	−1.06	.1446	−0.08	.4681	0.90	.8159	1.88	.9699
−2.05	.0202	−1.04	.1492	−0.06	.4761	0.92	.8212	1.90	.9713
−2.00	.0228	−1.02	.1539	−0.04	.4841	0.94	.8264	1.92	.9726
−1.98	.0239	−1.00	.1587	−0.02	.4920	0.96	.8315	1.94	.9738
−1.96	.0250	−0.98	.1635	0.00	.5000	0.98	.8365	1.96	.9750
−1.94	.0262	−0.96	.1685	0.02	.5080	1.00	.8414	1.98	.9761
−1.92	.0274	−0.94	.1736	0.04	.5160	1.02	.8461	2.00	.9772
−1.90	.0287	−0.92	.1788	0.06	.5239	1.04	.8508	2.05	.9798
−1.88	.0301	−0.90	.1841	0.08	.5319	1.06	.8554	2.10	.9821
−1.86	.0314	−0.88	.1894	0.10	.5398	1.08	.8599	2.15	.9842
−1.84	.0329	−0.86	.1949	0.12	.5478	1.10	.8643	2.20	.9861
−1.82	.0344	−0.84	.2005	0.14	.5557	1.12	.8686	2.25	.9878
−1.80	.0359	−0.82	.2061	0.16	.5636	1.14	.8729	2.30	.9893
−1.78	.0375	−0.80	.2119	0.18	.5714	1.16	.8770	2.35	.9906
−1.76	.0392	−0.78	.2177	0.20	.5793	1.18	.8810	2.40	.9918
−1.74	.0409	−0.76	.2236	0.22	.5871	1.20	.8849	2.45	.9929
−1.72	.0427	−0.74	.2297	0.24	.5948	1.22	.8888	2.50	.9938
−1.70	.0446	−0.72	.2358	0.26	.6026	1.24	.8925	2.55	.9946
−1.68	.0465	−0.70	.2420	0.28	.6103	1.26	.8962	2.60	.9953
−1.66	.0485	−0.68	.2483	0.30	.6179	1.28	.8997	2.65	.9960
−1.64	.0505	−0.66	.2546	0.32	.6255	1.30	.9032	2.70	.9965
−1.62	.0526	−0.64	.2611	0.34	.6331	1.32	.9066	2.75	.9970
−1.60	.0548	−0.62	.2676	0.36	.6406	1.34	.9099	2.80	.9974
−1.58	.0571	−0.60	.2743	0.38	.6480	1.36	.9131	2.85	.9978
−1.56	.0594	−0.58	.2810	0.40	.6554	1.38	.9162	2.90	.9981
−1.54	.0618	−0.56	.2877	0.42	.6628	1.40	.9192	2.95	.9984
−1.52	.0643	−0.54	.2946	0.44	.6700	1.42	.9222	3.00	.9986
−1.50	.0668	−0.52	.3015	0.46	.6773	1.44	.9251	3.05	.9989
−1.48	.0694	−0.50	.3085	0.48	.6844	1.46	.9279		
−1.46	.0721	−0.48	.3156	0.50	.6915	1.48	.9306		
−1.44	.0749	−0.46	.3228	0.52	.6985	1.50	.9332		

price, and time to maturity may be read directly from the option pages. The interest rate used is the money market rate for a maturity equal to that of the option. The last input, however, the standard deviation of the stock return, is not directly observable. It must be estimated from historical data, from scenario analysis, or from the prices of other options, as we will describe momentarily.

We saw in Chapter 5 that the historical variance of stock market returns can be calculated from n observations as follows:

$$\sigma^2 = \frac{n}{n-1} \sum_{t=1}^{n} \frac{(r_t - \bar{r})^2}{n}$$

where $\bar{r}$ is the average return over the sample period. The rate of return on day t is defined to be consistent with continuous compounding as $r_t = \ln(S_t/S_{t-1})$. (We note again that the natural logarithm of a ratio is approximately the percentage difference between the numerator and denominator so that $\ln(S_t/S_{t-1})$ is a measure of the rate of return of the stock from time $t - 1$ to time t.) Historical variance commonly is computed using daily returns over periods of several months. Because the standard deviation of stock returns must be estimated, however, it is always possible that discrepancies between an option price and its Black-Scholes value are simply artifacts of error in the estimation of the stock's volatility.

In fact, market participants often give the option valuation problem a different twist. Rather than calculating a Black-Scholes option value for a given stock standard deviation, they ask instead, "What standard deviation would be necessary for the option price that I can see to be consistent with the Black-Scholes formula?" This is called the **implied volatility** of the option, the volatility level for the stock that the option price implies. From the implied standard deviation, investors judge whether they think the actual stock standard deviation exceeds the implied volatility. If it does, the option is considered a good buy; if actual volatility seems greater than the implied volatility, its fair price would exceed the observed price.

CONCEPT CHECK

4. Consider the option in the example selling for $15 with Black-Scholes value of $13.70. Is its implied volatility more or less than .5?

Another variation is to compare two options on the same stock with equal expiration dates but different exercise prices. The option with the higher implied volatility would be considered relatively expensive, because a higher standard deviation is required to justify its price. The analyst might consider buying the option with the lower implied volatility and writing the option with the higher implied volatility.

Figure 18.6 presents plots of the historical and implied standard deviation of the rate of return on the S&P 500 Index. The implied volatility is derived from prices of option contracts traded on the index. Notice that although both series have considerable tendency to move together, there is some slippage between the two estimates of volatility. Notice also that both volatility series vary considerably over time. Therefore, choosing the proper volatility value to use in any option-pricing model always presents a formidable challenge. A considerable amount of recent research has been devoted to new techniques to predict changes in volatility. These techniques, which go by the name ARCH models, posit that changes in stock volatility are partially predictable, and that by analyzing recent levels and trends in volatility, one can improve predictions of future volatility.

The Black-Scholes valuation formula, as well as implied volatilities, are easily calculated using an Excel spreadsheet, as in Figure 18.7. The model inputs are listed in column A, and the outputs are given in column E. The formulas for d_1 and d_2 are provided in the spreadsheet, and the Excel formula NORMSDIST(d_1) is used to calculate $N(d_1)$. Cell G6 contains the Black-Scholes formula.

Figure 18.6 S&P 500 implied and historical volatility comparison.

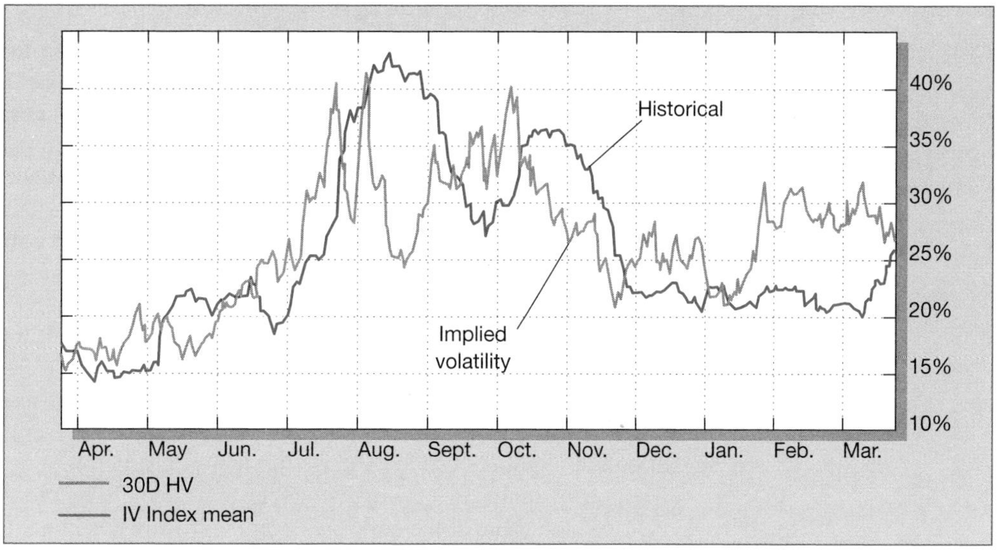

Source: IVolatility.com site, www.ivolatility.com.

To compute an implied volatility, we can use the Goal Seek command from the Tools menu in Excel. Goal Seek asks us to change the value of one cell to make the value of another cell (called the target cell) equal to a specific value. For example, if we observe a call option selling for $7 with other inputs as given in the spreadsheet, we can use Goal Seek to find the value for cell B2 (the standard deviation of the stock) that will make the option value in cell E6 equal to $7. In this case, the target cell, E6, is the call price, and spreadsheet manipulates cell B2. When you ask the spreadsheet to "Solve," it finds that a standard deviation equal to .2783 is consistent with a call price of $7; this would be the option's implied volatility if it were selling at $7.

Dividends and Call Option Valuation

We noted earlier that the Black-Scholes call option formula applies to stocks that do not pay dividends. When dividends are to be paid before the option expires, we need to adjust the formula. The payment of dividends raises the possibility of early exercise, and for most realistic dividend payout schemes the valuation formula becomes significantly more complex than the Black-Scholes equation.

We can apply some simple rules of thumb to approximate the option value, however. One popular approach, originally suggested by Black, calls for adjusting the stock price downward by the present value of any dividends that are to be paid before option expiration.[5] Therefore, we would

Figure 18.7 Spreadsheet to calculate Black-Scholes call option values.

	A	B	C	D	E	F	G	H	I	J
1	INPUTS			OUTPUTS			FORMULA FOR OUTPUT IN COLUMN E			
2	Standard deviation (annual)	0.2783		d1	0.0029		(LN(B5/B6)+(B4+.5*B2^2)*B3)/(B2*SQRT(B3))			
3	Maturity (in years)	0.5		d2	-0.1939		E2-B2*SQRT(B3)			
4	Risk-free rate (annual)	0.06		N(d1)	0.5012		NORMSDIST(E2)			
5	Stock price	100		N(d2)	0.4231		NORMSDIST(E3)			
6	Exercise price	105		B/S call value	7.0000		B5*E4-B6*EXP(-B4*B3)*E5			
7	Dividend yield (annual)	0		B/S put value	8.8968		B6*EXP(-B4*B3)*(1-E5)-B5*(1-E4)			

[5]Fischer Black, "Fact and Fantasy in the Use of Options," *Financial Analysts Journal* 31 (July/August 1975).

simply replace S_0 with S_0 − PV(dividends) in the Black-Scholes formula. Such an adjustment will take dividends into account by reflecting their eventual impact on the stock price. The option value then may be computed as before, assuming that the option will be held to expiration.

In one special case, the dividend adjustment takes a simple form. Suppose the underlying asset pays a continuous flow of income. This might be a reasonable assumption for options on a stock index, where different stocks in the index pay dividends on different days, so that dividend income arrives in a more or less continuous flow. If the dividend yield, denoted δ, is constant, one can show that the present value of that dividend flow accruing until the option maturity date is $S_0(1 - e^{-\delta T})$. (For intuition, notice that $e^{-\delta T}$ approximately equals $1 - \delta$, so the value of the dividend is approximately $\delta T S_0$.) In this case, $S_0 - \text{PV(Div)} = S_0 e^{-\delta T}$, and we can derive a Black-Scholes call option formula on the dividend-paying asset simply by substituting $S_0 e^{-\delta T}$ for S_0 in the original formula. This approach is used in Figure 18.7.

These procedures would yield a very good approximation of option value for European call options that must be held until maturity, but they do not allow for the fact that the holder of an American call option might choose to exercise the option just before a dividend. The current value of a call option, assuming that the option will be exercised just before the ex-dividend date, might be greater than the value of the option—assuming it will be held until maturity. Although holding the option until maturity allows greater effective time to expiration, which increases the option value, it also entails more dividend payments, lowering the expected stock price at maturity and thereby lowering the current option value.

For example, suppose that a stock selling at $20 will pay a $1 dividend in four months, whereas the call option on the stock does not expire for six months. The effective annual interest rate is 10 percent, so that the present value of the dividend is $\$1/(1.10)^{1/3} = \$0.97$. Black suggests that we can compute the option value in one of two ways:

1. Apply the Black-Scholes formula assuming early exercise, thus using the actual stock price of $20 and a time to expiration of four months (the time until the dividend payment).
2. Apply the Black-Scholes formula assuming no early exercise, using the dividend-adjusted stock price of $20 – $0.97 = $19.03 and a time to expiration of six months.

The greater of the two values is the estimate of the option value, recognizing that early exercise might be optimal. In other words, the so-called **pseudo-American call option value** is the maximum of the value derived by assuming that the option will be held until expiration and the value derived by assuming that the option will be exercised just before an ex-dividend date. Even this technique is not exact, however, for it assumes that the option holder makes an irrevocable decision now on when to exercise, when in fact the decision is not binding until exercise notice is given.[6]

Put Option Valuation

We have concentrated so far on call option valuation. We can derive Black-Scholes European put option values from call option values using the put-call parity theorem. To value the put option, we simply calculate the value of the corresponding call option in equation 18.2 from the Black-Scholes formula, and solve for the put option value as

$$\begin{aligned} P &= C + \text{PV}(X) - S_0 \\ &= C + Xe^{-rT} - S_0 \end{aligned} \quad (18.2)$$

[6]An exact formula for American call valuation on dividend-paying stocks has been developed in Richard Roll, "An Analytic Valuation Formula for Unprotected American Call Options on Stocks with Known Dividends," *Journal of Financial Economics* 5 (November 1977). The technique has been discussed and revised in Robert Geske, "A Note on an Analytical Formula for Unprotected American Call Options on Stocks with Known Dividends," *Journal of Financial Economics* 7 (December 1979); Robert E. Whaley, "On the Valuation of American Call Options on Stocks with Known Dividends," *Journal of Financial Economics* 9 (June 1981); and Giovanni Barone-Adesi and Robert E. Whaley, "Efficient Analytic Approximations of American Option Values," *Journal of Finance* 42, no. 2 (June 1987). These are difficult papers, however.

We must calculate the present value of the exercise price using continuous compounding to be consistent with the Black-Scholes formula.

Sometimes, it is easier to work with a put option valuation formula directly. If we substitute the Black-Scholes formula for a call in equation 18.7, we obtain the value of a European put option as

$$P = Xe^{-rT}[1 - N(d_2)] - S_0[1 - N(d_1)] \tag{18.3}$$

EXAMPLE 18.2 Black-Scholes Put Valuation

Using data from the Black-Scholes call option example ($C = \$13.70$; $X = \$95$; $S = \$100$; $r = .10$; and $T = .25$), we find that a European put option on that stock with identical exercise price and time to maturity is worth

$$P = \$13.70 + \$95e^{-.10 \times .25} - \$100 = \$6.35$$

As we noted traders can do, we might then compare this formula value to the actual put price as one step in formulating a trading strategy.

Equation 18.2 is valid for European puts on non-dividend-paying stocks. Listed put options are American options that offer the opportunity of early exercise, however, and we have seen that the right to exercise puts early can turn out to be valuable. This means that an American option must be worth more than the corresponding European option. Therefore, equation 18.2 describes only the lower bound on the true value of the American put. However, in many applications the approximation is very accurate.[7]

18.4 USING THE BLACK-SCHOLES FORMULA

Hedge Ratios and the Black-Scholes Formula

www.alcan.com

In Chapter 17, Section 17.2, we considered two investments in Alcan: 200 shares of Alcan stock or 2,000 call options on Alcan. We saw that the call option position was more sensitive to swings in Alcan's stock price than the all-stock position. To analyze the overall exposure to a stock price more precisely, however, it is necessary to quantify these relative sensitivities. A tool that enables us to summarize the overall exposure of portfolios of options with various exercise prices and times to maturity is the **hedge ratio**. An option's hedge ratio is the change in the price of an option for a $1 increase in the stock price. Therefore, a call option has a positive hedge ratio and a put option has a negative hedge ratio. The hedge ratio is commonly called the option's **delta**.

If you were to graph the option value as a function of the stock value as we have done for a call option in Figure 18.8, the hedge ratio is simply the slope of the value function evaluated at the current stock price. For example, suppose that the slope of the curve at $S_0 = \$120$ equals .60. As the stock increases in value by $1, the option increases by approximately $.60, as the figure shows.

For every call option written, .60 shares of stock would be needed to hedge the investor's portfolio. For example, if one writes 10 options and holds six shares of stock, according to the hedge ratio of .6, a $1 increase in stock price will result in a gain of $6 on the stock holdings, whereas the loss on the 10 options written will be $10 \times \$0.60$, an equivalent $6. The stock price movement leaves total wealth unaltered, which is what is required of a hedged position. The investor holding the stock and option in proportions dictated by their relative price movements hedges the portfolio.

[7] For a more complete treatment of American put valuation, see R. Geske and H. E. Johnson, "The American Put Valued Analytically," *Journal of Finance* 39 (December 1984), pp. 1511–1524.

Figure 18.8 Call option value and hedge ratio.

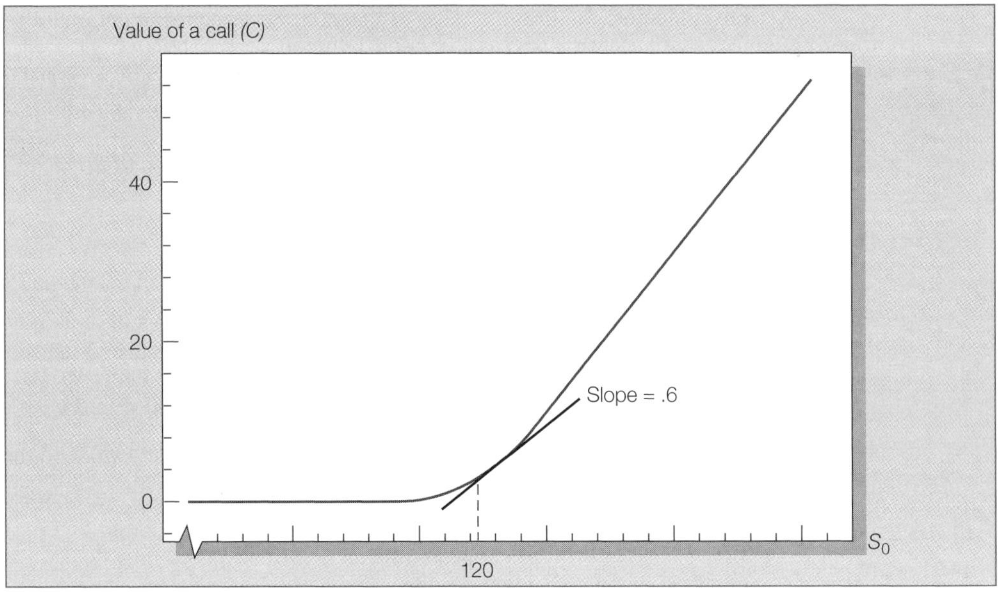

Black-Scholes hedge ratios are particularly easy to compute. It turns out that the hedge ratio for a call is $N(d_1)$, and the hedge ratio for a put is $N(d_1) - 1$. We defined $N(d_1)$ as part of the Black-Scholes formula (equation 18.1). Recall that $N(d)$ stands for the area under the standard normal curve up to d. Therefore, the call option hedge ratio must be positive and less than 1, whereas the put option hedge ratio is negative and of smaller absolute value than 1.

Figure 18.8 verifies the insight that the slope of the call option valuation function is indeed less than 1, approaching 1 only as the stock price becomes much greater than the exercise price. This tells us that option values change less than one-for-one with changes in stock prices. Why should this be? Suppose that an option is so far in the money that you are absolutely certain it will be exercised. In that case, every dollar increase in the stock price would indeed increase the option value by $1. However, if there is a reasonable chance that the call option will expire out of the money even after a moderate stock price gain, a $1 increase in the stock price will not necessarily increase the ultimate payoff to the call; therefore, the call price will not respond by a full dollar.

The fact that hedge ratios are less than 1 does not conflict with our earlier observation that options offer leverage and are quite sensitive to stock price movements. Although *dollar* movements in option prices are slighter than dollar movements in the stock price, the *rate of return* volatility of options remains greater than stock return volatility because options sell at smaller prices. In our example, with the stock selling at $120 and a hedge ratio of 0.6, an option with exercise price $120 may sell for $5. If the stock price increases to $121, the call price would be expected to increase by only $.60, to $5.60. The percentage increase in the option value is $.60/$5.00 = 12 percent, however, whereas the stock price increase is only $1/$120 = .83 percent. The ratio of the percentage changes is 12 percent/.83 percent = 14.4. For every 1 percent increase in the stock price, the option price increases by 14.4 percent. This ratio, the percent change in option price per percent change in stock price, is called the **option elasticity**.

CONCEPT CHECK

5. What is the elasticity of a put option currently selling for $4 with exercise price $120 and hedge ratio –.4, if the stock price is currently $122?

The hedge ratio is an essential tool in portfolio management and control. An example will illustrate.

Consider two portfolios, one holding 750 Alcan calls and 200 shares of Alcan, and the other holding 800 shares of Alcan. Which portfolio has greater dollar exposure to Alcan price movements? You can answer this question easily using the hedge ratio.

Each option changes in value by H dollars for each dollar change in stock price, where H stands for the hedge ratio. Thus, if H equals 0.6, the 750 options are equivalent to 450 ($.6 \times 750$) shares in terms of the response of their market value to Alcan's stock price movements. The first portfolio has less dollar sensitivity to Alcan, because the 450 share-equivalents of the options plus the 200 shares actually held are less than the 800 shares held in the second portfolio.

This is not to say, however, that the first portfolio is less sensitive to Alcan in terms of its rate of return. As we noted in discussing option elasticities, the first portfolio may be of lower total value than the second, so despite its lower sensitivity in terms of total market value, it might have greater rate of return sensitivity. Because a call option has a lower market value than the stock, its price changes more than proportionally with stock price changes, even though its hedge ratio is less than 1.

Portfolio Insurance

In Chapter 17 we showed that protective put strategies offer a sort of insurance policy on an asset. The protective put has proved to be extremely popular with investors. Even if the asset price falls, the put conveys the right to sell the asset for the exercise price, which is a way to lock in a minimum portfolio value. With an at-the-money put ($X = S_0$), the maximum loss that can be realized is the cost of the put. The asset can be sold for X, which equals its original value, so even if the asset price falls, the investor's net loss over the period is just the cost of the put. If the asset value increases, however, upside potential is unlimited. Figure 18.9 graphs the profit or loss on a protective put position as a function of the change in the value of the underlying asset.

Although the protective put is a simple and convenient way to achieve **portfolio insurance**, there are practical difficulties in trying to insure a portfolio of stocks. First, unless the investor's portfolio corresponds to a standard market index for which puts are traded, a put option on the portfolio will not be available for purchase. In addition, if index puts are used to protect a nonindexed portfolio, tracking errors can result. For example, if the portfolio falls in value while the

Figure 18.9
Profit on a protective put strategy.

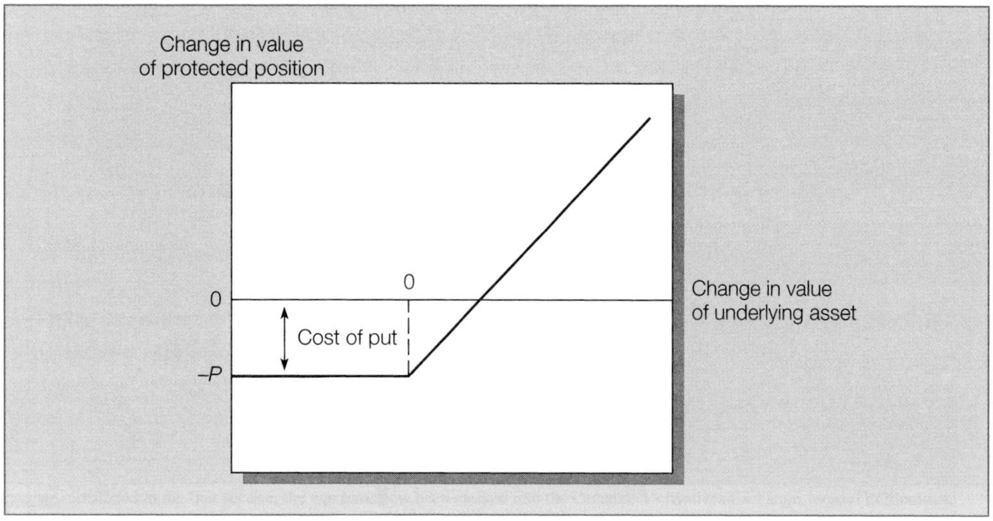

market index rises, the put will fail to provide the intended protection. Tracking error limits the investor's freedom to pursue active stock selection, because such error will be greater as the managed portfolio departs more substantially from the market index.

www.cboe.com

Moreover, the desired horizon of the insurance program must match the maturity of a traded put option in order to establish the appropriate protective put position. Today long-term options on market indexes and several larger stocks called LEAPS (for *long-term equity anticipation securities*) trade on the CBOE and the Canadian Derivatives Exchange with maturities of several years. However, this market has been active only for a few years. In the mid-1980s, while most investors pursuing insurance programs had horizons of several years, actively traded puts were limited to maturities of less than a year. Rolling over a sequence of short-term puts, which might be viewed as a response to this problem, introduces new risks because the prices at which successive puts will be available in the future are not known today.

Providers of portfolio insurance with horizons of several years, therefore, could not rely on the simple expedient of purchasing protective puts for their clients' portfolios. Instead, they followed trading strategies to replicate the payoffs to the protective put position.

Here is the general idea: Even if a put option on the desired portfolio with the desired expiration date does not exist, a theoretical option pricing model (such as the Black-Scholes model) can be used to determine how that option's price would respond to the portfolio's value if the option did in fact trade. For example, if stock prices were to fall, the put option would increase in value. The option model could quantify this relationship. The next exposure of the (hypothetical) protective put portfolio to swings in stock prices is the sum of the exposures of the two components of the portfolio, the stock and the put. The net exposure of the portfolio equals the equity exposure less the (offsetting) put option exposure. We can create "synthetic" protective put positions by holding a quantity of stocks with the same net exposure to market swings as the hypothetical protective put position. The key to this strategy is the option's delta or hedge ratio, that is, the change in the price of the protective put option per change in the value of the underlying stock portfolio.

EXAMPLE 18.3 Synthetic Protective Put Options

Suppose that a portfolio is currently valued at \$100 million. An at-the-money put option on the portfolio might have a hedge ratio or delta of –.6, meaning that the option's value swings \$.60 for every dollar change in portfolio value, but in an opposite direction. Suppose the stock portfolio falls in value by 2 percent. The profit on a hypothetical protective put position (if the put existed) would be as follows (in millions of dollars):

Loss on stocks: 2% of \$100	= \$2.00
Gain on put: .6 × \$2	= \$1.20
Net loss:	= \$ .80

We create the synthetic option position by selling a proportion of shares equal to the put option's delta (that is, selling 60 percent of the shares), and placing the proceeds in risk-free T-bills. The rationale is that the hypothetical put option would have offset 60 percent of any change in the stock portfolio's value, so one must reduce portfolio risk directly by selling off 60 percent of the equity and putting the proceeds into a risk-free asset. Total return on a synthetic protective put position with \$60 million in risk-free investments, such as T-bills, and \$40 million in equity is

Loss on stocks: 2% of \$40	= \$.80
Loss on bills:	= 0
Net loss:	= \$.80

The synthetic and actual protective put positions have equal returns. We conclude that if you sell a proportion of shares equal to the put option's delta and place the proceeds in cash equivalents, your exposure to the stock market will equal that of the desired protective put position.

The difficulty with this procedure is that deltas constantly change. Figure 18.10 shows that, as the stock price falls, the magnitude of the appropriate hedge ratio increases. Therefore, market declines require extra hedging, that is, additional conversions of equity into cash. This constant updating of the hedge ratio is called **dynamic hedging**.

Dynamic hedging is one reason portfolio insurance has been said to contribute to market volatility. Market declines trigger additional sales of stock as portfolio insurers strive to increase their hedging. These additional sales are seen as reinforcing or exaggerating market downturns.

In practice, portfolio insurers do not actually buy or sell stocks directly when they update their hedge positions. Instead, they minimize trading costs by buying or selling stock index futures as a substitute for sale of the stocks themselves. As you will see in the following chapter, stock prices and index futures prices usually are very tightly linked by cross-market arbitrageurs so that futures transactions can be used as reliable proxies for stock transactions. Instead of selling equities based on the put option's delta, insurers will sell an equivalent number of futures contracts.[8]

Several U.S. portfolio insurers suffered great setbacks on October 19, 1987, when the market suffered an unprecedented one-day loss of about 20 percent. We can describe what happened then so you can appreciate the complexities of applying a seemingly straightforward hedging concept:

1. Market volatility was much greater than ever encountered before. Put option deltas based on historical experience were too low, and insurers underhedged, held too much equity, and suffered excessive losses.

Figure 18.10 Hedge ratios change as the stock price fluctuates.

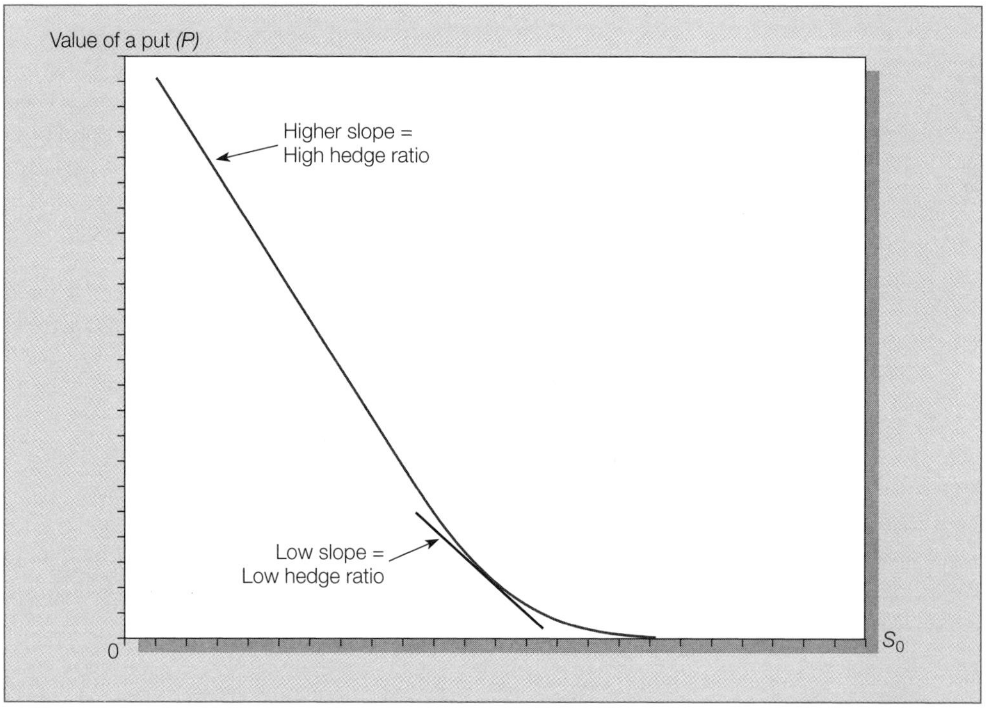

[8]Notice, however, that the use of index futures reintroduces the problem of tracking error between the portfolio and the market index.

2. Prices moved so fast that insurers could not keep up with the necessary rebalancing. They were chasing deltas that kept getting away from them. In addition, the futures market saw a "gap" opening, where the opening price was nearly 10 percent below the previous day's close. The price dropped before insurers could update their hedge ratios.
3. Execution problems were severe. First, current market prices were unavailable, with the trade execution and price quotation system hours behind, which made computation of correct hedge ratios impossible. Moreover, trading in stocks and stock futures ceased altogether during some periods. The continuous rebalancing capability that is essential for a viable insurance program simply vanished during the precipitous market collapse.
4. Futures prices traded at steep discounts to their proper levels compared to reported stock prices, thereby making the sale of futures (as a proxy for equity sales) to increase hedging seem expensive. Although we will see in the next chapter that stock index futures prices normally exceed the value of the stock index, on October 19, 1987, futures sold far below the stock index level. The so-called cash-to-futures spread was negative most of the day. When some insurers gambled that the futures price would recover to its usual premium over the stock index and chose to defer sales, they remained underhedged. As the market fell further, their portfolios experienced substantial losses.

Although most observers believe that the portfolio insurance industry will never recover from the market crash, the boxed article here points out that delta hedging is still alive and well on Wall Street. Dynamic hedges are widely used by large firms to hedge potential losses from the options they write. The article points out, however, that these traders are increasingly aware of the practical difficulties in implementing dynamic hedges in very volatile markets.

Hedging Bets on Mispriced Options

Suppose you believe that the standard deviation of IBM stock returns will be 35 percent over the next few weeks, but IBM put options are selling at a price consistent with a volatility of 33 percent. Because the put's implied volatility is less than your forecast of the stock volatility, you believe the option is underpriced. Using your assessment of volatility in an option-pricing model like the Black-Scholes formula, you would estimate that the fair price for the puts exceeds the actual price.

Does this mean that you ought to buy put options? Perhaps it does, but by doing so, you risk great losses if IBM stock performs well, *even if* you are correct about the volatility. You would like to separate your bet on volatility from the "attached" bet inherent in purchasing a put that IBM's stock price will fall. In other words, you would like to speculate on the option mispricing by purchasing the put option, but hedge the resulting exposure to the performance of IBM stock.

We've seen that the option *delta* is in fact a hedge ratio that can be used for this purpose. The delta was defined as

$$\text{Delta} = \frac{\text{Change in value of option}}{\text{Change in value of stock}}$$

Therefore, delta is the slope of the option-pricing curve.

This ratio tells us precisely how many shares of stock we must hold to offset our exposure to IBM. For example, if the delta is $-.6$, then the put will fall by \$.60 in value for every one-point increase in IBM stock, and we need to hold .6 share of stock to hedge each put. If we purchase 10 option contracts, each for 100 shares, we would need to buy 600 shares of stock. If the stock price rises by \$1, each put option will decrease in value by \$.60, resulting in a loss of \$600. However, the loss on the puts will be offset by a gain on the stock holdings of \$1 per share $\times$ 600 shares.

To see how the profits on this strategy might develop, let's use the following example.

DELTA-HEDGING: THE NEW NAME IN PORTFOLIO INSURANCE

Portfolio insurance, the high-tech hedging strategy that helped grease the slide in the 1987 stock-market crash, is alive and well.

And just as in 1987, it doesn't always work out as planned, as some financial institutions found out in the recent European bond-market turmoil.

Banks, securities firms, and other big traders rely heavily on portfolio insurance to contain their potential losses when they buy and sell options. But since portfolio insurance got a bad name after it backfired on investors in 1987, it goes by an alias these days—the sexier, Star Trek moniker of "delta-hedging."

Whatever you call it, the recent turmoil in European bond markets taught some practitioners—including banks and securities firms that were hedging options sales to hedge funds and other investors—the same painful lessons of earlier portfolio insurers: delta-hedging can break down in volatile markets, just when it is needed most.

What's more, at such times, it can actually feed volatility. The complexities of hedging certain hot-selling "exotic" options may only compound such glitches.

"The tried-and-true strategies for hedging [these products] work fine when the markets aren't subject to sharp moves or large shocks," says Victor S. Filatov, president of Smith Barney Global Capital Management in London. But turbulent times can start "causing problems for people who normally have these risks under control."

Options are financial arrangements that give buyers the right to buy, or sell, securities or other assets at prearranged prices over some future period. An option can gyrate wildly in value with even modest changes in the underlying security's price; the relationship between the two is known as the option's "delta." Thus, dealers in these instruments need some way to hedge their delta to contain the risk.

How you delta-hedge depends on the bets you're trying to hedge. For instance, delta-hedging would prompt options sellers to sell into falling markets and buy into rallies. It would give the opposite directions to options buyers, such as dealers who might hold big options inventories.

In theory, delta-hedging takes place with computer-timed precision, and there aren't any snags. But in real life, it doesn't always work so smoothly.

"When volatility ends up being much greater than anticipated, you can't get your delta trades off at the right points," says an executive at one big derivatives dealer.

A Scenario in Treasuries

How does this happen? Take the relatively simple case of dealers who sell "call" options on long-term Treasury bonds. Such options give buyers the right to buy bonds at a fixed price over a specific time period. And compared with buying bonds outright, these options are much more sensitive to market moves.

Because selling the calls made those dealers vulnerable to a rally, they delta-hedged by buying bonds. As bond prices turned south [and option deltas fell] the dealers shed their hedges by selling bonds, adding to the selling orgy. The plunging markets forced them to sell at lower prices than expected, causing unexpected losses on their hedges.

To be sure, traders say delta-hedging wasn't the main source of selling in the markets' fall. That dubious honor goes to the huge dumping by speculators of bond and stock holdings that were purchased with borrowed money. While experts may agree that delta-hedging doesn't actually cause crashes, in some cases it can speed the decline once prices slip.

By the same token, delta-hedging also tends to buoy prices once they turn up—which may be one reason why markets correct so suddenly these days.

Source: Barbara Donnelly Granito, "Delta-Hedging: The New Name in Portfolio Insurance," *The Wall Street Journal*, March 17, 1994.

EXAMPLE 18.4 Speculating on Mispriced Options

Option maturity, T	60 days
Put price, P	\$4.495
Exercise price, X	\$90
Stock price, S	\$90
Risk-free rate, r	4%

We assume that the stock will not pay a dividend in the next 60 days. Given these data, the implied volatility on the option is 33 percent, as we posited. However, you believe the true volatility is 35 percent, implying that the fair put price is \$4.785. Therefore, if the market assessment of volatility is revised to the value you believe is correct, your profit will be \$.29 per put purchased.

Recall that the hedge ratio, or delta, of a put option equals $N(d_1) - 1$, where $N(\bullet)$ is the cumulative normal distribution function and

BLACK-SCHOLES OPTION VALUATION

The spreadsheet below can be used to determine option values using the Black-Scholes model. The inputs are the stock price, standard deviation, maturity of the option, exercise price, and risk-free rate. The call option is valued using equation 18.1 and the option is valued using equation 18.3. For both calls and puts, the dividend-adjusted Black-Scholes formula substitutes Se^{-rq} for S, as outlined earlier under "Dividends and Call Option Valuation." The model also calculates the intrinsic and time value for both puts and calls.

The model presents sensitivity analysis using the one-way data table. For most of the variables that are used in the Black-Scholes model, ranges of the variables are simulated so that sensitivity of option values and time premiums to these variables can be evaluated.

The first workbook presents the analysis of calls; the second presents similar analysis of puts. You can find these spreadsheets at www.mcgrawhill.ca/college/bodie.

	A	B	C	D	E	F	G	H	I	J	K	L	M	N
1	**Black-Scholes Option Pricing**													
2	**Call Valuation & Call Time Premiums**													
3														
4														
5	***Inputs***													
6	Standard Deviation	0.2783												
7	Variance	0.07745089		**Standard Deviation of Returns**	**Call Option Value**		**Standard Deviation of Returns**	**Call Time Value**		**Stock Price**	**Call Option Value**		**Stock Price**	**Call Time Value**
8	Maturity in Years	0.5									6.99991736			6.99991736
9	Risk-Free Rate (Annual)	0.06			6.99991736			6.99991736		60	0.01670918		60	0.01670918
10	Stock Price	100		0.15	3.38791003		0.15	3.38791003		65	0.0611049		65	0.0611049
11	Exercise Price	105		0.175	4.08913153		0.175	4.08913153		70	0.17928127		70	0.17928127
12	Dividend Yield	0		0.2	4.7923313		0.2	4.7923313		75	0.44023735		75	0.44023735
13	***Outputs***			0.225	5.49667006		0.225	5.49667006		80	0.93505127		80	0.93505127
14	d1	0.00290952		0.25	6.20162034		0.25	6.20162034		85	1.76318603		85	1.76318603
15	d2	-0.1938783		0.275	6.90682567		0.275	6.90682567		90	3.01402809		90	3.01402809
16	N(d1)	0.50116074		0.3	7.61202812		0.3	7.61202812		95	4.75048306		95	4.75048306
17	N(d2)	0.42313561		0.325	8.31703221		0.325	8.31703221		100	6.99991736		100	6.99991736
18	Black-Scholes Call Value	6.99991736		0.35	9.02168403		0.35	9.02168403		105	9.75365947		105	9.75365947
19	Black-Scholes Put Value	8.89669838		0.375	9.7258562		0.375	9.7258562		110	12.9735425		110	7.97354246
20				0.4	10.4294397		0.4	10.4294397		115	16.6018522		115	6.60185217
21				0.425	11.1323386		0.425	11.1323386		120	20.5719132		120	5.57191315
22	Intrinsic Value of Call	0		0.45	11.8344663		0.45	11.8344663		125	24.8166994		125	4.8166994
23	Time Value of Call	6.99991736		0.475	12.5357435		0.475	12.5357435		130	29.2747208		130	4.27472078
24				0.5	13.236096		0.5	13.236096		135	33.8932551		135	3.89325512
25	Intrinsic Value of Put	5												
26	Time Value of Put	3.89669838												

$$d_1 = \frac{\ln(S/X) + (r + \sigma^2/2)T}{\sigma\sqrt{T}}$$

Using your estimate of $\sigma = .35$, you find that the hedge ratio $N(d_1) - 1 = -.453$.

Suppose, therefore, that you purchase 10 option contracts (1,000 puts) and purchase 453 shares of stock. Once the market "catches up" to your presumably better volatility estimate, the put options purchased will increase in value. If the market assessment of volatility changes as soon as you purchase the options, your profits should equal $1{,}000 \times \$.29 = \$290$. The option price will be affected as well by any change in the stock price, but this part of your exposure will be eliminated if the hedge ratio is chosen properly. Your profit should be based solely on the effect of the change in the implied volatility of the put, with the impact of the stock price hedged away.

Table 18.3 illustrates your profits as a function of the stock price assuming that the put price changes to reflect *your* estimate of volatility. Panel B shows that the put option alone can provide profits or losses depending on whether the stock price falls or rises. We see in panel C, however, that each *hedged* put option provides profits nearly equal to the original mispricing, regardless of the change in the stock price.[9]

CONCEPT CHECK

6. Suppose you bet on volatility by purchasing calls instead of puts. How would you hedge your exposure to stock-price fluctuations? What is the hedge ratio?

A variant of this strategy involves cross-option speculation. Suppose you observe a 45-day maturity call option on IBM with strike price 95 selling at a price consistent with a volatility of $\sigma = 33$ percent while another 45-day call with strike price 90 has an implied volatility of only 27 percent. Because the underlying asset and maturity date are identical, you conclude that the call with the higher implied volatility is relatively overpriced. To exploit the mispricing, you might buy the cheap calls (with strike price 90 and implied volatility of 27 percent) and write the expensive calls (with strike price 95 and implied volatility 33 percent). If the risk-free rate is 4 percent and IBM is selling at $90 per share, the calls purchased will be priced at $3.6202 and the calls written will be priced at $2.3735.

Despite the fact that you are long one call and short another, your exposure to IBM stock-price uncertainty will not be hedged using this strategy. This is because calls with different strike prices have different sensitivities to the price of the underlying asset. The lower-strike-price call has a higher delta and therefore greater exposure to the price of IBM. If you take an equal number of positions in these two options, you will inadvertently establish a bullish position in IBM, as the calls you purchase have higher deltas than the calls you write. In fact, you may recall from Chapter 17 that this portfolio (long call with low exercise price and short call with high exercise price) is called a *bullish spread.*

Table 18.3 Profit on Hedged Put Portfolio

A. Cost to establish hedged position			
1,000 put options @ $4.495/option	$ 4,495		
453 shares @ $90/share	40,770		
Total outlay	$45,265		
B. Value of put option as a function of the stock price at implied volatility of 35%			
Stock Price:	**89**	**90**	**91**
Put price	$5.254	$4.785	$4.347
Profit (loss) on each put	0.759	0.290	(0.148)
C. Value of and profit on hedged put portfolio			
Stock Price:	**89**	**90**	**91**
Value of 1,000 put options	$ 5,254	$ 4,785	$ 4,347
Value of 453 shares	40,317	40,770	41,223
Total	$45,571	$45,555	$45,570
Profit (= Value − Cost from panel A)	306	290	305

[9]The profit is not exactly independent of the stock price. This is because as the stock price changes, so do the deltas used to calculate the hedge ratio. The hedge ratio in principle would need to be continually adjusted as deltas evolve. The sensitivity of the delta to the stock price is called the *gamma* of the option. Option gammas are analogous to bond convexity. In both cases, the curvature of the value function means that hedge ratios or durations change with market conditions, making rebalancing a necessary part of hedging strategies.

To establish a hedged position, we can use the hedge ratio approach as follows. Consider the 95-strike-price options you write as the asset that hedges your exposure to the 90-strike-price options your purchase. Then the hedge ratio is

$$H = \frac{\text{Change in value of 90-strike-price call for \$1 change in IBM}}{\text{Change in value of 95-strike-price call for \$1 change in IBM}}$$

$$= \frac{\text{Delta of 90-strike-price call}}{\text{Delta of 95-strike-price call}} > 1$$

You need to write *more* than one call with the higher strike price to hedge the purchase of each call with the lower strike price. Because the prices of higher-strike-price calls are less sensitive to IBM prices, more of them are required to offset the exposure.

Suppose the true annual volatility of the stock is midway between the two implied volatilities, so $\sigma = 30$ percent. We know that the delta of a call option is $N(d_1)$. Therefore, the deltas of the two options and the hedge ratio are computed as follows:

Option with strike price 90:

$$d_1 = \frac{\ln(90/90) + (.04 + .30^2/2) \times 45/365}{.30\sqrt{45/365}} = .0995$$

$$N(d_1) = .5396$$

Option with strike price 95:

$$d_1 = \frac{\ln(90/95) + (.04 + .30^2/2) \times 45/365}{.30\sqrt{45/365}} = -.4138$$

$$N(d_1) = .3395$$

Hedge ratio:

$$\frac{.5396}{.3395} = 1.589$$

Therefore, for every 1,000 call options purchased with strike price 90, we need to write 1,589 call options with strike price 95. Following this strategy enables us to bet on the relative mispricing of the two options without taking a position on IBM. Panel A of Table 18.4 shows that the position will result in a cash inflow of $151.30. The premium income on the calls written exceeds the cost of the calls purchased.

When you establish a position in stocks and options that is hedged with respect to fluctuations in the price of the underlying asset, your portfolio is said to be **delta-neutral**, meaning that the portfolio has no tendency to either increase or decrease in value when the stock price fluctuates.

Let's check that our options position is in fact delta-neutral. Suppose that the implied volatilities of the two options come back into alignment just after you establish your position, so that both options are priced at implied volatilities of 30 percent. You expect to profit from the increase in the value of the call purchased as well as from the decrease in the value of the call written. The option prices at 30 percent volatility are given in panel B of Table 18.4 and the values of your position for various stock prices are presented in panel C. Although the profit or loss on each option is affected by the stock price, the value of the delta-neutral option portfolio is positive and essentially independent of the price of IBM. Moreover, we saw in panel A that the portfolio would have been established without ever requiring a cash outlay. You would have cash inflows both when you establish the portfolio *and* when you liquidate it after the implied volatilities converge to 30 percent.

This unusual profit opportunity arises because you have identified prices out of alignment. Such opportunities could not arise if prices were at equilibrium levels. By exploiting the pricing

Table 18.4 Profits on Delta-Neutral Options Portfolio

A. Cash flow when portfolio is established			
Purchase 1,000 calls ($X = 90$) @ $3.6202 (option priced at implied volatility of 27%)	$3,620.20 cash outflow		
Write 1,589 calls ($X = 95$) @ $2.3735 (option priced at implied volatility of 33%)	3,771.50 cash inflow		
Total	$ 151.30 net cash inflow		
B. Option prices at implied volatility of 30%			
Stock Price:	**89**	**90**	**91**
90-strike-price calls	$3.478	$3.997	$4.557
95-strike-price calls	1.703	2.023	2.382
C. Value of portfolio after implied volatilities converge to 30%			
Stock Price:	**89**	**90**	**91**
Value of 1,000 calls held	$3,478	$3,997	$4,557
− Value of 1,589 calls written	2,705	3,214	3,785
Total	$ 773	$ 783	$ 772

discrepancy using a delta-neutral strategy, you should earn profits regardless of the price movement in IBM stock.

Delta-neutral hedging strategies are also subject to practical problems, the most important of which is the difficulty in assessing the proper volatility for the coming period. If the volatility estimate is incorrect, so will be the deltas, and the overall position will not truly be hedged. Moreover, option or option-plus-stock positions generally will not be neutral with respect to changes in volatility. For example, a put option hedged by a stock might be delta-neutral, but it is not volatility neutral. Changes in the market assessments of volatility will affect the option price even if the stock price is unchanged.

These problems can be serious, because volatility estimates are never fully reliable. First, volatility cannot be observed directly, and must be estimated from past data which imparts measurement error to the forecast. Second, we've seen that both historical and implied volatilities fluctuate over time. Therefore, we are always shooting at a moving target. Although delta-neutral positions are hedged against changes in the price of the underlying asset, they still are subject to **volatility risk**, the risk incurred from unpredictable changes in volatility. Thus, although delta-neutral option hedges might eliminate exposure to risk from fluctuations in the value of the underlying asset, they do not eliminate volatility risk.

18.5 BINOMIAL OPTION PRICING

Two-State Option Pricing

A complete understanding of the Black-Scholes formula is difficult without a substantial mathematics background. Nevertheless, we can develop valuable insight into option valuation by considering a particularly simple special case. Assume that a stock price can take only two possible values at option expiration: the stock will either increase to a given higher price or decrease to a given lower price. Although this may seem an extreme simplification, it allows us to come closer to understanding more complicated and seemingly more realistic models. Moreover, we can extend this approach to accept far more reasonable specifications of stock price behaviour. In fact, several major financial firms employ variants of this simple model to value options and securities with option-like features.

Suppose that the stock currently sells at S_0 = $100 and that by year-end the price will either increase by a factor of $u = 2$ to $200 or fall by a factor of $d = .5$ to $50. A call option on the stock might specify an exercise price of $125 and a time to expiration of one year. Suppose the interest rate is 8 percent. At year-end, the payoff to the holder of the call option either will be zero if the stock falls or $75 if the stock price goes to $200.

Compare this payoff to that of a portfolio consisting of one share of the stock and borrowing of $46.30 at the interest rate of 8 percent. The payoff to this portfolio also depends on the stock price at year-end:

Value of stock	$50	$200
–Repayment of loan with interest	–$50	–$ 50
Total	$ 0	$150

The payoff of this portfolio is exactly twice the option value regardless of the stock price. In other words, two call options will exactly replicate the payoff to the portfolio; two call options, therefore, should have the same price as the cost of establishing the portfolio. We know the cost of establishing the portfolio is $100 for the stock, less the $46.30 proceeds from borrowing. Hence, the two calls should sell at

$$2C = \$100 - \$46.30 = \$53.70$$

or each call should sell at C = $26.85. Thus, given the stock price, exercise price, interest rate, and volatility of the stock price (as represented by the magnitude of the up or down movements), we can derive the fair value for the call option.

This valuation approach relies heavily on the notion of replication. With only two possible end-of-year values of the stock, the returns to the leveraged stock portfolio replicate the returns to the call option and therefore command the same market price. This notion of replication is behind most option pricing formulas. For more complex price distributions for stocks, the replication technique is correspondingly more complex, but the principles remain the same.

One way to view the role of replication is to note that, using the numbers assumed for this example, a portfolio made up of one share of stock and two call options written is perfectly hedged. Its year-end value is independent of the ultimate stock price:

Stock value	$50	$200
–Obligations from two calls written	– 0	–$150
Net payoff	$50	$ 50

The investor has formed a risk-free portfolio, with a payout of $50. Its value must be the present value of $50, or $50/1.08 = $46.30. The value of the portfolio, which equals $100 from the stock held long, minus $2C$ from the two calls written, should equal $46.30. Hence, $100 – $2C$ = $46.30, or C = $26.85.

The ability to create a perfect hedge is the key to this argument. The hedge guarantees the end-of-year payout, which can be discounted using the risk-free interest rate. To find the value of the option in terms of the value of the stock, we do not need to know the option's or the stock's beta or expected rate of return. (Recall that this also was true of Black-Scholes option valuation.) The perfect hedging, or replication, approach enables us to express the value of the option in terms of the current value of the stock without this information. With a hedged position the final stock price does not affect the investor's payoff, so the stock's risk-and-return parameters have no bearing.

The hedge ratio of this example is one share of stock to two calls, or one-half. For every option written, one half-share of stock must be held in the portfolio to hedge away risk. This ratio has an easy interpretation in this context: it is the ratio of the range of the values of the option to those of the stock across the two possible outcomes. The option is worth either zero or $75, for a range of $75. The stock is worth either $50 or $200, for a range of $150. The ratio of ranges, 75/150, is one-half, which is the hedge ratio we have established.

The hedge ratio equals the ratio of ranges because the option and stock are perfectly correlated in this two-state example. When the returns of the option and stock are perfectly correlated, a perfect hedge requires that option and stock be held in a fraction determined only by relative volatility.

The generalization of the hedge ratio for the other two-state option problems is

$$H = \frac{C_u - C_d}{uS_0 - dS_0}$$

where C_u and C_d refer to the call option's value when the stock goes up or down, respectively, and uS_0 and dS_0 are the stock prices in the two states. The hedge ratio, H, is thus the ratio of the swings in the possible end-of-period values of the option and the stock. If the investor writes one option and holds H shares of stock, the value of the portfolio will be unaffected by the stock price. In this case, option pricing is easy: simply set the value of the hedged portfolio equal to the present value of the known payoff.

Using our example, the option pricing technique would proceed as follows:

1. Given the possible end-of-year stock prices, $uS_0 = 200$ and $dS_0 = 50$, and the exercise price of $125, calculate that $C_u = 75$ and $C_d = 0$. The stock price range is thus $150, while the option price range is $75.
2. Find that the hedge ratio is 75/150 = .5.
3. Find that a portfolio made up of .5 shares with one written option would have an end-of-year value of $25 with certainty.
4. Show that the present value of $25 with a one-year interest rate of 8 percent is $23.15.
5. Set the value of the hedged position to the present value of the certain payoff:

$$.5S_0 - C_0 = 23.15$$
$$\$50 - C_0 = \$23.15$$

6. Solve for the call's value, $C_0 = \$26.85$.

What if the option were overpriced, perhaps selling for $30? Then you can make arbitrage profits. Here is how:

	Initial Cash Flow	Cash Flow in 1 Year for Each Possible Stock Price: S = 50	S = 200
1. Write two options	60	0	−150
2. Purchase one share	−100	50	200
3. Borrow $40 at 8% interest, and repay in 1 year	40	−43.20	− 43.20
Total	0	6.80	6.80

Although the net initial investment is zero, the payoff in one year is positive and riskless. If the option were underpriced, one would simply reverse this arbitrage strategy: buy the option, and short-sell the stock to eliminate price risk. Note, by the way, that the present value of the profit to the arbitrage strategy above exactly equals twice the amount by which the option is overpriced. The present value of the risk-free profit of $6.80 at an 8 percent interest rate is $6.30. With two options written in this strategy, this translates to a profit of $3.15 per option, exactly the amount by which the option was overpriced: $30 versus the "fair value" of $26.85.

CONCEPT CHECK

7. Suppose the call option in the above example had been underpriced, selling at $24. Formulate the arbitrage strategy to exploit the mispricing, and show that it provides a riskless cash flow in one year of $3.08 per option purchased.

Generalizing the Two-State Approach

Although the two-state stock price model seems simplistic, we can generalize it to incorporate more realistic assumptions. To start, suppose that we were to break up the year into two six-month segments, and then assert that over each half-year segment the stock price could take on two values. In this case we will say it can increase 10 percent or decrease 5 percent (i.e., $u = 1.10$ and $d = .95$. A stock initially selling at 100 could follow these possible paths over the course of the year:

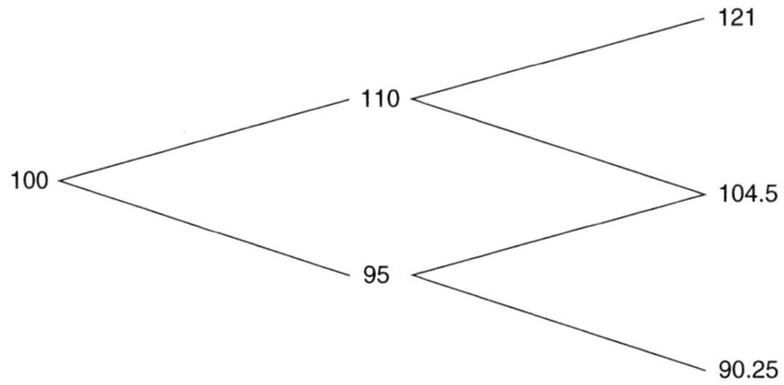

The midrange value of 104.5 can be attained by two paths: an increase of 10 percent followed by a decrease of 5 percent, or a decrease of 5 percent followed by a 10 percent increase.

There are now three possible end-of-year values for the stock and three for the option.

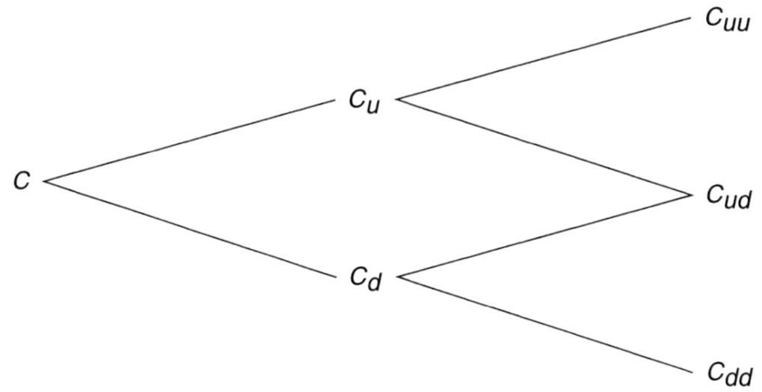

Using methods similar to those we followed above, we could value C_u from knowledge of C_{uu} and C_{ud} then value C_d from knowledge of C_{du} and C_{dd} and finally value C from knowledge of C_u

and C_d. There is no reason to stop at six-month intervals. We could next break up the year into 4 three-month units, or 12 one-month units, or 365 one-day units, each of which would be posited to have a two-state process. Although the calculations become quite numerous and correspondingly tedious, they are easy to program into a computer, and such computer programs are used widely by participants in the options market.

EXAMPLE 18.5 Binomial Option Pricing

Suppose that the risk-free interest rate is 5 percent per six-month period and we wish to value a call option with exercise price \$110 on the stock described in the two-period price tree just above. We start by finding the value of C_u. From this point, the call can rise to an expiration-date value of C_{uu} = \$11 (since at this point the stock price is $u \times u \times S_0$ = \$121) or fall to a final value of $C_{ud} = 0$ (since at this point, the stock price is $u \times d \times S_0$ = \$104.50, which is less than the \$110 exercise price). Therefore the hedge ratio at this point is

$$H = \frac{C_{uu} - C_{ud}}{uuS_0 - udS_0} = \frac{\$11 - \$0}{\$121 - \$104.50} = \frac{2}{3}$$

Thus, the following portfolio will be worth \$209 at option expiration regardless of the ultimate stock price:

	udS_0 = \$104.50	uuS_0 = \$121
Buy 2 shares at price uS_0 = \$110	\$209	\$242
Write 3 calls at price C_u	0	−33
Total	\$209	\$209

The portfolio must have a current market value equal to the present value of \$209:

$$2 \times 110 - 3C_u = \$209/1.05 = \$199.047$$

Solve to find that C_u = \$6.984.

Next we find the value of C_d. It is easy to see that this value must be zero. If we reach this point (corresponding to a stock price of \$95), the stock price at option maturity will be either \$104.50 or \$90.25; in either case, the option will expire out of the money. (More formally, we could note that with $C_{ud} = C_{dd} = 0$, the hedge ratio is zero, and a portfolio of *zero* shares will replicate the payoff of the call!)

Finally, we solve for C using the values of C_u and C_d. Concept Check 8 leads you through the calculations that show the option value to be \$4.434.

CONCEPT CHECK

8. Show that the initial value of the call option in Example 18.5 is \$4.434.
   a. Confirm that the spread in option values is $C_u - C_d$ = \$6.984.
   b. Confirm that the spread in stock values is $uS_0 - dS_0$ = \$15.
   c. Confirm that the hedge ratio is .4656 shares purchased for each call written.
   d. Demonstrate that the value in one period of a portfolio comprising .4656 shares and one call written is riskless.
   e. Calculate the present value of this payoff.
   f. Solve for the option value.

As we break the year into progressively finer subintervals, the range of possible year-end stock prices expands and, in fact, will ultimately take on a lognormal distribution.[10] This can be seen from an analysis of the event tree for the stock for a period with three subintervals:

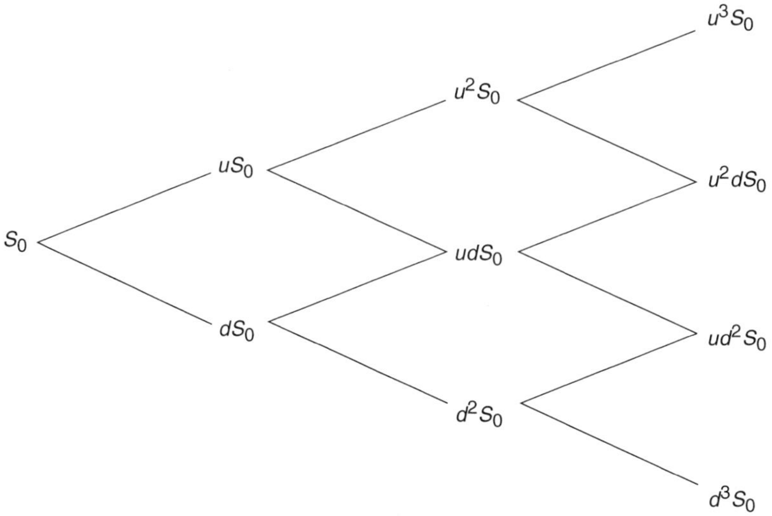

First, notice that as the number of subintervals increases, the number of possible stock prices also increases. Second, notice that extreme events such as u^3S_0 or d^3S_0 are relatively rare, since they require either three consecutive increases or decreases in the three subintervals. More moderate, or midrange, results such as u^2dS_0 can be arrived at by more than one path—any combination of two price increases and one decrease will result in stock price u^2dS_0. Thus the midrange values will be more likely, and the stock price distribution will acquire the familiar bell-shaped pattern discussed in Chapter 5. The probability of each outcome is described by the binomial distribution, and this multiperiod approach to option pricing is therefore called the **binomial model**.

For example, using our initial stock price of \$100, equal probability of stock price increases or decreases, and three intervals for which the possible price increase is 5 percent and the possible price decrease is 3 percent, we would obtain the probability distribution of stock prices from the following calculations. There are eight possible combinations for the stock price movements in the three periods: *uuu*, *uud*, *udu*, *duu*, *udd*, *dud*, *ddu*, *ddd*. Each has probability of $\frac{1}{8}$. Therefore the probability distribution of stock prices at the end of the last interval would be as follows:

Event	Probability	Stock Price
3 up movements	$\frac{1}{8}$	$100 \times 1.05^3 = 115.76$
2 up and 1 down	$\frac{3}{8}$	$100 \times 1.05^2 \times .97 = 106.94$
1 up and 2 down	$\frac{3}{8}$	$100 \times 1.05 \times .97^2 = 98.79$
3 down movements	$\frac{1}{8}$	$100 \times .97^3 = 91.27$

The midrange values are three times as likely to occur as the extreme values. Figure 18.11, panel A is a graph of the frequency distribution for this example. The graph approaches the familiar

[10]Actually, more complex considerations enter here. The limit of this process is lognormal only if we assume also that stock prices move continuously, by which we mean that over small time intervals only small price movements can occur. This rules out rare events such as sudden, extreme price moves in response to dramatic information (like a takeover attempt). For a treatment of this type of "jump process," see John C. Cox and Stephen A. Ross, "The Valuation of Options for Alternative Stochastic Processes," *Journal of Financial Economics* 3 (January–March 1976); or Robert C. Merton, "Option Pricing When Underlying Stock Returns Are Discontinuous," *Journal of Financial Economics* 3 (January–March 1976).

Figure 18.11 Probability distributions. Panel A: Possible outcomes and associated probabilities for stock prices after three periods. The stock price starts at $100, and in each period it can increase by 5% or decrease by 3%. Panel B: Each period is subdivided into two smaller subperiods. Now there are six periods, and in each of these the stock price can increase by 2.5% or fall by 1.5%. Notice that as the number of periods increases the stock price distribution approaches the familiar bell-shaped curve.

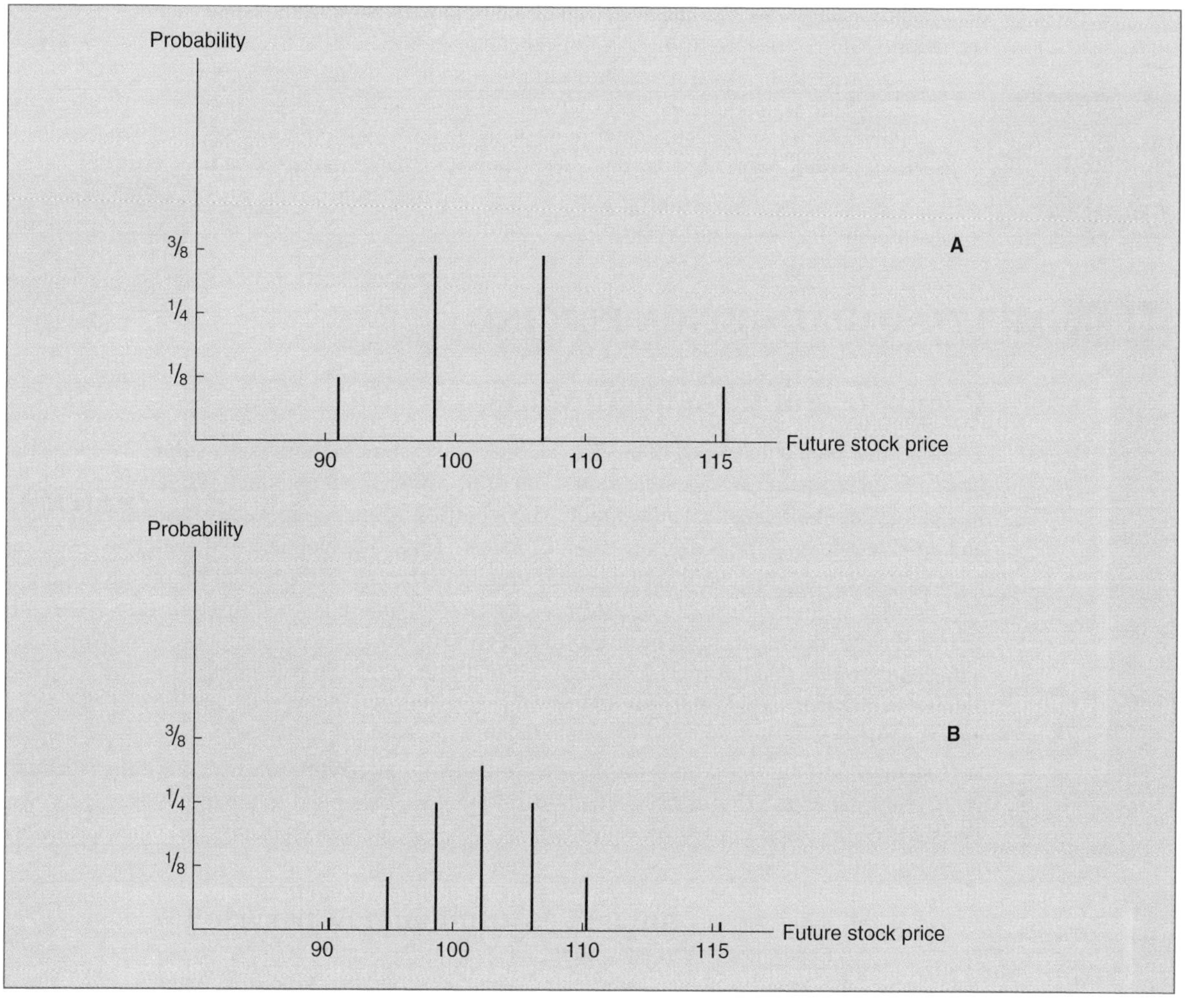

appearance of the bell-shaped curve. In fact, as the number of intervals increases, as in panel B, the frequency distribution progressively approaches the lognormal distribution rather than the normal distribution. (Recall our discussion in the appendix to Chapter 5 on why the lognormal distribution is superior to the normal as a means of modelling stock prices.)

Suppose that we were to continue subdividing the interval in which stock prices are posited to move up or down. Eventually, each node of the event tree would correspond to an infinitesimally small time interval. The possible stock price movement within that time interval would be correspondingly small. As those many intervals pass, the end-of-period stock price would more and more closely resemble a lognormal distribution. Thus the apparent oversimplification of the two-state model can be overcome by progressively subdividing any period into many subperiods.

At any node, one still could set up a portfolio that would be perfectly hedged over the next tiny time interval. Then, at the end of that interval, upon reaching the next node, a new hedge ratio could be computed and the portfolio composition could be revised to remain hedged over the coming small interval. By continuously revising the hedge position, the portfolio would remain hedged and would earn a risk-free rate of return over each interval. This is dynamic hedging, which calls for continued updating of the hedge ratio as time passes. In fact, Black and Scholes used a dynamic hedge approach to derive their option valuation formula. It can be shown that, under certain assumptions, the limiting form of the binomial model is the Black-Scholes expression (equation 18.1).

CONCEPT CHECK

9. Would you expect the hedge ratio to be higher or lower when the call option is more in the money? (*Hint:* Remember that the hedge ratio is the change in the option price divided by the change in the stock price. When is the option price most sensitive to the stock price?)

18.6 MULTINOMIAL OPTION PRICING

Complete and Incomplete Markets

The binomial model described in the previous section assumes that in every subinterval the stock price can take exactly two possible values, up or down by given amounts. We saw that in such a model it is possible to replicate the option with a portfolio containing exactly two assets, the stock and a riskless loan at the prevailing rate of interest. This correspondence of available assets and possible stock values in every subinterval is crucial to the use of the model for option pricing.

Consider again the example of the previous section, where a stock that sells at $100 can by year-end either double to $200 or be cut in half to $50. Now, however, suppose that there is also a third possibility, that the stock keeps the original price of $100. If the interest rate is 8 percent, can we still use the replication method to value the option with exercise price of $125 and one year time to expiration?

The answer to this question is no. At year-end, the option payoff is either zero if the stock falls or stays the same or $75 if it rises. The portfolio that we examined in the previous section, with one share of the stock and borrowing of $46.30 at 8 percent, now yields the following contingent payoffs:

Value of stock	$50	$100	$200
Repayment of loan with interest	–50	–50	–50
Total	$ 0	$ 50	$150

The holder of this portfolio would get twice the option value when the stock goes up or down, *plus* $50 whenever the stock stays the same. Hence, the value of the portfolio can no longer be equal to twice that of the option, since it is clearly greater.

In fact, it can be shown that there is no portfolio involving only the stock and borrowed funds capable of replicating this option. Suppose that a replicating portfolio contains x shares and $\$y$ of borrowed funds. Its future value must be equal to that of the option for all possible values of the stock. This means that

$$50x - 1.08y = 0,\ 100x - 1.08y = 0,\ 200x - 1.08y = 75$$

This system has no solution, since it has three equations and only two unknowns. This implies that there is no portfolio capable of replicating the option. The reason for this is that there are more possible future values of the stock than there are assets to form a replicating portfolio.

In the binomial model, there are only two future "states of the world" as far as the stock price is concerned. In our example, the stock can only go down to \$50 (state 1), or up to \$200 (state 2). Suppose also that we have two assets, also numbered 1 and 2, each one of them yielding a payoff equal to \$1 if the corresponding state occurs, and 0 otherwise; their respective values are v_1 and v_2. These assets are known as *elementary* or *primitive* securities, and they are a very convenient analytical tool in valuing options or other derivative assets.

With these elementary assets we now can replicate every other asset in our binomial model. Thus, the stock is equivalent to a portfolio of 50 units of asset 1 and 200 units of asset 2, and any riskless investment corresponds to portfolios having equal numbers of units of assets 1 and 2. This helps us determine the two elementary assets' values, v_1 and v_2:

$$\begin{aligned} 50v_1 + 200v_2 &= 100 \\ v_1 + v_2 &= 1/1.08 \end{aligned}$$

Solving this system, we find $v_1 = 0.5679$, and $v_2 = 0.358$. With these prices it is now very easy to price the option with exercise price \$125: it is simply equal to $75v_2 = 75 \times 0.358 = 26.85$, which is the value found in the previous section.

We now can see why the notion of replication can be applied to the binomial model but breaks down when there is a third "state of the world." In such a case we have three elementary assets, each one paying \$1 when the corresponding state of the world occurs, and zero otherwise. Let us number them 1, 2, and 3, corresponding to the ascending order of future stock price, and denote their corresponding values by v_1, v_2, and v_3; then one share would be equivalent to a portfolio of 50 units of asset 1, 100 units of asset 2, and 200 units of asset 3. However, we now have only *two* equations to determine the three unknown elementary asset values v_1, v_2, and v_3:

$$\begin{aligned} 50v_1 + 100v_2 + 200v_3 &= 100 \\ v_1 + v_2 + v_3 &= 1/1.08 \end{aligned} \tag{18.3}$$

Here, the observable stock price and rate of interest are insufficient to give us unique values of the three elementary assets. There are more states of the world (and, hence, elementary assets) than there are observable assets. This indeterminacy is the mirror image of the impossibility to find a portfolio replicating a given option.

A market that has as many independent observable assets as there are future states of the world is said to be *complete.* By contrast, **incomplete markets** are those that have fewer such assets than there are states of the world; real-world markets generally are assumed to be incomplete.[11] The binomial model is the only complete market model if our states of the world are classified by a stock's future payoffs and if we observe only the optioned stock and the riskless rate of interest.

Generalizing the Binomial Option Pricing Model

A unique set of elementary asset values consistent with the observed stock price and rate of interest does not exist in incomplete markets. Consequently, a unique option price cannot be derived by the replication method. For instance, there are infinitely many values of v_3, the elementary asset that pays \$1 when the stock goes up and zero otherwise, that satisfy the two equations of equation 18.3 corresponding to the stock price and rate of interest. Each one of these v_3 values would yield a different value of the option with exercise price equal to \$125, since the option's payoff is zero in all other states of the world.

---

[11]See the remarks in W. Sharpe, *Investments*, 2nd ed. (Englewood Cliffs, NJ: Prentice Hall, 1988), pp. 99–101.

This indeterminacy is rather disturbing, given that a stock price model with three (or more) states is otherwise very similar to the two-state model. In both types of models we can subdivide the year into progressively finer subintervals, approaching at the limit *the same* lognormal distribution. For such a distribution, the appropriate option value is given by the Black-Scholes formula. Do all admissible option values, derived from the values of v_3 satisfying the two equations in equation 18.3 similarly approach the Black-Scholes option price at the limit?

The answer is again no. While there are infinitely many option values consistent with the observed stock price and rate of interest, only a given subset of them, contained between an upper and a lower bound, converge at the limit to the Black-Scholes option value. This set of option values constitutes, therefore, the appropriate generalization of the binomial model when the number of possible future stock prices exceeds two.

The two bounds that define the appropriate option values depend not only on the size of the future stock prices, but also on their probabilities. Suppose, for instance, that in our previous example the stock price either could double or be cut in half, each with probability equal to $\frac{1}{4}$, and could stay the same with probability equal to $\frac{1}{2}$. The expected value of the stock price would be equal to

$$.25 \times 50 + .5 \times 100 + .25 \times 200 = 112.5$$

This corresponds to a return of 12.5 percent, which is higher than the rate on interest of 8 percent. For stock price distributions with expected returns higher than the rate of interest, it can be shown that upper and lower bounds on the admissible option values are equal to the expected present values of the call payoff with the expectations taken over transformed[12] stock price distributions. In this example, the transformed probabilities for the upper bound are .304, .464, and .232 for stock prices of 50, 100, and 200, respectively; they give an upper bound equal to $75 \times .232/1.08 = \$16.11$. The corresponding transformed probabilities for the lower bound are .263, .526, and .211, yielding a lower bound equal to $75 \times .211/1.08 = \$14.65$.

Thus, option prices with an exercise price of \$125 must lie between \$15.86 and \$16.11 in this three-state option pricing model. As we subdivide the time period into increasingly finer partitions, the distance between the two bounds tends to decrease. At the limit, both bounds become equal to the Black-Scholes option value.

18.7 EMPIRICAL EVIDENCE

There have been an enormous number of empirical tests of the option pricing model. For the most part, the results of the studies have been positive in that the Black-Scholes model generates option values fairly close to the actual prices at which options trade. At the same time, some regular empirical failures of the model have been noted.

Whaley[13] examines the performance of the Black-Scholes formula relative to that of more complicated option formulas that allow for early exercise. His findings also indicate that formulas

---

[12]Let p_1, p_2, and p_3 denote the three probabilities corresponding to the down, stay-the-same, and up states, respectively. Then for the upper bound the probabilities are transformed into $p_1 = Q + (1 - Q)p_1$, $p_2 = (1 - Q)p_2$, $p_3 = (1 - Q)p_3$, where Q is equal to $(112.5 - 108)/(112.5 - 50)$ in our example, the ratio of the difference between the expected future stock price and the rate of interest, to the difference between the expected stock price and the lowest possible stock value. The transformation for the lower bound is slightly more complicated. See S. Perrakis, "Preference-Free Option Prices When the Stock Return Can Go Up, Go Down, or Stay the Same," *Advances in Futures and Options Research,* 1988.

[13]Robert E. Whaley, "Valuation of American Call Options on Dividend-Paying Stocks: Empirical Tests," *Journal of Financial Economics* 10 (1982).

allowing for the possibility of early exercise do better at pricing than does the Black-Scholes formula. The Black-Scholes formula seems to perform worst for options on stocks with high dividend payouts. The true American call option formula, on the other hand, seems to fare equally well in the prediction of option prices on stocks with high or low dividend payouts.

Rubinstein[14] has pointed out that the performance of the Black-Scholes model has deteriorated in recent years in the sense that options on the same stock with the same strike price which *should* have the same implied volatility actually exhibit progressively different implied volatilities. He attributes this to an increasing fear of another market crash like that experienced in 1987, and notes that, consistent with this hypothesis, out-of-the-money put options are priced higher (i.e., with higher implied volatilities) than other puts. The market prices these options as though there is a bigger chance of a large drop in the stock price than would be suggested by the Black-Scholes assumptions.

Figure 18.12, which considers implied volatility of options on the S&P 500, is typical of recent empirical studies. The implied volatility as a function of exercise price would be flat if the Black-Scholes model were perfect. All S&P options with identical expiration dates would have identical implied volatilities since they are all written on the same index for the same horizon. Instead, the figure shows that the implied volatility curve declines as a function of exercise price. Clearly the Black-Scholes model is missing something, and that seems to be related to the probability of a big negative jump in stock prices.

A different type of empirical test on option pricing examines whether the observed call option prices satisfy the general restrictions stated in the first section of this chapter. These restrictions are independent of any particular option pricing model. The major difficulty in carrying out the tests is the simultaneous observation of corresponding stock and option prices. A Canadian study by Halpern and Turnbull[15] examined whether traded stock and call option prices on the TSX, together with the prevailing rates of interest, did satisfy the appropriate conditions in 1978–1979. They found several violations of these restrictions, which should have allowed traders to realize riskless profits. There are, however, indications that these violations were due to the comparative novelty of option trading on the TSX and did not persist in more recent years.

Figure 18.12 Black-Scholes implied volatilities for options with 30, 45, and 60 days to maturity on May 16, 1996.

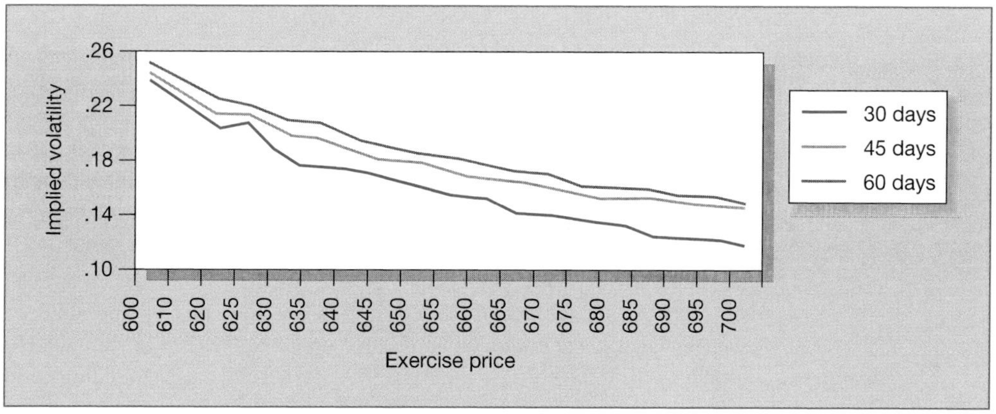

Source: Shiheng Wang, "An Empirical Study on the Implied Volatility Function of S&P 500 Options," dissertation, Queen's University, Ontario, August 2002.

[14]Mark Rubinstein, "Implied Binomial Trees," *Journal of Finance* 49 (July 1994), pp. 771–818.

[15]Paul Halpern and Stuart Turnbull, "Empirical Tests of Boundary Conditions for Toronto Stock Exchange Options," *Journal of Finance* 40, no. 2 (June 1985).

SUMMARY

1. Option values may be viewed as the sum of intrinsic value plus time or "volatility" value. The volatility value is the right to choose not to exercise if the stock price moves against the holder. Thus, option holders cannot lose more than the cost of the option regardless of stock price performance.
2. Call options are more valuable when the exercise price is lower, when the stock price is higher, when the interest rate is higher, when the time to maturity is greater, when the stock's volatility is greater, and when dividends are lower.
3. Call options must sell for at least the stock price less the present value of the exercise price and dividends to be paid before maturity. This implies that a call option on a non-dividend-paying stock may be sold for more than the proceeds from immediate exercise. Thus, European calls are worth as much as American calls on stocks that pay no dividends because the right to exercise the American call early has no value.
4. The Black-Scholes formula is valid for options on stocks that pay no dividends. Dividend adjustments may be adequate to price European calls on dividend-paying stocks, but the proper treatment of American calls on dividend-paying stocks requires more complex formulas.
5. Put options may be exercised early whether the stock pays dividends or not. Therefore, American puts generally are worth more than European puts.
6. European put values can be derived from the call value and the put-call parity relationship. This technique cannot be applied to American puts for which early exercise is a possibility.
7. The hedge ratio refers to the number of shares of stock required to hedge the price risk involved in writing one option. Hedge ratios are near zero for deep out-of-the-money call options, and approach 1 for deep in-the-money calls.
8. Although hedge ratios are less than 1, call options have elasticities greater than 1. The rate of return on a call (as opposed to the dollar return) responds more than one-for-one with stock price movements.
9. Portfolio insurance can be obtained by purchasing a protective put option on an equity position. When the appropriate put is not traded, portfolio insurance entails a dynamic hedge strategy in which a fraction of the equity portfolio equal to the desired put option's delta is sold and placed in risk-free securities.
10. The option delta is used to determine the hedge ratio options positions. Delta-neutral portfolios are independent of price changes in the underlying asset. Even delta-neutral option portfolios are subject to volatility risk, however.
11. Options may be priced relative to the underlying stock price using a simple two-period, two-state pricing model. As the number of periods increases, we may approximate more realistic stock price distributions. The Black-Scholes formula may be seen as a limiting case of the binomial option model as the holding period is divided into progressively smaller subperiods.
12. The simple two-state pricing model is the only model where an exact option price can be derived from the stock and the rate of interest. If there are more than two possible stock prices, then only an upper and a lower bound on admissible option values can be defined. However, both bounds become, at the limit, equal to the Black-Scholes formula, as the holding period is subdivided into progressively finer subintervals.

KEY TERMS

intrinsic value 684
Black-Scholes pricing formula 690
implied volatility 694
pseudo-American call option value 696
hedge ratio 697
delta 697
option elasticity 698
portfolio insurance 699
dynamic hedging 701
delta-neutral 706
volatility risk 707
binomial model 712
incomplete markets 715

SELECTED READINGS

The breakthrough articles in option pricing are:

Black, Fischer, and Myron Scholes. "The Pricing of Options and Corporate Liabilities." *Journal of Political Economy* 81 (May/June 1973).

Merton, Robert C. "Theory of Rational Option Pricing." *Bell Journal of Economics and Management Science* 4 (Spring 1973).

Articles on portfolio insurance and replication strategies may be found in:

McCallum, John S. "On Portfolio Insurance, the Stock Market Crash, and Avoiding a Repeat." *Business Quarterly* 53, no. 2 (Fall 1989).

The January/February 1988 edition of *Financial Analysts Journal* is devoted to issues surrounding portfolio insurance.

Several applications of option-type analysis to various financial instruments are surveyed in:

Hull, John, and Alan White. "An Overview of Contingent Claims Pricing." *Canadian Journal of Administrative Sciences* 5, no. 3 (September 1988).

Other relevant references are:

Bigger, Nahum, and John Hull. "The Valuation of Currency Options." *Financial Management* 12 (1993).

Boyle, Phelim, and Eric P. Kirzner. "Pricing Complex Options: Echo-Bay Ltd. Gold Purchase Warrants." *Canadian Journal of Administrative Sciences* 2, no. 4 (December 1985).

Hull, John, and Alan White. "Hedging the Risks from Writing Foreign Currency Options." *Journal of International Money and Finance,* June 1987.

Reich, Alan L. "Market Efficiency of IOCC Gold Options Traded on the Montreal Exchange." *International Options Journal* 1, no. 1 (Fall 1984).

The two-state approach was first suggested in:

Sharpe, William F. *Investments.* Englewood Cliffs, NJ: Prentice Hall, 1978.

The approach was developed more fully in:

Cox, John C., Stephen A. Ross, and Mark Rubinstein. "Option Pricing: A Simplified Approach." *Journal of Financial Economics* 7 (September 1979).

Rendleman, Richard J. Jr., and Brit J. Bartter. "Two-State Option Pricing." *Journal of Finance* 34 (December 1979).

The extension of the two-state option pricing was introduced in:

Perrakis, Stylianos, and Peter Ryan. "Option Pricing Bounds in Discrete Time." *Journal of Finance* 39 (June 1984).

Ritchken, Peter. "On Option Pricing Bounds." *Journal of Finance* 40 (September 1985).

The approach was developed more fully in:

Perrakis, Stylianos. "Option Pricing Bounds in Discrete Time: Extensions and the Pricing of the American Put." *Journal of Business* 59 (February 1986).

Perrakis, Stylianos. "Preference-Free Option Pricing When the Stock Returns Can Go Up, Go Down, or Stay the Same." *Advances in Futures and Options Research* 3 (1988).

Ritchken, Peter, and S. Kuo. "Option Bounds with Finite Revision Opportunities." *Journal of Finance* 43 (June 1988).

Empirical work in Canadian option markets is contained in:

Halpern, Paul, and Stuart Turnbull. "Empirical Tests on Boundary Conditions for Toronto Stock Exchange Options." *Journal of Finance* 40, no. 3 (June 1985).

Mandron, Alix. "Some Empirical Evidence About Canadian Stock Options, Part I: Valuation; and Part II: Market Structure." *Canadian Journal of Administrative Sciences* 5, no. 2 (June 1988).

Gendron, Michel, Nabil Khoury, and Pierre Yourougou. "Probability of Price Reversal and Relative Noise in Stock and Option Markets." *The Journal of Financial Research* 17, no. 2 (Summer 1994).

Ramsey, John. "When Is Delta Hedging Rational?"; and Masse, C., J. Kushner, J. Hanrahun, and R. L. Welch. "The Effect of Option Introduction on the Risk and Return of Canadian Equity Securities for 1975–91." Both articles can be found in *Proceedings of the Annual Conference of the Administrative Sciences Association of Canada, Finance Division* 15, no. 1 (1994).

Gagnon, Louis, and Greg Lypny. "The Benefits of Dynamically Hedging the Toronto 35 Stock Index." *Canadian Journal of Administrative Sciences* 14, no. 1 (March 1997).

Wei, Jason, and Craig Doidge, "Volatility Forecasting and the Efficiency of the Toronto 35 Index Option Market," *Canadian Journal of Administrative Sciences* 15, no. 1 (March 1998).

The March 1994 issue of the Canadian Journal of Administrative Sciences *was devoted to Canadian financial markets and institutions. The following articles in that issue contain empirical work on various aspects of Canadian options markets:*

Gagnon, Louis. "Empirical Investigation of the Canadian Government Bond Options Market."
Wei, Jason Z. "Market Efficiency: Experience with Nikkei Put Warrants."
Perrakis, Stylianos, and Peter J. Ryan. "Options on Thinly-Traded Stocks: Theory and Empirical Evidence."

PROBLEMS

1. We showed in the text that the value of a call option increases with the volatility of the stock. Is this also true of put option values? Use the put-call parity theorem as well as a numerical example to prove your answer.
2. In each of the following questions, you are asked to compare two options with parameters as given. The risk-free interest rate for *all* cases should be assumed to be 6 percent. Assume the stocks on which these options are written pay no dividends.

a.

Put	T	X	σ	Price of Option
A	.5	50	.20	$10
B	.5	50	.25	$10

Which put option is written on the stock with the lower price?
i. A
ii. B
iii. Not enough information

b.

Put	T	X	σ	Price of Option
A	.5	50	.2	$10
B	.5	50	.2	$12

Which put option must be written on the stock with the lower price?
i. A
ii. B
iii. Not enough information

c.

Call	S	X	σ	Price of Option
A	50	50	.20	$12
B	55	50	.20	$10

Which call option must have the lower time to maturity?
i. A
ii. B
iii. Not enough information

d.

Call	T	X	S	Price of Option
A	.5	50	55	$10
B	.5	50	55	$12

Which call option is written on the stock with higher volatility?
i. A
ii. B
iii. Not enough information

e.

Call	T	X	S	Price of Option
A	.5	50	55	\$10
B	.5	55	55	\$ 7

Which call option is written on the stock with higher volatility?

i. A

ii. B

iii. Not enough information

3. Reconsider the determination of the hedge ratio in the two-state model (in Section 18.5), where we showed that one-half share of stock would hedge one option. What is the hedge ratio at the following exercise prices: 115, 100, 75, 50, 25, 10? What do you conclude about the hedge ratio as the option becomes progressively more in the money?

4. Show that Black-Scholes call option hedge ratios also increase as the stock price increases. Consider a one-year option with exercise price \$50 on a stock with annual standard deviation of 20 percent. The T-bill rate is 8 percent per year. Find $N(d_1)$ for stock prices \$45, \$50, and \$55.

5. We will derive a two-state put option value in this problem. Data: $S_0 = 100$; $X = 110$; and $1 + r = 1.1$. The two possibilities for S_T are 130 and 80.

a. Show that the range of S is 50 while that of P is 30 across the two states. What is the hedge ratio of the put?

b. Form a portfolio of three shares of stock and five puts. What is the (nonrandom) payoff to this portfolio? What is the present value of the portfolio?

c. Given that the stock currently is selling at \$100, solve for the value of the put.

6. Calculate the value of the call option on the stock in problem 5 with an exercise price of \$110. Verify that the put-call parity theorem is satisfied by your answers to problems 5 and 6. (Do not use continuous compounding to calculate the present value of X in this example because we are using a two-state model here, not a continuous-time Black-Scholes model.)

7. Use the Black-Scholes formula to find the value of a call option on the following stock:

Time to maturity	=	6 months
Standard deviation	=	50 percent per year
Exercise price	=	50
Stock price	=	50
Interest rate	=	10 percent

8. Recalculate the value of the option in problem 7, successively substituting one of the changes below while keeping the other parameters as in problem 7:

a. Time to maturity = 3 months

b. Standard deviation = 25 percent per year

c. Exercise price = \$55

d. Stock price = \$55

e. Interest rate = 15 percent

Consider each scenario independently. Confirm that the option value changes in accordance with the prediction of Table 18.1.

9. A call option with $X = \$50$ on a stock currently priced at $S = \$55$ is selling for \$10. Using a volatility estimate of $\sigma = .30$, you find that $N(d_1) = .6$ and $N(d_2) = .5$. The risk-free interest rate is zero. Is the implied volatility based on the option price more or less than .30? Explain.

10. Would you expect a \$1 increase in a call option's exercise price to lead to a decrease in the option's value of more or less than \$1?

11. Is a put option on a high-beta stock worth more than one on a low-beta stock? The stocks have identical firm-specific risk.

12. All else being equal, is a call option on a stock with a lot of firm-specific risk worth more than one on a stock with little firm-specific risk? The betas of the two stocks are equal.

13. All else equal, will a call option with a high exercise price have a higher or lower hedge ratio than one with a low exercise price?

14. Should the rate of return of a call option on a long-term Treasury bond be more or less sensitive to changes in interest rates than the rate of return of the underlying bond?

15. If the stock price falls and the call price rises, then what has happened to the call option's implied volatility?

16. If the time to maturity falls and the put price rises, then what has happened to the put option's implied volatility?

17. According to the Black-Scholes formula, what will be the value of the hedge ratio of a call option as the stock price becomes infinitely large? Explain briefly.

18. According to the Black-Scholes formula, what will be the value of the hedge ratio of a put option for a very small exercise price?

19. The hedge ratio of an at-the-money call option on IBM is .4. The hedge ratio of an at-the-money put option is –.6. What is the hedge ratio of an at-the-money straddle position on IBM?

20. A collar is established by buying a share of stock for $50, buying a six-month put option with exercise price $45, and writing a six-month call option with exercise price $55. Based on the volatility of the stock, you calculate that for a strike price of $45 and maturity of six months, $N(d_1) = .60$, while for the exercise price of $55, $N(d_1) = .35$.

a. What will be the gain or loss on the collar if the stock price increases by $1?

b. What happens to the delta of the portfolio if the stock price becomes very large? Very small?

21. These three put options all are written on the same stock. One has a delta of –.9, one a delta of –.5, and one a delta of –.1. Assign deltas to the three puts by filling in this table.

Put	X	Delta
A	10	
B	20	
C	30	

22. You are *very* bullish (optimistic) on stock EFG, much more so than the rest of the market. In each question, choose the portfolio strategy that will give you the biggest dollar profit if your bullish forecast turns out to be correct. Explain your answer.

a. Choice A. $10,000 invested in calls with $X = 50$
Choice B. $10,000 invested in EFG stock

b. Choice A. 10 call options contracts (for 100 shares each), with $X = 50$
Choice B. 1,000 shares of EFG stock

23. Imagine you are a provider of portfolio insurance. You are establishing a four-year program. The portfolio you manage is currently worth $100 million, and you hope to provide a minimum return of 0 percent. The equity portfolio has a standard deviation of 25 percent per year, and T-bills pay 5 percent per year. Assume for simplicity that the portfolio pays no dividends (or that all dividends are reinvested).

a. What fraction of the portfolio should be placed in bills? What fraction in equity?

b. What should the manager do if the stock portfolio falls by 3 percent on the first day of trading?

CFA® PROBLEMS

24. Joel Franklin is a portfolio manager responsible for derivatives. Franklin observes an American-style option and a European-style option with the same strike price, expiration, and underlying stock. Franklin believes that the European-style option will have a higher premium than the American-style option.

a. Critique Franklin's belief that the European-style option will have a higher premium.

Franklin is asked to value a 1-year European-style call option for Abaco Ltd. common stock, which last traded at \$43. He has collected the information in the following table.

Closing stock price	\$43.00
Call and put option exercise price	45.00
1-year put option price	4.00
1-year Treasury bill rate	5.50%
Time to expiration	One year

b. Calculate, using put-call parity and the information provided in the table, the European-style call option value.

c. State the effect, if any, of each of the following three variables on the value of a call option. (No calculations required.)

i. An increase in short-term interest rate

ii. An increase in stock price volatility

iii. A decrease in time to option expiration

25. You would like to be holding a protective put position on the stock of XYZ Co. to lock in a guaranteed minimum value of \$100 at year-end. XYZ currently sells for \$100. Over the next year, the stock price will increase by 10 percent or decrease by 10 percent. The T-bill rate is 5 percent. Unfortunately, no put options are traded on XYZ Co.

a. Suppose the desired put option were traded. How much would it cost to purchase?

b. What would have been the cost of the protective put portfolio?

c. What portfolio position in stock and T-bills will ensure you a payoff equal to the payoff that would be provided by a protective put with $X = 100$? Show that the payoff to this portfolio and the cost of establishing the portfolio matches that of the desired protective put.

CFA® PROBLEMS

26. A stock index is currently trading at 50. Paul Tripp, CFA wants to value two-year index options using the binomial model. The stock will either increase in value by 20 percent or fall in value by 20 percent. The annual risk-free interest rate is 6 percent. No dividends are paid on any of the underlying securities in the index.

a. Construct a two-period binomial tree for the value of the stock index.

b. Calculate the value of a European call option on the index with an exercise price of 60.

c. Calculate the value of a European put option on the index with an exercise price of 60.

d. Confirm that your solutions for the values of the call and the put satisfy put-call parity.

27. Suppose that the risk-free interest rate is zero. Would an American put option ever be exercised early? Explain.

28. Let $p(S,T,X)$ denote the value of a European put on a stock selling at S dollars, with time to maturity T, and with exercise price X, and let $P(S,T,X)$ be the value of an American put.

a. Evaluate $p(0,T,X)$.

b. Evaluate $P(0,T,X)$.

c. Evaluate $p(S,T,0)$.

d. Evaluate $P(S,T,0)$.

e. What does your answer to (*b*) tell you about the possibility that American puts may be exercised early?

29. You are considering the sale of a call option with an exercise price of \$100 and one year to expiration. The underlying stock pays no dividends, its current price is \$100, and you believe it has a 50 percent chance of increasing to \$120 and a 50 percent chance of decreasing to \$80. The risk-free rate of interest is 10 percent. Calculate the call option's value using the two-state stock price model.

30. Consider an increase in the volatility of the stock in problem 29. Suppose that if the stock increases in price, it will increase to \$130, and that if it falls, it will fall to \$70. Show that the value of the call option is now higher than the value derived in problem 29.

31. Calculate the value of a put option with exercise price \$100 using the data in problem 29. Show that put-call parity is satisfied by your solution.

32. XYZ Corp. will pay a \$2 per share dividend in two months. Its stock price currently is \$60 per share. A call option on XYZ has an exercise price of \$55 and three-month time to maturity. The risk-free interest rate is .5 percent per month, and the stock's volatility (standard deviation) = 7 percent per month. Find the pseudo-American option value. (*Hint:* Try defining one "period" as a month, rather than as a year.)

33. "The beta of a call option on General Motors is greater than the beta of a share of General Motors." True or false?

34. "The beta of a call option on the S&P 500 index with an exercise price of 1030 is greater than the beta of a call on the index with an exercise price of 1040." True or false?

35. What will happen to the hedge ratio of a convertible bond as the stock price becomes very large?

CFA® PROBLEMS

36. Ken Webster manages a \$100 million equity portfolio benchmarked to the S&P 500 index. Over the past two years, the S&P 500 Index has appreciated 60 percent. Webster believes the market is overvalued when measured by several traditional fundamental/economic indicators. He is concerned about maintaining the excellent gains the portfolio has experienced in the past two years but recognizes that the S&P 500 Index could still move above its current 668 level.

Webster is considering the following *option collar* strategy:

- Protection for the portfolio can be attained by purchasing an S&P 500 Index put with a strike price of 665 (just out of the money).
- The put can be financed by selling two 675 calls (further out-of-the-money) for every put purchased.
- Because the combined delta of the two calls is less than 1 (i.e., $2 \times .36 = .72$) the options will not lose more than the underlying portfolio will gain if the market advances.

The information in the following table describes the two options used to create the collar.

Options to Create the Collar

Characteristics	675 Call	665 Put
Option price	\$4.30	\$8.05
Option implied volatility	11.00%	14.00%
Option's delta	0.36	−0.44
Contracts needed for collar	602	301

Notes:
- Ignore transaction costs.
- S&P 500 historical 30-day volatility = 12.00%.
- Time to option expiration = 30 days.

a. Describe the potential returns of the combined portfolio (the underlying portfolio plus the option collar) if after 30 days the S&P 500 index has:

i. Risen approximately 5 percent to 701.00

ii. Remained at 668 (no change)

iii. Declined by approximately 5 percent to 635.00

(No calculations are necessary.)

b. Discuss the effect on the hedge ratio (delta) of *each* option as the S&P 500 approaches the level for *each* of the potential outcomes listed in part (*a*).

c. Evaluate the pricing of *each* of the following in relation to the volatility data provided:

i. The put

ii. The call

37. Salomon Brothers believes that market volatility will be 20 percent annually for the next three years. Three-year at-the-money call and put options on the market index sell at an implied volatility of 22 percent. What options portfolio can Salomon Brothers establish to speculate on its volatility belief without taking a bullish or bearish position on the market? Using Salomon's estimate of volatility, three-year at-the-money options have $N(d_1) = .6$.

38. Suppose that call options on Exxon stock with time to maturity three months and strike price $60 are selling at an implied volatility of 30 percent. Exxon stock currently is $60 per share, and the risk-free rate is 4 percent. If you believe the true volatility of the stock is 32 percent, how can you trade on your belief without taking on exposure to the performance of Exxon? How many shares of stock will you hold for each option contract purchased or sold?

39. Using the data in problem 38, suppose that three-month put options with a strike price of $60 are selling at an implied volatility of 34 percent. Construct a delta-neutral portfolio comprising positions in calls and puts that will profit when the option prices come back into alignment.

40. Suppose that Salomon Brothers sells call options on $1.25 million worth of a stock portfolio with beta = 1.5. The option delta is .8. It wishes to hedge out its resultant exposure to a market advance by buying market index futures contracts.

a. If the current value of the market index is 1,000 and the contract multiplier is $250, how many contracts should it buy?

b. What if Salomon instead uses market index puts to hedge its exposure? Should it buy or sell puts? Each put option is on 100 units of the index, and the index at current prices represents $1,000 worth of stock.

41. You are holding call options on a stock. The stock's beta is .75, and you are concerned that the stock market is about to fall. The stock is currently selling for $5 and you hold 1 million options on the stock (i.e., you hold 10,000 contracts for 100 shares each). The option delta is .8. How many market index futures contracts must you buy or sell to hedge your market exposure if the current value of the market index is 1,000 and the contract multiplier is $250?

STANDARD &POOR'S

Option traders love stock volatility. (Why?) From the Market Insight entry page (**www.mcgrawhill.ca/edumarketinsight**), link to *Industry,* then pull down to the airlines industry. Review the *Industry Profile* for a measure of recent stock price volatility. Then review the S&P Industry Survey for the airlines industry. What factors associated with the industry have produced the recent stock volatility? In the Black-Scholes valuation model, how is volatility associated with option value? What options strategies exploit volatility?

E-INVESTMENTS
Black-Scholes Option Pricing

Go to options calculator available at **www.schaeffersresearch.com/streetools/options/calculator.aspx**.

Use a Canadian firm, Alcan (AL), Canadian Pacific (CP), or Nortel (NT), for the firm. Enter the ticker symbol and click on *Get Quote* for the latest price and the dividend for the firm. Make sure the company is not paying a cash dividend in the near future and enter 0.0 for the quarterly dividend. The calculator will display the current interest rate. Find the prices for call and put options in the two months following the closest expiration month. (You can request the options prices directly in the calculator.) For example, if you are in February, you would use the April and July options. Use the options that are closest to being at the money. For example, if the most recent price of AL was $43.30, you would select the 45 strike price.

Once you have entered the options prices and other data, hit the *Go Figure* button and analyze the results.

Are the calculated prices in line with observed prices? Compare the implied volatility with the historical volatility.

FUTURES AND FORWARD MARKETS

Futures and forward contracts are similar to options in that they specify the purchase or sale of some underlying security at some future date. The key difference is that the holder of an option to buy is not compelled to buy and will not do so if it is to his or her disadvantage. A futures or forward contract, on the other hand, carries the obligation to go through with the agreed-upon transaction.

A forward contract is not an investment in the strict sense that funds are paid for an asset—it is only a commitment today to transact in the future. Forward arrangements are part of our study of investments, however, because they offer a powerful means to hedge other investments and generally modify portfolio characteristics.

Forward markets for future delivery of various commodities go back in time at least to ancient Greece. Organized *futures markets*, though, are a relatively modern development, dating only to the nineteenth century. Futures markets replace informal forward contracts with highly standardized, exchange-traded securities.

This chapter describes the workings of futures markets and the mechanics of trading in these markets. We show how futures contracts are useful investment vehicles for both hedgers and speculators and how the futures price relates to the spot price of an asset.

This chapter deals with both principles of futures markets in general and specific futures markets in some detail.

19.1 THE FUTURES CONTRACT

To see how futures and forwards work and how they might be useful, consider the portfolio diversification problem facing a farmer growing a single crop, let us say wheat. The entire planting season's revenue depends critically on the highly volatile crop price. The farmer can't easily diversify his position because virtually his entire wealth is tied up in the crop.

The miller who must purchase wheat for processing faces a portfolio problem that is the mirror image of the farmer's. He is subject to profit uncertainty because of the unpredictable future cost of the wheat.

Both parties can reduce this source of risk if they enter into a **forward contract** requiring the farmer to deliver the wheat when harvested at a price agreed upon now, regardless of the market price at harvest time. No money need change hands at this time. A forward contract is simply a deferred-delivery sale of some asset with the sales price agreed on now. All that is required is that each party be willing to lock in the ultimate price to be paid or received for delivery of the commodity. A forward contract protects each party from future price fluctuations.

Futures markets formalize and standardize forward contracting. Buyers and sellers trade in a centralized futures exchange. The exchange standardizes the types of contracts that may be traded: it establishes contract size, the acceptable grade of commodity, contract delivery dates, and so forth. Although standardization eliminates much of the flexibility available in forward contracting, it has the offsetting advantage of liquidity because many traders will concentrate on the same small set of contracts. Futures contracts also differ from forward contracts in that they call for a daily settling up of any gains or losses on the contract. In the case of forward contracts, no money changes hands until the delivery date.

The centralized market, standardization of contracts, and depth of trading in each contract allows futures positions to be liquidated easily through a broker rather than personally renegotiated with the other party to the contract. Because the exchange guarantees the performance of each party to the contract, costly credit checks on other traders are not necessary. Instead, each trader simply posts a good-faith deposit, called the *margin*, in order to guarantee contract performance.

The Basics of Futures Contracts

The **futures contract** calls for delivery of a commodity at a specified delivery or maturity date, for an agreed-upon price (called the **futures price**), to be paid at contract maturity. The contract specifies precise requirements for the commodity. For agricultural commodities, allowable grades (e.g., No. 2 hard winter wheat, or No. 1 soft red wheat) are set by the exchange. The place or means of delivery of the commodity is specified as well. For agricultural commodities, delivery is made by transfer of warehouse receipts issued by approved warehouses. For financial futures, delivery may be made by wire transfer; in the case of index futures, delivery may be accomplished by a cash settlement procedure similar to those for index options. (Although the futures contract technically calls for delivery of an asset, delivery in fact rarely occurs. Instead, traders much more commonly close out their positions before contract maturity, taking gains or losses in cash.)

Because the futures exchange completely specifies the terms of the contract, the traders need bargain only over the futures prices. The trader taking the **long position** commits to purchasing the commodity on the delivery date, while the trader who takes the **short position** commits to delivering the commodity at contract maturity. The trader in the long position is said to "buy" a contract; the short-side trader "sells" a contract. The words *buy* and *sell* are figurative only, because a contract is not really bought or sold like a stock or bond, but is entered into by mutual agreement. At the time the contract is entered into, no money changes hands.

Figure 19.1 shows prices for several agricultural futures contracts on the Winnipeg Commodity Exchange as they appear in *The Globe and Mail.* The boldface lines list the commodity, the

Figure 19.1 Prices for Canadian commodity futures.

MONTREAL EXCHANGE FUTURES & OPTIONS

r = not traded; s = no option offered

Futures

3-month bankers' acceptances $1M, pts. of 100%

sea hi	sea lo	mth.	open	high	low	settle	chg.	op int
97.91	97.86	Jun04	97.89	97.89	97.88	97.89	+0.02	79171
97.69	97.54	Sep04	97.58	97.65	97.58	97.65	+0.08	98523
97.40	97.19	Dec04	97.27	97.30	97.26	97.29	+0.07	43953
97.03	96.82	Mar05	96.88	96.93	96.88	96.93	+0.08	20691
96.67	96.47	Jun05	96.56	96.56	96.54	96.57	+0.08	7073
96.29	96.12	Sep05	96.19	96.20	96.18	96.22	+0.09	3788

Est sales	Prv sales	Open Int	Chg
20253	29467	257174	+4756

2-year Cda bonds $100K, pts of 100%, 1 pt = $10

sea hi	sea lo	mth.	open	high	low	settle	chg.	op int
104.67	104.50	Jun04	104.59	104.61	104.57	104.61	+0.11	6776

Est sales	Prv sales	Open Int	Chg
1012	1075	6776	−192

10-year Cda bonds $100K, pts of 100%, 1 pt = $10

sea hi	sea lo	mth.	open	high	low	settle	chg.	op int
108.45	107.32	Jun04	107.81	108.15	107.81	108.14	+0.39	90255

Est sales	Prv sales	Open Int	Chg
3854	9215	90255	−3775

S&P/TSX 60 200 X index pts, pts of 100%, 5 pts=$10

sea hi	sea lo	mth.	open	high	low	settle	chg.	op int
457.80	447.80	Jun04	452.50	455.00	448.50	448.70	−4.10	88021

Est sales	Prv sales	Open Int	Chg
3779	5137	88236	+138

S&P/TSX Info Tech Index 500 X index pts, pts of 100%, 5 pts=$10

Est sales	Prv sales	Open Int	Chg
		0	+0

S&P/TSX Energy Index 200 X index pts, pts of 100%, 1 pt=$20

Est sales	Prv sales	Open Int	Chg
	15	30	+15

S&P/TSX Financial Index 200 X index pts, pts of 100%, 1 pt=$20

Est sales	Prv sales	Open Int	Chg
		62	+0

S&P/TSX Gold Index 200 X index pts, pts of 100%, 1 pt=$20

Est sales	Prv sales	Open Int	Chg
		2	+0

Nortel 100 shares, pts of 100%, 1 pt=$1

Est sales	Prv sales	Open Int	Chg
		0	+0

30-day Overnight repo rate $5M, pts of 100%, 1 pt=$41.10

Est sales	Prv sales	Open Int	Chg
		0	+0

Options

3-mo. bankers' acceptances futures$1M,pts of 100%

price	calls-last Jun	calls-last Sep	calls-last Dec	puts-last Jun	puts-last Sep	puts-last Dec
9550.00	s	2.15	1.795	s	r	.005
9562.00	s	2.025	1.67	s	r	.005
9575.00	s	1.90	1.55	s	r	0.01
9587.00	s	1.775	1.43	s	r	.015
9600.00	1.89	1.65	1.31	r	r	0.02
9612.00	1.765	1.525	1.19	r	r	.025
9625.00	1.64	1.40	1.07	r	r	0.03
9637.00	1.515	1.275	.955	r	r	0.04
9650.00	1.39	1.15	.845	r	r	.055
9662.00	1.265	1.025	.735	r	r	0.07
9675.00	1.14	0.90	.635	r	r	.095
9687.00	1.015	.775	.535	r	r	0.12
9700.00	0.89	.655	.445	r	.005	.155
9712.00	.765	.535	0.36	r	0.01	.195
9725.00	0.64	0.42	0.28	r	0.02	0.24
9737.00	.515	.315	.215	r	0.04	0.30
9750.00	0.39	0.22	0.16	r	0.07	0.37
9762.00	.265	0.14	0.11	r	.115	.445
9775.00	0.14	0.08	.075	r	0.18	.535
9787.00	.045	0.04	.045	0.03	.265	0.63
9800.00	.005	.015	0.03	.115	.365	0.74
9812.00	r	.005	.015	.235	0.48	0.85
9825.00	r	r	.005	0.36	0.60	.965
9837.00	r	r	.005	.485	.725	1.09
9850.00	r	r	r	0.61	0.85	1.21

Prev day call vol	0	Open Int	47000
Prev day put vol	0	Open Int	21740

WINNIPEG FUTURES

CANOLA 20 tonnes $Cdn/tonne

sea hi	sea lo	mth.	open	high	low	settle	chg.	op int
448.30	347.50	Jul04	374.00	374.00	368.50	371.70	−3.00	30567
408.00	331.20	Nov04	373.50	373.50	366.50	369.40	−5.00	36045

Est sales	Prv sales	Open Int	Chg
		68721	+36

FLAXSEED 20 tonnes $US/tonne

Est sales	Prv sales	Open Int	Chg
		0	+0

WESTERN BARLEY 20 tonnes $Cdn/tonne

sea hi	sea lo	mth.	open	high	low	settle	chg.	op int
168.50	135.50	Jul04	158.50	158.50	157.10	157.40	−1.90	6344
166.00	136.00	Oct04	157.00	157.50	157.00	157.00	−1.90	2435

Est sales	Prv sales	Open Int	Chg
		10477	−97

WHEAT 20 tonnes $Cdn/tonne

sea hi	sea lo	mth.	open	high	low	settle	chg.	op int
166.00	139.00	Jul04	163.50	163.50	162.00	163.20	−0.60	3234
170.50	136.00	Oct04	163.00	163.20	162.00	163.20		1812

Est sales	Prv sales	Open Int	Chg
		5562	−36

Source: *The Globe and Mail*, May 21, 2004. Reprinted by permission of The Globe and Mail.

www.wce.ca

contract size, and the pricing unit. Under "Winnipeg Futures," the first contract listed is for canola. Each contract calls for delivery of 20 tonnes, and prices are quoted in dollars per tonne. The next several rows detail price data for contracts expiring on various dates. The November 2004 maturity canola contract, for example, opened during the date at a futures price of $373.50 per tonne. The highest futures price during the day was $373.50, the lowest was $366.50, and the settlement price (a representative trading price during the last few minutes of trading) was $369.40. The settlement price decreased by $5 from the previous trading day. The highest futures price over the contract's life to date was $408, and the lowest was $331.20. Finally, open interest, or the number of outstanding contracts, was 36,045. Similar information is given for each maturity date for all commodities traded on the exchange.

The trader holding the long position, who will purchase the good, profits from price increases. Suppose that in November the price of canola turns out to be $375 per tonne. The long-position trader who entered into the contract at the futures price of $369.40 on May 20 would pay the agreed-upon $369.40 per tonne to receive canola that, at contract maturity, is worth $375 per tonne in the market. Since each contract calls for delivery of 20 tonnes, ignoring brokerage fees, the profit to the long position equals 20($375 – $369.40) = $112. Conversely, the short position must deliver 20 tonnes of canola, each with value $375, for the previously agreed-upon futures price of only $369.40. The short position's loss equals the long position's gain.

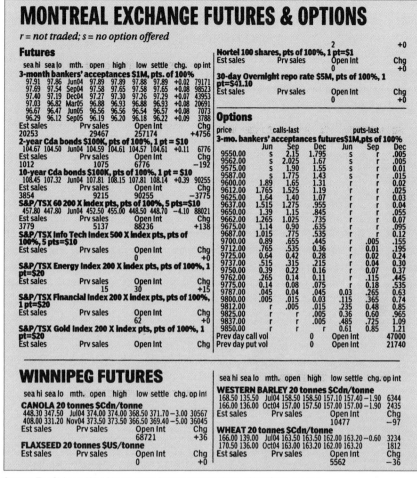

To summarize, at maturity:

$$\text{Profit to long} = \text{Spot price at maturity} - \text{Original futures price}$$
$$\text{Profit to short} = \text{Original futures prices} - \text{Spot price at maturity}$$

where the spot price is the actual market price of the commodity at the time of delivery.

The futures contract is therefore a zero-sum game, with losses and gains to all positions netting out to zero. Every long position is offset by a short position. The aggregate profits to futures trading, summing over all investors, also must be zero, as is the net exposure to changes in the commodity price. For this reason, the establishment of a futures market in a commodity should not have a major impact on the spot market for that commodity.

Figure 19.2, panel A, is a plot of the profits realized by an investor who enters the long side of a futures contract as a function of the price of the asset on the maturity date. Notice that profit is zero when the ultimate spot price, P_T, equals the initial futures price, F_0. Profit per unit of the underlying asset rises or falls one-for-one with changes in the final spot price. Unlike the payoff of a call option, the payoff of the long futures position can be negative: this will be the case if the spot price falls below the original futures price. Unlike the holder of a call, who has an *option* to buy, the long futures position trader cannot simply walk away from the contract. Also unlike options, in the case of futures there is no need to distinguish gross payoffs from net profits. This is because the futures contract is not purchased; it is simply a contract that is agreed to by two parties. The futures price adjusts to make the present value of either side of the contract equal to zero.

The distinction between futures and options is highlighted by comparing panel A of Figure 19.2 to the payoff and profit diagrams for an investor in a call option with exercise price, X, chosen equal to the futures price F_0 (see panel C). The futures investor is exposed to considerable losses if the asset price falls. In contrast, the investor in the call cannot lose more than the cost of the option.

Figure 19.2, panel B, is a plot of the profits realized by an investor who enters the short side of a futures contract. It is the mirror image of the profit diagram for the long position.

CONCEPT CHECK

1. *a.* Compare the profit diagram in Figure 19.2B to the payoff diagram for a long position in a put option. Assume the exercise price of the option equals the initial futures price.
   b. Compare the profit diagram in Figure 19.2B to the payoff diagram for an investor who writes a call option.

Figure 19.2 Profits to buyers and sellers of futures and options contracts.

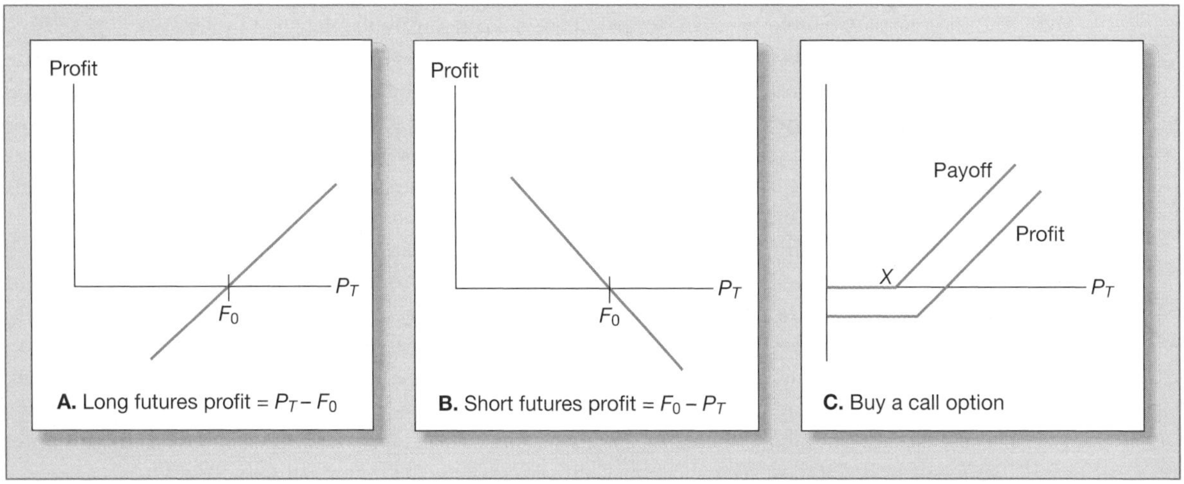

Existing Contracts

Futures and forward contracts are traded on a wide variety of goods in four broad categories: agricultural commodities, metals and minerals (including energy commodities), foreign currencies, and financial futures (fixed-income securities and stock market indexes). Innovation in financial futures has been rapid and is ongoing. Figure 19.3 illustrates both the tremendous growth in futures trading in the last decade and the preeminent role of financial futures. Table 19.1 enumerates some of the various contracts trading in the U.S. in 2002. Contracts now trade on items that would not have been considered possible only a few years ago. For example, there are now electricity as well as weather futures and options contracts. Weather derivatives (which trade on the Chicago Mercantile Exchange) have payoffs that depend on the number of degree-days by which the temperature in a region exceeds or falls short of 65 degrees Fahrenheit. The potential use of these derivatives in managing the risk surrounding electricity or oil and natural gas use should be evident. The boxed article here provides more examples of the use of such instruments.

In Canada, futures contracts for several major agricultural commodities have been trading for a long time at the Winnipeg Commodity Exchange (WCE). All other futures contracts, as well as all option contracts, have been trading since 1999 at the Montreal Exchange, which was renamed the Canadian Derivatives Exchange. The early 1980s saw the introduction of several precious metal, stock index, and interest rate futures, together with options on stock indices, foreign currencies, and bonds. By the end of the decade, most of these instruments had failed. By 2004, apart from the WCE the only active futures trading in Canada was in S&P/TSX 60 contracts, various S&P/TSX sectoral indices, bankers' acceptances, the overnight repo rate,

Figure 19.3 CBOT trading volume in futures contracts.

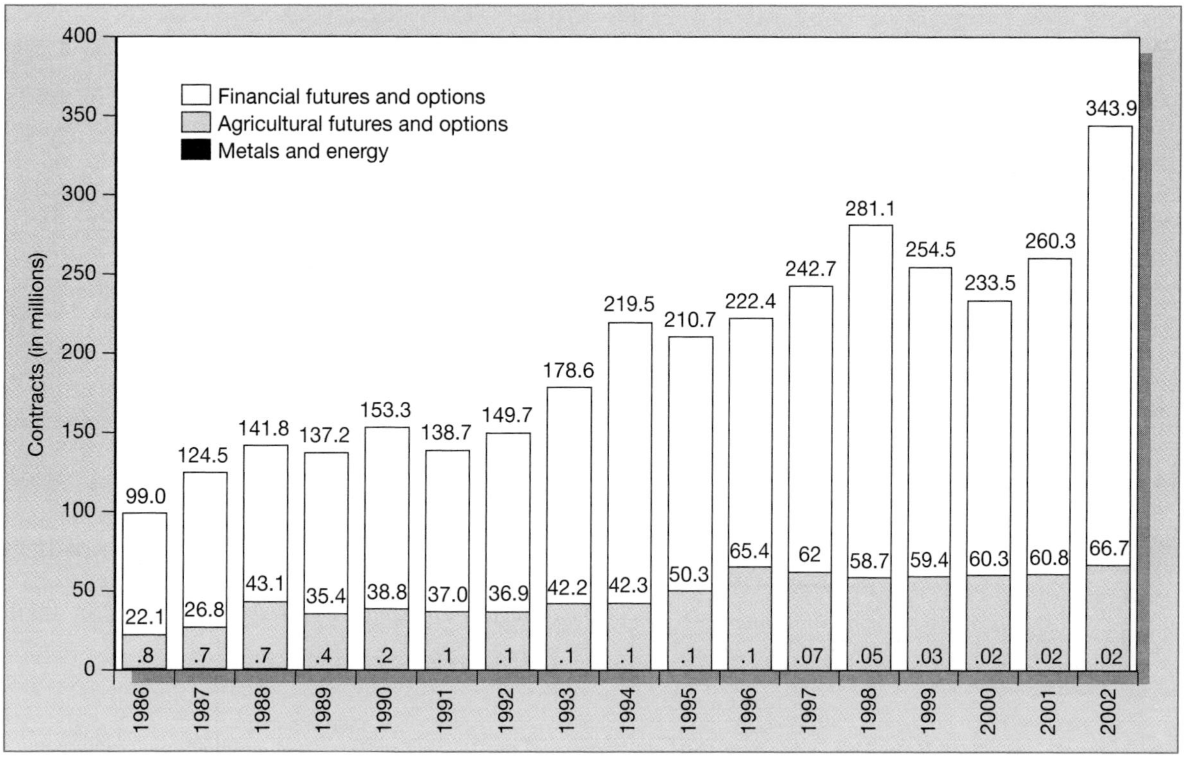

Note: Totals subject to rounding error.

Source: Chicago Board of Trade.

WEATHER DERIVATIVES

It is estimated that one-seventh of the U.S. economy is affected by weather risk. Weather impacts are the most pronounced for energy and power firms. For instance, the consumption volume of natural gas depends heavily on how cold the winter season is. Weather derivatives are perfect instruments for hedging volume risk.

Since its inception in the fall of 1997, the over-the-counter weather derivatives market has been growing steadily. The global market size is currently estimated at US$8 billion. In the fall of 1999, the Chicago Mercantile Exchange introduced temperature futures for a dozen cities in the United States. That same year, an Internet-based trading consortium, I-Wex, began in Europe. Virtually all of the market growth in this area occurred in the U.S., with Europe and Asia trailing far behind.

The contracted weather variables include temperature, precipitation, wind speed, and humidity. The vast majority of the contracts are temperature-based, which typically cover a season or a month. The contract variable is either heating degree days (HDDs) for the winter, or cooling degree days (CDDs) for the summer. HDDs (or CDDs) measure how many degrees the average daily temperature is below (or above) 65°F. The colder the day, the higher the HDDs; the warmer the day, the higher the CDDs. The daily HDDs or CDDs are then accumulated for the contract period. To illustrate, suppose the daily average temperature in Fahrenheit for June 1st, 2nd, 3rd, 4th, ..., and 30th are 67, 69, 65, 68, ..., and 72, respectively. The daily CDDs would then be 2, 4, 0, 3, ..., and 7. The monthly CDDs for June would be the sum of 2, 4, 0, 3, ..., and 7. If it turns out to be 180, then, depending on what the contracted level of CDDs is, one party will pay the other according to the difference between the contract level and the realized level of CDDs.

Contracts have also been struck based on custom-tailored variables. For instance, in May 2000, Corney & Barrow, a wine bar chain in London, England, entered into a temperature contract to hedge against low sales on cool summer days. The chain found that when the temperature is below 24°C, customer volume starts to dwindle. To hedge against unfavourable temperatures, Corney & Barrow purchased a derivative contract for the June–September season, which entails a payoff of £1,000 (24°C – T) per day for the days when the temperature (T) is below 24°C. Similar contracts have been used by restaurants.

As an alternative asset class, weather derivatives also hold their appeal. Given the relative youth of the instruments, very little is known about their true role and potential in general investments. But risk reduction or diversification ought to be the main focus. Our limited research shows that the correlation between stock market indices and local temperatures is, typically, very low. This suggests diversification potential in a portfolio's context. Indeed, in Europe, several hedge funds have been set up that are dedicated to weather derivatives.

The current state of the weather derivatives market is still typified by high bid-ask spreads and low liquidity. I-Wex has launched three temperature indices for Paris, Berlin, and London, respectively. The London International Financial Futures Exchange (LIFFE) plans to launch futures contracts on these indices. With more such broadly based contracts being formally traded and increasing public awareness of this new breed of financial instrument, there is potential for broader participation in the market. This growing interest will eventually make weather derivatives a truly alternative class of investment assets.

Source: Jason Wei, "Weather Derivatives: A Truly Alternative Asset Class for Investors," *Canadian Investment Review* 15, no. 1 (Spring 2002), p. 51. Reprinted by permission of Canadian Investment Review.

Canada bond futures, and options on Canada bond futures and bankers' acceptances, as well as futures on Nortel stock. Low liquidity, thin trading, and the ready availability of comparable financial instruments in the United States are major reasons for the relative failure of financial innovations in Canadian futures markets.[1]

Outside the futures markets, a fairly developed network of banks and brokers has established a forward market in foreign exchange. This forward market is not a formal exchange in the sense that the exchange specifies the terms of the traded contract. Instead, participants in a forward contract may negotiate for delivery of any quantity of goods, as distinguished from futures markets where contract size is set by the exchange. In forward arrangements, banks and brokers simply negotiate contracts for clients (or themselves) as needed.

[1]A more extensive treatment of the reasons for the failure of many new Canadian futures instruments can be found in E. Kirzner, "The Evolving Derivatives Story," *Canadian Investment Review* 11 (Winter 1998).

Table 19.1 Sample of Futures Contracts

Foreign Currencies	Agricultural	Metals and Energy	Interest Rate Futures	Equity Indices
British pound	Corn	Copper	Eurodollars	S&P 500
Canadian dollar	Oats	Aluminum	Euroyen	Dow Jones Industrials
Japanese yen	Soybeans	Gold	Euro-denominated bond	S&P Mid-Cap 400
Euro	Soybean meal	Platinum	Euroswiss	Nasdaq 100
Swiss franc	Soybean oil	Palladium	Sterling	NYSE index
Australian dollar	Wheat	Silver	Gilt†	Russell 2000 index
Mexican peso	Barley	Crude oil	German government bond	Nikkei 225 (Japanese)
Brazilian real	Flaxseed	Heating oil	Italian government bond	FTSE index (British)
	Canola	Gas oil	Canadian government bond	CAC-40 (French)
	Rye	Natural gas	Treasury bonds	DAX-30 (German)
	Cattle	Gasoline	Treasury notes	All ordinary (Australian)
	Hogs	Propane	Treasury bills	S&P/TSX 60 (Canadian)
	Pork bellies	CRB index*	LIBOR	Dow Jones Euro STOXX 50
	Cocoa	Electricity	EURIBOR	
	Coffee	Weather	Euroswiss	
	Cotton		Municipal bond index	
	Milk		Federal funds rate	
	Orange juice		Bankers' acceptance	
	Sugar			
	Lumber			
	Rice			

*The Commodity Research Bureau's index of futures prices of agricultural and metal and energy prices.

†*Gilts* are British government bonds.

19.2 MECHANICS OF TRADING IN FUTURES MARKETS

The Clearinghouse and Open Interest

Trading in futures contracts is more complex than making ordinary stock transactions. If you want to make a stock purchase, your broker simply acts as an intermediary to enable you to buy shares from or sell to another individual through the stock exchange. In futures trading, however, the exchange plays a more active role.

When an investor contacts a broker to establish a futures position, the brokerage firm wires the order to the firm's trader on the floor of the futures exchange. In contrast to stock trading, which involves specialists or market makers in each security, most futures trades take place among floor traders in the "trading pit" for each contract. Traders use voice or hand signals to signify their desire to buy or sell. Once a trader willing to accept the opposite side of a trade is located, the trade is recorded and the customer is notified.

At this point, just as is true for options contracts, the **clearinghouse** enters the picture. Rather than having the long and short traders hold contracts with each other, the clearinghouse becomes the seller of the contract for the long position and the buyer of the contract for the short position. The clearinghouse is obligated to deliver the commodity to the long position and to pay for delivery from the short; consequently, the clearinghouse's position nets to zero. This arrangement makes the clearinghouse the trading partner of each trader, both long and short. The clearinghouse, bound to perform on its side of each contract, is the only party that can be hurt by the failure of any trader to fulfill the obligations of the futures contract. This arrangement is necessary, because a futures contract calls for future performance, which cannot be guaranteed as easily as an immediate stock transaction.

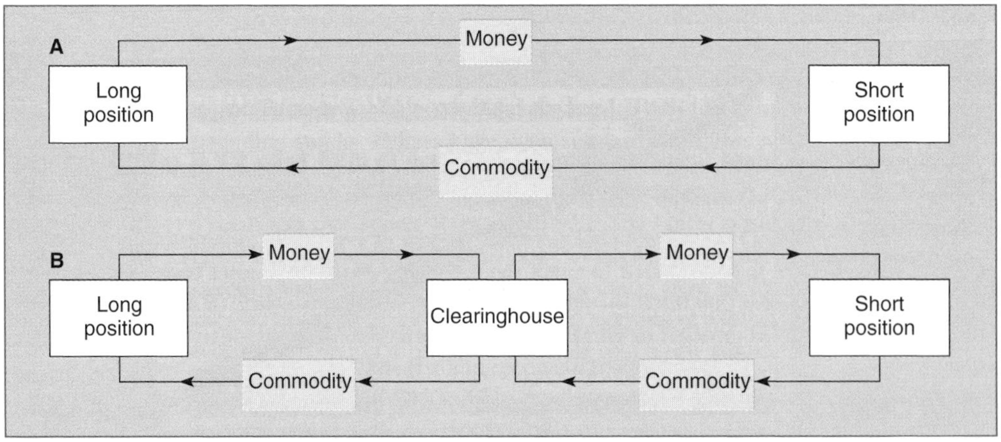

Figure 19.4 Panel A: Trading without the clearinghouse. Panel B: Trading with the clearinghouse.

Figure 19.4, panel A illustrates what would happen in the absence of the clearinghouse. The trader in the long position would be obligated to pay the futures price to the short position trader; the trader in the short position would be obligated to deliver the commodity. Panel B shows how the clearinghouse becomes an intermediary, acting as the trading partner for each side of the contract. The clearinghouse's position is neutral, since it takes a long and a short position for each transaction.

The clearinghouse makes it possible for traders to liquidate positions easily. If you are currently long in a contract and want to undo your position, you simply instruct your broker to enter the short side of a contract to close out your position. This is called a **reversing trade**. The exchange nets out your long and short positions, reducing your net position to zero. Your zero net position with the clearinghouse eliminates the need to fulfill at maturity either the original long or the reversing short position.

The **open interest** on the contract is the number of contracts outstanding. (Long and short positions are not counted separately, meaning that open interest can be defined as the number of either long or short contracts outstanding.) The clearinghouse's position nets out to zero, of course, and so is not counted in the computation of open interest. When contracts begin trading, open interest is zero. As time passes, open interest increases as progressively more contracts are entered. Almost all traders, however, liquidate their positions before the contract maturity date. Instead of actually taking or making delivery of the commodity, virtually all traders enter reversing trades to cancel their original positions, thereby realizing the profits or losses on the contract. Actual deliveries and purchases of commodities are then made via regular channels of supply. The percentage of contracts that result in actual delivery is estimated to range from less than 1 percent to 3 percent, depending on the commodity and the activity in the contract. The image of a trader awakening one delivery date with a hog in the front yard is amusing, but unlikely.

You can see the typical pattern of open interest in Figure 19.1. In the three-month bankers' acceptances contracts, for example, the June and September contracts have significant open interest. The most distant September 2005 maturity contract has relatively little open interest, because the contract has only recently been available for trading.

Marking to Market and the Margin Account

Anyone who saw the film *Trading Places* knows that Eddie Murphy as a trader in orange juice futures had no intention of purchasing or delivering orange juice. Traders simply bet on the future price of juice. The total profit or loss realized by the long trader who buys a contract at time zero and closes, or reverses, it at time t is just the change in the futures price over the period $F_t - F_0$. Symmetrically, the short trader earns $F_0 - F_t$.

The process by which profits or losses accrue to traders is called **marking to market**. At initial execution of a trade, each trader establishes a margin account. The margin is a security account consisting of cash and/or near-cash securities, such as Treasury bills, which ensure that the trader is able to satisfy the obligations of the futures contract. Because both parties to a futures contract are exposed to losses, both must post margin. This is in contrast to options, where only the option writer has an obligation and thus needs to post margin. If the initial margin for canola, for example, is 10 percent, then the trader must post $738.80 per contract of the margin account. This is 10 percent of the contract value of $738.80 per tonne × 20 tonnes per contract. Because the margin may be satisfied with interest-earning securities, posting the margin does not impose a significant opportunity cost of funds on the trader. The initial margin usually is set between 5 percent and 15 percent of the total value of the contract. Contracts written on assets with more volatile prices require higher margins.

On any day that futures markets trade, futures prices may rise or fall. Instead of waiting until the maturity date for traders to realize all gains and losses, the clearinghouse requires all positions to recognize profits as they accrue daily. If the futures price of canola at the WCE rises from $369.40 to $371.40 per tonne, the clearinghouse credits the margin account of the long position for 20 tonnes (which is the standard size of the canola-futures contract) multiplied by $2 per tonne, or $40 per contract. Conversely, for the short position the clearinghouse takes this amount from the margin account for each contract held. This daily settling is marking to market.

Therefore, the maturity date of the contract does not govern realization of profit or loss. Marking to market ensures that, as futures prices change, the proceeds accrue to the trader's margin account immediately.

CONCEPT CHECK

2. What must be the net inflow or outlay from marking to market for the clearinghouse?

If a trader accrues sustained losses from daily marking to market, the margin account may fall below a critical value called the **maintenance margin** or **variation margin**. Once the value of the account falls below this value, the trader receives a margin call. Either new funds must be transferred into the margin account, or the broker will close out enough of the trader's position to reduce the required margin for that position to a level at or below the trader's remaining margin. This procedure safeguards the position of the clearinghouse. Positions are closed out before the margin account is exhausted—the trader's losses are covered and the clearinghouse is not affected.

Marking to market is the major way in which futures and forward contracts differ, besides contract standardization. Futures follow a pay- (or receive-) as-you-go-method. Forward contracts are simply held until maturity, and no funds are transferred until that date, although the contracts may be traded.

It is important to note that the futures price on the delivery date will equal the spot price of the commodity on that date. Since a maturing contract calls for immediate delivery, the futures price on that day must equal the spot price—the cost of the commodity from the two competing sources is equalized in a competitive market.[2] You may obtain the delivery of the commodity either by purchasing it directly in the spot market or by entering the long side of a futures contract.

A commodity available from two sources (spot or futures market) must be priced identically, or else investors will rush to purchase it from the cheap source in order to sell it in the higher-priced market. Such arbitrage activity could not persist without prices adjusting to eliminate the arbitrage opportunity. Therefore, the futures price and spot price must converge at maturity. This is called the **convergence property**.

[2]Small differences between the spot and futures prices at maturity may persist because of transportation costs, but this is a minor factor.

For an investor who establishes a long position in a contract now (time 0) and holds that position until maturity (time T), the sum of all daily settlements will equal $F_T - F_0$, where F_T stands for the futures price at contract maturity. We have noted, however, that the futures price at maturity equals the spot price, P_T, so total futures profits also may be expressed as $P_T - F_0$. Summing the daily marking-to-market settlements results in a profit formula identical to that of a forward contract.

Because these payments accrue continually, we should not, strictly speaking, simply add them up to obtain total profits without first adjusting for interest on interim payments. Some empirical evidence, however, suggests that interest earnings on daily settlements have only a small effect on the determination of futures and forward prices. For this reason, we often ignore this fine point and simply take the profits or losses on a futures contract held to maturity to be $P_T - F_0$ for the long position, and $F_0 - P_T$ for the short.

EXAMPLE 19.1 Marking to Market

Assume the current futures price for silver for delivery five days from today is $7.60 per ounce (in U.S. dollars). Suppose that over the next five days the futures price evolves as follows:

Day	Futures Price
0 (today)	$7.60
1	$7.70
2	$7.75
3	$7.68
4	$7.68
5 (delivery)	$7.71

The spot price of silver on the delivery day is $7.71: the convergence property implies that the price of silver in the spot market must equal the futures price on delivery day.

The daily marking-to-market settlements for each contract held by the long position will be as follows:

Day	Profit (Loss) per Ounce	× 5,000 Ounces/Contract = Daily Proceeds
1	7.70 – 7.60 = .10	$500
2	7.75 – 7.70 = .05	250
3	7.68 – 7.75 = –.07	–350
4	7.68 – 7.68 = 0	0
5	7.71 – 7.68 = .03	150
		$550

The profit on day 1 is the increase in the futures price from the previous day, or ($7.70 – $7.60) per ounce. Because each silver contract on the Commodity Exchange (CMX) calls for purchase and delivery of 5,000 ounces, the total profit per contract is 5,000 multiplied by $.10, or $500. On day three, when the futures price falls, the long position's margin account will be debited by $350. By day five, the sum of all daily proceeds is $550. This is exactly equal to 5,000 times the difference between the final futures price of $7.71 and the original futures price of $7.60. Thus the sum of all the daily proceeds (per ounce of silver held long) equals $P_T - F_0$.

Cash Versus Actual Delivery

Most futures markets call for delivery of an actual commodity, such as a particular grade of wheat or a specified amount of foreign currency, if the contract is not reversed before maturity. For agricultural commodities where quality of the delivered good may vary, the exchange sets quality standards as part of the futures contract. In some cases, contracts may be settled with higher- or lower-grade commodities. In these cases, a premium or discount is applied to the delivered commodity to adjust for the quality difference.

Some futures contracts call for **cash delivery**. An example is a stock index futures contract where the underlying asset is an index such as the S&P/TSX 60 or the S&P 500 index. Delivery of every stock in the index clearly would be impractical. Hence the contract calls for "delivery" of a cash amount equal to the value that the index attains on the maturity date of the contract. The sum of all the daily settlements from marking to market results in the long position realizing total profits or losses of $S_T - F_0$, where S_T is the value of the stock index on the maturity date T, and F_0 is the original futures price. Cash settlement closely mimics actual delivery, except the cash value of the asset rather than the asset itself is delivered by the short position in exchange for the futures price.

More concretely, the S&P/TSX 60 index contract calls for delivery of $200 multiplied by the value of the index. At maturity, the index might list at 400, a market-value-weighted index of the prices of all 60 stocks in the index. The cash settlement contract calls for delivery of $\$200 \times 400$, or $80,000, in return for 200 times the futures price. This yields exactly the same profit as would result from directly purchasing 200 units of the index for $80,000 and then delivering it for 200 times the original futures price.

Regulations

Futures markets in Canada are under the jurisdiction of the provincial securities commissions, with the exception of grain futures traded on the WCE, which are subject to federal law. Most futures trading is self-regulated, although some provinces have passed commodity futures acts.

In the United States, futures markets are regulated by the Commodities Futures Trading Commission (CFTC), a federal agency. The CFTC sets capital requirements for member firms of the futures exchanges, authorizes trading in new contracts, and oversees maintenance of daily trading records.

The futures exchange may set limits on the amount by which futures prices may change from one day to the next. In the S&P/TSX 60 the Montreal Exchange halts trading in conjunction with the triggering of "circuit breakers" set in coordination with the NYSE and the TSX. Suppose, for example, the price limit on the S&P/TSX 60 futures contract is set at $2,000, corresponding to a change of 10 ($2,000/$200) in the index. This means that if S&P/TSX 60 futures close today at 400, trades tomorrow in the S&P/TSX 60 index may vary only between 410 and 390. Likewise, if the price limit on silver contracts traded on the Chicago Board of Trade is $1, this means that if silver futures close today at $7.40 per ounce, trades in silver tomorrow may vary only between $6.40 and $8.40 per ounce. The exchanges may increase or reduce price limits in response to perceived increases or decreases in price volatility of the contract. Price limits often are eliminated as contracts approach maturity, usually in the last month of trading.

Price limits traditionally are viewed as a means to limit violent price fluctuations. This reasoning seems dubious. Suppose that an international monetary crisis overnight drives up the spot price of silver to $10.50. No one would sell silver futures at prices for future delivery as low as $7.40. Instead, the futures price would rise each day by the $1 limit, although the quoted price would represent only an unfilled bid order—no contracts would trade at the low quoted price. After several days of limit moves of $1 per day, the futures price would finally reach its equilibrium level, and trading would occur again. This process means no one could unload a position until the price reached its equilibrium level. This example shows that price limits offer no real protection against price fluctuation.

Taxation

Because of the marking-to-market procedure, investors do not have control over the tax year in which they realize gains or losses. Instead, price changes are realized gradually, with each daily settlement. Therefore, taxes are paid at year-end on accumulated profits or losses, regardless of whether the position has been closed out.

19.3 FUTURES MARKETS STRATEGIES

Hedging and Speculating

Hedging and speculating are two polar uses of futures markets. A speculator uses a futures contract to profit from movements in futures prices; a hedger, to protect against price movement. If speculators believe that prices will increase, they will take a long position for expected profits. Conversely, they will exploit expected price declines by taking a short position.

EXAMPLE 19.2 Speculating with Bond Futures

Let's consider the use of the 10-year Canada bond futures contract, the listing for which appears in Figure 19.1. Each Canada bond contract on the Montreal Exchange calls for delivery of \$100,000 par value of bonds. The listed futures price of 108.14 means the market price of the underlying bonds is 108.14 percent of par, or \$108,140. Therefore, for every increase of one point in the Canada bond futures price (e.g., to 109.14), the long position gains \$1,000, and the short loses that amount. Therefore, if you are bullish on bond prices, you might speculate by buying Canada bond futures contracts.

If the Canada bond futures price increases by one point to 109.14, then you profit by \$1,000 per contract. If the forecast is incorrect, and Canada bond futures prices decline, you lose \$1,000 times the decrease in the futures price for each contract purchased. Speculators bet on the direction of futures price movements.

Why does a speculator buy a Canada bond futures contract? Why not buy Canada bonds directly? One reason lies in transaction costs, which are far smaller in futures markets.

Another important reason is the leverage futures trading provides. Recall that each Canada bond contract calls for delivery of \$100,000 par value, worth \$108,140 in our example. The initial margin required for this account might be only \$10,000. The \$1,000 per contract gain translates into a \$1,000/\$10,000 = 10 percent return on the money put up, despite the fact that the Canada bond futures price increases only 1/108.14 = .0925%. Futures margins, therefore, allow speculators to achieve much greater leverage than is available from direct trading in a commodity.

Hedgers by contrast use futures markets to protect themselves against price movements. An investor holding a Canada bond portfolio, for example, might anticipate a period of interest rate volatility and want to protect the value of the portfolio against price fluctuations. In this case, the investor has no desire to bet on price movements in either direction. To achieve such protection, a hedger takes a short position in Canada bond futures, which obligates him to deliver Canada bonds at the contract maturity date for the current futures price. This locks in the sales price for the bonds and guarantees that the total value of the bond-plus-futures position at the maturity date is the futures price.[3]

EXAMPLE 19.3 Hedging with Bond Futures

Suppose as in Figure 19.1 that the futures price for June 2004 delivery (rounding to the nearest dollar) is \$108 per \$100 par value, and that the only three possible Canada bond prices in June are \$107, \$108, and \$109. If the investor currently holds 200 bonds, each with par value \$1,000, he would take short positions in two contracts, each for \$100,000 par value. Protecting the value of a portfolio with short futures positions is called *short hedging*. Taking the futures position requires no current investment. (The initial margin requirement is small relative to the size of the contract, and because it may be posted in interest-bearing securities, it does not represent a time-value or opportunity cost.)

The profits in June from each of the two short futures contracts will be 1,000 times any decrease in the futures price. At maturity, the convergence property ensures that the final futures price will equal the spot price of the Canada bonds. Hence the futures profit will be 2,000 times $(F_0 - P_T)$, where P_T is the price of the bonds on the delivery date and F_0 is the original futures price, \$108.

Now consider the hedged portfolio consisting of the bonds and the short futures positions. The portfolio value as a function of the bond price in June can be computed as follows:

	Canada Bond Price in June		
	\$107	\$108	\$109
Bond holdings (value = $2{,}000P_T$)	\$214,000	\$216,000	\$218,000
Futures profits or losses	2,000	0	−2,000
Total	\$216,000	\$216,000	\$216,000

The total portfolio value is unaffected by the eventual bond price, which is what the hedger wants. The gains or losses on the bond holdings are exactly offset by those on the two contracts held short.

For example, if bond prices fall to \$107, the losses on the bond portfolio are offset by the \$2,000 gain on the futures contracts. That profit equals the difference between the futures price on the maturity date (which equals the spot price on that date of \$107) and the originally contracted futures price of \$108. For short contracts, a profit of \$1 per \$100 par value is realized from the fall in the spot price. Because two contracts call for delivery of \$200,000 par value, this results in a \$2,000 gain that offsets the decline in the value of the bonds held in portfolio. In contrast to a speculator, a hedger is indifferent to the ultimate price of the asset. The short hedger who has in essence arranged to sell the asset for an agreed-upon price need not be concerned about further developments in the market price.

To generalize this example, you can note that the bond will be worth P_T at maturity, whereas the profit on the futures contract is $F_0 - P_T$. The sum of the two positions is F_0 dollars, which is independent of the eventual bond price.

A *long hedge* is the analogue to a short hedge for a purchaser of an asset. Consider, for example, a pension fund manager who anticipates a cash inflow in two months that will be invested in fixed-income securities. The manager views Canada bonds as very attractively priced now and

[3]To keep things simple, we will assume that the Canada bond futures contract calls for delivery of a bond with the same coupon and maturity as that in the investor's portfolio. In practice, a variety of bonds may be delivered to satisfy the contract, and a "conversion factor" is used to adjust for the relative values of the eligible delivery bonds. We will ignore this complication.

would like to lock in current prices and yields until the investment actually can be made two months hence. The manager can lock in the effective cost of the purchase by entering the long side of a contract, which commits her to purchasing at the current futures price.

CONCEPT CHECK

3. Suppose, as in our example, that Canada bonds will be priced at \$110, \$111, or \$112 in two months. Show that the cost in June of purchasing \$200,000 par value of Canada bonds net of the profit/loss on two long Canada bond contracts will be \$222,000 regardless of the eventual bond price.

Exact futures hedging may be impossible for some goods because the necessary futures contract is not traded. For example, a portfolio manager might want to hedge the value of a diversified, actively managed portfolio for a period of time. However, futures contracts are listed only on indexed portfolios. Nevertheless, because returns on the manager's diversified portfolio will have a high correlation with returns on broad-based indexed portfolios, an effective hedge may be established by selling index futures contracts. Hedging a position using futures on another asset is called *cross-hedging*.

CONCEPT CHECK

4. What are the sources of risk to an investor who uses aluminum futures to hedge an inventory of bauxite.

Futures contracts may also be used as general portfolio hedges. Bodie and Rosansky[4] show that commodity futures returns have had a negative correlation with the stock market. Investors may add a diversified portfolio of futures contracts to a diversified stock portfolio to lower the standard deviation of the overall rate of return.

In their study the correlation coefficient between the two portfolios during the estimation period was –.24. This implies that long positions in commodity futures would add substantial diversification benefits to a stock portfolio.

Commodity futures also are inflation hedges. When commodity prices increase because of unanticipated inflation, returns from long futures positions will increase because the contracts call for delivery of goods for the price agreed upon before the high inflation rate became a reality.

Basis Risk and Hedging

The **basis** is the difference between the futures price and the spot price.[5] As we have noted, on the maturity date of a contract the basis must be zero: The convergence property implies that $F_T - P_T = 0$. Before maturity, however, the futures price for later delivery may differ substantially from the current spot price.

We discussed the case of a short hedger who holds an asset and a short position to deliver that asset in the future. If the asset and futures contract are held until maturity, the hedger bears no risk, because the ultimate value of the portfolio on the delivery date is determined completely by the current futures price. Risk is eliminated because the futures price and spot price at contract maturity must be equal: gains and losses on the futures and the commodity position will exactly cancel. If the contract and asset are to be liquidated early, however, the hedger bears **basis risk**, because the futures price and spot price need not move in perfect lockstep at all times before the delivery date. In this case, gains and losses on the contract and the asset need not exactly offset each other.

---

[4]Zvi Bodie and Victor Rosansky, "Risk and Return in Commodity Futures," *Financial Analysts Journal*, May/June 1980.

[5]Usage of the word *basis* is somewhat loose. It sometimes is used to refer to F-P and sometimes to P-F. We will consistently call the basis F-P.

Some speculators try to profit from movements in the basis. Rather than betting on the direction of the futures or spot prices per se, they bet on the changes in the difference between the two. A long spot–short futures position will profit when the basis narrows.

EXAMPLE 19.4 Speculating on the Basis

Consider an investor holding 5,000 ounces of silver, who is short one silver futures contract. Silver might sell for $7.20 per ounce, while the futures price for next-year delivery is $7.80. The basis is therefore 60 cents. Tomorrow, the silver spot price might increase to $7.24, while the futures price might increase to $7.81. The basis has narrowed from 60 cents to 57 cents. The investor realizes a capital gain of 4 cents per ounce on her silver holdings and a loss of 1 cent per ounce from the increase in the futures price. The net gain is the decrease in basis, or 3 cents per ounce.

A related strategy is a calendar **spread** position where the investor takes a long position in a futures contract of one maturity and a short position in a contract on the same commodity, but with a different maturity. Profits accrue if the difference in futures prices between the two contracts changes in the hoped-for direction; that is, if the futures price on the contract held long increases by more (or decreases by less) than the futures price on the contract held short.

Other Hedging Strategies

Futures contracts are used for hedging purposes in a large variety of situations. Some of these will be examined in this chapter, while others will be seen in subsequent chapters.

We already saw how commodity futures can be used to hedge producer or consumer risks arising from spot price fluctuations. Similarly, interest rate futures can be used to hedge interest rate risk. Such a risk is present in underwriting bond issues or in managing bond portfolios. Hedging strategies for dealing with such risk will be examined later in this chapter.

Stock index futures can be used to modify the systematic risk of stock portfolios. The corresponding appropriate techniques are examined in Chapter 21. Similarly, foreign exchange futures are important tools to manage the risk arising from fluctuations in the exchange rate. Such risk appears in investors holding financial instruments denominated in Foreign currencies, or in firms whose receipts or costs are dependant on the exchange rate with foreign currency. We examine how to hedge it in Chapter 22.

19.4 THE DETERMINATION OF FUTURES PRICES

The Spot-Futures Parity Theorem

We have seen that a futures contract can be used to hedge changes in the value of the underlying asset. If the hedge is perfect, meaning that the asset-plus-futures portfolio has no risk, then the hedged position must provide a rate of return equal to the rate on other risk-free investments. Otherwise, there will be arbitrage opportunities that investors will exploit until prices are brought back into line. This insight can be used to derive the theoretical relationship between a futures price and the price of its underlying asset.

Suppose, for example, that the S&P/TSX 60 index currently is at 400 and an investor who holds $400 in a mutual fund indexed to the S&P/TSX 60 wishes to temporarily hedge her exposure to market risk. Assume that the indexed portfolio pays dividends totalling $5 over the course of the year and, for simplicity, that all dividends are paid at year-end. Finally, assume that the futures price for year-end delivery on the S&P/TSX 60 contract is 408.[6] Let's examine the end-of-year proceeds for various values of the stock index if the investor hedges her portfolio by entering the short side of the futures contract.

Value of stock portfolio	380	390	400	405	410	420
Payoff from short futures position (equals $F_0 - F_T = \$408 - S_T$)	28	18	8	3	−2	−12
Dividend income	5	5	5	5	5	5
Total	$413	$413	$413	$413	$413	$413

The payoff from the short futures position equals the difference between the original futures price, $408, and the year-end stock price. This is due to convergence: the futures price at contract maturity will equal the stock price at that time.

Notice that the overall position is perfectly hedged. Any increase in the value of the indexed stock portfolio is offset by an equal decrease in the payoff of the short futures position, resulting in a final value independent of the stock price. The $413 payoff is the sum of the current futures price, $F_0 = \$408$, and the $5 dividend. It is as though the investor arranged to sell the stock at year-end for the current futures price, thereby eliminating price risk and locking in total proceeds equal to the sales price plus dividends paid before the sale.

What rate of return is earned on this riskless position? The stock investment requires an initial outlay of $400, while the futures position is established without an initial cash outflow. Therefore, the $400 portfolio grows to a year-end value of $413, providing a rate of return of 3.25 percent. More generally, a total investment of S_0, the current stock price, grows to a final value of $F_0 + D$, where D is the dividend payout on the portfolio. The rate of return is therefore

$$\text{Rate of return on perfectly hedged stock portfolio} = \frac{(F_0 + D) - S_0}{S_0}$$

This return is essentially riskless. We observe F_0 at the beginning of the period when we enter the futures contract. While dividend payouts are not perfectly riskless, they are highly predictable over short periods, especially for diversified portfolios. Any uncertainty is *extremely* small compared to the uncertainty of stock prices.

Presumably, 3.25 percent must be the rate of return available on other riskless investments. If not, then investors would face two competing risk-free strategies with different rates of return, a situation that could not last. Therefore, we conclude that

$$\frac{(F_0 + D) - S_0}{S_0} = r_f$$

Rearranging, we find that the futures price must be

$$F_0 = S_0(1 + r_f) - D = S_0(1 + r_f - d) \tag{19.1}$$

where d is the dividend yield on the stock portfolio, defined as D/S_0. This result is called the **spot-futures parity theorem**. It gives the normal or theoretically correct relationship between spot and futures prices.

[6]Actually, the futures contract calls for delivery of $200 times the value of the S&P/TSX 60 index, so that each contract would be settled for $200 times 408. We will simplify by assuming that you can buy a contract for one unit rather than 500 units of the index. In practice, one contract would hedge about $200 × 400 = $80,000 worth of stock. Of course, institutional investors would consider a stock portfolio of this size to be quite small.

EXAMPLE 19.5 Futures Market Arbitrage

Suppose that parity were violated. For example, suppose the risk-free interest rate in the economy were only 3 percent, so that according to parity, the futures price should be $400(1 + .03) – $5 = $407. The actual futures price, F_0 = $408, is $1 higher than its "appropriate" value. This implies that an investor can make arbitrage profits by shorting the relatively overpriced futures contract and buying the relatively underpriced stock portfolio using money borrowed at the 3 percent market interest rate. The proceeds from this strategy would be as follows:

Action	Initial Cash Flow	Cash Flow in One Year
Borrow $400, repay with interest in one year	+$400	–400(1.03) = –$412
Buy stock for $400	–$400	S_T + $5 dividend
Enter short futures position (F_0 = $408)	0	$408 – S_T
Total	0	$1

The net initial investment of the strategy is zero. But its cash flow in one year is positive and riskless. The payoff is $1 regardless of the stock price. This payoff is precisely equal to the mispricing of the futures contract relative to its parity value.

When parity is violated, the strategy to exploit the mispricing produces an arbitrage profit—a riskless profit requiring no initial net investment. If such an opportunity existed, all market participants would rush to take advantage of it. The results? The stock price would be bid up, and/or the futures price offered would be bid down until equation 19.1 was satisfied. A similar analysis applies to the possibility that F_0 is less than $407. In this case, you simply reverse the strategy above to earn riskless profits. We conclude, therefore, that in a well-functioning market in which arbitrage opportunities are competed away, $F_0 = S_0(1 + r_f) - D$.

CONCEPT CHECK

5. What are the three steps of the arbitrage strategy if F_0 is equal to $405? Work out the cash flows of the strategy now and in one year in a table like the one above.

The parity relationship also is called the **cost-of-carry relationship** because it asserts that the futures price is determined by the relative costs of buying a stock with deferred delivery in the futures market versus buying it in the spot market with immediate delivery and "carrying" it in inventory. If you buy the stock now, you tie up your funds and incur a time-value-of-money cost of r_f per period. On the other hand, you receive dividend payments with a current yield of d. The net carrying-cost advantage of deferring delivery of the stock is therefore $r_f - d$ per period. This advantage must be offset by a differential between the futures price and the spot price. The price differential just offsets the cost-of-carry advantage when $F_0 = S_0(1 + r_f - d)$.

The parity relationship is easily generalized to multiperiod applications. We simply recognize that the difference between the futures and spot prices will be larger as the maturity of the contract is longer. This reflects the longer period to which we apply the net cost of carry. For contract maturity of T periods, the parity relationship is

$$F_0 = S_0(1 + r_f - d)^T \tag{19.2}$$

Although we have described parity in terms of stocks and stock index futures, it should be clear that the logic applies as well to any financial futures contract. For gold futures, for example, we would simply set the dividend yield to zero. For bond contracts, we would let the coupon income on the bond play the role of dividend payments. In both cases, the parity relationship would be essentially the same as equation 19.2.

The arbitrage strategy described above should convince you that these parity relationships are more than just theoretical results. Any violations of the parity relationship give rise to arbitrage opportunities that can provide large profits to traders. We will see shortly that index arbitrage in the stock market is a tool to exploit violations of the parity relationship for stock index futures contracts.

Spreads

Just as we can predict the relationship between spot and futures prices, there are similar methods to determine the proper relationships among futures prices for contracts of different maturity dates. These relationships are simple generalizations of the spot-futures parity relationship. We will restrict ourselves to stock futures in this discussion and thus avoid the additional complications that arise from non-interest-carrying costs.

Call $F(T_1)$ the current futures price for delivery at date T_1, and $F(T_2)$ the futures price for delivery at T_2. Let d be the dividend yield of the stock between T_1 and T_2. We know from the parity equation 19.2 that[7]

$$F(T_1) = S_0(1 + r_f - d)^{T_1}$$

$$F(T_2) = S_0(1 + r_f - d)^{T_2}$$

As a result,

$$F(T_2)/F(T_1) = (1 + r_f - d)^{(T_2 - T_1)}$$

Therefore, the basic parity relationship for spreads is

$$F(T_2) = F(T_1)(1 + r_f - d)^{(T_2 - T_1)} \tag{19.3}$$

Note that equation 19.3 is quite similar to the spot-futures parity relationship. The major difference is in the substitution of $F(T_1)$ for the current spot price. The intuition also is similar. Delaying delivery from T_1 to T_2 provides the long position with the knowledge that the stock will be purchased for $F(T_2)$ dollars at T_2 but does not require that money be tied up in the stock until T_2. The savings realized are the cost of carry between T_1 and T_2 of the money that would have been paid at T_1. Delaying delivery from T_1 until T_2 frees up $F(T_1)$ dollars, which earn risk-free interest at rate r_f. The delayed delivery of the stock also results in the lost dividend yield between T_1 and T_2. The net cost of carry saved by delaying the delivery is thus $r_f - d$. This gives the proportional increase in the futures price that is required to compensate market participants for the delayed delivery of the stock and postponement of the payment of the futures price. If the parity condition for spreads is violated, arbitrage opportunities will arise. (Problem 5 at the end of the chapter explores this phenomenon.)

EXAMPLE 19.6 Spread Pricing

To see how to use equation 19.3, consider the following data for a hypothetical contract:

Contract Maturity Date	Futures Price
January 15	105
March 15	105.10

[7]We also assume that r_f is the same for all maturities, which implies that the pure yield curve that we saw in Chapter 12 is "flat."

Suppose that the effective annual T-bill rate is expected to persist at 5 percent and that the dividend yield is 4 percent per year. The "correct" March futures price relative to the January price is, according to equation 19.3,

$$105(1 + .05 - .04)^{1/6} = 105.174$$

The actual March futures price is 105.10, meaning that the March futures contract is slightly underpriced compared to the January futures contract, and that, aside from transaction costs, an arbitrage opportunity seems to be present.

Equation 19.3 shows that futures prices should all move together. Actually, it is not surprising that futures prices for different maturity dates move in unison, because all are linked to the same spot price through the parity relationship. Figure 19.5 plots futures prices on gold for three maturity dates. It is apparent that the prices move in virtual lockstep and that the more distant delivery dates require higher futures prices, as equation 19.3 predicts.

Figure 19.5 Gold futures prices, October 2000.

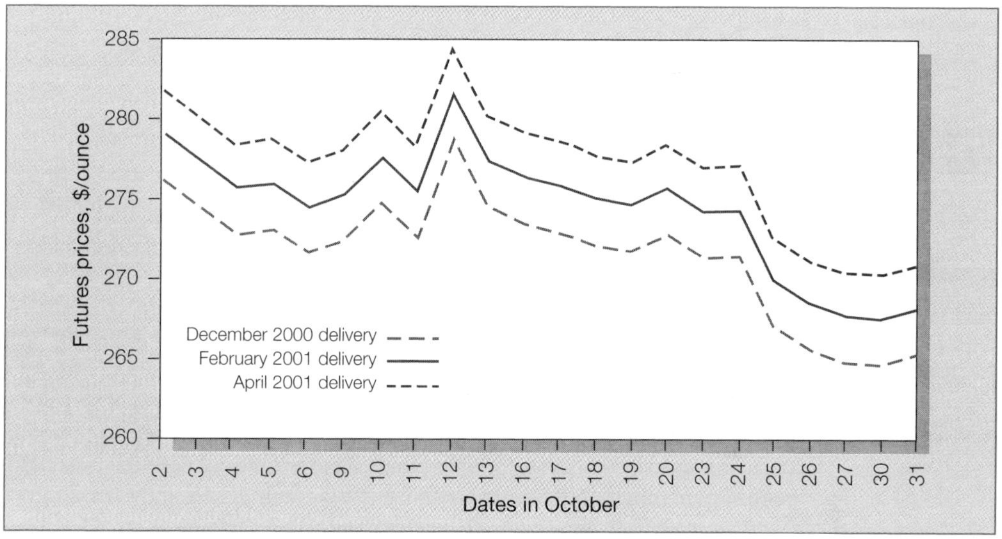

Forward Versus Futures Pricing

Until now we have paid little attention to the differing time profile of returns of futures and forward contracts. Instead, we have taken the sum of daily marking-to-market proceeds to the long position as $P_T - F_0$ and assumed for convenience that the entire profit to the futures contract accrues on the delivery date. The parity theorems we have derived apply strictly to forward pricing because they are predicated on the assumption that contract proceeds are realized only on delivery. Although this treatment is appropriate for a forward contract, the actual timing of cash flows influences the determination of the futures price.

Futures prices will deviate from parity values when marking to market gives a systematic advantage to either the long or short position. If marking to market tends to favour the long position, for example, the futures price should exceed the forward price, since the long position will be willing to pay a premium for the advantage of marking to market.

When will marking to market favour either the long or short trader? A trader will benefit if daily settlements are received when the interest rate is high and paid when the interest rate is low. Receiving payments when the interest rate is high allows investment of proceeds at a high rate; traders therefore prefer a high correlation between the level of the interest rate and the payments received from marking to market. The long position will benefit if futures prices tend to rise when interest rates are high. In such circumstances, the long trader will be willing to accept a higher futures price. Whenever there is a positive correlation between interest rates and changes in futures prices, the "fair" futures price will exceed the forward price. Conversely, a negative correlation means that marking to market favours the short position and implies that the equilibrium futures price should be below the forward price.

For most contracts, it appears that the covariance between futures prices and interest rates is low enough so that futures prices and forward prices differ by negligible amounts. Contracts on long-term fixed-income securities, however, may exhibit a significant spread between forward and futures prices because prices have a high correlation with interest rates.

S&P's Institutional Market Services www.compustat.com

On the other hand, the difference between futures prices and forward prices also is influenced by transaction costs. For a forward contract, any violation of the spot-futures parity theorem can be exploited by a simple buy-and-hold portfolio strategy. The marking-to-market feature of the futures contract, on the other hand, implies that the corresponding strategy for such contracts must be dynamic, involving many more purchases and sales of the assets in the portfolio. These activities may raise total transaction costs to the point of eliminating the arbitrage profits. In such cases, the parity relationship may be violated, even though no profitable arbitrage may be feasible.

19.5 COMMODITY FUTURES PRICING

In commodity futures the cost of carrying is greater than for financial assets, especially for items subject to spoilage. Moreover, spot prices for some commodities demonstrate marked seasonal patterns that can affect futures pricing.

Pricing with Storage Costs

The cost of carrying commodities includes (in addition to interest costs) storage costs, insurance costs, and an allowance for spoilage of goods in storage. To price commodity futures, let us reconsider the earlier arbitrage strategy that calls for holding both the asset and a short position in the futures contract on the asset. In this case, we will denote the price of the commodity at time T as P_T, and assume for simplicity that all noninterest carrying costs (C) are paid in one lump sum at time T, the contract maturity. Carrying costs appear in the final cash flow.

Action	Initial Cash Flow	Cash Flow at Time T
Buy asset; pay carrying costs at T	$-P_0$	$P_T - C$
Borrow P_0; repay with interest at time T	P_0	$-P_0(1 + r_f)$
Short futures position	0	$F_0 - P_T$
Total	0	$F_0 - P_0(1 + r_f) - C$

Because market prices should not allow for arbitrage opportunities, the terminal cash flow of this zero net investment, risk-free strategy should be zero.

If the cash flow were positive, this strategy would yield guaranteed profits for no investment. If the cash flow were negative, the reverse of this strategy also would yield profits. In practice, the reverse strategy would involve a short sale of the commodity. This is unusual but may be done as long as the short sale contract appropriately accounts for storage costs.[8] Thus we conclude that

$$F_0 = P_0(1 + r_f) + C$$

[8]Robert A. Jarrow and George S. Oldfield, "Forward Contracts and Futures Contracts," *Journal of Financial Economics* 9 (1981).

Finally, if we call $c = C/P_0$, and interpret c as the percentage "rate" of carrying costs, we may write

$$F_0 = P_0(1 + r_f + c) \tag{19.4}$$

which is a (one-year) parity relationship for futures involving storage costs. Compare equation 19.4 to the first parity relationship for stocks, equation 19.2, and you will see that they are extremely similar. In fact, if we think of carrying costs as a "negative dividend," the equations are identical. This treatment makes intuitive sense because, instead of receiving a dividend yield of *d*, the storer of the commodity must pay a storage cost of *c*. Obviously, this parity relationship is simply an extension of those we have seen already.

It is vital to note that we derive equation 19.4 assuming that the asset will be bought and stored; it therefore applies only to goods that currently *are* being stored. Two kinds of commodities cannot be expected to be stored. The first kind is commodities such as electricity or highly perishable goods, for which storage is technologically not feasible. The second includes goods that are not stored for economic reasons. For example, it would be foolish to buy wheat now, planning to store it for ultimate use in three years. Instead, it is clearly preferable to delay the purchase of the wheat until after the harvest of the third year. The wheat is then obtained without incurring the storage costs. Moreover, if the wheat harvest in the third year is comparable to this year's, you could obtain it at roughly the same price as you would pay this year. By waiting to purchase, you avoid both interest and storage costs.

In fact, it is generally not reasonable to hold large quantities of agricultural goods across a harvesting period. Why pay to store this year's wheat, when you can purchase next year's wheat when it is harvested? Maintaining large wheat inventories across harvests makes sense only if such a small wheat crop is forecast that wheat prices will not fall when the new supply is harvested.

CONCEPT CHECK

6. People are willing to buy and "store" shares of stock despite the fact that their purchase ties up capital. Most people, however, are not willing to buy and store wheat. What is the difference in the properties of the expected evolution of stock prices versus wheat prices that accounts for this result?

Because storage across harvests is costly, equation 19.4 should not be expected to apply for holding periods that span harvest times, nor should it apply to perishable goods that are available only "in season." You can see that this is so if you look at the U.S. futures markets page of the newspaper. Figure 19.6, for example, gives futures prices for several times to maturity for soybeans and for gold. Whereas the futures price for gold, which is a stored commodity, increases steadily

Figure 19.6 Futures prices for corn and gold.

Soybeans (CBOT)

5,000 bushels, US cents per contract; 1/4 cent = $12.50 per contract

9998.000	515.500	May04	988.000	1014.000	987.000	1013.000	+21.500	2,130
1064.000	517.500	July04	965.000	985.000	962.000	982.500	+10.250	135,682
1024.000	521.000	Aug04	905.000	919.500	901.000	917.750	+13.250	20,457
904.500	522.000	Sept04	786.000	794.000	778.500	792.500	+9.500	11,902
799.000	483.000	Nov04	733.000	740.500	725.000	736.000	+5.500	55,658
799.000	572.000	Jan05	736.000	741.000	730.000	738.500	+6.000	4,225
787.000	550.000	Mar05	730.000	733.000	725.000	732.000	+6.500	2,952
776.000	636.000	May05	715.000	721.000	712.000	717.000	+5.750	1,274

Prev. vol. 126,527 Prev. open int. 235,582

METAL

Gold (COMEX)

100 troy ozs., US$ per troy oz.; 10 cents = $10 per contract

433.00	287.00	June04	378.90	379.20	373.00	374.90	-2.80	153,234
433.00	324.70	Aug04	379.60	380.00	374.00	375.90	-2.80	24,624
432.00	332.00	Oct04	380.70	381.00	376.20	377.00	-2.80	6,411
436.50	290.00	Dec04	382.00	382.60	376.00	378.30	-2.80	30,837
435.00	331.50	Feb05	379.00	379.00	379.00	379.70	-2.90	3,079
437.50	380.70	Apr05	...	...	...	381.20	-3.00	3,471
436.60	302.00	June05	...	...	...	382.90	-3.10	13,433
414.00	379.00	Aug05	...	...	...	384.80	-3.30	1,888
441.50	298.40	Dec05	389.00	392.50	388.00	388.80	-3.70	6,470
447.00	312.00	June06	...	...	...	396.10	-4.00	6,325
450.50	338.00	Dec06	405.00	405.00	405.00	404.30	-4.10	1,815
450.00	367.00	June07	...	...	...	413.30	-3.90	1,141
467.00	368.00	Dec07	...	...	...	422.70	-3.90	1,246

Prev. vol. 62,082 Prev. open int. 255,488

Source: *The Financial Post*, May 14, 2004. Reprinted by permission.

with the maturity of the contract, the futures price for soybeans is seasonal; it rises within a harvest period as equation 19.4 would predict, but the price then falls across harvests as new supplies become available.

Futures pricing across seasons requires a different approach that is not based on storage across harvest periods. In place of general no-arbitrage restrictions we rely instead on risk premium theory and discounted cash flow (DCF) analysis.

Discounted Cash Flow Analysis for Commodity Futures

We have said that most agricultural commodities follow seasonal price patterns; prices rise before a harvest and then fall at the harvest when the new crop becomes available for consumption. Figure 19.7 graphs this pattern. The price of the commodity following the harvest must rise at the rate of the total cost of carry (interest plus noninterest carrying costs) to induce holders of the commodity to store it willingly for future sale instead of selling it immediately. Inventories will be run down to near zero just before the next harvest.

Clearly, this pattern differs sharply from financial assets, such as stocks or gold, for which there is no seasonal price movement. For financial assets, the current price is set in market equilibrium at a level that promises an expected rate of capital gains plus dividends equal to the required rate of return on the asset. Financial assets are stored only if their economic rate of return compensates for the cost of carry. In other words, financial assets are priced so that storing them produces a fair return. Agricultural prices, by contrast, are subject to steep periodic drops as each crop is harvested, which makes storage across harvests consequently unprofitable.

Of course, neither the exact size of the harvest nor the demand for the good is known in advance, so the spot price of the commodity cannot be perfectly predicted. As weather forecasts change, for example, the expected size of the crop and the expected future spot price of the commodity are updated continually.

Given the current expectation of the spot price of the commodity at some future date and a measure of the risk characteristics of that price, we can measure the present value of a claim to receive the commodity at that future date. We simply calculate the appropriate risk premium from

Figure 19.7 Typical commodity price pattern over the season. Prices adjusted for inflation.

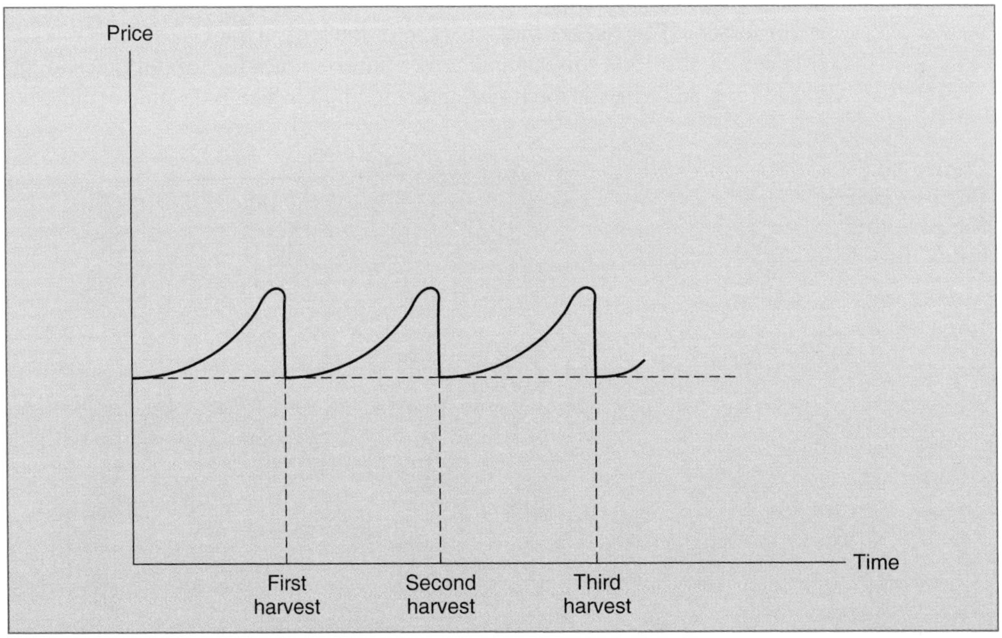

a model such as the CAPM or APT and discount the expected spot price at the appropriate risk-adjusted interest rate.

EXAMPLE 19.7 Commodity Futures Pricing

Table 19.2, which presents betas on a variety of commodities, shows that the beta of orange juice, for example, was estimated to be .117 over the period. If the T-bill rate is currently 5.5 percent, and the historical market risk premium has been about 8.5 percent, the appropriate discount rate for orange juice would be given by the CAPM as

$$5.5\% + .117(8.5\%) = 6.49\%$$

If the expected spot price for orange juice six months from now is $1.45 per pound, the present value of a six-month deferred claim to a pound of orange juice is simply

$$\$1.45/(1.0649)^{1/2} = \$1.405$$

What would the proper futures price for orange juice be? The contract calls for the ultimate exchange of orange juice for the futures price. We have just shown that the present value of the juice is $1.405. This should equal the present value of the futures price that will be paid for the juice. A commitment to a payment of F_0 dollars in six months has a present value of $F_0/(1.055)^{1/2} = .974 \times F_0$.

Table 19.2 Commodity Betas

Commodity	Beta
Wheat	−0.370
Corn	−0.429
Oats	0.000
Soybeans	−0.266
Soybean oil	−0.650
Soybean meal	0.239
Broilers	−1.692
Plywood	0.660
Potatoes	−0.610
Platinum	0.221
Wool	0.307
Cotton	−0.015
Orange juice	0.117
Propane	−3.851
Coca	−0.291
Silver	−0.272
Copper	0.005
Cattle	0.365
Hogs	−0.148
Pork bellies	−0.062
Eggs	−0.293
Lumber	−0.131
Sugar	−2.403

Source: Zvi Bodie and Victor Rosansky, "Risk and Return in Commodity Futures," *Financial Analysts Journal* 36 (May/June 1980). © 1980, Association for Investment Management and Research. Reproduced and republished from Financial Analysts Federation with permission from AIMR. All rights reserved.

(Note that the discount rate is the risk-free rate of 5.5 percent, because the promised payment is fixed and therefore independent of market conditions.)

To equate the present values of the promised payment of F_0 and the promised receipt of orange juice, we would set

$$.974F_0 = \$1.405$$

or

$$F_0 = \$1.443$$

The general rule, then, to determine the appropriate futures price is to equate the present value of the future payment of F0 and the present value of the commodity to be received. This gives us

$$\frac{F_0}{(1 + r_f)^T} = \frac{E(P_T)}{(1 + k)^T}$$

or

$$F_0 = E(P_T)\left(\frac{1 + r_f}{1 + k}\right)^T \qquad (19.5)$$

where k is the required rate of return on the commodity, which may be obtained from a model of asset market equilibrium such as the CAPM.

Note that equation 19.5 is perfectly consistent with the spot-futures parity relationship. For example, apply equation 19.5 to the futures price for a stock paying no dividends. Because the entire return on the stock is in the form of capital gains, the expected rate of capital gains must equal k, the required rate of return on the stock. Consequently, the expected price of the stock will be its current price times $(1 + k)^T$, or $E(P_T) = P_0(1 + k)^T$. Substituting this expression into equation 19.5 results in $F_0 = P_0(1 + r_f)^T$, which is exactly the parity relationship. This equilibrium derivation of the parity relationship simply reinforces the no-arbitrage restrictions we derived earlier. The spot-futures parity relationship may be obtained from the equilibrium condition that all portfolios earn fair expected rates of return.

The advantage of the arbitrage proofs that we have explored is that they do not rely on the validity of any particular model of security market equilibrium. The absence of arbitrage opportunities is a much more robust basis for argument than the CAPM, for example. Moreover, arbitrage proofs clearly demonstrate how an investor can exploit any misalignment in the spot-future relationship. To their disadvantage, arbitrage restrictions may be less precise than desirable in the face of storage costs or costs of short selling.

We can summarize by saying that the actions of arbitrageurs force the futures prices of financial assets to maintain a precise relationship with the price of the underlying financial asset.[9] This relationship is described by the spot-futures parity formula. Opportunities for arbitrage are more limited in the case of commodity futures, because such commodities often are not stored. Hence, to make a precise prediction for the correct relationship between futures and spot prices, we must rely on a model of security market equilibrium, such as the CAPM or APT, and estimate the unobservables, the expected spot price, and the appropriate rate of return. Such models will be perfectly consistent with the parity relationships in the benchmark case where investors willingly store the commodity.

? CONCEPT CHECK

7. Suppose that the systematic risk of orange juice were to increase, holding the expected time T price of juice constant. If the expected spot price is unchanged, would the futures price change? In what direction? What is the intuition behind your answer?

---

[9]Recall, however, the qualifications to this statement mentioned at the end of Sections 19.4 and 19.6.

Futures Prices Versus Expected Spot Prices

The above analysis sheds light upon one of the oldest controversies in the theory of futures pricing: the relationship between the futures price and the expected value of the spot price of the commodity at some *future* date. Three traditional theories have been put forth: the expectations hypothesis, normal backwardation, and contango. Today's consensus is that all of these traditional hypotheses are subsumed by the insights provided by modern portfolio theory. Figure 19.8 shows the expected path of futures prices under the three traditional hypotheses.

Expectations Hypothesis

The *expectations hypothesis* is the simplest theory of futures pricing. It states that the futures price equals the expected value of the future spot price of the asset: $F_0 = E(P_T)$. Under this theory, the expected profit to either position of a futures contract would equal zero: the short position's expected profit is $F_0 - E(P_T)$, while the long's is $E(P_T) - F_0$. With $F_0 = E(P_T)$, the expected profit to either side is zero. This hypothesis relies on a notion of risk neutrality. If all market participants are risk-neutral, they should agree on a futures price that provides an expected profit of zero to all parties.

The expectations hypothesis bears a resemblance to market equilibrium in a world with no uncertainty; that is, if prices of goods at all future dates are currently known, then the futures price for delivery at any particular date would simply equal the currently known future spot price for that date. It is a tempting but incorrect leap to assert next that under uncertainty the futures price should equal the currently expected spot price. This view ignores the risk premiums that must be built into futures prices when ultimate spot prices are uncertain.

Figure 19.8 Futures price over time in the special case that the expected spot price remains unchanged.

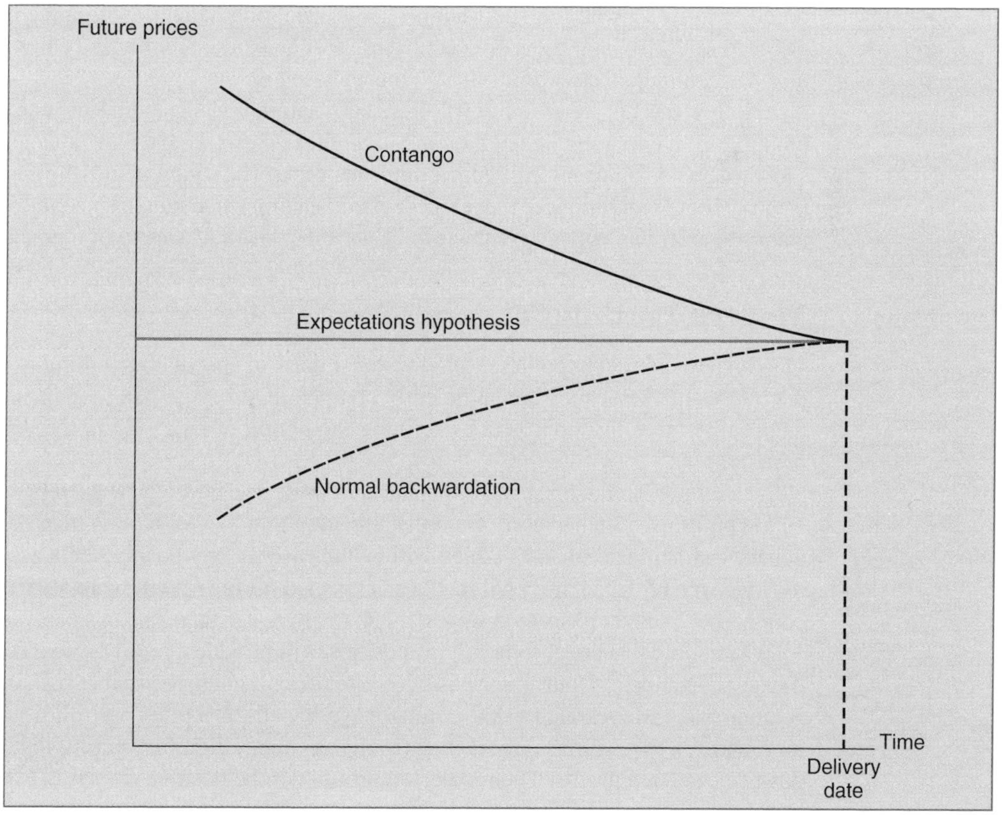

Normal Backwardation

This theory is associated with the famous British economists, John Maynard Keynes and John Hicks. They argued that for most commodities there are natural hedgers who desire to shed risk. For example, wheat farmers will desire to shed the risk of uncertain wheat prices. These farmers will take short positions to deliver wheat in the future at a guaranteed price; they will short hedge. In order to induce speculators to take the corresponding long positions, the farmers need to offer them an expectation of profit. Speculators will enter the long side of the contract only if the futures price is below the expected spot price of wheat, for an expected profit of $E(P_T) - F_0$. The speculator's expected profit is the farmer's expected loss, but farmers are willing to bear the expected loss on the contract in order to shed the risk of uncertain wheat prices. The theory of *normal backwardation* thus suggests that the futures price will be bid down to a level below the expected spot price and will rise over the life of the contract until the maturity date, at which point $F_T = P_T$.

Although this theory recognizes the important role of risk premiums in futures markets, it is based on total variability rather than on systematic risk. (This is not surprising, as Keynes wrote almost 40 years before the development of modern portfolio theory.) The modern view refines the measure of risk used to determine appropriate risk premiums.

Contango

The polar hypothesis to backwardation holds that the natural hedgers are the purchasers of a commodity, rather than the suppliers. In the case of wheat, for example, we would view grain processors as willing to pay a premium to lock in the price that they must pay for wheat. These processors hedge by taking a long position in the futures market; they are long hedgers, as opposed to farmers, who are short hedgers. Because long hedgers will agree to pay high futures prices to shed risk, and because speculators must be paid a premium to enter into the short position, the *contango* theory holds that F_0 must exceed $E(P_T)$.

It is clear that any commodity will have both natural long hedgers and short hedgers. The compromise traditional view, called the *net hedging hypothesis,* is that F_0 will be less than $E(P_T)$ when short hedgers outnumber long hedgers, and vice versa. The strong side of the market will be the side (short or long) that has more natural hedgers. The strong side must pay a premium to induce speculators to enter into enough contracts to balance the "natural" supply of long and short hedgers.

Modern Portfolio Theory

The three traditional hypotheses all envision a mass of speculators willing to enter either side of the futures market if they are sufficiently compensated for the risk they incur. Modern portfolio theory fine-tunes this approach by refining the notion of risk used in the determination of risk premiums.

As we saw, futures price and expected spot price at a future date are related through equation 19.5. You can see immediately from that equation that F_0 will be less than the expectation of P_T whenever k is greater than r_f, which will be the case for any positive-beta asset. This means that the long side of the contract will make an expected profit (F_0 will be lower than $E(P_T)$) when the commodity exhibits positive systematic risk (k is greater than r_f).

Why should this be? A long futures position will provide a profit (or loss) of $P_T - F_0$. If the ultimate realization of P_T involves positive systematic or nondiversifiable risk, the profit to the long position also involves such risk. Speculators with well-diversified portfolios will be willing to enter long futures positions only if they receive compensation for bearing that risk in the form of positive expected profits. Their expected profits will be positive only if $E(P_T)$ is greater than F_0.

The converse is that the short position's profit is the negative of the long's and will have negative systematic risk. Diversified investors in the short position will be willing to suffer an expected loss in order to lower portfolio risk and will be willing to enter the contract even when F_0 is less than $E(P_T)$. Therefore, if P_T has positive beta, F_0 must be less than the expectation of P_T. The analysis is reversed for negative-beta commodities.

CONCEPT CHECK

8. What must be true of the risk of the spot price of an asset if the futures price is an unbiased estimate of the ultimate spot price?

19.6 STOCK INDEX FUTURES

The Contracts

In contrast to most futures contracts, which call for delivery of a specified commodity, stock index contracts are settled by a cash amount equal to the value of the stock index in question on the contract maturity date times a multiplier that scales the size of the contract. The total profit to the long position is $S_T - F_0$, where S_T is the value of the stock index on the maturity date. Cash settlement avoids the costs that would be incurred if the short trader had to purchase the stocks in the index and deliver them to the long position, and if the long position then had to sell the stock for cash. Instead, the long trader's profit is $S_T - F_0$ dollars, and the short trader's is $F_0 - S_T$ dollars. These profits duplicate those that would arise with actual delivery.

As noted earlier, there are several index futures contracts currently trading in Canada, including the S&P/TSX 60, which trades in the Montreal Exchange (ME) with a multiplier equal to $200. Several sectoral index futures, the Info Tech, Financial, Energy, and Gold Index futures, also trade in the ME. In the United States there are many more stock index futures contracts currently traded. Table 19.3 lists the major ones, showing under contract size the multiplier used to calculate contract settlements. An S&P 500 contract, for example, with a futures price of 1,300 and a final index value of 1,305 would result in a profit for the long side of $250 × (1,305 – 1,300) = $1,250.

www.me.org

The broad-based U.S. stock market indices are all highly correlated. Table 19.4 presents a correlation matrix for four indices. The lowest correlation is .944.

Creating Synthetic Stock Positions: An Asset Allocation Tool

One reason why stock index futures are so popular is that they substitute for holdings in the underlying stocks themselves. Index futures let investors participate in broad market movements without actually buying or selling large numbers of stocks.

Because of this, we say futures represent "synthetic" holdings of the market portfolio. Instead of holding the market directly, the investor takes a long futures position in the index. Such a strategy is attractive because the transaction costs involved in establishing and liquidating futures positions are much lower than taking actual spot positions. Investors who wish to frequently buy and sell market positions find it much less costly to play the futures market rather than the underlying spot market. "Market timers," who speculate on broad market moves rather than on individual securities, are large players in stock index futures for this reason.

One means to market time, for example, is to shift between Treasury bills and broad-based stock market holdings. Timers attempt to shift from bills into the market before market upturns and to shift back into bills to avoid market downturns, thereby profiting from broad market movements.

Table 19.3 Major Stock-Index Futures

Contract	Underlying Market Index	Contract Size	Exchange
S&P 500	Standard & Poor's 500 index; a value-weighted arithmetic average of 500 stocks	$250 times the S&P 500 index	Chicago Mercantile Exchange
Dow Jones Industrial Average	Dow Jones Industrial Average; price-weighted average of 30 firms	$10 times the index	Chicago Board of Trade
Russell 2000	Index of 2,000 smaller firms	$500 times the index	Chicago Mercantile Exchange
S&P Mid-Cap	Index of 400 firms of midrange market value	$500 times the index	Chicago Mercantile Exchange
Nasdaq 100	Value-weighted arithmetic average of 100 of the largest over-the-counter stocks	$100 times the index	Chicago Mercantile Exchange
Nikkei	Nikkei 225 stock average	$5 times the Nikkei Index	Chicago Mercantile Exchange
FT-SE 100	Financial Times–Share Exchange Index of 100 U.K. firms	£10 times the FT-SE Index	London International Financial Futures Exchange
DAX-30	Index of 30 German stocks	25 Euros times the index	Eurex
CAC-40	Index of 40 French stocks	10 Euros times the index	MATIF (*Marché à Terme International de France*)
DJ Euro Stoxx 50	Index of blue-chip Euro-zone stocks	10 Euros times the index	Eurex

Market timing of this sort, however, can result in huge brokerage fees with the frequent purchase and sale of many stocks. An attractive alternative is to invest in Treasury bills and hold varying amounts of market index futures contracts.

The strategy works like this: When timers are bullish, they will establish many long futures positions that they can liquidate quickly and cheaply when expectations turn bearish. Rather than shifting back and forth between T-bills and stocks, they buy and hold T-bills, and adjust only the futures position. This minimizes transaction costs. An advantage of this technique for timing is that investors can implicitly buy or sell the market index in its entirety, whereas market timing in the spot market would require the simultaneous purchase or sale of all the stocks in the index. This is technically difficult to coordinate and can lead to slippage in execution of a timing strategy.

You can construct a T-bill plus index futures position that duplicates the payoff to holding the

Table 19.4 Correlations Among Major U.S. Stock Market Indices

	S&P	NYSE	Nasdaq	DJIA
S&P	1	0.988	0.980	0.992
NYSE		1	0.944	0.994
Nasdaq			1	0.960
DJIA				1

Note: Correlations were computed from monthly percentage rates of price appreciation between 1992 and 1999.

stock index itself. Here is how:

1. Hold as many market index futures contracts long as you need to purchase your desired stock position. A desired holding of $1,000 multiplied by the S&P/TSX 60 index, for example, would require the purchase of five contracts because each contract calls for delivery of $200 multiplied by the index.
2. Invest enough money in T-bills to cover the payment of the futures price at the contract's maturity date. The necessary investment will equal the present value of the futures price that will be paid to satisfy the contracts. The T-bill holdings will grow by the maturity date to a level equal to the futures price.

EXAMPLE 19.8 Synthetic Positions Using Stock Index Futures

Suppose that an institutional investor wants to invest $40 million in the Canadian equity market for one month and, to minimize trading costs, chooses to buy the S&P/TSX 60 futures contract as a substitute for actual stock holdings. If the index is now at 400, the one-month delivery futures price is 404, and the T-bill rate is 1 percent per month, the investor would buy 500 contracts. (Each contract controls $200 × 400 = $80,000 worth of stock, and $40 million/$80,000 = 500.) The institution thus has a long position of 100,000 × the S&P/TSX 60 index (500 contracts × the contract multiplier of $200). To cover payment of the futures price, it must invest 100,000 × the present value of the futures price in T-bills. This equals 100,000 × (404/1.01) = $40 million market value of bills. Notice that the $40 million outlay in bills is precisely equal to the amount that would have been needed to buy the stock directly. The bills will increase in value in one month to $40.4 million.

This is an artificial, or synthetic, stock position. What is the value of this portfolio at the maturity date? Call S_T the value of the stock index on the maturity date T, and, as usual, let F_0 be the original futures price:

	In General (per unit of the index)	Our Numbers
1. Profits from contract	$(S_T - F_0)$	$100{,}000(S_T - 404)$
2. Value of T-bills	F_0	40,400,000
Total	S_T	$100{,}000S_T$

The total payoff on the contract maturity date is exactly proportional to the value of the stock index. In other words, adopting this portfolio strategy is equivalent to holding the stock index itself, aside from the issue of interim dividend distributions and tax treatment.

The bills-plus-futures strategy may be viewed as a 100 percent stock strategy. At the other extreme, investing in zero futures results in a 100 percent bills position. Moreover, a short futures position will result in a portfolio equivalent to that obtained by short selling the stock market index, because in both cases the investor gains from decreases in the stock price. Bills-plus-futures mixtures clearly allow for a flexible and low transaction-cost approach to market timing. The futures positions may be established or reversed quickly and cheaply. Also, since the short futures position allows the investor to earn interest on T-bills, it is superior to a conventional short sale of the stock, where the investor typically earns no interest on the proceeds of the short sale.

CONCEPT CHECK

9. As the payoffs of the synthetic and actual stock positions are identical, so should be the costs. What does this say about the spot-futures parity relationship?

MAXIMIZING YOUR GLOBAL EXPOSURE

Foreign stock markets can offer Canadian investors diversification, exposure to successful international companies or emerging economies and wide stock selection opportunities.

This is particularly true for RRSP investors who wish to maximize their long-term retirement savings and broaden their base for portfolio growth.

But the global equity market is a big place, with Canada making up just over 2 per cent of world stock markets. And finding the right international investment is not as easy as booking an airline ticket.

Even if you could identify which foreign market provides the best growth potential, you must then determine which companies or stocks within the local economy will deliver good returns.

An easier route can be to choose mutual funds based on equity market index futures. These futures directly reflect the price movement of the chosen country's market index. A fund composed of these futures, when fully backed by treasury bills, essentially tracks the performance of the country's primary equity market, like the TSE 300, the S&P 500 in the United States or the FTSE 100 in London.

By doing so, investors can at least obtain investment returns that are very similar to the stock markets the fund mimics.

Index futures have become widely used by major pension fund managers who have the large sums to purchase the appropriate basket of futures contracts.

Today, futures are available to individual investors in the form of mutual funds for as little as $500, or less through frequent purchase plans.

Index futures mutual funds can be of particular interest to RRSP investors. Revenue Canada requires investors to limit their foreign holdings to 20 per cent of their total RRSP portfolio but futures contracts have almost a zero cost base for tax purposes.

By using Canadian treasury bills to fully back their commitments to futures contracts on foreign market indexes, the funds' investment dollars are considered "Canadian content" and are thus 100 per cent RRSP eligible. In fact, these mutual funds are best held inside an RRSP for tax reasons, since your total return is taxed as interest income.

Another benefit of index futures funds is that they typically have below-average management costs. Since they purchase a limited number of futures contracts rather than numerous individual stocks, trading, custody and management costs tend to be lower and these savings can be passed on to investors.

Some people might describe the use of equity index futures to be "passive" investing, since it seeks to track the index and not outperform it, as the "active" stock-picking within the market.

But buying a basket of global indexes doesn't have to be passive. If you're a confident, sophisticated investor with the time and knowledge to research the markets, you might take a more active approach by carefully acquiring a number of equity index futures mutual funds representing various geographic regions, and periodically reweight them according to their expected market performance.

Alternatively, some funds offer investment vehicles where the amounts allocated to each region or country are strategically adjusted by a professional manager.

As in all prudent investment strategies, investors should diversify their total portfolio to match investment needs and risk tolerance.

Whether you take an active approach to equity index futures investing or, as with many RRSP investors, employ index futures funds as a way to boost your international market exposure, these innovative funds can be an important part of a well-balanced portfolio.

Source: Colin Carlton, *The Globe and Mail*, February 20, 1999, p. C9. Reprinted with permission of Colin G. Carlton, Chief Investment Officer, Canada Trust Investment Management Group.

The boxed article here illustrates the use of futures contracts to create synthetic equity positions in stock markets. The article notes the advantages to RRSP investors of using Canadian T-bills in combination with futures contracts on foreign market indices.

Empirical Evidence on Pricing of Stock Index Futures

Recall equation 19.2, the spot-futures parity relationship between the futures and spot stock price:

$$F_0 = S_0(1 + r_f - d)^T$$

Several investigators have tested this relationship empirically. The general procedure has been to calculate the theoretically appropriate futures price using the current value of the stock index and equation 19.2. The dividend yield of the index in question is approximated using historical data. Although dividends of individual securities may fluctuate unpredictably, the annualized dividend yield of a broad-based index such as the S&P 500 is fairly stable, recently in the neighbourhood of 1.5 percent per year. The yield is seasonal with regular and predictable peaks and troughs, however, so the dividend yield for the relevant months must be the one used. Figure 19.9 illustrates the dividend yield of the S&P 500 index from 1997 to 2001.

Figure 19.9 Monthly dividend yield of the S&P 500.

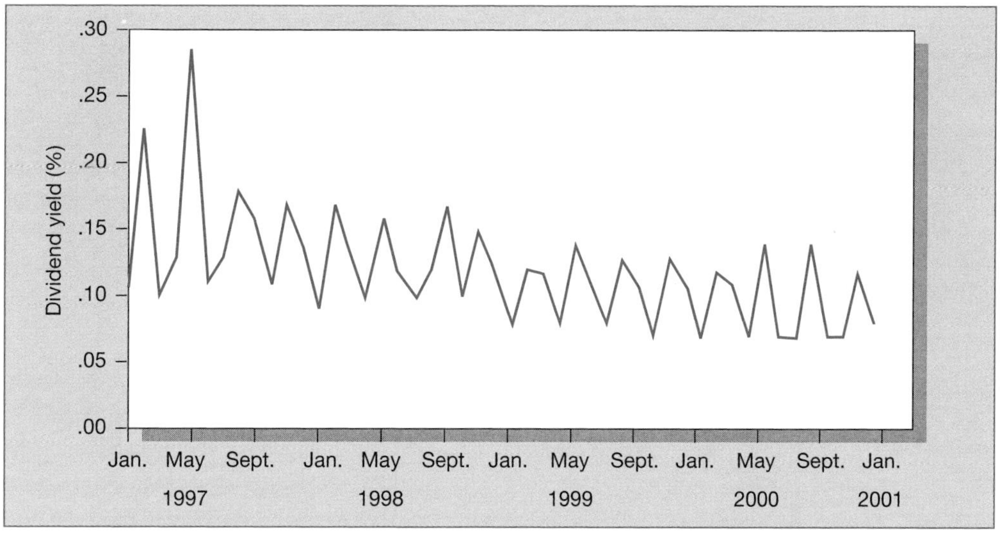

If the actual futures price deviates from the value dictated by the parity relationship, then (forgetting transaction costs) an arbitrage opportunity arises. Given an estimate of transaction costs, we can bracket the theoretically correct futures price within a band. If the actual futures price lies within that band, the discrepancy between the actual and the proper futures prices is too small to exploit because of the transaction costs; if the actual price lies outside the no-arbitrage band, profit opportunities are worth exploiting.

Modest and Sundaresan[10] constructed such a test using the April and June 1982 S&P 500 contracts. Figure 19.10 replicates an example of their results. The figure shows that the futures prices generally did lie in the theoretically determined no-arbitrage band, but that profit opportunities occasionally were possible for low-cost transactors.

Modest and Sundaresan point out that much of the cost of short-selling shares is attributable to the investor's inability to invest the entire proceeds from the short sale. Proceeds must be left

Figure 19.10 Prices of S&P 500 contracts maturing June 1982. Data plotted for April 21–June 16, 1982.

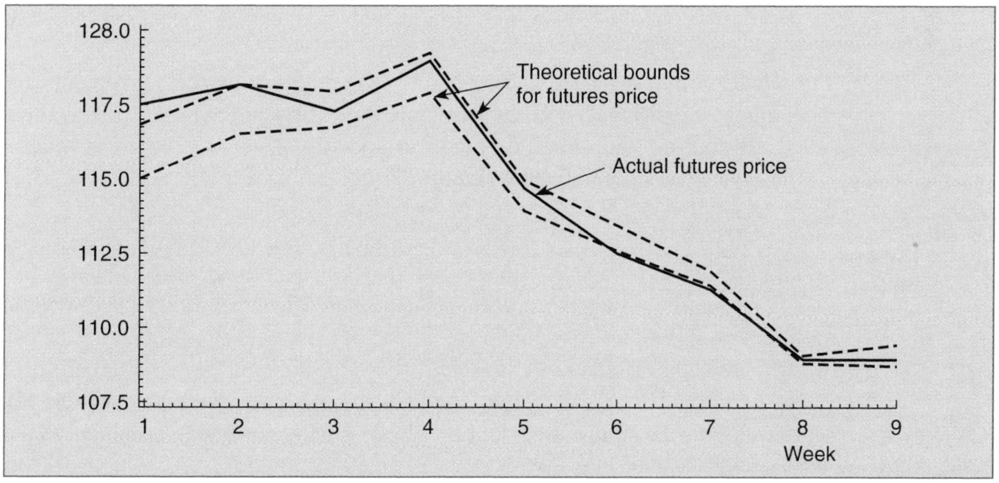

Source: David Modest and Mahadevan Sundaresan, "The Relationship Between Spot and Futures Prices in Stock Index Futures Markets: Some Preliminary Evidence," *Journal of Futures Markets* 3 (Spring 1983). © John Wiley & Sons, Inc., 1983. Reprinted by permission of The Globe and Mail.

[10]David Modest and Mahadevan Sundaresan, "The Relationship Between Spot and Futures Prices in Stock Index Futures Markets: Some Preliminary Evidence," *Journal of Futures Markets* 3 (Spring 1983).

on margin account, where they do not earn interest. Arbitrage opportunities, or the width of the no-arbitrage band, therefore depend upon assumptions regarding the use of short-sale proceeds. Figure 19.10 assumes that one-half of the proceeds are available to the short seller.

CONCEPT CHECK

10. What (if anything) would happen to the top of the no-arbitrage band if short-sellers could obtain full use of the proceeds from the short sale? What would happen to the low end of the band? (*Hint*: When do violations of parity call for a long futures–short stock position versus short futures–long stock position?)

Index Arbitrage and the Triple Witching Hour

Whenever the actual futures price falls outside the no-arbitrage band, there is an opportunity for profit. This is why the parity relationships are so important. Far from being theoretical academic constructs, they are in fact a guide to trading rules that can generate large profits. One of the most notable developments in trading activity has been the advent of **index arbitrage**, an investment strategy that exploits divergences between the actual futures price and its theoretically correct parity value.

In theory, index arbitrage is simple. If the futures price is too high, short the futures contract and buy the stocks in the index. If it is too low, go long in futures and short the stocks. You can perfectly hedge your position and should earn arbitrage profits equal to the mispricing of the contract.

In practice, however, index arbitrage can be difficult to implement. The problem lies in buying "the stocks in the index." Selling or purchasing shares in all stocks in an index is impractical for two reasons. The first is transaction costs, which may outweigh any profits to be made from the arbitrage. Second, it is extremely difficult to buy or sell stock of many different firms simultaneously, and any lags in the execution of such a strategy can destroy the effectiveness of a plan to exploit temporary price discrepancies.

Arbitrageurs need to trade an entire portfolio of stocks quickly and simultaneously if they hope to exploit disparities between the futures price and its corresponding stock index. For this they need a coordinated trading program; hence the term **program trading**, which refers to coordinated purchases or sales of entire portfolios of stocks. The response has been the designated order turnaround (DOT) system, which enables traders to send coordinated buy or sell programs to the floor of the stock exchange via computer.

Index arbitrage seems to have had its own effect on market movements. Four times a year, for example, the S&P/TSX 60 futures contract expires at the same time as the S&P/TSX 60 index option contract and option contracts on individual stocks. The great volatility of the market at these periods has led people to call the simultaneous expirations the **triple witching hour**.

Expiration-day volatility can be explained by program trading to exploit arbitrage opportunities. Suppose that before a stock index future contract matures, the futures price is a little above its parity value. Arbitrageurs will attempt to lock in superior profits by buying the stocks in the index (the program trading buy order) and taking an offsetting short futures position. If and when the pricing disparity reverses, the position can be unwound at a profit. Alternatively, arbitrageurs can wait until contract maturity day and realize a profit by closing out the offsetting stock and futures positions with "marked-on-close" orders, that is, closing out both positions at prices in the closing range of the day. By waiting until the close of the maturity day, arbitrageurs can be assured that the futures price and stock index price will be aligned—they rely on the convergence property.

Obviously, when many program traders follow such a strategy at market close, a wave of program selling passes over the market. The result? Prices go down. This is the expiration-day effect. If execution of the arbitrage strategy calls for a sale (or short sale) of stocks, unwinding on expiration day requires repurchase of the stocks, with the opposite effect: prices will increase.

The success of these arbitrage positions and associated program trades depends on only two things: the relative levels of spot and futures prices and synchronized trading in the two markets. Because arbitrageurs exploit disparities in futures and spot prices, absolute price levels are unimportant. This means that large buy or sell programs can hit the floor even if stock prices are at "fair" levels, that is, at levels consistent with fundamental information. The markets in individual stocks may not be sufficiently deep to absorb the arbitrage-based program trades without significant price movements, despite the fact that those trades are not informationally motivated.

In an investigation of expiration-day effects, Stoll and Whaley[11] found that the market is in fact more volatile at contract expirations. For example, the standard deviation of the last-hour return on the S&P 500 index is .641 on expirations of the S&P 500 futures contract, whereas it is only .211 on nonexpiration days. Interestingly, the last-hour volatility of non-S&P 500 stocks appears unaffected by expiration days, consistent with the hypothesis that the effect is related to program trading of the stocks in the index. In a subsequent study, however, these same authors found that any expiration-day effects detected in their sample were quite mild. Hence, index arbitrage probably does not have a major impact on stock prices, and any impact it does have appears to be short-lived.

19.7 FOREIGN EXCHANGE FUTURES

The Markets

Exchange rates between currencies vary continually and often quite substantially. This variability can be a source of concern for anyone involved in international business. A Canadian exporter who sells goods in England, for example, will be paid in British pounds, and the dollar value of those pounds depends on the exchange rate at the time payment is made. Until that date, the Canadian exporter is exposed to foreign exchange rate risk. This risk, however, is easily hedged through currency futures or forward markets.

The forward market in foreign exchange is fairly informal. It is simply a network of banks and brokers that allows customers to enter forward contracts to purchase or sell currency in the future at a currently agreed-upon rate of exchange. Unlike those in futures markets, these contracts are not standardized in a formal market setting. Instead, each is negotiated separately. Moreover, there is no marking to market as would occur in futures markets. The contracts call only for execution at the maturity date.

Chicago Mercantile Exchange www.cme.com

For currency futures, however, there are formal markets. As already noted, trading in such futures was introduced by the Montreal Exchange but did not meet with any success; by 1991, it had been eliminated. Elsewhere, however, currency futures markets were established by the Chicago Mercantile Exchange (International Monetary Market), or the London International Financial Futures Exchange. In these exchanges, contracts are standardized by size, and daily marking to market is observed. Moreover, there are standard clearing arrangements that allow traders to enter or reverse positions easily.

Figure 19.11 reproduces a listing of foreign exchange spot and forward rates from *The Globe and Mail.* The listing gives the number of both Canadian and U.S. dollars required to purchase some unit of foreign currency. Figure 19.12 reproduces futures listings from *The Financial Post,* which show the number of dollars needed to purchase a given unit of foreign currency. In Figure 19.9, both spot and forward exchange rates are listed for various delivery dates for several major

[11]Hans R. Stoll and Robert E. Whaley, "Program Trading and Expiration Day Effects," *Financial Analysts Journal*, March/April 1987; and "Expiration-Day Effects: What Has Changed?" *Financial Analysts Journal*, January/February 1991.

Figure 19.11 Foreign exchange listing.

FOREIGN EXCHANGE

Cross rates

	Canadian dollar	U.S. dollar	British pound	Japanese yen	Swiss franc	Euro
Canadian dollar	—	1.3731	2.4559	0.012252	1.0735	1.6492
U.S. dollar	0.7283	—	1.7886	0.008923	0.7818	1.2011
British pound	0.4072	0.5591	—	0.004989	0.4371	0.6715
Japanese yen	81.62	112.07	200.45	—	87.62	134.61
Swiss franc	0.9315	1.2791	2.2878	0.011413	—	1.5363
Euro	0.6064	0.8326	1.4891	0.007429	0.6509	—

Mid-market rates in Toronto at noon, May. 21, 2004. Prepared by BMO Nesbitt Burns, Capital Markets.

	$1 U.S. in Cdn. $=	$1 Cdn. in U.S. $=
U.S./Canada spot	1.3731	0.7283
1 month forward	1.3743	0.7276
2 months forward	1.3753	0.7271
3 months forward	1.3761	0.7267
6 months forward	1.3778	0.7258
12 months forward	1.3795	0.7249
3 years forward	1.3836	0.7228
5 years forward	1.3576	0.7366
7 years forward	1.3936	0.7176
10 years forward	1.3991	0.7147
Cdn. dollar in 2004: High	1.2683	0.7885
Low	1.4003	0.7141
Average	1.3327	0.7503

country	currency	Cdn.$ per unit	U.S.$ per unit
Britain	Pound	2.4559	1.7886
1 month forward		2.4510	1.7835
2 months forward		2.4461	1.7786
3 months forward		2.4410	1.7739
6 months forward		2.4248	1.7599
12 months forward		2.3952	1.7363
Europe	Euro	1.6492	1.2011
1 month forward		1.6493	1.2001
3 months forward		1.6492	1.1985
6 months forward		1.6497	1.1974
12 months forward		1.6525	1.1979
Japan	Yen	0.012252	0.008923
1 month forward		0.012275	0.008932
3 months forward		0.012321	0.008953
6 months forward		0.012395	0.008996
12 months forward		0.012567	0.009110
Algeria	Dinar	0.01976	0.0144
Antigua,Grenada &St.Lucia	EC.dollar	0.5143	0.3745
Argentina	Peso	0.46625	0.33956
Australia	Dollar	0.9624	0.7009

country	currency	Cdn. $ per unit	U.S. $ per unit
Austria	Euro	1.6492	1.2011
Bahamas	Dollar	1.3731	1.0000
Barbados	Dollar	0.6900	0.5025
Belgium	Euro	1.6492	1.2011
Bermuda	Dollar	1.3731	1.0000
Brazil	Real	0.4313	0.3141
Bulgaria	Lev	0.847227	0.6170
Chile	Peso	0.002139	0.001558
China	Renminbi	0.1659	0.1208
Cyprus	Pound	2.8149	2.0500
Czech Rep	Koruna	0.0518	0.0377
Denmark	Krone	0.2217	0.1615
Egypt	Pound	0.2216	0.1614
Fiji	Dollar	0.7658	0.5577
Finland	Euro	1.6492	1.2011
France	Euro	1.6492	1.2011
Germany	Euro	1.6492	1.2011
Greece	Euro	1.6492	1.2011
Hong Kong	Dollar	0.1763	0.1284
Hungary	Forint	0.00652	0.00474
Iceland	Krona	0.01879	0.01368
India	Rupee	0.03034	0.02209
Indonesia	Rupiah	0.000152	0.000110
Ireland	Euro	1.6492	1.2011
Israel	N Shekel	0.3001	0.2186
Italy	Euro	1.649200	1.201078
Jamaica	Dollar	0.02287	0.01665
Jordan	Dinar	1.9394	1.4124
Lebanon	Pound	0.000907	0.000661
Luxembourg	Euro	1.64920	1.20108
Malaysia	Ringgit	0.3614	0.2632
Mexico	N Peso	0.1189	0.0866
Netherlands	Euro	1.6492	1.2011
New Zealand	Dollar	0.8387	0.6108
Norway	Krone	0.2007	0.1462
Pakistan	Rupee	0.02382	0.01735

country	currency	Cdn. $ per unit	U.S. $ per unit
Panama	Balboa	1.3731	1.0000
Philippines	Peso	0.02457	0.01790
Poland	Zloty	0.3531	0.2571
Portugal	Euro	1.64920	1.20108
Romania	Leu	0.000041	0.000030
Russia	Ruble	0.047392	0.034515
Saudi Arabia	Riyal	0.3662	0.2667
Singapore	Dollar	0.8013	0.5836
Slovakia	Koruna	0.0410	0.0299
South Africa	Rand	0.2043	0.1488
South Korea	Won	0.001169	0.000851
Spain	Euro	1.64920	1.20108
Sudan	Dinar	0.00529	0.0038
Sweden	Krona	0.1819	0.1325
Switzerland	Franc	1.0735	0.7818
Taiwan	Dollar	0.04109	0.0299
Thailand	Baht	0.03374	0.0246
Trinidad, Tob	Dollar	0.2233	0.1626
Turkey	Lira	0.0000009	0.0000006
Venezuela	Bolivar	0.000717	0.00052
Zambia	Kwacha	0.000294	0.000214
Sp Draw Rt	S.D.R.	1.9966	1.4541

Closing rates

The U.S dollar closed at $1.3733 in terms of Canadian funds, up $0.0052 from Thursday. The pound sterling closed at $2.4564, up $0.0261.

In New York, the Canadian dollar closed down $0.0027 at $0.7282 in terms of U.S. funds. The pound sterling was up $0.0123 to $1.7887.

Source: *The Globe and Mail*, May 22, 2004. Reprinted by permission of The Globe and Mail.

currencies. The forward quotations always apply to delivery in 1 month, 3 months, 6 months, or 1 year. Thus, tomorrow's forward listings will apply to a maturity date one day later than today's listing. In contrast, the futures contracts mature in March, June, September, and December, and these four maturity days are the only dates each year when futures contracts settle.

Interest Rate Parity

As is true of stocks and stock futures, there is a spot-futures exchange rate relationship that will prevail in well-functioning markets. Should this so-called interest rate parity relationship be violated, arbitrageurs will be able to make risk-free profits in foreign exchange markets with zero net investment. Their actions will force futures and spot exchange rates back into alignment.

We can illustrate the **interest rate parity theorem** by using two currencies, the Canadian dollar and the British (U.K.) pound. Call E_0 the current exchange rate between the two currencies, that is, E_0 dollars are required to purchase one pound. F_0, the forward price, is the number

Figure 19.12
Foreign exchange futures.

—Lifetime—				—Daily—				Prev
High	Low	Mth	Open	High	Low	Settle	Chg	op.int
CURRENCY								
Australian Dollar (IMM)								
A$100,000, US$ per A$; 0.0001 = $10 per contract								
0.7875	0.5645	June04	0.6833	0.6970	0.6820	0.6862	-0.0072	35,912
0.7780	0.5756	Sept04	0.6762	0.6880	0.6760	0.6792	-0.0071	1,177
Est. vol. 1,169		Prev. vol. 9,508			Prev. open int. 37,316			
British Pound (IMM)								
62,500 pounds, US$ per pound; 0.0002 = $12.50 per contract								
1.8946	1.6080	June04	1.7599	1.7698	1.7523	1.7572	-0.0107	44,530
Est. vol. 2,349		Prev. vol. 18,613			Prev. open int. 45,365			
Canadian Dollar (IMM)								
C$100,000, US$ per C$; 0.0001 = $10 per contract								
0.7850	0.6201	June04	0.7178	0.7210	0.7140	0.7179	-0.0014	77,583
0.7815	0.6505	Sept04	0.7172	0.7187	0.7130	0.7167	-0.0014	5,291
0.7800	0.6940	Dec04	0.7162	0.7162	0.7124	0.7161	-0.0014	3,730
0.7775	0.7150	Mar05	...	...	0.7150	0.7156	-0.0014	383
0.7760	0.7150	June05	...	0.7155	0.7150	0.7152	-0.0014	152
Est. vol. 4,748		Prev. vol. 11,498			Prev. open int. 87,177			
European Currency (CME)								
125,000 ECUs, US$ per unit; 0.0001 = $12.50 per contract								
1.2875	1.0570	June04	1.1816	1.1919	1.1760	1.1811	-0.0087	130,577
1.2800	1.0500	Sept04	1.1809	1.1890	1.1744	1.1790	-0.0087	1,213
Est. vol. 13,508		Prev. vol. 71,700			Prev. open int. 132,375			
Japanese Yen (IMM)								
12.5 million yen, US$ per yen (scaled .00); 0.0001 = $12.50 per contract								
0.9695	0.8496	June04	0.8755	0.8872	0.8730	0.8740	-0.0100	107,546
Est. vol. 6,624		Prev. vol. 21,159			Prev. open int. 108,536			
Mexican Peso (IMM)								
500,000 new pesos, US$ per peso; 0.000025 = $12.50 per contract								
0.0913	0.0848	June04	0.0855	0.0859	0.0854	0.0855	-0.0001	62,219
0.0894	0.0837	Sept04	0.0843	0.0843	0.0842	0.0842	-0.0001	1,245
Est. vol. 3,674		Prev. vol. 6,060			Prev. open int. 65,660			
Swiss Franc (IMM)								
125,000 francs, US$ per franc; 0.0001 = $12.50 per contract								
0.8248	0.7117	June04	0.7693	0.7757	0.7644	0.7685	-0.0059	37,644
Est. vol. 4,276		Prev. vol. 11,284			Prev. open int. 38,180			
U.S. Dollar Index (FINEX)								
1000 x index points and US cents; 0.01 = $10 per contract								
100.60	85.21	June04	91.41	92.45	91.41	92.15	+0.71	13,071
95.37	85.85	Sept04	91.77	92.81	91.77	92.55	+0.71	2,148
		Prev. vol. 2,422			Prev. open int. 15,253			

Source: *The Financial Post* (*National Post*), May 14, 2004. Reprinted by permission.

of dollars that is agreed to today for purchase of one pound at time T in the future. Call the risk-free interest rates in Canada and the United Kingdom r_{CAN} and r_{UK}, respectively.

The interest rate parity theorem then states that the proper relationship between E_0 and F_0 is given as

$$F_0 = E_0\left(\frac{1 + r_{CAN}}{1 + r_{UK}}\right)^T \tag{19.6}$$

For example, if $r_{CAN} = .06$ and $r_{UK} = .05$ annually, while $E_0 = \$2.10$ per pound, then the proper futures price for a one-year contract would be

$$\$2.10\left(\frac{1.06}{1.05}\right) = \$2.12 \text{ per pound}$$

Consider the intuition behind this result. If r_{CAN} is greater than r_{UK}, money invested in Canada will grow at a faster rate than money invested in the United Kingdom. If this is so, why wouldn't all investors decide to invest their money in Canada? One important reason why not is that the dollar may be depreciating relative to the pound. Although dollar investments in Canada grow faster than pound investments in the United Kingdom, each dollar is worth progressively fewer pounds as time passes. Such an effect will exactly offset the advantage of the higher Canadian interest rate.

To complete the argument, we need only determine how a depreciating dollar will show up in equation 19.6. If the dollar is depreciating, meaning that progressively more dollars are required to purchase each pound, then the forward exchange rate F_0 (which equals the dollars required to purchase one pound for delivery in one year) must exceed E_0, the current exchange rate. This is exactly what equation 19.6 tells us: When r_{CAN} exceeds r_{UK}, F_0 must exceed E_0. The depreciation of the dollar embodied in the ratio of F_0 to E_0 exactly compensates for the difference in interest rates available in the two countries. Of course, the argument also works in reverse; if r_{CAN} is less than r_{UK}, then F_0 is less than E_0.

EXAMPLE 19.9 Covered Interest Arbitrage

What if the interest rate parity relationship is violated? For example, suppose the futures price is \$2.11 instead of \$2.12. You could adopt the following strategy to reap arbitrage profits. In this example, let E_1 denote the exchange rate that will prevail in one year. E_1 is, of course, a random variable from the perspective of today's investors.

Action	Initial Cash Flow (\$)	Cash Flow in One Year (\$)
1. Borrow one U.K. pound in London. Convert to dollars.	2.10	$-E_1(1.05)$
2. Lend \$2.10 in Canada.	–2.10	2.10(1.06)
3. Enter a contract to purchase 1.05 pounds at a (futures) price of $F_0 = \$2.11$.	0	$1.05(E_1 - 2.11)$
Total	0	\$.0105

In step 1, you exchange the one pound borrowed in the United Kingdom for \$2.10 at the current exchange rate. After one year you must repay the pound borrowed with interest. Since the loan is made in the United Kingdom at the U.K. interest rate, you would repay 1.05 pounds, which would be worth $E_1(1.05)$ dollars. The Canadian loan in step 2 is made at the Canadian interest rate of 6 percent. The futures position in step 3 results in receipt of 1.05 pounds, for which you would first pay F_0 dollars each, and then trade into dollars at rate E_1.

Note that the exchange rate risk here is exactly offset between the pound obligation in step 1 and the futures position in step 3. The profit from the strategy is therefore risk-free and requires no net investment.

To generalize this strategy:

Action	Initial Cash Flow (\$)	Cash Flow in One Year (\$)
1. Borrow one U.K. pound in London. Convert to \$.	$\$E_0$	$-\$E_1(1 + r_{UK})$
2. Use proceeds of borrowing in London to lend in Canada.	$-\$E_0$	$\$E_0(1 + r_{CAN})$
3. Enter $(1 + r_{UK})$ futures positions to purchase one pound for F_0 dollars.	0	$(1 + r_{UK})(E_1 - F_0)$
Total	0	$E_0(1 + r_{CAN}) - F_0(1 + r_{UK})$

Let us again review the stages of the arbitrage operation. The first step requires borrowing one pound in the United Kingdom. With a current exchange rate of E_0, the one pound is converted into E_0 dollars, which is a cash inflow. In one year the British loan must be paid off with interest, requiring a payment in pounds of $(1 + r_{UK})$, or in dollars $E_1(1 + r_{UK})$. In the second step the proceeds of the British loan are invested in Canada. This involves an initial cash outflow of $\$E_0$, and a cash inflow of $\$E_0(1 + r_{CAN})$ in one year. Finally, the exchange risk involved in the British borrowing is hedged in step 3. Here, the $(1 + r_{UK})$ pounds that will need to be delivered to satisfy the British loan are purchased ahead in the futures contract.

The net proceeds to the arbitrage portfolio are risk-free and given by $E_0(1 + r_{CAN}) - F_0(1 + r_{UK})$. If this value is positive, borrow in the United Kingdom, lend in Canada, and enter a long futures position to eliminate foreign exchange risk. If the value is negative, borrow in Canada, lend in the United Kingdom, and take a short position in pound futures. When prices are aligned properly to preclude arbitrage opportunities, the expression must equal zero. If it were positive, investors would pursue the arbitrage portfolio. If it were negative, they would pursue the reverse positions.

Rearranging this expression gives us the relationship

$$F_0 = \frac{1 + r_{\text{CAN}}}{1 + r_{\text{UK}}} E_0 \tag{19.7}$$

which is the interest rate parity theorem for a one-year horizon, known also as the **covered interest arbitrage relationship**.

CONCEPT CHECK

11. What are the arbitrage strategy and associated profits if the initial futures price is F_0 = $2.14/pound?

Ample empirical evidence bears out this theoretical relationship. For two other currencies, for example, on May 21, 2004, *The Globe and Mail* listed the one-year U.S. interest rate at 1.83 percent and the one-year Canadian rate at 2.46 percent. The U.S. dollar was then worth 1.3731 Canadian dollars. Substituting these values into equation 19.7 gives $F_0 = 1.3731 \times (1.0246/1.0183) = 1.3816$. The actual forward price at that time for six-month delivery was $1.3795 per U.S. dollar, so close to the parity value that transaction costs would prevent arbitrageurs from profiting from the discrepancy.

19.8 INTEREST RATE FUTURES

The Markets

The late 1970s and 1980s saw a dramatic increase in the volatility of interest rates, leading to investor desire to hedge returns on fixed-income securities against changes in interest rates. As one example, thrift institutions that had loaned money on home mortgages before 1975 suffered substantial capital losses on those loans when interest rates later increased. An interest rate futures contract could have protected banks against such large swings in yields. The significance of these losses has spurred trading in interest rate futures.

www.me.org

As with other futures contracts, several Canadian interest rate futures were introduced in the past by the TFE and Montreal Exchange.[12] Very few of them survive today. Figure 19.1 shows the futures contracts that traded on the Canadian Derivatives Exchange in May 2004. Only bankers' acceptances and Canada bond and overnight repo rate futures had survived by that date.

Interest rate futures contracts call for delivery of a bond, bill, or note. Should interest rates rise, the market value of the security at delivery will be less than the original futures price, and the deliverer will profit. Hence, the short position in the interest rate futures contract gains when interest rates rise.

In the United States, the major interest rate contracts currently traded are on Treasury bills, Treasury notes, Treasury bonds, and a municipal bond index. These securities thus provide an opportunity to hedge against a wide spectrum of maturities from very short- (T-bills) to long-term (T-bonds). In addition, futures contracts trade on Eurodollar rates and interest rates in Germany, Japan, Switzerland, Italy, Canada, and the United Kingdom and are listed in the major U.S. financial publications.

[12]As we mentioned in the first section, the two have now been merged into the Canadian Derivatives Exchange, located in Montreal.

Hedging Interest Rate Risk

Like equity managers, fixed-income managers may desire to separate security-specific decisions from bets on movements in the entire structure of interest rates. Consider, for example, these problems:

1. A fixed-income manager holds a bond portfolio on which capital gains have been earned. She foresees an increase in interest rates but is reluctant to sell her portfolio and replace it with a lower-duration mix of bonds because such rebalancing would result in large trading costs as well as realization of capital gains for tax purposes. Still, she would like to hedge her exposure to interest rate increases.
2. A corporation plans to issue bonds to the public. It believes that now is a good time to act, but it cannot issue the bonds for another three months because of the lags inherent in SEC registration. It would like to hedge the uncertainty surrounding the yield at which it eventually will be able to sell the bonds.
3. A pension fund will receive a large cash inflow next month that it plans to invest in long-term bonds. It is concerned that interest rates may fall by the time it can make the investment, and would like to lock in the yield currently available on long-term issues.

In each of these cases, the investment manager wishes to hedge interest rate uncertainty. This hedging takes place by using two properties of fixed-income securities that we saw in Chapter 13. The first one is that the sensitivity of these securities to changes in the rate of interest is approximately proportional to the size of their *modified duration*. The second one is that the duration of a portfolio of fixed-income securities is equal to the "portfolio" of durations, the weighted average of the durations of the securities in the portfolio. Hedging interest rate risk, therefore, is the process of changing the duration of our fixed-income portfolio, by taking an appropriate position (long or short) in interest rate futures contracts. This combination of the futures contract position and the original portfolio would have duration equal to the weighted average of the durations of the position and the portfolio.

The hedge ratio, the appropriate number of long or short contracts, depends on the ratios of the sizes and the modified durations of the portfolio and the instrument underlying the futures contract. The exact procedure will be illustrated in detail when we discuss hedging in Chapter 21 by an example of a bond portfolio manager, as in case 1 above. Hedging interest rate risk can either set the duration equal to zero or reduce it to a desired value. An example where this last case arises is in a financial corporation in which the duration of the assets is lower than that of its liabilities. By taking appropriate positions in interest rate futures it is possible to reduce the duration of the liabilities to match that of the assets and reduce the balance sheet exposure to interest rate risk.

Other Interest Rate Futures

We have just seen how futures contracts on long-term Treasury bonds can be used to manage interest rate risk. These contracts are on the *prices* of interest-rate-dependent securities. All Canadian interest rate futures are of this form. U.S. futures contracts, however, also trade on *interest rates* themselves. The biggest of these contracts in terms of trading volume is the Eurodollar contract, the listing for which we reproduce as Figure 19.13. The profit on this contract is proportional to the difference between the LIBOR rate at contract maturity and the contract rate entered into at contract inception. Recall that "LIBOR" stands for the London Interbank Offered Rate. It is the rate at which large banks in London are willing to lend money among themselves, and it is the premier short-term interest rate quoted in the European dollar-denominated money market. There are analogous rates on interbank loans in other currencies. For example, one close cousin of LIBOR is EURIBOR, which is the rate at which Euro-denominated interbank loans within the Euro zone are offered by one prime bank to another.

Figure 19.13 The Eurodollar futures contract.

Eurodollar (CME)-$1,000,000; pts of 100%

	OPEN	HIGH	LOW	SETTLE	CHG	YIELD	CHG	OPEN INT
Mar	98.69	98.70	98.69	98.69	...	1.31	...	668,180
Apr	98.73	98.74	98.73	98.74	...	1.26	...	19,854
May	98.78	98.78	98.77	98.78	.01	1.22	-.01	3,105
June	98.78	98.81	98.78	98.79	...	1.21	...	728,843
July	98.80	98.80	98.79	98.80	.02	1.20	-.02	201
Sept	98.76	98.79	98.75	98.77	...	1.23	...	621,423
Dec	98.61	98.64	98.59	98.62	...	1.38	...	573,959
Mr04	98.36	98.39	98.33	98.36	-.01	1.64	.01	402,207
June	98.05	98.07	98.01	98.04	-.02	1.96	.02	278,510
Sept	97.72	97.75	97.67	97.71	-.03	2.29	.03	218,632
Dec	97.38	97.42	97.33	97.36	-.05	2.64	.05	196,799
Mr05	97.09	97.13	97.04	97.08	-.05	2.92	.05	138,429
June	96.86	96.88	96.79	96.82	-.06	3.18	.06	119,414
Sept	96.62	96.64	96.55	96.58	-.06	3.42	.06	110,403
Dec	96.39	96.41	96.32	96.35	-.06	3.65	.06	97,741
Mr06	96.20	96.22	96.13	96.17	-.06	3.83	.06	81,040
June	96.02	96.04	95.95	95.99	-.06	4.01	.06	70,071
Sept	95.86	95.88	95.79	95.82	-.06	4.18	.06	64,099
Dec	95.69	95.71	95.62	95.65	-.06	4.35	.06	51,260
Mr07	95.55	95.55	95.47	95.51	-.06	4.49	.06	49,232
June	95.42	95.42	95.33	95.37	-.07	4.63	.07	35,148
Sept	95.30	95.30	95.21	95.25	-.07	4.75	.07	27,409
Dec	95.17	95.17	95.09	95.13	-.07	4.87	.07	23,368
Mr08	95.06	95.06	95.00	95.02	-.07	4.98	.07	9,598
Sp09	94.49	94.49	94.46	94.46	-.06	5.54	.06	7,974

Est vol 698,991; vol Wed 752,080; open int 4,684,399, +30,901.

Source: *The Wall Street Journal,* March 7, 2003. Reprinted by permission of The Wall Street Journal,

The listing conventions for this contract are a bit peculiar. Consider, for example, the first contract listed, which matures in March 2003. The current futures price is presented as $F_0 = 98.69$. However, this value is not really a price. In effect, participants in the contract negotiate over the contract interest rate, and the so-called "futures price" is actually set equal to 100 – Contract rate. Since the contract rate is 1.31 percent (see the next-to-last column), the futures price is listed as $100 - 1.31 = 98.69$. Similarly, the final futures price on contract maturity date will be marked to $F_T = 100 - \text{LIBOR}_T$. Thus, profits to the buyer of the contract will be proportional to

$$F_T - F_0 = (100 - \text{LIBOR}_T) - (100 - \text{Contract rate}) = \text{Contract rate} - \text{LIBOR}_T$$

Thus, the contract design allows participants to trade directly on the LIBOR rate. The contract multiplier is $1 million, but the LIBOR rate on which the contract is written is a three-month (quarterly) rate; for each basis point that the (annualized) LIBOR increases, the quarterly interest rate increases by only ¼ of a basis point, and the profit to the buyer decreases by

$$.0001 \times \tfrac{1}{4} \times \$1{,}000{,}000 = \$25$$

Examine the payoff on the contract, and you will see that, in effect, the Eurodollar contract allows traders to "swap" a fixed interest rate (the contract rate) for a floating rate (LIBOR). This exchange of interest rates is the building block for long-term interest rate swaps, which is the subject of the next section. Notice in Figure 19.13 that the total open interest on this contract is enormous—almost five million contracts—and that contracts with open interest extend out to ten years' maturity. Contracts with such long-term maturities are quite unusual. They reflect the fact that the Eurodollar contract is used by dealers in long-term interest rate swaps as a hedging tool.

19.9 SWAPS

We noted in Chapter 13 that interest rate swaps have become common tools for interest rate risk management. A large and active market also exists for foreign exchange swaps. Recall that a swap arrangement obligates two counterparties to exchange cash flows at one or more future dates. To illustrate, a **foreign exchange swap** might call for one party to exchange $2 million for 1 million British pounds in each of the next five years. An **interest rate swap** with notional principal of

$1 million might call for one party to exchange a variable cash flow equal to $1 million times the LIBOR rate for $1 million times a fixed rate of 8 percent. In this way, the two parties exchange the cash flows corresponding to interest payments on a fixed-rate 8 percent coupon bond for those corresponding to payments on a floating-rate bond paying LIBOR.

EXAMPLE 19.10 Balance Sheet Restructuring Using Swaps

Swaps offer participants easy ways to restructure their balance sheets. Consider, for example, a firm that has issued long-term bonds with total par value of $10 million at a fixed coupon rate of 8 percent. The firm is obligated to make interest payments of $800,000 per year. However, it can change the nature of its interest obligations from fixed rate to floating rate by entering a swap agreement to pay a floating rate of interest and receive a fixed rate.

A swap with notional principal of $10 million that exchanges LIBOR for an 8 percent fixed rate will bring the firm fixed cash inflows of $800,000 per year and obligate it to pay instead $10 million × LIBOR. The net cash flow from the swap is $10 million × (.08 − LIBOR). The receipt of the fixed payments from the swap agreement offsets the firm's interest obligations on the outstanding bond issue, leaving it with a net obligation to make floating-rate payments. The swap, therefore, is a way for the firm to effectively convert its outstanding fixed-rate debt into synthetic floating-rate debt.

Suppose that the swap is for three years and the LIBOR rates turn out to be 7 percent, 8 percent, and 9 percent in the next three years. The firm's cash flows would be as illustrated in Table 19.4. The top line of the table shows the cash flow on the fixed-rate debt, equal to 8 percent of the $10 million bond principal. The cash flow on its $10 million swap position (pay floating, receive fixed rate) equals (.08 − LIBOR) × $10 million. The swap therefore contributes a positive cash flow when LIBOR is only 7 percent but a negative cash flow when LIBOR rises to 9 percent. The firm's net payment, in the last line of the table, is simply LIBOR × $10 million. The swap has therefore transformed the firm's fixed rate debt into synthetic floating-rate debt. To see this more generally, note that the firm's net cash flow after entering the swap is as follows:

− .08 × principal	Payment on bond
+ (.08 − LIBOR) × principal	Net cash flow from swap (pay LIBOR, receive 8%)
= −LIBOR × principal	

Therefore, the firm's net cash outflow equals the LIBOR rate times bond principal, just as if it had issued a floating rate bond tied to LIBOR.

CONCEPT CHECK

12. Show how a firm that has issued a floating-rate bond with a coupon equal to the LIBOR rate can use swaps to convert that bond into synthetic fixed-rate debt. Assume the terms of the swap allow an exchange of LIBOR for a fixed rate of 8 percent.

Table 19.4 Balance Sheet Restructuring (the firm converts an 8% fixed-rate bond into a synthetic floating-rate bond with coupon equal to the LIBOR rate)

	LIBOR		
	7%	8%	9%
As debt payer (8% of $10 million)	–$800,000	–$800,000	–$800,000
As floating payer receives $10 million × (.08 – LIBOR)	+$100,000	+0	+ –$100,000
Net cash flow	–$700,000	–$800,000	–$900,000

As the example shows, an interest rate swap agreement is a cheap and quick way to restructure the balance sheet. The swap does not entail trading costs to buy back outstanding bonds or underwriting fees and lengthy registration procedures to issue new debt. In addition, if the firm perceives price advantages in either the fixed or floating rate market, the swap market allows it to issue its debt in the cheaper of the two markets and then "convert" to the financing mode that best suits its business needs.

Foreign exchange swaps also enable the firm to quickly and cheaply restructure its balance sheet. Suppose, for example, that the firm issues $10 million in debt at 8 percent, but it actually prefers that its interest obligations be denominated in British pounds. For example, the issuing firm might be a British corporation that perceives advantageous financing opportunities in Canada but prefers pound-denominated liabilities. Then the firm, whose debt currently obliges it to make dollar-denominated payments of $800,000, can agree to swap a given number of pounds each year for $800,000. By so doing, it effectively covers its dollar obligation and replaces it with a new pound-denominated obligation.

How can the fair swap rate be determined? For example, do we know that an exchange of LIBOR is a fair trade for a fixed rate of 8 percent? Or what is the fair swap rate between dollars and pounds for the foreign exchange swap we considered? To answer these questions we can exploit the analogy between a swap agreement and a forward or futures contract.

Consider a swap agreement to exchange dollars for pounds for one period only. Next year, for example, one might exchange $1 million for £.5 million. This is no more than a simple forward contract in foreign exchange. The dollar-paying party is contracting to buy British pounds in one year for a number of dollars agreed upon today. The forward exchange rate for one year delivery is $F_1 =$ \$2/pound. We know from the interest rate parity relationship that this forward price should be related to the spot exchange rate, E_0, by the formula $F_1 = E_0(1 + r_{CAN})/(1 + r_{UK})$. Because a one-period swap is in fact a forward contract, the fair swap rate also is given by the parity relationship.

Now consider an agreement to trade foreign exchange for two periods. This agreement could be structured as a portfolio of two separate forward contracts. If so, the forward price for the exchange of currencies in one year would be $F_1 = E_0(1 + r_{CAN})/(1 + r_{UK})$, while the forward price for the exchange in the second year would be $F_2 = E_0[(1 + r_{CAN})/(1 + r_{UK})]^2$. As an example, suppose that $E_0 = \$2.038/\text{pound}$, $r_{CAN} = 5$ percent, and $r_{UK} = 7$ percent. Then, using the parity relationship, we would have prices for forward delivery of $F_1 = \$2.038/£ \times (1.05/1.07) = \$2.00/£$ and $F_2 = \$2.038/£ \times (1.05/1.07)^2 = \$1.9625/£$. Figure 19.14, panel A illustrates this sequence of cash exchanges assuming that the swap calls for delivery of one pound in each year. While the dollars to be paid in each of the two years are known today, they vary from year to year.

In contrast, a swap agreement to exchange currency for two years would call for a fixed exchange rate to be used for the duration of the swap. This means that the same number of dollars would be paid per pound in each year, as illustrated in panel B. Because the forward prices for delivery in each of the next two years are $2/£ and $1.9625/£, the fixed exchange rate that makes the two-period swap a fair deal must be between these two values. Therefore, the dollar payer underpays for the pound in the first year (compared to the forward exchange rate) and overpays in the second year. Thus, the swap can be viewed as a portfolio of forward transactions, but instead of each transaction being priced independently, one forward price is applied to all of the transactions.

Given this insight, it is easy to determine the fair swap price. If we were to purchase one pound per year for two years using two independent forward rate agreements, we would pay F_1 dollars in one year and F_2 dollars in two years. If, instead, we enter a swap, we pay a constant rate of F^* dollars per pound. Because both strategies must be equally costly, we conclude that

$$\frac{F_1}{1 + y_1} + \frac{F_2}{(1 + y_2)^2} = \frac{F^*}{1 + y_1} + \frac{F^*}{(1 + y_2)^2}$$

Figure 19.14 Forward contracts versus swaps. Panel A: Two forward contracts, each priced independently. Panel B: Two-year swap agreement.

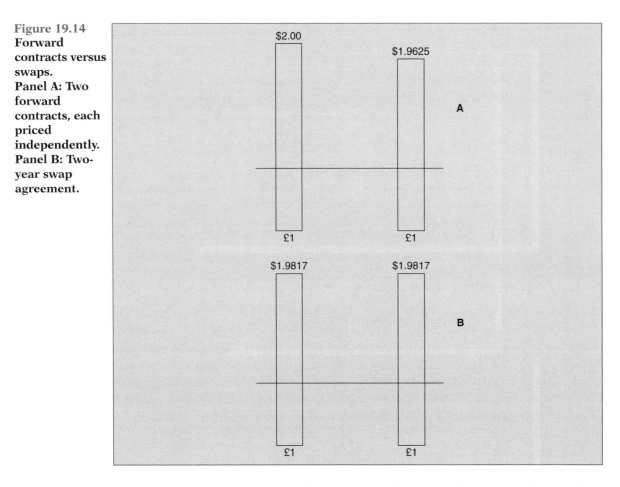

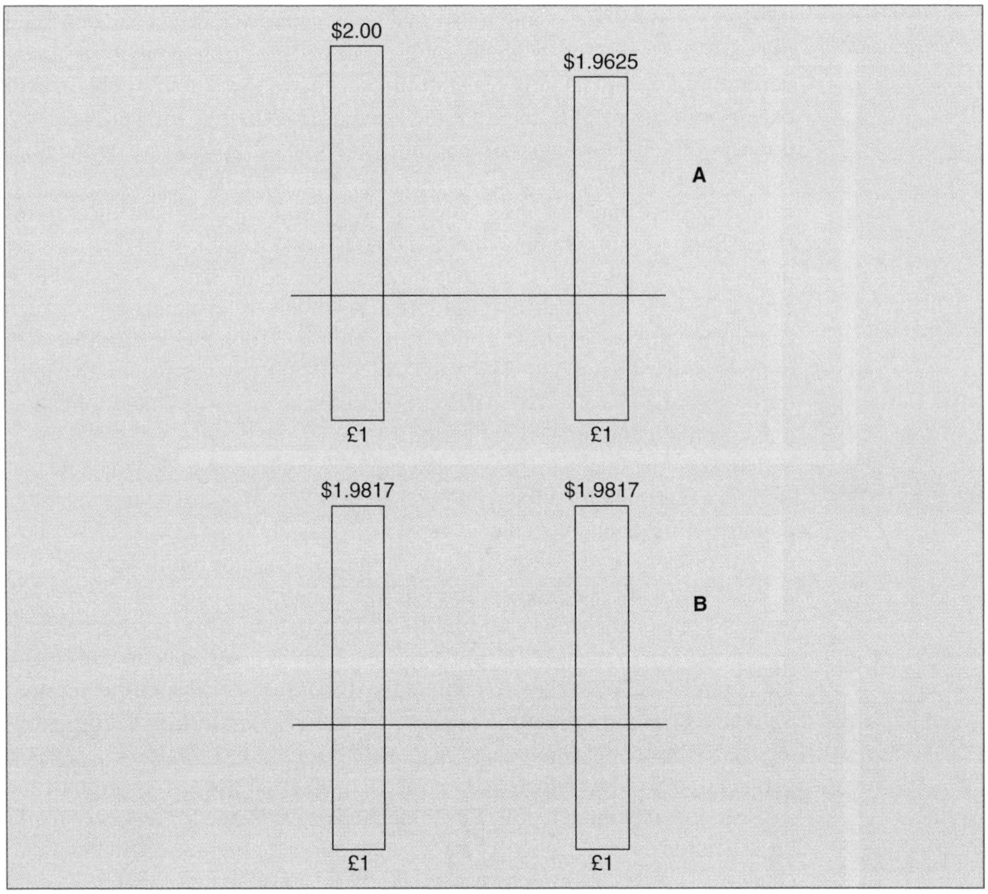

where y_1 and y_2 are the appropriate yields from the yield curve for discounting dollar cash flows of one and two years' maturity, respectively. In our example, where we have assumed a flat Canadian yield curve at 5 percent, we would solve

$$\frac{2.00}{1.05} + \frac{1.9625}{1.05^2} = \frac{F^*}{1.05} + \frac{F^*}{1.05^2}$$

which implies that $F^* = 1.9817$. The same principle would apply to a foreign exchange swap of any other maturity. In essence, we need to find the level annuity, F^*, with the same present value as the sequence of annual cash flows that would be incurred in a sequence of forward rate agreements.

Interest rate swaps can be subjected to precisely the same analysis. Here, the forward contract is on an interest rate. For example, if you swap LIBOR for an 8 percent fixed rate with notional principal of \$100, then you have entered a forward contract for delivery of \$100 times r_{LIBOR} for a fixed "forward" price of \$8. If the swap agreement is for many periods, the fair spread will be determined by the entire sequence of interest rate forward prices over the life of the swap.

Credit Risk in the Swap Market

The rapid growth of the swap market has given rise to increasing concern about credit risk in these markets. Actually, although credit risk in the swap market is certainly not trivial, it is not nearly as large as the magnitude of the notional principal in these markets would suggest. To see why, consider a simple interest rate swap of LIBOR for a fixed rate. At the time the transaction is initiated, it has zero net present value to both parties for the same reason that a futures contract has zero value at inception: both are simply contracts to exchange cash in the future at terms established today that make both parties willing to enter into the deal. Even if one party were to back out of the deal at this moment, it would not cost the counterparty anything, because another trader could be found to take its place.

Once interest or exchange rates change, however, the situation is not as simple. Suppose, for example, that interest rates increase shortly after an interest-rate swap agreement has begun. The floating-rate payer therefore suffers a loss, while the fixed-rate payer enjoys a gain. If the floating-rate payer reneges on its commitment at this point, the fixed-rate payer suffers a loss. However, that loss is not as large as the notional principal of the swap, for the default of the floating-rate payer relieves the fixed-rate payer from its obligation as well. The loss is only the *difference* between the values of the fixed-rate and floating-rate obligations, not the *total* value of the payments that the floating-rate payer was obligated to make.

EXAMPLE 19.11 Credit Risk in Swaps

Consider a swap written on \$1 million of notional principal that calls for exchange of LIBOR for a fixed rate of 8 percent for five years. Suppose, for simplicity, that the yield curve is currently flat at 8 percent. With LIBOR thus equal to 8 percent, no cash flows will be exchanged unless interest rates change. But now suppose that the yield curve immediately shifts up to 9 percent. The floating-rate payer now is obligated to pay a cash flow of $(.09 - .08) \times \$1$ million = \$10,000 each year to the fixed-rate payer (as long as rates remain at 9 percent). If the floating-rate payer defaults on the swap, the fixed-rate payer loses the prospect of that five-year annuity. The present value of that annuity is \$10,000 × Annuity factor(9%, 5 years) = \$38,897. This loss may not be trivial, but it is less than 4 percent of notional principal. We conclude that the credit risk of the swap is far less than notional principal. Again, this is because the default by the floating-rate payer costs the counterparty only the net difference between the LIBOR rate and the fixed rate.

Swap Variations

Swaps have given rise to a wide range of spinoff products. Many of these add option features to the basic swap agreement. For example, an *interest rate cap* is an agreement in which the cap buyer makes a payment today in exchange for possible future payments if a "reference" interest rate (usually LIBOR) exceeds a "limit rate" on a series of settlement dates. For example, if the limit rate is 7 percent, then the cap holder receives $(r_{\text{LIBOR}} - 0.07)$ for each dollar of notional principal if the LIBOR rate exceeds 7 percent. The purchaser of the cap in effect has entered a swap agreement to exchange the LIBOR rate for a fixed rate of 7 percent with an option to not execute the swap in any period that the transaction is unprofitable. The payoff to the holder of the cap is

(Reference rate – Limit rate) × Notional principal *if* this value is positive and zero otherwise

This, of course, is the payoff of an option to purchase a cash flow proportional to the LIBOR rate for an exercise price proportional to the limit rate.

Similar to caps, an *interest rate floor* pays its holder in any period that the reference interest rate falls *below* some limit. This is analogous to a sequence of options to sell the reference rate for a stipulated "strike rate."

A *collar* combines interest rate caps and floors. A collar entails the purchase of a cap with one limit rate and the sale of a floor with a lower limit rate. If a firm starts with a floating-rate liability and buys the cap, it achieves protection against rates rising. If rates do rise, the cap provides a cash flow equal to the reference interest rate for a payment equal to the limit rate. Therefore, the cap places an upper bound equal to the limit rate on the firm's interest rate expense. The written floor places a limit on how much the firm can benefit from rate declines. Even if interest rates fall dramatically, the firm's savings on its floating-rate obligation will be offset by its obligation to pay the difference between the reference rate and the limit rate. Therefore, the collar limits the firm's net cost of funds to a value between the limit rate on the cap and the limit rate on the floor.

Other option-based variations on the basic swap arrangement are *swaptions.* A swaption is an option on a swap. The buyer of the swaption has the right to enter an interest rate swap on some reference interest rate at a prespecified fixed interest rate on or before some expiration date. A *call swaption* (often called a *payer swaption*) is the right to pay the fixed rate in a swap and receive the floating rate. A *put swaption* is the right to receive the fixed rate and pay the floating rate. An exit option is the right to walk away from a swap without penalty. Swaptions can be European or American.

There also are futures and forward variations on swaps. A forward swap, for example, obligates both traders to enter a swap at some date in the future with terms agreed to today.

SUMMARY

1. Forward contracts are arrangements that call for future delivery of an asset at a currently agreed-upon price. The long trader is obligated to purchase the good, and the short trader is obligated to deliver it. If the price of the asset at the maturity of the contract exceeds the forward price, the long side benefits by virtue of acquiring the good at the contract price.
2. A futures contract is similar to a forward contract, differing most importantly in the aspects of standardization and marking to market, which is the process by which gains and losses on futures contract positions are settled daily. In contrast, forward contracts call for no cash transfers until contract maturity.
3. Futures contracts are traded on organized exchanges that standardize the size of the contract, the grade of the deliverable asset, the delivery date, and the delivery location. Traders negotiate only over the contract price. This standardization creates increased liquidity in the marketplace and means buyers and sellers can easily find many traders for a desired purchase or sale.
4. The clearinghouse represents an intermediary between each pair of traders, acting as the short position for each long, and as the long position for each short. In this way, traders need not be concerned about the performance of the trader on the opposite side of the contract. In turn, traders post margins to guarantee their own performance on the contracts.
5. The gain or loss to the long side for a futures contract held between time 0 and t is $F_t - F_0$. Because $F_T = P_T$, the long's profit if the contract is held until maturity is $P_T - F_0$, where P_T is the spot price at time T and F_0 is the original futures price. The gain or loss to the short position is $F_0 - P_T$.
6. Futures contracts may be used for hedging or speculating. Speculators use the contracts to take a stand on the ultimate price of an asset. Short hedgers take short positions in contracts to offset any gains or losses on the value of an asset already held in inventory. Long hedgers take long positions to offset gains or losses in the purchase price of a good.
7. The spot-futures parity relationship states that the equilibrium futures price on an asset providing no services or payments (such as dividends) is $F_0 = P_0(1 + r_f)^T$. If the futures price deviates from this value, then market participants can earn arbitrage profits.
8. If the asset provides services or payments with yield d, the parity relationship becomes $F_0 = P_0(1 + r_f - d)^T$. This model also is called the cost-of-carry model, because it states that the futures price must exceed the spot price by the net cost of carrying the asset until maturity date T.
9. Commodity futures pricing is complicated by costs for storage of the underlying commodity. When the asset is willingly stored by investors, then the storage costs enter the futures pricing equation as follows:

$$F_0 = P_0(1 + r_f + c)^T$$

The non-interest-carrying costs, c, play the role of a "negative dividend" in this context.

10. When commodities are not stored for investment purposes, the correct futures price must be determined using general risk-return principles. In this event

$$F_0 = E(P_T)\left(\frac{1 + r_f}{1 + k}\right)^T$$

The equilibrium (risk-return) and the no-arbitrage predictions of the proper futures price are consistent with one another.

11. The equilibrium futures price will be less than the currently expected time T spot price if the spot price exhibits systematic risk, in which case $k > r_f$. This provides an expected profit for the long position that bears the risk and imposes an expected loss on the short position that is willing to accept that expected loss as a means to shed risk.

12. Futures contracts calling for cash settlement are traded on the S&P/TSX 60 in Canada and in various U.S. stock market indices. The contracts may be mixed with Treasury bills to construct artificial equity positions, which makes them potentially valuable tools for market timers. Market index contracts also are used by arbitrageurs who attempt to profit from violations of the parity relationship.

13. Foreign exchange futures trade in the United States. on several foreign currencies, as well as on a European currency index. The interest rate parity relationship for foreign exchange futures is

$$F_0 = E_0\left(\frac{1 + r_{\text{US}}}{1 + r_{\text{foreign}}}\right)^T$$

Deviations of the futures price from this value imply arbitrage opportunity. Empirical evidence, however, suggests that generally the parity relationship is satisfied.

14. Interest rate futures allow for hedging against interest rate fluctuations in several different markets. Currently, few of them are actively traded in Canada. When they are used for hedging fixed-income portfolios, the hedge ratio is proportional to the ratios of modified duration and the size of the portfolio.

15. Swaps, which call for the exchange of a series of cash flows, may be viewed as portfolios of forward contracts. Each transaction may be viewed as a separate forward agreement. However, instead of pricing each exchange independently, the swap sets one "forward price" that applies to all of the transactions. Therefore, the swap price will be an average of the futures prices that would prevail if each exchange were priced separately.

KEY TERMS

forward contract 728
futures contract 728
futures price 728
long position 728
short position 728
clearinghouse 733
reversing trade 734
open interest 734
marking to market 735
maintenance margin (variation margin) 735
convergence property 735
cash delivery 737
basis 740
basis risk 740
spread 741
spot-futures parity theorem 742
cost-of-carry relationship 743
index arbitrage 758
program trading 758
triple witching hour 758
interest rate parity theorem 760
covered interest arbitrage relationship 763
foreign exchange swap 765
interest rate swap 765

SELECTED READINGS

Extensive treatments of the institutional background of several futures markets in the United States and Canada are provided in:

Hull, John C. *Options, Futures and Other Derivatives*, 5th ed. Englewood Cliffs, NJ: Prentice Hall, 2003.

Khoury, Nabil, and Pierre Laroche. *Options et Contracts à Terme* (in French), 2nd ed. Quebec: Les Presses de l'Université Laval, 1995.

Excellent, although challenging, treatments of the differences between futures and forward markets and the pricing of each type of contract are in:

Black, Fischer. "The Pricing of Commodity Contracts." *Journal of Financial Economics* 3 (January–March 1976).

Cox, John, Jonathan Ingersol, and Stephen A. Ross. "The Relation Between Forward Prices and Futures Prices." *Journal of Financial Economics* 9 (December 1981).

Jarrow, Robert, and George Oldfield. "Forward Contracts and Futures Contracts." *Journal of Financial Economics* 9 (December 1981).

For treatments of the backwardation/contango debate, see:

Cootner, Paul H. "Speculation and Hedging." Standford, CA: Food Research Institute Studies, Supplement, 1967.

Hicks, J. R. *Value and Capital*, 2nd ed. London: Oxford University Press, 1946.

Keynes, John Maynard. *Treatise on Money*, 2nd ed. London: Macmillan, 1930.

Working, Holbrook. "The Theory of Price of Storage." *American Economic Review* 39 (December 1949).

Two empirical studies on Canadian index futures markets are:

Park, Tae H., and Lorne N. Switzer. "Bivariate GARCH Estimation of the Optimal Hedge Ratios for Stock Index Futures: A Note." *Journal of Futures Markets* 15, no. 1 (1995); and "Index Participation Units and the Performance of the Index Futures Markets: Evidence from the Toronto 35 Index Participation Units Market." *Journal of Futures Markets* 15, no. 2 (1995).

Canadian studies of the use of financial futures to hedge interest rate risk are:

Fortin, Michel, and Nabil Khoury. "Hedging Interest Rate Risks with Financial Futures." *Canadian Journal of Administrative Sciences* 1, no. 2 (December 1984).

Gagnon, Louis, Samuel Mensah, and Edward H. Blinder. "Hedging Canadian Corporate Debt: A Comparative Study of the Hedging Effectiveness of Canadian and U.S. Bond Futures." *Journal of Futures Markets* 9, no. 1 (1989).

Gagnon, Louis, and Greg Lypny. "Hedging Short-Term Interest Risk Under Time-Varying Distributions." *Journal of Futures Markets*, 15, no. 7 (1995).

Analyses of risk and return in commodity futures are in:

Dusak, Katherine. "Futures Trading and Investor Returns: An Investigation of Commodity Market Risk Premiums." *Journal of Political Economy* 81 (December 1973).

Khoury, Nabil T., and Jean-Marc Martel. "Optimal Futures Hedging in the Presence of Asymmetric Information." *Journal of Futures Markets* 5, no. 4 (1985).

The issue of the storage of commodities is treated in:

Brennan, Michael. "The Supply of Storage." *American Economic Review* 47 (March 1958).

Khoury, Nabil T., and Jean-Marc Martel. "A Supply of Storage Theory with Asymmetric Information." *Journal of Futures Markets* 9, no. 6 (1989).

Empirical studies on Canadian Commodity futures markets include:

Khoury, Nabil T., and Pierre Yourougou. "Price Discovery Performance and Maturity Effect in the Canadian Feed Wheat Market." *Review of Futures Markets* 8, no. 3 (1989).

———. "The Informational Content of the Basis: Evidence from Canadian Barley, Oats, and Canola Futures Markets." *Journal of Futures Markets* 11, no. 1 (1991).

Perrakis, Stylianos, and Nabil Khoury. "Asymmetric Information in Commodity Futures Markets: Theory and Empirical Evidence," *Journal of Futures Markets* 18, no. 7 (1998).

A good introduction to swaps is:

Brown, Keith C., and Donald J. Smith. *Interest Rate and Currency Swaps: A Tutorial.* Charlottesville, VA: Institute of Chartered Financial Analysts, 1995.

PROBLEMS

1. Why is there no futures market in cement?
2. Why might an investor choose to purchase futures contracts rather than the underlying asset?
3. What is the difference in cash flow between short selling an asset and entering a short futures position?
4. In each of the following cases discuss how you, as a portfolio manager, would use financial futures to protect the portfolio.
   a. You own a large position in a relatively illiquid bond that you want to sell.

b. You have a large gain on one of your long Treasuries and want to sell it, but you would like to defer the gain until the next accounting period, which begins in four weeks.

c. You will receive a large contribution next month that you hope to invest in long-term corporate bonds on a yield basis as favourable as is now available.

5. Consider this arbitrage strategy to derive the parity relationship for spreads: (1) enter a long futures position with maturity date T_1 and futures price $F(T_1)$; (2) enter a short position with maturity T_2 and futures price $F(T_2)$; and (3) at T_1, when the first contract expires, buy the asset and borrow $F(T_1)$ dollars at rate r_f and pay back the loan with interest at time T_2.

a. What are the total cash flows to this strategy at times 0, T_1, and T_2?

b. Why must profits at time T_2 be zero if no arbitrage opportunities are present?

c. What must be the relationship between $F(T_1)$ and $F(T_2)$ for the profits at T_2 to be equal to zero? This relationship is the parity relationship for spreads.

6. Consider a stock that pays no dividends on which a futures contract, a call option, and a put option trade. The maturity date for all three contracts is T, the exercise price of the put and the call are both X, and the futures price is F. Show that if $X = F$, then the call price equals the put price. Use parity conditions to guide your demonstration.

7. Suppose that an investor in a 50 percent tax bracket purchases three soybean futures contracts at a price of $5.40 a bushel and closes them out at a price of $5.80. What are the after-tax profits to the position?

8. These questions address stock futures contracts:

a. A hypothetical futures contract on a nondividend-paying stock with current price $150 has a maturity of one year. If the T-bill rate is 6 percent, what is the futures price?

b. What should be the futures price if the maturity of the contract is three years?

c. What if the interest rate is 8 percent and the maturity of the contract is three years?

9. You suddenly receive information that indicates to you that the stock market is about to rise substantially. The market is unaware of this information. What should you do?

10. Suppose the value of the S&P/TSX 60 stock index is currently 400. If the one-year T-bill rate is 6 percent and the expected dividend yield on the S&P/TSX 60 is 2 percent, what should the one-year maturity futures price be?

11. It is now January. The current interest rate is 5 percent annually. The June futures price for gold is $346.30, while the December futures price is $360. Is there an arbitrage opportunity here? If so, how would you exploit it?

12. The Montreal Exchange has just introduced a new futures contract on Brandex stock, a company that currently pays no dividends. Each contract calls for delivery of 1,000 shares of stock in one year. The T-bill rate is 6 percent per year.

a. If Brandex stock now sells at $120 per share, what should be the futures price?

b. If Brandex stock immediately decreases by 3 percent, what will be the change in the futures price and the change in the investor's margin account?

c. If the margin on the contract is $12,000, what is the percentage return on the investor's position?

13. The multiplier for a futures contract on the stock market index is 200. The maturity of the contract is one year, the current level of the index is 400, and the risk-free interest rate is 0.5 percent per month. The dividend yield on the index is .2 percent per month. Suppose that after one month, the level of the stock index is 410.

a. Find the cash flow from the marking-to-market proceeds on the contract. Assume that the parity condition always holds exactly.

b. Find the holding-period return if the initial margin on the contract is $15,000.

CFA® PROBLEMS

14. Michelle Industries issued a Swiss franc–denominated five-year discount note for SFr200 million. The proceeds were converted to U.S. dollars to purchase capital equipment in the United States.

The company wants to hedge this currency exposure and is considering the following alternatives:

- At-the-money Swiss franc call options
- Swiss franc forwards
- Swiss franc futures

a. Contrast the essential characteristics of each of these three derivative instruments.

b. Evaluate the suitability of each in relation to Michelle's hedging objective, including both advantages and disadvantages.

15. You are a corporate treasurer who will purchase $1 million of bonds for the sinking fund in three months. You believe rates will soon fall, and you would like to repurchase the company's sinking fund bonds (which currently are selling below par) in advance of requirements. Unfortunately, you must obtain approval from the board of directors for such a purchase, and this can take up to two months. What action can you take in the futures market to hedge any adverse movements in bond yields and prices until you can actually buy the bonds? Will you be long or short? Why? A qualitative answer is fine.

16. Consider the futures contract written on the S&P 500 index and maturing in six months. The interest rate is 3 percent per six-month period, and the future value of dividends expected to be paid over the next six months is $10. The current index level is 950. Assume that you can short sell the S&P 500 index.

a. Suppose the expected rate of return on the market is 6 percent per six-month period. What is the expected level of the index in six months?

b. What is the theoretical no-arbitrage price for a six-month futures contract on the S&P 500 stock index?

c. Suppose the futures price is 948. Is there an arbitrage opportunity here? If so, how would you exploit it?

17. Suppose that the value of the S&P 500 stock index is 900.

a. If each futures contract costs $25 to trade with a discount broker, how much is the transaction cost per dollar of stock controlled by the futures contract?

b. If the average price of a share on the NYSE is about $40, how much is the transaction cost per "typical share" controlled by one futures contract?

c. For small investors, the typical transaction cost per share in stocks directly is about 30 cents per share. How many times the transactions costs in futures markets is this?

18. The one-year futures price on a stock-index portfolio is 406, the level of the stock index currently is 400, the one-year risk-free interest rate is 3 percent, and the year-end dividend that will be paid on a $400 investment in the market index portfolio is $5.

a. By how much is the contract mispriced?

b. Formulate a zero net-investment arbitrage portfolio and show that you can lock in riskless profits equal to the futures mispricing.

c. Now assume (as is true for small investors) that if you short-sell the stocks in the market index, the proceeds of the short sale are kept with the broker, and you do not receive any interest income on the funds. Is there still an arbitrage opportunity (assuming you don't already own the shares in the index)? Explain.

d. Given the short-sale rules, what is the no-arbitrage band for the stock-futures price relationship? That is, given a stock index level of 400, how high and how low can the futures price be without giving rise to arbitrage opportunities?

19. Consider these futures market data for the June delivery S&P 500 contract, exactly six months hence. The S&P 500 index is at 900, and the June maturity contract is at $F_0 = 901$.

a. If the current interest rate is 2.2 percent semiannually, and the average dividend rate of the stocks in the index is 1.2 percent semiannually, what fraction of the proceeds of stock short sales would need to be available for you to earn arbitrage profits?

b. Suppose that you, in fact, have access to 90 percent of the proceeds from a short sale. What is the lower bound on the futures price that rules out arbitrage opportunities? By how much does the actual futures price fall below the no-arbitrage bound? Formulate the appropriate arbitrage strategy and calculate the profits to that strategy.

CFA® PROBLEMS

20. Janice Delsing, a U.S.-based portfolio manager, manages an $800 million portfolio ($600 million in stocks and $200 million in bonds). In reaction to anticipated short-term market events, Delsing wishes to adjust the allocation to 50 percent stock and 50 percent bonds through the use of futures. Her position will be held only until "the time is right to restore the original asset allocation." Delsing determines a financial futures-based asset allocation strategy is appropriate. The stock futures index multiplier is $250 and the denomination of the bond futures contract is $100,000. Other information relevant to a futures-based strategy is given in the following exhibit:

Bond portfolio modified duration	5 years
Bond portfolio yield to maturity	7%
Basis point value (BPV) of bond futures	$97.85
Stock index futures price	1378
Stock portfolio beta	1.0

a. Describe the financial futures-based strategy needed and explain how the strategy allows Delsing to implement her allocation adjustment. No calculations are necessary.

b. Compute the number of each of the following needed to implement Delsing's asset allocation strategy:

i. Bond futures contracts

ii. Stock index futures contracts

21. What is the difference between the futures price and the value of the futures contract?

22. If the spot price of gold is $350 per troy ounce, the risk-free interest rate is 10 percent, and storage and insurance costs are zero, what should the forward price of gold be for delivery in one year? Use an arbitrage argument to prove your answer, and include a numerical example showing how you could make risk-free arbitrage profits if the forward price exceeded its upper-bound value.

23. If the wheat harvest today is poor, would you expect this fact to have any effect on today's futures prices for wheat to be delivered (post-harvest) two years from today? Under what circumstances will there be no effect?

24. Suppose that the price of corn is risky, with a beta of .5. The monthly storage cost is $.03, and the current spot price is $2.75, with an expected spot price in three months of $2.94. If the expected rate of return on the market is 1.8 percent per month, with a risk-free rate of 1 percent per month, would you store corn for three months?

CSI

25. Use the information below in solving this problem.

Issue	Price	Yield to Maturity	Modified Duration*
U.S. Treasury bond 11% maturing Nov. 15, 2014	100	11.75%	7.6 years
U.S. Treasury long bond futures contract (contract expiration date December 1986)	63.33	11.85%	8.0 years
XYZ Corporation bond $12\frac{1}{2}$% maturing June 1, 2005 (sinking fund debenture, rated AAA)	93	13.50%	7.2 years
Volatility of AAA corporate bond yields relative to U.S. Treasury bond yields = 1.25 to 1.0 (1.25 times)			
Assume no commission and no margin requirements on U.S. Treasury long bond futures contracts.			
Assume no taxes.			
One U.S. Treasury long bond futures contract is a claim on $100,000 par value long-term U.S. Treasury bonds.			

*Modified duration = Duration/(1 + *y*).

- *Situation A.* A fixed-income manager holding a \$20 million market value position of U.S. Treasury $11\frac{3}{4}$ percent bonds maturing November 15, 2014 expects the economic growth rate and the inflation rate to be above market expectations in the near future. Institutional rigidities prevent any existing bonds in the portfolio from being sold in the cash market.
- *Situation B.* The treasurer of XYZ Corporation has recently become convinced that interest rates will decline in the near future. He believes it is an opportune time to purchase his company's sinking fund bonds in advance of requirements since these bonds are trading at a discount from par value. He is preparing to purchase in the open market \$20 million par value XYZ Corporation $12\frac{1}{2}$ percent bonds maturing June 1, 2005. A \$20 million par value position of these bonds is currently offered in the open market at 93. Unfortunately, the treasurer must obtain approval from the board of directors for such a purchase, and this approval process can take up to two months. The board of directors' approval in this instance is only a formality.

For each of these two situations, outline and calculate how the interest rate risk can be hedged using the Treasury long bond futures. Show all calculations, including the total number of futures contracts used.

26. You ran a regression of the yield of KC Company's 10-year bond on the 10-year U.S. Treasury benchmark's yield using month-end data for the past year. You found the following result:

$$\text{Yield}_{\text{KC}} = .54 + 1.22\ \text{Yield}_{\text{Treasury}}$$

Where Yield_{KC} is the yield on the KC bond and $\text{Yield}_{\text{Treasury}}$ is the yield on the U.S. Treasury bond.

The modified duration on the 10-year U.S. Treasury is 7.0 years, and modified duration on the KC bond is 6.93 years.

a. Calculate the percentage change in the price of the 10-year U.S. Treasury, assuming a 50-basis-point change in the yield on the 10-year U.S. Treasury.

b. Calculate the percentage change in the price of the KC bond, using the regression equation above, assuming a 50-basis-point change in the yield on the 10-year U.S. Treasury.

27. Futures contracts and options contracts can be used to modify risk. Identify the fundamental distinction between a futures contract and an option contract, and briefly explain the difference in the manner that futures and options modify portfolio risk.

CFA® PROBLEMS

28. Suppose your client says, "I am invested in Japanese stocks but want to eliminate my exposure to this market for a period of time. Can I accomplish this without the cost and inconvenience of selling out and buying back in again if my expectations change?"

a. Briefly describe a strategy to hedge both the local market risk and the currency risk of investing in Japanese stocks.

b. Briefly explain why the hedge strategy you described in part (*a*) might not be fully effective.

29. Suppose that the spot price of the Euro is currently 90 cents. The one-year futures price is 93 cents. Is the interest rate higher in the United States or the Euro zone?

30. *a.* The spot price of the British pound is currently \$1.60. If the risk-free interest rate on one-year government bonds is 4 percent in the United States and 8 percent in the United Kingdom, what must be the forward price of the pound for delivery one year from now?

b. How could an investor make risk-free arbitrage profits if the forward price were higher than the price you gave in answer to (*a*)? Give a numerical example.

31. Consider the following information:

$$r_{\text{US}} = 4\% \qquad r_{\text{UK}} = 7\%$$
$$E_0 = 1.60 \text{ dollars per pound}$$
$$F_0 = 1.58 \text{ (1-year delivery)}$$

where the interest rates are annual yields on U.S. or U.K. bills. Given this information,

a. Where would you lend?
b. Where would you borrow?
c. How could you arbitrage?

CFA® PROBLEMS

32. René Michaels, CFA plans to invest $1 million in U.S. government cash equivalents for the next 90 days. Michaels's client has authorized her to use non–U.S. government cash equivalents, but only if the currency risk is hedged to U.S. dollars by using forward currency contracts.
a. Calculate the U.S. dollar value of the hedged investment at the end of 90 days for each of the two cash equivalents in the table below. Show all calculations.
b. Briefly explain the theory that best accounts for your results.
c. Based on this theory, estimate the implied interest rate for a 90-day U.S. government cash equivalent.

Interest Rates
90-Day Cash Equivalents

Japanese government	7.6%
Swiss government	8.6%

Exchange Rates
Currency Units per U.S. Dollar

	Spot	90-Day Forward
Japanese yen	133.05	133.47
Swiss franc	1.5260	1.5348

33. The U.S. yield curve is flat at 5 percent and the Euro yield curve is flat at 8 percent. The current exchange rate is $.85 per Euro. What will be the swap rate on an agreement to exchange currency over a three-year period? The swap will call for the exchange of one million Euros for a given number of dollars in each year.

34. Firm ABC enters a five-year swap with firm XYZ to pay LIBOR in return for a fixed 8 percent rate on notional principal of $10 million. Two years from now, the market rate on three-year swaps is LIBOR for 7 percent; at this time, firm XYZ goes bankrupt and defaults on its swap obligation.
a. Why is firm ABC harmed by the default?
b. What is the market value of the loss incurred by ABC as a result of the default?
c. Suppose instead that ABC had gone bankrupt. How do you think the swap would be treated in the reorganization of the firm?

35. At the present time, one can enter five-year swaps that exchange LIBOR for 8 percent. Five-year caps with limit rates of 8 percent sell for $.30 per dollar of notional principal. What must be the price of five-year floors with a limit rate of 8 percent?

36. At the present time, one can enter five-year swaps that exchange LIBOR for 8 percent. An *off-market swap* would then be defined as a swap of LIBOR for a fixed rate other than 8 percent. For example, a firm with 10 percent coupon debt outstanding might like to convert to synthetic floating-rate debt by entering a swap in which it pays LIBOR and receives a fixed rate of 10 percent. What up-front payment will be required to induce a counterparty to take the other side of this swap? Assume notional principal is $10 million.

CSI

The following questions are adapted from the Canadian Securities Course.

37. "Buying futures contracts on an underlying commodity allows the buyer to lock in a future price." True or false?

38. Which of the following statements is/are correct regarding futures and forwards?
a. A futures contract entails an immediate transfer of ownership of the underlying security.

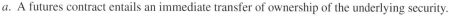

b. A forward allows the holder to make or take delivery of the underlying commodity or financial instrument, in the future, at the going price on that future date.

c. Because of the associated risks, the margins requirements (in percentage terms) are set higher than most financial instruments.

d. Both futures and forward contracts are derivative instruments used extensively as a risk management tool by portfolio managers and other hedgers.

STANDARD &POOR'S

From the Market Insight entry page (**www.mcgrawhill.ca/edumarketinsight**), link to *Industry*, then pull down to the soft drink industry. Open the S&P industry survey for food and nonalcoholic beverages and review the *Key Industry Ratios and Statistics*. What futures contract might this industry use to hedge its price risk? Where is this contract traded? For information on this market see **www.chdwk.com/sugar.cfm**.

STANDARD &POOR'S

From the Market Insight entry page (**www.mcgrawhill.ca/edumarketinsight**), link to Coca-Cola (KO). From the *EDGAR* link and the latest 10K report, find the proportion of Coke's revenue derived from sales outside the United States. If Coke expects to transfer funds from Europe to the United States in 90 days, how might it hedge this transaction with currency futures and options on futures contracts? (What contracts might Coke buy or sell? Why?)

E-INVESTMENTS
Describing Different Swaps

Go to **www.finpipe.com/derprem.htm**. Finpipe.com contains excellent discussions on the derivatives markets. From this site, access the descriptions on interest rate swaps, equity swaps, and commodity swaps.

Describe each of the swaps. Give an example of how each might be used to hedge risk.

PART SEVEN

ACTIVE PORTFOLIO MANAGEMENT

20 Active Management and Performance Measurement

21 Portfolio Management Techniques

22 International Investing

ACTIVE MANAGEMENT AND PERFORMANCE MEASUREMENT

In the first parts of this book, we presented the concept of asset pricing under a portfolio theory approach that led to the notion of efficient markets. This demonstrated why assets should be efficiently priced and why the market portfolio represents the appropriate equity investment choice. The theory implies that a passive strategy of holding the market portfolio of equities, in conjunction with investments in bonds and cash, is optimal. Chapter 9 on market efficiency summarized this conclusion. Subsequently, we investigated techniques for evaluating stocks, bonds and derivatives; the result of this valuation process should be the prices that these assets would command in the efficient market. Were the results of these analyses to produce values that differed from observed market prices, we would have to reject either our analysis or the notion of rigid market efficiency; in the latter case, this would give rise to active rather than passive management.

Despite the efficient market hypothesis, there are reasons to believe that active management can have effective results, but these need to be verified after the fact. It is possible to evaluate the performance of a portfolio manager, but it is not a simple matter; what the manager is trying to do as an investment strategy, and how this relates to individual investors, will cause different measures of performance to apply. Although the subject may seem technical, a close and accurate appraisal of performance is needed to cut through the arbitrary or nonspecific claims of success made by many professional managers.

We begin with a discussion of what one might expect from active management but illustrate how active management causes problems in evaluation. We then review the conventional approaches to risk adjustment for performance evaluation. We show the problems inherent in these approaches, even though they involve the use of specific theoretical measures, when they are applied in a complex world. We also present some newer alternatives to performance appraisal. Next we deal specifically with the issue of market timing, in which asset allocations between the three components are modified in response to macroeconomic factors. We conclude with some results and a discussion regarding the evaluation of actual performance. The appendices to this chapter present some technical details of measuring investment returns and an advanced analysis for assessing timing ability as an option.

20.1 THE OBJECTIVE OF ACTIVE MANAGEMENT

How can a theory of active portfolio management be reconciled with the notion that markets are in equilibrium? Market efficiency prevails when many investors are willing to depart from maximum diversification, or a passive strategy, by adding mispriced securities to their portfolios in the hope of realizing abnormal returns. The competition for such returns ensures that prices will be near their "true" values. Most managers will not beat the passive strategy on a risk-adjusted basis. However, in the competition for rewards to investing, exceptional managers might beat the average forecasts built into market prices.

There is both economic logic and some empirical evidence to indicate that exceptional portfolio managers can beat the average forecast. Let us discuss economic logic first. We must assume that, if no analyst can beat the passive strategy, investors will be smart enough to divert their funds from strategies entailing expensive analysis to less expensive passive strategies. With less capital under active management and less research being produced, prices will no longer reflect sophisticated forecasts. The potential profit resulting from research will then increase and active managers using this research will again have superior performance.[1]

As for empirical evidence, consider the following: (1) some portfolio managers have produced streaks of abnormal returns that are hard to label as lucky outcomes; (2) the "noise" in realized rates is enough to prevent us from rejecting outright the hypothesis that some money managers have beaten the passive strategy by a statistically small, yet economically significant, margin; and (3) some anomalies in realized returns have been sufficiently persistent to suggest that portfolio managers who identified them in a timely fashion could have beaten the passive strategy over prolonged periods.

These conclusions persuade us that there is a role for a theory of active portfolio management. Active management has an inevitable lure even if investors agree that security markets are nearly efficient.

Suppose that capital markets are perfectly efficient, an easily accessible market index portfolio is available, and this portfolio is, for all practical purposes, the efficient risky portfolio.

[1]This point is worked out fully in Sanford J. Grossman and Joseph E. Stiglitz, "On the Impossibility of Informationally Efficient Markets," *American Economic Review* 70 (June 1980).

Clearly, in this case security selection would be a futile endeavour. You would be better off with a passive strategy of allocating funds to a money market fund (the safe asset) and the market index portfolio. Under these simplifying assumptions the optimal investment strategy seems to require no effort or know-how.

Such a conclusion, however, is too hasty. Recall that the proper allocation of investment funds to the risk-free and risky portfolios requires some analysis because *y*, the fraction to be invested in the risky market portfolio, *M*, is given by

$$y = \frac{E(r_M) - r_f}{.01A\sigma_M^2} \tag{20.1}$$

where $E(r_M) - r_f$ is the risk premium on *M*, σ_M^2 its variance, and *A* is the investor's coefficient of risk aversion. Any rational allocation therefore requires an estimate of σ_M and $E(r_M)$. Even a passive investor needs to do some forecasting, in other words.

Forecasting $E(r_M)$ and σ_M is further complicated by the existence of security classes that are affected by different environmental factors. Long-term bond returns, for example, are driven largely by changes in the term structure of interest rates, whereas equity returns depend on changes in the broader economic environment, including macroeconomic factors beyond interest rates. Once our investor determines relevant forecasts for separate sorts of investments, she might as well use an optimization program to determine the proper mix for the portfolio. It is easy to see how the investor may be lured away from a purely passive strategy, and we have not even considered temptations such as international stock and bond portfolios or sector portfolios.

In fact, even the definition of a "purely passive strategy" is problematic, because simple strategies involving only the market-index portfolio and risk-free assets now seem to call for market analysis. For our purposes we define purely passive strategies as those that use only index funds *and* weight those funds by fixed proportions that do not vary in response to perceived market conditions. For example, a portfolio strategy that always places 60 percent in a stock market index fund, 30 percent in a bond index fund, and 10 percent in a money market fund is a purely passive strategy.

More important, the lure into active management may be extremely strong because the potential profit from active strategies is enormous. At the same time, competition among the multitude of active managers creates the force driving market prices to near-efficiency levels. Although enormous profits may be increasingly difficult to earn, decent profits to the better analysts should be the rule rather than the exception. For prices to remain efficient to some degree, some analysts must be able to eke out a reasonable profit. Absence of profits would decimate the active investment management industry, eventually allowing prices to stray from informationally efficient levels. The theory of managing active portfolios is the concern of this chapter.

What does an investor expect from a professional portfolio manager, and how does this expectation affect the operation of the manager? If the client were risk-neutral, that is, indifferent to risk, the answer would be straightforward. The investor would expect the portfolio manager to construct a portfolio with the highest possible expected rate of return. The portfolio manager follows this dictum and is judged by the realized average rate of return.

When the client is risk-averse, the answer is more difficult. Without a normative theory of portfolio management, the manager would have to consult each client before making any portfolio decision in order to ascertain that reward (average return) is commensurate with risk. Massive and constant input would be needed from the client-investors, and the economic value of professional management would be questionable.

Fortunately, the theory of mean-variance efficient portfolio management allows us to separate the "product decision," which is how to construct a mean-variance efficient risky portfolio, and the "consumption decision," or the investor's allocation of funds between the efficient risky portfolio and the safe asset. We have seen that construction of the optimal risky portfolio is purely a technical problem, resulting in a single optimal risky portfolio appropriate for all investors. Investors will differ only in how they apportion investment to that risky portfolio and the safe asset.

Another feature of the mean-variance theory that affects portfolio management decisions is the criterion for choosing the optimal risky portfolio. In Chapter 8 we established that the optimal risky portfolio for any investor is the one that maximizes the reward-to-variability ratio, or the expected excess rate of return (over the risk-free rate) divided by the standard deviation. A manager who uses this Markowitz methodology to construct the optimal risky portfolio will satisfy all clients regardless of risk aversion. Clients, for their part, can evaluate managers using statistical methods to draw inferences from realized rates of return about prospective, or ex ante, reward-to-variability ratios.

William Sharpe's assessment of mutual fund performance[2] is the seminal work in the area of portfolio performance evaluation. Sharpe's measure, the reward-to-variability ratio or excess return over standard deviation, $(\bar{r}_P - \bar{r}_f)/\sigma_P$, is now a common criterion for tracking performance of professionally managed portfolios. We will define it formally in the next section, but for now, we assume that it is a suitable basis for comparison.

Briefly, mean-variance portfolio theory implies that the objective of professional portfolio managers is to maximize the (ex ante) Sharpe measure, which entails maximizing the slope of the capital allocation line (CAL). A "good" manager is one whose CAL is steeper than the CAL representing the passive strategy of holding a market index portfolio. Clients can observe rates of return and compute the realized Sharpe measure (the ex post CAL) to evaluate the relative performance of their manager.

Ideally, clients would like to invest their funds with the most able manager, one who consistently obtains the highest Sharpe measure and presumably has real forecasting ability. This is true for all clients, regardless of their degree of risk aversion. At the same time, each client must decide what fraction of investment funds to allocate to this manager, placing the remainder in a safe fund. If the manager's Sharpe measure is constant over time (and can be estimated by clients), the investor can compute the optimal fraction to be invested with the manager from equation 6.3, based on the portfolio long-term average return and variance. The remainder will be invested in a money market fund.

The manager's ex ante Sharpe measure from updated forecasts will be constantly varying. Clients may wish to increase their allocation to the risky portfolio when the forecasts are optimistic, and vice versa. However, it would be impractical to constantly communicate updated forecasts to clients and for them to constantly revise their allocation between the risky portfolios and risk-free asset.

Allowing managers to shift funds between their optimal risky portfolio and a safe asset according to their forecasts alleviates the problem. Indeed, many stock funds allow the managers reasonable flexibility to do just that. Managers can be assessed on their decisions of timing, when to invest in risky or safe portfolios, and selectivity (i.e., which risky assets to choose). For a discussion on active management, see the boxed article here.

Performance Measurement Under Active Management

We know that the high variance of stock returns requires a very long observation period to determine performance levels with any statistical significance, even if portfolio returns are distributed

[2]William F. Sharpe, "Mutual Fund Performance," *Journal of Business, Supplement on Security Prices* 39 (January 1966).

DEBUNKING THE MYTHS OF PASSIVE MANAGEMENT

Over the last several years, passive management has enjoyed impressive growth. While active managers used to ignore their boring indexing cousins, times have changed. Indexing is gaining market share. It often outperforms the majority of active managers. Now the active world has raised a variety of arguments against the use of passive management. I present below my response to a series of myths that have come to the fore in recent months.

- Active management is preferable to indexing because indexing requires that you be fully invested. This hurts you in down markets. This argument is used most often in the U.S. equity context.

The problem with this argument is that historically, it has not been true. According to a study by Lipper services, the Standard & Poor's (S&P) 500 has outperformed the median manager in five of the last seven significant market downturns. Over 75% of managers have failed to beat the S&P 500 index in recent years.

Active managers must make two market timing calls correctly: knowing when to get into cash at the market peak and knowing when to get back into stocks when the market bottoms. Research and history show that active managers are not good at market timing calls. Even if active managers knew when to increase cash just in time for down markets, there are many more up markets than down markets. Unless their timing is perfect in both directions, remaining fully invested is a better overall strategy.

- The equity bull market has been due to the success of large-cap stocks. As soon as mid- and small-cap stocks performbetter, active managers will outperform. This is because they often hold some mid- and small-cap stocks.

There is no question that large-cap indexes have outperformed, particularly in the U.S. Active managers have been free to invest in these companies throughout the cycle. Some have chosen to underweight these names, with poor results. This is not the fault of the large-cap index. Active managers as a group simply made the wrong choices.

- The surge of the equity markets, particularly in the U.S. has been exacerbated by large flows into retail index funds during a bull market. When markets weaken, retail investors will flee these funds, which will have a downward spiralling effect on the index and index funds.

Equity markets around the world have been fed by flows from retail investors. In the case of North America, many of these assets are coming from defined contribution plans and other long-term retirement arrangements. These investors generally put their money into mutual funds and wait. Only a small minority moves assets frequently between investment options to catch the latest market swing. As well, retail investors are much better informed than they were a decade ago. There is no evidence that they have liquidated en masse when markets fall. For these reasons, it is unlikely that massive panic selling will occur, with retail investors fleeing in droves from index funds.

- Many indexes are problematic and have diversification problems. The Toronto Stock Exchange (TSE) 300 is heavily weighted in a few names, such as Nortel and BCE. The Europe and Australia, Far East (EAFE) index has been weighted heavily in Japan and now has a large exposure to Europe and the U.K. On the bond side, the Scotia Capital Markets Universe (SCMU) index does not hold smaller issues, which eliminates an important part of the market.

Despite the imperfections of the various indexes around the world, indexing remains a prudent investment strategy. Active portfolios are generally less diversified than indexed portfolios. Some may argue that a 10% weighting in Nortel is large in nominal terms. But underweighting Nortel by a large amount in this context represents a significant bet.

Interestingly, we most often hear complaints about the indexes when managers as a group have underperformed. Indexes remain an important performance benchmark.

- While most bond managers have produced near-index returns, new opportunities for outperformance are opening up as corporate issuance increases.

With the SCMU index now holding nearly 20% in corporate bonds (up from 11% just three years ago), the relative overall yield of the SCMU index is higher. This only raises the bar for active managers. The higher the overall credit quality of an index, the easier it is to beat: just add credit product. Active managers now must make three credit bets to add value: take on more credit risk, make the right specific credit bets and make market timing bets as to when to overweight or underweight corporates. This will prove to be a challenge.

While everyone loves a good controversy, most people agree that active and passive management work well together in a variety of fund structures. Investors are continuing to strike the optimal balance of indexing and other quantitative strategies within their total fund structure.

Source: Marcia L. Brown, *Benefits Canada* 23, no. 12 (December 1999), pp. 17, 19. Reprinted with permission from the December 1999 edition of *Benefits Canada*.

with constant mean and variance. Imagine how this problem is compounded when portfolio return distributions are constantly changing.

It is acceptable to assume that the return distributions of passive strategies have constant mean and variance when the measurement interval is not too long. However, under an active strategy return distributions change by design, as the portfolio manager updates the portfolio in accordance with the dictates of financial analysis. In such a case, estimating various statistics from a sample period assuming a constant mean and variance may lead to substantial errors. Let us look at an example.

Suppose that the Sharpe measure of the passive strategy is .4. Over an initial period of 52 weeks, the portfolio manager executes a low-risk strategy with an annualized mean excess return of 1 percent and standard deviation of 2 percent. This makes for a Sharpe measure of .5, which beats the passive strategy. Over the next 52-week period this manager finds that a *high*-risk strategy is optimal, with an annual mean excess return of 9 percent and standard deviation of 18 percent. Here again, the Sharpe measure is .5. Over the two-year period our manager maintains a better-than-passive Sharpe measure.

Figure 20.1 shows a pattern of (annualized) quarterly returns that are consistent with our description of the manager's strategy over two years. In the first four quarters the excess returns are –1 percent, 3 percent, –1 percent, and 3 percent, making for an average of 1 percent and standard deviation of 2 percent. In the next four quarters the returns are: –9 percent, 27 percent, –9 percent, and 27 percent, making for an average of 9 percent and a standard deviation of 18 percent. Since Sharpe's measure is average excess return divided by standard deviation, both years yield a ratio of 0.5. However, if we take the eight-quarter sequence as a single measurement period and measure the portfolio's mean and standard deviation over that full period, we will obtain an average excess return of 5 percent and standard deviation of 13.42 percent, making for a Sharpe measure of only .37. Since a higher Sharpe ratio is considered better, the active strategy is apparently inferior to the passive strategy!

What happened? The shift in the mean from the first four quarters to the next was not recognized as a shift in strategy. Instead, the difference in mean returns in the two years added to the

Figure 20.1 Portfolio returns.

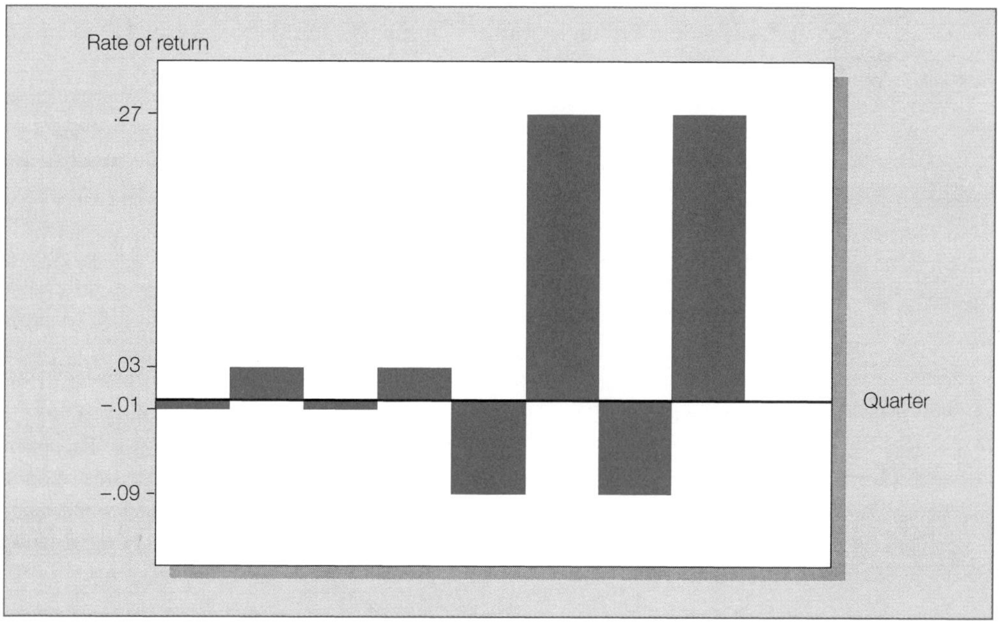

appearance of volatility in portfolio returns. The active strategy with shifting means appears riskier than it really is and biases the estimate of the Sharpe measure downward. We conclude that for actively managed portfolios it is crucial to keep track of portfolio composition and changes in portfolio mean and risk.

20.2 RISK-ADJUSTED PERFORMANCE MEASURES

In order to evaluate the performance of a portfolio manager, we will need both a measurement of the returns of the portfolio and a way of comparing those returns to one or more benchmarks considering the risk involved. The first problem is not quite as trivial as it might seem, as it also implies the question of whether the past performance is indicative of future performance. The second process depends greatly on the context in which the comparison is made.

Measuring Returns

We have already defined the holding period return as the difference between the end-of-period and initial values plus interim cash flows (dividends or interest), divided by the initial value. This concept is clear for a single period, as we see from the simple example that follows. Suppose you purchase today for $50 a stock paying a $2 dividend; if in one year you sell it for $53, your rate of return is simply the gain ($53 $50), plus a dividend of $2 divided by cost ($50). Then (3 + 2)/50 gives a return of 10 percent. The financial mathematics technique of internal rate of return yields the same result. Equating the initial investment ($50) to the end-of-year proceeds of ($53 + $2) discounted by $1 + r$ (the unknown rate) gives the solution $r = .10$ again.

This simple result is confused by the complication of changing the dollar investment in the portfolio over time. For instance, suppose you were to increase your holding of the stock after one period; how do you calculate your return at the end of the second period? The answer is to calculate the **dollar-weighted rate of return** by using the discounted cash flow approach. Yet the performance of a manager cannot be assessed on the basis of an individual's choice of contributing or withdrawing funds from a portfolio. For this reason, we tend to use the **time-weighted rate of return** for assessing professional management.

A second aspect of the problem relates to the method of averaging over many holding periods. This can be done in the conventional way of a simple arithmetic average, in which we sum the annual returns and divide by the number of years. Yet we should also recall from interest rate calculations that we often multiply the annual returns (plus one) and take the *n*th root for the geometric average.

Both of these questions are addressed in depth in Appendix 20A, which you should review to clarify the issue if you are not completely familiar with the techniques and which illustrates the technical issues involved in using different techniques of averaging. As an individual, you will probably be interested in how much your portfolio has grown under your personal history of contributing excess funds, and for this purpose your performance will be best reflected by the dollar-weighted return and by using geometric averaging. For our purposes here, which concern the appraisal of professionals, it is the time-weighted return that we use. This is combined with arithmetic averaging when we measure their past performance and use this in choosing to retain their services for the future. The simplest calculation of their performance that appears in popular surveys will be the ratio of their current portfolio values to the starting value at various intervals, leading to the geometric average as the measure of their annual returns.

Risk Adjustment Techniques

Calculating average portfolio returns does not mean the task is done—returns must be adjusted for risk before they can be compared meaningfully. The simplest and most popular way to adjust returns for portfolio risk is to compare rates of return with those of other investment funds with similar risk characteristics. For example, high-yield bond portfolios are grouped into one "universe," growth stock, equity funds are grouped into another universe, and so on. Then the (usually time-weighted) average returns of each fund within the universe are ordered, and each portfolio manager receives a percentile ranking depending on relative performance within the **comparison universe**. For example, the manager with the ninth-best performance in a universe of 100 funds would be the 90th percentile manager: his performance was better than 90 percent of all competing funds over the evaluation period.

www.tsx.com

These relative rankings usually are displayed in a chart such as that in Figure 20.2. The chart summarizes performance rankings over five periods: one quarter, one year, three years, five years, and ten years. The top and bottom lines of each box are drawn at the rate of return of the 95th and 5th percentile managers. The three dotted lines correspond to the rates of return of the 75th, 50th (median), and 25th percentile managers. The diamond is drawn at the average return of a particular fund and the rectangle is drawn at the return of a benchmark index such as the S&P/TSX Composite. The placement of the diamond within the box is an easy-to-read representation of the performance of the fund relative to the comparison universe.

This comparison of performance with other managers of similar investment style is a useful first step in evaluating performance. However, such rankings can be misleading. For example, within a particular universe, some managers may concentrate on particular subgroups, so that portfolio characteristics are not truly comparable. For example, within the equity universe, one manager may concentrate on high-beta stocks. Also, refinements are occurring. More sophisticated measures are being created, for example, indices based on fairly precise characterizations, such as small-capitalization firms or biotechnology firms. These measures help to establish standards for comparison, but they are generally not presented to the average

Figure 20.2 Universe comparison (periods ending December 31, 2004).

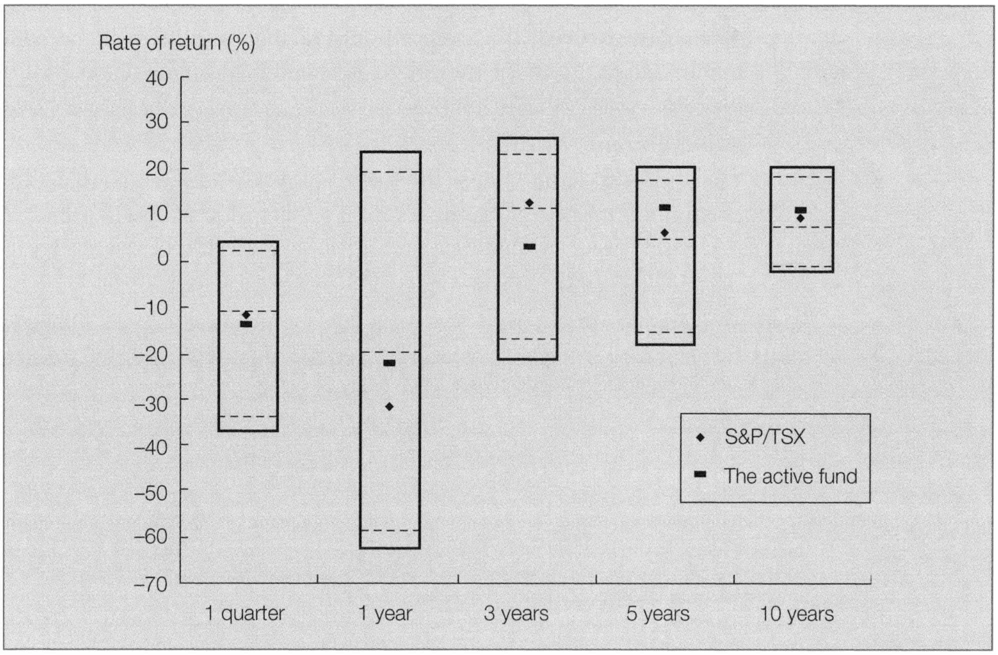

investor in mass-circulation tabulations. Within fixed-income universes, durations can vary across managers. These considerations suggest that a more precise means for risk adjustment is desirable.

Methods of risk-adjusted performance evaluation using mean-variance criteria came on stage simultaneously with the capital asset pricing model. Jack Treynor,[3] William Sharpe,[4] and Michael Jensen[5] recognized immediately the implications of the CAPM for rating the performance of managers. Within a short time, academicians were in command of a battery of performance measures, and a bounty of scholarly investigation of mutual fund performance was pouring from ivory towers. Shortly thereafter, agents emerged who were willing to supply rating services to portfolio managers eager for regular feedback. This trend has since lost some of its steam.

One explanation for the lagging popularity of risk-adjusted performance measures is the generally negative cast to the performance statistics. In nearly efficient markets it is extremely difficult for analysts to perform well enough to overcome costs of research and transaction costs. Indeed, we have seen that the most professionally managed equity funds generally underperform the S&P/TSX Composite index on both risk-adjusted and raw return measures. Another reason mean-variance criteria may have suffered relates to intrinsic problems in these measures, such as the one illustrated in the previous section.[6]

Let us begin by cataloguing some possible risk-adjusted performance measures and examining the circumstances in which each measure might be most relevant.

1. *Sharpe's measure:* $(\bar{r}_P - \bar{r}_f)/\sigma_P$

   Sharpe's measure divides average portfolio excess return over the sample period by the standard deviation of returns over that period. It measures the reward to-(total-) volatility tradeoff.[7]

2. *Treynor's measure:* $(\bar{r}_P - \bar{r}_f)/\beta_P$

   Like Sharpe's, **Treynor's measure** gives excess return per unit of risk, but uses systematic risk instead of total risk.

3. *Jensen's measure:* $\alpha_P = \bar{r}_P - [\bar{r}_f + \beta_P(\bar{r}_M - \bar{r}_f)]$

   Jensen's measure is the average return on the portfolio over and above that predicted by the CAPM, given the portfolio's beta and the average market return. Jensen's measure is the portfolio's alpha value.

4. *Appraisal ratio:* $\alpha_P/\sigma(e_P)$

   The **appraisal ratio** divides the alpha of the portfolio by the nonsystematic risk of the portfolio. It measures abnormal return per unit of risk that in principle could be diversified away by holding a market index portfolio. (The industry also calls this the "information ratio" and refers to $\sigma(e_P)$ as the "tracking error.")

Each measure has some appeal. But each does not necessarily provide consistent assessments of performance, since the risk measures used to adjust returns differ substantially.

---

[3]Jack L. Treynor, "How to Rate Management Investment Funds," *Harvard Business Review* 43 (January/February 1966).

[4]William F. Sharpe, "Mutual Fund Performance," *Journal of Business* 39 (January 1966).

[5]Michael C. Jensen, "The Performance of Mutual Funds in the Period 1945–1964," *Journal of Finance*, May 1968; and "Risk, the Pricing of Capital Assets, and the Evaluation of Investment Portfolios," *Journal of Business*, April 1969.

[6]A statistical analysis of the subject is presented in J. D. Jobson and R. M. Korkie, "Performance Hypothesis Testing with the Sharpe and Treynor Measures," *Journal of Finance* 36, no. 4 (September 1981).

[7]We place bars over r_f as well as r_P to denote the fact that since the risk-free rate may not be constant over the measurement period, we are taking a sample average, just as we do for r_P.

? CONCEPT CHECK

1. Consider the following data for a particular sample period:

	Portfolio P	Market M
Average return	.35	.28
Beta	1.20	1.00
Standard deviation	.42	.30
Nonsystematic risk, $\sigma(e)$	.18	0.00

Calculate the following performance measures for portfolio P and the market: Sharpe, Jensen (alpha), Treynor, and appraisal ratio. The T-bill rate during the period was .06. By which measures did portfolio P outperform the market?

The M^2 Measure of Performance

While the Sharpe ratio can be used to rank portfolio performance, its numerical value is not easy to interpret. Comparing the ratios for portfolios M and P in Concept Check 1, you should have found that $S_P = .69$ and $S_M = .73$. This suggests that portfolio P underperformed the market index. But is a difference of .04 in the Sharpe ratio economically meaningful? We are used to comparing rates of return, but these ratios are difficult to interpret.

A variant of Sharpe's measure was recently introduced by Leah Modigliani of Morgan Stanley and her grandfather Franco Modigliani, past winner of the Nobel Prize for economics.[8] Their approach has been dubbed the M^2 measure (for Modigliani-squared). Like the Sharpe ratio, the M^2 measure focuses on total volatility as a measure of risk, but its risk-adjusted measure of performance has the easy interpretation of a differential return relative to the benchmark index.

To compute the M^2 measure, we imagine that a managed portfolio, P, is mixed with a position in T-bills so that the complete, or "adjusted," portfolio matches the volatility of a market index such as the S&P/TSX Composite. For example, if the managed portfolio has 1.5 times the standard deviation of the index, the adjusted portfolio would be two-thirds invested in the managed portfolio and one-third invested in bills. The adjusted portfolio, which we call P^*, would then have the same standard deviation as the index. (If the managed portfolio had *lower* standard deviation than the index, it would be leveraged by borrowing money and investing the proceeds in the portfolio.) Because the market index and portfolio P^* have the same standard deviation, we may compare their performance simply by comparing returns. This is the M^2 measure:

$$M^2 = r_{P*} - r_M \tag{20.2}$$

EXAMPLE 20.1 M^2 Measure

Using the data of Concept Check 1, P has a standard deviation of 42 percent versus a market standard deviation of 30 percent. Therefore, the adjusted portfolio P^* would be formed by mixing bills and portfolio P with weights 30/42 = .714 in P and 1 – .714 = .286 in bills. The expected return on this portfolio would be (.286 × 6%) + (.714 × 35%) = 26.7 percent, which is 1.3 percent less than the market return. Thus portfolio P has an M^2 measure of –1.3 percent.

A graphical representation of the M^2 measure appears in Figure 20.3. We move down the capital allocation line corresponding to portfolio P (by mixing P with T-bills) until we reduce the standard deviation of the adjusted portfolio to match that of the market index. The M^2 measure is then the vertical distance (i.e., the difference in expected returns) between portfolios P^* and M.

[8]Franco Modigliani and Leah Modigliani, "Risk-Adjusted Performance," *Journal of Portfolio Management*, Winter 1997, pp. 45–54.

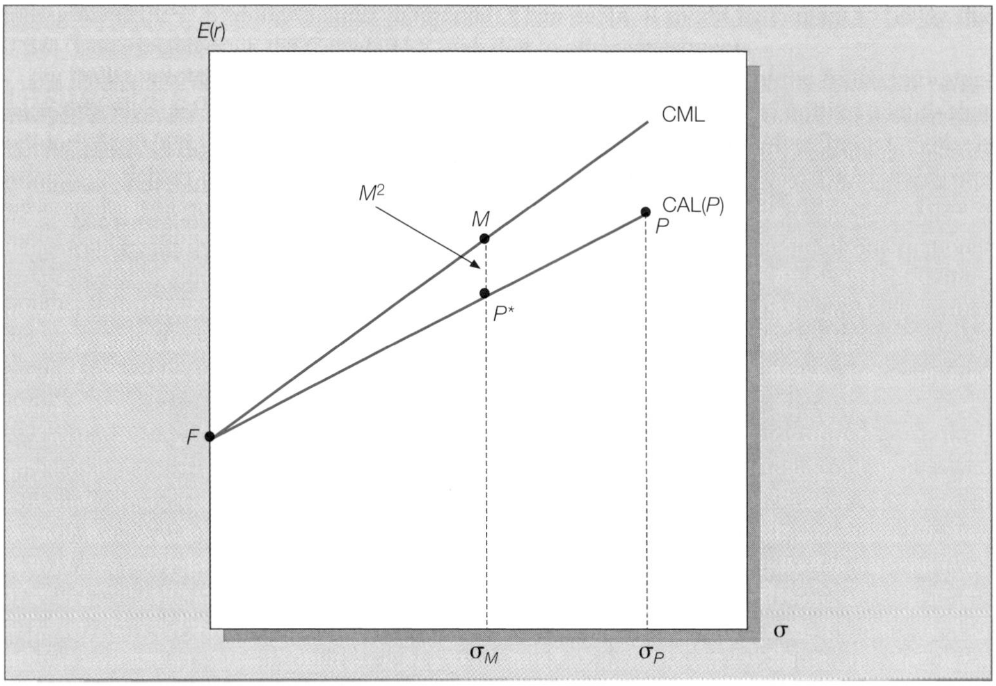

Figure 20.3 ***M*² of portfolio *P*.**

You can see from Figure 20.3 that P will have an M^2 measure below that of the market when its capital allocation line is less steep than the capital market line, that is, when its Sharpe ratio is less than that of the market index.

Relationships Between the Measures

It is interesting to see how these measures are related to one another. Beginning with Treynor's measure, note that as the market index beta is 1.0, Treynor's measure for the market index is

$$T_M = \bar{r}_M - \bar{r}_f$$

The mean excess return of portfolio P is

$$\bar{r}_P - \bar{r}_f = \alpha_P + \beta_P(\bar{r}_M - \bar{r}_f)$$

and thus its Treynor measure is

$$\begin{aligned} T_P &= \frac{\alpha_P + \beta_P(\bar{r}_M - \bar{r}_f)}{\beta_P} \\ &= \frac{\alpha_P}{\beta_P} + \bar{r}_M - \bar{r}_f \\ &= \frac{\alpha_P}{\beta_P} + T_M \end{aligned}$$

Treynor's measure compares portfolios on the basis of the alpha-to-beta ratio.[9] Note that this is very different in numerical value *and spirit* from the appraisal ratio, which is the ratio of alpha to residual risk.

[9]Interestingly, although our definition of the Treynor measure is conventional, Treynor himself initially worked with the alpha-to-beta ratio. In this form, the measure is independent of the market. Both measures will rank-order portfolio performance identically, because they differ by a constant (the market's Treynor value). Some call the ratio of alpha-to-beta "modified alpha" or "modified Jensen's measure," not realizing that this is really Treynor's measure.

The Sharpe measure for the market index portfolio is

$$S_M = \frac{\bar{r}_M - \bar{r}_f}{\sigma_M}$$

For portfolio P we have

$$S_P = \frac{\bar{r}_P - \bar{r}_f}{\sigma_P} = \frac{\alpha_P + \beta_P(\bar{r}_M - \bar{r}_f)}{\sigma_P}$$

With some algebra that relies on the fact that ρ^2 between P and M is

$$\rho^2 = \frac{\beta^2\sigma^2{}_M}{\beta^2\sigma^2{}_M + \sigma^2(e)} = \frac{\beta^2\sigma^2{}_M}{\sigma^2{}_P}$$

we find that

$$S_P = \frac{\alpha_P}{\sigma_P} + \frac{\beta_P(\bar{r}_M - \bar{r}_f)}{\sigma_P}$$

$$= \frac{\alpha_P}{\sigma_P} + \rho S_M$$

This expression yields some insight into the process of generating valuable performance with active management. It is obvious that one needs to find significant-alpha stocks to establish potential value. A higher portfolio alpha, however, has to be tempered by the increase in standard deviation that arises when one departs from full diversification. The more we tilt toward high alpha stocks, the lower the correlation with the market index, ρ, and the greater the potential loss of performance value.

Finally, the M^2 and Sharpe measures are directly related. From Figure 20.3, R_{p*} (the excess return on the adjusted portfolio) equals $S_p\sigma_M$; hence

$$M^2 = r_{p*} - r_M = R_{p*} - R_M = S_p\sigma_M - R_M$$

For superior performance, a positive alpha is required. However, the different measures will, in general, rank portfolios differently than alpha. It is important to use the performance measure that fits the relevant scenario.

Sharpe's Measure as the Criterion for Overall Portfolios

Suppose that Jane d'Arque constructs a portfolio and holds it for a considerable period of time. She makes no changes in portfolio composition during the period. In addition, suppose that the daily rates of return on all securities have constant means, variances, and covariances. This assures that the portfolio rate of return also has a constant mean and variance. These assumptions are unrealistic, but they will help us to focus on the key issue. They also are crucial to understanding the shortcoming of conventional applications of performance measurement.

Now we want to evaluate the performance of Jane's portfolio. Has she made a good choice of securities? This is really a three-pronged question. First, good choice compared with what alternatives? Second, in choosing between two distinct alternatives, what are the appropriate criteria to use to evaluate performance? Finally, having identified the alternatives and the performance criteria, is there a rule that will separate basic ability from the random luck of the draw?

Earlier chapters of this text help to determine portfolio choice criteria. If investor preferences can be summarized by a mean-variance utility function such as that introduced in Chapter 5, we can arrive at a relatively simple criterion. The particular utility function that we have used in this text is

$$U = E(r_P) - \tfrac{1}{2}A\sigma^2{}_P$$

where A is the coefficient of risk aversion. With mean-variance preferences, Jane will want to maximize her Sharpe measure (i.e., the ratio $[E(r_P) - r_f]/\sigma_P$) of her *complete* portfolio of assets. Recall that this is the criterion that led to the selection of the tangency portfolio in Chapter 6. Jane's problem reduces to that of whether her overall portfolio is the one with the highest possible Sharpe ratio.

Appropriate Performance Measures in Three Scenarios

To evaluate Jane's portfolio choice, we first ask whether she intends this portfolio to be her exclusive investment vehicle. If the answer is no, we need to know what her "complementary" portfolio is—the portfolio to which she is adding the one in question. The appropriate measure of portfolio performance depends critically on whether the portfolio is the entire investment fund or only a portion of the investor's overall wealth.

Jane's Choice Portfolio Represents Her Entire Risky Investment Fund In this simplest case, we need to ascertain only whether Jane's portfolio has the highest possible Sharpe measure. We can proceed in three steps:

1. Assume that her past security performance is representative of expected future performance, meaning that security returns over Jane's holding period exhibit averages and sample covariances that Jane might have anticipated.
2. Determine the benchmark (alternative) portfolio that Jane would have held if she had chosen a passive strategy (e.g., the S&P/TSX Composite).
3. Compare Jane's Sharpe measure to that of the alternative.

In essence, when Jane's portfolio represents her entire investment fund, the benchmark alternative is the market index or another specific portfolio. The performance criterion is the Sharpe measure of the actual portfolio versus that of the benchmark portfolio.

Jane's Portfolio Is an Active Portfolio and Is Mixed with the Passive Market Index Portfolio How do we evaluate the optimal mix in this case? Call Jane's portfolio *P*, and denote the market portfolio by *M*. When the two portfolios are mixed optimally, it turns out (as we shall examine more closely in Section 21.3) that the square of the Sharpe measure of the composite portfolio, *C*, is given by

$$S^2{}_C = S^2{}_M + \left[\frac{\alpha_P}{\sigma(e_P)}\right]^2$$

where α_P is the abnormal return of the active portfolio, relative to the passive market portfolio, and $\sigma(e_P)$ is the diversifiable risk. The ratio $\alpha_P/\sigma(e_P)$ is thus the correct performance measure for *P* for this case, since it gives the improvement in the Sharpe measure of the overall portfolio attributable to the inclusion of *P*.

To see the intuition of this result, recall the single-index model:

$$r_P - r_f = \alpha_P + \beta_P(r_M - r_f) + e_P$$

If *P* is fairly priced, the $\alpha_P = 0$, and e_P is just diversifiable risk that can be avoided. If *P* is mispriced, however, α_P no longer equals zero. Instead, it represents the expected abnormal return. Holding *P* in addition to the market portfolio thus brings a reward of α_P against the nonsystematic risk voluntarily incurred, $\sigma(e_P)$. Therefore, the ratio of $\alpha_P/\sigma(e_P)$ is the natural benefit-to-cost ratio for portfolio *P*.

Jane's Choice Portfolio Is One of Many Portfolios Combined into a Large Investment Fund This third case might describe the situation where Jane, as a corporate financial officer, manages the corporate pension fund. She parcels out the entire fund to a number of portfolio managers. Then she evaluates the performance of individual managers to reallocate parts of the fund to improve future performance. What is the correct performance measure?

Table 20.1 Portfolio Performance

	Portfolio *P*	Portfolio *Q*	Market
Beta	.90	1.60	1.0
Excess return ($\bar{r} - \bar{r}_f$)	.11	.19	.10
Alpha*	.02	.03	0

*Alpha = Excess return − (Beta × Market excess return)

$= (\bar{r} - \bar{r}_f) - \beta(\bar{r}_M - \bar{r}_f)$

$= \bar{r} - [\bar{r}_f + \beta(\bar{r}_m - \bar{r}_f)]$

We could use the appraisal ratio if the complementary portfolio to *P* is approximately equal to the market index portfolio by virtue of its being spread among many managers and thus well diversified. But you can imagine that the portfolio managers would take offense at this assumption. Jane, too, is likely to respond, "Do you think I am exerting all this effort just to end up with a passive portfolio?"

We could estimate the benefit of portfolio *P* to the entire diversified fund by *P*'s alpha value. α_P would give Jane some indication of *P*'s potential contribution to the overall portfolio. A better solution, however, is to use Treynor's measure.

Suppose you determine that portfolio *P* exhibits an alpha value of 2 percent. "Not bad," you tell Jane. But she pulls out of her desk a report and informs you that another portfolio, *Q*, has an alpha of 3 percent. "One hundred basis points is significant," says Jane. "Should I transfer some of my funds from *P*'s manager to *Q*'s?"

You tabulate the relevant data, as in Table 20.1 and graph the results as in Figure 20.4. Note that we plot *P* and *Q* in the mean return–beta (rather than the mean–standard deviation) plane, because we assume that *P* and *Q* are two of many subportfolios in the fund, and thus that nonsystematic risk will be largely diversified away, leaving beta as the appropriate risk measure. The security market line (SML) shows the value of α_P and α_Q as the distance of *P* and *Q* above the SML.

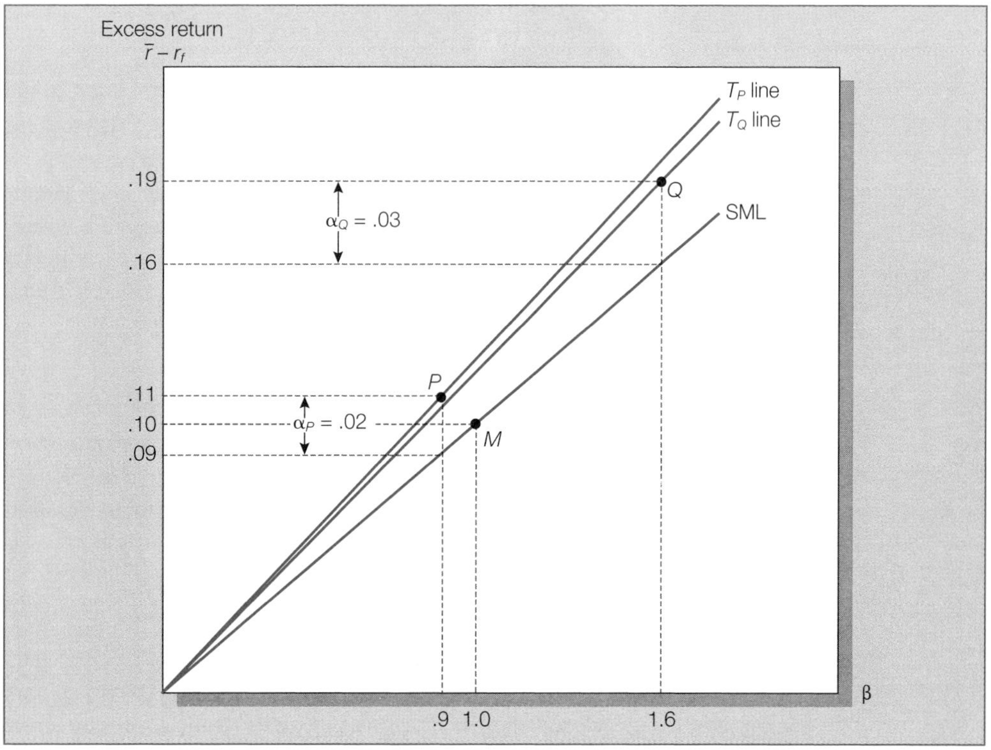

Figure 20.4 Treynor measure.

Suppose that portfolio Q can be mixed with T-bills. Specifically, if we invest w_Q in Q and $w_F = 1 - w_Q$ in T-bills, the resulting portfolio, Q^*, will have alpha and beta values proportional to Q's alpha and beta and to w_Q:

$$\alpha_{Q^*} = w_Q \alpha_Q$$
$$\beta_{Q^*} = w_Q \beta_Q$$

Thus, all portfolios Q^* generated from mixes of Q and T-bills plot on a straight line from the origin through Q. We call it the T-line for the Treynor measure, which is the slope of this line.

Figure 20.4 shows the T-line for portfolio P as well. P has a steeper T-line; despite its lower alpha, P is a better portfolio in this case after all. For any *given* beta, a mixture of P with T-bills will give a better alpha than a mixture of Q with T-bills.

EXAMPLE 20.2 Equalizing Beta

Suppose that we choose to mix Q with T-bills to create a portfolio Q^* with a beta equal to that of P. We find the necessary proportion by solving for w_Q:

$$w_Q \beta_Q = 1.6 w_Q = \beta_P = .9$$
$$w_Q = \tfrac{9}{16}$$

Portfolio Q^* therefore has an alpha of

$$\alpha_{Q^*} = \tfrac{9}{16} \times 3 = 1.69\%$$

which, in fact, is less than that of P.

In other words, the slope of the T-line is the appropriate performance criterion for the third case. The slope of the T-line for P, denoted by T_P, is given by

$$T_P = \frac{\bar{r}_P - \bar{r}_f}{\beta_P}$$

Treynor's performance measure is appealing in the sense that it shows that when an asset is part of a large investment portfolio, one should weigh its mean excess return, $\bar{r}_P - \bar{r}_f$, against its *systematic* risk (as measured by beta), rather than against total or diversifiable risk (as measured by its standard deviation) to evaluate its contribution to performance.

Like M^2, Treynor's measure is a percentage. If you subtract the market excess return from Treynor's measure, you will obtain the difference between the return on the T_p line in Figure 20.4 and the SML, at the point where $\beta = 1$. We might dub this difference the Treynor-square, or T^2, measure (analogous to M^2). Be aware though that M^2 and T^2 are as different as Sharpe's measure is from Treynor's measure. They may well rank portfolios differently.

Actual Performance Measurement: An Example

Now that we have examined possible criteria for performance evaluation, we need to deal with a statistical issue: How can we derive an appropriate performance measure for ex ante decisions using ex post data? Before we plunge into a discussion of this problem, let us look at the rate of return on Jane's portfolio over the last 12 months. Table 20.2 shows the excess return recorded each month for Jane's portfolio P, one of her alternative portfolios, Q, and the benchmark market index portfolio M. The last rows in Table 20.2 give sample averages and standard deviations. From these, and regressions of P and Q on M, we obtain the necessary performance statistics.

The performance statistics in Table 20.3 show that portfolio Q is more aggressive than P, in the sense that its beta is significantly higher (1.40 versus .69). On the other hand, P appears better diversified from its residual standard deviation (1.95 percent versus 8.98 percent). Both portfolios

Table 20.2 Excess Returns for Portfolios *P* and *Q* and the Benchmark *M* over 12 Months

Month	Jane's Portfolio *P*	Alternative *Q*	Benchmark *M*
1	3.58	2.81	2.20
2	−4.91	−1.15	−8.41
3	6.51	2.53	3.27
4	11.13	37.09	14.41
5	8.78	12.88	7.71
6	9.38	39.08	14.36
7	−3.66	−8.84	−6.15
8	5.56	.83	2.74
9	−7.72	.85	−15.27
10	7.76	12.09	6.49
11	−4.01	−5.68	−3.13
12	.78	−1.77	1.41
Year's average	2.76	7.56	1.63
Standard deviation	6.17	14.89	8.48

have outperformed the benchmark market index portfolio, as is evident from their larger Sharpe measures and positive alphas.

Which portfolio is more attractive on the basis of reported performance? If *P* or *Q* represents the entire investment fund, *Q* would be preferable on the basis of its higher Sharpe measure (.51 vs. .45) and better M^2 (2.69 percent vs. 2.19 percent). On the other hand, as an active portfolio to be mixed with the market index, *P* is preferable to *Q*, as is evident from its appraisal ratio (.84 vs. .59). For the third scenario, where *P* and *Q* are competing for a role as one of a number of subportfolios, *Q* has the superior Treynor measure (5.40 vs. 4.00).

This analysis is based on 12 months of data only, a period too short to lend statistical significance to the conclusions. Even longer observation intervals may not be enough to make the decision clear-cut, which represents a further problem. For an Excel model that calculates these measures, go to www.mhhe.com/bkm.

Realized Returns Versus Expected Returns

When evaluating a portfolio, the evaluator knows neither the portfolio manager's original expectations nor whether those expectations made sense. One can only observe performance after the fact and hope that random results are not taken for, or do not hide, true underlying ability. But

Table 20.3 Performance Statistics

	Portfolio *P*	Portfolio *Q*	Portfolio *M*
Sharpe's measure	.45	.51	.19
M^2	2.19	2.69	.00
SCL regression statistics			
Alpha	1.63	5.28	.00
Beta	.69	1.40	1.00
Treynor	4.00	5.40	1.63
T^2	2.37	3.77	.00
$\sigma(e)$	1.95	8.98	.00
Appraisal ratio	.84	.59	.00
R-square	.91	.64	1.00

PERFORMANCE MEASUREMENT

The following performance measurement spreadsheet computes all the performance measures discussed in this section. You can see how relative ranking differs according to the criterion selected. This Excel model is available at the Online Learning Centre (www.mcgrawhill.ca/college/bodie).

	A	B	C	D	E	F	G	H	I	J	K
1	**Performance Measurement**							**LEGEND**			
2								Enter data			
3								Value calculated			
4								See comment			
5											
6					**Non-**						
7		**Average**	**Standard**	**Beta**	**systematic**	**Sharpe's**	**Treynor's**	**Jensen's**	**M2**	**T2**	**Appraisal**
8	**Fund**	**Return**	**Deviation**	**Coefficient**	**Risk**	**Measure**	**Measure**	**Measure**	**Measure**	**Measure**	**Ratio**
9	Alpha	28.00%	27.00%	1.7000	5.00%	0.8148	0.1294	-0.0180	-0.0015	-0.0106	-0.3600
10	Omega	31.00%	26.00%	1.6200	6.00%	0.9615	0.1543	0.0232	0.0235	0.0143	0.3867
11	Omicron	22.00%	21.00%	0.8500	2.00%	0.7619	0.1882	0.0410	-0.0105	0.0482	2.0500
12	Millennium	40.00%	33.00%	2.5000	27.00%	1.0303	0.1360	-0.0100	0.0352	-0.0040	-0.0370
13	Big Value	15.00%	13.00%	0.9000	3.00%	0.6923	0.1000	-0.0360	-0.0223	-0.0400	-1.2000
14	Momentum Watcher	29.00%	24.00%	1.4000	16.00%	0.9583	0.1643	0.0340	0.0229	0.0243	0.2125
15	Big Potential	15.00%	11.00%	0.5500	1.50%	0.8182	0.1636	0.0130	-0.0009	0.0236	0.8667
16	S&P Index Return	20.00%	17.00%	1.0000	0.00%	0.8235	0.1400	0.0000	0.0000	0.0000	0.0000
17	T-Bill Return	6.00%		0.0000							
18											
19	**Ranking By Sharpe's Measure**				**Non-**						
20		**Average**	**Standard**	**Beta**	**systematic**	**Sharpe's**	**Treynor's**	**Jensen's**	**M2**	**T2**	**Appraisal**
21	**Fund**	**Return**	**Deviation**	**Coefficient**	**Risk**	**Measure**	**Measure**	**Measure**	**Measure**	**Measure**	**Ratio**
[illegible]	Millennium	[illegible]	33.00%	[illegible]	27.00%	[illegible]	[illegible]	-0.0100	[illegible]	[illegible]	-0.0370

risky asset returns are "noisy," which complicates the inference problem. To avoid making mistakes, we have to determine the "significance level" of a performance measure to know whether it reliably indicates ability.

Consider Joe Dark, a portfolio manager. Suppose that his portfolio has an alpha of 20 basis points per month, which makes for a hefty 2.4 percent per year before compounding. Let us assume that the return distribution of Joe's portfolio has constant mean, beta, and alpha, a heroic assumption, but one that is in line with the usual treatment of performance measurement. Suppose that for the measurement period Joe's portfolio beta is 1.2 and the monthly standard deviation of the residual (nonsystematic risk) is .02 (2 percent). With a market index standard deviation of 6.5 percent per month (22.5 percent per year), Joe's portfolio systematic variance is

$$\beta^2\sigma_M^2 = 1.2^2 \times 6.5^2 = 60.84$$

and hence the correlation coefficient between his portfolio and the market index is

$$\rho = \left[\frac{\beta^2\sigma_M^2}{\beta^2\sigma_M^2 + \sigma^2(e)}\right]^{1/2} = \left[\frac{60.84}{60.84 + 4}\right]^{1/2} = .97$$

which shows that his portfolio is quite well diversified.

To estimate Joe's portfolio alpha from the security characteristic line (SCL), we regress the portfolio excess returns on the market index. Suppose that we are in luck and the regression estimates yield the true parameters. That means that our SCL estimates for the N months are

$$\hat{\alpha} = .2\%, \qquad \hat{\beta} = 1.2, \qquad \hat{\sigma}(e) = 2\%$$

The evaluator who runs such a regression, however, does not know the true values, and hence must compute the t-statistic of the alpha estimate to determine whether to reject the hypothesis that Joe's alpha is zero, that is, that he has no superior ability.

The standard error of the alpha estimate in the SCL regression is approximately

$$\sigma(\hat{\alpha}) = \frac{\hat{\sigma}(e)}{\sqrt{N}}$$

where N is the number of observations and $\hat{\sigma}(e)$ is the sample estimate of nonsystematic risk. The t-statistic for the alpha estimate is then

$$t(\hat{\alpha}) = \frac{\hat{\alpha}}{\hat{\sigma}(\alpha)} = \frac{\hat{\alpha}\sqrt{N}}{\hat{\sigma}(e)} \tag{20.3}$$

Suppose that we require a significance level of 5 percent. This requires a $t(\hat{\alpha})$ value of 1.96 if N is large. With $\hat{\alpha} = .2$ and $\hat{\sigma}(e) = 2$, we solve equation 20.3 for N and find that

$$1.96 = \frac{.2\sqrt{N}}{2}$$

$$N = 384 \text{ months}$$

or 32 years!

What have we shown? Here is an analyst who has very substantial ability. The example is biased in his favour in the sense that we have assumed away statistical problems. Nothing changes in the parameters over a long period of time. Furthermore, the sample period "behaves" perfectly. Regression estimates are all perfect. Still, it will take Joe's entire working career to get to the point where statistics will confirm his true ability. We have to conclude that the problem of statistical inference makes performance evaluation extremely difficult in practice.

CONCEPT CHECK

2. Suppose an analyst has a measured alpha of .2 percent with a standard error of 2 percent, as in our example. What is the probability that the positive alpha is due to luck of the draw and that true ability is zero?

20.3 ALTERNATIVES TO MEAN-VARIANCE MEASURES

Morningstar's Risk-Adjusted Rating

The commercial success of Morningstar, Inc., the premier source of information on mutual funds, has made its *Risk Adjusted Rating* (RAR) among the most widely used performance measures. The Morningstar five-star rating is coveted by the managers of the thousands of funds covered by the service. We reviewed the rating system in Chapter 4.

Morningstar calculates a number of RAR performance measures that are similar, although not identical, to the standard mean/variance measures we discussed in this chapter. The most distinct measure, the Morningstar Star Rating, is based on comparison of each fund to a peer group. The peer group for each fund is selected on the basis of the fund's investment universe (e.g., international, growth versus value, fixed income, and so on) as well as portfolio characteristics such as average price-to-book value, price-earnings ratio, and market capitalization.

Morningstar computes fund returns (adjusted for loads) as well as a risk measure based on fund performance in its worst years. The risk-adjusted performance is ranked across funds in a style group and stars are awarded according to the following table:

Percentile	Stars
0–10	1
10–32.5	2
32.5–67.5	3
67.5–90	4
90–100	5

Figure 20.5 Ranking based on Morningstar's category RARs and excess return Sharpe ratios.

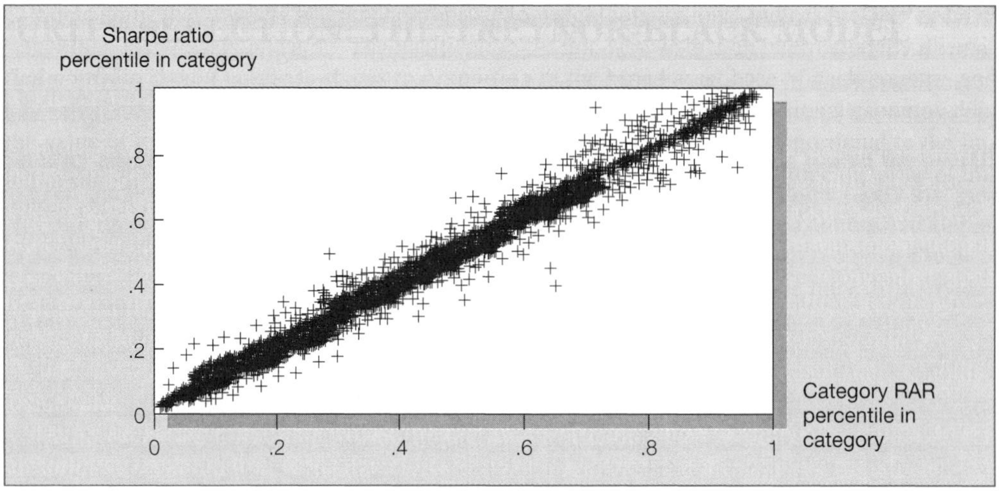

Source: William F. Sharpe, "Morningstar's Performance Measures: Category Ratings," January 15, 1999, accessed March 14, 2002, www.wsharpe.com.

The Morningstar RAR method produces results that are similar but not identical to that of the mean/variance-based Sharpe ratios. Figure 20.5 demonstrates the fit between ranking by RAR and by Sharpe ratios from the performance of 1,286 diversified equity funds over the period 1994–1996. Sharpe notes that this period is characterized by high returns that contribute to a good fit.

Style Analysis

Style analysis was introduced by Nobel laureate William Sharpe.[10] The popularity of the concept was aided by a well-known study[11] concluding that 91.5 percent of the variation in returns of 82 mutual funds could be explained by the funds' asset allocation to bills, bonds, and stocks. Later studies that considered asset allocation across a broader range of asset classes found that as much as 97 percent of fund returns can be explained by asset allocation alone.

Sharpe considered 12 asset class (style) portfolios. His idea was to regress fund returns on indices representing a range of asset classes. The regression coefficient on each index would then measure the implicit allocation to that "style." Because funds are barred from short positions, the regression coefficients are constrained to be either zero or positive and to sum to 100 percent, so as to represent a complete asset allocation. The R-square of the regression would then measure the percentage of return variability attributed to the effects of security selection.

To illustrate the approach, consider Sharpe's study of the monthly returns on Fidelity's Magellan Fund over the period January 1985 through December 1989, shown in Table 20.4. While there are 12 asset classes, each one represented by a stock index, the regression coefficients are positive for only 4 of them. We can conclude that the fund returns are well explained by only four style portfolios. Moreover, these three style portfolios alone explain 97.3 percent of returns.

The proportion of return variability *not* explained by asset allocation can be attributed to security selection within asset classes. For Magellan, this was $100 - 97.3 = 2.7$ percent. To evaluate the average contribution of stock selection to fund performance we track the residuals from the regression, displayed in Figure 20.6. The figure plots the cumulative effect of these

[10] William F. Sharpe, "Asset Allocation: Management Style and Performance Evaluation," *Journal of Portfolio Management,* Winter 1992, pp. 7–19.

[11] Gary Brinson, Brian Singer, and Gilbert Beebower, "Determinants of Portfolio Performance," *Financial Analysts Journal,* May/June 1991.

Table 20.4 Sharpe's Style Portolios for the Magellan Fund

	Regression Coefficient*
Bills	0
Intermediate bonds	0
Long-term bonds	0
Corporate bonds	0
Mortgages	0
Value stocks	0
Growth stocks	47
Medium-cap stocks	31
Small stocks	18
Foreign stocks	0
European stocks	4
Japanese stocks	0
Total	100.00
R-square	97.3

*Regressions are constrained to have nonnegative coefficients and to have coefficients that sum to 100 percent.

Source: William F. Sharpe, "Asset Allocation: Management Style and Performance Evaluation," *Journal of Portfolio Management,* Winter 1992, pp. 7–19.

residuals; the steady upward trend confirms Magellan's success at stock selection in this period. Notice that the plot in Figure 20.6 is far smoother than the plot in Figure 20.7, which shows Magellan's performance compared to a standard benchmark, the S&P 500. This reflects the fact that the regression-weighted index portfolio tracks Magellan's overall style much better than the S&P 500. The performance spread is much noisier using the S&P as the benchmark.

Of course, Magellan's consistently positive residual returns (reflected in the steadily increasing plot of cumulative return difference) is hardly common. Figure 20.8 shows the frequency distribution of average residuals across 636 mutual funds.

Figure 20.6 Fidelity Magellan Fund cumulative return difference: fund versus style.

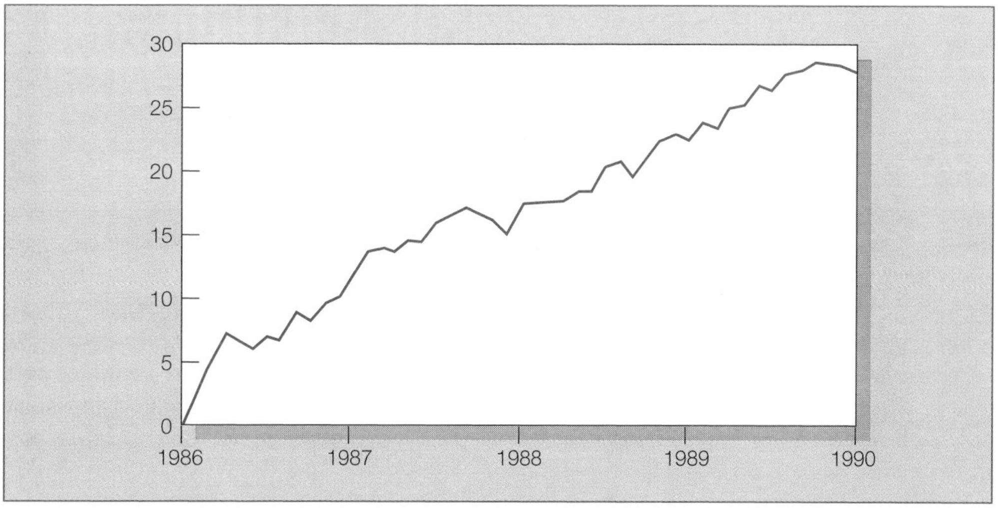

Source: William F. Sharpe, "Asset Allocation: Management Style and Performance Evaluation," *Journal of Portfolio Management,* Winter 1992, pp. 7–19.

Figure 20.7 Fidelity Magellan Fund cumulative return difference: fund versus benchmark.

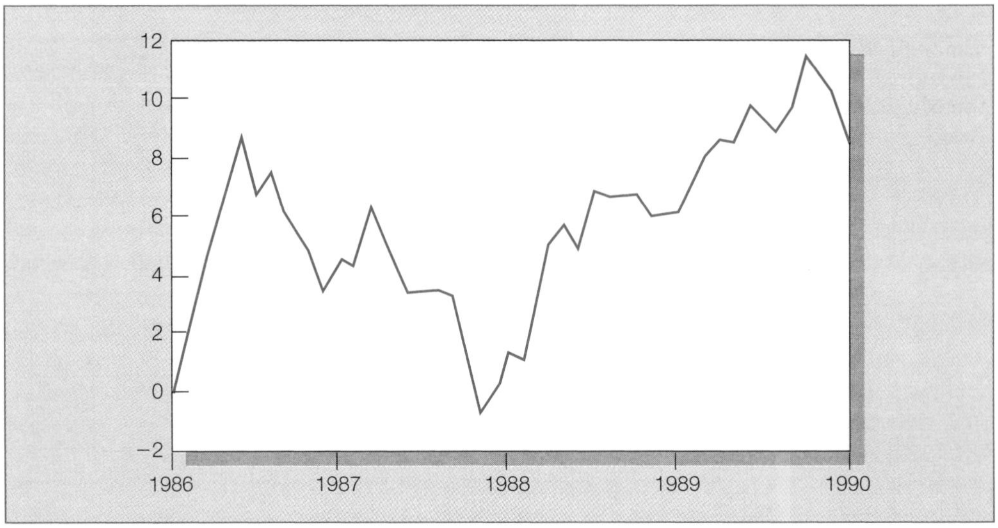

Source: William F. Sharpe, "Asset Allocation: Management Style and Performance Evaluation," *Journal of Portfolio Management,* Winter 1992, pp. 7–19.

Figure 20.8 Average tracking error, 636 mutual funds, 1985–1989.

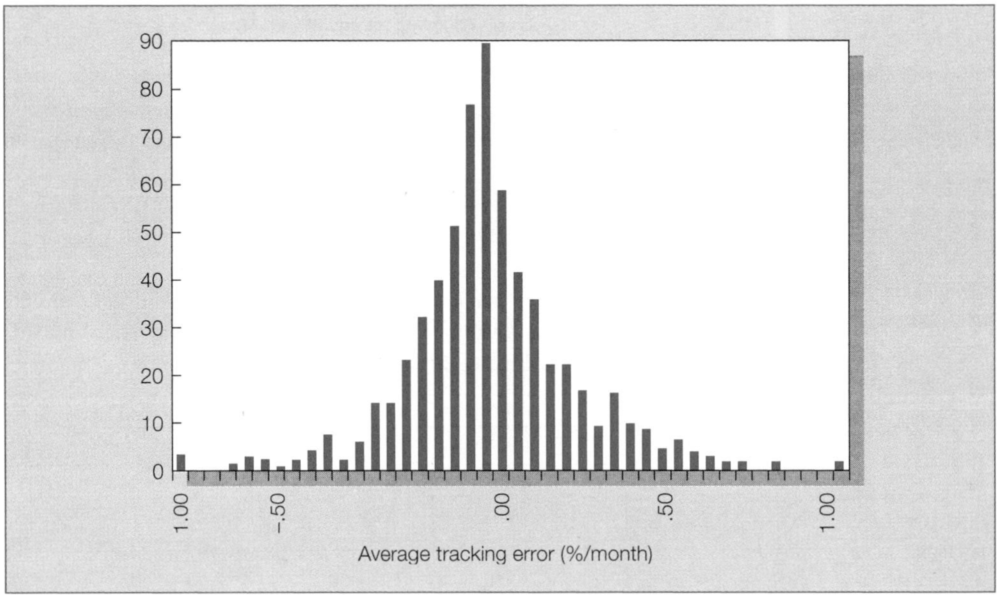

Source: William F. Sharpe, "Asset Allocation: Management Style and Performance Evaluation," *Journal of Portfolio Management,* Winter 1992, pp. 7–19.

Alternative Performance Measures

Increasingly, the traditional mean-variance measures of performance are coming under attack. The assumption that these first two moments of the return distributions are the only factors in investors' risk aversion is often challenged. Furthermore, the normality or log-normality of returns is also questioned. Earlier work has considered third and fourth moments (i.e., skewness and kurtosis) in appraising portfolios. Reactions to anomalous findings, according to the CAPM, in returns lead to alternative explanations for valuation. For example, the Fama and French studies have pointed to the inability of the CAPM to determine returns. Consequently,

OPTIMIZING A PORTFOLIO THROUGH MANAGER SELECTION

It is unfortunate that, to date, plan sponsors have received minimal direction with respect to manager structure. No well-developed framework has been available to answer such questions as:

- How do you allocate and control active risk between managers?
- How many managers should you have and what should the allocation be to each?
- What should the mix between passive and active be?

This discussion focuses on the most typical application of this problem within a single asset class. One can achieve returns almost identical to the benchmark by investing in an index fund replicating that benchmark return. Many investors feel that added returns are possible and attainable by selecting active managers. When an investor hires an active manager, the plan sponsor is accepting the risk that the active manager may not outperform the benchmark. Our objective function, therefore, is to maximize the expected active return for a given level of active risk.

As with any optimization, the issue is to identify the appropriate risk budget, or the level of risk aversion that is appropriate. One can budget at a risk equal to zero (index fund) or as high as the single manager exhibiting the highest level of risk among other potential managers. Wherever the plan sponsor chooses to be along this continuum is a matter of setting the risk budget.

Invariably, they usually discover two attributes:

- The allocation between managers is suboptimal.
- The actual risk budget they have assumed is either higher (most times) or lower (less frequent) than they desired.

For instance, our experience is that a fund with a structure that includes only traditional active managers will likely have active risk levels over 4 per cent at the total asset class level, an uncomfortable (and reducible) amount of risk.

The investor will need to identify either their risk aversion factor or (most likely) the absolute level of active risk they are willing to tolerate—the "risk budget." A simple way to do this is to ask, "If a 4 per cent active risk budget means that, in one year out of six, the asset class as implemented will underperform by 4 per cent or more, would I be comfortable communicating such bad new to the fund's stakeholders with that frequency? Would I be better off with a risk budget closer to, say, 2 per cent? Or some other amount?"

A related question addressing the perception that investors need to hedge against the possibility that they lack skill in manager selection is: "If I doubt my skill at selecting managers, just how big a loss am I willing to take to exercise it?" Note that the investor has a risk control "dial"; the more it is turned to the left, to a lower level of risk, the more the allocation to core managers increases. The inverse is also true; the higher the risk level, the greater the allocation to traditional active managers.

As long as investors continue to use active managers, and no doubt they will, they are implicitly making alpha estimates. A better, more disciplined approach is to make explicit estimates that can be held up to the light of day, that will appear reasonable and will be defendable in debate. An effort to build a strong structure of managers should be made with the most transparent methods possible.

Source: Bill Chinery, "Maximizing Your Plan's Efficiency: Risk Budgeting," *Canadian Investment Review* 15, no. 2 (Summer 2002), p. 35.

researchers have looked for other measures that might reveal superior management. The boxed article here also suggests aspects of the choice faced by investors.

In the list of suggested readings, we refer to a short article by Wilfred Vos, who examines measures that also capture skewness and proposes his own rating system, the Vos Value Ratio (VVR), which is broken down into three different modules: a performance module (VVR P), a risk module (VVR R), and a best balance module (VVR B), combining the previous two.[12] He states:

> Post Modern Portfolio Theory, which is gaining acceptance with institutional investors worldwide, replaces standard deviation with downside risk, which differentiates between upside and downside variability. In so doing, it treats as risky only those returns that have fallen below some target or benchmark return. ... Intuitively, short-fall probability is perhaps most closely related to what risk is for the mutual fund investor. This is the idea that the probability of making a gain in any standardized time period is what is most relevant.

[12]See the suggested reading "Measuring Mutual Fund Performance" and also articles referenced by him: Brian M. Rom and Kathleen W. Ferguson, "New Breed of Tools Available to Assess Risk," *Pensions & Investments*, November 13, 1995; and Lawrence Kryzanowski and Simon Lalancette, "Conditioning for Better Performance Evaluations," *Canadian Investment Review*, Fall 1997.

20.4 MARKET TIMING

Consider the results of the following two different investment strategies:

1. An investor who put $1,000 in 30-day commercial paper on January 1, 1927, and rolled over all proceeds into 30-day paper (or into 30-day T-bills after they were introduced) would have ended on December 31, 1978, 52 years later, with $3,600.
2. An investor who put $1,000 in the NYSE index on January 1, 1927, and reinvested all dividends in that portfolio would have ended on December 31, 1978, with $67,500.

www.nyse.com

Suppose we define **market timing** as the ability to tell (with certainty) at the beginning of each month whether the NYSE portfolio will outperform the 30-day paper portfolio. Accordingly, at the beginning of each month, the market timer shifts all funds into either cash equivalents (30-day paper) or equities (the NYSE portfolio), whichever is predicted to do better. Professor Robert Merton asked a group of finance professors at a seminar to estimate what, beginning with $1,000 on the same date, the perfect timer would have amassed 52 years later. Out of the collected responses, the boldest guess was a few million dollars. The correct answer: $5.36 *billion.*

CONCEPT CHECK

3. What was the monthly and annual compounded rate of return for the three strategies over the period 1926–1978?

These numbers have some lessons for us. The first has to do with the power of compounding. Its effect is particularly important because more and more of the funds under management represent pension savings. The horizons of such investments may not be as long as 52 years, but by and large they are measured in decades, making compounding a significant factor.

Another result that may seem surprising at first is the huge difference between the end-of-period value of the all-safe asset strategy ($3,600) and that of the all-equity strategy ($67,500). Why would anyone invest in safe assets given this historical record? If you have internalized the lessons of previous chapters, you know the reason: risk. The average rates of return and the standard deviations on the all-bills and all-equity strategies presented by Merton are:

	Arithmetic Mean	Standard Deviation
Bills	2.55	2.10
Equities	10.70	22.14

The significantly higher standard deviation of the rate of return on the equity portfolio is commensurate with its significantly higher average return.

Can we also view the rate of return premium on the perfect-timing fund as a risk premium? The answer must be no, because the perfect timer never does worse than either bills or the market. The extra return is not compensation for the possibility of poor returns but is attributable to superior analysis. It is the value of superior information that is reflected in the tremendous end-of-period value of the portfolio.

Merton[13] pursued the issue of value of information by simulating the returns, using the actual monthly return data, given perfect timing and also incorporating a charge for this timing ability. The monthly rate-of-return statistics for the all-equity portfolio and the timing portfolio are:

[13]Robert C. Merton, "On Market Timing and Investment Performance: An Equilibrium Theory of Value for Market Forecasts," *Journal of Business*, July 1981.

Per Month	All Equities (%)	Perfect Timer, No Charge (%)	Perfect Timer, Fair Charge (%)
Average rate of return	.85	2.58	.55
Average excess return over return on safe asset	.64	2.37	.34
Standard deviation	5.89	3.82	3.55
Highest return	38.55	38.55	30.14
Lowest return	−29.12	.06	−7.06
Coefficient of skewness	.42	4.28	2.84

Ignore for the moment the last column ("Perfect Timer, Fair Charge"). The first two rows of results are self-explanatory. The third item, standard deviation, requires some discussion. The standard deviation of the rate of return earned by the perfect market timer was 3.82 percent, far greater than the volatility of T-bill returns over the same period. Does this imply that (perfect) timing is a riskier strategy than investing in bills? No. For this analysis, standard deviation is a misleading measure of risk.

To see why, consider how you might choose between two hypothetical strategies: the first offers a sure rate of return of 5 percent; the second strategy offers an uncertain return that is given by 5 percent *plus* a random number that is zero with probability .5 and 5 percent with probability .5. The characteristics of each strategy are

	Strategy 1 (%)	Strategy 2 (%)
Expected return	5	7.5
Standard deviation	0	2.5
Highest return	5	10.0
Lowest return	5	5.0

Clearly, strategy 2 dominates strategy 1 since its rate of return is *at least* equal to that of strategy 1 and sometimes greater. No matter how risk-averse you are, you will always prefer strategy 2 to strategy 1, despite the significant standard deviation of strategy 2. Compared to strategy 1, strategy 2 provides only "good surprises," so the standard deviation in this case cannot be a measure of risk.

These results are analogous to the case of the perfect timer compared with an all-equity or all-bills strategy. In every period, the perfect timer obtains at least as good a return and, in some cases, a better one. Therefore, the timer's standard deviation is a misleading measure of risk compared to an all-equity or all-bills strategy.

Returning to the empirical results, you can see that the highest rate of return is identical for the all-equity and the timing strategies, whereas the lowest rate of return is positive for the perfect timer and disastrous for the all-equity portfolio. Another reflection of this is seen in the coefficient of skewness, which measures the asymmetry of the distribution of returns. Because the equity portfolio is almost (but not exactly) normally distributed, its coefficient of skewness is very low at .42. In contrast, the perfect timing strategy effectively eliminates the negative tail of the distribution of portfolio returns (the part below the risk-free rate). Its returns are "skewed to the right," and its coefficient of skewness is therefore quite large, 4.28.

Now for the last column, "Perfect Timer, Fair Charge," which is perhaps the most interesting. Most assuredly, the perfect timer will charge clients for such a valuable service. (The perfect timer may have otherworldly predictive powers, but saintly benevolence is unlikely.)

Subtracting a fair fee from the monthly rate of return of the timer's portfolio gives us an average rate of return lower than that of the passive, all-equity strategy. However, because the fee is *assumed* to be fair, the two portfolios (the all-equity strategy and the market timing with fee strategy) must be equally attractive after risk adjustment. In this case, again, the standard deviation of the market timing strategy (with fee) is of no help in adjusting for risk, because the coefficient of skewness remains high, 2.84. In other words, standard mean-variance analysis is quite complicated for valuing market timing. An alternative, option-based approach is given in Appendix 20B.

The Value of Imperfect Forecasting

Unfortunately, managers are not perfect forecasters, as you and Merton know. It seems pretty obvious that if managers are right most of the time they are doing very well. However, when we say right "most of the time," we cannot refer merely to the percentage of time a manager is right. The weather forecaster in Timbuktu, who *always* predicts no rain, may be right 90 percent of the time, but a high success rate for a "stopped-clock" strategy clearly is not evidence of forecasting ability.

Similarly, the appropriate measure of market forecasting ability is not the overall proportion of correct forecasts. If the market is up two days out of three and a forecaster always predicts a market advance, the two-thirds success rate is not a measure of forecasting ability. We need to examine both the proportion of bull markets ($r_M > r_f$) correctly forecast *and* the proportion of bear markets ($r_M < r_f$) correctly forecast.

If we call P_1 the proportion of the correct forecasts of bull markets and P_2 the proportion for bear markets, then $P_1 + P_2 - 1$ is the correct measure of timing ability. For example, a forecaster who always guesses correctly will have $P_1 = P_2 = 1$ and will show ability of 1 (100 percent). An analyst who always bets on a bear market will mispredict all bull markets ($P_1 = 0$), correctly "predict" all bear markets ($P_2 = 1$), and end up with timing ability of $P_1 + P_2 - 1 = 0$. If C denotes the (call option) value of a perfect market timer, then $(P_1 + P_2 - 1)C$ measures the value of imperfect forecasting ability.

CONCEPT CHECK

4. What is the market timing score of someone who flips a fair coin to predict the market?

Identifying Timing Ability

In its pure form, market timing involves shifting funds between a market index portfolio and a safe asset, such as T-bills or a money market fund, depending on whether the market as a whole is expected to outperform the safe asset. In practice, of course, most managers do not shift fully between T-bills and the market. How might we measure partial shifts into the market when it is expected to perform well?

To simplify, suppose that the investor holds only the market index portfolio and T-bills. If the weight on the market were constant, for example, 0.6, then the portfolio beta also would be constant, and the portfolio characteristic line would plot as a straight line with slope 0.6, as in Figure 20.9, panel A. If, however, the investor could correctly time the market, and shift funds into it in periods when the market does well, the characteristic line would plot as in panel B. A timer who can predict bull and bear markets will shift more into the market when the market is about to go up. The portfolio beta and the slope of the characteristic line will be higher when r_M is higher, resulting in the curved line that appears in panel B.

Treynor and Mazuy[14] proposed that such a line can be estimated by adding a squared term to the usual linear index model:

$$r_P - r_f = a + b(r_M - r_f) + c(r_M - r_f)^2 + e_P$$

[14]Jack L. Treynor and Kay Mazuy, "Can Mutual Funds Outguess the Market?" *Harvard Business Review* 43 (July/August 1966).

Figure 20.9 Characteristic lines. Panel A: No market timing, beta is constant. Panel B: Market timing, beta increases with expected market excess return. Panel C: Market timing with only two values of beta.

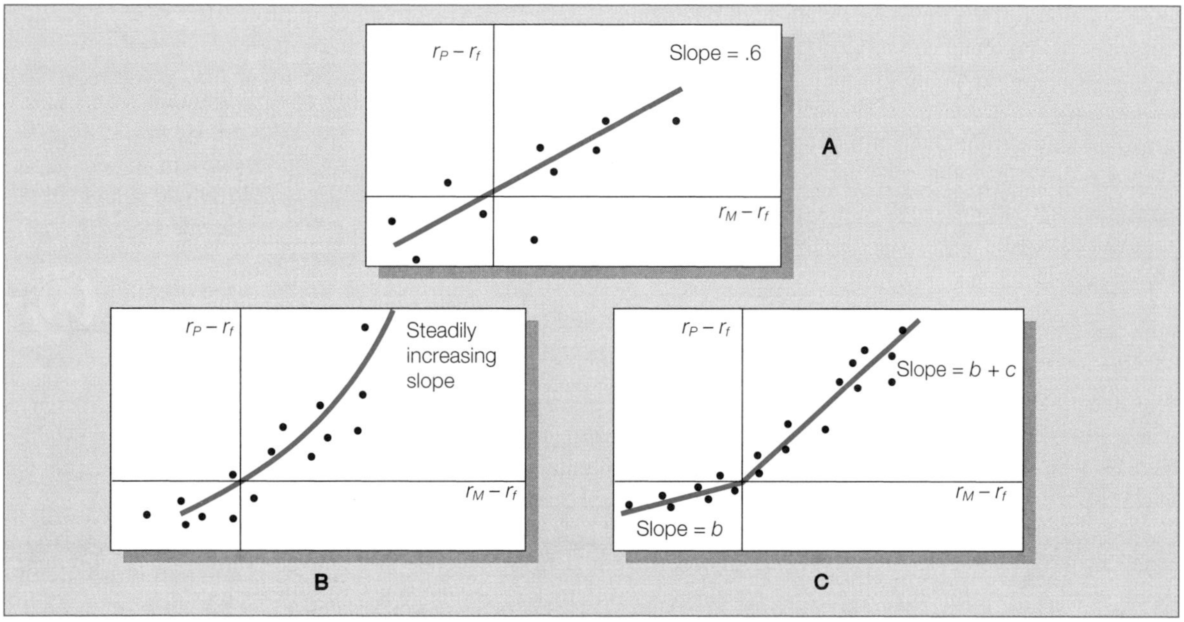

where r_P is the portfolio return, and *a, b,* and *c* are estimated by regression analysis. If *c* turns out to be positive, we have evidence of timing ability, because this last term will make the characteristic line steeper as $r_M - r_f$ is larger. Treynor and Mazuy estimated this equation for a number of mutual funds but found little evidence of timing ability.

A similar and simpler methodology was proposed by Henriksson and Merton.[15] These authors suggested that the beta of the portfolio can take only two values: a large value if the market is expected to do well and a small value otherwise. Under this scheme, the portfolio characteristic line appears as panel C. Such a line appears in regression form as

$$r_P - r_f = a + b(r_M - r_f) + c(r_M - r_f)D + e_P$$

where D is a dummy variable that equals 1 for $r_M > r_f$ and zero otherwise. Hence the beta of the portfolio is b in bear markets and $b + c$ in bull markets. Again, a positive value of c implies market timing ability.

Henriksson[16] estimated this equation for 116 mutual funds over the period 1968–1980. He found that the average value of *c* for the funds was *negative,* and equal to –.07, although the value was not statistically significant at the conventional 5 percent level. Eleven funds had significantly positive values of *c,* while eight had significantly negative values. Overall, 62 percent of the funds had negative point estimates of timing ability. In sum, the results showed little evidence of market timing ability. Perhaps this should be expected; given the tremendous values to be reaped by a successful market timer, it would be surprising in nearly efficient markets to uncover clear-cut evidence of such skills.[17]

---

[15] Roy D. Henriksson and R. C. Merton, "On Market Timing and Investment Performance. II. Statistical Procedures for Evaluating Forecasting Skills," *Journal of Business* 54 (October 1981).

[16] Roy D. Henriksson, "Market Timing and Mutual Fund Performance: An Empirical Investigation," *Journal of Business* 57 (January 1984).

[17] See John Rumsey, "Can We Detect Market Timing Ability Using an Option Model?" *Canadian Journal of Administrative Sciences* 17, no. 3 (September 2000), pp. 269–279; the author finds the answer is negative, even if timing is successful.

EXAMPLE 20.3 A Test of Market Timing

Using Table 20.2 and regressing the excess returns of portfolios P and Q on the excess returns on M and the square of these returns,

$$r_P - r_f = a_P + b_P(r_M - r_f) + c_P(r_M - r_f)^2 + e_P$$
$$r_Q - r_f = q_Q + b_Q(r_M - r_f) + c_Q(r_M - r_f)^2 + e_Q$$

we derive the following statistics:

	Portfolio	
Estimate	***P***	***Q***
Alpha (*a*)	1.77 (1.63)	−2.29 (5.28)
Beta (*b*)	.70 (.69)	1.10 (1.40)
Timing (*c*)	.00	.10
R-square	.91 (.91)	.98 (.64)

The numbers in parentheses are the regression estimates from the single variable regression reported in Table 20.3. The results reveal that portfolio P shows no timing. It is not clear whether this is a result of Jane's making no attempt at timing or that the effort to time was in vain and served only to increase portfolio variance unnecessarily.

The results for portfolio Q, however, reveal that timing has, in all likelihood, successfully been attempted. The timing coefficient, c, is estimated at .10. This describes a successful timing effort that was offset by unsuccessful stock selection. Note that the alpha estimate, a, is now −2.29 percent, as opposed to the 5.28 percent estimate derived from the regression equation that did not allow for the possibility of timing activity.

The example shows the inadequacy of conventional performance evaluation techniques that assume constant mean returns and constant risk. The market timer constantly shifts beta and mean return, moving into and out of the market. Whereas the expanded regression captures this phenomenon, the simple SCL does not. The relative desirability of portfolios P and Q remains unclear in the sense that the value of the timing success and selectivity failure of Q compared with P has yet to be evaluated. The important point for performance evaluation, however, is that expanded regressions can capture many of the effects of portfolio composition change that would confound the more conventional mean-variance measures.

20.5 PERFORMANCE EVALUATION

Performance evaluation has two very basic problems:

1. Many observations are needed for significant results even when portfolio mean and variance are constant.
2. Shifting parameters when portfolios are actively managed make accurate performance evaluation all the more elusive.

Although these objective difficulties cannot be overcome completely, it is clear that to obtain reasonably reliable performance measures we need to do the following:

1. Maximize the number of observations by taking more frequent return readings.
2. Specify the exact make-up of the portfolio to obtain better estimates of the risk parameters at each observation period.

Suppose an evaluator knows the exact portfolio composition at the opening of each day. Because the daily return on each security is available, the total daily return on the portfolio can be calculated. Furthermore, the exact portfolio composition allows the evaluator to estimate the risk characteristics (variance, beta, residual variance) for each day. Thus, daily risk-adjusted rates of return can be obtained. Although a performance measure for one day is statistically unreliable, the number of days with such rich data accumulates quickly. Performance evaluation that accounts for frequent revision in portfolio composition is superior by far to evaluation that assumes constant risk characteristics over the entire measurement period.

What sort of evaluation takes place in practice? Performance reports for portfolio managers traditionally have been based on quarterly data over 5–10 years. Currently, managers of mutual funds are required to disclose the exact composition of their portfolios only quarterly. Trading activity that immediately precedes the reporting date is known as "window dressing." Rumour has it that window dressing involves changes in portfolio composition to make it look as if the manager chose successful stocks. If Bombardier performed well over the quarter, for example, a portfolio manager will make sure that his or her portfolio includes a lot of Bombardier on the reporting date, whether or not it did during the quarter and whether or not Bombardier is expected to perform as well over the next quarter. Of course, portfolio managers deny such activity, and we know of no published evidence to substantiate the allegation. However, if window dressing is quantitatively significant, even the reported quarterly composition data can be misleading. Mutual funds publish portfolio values on a daily basis, which means the rate of return for each day is publicly available, but portfolio composition is not.

Moreover, mutual fund managers have had considerable leeway in the presentation of both past investment performance and fees charged for management services. The resultant noncomparability of net-of-expense performance numbers has made meaningful comparison of funds difficult. This may be changing, however; the OSC has moved toward greater disclosure in the reporting of fees. Awareness of the fees may help to evaluate performance based on the actual invested capital.

Portfolio managers reveal their portfolio composition only when they have to, which so far is quarterly. This is not nearly sufficient for adequate evaluation. However, current computer and communication technology makes it easy to use daily composition data for evaluation purposes. If the technology required for meaningful evaluation is in place, implementation of more accurate performance measurement techniques could improve welfare by enabling the public to identify the truly talented investment managers. In the United States, the Association of Investment Management and Research has published an extensive set of performance presentation standards encouraging the presentation of regular reporting periods and intervals, comparative indices, and expense effects.

An additional problem in performance evaluation has received considerable attention from researchers in recent years. The issue is known as **survivorship bias**, which refers to the measurement of results from a population whose membership varies over time; put more simply, badly performing funds disappear, and their poor results are not counted in determining average performance. In consequence, the reported average for mutual fund performance exceeds the ex ante results that an investor can expect from a randomly selected fund. Brown et al.[18] exposed the problem in a 1992 article. A number of articles have examined the question of performance persistence by mutual fund managers, with Brown and Goetzmann[19] reporting on the effect of survival bias in such studies. A 1995 study of this phenomenon for Canadian funds is summarized by Curwood et al.[20]

---

[18]S. J. Brown, W. N. Goetzmann, R. G. Ibottson, and S. A. Ross, "Survivorship Bias in Performance Studies," *Review of Financial Studies* 5 (1992), pp. 553–580.

[19]S. J. Brown and W. N. Goetzmann, "Performance Persistence," *The Journal of Finance* 50 (June 1995), pp. 679–698.

[20]B. Curwood, S. Hadjiyannakis, P. Halpern, and K. Taylor, "How Survivorship Bias Skews Results of Comparative Measurement Universes," *Canadian Investment Review* 8 (Winter 1995/1996), pp. 9–12.

Empirical Studies of Canadian Performance

A number of studies of the general performance of Canadian mutual funds have been conducted, using a variety of techniques and investigating different phenomena. Researchers have investigated the stability of the funds' betas, the effects of inflation and fund size, performance in good and bad markets, and the general question of the value of managerial expertise.

An early study by Grant[21] used Jensen's measure to compare performance over the period 1960–1974. By examining the stability of the risk measure beta and performance, Grant found that funds were unable to satisfy the objectives that they set for themselves; that is, the revealed instability meant that an investor could not guarantee either high or low growth and risk by investing in funds with defined objectives. Similarly, Dhingra found that both average returns and volatility for fund portfolios were unstable over time.[22]

Calvet and Lefoll[23] investigated the inflationary effect on returns and concluded that the real returns of funds were not superior to those of the then TSE 300. They used 17 mutual funds quarterly returns over the period 1966–1975 selected because they had less than 10 percent of their capital invested in foreign securities. The study also developed its own methodology in order to evaluate performance under inflationary conditions. Of the 17 funds, only one had a significantly positive alpha, indicating a slightly better performance than the market index if management fees are ignored. All other funds' performance measures were not significantly different from zero. These results remained virtually unchanged when performance was estimated with the "traditional" method that ignores inflation.

Standard & Poor's www.sandp.com

Khoury and Martel[24] used a multicriterion evaluation of return and risk measures in a study to determine the effect of fund size. The data were drawn from a sample of 34 funds from 1981–1986, and they identified a combined index incorporating the then TSE 300, the S&P 500 and the EAFE (for international effects). They concluded that for this sample, fund size was associated with superior performance when more weight was placed on risk than on returns.

Fund performance for the period 1967–1984 was analyzed by Bishara,[25] who concluded that Canadian funds could not outperform the market. He subdivided his fund universe into balanced, income, and growth funds and considered their returns over boom and recession periods. His findings concluded that while growth funds managed to match the index return, the balanced and income funds were inferior to the index over the whole period and during one boom.[26]

The more specific issue of identifying timing and selectivity ability has received less attention. There is difficulty in defining the two skills where these tend to be related to the regression characteristics rather than to their intuitive, economic characteristics. Admati et al.[27] have presented two alternative structures for testing these abilities, based on the alternative definitions. The normal regression-based approach is identified as a portfolio approach; this stresses the use of obvious portfolios to be used for timing decisions, such as the T-bill and index fund portfolios, and examines the regression residuals for different managers. A newer approach is to use a factor model that will relate to the economic factors giving rise to timing and selecting decisions. In both cases, the issue is the quality of information possessed by the manager; the information will

---

[21]D. Grant, "Investment Performance of Canadian Mutual Funds: 1960–1974," *Journal of Business Administration* 8 (Fall 1976).

[22]H. L. Dhingra, "Portfolio Volatility Adjustment by Canadian Mutual Funds," *Journal of Business Finance and Accounting* 5, no. 4 (1978).

[23]A. L. Calvet and J. Lefoll, "The CAPM Under Inflation and the Performance of Canadian Mutual Funds," *Journal of Business Administration* 12, no. 1 (Fall 1980).

[24]N. T. Khoury and J.-M. Martel, "The Relationship Between Risk-Return Characteristics of Mutual Funds and Their Size," *Finance* 11, no. 2 (1990). See also J.-M. Martel, N. T. Khoury, and M. Bergeron, "An Application of a Multicriteria Approach to Portfolio Comparisons," *Journal of the Operations Research Society* 39, no. 7 (1988).

[25]Halim Bishara, "Evaluation of the Performance of Canadian Mutual Funds (1967–1984)," *Finance Proceedings*, Administrative Sciences Association of Canada 9 (1988).

[26]These statements must be appreciated in the light of the diminishing statistical significance that accompanies sample size reduction; each of the stated results is significant.

[27]A. R. Admati, S. Bhattacharya, P. Pfleiderer, and S. A. Ross, "On Timing and Selectivity," *Journal of Finance* 41, no. 3 (July 1986).

affect the performance of individual assets and the portfolios either directly, by analysis of the assets, or through the factors that generate returns on the assets and portfolios.

Few Canadian studies have focused on the timing issue, although Dhingra related volatility changes to the passage of time, as noted previously. A recent study, however, by Weigel and Ilkiw[28] investigated market timing effected by two methods: **tactical asset allocation** (TAA) models and **swing fund management**. They have a very specific interpretation of the two terms, where TAA is generally used for both. Swing fund management describes the more traditional practice of switching weights in response to intuitive appraisal of the economy and asset class response. TAA is the result of computerized decision rules and relies on the use of options and other derivative instruments to effect rapid and cost-effective adjustments to the portfolio mix. The study found TAA to be a superior approach, but the authors qualified the reliability of their results due to data limitations.

In further research of the subject, Carlton and Osborn investigated the choice of the base portfolio from which tactical switches were made as a result of timing decisions.[29] They found this factor to be unimportant in assessing managerial ability.

A thorough study of performance attribution by Kryzanowski, Lalancette, and To used an intertemporal asset pricing model to investigate returns, risk, and performance in Canadian mutual fund portfolios.[30] They concluded that Canadian managers had significant performance in stock-picking and timing; unfortunately, in both abilities their results were negative.

SUMMARY

1. A truly passive portfolio strategy entails holding the market index portfolio and a money market fund. Determining the optimal allocation to the market portfolio requires an estimate of its expected return and variance, which in turn suggests delegating some analysis to professionals.
2. Active portfolio managers attempt to construct a risky portfolio that maximizes the reward-to-variability (Sharpe) ratio.
3. The shifting mean and variance of actively managed portfolios make it even harder to assess performance. A typical example is the attempt of portfolio managers to time the market, resulting in ever-changing portfolio betas.
4. The appropriate performance measure depends on the role of the portfolio to be evaluated. Appropriate performance measures are as follows:
   a. *Sharpe.* When the portfolio represents the entire investment fund
   b. *Appraisal ratio.* When the portfolio represents the active portfolio to be optimally mixed with the passive portfolio
   c. *Treynor.* When the portfolio represents one subportfolio of many
5. Many observations are required to eliminate the effect of the "luck of the draw" from the evaluation process, because portfolio returns commonly are very "noisy."
6. The value of perfect market timing ability is considerable. The rate of return to a perfect market timer will be uncertain. However, its risk characteristics are not measurable by standard measures of portfolio risk, because perfect timing dominates a passive strategy, providing "good surprises" only.
7. With imperfect timing, the value of a timer who attempts to forecast whether stocks will outperform bills is given by the conditional probabilities of the true outcome given the forecasts: $P_1 + P_2 - 1$. Thus, if the value of perfect timing is given by the option value, C, then imperfect timing has the value $(P_1 + P_2 - 1)C$.

[28]Eric J. Weigel and John H. Ilkiw, "Market Timing Skill in Canada: An Assessment," *Canadian Investment Review* 4, no. 1 (Spring 1991).
[29]Colin G. Carlton and John C. Osborn, "The Determinants of Balanced Fund Performance," *Canadian Investment Review* 4, no. 1 (Spring 1991).
[30]Lawrence Kryzanowski, Simon Lalancette, and Minh Chau To, "Performance Attribution Using a Multivariate Intertemporal Asset Pricing Model with One State Variable," *Canadian Journal of Administrative Sciences* II, no. 1 (March 1994).

8. The Morningstar rating method compares each fund to a peer group represented by a style portfolio within four asset classes. Risk-adjusted ratings (RAR) are based on fund returns relative to the peer group and used to award each fund one to five stars based on the rank of its RAR.
9. Style analysis uses a multiple regression model where the factors are category (style) portfolios such as bills, bonds, and stocks. A regression of fund returns on the style portfolio returns generates residuals that represent the value added of stock selection in each period. These residuals can be used to gauge fund performance relative to similar-style funds.
10. A simple way to measure timing and selection success simultaneously is to estimate an expanded SCL, with a quadratic term added to the usual index model.
11. The value of perfect market timing ability is considerable. The rate of return to a perfect market timer will be uncertain. Its risk characteristics, however, are not measurable by standard measures of portfolio risk, because perfect timing dominates a passive strategy, providing "good" surprises only.
12. Empirical studies of mutual fund performance have not revealed any ability to outperform the market index or time market swings.

KEY TERMS

dollar-weighted rate of return 786
time-weighted rate of return 786
comparison universe 787
Sharpe's measure 788
Treynor's measure 788
Jensen's measure 788
appraisal ratio 788
market timing 802
survivorship bias 807
tactical asset allocation 809
swing fund management 809

SELECTED READINGS

The mean-variance based performance evaluation literature is based on early papers by:

Sharpe, William F. "Mutual Fund Performance." *Journal of Business* 39 (January 1966).

Treynor, Jack L. "How to Rate Management Investment Funds." *Harvard Business Review* 43 (January/February 1966).

Jensen, Michael C. "The Performance of Mutual Funds in the Period 1945–1964." *Journal of Finance*, May 1968.

Jensen, Michael C. "Risk, the Pricing of Capital Assets, and the Evaluation of Investment Portfolios." *Journal of Business*, April 1969.

A recent review of investment performance is given by a number of notable researchers in the twentieth anniversary edition of the Journal of Portfolio Management including:

Sharpe, William F. "The Sharpe Ratio." *Journal of Portfolio Management* 21 (Fall 1994).

A multicriterion approach to fund performance measurement is described in:

Vos, Wilfred. "Measuring Mutual Fund Performance." *Canadian Investment Review*, Winter 1998.

The problems that arise when conventional mean-variance measures are calculated in the presence of a shifting-return distribution are treated in:

Dybvig, Philip H., and Stephen A. Ross. "Differential Information and Performance Measurement Using a Security Market Line." *Journal of Finance* 40 (June 1985).

The separation of investment ability into timing versus selection activity derives from:

Fama, Eugene F. "Components of Investment Performance." *Journal of Finance* 25 (June 1970).

Key empirical papers on timing versus selection are:

Admati, A. R., S. Bhattacharya, P. Pfleiderer, and S. A. Ross. "On Timing and Selectivity." *Journal of Finance* 41, no. 3 (July 1986).

Henriksson, Roy D. "Market Timing and Mutual Fund Performance: An Empirical Investigation." *Journal of Business* 57 (January 1984).

Henriksson, Roy D., and R. C. Merton. "On Market Timing and Investment Performance. II. Statistical Procedures for Evaluating Forecasting Skills." *Journal of Business* 54 (October 1981).

Kon, S. J., and F. D. Jen. "The Investment Performance of Mutual Funds: An Empirical Investigation of Timing, Selectivity, and Market Efficiency." *Journal of Business* 52 (April 1979).

Lee, Cheng-Few, and Shafiqur Rahman. "Market Timing, Selectivity, and Mutual Fund Performance: An Empirical Investigation." *Journal of Business* 63, no. 2 (April 1990).

Treynor, Jack, L., and Kay Mazuy. "Can Mutual Funds Outguess the Market?" *Harvard Business Review* 43 (July/August 1966).

The valuation of market timing ability using the option pricing framework was developed in:

Merton, Robert C. "On Market Timing and Investment Performance: An Equilibrium Theory of Value for Market Forecasts." *Journal of Business*, July 1981.

PROBLEMS

1. The five-year history of annual rates of return in excess of the T-bill rate for two competing stock funds is:

The Bull Fund	The Unicorn Fund
–21.7	–1.3
28.7	15.5
17.0	14.4
2.9	–11.9
28.9	25.4

a. How would these funds compare in the eye of the risk-neutral potential client?

b. How would these finds compare by Sharpe's measure?

c. If a risk-averse investor (with a coefficient of risk aversion $A = 3$) had to choose one of these funds to mix with T-bills, which fund would be better to choose, and how much should be invested in that fund on the basis of the available data?

2. Based on current dividend yields and expected capital gains, the expected rates of return on portfolios *A* and *B* are .12 and .16, respectively. The beta of *A* is 0.7, while that of *B* is 1.4. The T-bill rate is currently .06, while the expected rate of return of the S&P/TSX index is .13. The standard deviation of portfolio *A* is .12 annually, that of *B* is .31, and that of the S&P/TSX index is .18.

a. If you currently hold a market-index portfolio, would you choose to add either of these portfolios to your holdings? Explain.

b. If instead you could invest *only* in T-bills and *one* of these portfolios, which would you choose?

3. Consider the two (excess return) index-model regression results for stocks A and B. The risk-free rate over the period was 6 percent, and the market's average return was 14 percent. Performance was measured using an index model regression on excess returns.

	Stock A	Stock B
Index model regression estimates	$1\% + 1.2(r_M - r_f)$	$2\% + .8(r_M - r_f)$
R-square	.576	.436
Residual standard deviation, $\sigma(e)$	10.3%	19.1%
Standard deviation of excess returns	21.6%	24.9%

a. Calculate the following statistics for each stock:

i. Alpha

ii. Appraisal ratio

iii. Sharpe measure

iv. Treynor measure

b. Which stock is the best choice under the following circumstances?

i. This is the only risky asset to be held by the investor.

ii. This stock will be mixed with the rest of the investor's portfolio, currently composed solely of holdings in the market index fund.

iii. This is one of many stocks that the investor is analyzing to form an actively managed stock portfolio.

4. Evaluate the timing and selection abilities of four managers whose performances are plotted in the following four scatter diagrams:

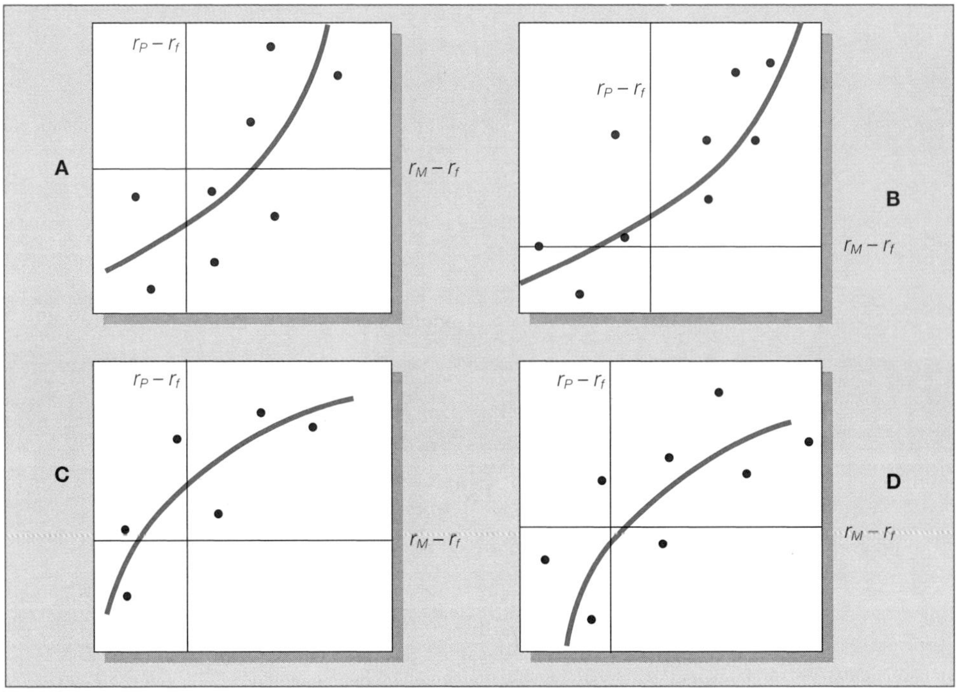

5. In scrutinizing the record of two market timers, a fund manager comes up with the following table:

Number of months that $r_M > r_f$	135	
Correctly predicted by timer *A*		78
Correctly predicted by timer *B*		86
Number of months that $r_M < r_f$	92	
Correctly predicted by timer *A*		57
Correctly predicted by timer *B*		50

What are the conditional probabilities, P_1 and P_2, and the total ability parameters for timers *A* and *B*?

Use the following data in solving problems 6 and 7.

The administrator of a large pension fund wants to evaluate the performance of three portfolio managers. Each portfolio manager invests only in U.S. common stocks. Assume that during the most recent five-year period, the average annual total rate of return including dividends on the S&P 500 was 14 percent, and the average nominal rate of return on government Treasury bills was 8 percent. The following table shows risk and return measures for each portfolio:

Portfolio	Average Annual Rate of Return	Standard Deviation	Beta
P	17%	20%	1.1
Q	24	18	2.1
R	11	10	0.5
S&P 500	14	12	1.0

CFA® PROBLEMS

6. The Treynor performance measure for portfolio *P* is:
   a. .082
   b. .099
   c. .155
   d. .450

CFA® PROBLEMS

7. The Sharpe performance measure for portfolio *Q* is:
   a. .076
   b. .126
   c. .336
   d. .888

CFA® PROBLEMS

8. An analyst wants to evaluate portfolio *X*, consisting entirely of U.S. common stocks, using both the Treynor and Sharpe measures of portfolio performance. The following table provides the average annual rate of return for portfolio *X*, the market portfolio (as measured by the S&P 500), and U.S. Treasury bills during the past eight years:

	Average Annual Rate of Return	Standard Deviation of Return	Beta
Portfolio *X*	10%	18%	0.60
S&P 500	12	13	1.00
T-bills	6	NA	NA

   a. Calculate the Treynor and Sharpe measures for both portfolio *X* and the S&P 500. Briefly explain whether portfolio *X* underperformed, equalled, or outperformed the S&P 500 on a risk-adjusted basis using both the Treynor measure and the Sharpe measure.
   b. In view of the performance of portfolio *X* relative to the S&P 500 calculated in part (*a*), briefly explain the reason for the conflicting results when using the Treynor measure versus the Sharpe measure.

CFA® PROBLEMS

9. During the annual review of Acme's pension plan, several trustees questioned their investment consultant about various aspects of performance measurement and risk assessment.
   a. Comment on the appropriateness of using each of the following benchmarks for performance evaluation:
      - Market index
      - Benchmark normal portfolio
      - Median of the manager universe
   b. Distinguish among the following performance measures:
      - The Sharpe ratio
      - The Treynor measure
      - Jensen's alpha

      i. Describe how each of the three performance measures is calculated.
      ii. State whether each measure assumes that the relevant risk is systematic, unsystematic, or total. Explain how each measure relates excess return and the relevant risk.

CFA® PROBLEMS

10. Trustees of the Pallor Corp. pension plan ask consultant Donald Millip to comment on the following statements. What should his response be?
    i. Median manager benchmarks are statistically unbiased measures of performance over long periods of time.

ii. Median manager benchmarks are unambiguous and are therefore easily replicated by managers wishing to adopt a passive/indexed approach.
iii. Median manager benchmarks are not appropriate in all circumstances because the median manager universe encompasses many investment styles.

CFA® PROBLEMS

11. James Chan is reviewing the performance of the global equity managers of the Jarvis University endowment fund. Williamson Capital is currently the endowment fund's only large-capitalization global equity manager. Performance data for Williamson Capital are shown in Table 20A.

Chan also presents the endowment fund's investment committee with performance information for Joyner Asset Management, which is another large-capitalization global equity manager. Performance data for Joyner Asset Management are shown in Table 20B. Performance data for the relevant risk-free asset and market index are shown in Table 20C.

a. Calculate the Sharpe ratio and Treynor measure for both Williamson Capital and Joyner Asset Management.

b. The Investment Committee notices that using the Sharpe ratio versus the Treynor measure produces different performance rankings of Williamson and Joyner. Explain why these criteria may result in different rankings.

Table 20A Williamson Capital Performance Data, 1990–2001

Average annual rate of return	22.1%
Beta	1.2
Standard deviation of returns	16.8%

Table 20B Joyner Asset Management Performance Data 1990–2001

Average annual rate of return	24.2%
Beta	0.8
Standard deviation of returns	20.2%

Table 20C Relevant Risk-Free Asset and Market Index Performance Data, 1990–2001

Risk-Free Asset	
Average annual rate of return	5.0%
Market Index	
Average annual rate of return	18.9%
Standard deviation of returns	13.8%

12. Conventional wisdom says that one should measure a manager's investment performance over an entire market cycle. What arguments support this contention? What arguments contradict it?

13. Does the use of universes of managers with similar investment styles to evaluate relative investment performance overcome the statistical problems associated with instability of beta or total variability?

14. During a particular year, the T-bill rate was 6 percent, the market return was 14 percent, and a portfolio manager with beta of .5 realized a return of 10 percent.

a. Evaluate the manager based on the portfolio alpha.

b. Reconsider your answer to part (*a*) in view of the Black-Jensen-Scholes finding that the security market line is too flat. Now how do you assess the manager's performance?

CFA® PROBLEMS

15. The chairperson provides you with the following data, covering one year, concerning the portfolios of two of the fund's equity managers (firm A and firm B). Although the portfolios consist primarily of common stocks, cash reserves are included in the calculation of both portfolio betas and performance. By way of perspective, selected data for the financial markets are included in the following table:

	Total Return (%)	Beta
Firm A	24.0	1.0
Firm B	30.0	1.5
S&P/TSX Composite	21.0	
ScotiaMcLeod Total Bond Index	31.0	
91-day Treasury bills	12.0	

a. Calculate and compare the risk-adjusted performance of the two firms relative to each other and to the S&P/TSX Composite.

b. Explain *two* reasons the conclusions drawn from this calculation may be misleading.

CFA® PROBLEMS

16. Carl Karl, a portfolio manager for the Alpine Trust Company, has been responsible since 1975 for the City of Alpine's Employee Retirement Plan, a municipal pension fund. Alpine is a growing community, and city services and employee payrolls have expanded in each of the past ten years. Contributions to the plan in fiscal 1980 exceeded benefit payments by a three-to-one ratio.

The plan's Board of Trustees directed Karl five years ago to invest for total return over the long term. However, as trustees of this highly visible public fund, they cautioned him that volatile or erratic results could cause them embarrassment. They also noted a state statute that mandates that not more than 25 percent of the plan's assets (at cost) be invested in common stocks.

At the annual meeting of the trustees in November 1980, Karl presented the following portfolio and performance report to the board:

Alpine Employee Retirement Plan

Asset Mix as of 9/30/80	At Cost (millions)		At Market (millions)	
Fixed-income assets				
Short-term securities	$ 4.5	11.0%	$ 4.5	11.4%
Long-term bonds and mortgages	26.5	64.7	23.5	59.5
Common stocks	10.0	24.3	11.5	29.1
	$41.0	100.0%	$39.5	100.0%

Investment Performance

	Annual Rates of Return for Period Ending 9/30/80	
	5 Years	1 Year
Total Alpine Fund:		
Time-weighted*	8.2%	5.2%
Dollar-weighted (internal)*	7.7%	4.8%
Assumed actuarial return	6.0%	6.0%
U.S. Treasury bills	7.5%	11.3%
Large sample of pension funds (average 60% equities, 40% fixed income)	10.1%	14.3%
Common stocks—Alpine Fund	13.3%	14.3%
Average portfolio beta coefficient	0.90	0.89
Standard & Poor's 500 stock index	13.8%	21.1%
Fixed income securities—Alpine Fund	6.7%	1.0%
Salomon Brothers' bond index	4.0%	–11.4%

*See Appendix 20A for an explanation of these terms.

Karl was proud of his performance, and thus he was chagrined when a trustee made the following critical observations:

a. "Our one-year results were terrible, and it's what you've done for us lately that counts most."

b. "Our total fund performance was clearly inferior compared to the large sample of other pension funds for the last five years. What else could this reflect except poor management judgment?"

c. "Our common stock performance was especially poor for the five-year period."

d. "Why bother to compare your returns to the return from Treasury bills and the actuarial assumption rate? What your competition could have earned for us or how we would have fared if invested in a passive index [which doesn't charge a fee] are the only relevant measures of performance."

e. "Who cares about time-weighted return? If it can't pay pensions, what good is it?"

Appraise the merits of each of these statements and give counterarguments that Mr. Karl can use.

CFA® PROBLEMS

17. The Retired Fund is an open-ended mutual fund composed of $500 million in U.S. bonds and U.S. Treasury bills. This fund has had a portfolio duration (including T-bills) of between three and nine years. Retired has shown first-quartile performance over the past five years, as measured by an independent fixed-income measurement service. However, the directors of the fund would like to measure the market timing skill of the fund's sole bond investment manager. An external consulting firm has suggested the following three methods:

i. Method I examines the value of the bond portfolio at the beginning of every year and then calculates the return that would have been achieved had that same portfolio been held throughout the year. This return would then be compared with the return actually obtained by the fund.

ii. Method II calculates the average weighting of the portfolio in bonds and T-bills for each year. Instead of using the actual bond portfolio, the return on a long-bond market index and T-bill index would be used. For example, if the portfolio on average was 65 percent in bonds and 35 percent in T-bills, the annual return on a portfolio invested 65 percent in a long-bond index and 35 percent in T-bills would be calculated. This return is compared with the annual return that would have been generated using the indices and the manager's actual bond/T-bill weighting for each quarter of the year.

iii. Method III examines the net bond purchase activity (market value of purchases less sales) for each quarter of the year. If net purchases were positive (negative) in any quarter, the performance of the bonds would be evaluated until the net purchase activity became negative (positive). Positive (negative) net purchases would be viewed as a bullish (bearish) view taken by the manager. The correctness of this view would be measured.

Critique *each* method with regard to market timing measurement problems.

CFA® PROBLEMS

18. A plan sponsor with a portfolio manager who invests in small-capitalization, high-growth stocks should have the plan sponsor's performance measured against which *one* of the following?

a. S&P 500 index

b. Wilshire 5000 index

c. Dow Jones Industrial Average

d. S&P 400 index

CFA® PROBLEMS

19. Strict market timers attempt to maintain a ________________ portfolio beta and a ________________ portfolio alpha.

a. Constant; shifting

b. Shifting; zero

c. Shifting; shifting

d. Zero; zero

CFA® PROBLEMS

20. Which of the following methods measures the reward-to-volatility tradeoff by dividing the average portfolio excess return over the standard deviation of return?

a. Sharpe's measure
b. Treynor's measure
c. Jensen's measure
d. Appraisal ratio

APPENDIX 20A: MEASURING INVESTMENT RETURNS

Dollar-Weighted Returns Versus Time-Weighted Returns

When we consider investments over a period during which cash has been added to or withdrawn from the portfolio, measuring the rate of return becomes more difficult. To continue our example from the beginning of Section 20.2, suppose that you were to purchase a second share of the same stock at the end of the first year and hold both shares until the end of year 2, at which point you sell each share for $54.

Total cash outlays are:

Time	Outlay
0	$50 to purchase first share
1	$53 to purchase second share a year later

Proceeds are:

Time	Proceeds
1	$2 dividend from initially purchased share
2	$4 dividend from the 2 shares held in the second year, plus $108 received from selling both shares at $54 each

Using the discounted cash flow (DCF) approach, we can solve the average return over the two years by equating the present values of the cash inflows and outflows:

$$50 + \frac{53}{1 + r} = \frac{2}{1 + r} + \frac{112}{(1 + r)^2}$$

resulting in $r = 7.117$ percent.

This value is called the **dollar-weighted rate of return** on the investment. It is "dollar-weighted" because the stock's performance in the second year, when two shares of stock are held, has a greater influence on the average overall return than the first-year return, when only one share is held.

This investment approach, buying an equal amount of shares each period with new cash, is not unrealistic. A popular variant, in fact, is called **dollar-cost averaging**. Instead of buying a second share, you invest another $50 after one year. Notice the effect of this is to buy fewer shares at a higher price, or more shares at a lower price if the price should fall. In the example above, you only purchase 1/1.06 shares and receive that portion of the dividend. Skipping the arithmetic details, we find that r rises to 7.145 percent with the revised cash flows. This strategy for investing ignores inflation and increased ability to invest, but it can be practised on a monthly basis, with periodic increases in the averaging quantity.

An alternative to the internal or dollar-weighted return is the **time-weighted return**. This method ignores the number of shares of stock held in each period. The stock return in the first year was 10 percent. (A $50 purchase provided $2 in dividends and $3 in capital gains.) In the second year, the stock had a starting value of \$53 and sold at year-end for \$54, for a total one-period rate of return of \$3 (\$2 dividend plus \$1 capital gain) divided by \$53 (the stock price at the start of the second year), or 5.66 percent. The time-weighted rate of return is the average of 10 percent and 5.66 percent, which is 7.83 percent. This average return considers only the period-by-period returns without regard to the amounts invested in the stock in each period.

Note that the dollar-weighted return is less than the time-weighted return in this example. The reason is that the stock fared relatively poorly in the second year, when the investor was holding more shares. The greater weight that the dollar-weighted average places on the second-year return results in a lower measure of investment performance. In general, dollar- and time-weighted returns will differ, and the difference can be positive or negative depending on the configuration of period returns and portfolio composition.

Which measure of performance is superior? They both have their place, depending on what the investment pattern is, and that depends upon who is doing the investing. In the money management industry, portfolio managers are subject to the withdrawal and contribution wishes of their clients. Specifically in open-ended funds, the total asset value is based both on investor net contributions and past performance; calculation of net asset value (NAV) per unit is the basis for redemptions or purchases, which is a result of the portfolio performance since the last calculation. Total portfolio value is adjusted by net contributions and net increases in component asset prices; for closed-end funds, only the latter is relevant. The same two effects occur in the case of pension fund management, as contributions are made and benefits paid. Consequently, the money management industry uses time-weighted returns for performance evaluation.

CONCEPT CHECK

A.1. Shares of XYZ Corp. pay a \$2 dividend at the end of every year on December 31. An investor buys two shares of the stock on January 1 at a price of \$20 each, sells one of those shares for \$22 a year later on the next January 1, and sells the second share an additional year later for \$19. Find the time- and dollar-weighted rates of return on the two-year investment.

Arithmetic Averaging Versus Geometric Averaging

Our example took the arithmetic average of the two annual returns for the time-weighted average of 7.83 percent. The principle of compounding lends itself to the computation of a geometric average instead. If stock had been purchased to yield the combined returns of growth with dividend reinvestment, the factors of 1.10 and 1.0566 lead to a compound growth rate of

$$(1 + r_G)^2 = (1.10)(1.0566)$$

Taking the square root of each side gives the result. In general terms, for an n-period investment, the geometric average rate of return is given by

$$1 + r_G = [(1 + r_1)(1 + r_2) \ldots (1 + r_n)]^{1/n} \quad (20A.1)$$

where r_t is the return in each time period. By contrast, the arithmetic average rate of return is given by

$$r_G = (r_1 + r_2 + \ldots + r_n) \times 1/n \quad (20A.2)$$

The geometric average return in this example, 7.81 percent, is slightly less than the arithmetic average return, 7.83 percent. This is a general property: geometric averages never exceed arithmetic averages, and the difference between the two becomes greater as the variability of period-by-period returns becomes greater. The general rule when returns are expressed as decimals, is

$$r_G \approx r_A - \sigma^2/2 \quad (20A.3)$$

where σ^2 is the variance of returns. Equation 20A.3 is exact when the returns are normally distributed.

For example, consider Table 20A.1, which presents arithmetic and geometric returns over the period 1949–1987 for a variety of investments. The arithmetic averages all exceed the geometric averages, and the difference is greatest for stocks of small firms, where annual returns exhibit the greatest standard deviation. Indeed, the difference between the two averages falls to zero only when there is no variation in yearly returns, although the table indicates that, by the time the standard deviation falls to a level characteristic of T-bills, the difference is quite small.

Here is another return question. In the case of time-weighted averages, which is the superior measure of investment performance, the arithmetic average or the geometric average? The geometric average has considerable appeal because it represents exactly the constant rate of return we would have needed to earn in each year to match actual performance over some past investment period. It is an excellent measure of *past* performance. However, if our focus is on future performance, then the arithmetic average is the statistic of interest because it is an unbiased estimate of the portfolio's expected future return (assuming, of course, that the expected return does not change over time). In contrast, because the geometric return over a sample period is always less than the arithmetic mean, it constitutes a downward-biased estimator of the stock's expected return in any future year.

To illustrate this concept, suppose that in any period a stock will either double in value (r = 100 percent) with probability of .5, or halve in value (r = –50 percent) with probability .5. The table following illustrates these outcomes:

Investment Outcome	Final Value of Each Dollar Invested	One-Year Rate of Return
Double	$2	100%
Halve	$0.50	–50%

Suppose that the stock's performance over a two-year period is characteristic of the probability distribution, doubling in one year, and halving in the other. The stock's price ends up exactly

Table 20A.1 Selected Canadian Annual Returns by Investment Class, 1949–1987

	Annual Returns				
	Geometric Average	Arithmetic Average	Maximum	Minimum	Standard Deviation
Equities (Value-Weighted)					
Small firms	15.08	18.93	46.41	–27.85	19.61
Large firms	11.07	12.45	51.40	–26.78	17.59
All firms	11.15	12.50	51.30	–28.29	17.82
Equities (Equal-Weighted)					
Small firms	20.23	23.83	80.72	–32.72	29.70
Large firms	12.22	13.93	46.41	–27.85	19.60
All firms	15.51	18.62	59.30	–27.35	23.83
Long-term industrial bonds	6.22	6.62	43.36	–7.60	9.69
Long-term Canada bonds	5.22	5.64	45.81	–5.82	10.17
Treasury bills	5.90	5.98	19.09	0.51	4.16
Inflation	4.69	4.76	12.32	–1.73	3.76

Source: Adapted from James E. Hatch and Robert W. White, *Canadian Stocks, Bonds, Bills, and Inflation: 1950–1987* (Charlottesville, VA: The Financial Analysts Research Foundation, 1988). © 1988, Association for Investment Management and Research. Reproduced and republished from Financial Analysts Federation with permission from CFA Institute. All rights reserved.

where it started, and the geometric average annual return is zero:

$$1 + r_G = [(1 + r_1)(1 + r_2)]^{1/2}$$
$$= [(1 + 1)(1 - .50)]^{1/2}$$
$$= 1$$

so that

$$r_G = 0$$

which confirms that a zero year-by-year return would have replicated the total return earned on the stock.

The expected annual future rate of return on the stock, however, is *not* zero: it is the arithmetic average of 100 percent and –50 percent: (100 – 50)/2 = 25 percent. To confirm this, note that there are two equally likely outcomes for each dollar invested: either a gain of \$1 (when $r = 100$ percent) or a loss of \$.50 (when $r = -50$ percent). The expected profit is (\$1 – \$.50)/2 = \$.25, for a 25 percent expected rate of return. The profit in the good year more than offsets the loss in the bad year, despite the fact that the geometric return is zero. The arithmetic average return thus provides the best guide to expected future returns from an investment.

You might question the assumption of a pattern of doubling or halving with equal probability. Why not plus or minus 50 percent, symmetrically? The answer is that plus 100 and minus 50 percent *is* symmetric, in a multiplicative or geometric sense. In fact, the prospects of plus or minus the same percent should not be considered equal; 100 percent is double or nothing, and nothing means you are out. Bringing utilities into the picture, you might be indifferent between plus 100 and minus 50 percent. The arithmetic average, your expected gain, is the wealth you will have and it will have a certain utility; but that is different from your expected utility for the gamble.

This argument carries forward into multiperiod investments. Consider, for example, all the possible outcomes over a two-year period:

Investment Outcome	Final Value of Each Dollar Invested	Total Return over Two Years
Double, double	\$4	300%
Double, halve	\$1	0
Halve, double	\$1	0
Halve, halve	\$.25	–75%

The expected final value of each dollar invested is (4 + 1 + 1 + .25)/4 = \$1.5625 for two years, again indicating an average rate of return of 25 percent per year, equal to the arithmetic average. Note that an investment yielding 25 percent per year with certainty will yield the same final compounded value as the expected final value of this investment, as $1.25^2 = 1.5625$. The arithmetic average return on the stock is [300 + 0 + 0 + (–75)]/4 = 56.25 percent per two years, for an effective annual return of 25 percent, that is, $1.5625^{1/2} - 1$. In contrast, the geometric mean return is zero:

$$[(1 + 3)(1 + 0)(1 + 0)(1 - .75)]^{1/4} = 1.0$$

Again, the arithmetic average is the better guide to *future* performance.

CONCEPT CHECK

A.2. Suppose that a stock now selling for \$100 will either increase in value by 15 percent by year-end with probability .5 or fall in value by 5 percent with probability .5. The stock pays no dividends.

a. What are the geometric and arithmetic mean returns on the stock?

b. What is the expected end-of-year value of the share?

c. Which measure of expected return is superior?

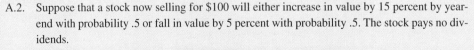

Appendix 20A Key Terms

dollar-weighted rate of return 817

dollar-cost averaging 817

time-weighted return 817

Appendix 20A Problems

1. Consider the rate of return of stocks ABC and XYZ.

Year	r_{ABC}	r_{XYZ}
1	.20	.30
2	.12	.12
3	.14	.18
4	.03	.00
5	.01	−.10

a. Calculate the arithmetic average return on these stocks over the sample period.
b. Which stock has greater dispersion around the mean?
c. Calculate the geometric average returns of each stock. What do you conclude?
d. If you were equally likely to earn a return of 20 percent, 12 percent, 14 percent, 3 percent, or 1 percent in each of the five annual returns for stock ABC, what would be your expected rate of return? What if the five outcomes were those of stock XYZ?

2. XYZ stock price and dividend history are as follows:

Year	Beginning-of-Year Price	Dividend Paid at Year-End
1995	$100	$4
1996	$120	$4
1997	$ 90	$4
1998	$100	$4

An investor buys three shares of XYZ at the beginning of 1995, buys another two shares at the beginning of 1996, sells one share at the beginning of 1997, and sells all four remaining shares at the beginning of 1998.

a. What are the arithmetic and geometric average time-weighted rates of return for the investor?
b. What is the dollar-weighted rate of return? (*Hint*: Carefully prepare a chart of cash flows for the *four* dates corresponding to the turn of the year for January 1, 1995, to December 31, 1998. If your calculator cannot calculate internal rate of return, you will have to use trial and error.)

3. A manager buys three shares of stock today, and then sells one of those shares each year for the next three years. His actions and the price history of the stock are summarized below. The stock pays no dividends.

Time	Price	Action
0	$ 90	Buy 3 shares
1	100	Sell 1 share
2	100	Sell 1 share
3	100	Sell 1 share

a. Calculate the time-weighted geometric average return on this "portfolio."
b. Calculate the time-weighted arithmetic average return on this portfolio.
c. Calculate the dollar-weighted average return on this portfolio.

CFA® PROBLEMS

4. In measuring the comparative performance of different fund managers, the preferred method of calculating rate of return is:

a. Internal
b. Time-weighted
c. Dollar-weighted
d. Income

CFA® PROBLEMS

5. Which *one* of the following is a valid benchmark against which a portfolio's performance can be measured over a given time period?

a. The portfolio's dollar-weighted rate of return
b. The portfolio's time-weighted rate of return
c. The portfolio manager's "normal" portfolio
d. The average beta of the portfolio

CFA® PROBLEMS

6. Assume you invested in an asset for two years. The first year you earned a 15 percent return, and the second year you earned a *negative* 10 percent return. What was your annual geometric return?

CFA® PROBLEMS

7. Assume you purchased a rental property for \$50,000 and sold it one year later for \$55,000 (there was no mortgage on the property). At the time of the sale, you paid \$2,000 in commissions and \$600 in taxes. If you received \$6,000 in rental income (all of it received at the end of the year), what annual rate of return did you earn?

a. 15.3 percent
b. 15.9 percent
c. 16.8 percent
d. 17.1 percent

CFA® PROBLEMS

8. A portfolio of stocks generates a –9 percent return in 1990, a 23 percent return in 1991, and a 17 percent return in 1992. The annualized return (geometric mean) for the entire period is

a. 7.2 percent
b. 9.4 percent
c. 10.3 percent
d. None of the above

CFA® PROBLEMS

9. A two-year investment of \$2,000 results in a return of \$150 at the end of the first year and a return of \$150 at the end of the second year, in addition to the return of the original investment. The internal rate of return on the investment is

a. 6.4 percent
b. 7.5 percent
c. 15.0 percent
d. None of the above

CFA® PROBLEMS

10. In measuring the performance of a portfolio, the time-weighted rate of return is superior to the dollar-weighted rate of return because

a. When the rate of return varies, the time-weighted return is higher.
b. The dollar-weighted return assumes all portfolio deposits are made on day 1.
c. The dollar-weighted return can only be estimated.
d. The time-weighted return is unaffected by the timing of portfolio contributions and withdrawals.

CFA® PROBLEMS

11. The annual rate of return for JSI's common stock has been:

	1995	1996	1997	1998
Return	14%	19%	–10%	14%

a. What is the arithmetic mean of the rate of return for JSI's common stock over the four years?
i. 8.62 percent

ii. 9.25 percent
iii. 14.25 percent
iv. None of the above

b. What is the geometric mean of the rate of return for JSI's common stock over the four years?
i. 8.62 percent
ii. 9.25 percent
iii. 14.21 percent
iv. Cannot be calculated due to the negative return in 1997

CFA® PROBLEMS

12. A pension fund portfolio begins with $500,000 and earns 15 percent the first year and 10 percent the second year. At the beginning of the second year, the sponsor contributes another $500,000. The time-weighted and dollar-weighted rates of return were:

a. 12.5 percent and 11.7 percent
b. 8.7 percent and 11.7 percent
c. 12.5 percent and 15.0 percent
d. 15.0 percent and 11.7 percent

CFA® PROBLEMS

13. The difference between an arithmetic average and a geometric average of returns

a. Increases as variability of the returns increases
b. Increases as the variability of the returns decreases
c. Is always negative
d. Depends on the specific returns being averaged, but is not necessarily sensitive to their variability

APPENDIX 20B: OPTION PRICING OF TIMING ABILITY

Merton's approach to analyzing the pattern of returns to the perfect market timer was to recognize that perfect foresight is equivalent to holding a call option on the equity portfolio. Recall that a call option is a right, but not an obligation, to acquire an asset at a predetermined "exercise" price. The perfect timer has the option here to invest 100 percent in either the safe asset or the equity portfolio, whichever will yield the higher return. This is shown in Figure 20B.1. The rate of return is bounded from below by r_f.

To see the value of information as an option, suppose that the market index currently is at S_0, and that a call option on the index has an exercise price of $X = S_0(1 + r_f)$. If the market outperforms bills over the coming period, S_T will exceed X, whereas it will be less than X otherwise. Now look at the payoff to a portfolio consisting of this option and S_0 dollars invested in bills:

	Payoff to Portfolio	
	$S_T < X$	$S_T \geq X$
Bills:	$S_0(1 + r_f)$	$S_0(1 + r_f)$
Option:	0	$S_T - X$
Total	$S_0(1 + r_f)$	S_T

The portfolio pays the risk-free return when the market is bearish (i.e., the market return is less than the risk-free rate) and pays the market return when the market is bullish and beats bills. Such a portfolio is a perfect market timer. Consequently, we can measure the value of perfect ability as the value of the call option, because a call enables the investor to earn the market return only when it exceeds r_f.

This insight lets Merton value timing ability using the theory of option valuation, and from this we calculate our fair charge for timing. Each month, we calculate the option value based on the current s_0 and r_f; this value is then subtracted from the portfolio payoff, which is converted to a rate of return to determine the monthly statistics.

Figure 20B.1
Rate of return of a perfect market timer.

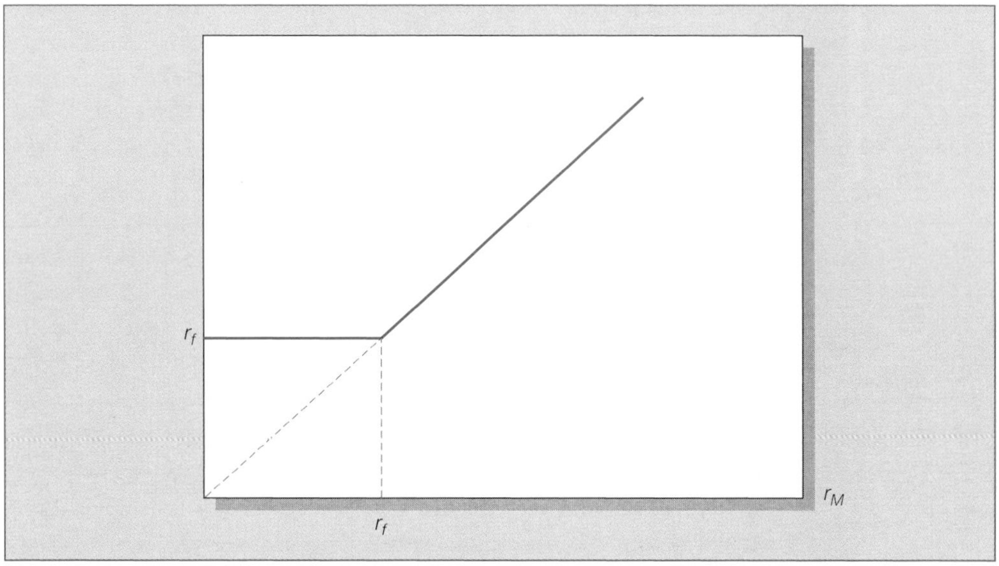

PORTFOLIO MANAGEMENT TECHNIQUES

In the previous chapter, we explored the concept of active portfolio management and of how the success of those who reject a passive approach can be assessed. Active management takes the form of either the selection of assets that are expected to outperform the market index or the allocation of funds between equities, bonds and cash so as to place capital where it will earn the highest return over shorter periods. In this chapter, we discuss just how active management is executed, that is, what specific techniques can be used to invest in accordance with the results of selectivity or timing analysis.

We shall begin the discussion by explaining the passive strategy of indexing, or how purchasing the market portfolio is achieved. Since this is passive only with respect to equities, we continue with the issue of asset allocation, which turns passive strategies with respect to selectivity into active timing. In the following section, we demonstrate how selectivity can be optimally conducted, while respecting the notions of portfolio optimization; this is effected by purchasing an index portfolio, but also adding specific equity positions that respond to security analysis decisions. Next we discuss how active or passive positions can be hedged by the use of derivatives. Finally, we describe how the success of a portfolio manager in asset allocation and security selection can be assessed by specific attribution of the results to particular skills.

21.1 INDEXING

Portfolio theory is substantiated by a considerable body of evidence that points to (1) the relatively accurate pricing of financial assets by the CAPM, (2) the lack of success of portfolio managers in beating the market, whether by timing or selectivity, and (3) the general refutation of apparent anomalies and violations of weak and semistrong forms of market efficiency. In consequence, investors have been advised to diversify and to buy-and-hold. Since perfect diversification is virtually impossible because of transactions costs, investors can either buy a relatively small portfolio that will still eliminate almost all diversifiable risk if chosen optimally, or they can purchase mutual funds (which unfortunately are likely to charge 1 to 2 percent per annum for the benefits of diversification, management and accounting services). As noted in Chapter 4, the average mutual fund will probably underperform the market approximately by the size of its management fee percentage.

Investors appear to be faced with the dismal prospect of doing worse than the well-known dartboard strategy by relying on mutual funds; in fact, they have a better option. A reasonable solution is to buy a low-cost mutual fund which does not charge for its management skills. Such funds may be relatively passive funds, which simply reduce their fees and probably have low portfolio turnover; this saves the investor transactions fees in their portfolios (even with low commissions to funds, the bid-asked spread will still impose a noticeable cost), and reduces the capital gains tax burden. Alternatively, the funds may be **index funds**, whose stated policy is to hold only those equities which compose one of the popular market indices, such as the S&P/TSX Composite or S&P 500. Some turnover still occurs, when the index is adjusted to replace one asset by another; at this point the index fund must sell and buy accordingly. Nevertheless, the major expense of maintaining a research team is eliminated as well as most of the transactions costs. Examples of such funds include the BMO Equity Index and its older and much larger U.S. equivalent, the Vanguard 500 Portfolio, which tracks the S&P 500 index. Added to these benefits is the evidence in the middle nineties that the market indices and index funds outperformed the vast majority of managed funds, giving them increasing publicity for unsophisticated investors.

A lower-cost alternative has emerged more recently. Investors in Canada can duplicate the S&P/TSX 60 index by purchasing iUnits; these securities are traded on the TSX as ordinary shares, but replicate the index in the same way as an index fund. This is achieved at almost no cost to the investor. The management expenses, for maintaining the portfolio and occasionally adjusting it in line with the index, are covered by retaining the dividends received on the stocks until the end of the quarter, at which time the aggregated dividends are paid to the investor's account; the interest earned on the funds is sufficient to cover the expense, with any excess also paid out. The U.S. equivalent goes by the name of "Spiders," from the name S&P Depositary Receipts, based on the S&P 500 index, but there are also "Diamonds" for the Dow-Jones Industrials, and "Cubes" for the Nasdaq 100.

In both Canada (through ETFs issued by BGI) and the United States, one can also invest in various sector indices, such as high-tech or energy sector indices based on the major representatives of those fields. These can be invested in as ETFs relatively inexpensively. As an alternative, one can buy mutual funds that are restricted to sectors, such as Fidelity's "Select" funds; this turns out to be an expensive alternative, with higher fees than the average funds. At this point, we are departing from the notion of replicating the market portfolio and turning to playing bets on sector performance; this represents a compromise position based on sector selectivity rather than individual stock selectivity, and can be explained (as we shall see) as a timing or asset allocation play.

For the equity component of a portfolio then, the efficient and low-cost method to holding the market portfolio has come to be known as **indexing**; it is achieved by purchasing some kind of index security whose performance will track almost perfectly that of the market portfolio. In the United States there are also a number of alternative indexes aimed at different slices of the whole market, namely the Russell 2000 and S&P 400, for the somewhat lower capitalization equities, or the Wilshire 5000, for almost the entire set of listed securities. These are intended as benchmarks for portfolio performance comparison purposes, but derivatives can also be based upon them and used for hedging purposes. The purchase of the index security fulfills the aim of acquiring a well-diversified proxy for the market portfolio. It allows an investor to follow the dictates of modern portfolio theory and has the added benefit of avoiding the realization of any capital gains through portfolio rebalancing.

In addition to the passive strategy of indexing, the index security and sector indexes can be used as part of an active management scheme. A basic strategy for risk reduction involves shorting an index security (either a future or index option) against a portfolio; this can be done for timing (after a sustained up-move) or for reducing the systematic risk of an active portfolio imperfectly correlated with the index. Similarly, a portfolio of securities drawn from a particular sector can be hedged by shorting the sector index securities. (This process is explained in Section 21.4.)[1]

As noted in the bond portfolio management chapter, bond indexing can be achieved through a cellular portfolio, but this is not really a practical investment. Instead the more traditional opportunities are personal construction of laddered or barbell portfolios, or the purchase of a professionally managed bond mutual fund; in the latter case, it is generally accepted that the lowest cost (management fees) fund is likely to be the best. (Others recommend the direct purchase of a medium-term bond, on issue, from the Bank of Canada, which is rolled over at maturity; this is claimed to have at least as good realized returns as mutual funds, whose portfolio durations are generally of similar length as the initial bond maturity.)

Finally for cash, a money market fund, invested either in government securities alone or in prime corporate issues as well, provides the best yields for the ultimate liquidity that a "cash" component is expected to have.

21.2 ASSET ALLOCATION

Market timing in its simplest form would entail buying an index fund of equities when the investor predicted that the market would be yielding higher than a money market fund and selling it when the prediction reversed. This was alluded to in the previous chapter when Robert Merton's demonstration was described. With fixed income securities added to the portfolio, the prediction would have to include whether bonds, stocks or cash would have the highest return and the resultant action would require switching to whichever asset was chosen. In fact, since perfect predictions are not expected, one is more likely to talk about the risk-adjusted returns predicted for each asset. Professional advisors determine the probabilities of each of the three assets outperforming the others, and then recommend portfolio proportions for the three assets which respond to the strength of the probabilities. The recommended proportions are then referred to as asset allocations.

A passive asset allocation approach would specify the three proportions and keep them unmodified under a long-term, buy-and-hold strategy. Such a strategy is, once again, supported by the empirical evidence describing the average results of those who try to time the market. The only question in that prescription is answered by our earliest conclusion in portfolio theory—that of the location along the capital allocation line representing the proportion of wealth placed in the risky portfolio. We would amplify that simple two-asset allocation as presented in Chapter 6, where risky capital was first allocated between what was described as a (less risky) bond portfolio and a (more risky) stock portfolio, and then the capital allocation question was resolved.

[1]See Lorne Switzer and Rana Zoghaib, "Index Participation Units, Market Tracking Risk, and Equity Market Demand," *Canadian Journal of Administrative Sciences* 16, no. 3 (September 1999), pp. 243–255.

We should note at this point that the prescription of Chapter 6 is not followed strictly in the markets. Essentially, the markets are segmented into bond and equity (and others), and optimal portfolios are constructed separately. The proportion in each of the two asset classes plus cash are determined as a distinct decision. The first result of determining an allocation of capital between cash, bonds, and equities is taken as a neutral or baseline allocation. The resultant weights designated as neutral will depend on the risk tolerance of the individual investor, and must be determined by a manager in consultation with the client. For example, risk-tolerant clients may place a large fraction of their capital in the equity market, perhaps directing the portfolio manager to set neutral weights of 75 percent equity, 15 percent bonds, and 10 percent cash equivalents. In contrast, more risk-averse clients may set neutral weights of 45/35/20 percent for the three markets; thus their portfolios in normal circumstances will be exposed to less risk than that of the risk-tolerant client. Any deviation from these weights, by either type of client, must be justified by a belief that one or the other market will either under- or overperform its usual risk-return profile. This would be an intentional departure from the neutral position based on macro analysis.

The previous risk tolerance approach to baseline portfolios applies to individual clients and their financial advisors. Brokerage houses tend to identify a broader portfolio for their general clients. This approach is defined by the establishment of a baseline portfolio position for at least two types of investors; thus there may exist model portfolios described as the "balanced portfolio" and the "growth portfolio." Each of these might hold the same bond and stock portfolios, but in different proportions. (There are opportunities for expansion at this point; the equity portfolio could be redefined for different representative investors having objectives of "preservation of capital" or "aggressive growth," but these objectives could also be satisfied simply by moving along the capital allocation line.)

The two portfolios above were described as baseline positions. Under an active asset allocation approach, proportions are adjusted from the **baseline allocation** in response to the predictions about asset performance. These predictions are initially based on a macroeconomic analysis indicating such results as (1) increasing activity leading to higher interest rates that would lower bond prices but perhaps increase corporate profits and equity prices, or (2) higher inflation leading to both higher interest rates with falling bond prices and squeezed profits with higher discount factors causing equity declines also. The resultant asset allocation decisions in these two cases would be switching funds out of bonds and into stocks, and reducing positions in both bonds and stocks and increasing the cash proportion.

Brokerage houses regularly report on the asset allocation proportions in their two-or-more-model portfolios, giving their current allocations and reminding their clients of the neutral positions. They also tend to indicate the maximum and minimum levels for each asset proportion to indicate the strength of their convictions about market prospects. Thus a balanced portfolio might have a neutral weighting of (stocks, bonds, cash) (60 percent, 30 percent, 10 percent) with a stated range of (30–70 percent, 20–40 percent, 5–25 percent); with a recommendation of (68 percent, 25 percent, 7 percent), the broker would be indicating a very bullish perspective on equities, while a (50 percent, 35 percent, 15 percent) posture would suggest a somewhat cautious outlook for equity performance.

In our review of empirical evidence on performance, we noted that asset allocation is also described more specifically as "swing fund management" and "tactical asset allocation," with the first term referring to a more general and subjective version based on economic conditions. Assessment of interest rates for short- and long-term debt instruments and predicted returns on the market index quickly leads to an increase or decrease in each of the current proportions to provide the next allocation. Subjectively, if the differences between predicted short and long rates and equity returns shrink, then capital will be moved toward bonds and cash, while if the differences are expanding the allocation will shift toward equities. This loose and intuitive approach is given the more impressive "tactical" label when more formal computational techniques are employed. Extensive analysis of time series and their changes, using sophisticated statistical techniques and even

LOOKING BEYOND HISTORICAL DATA IN SECURITY SELECTION

When it comes to the relative importance of asset allocation and security selection, the overwhelming consensus is that asset allocation is more important. This is because many investors fail to distinguish between the consequences of investor behaviour and the opportunities offered by the capital markets.

The widely held view that asset allocation is more important arises, in part, from a 1986 study by Brinson, Hood and Beebower called "Determinants of Portfolio Performance" which attributes the performance of 91 large corporate pension funds to three investment activities: policy, timing and security selection. The analysis revealed that asset allocation policy accounted for 93.6 per cent of total return variation over time.

Yet selecting stocks for the equity portion of a portfolio is substantially more important than choosing a portfolio's exposure among stocks, bonds and cash. It is important to look beyond the historical performance of actual funds because these results depend on two separate factors: the opportunities that arise from a variation in asset class and security returns, as well as the extent to which investors exercise discretion in exploiting these opportunities.

For this study, the term "importance" is defined as the extent to which a particular investment activity causes dispersion in wealth. Using a bootstrap* methodology, the importance of security selection is measured by holding a consistent asset mix at a 60/30/10 among stocks, bonds and cash, and calculating the variation in return on the basis of the variation among randomly diversified stock portfolios. The next step is to measure the importance of asset allocation by holding constant individual security weights and calculating variation in return due purely to asset allocation variation around an expected allocation of 60/30/10 to stocks, bonds and cash.

Random variation among individual securities within the stock component of a portfolio causes substantially more return variation than random asset allocation among stocks, bonds and cash, holding constant the individual security weights within the stock component. In fact, the dispersion around average performance arising from security selection is substantially greater than the dispersion arising from asset allocation in every major developed country.

It can be argued that annualized cumulative return is not an appropriate metric because it ignores risk. This concern is addressed by ranking the asset allocation and security selection portfolios by utility, which encompasses both return and risk. This involves the use of a mean-variance approximation of log-wealth utility. The results show that the dispersion of utility, as well as return, is much greater among portfolios that vary by security composition than it is for portfolios varying by asset class.

Overall, the simulation results and actual fund performance highlight an often ignored, yet important, feature in the institutional investment industry. Security selection strategies do not offer as wide a distribution of opportunities as the distribution that arises naturally from security returns. In fact, it is believed that managers compress the natural opportunity set to reduce their exposure to risk.

A log-wealth utility function assumes utility is equal to the logarithm of wealth which, in turn, implies that utility increases with wealth, but at a decreasing rate. It is one of a family of utility functions that assume investors have constant relative risk aversion.

*Bootstrapping is a procedure by which new samples are generated from an original data set by randomly selecting observations from the original data set. It differs from Monte Carlo simulation in that it draws randomly from an empirical sample, whereas Monte Carlo simulation draws randomly from a theoretical distribution.

Source: Sébastien Page, "Asset Allocation Versus Security Selection: Looking Beyond Historical Data Raises the Status of Security Selection," *Canadian Investment Review* 15, no. 4 (Winter 2002), p. 37.

the latest technologies such as neural networks and chaos theory, requires extensive sessions on higher powered computers to produce (perhaps) more reliable estimates of the optimal proportions. One should note, however, that research in this area by some foremost financial researchers concludes that the essential ingredients in the analysis are still the predicted returns on short- and long-term debt securities and on the market index, with much attention paid to their relative levels both to each other and to their historical values, as well as current economic conditions.

The economic analysis can be extended further, using the fundamental approach previously described in Chapter 14. This would reveal that certain sectors of the market are expected to perform better at different stages of the economic cycle in general, which is linked to the assessment of where the cycle currently is to identify superior prospects; alternatively, specific sectors can be expected to outperform due to particular economic conditions that are occurring. Such predictions would lead to overweighting of these sectors, either through their representative companies or through a sector fund or index, with a corresponding underweighting of all other sectors or of some predicted to underperform. This adjustment of the equity portfolio would constitute a finer level of asset allocation, which is assessed specifically by the techniques presented in Section 21.5.

21.3 SECURITY SELECTION: THE TREYNOR-BLACK MODEL

Overview of the Treynor-Black Model

Security analysis is the other form of active portfolio management besides timing the overall market. Suppose that you are an analyst studying individual securities. It is quite likely that you will turn up several securities that appear to be mispriced. They offer positive anticipated alphas to the investor. But how do you exploit your analysis? Concentrating a portfolio on these securities entails a cost, namely, the firm-specific risk that you could shed by more fully diversifying. As an active manager you must strike a balance between aggressive exploitation of perceived security mispricing and diversification motives that dictate that a few stocks should not dominate the portfolio.

Treynor and Black[2] developed an optimizing model for portfolio managers who use security analysis. It represents a portfolio management theory that assumes security markets are *nearly* efficient. The essence of the model is this:

1. Security analysts in an active investment management organization can analyze in depth only a relatively small number of stocks out of the entire universe of securities. The securities not analyzed are assumed to be fairly priced.
2. For the purpose of efficient diversification, the market index portfolio is the baseline portfolio, which the model treats as the passive portfolio.
3. The macro forecasting unit of the investment management firm provides forecasts of the expected rate of return and variance of the passive (market index) portfolio.
4. The objective of security analysis is to form an active portfolio of a necessarily limited number of securities. Perceived mispricing of the analyzed securities is what guides the composition of this active portfolio.
5. Analysts follow several steps to make up the active portfolio and evaluate its expected performance:
   a. Estimate the beta of each analyzed security and its residual risk. From the beta and the macro forecast, $E(r_M) - r_f$, determine the *required* rate of return of the security.
   b. Given the degree of mispricing of each security, determine its expected return and expected *abnormal* return (alpha).
   c. Calculate the cost of less than full diversification. The nonsystematic risk of the mispriced stock, the variance of the stock's residual, offsets the benefit (alpha) of specializing in an underpriced security.
   d. Use the estimates for the values of alpha, beta, and residual risk to determine the optimal weight of each security in the active portfolio.
   e. Estimate the alpha, beta, and residual risk for the active portfolio according to the weights of the securities in the portfolio.
6. The macroeconomic forecasts for the passive index portfolio and the composite forecasts for the active portfolio are used to determine the optimal risky portfolio, which will be a combination of the passive and active portfolios.

Just as even imperfect market timing ability has enormous value, security analysis of the sort Treynor and Black propose has similar potential value. Even with far from perfect security analysis, proper active management can add value.

---

[2]Jack L. Treynor and Fischer Black, "How to Use Security Analysis to Improve Portfolio Selection," *Journal of Business*, January 1973.

Although the Treynor-Black model is conceptually easy to implement, it has not been successful in the portfolio management industry. Yet its fundamental assumption is being accepted by managers who are uncomfortable with performance comparisons against the index. They are acknowledging that index portfolios and securities should form the basis of an individual portfolio, but they recommend the use of their advice for an active component of the total portfolio. Essentially, they are sacrificing risk-return improvement by not using the details of the procedure that follows.

Portfolio Construction

Assuming that all securities are fairly priced, and using the index model as a guideline for the rate of return on fairly priced securities, the rate of return on the *i*th security is given by

$$r_i = r_f + \beta_i(r_M - r_f) + e_i \tag{21.1}$$

where e_i is the zero-mean, firm-specific disturbance.

Absent security analysis, Treynor and Black (TB) take equation 21.1 to represent the rate of return on all securities and assume that the market portfolio, *M,* is the efficient portfolio. For simplicity, they also assume that the nonsystematic components of returns, e_i, are independent across securities. As for market timing, TB assume that the forecast for the **passive portfolio** already has been made, so that the expected return on the market index, r_M, as well as its variance, σ^2_M, has been assessed.

Now a portfolio manager unleashes a team of security analysts to investigate a subset of the universe of available securities. The objective is to form an active portfolio of positions in the analyzed securities to be mixed with the index portfolio. For each security, *k,* that is researched, we write the rate of return as

$$r_k = r_f + \beta_k(r_M - r_f) + e_k + \alpha_k \tag{21.2}$$

where α_k represents the extra expected return (called the *abnormal return*) attributable to any perceived mispricing of the security. Thus for each security analyzed the research team estimates the parameters α_k, β_k, $\sigma^2(e_k)$. If all the α_k turn out to be zero, there would be no reason to depart from the passive strategy and the index portfolio *M* would remain the manager's choice. However, this is a remote possibility. In general, there will be a significant number of non-zero alpha values, some positive and some negative.

One way to get an overview of the TB methodology is to examine what we should do with the active portfolio once we get it. Suppose that the **active portfolio** (*A*) has been constructed somehow and has the parameters α_A, β_A, $\sigma^2(e_A)$. Its total variance is the sum of its systematic variance, $\beta^2_A\sigma^2_M$, plus the non-systematic variance $\sigma^2(e_A)$. Its covariance with the market index portfolio, *M,* is

$$\text{Cov}(r_A, r_M) = \beta_A\sigma^2_M$$

Figure 21.1 shows the optimization process with the active and passive portfolios. The dashed efficient frontier represents the universe of all securities assuming that they are all fairly priced, that is, that all alphas are zero. By definition, the market index, *M,* is on this efficient frontier and is tangent to the (broken) capital market line (CML). In practice the analysts do not need to know this frontier. They need only to observe the market index portfolio and construct a portfolio resulting in a capital allocation line that lies above CML. Given their perceived superior analysis, they will view the market index portfolio as inefficient: the active portfolio, *A,* constructed from mispriced securities must lie, by design, above the CML.

To locate the active portfolio *A* in Figure 21.1, we need its expected return and standard deviation. The standard deviation by equation 8.7 is

$$\sigma_A = [\beta^2_A\sigma^2_M + \sigma^2(e_A)]^{1/2}$$

Figure 21.1 The optimization process with active and passive portfolios.

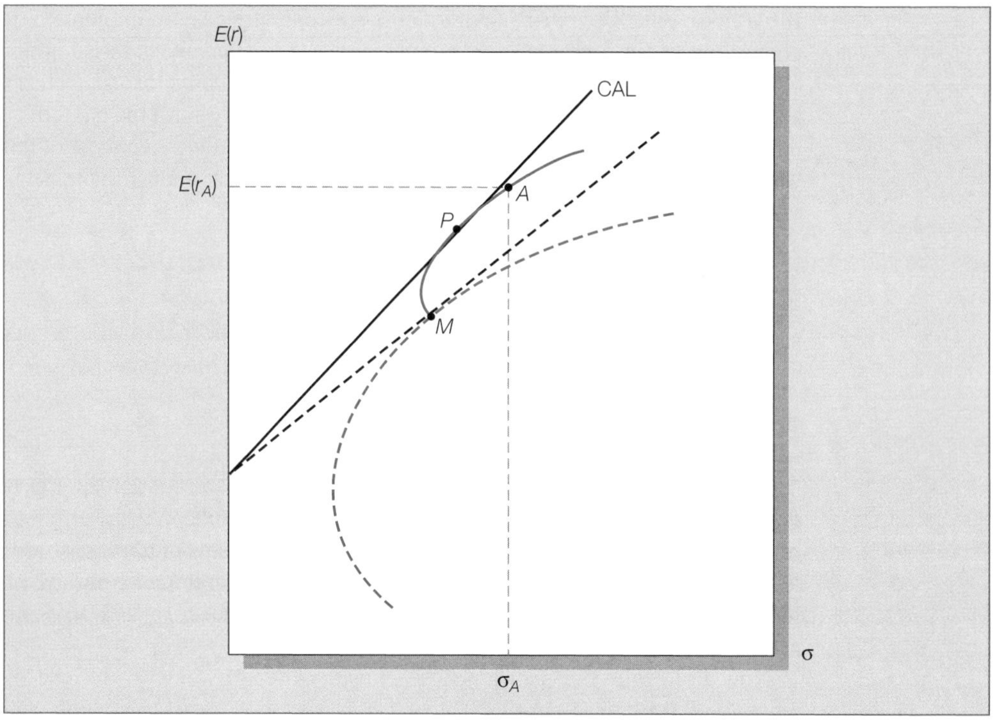

Because of the positive alpha value that is forecast for *A,* it plots above the (broken) CML with expected return

$$E(r_A) = \alpha_A + r_f + \beta_A[E(r_M) - r_f]$$

The optimal combination of the active portfolio, *A,* with the passive portfolio, *M,* is a simple application of the construction of optimal risky portfolios from two component assets that we first encountered in Chapter 6. Because the active portfolio is not perfectly correlated with the market index portfolio, we need to account for their mutual correlation in the determination of the optimal allocation between the two portfolios. This is evident from the solid efficient frontier that passes through *M* and *A.* It supports the optimal capital allocation line (CAL) and identifies the optimal risky portfolio, *P,* which combines portfolios *A* and *M,* and is the tangency point of the CAL to the efficient frontier. The active portfolio *A* in this example is not the ultimately efficient portfolio, because we need to mix *A* with the passive market portfolio to achieve greater diversification.

Let us now outline the algebraic approach to this optimization problem. If we invest a proportion, *w,* in the active portfolio and $1 - w$ in the market index, the portfolio return will be

$$r_p(w) = wr_A + (1 - w)r_M$$

We can use this equation to calculate Sharpe's measure (dividing the mean excess return by the standard deviation of the return) as a function of the weight, *w,* then find the optimal weight, w^*, that maximizes the measure. This is the value of *w* that makes *P* the optimal tangency portfolio in Figure 21.1.

What is the reward-to-variability ratio of the optimal risky portfolio once we find the best mix, w^*, of the active and passive index portfolio? First let us re-express the Sharpe ratio as:

$$S_P = \frac{E(r_P) - r_f}{\sigma_P} = \frac{R_P}{\sigma_P}$$

If we compute the square of Sharpe's measure of the risky portfolio, we can separate the contributions of the index and active portfolios as follows:

$$S^2_P = S^2_M + \frac{\alpha^2_A}{\sigma^2(e_A)} = \left[\frac{R_M}{\sigma_M}\right]^2 + \left[\frac{\alpha_A}{\sigma(e_A)}\right]^2 \tag{21.3}$$

This decomposition of the Sharpe measure of the optimal risky portfolio, which by the way is valid *only* for the optimal portfolio, tells us how to construct the active portfolio. Equation 21.3 shows that the highest Sharpe measure for the risky portfolio will be attained when we construct an active portfolio that maximizes the value of $\alpha_A/\sigma(e_A)$. The ratio of alpha to residual standard deviation of the active portfolio will be maximized when we choose a weight for the kth analyzed security as follows:

$$w_k = \frac{\alpha_k/\sigma^2(e_k)}{\sum_{i=1}^{n} \alpha_i/\sigma^2(e_i)} \tag{21.4}$$

This makes sense: the weight of a security in the active portfolio depends on the ratio of the degree of mispricing, α_k, to the nonsystematic risk, $\sigma^2(e_k)$, of the security. The denominator, the sum of the ratio across securities, is a scale factor to guarantee that the weights sum to one.

Note from equation 21.3 that the square of Sharpe's measure of the optimal risky portfolio is increased over the square of the Sharpe measure of the passive (market-index) portfolio by the amount

$$\left[\frac{\alpha_A}{\sigma(e_A)}\right]^2$$

The ratio of the degree of mispricing, α_A, to the nonsystematic standard deviation, $\sigma(e_A)$, becomes a natural performance measure of the active component of the risky portfolio. In Section 20.2, we identified this as the appraisal ratio.

We can also calculate the contribution of a single security in the active portfolio to the portfolio's overall performance. When the active portfolio contains n analyzed securities, the total improvement in the squared Sharpe measure equals the sum of the squared appraisal ratios of the analyzed securities,

$$\left[\frac{\alpha_A}{\sigma(e_A)}\right]^2 = \sum_{i=1}^{n}\left[\frac{\alpha_i}{\sigma(e_i)}\right]^2 \tag{21.5}$$

The appraisal ratio for each security, $\alpha_i/\sigma(e_i)$, is a measure of the contribution of that security to the performance of the active portfolio.

Once the optimal active portfolio composition has been identified, its weight w^* in the optimal tangency portfolio P (on the opportunity curve APM in Figure 21.1) is found, as noted above, by maximizing the Sharpe measure as a function of w. In other words, we want the weight w that provides the steepest CAL (in Figure 21.1), which was determined by equation 6.11 for a portfolio of two risky assets, given a risk-free asset:

$$w_A = \frac{[E(r_A) - r_f]\sigma^2_M - [E(r_M) - r_f]\text{Cov}(r_A, r_M)}{[E(r_A) - r_f]\sigma^2_M + [E(r_M) - r_f]\sigma^2_A - [E(r_A) - r_f + E(r_M) - r_f]\text{Cov}(r_A, r_M)} \tag{6.11}$$

Now recall that for $R_P = E(r_P) - r_f$,

$$\begin{aligned} E(r_A) - r_f &= \alpha_A + \beta_A R_M \\ \text{Cov}(R_A, R_M) &= \beta_A \sigma^2_M \\ \sigma^2_A &= \beta^2_A \sigma^2_M + \sigma^2(e_A) \end{aligned}$$

$$[E(r_A) - r_f] + [E(r_M) - r_f] = (\alpha_A + \beta R_M) + R_M = \alpha_A + R_M(1 + \beta_A)$$

Substituting these expressions into equation 6.11, dividing both numerator and denominator by σ_M^2, and collecting terms yields the expression for the optimal weight in portfolio A, w^*,

$$w^* = \frac{\alpha_A}{\alpha_A(1 - \beta_A) + R_M \dfrac{\sigma^2(e_A)}{\sigma_M^2}} \tag{21.6}$$

Let's begin with the simple case where $\beta_A = 1$ and substitute into equation 21.6. Then the optimal weight, w_0, is

$$w_0 = \frac{\alpha_A/R_M}{\sigma^2(e_A)/\sigma^2_M} \tag{21.7}$$

This is a very intuitive result. If the systematic risk of the active portfolio is average, that is, $\beta_A = 1$, then the optimal weight is the "relative advantage" of portfolio A as measured by the ratio: alpha/(market excess return), divided by the "disadvantage" of A, that is the ratio: (nonsystematic risk of A)/(market risk). Some algebra applied to equation 21.6 reveals the relationship between w_0 and w^*:

$$w^* = \frac{w_0}{1 + (1 - \beta_A)w_1} \tag{21.8}$$

w^* increases when β_A increases because the larger the systematic risk, β_A, of the active portfolio, A, the smaller the benefit from diversifying it with the index, M, and the more beneficial it is to take advantage of the mispriced securities. However, we expect the beta of the active portfolio to be in the neighbourhood of 1.0 and the optimal weight, w^*, to be close to w_0.

EXAMPLE 21.1 Treynor-Black Process

Suppose that the macroforecasting unit of Drex Portfolio Inc. (DPF) issues a forecast for a 15 percent market return. The forecast's standard error is 20 percent. The risk-free rate is 7 percent. The macro data can be summarized as follows:

$$E(r_M) - r_f = .08;\ \sigma_M = .20$$

At the same time, the security analysis division submits to the portfolio manager the following forecast of annual returns for the three securities that it covers:

Stock	α	β	$\sigma(e)$	$\alpha/\sigma(e)$
1	7%	1.6	45%	.1556
2	−5	1.0	32	−.1563
3	3	0.5	26	.1154

Note that the alpha estimates appear reasonably moderate. The estimates of the residual standard deviations are correlated with the betas, just as they are in reality. The magnitudes also reflect typical values for NYSE stocks. Equations 21.5 and 21.3 and the analyst input table allow a quick calculation of the DPF portfolio's Sharpe measure:

$$S_P = [(8/20)^2 + .1556^2 + .1563^2 + .1154^2]^{1/2} = \sqrt{.2220} = .4711$$

Compare the result with the Sharpe ratio for the market-index portfolio, which is only 8/20 = .40. We now proceed to compute the composition and performance of the active portfolio.

First, let us construct the optimal active portfolio implied by the security analyst input list. To do so we compute the ratios as follows (remember to use decimal representations of returns in the formulas):

Stock	$\alpha/\sigma^2(e)$	$\frac{\alpha_k}{\sigma^2(e_k)} \Big/ \sum_{i=1}^{3} \frac{\alpha_i}{\sigma^2(e_i)}$
1	$.07/.45^2 = .3457$	$.3457/.3012 = 1.1477$
2	$-.05/.32^2 = -.4883$	$-.4883/.3012 = -1.6212$
3	$.03/.26^2 = .4438$	$.4438/.3012 = 1.4735$
Total	.3012	1.0000

The last column presents the optimal positions of each of the three securities in the active portfolio. Obviously, stock 2 has a negative weight. The magnitudes of the individual positions in the active portfolio (e.g., 114.77 percent in stock 1) seem quite extreme. However, this should not concern us because the active portfolio will later be mixed with the well-diversified market index portfolio, resulting in much more moderate positions, as we shall see shortly.

The forecasts for the stocks, together with the proposed composition of the active portfolio, lead to the following parameter estimates for the active portfolio:

$$\alpha_A = 1.1477 \times .07 + (-1.6212) \times (-.05) + 1.4735 \times .03 = .2056$$
$$\beta_A = 1.1477 \times 1.6 + (-1.6212) \times 1.0 + 1.4735 \times .5 = .9519$$
$$\sigma(e_A) = [1.1477^2 \times .45^2 + (-1.6212)^2 \times .32^2 + 1.4735^2 \times .26^2]^{1/2} = .8262$$
$$\sigma^2(e_A) = .8262^2 = .6826$$

Note that the negative weight (short position) on the negative alpha stock results in a positive contribution to the alpha of the active portfolio. Note also that because of the assumption that the stock residuals are uncorrelated, the active portfolio's residual variance is simply the weighted sum of the individual stock residual variances, with the squared portfolio proportions as weights.

The parameters of the active portfolio are now used to determine its proportion in the overall risky portfolio:

$$w_0 = \frac{\alpha_A/\sigma^2(e_A)}{[E(r_M) - r_f]/\sigma^2_M} = \frac{.2056/.6826}{.08/.04} = .1506$$

$$w^* = \frac{w_0}{1 + (1 - \beta_A)w_0} = \frac{.1506}{1 + (1 - .9519) \times .1506} = .1495$$

Although the active portfolio's alpha is impressive (20.56 percent), its proportion in the overall risky portfolio, before adjustment for beta, is only 15.06 percent, because of its large nonsystematic risk (82.62 percent). Such is the importance of diversification. As it happens, the beta of the active portfolio is almost 1.0, and hence the correction for beta (from w_0 to w^*) is small, from 15.06 percent to 14.95 percent. The direction of the change makes sense. If the beta of the active portfolio is low (less than 1.0), there are more potential gains from diversification. Hence a smaller position in the active portfolio is called for. If the beta of the active portfolio were significantly greater than 1.0, a larger correction in the opposite direction would be called for.

The proportions of the individual stocks in the active portfolio, together with the proportion of the active portfolio in the overall risky portfolio, determine the proportions of each individual stock in the overall risky portfolio.

Stock	Final Position
1	$.1495 \times 1.1477 = .1716$
2	$.1495 \times (-1.6212) = -.2424$
3	$.1495 \times 1.4735 = .2202$
Active portfolio	.1495
Market portfolio	.8505
	1.0000

Another measure of the gain from using this portfolio is the M^2 statistic, as described in Chapter 20. M^2 is calculated by comparing the expected return of a portfolio on the capital allocation line supported by portfolio P, CAL(P), with a standard deviation equal to that of the market index, to the expected return on the market index. In other words, we mix portfolio P with the risk-free asset to obtain a new portfolio P^* that has the same standard deviation as the market portfolio. Since both portfolios have equal risk, we can compare their expected returns. The M^2 statistic is the difference in expected returns. Portfolio P^* can be obtained by investing a fraction σ_M/σ_P in P and a fraction $(1 - \sigma_M/\sigma_P)$ in the risk-free asset.

The risk premium on CAL(P^*) with total risk σ_M is given by

$$E(r_{P*}) - r_f = S_P\sigma_M = .4711 \times .20 = .0942, \text{ or } 9.42\% \tag{21.9}$$

and

$$M^2 = [E(r_{P*}) - r_f] - [E(r_M) - r_f] = 9.42 - 8 = 1.42\% \tag{21.10}$$

At first blush, an incremental expected return of 1.42 percent seems paltry compared with the alpha values submitted by the analyst. This seemingly modest improvement is the result of diversification motives: to mitigate the large risk of individual stocks (verify that the standard deviation of stock 1 is 55 percent) and maximize the portfolio Sharpe measure (which compares excess return to total volatility), we must diversify the active portfolio by mixing it with M. Note also that this improvement has been achieved with only three stocks, and with forecasts and portfolio rebalancing only once a year. Increasing the number of stocks and the frequency of forecasts can improve the results dramatically.

For example, suppose the analyst covers three more stocks that turn out to have alphas and risk levels identical to the first three. Use equation 21.5 to show that the squared appraisal ratio of the active portfolio will double. By using equation 21.3, it is easy to show that the new Sharpe measure will rise to .5327. Equation 21.10 then implies that M^2 rises to 2.65 percent, almost double the previous value. Increasing the frequency of forecasts and portfolio rebalancing will deploy the power of compounding to improve annual performance even more.

CONCEPT CHECK ?

1. *a.* When short positions are prohibited, the manager simply discards stocks with negative alphas. Using the preceding example, what would be the composition of the active portfolio if short sales were disallowed? Find the cost of the short-sale restriction in terms of the decline in performance (M^2) of the new overall risky portfolio.

   b. How would your answer change if the macro forecast is adjusted upward, for example, to $E(r_M) = 12$ percent, and short sales are again allowed?

Imperfect Forecasts of Alpha Values

Suppose an analyst is assigned to a security and provides you with a forecast of $\alpha = 20\%$. It looks like a great opportunity! Using this forecast in the Treynor-Black algorithm, we'll end up tilting our portfolio heavily toward this security. Should we go out on a limb? Before doing so, any reasonable manager would ask: "How good is the analyst?" Unless the answer is a resounding "good," a reasonable manager would discount the forecast. We can quantify this notion.

Suppose we have a record of an analyst's past forecast of alpha, α^f. Relying on the index model and obtaining reliable estimates of the stock beta, we can estimate the true alphas (after the fact) from the average realized excess returns on the security, $\bar{R}$, and the index, $\bar{R}_M$, that is,

$$\alpha = \bar{R} - \beta\bar{R}_M$$

To measure the forecasting accuracy of the analyst, we can estimate a regression of the forecasts on the realized alpha:

$$\alpha^f = a_0 + a_1\alpha + \varepsilon$$

The coefficients a_0 and a_1 reflect potential bias in the forecasts, which we will ignore for simplicity; that is, we will suppose $a_0 = 0$ and $a_1 = 1$. Because the forecast errors are uncorrelated with the true alpha, the variance of the forecast is

$$\sigma^2_{\alpha^f} = \sigma^2_\alpha + \sigma^2_\varepsilon$$

The quality of the forecasts can be measured by the squared correlation coefficient between the forecasts and realization, equivalently, the ratio of explained variance to total variance

$$\rho^2 = \frac{\sigma^2_\alpha}{\sigma^2_\alpha + \sigma^2_\varepsilon}$$

This equation shows us how to "discount" analysts' forecasts to reflect their precision. Knowing the quality of past forecasts, ρ^2, we "shrink" any new forecast, α^f, to $\rho^2\alpha^f$, to minimize forecast error. This procedure is quite intuitive. If the analyst is perfect, that is, $\rho^2 = 1$, we take the forecast at face value. If analysts' forecasts have proven to be useless, with $\rho^2 = 0$, we ignore the forecast. The quality of the forecast gives us the precise shrinkage factor to use.

Suppose the analysts' forecasts of the alpha of the three stocks in our previous example are all of equal quality, $\rho^2 = .2$. Shrinking the forecasts of alpha by a factor of .2 and repeating the optimization process, we end up with a much smaller weight on the active portfolio (.03 instead of .15), a much smaller Sharpe measure (.4031 instead of .4711), and a much smaller M^2 (.06% instead of 1.42%).

The reduction in portfolio expected performance does not reflect an inferior procedure. Rather, accepting alpha forecasts without acknowledging and adjusting for their imprecision would be naïve. We must adjust our expectations to the quality of the forecasts.

In reality, we can expect the situation to be much worse. A forecast quality of .2, that is, a correlation coefficient of $\sqrt{.2} = .45$ between alpha forecasts and realizations is most likely unrealistic in nearly efficient markets. Moreover, we don't even know this quality, and its estimation introduces yet another potential error into the optimization process. Finally, the other parameters we use in the TB model: market expected return and variance, and security betas and residual variances, are also estimated with errors. Thus, under realistic circumstances, we would be fortunate to obtain even the meager results we have just uncovered.

So, should we ditch the TB model? Before we do, let's make one more calculation. The "meagre" Sharpe measure of .4031 squares to .1625, larger than the market's squared Sharpe measure of .16 by .0025. Suppose we cover 300 securities instead of three, that is, 100 sets identical to the one we analyzed. From equations 21.3 and 21.5 we know that the increment to the squared Sharpe measure will rise to $100 \times .0025 = .25$. The squared Sharpe measure of the risky portfolio will rise to $.16 + .25 = .41$, a Sharpe measure of .64, and an M^2 of 4.8 percent! Moreover, some of the estimation errors of the other parameters that plague us when we use three securities will offset one another and be diversified away with many more securities covered.[3]

What we see here is a demonstration of the value of security analysis we mentioned at the outset. In the final analysis, the value of the active management depends on forecast quality. The vast demand for active management suggests that this quality is not negligible. The optimal way to exploit analysts' forecasts is with the TB model.

---

[3]Empirical work along these lines can be found in Alex Kane, Tae-Hwan Kim, and Halbert White, "The Power of Portfolio Optimization," UCSD Working Paper, July 2000.

21.4 HEDGING

We have seen two methods of reacting to information based on analysis of either macroeconomic scenarios or individual security returns, recognizing powers of either timing or selectivity. In both cases, underlying portfolios are based on index replication. Under these strategies, investors remain exposed to market risk and its effect on their total portfolios, tempered as they may be by the adjustments made through active management. By using derivatives, this market risk can be further reduced; stock index futures can be sold short against the value of the equity portfolio, while interest rate futures can be shorted against the value of the bond portfolio. In this section we describe the actual construction of the hedges based on the size and beta or duration of the two portfolios.

Hedging Systematic Risk

We saw in Chapter 19 that pure market timers might use a combination of money market securities and stock index futures contracts to adjust market exposure in response to changing forecasts about stock market performance. When the outlook is bullish, more contracts would be added to the fixed position in cash equivalents.

This form of timing is a bit restrictive, however, in that it allows for equity positions in only the stock index. How might a manager of a more actively constructed portfolio hedge market exposure? Suppose, for example, that you manage a \$30 million portfolio with a beta of .8. You are bullish on the market over the long term, but you are afraid that over the next two months, the market is vulnerable to a sharp downturn. If trading were costless, you could sell your portfolio, place the proceeds in T-bills for two months, and then reestablish your position after you perceive that the risk of the downturn has passed. In practice, however, this strategy would result in unacceptable trading costs, not to mention tax problems resulting from the realization of capital gains or losses on the portfolio. An alternative approach would be to use stock index futures to hedge your market exposure.

EXAMPLE 21.2A Hedging Market Risk

Suppose that the S&P/TSX 60 index currently is at 400. A decrease in the index to 390 would represent a drop of 2.5 percent. Given the beta of your portfolio, you would expect a loss of $.8 \times 2.5\%$ $= 2$ percent, or in dollar terms, $.02 \times \$30$ million = \$600,000. Therefore, the sensitivity of your portfolio value to market movements is \$600,000 per 10-point movement in the S&P 60 index.

To hedge this risk, you could sell stock index futures. When your portfolio falls in value along with declines in the broad market, the futures contract will provide an offsetting profit.

The sensitivity of a futures contract to market movements is easy to determine. With its contract multiplier of \$200, the profit on the S&P/TSX 60 futures contract varies by \$2,000 for every 10-point swing in the index. Therefore, to hedge your market exposure for two months, you could calculate the **hedge ratio** as follows:

$$H = \frac{\text{Change in portfolio value}}{\text{Profit on one futures contract}} = \frac{\$600{,}000}{\$2{,}000} = 300 \text{ contracts (short)}$$

You would enter the short side of the contracts, because you want profits from the contract to offset the exposure of your portfolio to the market. Because your portfolio does poorly when the market falls, you need a position that will do well when the market falls.

We also could approach the hedging problem using the regression procedure illustrated above. The predicted value of the portfolio is graphed in Figure 21.2 as a function of the value of the S&P/TSX 60 index. With a beta of .8, the slope of the relationship is 60,000: a 2.5 percent in-

Figure 21.2 Predicted value of the portfolio as a function of the market index.

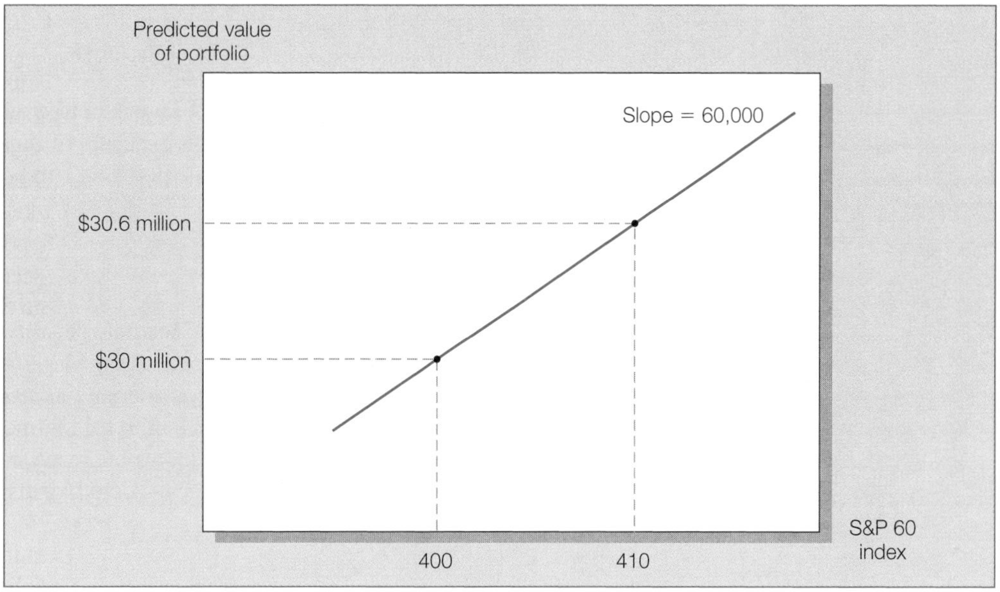

crease in the index, from 400 to 410 results in a capital gain of 2 percent of \$30 million, or \$600,000. Therefore, your portfolio will increase in value by \$60,000 for each increase of one point in the index. As a result, you should enter a short position on 60,000 units of the S&P 60 index to fully offset your exposure to marketwide movements. Because the contract multiplier is \$200 times the index, you need to sell 60,000/200 = 300 contracts.

Notice that when the slope of the regression line relating your unprotected position to the value of an asset is positive, your hedge strategy calls for a *short* position in that asset. The hedge ratio is the negative of the regression slope. This is because the hedge position should offset your initial exposure. If you do poorly when the asset value falls, you need a hedge vehicle that will do well when the asset value falls. This calls for a short position in the asset.

Active managers sometimes believe that a particular asset is underpriced, but that the market as a whole is about to fall. Even if the asset is a good buy relative to other stocks in the market, it still might perform poorly in a broad market downturn. To solve this problem, the manager would like to separate the bet on the firm from the bet on the market: the bet on the company must be offset with a hedge against the market exposure that normally would accompany a purchase of the stock.

EXAMPLE 21.2B Hedging an Active Portfolio

Here again, the stock's beta is the key to the hedging strategy. Suppose the beta of the stock is 2/3, and the manager purchases \$600,000 worth of the stock. For every 3 percent drop in the broad market, the stock would be expected to respond with a drop of $2/3 \times 3\% = 2$ percent, or \$12,000. The S&P/TSX 60 contract will fall by 12 points from a current value of 400 if the market drops 3 percent. With the contract multiplier of \$200, this would entail a profit to a short futures position of $12 \times \$200 = \$2{,}400$ per contract. Therefore, the market risk of the stock can be offset by shorting five S&P/TSX 60 contracts. More formally, we could calculate the hedge ratio as

$$H = \frac{\text{Expected change in stock value per 3\% market drop}}{\text{Profit on one short contract per 3\% market drop}}$$

$$= \frac{\text{\$12,000 swing in unprotected position}}{\text{\$2,400 profit per contract}}$$

$$= 5 \text{ contracts}$$

Now that market risk is hedged, the only source of variability in the performance of the stock-plus-futures portfolio will be the firm-specific performance of the stock.

By allowing investors to bet on market performance, the futures contract allows the portfolio manager to make stock picks without concern for the market exposure of the stocks chosen. After the stocks are chosen, the resulting systematic risk of the portfolio can be modulated to any degree using the stock futures contracts.

Hedging Interest Rate Risk

Like equity managers, fixed-income managers also desire to separate security-specific decisions from bets on movements in the entire structure of interest rates. Consider, for example, a fixed-income manager who holds a bond portfolio on which considerable capital gains have been earned. She foresees an increase in interest rates but is reluctant to sell her portfolio and replace it with a lower-duration mix of bonds because such rebalancing would result in large trading costs as well as realization of capital gains for tax purposes. Still, she would like to hedge her exposure to interest rate increases.

EXAMPLE 21.3 Hedging a Bond Portfolio

Suppose that the portfolio manager has a \$10 million bond portfolio with a modified duration of nine years.[4] If, as feared, market interest rates increase and the bond portfolio's yield also rises, say by ten basis points (.1 percent), the fund will suffer a capital loss. Recall from Chapter 13 that the capital loss in percentage terms will be the product of modified duration, D^*, and the change in the portfolio yield. Therefore, the loss will be

$$D^* \times \Delta y = 9 \times .1\% = .9\%$$

or \$90,000. This establishes that the sensitivity of the value of the unprotected portfolio to changes in market yields is \$9,000 per one-basis-point change in the yield. Market practitioners call this ratio the **price value of a basis point**, or PVBP. The PVBP represents the sensitivity of the dollar value of the portfolio to changes in interest rates. Here, we've shown that

$$\text{PVBP} = \frac{\text{Change in portfolio value}}{\text{Predicted change in yield}} = \frac{\$90{,}000}{10 \text{ basis points}} = \$9{,}000 \text{ per basis point}$$

One way to hedge this risk is to take an offsetting position in an interest rate futures contract. The Canada bond contract nominally calls for delivery of \$100,000 par value bonds with 9 percent coupons and 10-year maturity. In practice, the contract delivery terms are fairly complicated because many bonds with different coupon rates and maturities may be substituted to settle the contract. However, we will assume that the bond to be delivered on the contract already is known and has a modified duration of 10 years. Finally, suppose that the futures price currently is \$90 per \$100 par value. Because the contract requires delivery of \$100,000 par value of bonds, the contract multiplier is \$1,000.

Given these data, we can calculate the PVBP for the futures contract. If the yield on the delivery bond increases by 10 basis points, the bond value will fall by $D^* \times .1\% = 10 \times .1\% =$ 1 percent. The futures price also will decline 1 percent from 90 to 89.10.[5] Because the contract

---

[4]Recall that modified duration, D^*, is related to duration, D, by the formula D^* $D/(1 + y)$, where y is the bond's yield to maturity. If the bond pays coupons semiannually, then y should be measured as a semiannual yield. For simplicity, we will assume annual coupon payments, and treat y as the effective annual yield to maturity.

[5]This assumes the futures price will be exactly proportional to the bond price, which ought to be nearly true.

multiplier is \$1,000, the gain on each short contract will be \$1,000 × .90 = \$900. Therefore, the PVBP for one futures contract is \$900/10-basis-point change, or \$90 for a change in yield of one basis point.

Now we can easily calculate the hedge ratio as follows:

$$H = \frac{\text{PVBP of portfolio}}{\text{PVBP of hedge vehicle}} = \frac{\$9{,}000}{\$90 \text{ per contract}} = 100 \text{ contracts}$$

Therefore, 100 bond futures contracts will serve to offset the portfolio's exposure to interest rate fluctuations.

CONCEPT CHECK

2. Suppose the bond portfolio is twice as large, \$20 million, but that its modified duration is only 4.5 years. Show that the proper hedge position in T-bond futures is the same as the value just calculated, 100 contracts.

Although the hedge ratio is easy to compute, the hedging problem in practice is more difficult. We assumed in our example that the yields on the T-bond contract and the bond portfolio would move perfectly in unison. Although interest rates on various fixed-income instruments do tend to vary in tandem, there is considerable slippage across sectors of the fixed-income market. For example, Figure 21.3 shows that the spread between long-term corporate and Treasury bond yields has fluctuated considerably over time. Our hedging strategy would be fully effective only if the yield spread across the two sectors of the fixed-income market were constant (or at least perfectly predictable) so that yield changes in both sectors were equal.

This problem highlights the fact that most hedging activity is in fact **cross-hedging**, meaning that the hedge vehicle is a different asset than the one to be hedged. To the extent that there is slippage between prices or yields of the two assets, the hedge will not be perfect. Nevertheless, even cross-hedges can eliminate a large fraction of the total risk of the unprotected portfolio.

Figure 21.3 Yield spread between long-term government and AA corporate bonds.

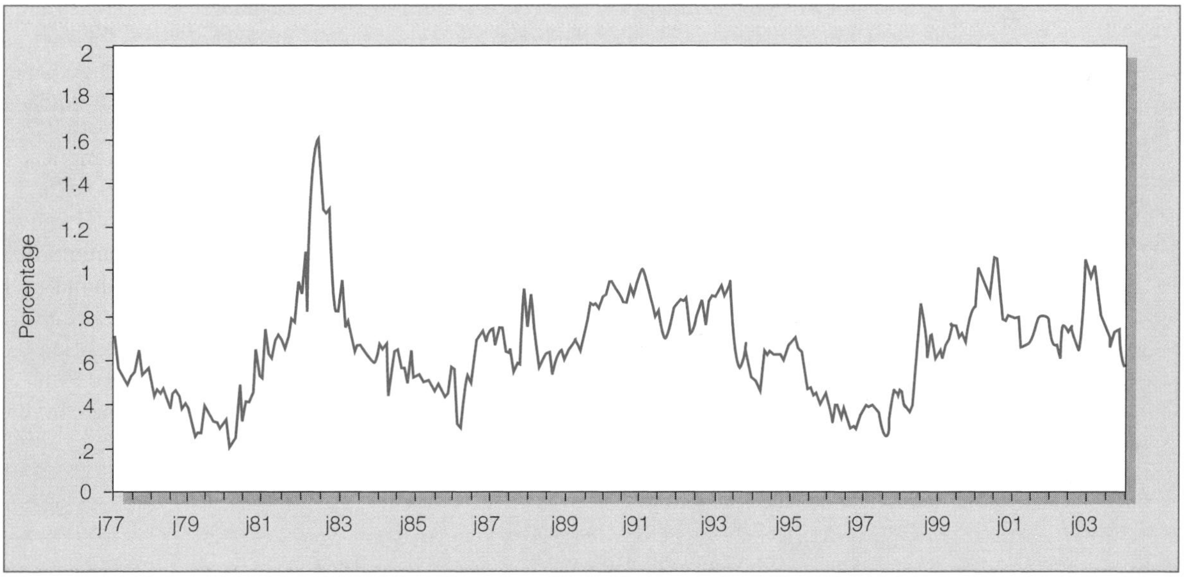

21.5 PERFORMANCE ATTRIBUTION PROCEDURES

Traditionally, portfolio managers have distinguished themselves as either market-timers or stock-pickers. In this way, some have claimed an aptitude for timing the broad market swings by macroeconomic analysis; others, doubting the feasibility of this, have relied on **selectivity**—identifying equities that would perform well in particular economic climates. More recently, we have seen the emergence of managers who despair of either ability and operate index funds. Chapter 20 described a number of measures used to assess the success of managers' efforts.

Rather than focus on risk-adjusted returns, practitioners often want simply to ascertain which decisions resulted in superior or inferior performance. Superior investment performance depends on an ability to be in the "right" securities at the right time. Such timing and selection ability may be considered broadly, for instance, being in equities as opposed to fixed-income securities when the stock market is performing well. Or it may be defined at a more detailed level, such as choosing the relatively better-performing stocks within a particular industry. Portfolio managers constantly make both broad-brush asset-market allocation decisions, as well as more detailed sector and security allocation decisions within markets. Performance attribution studies attempt to break down overall performance into discrete components that may be identified with a particular level of the portfolio selection process.

Recent characterizations of performance ability have extended the simpler timing–selectivity dichotomy by adding a policy variable representing asset allocation. As we have noted, market-timers do not actually switch from T-bills to index funds; rather, they have a standard or base allocation of portfolio weights to T-bills, government bonds, corporate bonds, domestic equities, foreign equities, and perhaps other assets. From this base allocation they shift weights as they see the various assets responding more favourably to changing market conditions.

Attribution studies start from the broadest asset allocation choices and progressively focus on ever-finer details of portfolio choice. The difference between a managed portfolio's performance and that of a benchmark portfolio then may be expressed as the sum of the contributions to performance of a series of decisions made at the various levels of the portfolio construction process. For example, one common attribution system breaks performance down into three components: (1) broad-asset market allocation choices across equity, fixed-income, and money markets, (2) industry (sector) choice within each market, and (3) security choice within each sector.

The attribution method explains the difference in returns between a managed portfolio, P, and a selected benchmark portfolio, B, called the **bogey**. Suppose that the universe of assets for P and B includes n asset classes such as equities, bonds, and bills. For each asset class, a benchmark index portfolio is determined. For example, the S&P/TSX 60 may be chosen as benchmark for equities. The bogey portfolio is set to have fixed weights in each asset class, and its rate of return is given by

$$r_B = \sum_{i=1}^{n} w_{Bi} r_{Bi}$$

where w_{Bi} is the weight of the bogey in asset class i, and r_{Bi} is the return on the benchmark portfolio of that class over the evaluation period. The portfolio managers choose weights in each class, w_{Pi}, based on their capital market expectations, and they choose a portfolio of the securities within each class on the basis of their security analysis, which earns r_{Pi} over the evaluation period. Thus the return of the managed portfolio will be

$$r_P = \sum_{i=1}^{n} w_{Pi} r_{Pi}$$

The difference between the two rates of return, therefore, is

$$r_P - r_B = \sum_{i=1}^{n} w_{Pi} r_{Pi} - \sum_{i=1}^{n} w_{Bi} r_{Bi} = \sum_{i=1}^{n} (w_{Pi} r_{Pi} - w_{Bi} r_{Bi}) \qquad (21.11)$$

Each term in the summation of equation 21.11 can be rewritten in a way that shows how asset allocation decisions versus security selection decisions for each asset class contributed to overall performance. We decompose each term of the summation into a sum of two terms as follows. Note that the two terms we have labelled contributions from asset allocation and security selection in the following decomposition do in fact sum to the total contribution of each asset class to overall performance.

Contribution from asset allocation	$(w_{Pi} - w_{Bi})r_{Bi}$
+ Contribution from security selection	$w_{Pi}(r_{Pi} - r_{Bi})$
= Total contribution from asset class i	$w_{Pi}r_{Pi} - w_{Bi}r_{Bi}$

The first term of the sum measures the impact of asset allocation because it shows how deviations of the actual weight from the benchmark weight for that asset class multiplied by the index return for the asset class added to or subtracted from total performance. The second term of the sum measures the impact of security selection because it shows how the manager's excess return *within* the asset class compared to the benchmark return for that class multiplied by the portfolio weight for that class added to or subtracted from total performance. Figure 21.4 presents a graphical interpretation of the attribution of overall performance into security selection versus asset allocation.

To illustrate this method, consider the attribution results for a hypothetical portfolio. The portfolio invests in stocks, bonds, and money market securities. An attribution analysis appears in Tables 21.1 to 21.4. The portfolio return over the month is 5.34 percent.

The first step is to establish a benchmark level of performance against which performance ought to be compared. This benchmark, again, is called the bogey. The bogey portfolio represents what the portfolio manager would have earned by a passive strategy. "Passive" has two attributes. First, the asset allocation is set to neutral as determined by some market consensus. Second, within each asset class the funds are invested in an indexed portfolio such as the S&P/TSX 60, the Scotia Capital index, and a money market index. Any departure from the benchmark's return by the manager's return must be due to either asset allocation (departure from the neutral allocation across markets) or security selection (departure from the passive index within asset classes), or both.

www.scotia capital.com

Figure 21.4 Performance attribution of *i*th asset class. Enclosed area indicates total rate of return.

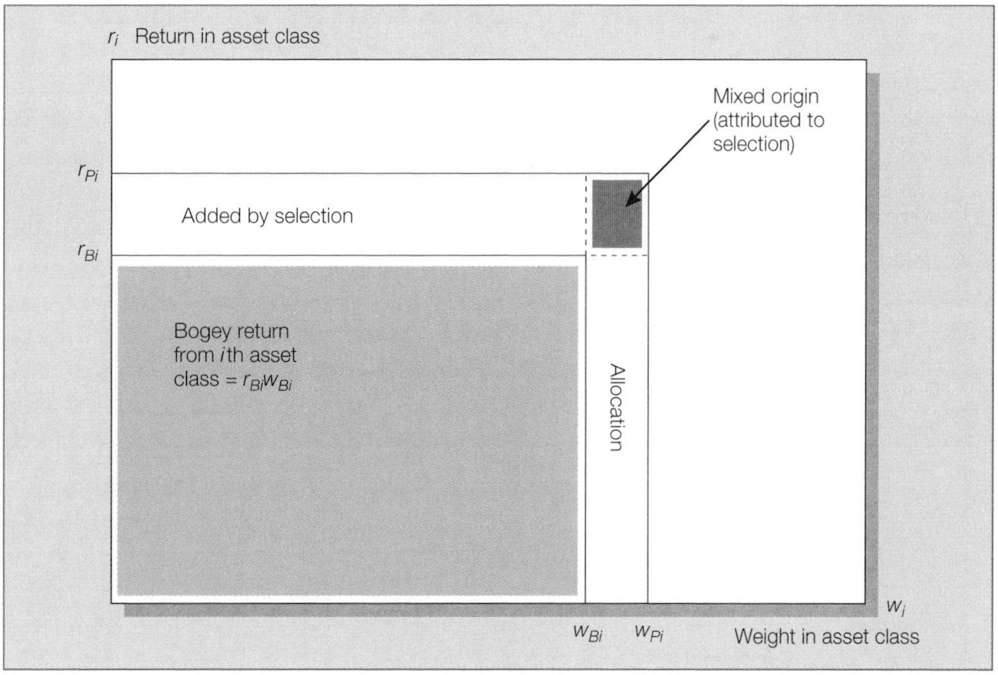

Table 21.1 Performance of the Managed Portfolio

Component	Benchmark Weight	Return of Index During Month (%)
Bogey Performance and Excess Return		
Equity (S&P/TSX 60)	.60	5.81
Bonds (Scotia Capital)	.30	1.45
Cash (money market)	.10	0.48
Bogey = (.60 × 5.81) + (.30 × 1.45) + (.10 × .48) = 3.97%		
Return of managed portfolio		5.34%
Return of bogey portfolio		3.97
Excess return of managed portfolio		1.37%

In Table 21.1, the neutral weights are 60 percent equity, 30 percent fixed-income, and 10 percent cash (money market securities). The bogey portfolio, composed of "investments" in each index with the 60/30/10 weights, returned 3.97 percent. The managed portfolio's measure of extra-market performance is positive and equal to its actual return less the return of the bogey: 5.34 – 3.97 = 1.37 percent. The next step is to allocate the 1.37 percent excess return to the separate decisions that contributed to it.

Asset Allocation Decisions

As shown in Table 21.2, our hypothetical managed portfolio was invested in the equity, fixed-income, and money markets with weights 70 percent, 7 percent, and 23 percent, respectively. The portfolio's performance can derive from the departure of this weighting scheme from the benchmark 60/30/10 weights, as well as from superior or inferior results *within* each of the three broad markets.

To isolate the effect of the manager's asset allocation choice, we measure the performance of a hypothetical portfolio that would have invested in the *indices* for each market with weights 70/7/23. This return measures the individual effect of the shift away from the benchmark 60/30/10 weights, without allowing for any effects attributable to active management of the securities selected within each market. Superior performance relative to the bogey is achieved by overweighting investments

Table 21.2 Performance Attribution

Market	(1) Actual Weight in Market	(2) Benchmark Weight in Market	(3) Excess Weight	(4) Market Return (%)	(5) = (3) × (4) Contribution to Performance (%)
A. Contribution of Asset Allocation to Performance					
Equity	.70	.60	.10	5.81	.5810
Fixed income	.07	.30	−.23	1.45	−.3335
Cash	.23	.10	.13	.48	−.0624
	Contribution of asset allocation				.3099
Market	**(1) Portfolio Performance (%)**	**(2) Index Performance (%)**	**(3) Excess Performance (%)**	**(4) Portfolio Weight**	**(5) = (3) × (4) Contribution (%)**
B. Contribution of Selection to Total Performance					
Equity	7.28	5.81	1.47	.70	1.03
Fixed income	1.89	1.45	.44	.07	.03
	Contribution of selection within markets				1.06

in markets that turn out to perform relatively well and by underweighting poorly performing markets. The contribution of asset allocation to superior performance equals the sum over all markets of the excess weight in each market multiplied by the return of the market index.

Panel A of Table 21.2 demonstrates that asset allocation contributed almost 31 basis points to the portfolio's overall excess return of 137 basis points. The major factor contributing to superior performance in this month was the heavy weighting of the equity market in a month when the equity market had an excellent return of 5.81 percent.

Sector and Security Allocation Decisions

If .31 percent of the excess performance can be attributed to advantageous asset allocation across markets, the remaining 1.06 percent must be attributable to sector and security selection within each market. Panel B of Table 21.2 details the contribution of the managed portfolio's sector and security selection to total performance.

Panel B shows that the equity component of the managed portfolio had a return of 7.28 percent versus a return of 5.81 percent for the S&P/TSX 60. The fixed-income return was 1.89 percent versus 1.45 percent for the Scotia Capital index. The superior performance in equity and fixed-income markets weighted by the portfolio proportions invested in each market sums to the 1.06 percent contribution to performance attributable to sector and security selection.

Table 21.3 documents the sources of the equity component performance by each sector within the market. The first three columns detail the allocation of funds to the sectors in the equity market compared with their (hypothetical) representation in the S&P/TSX 60. Column 4 shows the rate of return of each sector, and column 5 documents the performance of each sector relative to the return of the S&P/TSX 60. The contribution of each sector's allocation presented in column 6 equals the product of the difference in the sector weight and the sector's relative performance.

Note that good performance (a positive contribution) derives from overweighting well-performing sectors, such as energy, or underweighting poorly performing sectors, such as transportation. The excess return of the equity component of the portfolio attributable to sector allocation alone is 1.01 percent. Since the equity component of the portfolio outperformed the S&P/TSX 60 by 1.47 percent (Table 21.2, panel B, column 3), we conclude that the effect of security selection within sectors must have contributed an additional 1.47 – 1.01 = .46 percent to the performance of the equity component of the portfolio.

A similar sector analysis can be applied to the fixed-income portion of the portfolio, but we do not show those results here.

Table 21.3 Sector Selection Within the Equity Market

	(1)	(2)	(3)	(4)	(5)	(6) = (3) × (5)
	Beginning-of-Month Weights (%)				Sector	Sector
Sector	Portfolio	S&P/TSX 60	Difference in Weights	Sector Return	Over-/Under-Performance*	Allocation Contribution
Interest-sensitive	29.72	31.99	−2.27	6.4	.9	−2.04
Consumer	9.54	17.46	−7.92	5.4	−.1	.79
Resource	10.31	21.52	−11.21	3.7	−1.8	20.18
Energy	24.29	9.31	14.98	8.4	2.9	43.44
Industrial products	19.03	9.83	9.2	8.3	2.8	25.76
Transportation	2.32	3.70	−1.38	−.2	−5.7	7.87
Management companies	4.79	6.19	−1.4	2.1	−3.4	4.76
Total						**100.76 basis points**

*S&P/TSX 60 performance, excluding dividends, was 5.5 percent. Returns compared net of dividends.

PERFORMANCE ATTRIBUTION

The performance attribution spreadsheet develops the attribution analysis that is presented in this section. Additional data can be used in the analysis of performance for other sets of portfolios. The model can be used to analyze performance of mutual funds and other managed portfolios.

You can find this Excel model on the Online Learning Centre (www.mcgrahill.ca/college/bodie).

	A	B	C	D	E	F
1	**Performance Attribution**					
2						
3						
4	**Bogey**					
5	**Portfolio**		**Benchmark**	**Return on**	**Portfolio**	
6	**Component**	**Index**	**Weight**	**Index**	**Return**	
7	Equity	S&P 500	0.60	5.8100%	3.4860%	
8	Bonds	Lehman Index	0.30	1.4500%	0.4350%	
9	Cash	Money Market	0.10	0.4800%	0.0480%	
10			Return on Bogey		3.9690%	
11						
12		**Managed**				
13		**Portfolio**	**Portfolio**	**Actual**	**Portfolio**	
14		**Component**	**Weight**	**Return**	**Return**	
15		Equity	0.70	5.8100%	5.0960%	
16		Bonds	0.07	1.4500%	0.1323%	
17		Cash	0.23	0.4800%	0.1104%	
18			Return on Managed		5.3387%	
19			Excess Return		1.3697%	

Summing Up Component Contributions

In this particular month, all facets of the portfolio selection process were successful. Table 21.4 details the contribution of each aspect of performance. Asset allocation across the major security markets contributes 31 basis points. Sector and security allocation within those markets contributes 106 basis points, for total excess portfolio performance of 137 basis points. The sector and security allocation of 106 basis points can be partitioned further. Sector allocation within the equity market results in excess performance of 100.76 basis points, and security selection within sectors contributes 46 basis points. (The total equity excess performance of 147 basis points is multiplied by the 70 percent weight in equity to obtain contribution to portfolio performance.) Similar partitioning could be done for the fixed-income sector.

Table 21.4 Portfolio Attribution: Summary

		Contribution (basis points)
1. Asset allocation		31.0
2. Selection		
a. Equity excess return		
i. Sector allocation	101	
ii. Security allocation	46	
	147 × .70 (portfolio weight) =	102.9
b. Fixed-income excess return	44 × .07 (portfolio weight) =	3.1
Total excess return of portfolio		**137.0 basis points**

? CONCEPT CHECK

3. *a.* Suppose the benchmark weights had been set at 70 percent equity, 25 percent fixed-income, and 5 percent cash equivalents. What then are the contributions of the manager's asset allocation choices?

   b. Suppose the S&P/TSX 60 return is 5 percent. Compute the new value of the manager's security selection choices.

SUMMARY

1. Indexing represents the adoption of a passive strategy with respect to the asset class; it is achieved by purchase of a proxy to the market such as an index mutual fund or an exchange-traded index security.
2. Asset allocation refers to the proportions of capital invested in the three asset classes of stocks, bonds and cash.
3. Passive asset allocation corresponds to a stable investment in the baseline allocation that suits an investor's risk preferences; in contrast, active asset allocation occurs when adjustments to the baseline position are adopted in response to macroeconomic forecasts.
4. The Treynor-Black security selection model envisions that a macroeconomic forecast for market performance is available and that security analysts estimate abnormal expected rates of return, α, for various securities. Alpha is the expected rate of return on a security beyond that explained by its beta and the security market line. In the Treynor-Black model, the weight of each analyzed security is proportional to the ratio of its alpha to its nonsystematic risk, $\sigma^2(e)$.
5. Once the active portfolio is constructed, its alpha value, nonsystematic risk, and beta can be determined from the properties of the component securities. The optimal risky portfolio, *P*, is then constructed by holding a position in the active portfolio according to the ratio of α_P to $\sigma^2(e_P)$, divided by the analogous ratio for the market index portfolio. Finally, this position is adjusted by the beta of the active portfolio.
6. When the overall risky portfolio is constructed using the optimal proportions of the active portfolio and passive portfolio, its performance, as measured by the square of Sharpe's measure, is improved (over that of the passive, market index portfolio) by the amount $[\alpha_A/\sigma(e_A)]^2$.
7. The contribution of each security to the overall improvement in the performance of the active portfolio is determined by its degree of mispricing and nonsystematic risk. The contribution of each security to portfolio performance equals $[\alpha_i/\sigma(e_i)]^2$, so that for the optimal risky portfolio,

$$S^2_P = \left[\frac{E(r_M) - r_f}{\sigma_M}\right]^2 + \sum_{i=1}^{n}\left[\frac{\alpha_i}{\sigma(e_i)}\right]^2$$

8. The hedge ratio is the number of hedging vehicles such as futures contracts required to offset the risk or the unprotected position.
9. The hedge ratio for systematic market risk is proportional to the size and beta of the underlying stock portfolio. The hedge ratio for fixed-income portfolios is proportional to the price value of a basis point, which in turn is proportional to modified duration and the size of the portfolio.
10. Common attribution procedures partition performance improvements to asset allocation, sector selection, and security selection. Performance is assessed by calculating departures of portfolio composition from a benchmark or neutral portfolio.

KEY TERMS

index fund 826	active portfolio 831	cross-hedging 841
indexing 826	hedge ratio 838	selectivity 842
baseline allocation 828	price value of a basis point 840	bogey 842
passive portfolio 831		

Visit us at www.mcgrawhill.ca/college/bodie

SELECTED READINGS

The separation of investment ability into timing versus selectivity derives from:

Fama, Eugene F. "Components of Investment Performance." *Journal of Finance* 25 (June 1970).

The Treynor-Black model was laid out in:

Treynor, Jack, and Fischer Black. "How to Use Security Analysis to Improve Portfolio Selection." *Journal of Business*, January 1973.

The applicability of the model is demonstrated in:

Ambachtsbeer, Keith. "Profit Potential in an Almost Efficient Market." *Journal of Portfolio Management*, Fall 1974.

A good book devoted to risk management is:

Smithson, Charles H., Clifford W. Smith, with D. Sykes Wilford. *Managing Financial Risk.* Burr Ridge, IL: Irwin Professional Publishing, 1995.

PROBLEMS

1. What are the implications of placing your entire equity portfolio in iUnits, or some management company's index mutual fund?

2. You have \$100,000 to invest in equities, and have decided to use iUnits (S&P/TSX 60s) as your index portfolio; use a newspaper listing or the Internet to determine how many units you could buy with your capital.

3. A portfolio manager summarizes the input from the macro and micro forecasters in the following table:

Micro Forecasts

Asset	Expected Return (%)	Beta	Residual Standard Deviation
Stock A	20	1.3	58
Stock B	18	1.8	71
Stock C	17	.7	60
Stock D	12	1.0	55

Macro Forecasts

Asset	Expected Return (%)	Standard Deviation
T-bills	8	0
Passive equity portfolio	16	23

a. Calculate expected excess returns, alpha values, and residual variances for these stocks.

b. Construct the optimal risky portfolio.

c. What is Sharpe's measure for the optimal portfolio, and how much of it is contributed by the active portfolio?

d. What should be the exact make-up of the complete portfolio for an investor with a coefficient of risk aversion of 2.8?

4. Recalculate problem 3 for a portfolio manager who is not allowed to short-sell securities.

a. What is the cost of the restriction in terms of Sharpe's measure?

b. What is the utility loss to the investor ($A = 2.8$) given his new complete portfolio?

5. Suppose that on the basis of an analyst's past record, you estimate that the relationship between forecast and actual alpha is:

$$\text{Actual abnormal return} = .3 \times \text{Forecast of alpha}$$

Use the alphas from problem 3. How much is expected performance affected by recognizing the imprecision of alpha forecasts?

6. A manager is holding a \$1 million stock portfolio with a beta of 1.25. She would like to hedge the risk of the portfolio using the TSE 35 stock index futures contract. How many dollars' worth of the index should she sell in the futures market to minimize the volatility of her position?

7. A manager is holding a \$1 million bond portfolio with a modified duration of eight years. She would like to hedge the risk of the portfolio by short-selling Canada bonds. The modified duration of Canadas is 10 years. How many dollars' worth of Canadas should she sell to minimize the variance of her position?

8. Yields on short-term bonds tend to be more volatile than yields on long-term bonds. Suppose that you have estimated that the yield on 20-year bonds changes by 10 basis points for every 15-basis-point move in the yield on five-year bonds. You hold a \$1 million portfolio of five-year maturity bonds with modified duration four years and desire to hedge your interest rate exposure with Canada bond futures, which currently have modified duration nine years and sell at $F_0 = \$95$. How many futures contracts should you sell?

9. You hold an \$8 million stock portfolio with a beta of 1.0. You believe that the risk-adjusted abnormal return on the portfolio (the alpha) over the next three months is 2 percent. The S&P/TSX 60 index currently is at 800 and the risk-free rate is 1 percent per quarter.
   a. What will be the futures price on the three-month maturity S&P/TSX 60 futures contract?
   b. How many S&P/TSX 60 futures contracts are needed to hedge the stock portfolio?
   c. What will be the profit on that futures position in three months as a function of the value of the S&P/TSX 60 index on the maturity date?
   d. If the alpha of the portfolio is 2 percent, show that the expected rate of return (in decimal form) on the portfolio as a function of the market return is $r_p = .03 + 1.0 \times (r_M - .01)$.
   e. Call S_T the value of the index in three months. Then $S_T/S_0 = S_T/800 = 1 + r_M$. (We are ignoring dividends here to keep things simple.) Substitute this expression in the equation for the portfolio return, r_p, and calculate the expected value of the hedged (stock-plus-futures) portfolio in three months as a function of the value of the index.
   f. Show that the hedged portfolio provides an expected rate of return of 3 percent over the next three months.
   g. What is the beta of the hedged portfolio? What is the alpha of the hedged portfolio?

www.ibm.ca

10. Suppose that the relationship between the rate of return on IBM stock, the market index, and a computer industry index can be described by the following regression equation: $r_{IBM} = .5r_M + .75r_{industry}$. If a futures contract on the computer industry is traded, how would you hedge the exposure to the systematic and industry factors affecting the performance of IBM stock? How many dollars' worth of the market and industry index contracts would you buy or sell for each dollar held in IBM?

11. Nesbitt Burns believes that market volatility will be 20 percent annually for the next three years. Three-year at-the-money call and put options on the market index sell at an implied volatility of 22 percent. What options portfolio can Nesbitt Burns establish to speculate on its volatility belief without taking a bullish or bearish position on the market? Using Nesbitt's estimate of volatility, three-year at-the-money options have $N(d_1) = .6$.

12. Suppose that Scotia Capital sells call options on \$1.25 million worth of a stock portfolio with beta = 1.5. The option delta is .8. It wishes to hedge out its resultant exposure to a market advance by buying market index futures contracts. If the current value of the market index is 1,000 and the contract multiplier is \$250, how many contracts should it buy?

13. Consider the following information regarding the performance of a money manager in a recent month. The table presents the actual return of each sector of the manager's portfolio in column 1, the fraction of the portfolio allocated to each sector in column 2, the benchmark or neutral sector allocations in column 3, and returns of sector indices in column 4.

	Actual Return	Actual Weight	Benchmark Weight	Index Return
Equity	.02	.70	.60	.025 (S&P 60)
Bonds	.01	.20	.30	.012 (Scotia Capital)
Cash	.005	.10	.10	.005

a. What was the manager's return for the month? What was her overperformance or underperformance?

b. What was the contribution of security selection to relative performance?

c. What was the contribution of asset allocation to relative performance? Confirm that the sum of selection and allocation contributions equals her total "excess" return relative to the bogey.

CFA® PROBLEMS

www.pg.com

14. On June 1, 1989, Byron Henry was examining a new fixed-income account that his firm, Hawaiian Advisors, had accepted. Included in the new portfolio was a $10 million par value position in Procter & Gamble (PG) $8\frac{5}{8}$ percent bonds due April 1, 2016.

Henry was concerned about this position for three reasons: (1) there was an unrealized loss on the PG bonds due to a widening in the yield spread between U.S. Treasuries and high-grade corporate bonds; (2) he felt that the PG bonds represented too large a portion of the $100 million portfolio; and (3) he feared that interest rates would move higher over the short term.

Hawaiian Advisors has the capability to do short sales and to use financial futures as well as options on futures. With this in mind, Henry collected some information on the PG bonds and on some alternative vehicles, shown in Tables 21.5 and 21.6.

Table 21.5
Bonds

Name	Coupon	Maturity	Price	Yield	Duration (years)	Price Value of a Basis Point
Procter & Gamble	$8\frac{5}{8}$%	4/1/16	86.36	10.10%	10.08	0.08286
U.S. Treasury bond	$9\frac{1}{8}$%	5/15/13	99.125	9.21%	9.25	0.08766

Henry recalled that the formula for calculating a hedge ratio is

$$\text{Hedge ratio} = \text{Yield beta} \times \frac{\text{PVBP}(y)}{\text{PVBP}(x)}$$

where

PVBP(y) = the price change for a one-basis-point change (PVBP) in the target vehicle (the PG bond)

PVBP(x) = the price change for a one-basis-point change (PVBP) in the hedge vehicle (the U.S. Treasury bond or the U.S. Treasury bond future)

Henry did a regression using Y (the dependent variable) as the yield of the PG bonds, and X (the independent variable) as the yield of the U.S. Treasury bonds. The result was the following equation:

$$Y = 1.75 + .89X \qquad (R\text{-square} = .81)$$

Henry did a second regression using Y (the dependent variable) as the yield of the PG bonds, and X (the independent variable) as the yield on the futures contract. The result was the following equation:

$$Y = 5.25 + .47X \qquad (R\text{-square} = .49)$$

Table 21.6 Futures (contract size = $100,000)

Contract	Expiration	Settlement Price	Yield	Price Value of a Basis Point	Conversion Factor
U.S. Treasury bond future	Dec. 1989	86.3125	9.51%	0.0902	1.1257

For tax reasons, Henry does not want to sell the PG bonds now but would like to protect the portfolio from any further price decline. Formulate two hedging strategies, using only the investment vehicles cited in Tables 21.5 and 21.6, that would protect against any further decline in the price of the PG bonds. Calculate the relevant hedge ratio for each strategy. Comment on the appropriateness of each of these strategies for this portfolio.

APPENDIX 21A: MULTIFACTOR MODELS AND ACTIVE PORTFOLIO MANAGEMENT

Perhaps in the foreseeable future a multifactor structure of security returns will be developed and accepted as conventional wisdom. So far, our analytical framework for active portfolio management seems to rest on the validity of the index model, that is, on a single-factor security model. Despite this appearance, a multifactor structure will not affect the construction of the active portfolio because the entire Treynor-Black analysis focuses on the residuals of the index model. If we were to replace the one-factor model with a multifactor model, we would continue to form the active portfolio by calculating each security's alpha relative to its fair return (give its betas on *all* factors) and again would combine the active portfolio with the portfolio that would be formed in the absence of security analysis. The multifactor framework, however, does raise several new issues in portfolio management.

You saw in Chapter 8 how the index model simplifies the construction of the input list necessary for portfolio optimization programs. If

$$r_i - r_f = \alpha_i + \beta_i(r_M - r_f) + e_i$$

adequately describes the security market, then the variance of any asset is the sum of systematic and nonsystematic risk: $\sigma^2(r_i) = \beta^2{}_i\sigma^2{}_M + \sigma^2(e_i)$, and the covariance between any two assets is $\beta_i\beta_j\sigma^2{}_M$.

How do we generalize this rule to use in a multifactor model? To simplify, let us consider a two-factor world, and let us call the two-factor portfolios M and H. Then we generalize the index model to

$$\begin{aligned} r_i - r_f &= \beta_{iM}(r_M - r_f) + \beta_{iH}(r_H - r_f) + \alpha_i + e_i \\ &= r_\beta + e_i \end{aligned} \qquad (21A.1)$$

β_M and β_H are the betas of the security relative to portfolios M and H. Given the rates of return on the factor portfolios, r_M and r_H, the fair excess rate of return over r_f on a security is denoted r_β and its expected abnormal return is α_i.

How can we use equation 21A.1 to form optimal portfolios? Suppose that investors simply wish to maximize the Sharpe measures of their portfolios. The factor structure of equation 21A.1 can be used to generate the inputs for the Markowitz portfolio selection algorithm. The variance and covariance estimates are now more complex, however:

$$\sigma^2(r_i) = \beta^2{}_{iM}\sigma^2{}_M + \beta^2{}_{iH}\sigma^2{}_H + 2\beta_{iM}\beta_{iH}\text{Cov}(r_M,r_H) + \sigma^2(e_i)$$
$$\text{Cov}(r_i,r_j) = \beta_{iM}\beta_{jM}\sigma^2{}_M + \beta_{iH}\beta_{jH}\sigma^2{}_H + (\beta_{iM}\beta_{jH} + \beta_{jM}\beta_{iH})\text{Cov}(r_M,r_H)$$

Nevertheless, the informational economy of the factor model still is valuable, because we can estimate a covariance matrix for an n-security portfolio from:

n estimates of β_{iM}
n estimates of β_{iH}
n estimates of $\sigma^2(e_i)$
1 estimate of $\sigma^2{}_M$
1 estimate of $\sigma^2{}_H$

rather than $n(n + 1)/2$ separate variance and covariance estimates. Thus, the factor structure continues to simplify portfolio construction issues.

The factor structure also suggests an efficient method to allocate research effort. Analysts can specialize in forecasting means and variances of different factor portfolios. Having established factor betas, they can form a covariance matrix to be used together with expected security returns generated by the CAPM or APT to construct an optimal passive risky portfolio. If active analysis of individual stocks also is attempted, the procedure of constructing the optimal active portfolio and its optimal combination with the passive portfolio is identical to that followed in the single-factor case.

It is likely, however, that the factor structure of the market has hedging implications. This means that clients will be willing to accept an inferior Sharpe measure (in terms of dollar returns) to maintain a risky portfolio that has the desired hedge qualities. Portfolio optimization for these investors obviously is more complicated, requiring specific information on client preferences. The portfolio manager will not be able to satisfy diverse clients with one portfolio.

In the case of the multifactor market, even passive investors (meaning those who accept market prices as "fair") need to do a considerable amount of work. They need forecasts of the expected return and volatility of each factor return, and they need to determine the appropriate weights on each factor portfolio to maximize their expected utility. Such a process is straightforward in principle, but quickly becomes analytically demanding.

INTERNATIONAL INVESTING

Although it is common in Canada to consider the S&P 60 as the market index portfolio, such practice is rather limited in scope. Equities actually make up 10 percent of total Canadian wealth and a far smaller percentage of world wealth. In one sense, international investing may be viewed as no more than a straightforward generalization of our earlier treatment of portfolio selection with a larger menu of assets from which to construct a portfolio. One faces similar issues of diversification, security analysis, security selection, and asset allocation. On the other hand, international investments pose some problems not encountered in domestic markets. Among these are the presence of exchange rate risk, restrictions on capital flows across national boundaries, an added dimension of political risk and country-specific regulations, and different accounting practices in different countries.

In this chapter we will see the importance of world markets and the benefits of diversification for risk-return tradeoffs; we also introduce the possibilities for making international investments. We then examine the effect of currency fluctuations on returns. Following this, we review the processes of appraising international investing, including the identification of factors underlying those returns and the determination of success in selecting areas and assets for portfolios in the context of active, rather than passive, international investment. Finally, we examine the issue of segmentation of markets, which underlies the expected benefits of diversification across national or regional borders.

22.1 INTERNATIONAL INVESTMENTS

The World Equity Portfolio

Canadian investors have shown themselves to be far less prone than their American neighbours to limit their investment horizons to the national boundaries. The presence and influence of foreign investors and markets serve to focus Canadian attention on alternatives to domestic investment; while the proximity of the United States makes it the dominant figure in our international perspective, European and Far Eastern nations already and increasingly are receiving substantial attention from investors. The internationalization of trade, beyond the traditional markets for major corporations such as Alcan, Inco, and the banks, implies that Canadians can and must diversify their portfolio holdings into foreign assets in order to hedge foreign currency and economic fluctuations.

The portfolio holdings of an investor in any country should serve to protect his or her future consumption opportunities, given the prices faced domestically; but these prices are affected by foreign economic conditions and pricing relative to the proportion that foreign trade represents in the domestic economy. Thus in the United States, where domestic production and consumption represent the vast majority of economic activity, foreign economic events have had less and later effect on domestic conditions; in contrast, Canadian conditions react swiftly and directly to external events, particularly those in the United States. Canadians, therefore, have far more need to link themselves to foreign financial markets in order to hedge their portfolios and their consumption opportunities from adverse international events.

Canadians, by nature, may be more inclined to underestimate the size of their securities markets rather than the opposite. The Canadian market values in 2003 represented only 2.9 percent; that left about $30 trillion (U.S.) of foreign securities for investment opportunities. As we noted in Chapter 1, Canadians can easily invest in U.S. securities; but these represented only some 45 percent of the equity markets. Furthermore, we shall see that for Canadian portfolios, U.S. securities offer little in the way of diversification, which is the key opportunity to be exploited in considering foreign securities.

International Diversification

The economic events of the end of the nineties might incline investors to believe that international markets are highly correlated. The "Asian flu" that began with Thailand's currency and stock market collapse swept around Asia and then to Europe and the Americas. One country's financial troubles indicated the potential for the same and led to the realization of those fears in a number of similar and supposedly healthier nations. Fears of a global financial crisis and the drastic retrenchment in Asian economies caused the stocks of multinational banks and firms to fall. As stability returned and fears subsided, a new crisis arose in Russia and Brazil; again the news struck multinationals and banks in various countries proportionately to their exposure. What was evident was that all the markets and economies were interlinked. What then was the point of trying to diversify risk by spreading investments across these different financial markets?

While the evidence of correlation was strong, the level of that correlation is demonstrably lower than one might suspect. The discussion of diversification in Chapter 6 indicates that any assets that are less than perfectly correlated will improve the reward-to-volatility ratio. The addition of foreign securities to a portfolio will, therefore, always serve to extend diversification. In considering their contribution, we usually distinguish between developed countries and emerging markets.

Developed (high-income) countries are defined as those with per capita income exceeding $9,300 (in 2000), and their broad stock indices are generally less risky than those of emerging markets. The World Bank listed 52 developed countries in 2000, many of them with very small exchanges. Our list includes 25 countries with the largest equity capitalization, the smallest of which is New Zealand with a capitalization of $19 billion in 2001. These countries made up 79 percent of world gross domestic product in 2001.

The first five columns of Table 22.1 show market capitalization over the years 1996–2001. The first line is capitalization for all world exchanges, showing total capitalization of corporate equity in 2001 as $25.7 trillion, of which U.S. stock exchanges made up $13.2 trillion (49 percent). The figures in these columns demonstrate the volatility of these markets; indeed, world capitalization in 2001 was less than it was two years earlier and in the entire Pacific Basin it was less than it was in 1996!

The next three columns of Table 22.1 show country equity capitalization as a percentage of the world's in 2001 and 1996 and the growth in capitalization over the five years 1996–2001. The large volatility of country stock indexes resulted in significant changes in relative size. For example, U.S. weight in the world equity portfolio increased from 37 percent in 1996 to 49 percent in 2001, while that of Japan decreased from 24 percent to 11 percent. The weights of the five largest countries behind the U.S. (Japan, U.K., France, Germany, and Switzerland) added up to 39.2 percent in 2001, so that in the universe of these six countries alone, the weight of the U.S. was only 62 percent [49/(49 + 39.2)]. Clearly, U.S. stocks may not comprise a fully diversified portfolio of equities.

Unlike the 1980s and early 1990s, the period 1996–2001 saw a decline in the value of equities of the Pacific Basin (growth of −4 percent), but a resurgence in North America (growth of 136%) and Europe (104 percent). These numbers show that economic position of countries is just as variable as the stock prices that capitalize the future value of the particular corporate sectors of these economies.

The last three columns of Table 22.1 show GDP, per capita GDP, and equity capitalization as a percentage of GDP for the year 2001. As we would expect, per capital GDP in developed countries is not as variable across countries as total GDP, which is determined in part by total population. But market capitalization as a percentage of GDP is quite variable, suggesting widespread differences in economic structure even across developed countries. We return to this issue in the next section.

For a passive strategy one could argue that a portfolio of equities of just the six countries with the largest capitalization would make up 79.2 percent (in 2001) of the world portfolio and may be sufficiently diversified. This argument will not hold for active portfolios that seek to tilt investments toward promising assets. Active portfolios will naturally include many stocks or even indices of emerging markets.

Table 22.2 makes the point. Surely, active portfolio managers must prudently scour stocks in markets such as China, Brazil, or Korea. The table shows data from the 20 largest emerging markets, the most notable of which is China with equity capitalization of $170 billion (.66 percent of world capitalization) in 2001, and growth of 651 percent over the five years 1996–2001. But managers also would not want to have missed a market like Poland (.09 percent of world capitalization) with a growth of 287 percent over the same years.

These 20 emerging markets make up 16 percent of the world GDP and, together with the 25 developed markets in Table 22.1, make up 95 percent of the world GDP. Per capita GDP in these countries in 2001 was quite variable, ranging from $470 (India) to $8,870 (Korea); still, no active

E-INVESTMENTS
International Fundamental Analysis

Research a country and/or an industry or company in a specific country at Wright Investor's Service (**www.wisi.com**). Pull down the menu bar under *Wright Research Center,* make your selection, and then review the companies. This is an excellent site for researching international companies and industries.

Table 22.1 Market Capitalization of Stock Exchanges in Developed Countries

	Market Capitalization										GDP per Capita	Capitalization as % of GDP
	U.S. Dollars (billions)						Percent of World		Growth	GDP		
	2001	2000	1999	1998	1997	1996	2001	1996	1996–2001	2001	2001	2001
World	**$25,711**	**$31,668**	**$26,198**	**$20,703**	**$17,966**	**$14,494**	**100%**	**100%**	**77%**	**30,960**	**5,450**	**83**
North America	**13,169**	**15,601**	**13,166**	**10,008**	**7,685**	**5,590**	**51.2**	**38.6**	**135.6**			
United States	12,597	14,882	12,623	9,528	7,271	5,294	49.0	36.5	137.9	10,208	35,900	123
Canada	572	719	543	479	413	295	2.2	2.0	94.0	700	22,525	82
Europe	**7,305**	**9,185**	**7,657**	**6,948**	**4,878**	**3,585**	**28**	**25**	**104**			
United Kingdom	2,256	2,639	2,475	2,179	1,635	1,206	8.8	8.3	87	1,424	23,750	158
France	1,119	1,356	937	843	518	427	4.4	2.9	162	1,307	21,910	86
Germany	896	1,204	1,062	992	709	481	3.5	3.3	86	1,848	22,500	48
Switzerland	633	712	662	596	447	303	2.5	2.1	109	247	34,019	256
Netherlands	559	723	634	607	479	339	2.2	2.3	65	381	23,810	147
Italy	556	736	526	464	247	214	2.2	1.5	160	1,090	18,950	51
Spain	336	337	310	311	212	150	1.3	1.0	124	582	14,590	58
Sweden	212	375	253	247	188	139	0.8	1.0	52	210	23,580	101
Finland	164	379	173	93	60	42	0.6	0.3	295	121	23,260	136
Belgium	130	158	152	173	105	82	0.5	0.6	58	230	22,420	56
Denmark	90	101	75	88	61	44	0.3	0.3	103	163	30,450	55
Ireland	76	75	58	59	36	27	0.3	0.2	185	103	27,140	73
Norway	69	54	52	56	47	35	0.3	0.2	100	165	36,600	42
Greece	55	88	83	51	27	17	0.2	0.1	224	116	11,000	47
Portugal	49	74	59	75	47	23	0.2	0.2	111	110	10,940	45
Israel	39	47	35	29	24	18	0.2	0.1	120	110	17,159	35
Austria	24	28	31	35	27	26	0.1	0.2	−8	189	23,078	13
New Zealand	19	23	26	26	36	29	0.1	0.2	−34	49	12,763	39
Pacific Basin	**4,642**	**6,184**	**4,764**	**3,201**	**4,729**	**4,830**	**18**	**33**	**−4**			
Japan	2,947	4,246	3,092	2,188	3,138	3,509	11	24	−16	4,148	32,720	71
Hong Kong	532	553	404	254	452	289	2.1	2.0	84	162	10,940	329
Australia	363	384	378	249	276	219	1.4	1.5	65	357	18,459	102
Taiwan	205	331	260	173	232	152	0.8	1.0	35	282	12,620	73
Singapore	113	143	133	72	116	138	0.4	0.9	−18	86	20,880	132

Source: Datastream, July 2002.

Table 22.2 Market Capitalization of Stock Exchanges in Emerging Markets

	Market Capitalization										GDP per Capita	Capitalization as % of GDP
	U.S. Dollars (billions)						Percent of World		Growth	GDP		
	2001	2000	1999	1998	1997	1996	2001	1996	1996–2001	2001	2001	2001
China	$170	$ 94	$ 78	$ 67	$ 48	$ 23	0.66%	0.16%	651%	1,180	928	14%
Brazil	169	220	155	135	175	86	0.66	0.59	97	503	2,810	34
Korea	151	218	181	35	95	104	0.59	0.72	45	423	8,870	36
Mexico	140	128	115	96	97	74	0.55	0.51	89	621	6,190	23
South Africa	101	123	126	121	148	124	0.39	0.86	−19	112	2,520	90
India	88	139	93	72	113	88	0.34	0.61	−1	485	470	18
Malaysia	76	98	90	50	170	167	0.30	1.15	−54	89	3,720	86
Russia	66	49	35	44	93	37	0.26	0.25	80	310	2,144	21
Chile	53	49	47	45	61	48	0.20	0.33	10	64	4,170	82
Turkey	36	75	39	54	36	24	0.14	0.16	50	148	2,230	24
Argentina	29	37	51	48	56	43	0.11	0.30	−31	267	7,120	11
Thailand	26	30	46	17	46	89	0.10	0.61	−71	115	1,820	23
Poland	22	29	25	14	7	6	0.09	0.04	287	176	4,566	13
Philippines	20	23	41	26	55	62	0.08	0.42	−68	71	862	28
Indonesia	19	32	39	12	76	60	0.07	0.41	−68	145	688	13
Czech Republic	10	13	12	13	11	13	0.04	0.09	−26	52	5,137	19
Hungary	9	14	14	15	8	4	0.04	0.03	128	56	5,482	16
Peru	6	8	7	8	11	10	0.02	0.07	−36	54	2,070	11
Colombia	6	5	7	10	22	17	0.02	0.12	−65	83	1,940	7
Venezuela	4	4	4	4	10	4	0.02	0.03	2	130	5,280	3

Source: Datastream, July 2002.

manager would want to ignore India in an international portfolio. Market capitalization as a percent of GDP, which ranges from 3 percent (Venezuela) to 90 percent (South Africa), suggests that these markets are expected to show significant growth over the coming years, even absent spectacular growth in GDP.

The growth of capitalization in emerging markets over 1996–2001 was much more volatile than growth in developed countries (as disastrous as −71 percent for Thailand), suggesting that both risk and rewards in this segment of the globe may be substantial.

Market Capitalization and GDP

The contemporary view of economic development (rigorously stated in deSoto[1]) holds that a major requirement for economic advancement is a developed code of business laws, institutions, and regulation that allows citizens to legally own, capitalize, and trade capital assets. As a corollary, we expect that development of equity markets will serve as catalysts for enrichment of the population, that is, that countries with larger relative capitalization of equities will tend to be richer.

Figure 22.1 is a simple (perhaps simplistic, since other relevant explanatory variables are omitted) rendition of the argument that a developed market for corporate equity contributes to the enrichment of the population. The *R*-square of the regression line shown in Figure 22.1 is 35 percent and the regression coefficient is .73, suggesting that an increase of 1 percent in the ratio of market capitalization to GDP is associated with an increase in per capita GDP of 0.73 percent. It is remarkable that not one of the 25 developed countries is below the regression line; only low-income emerging markets lie below the line. Countries like Venezuela and Norway that lie above the line, that is, exhibit higher per capita GDP than predicted by the regression, enjoy oil wealth that contributes to population income. Countries below the line, such as Indonesia, South Africa, Philippines, and India, suffered from deterioration of the business environment due to political strife and/or government policies that restricted the private sector. China's policies of freeing up economic activities contributed to the remarkable growth in market capitalization over 1996–2001. The expected continuation of this process will likely move China toward the predicted relationship in coming years.

Figure 22.1
Per capita GDP tends to be higher when market capitalization as a percentage of GDP is higher (log scale).

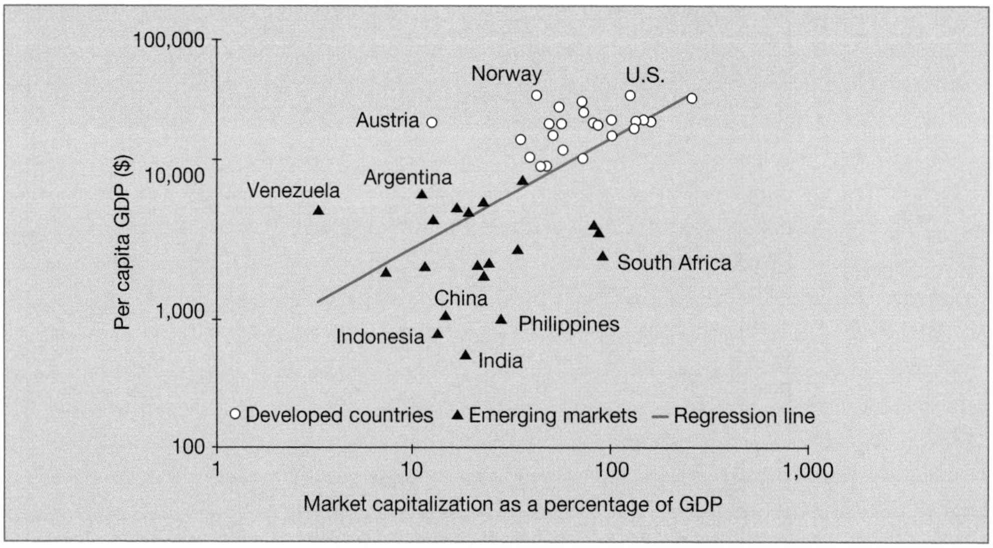

[1]Hernando de Soto, *The Mystery of Capital* (New York: Basic Books, 2000).

Techniques for Investing Internationally

Investors have a number of alternatives for achieving international exposure in their portfolios, the most direct being difficult for individuals. Large, or institutional, investors can invest directly in shares of companies trading on foreign exchanges, except in certain developing markets where foreign investment is restricted. Small investors still have satisfactory opportunities that include the purchase of

1. Foreign shares on U.S. markets
2. International closed-end mutual funds
3. International open-end mutual funds
4. International ETFs

www.ibm.com

Before describing these options, we should recall that among the stocks available for investment, there are both domestic and foreign companies, which are commonly known as *multinational firms.* Almost all large banks would qualify for this label, but there are also numerous nonfinancial enterprises, such as Alcan, Nestlé, IBM, and Unilever. Such firms can be characterized as conducting many, if not all, of their primary activities, including obtaining raw materials, production, sales, and financing, in a large number of countries. Typically, these firms derive a majority of their profits from foreign sales. Hence, we can conclude that their financial results will depend on the economic conditions all around the world, and thus are themselves internationally diversified. Analysis of multinationals requires a more widely based approach than does analysis of purely domestic firms.[2]

www.nyse.com

These firms may be bought on Canadian or U.S. exchanges in most cases, with the largest Canadian multinationals trading on both. In addition to the U.S. multinationals, one can, of course, purchase other U.S. firms for specific U.S. exposure. There are also a number of the largest European, Japanese, and Mexican companies that trade on the NYSE in the form of **American Depository Receipts**, or **ADRs**. ADRs are issued by U.S. financial institutions, or by the firms themselves, and represent claims to a number of shares in the foreign firm, issued abroad but held on deposit in the United States. A U.S. financial institution like a bank will purchase shares of a foreign firm in that firm's country, then issue claims to those shares in the United States. Each ADR is then a claim on a given number of the shares of stock held by the bank. In this way, the stock of foreign companies can be traded on U.S. stock exchanges. Trading foreign stocks with ADRs has become increasingly easy.

Tokyo Stock Exchange www.tse.or.jp

There are also a wide array of mutual funds with an international focus. **Single-country funds** are mutual funds that invest in the shares of only one country. These tend to be closed-end funds, as listed in Table 22.3. Many of the large mutual fund families have a variety of open-end funds with an international focus. A new trend is to focus on global sector diversification; rather than a domestic fund for pharmaceuticals or high tech, or a fund for regional or single-country large-cap firms, portfolios are designed by internationally diversifying holdings in pharmaceuticals or high-tech companies.

Just as returns on actively managed domestic funds are dominated by index securities, so in general are the open- and closed-end international funds. Morgan Stanley's iShares are a set of passive investments based on foreign market indices which can be bought on U.S. exchanges like stocks. (See the boxed article here.)

U.S. investors also can trade derivative securities based on prices in foreign security markets. For example, they can trade options and futures on the Nikkei stock index of 225 stocks traded

[2] A study on the effectiveness of diversification through multinationals reveals, however, that the price of this diversification may be lower risk-adjusted performance; see S. Foerster, R. Reinders, and M. Thorfinnson, "Are Investors Rewarded for the Foreign Exposure of Canadian Corporations?" *Canadian Investment Review* 5, no. 1 (Spring 1992).

GOING GLOBAL PROVIDES SHELTER AT HOME

John Templeton, founder of the Templeton family of mutual funds, including the flagship Templeton Growth Fund, remains an ardent proponent of value-based investing.

In particular, Sir John, who now lives in Nassau having retired many years ago from participation in portfolio management, believes in the virtues of global diversification.

Templeton Growth Fund wasn't the first global investment fund; global funds existed in Europe in the 19th century. It was, however, one of the first North America-based global funds—and it is probably the most famous. Although value investing is not currently in vogue, the Templeton global investing heritage is a bedrock of finance.

Twenty-five years ago Bruno Solnik articulated the global approach in a rigorous manner. He demonstrated that much of the variance in stock indexes is caused by the unique risk of each country and can be diversified away in an international portfolio of securities.

Markets and regions reflect local conditions rather than systematic world events. It is true that markets tend to move together during major economic or political shocks, such as the 1997 Asian flu and the April, 2000, high-tech collapse.

But in general, given differing political and social policies, the relationships among the markets of different countries remains low.

Canada has been a global market leader over the past two years. However over the past three decades, it has been one of the most disappointing, often ranking in the bottom third of developed markets.

Since Canadian stocks are subject to domestic economic, political and social factors that can't be diversified away inside Canada, you have to go global to do so.

There are two approaches to global investing. The top-down method means selecting specific countries, and then identifying appropriate investments within the country. Bottom-up investing means starting with individual company selection, then selecting industries and finally examining the overall country allocation.

From my experience, the top-down approach is best, at least for retail investors. Studies demonstrate that the country factor is the most important in global investments and that it dominates world, currency and industry systematic influences.

Diversifying by country or region is easier than picking individual country stocks. Much of the total global returns are generated by country indexes while currency and individual stock movements have a substantially lesser effect on performance.

The FPX indexes are globally diversified. The product of choice is the index participation unit or IPU.

IPUs are exchange-traded securities that represent a specific underlying market index. IPUs trade on exchanges just like stocks at a specific designated IPU to index ratio. Their design allows them to track underlying indexes very closely.

For the FPX indexes, we currently use two foreign IPUs: SPDRs and iShares.

SPDRs, based on the Standard and Poor's 500 composite index, were introduced in the United States on Jan. 29, 1993. SPDRs are quoted and traded in one-tenth the value of the underlying S&P 500 index. The dividends and other distributions of the 500 companies of the S&P 500 are collected and invested by the trust and then distributed on a quarterly basis to the unitholders. SPDRs dividends are not eligible for the dividend tax credit. The SPDR trust has a term of 25 years and will expire in 2018.

Non-U.S. IPUs are available in the form of iShares Morgan Stanley Capital International (MSCI) index funds. Originally issued as MSCI World Equity Benchmark Shares (WEBS) in May, 1996, iShares represent a basket of securities that replicates the total return performance of a specific MSCI market index. All MSCI indexes are total return indexes with net dividends (after withholding taxes) deemed to be reinvested.

The MSCI World Composite index, which was launched in 1969, is the most widely used index of world market performance.

There are currently 21 different series of iShares MSCI series outstanding. They include Australia, Austria, Belgium, Canada, European monetary union, France, Germany, Hong Kong, Italy, Japan, Malaysia, Mexico, the Netherlands, Singapore, South Africa, South Korea, Spain, Sweden, Switzerland, Taiwan and the United Kingdom.

As a result of the burgeoning popularity of IPUs, there is greater competition and lots of new products—either already trading or in the incubation stage.

As sponsors compete to attract investors' attention and dollars, we should see enhanced investment opportunities as well as lower management expense ratios. For example, in May, a series of new iShares based on the various S&P Barra and Russell value and growth indexes made its debut. These IPUs are traded on the American Stock Exchange and have MERs of 0.18% to 0.20%. Additional IPUs will soon debut.

Although IPU investing is hardly consistent with the Templeton way of active search for value, it certainly is a convenient way to add global securities to your portfolio.

Source: Eric Kirzner, "Going Global Provides Shelter at Home: Diversification. Top-Down Approach Is Easier for Retail Investors," *Financial Post* (*National Post*), July 31, 2001, p. C8.

Table 22.3 Closed-End International Funds Listed on the NYSE

Ticker Symbol	Name	Ticker Symbol	Name
Australia and Asia		**Europe and Middle East**	
APB	Asia Pacific Fund	OST	Austria Fund
APF	Morgan Stanley Asia Pacific	FRG	Emerging Germany Fund
GRR	Asia Tigers Fund	EF	Europe Fund
TGF	Emerging Tigers Fund	IBF	1st Iberian Fund
FAE	Fidelity Advisors Emerging Asia	FRF	France Growth Fund
SHF	Schroder Asian Growth	FGF	Future Germany Fund
SAF	Scudder New Asia Fund	GER	Germany Fund
CHN	China Fund	GSP	Growth Fund of Spain
GCH	Greater China Fund	IRL	Irish Investment Fund
JFC	Jardine Fleming China	ITA	Italy Fund
TCH	Templeton China World	GF	New Germany Fund
TDF	Templeton Dragon Fund	PGF	Portugal Fund
TVF	Templeton Vietnam Fund	SNF	Spain Fund
IAF	1st Australia Fund	SWZ	Swiss Helvetia Fund
FPF	1st Philippine	TKF	Turkish Investment Fund
IFN	India Fund	UKM	U.K. Fund
IGF	India Growth Fund	ISL	1st Israel Fund
JFI	Jardine Fleming India Fund	EME	For. & Col. Em. Middle East
IIF	Morgan Stanley India Fund	**Latin America**	
IF	Indonesia Fund	AF	Argentina Fund
JGF	Jakarta Growth Fund	BZF	Brazil Fund
JOF	Japan OTC Equity Fund	BZL	Brazilian Equity Fund
JEQ	Japan Equity Fund	CH	Chile Fund
KF	Korea Fund	MEF	Emerging Mexico Fund
KEF	Korea Equity Fund	LDF	Latin America Discovery Fund
KIF	Korean Investment Fund	LAQ	Latin America Equity Fund
FAK	Fidelity Advisors Korea Fund	MXF	Mexico Fund
MF	Malaysia Fund	MXE	Mexico Equity & Income
PKF	Pakistan Investment Fund	**Global Funds**	
ROC	R.O.C. Taiwan Fund	CLM	Clemente Global Growth
SGF	Singapore Fund	ETF	Emerging Markets Telecom
TWN	Taiwan Fund	EMG	Emerging Markets Infrastructure
TYW	Taiwan Equity Fund	GPF	Global Privatization Fund
TTF	Thai Fund	GTD	GT Global Developing Markets
TC	Thai Capital Fund	MSF	Morgan Stanley Emerging Markets
South Africa			
ASA	ASA Ltd.	EMF	Templeton Emerging Markets
AFF	Morgan Stanley Africa Fund	VLU	Worldwide Value Fund
NSA	New South Africa Fund		
SOA	Southern Africa Fund		

on the Tokyo stock exchange, or on FTSE (Financial Times Share Exchange) indices of U.K. and European stocks.

Although closed-end funds typically trade at a discount to asset value, foreign funds tend to trade at a premium as they offer a service, diversification, that investors cannot provide themselves in foreign markets.[3] In this case, it would seem better to invest in open-end funds, which sell at asset value. As an interesting note on the investment policies of closed- and open-end funds, Franklin Templeton and Morgan Stanley offer both types of funds managed by the same advisors. On one occasion, it was observed that, for both these firms, the performance of the closed-end versions exceeded the open-end fund results by almost exactly the amount of the premium, suggesting excellent market efficiency in pricing. How could this happen? Closed-end funds are able to be fully invested if desired, since the investors' funds have been collected and need not be refunded. The open-end funds, on the other hand, must always maintain a cash reserve for investors who wish to cash in, so their returns must be lower due to the short-term rates; given the higher volatility of foreign markets, and the investor reactions, cash reserves for international funds are quite high.

22.2 RISK ISSUES IN INTERNATIONAL INVESTING

International investing poses unique challenges and a variety of new risks for Canadian investors. Assessment of foreign assets is impeded when information is less timely and more difficult to come by, as well as being reported according to standards and regulations that may differ from North American practice. Transactions costs are usually higher due to direct commissions or in many cases taxes on purchase or sale (in addition to capital gains taxes), as illustrated in Figure 22.2.

Figure 22.2
Cost estimates for one-way trades.

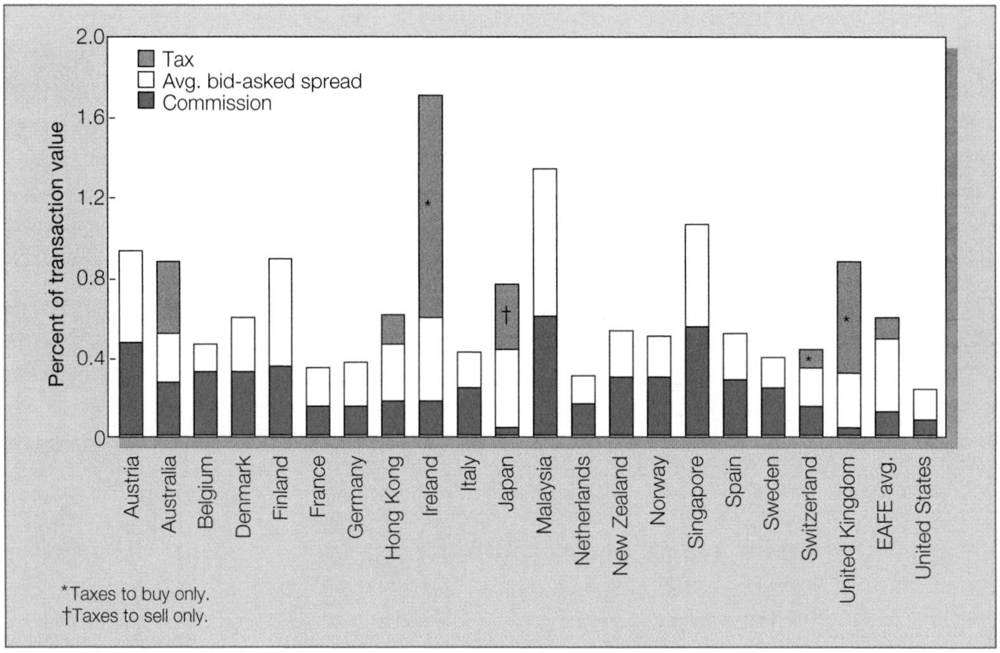

Source: Bruno Solnik, *International Investments*, 3rd ed. (Reading, MA: Addison-Wesley, 1996).

[3]On the other hand, the premium on foreign funds appears to be related to investment restrictions in the particular countries involved. See C. Bonser-Neal, G. Brauer, R. Neal, and S. Wheatley, "International Investment Restrictions and Closed-End Country Fund Prices," *Journal of Finance* 45 (June 1990).

Country-Specific Risk

One particular concern is referred to as **political risk**. The term is used to describe the possibility of the expropriation of assets, changes in tax policy, the institution of restrictions on the exchange of foreign currency for domestic currency and the repatriation of profits, or other changes in the business climate of a country. An extreme example of this happened to a Canadian company engaged in diamond mining in Angola in 1998. The mine operators found themselves under attack by guerillas wanting to either take over the property or extract a "royalty" to permit the operation to continue. Protection money or slightly less obvious taxes imposed by forms of corruption are common in less developed countries. Multinationals and foreign companies may be forced to deliver a percentage of their returns to local influences, and must weigh these and additional uncertainty against the potential profits.

In the past, when international investing was novel, assessment of political risk was an art. As cross-border investment has increased and more resources have been utilized, the quality of related analysis has improved. A leading organization in the field (which is quite competitive) is the PRS (Political Risk Services) Group and the presentation here follows the PRS methodology.[4]

PRS's country risk analysis results in a country composite risk rating on a scale of 0 (most risky) to 100 (least risky). Countries are then ranked by composite risk measure and divided into five categories: very low risk (100–80), low risk (79.9–70), moderate risk (69.9–60), high risk (59.9–50), and very high risk (less than 50). To illustrate, Table 22.4 shows the placement of five countries in the September 2001 issue of the PRS *International Country Risk Guide.* The countries shown are the two largest capitalization countries (U.S. and Japan) and the three most populous emerging markets (China, India, and Indonesia). Surprisingly, Table 22.4 shows that the U.S. ranked only 20th in September of 2001, having deteriorated from the 11th rank in the previous year. Japan actually ranked higher at 13. Both these developed countries placed in the "very low risk" category. Of the three emerging markets, it is not surprising to see Indonesia ranked 115th of 140 countries, placing it in the "high risk" category, while China ranked 60th, in the "low risk" category, and India ranked 92nd, in the "moderate risk" category.

The composite risk rating is an average of three measures: political risk, financial risk, and economic risk. Political risk is measured on a scale of 100–0, while financial and economic risk are measured on a scale of 50–0. The three measures are added and divided by two to obtain the composite rating. This amounts to a weighted average of the three measures with a weight of .5

Table 22.4 Composite Risk Ratings for October 2000 and September 2001

Rank, Sept. 2001	Country	Composite Risk Rating, Sept. 2001	Composite Risk Rating, Oct. 2000	Sept. 2001 Rating Minus Oct. 2000 Rating	Rank, Oct. 2000
	Very low risk				
13	Japan	86.5	83.5	3	12
20	United States	83.3	83.8	−0.5	11
	Low risk				
60	China	72.5	73.5	−1	47
	Moderate risk				
92	India	64.8	63.3	1.5	89
	High risk				
115	Indonesia	59.8	56.5	3.3	118

Source: *International Country Risk Guide*, September 2001, Table1.

[4]You can find more information at www.prsgroup.com.

Table 22.5 Variables Used in PRS's Political Risk Score

Political Risk Variables	Financial Risk Variables	Economic Risk Variables
Government stability	Foreign debt (% of GDP)	GDP per capita
Socioeconomic conditions	Foreign debt service (% of GDP)	Real annual GDP growth
Investment profile	Current account (% of exports)	Annual inflation rate
Internal conflicts	Net liquidity in months of imports	Budget balance (% of GDP)
External conflicts	Exchange rate stability	Current account balance (% GDP)
Corruption		
Military in politics		
Religious tensions		
Law and order		
Ethnic tensions		
Democratic accountability		
Bureaucracy quality		

on political risk and .25 each on financial and economic risk. The variables used by PRS to determine the composite risk rating of the three measured are shown in Table 22.5.

Table 22.6 shows the three risk measures for the five countries in Table 22.4, in order of the September 2001 ranking of the composite risk ratings. The table shows that by political risk, the five countries ranked in the same order. But in the financial risk measure, the U.S. ranked below China and India (!), and by the economic risk measure, the United States ranked above Japan, and India ranked below Indonesia. More interesting are the ratings forecasts for one and five years. These forecasts are quite pessimistic about the United States, whose composite rating is expected to continue to deteriorate over the years 2002–2006. (This may have been prescient, since it appears this report was prepared prior to the September 11, 2001, attacks.) At the same time, the ratings of three of the other four countries were expected to improve over the next five years.

The country risk is captured in greater depth by scenario analysis for the composite measure and each of its components. Table 22.7 (A and B) shows one- and five-year worst-case and best-case scenarios for the composite ratings and for the political risk measure. Risk stability is defined as the difference in the rating between the best- and worst-case scenarios and is quite large in most cases. The worst-case scenario is in some cases sufficient to move a country to a higher risk category. Table 22.7B shows that U.S. political risk was forecast to deteriorate in five years (2006) to the level of Japan.

Finally, Table 22.8 shows ratings of political risk by each of its 12 components. Corruption (variable F) in China is rated worse than in India and equal to that of Indonesia. In democratic accountability (variable K), China ranked worst and India best, while Indonesia ranked better than both in external conflict (variable E).

Table 22.6 Current Risk Ratings and Composite Risk Forecasts

	Current Ratings			Composite Ratings			
Country	Political Risk, Sept. 2001	Financial Risk, Sept. 2001	Economic Risk, Sept. 2001	1 Year Ago, Oct. 2000	Current, Sept. 2001	1-Year Forecast	5-Year Forecast
Japan	90	45.5	37.5	83.5	86.5	84.5	85.5
United States	89.5	37.5	39.5	83.8	83.3	82.5	80.5
China	62	45	38	73.5	72.5	72.5	76.5
India	56	40.5	33	63.3	64.8	64	68
Indonesia	49.5	35	35	56.5	59.8	52.5	64.5

Source: *International Country Risk Guide,* September 2001, Table 2B.

Table 22.7 Composite and Political Risk Forecasts

A. Composite Risk Forecasts

		1 Year Ahead				5 Years Ahead			
	Current Rating	Worst Case	Most Probable	Best Case	Risk Stability	Worst Case	Most Probable	Best Case	Risk Stability
Japan	**86.5**	79.5	84.5	88	8.5	78.5	85.5	91	12.5
United States	**83.3**	75	82.5	85.5	10.5	73	80.5	84	11
China	**72.5**	68	72.5	74.5	6.5	67	76.5	81	14
India	**64.8**	58	64	66.5	8.5	60	68	70.5	10.5
Indonesia	**59.8**	45	52.5	55	10	46.5	64.5	68.5	22

B. Political Risk Forecasts

		1 Year Ahead				5 Years Ahead			
	Current Rating	Worst Case	Most Probable	Best Case	Risk Stability	Worst Case	Most Probable	Best Case	Risk Stability
Japan	**90**	76	83	88	12	76	85	94	18
United States	**89.5**	78	90	93	15	80	85	88	8
China	**62**	58	63	65	7	60	70	74	14
India	**56**	50	60	63	13	58	65	67	9
Indonesia	**49.5**	40	48	50	10	40	60	64	24

Sources: A: *International Country Risk Guide,* September 2001, Table 2C; B: *International Country Risk Guide,* September 2001, Table 3C.

Each monthly issue of the *International Country Risk Guide* of the PRS Group includes great detail and holds some 250 pages. Other organizations compete in supplying such evaluations. The result is that today's investor can become well equipped to properly assess the risks involved in international investing.

Table 22.8 Political Risk Points by Component, September 2001

This table lists the total points for each of the following political risk components out of the maximum points indicated. The symbol ↑ indicates a rise in the points awarded to that specific risk component from the previous month (an improving risk), while the symbol ↓ indicates a decrease (deteriorating risk). The final columns in the table show the overall political risk rating (the sum of the points awarded to each component) and the change from the preceding month.

A	*Government stability*	*12*	*E*	*External conflict*	*12*	*I*	*Law and order*	*6*
B	*Socioeconomic conditions*	*12*	*F*	*Corruption*	*6*	*J*	*Ethnic tensions*	*6*
C	*Investment profile*	*12*	*G*	*Military in politics*	*6*	*K*	*Democratic accountability*	*6*
D	*Internal conflict*	*12*	*H*	*Religious tensions*	*6*	*L*	*Bureaucracy quality*	*4*

Country	A	B	C	D	E	F	G	H	I	J	K	L	Political Risk Rating	
United States	10	10.5	11	12	10.5	4	5.5	6	6	5	5	4	**89.5**	0
Japan	10.5	8.5	↑12.0	12	↓11.0	3	6	5	5	6	5	4	**88**	−0.5
China	10	7	↓7.5	10	9.5	1	2	4	4	4	1	2	**62**	−0.5
India	↑7.5	3.5	↓8.0	↓7.0	↓8.0	2	3	2	4	2	6	3	**56**	−1.5
Indonesia	↑9.5	2	↑7.0	6.5	10	1	2.5	1	2	2	4	2	**49.5**	2

Exchange Rate Risk

Beyond these risks, international investing entails **exchange rate risk**. The dollar return from a foreign investment depends not only on the returns in the foreign currency, but also on the exchange rate between the dollar and that currency, as we see from the following example.

EXAMPLE 22.1 Exchange Rate Risk

Consider an investment in England in risk-free British government bills paying 10 percent annual interest in British pounds. Although these U.K. bills would be the risk-free asset to a British investor, this is not the case for a Canadian investor. Suppose, for example, the current exchange rate is \$2 per pound, and the Canadian investor starts with \$20,000. That amount can be exchanged for £10,000 and invested at a riskless 10 percent rate in the United Kingdom to provide £11,000 in one year.

What happens if the dollar-pound exchange rate varies over the year? Say that during the year, the pound depreciates relative to the dollar, so that by year-end only \$1.80 is required to purchase £1. The £11,000 can be exchanged at the year-end exchange rate for only \$19,800 (£11,000 × \$1.80/£), resulting in a loss of \$200 relative to the initial \$20,000 investment. Despite the positive 10 percent pound-denominated return, the dollar-denominated return is –1 percent.

We can generalize from these results. The \$20,000 is exchanged for \$20,000/E_0 pounds, where E_0 denotes the original exchange rate (\$2/£). The U.K. investment grows to $(20{,}000/E_0)[1 + r_f(\text{UK})]$ British pounds, where $r_f(\text{UK})$ is the risk-free rate in the United Kingdom. The pound proceeds ultimately are converted back to dollars at the subsequent exchange rate E_1, for total dollar proceeds of $20{,}000(E_1/E_0)[1 + r_f(\text{UK})]$. The dollar-denominated return on the investment in British bills, therefore, is

$$1 + r(\text{C}) = [1 + r_f(\text{UK})]E_1/E_0 \qquad (22.1)$$

We see in equation 22.1 that the dollar-denominated return for a Canadian investor equals the pound-denominated return times the exchange rate "return." For a Canadian investor, the investment in the British bill is a combination of a safe investment in the United Kingdom and a risky investment in the performance of the pound relative to the dollar. Here, the pound fared poorly, falling from a value of \$2 to only \$1.80. The loss on the pound more than offsets the earnings on the British bill.

Figure 22.3 illustrates this point. It presents returns on stock market indices in some of the larger foreign stock markets during 2001. The upper boxes depict returns in local currencies, whereas the lower boxes depict returns in U.S. dollars, adjusting for exchange rate movements. It is clear that exchange rate fluctuations over this period had large effects on dollar-denominated returns. For example, Australia showed a 9.1 percent gain in dollars, and a 0.5 percent gain in local currency.

? CONCEPT CHECK

1. Calculate the rate of return in dollars to a Canadian investor holding the British bill if the year-end exchange rate is: (*a*) E_1 = \$2/£; (*b*) E_1 = \$2.20/£.

Pure exchange rate risk is the risk borne by investments in foreign safe assets. The investor in U.K. bills of Example 22.1 bears only the risk of the U.K./Canadian exchange rate. We can assess the magnitude of exchange rate risk by examination of historical rates of change in various exchange rates and their correlations.

Figure 22.3 Stock market returns in dollars and local currencies for 2001.

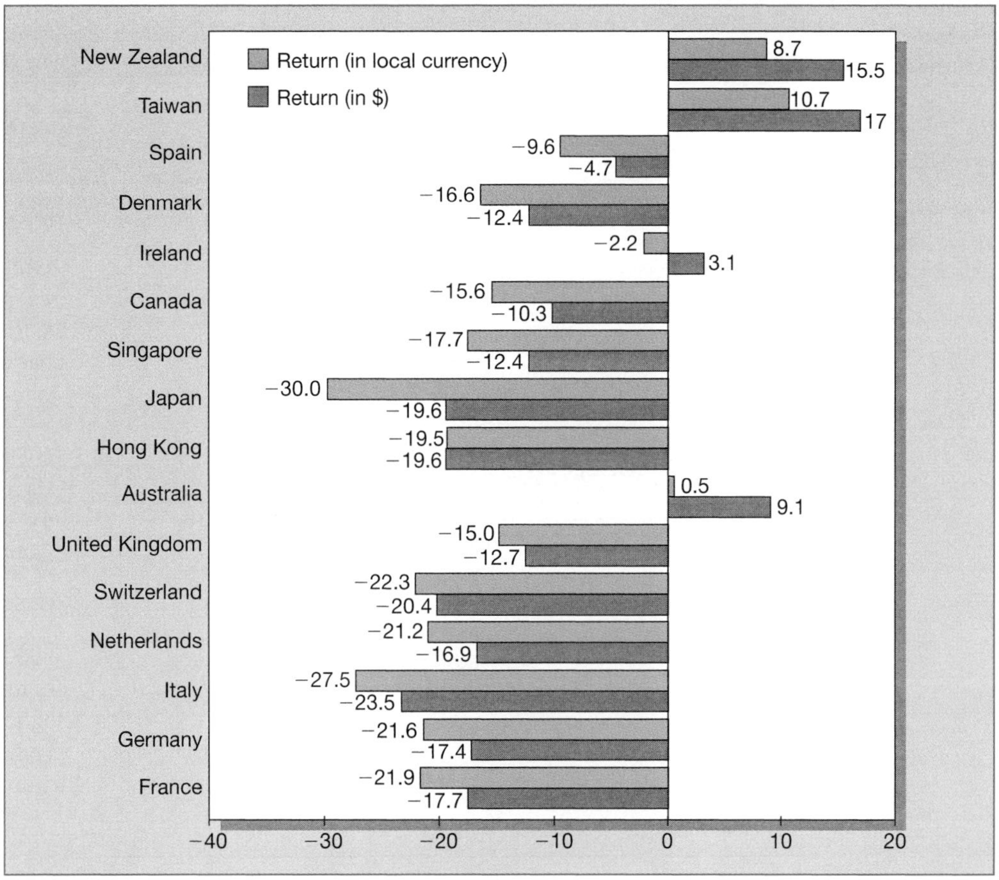

Source: Datastream.

Table 22.9A shows historical exchange rate risk measured from monthly percent changes in the exchange rates of major currencies over the period 1997–2001.[5] The data shows that currency risk is quite high. The annualized standard deviation of the percent changes in the exchange rate ranged from 5.01 percent (Canadian dollar) to 14.18 percent (Japanese yen). The standard deviation of monthly returns on U.S. large stocks for the same period was 18.81 percent. Hence, currency exchange risk alone would amount to between 27 percent (5.01/18.81) and 75 percent (14.18/18.81) of the risk on stocks. Clearly, an active investor who believes that Japanese stocks are underpriced, but has no information about any mispricing of the Japanese yen, would be advised to hedge the yen risk exposure when tilting the portfolio toward Japanese stocks. Exchange rate risk of the major currencies is quite stable over time. For example, a study by Solnik[6] for the period 1971–1998 finds similar standard deviations, ranging from 4.8 percent (Canadian dollar) to 12.0 percent (Japanese yen).

In the context of international portfolios, exchange rate risk may be mostly diversifiable. This is evident from the low correlation coefficients in Table 22.9B. (This observation will be reinforced when we compare the risk of hedged and unhedged country portfolios in a later section.) Thus, passive investors with well-diversified international portfolios need not be concerned with hedging exposure to foreign currencies.

[5]Note that currencies and returns are in U.S. dollars; the discussion proceeding from Table 22.3 is from the perspective of a U.S. dollar portfolio.

[6]B. Solnick, *International Investing*, 4th ed. (Reading, MA: Addison-Wesley, 1999).

Table 22.9 Rates of Change in the Value of the U.S. Dollar Against Major World Currencies, 1997–2001 (monthly data)

A. Standard Deviation (annualized)					
Country Currency	Euro (€)	U.K. (£)	Japan (¥)	Australia ($A)	Canada ($C)
Standard dev.	9.61	6.61	14.18	11.44	5.01

B. Correlation Matrix					
	Euro	U.K.	Japan	Australia	Canada
Euro	1.00				
U.K.	0.64	1.00			
Japan	0.29	0.21	1.00		
Australia	0.29	0.22	0.35	1.00	
Canada	−0.02	0.02	0.13	0.53	1.00

C. Average Increases			
	Average Annualized Dollar Return on Cash Investments		Average Annualized % Increase in the Value of the U.S. Dollar
U.S.	5.67		
France	−2.64	Euro	7.28
Germany	−2.82	Euro	7.28
Italy	−1.81	Euro	7.28
Netherlands	−2.88	Euro	7.28
Switzerland	−1.48	Euro	7.28
U.K.	3.34	U.K.	3.47
Australia	−2.74	Australia	9.46
Japan	−0.97	Japan	3.44
Canada	1.90	Canada	3.17

The annualized average monthly increase in the value of the U.S. dollar against the major currencies over the five-year period and dollar returns on foreign bills (cash investments) appear in Table 22.9C. The table shows that the value of the U.S. dollar consistently increased in this particular period. For example, the total increase against the Japanese yen over the five years was 18 percent and against the Australian dollar, 57 percent. This currency appreciation of the U.S. dollar was not offset by higher interest rates available in other countries. Had an investor been able to forecast the large exchange rate movements, it would have been a source of great profit. The currency market thus provided attractive opportunities for investors with superior information or analytical ability.

The investor in our example could have hedged the exchange rate risk using a forward or futures contract in foreign exchange. Recall that a forward or futures contract on foreign exchange calls for delivery or acceptance of one currency for another at a stipulated exchange rate. Here, the Canadian investor would agree to deliver pounds for dollars at a fixed exchange rate, thereby eliminating the future risk involved with conversion of the pound investment back into dollars.

EXAMPLE 22.2 Hedging Exchange Rate Risk

If the futures exchange rate had been $F_0 = \$1.93/£$ when the investment was made, the Canadian investor could have assured a riskless dollar-denominated return by locking in the year-end exchange rate at \$1.93/£. In this case, the riskless U.S. return would have been 6.15 percent:

$$[1 + r_f(\text{UK})]F_0/E_0 = (1.10)\ 1.93/2 = 1.0615$$

Here are the steps to take to lock in the dollar-denominated returns. The futures contract entered in the second step exactly offsets the exchange rate risk incurred in step 1.

Initial Transaction	End-of-Year Proceeds in Dollars
Exchange \$20,000 for £10,000 and invest at 10% in the United Kingdom	£11,000 × E_1
Enter a contract to deliver £11,000 for dollars at the (forward) exchange rate \$1.93/£	£11,000(1.93 – E_1)
Total	£11,000 × \$1.93/£ = \$21,320

You may recall that this is the same type of hedging strategy at the heart of the interest rate parity relationship discussed in Chapter 19, where futures markets are used to eliminate the risk of holding another asset. The Canadian investor can lock in a riskless dollar-denominated return either by investing in the United Kingdom and hedging exchange rate risk or by investing in riskless Canadian assets. Because the returns on two riskless strategies must provide equal returns, we conclude

$$[1 + r_f(\text{UK})]\,\frac{F_0}{E_0} = 1 + r_f(\text{C})$$

This leads to the **interest rate parity theorem** of Chapter 19.

Unfortunately, such perfect exchange rate hedging is usually not so easy. In our example, we knew exactly how many pounds to sell in the forward or futures market because the pound-denominated proceeds in the United Kingdom were riskless. If the U.K. investment had not been in bills, but instead had been in risky U.K. equity, we would know neither the ultimate value in pounds of our U.K. investment nor how many pounds to sell forward. That is, the hedging opportunity offered by foreign exchange forward contracts would be imperfect.

To summarize, the generalization of equation 22.1 is

$$1 + r(\text{C}) = [1 + r(\text{foreign})]E_1/E_0 \qquad (22.2)$$

where r(foreign) is the possibly risky return earned in the currency of the foreign investment. You can set up a perfect hedge only in the special case that r(foreign) is itself a known number. In that case, you know you must sell in the forward or futures market an amount of foreign currency equal to [1 + r(foreign)] for each unit of that currency you purchase today.

CONCEPT CHECK

2. How many pounds would need to be sold forward to hedge exchange rate risk in the above example if: (*a*) r(UK) = 20 percent; (*b*) r(UK) = 30 percent?

Using Futures to Manage Exchange Rate Risk

We have just seen an illustration of using the futures exchange rate to lock in the return on the investment in U.K. bills. Using futures is a more precise operation, as we saw in Chapter 19, and there are some details to clarify for foreign exchange hedging. International currencies are quoted in cross rates against each other, particularly for major currencies; futures, however, are traded on the International Monetary Market (IMM, a division of the Chicago Mercantile Exchange) on the basis of individual currencies against the U.S. dollar. Suppose that a Canadian institution has made an investment in the United Kingdom and wishes to hedge the returns against dollar-pound exchange fluctuations. Instead of using forwards between the Canadian dollar and British pound, the firm could use futures of the Canadian dollar against the U.S. dollar, and again of the U.S. dollar against the pound. Then again, it might be content to hedge the U.S./U.K. risk and retain the Canada/U.S. risk due to other investments.

Let us examine the use of futures to control the U.S./U.K. risk, so that the following references to dollars are in U.S. currency. The institution has a portfolio of two million pounds that will lose $200,000 for every $.10 depreciation in the pound against the dollar. To hedge this, it arranges to deliver pounds for dollars at an exchange rate determined today. Thus, in delivering pounds, it is on the short side of the pound futures contract, which will benefit from a pound depreciation.

For example, suppose that the futures price is currently $1.50 per pound for delivery in three months. If the firm enters a futures contract with a futures price of $1.50 per pound, and the exchange rate in three months is $1.40 per pound, then the profit on the transaction is $.10 per pound. The futures price converges at the maturity date to the spot exchange rate of $1.40 and the profit to the short position is therefore $F_0 - F_T = \$1.50 - \$1.40 = \$.10$ per pound.

How many pounds should be sold in the futures market to most fully offset the exposure to exchange rate fluctuations? We need to find the number of pounds we should commit to delivering in order to provide a $200,000 profit for every $.10 that the pound depreciates. Therefore, we need a futures position to deliver 2,000,000 pounds. As we have just seen, the profit per pound on the futures contract equals the difference in the current futures price and the ultimate exchange rate; therefore, the foreign exchange profits resulting from a $.10 depreciation[7] will equal $\$.10 \times 2{,}000{,}000 = \$200{,}000$.

The proper hedge position in pound futures is independent of the actual depreciation in the pound as long as the relationship between profits and exchange rates is approximately linear. For example, if the pound depreciates by only half as much, $.05, the investment would lose only $100,000. The futures position would also return half the profits: $\$.05 \times 2{,}000{,}000 = \$100{,}000$, again just offsetting the exposure. If the pound *appreciates,* the hedge position still (unfortunately in this case) offsets the exposure. If the pound appreciates by $.05, the firm might gain $100,000 from the enhanced value of the pound; however, it will lose that amount on its obligation to deliver the pounds for the original futures price.

The hedge ratio is the number of futures positions necessary to hedge the risk of the unprotected portfolio. In general, we can think of the hedge ratio as the number of hedging vehicles (e.g., futures contracts) one would establish to offset the risk of a particular unprotected position. The hedge ratio, H, in this case is

$$H = \frac{\text{Change in value of unprotected position for a given change in exchange rate}}{\text{Profit derived from one futures position for the same change in exchange rate}}$$

$$= \frac{\$200{,}000 \text{ per } \$.10 \text{ change in \$/£ exchange rate}}{\$.10 \text{ profit } \textit{per pound} \text{ delivered per } \$.10 \text{ change in \$/£ exchange rate}}$$

$$= 2{,}000{,}000 \text{ pounds to be delivered}$$

Because each pound-futures contract on the IMM calls for delivery of 62,500 pounds, you would need to short 2,000,000/62,500 per contract = 32 contracts.

One interpretation of the hedge ratio is as a ratio of sensitivities to the underlying source of uncertainty. The sensitivity of operating profits is $200,000 per swing of $.10 in the exchange rate. The sensitivity of futures profits is $.10 per pound to be delivered per swing of $.10 in the exchange rate. Therefore, the hedge ratio is 200,000/.10 = 2,000,000 pounds.

We could just as easily have defined the hedge ratio in terms of futures contracts rather than in terms of pounds. Because each contract calls for delivery of 62,500 pounds, the profit on

[7]Actually, the profit on the contract depends on the changes in the futures price, not the spot exchange rate. For simplicity, we call the decline in the futures price the depreciation in the pound.

Table 22.10 Domestic and Foreign Investments: Annualized Returns and Return Standard Deviations for 1973–1987

Period	TSE 300	Unhedged EAFE	Local EAFE	Hedged EAFE	Unhedged S&P 500	Local S&P 500	Hedged S&P 500	Canadian Paper	Canadian Bonds
1973–1987									
Return	11.0	17.7	12.0	16.0	11.8	9.8	10.7	10.8	9.7
Standard deviation	22.2	27.2	17.3	19.3	17.8	18.0	18.5	1.2	14.5
1973–1977									
Return	1.6	4.6	−0.2	0.2	1.7	−0.2	0.8	8.6	7.2
Standard deviation	12.4	21.6	18.0	19.5	18.8	18.2	19.2	1.7	8.5
1978–1982									
Return	18.3	14.5	13.8	20.8	16.8	14.0	14.5	14.0	8.1
Standard deviation	26.1	18.6	7.9	7.6	12.4	12.8	12.3	4.1	13.9
1983–1987									
Return	13.8	36.2	23.7	29.0	17.5	16.4	17.7	9.9	13.9
Standard deviation	20.4	27.1	11.6	12.4	14.4	15.5	16.0	1.5	14.9

Source: Robert Auger and Denis Parisien, "The Risks and Rewards of Global Investing," *Canadian Investment Review* 2, no. 1 (Spring 1989). Reprinted by permission.

each contract per swing of $.10 in the exchange rate is $6,250. Therefore, the hedge ratio defined in units of futures contracts is $200,000/$6,250 = 32 contracts, as derived above.

Although one may well wish to hedge the exchange rate risk, another opinion maintains that domestic consumption is dependent upon the prices of foreign goods and thus, currency fluctuations in one's portfolio actually help to hedge this risk to consumption. As such, once a foreign component has been determined for a portfolio, it is best to leave it unhedged. In fact, a study by Auger and Parisien[8] for 1973–1987 data including Canadian assets, U.S. equities (S&P 500), and international equities (Morgan Stanley's EAFE index, described in the following section) analyzes the effect of foreign currency hedging on internationally diversified portfolios for Canadian investors. While the unhedged EAFE portfolio had a slightly higher rate of return of 17.7 percent for volatility of 27.2 percent, the hedged equivalent return of 16.0 percent was obtained for a volatility of only 19.3 percent. Table 22.10, reproduced from their study, shows the returns and volatilities for various portfolios and periods; the results show the local currency returns and the Canadian dollar equivalents, with and without hedging. Note that the TSE 300 (now known as the S&P/TSX Composite) is clearly dominated by the hedged EAFE portfolio.

Diversification of Risk

Expanding the universe of assets is expected to reduce the overall risk of a portfolio. Before arriving at that conclusion, however, we should first examine the statistics of returns from individual country assets. Figures 22.4–22.6 and Tables 22.11–22.13 present a cross-sectional analysis and a historical look at returns from different markets together with an appraisal of the diversification effects. As usual, the reference currency is the U.S. dollar.

Table 22.11 gives the statistics in local currency and U.S. dollars for monthly returns over the five-year period 1997–2001, segregated into developed and emerging markets. Figure 22.4 shows the risk as countries are ranked by increasing standard deviation; analogously, Figure 22.5 shows the returns in decreasing order. Emerging markets show a pattern of *higher risk* and

[8]Robert Auger and Denis Parisien, "The Risks and Rewards of Global Investing," *Canadian Investment Review* 2, no. 1 (Spring 1989).

Figure 22.4 Annualized standard deviation of investments across the globe, 1997–2001

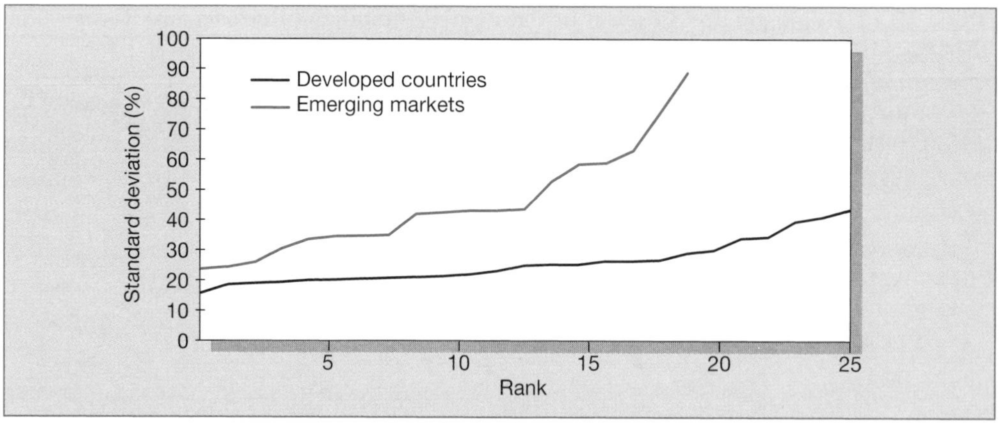

Countries in developed and emerging markets are ranked from low to high standard deviation.

lower return. Yet that observation is incomplete before the correlations are examined. First we examine the effect of currency risk, by looking at Figure 22.6; this shows that there is little difference in the overall risk between domestic currency and U.S. dollar returns. (This reflects low correlations across countries between changes in exchange rates, and low correlation between the exchange rate changes versus the U.S. dollar and stock returns in local currencies.)

Figure 22.5 Annualized average return of investments across the globe, 1997–2001

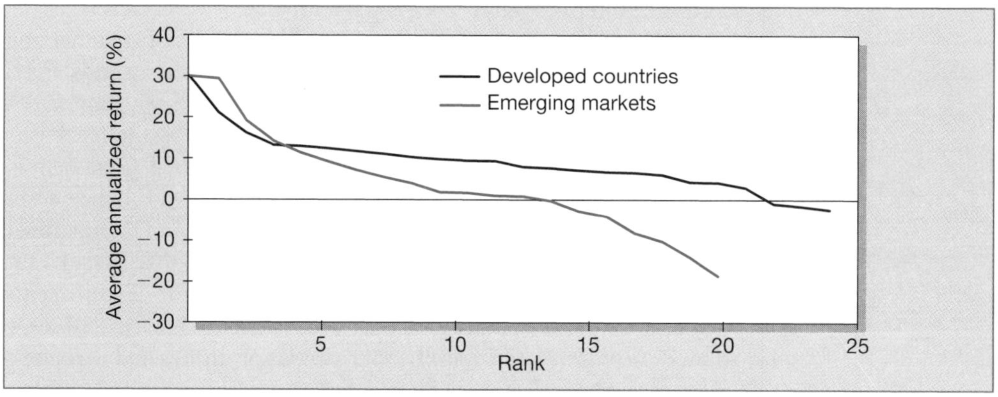

Countries in developed and emerging markets are ranked from high to low average return.

Figure 22.6 Standard deviation of investments across the globe in U.S. dollars versus local currency, 1997–2001.

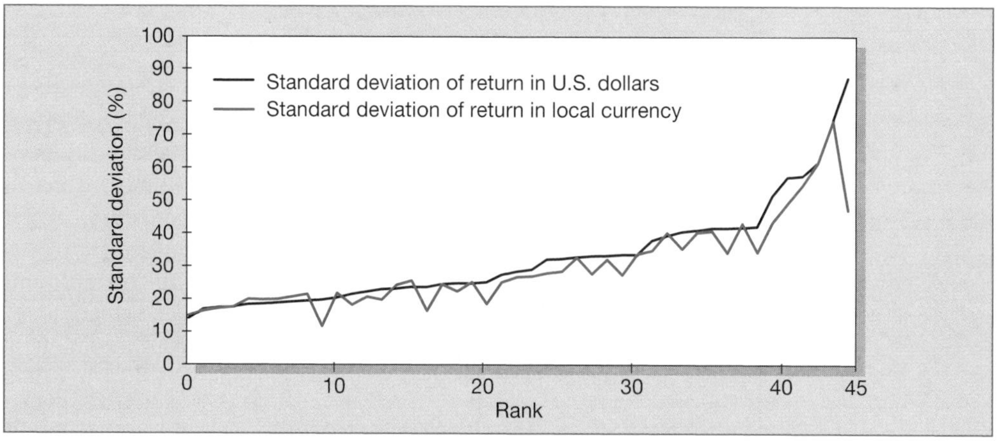

Countries ranked from low to high standard deviation of returns in U.S. dollars.

Table 22.11 Risk and Return Across the Globe, 1997–2001

	% per Annum in U.S. Dollars		% per Annum in Local Currency	
Country	Average	Standard Dev.	Average	Standard Dev.
A. Developed Countries				
U.K.	5.97	15.24	9.39	16.23
Belgium	5.36	17.98	12.42	17.58
Austria	−3.09	18.41	4.00	18.32
U.S.	11.98	18.78	11.98	18.78
Denmark	8.30	19.38	15.62	21.04
Netherlands	6.84	19.55	14.34	20.87
Switzerland	8.74	19.86	13.31	21.05
Ireland	10.73	20.16	19.21	21.73
Germany	5.55	20.43	13.13	22.49
Australia	4.86	20.74	12.42	13.01
France	11.45	21.36	18.84	22.81
Canada	10.08	22.41	12.51	19.37
Spain	8.38	24.20	15.94	25.20
Italy	12.30	24.50	20.02	26.47
New Zealand	−3.17	24.51	5.99	17.65
Norway	1.57	25.61	7.80	23.34
Portugal	6.51	25.63	14.12	26.10
Japan	−3.96	25.96	−2.84	19.68
Israel	15.37	28.13	20.98	26.04
Sweden	9.25	29.10	17.45	27.61
Singapore	−2.47	32.86	1.98	29.26
Hong Kong	3.01	33.34	3.17	33.32
Taiwan	2.89	38.28	6.67	35.41
Greece	20.50	39.70	28.83	40.64
Finland	29.99	42.09	38.10	43.33
B. Emerging Markets				
Peru	−5.61	23.15	−0.36	21.74
Chile	0.39	23.85	8.64	20.89
China	8.23	25.37	8.17	25.37
Colombia	−15.96	29.67	−0.66	27.81
Czech Rep.	0.54	32.66	4.60	28.71
Mexico	13.44	33.65	14.76	28.49
India	4.36	33.78	9.93	32.75
South Africa	−0.33	34.06	16.77	28.22
Argentina	−0.47	34.08	−0.41	34.29
Poland	2.78	40.83	7.17	35.88
Hungary	10.45	41.29	20.76	40.73
Venezuela	−9.81	41.90	−1.10	41.14
Philippines	−20.63	41.91	−9.81	34.76
Brazil	6.09	42.40	19.38	34.91
Malaysia	−4.25	51.37	0.49	43.70
Korea	18.56	56.85	22.84	49.30
Thailand	−11.92	57.27	−3.08	54.66
Russia	29.23	61.25	29.23	61.25
Turkey	29.43	73.54	81.40	73.56
Indonesia	−1.67	86.11	−2.41	47.37

Table 22.12 Correlations for Asset Returns; Unhedged and Hedged Currencies

A. Correlation of Monthly Asset Return 1997–2001 in $US (unhedged currencies)

	Stocks							Bonds						
Asset/Country	**U.S.**	**Germany**	**U.K.**	**Japan**	**Australia**	**Canada**	**France**	**U.S.**	**Germany**	**U.K.**	**Japan**	**Australia**	**Canada**	**France**
U.S.	1.00													
Germany	0.75	1.00												
U.K.	0.83	0.80	1.00											
Japan	0.58	0.45	0.57	1.00										
Australia	0.71	0.62	0.73	0.60	1.00									
Canada	0.82	0.74	0.73	0.52	0.67	1.00								
France	0.70	0.89	0.82	0.49	0.57	0.70	1.00							
U.S. Treasury	0.09	0.17	0.08	0.00	−0.11	0.11	0.08	1.00						
Germany	0.00	0.06	−0.03	−0.25	−0.19	−0.01	−0.02	0.77	1.00					
U.K.	0.11	0.17	0.13	−0.07	−0.08	0.00	0.06	0.83	0.76	1.00				
Japan	0.02	0.09	0.12	−0.04	−0.06	0.04	0.02	0.80	0.57	0.72	1.00			
Australia	0.00	0.12	0.04	−0.01	−0.08	0.15	−0.01	0.88	0.70	0.71	0.71	1.00		
Canada	0.00	0.08	0.00	−0.03	−0.05	0.12	−0.03	0.88	0.75	0.65	0.64	0.90	1.00	
France	−0.06	0.03	−0.07	−0.24	−0.18	−0.04	−0.05	0.69	0.98	0.66	0.46	0.63	0.72	1.00

B. Correlation of Monthly Asset Return 1997–2001 in Local Currency (hedged currencies)

	Stocks							Bonds						
Asset/Country	**U.S.**	**Germany**	**U.K.**	**Japan**	**Australia**	**Canada**	**France**	**U.S.**	**Germany**	**U.K.**	**Japan**	**Australia**	**Canada**	**France**
Stocks														
U.S.	1.00													
Germany	0.78	1.00												
U.K.	0.83	0.78	1.00											
Japan	0.55	0.51	0.46	1.00										
Australia	0.72	0.60	0.73	0.47	1.00									
Canada	0.80	0.75	0.77	0.47	0.66	1.00								
France	0.75	0.90	0.82	0.51	0.56	0.74	1.00							
Bonds														
U.S.	0.09	0.22	0.06	0.05	−0.03	0.12	0.13	1.00						
Germany	−0.02	0.11	−0.01	−0.19	−0.08	0.01	0.03	0.82	1.00					
U.K.	0.13	0.18	0.12	−0.07	0.02	0.05	0.10	0.85	0.79	1.00				
Japan	0.06	0.18	0.12	−0.01	−0.02	0.06	0.11	0.82	0.66	0.78	1.00			
Australia	0.05	0.19	0.06	−0.01	0.04	0.16	0.10	0.92	0.81	0.77	0.77	1.00		
Canada	0.02	0.12	0.01	−0.03	0.01	0.11	0.04	0.89	0.85	0.71	0.67	0.95	1.00	
France	−0.05	0.08	−0.05	−0.20	−0.09	0.00	0.00	0.76	0.98	0.70	0.57	0.76	0.83	1.00

IS INTERNATIONAL INVESTING DEAD?

Newspaper articles and academic papers have recently questioned the benefits of international investing. International returns have not been attractive and, to make matters worse, correlations between international and domestic markets have been increasing. Is this a new secular trend? Is international investing dead? This article explains why currently it appears that "the king is dead," but also why we will most likely exclaim "long live the king" again soon.

Over the past 10 years the correlation between international and Canadian equities has increased dramatically. For example, using three-year monthly returns, the correlation between international and Canadian equities touched 0.34 in 1990, 0.56 in 1995 and 0.70 in 2002.

Over the past three years, non-Canadian equity markets have substantially underperformed Canadian equities, making the case for investing outside of Canada look like a losing battle.

Global Synchronized Bear Market

While these performance results are not pretty, they should not be surprising given that we have been living through a global synchronized bear market that was caused by the following factors:

- The bursting of the global technology, media and telecommunications stock bubble
- Corporate scandals
- Oil price shock and geopolitical uncertainty

It's important to remember that bear markets are a natural part of stock market cycles. They can hurt, but out of every bear market is eventually born a bull market. The difficulty most investors have is seeing through the bottom of the cycle. For example, if you were back in June 1970, after the market had compressed almost 24%, do you believe you would have foreseen the market's rise by almost 82% over the next three years?

Asset allocation is a three-dimensional problem where the ingredients are expected returns, risk and correlations. Some important observations are as follows:

- Returns, risk and correlations are all time-varying, which makes assumptions about these variables treacherous;
- Volatility appears to shift over time through low, moderate and high volatility regimes; and
- The correlation between Canadian and international equities has indeed varied over time but its recent high water mark is more an artifact of "this statistician" selecting a data point as opposed to representing a specific trend—that is to say, statistics don't lie but know your statistician.

Over time, there have not been particular secular trends. Instead, the evidence suggests that the behavior of this correlation is "cyclical" or regime-like in nature.

Shifts Are Difficult to Forecast

The behavior of markets changes over time, as they transition from one regime to another. These regime shifts are extremely difficult to anticipate. For example, not too long ago the popular investment books had such titles as *Dow 36,000 and Electronic Day Trading Made Easy*.

What makes regime shifts so difficult to forecast is the fact that asset class returns are not normally distributed but are better described as being "lumpy" or having outliers, that is, suffering from skewness.

Perhaps another way to examine the challenge of predicting regime shifts is displayed in Table 1. Three or four different economic regimes, can be identified between 1972 and 1993 depending on how one interprets the period. Of course, there could be other opinions on how to classify these regimes, which supports the sage saying: "history is almost forecastable from the future."

Successful asset allocation decisions are strategic in nature and based on the following premises:

- Stocks outperform bonds.
- Bonds outperform cash.
- Correlations are relatively stable.

The first two assumptions are based on the belief that, in the long term, capitalism works, while the spreads between asset classes should reflect where interest rates are today and one's view on productivity growth and inflation.

Generally speaking, the excess returns for stocks have been positive for five out of six economic regimes since 1924. Only in coming out of a disinflation regime where bond yields had hit new records did "capitalism appear to fail."

We do not believe that the correlation between Canadian and international stocks has permanently increased to a significant degree but is instead an artifact of this temporary regime shift where equity correlations have increased reflecting the global synchronized bear market regime.

Hence, the principles for benefits of international investing are still there, including:

1. International markets have become a significant portion of world markets, while Canada has indeed shrunk over time. Today, international companies compose a larger proportion of the opportunity set for investors than they did in 1970, according to FactSet Research Systems.
2. International equities offer access to a broader spectrum of economies and opportunities that can provide for further diversification benefits.
3. Sector and country correlations still vary: From an investment manager perspective, international markets are thought of less from an EAFE perspective and more from a sector and country viewpoint. From a Canadian investor perspective there are a wide variety of diversification benefits available across sectors with correlations as low as 0.10, and countries with correlations of less than 0.20.

In conclusion:

- The bear market will end if it hasn't already; and
- Market volatility will stabilize; while
- Correlations between equities will stabilize; and consequently
- International investing will continue to provide superior returns adjusted for risk.

And recall the observations of Nobel Prize–winning economist Harry Markowitz: "Diversificaiton is both observed and sensible; a rule of behavior which does not imply the superiority of diversification must be rejected both as a hypothesis and a maxim."

Source: Harry S. Marmer, *Canadian Investment Review* 16, no. 2 (Summer 2003), p. 43. Reprinted by permission of Canadian Investment Review.

Table 22.13 Correlations of U.S. Equity Returns with Country Equity Returns

	Sample Period (monthly excess returns in $U.S.)	
	1967–2001*	**1970–1989†**
World	0.95	0.86
United Kingdom	0.83	0.49
Canada	0.82	0.72
Germany	0.75	0.33
Sweden	0.73	0.38
Netherlands	0.71	0.56
Australia	0.71	0.47
France	0.70	0.42
Denmark	0.67	0.33
Hong Kong	0.67	0.29
Spain	0.65	0.25
Switzerland	0.65	0.49
Norway	0.63	0.44
Japan	0.58	0.27
Italy	0.55	0.22
Austria	0.46	0.12
Belgium	0.46	0.41

***Source:** Datastream.

†**Source:** Campbell R. Harvey, "The World Price of Covariance Risk," *Journal of Finance,* March 1991.

Table 22.12 presents correlations between individual country returns and U.S. returns. First we see the correlations for both stock and bond investments in un-hedged returns (panel A) and hedged returns (panel B); the key result is that correlations between stock returns and bond returns of different countries are very low and frequently negative. Next, the correlation between the stock returns of different countries is quite high, and hedging does not play much of a part. It appears that cross-border correlation of stock indices has risen greatly; this conclusion is substantiated by Table 22.13, which shows from two independent studies how international correlations have risen substantially in recent years; globalization of economic activity and market integration are seen to be the causes of this increase in correlation, as discussed in the boxed article here.

22.3 MEASUREMENT OF INTERNATIONAL INVESTING

Passive and Active International Investing

Passive Benchmarks When we discussed investment strategies in the purely domestic context, we used a market index portfolio like the S&P 60 as a benchmark passive equity investment. This suggests a world market index might be a useful starting point for a passive international strategy.

One widely used index of non-U.S. stocks is the **Europe, Australia, Far East (EAFE) index** computed by Morgan Stanley. Additional indices of world equity performance are published by Salomon Brothers, First Boston, and Goldman, Sachs. Portfolios designed to mirror or even replicate the country, currency, and company representation of these indices would be the obvious generalization of the purely domestic passive equity strategy.

An issue that sometimes arises in the international context is the appropriateness of market-capitalization weighting schemes in the construction of international indices. Capitalization weighting is far and away the most common approach. However, some argue that it might not be the best weighting scheme in an international context. This is in part because different countries have differing proportions of their corporate sector organized as publicly traded firms.

Table 22.14 shows 1996 and 2001 data for market capitalization weights versus the GNP for countries in the EAFE index. These data reveal substantial disparities between the relative sizes of market capitalization versus GNP. Since market capitalization is a stock figure (the value of equity at one point in time), while GNP is a flow figure (production of goods and services during the entire year), we expect capitalization to be more volatile and the relative shares to be variable over time. Some discrepancies are persistent, however. For example, the United Kingdom's share of capitalization is about double its share of GNP, while Germany's share of capitalization is much less than its share of GNP. These disparities indicate that a greater proportion of economic activity is conducted by publicly traded firms in the United Kingdom than in Germany. Table 22.14 also illustrates the influence of stock market volatility on market-capitalization weighting schemes. For example, as its stock market swooned in the 1990s, Japan's share of EAFE capitalization declined from about 44 percent more than its share of GNP in 1996 to 26 percent below its share in 2001.

Table 22.14 Weighting Schemes for EAFE Countries

Country	2001		1996	
	% of EAFE Market Capitalization	% of EAFE GNP	% of EAFE Market Capitalization	% of EAFE GNP
Japan	25.8	31.0	43.5	31.5
United Kingdom	19.6	10.6	15.5	8.0
Germany	7.9	13.8	6.3	16.0
France	9.8	9.8	5.6	10.4
Netherlands	5.0	2.8	4.4	2.8
Switzerland	5.5	1.8	3.9	2.0
Hong Kong	4.7	1.2	3.8	1.0
Australia	3.2	2.7	2.8	2.7
Italy	5.0	8.1	2.7	8.3
Taiwan	1.7	2.1	2.0	1.9
Spain	2.9	4.3	1.9	4.1
Sweden	1.9	1.6	1.8	1.8
Singapore	1.0	0.6	1.7	0.6
Belgium	1.2	1.7	1.1	1.8
Denmark	0.8	1.2	0.6	1.2
Finland	1.4	0.9	0.5	0.9
Norway	0.6	1.2	0.4	1.1
New Zealand	0.2	0.4	0.4	0.4
Ireland	0.7	0.8	0.3	0.5
Austria	0.2	1.4	0.3	1.5
Portugal	0.4	0.8	0.3	0.8
Greece	0.5	0.9	0.2	0.8
Luxemburg	0.2	0.1	0.1	0.1

Source: Datastream.

Some argue that it would be more appropriate to weight international indices by GNP or GDP rather than market capitalization. The justification for this view is that an internationally diversified portfolio should purchase shares in proportion to the broad asset base of each country, and GDP might be a better measure of the importance of a country in the international economy than the value of its outstanding stocks. Others have even suggested weights proportional to the import share of various countries. The argument is that investors who wish to hedge the price of imported goods might choose to hold securities in foreign firms in proportion to the goods imported from those countries.

Performance Attribution Active portfolio management in an international context may be viewed similarly as an extension of active domestic management. In principle, one would form an efficient frontier from the full menu of world securities and determine the optimal risky portfolio. We saw in Chapter 6 that even in the domestic context, the need for specialization in various asset classes usually calls for a two-step procedure in which asset allocation is fixed initially, and then security selection within each asset class is determined. The complexities of the international market argue even more strongly for the primacy of asset allocation, and this is the perspective often taken in the evaluation of active portfolio management. Performance attribution of international managers focuses on these potential sources of abnormal returns: currency selection, country selection, stock selection within countries, and cash-bond selection within countries.

We can measure the contribution of each of these factors following a manner similar to the performance attribution techniques introduced in Chapter 21.

1. **Currency selection** measures the contribution to total portfolio performance attributable to exchange rate fluctuations relative to the investor's benchmark currency, which we will take to be the U.S. dollar. We might use a benchmark like the EAFE index to compare a portfolio's currency selection for a particular period to a passive benchmark. EAFE currency selection would be computed as the weighted average of the currency appreciation of the currencies represented in the EAFE portfolio using as weights the fraction of the EAFE portfolio invested in each currency.
2. **Country selection** measures the contribution to performance attributable to investing in the better-performing stock markets of the world. It can be measured as the weighted average of the equity *index* returns of each country using as weights the share of the manager's portfolio in each country. We use index returns to abstract from the effect of security selection within countries. To measure a manager's contribution relative to a passive strategy, we might compare country selection to the weighted average across countries of equity index returns using as weights the share of the EAFE portfolio in each country.
3. **Stock selection** ability may, as in Chapter 21, be measured as the weighted average of equity returns *in excess of the equity index* in each country. Here, we would use local currency returns and use as weights the investments in each country.
4. **Cash/bond selection** may be measured as the excess return derived from weighting bonds and bills differently from some benchmark weights.

Table 22.15 gives an example of how to measure the contribution of the decisions an international portfolio manager might make.

CONCEPT CHECK

3. Using the data in Table 22.15, compute the manager's country and currency selection if portfolio weights had been 40 percent in Europe, 20 percent in Australia, and 40 percent in the Far East.

Table 22.15 Example of Performance Attribution: International

	EAFE Weight	Return on Equity Index	Currency Application $E_1/E_0 - 1$	Manager's Weight	Manager's Return
Europe	.30	10%	10%	.35	8%
Australia	.10	5	−10	.10	7
Far East	.60	15	30	.55	18

Currency Selection

EAFE: (.30 × 10%) + (.10 × −10%) + (.60 × 30%) = 20% appreciation

Manager: (.35 × 10%) + (.10 × −10%) + (.55 × 30%) = 19% appreciation

Loss of 1% relative to EAFE

Country Selection

EAFE: (.30 × 10%) + (.10 × 5%) + (.60 × 15%) = 12.5%

Manager: (.35 × 10%) + (.10 × 5%) + (.55 × 15%) = 12.25%

Loss of .25% relative to EAFE

Stock Selection

(8% − 10%).35 + (7% − 5%).10 + (18% − 15%).55 = 1.15%

Contribution of 1.15% relative to EAFE

Security Analysis Security analysis of non-U.S. companies is complicated by noncomparabilities in accounting data. Security analysts must attempt to place accounting statements on an equal footing before comparing companies. Some of the major issues are:

1. *Depreciation.* Canada allows firms to use different financial reports for tax and reporting purposes. As a result, even firms that use accelerated depreciation for tax purposes in Canada often use straight-line depreciation for reporting purposes. This use of dual statements is uncommon elsewhere. Outside North America, firms tend to use accelerated depreciation for reporting as well as taxes, which affects both earnings and book values of assets.
2. *Reserves.* Canadian standards may permit lower allowances for possible losses, resulting in higher reported earnings than in other countries. There are also big differences in how firms reserve for pension liabilities.
3. *Consolidation.* Accounting practice in some countries does not call for all subsidiaries to be consolidated in the corporation's income statement.
4. *Taxes.* Taxes may be reported either as paid or accrued.
5. *P/E ratios.* There may be different practices for calculating the number of shares used to calculate P/E ratios. Firms may use end-of-year shares, year-average shares, or even beginning-of-year shares.

Factor Models and International Investing

International investing presents a good opportunity to demonstrate an application of multifactor models of security returns such as those considered in connection with the arbitrage pricing model. Natural factors might include

1. A world stock index
2. A national (domestic) stock index
3. Industrial-sector indexes
4. Currency movements

Solnik and de Freitas[9] used such a framework, and Table 22.16 shows some of their results for several countries. The first four columns of numbers present the *R*-square of various one-factor regressions. Recall that the *R*-square, or R^2, measures the percentage of return volatility of a company's stock that can be explained by the particular factor treated as the independent or explanatory variable. Solnik and de Freitas estimated the factor regressions for many firms in a given country and reported the average *R*-square across the firms in that country.

In this case, the table reveals that the domestic factor seems to be the dominant influence on stock returns. While the domestic index alone generates an average *R*-square of .42 across all countries, adding the three additional factors (in the last column of the table) increases average *R*-square only to .46.

At the same time, there is clear evidence of a world market factor in results of the market crash of October 1987. Even though we have said equity returns across borders show only moderate correlation, a study by Richard Roll[10] showed negative October 1987 equity index returns in all 23 countries considered. Figure 22.7, reproduced from Roll's study, shows the values he found for regional equity indices during that month. The obvious correlation among returns suggests some underlying world factor common to all economies. Roll found that the beta of a country's equity index on a world index (estimated through September 1987) was the best predictor of that index's response to the October 1987 crash, which lends further support to the presence of a world factor.

Table 22.16 Relative Importance of World, Industrial, Currency, and Domestic Factors in Explaining Return of a Stock

	Average *R*-Square of Regression on Factors				
	Single-Factor Tests				
Locality	World	Industrial	Currency	Domestic	Joint Test All Four Factors
Switzerland	.18	.17	.00	.38	.39
West Germany	.08	.10	.00	.41	.42
Australia	.24	.26	.01	.72	.72
Belgium	.07	.08	.00	.42	.43
Canada	.27	.24	.07	.45	.48
Spain	.22	.03	.00	.45	.45
United States	.26	.47	.01	.35	.55
France	.13	.08	.01	.45	.60
United Kingdom	.20	.17	.01	.53	.55
Hong Kong	.06	.25	.17	.79	.81
Italy	.05	.03	.00	.35	.35
Japan	.09	.16	.01	.26	.33
Norway	.17	.28	.00	.84	.85
Netherlands	.12	.07	.01	.34	.31
Singapore	.16	.15	.02	.32	.33
Sweden	.19	.06	.01	.42	.43
All countries	.18	.23	.01	.42	.46

Source: Bruno Solnik, *International Investments*, 3rd ed. (Reading, MA: Addison-Wesley, 1996), p. 37. © 1996 by Addison-Wesley Publishing Company, Inc. Reprinted by permission of the publisher.

[9]Bruno Solnik and A. de Freitas, "International Factors of Stock Price Behavior," in S. Khoury and A. Ghosh, eds., *Recent Developments in International Finance and Banking* (Lexington, MA: Lexington Books, 1988). Cited in Bruno Solnik, *International Investments*, 2nd ed. (Reading, MA: Addison-Wesley, 1991).

[10]Richard Roll, "The International Crash of October 1987," *Financial Analysts Journal*, September/October 1988.

Figure 22.7 Regional indices around the crash of October 14 –October 26, 1987.

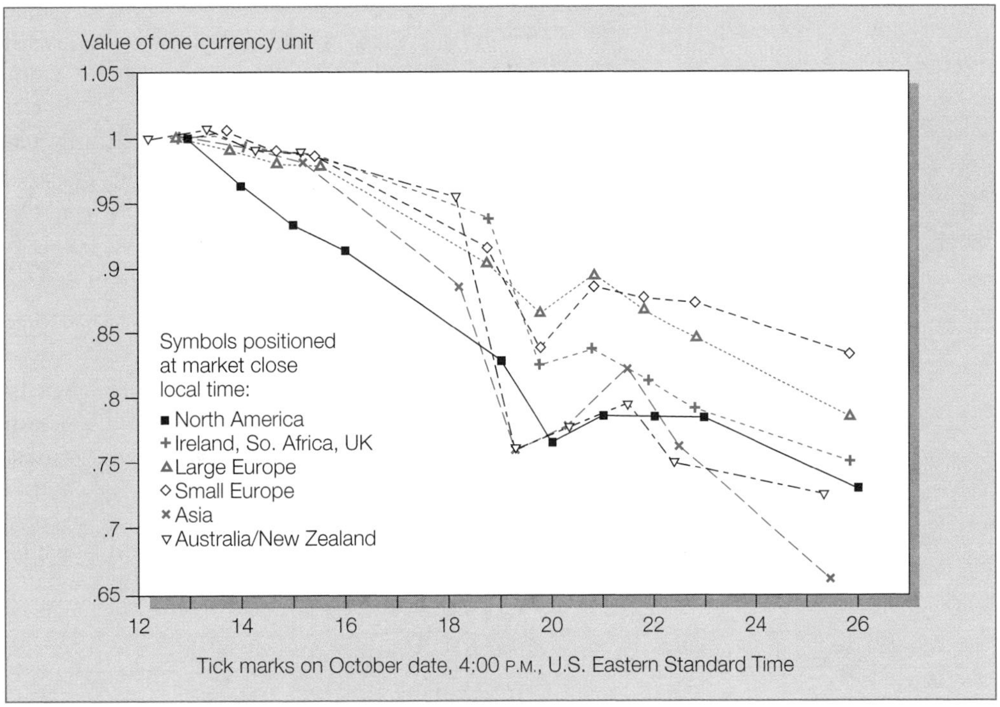

Source: Richard Roll, "The International Crash of October 1987," *Financial Analysts Journal*, September/October 1988. © 1988, Association for Investment Management and Research. Reproduced and republished from Financial Analysts Federation with permission from CFA Institute. All rights reserved.

Equilibrium in International Capital Markets

We can use the CAPM or the APT to predict expected rates of return in an international capital market equilibrium, just as we can for domestic assets. The models need some adaptation for international use, however.

For example, one might expect that a world CAPM would result simply by replacing a narrow domestic market portfolio with a broad world market portfolio and measuring betas relative to the world portfolio. This approach was pursued in part of a paper by Ibbotson, Carr, and Robinson,[11] who calculated betas of equity indices of several countries against a world equity index. Their results appear in Table 22.17. The betas for different countries show surprising variability.

Although such a straightforward generalization of the simple CAPM seems like a reasonable first step, it is subject to some problems:

1. Taxes, transaction costs, and capital barriers across countries make it difficult and not always attractive for investors to hold a world index portfolio. Some assets are simply unavailable to foreign investors.
2. Investors in different countries view exchange rate risk from the perspective of their different domestic currencies. Thus they will not agree on the risk characteristics of various securities and therefore will not derive identical efficient frontiers.
3. Investors in different countries tend to consume different baskets of goods, either because of differing tastes or because of tariffs, transportation costs, or taxes. If relative prices of

[11] Roger G. Ibbotson, Richard C. Carr, and Anthony W. Robinson, "International Equity and Bond Returns," *Financial Analysts Journal*, July/August 1982.

Table 22.17 Equity Returns, 1960–1980

	Average Return	Standard Deviation of Return	Beta	Alpha
Australia	12.20	22.80	1.02	1.52
Austria	10.30	16.90	0.01	4.86
Belgium	10.10	13.80	0.45	2.44
Canada	12.10	17.50	0.77	2.75
Denmark	11.40	24.20	0.60	2.91
France	8.10	21.40	0.50	0.17
Germany	10.10	19.90	0.45	2.41
Italy	5.60	27.20	0.41	–1.92
Japan	19.00	31.40	0.81	9.49
Netherlands	10.70	17.80	0.90	0.65
Norway	17.40	49.00	–0.27	13.39
Spain	10.40	19.80	0.04	4.73
Sweden	9.70	16.70	0.51	1.69
Switzerland	12.50	22.90	0.87	2.66
United Kingdom	14.70	33.60	1.47	1.76
United States	10.20	17.70	1.08	–0.69

Source: Roger G. Ibbotson, Richard C. Carr, and Anthony W. Robinson, "International Equity and Bond Returns," *Financial Analysts Journal*, July/August 1982.

goods vary over time, the inflation risk perceived by investors in different countries will also differ.

These problems suggest that the simple CAPM will not work as well in an international context as it would if all markets were fully integrated. Some evidence suggests that assets that are less accessible to foreign investors carry higher risk premiums than a simple CAPM would predict.[12]

The APT seems better designed for use in an international context than the CAPM, as the special risk factors that arise in international investing can be treated much like any other risk factor. World economic activity and currency movements might simply be included in a list of factors already used in a domestic APT model.

22.4 INTEGRATION WITH INTERNATIONAL MARKETS

Integration Versus Segmentation in Markets

Investigation of the benefits of international investment leads immediately to the question of whether assets listed in different capital markets offer the same risk-return characteristics. Interlisting of stocks on various world exchanges makes them accessible to investors in those markets and places them in direct competition as financial assets with the domestic securities of those markets. One might suspect that the inevitable result of this would be that all assets in all markets would display the same risk-return characteristics, at least relative to some world index or common factors. Were this the case, we would describe the markets as being fully **integrated**. In contrast to this, if assets in different markets retained different risk-return

[12] Vihang Errunza and Etienne Losq, "International Asset Pricing Under Mild Segmentation: Theory and Test," *Journal of Finance* 40 (March 1985), pp. 105–124.

EXCEL APPLICATION

INTERNATIONAL DIVERSIFICATION

The graph shown below appears in a spreadsheet available on our Online Learning Centre at www.mcgrawhill.ca/college/bodie. It can be used to find efficient combinations of individual securities or funds. To use the model and approach, you must have estimates of expected returns for the securities or funds, estimates of the standard deviation of returns, and pairwise correlations of the securities or funds.

The data for the analysis is contained in a file called Web Portfolio. The Web Portfolio model contains returns, variance in return, and correlations for all of the World Equity Benchmark Shares (WEBS; now iShares) that have been trading for a 48-month period through December 2000. The monthly returns have been annualized. The model constructs an efficient frontier for a subset of eight Web securities. The model was built using the methodology described in Chapter 6. We have constrained allocations to the various indices to be zero or positive. This restricts the use of short sales. The model can be modified to allow short sales by making appropriate changes to the weights.

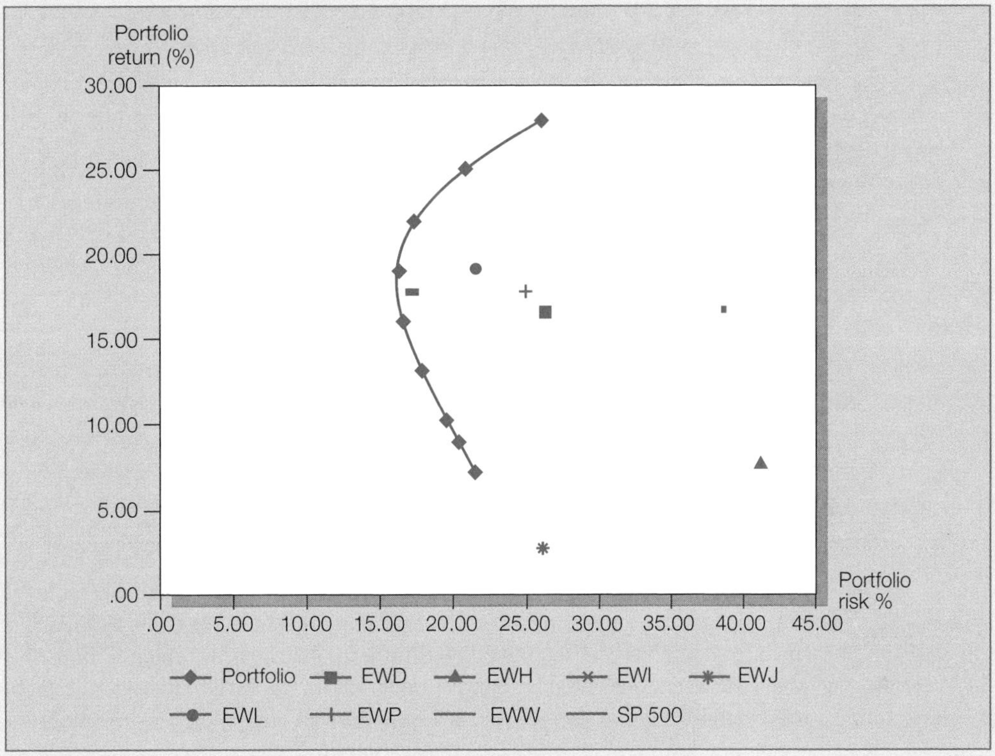

characteristics or were priced according to different and country-specific factors, we would describe these markets as **segmented**.

The existence of market segmentation is ascribed to both indirect and legal barriers to investment by all potential investors in all potential assets. Indirect barriers are defined as those previously mentioned problems besetting the foreign investor, such as lack of access to financial information or ability to trade efficiently in the securities. Legal barriers include restrictions on foreign ownership or of foreign investment by individuals or institutions, such as the limitation placed on Canadian pension funds. Interlisting of securities tends to alleviate the indirect barriers but usually cannot solve legal barriers.

Studies indicate that various important financial ratios vary widely across the different markets. This might be taken as evidence of clear segmentation of the many markets, possibly excepting the Canadian and U.S. markets with their similar ratios, given the relevance of these ratios to market valuation. Yet these statistics must be recognized as dependent upon the market conditions under which they were compiled; prices are high relative to earnings during recessions. Furthermore, the different markets are not homogeneous in terms of the firms that comprise the indices; the Canadian market is disproportionately high in natural resource companies. Financial ratios vary appropriately across different industries, and the different comparisons of specific national markets leads to a variety of aggregates of ratios.

Consideration of financial ratios is a dated approach to valuation, however, and cannot provide reliable evidence as to market segmentation. Modern financial theory prescribes the comparison of ex post risk-return measures and the sensitivity to market factors as evidence. Recent interest in the subject of market integration and segmentation has led to a number of theoretical and empirical studies to test which of the two descriptions is accurate. Generally, these tests involve attempts to price international assets by appeal to multifactor models, as described in the previous section; both multifactor CAPM and APT models have been used. Modelling the effects of barriers causing segmentation is difficult, however, given the problem of defining and quantifying imperfections in the markets. Hence, the risk premiums for the various factors cannot be reliably established. Alternatively, theory suggests that the integration of a smaller market with larger markets will result in a lowering of expected returns in the smaller market, due to increased liquidity and demand, but more importantly, due to a lowering of the risk premium. Interlisting of securities should produce a lowering of risk premiums for these securities at least; thus the event of interlisting can be studied to test for an observed reduction as of the occurrence of the event.[13]

Integration of Canadian and U.S. Markets

Canadian markets offer a unique opportunity to researchers to study the question of segmentation versus integration since they are close to U.S. markets both institutionally and geographically; the economies are closely linked, corporations are governed by essentially similar rules and practices, and both debt and equity instruments of both countries are sold to and traded by investors of both countries, with interlisting of many stocks. Yet the different tax treatment of dividends in the two countries implies that ex-dividend day returns should differ for stocks in the two markets; interlisted stocks were shown by Booth and Johnston[14] to behave differently from domestically traded stocks. Comparison of interlisted and domestic stocks can provide statistically significant results to demonstrate segmentation. Furthermore, a case for integration between the two markets can be made more strongly than for integration of a third market with either of the two. Statistical methods can be used to test for the different characteristics of integration as would be expected under the closely linked versus distant markets.

Most empirical studies of Canadian and U.S. returns differ in their conclusions as to whether the two markets are truly integrated. Hatch and White[15] examined the comparative returns of U.S. and Canadian stock markets, and noted that U.S. stocks had a higher return than did Canadian but had a slightly lower risk; they rationalized this as resulting from a lower beta

---

[13] Gordon J. Alexander, Cheol S. Eun, and S. Janakiramanan, "Asset Pricing and Dual Listing on Foreign Capital Markets: A Note," *Journal of Finance* 42 (March 1987).

[14] L. D. Booth and D. J. Johnston, "The Ex-Dividend Day Behavior of Canadian Stock Prices: Tax Changes and Clientele Effects," *Journal of Finance* 39 (June 1984).

[15] J. E. Hatch and R. W. White, "A Canadian Perspective on Canadian and United States Capital Market Returns: 1950–1983," *Financial Analysts Journal* 42 (May/June 1986).

for Canadian stocks, relative to a world index. Brennan and Schwartz[16] rejected integration of the two markets over the period 1968–1980 based on a combined index, but their analysis does not correct for the substantial double-counting of interlisted stocks. Extending the period to 1982, Jorion and Schwartz[17] found the same result by using a two-factor CAPM approach; the model was designed to eliminate the commonality between the domestic and international components. They found that the international index did not account for all the returns in Canadian stocks, leaving a priceable national component; hence, they concluded there was evidence of segmentation. A recent study by Mittoo[18] finds evidence that both time and interlisting are significant in explaining the segmentation issue. Using both CAPM and APT approaches, it is revealed that data prior to 1982 support segmentation, while integration is indicated afterward; furthermore, interlisted stocks after 1982 show integration, but domestically listed stocks suggest segregation. The data were restricted to TSE 35 companies to avoid thin-trading problems and natural resource factor loading, and to a time period where regulatory impediments to integration were absent. Alexander, Eun, and Janakiramanan[19] tested the reduction in expected required returns following interlisting for the period 1969–1982. They investigated both Canadian and non–North American stocks that were listed on the NYSE, AMEX, or Nasdaq, and found a significant distinction between the Canadian and non-Canadian groups; as hypothesized, the Canadian stocks experienced a much smaller return reduction than did the others. In fact, the Canadian results were found to be insignificant, leading them to the conclusion that the foreign markets are definitely segmented from the U.S., but that the Canadian market may not have been.

www.nasdaq.com

In conclusion, we can say that there are institutional and sectoral explanations for an apparent segmentation of Canadian and U.S. markets; at the same time, similarities and accessibility of the two markets suggest little if any differential pricing is likely and that virtual integration is possible.

SUMMARY

1. Canadian assets make up only a small fraction of the world wealth portfolio. International capital markets offer important opportunities for portfolio diversification with enhanced risk-return characteristics.
2. Investors can diversify internationally by buying multinational firms on Canadian or U.S. markets or by buying closed- or open-ended mutual funds that invest in specific countries, regions, or internationally in general.
3. Exchange rate risk imparts an extra source of uncertainty to investments denominated in foreign currencies. Much of that risk can be hedged in foreign exchange futures or forward markets, but unless the foreign currency rate of return is known, a perfect hedge is not feasible.
4. Several world market indices can form a basis for passive international investing. Active international management can be partitioned into currency selection, country selection, stock selection, and cash/bond selection.
5. A factor model applied to international investing would include a world factor, as well as the usual domestic factors. Although some evidence suggests that domestic factors dominate stock returns, the October 1987 crash provides evidence of an important international factor.
6. Financial markets in different countries may be integrated or segmented, depending on whether factors that influence security prices are universal or specific to the countries.

[16] M. J. Brennan and E. Schwartz, "Asset Pricing in a Small Economy: A Test of the Omitted Assets Model," in Spremann, ed., *Survey of Developments in Modern Finance* (New York: Springer-Verlag, 1986).

[17] P. Jorion and E. Schwartz, "Integration vs. Segmentation in the Canadian Stock Market," *Journal of Finance* 41 (July 1986).

[18] Usha R. Mittoo, "Additional Evidence on Integration in the Canadian Stock Market," *Journal of Finance* 47 (December 1992).

[19] Gordon J. Alexander, Cheol S. Eun, and S. Janakiramanan, "International Listings and Stock Returns: Some Empirical Evidence," *Journal of Financial and Quantitative Analysis* 23 (1988). This is a typical example of the event study methodology, described in Chapter 9.

7. The benefits of international diversification are increased if market segmentation exists. Studies indicate that Canadian markets are at most mildly segmented from U.S. markets. For Canadian investors, overseas investment offers the greatest diversification opportunities.

KEY TERMS

American Depository Receipt (ADR) 859
single-country fund 859
political risk 863
exchange rate risk 866
interest rate parity theorem 869
Europe, Australia, Far East (EAFE) index 876
currency selection 878
country selection 878
stock selection 878
cash/bond selection 878
integrated 882
segmented 883

SELECTED READINGS

Comprehensive textbooks on international facets of investing are:

Solnik, Bruno. *International Investments,* 3rd ed. Reading, MA: Addison-Wesley Publishing, Co., Inc., 1996.

Grabbe, J. Orlin. *International Financial Markets,* 2nd ed. New York: Elsevier Science Publishers, 1991.

A text with a greater emphasis on corporate applications and foreign exchange risk management is:

Shapiro, Alan C. *Multinational Financial Management.* Boston: Allyn & Bacon, Inc., 1986.

A good book of readings is:

Lessard, Donald R., ed., *International Financial Management: Theory and Application.* New York: John Wiley & Sons, 1985.

Some recent Canadian empirical studies on international diversification include the works mentioned in the footnotes and:

Marmer, Harry S. "International Investing: A New Canadian Perspective." *Canadian Investment Review* 4, no. 1 (Spring 1991).

Foerster, Stephen R. and W. Andrew Karolyi. "The Effect of Market Segmentation and Investor Recognition on Asset Prices: Evidence from Foreign Stock Listings in the U.S." *Journal of Finance* 54(1999), pp. 981–1013.

Two textbooks on international investing and capital markets are:

Giddy, Ian H. *Global Financial Markets.* Lexington, MA: D.C. Heath, 1993.

Solnik, Bruno. *International Investments,* 3rd ed. Reading, MA: Addison-Wesley, 1996.

PROBLEMS

CFA® PROBLEMS

1. You are a U.S. investor who purchased British securities for £2,000 one year ago when the British pound cost US$1.50. What is your total return (based on U.S. dollars) if the value of the securities is now £2,400 and the pound is worth $1.75? No dividends or interest was paid during this period.
   a. 16.7 percent
   b. 20.0 percent
   c. 28.6 percent
   d. 40.0 percent

CFA® PROBLEMS

2. The correlation coefficient between the returns on a broad index of U.S. stocks and the returns on indices of the stocks of other industrialized countries is mostly __________, and the correlation coefficient between the returns on various diversified portfolios of U.S. stocks is mostly __________.
   a. less than .8; greater than .8
   b. greater than .8; less than .8
   c. less than 0; greater than 0
   d. greater than 0; less than 0

CFA® PROBLEMS

3. An investor in the common stock of companies in a foreign country may wish to hedge against the ______________ of the investor's home currency and can do so by ______________ the foreign currency in the forward market.

a. depreciation; selling
b. appreciation; purchasing
c. appreciation; selling
d. depreciation; purchasing

4. Suppose a Canadian investor wishes to invest in a British firm currently selling for £40 per share. The investor has $10,000 to invest, and the current exchange rate is $2/£.

a. How many shares can the investor purchase?
b. Fill in the table below for rates of return after one year in each of the nine scenarios (three possible prices per share in pounds times three possible exchange rates).

		Dollar-Denominated Return for Year-End Exchange Rate		
Price per Share (£)	**Pound-Denominated Return (%)**	**$1.80/£**	**$2/£**	**$2.20/£**
£35				
£40				
£45				

c. When is the dollar-denominated return equal to the pound-denominated return?

5. If each of the nine outcomes in problem 4 is equally likely, find the standard deviation of both the pound- and dollar-denominated rates of return.

6. Now suppose that the investor in problem 4 also sells forward £5,000 at a forward exchange rate of $2.10/£.

a. Recalculate the dollar-denominated returns of each scenario.
b. What happens to the standard deviation of the dollar-denominated return? Compare it both to its old value and the standard deviation of the pound-denominated return.

7. Calculate the contribution to total performance from currency, country, and stock selection for the manager in the example below. (E_1/E_0 is foreign currency units per dollar.)

	EAFE Weight	Return on Equity Index	$E_1/E_0 - 1$	Manager's Weight	Manager's Return
Europe	.30	20%	–10%	.35	18%
Australia	.10	15	0	.15	20
Far East	.60	25	+10	.50	20

8. If the current exchange rate is $1.75/£, the one-year forward exchange rate is $1.85/£, and the interest rate on British government bills is 8 percent per year, what risk-free dollar-denominated return can be locked in by investing in the British bills?

9. If you were to invest $10,000 in the British bills of problem 8, how would you lock in the dollar-denominated return?

CFA® PROBLEMS

10. John Irish, CFA, is an independent investment advisor who is assisting Alfred Darwin, the head of the Investment Committee of General Technology Corporation, to establish a new pension fund. Darwin asks Irish about international equities and whether the Investment Committee should consider them as an additional asset for the pension fund.

a. Explain the rationale for including international equities in General's equity portfolio. Identify and describe three relevant considerations in formulating your answer.

b. List three possible arguments against international equity investment and briefly discuss the significance of each.

c. To illustrate several aspects of the performance of international securities over time, Irish shows Darwin the following graph of investment results experienced by a U.S. pension fund in the recent past. Compare the performance of the U.S. dollar and non-U.S. dollar equity and fixed-income asset categories, and explain the significance of the result of the Account Performance Index relative to the results of the four individual asset class indices.

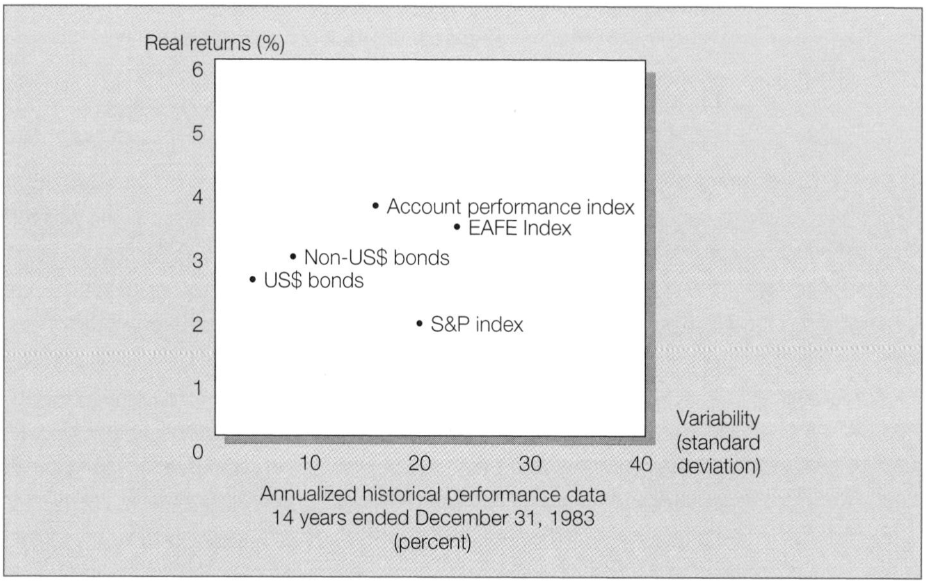

CFA® PROBLEMS

11. You are a U.S. investor considering purchase of one of the following securities. Assume that the currency risk of the German government bond will be hedged, and the six-month discount on Canadian dollar forward contracts is –.75% versus the U.S. dollar.

Bond	Maturity	Coupon	Price
U.S. government	June 1, 2003	6.50%	100.00
Canadian government	June 1, 2003	7.50%	100.00

Calculate the expected price change required in the Canadian government bond which would result in the two bonds having equal total returns in U.S. dollars over a six-month horizon. Assume that the yield on the U.S. bond is expected to remain unchanged.

CFA® PROBLEMS

12. A global manager plans to invest $1 million in U.S. government cash equivalents for the next 90 days. However, she is also authorized to use non-U.S. government cash equivalents, as long as the currency risk is hedged to U.S. dollars using forward currency contracts.

a. What rate of return will the manager earn if she invests in money market instruments in either Canada or Japan and hedges the dollar value of her investment? Use the data in the following tables.

b. What must be the approximate value of the 90-day interest rate available on U.S. government securities?

Interest Rates (APR) 90-Day Cash Equivalents		
Japanese government	2.52%	
Canadian government	6.74%	
Exchange Rates Dollars per Unit of Foreign Currency		
	Spot	**90-Day Forward**
Japanese yen	.0119	.0120
Canadian dollar	.7284	.7269

13. Suppose two all-equity-financed firms, ABC and XYZ, both have $100 million of equity outstanding. Each firm now issues $10 million of new stock and uses the proceeds to purchase the other's shares.

a. What happens to the sum of the value of outstanding equity of the two firms?

b. What happens to the value of the equity in these firms held by the noncorporate sector of the economy?

c. Prepare the balance sheet for these two firms before and after the stock issues.

d. If both of these firms were in an index, what would happen to their weights in the index?

CFA® PROBLEMS

14. After much research on the developing economy and capital markets of the country of Otunia, your firm, GAC, has decided to include an investment in the Otunia stock market in its Emerging Markets Commingled Fund. However, GAC has not yet decided whether to invest actively or by indexing. Your opinion on the active-versus-indexing decision has been solicited. The following is a summary of the research findings:

Otunia's economy is fairly well diversified across agricultural and natural resources, manufacturing (both consumer and durable goods), and a growing finance sector. Transaction costs in securities markets are relatively large in Otunia because of high commissions and government "stamp taxes" on securities trades. Accounting standards and disclosure regulations are quite detailed, resulting in wide public availability of reliable information about companies' financial performance.

Capital flows into and out of Otunia, and foreign ownership of Otunia securities is strictly regulated by an agency of the national government. The settlement procedures under these ownership rules often cause long delays in settling trades made by nonresidents. Senior finance officials in the government are working to deregulate capital flows and foreign ownership, but GAC's political consultant believes that isolationist sentiment may prevent much real progress in the short run.

a. Briefly discuss aspects of the Otunia environment that favour investing actively, and aspects that favour indexing.

b. Recommend whether GAC should invest in Otunia actively or by indexing. Justify your recommendation based on the factors identified in part (*a*).

15. A global equity manager is assigned to select stocks from a universe of large stocks throughout the world. The manager will be evaluated by comparing her returns to the return on the MSCI World Market Portfolio, but she is free to hold stocks from various countries in whatever proportions she finds desirable. Results for a given month are contained in the following table:

Country	Weight in MSCI Index	Manager's Weight	Manager's Return in Country	Return of Stock Index for That Country
United Kingdom	.15	.30	20%	12%
Japan	.30	.10	15	15
United States	.45	.40	10	14
Germany	.10	.20	5	12

a. Calculate the total value added of all the manager's decisions this period.

b. Calculate the value added (or subtracted) by her *country* allocation decisions.

c. Calculate the value added from her stock selection ability within countries. Confirm that the sum of the contributions to value added from her country allocation plus security selection decisions equals total over- or underperformance.

CFA® PROBLEMS

16. You and a prospective client are considering the measurement of investment performance, particularly with respect to international portfolios for the past five years. The data you discussed are presented in the following table:

International Manager or Index	Total Return	Country and Security Return	Currency Return
Manager A	–6.0%	2.0%	–8.0%
Manager B	–2.0	–1.0	–1.0
International Index	–5.0	0.2	–5.2

a. Assume that the data for manager A and manager B accurately reflect their investment skills and that both managers actively manage currency exposure. Briefly describe one strength and one weakness for each manager.

b. Recommend and justify a strategy that would enable your fund to take advantage of the strengths of each of the two managers while minimizing their weaknesses.

abnormal return. Return on a stock beyond what would be predicted by market movements alone. See also ***cumulative abnormal return (CAR)***.

accounting earnings. Earnings of a firm as reported on its ***income statement***.

acid test ratio. See ***quick ratio***.

active management. Attempts to achieve portfolio returns more than commensurate with risk, either by forecasting broad market trends or by identifying particular mispriced sectors of a market or securities in a market.

active portfolio. In the context of the Treynor-Black model, the portfolio formed by mixing analyzed stocks of perceived non-zero alpha values. This portfolio is ultimately mixed with the passive market index portfolio.

advance-decline line. A graph of the net difference between the number of stock prices advancing and the number declining; a technical indicator of market breadth.

agency theory. The study of conflicts of interest between stockholders, bondholders, and managers of a firm.

alpha. The abnormal rate of return on a security in excess of what would be predicted by an equilibrium model such as the ***capital asset pricing model (CAPM) or arbitrage pricing theory (APT).***

American Depository Receipt (ADR). The instrument traded on the NYSE which represents an equity interest in a (foreign) company; ADRs are equivalent to a number of shares in the company, as traded in that company's home market, and are entitled to proportional payments of dividends.

American option. An option that can be exercised before and up to its expiration date. See also ***European option***.

announcement date. Date on which particular news concerning a given company is announced to the public. Used in ***event studies***, which researchers use to evaluate the economic impact of events of interest.

anomalies. Patterns of returns that seem to contradict the ***efficient market hypothesis***.

appraisal ratio. The signal-to-noise ratio of an analyst's forecasts. The ratio of ***alpha*** to residual ***standard deviation***.

arbitrage pricing theory (APT). An asset pricing theory that is derived from a ***factor model***, using diversification and ***arbitrage*** arguments. The theory describes the relationship between ***expected returns*** on securities, given that there are no opportunities to create wealth through risk-free arbitrage investments.

arbitrage. A zero-risk, zero-net investment strategy that still generates profits.

asked price. The price at which a dealer will sell a security.

asset allocation decision. Choosing among broad asset classes such as stocks versus bonds.

asset turnover (ATO). The annual sales generated by each dollar of assets (sales/assets).

at the money. Said of an option whose ***exercise price*** equals its asset value. See also ***in the money*** and ***out of the money***.

auction market. A market where all traders in an asset meet at one place to buy or sell. The TSX is an example.

average collection period, or **days' receivables.** The ratio of accounts receivable to sales, or the total amount of credit extended per dollar of daily sales (Average AR/Sales × 365).

balance sheet. A financial statement of the assets, liabilities, and net worth of the firm as of a particular date.

bank discount yield. An annualized ***interest rate*** assuming simple interest and a 360-day year, and using the ***face value*** of the security rather than purchase price to compute return per dollar invested.

bankers' acceptance. A money market instrument consisting of an order to a bank by a customer to pay a fixed amount at a future debt; the bank has "accepted" this order.

baseline allocation. Neutral allocation of funds to equities, fixed income, and cash used as a portfolio starting point from which modifications are made in response to predictions of asset performance.

basis risk. Risk attributable to uncertain movements in the ***spread*** between a ***futures price*** and a spot price.

basis. The difference between the ***futures price*** and the spot price.

bear CD. Pays the holder a fraction of any fall in a given market index. See also ***bull CD***.

bearer deposit note (BDN). A negotiable bank time deposit (in Canada).

bearish. Pessimistic; used to describe investor attitudes. Also used in the term *bear market*. See also ***bullish***.

behavioural finance. A set of theoretical hypotheses that attribute departures from market efficiency to systematic patterns of investor behaviour that seemingly contradict rationality.

benchmark error. Use of an inappropriate ***proxy*** for the true ***market portfolio***.

beta. The measure of the systematic risk of a security. The tendency of a security's returns to respond to swings in the broad market.

bid price. The price at which a dealer is willing to purchase a security.

bid-asked spread. The difference between a dealer's ***bid price*** and ***asked price***.

binomial model. An option valuation model predicated on the assumption that stock prices can move to only two values over any short time period.

Black-Scholes pricing formula. An equation to value a ***call option*** that uses the stock price, the ***exercise price***, the risk-free ***interest rate***, the time to maturity, and the ***standard deviation*** of the stock return.

block house. Brokerage firms that help to find potential buyers or sellers of large block trades.

block sale. A sale of more than 10,000 shares of stock.

block transactions. Large transactions in which at least 10,000 shares of stock are bought or sold. Brokers or ***block houses*** often search directly for other large traders rather than bringing the trade to the ***stock exchange***.

board lot. A standard volume of traded securities, generally equal to 100 shares. It can be larger (smaller) for low-priced (high-priced) securities.

bogey. The return an investment manager is compared to for performance evaluation.

bond. A security issued by a borrower that obligates the issuer to make specified payments to the holder over a specified period. A *coupon bond* obligates the issuer to make interest payments called coupon payments over the life of the bond, then to repay the ***principal*** at maturity.

bond equivalent yield. Bond yield calculated on an annual percentage rate method. Differs from ***effective annual yield***.

bond indenture. See ***indenture***.

bond index portfolio. A portfolio of bonds stratified to include representatives of available grades, coupons, and maturities in weights proportional to the actual bond universe.

book value. An accounting measure describing the net worth of common equity according to a firm's ***balance sheet***.

book-to-market effects. The ratio of the ***book value*** of the firm's equity to the market value of the equity, used as a predictor of the return on the firm's securities.

bootstrapping. A technique for the derivation of the ***spot rates*** for various maturities from observed market prices of coupon bonds of different maturities.

breadth. A technical indicator measuring the extent to which movement in a market index is reflected in the price movements of all stocks.

brokered market. A market where an intermediary (a broker) offers search services to buyers and sellers.

bull CD. Pays its holder a specified percentage of the increase in return on a specified market index while guaranteeing a minimum rate of return. See also ***bear CD***.

bullish. Optimistic; used to describe investor attitudes. Also used in the term *bull market*. See also ***bearish***.

bundling, unbundling. The creation of securities either by combining ***primitive*** and ***derivative securities*** into one hybrid or by separating returns on an asset into classes.

business cycle. The sequence of expansion and contraction of activity in the economy, observable after the fact.

call option. The right to buy an asset at a specified ***exercise price*** on or before a specified expiration date.

callable. The feature of ***bonds*** or preferred shares allowing the issuer to repurchase the security at a fixed price in some specified period.

callable bond. A ***bond*** that the issuer may repurchase at a given price in some specified period.

candlestick chart. A ***technical analysis*** tool recording high, low, open and close prices in a period of trading.

capital allocation decision. The choice of the proportion of the overall portfolio to place in safe ***money market*** securities, versus risky but higher-return securities like stocks.

capital allocation line (CAL). A graph showing all feasible risk-return combinations of a ***risky*** and ***risk-free asset***.

capital asset pricing model (CAPM). A model of financial market equilibrium that allows the computation of the risk-adjusted equilibrium rates of return for various ***financial assets***.

capital gains. The amount by which the sale price of a security exceeds the purchase price.

capital market line (CML). A ***capital allocation line (CAL)*** provided by the market index portfolio.

capital markets. The markets for longer-term, relatively riskier securities.

cash delivery. The provision of some ***futures contracts*** that requires no delivery of the underlying assets (as in agricultural futures) but settlement according to the cash value of the asset.

cash equivalents. Short-term ***money market*** securities.

cash flow matching. A form of ***immunization***, matching cash flows from a bond with an obligation.

cash settlement. The provision of certain options (***index options***) or ***futures contracts*** that requires, not delivery of the underlying asset, but settlement by the cash value of the asset.

cash/bond selection. Asset allocation in which the choice is between short-term ***cash equivalents*** and longer-term bonds.

certainty equivalent. The certain return providing the same utility as a risky portfolio.

certainty equivalent rate. A rate that risk-free investments would need to offer with certainty to be considered equally attractive to a particular risky portfolio.

certificate of deposit. A bank time deposit.

clearinghouse. Established by ***exchanges*** to facilitate transfer of securities resulting from trades. For options and ***futures contracts***, the clearinghouse may interpose itself as a middleman between two traders.

closed-end (mutual) fund. A fund whose shares are traded through brokers at market prices; the fund will not redeem shares at their ***net asset value (NAV)***. The market price of the fund can differ from the net asset value.

collar. An option strategy that brackets the value of the underlying asset between two bounds.

collateral. A specific asset pledged against possible default on a bond. *Mortgage* bonds are backed by claims on property. *Collateral trust bonds* are backed by claims on other securities. *Equipment obligation bonds* are backed by claims on equipment.

collateralized mortgage obligation (CMO). A mortgage ***pass-through security*** that partitions cash flows from underlying mortgages into successive maturity groups, called ***tranches***, that receive ***principal*** payments according to different maturities.

commercial paper. Short-term unsecured paper (or note) issues by large corporations.

commingled funds. Investment pools of funds for accounts that are too small for individual attention and are managed as a group.

commission broker. A broker on the floor of the ***exchange*** who executes orders for other members.

common stock. Equities, or equity securities, issued as ownership shares in a publicly held corporation. Shareholders have voting rights and may receive dividends based on their proportionate ownership.

comparison universe. The collection of money managers of similar investment style used for assessing relative performance of a portfolio manager.

complete portfolio. The entire portfolio, including ***risky*** and ***risk-free assets***.

confidence index. The ratio of the average yield on ten top-rated ***corporate bonds*** divided by the average yield on ten intermediate-grade corporate bonds; a technical indicator that is ***bullish*** when the index approaches 100 percent, implying low-risk premiums.

constant-growth DDM. A form of the ***dividend discount model (DDM)*** that assumes dividends will grow at a constant rate.

contango theory. Holds that the ***futures price*** must exceed the expected future spot price.

contingent claim. Claim whose value is directly dependent on or is contingent on the value of some underlying assets.

contingent immunization. A mixed passive-active strategy that immunizes a portfolio if necessary to guarantee a minimum acceptable return but otherwise allows ***active management***.

convergence property. The convergence of ***futures prices*** and spot prices at the maturity of the ***futures contract***.

convertible bond. A bond with an option allowing the bondholder to exchange the bond for a number of shares. The *market conversion price* is the current value of the shares for which the bond may be exchanged. The *conversion premium* is the excess of the bond's value over the conversion price.

convexity. The property of curvature in the graph which expresses the rate of change in bond value in response to changes in the ***interest rate***; higher ***coupon bonds*** have greater convexity than lower or ***zero-coupon bonds*** of the same duration.

corporate bonds. Long-term debt issued by private corporations typically paying semiannual coupons and returning the ***face value*** of the bond at maturity.

correlation coefficient. A statistic that scales the **covariance** to a value between minus one (perfect negative correlation) and plus one (perfect positive correlation).

cost-of-carry relationship. See ***spot-futures parity theorem***.

country selection. A type of active international management that measures the contribution to performance attributable to investing in the better-performing stock markets of the world.

coupon bond. Obligates the issuer to make interest payments called *coupon* payments over the life of the bond, then to repay the ***principal*** at maturity.

coupon rate. A bond's interest payments per dollar of ***par value***.

covariance. A measure of the degree to which returns on two ***risky assets*** move in tandem. A *positive* covariance means that asset returns move together. A *negative* covariance means they vary inversely.

covered call. A combination of selling a call on a stock together with buying the stock.

covered interest arbitrage relationship. See ***interest rate parity relationship***.

credit enhancement. Purchase of the financial guarantee of a large insurance company to raise funds.

cross-hedging. Hedging a position in one asset using futures on another commodity.

cumulative abnormal return (CAR). The total ***abnormal return*** for the period surrounding an announcement or the release of information.

currency selection. Asset allocation in which the investor chooses among investments denominated in different currencies.

current ratio. A ratio representing the ability of the firm to pay off its current liabilities by liquidating current assets (current assets/current liabilities).

days' receivables. See ***average collection period***.

dealer market. A market where traders specializing in particular commodities buy and sell assets for their own accounts. The OTC market is an example.

debenture, or **unsecured bond.** A bond not backed by specific ***collateral***.

dedication strategy. Refers to multiperiod ***cash flow matching***.

default premium. A differential in promised yield that compensates the investor for the risk inherent in purchasing a corporate bond that entails some risk of default.

deferred annuities. Tax-advantaged life insurance product. Deferred annuities offer deferral of taxes with the option of withdrawing one's funds in the form of a life annuity.

defined-benefit plans. Pension plans in which retirement benefits are set according to a fixed formula.

defined-contribution plans. Pension plans in which the corporation is committed to making contributions according to a fixed formula.

delta (of option). See ***hedge ratio (for an option)***.

delta-neutral. A position in options and the underlying stock that is insensitive to changes in the price of the stock.

demand shock. An event affecting the aggregate demand for goods and services, thereby influencing the state of the economy.

derivative asset, or **contingent claim.** Securities providing payoffs that depend on or are contingent on the values of other assets such as commodity prices, bond and stock prices, or market index values. Examples are futures and options.

derivative security. See ***primitive security***.

desk trader. Representatives of securities firms who are limited to executing trades on behalf of clients of the firms; they may not trade for their firms accounts.

direct search market. A market in which buyers and sellers seek each other directly and transact directly.

disclosure. The requirement by securities and accounting bodies of fairness and truthfulness in information presented.

discretionary account. An account of a customer who gives a broker the authority to make buy-and-sell decisions on the customer's behalf.

diversifiable risk. Risk attributable to ***firm-specific risk***, or non-market risk. ***Nondiversifiable risk*** refers to ***systematic*** or ***market risk***.

diversification. Spreading a portfolio over many investments to avoid excessive exposure to any one source of risk.

dividend discount model (DDM). A formula to estimate the intrinsic value of shares by calculating the present value of all expected future dividends.

dividend payout ratio. Percentage of earnings paid out as dividends.

dollar-cost averaging. A strategy for investing by which the same sum of money is invested at regular time intervals; as an alternative to buying the same number of shares, this results in lower average cost for the portfolio.

dollar-weighted rate of return. An average giving the internal rate of return on an investment.

Dow theory. A long-standing approach to forecasting stock market direction by identification of long-term trends; the Dow Jones Industrial and Transportation Averages were used by Charles Dow to identify and confirm underlying trends.

duration. A measure of the average life of a bond, defined as the weighted average of the times until each payment is made, with weights proportional to the present value of the payment.

dynamic hedging. Constant updating of hedge positions as market conditions change.

earnings management. The practice of using flexibility in accounting rules to manipulate the reported profitability of a firm.

earnings retention ratio. See ***plowback ratio***.

earnings yield. The ratio of earnings to price, E/P.

economic earnings. The real flow of cash that a firm could pay out forever in the absence of any change in the firm's productive capacity.

economic value added (EVA). The dollar value of a firm's return in excess of its opportunity cost measured by the ***spread*** between ***return on assets (ROA)*** and the opportunity cost of capital, times the capital invested in the firm.

effective annual yield. Annualized ***interest rate*** on a security computed using compound interest techniques.

effective duration. The proportional change in a bond price per unit change in market interest rates for bonds with embedded options.

efficient diversification. The organizing principle of ***modern portfolio theory***, which maintains that any ***risk-averse*** investor will search for the highest ***expected return*** for any level of portfolio risk.

efficient frontier. Graph representing a set of portfolios that maximize ***expected return*** at each level of portfolio risk.

efficient market hypothesis (EMH). The prices of securities fully reflect available information. Investors buying securities in an efficient market should expect to obtain an equilibrium rate of return. *Weak-form* EMH asserts that stock prices already reflect all information contained in the history of past prices. The *semistrong-form* hypothesis asserts that stock prices already reflect all publicly available information. The *strong-form* hypothesis asserts that stock prices reflect all relevant information including insider information.

electronic communication network (ECN). A direct link between traders that avoids the formal ***exchanges*** and dealer markets.

endowment funds. Organizations chartered to invest money for specific purposes.

equities. See ***common stock***.

Eurodollars. US.-dollar-denominated deposits at foreign banks or foreign branches of American banks.

European option. A European option can be exercised only on the expiration date. See also ***American option***.

European, Australian, Far East (EAFE) index. A widely used index of non-U.S. stocks computed by Morgan Stanley.

event study. Research methodology designed to measure the impact of an event of interest on stock returns.

excess return. The difference between the actual rate of return on a ***risky asset*** and the ***risk-free rate***.

exchange rate risk. The uncertainty in asset returns due to movements in the ***exchange rates*** between the dollar and foreign currencies.

exchange. A national or regional auction market providing a facility for members to trade securities. A *seat* is a ***membership on an exchange.***

exchange rate. Price of a unit of one country's currency in terms of another country's currency.

exchange-traded funds (ETFs). Investment securities designed to represent an index or sub-index that are exchange-traded; an alternative to open- or ***closed-end mutual funds.***

exercise or **strike price.** Price set for calling (buying) an asset or putting (selling) an asset.

expectations hypothesis (of interest rates). Theory that ***forward interest rates*** are unbiased estimates of expected future interest rates.

expected return. The probability-weighted average of the possible outcomes.

expected return–beta relationship. Implication of the ***capital asset pricing model (CAPM)*** that security ***risk premiums*** (expected ***excess returns)*** will be proportional to ***beta***.

extendible bond. A bond that the holder may choose either to redeem for ***par value*** at maturity, or to extend for a given number of years; it is known as a put bond in the United States.

face value. See ***par value***.

factor model. A way of decomposing the factors that influence a security's rate of return into common and firm-specific influences.

factor portfolio. A ***well-diversified portfolio*** constructed to have a ***beta*** of 1.0 on one factor and a beta of zero on any other factor.

FIFO. The first-in, first-out accounting method of inventory valuation. See also ***LIFO***.

filter rule. A technical analysis technique stated as a rule for buying or selling stock according to past price movements.

financial assets. Claims to the income generated by real assets or claims on income from the government. See also ***real assets***.

financial engineering. Innovative security design and repackaging of investments.

financial intermediary. An institution such as a bank, ***mutual fund***, investment company, or insurance company that serves to connect the household and business sectors so households can invest and businesses can finance production.

financial investment. The investment of capital in financial instruments and asset, rather than in real, physical goods (real investment).

firm-specific risk. Risk peculiar to an individual firm that is independent of ***market risk***.

first-pass regression. A time series regression to estimate the ***betas*** of securities or portfolios.

fiscal policy. The use of taxes and government spending to affect aggregate demand as well as other objectives of macroeconomic policy.

fixed annuities. Annuity contracts in which the insurance company pays a fixed dollar amount of money per period.

fixed-income security. A security such as a bond that pays a specified cash flow over a specific period.

flight to quality. Describes the tendency of investors to require larger default premiums on investments under uncertain economic conditions.

float. Used to indicate the sale of new securities by firms to the public; the term also refers to the amount of stock available for public trading.

floating-rate bond. A bond whose ***interest rate*** is reset periodically according to a specified market rate.

floor broker. A member of the exchange who can execute orders for ***commission brokers***.

foreign exchange swap. The exchange of cash flows denominated in one currency for cash flows denominated in another currency, in order to manage the foreign exchange risk.

forward contract. An arrangement calling for future delivery of an asset at an agreed-upon price. Also see ***futures contract***.

forward interest rate. Rate of interest for a future period that would equate the total return of a long-term bond with that of a strategy of rolling over shorter-term bonds. The forward rate is inferred from the term structure.

fourth market. Direct trading in exchange-listed securities between one investor and another without the benefit of a broker.

fundamental analysis. Research to predict stock value that focuses on such determinants as earnings and dividends prospects, expectations for future ***interest rates***, and risk evaluation of the firm.

futures contract. Obliges traders to purchase or sell an asset at an agreed-upon price on a specified future date. The ***long position*** is held by the trader who commits to purchase. The ***short position*** is held by the trader who commits to sell. Futures differ from forward contracts in their standardization, exchange trading, ***margin*** requirements, and daily settling (marking to market).

futures option. The right to enter a specified ***futures contract*** at a ***futures price*** equal to the stipulated ***exercise price***.

futures price. The price at which a futures trader commits to make or take delivery of the underlying asset.

Global Industry Classification Standard (GICS). A classification of business sectors by industry grouping useful when building portfolios (replaces the U.S. government Standard Industry Classification—SIC).

globalization. Tendency toward a worldwide investment environment, and the ***integration*** of national capital markets.

growth company. A company for which the growth rate is greater than the market average due to superior opportunities for reinvestment.

guaranteed investment certificate. A fixed-term deposit with a trust company that pays interest and ***principal*** upon maturity and is nontransferable. See also ***certificate of deposit***.

hedge ratio (for a bond). The number of contracts held to offset a bond portfolio's risk.

hedge ratio (for an option). The number of stocks required to hedge against the price risk of holding one option. Also called the option's ***delta***.

hedging. Investing in an asset to reduce the overall risk of a portfolio.

holding period return. The rate of return over a given period.

homogenous expectations. The assumption that all investors use the same ***expected returns*** and ***covariance*** matrix of security returns as inputs in ***security analysis***.

horizon analysis. The forecasting of the realized compound yield over various holding periods or investment horizons.

illiquidity premium. Increase in the ***expected return*** of illiquid assets to compensate for their higher transaction costs.

immunization. A strategy that matches durations of assets and liabilities so as to make net worth unaffected by ***interest rate*** movements.

implied volatility. The ***standard deviation*** of stock returns that is consistent with an option's market value.

in the money. Said of an option whose exercise would produce profits. See ***also at the money*** and ***out of the money***.

income statement. A financial statement summarizing the profitability of the firm over a period of time, such as a year; revenues and expenses are listed and their difference is calculated as net income.

income trust. A pooled investment held in trust that generates high current income through distribution of income from assets held by a firm, often including non-taxable distributions of capital.

incomplete markets. Financial markets in which the number of available independent securities is less than the number of distinct future states of the world.

indenture. The document defining the contract between the bond issuer and the bondholder.

index arbitrage. An investment strategy that exploits divergences between actual ***futures prices*** and their theoretically correct parity values to make a profit.

index fund. A ***mutual fund*** holding shares in proportion to their representation in a market index such as the S&P/TSX composite.

index model. A model of stock returns using a market index such as the S&P/TSX composite to represent common or ***systematic risk*** factors.

index option. A ***call option*** or ***put option*** based on a stock market index.

indexing. Holding a portfolio composed of the ***market portfolio*** in the case of equities (or a cellular bond portfolio).

indifference curve. A curve connecting all portfolios with the same utility according to their means and ***standard deviations***.

industry life cycle. The set of stages in the evolution of an industry from innovative development to maturity and decline, which define the expectable returns for member firms.

initial public offering. Stock issued to the public for the first time by a formerly privately owned company.

input list. The set of estimates of expected rates of return and ***covariances*** for the securities that will constitute portfolios forming the efficient frontier.

inside information. Non-public knowledge about a corporation possessed by corporate officers, major owners, or other individuals with privileged access to information about a firm.

insider transactions. Transactions by officers, directors, and major stockholders in their firm's securities; these transactions must be reported publicly at regular intervals.

insurance principle. The law of averages. The average outcome for many independent trials of an experiment will approach the expected value of the experiment.

insured defined-benefit pension. A firm sponsoring a pension plan enters into a contractual agreement by which an insurance company assumes all liability for the benefits accrued under the plan.

integrated. Said of financial markets in which all assets exhibit the same risk-return characteristics relative to some common factor or index. See also ***segmented***.

integration. See ***integrated***.

interest coverage ratio, or **times interest earned.** A financial leverage measure (EBIT divided by interest expense).

interest rate parity relationship. The spot-futures ***exchange rate*** relationship that prevails in well-functioning markets.

interest rate. The number of dollars earned per dollar invested per period.

interest rate parity theorem. An equation—which should hold in well-functioning financial markets—yielding the futures exchange rate as a function of the ***spot rate*** and the ***interest rates*** prevailing in the two countries.

interest rate swaps. A method to manage ***interest rate*** risk where parties trade the cash flows corresponding to different securities without actually exchanging securities directly.

intermarket spread swap. Switching from one segment of the bond market to another (from Treasuries to corporates, for example).

intrinsic value (of a firm). The present value of a firm's expected future net cash flows discounted by the required rate of return.

intrinsic value (of an option). Stock price minus ***exercise price***, or the profit that could be attained by immediate exercise of an in-the-money option.

intrinsic value (of a share of stock). The present value of a firm's expected future net cash flows discounted by the required rate of return less the market value of debt, then divided by the number of shares outstanding.

investment company. Firm managing funds for investors. An investment company may manage several ***mutual funds***.

investment dealers. Firms that specialize in the sale of new securities to the public, typically by ***underwriting*** the issue; they are known as investment bankers in the United States.

investment horizon. The planned liquidation date of an investment portfolio or part of it; it plays a role in the choice of assets.

investment-grade bond. Bond rated BBB and above or Baa and above. Lower-rated bonds are classified as speculative-grade or junk bonds.

Jensen's measure. The alpha of an investment.

junk bond. See ***speculative-grade bond***.

Law of One Price. The rule stipulating that securities or portfolios with equal returns under all circumstances must sell at equal prices to preclude ***arbitrage*** opportunities.

leading economic indicators. A collection of economic series shown to precede changes in overall economic activity; these include retail sales, financial, manufacturing, house sales measures, and the U.S. index.

leverage ratio. Measure of debt to total capitalization of a firm.

LIFO. The last-in, first-out accounting method of valuing inventories. See also ***FIFO***.

limit order. An order specifying a price at which an investor is willing to buy or sell a security.

limited liability. The fact that shareholders have no personal liability to the creditors of the corporation in the event of failure.

liquidation value. Net amount that could be realized by selling the assets of a firm after paying the debt.

liquidity preference theory. Theory that the forward rate exceeds expected future ***interest rates***.

liquidity. The ease with which an asset can be converted to cash.

liquidity premium. Forward rate minus expected future short ***interest rate***.

load. The fee charged as a commission for purchasing a ***mutual fund***.

load fund. A ***mutual fund*** with a sales commission, or load.

London Interbank Offered Rate (LIBOR). Rate that most creditworthy banks charge one another for large loans of ***Eurodollars*** in the London market.

long position, or **long hedge.** Protecting the future cost of a purchase by taking a long futures position to protect against changes in the price of the asset.

maintenance or variation margin. An established value below which a trader's ***margin*** cannot fall. Reaching the maintenance margin triggers a margin call.

managed funds. A generic term for funds under the administration of investment companies.

management expense ratio. The combination of operating expenses and other charges expressed as a ratio of total assets in a ***mutual fund***.

margin. Describes securities purchased with money borrowed from a broker. Current maximum margin is 50 percent.

market capitalization rate. The market-consensus estimate of the appropriate discount rate for a firm's cash flows.

market making. The act of receiving orders to buy and sell securities and dealing in those securities, thereby establishing market ***liquidity*** and a price for the securities.

market risk, or **systematic risk.** Risk attributable to common macroeconomic factors. See also ***firm-specific risk***.

market order. A buy or sell order to be executed immediately at current market prices.

market portfolio. The portfolio for which each security is held in proportion to its market value.

market price of risk. A measure of the extra return, or ***risk premium***, that investors demand to bear risk. The reward-to-risk ratio of the ***market portfolio***.

market timing. Asset allocation in which the investment in the market is increased if one forecasts that the market will outperform ***Treasury bills***.

market value–weighted index. An index of a group of securities computed by calculating a weighted average of the returns of each security in the index, with weights proportional to outstanding market value.

market-to-book-value ratio. Market price of a share divided by ***book value*** per share.

marking to market. The daily settlement of obligations on futures positions.

mean return. See ***expected return***.

mean-variance criterion. The selection of portfolios on the basis of the means and ***variances*** of their returns. The choice of the higher ***expected return*** portfolio for a given level of variance or the lower variance portfolio for a given expected return.

membership or **seat on an exchange.** A limited number of ***exchange*** positions that enable the holder to trade for the holder's own accounts and charge clients for the execution of trades for their accounts.

minimum-variance frontier. Graph of the lowest possible portfolio ***variance*** that is attainable for a given portfolio ***expected return***.

minimum-variance portfolio. The portfolio of risk assets with lowest ***variance***.

modern portfolio theory (MPT). Principles underlying analysis and evaluation of rational portfolio choices on the basis of ***risk-return tradeoffs*** and ***efficient diversification***.

modified duration. Macaulay's duration divided by (1 + Yield to maturity). Measures interest rate sensitivity of the ***bond***.

monetary policy. The manipulation of the money supply to influence economic activity and the level of ***interest rates***.

money market. Includes short-term, highly liquid, and relatively low-risk debt instruments.

mortality tables. Tables of probabilities that individuals of various ages will die within a year.

mortgage funds. Pools of investment capital used to invest directly in mortgages, usually managed by banks or trust companies.

mortgage-backed security. Ownership claim in a pool of mortgages or an obligation that is secured by such a pool. Also called a ***pass-through security***, because payments are passed along from the mortgage originator to the purchaser of the mortgage-backed security.

moving average. A rolling average of stock prices, based on a short, intermediate, or long period, serving as a reference point for the current price; displayed on a chart.

multifactor models. Models of stock returns that decompose the factors that affect the returns into more than one common influence, as well as a firm-specific influence.

mutual fund. A firm pooling and managing funds of investors.

mutual fund theorem. A result associated with the ***capital asset pricing model (CAPM)***, asserting that investors will choose to invest their entire risky portfolio in a market-index ***mutual fund***.

naked option writing. Writing an option without an offsetting stock position.

Nasdaq. The automated quotation system for the OTC market, showing current bid-asked prices for thousands of stocks.

neglected-firm effect. That investments in stock of less-well-known firms have generated ***abnormal returns***.

net asset value (NAV). The value per share or unit of an investment in a pool of investments, determined as assets minus liabilities divided by the number of shares outstanding.

nominal interest rate. The ***interest rate*** in terms of nominal (not adjusted for purchasing power) dollars.

nondiversifiable risk. See ***systematic risk***.

nonsystematic risk. Non-market or ***firm-specific risk*** factors that can be eliminated by diversification. Also called ***unique risk*** or ***diversifiable risk***. ***Systematic risk*** refers to risk factors common to the entire economy.

normal backwardation theory. Holds that the ***futures price*** will be bid down to a level below the expected spot price.

normal distribution. A statistical distribution that has these properties: (1) it is symmetric and completely described by two parameters, its mean and standard deviation; (2) a weighted average of variables that are normally distributed will also be normally distributed. Can be applied to stock returns.

notional principal. An indicator of the size of an ***interest rate swap***, the amount of money that ***interest rates*** are multiplied with in order to determine the size of the cash flows that are being exchanged.

odd-lot theory. Assessment of market tops and bottoms by observation of the net buying and selling of odd-lots (shares sold in less than round or ***board lots***); used as a contrarian measure so that odd-lot buying suggests a top.

on the run. Recently issued ***bond***, selling at or near ***par value***.

open interest. The number of ***futures contracts*** outstanding.

open-end (mutual) fund. A fund that issues or redeems its own shares at their ***net asset value (NAV)***.

optimal risky portfolio. An investor's best combination of ***risky assets*** to be mixed with safe assets to form the complete portfolio.

option elasticity. The percentage increase in an option's value given a 1 percent change in the value of the underlying security.

original issue discount bond. A bond issued with a low ***coupon rate*** that sells at a discount from ***par value***.

out of the money. Said of an option whose exercise would not be profitable. See also ***in the money*** and ***at the money***.

over-the-counter market. An informal network of brokers and dealers who negotiate sales of securities (not a formal ***exchange***).

P/E effect. That portfolios of low P/E stocks have exhibited higher average risk-adjusted returns than high P/E stocks.

par value. The ***face value*** of the bond.

passive investment strategy. See ***passive management***.

passive management. Buying a ***well-diversified portfolio*** to represent a broad-based market index without attempting to search out mispriced securities.

passive portfolio. A market index portfolio.

passive strategy. See ***passive management***.

pass-through. A pool of loans (such as mortgages) sold in a package, and entitling the owner to receive all ***principal*** and interest payments made by the borrowers.

pass-through security. Pools of loans (such as home mortgage loans) sold in one package. Owners of pass-throughs receive all ***principal*** and interest payments made by the borrowers.

personal trust. An interest in an asset held by a trustee for the benefit of another person.

plowback or **earnings retention ratio.** The proportion of the firm's earnings reinvested in the business (and not paid out as dividends). The plowback ratio equals 1 minus the ***dividend payout ratio***.

point and figure chart. A ***technical analysis*** tool recording runs of price rises and falls with X's and O's.

political risk. Possibility of the expropriation of assets, changes in tax policy, restrictions on the exchange of foreign currency for domestic currency, or other changes in the business climate of a country.

portfolio insurance. The practice of using options or ***dynamic hedging*** strategies to provide protection against investment losses while maintaining upside potential.

portfolio management. Process of combining securities in a portfolio tailored to the investor's preferences and needs, monitoring that portfolio, and evaluating its performance.

portfolio opportunity set. The possible ***expected return–standard deviation*** pairs of all portfolios that can be constructed from a given set of assets.

preferred stock. Non-voting shares in a corporation, paying a fixed or variable stream of dividends.

premium. The purchase price of an option.

price value of a basis point. The change in the value of a fixed-income asset resulting from a one-basis-point change in the asset's ***yield to maturity***.

price-earnings multiple. See ***price-earnings ratio***.

price-earnings ratio. The ratio of a stock's price to its earnings per share. Also referred to as the *P/E multiple*.

price-weighted average. Computed by adding the prices of 30 companies and dividing by the divisor.

primary market. A market in which issues of securities are offered to the public.

primitive security, or **derivative security.** A *primitive security* is an instrument such as a stock or bond for which payments depend only on the financial status of its issuer. A *derivative security* is created from the set of primitive securities to yield returns that depend on factors beyond the characteristics of the issuer and that may be related to prices of other assets.

principal. The outstanding balance on a loan.

private placement. See ***public offering***.

profit margin (return on sales). Profit percentage defined as EBIT divided by total sales.

program trading. Coordinated buy orders and sell orders of entire portfolios, usually with the aid of computers, and often to achieve index ***arbitrage*** objectives.

prospectus. A final and approved ***registration statement*** including the price at which a security issue is offered.

protective put. Purchase of stock combined with a ***put option*** that guarantees minimum proceeds equal to the put's ***exercise price***.

proxy. An instrument empowering an agent to vote in the name of a shareholder.

prudent person. A phrase implying the conduct of conservative investment practices by professional and institutional investors when managing others' funds.

pseudo-American call option value. The maximum of the value derived by assuming that the option will be held until expiration and the value derived by assuming that the option will be exercised just before an ex-dividend date.

public offering or **private placement.** A *public offering* consists of bonds sold in the primary market to the general public; a *private placement* is sold directly to a limited number of institutional investors.

pure yield curve. A curve that shows the ***spot rates***, the yields on ***zero-coupon bonds***, as functions of the maturities of those bonds.

pure yield pickup swap. Moving to higher-yield bonds.

put option. The right to sell an asset at a specified ***exercise price*** on or before a specified expiration date.

put/call ratio. The ratio of outstanding ***put options*** to outstanding ***call options***, used as an indicator of market sentiment.

put-call parity theorem. An equation representing the proper relationship between put and call prices. Violation of parity allows ***arbitrage*** opportunities.

quality of earnings. The extent to which one can expect the reported level of a firm's earnings to be continued.

quick ratio. A measure of ***liquidity*** similar to the ***current ratio*** except for exclusion of inventories (cash plus receivables divided by current liabilities).

random walk. The notion that stock price changes are random and unpredictable.

rate anticipation swap. A switch made in response to forecasts of ***interest rates***.

real assets. Land, buildings, and equipment used to produce goods and services. See also ***financial assets***.

real estate limited partnership. A pool of funds that uses leverage to purchase real estate, and hence must be structured as a partnership rather than a ***mutual fund***.

real interest rate. The excess of the ***interest rate*** over the inflation rate. The growth rate of purchasing power derived from an investment.

real investment. The investment of capital in physical goods, such as equipment or plant, resulting in expansion of the productive base of the economy.

rebalancing. Realigning the proportion of assets in a portfolio as needed.

registered trader. A trader who makes a market in the shares of one or more firms and who maintains a "fair and orderly market" by dealing personally in the stock; known as *specialists* in the United States.

registration statement. A document required to be filed with the SEC to describe the issue of a new security.

regression equation. An equation that describes the average relationship between a dependent variable and a set of explanatory variables.

REIT. Real estate investment trust, which is similar to a closed-end ***mutual fund***. REITs invest in real estate or loans secured by real estate and issue shares in such investments.

relative strength. The ratio of an individual stock price to a price index for the relevant industry; a technical indicator of the out- or underperformance of a company relative to the industry or market.

replacement cost. Cost to replace a firm's assets. "Reproduction" cost.

repo (RP). See ***repurchase agreements***.

repurchase agreements (repos or **RPs).** Short-term, often overnight, sales of government securities with an agreement to repurchase the securities at a slightly higher price. A *reverse repo* is a purchase with an agreement to resell at a specified price on a future date.

residual income. See ***economic value added (EVA)***.

residuals. Parts of stock returns not explained by the explanatory variable (the market-index return). They measure the impact of firm-specific events during a particular period.

resistance level. A price level above which it is supposedly difficult for a stock or stock index to rise.

restricted shares. A special type of shares that have no voting rights, or only limited voting rights, but otherwise participate fully in the financial benefits of share ownership.

retractable bond. A bond that gives the right to the holder to redeem early at ***par value***, instead of holding it till maturity date.

return on assets (ROA). A profitability ratio; earnings before interest and taxes divided by total assets.

return on equity (ROE). An accounting ratio of net profits divided by equity.

return on sales. See ***profit margin***.

reversing trade. Entering the opposite side of a currently held futures position to close out the position.

reward-to-variability ratio. The excess ***expected return*** of a portfolio over the riskless rate of interest, divided by the ***standard deviation*** of the portfolio return.

reward-to-volatility ratio. Ratio of ***excess return*** to portfolio ***standard deviation***.

risk arbitrage. ***Speculation*** on perceived mispriced securities, usually in connection with merger and acquisition targets.

risk aversion. The preference of investors for assets with certain returns over assets with risky returns whose expectation is equal to the certain return.

risk lover. See ***risk-averse***.

risk premium. An ***expected return*** in excess of that on risk-free securities. The premium provides compensation for the risk of an investment.

risk-averse, risk-neutral, risk-lover. A *risk-averse* investor will consider risky portfolios only if they provide compensation for risk via a ***risk premium***. A *risk-neutral* investor finds the level of risk irrelevant and considers only the ***expected return*** of risk prospects. A *risk-lover* is willing to accept lower ***expected returns*** on prospects with higher amounts of risk.

risk-free asset. An asset with a certain rate of return; often taken to be short-term ***Treasury bills***.

risk-free rate. The ***interest rate*** that can be earned with certainty.

risk-lover. See ***risk-averse***.

risk-neutral. See ***risk-averse***.

risk-return tradeoff. If an investor is willing to take on risk, there is the reward of higher ***expected returns***.

risky asset. An asset with an uncertain rate of return.

scatter diagram. A plot of the observed values of the dependent variable versus those of the independent variable of a regression equation.

seasoned new issue. Stock issued by companies that already have stock on the market.

seat. See ***membership on an exchange***.

secondary market. Already-existing securities are bought and sold on the exchanges or in the OTC market.

secondary offering. Sale of a security by the issuer in the secondary market, so that a market price has been established; in Canada, a second issue which raises new funds for real investment is also classified as secondary.

second-pass regression. A cross-sectional regression of portfolio returns on ***betas***. The estimated slope is the measurement of the reward for bearing ***systematic risk*** during the period.

sector rotation. ***Rebalancing*** of a portfolio to emphasize economic sectors expected to outperform the market index.

securitization. Pooling loans for various purposes into standardized securities backed by those loans, which can then be traded like any other security.

security analysis. Determining the correct value of a security in the marketplace.

security characteristic line. A plot of the expected ***excess return*** on a security over the ***risk-free rate*** as a function of the excess return on the market.

security market line. Graphical representation of the ***expected return–beta relationship*** of the ***capital asset pricing model (CAPM)***.

segmentation. See ***segmented***.

segmented. Said of financial markets that are relatively independent of one another, and respond differently to the same factors. See also ***integrated***.

segregated funds. ***Mutual funds*** (usually issued by insurance companies) with an attached guarantee for a minimum payment.

selectivity. The ability to select individual stocks that will perform well in particular economic climates.

semistrong-form EMH. See ***efficient market hypothesis***.

separation property. The property that portfolio choice can be separated into two independent tasks: (1) determination of the optimal risky portfolio, which is a purely technical problem and (2) the personal choice of the best mix of the risky portfolio and the ***risk-free asset***.

serial bond issue. An issue of bonds with staggered maturity dates that spreads out the ***principal*** repayment burden over time.

settlement date. The date at which capital gains are recognized for tax purposes; usually five business days after the actual trade date.

Sharpe's measure. ***Reward-to-volatility ratio***; ratio of portfolio ***excess return*** to ***standard deviation***.

shelf registration. Advance registration of securities with the SEC for sale up to two years following initial registration.

short hedge. See ***short position***.

short interest. The total number of shares of stock held short in the market; considered ***bullish*** in that short holdings must be covered by purchases (latent demand), but ***bearish*** in that sophisticated traders (who are more likely to short) predict better.

short interest rate. A one-period ***interest rate***.

short position, or **short hedge.** Protecting the value of an asset held by taking a short position in a ***futures contract***.

short sale. The sale of shares not owned by the investor but borrowed through a broker and later repurchased to replace the loan. Profit comes from initial sale at a higher price than the repurchase price.

simple prospect. An investment opportunity in which a certain initial wealth is placed at risk and only two outcomes are possible.

single-country fund. A ***mutual fund*** that invests solely in the securities of a single country.

single-factor model. The model of security returns that acknowledges only one common factor. See ***factor model***.

single-index model. A model of stock returns that decomposes influences on returns into a systematic factor, as measured by the return on a broad market index, and firm-specific factors.

sinking fund. A procedure that allows for the repayment of ***principal*** at maturity by calling for the bond issuer to repurchase some proportion of the outstanding bonds either in the open market or at a special call price associated with the sinking fund provision.

skip-day settlement. A convention for calculating yield that assumes a ***Treasury bill*** sale is not settled until two days after quotation of the ***Treasury bill*** price.

small-firm effect. That investments in stocks of small firms appear to have earned ***abnormal returns***.

soft dollars. The value of research services that brokerage houses supply to investment managers "free of charge" in exchange for the investment manager's business.

speculation. Undertaking a risky investment with the objective of earning a positive profit compared with investment in a risk-free alternative (a ***risk premium***).

speculative-grade bond. Bond rated Ba or lower by Moody's, or BB or lower by Standard & Poor's, or an unrated bond.

split share. An equity security derived from a common share by splitting it into income and capital shares which return respectively, the original investment plus a stream of dividends and the capital gain portion since the time of splitting.

spot-futures parity theorem, or **cost-of-carry relationship.** Describes the theoretically correct relationship between spot and ***futures prices***. Violation of the parity relationship gives rise to ***arbitrage*** opportunities.

spot prices. Current, as opposed to future, prices of commodities, shares, currencies, etc.

spot rate. The current ***interest rate*** appropriate for discounting a cash flow of some given maturity.

spread (futures). Taking a ***long position*** in a ***futures contract*** of one maturity and a ***short position*** in a contract of different maturity, both on the same commodity.

spread (options). A combination of two or more ***call options*** or ***put options*** on the same stock with differing ***exercise prices*** or times to expiration. A *vertical* or *money spread* refers to a spread with different exercise price; a *horizontal* or *time spread* refers to differing expiration date.

standard deviation. Square root of the ***variance***.

statement of changes in financial position. A listing of the sources and uses of funds through operations, financing, and investments; over the specific time period, the net addition to the cash position is determined.

stock exchanges. Secondary markets where already issued securities are bought and sold by members.

stock selection. An active ***portfolio management*** technique that focuses on advantageous selection of particular stocks rather than on broad asset allocation choices.

stock split. Issue by a corporation of a given number of shares in exchange for the current number of shares held by stockholders. Splits may go in either direction, either increasing or decreasing the number of shares outstanding. A *reverse split* decreases the number outstanding.

straddle. A combination of buying both a call and a put, each with the same ***exercise price*** and expiration date. The purpose is to profit from expected volatility in either direction.

strap, strip. Variants of a straddle. A *strip* is two puts and one call on a stock; a *strap* is two calls and one put, both with the same ***exercise price*** and expiration date.

street name. Describes securities held by a broker on behalf of a client but registered in the name of the firm.

strike price. See ***exercise price***.

strip. See ***strap***.

stripped of coupons. Describes the practice of some investment banks that sell "synthetic" ***zero-coupon bonds*** by marketing the rights to a single payment backed by a coupon-paying ***Treasury bond***.

strong-form EMH. See ***efficient market hypothesis***.

subordinated debentures. Unsecured bonds that have been made inferior as claims to higher-ranked borrowings of a firm.

subordination clause. A provision in a ***bond indenture*** that restricts the issuer's future borrowing by subordinating the new leaders' claims on the firm to those of the existing bondholders. Claims of ***subordinated*** or ***junior*** debtholders are not paid until the prior debt is paid.

substitution swap. Exchange of one bond for a bond with similar attributes but more attractively priced.

superficial loss rule. A tax regulation that prohibits the recognition of capital losses if a security is purchased within 30 days of its sale.

superficial loss rule. The deferral of capital losses incurred on investments which are repurchased within 30 days of a sale at less than the original purchase price.

supply shock. An event affecting the aggregate supply of goods and services, thereby influencing the state of the economy.

support level. A price level below which it is supposedly difficult for a stock or stock index to fall.

survivorship bias. An upward bias to measured returns of a group of ***mutual funds*** that stems from the fact that failed funds are automatically excluded from the group.

swaps. Arrangements between firms to exchange the payments associated with debt contracts (made with other parties), without actually exchanging the underlying contract.

swing fund management. The practice of active ***portfolio management*** through the switching of weights for asset classes in response to predictions of economic changes.

systematic risk. Risk factors common to the whole economy, for example ***nondiversifiable risk***; see ***market risk***.

tactical asset allocation. Active ***portfolio management*** achieved by the use of options and derivatives to alter the response of asset classes to economic changes; rapid and cost-effective changes to asset class sensitivity are produced by computer analysis.

tax-deferral option. The feature of the U.S. Internal Revenue Code that the capital gains tax on an asset is payable only when the gain is realized by selling the asset.

tax-deferred retirement plans. Employer-sponsored and other plans that allow contributions and earnings to be made and accumulate tax free until they are paid out as benefits.

tax shelters. Investment opportunities whereby most, if not all, of the investment can be deducted from ordinary income for tax purposes over a year's horizon.

tax swap. Swapping two similar bonds to receive a tax benefit.

technical analysis. Research to identify mispriced securities that focuses on recurrent and predictable stock price patterns and on ***proxies*** for buy or sell pressure in the market.

term insurance. Provides a death benefit only, no buildup of cash value.

term premiums. Excess of the yields to maturity on long-term bonds over those of short-term bonds.

term structure of interest rates. The pattern of ***interest rates*** appropriate for discounting cash flows of various maturities.

thin trading. Persistently infrequent trading, including long intervals without any recorded transactions, for a given security.

third market. Trading of ***exchange***-listed securities on the OTC market.

time value (of an option). The part of the value of an option that is due to its positive time to expiration. Not to be confused with present value or the time value of money.

times interest earned. See ***interest coverage ratio***.

time-weighted rate of return. An average of the period-by-period ***holding period returns*** of an investment.

Tobin's *q*. Ratio of market value of the firm to ***replacement cost***.

tracking portfolio. A portfolio constructed to have returns with the highest possible correlation with a systematic risk factor.

tranche. See ***collateralized mortgage obligation***.

Treasury bill (T-bill). Short-term, highly liquid government securities issued at a discount from the ***face value*** and returning the face amount at maturity.

Treasury bond or **note.** Debt obligations of the U.S. federal government that make semiannual coupon payments and are sold at or near ***par value*** in denominations of $1,000 or more.

Treynor's measure. Ratio of ***excess return*** to ***beta***.

trin statistic. The ratio of the number of advancing to declining stocks divided by the ratio of volume in advancing versus declining stocks; a technical indicator of market strength that is ***bullish*** when the value is less than one.

triple witching hour. The four times a year that the S&P 500 ***futures contract*** expires at the same time as the S&P 100 ***index option*** contract and option contracts on individual stocks.

turnover. The ratio of trading activity in a portfolio to the assets of the portfolio.

unbundling. See ***bundling***.

underwriting, or **underwriting syndicate.** Underwriters (investment bankers) purchase securities from the issuing company and resell them. Usually a syndicate of investment bankers is organized behind a lead firm.

unique risk. See ***diversifiable risk***.

universal life policy. An insurance policy that allows for a varying death benefit and premium level over the term of the policy, with an ***interest rate*** on the cash value that changes with market interest rates.

unsecured bond. See ***debenture***.

utility. The measure of the welfare or satisfaction of an investor.

utility value. The welfare a given investor assigns to an investment with a certain return and risk.

value at risk. A risk measure that highlights the potential loss from extreme negative returns; another name for the quantile of a distribution. Abbreviated *Va*R.

VaR. See ***value at risk***.

variable annuities. Annuity contracts in which the insurance company pays a periodic amount linked to the investment performance of an underlying portfolio.

variable life policy. An insurance policy that provides a fixed death benefit plus a cash value that can be invested in a variety of funds from which the policyholder can choose.

variable rate mortgage. A conventional mortgage loan with interest payment varying in response to market rates.

variance. A measure of the dispersion of a random variable. Equals the expected value of the squared deviation from the mean.

variation margin. See ***maintenance margin***.

volatility risk. The risk of a portfolio containing options that arises from unpredictable changes in the volatility of the underlying asset.

warrant. An option issued by the firm to purchase shares of the firm's stock.

weak-form EMH. See ***efficient market hypothesis***.

well-diversified portfolio. A portfolio spread out over many securities in such a way that the weight in any one security is close to zero.

whole-life insurance policy. An insurance policy that provides a death benefit and a kind of savings plan that builds up cash value for possible future withdrawal.

workout period. Realignment period of a temporary misaligned yield relationship.

writing a call. Selling a ***call option***.

yield curve. A graph of ***yield to maturity*** as a function of time to maturity.

yield to maturity. A measure of the average rate of return that will be earned on a bond if held to maturity.

zero-beta portfolio. The ***minimum-variance portfolio*** uncorrelated with a chosen efficient portfolio.

zero-coupon bond (zero). A bond paying no coupons that sells at a discount and provides payment of the ***principal*** only at maturity.

NAME INDEX

A

Acker, Brian, 529
Ackert, L., 340n
Admati, A.R., 808
Aharony, J., 91n
Alexander, Craig, 523
Alexander, Gordon J., 884n, 885
Alexander, Sidney, 336
Altman, Edward, 416
Amihud, Yakov, 267, 268, 269n, 272, 341
Appelt, Tim, 395n
Arbel, Avner, 341
Assoe, K., 339n
Astle, Tom, 19
Athanassakos, G., 336n, 340n
Auger, Robert, 871

B

Baesel, Jerome, 91, 343
Baldwin, Warren, 34
Baltazar, Raman, 333n
Banz, Rolf, 339
Barber, Brad, 346
Barberis, Nicholas, 345n
Barnes, Martin, 523
Barnes, Tom, 415
Barone-Adesi, Giovanni, 340, 696n
Basu, Sanjoy, 338
Bavishi, Vinod, 596–597
Beebower, Gilbert, 798n, 829
Belisle, Geoffrey, 415
Benveniste, Lawrence, 64
Bergeron, M., 808n
Berges, Angel, 340
Bernard, Victor L., 575
Bernhard, Arnold, 630
Bernoulli, Daniel, 189–190
Bhabia, H., 333n
Bhattacharya, S., 808n
Bicksler, J., 301n
Bierwag, G.O., 483
Bishara, H., 120, 343, 808
Black, Fischer, 264, 311–312, 365, 369, 690, 695–696, 714, 830–831
Blake, Christopher R., 352
Blume, Marshall, 207, 336, 339, 632
Boabang, F., 66n
Bodie, Ziv, 134n, 667n
Bogle, Jack, 334
Bonsall, Matthew, 415n
Bonser-Neal, C., 862n
Booth, Lawrence D., 381n, 884
Bourgeois, J., 338n
Bowman, Melanie F., 614–615n
Brauer, G., 862n
Brealey, Richard A., 530n
Brennan, Michael J., 259, 597, 885
Brinson, Gary, 798n, 829
Brock, William, 625, 633n
Brockman, Paul, 597
Brown, David, 633
Brown, Lawrence D., 576
Brown, Marcia L., 784n
Brown, Stephen J., 385, 807
Buffet, Warren, 352
Byng, Tom, 415

C

Caldwell, Brendan, 529
Calvet, A. Louis, 120, 365, 380, 808
Campbell, John Y., 337, 379, 543
Carhart, Mark M., 351–352
Carlton, Colin G., 756n, 809
Carr, Richard C., 881
Carrick, Rob, 672n
Chen, Nai-Fu, 310, 373–374, 375
Cheng, Ben, 414, 415
Chevreau, Jonathan, 34
Chinery, Bill, 801n
Chopra, Navin, 337, 346n
Chordia, Tarun, 267
Chow, Jason, 612n
Chung, Richard, 66n
Clayman, Michelle, 586
Cleary, S., 336
Cohn, Richard, 534n
Conrad, Jennifer, 336
Constantinides, G., 345n
Cooper, Sherry, 539n
Cormier, Elise, 343
Coupland, Todd, 18
Cox, John C., 712n
Croft, Richard, 196n
Currier, Chet, 334
Curwood, B., 807

D

Damato, Karen, 212n
Daniel, Kent, 344, 378n
Das, S., 350n, 351
Davis, James L., 375, 376n, 377n
De Bondt, Werner F.M., 337, 345n, 346, 347
de Freitas, A., 880
De Long, J. Bradford, 348n
de Vassal, Vladimir, 334
Dhingra, H.L., 808
Dimson, E., 366
Dodd, David, 528
Donnelly, Barbara, 268n
Donville, Jason, 18
Dow, Charles, 613
Dresch, Stephen, 334

E

Easley, David, 632
Ebbers, Bernie, 64
Eckbo, B. Espen, 342
Edur, Oleu, 123n
Eleswrapu, Venkat, 267n
Elton, Edwin J., 311n, 350n, 351–352
Engle, Robert F., 378–379
Errunza, Vihang, 882n
Eun, Cheol S., 884n, 885

F

Fama, Eugene, 161n, 267, 268, 310–312, 336–338, 341, 342n, 343, 344, 349, 365, 369–370, 374, 375, 376n, 377n, 379, 382–383, 534n
Farmer, Patrick, 415
Fattouche, Michel, 18
Feldstein, Martin, 534n
Ferguson, Kathleen W., 801n
Ferson, Wayne, 371n
Fields-White, Monee, 461
Filatov, Victor S., 703
Fischer, Stanley, 540n
Fisher, Irving, 148
Foerster, S., 336n, 632, 859n
Folk, Levi, 414–415
Fooladi, I., 483
Foster, George, 91n, 574
Fowler, David J., 343, 365, 366n
French, Cameron, 68
French, Kenneth R., 161n, 310–312, 336–338, 341, 342n, 343, 344, 375, 376n, 377n, 379, 382–383
Friend, I., 207

G

Gagnon, Louis, 483n
Galler, M., 632n
Gauthier, James, 672
Geske, Robert, 696–697n
Givoly, D., 342, 576n
Goetzmann, William N., 119, 383, 385–386, 807
Gordon, Myron J., 508, 565
Gosh, A., 880n
Graham, Benjamin, 528–529
Granito, Barbara Donnelly, 703n
Grant, D., 808
Greenbaum, Gary, 212
Gross, Bill, 461
Grossman, Sanford J., 324, 781n
Gruber, Martin J., 311n, 350n, 351–352
Grubman, Jack, 64

H

Hadjiyannakis, S., 807n
Hallet, D., 414, 415
Halpern, Paul, 329n, 717, 807n
Hanrahan, Robert, 3442
Harris, M., 345n
Hartle, Thom, 614–615n
Harvey, Campbell, 371n
Hatch, J.E., 884
Hatch, James E., 819n
Haugen, Robert A., 337
Heinkel, Robert, 343
Henriksson, Roy D., 805
Hill, Chuck, 523
Hlavka, M., 350n, 351
Homer, Sidney, 460, 484
Hood, 829
Hulbert, Mark, 543n
Humbach, John, 334

I

Ibbotson, Roger G., 119, 385–386, 807n, 881
Ilkiw, John H., 809
Inglis, M., 336

J

Jacquier, Eric, 161n
Jaffe, Jeffrey F., 342, 344, 530n
Jaganathan, Ravi, 161n, 371
Janakiramanan, S., 884n, 885
Jarrow, Robert A., 345n, 746n
Jegadeesh, Narasimhan, 336, 352, 626, 632
Jennings, Robert H., 633
Jensen, Michael, 365, 369, 788
Jobson, J.D., 365n, 788n
Jog, Vijay, 40n, 66n, 336n, 340, 352, 365, 366n, 632n
Johnson, H.E., 697n
Johnson, Lewis D., 483n
Johnston, D.J., 884
Jones, C.P., 574
Jorion, Phillipe, 383, 885

K

Kahneman, D., 345, 347
Kalawsky, Keith, 19
Kan, R., 336n
Kandel, Schmuel, 367
Kane, Alex, 161n, 380, 837n
Kaplan, Robert S., 667n
Kaplin, Andy, 285n
Kaufman, G.C., 483n
Kaul, Gautam, 336
Kedrosky, Paulmuel, 628n
Keim, Donald B., 336n, 337, 339, 340
Kendall, Maurice, 322
Khoury, Nabil T., 148n, 808
Khoury, S., 880n
Kim, Tae-Hwan, 837n
Kirikos, G., 336n
Kirzner, Eric, 732n, 860n
Knight, Doug, 415
Kondratieff, 615–616
Kooli, M., 65n
Korajczyk, Robert, 371n
Korkie, R.M., 365n, 788n
Kothari, S.P., 341n

Kotlikoff, Laurence, 133n
Kraus, Alan, 343
Krishnan, Ramaswamy, 395n
Kryzanowski, Lawrence, 66n, 332, 374n, 416, 485n, 632n, 801n, 809
Kushner, Joseph, 342

L

L'Her, Jean-Francois, 576
La Porta, Raphael, 344
Lakonishok, Josef, 337, 344, 346n, 576n, 625, 633n
Lalancette, Simon, 801n, 809
Latane, H.A., 574
Lavalee, Marion Y., 416
Lavenstein, Roger, 479n
Lawson, William M., 349
LeBaron, Blake, 625, 633n
Lee, M.H., 343
Leeson, Nick, 13
Lefoll, J., 120, 365, 808
Lehman, Bruce, 632
Lel, U., 333n
Lepine, Vincent, 612
Lev, Baruch, 595
Levitt, Arthur, 88
Liebowitz, Martin L., 460, 484, 486
Lintner, John, 253, 364
Little, I.M.D., 528
Lo, Andrew W., 336
Londerville, J., 66n
Losq, Etienne, 882n
Loughran, T., 63n
Lussier, J., 338n
Lynch, Peter, 113, 335, 352, 518, 549

M

Macauley, Frederick, 462
MacBeth, James, 365, 369–370, 374
Macdonald, Don, 294n
MacKinlay, A. Craig, 336
Maksimovic, V., 345n
Malkiel, Burton G., 5, 120, 350, 460, 534n
Marcus, Alan J., 161n, 380
Markowitz, Harry, 196, 225–226, 253
Martel, J.M., 808
Mason, Scott, 567n
Masse, Isadore, 342
Matthews, Keith, 294
Mayers, David, 259, 371
Maynes, Elizabeth, 40n
Mazuy, Kay, 804
McConnell, John J., 340
McCullogh, J. Huston, 449n
McGough, Robert, 113n
McGrattan, Ellen R., 161n
McLeod, Guy, 148n
Meeker, Mary, 64
Mehra, Jarnish, 381
Mei, Jianping, 311n
Meier, Ron, 166
Mendelson, Haim, 267, 268, 269n, 272, 341
Merton, Robert C., 312, 540n, 567n, 667n, 690, 712n, 802, 805, 823–824, 827
Michalowski, Wojtek, 623n
Milken, Michael, 413
Miller, Merton, 272n, 364, 369, 530
Millham, Robert, 18
Mitchell, Mark, 332n
Mittoo, Usha R., 68n, 381n, 885
Modest, David, 757
Modigliani, Franco, 272n, 530, 534n, 543, 789
Modigliani, Leah, 789
Morgenstern, 190
Morin, Roger A., 364
Mossin, Jan, 253
Mossman, Charles, 597
Muelbroek, Lisa K., 91
Myers, Stewart C., 530n

N

Neff, John, 352
Nemiroff, Howard, 332
Netter, Jeffry, 332n
Newman, David, 34
Noh, Jaesun, 380

O

O'Hara, Maureen, 623
Odean, Terrance, 346, 347
Oldfield, George S., 746n
Olsen, Chris, 91n, 574
Olson, Dennis, 597
Osborn, John C., 809
Otuteye, E., 375
Ou, Jane A., 597

P

Pagan, Adrian, 378
Page, Sebastian, 829n
Palmon, Dan, 342
Parisien, Denis, 871
Parkhill, Rik, 68
Partch, M., 40n
Penman, Stephen H., 597
Perrakis, S., 716n
Pesando, James E., 134n
Pfleiderer, P., 808n
Pontiff, Jeffrey, 348
Porter, Doug, 612
Poterba, James M., 336n
Potvin, Paul, 206n
Pratt, Shannon, 267n
Prescott, Edward, 381
Press, Kevin, 5
Prihar, Anoop, 623
Pring, Martin, 611n

Q

Quattrone, Frank, 64

R

Rahman, Abdul, 380
Rakita, Ian, 66n
Ramaswamy, Krishna, 395n
Ready, M.J., 625
Redington, F.M., 477
Reinders, R., 859n
Reinganum, Marc R., 339, 340, 341
Richardson, Gordon, 576
Richardson, John, 18
Riding, Allan, 40n
Ritter, Jay R., 63n, 65n, 337, 340, 346n, 543
Roberts, Gordon, 483, 530n
Roberts, Harry, 336, 619–621
Robinson, Anthony W., 881
Robinson, Chris, 40n
Robinson, M.J., 365n
Roll, Richard, 154, 267, 310, 366, 367, 368n, 369, 371, 373–375, 696n, 880
Rom, Brian M., 801n
Rorke, C. Harvey, 343, 365, 366n
Rosenberg, David, 612
Ross, K., 74n
Ross, Stephen A., 301n, 310, 348, 367, 368n, 373–375, 385, 530n, 712n, 807n, 808n
Roth, John, 19
Rozeff, Michael, 576
Rubinstein, M., 717
Rumsey, John, 395n, 805n
Rydquist, K., 63n

S

Samuelson, Paul A., 185, 248–250, 352
Sanford, Jeff, 523n
Santos, Michael, 333n
Schatsky, Gary, 166
Scherbina, Anna, 161n
Schlarbaum, Gary G., 340
Schmitz, John, 623
Scholes, Myron, 364, 365, 366, 369, 690, 714
Schwartz, E., 885
Schwert, G. William, 378
Seyhun, H. Nejat, 342
Shanken, Jay, 341
Shapiro, J., 74n
Sharpe, William, 253, 290, 715n, 783, 788, 798
Shevlin, Terry, 91n, 574
Shiller, Robert, 337
Shliefer, Andrei, 344, 348n
Shoven, J.B., 134n
Siegel, Jeremy J., 88n
Singer, Brian, 798n
Sloan, Richard G., 341n
Smith, K., 74n
Solnik, Bruno, 860, 867, 880
Speidell, Lawrence S., 596–597
Spivak, Avia, 133n
Srivastava, Atul, 623n
Stambaugh, Robert F., 337, 339, 367
Stansky, Robert, 113
Statman, Moir, 347
Stein, Garry, 91, 343
Stein, Jeremy, 264
Stephens, Robertson, 64
Stiglitz, Joseph E., 324, 781n
Stoll, Hans R., 759
Strebel, Paul J., 341
Stulz, R., 345n
Subrahmanyam, Avanidhar, 267
Summers, Lawrence A., 336n, 348n
Sundaresan, Mahadevan, 757
Suret, Jean-Marc, 65n, 343, 576
Swary, I., 91n
Switzer, Lorne, 68n, 827n
Sy, O., 339n

T

Taylor, K., 807n
Taylor, Stephen J., 629n
Templeton, John, 352, 860
Thaler, Richard H., 337, 345n, 346, 347
Thomas, Jacob K., 575, 623n
Thomas, Roland, 623n
Thorfinnson, M., 859n
Tinic, Seha M., 340
Tirtiroglu, D., 333n
Titman, Sheridan, 336, 344, 352, 378n, 626
To, Minh Chau, 416, 809
Tobin, James, 506
Toevs, A., 483n
Train, John, 528n
Trepanier, David J., 62n
Treynor, Jack, 788, 805, 830–831
Trzcinka, Charles, 576
Turnbull, Stuart, 717
Tversky, A., 345, 347

U

Ursel, Nancy D., 62n

V

Vassalou, Maria, 378n
Vinik, Jeffrey, 113
Vishny, Robert W., 344, 348n
Von Neumann, 190
Vos, Wilfred, 801
Vuolteenaho, Tuomo, 379, 543

W

Waldman, Robert J., 348n
Wang, L., 66n
Warr, Richard S., 543
Wei, Jason, 732n
Weigel, Eric J., 809
Weinberger, Alfred, 486
West, Richard R., 340
Westerfield, Randolph W., 530n
Whaley, Robert E., 696n, 716, 759
Wheatley, S., 862n
Whipp, Rob, 34
White, Alan, 40n
White, Halbert, 837n
White, Robert W., 819n, 884
Whitelaw, Robert F., 380
Wilhelm, William, 64
Williams, J., 366
Wright, D.W., 623n

X

Xing, Yuhang, 378n

Y

Yardeni, Ed, 543

Z

Zaghloul, Hatim, 18
Ziemba, W.T., 336n, 345n
Zoghaib, Rana, 827n

INDEX

A

abnormal return, 326, 330
accounting, international conventions, 594–597
accounting earnings, 573
accounting information. *See* financial statements
accounts receivable to sales ratio, 582–583
accrued interest, 395
acid test ratio, 584
active portfolio, 832
active portfolio management, 207, 326–327, 458
  all-equity strategy, 802–804
  asset allocation. *See* asset allocation
  bonds, 484–488
  bonds swaps, 484
  contingent immunization, 138–139, 486–487
  horizon analysis, 486
  indexing, 458, 827–828
  intermarket spread swap, 484
  international investment, 853
  market timing, 802–804
  mean-variance portfolio theory, 783
  multifactor models, 851–852
  objective of, 781–786
  passive investment, vs., 784
  performance measure, 783–786
  portfolio mean and risk, 786
  pure yield pickup swap, 485
  rate anticipation swap, 485
  strategies, 207, 458
  substitution swap, 484
  tax swap, 486
adjustable-rate mortgage, 476
adjusted beta, 295–296
age, 10
agency problem, 16–21
agency theory, 20
AGF Management Ltd., 105
aggregate stock market, 541–542
Alcan Aluminum, 50, 68, 521–525, 859
alpha, 261, 836–837
alternate trading systems (ATS), 67
Amazon.com, 5
American Depository Receipts (ADRs), 22, 859
American Exchange, 648
American options, 643
American Stock Exchange, 46–48
AMEX. *See* American Stock Exchange
amortization, 569, 592
analysts' forecasts, 575–577
analysts, and agency problem, 16–21
analytics, 11
Angiotech Pharmaceuticals, 68
animal spirits, 322
announcement date, 233, 330
annual percentage rate (APR), 33, 36, 405
annuities, 102, 132–135, 467–468
appraisal ratio, 788, 791, 793, 794, 809
APT. *See* arbitrage pricing theory
arbitrage, 284, 743
  covered interest arbitrage relationship, 763
  index, 758–759
  opportunities, 301–303
  profits, 301–302
  program trading, 758–759
  proofs, 750
  risk, 302
  short-sale proceeds, 758
  zero investment portfolio, 301
arbitrage pricing theory, 284, 302
  betas, 304–306
  cost of capital, 311
  empirical evidence, 361–386
  and expected returns, 304–306
  international investment, 881–882
  multifactor, 308–309, 371–375
  security market line, 306–307
  and single assets, 307–308
  single-factor, 286
  well-diversified portfolios, 302–307
arbitrageur, 302
arithmetic averaging, 818–820
Asian
  flu, 854
  options, 671
asked price, 70, 76
asset, 569
  allocation. *See* asset allocation
  "call away", 50, 640
  expected return, 150, 170
  financial, 6
  income generating, 6
  and liability management, 476
  personal, 9
  plays, 548
  real, 6
  risk, 169
  risk-free, 198–199, 233–237
  risky, 195
  turnover, 580
  utilization ratios, 582–583
asset allocation
  baseline allocation, 828
  capital allocation decision. *See* capital
  decisions, 195, 844–845
  funds, 110
  international investment, 22, 878–881
  optimal risky portfolio, 217–221
  passive approach, 827
  risk tolerance, 203–206
  and security selection, 232–233
  tactical asset allocation models, 809
asset-backed bonds, 398
asset-return volatility, 378–381
Association for Investment Management and Research (AIMR), 100
assumed investment return, 133
ATI Technologies Inc., 68
attribution studies, 842
auction markets, 28, 67, 76, 79
auditors, 19–20
  and agency problems, 16–21
average collection period, 582–583

B

bad debt, 593
balance sheets, 6, 569–571
balanced funds, 110
bank, 10
bank deposits, 29
bank discount yield, 32–33
Bank of Canada, 8, 147, 537
Bank of Montreal, 61
Bankers Trust, 491
bankers' acceptances, 29
bankruptcy, 37, 504
Barclays Capital Group, 121
Barings Investment Bank, 13, 640
Barrick Gold, 50, 52, 68
barrier options, 672
baseline allocation, 828
basis, 740
bear CD, 671
bear market, 4
bearer
  bonds, 395
  deposit notes, 29, 198
behavioural finance, 345
Bell Canada Enterprises, 13
benchmark error, 367
benchmarks, 586
Berkshire Hathaway, 352
best-efforts underwriting agreement, 62
beta, 254, 258–259
  adjusted, 295–296
  estimates, 293–295
  estimating coefficients, 297
  and expected returns, 304–306
  measurement error in, 368–370
bid price, 70
bid-ask spreads, 66, 76, 85, 86
bills-plus-futures strategy, 755
binary options, 673
binomial model, 712
binomial option pricing, 707–714
Black-Scholes pricing formula, 690–707
  dividends, 695–696
  and hedge ratios, 697–699
  implied volatility, 694–695
  portfolio insurance, 699–702
block
  houses, 77
  sales, 77
  transactions, 66, 77
BMO Equity Index, 826
BMO Nesbitt Burns Inc., 61, 293, 294
board lots, 42
board of directors, 12, 19, 20
bogey, 842
Bombardier, 52
bond equivalent yield, 31, 36
bond floor, 664–665
bond indentures, 393, 417–419
  contract, 393
  dividend restrictions, 418
  double option, 418
  me-first rule, 418
  protective covenants, 417
  sinking funds, 417
  subordination clauses, 418
bond index funds, 474–475
bond index portfolio, 474
bond market, 393, 612
  indicators, 48
  innovation in, 398–399
bond pricing, 399–404
  after-tax returns, 411–412
  annuity factor, 400
  between coupon dates, 403–404
  convexity, 401, 459, 469–474
  coupon rates, 393, 459
  and duration, 465–469
  example, 400–404
  flat prices, 403–404
  holding-period return. *See* holding-period return
  interest rate sensitivity, 459–461
  invoice prices, 403–404
  over time, 408–412
  present value, 399–400, 462
  PV factor, 400
  quoted prices, 395
  sensitivity, 401–404
  and taxation, 411–412, 449–450
  term structure of interest rates, 431–434
  and yields, 404–408, 459
  zero-coupon bonds, 410–411
bond stripping, 434
bond swaps, 484
bonds, 5
  accrued interest, 395
  asset-backed, 398
  bearer, 395
  bid-asked spread, 66, 76, 85, 86
  bootstrapping, 448
  bulldog, 397
  call price, 395–396

call provisions, 395–386
callable, 33, 37, 396, 405–406, 472–473, 663–664
Canadian, 393–395
catastrophe, 398
characteristics, 393–399
collateral, 418–419
collateral trust, 418
convertible, 13, 37, 396, 664–666
convexity of, 469–474
corporate, 12, 36, 71, 395–396
coupon, 393, 434
current yield, 395, 405
debenture, 418
default premium, 419–420
default risk, 37, 412–421
default-free, 198
deferred callable, 396
detachable warrant, 666
duration, 462–469
effective annual yield, 405
equipment obligation, 418
Eurobonds, 16, 30, 397
Eurodollar, 30–31, 397
extendible, 37, 396
face value, 393
flight to quality, 420
floating-rate, 396–397
foreign, 397
futures, 731
Government of Canada, 33–36
high-yield, 412–417
historical record, 151–156
holding period return, 410
indexed, 398–399
international, 397
investment grade, 412
junk, 412–417
liquidity risk, 71
long-term deep discount, 13
mortgage, 418
municipal, 36
original issue discount, 410, 411
other issuers, 397
over-the-counter-market, 71
par value, 393, 449, 450
passive management, 474–483
pay-in-kind, 398
premium, 405, 406
pricing, 434
provincial, 36
public offering, 61–62
put, 396
rating, 412–418
real return, 146, 398
realized compound yield, 407–408
refunding, 396
registered, 395
retractable, 37, 396
reverse floaters, 398
risk structure of interest rates, 420
safety, 412, 414–417
Samurai, 397
secured, 36
speculative grade, 412
straight, 405, 406, 663–664
stripped, 13, 16, 410
unsecured, 37, 418
Yankee, 397, 474
yield to call, 405–406
yield to maturity, 36, 404–405, 407–408, 410
zero-coupon. *See* zero-coupon bonds
book, 76
book value, 504, 584
book-to-market effects, 337
book-to-market ratios, 341
bootstrapping, 448, 829
bottom line, 569
bought deal, 61
Box-Jenkins model, 576
BPI Corporate Bond Fund, 414, 415
Brane v. Roth, 655
Brascan, 505
breadth of market, 626
brokerage firms, 11, 67, 73, 77
brokered, 66
brokered market, 66
brokers' call loans, 30, 80
bubble, 3, 23
internet, 4–5
budget deficit, 536–537
bull CDs, 671
bull market, 4
bulldog bonds, 397
bullish spread, 659, 705
bundling, 14
business
cycle, 538–541, 542–549
risk, 155
sector, 8
buy-and-hold strategy, 827
See also passive investment strategy

C

call
options, 50, 53, 640–641
price, 395–396
protection, 406
swaption, 770
valuation. *See* option valuation
callable bonds, 33, 37, 396, 405–406, 472–473, 663–664
Canada Bonds, 33, 393–395, 541, 646
Canada Business Corporations Act, 88
Canada Deposit Insurance Corporation, 29
Canada Mortgage and Housing Corporation, 11–12, 38
Canada Pension Plan, 137
Canada Premium Bonds, 33
Canada Revenue Agency, 411
Canada Savings Bonds, 33
Canadian Bond Rating Service, 415–416
Canadian Dealer Network, 70
Canadian Deposit Insurance Corporation, 89
Canadian Derivatives Clearing Corporation, 645–646
Canadian Derivatives Exchange, 54, 67, 73, 645, 646–648, 700, 731, 763
Canadian Index Plus fund, 328
Canadian Institute of Chartered Accountants (CICA), 593
Canadian Investor Protection Fund, 89
Canadian Natural Resources Ltd., 68
Canadian Pacific, 61
Canadian Securities Administrators, 89
Canadian Securities Institute, 90
Canadian tax system, 129–131
Canadian Tire, 40–42
Canadian Unlisted Board, 70
Canadian Utilities, 42
Canadian Venture Exchange (CDNX), 67
candlestick chart, 617–618
capital, 2, 27
gains, 41, 104, 110, 112, 113, 130–131, 327–329
human, 9
losses, 130
market line, 206–207, 254, 255
markets, 2, 27
need for, 4–10
preservation of, 8
reputational, 11
capital allocation
decision, 195–197
line, 201, 254, 783
and separation property, 231–232
capital allocation decision, 194
capital asset pricing model, 252, 253–272
capital budgeting decisions, 263–264
dominance argument, 302
and efficient market hypothesis, 371
empirical evidence, 361–386
and equilibrium prices, 253, 283
expected return-beta relationship. *See* expected return-beta
expected returns, 256–260
extensions of, 262–267
international investment, 881–882
lifetime consumption, 267
and liquidity, 267–272
market portfolio. *See* market portfolio
multifactor, 258–260, 312–313, 371–375
passive strategy, 255
and performance measurement, 787–788
restricted borrowing, 262–265
security market line, 260–262
tests of, 364
zero-beta model, 262–265
capital cost allowance, 592
capital gain, 150
CAPM. *See* capital asset pricing model
cash cows, 512
cash delivery, 737
cash dividends, 643–644
cash equivalents, 27
cash flow approach, 529–531
cash flow matching, 482–483
cash settlement options, 53
cash-flow-to-debt ratio, 415
cash/bond selection, 878
catastrophe bonds, 398
CDNX. *See* Canadian Venture Exchange
cellular approach, 475
Central Limit Theorem, 157n
certainty equivalent rate, 165, 205
certificates of deposit, 29, 476, 669–671
chaos theory, 632, 829
Chartered Financial Analysts, 89
charting, 613–622, 633
candlestick chart, 617–618
congestion area, 617
data mining, 620
Dow theory, 613–615
Elliot wave theory, 615–616
Internet resources, 629
Kondratieff wave theory, 615–616
limitations, 619–622
point and figure chart, 616
pure trend analysis, 616
Superbowl rule, 620–622
chartists, 325, 613
Chicago Board of Trade, 737
Chicago Board Options Exchange, 639, 700
Chicago Mercantile Exchange, 759
CIBC Canadian Index Fund, 111
CIBC World Markets Inc., 18
circuit breakers, 90–91, 737
Cisco Systems, 3
clearinghouse, 78, 733–734
closed-end funds, 105–106, 861
closely-held corporation, 40
closet indexers, 329
CNBC, 3
coefficient of determination, 294
collar, 90, 660, 769
collateral, 418–419
collateralized loans, 667–669
collateralized mortgage obligation, 12n, 491
College Retirement Equity Fund, 632
commensurate gain, 163
commercial paper, 29, 198
commingled funds, 106
commission broker, 73
commissions, 42, 71, 84, 87, 111, 117, 737
commodities. *See* futures
Commodities Futures Trading Commission, 89, 737
commodity trading, 629
See also futures
common stocks, 39–40
limited liability, 39
residual claim, 40
comparison universe, 787
competition, 323–324
competitive bids, 28
complete markets, 715
complete portfolio, 196
compound leverage factor, 581
compounding, 181–183, 802
COMPUSTAT, 504
conditional variance, 379
confidence index, 623

conservatism, 346
considerable risk, 163
consolidation, 879
constant growth DDM, 508–509, 565–566
Constat Capital Sciences, 113
consumer price index, 146
contango, 752
contingent claims, 50, 567, 639
See also derivatives
contingent immunization, 138–139, 486–487
contingent liabilities, 504
continuous compounding, 181–183
contrarian investment strategy, 337
contributed surplus, 571
convergence property, 735
conversion premium, 396
conversion ratios, 396
convertible bonds, 13, 37, 396, 664–666
convertible securities, 664–666
convexity, 479–474
corporate
bonds, 12, 36, 71, 395–396, 412
finance, 529–531
correlation coefficient, 173, 210–211, 212, 215–216
cost of capital and arbitrage pricing theory, 311
cost of goods sold, 569
cost-of-carry relationship, 743
costs
liquidation, 269–271
mutual funds, 115–117
storage, 746–748
country selection, 878
coupon bonds, 434
covariance, 172, 210
covariance matrix, 223–224
coverage ratios, 414, 583–584
covered call, 655–657
covered interest arbitrage relationship, 763
covering the short position, 82
crash of October 1987, 3, 186, 701–702
credit risk, 766
credit union, 10
Criminal Code of Canada, 88
cross-hedgings, 740, 841
cross-holdings, 869–870
CTUCS, 113
cumulative abnormal return, 331–333
currency selection, 878
currency-translated options, 673
current account, 537
current ratio, 414, 583–584
cyclical industries, 538
cyclicals, 548

D

Daimler-Benz AG, 594
data mining, 344–345, 620
David Bowie bonds, 398
DAX, 48
days receivables, 582–583
dealer, 66, 78–79
dealer markets, 66, 78–79
Deans Knight Capital Management Ltd., 415
debentures, 36
dedication strategy, 482–483
default premium, 419–420
default risk, 37, 164, 412–421
defensive industries, 538
deferred annuities, 132–134
defined benefit pension plans, 101, 137–139
defined contribution pension plans, 101, 137–139
Dell Computers, 3, 17
delta, 697, 702
delta-hedging, 703
delta-neutral, 706
demand shock, 537
deposits. *See* bank deposits
depreciation, 504, 507, 569, 573, 592–593, 879
derivative assets, 50
derivative markets, 50–54, 73
contingent claims, 50, 639
derivative assets, 50
futures contracts, 52
options, 50–54
swaps, 12, 54
warrants, 54, 666
derivative zeros, 13
derivatives. *See also* derivative markets
futures. *See* futures
interest rate, 12, 490–491
issuance, 12
markets, 50–54
mortgage, 491
options. *See* options
and risk management, 13, 655
role of, 12
securities, 12
trading, 731
desk traders, 77
detachable warrant, 666
Deutsche Bourse, 69
direct search market, 66
directors. *See* board of directors
disclosure, 8, 17, 19
discount brokerage houses, 71, 84
discount brokers, 11, 71, 84
discounted cash flow analysis, 749–751
discretionary account, 84
discriminant analysis, 416–417
diversifiable risk, 208, 291
diversification, 22, 169
effect of, 246–248
and index models, 290–292
international, 853, 854–862
investment, 164
market risk, 208
and portfolio risk, 169, 195–197, 207–209
power, 246–248
dividend discount model, 504, 508–516
constant growth DDM, 508–509, 565–566
derivation of, 564–565
Gordon model, 508–509, 565
life cycles, 512–516
multistage growth models, 512–516
and price-earnings ratio, 525–526
stock prices, 564, 565
dividend payout ratio, 510
dividend yield, 150
dividends, 42
cash, 643
cumulative, 42
and option valuation, 686, 688–689, 695–696
restrictions, 418
stock, 643–644
taxation of, 22
DJ Canada 40 index, 44–45
dollar-cost averaging, 817
dollar-weighted returns, 817–818
dominance argument, 302
Dominion Bond Rating Service, 412
Dow, 3
Dow Jones & Company, 46
Dow Jones Industrial Average, 43, 45–46, 53, 90, 613, 614, 615, 826
Dow Jones Transportation Average, 613, 615
Dow theory, 613–615, 631–633
downtick, 77
Drexel Burnham Lambert, 413–414
Du Pont system, 580n
Dun & Bradstreet, 588
duration, 462–469
modified, 464
dynamic hedging, 701

E

e-brokers, 86
earnings, 516–526
accounting, 573–577
announcement date, 574
economic, 593
forecast errors, 574
forecasts, 541–542
per share, 666
and price-earning ratio, 592
quality of, 593–594
standardized unexpected, 574–576
yield, 541–542, 586
earnings retention ratio, 510
economic shocks, 534
economic system, sectors, 7–8
economic value added, 588–589
economies of scale, 11
effective annual yield, 32, 405
effective duration, 473
effects. *See* market anomalies
efficiency. *See* market efficiency
efficient frontier, 222–223, 226, 227–231
efficient market. *See* efficient market hypothesis; market efficiency
efficient market hypothesis
active vs. passive portfolio management, 326–327
and capital asset pricing model, 371
competition, 323–324
event studies, 329–333
financial statement analysis, 596
fundamental analysis, 326
and mutual fund performance, 349–352
portfolio management role, 327–329
and random walks. 323–327
semistrong-form, 324
strong-form, 325
technical analysis, 325–326, 610, 611
versions of, 324–327
weak-form, 324–327
electronic communication networks (ECNs), 67–68, 71–72, 87, 88
Elliot wave theory, 615–616
endowment funds, 101
equally weighted indices, 46–48
equilibrium
illiquidity premiums, 271
market prices, 252, 253–254
nominal rate of interest, 148
real rate of interest, 147
equities. *See* equity securities
equity
funds, 110
levered, 669
risk, 155
securities. *See* equity securities
valuation, 506, 567
equity carve-out, 42
equity premium puzzle, 381–384
equity securities, 39–43
common stocks, 39–40
preferred stocks, 42
stock market indices, 43–50
stock market listings, 40–42
equity spinoff, 42
ethical issues, 20, 91, 227
EURIBOR, 764
Euro-Canadian dollars, 30
Eurobonds, 16, 30, 397
Eurodollar, 13, 30, 397
Eurodollar futures contracts, 764–765
Euronext, 69, 72
Europe, Australia, Far East (EAFE) index, 784, 876, 878
European Monetary Union, 536
European option, 643, 688
event studies, 329–333
excess return, 151
exchange rate, 536–537, 759
exchange rate risk, 759, 762, 866–869
exchange-traded funds, 121, 130–131, 294
exercise price, 50, 640–641
exit option, 769
exotic options, 671–673
expectations hypothesis, 439, 751
expected return, 150, 170, 227–305
expected return-beta relationship, 362–363
capital asset pricing model, 258–259, 262, 265–267
capital budgeting decisions, 362
index model, 362–363

and professional management, 362
and regulatory commissions, 362
sample data set-up, 362
thin trading, 365–366
tort cases, 362
expense ratios. *See* management expense ratios
expenses, 569
expiration day effects, 758–759
Export Development Corporation, 14–15, 669
extendible bonds, 37, 396

F

face value, 393
factor model, 286–287
factor portfolios, 308, 372
fair and orderly market, 76
fair game, 164
Fama-French Three-Factor Model, 375–378
fast growers, 548
Fed's Stock Valuation Model (FSVM), 543
Federal reserve, 539
Federal Reserve Bank of New York, 17, 89
Federal Reserve Board, 30
Fidelity Magellan Fund, 113, 335, 798–799
FIFO (first-in, first-out), 591, 592
fill or kill orders, 75
filter rules, 336–337, 349
financial. *See* financial markets
Financial Analysts Federation (FAF), 100
financial assets, 6, 749
financial engineering, 12–16, 490–491, 669–671
financial intermediaries, 10–11
financial investment, 6
financial leverage, 546, 577–579
financial markets
brokerage services, 11
financial engineering, 12–16
financial intermediation, 10–11
investment banking, 11, 12
responses to clientele, 10–11
taxation and regulation, 16
Financial Post Information Service, The, 48, 576
financial ratios, 576, 586
See also ratios
financial risk, 155
financial scandals, 640
financial statement analysis
accounting earnings, 573–574
analysts' forecasts, 576
comparability, 591–597
depreciation, 573, 592–593
discrepancies in reported figures, 591
financial statements. *See* financial statements
illustration of, 589–590
inflation, 592–593
interest expense, 592–593
inventory valuation, 591
limitations, 591
ratio analysis, 580–588
return on equity, 577–579
financial statements, 569–573
balance sheet, 569–571
common-size balance sheet, 571
expenses, 569
flow of funds statement, 571
income statement, 569
limitations, 597
net income, 569
shareholders' equity, 569–571
statement of cash flows, 571–573
statement of changes in financial position, 571–573
financial system
clients of, 7–8
participants, 4
Financial Times Index of London, 43, 48
Financial Times of London, 43, 48
Financial Times Share exchange, 862
firm commitment underwriting arrangement, 61
firm-specific risk, 208, 258–259, 285–288
First Canadian Equity Index Fund, 207
first-pass regression, 363
fiscal policy, 537–538
Fisher equation, 148
fixed annuities, 133
fixed-asset turnover ratio, 582–583
fixed-charge coverage ratio, 414
fixed-income capital market, 33–39
corporate bonds, 36
Government of Canada bonds, 33–36
mortgage-backed securities, 37–39
mortgages, 37–39
municipal bonds, 36
provincial bonds, 36
fixed-income funds, 110
fixed-income securities, 392
bonds. *See* bonds
duration, 462–469
preferred stock, 42, 397
float, 61
floating-rate bonds, 396–397
floor traders, 73
flow of funds, 624
flow of funds statement, 571
flow-through shares, 135
forecasting errors, 345
forecasts, 576
alpha values, 836–837
analysts, 576
earnings, 541–542
inflation, 148–149, 161
interest rates, 458, 484, 488
market timing, 804
stock market, 541–542
value or imperfect, 804
foreign
bank deposits, 30
bonds, 397
currencies, 14–15
currency options, 643, 646
exchange futures, 759–763
exchange swaps, 765–770
index funds, 859, 878
indices, 48
markets, 72–73
multinational firms, 61, 859
sector, 7
securities, 22
stock exchange indices, 43, 48
forward
contract, 727, 728
markets, 759
prices, 745–746
rates, 436–439, 445–446, 450
fourth market, 71–72
FPX indexes, 860, 878
framing, 347
Frankfurt Exchange, 72
Franklin Templeton, 862
fraud, 19
free cash flow approach, 529–531
free-rider benefit, 207
FTSE, 48
full-service brokers, 84
fully diluted earnings per share, 666
Fund Counsel, 414
fundamental analysis, 326, 503
aggregate stock market, 541–549
balance sheet approach to valuation, 505
corporate finance, 529–531
dividend discount models, 508–516
earnings, 516–526
equity valuation, 531–534
free cash flow approach, 529–531
Graham technique, 528
growth, 516–526
growth investing, 527–529
industry analysis, 542–549
inflation, 531–534
macroeconomic analysis, 534–541
price-earnings ratio, 516–526
value investing, 527–529
Fundamental Approximation Theorem of Portfolio Analysis and Higher Moments, 185n
future short rate, 437
futures, 16
basic risk, 740
basis, 740
bond, 731
cash delivery, 737
cash settlement contract, 753
clearinghouse, 733–734
contracts, 52, 727, 728–733
convergence property, 735
covered interest arbitrage relationship, 763
cross hedging, 740
currency, 759
determination of price. *See* futures pricing
existing contracts, 731
foreign exchange, 759–763
hedging, 738–741
innovation in, 731
interest rate, 763–765
interest rate parity theorem, 759–763
long hedge, 739
long position, 52, 53, 728
margin account, 734–736
markets, 73, 727, 763
marking to market, 734–736
open interest, 734
options, 648
price, 52, 728
price limits, 737–738
regulations, 737–738
reversing trade, 734
short hedge, 739
short position, 52, 728
speculation, 738–740
spot price, 735, 751
spread position, 741
stock index. *See* stock index futures
taxation, 738
futures pricing, 741–746
and arbitrageurs, 758–759
commodity, 746–753
contango, 752
cost-of-carry relationship, 743
discounted cash flow analysis, 749–751
expectations hypothesis, 751
expected spot prices, 751
and interest rates, 763–765
modern portfolio theory, 752–753
normal backwardation, 752
spot-futures parity theorem, 741–744
spreads, 744–745
stock index futures, 753–759
storage costs, 746–748
vs. forward pricing, 745–746

G

GAAP guidelines, 594
gambling, 163–164
gap management, 476
GARCH model, 379–381, 633
generalized autoregressive conditional heteroskedasticity model, 378–381
generalized lest squares, 367
generally accepted accounting principles (GAAP), 591, 594
geometric average, 818–820
Glenmede Trust Co., 334
global economy, 534–536
Global Industry Classification Standard (GICS), 545
globalization, 22
Globe and Mail's Report on Business, The, 113
Globe and Mail, The, 28, 33, 39, 40, 44, 46, 48, 50, 52, 91, 105, 108, 327, 333, 335, 393–395, 642, 759
Goldman, Sachs, 876
goodwill, 596
Gordon model, 508–509, 565
Government of Canada, 13

Government of Canada bonds, 33–36
governments, 8
fiscal policy, 537–538
monetary policy. *See* monetary policy
Graham technique, 528
Graphoscope, 629
gross domestic product, 536–537, 540, 611, 858
growth
company, 527
investing, 527–529
and price-earnings ratio, 516–526
stocks, 21, 110
growth funds, 110
guaranteed investment certificates (GICs), 29, 145

H

hedge funds, 298
market-neutral, 107
hedge ratios, 697–699, 838
hedging, 169
and basic risk, 740
Black-Scholes formula, 697–699
and bond futures, 764
cross-hedging, 740, 841
derivatives, 13, 640
futures, 738–740
interest rate risk, 764, 840–841
perfect, 708
systematic risk, 838–840
heterogeneous expectations, 164
hidden agendas, 18
high-tech market, 18, 22
bubble and collapse, 3–4, 16–17
historical cost, 533
historical record, 151–156
hoarders, 9n
holding-period immunization, 481
holding-period return, 150, 151–156, 410
homogeneous expectations, 253
Hong Kong stock market, 535
horizon analysis, 408, 486
hot hands phenomenon, 352
households, 7–8
human capital, 9
human issues, 227
hybrid securities, 54

I

i60s, 121, 328
IBM, 660
illiquidity premiums, 267–272
immunization, 474, 475–483
cash flow matching, 482–483
contingent, 138, 486–487
dedication strategy, 482–483
net worth, 476–482
problems, 483
rebalancing, 480
target date, 477
implied volatility, 694–695
Inco Ltd., 68
income funds, 110
income statement. *See* taxation
income trust, 42
taxation, 43
incomplete markets, 715
indenture, 417
Independent Survey Co., 629
index arbitrage, 758–759
index funds, 45, 327–329, 334, 826
demand for stock, 282
index model, 285, 286–288, 296–298
cost of, 288
and diversification, 290–292
estimating, 364–365
estimating, 288–290
expected return-beta relationship, 362–363
industry version, 293–296
multifactor models, 298–301
regression equation, 289
security characteristic line, 289, 299–300
single-index model, 286
specialization of effort in security analysis, 288
tracking portfolio, 296–298
two-factor model, 298
index options, 646
Index Participation Units (IPUs), 328
index security, 827
index-linked CD, 669–671
indexed bonds, 398–399
indexing, 458, 474, 826–827
indices. *See* stock market indices
indifference curve, 168–169
industry analysis, 542–549
industry life cycle, 548–549
inflation
depreciation, 592
and equity valuation, 531–534
forecasts, 148–149, 161
and interest expense, 592–593
macroeconomic analysis, 536–537
"neutral", 532
and price-earning ratio, 533
rate, 146, 148, 149
and rates of return, 148
and stocks, 533
T-bill rate of return, 148–149
inflation illusion, 543
information
accounting. *See* financial statements
inside, 91, 342–343
Internet, 629
leakage, 331
mutual funds, 112–115
private, 633
superior, 802
value of, 802, 809
informationally efficient market, 323n
initial public offerings, 61, 62–66
underpricing, 63–65
innovative instruments, 13–15
input list, 226
inside information, 91, 342–343
inside the quoted spread, 74
insider trading, 91, 342–343, 653
Institute of Chartered Financial Analysts (ICFA), 100
Institutional Brokers Estimate System, 576
institutions
constraints, 102–103
management by, 100–103
portfolio objectives, 100–102
regulation, 103
unique needs, 103
insurance. *See* life insurance
insurance company, 10
insurance principle, 208, 248–250
insured defined benefit pension, 102
intangibles, 596
integrated markets, 882
interest coverage ratio, 584
interest expense, 592–593
interest rate cap, 769
interest rate floor, 769
interest rate parity theorem, 760–763, 869
interest rates
and bond prices, 458, 459–461, 465–469, 484, 491
cuts by Federal Reserve, 539
derivatives, 490–491
determinants of level, 145–149
equilibrium nominal, 148
equilibrium real, 147
forecasting, 458, 484, 488
forward rates, 436–439, 445–446
futures, 763–765
horizon analysis, 486
life insurance, 102
macroeconomic analysis, 536–537
management of risk, 477
nominal, 145–146
options, 648
real, 145–146
risk, 459–461
risk structure of, 420
short, 431
swaps, 488–489, 765
and taxes, 149
term structure. *See* term structure
uncertainty, 436–439
interest-burden ratio, 581
interest-only strip, 491
intermarket spread swap, 484
Intermarket Trading Systems (ITS), 71–72
internal rate of return, 249
international accounting conventions, 594–597
International Accounting Standards, 596
international bonds, 397
international diversification, 853, 854–862
international indices, 48
international investment
American Depository Receipts (ADRs), 22, 859
arbitrage pricing theory, 881–882
asset allocation, 22, 878–881
capital asset pricing model, 881–882
cash/bond selection, 878
country selection, 878
covered interest arbitrage relationship, 765
cross-holdings, 869–870
currency selection, 878
diversification, 854–862, 882
equilibrium in international capital markets, 881–882
exchange rate risk. *See* exchange rate risk
financial ratios, 882
integrated markets, 882–883
interest rate parity theorem, 869
measurement, 876–882
multifactor models, 879–881
passive benchmarks, 876–882
political risk, 535, 863
risk issues, 862–868
security analysis, 879–880
segmented markets, 882
single-country funds, 859
stock selection, 878
techniques, 859
world equity portfolio, 854
International Monetary Fund, 535
International Monetary Market, 759
internet
bubble, 4–5
charting resources, 629
trading, 88
Intersec Research Corp., 113
intrinsic value, 252, 507–508, 684
inventories, 573
inventory turnover ratio, 582–583
inventory valuation, 520, 533, 591
inverse floater, 490–491
inverse multiplier, 670
investment
bankers, 61–62
banking, 11
companies, 104–105, 114
dealers, 11, 61
diversification, 164
financial, 6
government encouragement of, 8
grade bonds, 412
horizon, 103
international. *See* international investment
objectives, 2–23
opportunity set, 201
real, 6
investment companies, 10, 114
Investment Dealers Association of Canada, 88–89
Investment Funds Institute of Canada, 106, 111
investment opportunity set, 218
investors
behaviour, 9, 349
high tax bracket, 7
objectives of, 4–5
rational, 262, 263–264
invoice price, 395
IPOs. *See* initial public offerings
IPUs, 859
iShares, 859–860
iUnits, 121, 826

J

January effect, 339–341
Jensen's measure, 788
junk bonds, 110, 412–417

K

Kondratieff wave theory, 615–616
kurtosis, 801

L

law of one price, 301–302
leading economic indicators, 540
leakage of information, 331
LEAPS, 52, 643, 700
Lehman Brothers, 48
Lehman Brothers Aggregate Index, 474
leverage, 81
  put-call parity, 666
leverage ratio, 414, 581
levered equity, 669
liabilities, 569
LIBOR, 30–31, 488–489, 764–765, 766, 769
life cycles, 9–10, 512–516
life expectancy, 9
life insurance, 9
  adjustable life, 102n
  insured defined benefit pension, 102
  interest rate, 102
  term insurance, 101, 102
  universal life, 102
  variable, 102, 134
  whole-life policy, 101–102
life insurance companies, immunization strategies, 477–478
lifetime consumption, 267
LIFO (last-in, first-out), 591
limit orders, 74
limit-buy order, 74
limit-sell order, 74
limited partnerships, 134–135
liquidation costs, 269–271
liquidation, value, 506
liquidity, 102–103
  bonds, 393–395
  and capital asset pricing model, 267–272
  preference theory, 440
  premium, 438, 440, 443
  ratios, 414, 583–584
load funds, 105
loans, 667–669
lognormal distributions, 186–188
London Interbank Offered Rate. *See* LIBOR
London International Financial Futures Exchange (LIFFE), 732, 759
London Stock Exchange, 69, 72
long hedge, 739
long position, 52, 728
Long Term Capital Management fund, 535
long-term deep discount bond, 13
long-term equity anticipation shares (LEAPS), 52, 643, 700
lookback options, 672
lucky events, 334–335

M

M^2 measure, 789–790
macro economy, 536–537
macroeconomic analysis, 534–541
  business cycle, 538–541
  demand shock, 537
  fiscal policy, 537–538
  global economy, 534–536
  macro economy, 536–537
  monetary policy, 537–538
  supply shock, 537
Magna International, 521–525, 549
magnitude issue, 333
maintenance margin, 735
Malkiel's bond-pricing relationships, 460
managed funds, 105
management, 19–20
management expense ratios, 115, 328
managers. *See* performance measurement
margin
  account, 734–736
  buying on, 80–82
  futures market, 728
  maintenance, 735
  options, 73, 613
  short sales, 82–84
  variation, 735
margin call, 80
margin purchases, 202
marginal price of risk, 258
mark to market, 612
market
  aggregate stock, 541–549
  auction, 28, 67, 76, 79
  beating the, 349, 352
  bond. *See* bond market
  breadth of, 626
  brokered, 66
  capital, 2, 66
  complete, 715
  crash of October 1987, 3, 186, 701–702
  dealer, 66, 78–79
  derivative. *See* derivative markets
  direct search, 66
  effects. *See* market anomalies
  efficiency. *See* market efficiency
  fixed-income capital. *See* fixed-income capital market
  foreign, 72
  fourth, 71–72
  futures, 73, 727, 763
  incomplete, 715
  index, 352, 366–368
  integration, 882
  models, 285
  money. *See* money market
  orders, 74–75
  over-the-counter. *See* over-the-counter market
  portfolio. *See* market portfolio
  price of risk, 257n
  price ratios, 584–586
  prices, 284, 302
  primary, 61
  risk, 208, 291, 293
  secondary, 61, 66, 67–70
  segmented, 882
  stock. *See* stock market
  third, 71–72
  timing. *See* market timing
  value-weighted index, 43, 44, 46
market anomalies, 338
  book-to-market effects, 337
  expiration-day effects, 758–759
  insider transactions, 342–343
  January effect, 339–341
  liquidity effects, 341
  market crash of October 1987, 3, 186, 701–702
  month-end effect, 340
  neglected-firm effect, 341
  post-earnings-announcement price drift, 344
  reversal effect, 337–338
  small-firm effect, 339–341
  three-factor model, 343
  vs. data mining, 344–345
  vs. risk premiums, 343
market capitalization, 858
market capitalization rate, 507, 588
market conversion value, 396
market efficiency
  Canada, in, 352
  hypothesis. *See* efficient market hypothesis
  lucky event issue, 334–335
  magnitude issue, 333
  market anomalies. *See* market anomalies
  selection bias issue, 333–334
  survivorship bias and tests of, 384–387
  and technical analysis, 631–633
  U.S., in, 352
market portfolio, 254
  passive strategy, 255
  risk premium, 256
market timing, 233, 753–755, 802–806
  identification of timing ability, 804–806
  imperfect forecasting, 804
  option pricing of, 823–824
  swing fund management, 809
  tactical asset allocation models, 809
market-makers, 73, 76, 77, 87
market-neutral hedge funds, 107
market-to-book value ratio, 584
marking to market, 734–736
Markowitz portfolio optimizer, 227
Markowitz portfolio selection model, 222–227, 253, 285
matrix prices, 50
mean absolute deviation, 184
mean return, 150, 170
mean-variance (M-V) criterion, 167
mean-variance analysis, 183–188
mean-variance portfolio theory, 783
measurement
  error in beta, 368–370
  international investment, 876–882
  performance. *See* performance measurement
  rate of return, 817–820
  term structure of interest rates, 447–450
memory bias, 345
mental accounting, 347
Merrill Lynch, 48, 122, 293n, 295
Merrill Lynch Domestic Master Index, 474
Methanex Corp., 68
Mexican stock market, 535
Microsoft, 504–506, 588
Microsoft Excel, 227–231
minimum-variance frontier, 222
minimum-variance portfolio, 213–215
modern portfolio theory, 186, 752–753
modified duration, 464
momentum, 337, 343
momentum investing, 21
monetary policy, 8, 31, 537–538
money illusion, 534
money market, 2, 27, 28–33
  bankers' acceptances, 30
  bearer deposit notes, 29, 198
  brokers' calls, 30
  certificate of deposit, 29
  commercial paper, 29, 198
  Eurodollars, 30, 397
  funds, 110, 198–199
  industry, 13
  instruments, 33
  LIBOR, 30–31
  repurchase agreements, 30
  treasury bills, 28–29
  yields, 33
money rates listing, 28
money spread, 658
month-end effect, 340
Montreal Exchange, 50, 67, 640, 731, 737, 759, 763
Moody's, 412
Moody's Industrial Manual, 419
Morgan Stanley, 859
Morgan Stanley Capital International, 545
Morgan Stanley Capital International-Europe index, 878
Morgan Stanley country indices, 122
Morgan Stanley Worldwide Equity Benchmark Shares, 859
Morningstar, 113–115, 212, 797
mortality tables, 133
mortgage funds, 106
mortgage-backed securities, 12, 37–39, 491
mortgages, 37–39
  derivatives, 491
  pass-throughs, 12, 36
  variable rate, 38
moving average, 624–625
multifactor models, 298–301, 851–852, 879–881
multinational firms, 22, 61, 859
multiple unit residential buildings (MURBs), 135

multiplier, 670
multistage growth models, 512–516
municipal bonds, 36
MURBs, 135
mutual fund LPs, 135
Mutual Fund Sourcebook, 116
mutual fund theorem, 255
mutual funds, 11, 108–109
  asset allocation funds, 110
  back-end load, 115
  balanced funds, 110
  cash positions, 623
  closed-end funds, 105–106, 861
  commissions, 111
  costs, 115–117
  dividend funds, 110
  equity funds, 110
  exchange-traded funds, 121
  fee structure, 115
  fees and returns, 116–117
  fixed-income funds, 110
  front-end load, 115
  global funds, 111, 859
  growth funds, 110
  "hot hands" phenomenon, 352
  income funds, 110
  index funds, 111
  index futures, 755–758
  information, 112–115
  investment policies, 110
  load, 195
  management expense ratios, 115, 328
  management performance analysis, 117–121
  money market funds, 110
  no-load funds, 115
  open-end funds, 105–106
  operating expenses, 115
  outperforming the index, 120
  performance, 117–121, 349–352, 784, 797, 808
  persistent performance, 119–121
  regional funds, 111
  returns, 116–117
  single-country, 859
  soft dollars, 116
  specialized sector funds, 111
  taxation of proceeds, 112
  trailer fees, 111

N

naked option writing, 651, 655
Nasdaq, 46, 104, 826
Nasdaq Stock market, 3, 4, 53, 67, 68–69, 70, 71–72, 78
National Bank Mutual Funds, 328
National Housing Act, 38
NEER, 263–264
neglected-firm effect, 341
net asset value (NAV), 104
net hedging hypothesis, 752
net present value, 249
net worth immunization, 476–482
neural networks, 632
new estimates of expected return (NEER), 263–264
New York Stock Exchange, 46, 67, 68, 72, 79, 86, 87, 186–188, 594, 627, 737
Nikkei index, 43, 48, 859
no-load funds, 115
non-diversifiable risk, 208
noncompetitive bids, 28
nonsystematic risk, 208
normal backwardation, 752
normal distribution, 158
Nortel Networks Corp., 17, 19, 20, 44–45, 784
North American Free Trade Agreement, 535
notional principal, 488

O

O'Donnell High Income Fund, 415
objective function, 218
objectives, 2–23
odd-lot theory, 623
Olympia and York, 29
on the run, 435
One Up On Wall Street, 518
Ontario Companies Act, 88
Ontario Securities Act, 30, 88
Ontario Securities Commission, 8, 62, 91
open interest, 734
open or good-till-cancelled orders, 75
open-end funds, 105–106
operating income, 507, 512
operating leverage, 546
optimal complete portfolio, 219
optimal risky portfolio, 217–221, 233–237
Option Clearing Corporation, 645–646
option elasticity, 698
option valuation, 684–686
  binomial option pricing, 707–714
  Black-Scholes pricing formula, 690–707
  call, 695–696
  call options, 649–650, 687
  complete markets, 714–715
  determinants, 685–686
  and dividend payout policy, 688–689
  dynamic hedging, 701
  early exercise, 688–690
  empirical evidence, 716–717
  expiration value, 684
  hedge ratios, 697–699
  implied volatility of option, 694–695
  incomplete markets, 714–715
  intrinsic value, 684
  multinomial option pricing, 714–716
  option elasticity, 698
  pseudo-American call, 695–696
  put options, 696–697
  replications, 708
  restrictions, 686–690
  time value, 684
  timing ability, 823–824
  two-state option pricing, 707–714
  volatility value, 684
  and volatility, 684, 707
options, 50–54, 640–648
  adjustment in contract terms, 643–644
  American, 643, 687, 689–690
  Asian, 671
  at the money, 642
  barrier, 672
  binary, 673
  call. *See* call
  cash dividends, 643–644
  cash settlement, 53
  certificates of deposit, 29, 669–671
  collar, 660
  covered call, 655–657
  currency-translated, 673
  "deliver the index", 646
  delta, 696–697, 702
  European, 643
  exercise price, 50, 640–641
  exit, 769
  exotic, 671–673
  financial engineering, 669–671
  foreign currency, 646
  futures, 648
  hedge ratio, 697–699
  in the money, 642
  index, 646
  interest rate, 648
  lookback, 672
  margin requirements, 646
  markets, 73
  naked option writing, 651, 655
  option-like securities, 663–669
  out of the money, 642
  premium, 53, 640–641
  pricing model, 671, 690–697
  protected index notes (PINs), 15, 669–671
  protective put, 653–655, 656, 699–700
  "purchase index", 646
  purchase price, 640
  put, 50–52, 53, 623, 641, 650, 696–697
  put-call parity theorem, 660–663
  spread, 658
  standardization of contract terms, 642
  stock index, 53, 645
  stock split, 645
  straddle, 657
  straps, 657
  strategies, 653–660
  strike price, 50, 640–641, 642
  strips, 657
  trading, 639–640, 642–643
  valuation. *See* option valuation
  vs. stocks, 651–653
orders
  competitive bid, 28
  fill or kill, 75
  limit, 74
  limit-sell, 74
  market, 74–75
  noncompetitive bid, 28
  open or good-till-cancelled, 75
  stop-buy, 75
  stop-loss, 74, 656
original-issue junk, 413
Outlook, 529
over-the-counter market, 54, 67, 68–70, 78–79, 642
overconfidence, 346

P

P/B ratio. *See* market-to-book value ratio
P/B screen, 584
P/E effect, 338
P/E ratio. *See* price-earnings ratio
PALTrak, 114–115
par value, 393, 449, 450
participation rate, 669
pass-through securities, 12, 36
passive core, 327
passive investment strategy, 206–207, 255, 326–327, 458
  asset allocation, 827
  bond index portfolio, 474
  bonds, 474–483
  buy-and-hold strategy, 827
  capital asset pricing model, 255
  cash flow matching, 482–483
  contingent immunization, 138, 486–487
  dedication strategy, 482–483
  equity index futures, 755–758
  immunization, 476–483
  indexing, 474, 826–827
  international investment, 876–882
  multifactor market, 852
  net worth immunization, 476–482
  target date immunization, 477
passive portfolio, 831
payer swaption, 770
paying for order flow, 87
peak, 547
peaks, 538
PEG ratio, 519
Penn Central, 31
pension funds
  defined benefit, 101, 137–139
  defined contribution, 101, 137–139
  fund appraisal, 139
  immunization of liability, 138, 476–477
  index futures, 755
  integrated, 137
  investment policy, 138
  tax status, 138
  use of indexing, 327, 784
performance attribution procedures, 842–846
performance measurement
  and active management, 783–786
  appraisal ratio, 788
  appropriate measure, 792–794
  Canadian, 808–809
  and capital asset pricing model, 787–788
  comparison of performance, 786–788
  comparison universe, 787
  empirical studies, 808–809
  example, 794–795

Jensen's measure, 788
kurtosis, 801
M2 measure, 789–790
management performance analysis, 113
mutual funds, 117–121, 349–352, 784, 797, 798
performance attribution procedures, 842–846
persistent performance, 119–121
problems, 806–808
and reporting requirements, 807
risk-adjusted method, 787–788
Sharpe's measure, 783, 786, 788, 791–792
shifting parameters, 806
skewness, 803
style analysis, 797–800
survivorship bias, 384–387, 807–808
Treynor's measure, 788, 790–791
Vos Value Ratio, 801
window dressing, 807
perpetuity, 397, 467–468, 478, 482, 565–566
personal trusts, 100
Piper Jaffray Companies, 13
Placer Dome Inc., 68
plowback ratio, 510
point and figure chart, 616
political risk, 535, 863
POP. *See* prompt offering prospectus
portfolio
active, 830–831, 832
active management. *See* active portfolio management
and arbitrage pricing theory, 302–307
barbell, 827
calculation of expected return and variance, 227–231
capital allocation, 195–197
capital market line, 206–207
cellular, 475
certainty equivalent rate, 165, 205
composition, 786, 807
constraints, 227
construction, 831–837
delta-neutral, 706
duration. *See* duration
efficient frontier. *See* efficient frontier
factor, 308, 372
immunization. *See* immunization
insurance, 16, 655, 699–702
laddered, 827
management, 825, 826–827
Markowitz selection model, 222–227
mathematics, 169–174
minimum-variance, 213–215
opportunity set, 215–216
optimal risky, 217–221, 232, 233–237
optimization process, 832–833
optimization technique, 232
P/E effect, 338
passive, 831, 843
performance measurement. *See* performance measurement
rate of return, 183
reporting requirements, 807
risk, 118, 169–174, 207–209, 256
risk-free asset, 233–237
spreadsheet model, 227–231
strategies. *See* portfolio strategies
theory. *See* portfolio theory
turnover rate, 112, 113
variance, 173–174
well-diversified, 302–303
window dressing, 807
world equity, 854
zero investment, 301
Portfolio Analytics Limited, 114
portfolio objectives, 100
portfolio strategies
active. *See* active portfolio management
contrarian, 337
January effect, 339–341
liquidity effects, 341
market efficiency, 352
month-end effect, 340
neglected-firm effect, 341
passive investment strategy. *See* passive investment strategy
reversal effect, 337–338
small-firm effect, 339–341
portfolio theory, 144
asset allocation. *See* asset allocation
lognormal distributions, 186–188
mean-variance analysis, 183–188
modern, 186, 752–753
normal distributions, 186–188
real vs. nominal risk, 156–157
risk and risk aversion, 162–169, 189–193
risk-return combinations. *See* risk-return combinations
utility value, 164–169, 189–193
post-earnings-announcement price drift, 344
Precision Drilling Corp., 68
predictability of returns, 322, 336–339
book-to-market ratios, 341
short horizons, 336–337
preferred stock, 42, 397
preliminary prospectus, 61
present value calculation, 399–400
present value of growth opportunities, 511
price adjustment process, 254
price continuity, 76
price discovery, 79
price improvement, 74
price priority, 79
price value of a basis point, 840
price-earnings effect, 338
price-earnings multiple, 516
price-earnings ratio, 41, 516–526
and dividend discount model, 525–526
financial statement-based, 584–586
and inflation, 533
international practices, 879
pitfalls, 520–525
return on equity, 516–518
and stock risk, 519
price-to-book ratio, 526
price-to-cash-flow ratio, 526
price-to-sales, 526
price-weighted average, 45
Priceline.com, 5, 519
primary market, 61
primitive security, 12, 715
principal-only strip, 491
private information, 633
private placement, 61
probability distributions, 149–150, 158, 183–188
Proctor & Gamble, 13, 491
profitability, 542–545
profitability ratio, 415
program trading, 78, 758–759
prospectus, 61, 62
protected index notes (PINs), 15, 669–671
protective put strategy, 653–655, 656, 699–700
provincial bonds, 36
proxy, 39
proxy flights, 39
prudent person law, 103
pseudo-American call, 695–696
public offering, 61
pure trend analysis, 616
pure yield curve, 435, 447
pure yield pickup swap, 485
put bonds, 396
put options, 50–52, 53, 623, 641, 650–651, 696–697
put swaption, 770
put/call ratio, 623

Q

quality of earnings, 593–594
Quebec Securities Commission, 67
quick ratio, 414, 584

R

random variable, 183
random walks, 323
rate anticipation swap, 485
rate of return
abnormal, 330
arithmetic averaging, 818–820
book-to-market ratios. *See* book-to-market ratios
bonds, 399, 404–412
capital asset pricing model, 256–260
comparison of, 786–789
cumulative abnormal, 331–333
dollar-weighted, 786, 817–818
excess, 151
expected, 150, 199
expected vs. realized, 382–384, 795–796
geometric average, 818–820
global, 159–160
historical, 159–160
historical record, 151–156
and inflation, 148, 533
mean, 150, 170
measurement of, 817–820
mutual funds, 116–117
nominal, 156–157
persistence, 632
portfolio, on, 171
predictability. *See* predictability of returns
probability distribution, 183
real, 148
research activity, on, 324
short horizons, 333–337
T-bill, 148–149
time-weighted, 786
time-weighted return, 817–818
rate-of-return analysis, 249–250
ratios
accounts receivable to sales ratio, 582–583
acid test ratio, 584
analysis, 580–588
appraisal, 788, 791, 793, 794, 809
asset utilization ratio, 582–583
book-to-market ratio, 263–264, 341, 584
cash-flow-to-debt ratio, 415
conversion, 396
coverage ratio, 414, 583–584
current ratio, 414, 583–584
dividend payout ratio, 510
earnings retention ratio, 510
financial. *See* financial ratios
fixed-asset turnover ratio, 582–583
fixed-charge coverage ratio, 414
hedge, 697–699, 838
interest coverage ratio, 583–584
interest-burden ratio, 581
international investment, 882
inventory turnover ratio, 582–583
leverage ratio, 414, 581
liquidity ratio, 414, 584
management expense ratio, 115, 328
market price, 584–586
PEG, 520
plowback ratio, 510
price value of a basis point, 840
price-earnings. *See* price-earnings ratio
price-to-book ratio, 526
price-to-cash-flow ratio, 526
price-to-sales, 526
profitability ratio, 415
put/call, 623
quick ratio, 414, 584
return on assets ratio, 415
reward-to-variability ratio. *See* reward-to-variability ratio
tax-burden, 580
times-interest-earned ratio, 414
turnover ratio, 112, 113, 582–583
Vos Value Ratio, 801
Reagan stimulus, 539
real assets, 6
real estate, 9
real estate investment trust (REIT), 107
real estate limited partnership, 107

real investment, 6
Real Return Bonds, 146, 157n, 398
rebalancing, 480
red herring, 61
redeemable preferred stock, 42
refunding, 396
registered bonds, 395
registered retirement income fund, 102
registered traders, 73, 76–77
regression equation, 289
regret avoidance, 347
regulation, 8
 and event studies, 332–333
 and expected return-beta relationship, 362
 futures markets, 737–738
 institutional investors, 103
 prudent person law, 103
 securities markets, 88–91
relative strength strategy, 325, 626–627
replacement value, 506
replication, 708, 715
repos. *See* repurchase agreements
representativeness, 346
repurchase agreements, 30
research, 324
Research Capital Corp., 18
Research Evaluation Service, 576
Research in Motion Ltd., 68
reserves, 594, 879
residence, 9
residual income, 588
residuals, 289
resistance level, 614
restricted
 borrowing, 262–265
 shareholders, 39
 shares, 39
retirement, 9
 See also tax-deferral retirement plans
retractable bonds, 37, 396
return on assets, 577–579
return on assets ratio, 415
return on equity, 577–579
 decomposition of, 580–582
 financial leverage, 577–579
 past vs. future, 577
 price-earnings ratio, 516–518
return on sales, 580
return requirements, 100
returns. *See* rate of return
reversal effect, 337–338, 632
reverse repo, 30
reversing trade, 734
reward-to-variability ratio, 201
risk, 149–151
 arbitrage, 302
 asset, 169
 aversion, 7, 151, 162–169, 189–193
 basic, 740
 bonds, 401–404, 414–417
 business, 155
 considerable, 163
 credit, 768–769
 default, 37, 164, 412–421
 derivatives, 13
 diversifiable, 208
 equity, 155
 exchange rate, 759, 762, 866–869
 financial, 155
 firm-specific. *See* firm-specific risk
 and gambling, 163–164
 and hedging, 169, 740
 holding-period return, 150
 interest rate, 459–461, 840–841
 and life cycle, 9–10
 lover, 166
 management, 655
 marginal price of, 258
 market, 208, 291, 293
 market price of, 257
 negative contribution, 257
 nominal, 156–157
 non-diversifiable, 208
 nonsystematic, 208
 political, 535, 863
 premiums, 151, 254, 256, 343–344
 price, 435, 438n, 478
 real, 156–157
 reinvestment rate, 478, 479, 480
 risk-neutral, 166
 and speculation, 163–164
 stock, 520
 systematic. *See* systematic risk
 tolerance, 7, 100–101, 166–167, 203–206
 unique, 208
 volatility, 707
 with simple prospects, 162–163
Risk Adjusted Rating (RAR), 797
risk arbitrage, 302
risk aversion, degree of, 204
risk premium, 151, 204
risk-free asset, 194, 198–199, 233–237
risk-free rate, 151
risk-pooling, 248–250
risk-return combinations
 one risky asset and one risk-free asset, 199–202
 optimal risky portfolio, 217–221, 233–237
 two risky assets, 209–216
risk-return trade-off, 100–101
risk-sharing, 248–250
risky asset, 170, 171, 194, 195
risky debt, 669
Roll's critique, 366–367
Rosenberg Institutional Equity Management Fund, 632
Royal Bank, 45
royalty trust, 42
RRSPs, 101, 102, 132, 755–756
Russell 2000 index, 827
Russsian currency, devaluation, 535

S

S&P 500, 334
S&P/TSE 60 index, 731, 737, 826
S&P/TSX 60 index, 53, 121
S&P/TSX Composite index, 45, 151, 293–297, 327, 333, 352, 541–542, 624–625
Salomon Brothers Broad Investment Grade Index, 474
Salomon Brothers Inc., 48, 876
Samurai bonds, 397
scatter diagram, 288
Scotia Capital, 62, 474, 475
Scotia Capital Markets Universe index, 784
Scotia McLeod, 48, 61, 475
Scotia McLeod Universe Bond index, 414
Scotiabank, 52
seal of approval, 11
SEAQ, 72
seasoned new issues, 61
seats, 67
second central moment, 184
second-pass regression, 363
secondary markets, 61, 66, 67–70
sector allocation decisions, 845–846
sector indexes, 827
sector rotation, 547
securities. *See also* stocks; trades
 asked price, 70, 76
 asset-backed, 12, 398
 bid price, 70
 convertible, 664–666
 derivative, 12
 equity. *See* equity securities
 exchange-listed, 71
 fixed-income. *See* fixed-income securities
 foreign, 22
 hybrid, 54
 issuance of, 6, 8, 61–66
 markets, 66–73, 88–91, 285–292
 mortgage-backed, 12, 37–39
 pass-through, 12, 36
 primitive, 12, 715
 "properly priced", 293
 relative strength, 626–627
 street name, 78
 underpricing, 63–65
Securities and Exchange Commission (SEC), 89, 332–333, 594, 596
Securities Exchange Act, 89
securitization, 12
security
 allocation decisions, 845–846
 analysis, 206, 232, 830–837, 879–880
 characteristic line, 289, 362
 market line, 260–262, 306–307, 362, 363
 selection, 222–227, 232–233
Security Analysis, 528
segmented markets, 882
segregated funds, 107
SEI Financial Services, 113
selection bias, 333–334
selectivity, 842
self-destructing patterns, 612, 631–633
"sell discipline", 656
semistrong-form efficient market hypothesis, 324
sensitivity
 business cycle, 542–549
 interest rate, 459–461
sensitivity to sales, 546
sentiment indicators, 622–623
separation property, 231–232, 255
serial bond issues, 418
serial correlation, of stock market returns, 336
settlement, 78
shareholders, 19, 39
shareholders' equity, 569–571
shares, 73
 See also stocks
Sharpe's measure, 783, 786, 788, 791–792
short
 hedge, 739
 horizon returns, 336–337
 interest, 624
 interest rate, 431
 position, 52, 82, 728
 sales, 82–84
short form prospectus system, 62
short interest rate, 431
simple prospects, 162–163
single-country funds, 859
single-factor APT. *See* arbitrage pricing theory
single-index model, 286
single-index security market, 285–292
sinking funds, 417
skewness, 176, 803
slow growers, 548
Small Order Execution System, 79
small-firm effect, 339–341
socially responsible investing, 227
soft dollars, 116–117
specialist, 73, 78–79, 86
specialization, 11
specialized sector funds, 111
speculation, 8, 163–164, 738–740
speculative grade bonds, 412
speculators, 9
Spiders, 121, 122, 328, 826, 860
split share, 13, 16
spot price, 735, 751
spot rate, 432, 450
spot-futures parity theorem, 741–744
spreads, 85, 658, 741, 744–745
St. Petersburg Paradox, 190
stabilizing trades, 77
stalwarts, 548
Standard & Poor's, 529, 542–545, 545
 S&P 100, 53
 S&P 400, 827
 S&P 500, 15, 53, 121, 328, 351, 352, 415, 784, 826
 S&P 500 futures contract, 756–759
 S&P Depository Receipts, 121, 826
 S&P/TSE 60 index, 731, 737, 826
 S&P/TSX 60 index, 53, 121
standard deviation, 150, 158, 170, 171, 199

standardized unexpected earnings, 574–576
statement of cash flows, 571–573
statement of changes in financial position, 571–573
Statistics Canada, 146, 540
stock dividends, 643–644
Stock Exchange Automated Quotations, 72
Stock Exchange Electronic Trading Service (SETS), 72
stock exchanges, 67, 68
  See also trades
  execution of trades, 76–77
  interlisting, 67–68, 68
  mergers of, 67
  orders, 74–75
  participants, 73
  seats, 67
stock index futures, 753–749
  bills-plus-futures strategy, 755–758
  cash settlement, 753
  contracts, 753
  empirical evidence on pricing, 758
  index arbitrage, 758–759
  synthetic stock positions, 753–758
  triple witching hour, 758–759
stock index options, 53, 645
stock market indices, 43–50
  equally weighted indices, 46–48
  foreign indices, 48
  international indices, 48
  market value-weighted index, 43
  price-weighted average, 45
stock markets
  aggregate, 541–549
  anomalies. *See* market anomalies
  boom of 1990s, 3
  breadth, 626
  crash of 1987, 3, 186, 701–702
  forecasts, 541–542, 576, 612
  high-tech, 3–4, 16–17, 18, 22
  indices. *See* stock market indices
  industry analysis, 542–549
  listings, 40–42
  past behaviour, 541–542
  predictability of returns. *See* predictability of returns
  price index, 540
  reversals, 337–338
  structure, 624–625
stock options, 593–594
stock prices
  dividend discount model of, 564, 565
  Dow theory, 613
  earnings announcement, 574
  and investment opportunities, 509–512
  random walk, 323
  resistance level, 614
  reversal effect, 337–338, 632
  support level, 614
  volatility and option values, 685–686
stock returns, 576
stock risk, 520
stock split, 643–644
stockbrokers, 11
stocks, 5, 73
  See also securities
  board lots, 42
  Canadian multinationals, 22
  common. *See* common stocks
  demand for, 279–282
  equilibrium prices, 279–282
  growth, 21
  historical record, 151–156
  and inflation, 533
  initial public offerings. *See* initial public offerings
  intrinsic value, 279–282
  issuance of, 61–66
  net asset value (NAV), 104
  new, 4–5
  preferred, 42, 397
  price-earnings ratio, 41
  seasoned new issues, 61
  secondary offering, 61
  split share, 13
  vs. options, 651–653
stop-buy orders, 75
stop-loss orders, 74, 656
storage costs, 746–748
straddle, 657
stratified sampling, 475
street name, 78
strike price, 50, 640–641, 642
strike rate, 769
strip bonds, 13, 16, 410
strong-form efficient market hypothesis, 325
style analysis, 797–799
submartingale, 323n
subordinated debentures, 36
subordination clauses, 418
substitution swap, 484
Suncor Energy Inc., 68
Superbowl rule, 620–622
SuperDot, 77–78
superficial loss rule, 130
superior information, 802
supply shock, 537
support level, 614
survivorship bias, 383–387, 807–808
suspensions, 332–333
swaps, 12, 54, 488, 765–770
  See also futures
  bonds, 484
  collar, 769
  fair swap price, 767–769
  foreign exchange, 765–770
  interest rate, 488–489, 765
  intermarket spread, 484
  notional principal, 488
  pure yield pickup, 485
  rate anticipation, 485
  reason for, 484
  spinoff products, 769
  substitution, 484
  swaptions, 770
  tax, 486
  workout period, 484
swaptions, 770
swing fund management, 706
Swiss Exchange, 69
syndicate, 61
synergy, 196
synthetic stock positions, 753–758
systematic risk, 208, 254, 272, 285–288, 838–840

T

T-bill yields, 31–33
takeovers
  abnormal return, 330, 331
  announcement date, 332–333
  check on management, 39–40
  closely-held corporation, 40
  cumulative abnormal return, 332–333
  event study, 332–333
target date immunization, 477
tax shelters, 134–136
tax swap, 486
tax-burden ratio, 580
tax-deferral option, 131–135
tax-deferral retirement plans, 101, 102, 132
taxation
  bond pricing, 411–412, 449–450
  bracket creep, 149
  Canadian tax system, 129–131
  capital gains. *See* capital
  deferred annuities, 132–134
  dividend income, 22, 42, 130
  and FIFO accounting, 591, 592
  futures, 738
  income trust, 43
  interest income, 130
  mutual fund proceeds, 112
  pension plans, 137–139
  preferred stock, 42
  and real rate of interest, 149
  response of financial market, 16
  settlement date, 131
  shelters, 134–136
  superficial loss rule, 130
  tax brackets, 7, 149
  tax-deferral options, 131–135
  tax-timing options, 449–450
  timing, 131
TD Asset Management, 121, 327
TD Evergreen, 415
TD TSE 300 Index Fund, 327
TD Waterhouse, 62
technical analysis, 325–326, 503, 610, 611–613
  breadth of market, 626
  Canadian investors, 627–629
  chaos theory, 632
  charting, 613–622
  commodity trading, 629
  credit balances in brokerage accounts, 624
  and efficient market, 631–633
  flow of funds, 624
  Internet resources, 629
  irrational factors, 347–349, 611
  market structure, 624–625
  moving average, 624–625
  neural networks, 632, 829
  private information, 633
  relative strength, 626–627
  self-destructing patterns, 612, 631–633
  sentiment indicators, 622–623
  short interest, 624
  smaller companies, 627
  technical indicators, 622–626
  Value Line ranking system, 629–631
  vs. efficient market hypothesis, 610, 611
technical indicators, 622–626
  confidence index, 623
  mutual fund cash positions, 623
  odd-lot theory, 623
  put/call ratio, 623
  sentiment indicators, 622–623
  trin statistic, 622
Templeton Funds, 352
Templeton Growth Fund, 860
tender offer, 39
term insurance, 101
term premiums, 444
term repo, 30
term structure, 430
  bond pricing, 431–434
  discount function, 449
  expectations hypothesis, 439
  forward rates, 436–439
  holding period returns, 435
  interpreting, 440–445
  liquidity, preference theory, 440
  measurement of, 447–450
  theories of, 439–440
  under certainty, 431–436
The Financial Post, 588, 627–629, 759
thin trading, 365–366
third capital moment, 176
third market, 71–72
time deposits, 16
time spread, 658
time value, 684
time-varying volatility, 378–381
time-weighted return, 817–818
times interest earned ratio, 414, 584
timing, 627
  See also market timing
timing of consumption, 9
TIPs. *See* Toronto 35 Index Participation
Tobin's *q*, 506
Tokyo Stock Exchange, 48, 69, 72–73, 862
top-down analysis, 534
Toronto 35 Index Participation (TIPs), 121
Toronto Stock Exchange, 40, 43, 67, 68, 72, 73, 87, 627
  daily trading volume, 68
  foreign securities, 22
  futures, 737
  indices, 43–45
  requirements for listing, 67, 70
Toronto Stock Exchange Composite Index, 43
Total Stock Market Portfolio, 46
tracking error, 329
tracking portfolio, 296–298, 308

trades
- block sales, 77
- costs, 84–83, 269–271
- desk, 77
- execution of, 76–77
- Internet, 86, 88
- margin, 79–84
- on-line, 86, 87, 629
- over-the-counter market, 78–79, 642
- program, 78, 758–759
- stabilizing, 77
- thin trading, 365–366

trading halts, 90
trading rules. *See* technical analysis
trading suspensions, 332–333
trading through, 79
trading volume, 632
trailer fees, 111
transaction costs, 826
TransCanada Options Inc., 640
treasury bills, 28–29, 151–156, 198, 410
trends
- analysis, 336–337, 614
- globalization, 22

Treynor's measure, 788, 790–791
Treynor-Black model, 830–837
Trimark Advantage Bond Fund, 415
Trimark Investment Management Inc., 415
trin statistic, 622
triple witching hour, 758–759
troughs, 538, 547
TSE 100 index, 45, 121, 294
TSE 300 Composite Index, 33, 151, 206, 293, 352, 414, 784
TSE 300 stock index, 541
TSE 35 index, 121, 624–625
TSX 60 index, 44–45
TSX Composite Index, 43, 111
TSX Group Inc., 68
TSX index, 45
TSX Venture, 44–45
TSX Venture Exchange (CDNX), 70
turnarounds, 548
turnover, 112, 113
turnover ratios, 112, 113, 582–583
two-state option pricing, 707–714

U

U.S. National Association of Securities Dealers Automated Quotation system. *See* Nasdaq Stock market
unbundling, 16
underpricing, 63–65
underwriting, 61, 63–65
underwriting syndicate, 61
unemployment rate, 536
unique risk, 208
unit investment trusts, 107
universal life insurance, 102
uptick, 77, 82
utility values, 164–169, 189–193, 203–206

V

VA Linux, 63–64
valuation
- balance sheet approach, 505
- bonds. *See* bond pricing
- book value, 504
- comparative valuation ratios, 526–527
- equity, 531–534, 567
- intrinsic value, 252, 507–508
- inventory, 520, 533, 591
- liquidation value, 506
- options. *See* option valuation
- replacement value, 506
- and shifting growth rates, 524–525
- stock prices, 509–512

value at expiration, 649–653, 684
- value of information, 823–824
- warrants. *See* warrants

value at risk, 159
value firms, 375–378
- equation, 376
- factor loadings, 376

value investing, 21, 527–529, 612
Value Line, 293n, 512–515
Value Line Investment Survey, 512, 529, 542–545, 576, 629
Value Line ranking system, 629–631
Vancouver Stock Exchange, 67, 640
Vanguard 500 Portfolio, 826
Vanguard Group, 118, 122
Vanguard Index Trust 500 Portfolio, 113
Vanguard Windsor Fund, 352
variable annuities, 133
variable life insurance, 102, 134
variance, 150, 170, 227
variation margin, 635
volatility
- appearance of, 786
- asset-return, 378–381
- expiration day, 684, 758–759
- GARCH model, 379–381
- and halt in trading, 90–91
- implied, 694–695
- NYSE stocks, 378
- option valuation, 684, 707
- time-varying, 378–381
- value, 684

Volcker tightening, 539
Vos Value Ratio, 801

W

W.R. Hambrecht & Co., 64
Wall Street Journal, The, 333, 335, 613, 614, 623
Walt Disney Company, 398
warrants, 666
weak-form efficient market hypothesis, 324–327
WEBS. *See* World Equity Benchmark Shares
Wheaton River Minerals Ltd., 68
whole-life insurance policy, 101–102
Wi-LAN Inc., 18
Wiesenberger Investment Company services, 114
Wilshire 5000 Index, 46, 118–119, 350, 827
window dressing, 807
Winnipeg Commodity Exchange, 53 73, 728–731, 737
World Equity Benchmark Shares (WEBS), 860
wrap accounts, 85
WT Capital, 64

Y

Yankee bonds, 397, 474
yield
- bank discount, 31–33
- bond, 404–408
- bond equivalent, 32, 36
- and bond pricing, 404–408
- bootstrapping, 448
- current, 395, 405
- curve, 432, 440–445, 447, 449, 450
- and default risk, 412, 419–420
- earnings, 541–542, 586
- effective annual, 32, 405
- maturity, to, 36, 404–405, 407–408, 410, 419–420
- money market instruments, 33
- pure yield curve, 447
- pure yield pickup swap, 485
- realized compound, 407–408
- spot rate, 450
- T-bill, 31–33
- to call, 405–406
- Treasury yield curve, 444

yield spread, 198

Z

zero-beta portfolio, 262–265
zero-coupon bonds, 13, 131, 393, 410–411
- duration, 463

zero-investment portfolio, 301
zeroes. *See* zero-coupon bonds